African Literature

To the literary tradition's writers, critics, readers,
and those yet to come

African Literature

An Anthology of Criticism and Theory

Edited by

Tejumola Olaniyan and Ato Quayson

Blackwell
Publishing

Editorial material and organization © 2007 by Blackwell Publishing Ltd

BLACKWELL PUBLISHING
350 Main Street, Malden, MA 02148-5020, USA
9600 Garsington Road, Oxford OX4 2DQ, UK
550 Swanston Street, Carlton, Victoria 3053, Australia

First published 2007 by Blackwell Publishing Ltd

3   2008

Library of Congress Cataloging-in-Publication Data

African literature : an anthology of criticism and theory / edited by Tejumola Olaniyan and Ato Quayson.
    p. cm.
  Includes bibliographical references and index.
  ISBN: 978-1-4051-1200-0 (hardcover : alk. paper)—ISBN: 978-1-4051-1201-7 (pbk. : alk. paper)
    1. African literature—History and criticism. I. Olaniyan, Tejumola. II. Quayson, Ato.

PL8010.A353 2007
809′.896—dc22

                              2006025799

A catalogue record for this title is available from the British Library.

Set in 10/12.5pt Dante
by SPi Publisher Services Private Ltd.
Printed and bound in Singapore
by COS Printers Pte Ltd

The publisher's policy is to use permanent paper from mills that operate a sustainable forestry policy, and which has been manufactured from pulp processed using acid-free and elementary chlorine-free practices. Furthermore, the publisher ensures that the text paper and cover board used have met acceptable environmental accreditation standards.

For further information on
Blackwell Publishing, visit our website:
www.blackwellpublishing.com

Contents

Acknowledgments

The editors would like to express their deep gratitude to Andrew McNeillie, our first editor at Blackwell. It goes without saying that the anthology would never have appeared from this source without his strong interest and belief in the project. And when Andrew McNeillie left Blackwell, Al Bertrand expertly took over with equal enthusiasm and conviction. At critical junctures of our extended haggling over length, Al was patient and professional all through. The anthology would have been much poorer without his understanding. Our thanks also go to Helen Gray for her very attentive editing of the manuscripts and to Karen Wilson for so deftly facilitating easy communication between us and the Blackwell office.

Tejumola Olaniyan would like to thank all the students in his "Theory of African Literature" course over the years for their critical and enthusiastic reception. Their varied responses helped shape both the nature of the materials gathered in the anthology and the arrangement of these. He also expresses his gratitude to Mojisola, Bolajoko and Olabimpe Olaniyan for their usual forbearance and also for their contributions to the indexing process. Finally, to the several colleagues he consulted with at length about the anthology, he sends his immense appreciation.

Ato Quayson would like to thank the students of his Commonwealth and International Literature courses at Cambridge, Tim Cribb of Churchill College, who was himself an expert at unearthing ignored critical masterpieces, and Jeeba Jehu-Appiah, for his role as friend, impromptu critic, interlocutor-at-large and spiritual mentor for many long years. One of Quayson's inspirations for his continuing interest in literary criticism is the idea of answering a question that Jeeba may never ask.

The editors and publisher gratefully acknowledge the permission granted to reproduce the copyright material in this book:

1. Alain Ricard, "Africa and Writing," pp. 153–63, in *The Cambridge History of African and Caribbean Literature*, Volume 1, ed. F. Abiola Irele and Simon Gikandi. Cambridge: Cambridge University Press, 2004. Copyright © Cambridge University Press, reprinted with permission of the publisher and author.

2. Albert S. Gérard, "Sub-Saharan Africa's Literary History in a Nutshell," pp. 24–31, in *Comparative Literature and African Literature*, ed. C. F. Swanepoel. Pretoria: Via Afrika, 1993.

3. Bernth Lindfors, "Politics, Culture, and Literary Form," pp. 135–50, in *African Textualities: Texts, Pre-Texts, and Contexts of African Literature*. Trenton: Africa World Press, 1997.

4. Russell G. Hamilton, "African Literature in Portuguese," pp. 603–10, in *The Cambridge History of African and Caribbean Literature*, Volume 2, ed. F. Abiola Irele and Simon Gikandi. Cambridge: Cambridge University Press, 2004. Copyright © Cambridge University Press, reprinted with permission of the publisher and author.

5. Anissa Talahite, "North African Writing," pp. 13–23, in *Writing and Africa*, ed. Mpalive-Hangson Msiska and Paul Hyland. London: Longman, 1997. © 1997. Reprinted by permission of Pearson Education Limited.

6. Jonathan Ngate, "A Continent and its Literatures in French," pp. 19–27, in *Francophone African Fiction: Reading a Literary Tradition*. Trenton: Africa World Press, 1988.

7. Simon Gikandi, "African Literature and the Colonial Factor," pp. 379–85 in *The Cambridge History of African and Caribbean Literature*, Volume 1, ed. F. Abiola Irele and Simon Gikandi. Cambridge: Cambridge University Press, 2004. Copyright © Cambridge University Press, reprinted with permission of the publisher and author.

8. V. Y. Mudimbe, "African Literature: Myth or Reality?," pp. 7–11, in *African Literature Studies: The Present State/L'etat present*, ed. Stephen Arnold. Washington, DC: Three Continents Press, 1985. © 1985 by V. Y. Mudimbe. Reprinted by permission of The African Literature Association and the author.

9. Liz Gunner, "Africa and Orality," pp. 1–5, 12–13, in *The Cambridge History of African and Caribbean Literature*, Volume 1, ed. F. Abiola Irele and Simon Gikandi. Cambridge: Cambridge University Press, 2004. Copyright © Cambridge University Press, reprinted with permission of the publisher and author.

10. F. Abiola Irele, "Orality, Literacy, and African Literature," 2pp. 23–34, in *The African Imagination: Literature in Africa and the Black Diaspora*. New York: Oxford University Press, 2001. Copyright © 2001 by F. Abiola Irele. Reprinted by permission of Oxford University Press, Inc.

11. Isidore Okpewho, "Oral Literature and Modern African Literature," pp. 293–6, 301–3, 314–16, in *African Oral Literature: Backgrounds, Character, and Continuity*. Bloomington, IN: Indiana University Press, 1992. Reprinted by permission of Indiana University Press and the author.

12. Mary E. Modupe Kolawole, "Women's Oral Genres," pp. 73–9, *Womanism and African Consciousness*. Trenton: Africa World Press, 1997.

13. Harold Scheub, "The Oral Artist's Script," pp. 16–20, in *The Poem in the Story: Music, Poetry and Narrative*. Madison: University of Wisconsin Press, 2002. Copyright © 2002. Reprinted by permission of the University of Wisconsin Press.

14. Chinua Achebe, "The Novelist as Teacher," pp. 42–5, in *Morning Yet on Creation Day: Essays*. London: Heinemann, 1975. © 1975 by Chinua Achebe. Reprinted by permission of David Higham Associates.

15. Chinua Achebe, "The Truth of Fiction," pp. 95–105, in *Hopes & Impediments: Selected Essays*. London: Heinemann, 1988. © 1988 by Chinua Achebe. Reprinted by permission of David Higham Associates.

16. Nadine Gordimer, "Three in a Bed: Fiction, Morals, and Politics," pp. 3–15, in *Living in Hope and History: Notes from our Century*. New York: Farrar, Straus & Giroux, 1999. © 1999

by Nadine Gordimer. Reprinted by permission of Farrar, Straus and Giroux, Bloomsbury Publishing, and Russell & Volkening, as agents for the author.

17. Naguib Mahfouz, Nobel Lecture, Dec 8, 1988, trans. Mohammed Salmawy. Nobel Foundation. Copyright © The Nobel Foundation 1998. Reprinted by permission of The Nobel Foundation.

18. Njabulo S. Ndebele, "Redefining Relevance, " pp. 60, 66–74, in *South African Literature and Culture: Rediscovery of the Ordinary.* Manchester: Manchester University Press, 1994. © 1994 by Njabulo S. Ndebele. Reprinted by permission of the author.

19. Albie Sachs, "Preparing Ourselves for Freedom," pp. 19–29, in *Spring is Rebellious: Arguments about Cultural Freedom.* Cape Town: Buchu Books, 1990.

20. Wole Soyinka, "A Voice That Would Not Be Silenced," pp. ix–xvi, Foreword to Tahar Djaout, *The Last Summer of Reason*, trans. Marjolijn de Jager. St Paul, MN: Ruminator Books, 2001. © 2001 by Wole Soyinka. Reprinted by permission of the author.

21. Micere Githae Mugo, "Exile and Creativity: A Prolonged Writer's Block," pp. 80–7, in *The Word Behind Bars and the Paradox of Exile*, ed. Kofi Anyidoho. Evanston: Northwestern University Press, 1997. © 1997. Reprinted by permission of Northwestern University Press.

22. Jack Mapanje, "Containing Cockroaches (Memories of Incarceration Reconstructed in Exile)," pp. 47–50, 53–6, 65–7, in *The Word Behind Bars and the Paradox of Exile,* ed. Kofi Anyidoho. Evanston: Northwestern University Press, 1997. © 1997. Reprinted by permission of Northwestern University Press.

23. Ngugi wa Thiong'O, "Writing Against Neo-colonialism," pp. 92–100, 102–3, in *Criticism and Ideology: Second African Writers' Conference, Stockholm, 1986*, ed. Kirsten H. Petersen. Uppsala: Scandinavian Institute of African Studies, 1988. © 1998 by Ngugi wa Thiong'O and Nordiska Afrikainstitutet. Reprinted by permission of The Nordic Africa Institute, Uppsala and the author.

24. Breyten Breytenbach, "The Writer and Responsibility," pp. 98–106, in *End Papers: Essays, Letters, Articles of Faith, Workbook Notes.* New York: Farrar, Straus & Giroux, 1986. © 1986 by Breyten Breytenbach. Reprinted by permission of Farrar, Straus and Giroux.

25. Nawal El Saadawi, "Dissidence and Creativity," pp. 152–60, 163–4, in *The Dissident Word: The Oxford Amnesty Lectures 1995*, ed. Chris Miller. New York: Basic Books, 1996. © 1996. Reprinted by permission of Basic Books, a member of Perseus Books, L.C.C.

26. Zoë Wicomb, "Culture Beyond Color? A South African Dilemma," *Transition* 60 (1993): 27–32.

27. Nurrudin Farah, "In Praise of Exile," pp. 64–7, in *Literature in Exile*, ed. John Glad. Durham: Duke University Press, 1990. Copyright © 1990 by Duke University Press. All rights reserved. Used by permission of the publisher.

28. D. Marechera, "The African Writer's Experience of European Literature," *Zambezia* 14.2 (1987): 99–105. © 1987. Reprinted by permission of University of Zimbabwe Publications.

29. Léopold Sédar Senghor, "Negritude: A Humanism of the Twentieth Century," pp. 179–92, in *The Africa Reader Vol. 1 and Vol. II*, ed. Wilfred G. Cartey and Martin Kilson. New York: Random House, 1970. Copyright © 1970 by Wilfred Cartey and Martin Kilson. Reprinted by permission of Random House, Inc.

30. F. Abiola Irele, "What is Négritude?," pp. 67–9, 74–9, in *The African Experience in Literature and Ideology.* London: Heinemann, 1981. Copyright © 1981 by F. Abiola Irele. Reprinted by permission of the author.

31. Peter S. Thompson, "Negritude and a New Africa: An Update," *Research in African Literatures* 33.4 (Winter 2002): 143–53. © 2002. Reprinted by permission of Indiana University Press.

32. Chinweizu, "Prodigals, Come Home!" *Okike: An African Journal of New Writing* 4 (1973): 1–10, 12.

33. Wole Soyinka, "Neo-Tarzanism: The Poetics of Pseudo-Tradition," pp. 315–21, 327–9, in *Art, Dialogue and Outrage: Essays on Literature and Culture*. Ibadan: New Horn Press, 1988. © 1988, 1993 by Wole Soyinka. Used by permission of Pantheon Books, a division of Random House, Inc.

34. Adéléké Adéèkó, "My Signifier is More Native Than Yours: Issues in Making a Literature African," excerpted from pp. 1–27, in *Proverbs, Textuality, and Nativism in African Literature*. Gainesville, FL: University Press of Florida, 1998. © 1988 by Adéléké Adéèkó. Reprinted with the permission of the University Press of Florida.

35. Kwame A. Appiah, "Out of Africa: Topologies of Nativism," *Yale Journal of Criticism* 2.1 (1988): 157–61, 169–76. © 1988 by Kwame A. Appiah. Reprinted by permission of the author.

36. Frantz Fanon. "On National Culture," pp.206–27 in *The Wretched of the Earth*, trans. C. Farrington. New York: Grove Press, 1963. Copyright © 1963 by Presence Africaine. Used by permission of Grove/Atlantic, Inc.

37. Paulin J. Hountondji, "True and False Pluralism," pp. 156–66, in *African Philosophy: Myth and Reality*, trans. Henri Evans, 2nd edition. Bloomington: Indiana University Press, 1996. © 1996. Reprinted by permission of Indiana University Press.

38. Sony Labou Tansi, " 'An Open Letter to Africans' c/o The Punic One-Party State," *Jeune Afrique Economie* 136 (1990): 8–9. Translated by John Conteh-Morgan. © 1990. Reprinted with permission of the translator, John Conteh-Morgan.

39. Benita Parry, "Resistance Theory/Theorizing Resistance or, Two Cheers for Nativism," pp. 40–3, in *Postcolonial Studies: A Materialist Critique*. London: Routledge, 2004. © 2004 by Benita Parry. Reprinted by permission of Taylor & Francis Books UK.

40. Obiajuna Wali, "The Dead End of African Literature?," *Transition* 10 (1963): 13–16.

41. Ngugi wa Thiong'O, "The Language of African Literature," pp. 4–33, in *Decolonising the Mind: The Politics of Language in African Literature*. London: James Currey, 1986. © 1986 by Ngugi wa Thiong'O. Reprinted by permission of James Currey Publishers.

42. Assia Djebar, "Anamnesis in the Language of Writing," trans. Anne Donadey with Christi Merrill. *Studies in Twentieth Century Literature* 23.1 (Winter 1999): 179–89. © 1999. Reprinted by permission of *Studies in Twentieth Century Literature*.

43. Daniel P. Kunene, "African Language Literature: Tragedy and Hope," *Research in African Literatures* 23.1 (1992): 7–15. © 1992. Reprinted by permission of Indiana University Press.

44. Emmanuel N. Obiechina, "Background to the West African Novel," pp. 3–12, in *Culture, Tradition and Society in the West African Novel*. Cambridge: Cambridge University Press, 1975. © 1975 by Emmanuel N. Obiechina. Reprinted by permission of the author.

45. André Brink, "Languages of the Novel: A Lover's Reflections," *New England Review* 19.3 (Summer 1998): 5–10, 15–17.

46. Neil Lazarus, "The Retrieval of Naturalism: The Politics of Narrative in Radical African Fiction," *Critical Exchange* 22 (Spring 1987): 55–60. © 1987 by Neil Lazarus. Reprinted by permission of the author.

47. Mineke Schipper, " 'Who am I?': Fact and Fiction in African First-Person Narrative," pp. 102–14, in *Beyond the Boundaries: African Literature and Literary Theory.* London: W. H. Allen & Co., 1989. Copyright © 1989 by Mineke Schipper. Reprinted by permission of Ivan R. Dee, Publisher, and the author.

48. Tejumola Olaniyan, "Festivals, Ritual, and Drama in Africa," pp. 35–48, in *The Cambridge History of African and Caribbean Literature,* Volume 1, ed. F. Abiola Irele and Simon Gikandi. Cambridge: Cambridge University Press, 2004. Copyright © Cambridge University Press, reprinted with permission of the publisher and author.

49. Wole Soyinka, "The Fourth Stage: Through the Mysteries of Ogun to the Origin of Yoruba Tragedy," pp. 140–60, in *Myth, Literature and the African World.* Cambridge: Cambridge University Press, 1976. Copyright © 1976 by Cambridge University Press, reprinted with permission of the publisher and author.

50. Tawfiq Al-Hakim, Introduction to King Oedipus, *Plays, Prefaces, and Postscripts, vol 1: Theatre of the Mind,* trans. William M. Hutchins, pp. 274–80. Washington, DC: Three Continents Press, 1981. Copyright © 1981 by Lynne Rienner Publishers, Inc. Reprinted with permission of the publisher.

51. Kofi Anyidoho, "Poetry as Dramatic Performance," *Research in African Literatures* 22.2 (Summer 1991): 41–8, 53–5. © 1991. Reprinted by permission of Indiana University Press.

52. Anne McClintock, " 'Azikwelwa' (We Will Not Ride): Politics and Value in Black South African Poetry," *Critical Inquiry* 13 (Spring 1987): 597–600, 610–13, 614–16, 619–23. Copyright © 1987 by The University of Chicago. Reprinted by permission of the University of Chicago Press.

53. Emmanuel Ngara, "Revolutionary Practice and Style in Lusophone Liberation Poetry," pp. 103–9, in Emmanuel Ngara, *Ideology and Forum in African Poetry: Implications for Communication.* London: James Currey, 1990. © 1990 by Emmanuel Ngara. Reprinted by permission of James Currey Publishers.

54. Eldred D. Jones, "Academic Problems and Critical Techniques," pp. 89–91, in *African Literature and the Universities,* ed. G. Moore. Ibadan: Ibadan University Press, 1965.

55. Rand Bishop, "The Making of a Literary Tradition," pp. 59–67, 68–9, in *African Literature, African Critics: The Forming of Critical Standards, 1947–1966.* New York: Greenwood Press, 1988. © 1988 by Rand Bishop. Reprinted by permission of Greenwood Publishing Group.

56. Kenneth W. Harrow, "A Formal Approach to African Literature," *Research in African Literatures* 29.3 (1997): 79–84. © 1997. Reprinted by permission of Indiana University Press and the author.

57. Ambroise Kom, "African Absence, A Literature Without a Voice," *Research in African Literatures* 29.3 (1997): 152–7. © 1997. Reprinted by permission of Indiana University Press and the author.

58. Biodun Jeyifo, "The Nature of Things: Arrested Decolonization and Critical Theory," *Research in African Literatures* 21.1 (Spring 1990): 33–48. © 1990. Reprinted by permission of Indiana University Press.

59. Christopher L. Miller, "Reading Through Western Eyes," pp. 1–6, in *Theories of Africans: Francophone Literature and Anthropology in Africa.* Chicago: University of Chicago Press, 1990. Copyright © 1990 by the University of Chicago. Reprinted by permission of the University of Chicago Press.

60. Olakunle George, "The Inherited Mandates in African Literary Criticism," pp. 85–91, in *Relocating Agency: Modernity and African Letters.* Albany: SUNY Press, 2003. Copyright

© 2003 by State University of New York. Reprinted by permission of State University of New York Press. All rights reserved.

61. Florence Stratton, "Exclusionary Practices in African Literary Criticism," pp. 1–7, in *Contemporary African Literature and the Politics of Gender*. New York: Routledge, 1994. Copyright © 1994 by Florence Stratton. Reprinted by permission of the publisher through the Copyright Clearance Center, www.copyright.com.

62. Omafume F. Onoge, "Towards a Marxist Sociology of African Literature," pp. 50–63, in *Marxism and African Literature*, ed. Georg M. Gugelberger. Trenton, NJ: Africa World Press, 1985.

63. Ngugi wa Thiong'O, "Writers in Politics: The Power of Words and the Words of Power," pp. 67–77, in *Writers in Politics: A Re-Engagement with Issues of Literature and Society*. Oxford: James Currey, 1997. © 1997 by Ngugi wa Thiong'O. Reprinted by permission of James Currey Publishers.

64. Amilcar Cabral, "National Liberation and Culture," pp. 139–47 and 149–50, in *Unity and Struggle: Speeches and Writings*, trans. Michael Wolfers. London: Heinemann, 1980. Copyright © 1980 by Michael Wolfers. Reprinted by permission of Michael Wolfers.

65. Agostinho Neto, "Concerning National Culture," *Ideologies and Literature* II.10 (Sept–Oct 1979): 12–15.

66. Ayi Kwei Armah, "Masks and Marx." *Presénce Africaine* 131 (1985): 37–49.

67. Chidi Amuta, "Marxism and African Literature," pp. 52–6 and 72–5, in *The Theory of African Literature: Implications for Practical Criticism*. London: Zed Books, 1989. © 1989 by Chidi Amuta. Reprinted by permission of Zed Books.

68. Ama Ata Aidoo, "To Be an African Woman Writer – An Overview and a Detail," pp. 157–65, in *Criticism and Ideology: Second African Writers' Conference, Stockholm 1986*, ed. Kirsten H. Petersen. Uppsala: Scandinavian Institute of African Studies, 1988. © 1998 by Ama Ata Aidoo and Nordiska Afrikainstitutet. Reprinted by permission of The Nordic Africa Institute, Uppsala.

69. Nawal El Saadawi, "The Heroine in Arab Literature," pp. 160–6, in *The Hidden Face of Eve*. London: Zed Books, 1980. Copyright © 1980 by Nawal El Saadawi. Reprinted by permission of Zed Books.

70. Flora Nwapa, "Women and Creative Writing in Africa," pp. 89–99, in *Sisterhood, Feminisms and Power: Feminism and Power from Africa to the Diaspora*, ed. O. Nnaemeka. Trenton, NJ: Africa World Press, 1998.

71. Lauretta Ngcobo, "African Motherhood – Myth and Reality," pp. 141–51, in *Criticism and Ideology: Second African Writers' Conference, Stockholm 1986*, ed. Kirsten H. Petersen. Uppsala: Scandinavian Institute of African Studies, 1988. © 1998 by Lauretta Ngcobo and Nordiska Afrikainstitutet. Reprinted by permission of The Nordic Africa Institute, Uppsala.

72. Molara Ogundipe-Leslie, " 'Stiwanism: Feminism in an African Context," pp. 214–26, 229–30, in *Recreating Ourselves: African Women and Critical Transformations*. Trenton, NJ: Africa World Press, 1994.

73. Buchi Emecheta, "Feminism with a small 'f'!," pp. 173–81, in *Criticism and Ideology: Second African Writers' Conference, Stockholm 1986*, ed. Kirsten H. Petersen. Uppsala: Scandinavian Institute of African Studies, 1988. © 1998 by Buchi Emecheta and Nordiska Afrikainstitutet. Reprinted by permission of The Nordic Africa Institute, Uppsala.

74. Yvonne Vera, "Writing Near the Bone," pp. 57–60, in *Word: On Being a (Woman) Writer*, ed. Jocelyn Burrell. New York: The Feminist Press, 2004. Feminist Press at CUNY. © 2004 by Yvonne Vera.

75. Carole Boyce Davies, "Some Notes on African Feminism," pp. 6–14, in *Ngambika: Studies of Women in African Literature*, ed. Carole Boyce Davies and Anne Adams Graves. Trenton: Africa World Press, 1986.

76. Obioma Nnaemeka, "Bringing African Women into the Classroom: Rethinking Pedagogy and Epistemology," pp. 304–9, 312–16, in *Borderwork: Feminist Engagements with Comparative Literature*, ed. Margaret R. Higonnet. Ithaca: Cornell University Press, 1994. Copyright © 1994 by Cornell University. Used by permission of the publisher, Cornell University Press.

77. Uzo Esonwanne, "Enlightenment Epistemology," pp. 88–95, in *The Politics of (M)Othering: Womanhood, Identity, and Resistance in African Literature*, ed. Obioma Nnaemeka. New York: Routledge, 1997. Copyright © 1997 by Uzo Esonwanne. Reprinted by permission of the publisher through the Copyright Clearance Center, www.copyright.com.

78. Ato Quayson, "Feminism, Postcolonialism and the Contradictory Orders of Modernity," pp. 103–6, 122–6, in *Postcolonialism: Theory, Practice or Process?* Cambridge: Polity, 2000. Copyright © 2000 by Ato Quayson. Reprinted by permission of Polity Press.

79. Sunday O. Anozie, "Genetic Structuralism as a Critical Technique (Notes Toward a Sociological Theory of the African Novel)," *The Conch* 3.1 (March 1971): 37–42.

80. Abiola Irele, "In Praise of Alienation," pp. 201–3, 214–24, in *The Surreptitious Speech: Présence Africaine and the Politics of Otherness*, 1947–1987, ed. V. Y. Mudimbe. Chicago: University of Chicago Press, 1992. Copyright © 1992 by the University of Chicago. Reprinted by permission of The University of Chicago Press.

81. Biodun Jeyifo, "In the Wake of Colonialism and Modernity," *Anglophonia/Caliban* 7 (2000): 78–84. Reprinted by permission of Éditions Presses Universitaires du Mirail.

82. Simon Gikandi, "Poststructuralism and Postcolonial Discourse," pp. 97–104, in *The Cambridge Companion to Postcolonial Literary Studies*, ed. Neil Lazarus. Cambridge: Cambridge University Press, 2004. Copyright © 2004 by Cambridge University Press, reprinted with permission of the publisher and author.

83. Robert J. C. Young, "Subjectivity and History: Derrida in Algeria," pp. 411–16, in *Postcolonialism: An Historical Introduction*. Oxford: Blackwell, 2001. Copyright © 2001 by Robert J. C. Young. Reprinted by permission of Blackwell Publishing.

84. Anne McClintock, "The Angel of Progress: Pitfalls of the Term 'Post-colonialism'," in *Social Text*, Volume 10, no. 2, pp. 1–15. Copyright © 1992 by Duke University Press. All rights reserved. Used by permission of the publisher.

85. Tejumola Olaniyan, "Postmodernity, Postcoloniality, and African Studies," pp. 39–53, in *Postmodernism, Postcoloniality, and African Studies*, ed. Zine Magubane. Trenton, NJ: Africa World Press, 2003.

86. Ato Quayson, "Postcolonialism and Postmodernism," pp. 132–41, in *Postcolonialism: Theory, Practice or Process?* Cambridge: Polity, 2000. © 2000 by Ato Quayson. Reprinted by permission of Polity Press.

87. Kwame A. Appiah, "Is the Post- in Postmodernism the Post- in Postcolonial?," *Critical Inquiry* 17.2 (Winter 1991): 336–44, 346–50, 352–4. Copyright © 1991 by The University of Chicago. Reprinted by permission of The University of Chicago Press.

88. Lewis Nkosi, "Postmodernism and Black Writing in South Africa," pp. 75–80, in *Writing South Africa: Literature, Apartheid, and Democracy, 1970–1995*, ed. Derek Attridge and Rosemary Jolly. Cambridge: Cambridge University Press, 1998. Copyright © 1998 Cambridge University Press, reprinted with permission of the publisher and author.

89. Karin Barber, "African Language Literature and Postcolonial Criticism," *Research in African Literatures* 26.4 (Winter 1995): 3–11. © 1995. Reprinted by permission of Indiana University Press and the author.

90. William Slaymaker, "Ecoing the Other(s): The Call of the Global Green and Black African Responses," *PMLA* 116.1 (2001): 129, 132–40. Copyright © 2001 by the Modern Language Association of America. Reprinted by permission of the Modern Language Association of America.

92. Juliana Makuchi Nfah-Abbenyi, "Ecological Postcolonialism in African Women's Literature," pp. 344–9, in *Literature of Nature: An International Sourcebook*, ed. Patrick Murphy. Chicago: Fitzroy Dearborn Publishers, 1998. Copyright © 1998 by Juliana Makuchi Nfah-Abbenyi. Reprinted by permission of Routledge/Taylor & Francis Group, LLC.

93. Rob Nixon, "Environmentalism and Postcolonialism," pp. 233–8, 242–4, 247–8, in *Postcolonial Studies and Beyond*, ed. A. Loomba, Suvir Kaul, M. Bunzl, A. Burton and J. Esty. Durham: Duke University Press, 2005. Copyright © 2005 by Duke University Press. All rights reserved. Used by permission of the publisher.

94. Chris Dunton, " 'Wheyting Be Dat?': The Treatment of Homosexuality in African Literature," *Research in African Literatures* 20.3 (Fall, 1989): 422–8, 444–5. Copyright © 1989. Reprinted by permission of Indiana University Press and the author.

95. Gaurav Desai, "Out in Africa," pp. 120–8, in *Sex Positives? The Cultural Politics of Dissident Sexualities (Genders 25)*, eds. Thomas Foster, Carol Siegel, and Ellen E. Berry. New York: New York University Press, 1997. © 1997 by New York University Press. Reprinted by permission of the author.

96. Juliana Makuchi Nfah-Abbenyi, "Toward a Lesbian Continuum? Or Reclaiming the Erotic," pp. 90–6, in *Gender in African Women's Writing: Identity, Sexuality and Difference*. Bloomington: Indiana University Press, 1997. Copyright © 1997 by Juliana Makuchi Nfah-Abbenyi. Reprinted by permission of Indiana University Press and the author.

Excerpt from Felix Mnthali, "Letter to a Feminist Friend." First published in *Marang*, Volume IV, 1983, pp. 48–49. © 1983 by Felix Mnthali. Reprinted by permission of the author.

Introduction

Tejumola Olaniyan and Ato Quayson

African literature today enjoys a reputation far wider than its age and circumstances would ordinarily suggest, and continues to be a major propelling force in the growth of more global studies such as postcolonial literary and cultural studies. Unfortunately, the same could not be said of African literary criticism and theory, which has been very much invisible in the current expanding interest in African literature, especially in Europe and North America. The invisibility is marked most significantly by the fact that while anthologies of African fiction, poetry, and drama and even republications of old and out-of-print literary texts are being produced, there is not a single anthology of African literary criticism and theory in existence, until this volume. Yet, *scholarly* speaking, African literary and critical production are not discrete entities but in a relationship of both supportive and critical, mutually affective intimacy. They are part of the same tradition of creative African letters growing out of and responding to the same contexts and pressures, and addressing similar concerns. African literary criticism and theory is the primary and immediate intellectual context for understanding African literature. Writing in a Nigerian newspaper about a dozen years ago, the distinguished critic, Biodun Jeyifo, lamented what he called the "homeless-ness" of the writings of African literary theorists and critics: the fact that such writings exist mainly in disparate journals, essay collections, and hard-to-find books scattered both inside and especially outside the continent. The resulting difficulty of easy access, both to scholars and students in training, has hampered a more lively and active intellectual environment, and, overall, the development of a more robust critical and theoretical tradition. It is the goal of the proposed anthology to redress the glaring lack, construct an easily accessible "home" for the canonical statements of African literary criticism and theory, and thereby help foster a more vigorous discursive tradition.

Like all excellent anthologies of its kind, the immediate and practical origin of this volume began in the classroom, which is also its ultimate destination. Its design has been influenced by a course on the subject that Tejumola Olaniyan, one of the co-editors, began teaching several years ago. The course was designed as a comprehensive introduction for both graduate and undergraduate students with or without prior experience in literary theory, African literary theory, or African literature. First, it took Olaniyan the whole of the preceding summer to track down relevant classic materials and investigate promising others.

And, second, a few weeks before the beginning of the semester, he began receiving emails from prospective students asking whether the course was or was not "really about New Criticism, postmodernism, new historicism, feminism, and the like." After all, what else could "theory" be? To them, it was as if, why give a strange title yoking "theory" and "African literature" together in a course? They had heard of "theory," of course, and also "African literature"; in fact, they knew or had taken courses that simply said "literary theory" or "literary theory and criticism," but they were not quite sure what a course adding "African" to these titles was or would look like. Because the two problems of the absence of a handy source of materials as obtains in other literary-critical traditions, and a widespread ignorance of the subject matter, are related, we have devised an anthology that usefully addresses them at both pedagogical and methodological levels.

Pedagogically, we have identified and gathered here a very wide array of themes, concerns, and preoccupations that are predominant in African literary discourse. And to critically and conceptually illustrate them is an even wider array of articles in each instance and from diverse points of view. To go through the anthology then is to get an in-depth training on the contexts and conditions of production and critical appreciation of African literature as an aesthetic object and as a social phenomenon. Methodologically, our selections both of themes and illustrative essays emphasize the history, production, circulation, circumstances, and preoccupations of modern African literary discourse that underscore the uniqueness of the tradition as well as its linkages and similarities to and with other traditions.

What we offer here is as strikingly comprehensive an anthology as possible in a first-time outing and given the existing conditions of access of African literary studies to major publishing outlets. This point needs no elaboration, but suffice to say that there are many essays we thought worthy but could not include due to space limitations. The selections we have made provide both a detailed overview as well as an extensive meticulous elaboration of African literary-critical and theoretical tradition. Partly because the anthology would be the first and only one of its kind for many years, and partly because it would remain as a main book of record on its subject, we have arranged the materials in such a way as to map a loose chronological development of the tradition. This has the advantage of providing a coherent, albeit contingent, narrative with a critical historical sense of emergence, trans-formations, and directions, as well as of the intricate relationships among the concerns and schools and critical orientations.

We are very much aware that "theory" is generally stereotyped for its "inaccessibility" and "unreadability" by many undergraduates, graduate students, and scholars. Hence, without sacrificing the profundity of insight, we also considered matters of style and, in fact, most of the authors of our selections are elegant prose stylists. Indeed, not a few of the students who have studied in class much of the materials collected here noted at the end – against the stereotype of "theory" they came to the class with – the lucidity with which complex conceptual issues are pondered and articulated in the readings. (Their confessed greatest revelation, though, was that the readings show them that there is actually some-thing "very substantive at stake in and behind the theories"; and that even when the language is difficult, the often "socially-oriented issues being addressed make the abstract discussions come alive and interesting." Perhaps, if English departments realize it, African literary theory and criticism can actually be used as an introduction to interest students in literary theory in general!) The anthology will give students a solid grounding in African literary criticism and theory as well as literary theory more generally. If the cited revelatory statements are at all representative, many students will value the unique perspectives on literary theory in general that African literary theory and criticism gives them, while the unpretentious "social interventionist" orientation of the tradition will teach them the fundamental reason why human beings think conceptually: to affect their reality in one way or the other. The current negative stereotypes of theory have been so enduring because of the general perception of its "distance" from or "irrelevance" to "real life." For teachers in the field, the anthology will be an indispensable compendium both for their teaching and their scholarship. Colleagues at conferences have lamented endlessly the absence of such a book, especially for teaching purposes. Now their search is over and they can begin to expand their course offerings.

A few notes of clarification are in order. First, we conceive of literary "criticism" as the systematic explication, analysis, and interpretation of literary works. Literary "theory," on the other hand, is a second order or meta-level reflection on literature and literary criticism; the philosophy of the emergence and evolution, analysis, interpretation and evaluation of literature and literary criticism. Both practices are united by certain levels of rigor, abstraction and extrapolation, even if in different degrees. Academic literary studies – as opposed to, say, newspaper reviews, for example – frequently shift gears from one to the other often in the same essay; hence to attempt to separate them is to fall into pedantry. Second, and finally, we have composed brief introductions to the chapters. Our goal is not to provide a summary of the listed selections. To do that judiciously in the short "headnote" space available is not only impossible but also counterproductive to the kind of rewarding engagement we imagined between the anthology and its readers. Instead, we have provided a portable summation of the many contexts of the section themes as a way of helping readers to make deeper historical and intellectual sense of the problematic in focus.

Part I

Backgrounds

One feature that makes African literary-critical discourse a most exciting but also complex area of study is its multiple determinations. The questions that demand immediate attention as preliminary introduction range from the obvious to the rarefied. How is it that most of what is known as "African literature," both within Africa itself and outside, is originally written in European languages? What are the other literary traditions on the continent? Given the predominance of orality in African cultures, what is the place of writing in Africa? What are the relations between African and European languages in the constitution of what most people know as African literature? And, given the imperial catalyst and context that brought the two bodies of languages together, what is the nature of that specific conjuncture and what is its impact, in both content and form, on the imaginative literature that emerged afterward? Beyond the literature itself, what is the effect of that epochal event on the way the literature is imagined as an area of study and on the protocols of its theorizing and criticism? These questions and more are addressed by the essays gathered in this part. They collectively paint a vast canvas of the rich contexts, historical and contemporary, of African literary production and their intricate diversity in terms of language, thematic and formal preoccupations. The scholarly study of African literature, criticism and theory has suffered from either too much or too little acknowledgment of their many contexts; the selections in this part insist on the recognition of those contexts without ignoring the aesthetic and conceptual achievements of African creative and critical literary enterprise.

Chapter 1

Africa and Writing

Alain Ricard

Africa is everywhere inscribed. From rocks to masks, sculptures, pyramids, and manuscripts one needs but a stubborn and narrow-minded commitment to alphabetic writing to deny that the continent has left graphic marks of its history everywhere. Graphic representation is indeed present, but is it writing? One of the best books on the topic, written from an Asian angle, *Visible Speech*, subtitled "The Diverse Oneness of Writing Systems," by John De Francis, will be my guide on what can be called the "African chapter in the history of writing" (see Figure 1.1). Speech communities always generate material means to keep and retrieve information – this is not always writing. I will then reflect on graphic representation of sounds and the competition generated between several systems of graphic representation, before considering the contribution of a new kind of artist, the alphabet inventor, who belongs to the history of art, and not to the history of literature.

De Francis makes two useful distinctions that have a practical bearing on the analysis of writing in Africa. He divides students of graphic systems into two camps, the inclusivists and exclusivists, using as a discriminating criterion their definition of writing:

> Partial writing is a system of graphic symbols that can be used to convey only some thought. Full writing is a system of graphic symbols that can be used to convey any and all thought. Inclusivists believe that both partial and full writing should be called writing; exclusivists believe that only full writing deserve this label. (De Francis 1989: 5)

Africa is the continent with the largest number of recorded rock art paintings: from the Drakensberg and the Matopos in Southern Africa to the Air in the Sahara, the continent seems to have been populated by crowds of painters eager to record, to pray, or to celebrate. A recent book, *L'art rupestre dans le monde*, by Emmanuel Anati, director of Unesco World Archive of Rock Art (WARA), based on an extensive survey of several millions of pictures and engravings, attempts to demonstrate that cave paintings are indeed a kind of writing, and that we have here a universal code. Studies by Henri Lhote on the Sahara and by Henri Breuil and Victor Ellenberger in southern Africa are of course part of this model that

First published in *The Cambridge History of African and Caribbean Literature*, vol. 1, ed. Abiola Irele and Simon Gikandi, pp. 153–63. Cambridge: Cambridge University Press, 2004.

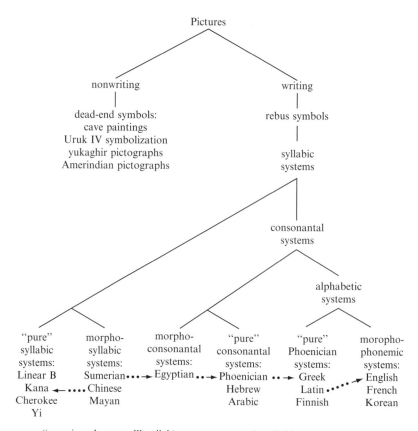

Figure 1.1   De Francis's Writing Classification Scheme. (From De Francis 1989.)

organizes graphic production according to two axes: a diachronic series taking into account the mode of subsistence of the artists and a synchronic dealing with the syntax of the pictograms. For Anati, some pictograms are ideograms and point to a universal code of graphic expression. In his view, Central Tanzania offers what is probably the longest sequence in the world of such images and is probably the "cradle" of this art (Anati 1997: 191–2). They are an exceptional testimony of the development process of thinking, of intellectual achievement, and of the cultural changes that have marked East Africa within the last 40,000 years. Especially impressive are the pictures of the Kundusi gatherers, with their heads masked, arranged in a triad, as if captivated by a special myth:

> Painted walls stand for a cathedral. In it are kept myths and legends, i.e., the capacity to keep a living relationship with the past or the future, which is usually done in palaces or sanctuaries.

> What is called the White Bantu style offers us a true historical archive, full of pictograms and ideograms, which remains to be interpreted. It provides extraordinary information on the concepts and beliefs of Bantu people.

(Anati 1997: 221; 223)

Anati's attempts to relate recent findings to Nyau ritual and dance are especially interesting: they allow us to read the paintings as pictograms of masks and dance and provide a bridge to present-day Chewa society (Anati 1997: 235; Probst 1997).

Africa is full of inscriptions of what the Angolan writer Luandino Vieira calls "illiterate writing." Paintings and engravings that encode stories and rituals belong to writing, if we adopt an inclusivist position. So does graphic symbolism in a different way. In her book, *Symboles graphiques en Afrique noire* (1992), C. Faik Nzuji undertakes a semiological analysis of the code of representation in different groups. This is an avenue that was explored long ago by Marcel Griaule and Germaine Dieterlen (1951). Dogon graphic symbolism has been the topic of several studies. It is indeed of the utmost importance because these symbols are in close relation to speech: they are produced within speech communities and demand interpretation by these communities. They fulfill one of the essential functions of writing: recording information and enabling its retrieval. They do this in a specialized way not available for any kind of messages. But many writing systems suffer from the same constraints. The "African Chapter in the History of Writing" (Raum 1943) is the study of ways to keep and retrieve information by graphic means:

> When Livingstone entered the country of the Lunda he observed that all trees along his route bore incisions, which are said to have resembled faces reminiscent of Egyptian pictures.
>
> (Raum 1943: 181)

These signs – incisions etched on trees and marked by colored dots on sticks – even if they are not pictographs (why not?) – fulfill some functions of writing, by reminding us of the words, spells, and prayers of those who inscribed them:

> Symbols are cultural creations that derive their meaning from rituals and cults, intense moments that punctuate the life of their users. In most cases, the body is marked, objects are carved, modeled to this end. Scarifications are thus messages sent to the ages.
>
> (Faik-Nzuji 1992: 122)

Marking of property, what Raum calls "crystallizing and registering thought processes" (1943: 9), as well as graphic and colored symbols are used by African peoples; they serve

> three main purposes: the perpetuation of expressions of emotional states and volitional tendencies in inscriptions which bear a magical, and sometimes religious, significance; the regulations of social relations by supplying distinguishing marks for private and clan property and by affording a medium of communication between individuals; finally graphic symbols serve to record the shape, name and number of objects as well as subjects of conversations and negotiations and thus act as instruments of intellectual processes.
>
> (1943: 187)

As is well known, graphic symbolism fulfills different functions: magical and numerical. Certain systems have been particularly well perfected, such as the Nsibidi script (Dalby 1986). Some objects elicit a verbal response and thus encapsulate a text. The systematic use of such objects can function like writing. It is especially important to recall these propositions to prevent a confusion of perspectives. These pictograms have been used for centuries. As David Dalby explains, the graphic symbolism of the Egyptian ideograms probably belongs to symbolic repertoires long used in Africa, whether on rock, on wood, or on skin. The Egyptian system of writing is of course full writing, capable of recording any thought: it recorded a literature used in an actual society. These pictographs have been enriched by what De Francis calls the rebus principle:

> Pictographs used as pictographs lead nowhere. Pictographs used as phonetic symbols lead to full writing... The rebus principle formed the basis of three systems of writing, generally thought to have been independently developed, which were created at intervals of about fifteen hundred years: first by the Sumerians about 3000 BC, then by the Chinese about 1500 BC, and last by the Mayas about the beginning of our era.
>
> (1989: 50)

As De Francis demonstrates convincingly – and paradoxically for those with a superficial and often ideological knowledge of Chinese writing – Chinese ideograms note essentially the sounds of syllables, while Egyptian hieroglyphs note the sounds of consonants. Of course not all the system is phonetically based but it has a central phonetic component, and it is precisely this that makes it capable of recording any kind of thought, of being full writing. The operation of the "rebus principle," substituting images of things to represent the sounds of their names, is the key to the development of a writing system. Pictograms serve to complete the picture, to enrich, to make the texts precise. The oldest written African language is thus Egyptian, to which we can add Nubian. The Meroe pyramids and the Sudan desert have yielded stones with inscriptions, allowing us to decipher Meroitic script but not to understand the language:

> In addition to its use in religious contexts, Meroitic was without doubt also the written language of both the administration and of daily life.
>   The variety of preserved inscribed monuments is so great that we can assume both knowledge and use of writing for a significant portion of the population . . . a comprehensive body of source material is now at hand for the Meroitic Period of the kingdom. Its value, however, is certainly weakened by the fact that the texts can be read, but not translated. A few basic rules of the linguistic structure are recognizable, showing that Meroitic might belong to a group of northern Sudanese languages to which Nubian is also ascribed. But the chronological and genetic distance from these languages is so great that not much help can be expected by making comparisons. The meaning of divine and personal names, place-names, and individual titles can be grasped, especially in those cases that stem from Egyptian. Among these are words like . . . *ato* ("water"), *at* ("bread").
>
> (Priese 1996: 253)

The Kingdom of Kush and its capital Kerma were in dynastic times (25–15 centuries BCE) at the center of an ancient Nubian empire and of the relations between Egypt and Black Africa. The inscriptions found are written in Egyptian, but Meroe, the successor kingdom, had its own written language. Written with a selection of Egyptian demotic hieroglyphs, it is indeed an African language, related to languages still spoken in the area. But it is also fascinating by reason of the mystery it presents: we know the consonants and the vowels but we cannot organize the discourse, as if the written image of the language were too far removed from an actual language. Many African languages have been written with rather inadequate systems: perhaps Meroe was the first one of the series and this is the cause of its present opacity.

The highly tonal, largely monosyllabic West African coastal languages would probably need something like the Chinese system to be efficiently written, whereas the class and tone languages of the Bantu would certainly be reduced to bare consonantal skeletons in the Egyptian writing system. In other words, these languages need another approach of representation where phonemic analysis would go along with symbolic representation. It is already difficult to write vowels, with aperture and length: how can we represent pitch as well in a phonemic (or alphabetic) system? The Vietnamese have succeeded in a context of an exceptionally strong feeling of national consciousness, ready to bear many sacrifices. The balance between phonemic and other kinds of representation (symbolic, pictographic) in a system is achieved over centuries: a writing system does not live divorced from a society. It is very important to realize, for instance, that a system which looks cumbersome and inefficient, like the hieroglyphs, had special advantages for the world within which it was required to function:

> The central complaint is that the Egyptians evidently lacking in imagination, failed to take what is deemed to be the obvious step: simply to use their uniconsonantal signs in the manner of an alphabet, abandoning the other types of signs. Such criticism, which is based essentially on the assumed superiority of alphabetic script over all others, is quite misplaced. It not only overrates the efficiency of alphabetic systems, it also undervalues the merits of others. The Egyptian system has the disadvantage of containing a relatively large number of signs. In compensation however, its mixed orthography creates visually distinctive word patterns that actually enhance legibility.
>
> (Davies 1987: 35)

In Africa only Egyptian, Nubian, Ge'ez, and Tamazight have, over the centuries, developed their own systems of full writing. A literature, a community of writers and readers were thus created. The Ethiopian syllabary (whether in Ge'ez or in Amharic) is the only syllabary still in practical use in Africa today. Other African languages have borrowed scripts, whether Arabic or Roman. In the last two centuries, inventions of specific syllabaries, in the Mande area for instance (Vai syllabary), have occurred in a context of intensive culture contact with Islam, but remained local and did not produce a literature (Dalby 1970). All these inventors should be remembered as graphic artists more than as writers or inventors. Only the Bamun sultan Njoya, at the beginning of the twentieth century, devised a syllabary in which original works of history were written; unfortunately the development of this original creation was stopped by the destruction of his printing shop at the time of French colonization. Arabic itself was probably the most commonly used written language in Africa up to the nineteenth century. It was written in Timbuktu in the fifteenth century and there still exists an Arabic literature in West Africa.

To borrow a script is not to borrow a language, and some adaptations are necessary. Arabic, for instance, has only three vowels, while many African languages have more (for instance, Kiswahili has five vowels) and some even have tones. Fula and Hausa were written in the Arabic script, using the *ajami* script created in the eighteenth century; as was Kiswahili on the Indian Ocean. But of course these adaptations are not without problems. As Amadou Hampaté Bâ, a well-known Islamic scholar as well as francophone writer put it:

> We do not even know for how long Fula was written in Arabic script... No linguistic study of the western system had been made to fix for each phoneme a specific sign... So writing varied

with each different area. The result was that a writer who did not know his text by heart had difficulties rereading his text six months later…The only known exception is the Futa Jallon where, thanks to a long practice of writing, people could reread themselves, not without difficulties.

(Bâ 1972: 28–9, my translation)

Arabic does not have certain phonemes, for instance -ng, so often present in Bantu languages. Tippu Tip, the famous slave dealer from Zanzibar wrote his autobiography in Kiswahili in 1899 using the Arabic script and the text was transliterated by the German Consul and published in romanized Kiswahili (Whiteley 1958) as well as in European languages; it is probably one of the first Swahili narratives in which Islam is not the dominant theme. Many Swahili Arabic-script manuscripts have been transliterated to become romanized books – Al Inkishafi, for instance, which is probably the greatest Swahili poem, written at the beginning of the nineteenth century – and spread in book form in 1939 thanks to W. Hitchens's work.

There has been a large movement towards romanization, along with the spread of colonial education and missionary Christian activity, not so much to convert Muslims to Christianity as to prevent the conversion of non-Muslim Africans to Islam by providing alternative ways of writing their languages, detached from any association with Arabic. This was the rationale for writing down in Roman script many African languages, in Nigeria especially. At the same time a romanized version of the Hausa script – boko – was printed and widely disseminated. It may have been a colonial plot in the 1930s, but its continuing success is due to other factors, especially its standardization. Let us also remember that the Turkish language was romanized at the same time. The same is true for Kiswahili, which was used as a medium by Catholic missionaries at the end of the nineteenth century, while Protestants were more reluctant to engage in the theological dialogue with Islam that this kind of linguistic appropriation required, since a large part of Swahili conceptual vocabulary came from Arabic. Finally, Somali was romanized in the 1970s and became the official language of the defunct Socialist Republic of Somalia.

The switch from Arabic to Roman script inspired a massive effort to write down previously unwritten languages. Some posed rather complex problems, as can be seen from the chart showing the different ways of writing down Khoi sounds such as clicks (see Figure 1.2). The creation of an International Phonetic Alphabet, in 1854, provided a useful comparative tool to compare different languages, previously recorded in rather haphazard ways, according to the different linguistic backgrounds of their students. French missionaries would write -ch while English would write -sh: Thomas Mofolo behaved as a proper student of the Paris Mission when he wrote the name of the Zulu hero Chaka (ch-French spelling of the Zulu fricative) and not Shaka.

The spread of writing and especially of printing has been the task of missions in Africa (see Coldham 1966) but without some measure of agreement on transcription, the dissemination of the written version of each African language is heavily handicapped. The Yoruba reached an agreement between themselves in 1875 (see Ade Ajayi 1960), thanks to the pioneering work of Bishop Samuel Ajayi Crowther, linguist, explorer, translator, and a Yoruba by birth: a fact that helped considerably the development of their written literature. Religious differences made for different writing systems, based on conventions of the European tongues. Sometimes nationalistic concerns were in force, and lasted long, as demonstrated

Nos.	TITLES.	Date.	Catal.	Dent	Lat.	Gutt.	Pal.
	PUBLICATIONS AND MANUSCRIPTS.			**CLICKS**			
1	Sir Thomas Harbert, Bart........	1638	28.	i s t			
2	G. Fr. Wrede, Compendium....	1664	*30.				
3	God Guil Leibnitii, Collect....	1717	35.	t ?		k ?	
4	M. P. Kolbe's Travels	1719	33.	⌒ (or) ~			
5	Andrew Sparrmann, M.D........	1782	23.	t '			
6	C. P. Thunberg, M.D..............	1789	24.	a	A	á	
7	F. Le Vaillnnt, Travels............	1790	25.	∧	V		Δ
8	John Barrow, F.R.S................	1801	26.	—		ᴗ	
9	Dr. van der Kemp, Catech.......	1805	*21.	By 6 differ. Numer.			
10	H. Lichtenstein, M.D..............	1808	18. .19.	t'¹	t'²		t'³
11	Kafix and Zulu Books. since...	1824	43.216.	o	x	q	(qo)
12	Will. J. Burcheil, Travels.........	1824	20.	)	(	((	
13	Joh. Leon. Ebner, Traveks	1829	*	——			
14	J. H. Schmelen, Mann., before	1830	10.	—	)	|	⌒
15	H. C. Knudsen, Spell-book......	1842	5. 6.	·	)	))	:
16	H. C. Knudsen, Luke's Gospel	1846	15.7.4.	·	)	(	:
17	C. F. Wuras, Catech., before...	1848	21.	·	)	(	
18	C. F. Wuras, Grammar...........	1850	16.	f	y	q	v
19	H. P. S. Schreuder, Zulu Gr....	1850	178.	⅄	≷	≶	
20	R. Lepains, Manuscript...........	1853		10	1X	(X)	10
21	Rich. Lepains, Stand Alphab...	1854		/	//	!	/
22	F. H. Vollmer, Spelling-book...	1854	8.12.	∇	q	q	x
23	Rhenish Mission Conference...	1856		/	//	⊬	≠
24	Henry Thindall, Grammar, &c	1856	2. 3.	c	x	q	v
25	Wm. H. L. Bleek., Rese., &c....	1857	215.56.	c	x	q	o
26	C. F. Wuras, Manuscript.........	1857	16.21.d	∧	π	⌒	
27	Manuscript Notes...................		6.	tg	kl	g kt	kt
28	J. W. Gibbe, Remarks, &c......	1852	174.	□	□]	吕	

Figure 1.2 Different ways of writing sounds. (From Bleek 1958.)

by the differences between South African and Lesotho spellings (*Shaka* or *Chaka*) of the same language, Sesotho. Today the size of the South African Sotho market is a powerful magnet that has helped to convert the orthography of Lesotho publishers, without any linguistic conference.

The issues in graphization leave us with a legacy of competition between churches and between states. The Gu people of Porto Novo (Benin Republic) never wrote their language like their Yoruba neighbors (Nigeria): to divide was a prerequisite of imperial rule and the invention of different graphic forms of mutually understandable languages was a great tool of division between competing powers (see Ricard 1995: 145–9).

In a typically romantic worldview, writing the language of an African group – of any group – meant, in the nineteenth century, bringing this group to light, making it emerge from the Dark Ages. The world was classified according to the "Great Divide": with Gutenberg the "Night has passed away and the Day has come," sings the choir in Mendelssohn's Second Symphony performed in 1840 to commemorate the four-hundredth anniversary of the invention of the movable type (Vail and White 1991: 1). A general theory of graphic expression cannot consider alphabetic writing to be the apex of human culture. It should reject well-known theories that have a rather ethnocentric bias: other paths have been followed by other cultures, in Asia or in Africa, for instance, but this is often forgotten. Misconceptions regarding non-alphabetic systems have long been the rule, such as believing in the totally non-phonetic nature of Chinese writing (Goody and Watt 1972: 349–52) and assigning, by contrast, to the alphabet the property of developing logical methods. As De Francis rightly comments: "There is in this approach [Goody and Watt's] no concrete analysis of why . . . the consonant-plus-vowel system should be singled out as the primary factor in the intellectual ascendancy of Greece over its Near Eastern neighbors, who had achieved their inferior literacy half a millennium earlier" (De Francis 1989: 245). These Manichean oppositions marked by remnants of an Orientalist posture have been even stronger in the African case and have prevented research from looking at the Egyptian data in an African context.

Going back to our inclusivist position we can safely say that the African chapter in the history of writing is probably one of the longest in human history and that the obsession with orality – what Leroy Vail and Landeg White (1991) call "the invention of oral man" – is more an ideological and political posture than a well-informed theoretical stand.

References

Ade Ajayi, J. F. 1960. "How Yoruba Was Reduced to Writing." *Odu* 8: 49–58.

Anati, Emmanuel. 1997. *L'art rupestre dans le monde. Imaginaire de la préhistoire.* Paris: Larousse.

Bâ, Amadou Hampaté. 1972. *Aspects de la civilisation africaine.* Paris: Présence Africaine.

Battestini, Simon. 1997. *Ecriture et texte.* Québec: Presses de l'Université Laval/Paris: Présence Africaine.

Bleek, Wm. H., comp. 1858. *The Library of His Excellency Sir George Grey, K. C. B., Vol. 1, Part I: Africa, Philology.* London, Leipzig.

Breuil, Henri. Preface to Ellenberger, Victor. 1952. *La fin tragique des Bushmen.* Paris: Amiot-Dumont.

Celenko, Theodore, ed. 1996. *Egypt in Africa.* Bloomington: Indiana University Press.

Coldham, Geraldine. 1966. *A Bibliography of Scriptures in African Languages.* 2 vols. London: British and Foreign Bible Society.

Dalby, David. 1984. *Le clavier international de Niamey.* Paris: ACCT. 1986. *L'Afrique et la lettre.* Lagos: Centre culturel français, Fête de la lettre/Paris: Karthala.

Dalby, David, ed. 1970. *Language and History in Africa.* London: Frank Cass.

Davies, W. V. 1987. *Reading the Past: Egyptian Hieroglyphs.* London: British Museum.

Deacon, Jeanette, and Thomas Dowson, eds. 1996. *Xam Bushmen and the Bleek and Lloyd Collection.* Johannesburg: Witwatersrand University Press.

De Francis, John. 1989. *Visible Speech: The Diverse Oneness of Writing Systems.* Honolulu: University of Hawaii Press.

Ellenberger, Victor. 1952. *La fin tragique des Bushmen*. Paris: Amiot-Dumont.

Faik-Nzuji, Clémentine Madiya. 1992. *Symboles graphiques en Afrique noire*. Paris: Karthala/Louvain: Ciltade.

Fishman, J., Charles Ferguson, and J. Das Gupta, eds. 1968. *Language Problems of Developing Nations*. New York: John Wiley.

Geary, Christraud. 1994. *King Njoya's Gift, a Beaded Sculpture from the Bamum Kingdom Cameroon in the National Museum of African Art*. Washington, DC: National Museum of African Art, Smithsonian Institution.

Gérard, Albert. 1981. *African Languages Literatures*. Harlow: Longman.

Goody, Jack, and Ian Watt. 1972. "The Consequences of Literacy." In *Language and Social Context: Selected Readings*. Ed. Pier Paolo Gilioli. Harmondsworth: Penguin: 311–57. Rpt. from *Comparative Studies in Society and History* 5 (1962–63): 304–26, 332–45.

Griaule, Marcel, and Germaine Dieterlen. 1951. *Signes graphiques soudanais*. Paris: Hermann.

Kendall, Timothy. 1997. *Kerma and the Kingdom of Kush 2500–1500 BC: The Archeological Discovery of an Ancient Nubian Empire*. Washington, DC: National Museum of African Art, Smithsonian Institution.

Kihore, Yaredi M. 1984. "Kiswahili katika hati za Kiarabu." *Mulika* 16: 38–45.

Lhote, Henri. 1972. *Les gravures du Nord Ouest de l'Aïr*. Paris: Arts et métiers graphiques.

Lacroix, P. F. 1965. *Poésie peule de l'Adamawa*. Classiques africains. Paris: Julliard.

Nasir, Sayyid Abdallah A. 1972. *Al Inkishafi, The Soul's Awakening*. Ed. W. Hitchens. Nairobi: Oxford University Press.

Niangoran-Bouah, G. 1984. *L'univers akan des poids à peser l'or*. Abidjan: Nouvelles éditions africaines.

Priese, Karl-Heinz. 1996. "Meroitic Writing and Language." In *Sudan: Ancient Kingdoms of the Nile*. Ed. Dietrich Wildung. Paris: Flammarion: 253–62.

Probst, Peter. 1997. "Danser le sida. Spectacle du nyau et culture populaire chewa dans le centre du Malawi." In *Les arts de la rue. Autrepart*, vol. 1. Ed. Michel Agier and Alain Ricard. *Cahiers des sciences humaines* (IRD): 91–112.

Raum, O. F. 1943. "The African Chapter in the History of Writing." *African Studies* 2: 178–92.

Ricard, Alain. 1995. *Littératures d'Afrique noire*. Paris: CNRS/Karthala.

Vail, Leroy, and Landeg White. 1991. *Power and the Praise Poem: Southern African Voices in History*. Charlottesville: University Press of Virginia; Oxford: James Currey.

Whiteley, Wilfred, trans. and ed. 1958. *Maisha ya Hamed bin Muhammed El Murjebi, yaani Tippu Pip*. Kampala, Nairobi, Dar es Salaam.

Wildung, Dietrich, ed. 1996. *Soudan, royaume sur le Nil*. Paris: Institut du monde arabe, Flammarion.

Yoruba Orthography Committee. 1969. *Kaaaro... oojiire, a Report on Yoruba Orthography*. Ibadan.

Zima, Petr. 1969. "Language, Script and Vernacular Literature in Africa." *African Language Review* 8: 212–24.

Chapter 2

Sub-Saharan Africa's Literary History in a Nutshell

Albert S. Gérard

[. . .]

The introduction of the writing skill to Africa was by no means a consequence of western colonisation. As a handful of historians and linguistic scholars have known all along, a substantial amount of poetry had been written in the Islamised areas of black Africa, using the Arabic script and language, or transliterating vernacular languages in the Arabic script. And prior to that, the written art had been known and widely practised in the oldest Christian country of the continent, Ethiopia. European influence thus found its proper place in initiating the third phase in a historical process that has lasted for nearly 2,000 years.

Several centuries before the beginning of the Christian era, Semitic migrants from southern Arabia came across the Red Sea and settled in the vicinity of Lake Tsana. They brought with them their own Sabaean script. Epigraphic evidence suggests that this was gradually altered to suit the new language that resulted from the fusion of the invaders' language with that of the original inhabitants. When the Ethiopian Christian Church was founded in the fourth century AD, political power was in the hands of the Aghazi people who had established the empire of Axum. It was their dialect, Ge'ez, which was used for translating the Gospels and other sacred books. As Ethiopia was Christianised by monks and missionaries belonging to the oriental churches, the country's religious life was under the control of the Coptic Patriarchate at Alexandria, and Ethiopian culture remained deeply religious, offering some resemblance to the spirit of Byzantine civilisation.

For a long time Ge'ez literature was limited to translations of religious books from the Greek: they included the Scriptures and the lives of the saints. Secular chronicles of the Ethiopian monarchs were also compiled. But the most important literary achievement in the language is a form of hymnal poetry known as *qenè*. It was appreciated as an edifying intellectual exercise because it was based on the 'wax and gold' principle, the gold being the esoteric meaning which is given poetic shape by being poured into the wax of the words.

First published in *Comparative Literature and African Literature*, ed. C. F. Swanepoel, pp. 24–31. Pretoria: Via Afrika, 1993.

By the 10th century AD, the centre of gravity of the empire had moved south to Amhara country. But although Amharic became the dominent dialect, Ge'ez remained in use for religious and scholarly writing. It was practised only by a thin layer of the population, an élite which was closely connected with the power of Church and State. As Ethiopia's culture tongue, its function was similar to that of Latin in western Europe and of Greek in the Byzantine empire.

Some writing was produced in Amharic in the 15th century. Because of its secular inspiration it differs highly from Ge'ez poetry. It consists mainly of war songs, praise poems in honour of the political and military rulers of the time. But at the end of the 19th century, emperor Tweodros realised that the conservative theocratic structure of the country was anachronistic and that if Ethiopia was to preserve her independence in the face of Europe's encroachments in Africa, some modernisation was called for. This remained the policy of his successors Menelik II and Haile Selassie.

One aspect of this process is of particular relevance to our topic: the fact that the Ethiopian emperors encouraged the growth of a Western-type literature in Amharic. Thanks to the introduction of the printing press, a few novels had been published by the time Ethiopia was conquered by Italy (1936). The massacres perpetrated by Marshall Graziani destroyed a large part of the Ethiopian élite, but after the Fascist defeat in 1941, a new generation of writers came to the fore and Amharic writing was resumed and flourished with a remarkable number of novels and plays reflecting the evolution of Ethiopian society.

While the written art was taking root in Christian Ethiopia, a second wave of literacy came from Arabia, this time as part of the stupendous expansion of Islam after *Hijra*. Western textbooks usually consider only one aspect of the spreading of the new religion: the conquest of Spain by Arab and Berber armies in the 7th century. But the Muslim creed and culture also spread over vast tracts of the African continent, bringing their language and script with them. The history of Islamic writing in black Africa exhibits two distinct patterns of development.

From time immemorial there must have been considerable trade going on between Arabia and the whole of the Indian Ocean area, especially the East African coast, Zanzibar and Madagascar. So far, however, we have little evidence regarding the early literary consequences of contact between Arab merchants and local cultures. That the Arabic script was known in Madagascar in the 15th century is established by the manuscripts which were brought to Europe by French explorers in the 17th century. Some of these texts are chronicles of important events in local political life. But it would seem that in later centuries the Arabic script was used chiefly for the making of talismans. On the other hand, many books may have been written by Islamic scholars and destroyed by the Christian missionaries in the 19th century, after King Radama I had opted in favour of the Roman script.

The most significant effects of Islamic influence in Eastern Africa occurred along the coastline and offshore islands of present-day Kenya and Tanzania. Here, close integration of immigrants of Arab stock into the native society and cultural cross-breeding between merchants and settlers from Arabia and the Persian Gulf area and the indigenous black population created a hybrid culture with its own, non-Arabic language, Swahili, which has a Bantu substratum with a strong admixture of Arabic elements.

There is much likelihood that writing was practised on the Swahili coast at an early date: the 14th-century Moroccan traveller Ibn Batuta mentions the presence of Islamic writers in the places he visited. No trace remains of such early writings, which may have been destroyed during the 16th and 17th centuries, when the Portuguese were controlling the Indian Ocean trade.

The earliest Swahili manuscripts we have can be dated from the early 18th century. In style and content they exhibit features which were to remain characteristic of imaginative writing in the language for two centuries: most 'classical' Swahili literature consists of verse epics known as *tendi*, dealing with the history of Islam and concentrating on events in the Prophet's life and on the holy wars of the 7th century. A few works recount episodes from the Old Testament. Much of this seems to be derived from popular chapbooks in Arabic which came from the Middle East. The function of such works was similar to that of much medieval literature in the West: to use the vernacular language in order to spread and popularise the history of the dominant religion. The first Swahili manuscripts were discovered and brought to Berlin by the missionary, explorer and linguist, Ludwig Krapf, in the mid-19th century, but they remained in obscurity until the Berlin Conference (1884–5) when the scramble for Africa gave them topical interest. Since then many of them have been published in Swahili and even translated into European languages.

While religious inspiration remained central to Swahili writing, a new orientation appeared at the beginning of the 19th century as a result of local political developments. The herald was one Muyaka who wrote polemical poetry directed against the suzerainty of the Omani sultans over the Swahili town of Mombasa. He is rightly claimed to have taken Swahili poetry from the mosque to the market-place, that is, he initiated poetic writing of purely secular inspiration. This poetry has often been regarded as nationalistic because its target was 'foreign' rule. But this is rather dubious as Muyaka was in the service of the governors of Mombasa, who were likewise of Omani origin. What matters is that from then on many writers also wrote about contemporary events, and in the course of the 19th century epic *tendi* were composed which dealt with the quarrels between coastal towns and the Sultan of Zanzibar.

This type of writing continued at the end of the century when Tanganyika had become a German colony; but the narrative verse composed about the resistance offered to the Germans by inland tribes which were not integrated into Swahili culture may have been commissioned by the German authorities. More significant, however, was the German's linguistic policy. They found that Swahili had become the *lingua franca* spread by Arab slave-traders over the whole of Tanganyika and beyond. Further, the ethnic structure of the colony was such that no other language could compete with Swahili for the status of administrative common language. They thus encouraged the teaching and writing of the language throughout the colony, paying the way for a nationalistic language policy in later days.

In Kenya, where Swahili literature had originated, it was developed spontaneously by the missionaries along the usual loose British lines, but when Tanganyika was taken over by the British after World War I, efforts were made to give Swahili the status of official *lingua franca* throughout British East Africa. In consequence of all this, Swahili literature, which had been of the *ajami* type – using the Arabic script for a non-Arab language – now resorted to the Roman script and a number of writers were encouraged to introduce western genres, especially the novel, which they did with limited success.

After independence the policy of interterritorial unity was soon abandoned. Under the leadership of Julius Nyerere, himself a noted scholar who had translated Shakespeare's *Julius Caesar* and *The Merchant of Venice*, Tanzania was the only country to adopt Swahili as its official language. The Institute of Swahili Research at the University of Dar es Salaam undertook to modernise the language so that it might become a suitable instrument for the expression and communication of 20th-century civilisation. One of the consequences of the encouragement given to the promotion of the language was the emergence of younger authors who have successfully rejected the conventions of traditional poetry. They have already produced a significant amount of original writing using a more personal style and dealing with topics of present-day interest.

Before closing this brief consideration of Islamic writing in eastern Africa, mention should be made of Somalia, a very special and exceptional case in the history of colonisation and of literacy. Although the Somali people are divided into a variety of often mutually hostile clans and sects, they are all Muslim nomads who speak closely-related dialects, thus forming an organic ethnic and cultural unity. Their oral art is important, but because of their nomadic habits, they had little opportunity to acquire literacy in the Arabic script, or, for that matter, in the Roman script.

The Somali-speaking populations were divided, at the end of the 19th century, between Italy, Britain, France (Djibouti) and Ethiopia (Ogaden). The small number of Somalis who became literate did so mostly in foreign languages. There were a few attempts at using the Arabic scripts in the late 19th century: the 'Mad Mullah' Abdille Hassan wrote *ajami-* type poetry as well as poetry in Arabic. The production of written works, however, remained very slight. It was only after the introduction of an official orthography in 1972 that Somalia could be expected to generate a written literature in her own language. Such a development is all the more likely to be encouraged by the government since a common literature would be a powerful factor of cohesion in a country which has suffered much by the divisiveness inherent in the colonial system. While the official language in the Republic of Djibouti is French, the civil servants in the early years of the Somali Republic were literate in Italian if they had been educated in the former Italian colony, or in English if they came from British Somaliland. While they communicated easily with one another orally since they all spoke some Somali dialect, written communications across the former colonial boundaries had to be translated from Italian into English and vice versa. It was obviously in the interest of national unity and practical efficiency that the Somali people – with their exceptional ethnic and linguistic homogeneousness – should be encouraged to use their own language for writing as well as for speaking. Such expectations have unfortunately failed to materialise.

In West Africa, the emergence and growth of Islamic writing followed an entirely different course. When the Muslims of the Maghreb were stopped at the battle of Poitiers (732) by an ancestor of Charlemagne, their attention turned southwards towards black Africa. The first black community to have been Islamised was the kingdom of Tekror in the Futa Toro near the mouth of the Senegal River. This was a prelude to the conquest of the Ghana empire in the late 11th century and to the Islamisation of the greater part of black West Africa.

There are many examples in history of military conquest leading to cultural (including linguistic and therefore literary) assimilation. The Romans spread Latin throughout Western Europe. The Spaniards and Portuguese imposed their languages throughout Latin America. In both cases, the vernacular languages were suppressed for several centuries. The Arabs likewise spread their language wherever they established their supremacy and they did so all the more fervently since Arabic was the sacred language used by God himself to dictate the Koran to the Prophet Mohammed.

During the decades following the Prophet's *hijra* in 622, military conquests by the Arabs in the Middle East and in North Africa had been synonymous with Islamisation and linguistic assimilation. Contrary to what had happened on the eastern coast, the literate culture that arose in the Sudanic area was in Arabic, one reason for this being that Sudanic Islam had inherited the strong fundamentalist trend that is central to Berber religion.

Two stages can be traced in the historical evolution of this West African literature. Until the late 18th century, the Arabic language remained the sole medium for the written art. This situation led to the emergence of Timbuctoo as a renowned centre of Islamic learning in the 14th, 15th and 16th centuries and to the composition of a large number of manuscripts there dealing, in Arabic verse, with the major disciplines of Muslim learning: religion, ethics, law, medicine, astronomy, logic, grammar, etc.

The impressive didactic literature which was produced in Timbuctoo was of multiracial authorship. The writers were a mixed lot, some originating from Egypt to Morocco, some from the West African empires of Mali, Songhay, Bornu and Kanem. Some were Negroes, some Arabs, some Berbers and some of hybrid origin. Together they were responsible for the flowering and international renown of the city as an intellectual centre, boasting a university which some have compared in its importance with the University of Louvain at the time. Many manuscripts have been discovered. Some have been translated into English or French, and more are still to be traced.

After the Moroccans had conquered Timbuctoo in 1591, a period of stagnation and decline set in. There was also a decline in Islamic fervour, especially among local rulers. It was as a reaction to this weakening of the faith that a Muslim revival started and grew throughout the 18th century. This initiated a new phase in the development of Islamic writing since the Fulani clerics who were the main agents of the revival realised that if they were to spread Islam to even deeper layers of the population and not only among the ruling and learned classes, it was necessary to give up the monopoly which Arabic had been enjoying for such a long time and to teach and preach in the languages actually spoken by the people. The habit presumably started in Arabic schools where the Koran was discussed in local parlance. This led to the emergence of written literature in several vernacular languages. The trend was started in the 18th century among the Fulani of the Futa Jalon in present-day Guinea. Their example was followed by other Fulani groups in the Sokoto empire, most notably in northern Nigeria and in the Adamawa region of northern Cameroon. But since the empire had superseded the Hausa kingdoms of northern Nigeria, Hausa was the second vernacular language to be used in writing. It has since grown to considerable proportions.

Present-day Hausa writers stick to their own language, which they transliterate either in the Arabic script (*ajami*) or the Roman script (*boko*). A number of them also compose verse in Arabic. But only an insignificant minority has found it advisable to resort to the European conqueror's language, English. Hausa can also boast an important literary journal, *Harsunan Nijeriya*, which is published at Admadu Bello University in Zaria.

At the end of the 19th century, a third West Africa language began to give rise to an *ajami*-type literature: this is Wolof, which has since become the *lingua franca* of Senegal. But contrary to what happened for Swahili and Hausa, Wolof writers have shown little inclination to modernise their medium: as in other former French colonies, creative authors prefer to resort to the European language.

In the main, however, it is to be observed that the Muslim cultures of black Africa have shown uncommon resilience to the impact of Europe, presumably because they are proudly grounded in one of the great religions of the world. Only two of those literatures – Swahili in the east and Hausa in the west – have submitted to various forms of modernisation, turning to the Roman script, availing themselves of the printing press, and adopting – although with great caution and even reluctance – such alien genres as prose fiction and stage drama. The reason for this special development seems to be that the territories where those literatures flourished were parts of the British Empire, whose representatives – unlike those of France, Portugal or Spain – gave genuine attention to the native languages and to the spreading of literacy in the African vernaculars.

This takes us to the third wave of literacy, which was to cover the whole of black Africa in the 19th and 20th centuries as a result of the European conquest. Actually, a beginning of a sort was made in the late 15th and early 16th centuries, when Portuguese sailors landed at the mouth of the Congo River and established relations with the local ruler, the Manicongo, in the name of their king. In a very short time, some of the subjects of the Manicongo had learned enough Portuguese to write official letters discussing co-operation between the two kingdoms. The Europeans were keen on ivory and the Africans on obtaining teachers.

On the other hand, some of the missionaries sent out to Christianise the 'pagans' tried to reduce the Kongo language to writing. They even had a vernacular catechism printed at the end of the 15th century. This promising type of relationship aborted, however, when it was discovered that it was more profitable to trade in slaves, since the Portuguese needed manpower for their plantations on Sao Tomé and even more in Brazil, where the Indians were adamant in their refusal to work for the white man.

[. . .]

Chapter 3

Politics, Culture, and Literary Form

Bernth Lindfors

The new literatures in English and French that have emerged in black Africa in the twentieth century have been profoundly influenced by politics. Indeed, one could argue that they have been generated and shaped by the same forces that have transformed much of the African continent during the past hundred years. Writers have served not only as chroniclers of contemporary political history but also as advocates of radical social change. Their works thus both reflect and project the course of Africa's cultural revolution.

Paradoxically, an African literature written in a European language is likely to be a more accurate barometer of fluctuations in national circumstances and mood than a literature written in an African language. One of the ironies of multilingualism in Africa is that the extraordinary number and variety of languages in most sub-Saharan nations make communication across ethnic and international boundaries difficult in anything but a colonial tongue. The writer who chooses to express himself in an African language will be addressing his message to a relatively small audience, merely a fraction of the total literate population in his country. Moreover, he may have to submit his work to prior censorship by church or state because missionary and government publishers may offer the only opportunities for publication in that language. Since such publishers tend to be interested primarily in providing reading matter for use in schools, an aspiring author may find himself compelled to write for young people instead of adults. In other words, he may be tongue-tied by the institutional constraints that inhibit open literary expression in his mother tongue.

An African author who chooses to write in a colonial language – particularly English or French – will be able to reach a much larger audience both at home and abroad and will not be prevented from articulating mature ideas that the church, state or school finds offensive. As a consequence, what he writes will be far more representative of the intellectual climate of his time and place than anything written in a local language for a smaller, younger and

First published in *African Textualities: Texts, Pre–texts, and Contexts of African Literature*, pp. 135–50. Trenton: Africa World Press, 1997.

less heterogeneous audience. He will be addressing a national audience because he will be communicating in a national language rather than an ethnic idiom (Achebe 1965: 27–30), and the international scope of his adopted tongue will carry his voice still farther. Only through European linguistic means will he be able to work effectively toward pan-African ends.

The Negritude writers were the first to prove this point. When asked why he and other francophone African poets wrote in French, Léopold Sédar Senghor replied:

> Because we are cultural half-castes, because, although we feel as Africans, we express ourselves as Frenchmen, because French is a language with a universal vocation, because our message is addressed to the Frenchmen of France as well as to other men, because French is a language of "graciousness and civility" . . . I know what its resources are because I have tasted and digested and taught it, and it is a language of the gods. Listen to Corneille, Lautréamont, Rimbaud, Péguy and Claudel. Listen to the great Hugo. The French language is a mighty organ capable of all tones and of all effects, from the softest mildness to the fulgurations of the storm. It is one by one, or all together, flute and oboe, trumpet and cannon. Again, French has given us the gift of its abstract words, so rare in our mother tongues, by which tears turn into precious stones. With us, words are naturally surrounded by an aura of sap and blood. French words are radiant with a thousand fires, like diamonds. Flares lighting up our night (94–5)

It was necessary to use such a combustible vehicle to bring home the explosive cultural message of Negritude "to the Frenchmen of France as well as to other men." Only a "language of the gods" could fully express the nuances of the new mythology that the "cultural half-castes" of French West Africa and the Antilles were beginning to propagate. Senghor and his apostles knew that one couldn't win converts to a syncretic pan-Negro faith by preaching only in Serer. The flares of French were needed to bring light to the entire black diaspora.

It is significant that the literary form chosen most often to carry this message was the surrealist poem. This form, with its powerful analogical strategies of rhythm, image and symbol, not only epitomized what Senghor regarded as the essence of African verbal art (Bâ), it also simultaneously linked African creativity with a respected, albeit once avant-garde, mode of European poetic expression. Negritude poetry was thus something both new and old, both freshly inventive yet recognizably imitative, a cross-cultural poetry in a quasi-familiar hybrid form that blended and synthesized two disparate artistic traditions into a harmoniously integrated whole. Like the poets themselves, Negritude poems were cultural assimilados readily accepted in French intellectual circles. They may have appeared quaint and picturesque to some European readers (Senghor 90–1), but their very accessible exoticism made them quite exciting to others. The ideology of Negritude probably would not have made such a strong impact on the French-speaking world had it not been packaged in such an impeccably "civilized" form. Surrealism was a very elegant mode of protest.

The Negritude poets were thus proving their right to be taken seriously by introducing new ideas in a manner Europe understood and appreciated. Their argument had philosophical depth, interesting cultural implications, and rock-hard Cartesian lucidity. Like leaders of earlier French intellectual movements, the founding fathers of Negritude had issued a manifesto and were proceeding to generate literary evidence to support their position. Since surrealist poetry alone could not convey their ideas with sufficient precision, they also wrote essays attempting to define and elaborate key concepts. These efforts paid off handsomely. In no time at all Negritude gained recognition as both an ideology and a mystique in the best French dialectical tradition.

Even latter-day critics of Negritude – and there are many, particularly in anglophone Africa – acknowledge its historical importance. Most would agree with Stanislas Adotevi's assertion that

> although certain aspects may seem old-fashioned and with frankly reactionary objectives, we should consider [the era of Negritude] as a primitive period necessary to the African renaissance … At a time when the whole world was given over to racialism … at a time when the whole of humanity raised voice in competitive cacophony, there was a single pistol-shot in the middle of this concert – negritude. It shook a few consciences and brought a few negroes together, and this was a good thing. (74–5)

However, it is doubtful that this shot would have made such an impact if the pistol had been manufactured entirely in Africa. It took a European instrument in skilled African hands to shock the world into greater awareness of the humanity of colonized black peoples.

After Negritude had done its work, the surrealist poem and philosophical essay gave way in French West Africa to another literary form: the satirical novel. Anti-colonial humor in fiction by Mongo Beti, Ferdinand Oyono, Bernard Dadié, and even Camara Laye (in some of the lugubriously hallucinated episodes in Le Regard du roi) set the dominant tone of the 1950s. The change in form and mood suited the temper of the times. Now that colonialism was moribund, one could afford to laugh at colonizer and colonized alike, pointing out absurd aspects of their interaction. Since it was no longer necessary to demonstrate that Africans were human beings, one could relax a bit and depict them as no better and no worse than Europeans, who certainly weren't saints. One didn't have to romanticize the past or pretend that villages in Africa were more wholesome morally than cities in Europe. The fact that independence was just around the corner made self-confident self-criticism and joking possible. Instead of striving to impress the colonial master, one now had license to tickle him, even if the last laugh was at his own expense. Satirical fiction may have helped to ease social and political tensions in French West Africa prior to independence by comically deflating some the issues that had been blown out of proportion during the Negritude era. The ironic needle now spoke louder than the pistol-shot.

In English-speaking West Africa the novel also emerged as the dominant literary form at the end of the colonial period, but it was a very different kind of novel. Writers there were more serious about their work and seldom cracked a smile. Like the earlier Negritude advocates, they sought to create a dignified image of the African past, but they were careful not to glorify the precolonial era as a Golden Age. According to Chinua Achebe, the most influential novelist of this period, the best way to "plead the cause of the past" was to project an "accurate but maybe unexciting image," not a romanticized one "which though beautiful is a distortion." It was simply a matter of effective tactics. Achebe felt that

> the credibility of the world [the writer] is attempting to recreate will be called to question and he will defeat his own purpose if he is suspected of glossing over inconvenient facts. We cannot pretend that our past was one long, technicolour idyll. We have to admit that like any other people's past ours had its good as well as its bad sides. ("Role" 158)

Yet the kind of objectivity that Achebe and his followers tried to achieve in depicting traditional African village life was not devoid of political commitment. The writer was expected to argue a case against colonialism by showing the damage it had done in Africa. The novelist in particular was regarded as a teacher whose primary task was to reeducate his society to an acceptance of itself. He could accomplish this by strongly affirming the value of African culture. Achebe believed that the "fundamental theme" of the African writer should be

> that African peoples did not hear of culture for the first time from Europeans; that their societies were not mindless but frequently had a philosophy of great depth and value and beauty, that they had poetry and, above all, they had dignity. It is this dignity that many African peoples all but lost during the colonial period, and it is this that they must now regain. The worst thing that can happen to any people is the loss of their dignity and self-respect. The writer's duty is to help them regain it by showing them in human terms what happened to them, what they lost. ("Role" 157)

He could do this best by writing realistic fiction.

Most of the early anglophone West African novelists wrote sad stories of culture conflict. They would either show how a well-knit African community became divided after exposure to Western institutions such as the church and school or else reveal how individuals suffered psychological distress because they had become "men of two worlds" who could not reconcile the African and Western elements of their personality. Either things fell apart in the villages or people fell apart in the cities. In both cases Africa was no longer at ease because a collision with Europe had knocked it off balance. The legacy of colonialism was cultural confusion, and it was virtually impossible to find stable moral values in societies or individuals mired in such a mess. Contrary to Western colonial mythology, Europe did not bring light, peace and justice to the Dark Continent; it brought chaos to what had once been a well-ordered world. This was the theme that preoccupied the first generation of anglophone West African novelists. They were attempting to rewrite African history in their fiction, and to do so effectively, they chose to express themselves in a manner that could not be misunderstood. Plain prose was a more powerful mode of protest for them than abstract poetry.

By the mid-1960s, only a few years after independence had been achieved, the popular mood in West Africa had changed to such an extent that new political institutions began to spring up to supplant the parliamentary forms of democracy hastily bequeathed to Africa as Europe departed. First it was the one-party state, then the military junta, that dominated the scene. Africans who had followed their nationalist leaders into independence became disenchanted with them afterwards and sought to bring them down. Since increasing centralization of power within the new nation-state made this difficult to accomplish through constitutional means, the army often played a key role in effecting political change. Bullets replaced ballots as instruments of governance, and in at least one country post-coup conflicts deteriorated into full-scale civil war. The pre-independence dream of a brave new world had turned into a nasty postcolonial nightmare.

During this period West African writers could not ignore what they saw around them. The novel remained their major literary outlet but they used it now as a vehicle of strong social and political satire. Instead of continuing to reconstruct the dignity of the African past, they turned their attention to the ugliness of the present and began to point the finger of blame at Africans themselves instead of Europeans. Wole Soyinka, who switched from drama to fiction during this period, exclaimed that "the African writer needs an urgent release from the fascination of the past" if he is to fulfill his function "as the record of the mores and experience of his society *and* as the voice of vision in his own time" (13). Chinua Achebe agreed, pointing out that

> Most of Africa today is politically free; there are thirty-six independent African States managing their own affairs – sometimes quite badly. A new situation has thus arisen. One of the writer's main functions has always been to expose and attack injustice. Should we keep at the old theme of racial injustice (sore as it still is) when new injustices have sprouted all around us? I think not.

The "black writer's burden," Achebe argued, was "to express our thought and feeling, even against ourselves, without the anxiety that what we say will be taken as evidence against our race" ("Burden" 138–9). In other words, the political battle at home was now far more important than the cultural struggle abroad.

This new emphasis continued into the 1970s, with novelists alternating between slice-of-life realism and sardonic satire. In Nigeria, where more novels were produced than in any other West African nation, the center of focus became the civil war experience. It is not surprising that most of this fiction was written by Ibos, many of whom used Biafran soldiers as their heroes and chose mercenaries and other war profiteers as their villains. But these novels were not propagandistic in the narrow sense of the word. They told of man's inhumanity to man but also of man's altruism, notably his willingness to sacrifice himself for others; in addition to human pettiness, stupidity, duplicity and greed, there were examples of human courage, compassion, and devotion to an ideal. These novelists seemed to be more concerned with comprehending the moral significance of actions taken during a civil war than with blaming the conflict on one side or another. This was a profoundly introspective literature even when attention was focused on surface details of combat and destruction. Themes of madness, terror and social dislocation served to underscore the fragility of human civilizations, particularly when subjected to the kind of irreversible devastation wrought by calculated brutality. In such novels things and people did not fall apart; they were pummeled into oblivion by forces too powerful for them to withstand or else they tried heroically to resist the cataclysmic dehumanization that was overtaking their world. It was not just groups of Africans backed by opposing European factions, not just Biafrans and Federalists, who were in conflict here; good and evil were at war.

Thus, in response to traumatic political and cultural changes since independence, anglophone West African writers have moved from an obsessive concern with the residual effects of colonialism in black Africa to a preoccupation with more universal themes rooted in more specific contemporary realities. In other words, there has been both a narrowing and a broadening of their range of interests. Instead of continuing to delineate the sociological and psychological damage suffered by Africans during the colonial encounter, they attempted to explore dimensions of the human condition by looking more closely at local examples of extreme situations. And they did this primarily through the medium of the novel, an elastic form that can accommodate many different approaches to reality but that has been exploited by these writers in basically two complementary ways: cynical satire (to deal with political corruption) and compassionate realism (to deal with the horrors of civil war).

As before, both approaches involved speaking truths plainly so that everyone could easily understand what was being said.

In East Africa, writing got off to a slower start than in West Africa, but production began to accelerate very rapidly in the late 1960s and early 1970s. The first major literary form to emerge was the novel, and in the hands of James Ngugi (now Ngugi wa Thiong'o) and his followers, it initially took essentially the same shape as its counterpart in West Africa. Ngugi's earliest novels, written just before independence, reexamined the colonial past, particularly the period that saw the rise of Gikuyu independent schools and the outbreak of the Mau Mau rebellion. Like Achebe, Ngugi felt that the novelist's work "is often an attempt to come to terms with 'the thing that has been', a struggle, as it were, to sensitively register his encounter with history, his people's history" (1972:39). The novelists who appeared immediately after Ngugi evidently shared this attitude for they too wrote historical fiction set in the relatively recent past.

Not long after independence, however, East Africa went through the same phase of political disillusionment that had infected West Africa, and novelists responded in the same way by turning their attention to contemporary times. Ngugi's analysis of this phenomenon echoes remarks by Soyinka and Achebe but adds an interesting economic perspective:

> The African writer was in danger of becoming too fascinated by the yesterday of his people and forgetting the present. Involved as he was in correcting his disfigured past, he forgot that his society was no longer peasant, with ownership of means of production, with communal celebration of joy and victory, communal sharing of sorrow and bereavement; his society was no longer organized on egalitarian principles. Conflicts between the emergent elitist middle-class and the masses were developing, their seeds being in the colonial pattern of social and economic development. And when he woke up to his task he was not a little surprised that events in post-independence Africa could take the turn they had taken. (1972: 44–5)

Ngugi was one of the first in East Africa to wake up and write a serious indictment of the turn his nation had taken. He was followed by others who exposed postcolonial political intrigues and social corruption in sharply satirical novels. As in West African fiction, the tendency now was to go beyond blaming Europe for introducing the cultural confusion that culminated in the collapse of modern Africa and begin accusing Africa of collaborating in its own destruction. The critical eye had turned inward.

The other major literary form that emerged in East Africa in the 1960s was the satirical song. In 1966 Okot p'Bitek published *Song of Lawino*, a long "lament" of an illiterate housewife deserted by her educated husband for an emancipated city girl. In registering her complaints against her husband and his "modern woman," Lawino strikes out at the nasty habits and illogical practices of Westernized Africans, contrasting them with the natural dignity of traditional ways. Her song is a hilarious put-down of African "apeman-ship" (p'Bitek, 1973: 1–5) and a defense of the integrity of indigenous culture, but p'Bitek added interesting piquancy to her argument by making Lawino herself a target of some of the satire. In this manner p'Bitek both revived and undercut the debate about Africa's cultural confusion by placing it in a new comic context. Indeed, he went further and had Lawino's husband reply to her charges in *Song of Ocol*, a book-length lyric in which the technique of reflexive satire is even more pronounced. Unlike the sober-sided West Africans who wrote on such subjects, p'Bitek was ready to laugh at the twisted victims of Africa's collision with Europe. He saw them as sad but funny creatures crushed by a colossal absurdity.

The light touch that p'Bitek introduced into the discussion of heavy cultural issues struck a very responsive chord in East Africa. Imitators immediately sprang up and started singing similar songs. A streak of zany comedy entered the literature, providing a refreshing alternative to the serious indictments of the postcolonial novelists. After p'Bitek the satirical song became one of the most popular literary forms in East Africa.

But it did not remain a static form. In the 1970s singers gradually moved away from cultural to political themes, focusing their attention on some of the same problems preoccupying the novelists. Again p'Bitek led the way, composing in *Song of Prisoner* and *Song of Malaya* eloquent broadsides against a multitude of social and civic sins. The tone of these verbal assaults was still basically humorous, but the humor, particularly in *Song of Prisoner*, now had a bitter aftertaste, reflecting deepened political disillusionment. Also, Europe had vanished; Africa itself was now the epicenter of quaking satire.

Although the literary histories of West and East Africa outlined here are quite similar in certain respects, one significant difference should be underscored: East African writers have had a greater propensity to laugh at evil. While West Africans brood or turn cynical when things go wrong in their society, East Africans seem to have a capacity to enjoy the incongruities of the moment, even when events conspire to work to their disadvantage. Nowhere is this better illustrated than in the popular literature on Idi Amin Dada that emerged in East Africa during and after his tenure as Uganda's Head of State. One of the most interesting specimens of this Idi-otic genre is a beast fable entitled *The Amazing Saga of Field Marshal Abdulla Salim Fisi, or How the Hyena Got His* written by a Ugandan author under the pseudonym "Alumidi Osinya." A brief foreword states:

> The point about the story that follows is that there really is perhaps no better way of talking about the rape of Africa by Africans themselves than the traditional African way of the "Why" or "How" animal story. This is how we told off our elders in the past . . . This is how they told each other off, in a gentle, mild way. . . Now, perhaps more than ever, when ruthless military dictators are the order of the day and shoot human beings as easily as they shoot the elephants in the National Parks (except that at least with elephants they get the tusks), now really is the time to try the mild, gentle way. Not though, in the Western sense, in the same way the British press, for instance, has regarded our excesses as buffoonery and just laughed them off while we continued needlessly to butcher each other. There is buffoonery, yes, but it's a mirthless, cruel buffoonery and although it may do us good to laugh at ourselves, let our eyes water too: this situation, partly of our own making, is so cruel that we need the sedative of laughter even to be able to look at it. And the effectiveness of the sedative can only be judged by the trickle of tears from the mirthless laughter. (ix–x)

One reason why East African writing differs from West African writing is that East African authors have resorted more often to the sedative of tearful laughter. Even the harshest subjects have been treated in this "mild, gentle way."

Black South African authors, faced with a different set of political circumstances, have produced a literature bearing little resemblance to East or West African writing. Their first major literary form in English was the short story, which flourished in the 1950s but was nearly obliterated in the mid-1960s by tough new censorship legislation. The writers themselves have explained that the pressures of life under apartheid rule, combined with extremely limited opportunities for publication in other forms, made the short story virtually the only literary outlet for "non-white" writers after 1948 (Mphahlele 186; Modisane 3; Nkosi 1962: 6). In the 1950s they wrote either romantic potboilers for *Drum* and other popular home magazines or else hard-hitting naturalistic vignettes for liberal, radical and communist publications. But both this frivolous escapist trash and this serious protest fiction fell victim to the repressive Publications and Entertainments Act of 1963, which gave the South African government power to ban anything it deemed immoral, objectionable or obscene. The most outspoken writers were blacklisted, placed under house arrest, and encouraged to leave South Africa permanently, and the publications that promoted blatant protest writing were quickly forced out of existence. Politically committed writers had to choose between silence and exile.

Those who opted for exile continued to write about South Africa but began to express themselves in a variety of literary forms. Foremost among these was the autobiography, which became the black refugee's favorite medium for articulating his outrage and frustration. Indeed, autobiographical writing almost turned into a tradition among newly exiled black South African intellectuals. Then, having got the experience of apartheid off their chest in this intensely personal way, they experimented with long fiction, drama and various types of poetry, sometimes commenting on the disorientations of exile but usually renewing their attacks on the evils of life back home. Escape from an oppressive environment and release of their long pent-up feelings of bitterness gave them the freedom to explore other modes of getting their message across. They had been liberated from the limitations of the short story.

Meanwhile, back in South Africa the urge for self-expression in English resurfaced in the 1970s in a new literary form – lyric poetry. The poetry movement got started in 1971 with the publication of Oswald Mtshali's *Sounds of a Cowhide Drum*, which sold more than ten thousand copies in its first year. This was followed by increasingly militant books of poetry by others – Mongane Wally Serote, James Matthews, Sydney Sipho Sepamla, to name only the most prominent. At first the South African censors seemed willing to ignore these poets, possibly because their messages were more obliquely stated than those of the short story writers. Poetry can be more difficult to interpret than prose, and it would have been absurd, even in the South Africa of that day, to have convicted a poet for achieving a splendid ambiguity.

[. . .]

However, as more black poetry was published in South Africa, the messages gradually grew cruder and more direct. Instead of carrying figurative titles with subtle political undertones such as *Sounds of a Cowhide Drum* (alluding to the percussive rhythm made by Zulu regiments as they marched into battle beating on their shields) or *Yakhal'inkomo* (the cry of cattle at the slaughter house), the books now had slogans for titles: *Cry Rage!* and *Black Voices Shout!* Soon the government stepped in and started banning such books. The most talented black poets – Mtshali and Serote – left the country for a spell. Thus, in the 1970s history repeated itself in South Africa: a literary movement that gave promise of articulating the discontents of blacks was again halted by heavy-handed government censorship. Black African poets appeared to have no alternative but to remain silent, turn to oral forms, or go into exile. Writing verse in their homeland would make them outlaws.

One significant factor conditioning all African literatures written in African languages has been the audience to whom they have been addressed. In colonial West and East Africa writers tended to speak to Europe first and to their own people second; only after the struggle for independence had been won in principle (if not in fact) did they relax and entertain their countrymen as well as the outside world by laughing at themselves. However as postcolonial disillusionment spread, this laughter turned bitter and self-criticism became the rule. Then African writers spoke primarily to their own people and were no longer greatly concerned about the negative image of Africa their writings might project to outsiders. In this way, East and West African literatures became decidedly more Afrocentric in the postcolonial era.

In South Africa, on the other hand, African authors who expressed themselves in English got their start by writing for popular magazines and newspapers aimed at an indigenous African reading public. Only after leaving South Africa did they concern themselves with writing for a foreign audience; this was more a matter of necessity than preference because as banned persons they could not get their works published or read in their motherland. Those who remained in South Africa continued to speak to their own people until the government made it virtually impossible for them to speak at all.

In black Africa, then, there have been basically two patterns of literary development in European languages since the second world war: the gradual Africanization of literary expression in West and East Africa as colonialism gave way to political self-determination, and the rapid de-Africanization of South African literary expression as repeated repression at home gave rise to a vigorous tradition of protest writing among exiled South Africans abroad. Writers in each area have chosen forms appropriate for conveying a political message to a particular audience and have switched to other forms when environmental conditions have altered. Thus, in morphology as well as ideology, literary art has been responsive to the winds of change that swept across sub-Saharan Africa in the mid-twentieth century. The intellectual history of a continent undergoing rapid cultural transformation can be discerned in the significant mutations such literatures manifest.

References

Achebe, Chinua. "The Role of the Writer in a New Nation." *Nigeria Magazine* 81 (1964): 157–60.
——. "English and the African Writer." *Transition* 18 (1965): 27–30.
——. "The Black Writer's Burden." *Présence Africaine* 59 (1966): 135–40.
Adotevi, Stanislas. "Negritude is Dead: The Burial. *Journal of the New African Literature and the Arts* 7–8 (1969–70): 70–81.
Bâ, Sylvia Washington. *The Concept of Negritude in the Poetry of Léopold Sédar Senghor.* Princeton, NJ: Princeton University Press, 1973.
Mphahlele, Ezekiel. *The African Image.* London: Faber, 1962.
Ngugi wa Thiong'O. *Homecoming: Essays on African and Caribbean Literature, Culture and Politics.* New York: Lawrence Hill, 1972.
Nkosi, Lewis. "African Fiction: Part One, South Africa: Protest." *Africa Report* 7, 9 (1962): 3–6.
P'Bitek, Okot. *Africa's Cultural Revolution.* Nairobi: Macmillan Books for Africa, 1973.
Senghor, Léopold Sédar. *Léopold Sédar Senghor: Prose and Poetry.* Ed. and trans. John Reed and Clive Wake. London: Oxford University Press, 1963.
Soyinka, Wole. "The Writer in an African State." *Transition* 31 (1967): 11–13.

Chapter 4

African Literature in Portuguese

Russell G. Hamilton

Portuguese was the first European language to reach sub-Saharan Africa. Thus, by the middle of the fifteenth century many Africans spoke Portuguese-based pidgins and creoles. As a consequence of this early presence, African writing in Portuguese appeared before anything comparable in English, French, and other European languages.

Literary precursors in the colonial period

With a few exceptions, documented as far back as the nineteenth century, precursors of a representative lusophone African literature did not come into being until the 1930s and 1940s. Joaquim Dias Cordeiro da Matta (1857–94) perhaps stands as Angolan literature's most important nineteenth-century precursor. A native of Icolo-e-Bengo, Cordeiro da Matta was a poet, the author of an unpublished novel, and the organizer of a Kimbundu–Portuguese dictionary.

António de Assis Júnior (1887–1960), a later precursor, was an "assimilated" African, according to the colonial Indigenous Law enacted by the Portuguese New State in the early twentieth century. In spite of his official social status of *assimilado*, Assis Júnior was transcultural, and he paid tribute to his Kimbundu ethnic origins. Like his predecessor Cordeiro da Matta, he compiled a Kimbundu–Portuguese dictionary. He established himself as a direct precursor of modern Angolan literature with *O segredo da morta* (1934) (The Dead Woman's Secret), subtitled *Romance de costumes angolenses* (A Romance of Angolan Customs). Although written in the style of Victor Hugo, Assis Júnior's early romance is a forerunner of the ethnographic Angolan prose fiction of the 1950s and 1960s.

Fernando Castro Soromenho (1910–68) is a unique precursor of Angolan prose fiction. Born to Portuguese parents in Mozambique and raised in Angola, Soromenho held an administrative position with the colonial diamond company. While living in eastern Angola, Soromenho launched his writing career in the tradition of colonial literature. After

First published in *The Cambridge History of African and Caribbean Literature*, vol. 2, ed. Abiola Irele and Simon Gikandi, pp. 603–10. Cambridge: Cambridge University Press, 2004.

publishing two collections of short stores and two novels that depict Africans as uncivilized and exotic, Soromenho experienced a *prise de conscience*. Coupled with a growing benevolence toward Africans and their culture, Soromenho's social consciousness led him to write *Terra morta* (1949) (Dead Earth), *Viragem* (1957) (The Turning), and the posthumously published *A chaga* (1970) (The Plague). So palpable was the social protest in these novels that the colonial authorities banned them, and Soromenho eventually went into exile in France and Brazil. Some see Soromenho not as a precursor, but as the father of Angolan prose fiction.

With the publication of *Sonetos* (1943) (Sonnets), Rui de Noronha (1909–43), of African and East Indian parentage, became a precursor with respect to Mozambican poetry. And when João Dias's (1926–49) *Godido e outros contos* (1950) (Godido and Other Stories) was issued posthumously, Dias became the first black Mozambican writer of prose fiction.

Foremost among Guinea-Bissau's precursors is Fausto Duarte (1903–53), a Cape Verdean who lived many years in then Portuguese Guinea, the setting of his four novels. All of Duarte's novels, including *Auá, novela negra* (1934) (Aua, a Black Novella), his best-known work, constitute what is an essentially benevolent, less exotic mode of colonial writing.

Caetano da Costa Alegre (1864–90) is one of the earliest precursors of modern São Tomense literature. At the age of ten this black 'native son,' or *filho da terra*, was sent to Portugal, where he spent the rest of his life. *Versos* (1916) (Verses), Costa Alegre's collected poems, was published in Lisbon sixteen years after his death. A number of Costa Alegre's poems invoke the land of his birth; others constitute sardonic glosses of the experiences of an African living in Europe.

The earliest prose fiction of note to be produced by a native São Tomense is *O preto do Charlestone* (1930) (The Black Man from Charlestone), a novella by Mário Domingues (1899–1977). Domingues, who, like Costa Alegre, lived most of his life in Portugal, is best remembered for *O menino entre gigantes* (1960) (The Boy among Giants), a novel of manners about an African boy coming of age in Lisbon. A prolific São Tomense novelist is Sum Marky, the creole pen name of José Ferreira Marques (b. 1921). A resident of Lisbon since 1960, Marky has written eight novels, five of which depict life in São Tomé.

Representative works and the emergence of literary-cultural movements in colonial times

For a number of historical reasons Cape Verde's colonial society gave rise to lusophone Africa's first indigenous intelligentsia or creole elite. Thus, during the 1930s and 1940s, when most writers in the other Portuguese-African colonies can be considered precursors, their Cape-Verdean counterparts were consciously establishing an autochthonous literary-cultural movement. Throughout Cape Verde's colonial history, a kind of national homogeneity was being forged in a crucible of biological, linguistic, and cultural hybridity. By the time of independence this legacy had coalesced into a sense of socially unifying Cape Verdeanness.

Although Portuguese continues to be independent Cape Verde's official language, virtually all Cape Verdeans, whatever their social status, also speak creole. Baltasar Lopes (da Silva) (1907–89), one of the founders, in 1936, of *Claridade* (Clarity), a landmark cultural/literary journal, declared Cape-Verdean creole to be a dialect of Portuguese. Along with other intellectuals of his generation, Baltasar Lopes, who authored *O dialecto crioulo de Cabo Verde* (1957) (The Creole Dialect of Cape Verde), sought to erase creole's pidgin stigma and to validate it as a literary language. Most linguists, of course, define a creole as a pidgin with native speakers, and a dialect is defined as a regional or social variation of a given language.

A Lisbon-educated philologist and lawyer, Baltasar Lopes was also a pioneering fiction writer. Many consider his *Chiquinho* (1947) to be the first authentically Cape-Verdean novel. Moreover, using the pen name Osvaldo Alcântara, Lopes also wrote poetry in a Portuguese sprinkled with creole expressions.

Baltasar Lopes belongs to a trio of *Claridade* poets, the others being Jorge Barbosa (1902–71) and Manuel Lopes (b. 1907). Barbosa set a durable standard for Cape-Verdean poets of his generation and beyond. And Manuel Lopes, although an admired poet, is best known for his prose fiction, especially *Chuva braba* (1956) (Wild Rain), a classic novel about the drought-stricken islands.

In the city of Mindelo, during colonial times the center of Cape Verde's literary-cultural activity, several other fiction writers of the *Claridade* and later the *Certeza* (Certainty) groups emerged in the 1940s. Two highly regarded writers of that era are António Aurélio Gonçalves (1902–84) and Henrique Teixeira de Sousa (b. 1918).

Younger writers respected and even admired their *Claridade* and *Certeza* predecessors. But unlike their elders, these younger writers focused more sharply on Cape Verde's endemic socioeconomic ills and they reclaimed what they saw as the islands' neglected African heritage. Chief among such writers are Ovídio Martins (b. 1928), Gabriel Mariano (b. 1928), Onésimo Silveira (b. 1935), and Kaoberdiano Dambara, pseudonym of Felisberto Vieira Lopes (b. 1937).

The advent of a literature of cultural revindication, social protest, and combativeness

In the 1950s and 1960s as the winds of change began to blow across Africa, socially conscious writers in the Portuguese colonies turned to modes of cultural expression that directly or indirectly challenged colonial rule. Growing anticolonialism led to liberation movements and, by the early 1960s, armed rebellion in Guinea-Bissau, Angola, and Mozambique. Writers from all five colonies increasingly produced works of cultural revindication, social protest, and combativeness. The colonial authorities reacted with censorship and repression. Dozens of militant writers went underground or into exile and not a few were arrested by the secret police. A number wrote clandestinely in their prison cells. Others succeeded in publishing their works abroad, including in Portugal, where, ironically, until the 1960s censorship was less strictly enforced than in the colonies.

By the early 1950s, Luanda had become the center of defiant cultural activity by the New Intellectuals of Angola. In 1951 this socially aware group launched *Mensagem* (Message), a literary journal, which the authorities banned within a year of its founding. Meanwhile, the House of Students from the Empire, a social and cultural association founded in Portugal in 1944, had published, between 1948 and 1964 (the year in which the authorities closed it down), a journal also called *Mensagem*. In October of 1952, numbers 2, 3, and 4 of the Luanda-based journal appeared in a combined and final issue. As did *Cultura* (Culture), another historic, short-lived Angolan journal, *Mensagem* brought together poems, short stories, and essays by aspiring writers, many of whom would become activists in the People's Movement for the Liberation of Angola (MPLA), founded in Luanda in 1956.

Agostinho Neto (1922–80), Aires de Almeida Santos (1922–92), Alexandre Dáskalos (1924–61), António Jacinto (1924–91), Viriato da Cruz (1928–73), Mário Pinto de Andrade (1928–90), Alda Lara (1930–62), Ernesto Lara Filho (1932–75), António Cardoso (b. 1933), Mário António (1934–89), Manuel dos Santos Lima (b. 1935), Fernando Costa Andrade (b. 1936), Arnaldo Santos (b. 1936), and the brothers Henrique (b. 1937), and Mário Guerra (b. 1939) are some of the principal writers among the multiracial New Intellectuals, who pledged to 'Discover Angola.'

As one of many examples of the interrelationship between cultural expression and political militancy, Agostinho Neto, who in 1975 would become Angola's first president, established himself in colonial times as a formidable poet. Neto, whose first arrest for political activism occurred in 1951, spent more than three years in Portuguese prisons. While interned in Lisbon's Caxias prison, Neto wrote the stirringly defiant 'Havemos de voltar' ('We Must Return'), which after independence became an Angolan anthem of nationalist resolve. A selection of Neto's poems in English translation was published in a volume entitled *Sacred Hope* (1974).

José Luandino Vieira (b. 1935) also paid dearly for his political activism. Born José Mateus Vieira da Graça in rural Portugal, when he was two years old he accompanied his settler parents to Angola, to the city of Luanda. Luandino, the sobriquet by which he is best known, was imprisoned for eleven years because of his opposition to colonial rule. Nine of those years were spent in the infamous Tarrafal, a prison located on the Cape-Verde island of Santiago. *Luuanda* (1964) (*Luuanda: Short Stories of Angola*, 1980) was published in the Angolan capital while Luandino was serving the third year of his sentence. The collection's three tales established Luandino as a quintessential Angolan writer. Moreover, Luandino's unique literary style influenced a generation of Angolan writers who also sought to validate the language, social norms, and culture of the white central city's black shanty towns. Luandino contributed to raising the creolized black Portuguese of the city's *musseques* (shanty towns) to the level of a literary language. All of Luandino's works, most written while he was interned, have influence such significant Luanda-based story-tellers as Jofre Rocha (b. 1941), Jorge Macedo (b. 1941), Manuel Rui (b. 1941), and Boaventura Cardoso (b. 1944).

In Portugal's East African colony of Mozambique, the 1950s and 1960s also witnessed increased literary activity. José Craveirinha (b. 1922), born in Lourenço Marques (now Maputo) to a Ronga mother and a Portuguese father, began his illustrious career as a poet in the 1950s. Craveirinha has the distinction of being the first African to receive, in 1991, the prestigious Camões prize, awarded annually since 1989, to a writer from one of the seven Portuguese-speaking countries.

A contemporary of Craveirinha is Noémia de Sousa (b.1927), whom Gerald Moore and Ulli Beier identify, in the 1968 edition of their *Modern Poetry from Africa*, as 'The first African woman to achieve a genuine reputation as a modern poet' (p. 253). Sousa is certainly the first black or mixed-race Mozambican woman to publish poems in Portuguese. Malangatana Ngwenya (b. 1936), although first and foremost a painter of international reputation, is probably the first Mozambican to have poems published in English translation. Two of Malangatana's poems appeared, in 1960, in the Nigerian journal *Black Orpheus*. Along with Craveirinha and Noémia de Sousa, Malangatana also has poems in the 1968 edition of

Modern Poetry from Africa. The artist's first book, entitled *Malangatana: vinte e quatro poemas* (1996) (Malangatana: Twenty-Four Poems), appeared nearly twenty-one years after Mozambique's independence.

Among socially conscious poets of pre-independence Mozambique the best known are Marcelino dos Santos (b. 1929), Rui Nogar (1932–93), Armando Guebuza (b. 1935), Fernando Ganhão (b. 1937), Jorge Rebelo (b. 1940), and Sérgio Vieira (b. 1941). These engagé writers composed many of the poems in *Poesia de combatte* (1971) (Poetry of Combat), issued in Lusaka, Zambia by the Mozambique Liberation Front (FRELIMO).

Orlando Mendes (1916–90) is a pioneering novelist of pre-independence Mozambique. Born to Portuguese parents in the northern city of Ilha de Moçambique, Mendes's *Portagem* (1965) (The Tollgate) is a novel in the tradition of South African Alan Paton's *Cry, the Beloved Country* (1948). A literary revelation indeed was Luís Bernardo Honwana (b. 1942), whose *Nós matamos o cão tinhoso* (1964) (*We Killed Mangy Dog and Other Mozambique Stories*, 1969) is the first lusophone African book to appear in English translation in the prestigious Heinemann's African Writers Series.

The predominantly white Association of Native Sons of Mozambique, founded in 1935 by Portuguese intellectuals, most born in the colony, assumed, by the 1960s, a nativistic cultural posture and a reformist, if not overtly liberationist, political agenda. A founding member of the Association, Rui Knopfli (1933–97) is arguably the best poet writing from what some call a Luso-Mozambican perspective. During the early 1970s Knopfli helped revitalize Lourenço Marques's quiescent literary scene with his poetry and as the editor of *Caliban*, a provocative literary journal.

One of *Caliban*'s principal collaborators was António Quadros (1933–94), a Portuguese-born poet who lived in Mozambique between 1968 and the early 1980s. Using the *nom de guerre* Mutemati Bernabé João, Quadros made an aesthetico-ideological impact with the poems of *Eu, o povo* (1975) (I, The People), issued shortly after independence by Mozambique's newly installed revolutionary government.

Few plays were written and even fewer staged in any of the Portuguese colonies. The authorities aggressively banned theatrical performances that might convey seditious messages, to which even the illiterate might have access. In late colonial Mozambique two exceptions were *Os noivos ou conferência dramática sobre o lobolo* (The Betrothed, or a Dramatic Lecture about the Bride Price) and *As trinta mulheres de Muzeleni* (The Thirty Wives of Muzeleni), by Lindo Nlhongo (1939–96). These plays, based on traditional African customs, apparently deemed to be harmless by the authorities, were allowed to be staged in Lourenço Marques in 1971 and 1974, respectively. (Neither play was published in its entirety until 1995.)

After Caetano da Costa Alegre's death in 1890, nearly fifty years would elapse before a comparable poet appeared. Francisco José Tenreiro (1921–63), the son of a Portuguese administrator and an African mother, like Costa Alegre, spent most of his short life in Portugal. In Lisbon he rose to unprecedented heights as a professor of geography and the first African to serve in the Portuguese National Assembly. He co-organized, with Mário Pinto de Andrade, the well-known Angolan poet, scholar, and militant, *Poesia negra de expressão portuguesa* (1953) (Black Poetry of Portuguese Expression), the first anthology of its kind. It should be noted parenthetically that Andrade lived in Paris from 1954 until 1959. During this self-imposed exile, the Angolan militant was private secretary to Alioune Diop, the Senegalese founder of the journal *Présence Africaine*, for which Andrade served as editor in chief. It was during his years in Paris, which Andrade called his 'great intellectual adventure,' that he came to know such Negritude writers as Aimé Césaire and Léopold Sédar Senghor. It was in fact Senghor's anthology of francophone African poetry that served as a model for Andrade's and Tenreiro's historic collection of lusophone African poetry. As for Tenreiro, who maintained contact with his Angolan collaborator, the São Tomense's own poems, characterized by some as early examples of a lusophone Negritude, were brought together in a posthumously issued volume titled *Coração em Africa* (1965) (With My Heart in Africa).

After Tenreiro's death, Alda Espírito Santo (b. 1926), Maria Manuela Margarido (b. 1926), and Tomaz Medeiros (b. 1931) breathed new life into São Tomense literary expression. Like Costa Alegre and Tenreiro before them, this trio of poets lived and wrote in Portugal. All three were active in the clandestinely anticolonialist, Lisbon-based House of Students from the Empire, which anthologized selections of their verse in *Poetas de São Tomé e Príncipe* (1963) (Poets of São Tomé and Príncipe).

Literature after independence

Anticolonialist forms and contents set the stage for the first years of post-independence literature in lusophone Africa. As revolutionary fervor abated, a body of less circumstantial literary expression began to appear in the former colonies.

[. . .]

Bibliography

Alegre, Caetano da Costa. [1916] 1951. 3rd edn. *Versos*. Lisbon: Ferin.

Alegre, Francisco Costa. 1990. *Madala*. São Tomé: EMAG.

Assis Júnior, António de. [1934] 1978. *O segredo da morta*. Luanda: A Luzitana; re-edited in Lisbon: Edições 70 for the União dos Escritores Angolanos.

Craveirinha, José. [1988] 1998. 2nd edn. *Maria*. Lisbon: Caminho.

Dias, João. 1952. *Godido e outros contos*. Lisbon: Casa dos Estudantes do Império.

Domingues, Mário. 1930. *O preto do Charlestone*. Lisbon: Ed. Guimarães & Cia.

—— 1960. *O menino entre gigantes*. Lisbon: Prelo.

Duarte, Fausto. 1934. *Auá: novela negra*. Lisbon: Livraria Clássica.

Lopes (da Silva), Baltasar. 1957. *O dialecto crioulo de Cabo Verde*. Lisbon: Junta das Missões Geográficas e de Investigação do Ultramar; 1961. 2nd edn. *Chiquinho*. Lisbon: Prelo.

Lopes, Manuel. [1956] 1985. 5th edn. *Chuva braba*. Lisbon: Edições 70.

Modern African Poetry. [1968] 1984. 3rd edn. (includes poems by six Angolans, one Cape Verdean, four Mozambicans, and one São-Tomense). Ed. Gerald Moore and Ulli Beier. Harmondsworth: Penguin.

Neto, Agostinho. 1974. *Sagrada esperança*. Lisbon: Sá da Costa.

—— 1974. *Sacred Hope*. Trans. Marga Holness. Dar-es-Salaam: Tanzania Publishing House.

Nlhongo, Lindo. 1995. *Dos peças de teatro: Os noivos ou conferência dramática sobre o lobolo; As trinta mulheres de Muzeleni*. Maputo: Associação dos Escritores Moçambicanos.

Noronha, Rui de. 1943. *Sonetos*. Lourenço Marques (Maputo): Minerva Central.

Santos, Arnaldo. 1992. *A boneca de Quilengues*. Porto: Asa.

—— 1999. *A casa velha das margens*. Luanda: Edições Chá de Caxinde.

Soromenho, Fernando. 1949. *Terra morta*. Rio de Janeiro: Casa do Estudante do Brasil.

—— 1957. *Viragem*. Lisbon: Ulisseia.

—— 1970. *A chaga*. Rio de Janeiro: Civilização Brasileira.

Tenreiro, Francisco José, and Mário Pinto de Andrade. 1953. *Poesia Negra de Expressão Portuguesa*. Lisbon: authors' edition.

Vieira, José Luandino. 1964. *Luuanda*. Luanda: ABC.

—— 1974. *A vida verdadeira de Domingos Xavier*. Lisbon: Edições 70.

—— 1978. *The Real Life of Domingos Xavier*. Trans. Michael Wolfers. London: Heinemann.

—— 1979. *João Vêncio: os seus amores*. Luanda: União dos Escritores Angolanos.

—— 1980. *Luuanda: Short Stories of Angola*. Trans. Tamara L. Bender. London: Heinemann.

—— 1991. *The Loves of João Vêncio*. Trans. Richard Zenith. New York: Harcourt Brace Jovanovich.

Chapter 5

North African Writing

Anissa Talahite

North African writing offers a perspective that cannot be strictly confined within the geographical boundaries of North Africa. From a linguistic and cultural point of view, it is part of Arabic literature, a category that includes the literature from the countries both of North Africa and the Middle East. North African writing is therefore determined by the sense of belonging to an Arab nation which shares the same language and culture, and to a certain extent, the same religion. Since North Africa became part of the Arab Muslim empire in the eighth century, the Arabic language and the Muslim religion have symbolised the force bringing the Arab people together in a common destiny. Today, North African writing is largely informed by this common Arab heritage which represents not only a way of connecting with the cultural tradition but also a way of understanding the present. Beyond their denomination as Arab and Muslim, North African countries are also shaped by the Berber culture and language, a tradition that preceded the introduction of Arab culture. In Morocco, for instance, Berber is the mother tongue of nearly half of the population.[1] The Berber oral tradition is an important component of North African culture despite the fact that it has been overshadowed by the dominant position occupied by the written languages. It has, however, recently been the focus of writers who have attempted to give Berber folk stories, songs and poems a more significant place within North African literature.[2]

The more recent history of North Africa saw the birth of a new literature that originated from the experience of French colonialism in the former colonies of the Maghreb (namely Morocco, Algeria and Tunisia). After some timid attempts to address the 'native question' in articles often published in colonial journals in the late nineteenth and early twentieth centuries, North African writing in French acquired a more definite shape in the 1950s with the emergence of a greater national consciousness. The French language became a channel through which writers could confront colonial authority. Thus, North African writers started experimenting with narratives and with poetic language as a way of forging a distinct identity. For North African writers, writing in French means reflecting on the

First published in *Writing and Africa*, ed. Mpalive–Hangson Msiska and Paul Hyland, pp. 13–23. London: Longman, 1997.

relationships between European and indigenous cultures in order to construct a North African voice which would integrate the different cultures inherited from the past.

The North African literary scene shows that it is difficult to regard North African writing as singular and homogeneous. Instead, it seems more appropriate to speak of North African *literatures* rather than of one literature: a literature in Arabic which extends beyond the confines of North Africa; an age-old Berber oral literature which has survived in certain areas; and a literature in French in the countries that were part of the former French empire. Given the range of North African writing, this survey concentrates only on the written literatures and on particular authors and texts that exemplify the main developments. Arabic and francophone literatures are dealt with in separate sections in order to highlight the importance of language in shaping modern literary forms.

Writing in Arabic

The countries of North Africa, from Morocco to Egypt, share the collective memory of their common Muslim Arab past, which survives today in their language and literature and which plays an important part in the shaping of an Arab identity. Although each country speaks its own variation of Arabic, the Arab world shares one official language (used in schools, the media, etc.) which is distinct from the spoken forms. This language, called 'fusha' in Arabic, but which in English is referred to as classical or sometimes literary Arabic, represents the crucible of Arab culture since it brings the Arab nation together as did Arab civilisation in the past. As far as writers are concerned, one of the great advantages of using classical Arabic is that it gives them access to a readership throughout the Arab world. However, modern writers have been increasingly confronted with the issue of bridging the gap between this higher form of Arabic, used by the educated minority, and the 'dialects' spoken by the majority.

The transformations of Arab society in the modern period brought about major changes in its literary expression. Arab societies at the beginning of the nineteenth century were faced with the need to reassess the heritage of Arab culture, incorporating technological and social change as well as making sense of the increasing contact of Arab culture with the West. A generation of writers, scholars and politicians started to formulate a debate on their society by exploring the intricacies of cultural transformation, the significance of religion in the face of scientific development and the political implications of social change. Their response to the increasing cultural and political impact of Europe on the Arab world was to redefine Arab culture and to create new forms of self-expression.

In Egypt, the cultural renaissance of the *Nahdah* in the late 1880s and the early 1900s was significant in shaping modern Arabic thinking as well as in influencing the development of literary forms. The *Nahdah* originated as an aesthetic movement in Lebanon but took on a political dimension in Egypt because of the particular historical circumstances brought about by the presence of European colonial powers. The invasion of Egypt by Napoleon in 1798 is seen as a crucial point in the modern history of the Arab world as it marks the beginning of increasing contacts between the East and the West. These contacts took the form of a military and cultural hegemony over Egypt and the rest of the Arab world. The military presence of European powers was accompanied by a particular interest in Arab culture: Orientalist scholars, archaeologists and painters identified with an exotic image of the 'Orient' which bore little in common with reality but which served to assert the supremacy of the West over Arab civilisation.[3] As a result of the increasing impact of European culture on the Arab way of life through the presence of traders, explorers, technicians and educationalists, a new class of Egyptians emerged, most having received an education in the schools set up by the colonial authorities. The writers who contributed to the cultural awakening of the *Nahdah* were scholars who were in close contact with European ideas and who had studied in European universities where they had become acquainted with European philosophy and literature. Rifa ah Rafi at-Tahtawi was one of the first modern Egyptian writers to write about European society.

At-Tahtawi and many of his contemporaries saw Europe's technological advance as a model of development for Arab societies. This idea, however, was not unambiguous and clashed with the Arab image of the past which symbolised, in many respects, civilisational progress. One of the ways in which some thinkers came to terms with this contradiction was to look at technological progress as distinct from moral superiority: the first an attribute of Europe; the second of the Arab world. Some writers tried to go beyond this dichotomy by analysing the changes that were affecting Islamic societies. The Tunisian politician and writer, Khayr ad-Din at-Tunisi provided an argument in favour of cultural borrowing from Europe. In his book, *Muqaddima*, he advocated a reform of Islamic institutions by arguing that Arab societies should learn from the experiences of European societies, mainly from the Industrial Revolution and from the democratic forms of political representation. His main contention was that, in the same way as the West had benefited from the scientific progress of the Arab world in the Middle Ages, it was now time for the Arabs to acquire knowledge from Europe. Others took a more nationalistic stand against European influence on the Islamic way of life. Although also calling for the need to adapt Islam to the demands of modern life, the leader of the Islamic Reformist movement, the Egyptian writer Jamal ad-Din al-Afghani, and later his follower, Muhammad Abduh, stressed the importance of religion in the spiritual life of a nation and the necessity to find strength in one's own cultural and spiritual heritage. Speaking against the cultural alienation threatening Arab societies, al-Afghani argued that reforms could only come from Islamic roots and not from a superficial imitation of European ways. In the same line of thought, another follower of the Reformist movement, Qasim Amin, suggested that one had to look at Islam itself in order to find a solution to gender inequalities. Arab women, according to him, had no status, not because of religion, but because autocratic rulers had determined a hierarchy whereby women were relegated to the lowest rank. Today, Qasim Amin's analysis seems to lack the depth of some of the more recent writings on gender in Arab societies by feminist authors, such as Nawal el-Saadawi and Fatima Mernissi. However, his position is to be interpreted in context: Qasim Amin's prime concern was not to analyse the question of gender but to formulate a critique of the social and symbolic structures in Arab society at a time of transition. The demands created by the economic, technological, social and political changes that were taking place at a very rapid pace forced writers to rethink their own cultural categories. This is clearly reflected in the literary production that has emerged since the *Nahdah*. The increasing contact with European culture and the internal dynamics of change that Arab societies were experiencing at the beginning of the century resulted in two main developments: the departure from classical poetry and the emergence of new narrative forms.

Arabic poetry, which pre-dates Islam, is the genre *par excellence* of classical Arabic literature. During the golden years of Arab Muslim civilisation, particularly under the Umayyad dynasty (660 AD), poetry reached the peak of its development and became a central element in the life of the Arabs. It was a means of recording history and celebrating battles and chivalrous rulers. Poetry played an important part in creating a sense of Arab national identity throughout the Arab world. The decline of this poetry in the nineteenth century coincided with the domination by the Ottoman empire and the stifling of Arab culture that resulted from it. One has to wait for the *Nahdah* in the early twentieth century to see a poetic revival in Arabic literature. The Egyptian poet Ahmad Shawqi symbolises the new spirit of the beginning of the century and is considered as the first poet who rescued Arabic poetry from decline. In line with the classical tradition of the *qasida* (the traditional ode with one rhyme), Shawqi's poetry recreates a harmonious world where the past and the present are one. Although celebrated as the 'Prince of Poets', Ahmad Shawqi was soon to be seen as failing to express the turmoil and the sense of displacement brought about by the deep transformations that the Arab world was experiencing. Still relying on the aesthetic conventions of the past, his poetry seemed unable to convey the urgency of the present.

The demands of the new era meant that poets had to find alternative poetic forms to express the deep transformations of Arab societies. The first generation of poets who broke away from the past found their inspiration in the European Romantic poets; but the main impulse came from those Arab poets who had emigrated to North America, the most celebrated of whom is probably the Lebanese-American Gibran Kahlil Gibran. The main contribution of the *Mahjar*, the literature in exile, was to introduce new techniques into Arabic poetry; namely, prose poems and free verse. The influence of the Mahjar poets was considerable, as in the case of the Tunisian, Abu al-Qasim al-Shabbi, a prominent figure of avant-garde Arabic poetry in the 1920s, whose romantic lyricism is the expression of a deeper yearning for freedom:

> O death, O fate that has no eyes,
> Stop where you are! Or turn aside,
> Let love and dream sing out for us[4]

Like his contemporaries, al-Shabbi is inspired by a desire to bring change and renewal to the old world. The poetic free flow of emotions is the expression of a need to break free from the constraints of classical poetry. This is made easier by the fact that the aesthetic conventions of Romantic poetry were borrowed from another tradition and therefore did not carry the weight of the Arabic past. Poets could therefore express themselves outside the social, political and aesthetic constraints of their culture.

Whether Arabic poetry in the first half of this century drew heavily on European romanticism, symbolism, or surrealism, it remained rooted in the Arab experience of a rapidly changing world. Technological and cultural changes brought about uncertainties which were to accentuate in the second half of the century with a series of events that affected the Arab world in a major way. The 1948 Palestine conflict, the creation of the state of Israel and the subsequent physical and symbolic displacement of the Palestinian people shattered the consciousness of Arab writers and marked a new turn in the way in which they perceived their place in the modern world. Disillusioned, they could no longer identify with the Romantic mood of the previous generation. Instead, they found an echo of their own gloom in the voices of poets in other parts of the world where people were experiencing similar situations of displacement, such as in the poetry of Pound, Eliot, Yeats, Aragon, Lorca, Neruda, and Hikmat.

After the 1950s, Arabic poetry took on a more vehement tone, denouncing injustice and oppression. This is shown in the writing by the Sudanese-Libyan poet Muhammad al-Faituri which reveals the evil of colonialism and racism by focusing on an image of Africa constructed around the idea of the struggle for freedom and dignity. In his later poems, al-Faituri uses the mythical figures of Bidpai and Dabshalim, taken from the Indian folk stories *Kalila wa Dimna*, which are also part of the Arabic folklore, to comment on the political situation in the Arab world following the defeat of 1967. Al-Faituri's work reflects the two-fold nature of Arabic poetry after the 1950s, as it moves between the outer world of politics on the one hand, and the inner world of the poet's dreams and aspirations, on the other. These dreams are often expressed through myths of resurrection which show, as Badawi put it, 'how deeply, and even tragically, concerned many of these poets are about the need to revive Arab culture and society, and drag it into the context of the fast-moving civilized western world'.[5]

The emergence of fiction in Arabic literature in the twentieth century also reflects the transition between the old world and the new age. Whether fiction and drama were part of Arabic literature prior to the introduction of European culture is an ongoing debate. Nevertheless, one could argue that they are new in the modern sense that is attributed to them today. Apart from the *maqama*, the traditional Arabic folk narrative which attracted writers as long ago as the tenth century, traditional folk stories were generally regarded as outside the literary canons which prevailed in the classical period. They did not generate any real interest among writers, who considered them as futile and as 'lower' forms of literature.[6]

Some critics have argued that the tradition of classical literature did not provide any framework for the development of narrative form and was even antagonistic to it. Bench-eikh, for example, explained that classical Arabic literature "neglected the individual for the benefit of the collective ideology... and privileged unifying abstractions to the expense of difference and reality.[7] Thus, according to this view, as genres that place the individual at their centre, fiction and drama could not have originated from the tradition of classical Arabic literature. It seems that what constituted the main impulse for the development of narrative genres was the influence of European fiction as well as the emergence of new concepts of history and human destiny in the modern period.

European works of fiction (mainly in French and in English) were first introduced to the Arabic-speaking public through translations but also in the original as, with the growing influence of European powers, the number of educated people who could read French and English was rising. Translations were part of the attempt to understand European culture, since the latter was becoming a model of technological as well as cultural progress. An important aspect of translation is the question that it raises about the difficulty of defining European concepts in Arabic and the necessity of adapting and transforming the original texts to comply with the specificities of Arab culture. The playwright Tawfiq al-Hakim, for example, describes how plots had to be altered when adapting European plays to the stage. At a time when tradition did not allow an Egyptian woman to appear unveiled in front of a person not related to her, translators had to change the plot so that male and female characters were related. As al-Hakim states, 'the alterations of social relations in accordance with the demands of our milieu in turn necessitated changes in the dialogue, the characterization and some of the situations of the play, adding up to considerable departures from the original'.[8] Thus, translations played an important part in introducing new ways of writing into Arabic literature.

The period of translation and adaptation of European texts was followed by the first attempts to write authentic Arabic narratives. The year 1923 saw the publication of what critics call the first significant novel in Arabic. Muhammad Husayn Haykal's *Zaynab* is the story of an Egyptian peasant forced to marry a man whom she does not love. Beyond the apparent simplicity of its theme, *Zaynab* addresses some important questions about Egyptian society which were not usually approached in literature, such as the life of the peasantry and the position of women. The novel is also innovative in its use of language as it attempts to break the barriers between high and low forms of Arabic by inserting colloquial patterns of speech into the dialogues. *Zaynab* marks the beginning of a search for authentic ways of translating the experiences of Arab people into narrative form.

The first novels to appear on the literary scene have a strong autobiographical flavour. Taha Husayn's *An Egyptian Childhood*, for example, portrays life in rural Egypt at the beginning of the century through the experiences of a boy who, struck by blindness in his early childhood (like the author himself), finds refuge in his thirst for learning. The novel uses the distance of the third-person narrative but at the same time tries to recreate the immediacy of the personal experiences. Like many of his contemporaries, Taha Husayn saw his individual life-story as part of the collective destiny of his people and, therefore, as a suitable subject for literature. The role of the novel in this early period was essentially to provide a framework for dealing with the individual experience as part of the wider social and historical changes that were happening in Arab society.

In the second half of the century, writers continued the experiments of the early novelists in a way more challenging and thematically diverse. The most prominent figure of this period is undoubtedly Naguib Mahfuz. It is interesting that Mahfuz's first novels attempt to resurrect history; not the history of the past Arab civilisation, but the ancient Pharaonic past. Set in Ancient Egypt, the novels are in fact a covert criticism of modern society. Evading censorship, Mahfuz uses the allegory of Ancient Egyptian history to make a critical comment about King Faruk's rule and the British protectorate. In his first novels, Mahfuz reinterprets the ancient past in order to analyse the present and establish historical continuity between the two. In his later novels, the Cairo trilogy, which is considered as his masterpiece, Mahfuz explores the recent past of Egyptian society by tracing the history of a Cairene family over several generations. This family is in many respects a microcosm of Egyptian society, and humanity in general. Beside being precisely located in time, the trilogy has a strong sense of place. The trilogy (each one named after a district of the old Cairo) focuses on the street as a social space, with its merchants, musicians and cafés. Critics have traditionally compared Mahfuz's realist descriptions with Dickens's London and Zola's Paris, emphasising the writer's debt to nineteenth-century European Realism. However, Mahfuz prefers to see his novels as part of a larger tradition, one that includes authors such as Dostoievsky, Tolstoi, Tchekhov, Maupassant, Shakespeare and Gide.[9]

European Realism has had a particular influence on Mahfuz and his contemporaries. It offered them a means of portraying the transformations of Arab society and the conflict between tradition and modernity by focusing on ordinary people: workers, shopkeepers, craftsmen, peasants, clerks, students. In Mahfuz's trilogy, the characters represent different

stages in the life of the nation. The central figure, Kamal Abdel Jawad, a largely autobiographical character, embodies the tensions between the old and the new. Kamal struggles to
come to grips with the contradictions between Arab traditional culture and a modernity that
is, in many respects, an 'imported' concept. Like his character, Mahfuz, as a writer using the
novel form, is involved in a similar process: the novel for him is a way of exploring new ways
of perceiving reality. The classical language of literature is modified through the play
between high and low forms of Arabic. Mahfuz's metaphors also show a desire to innovate;
the presence of similes referring to science, technology and modern communication
suggests, Somekh observes, that the novelist is attempting to create 'a language striving to
become one which befits a modern urban writer'.[10] As one of Mahfuz's characters remarks,
religion used to be a way of asserting truths, but now there is 'a new language, which is
Science, and there is no way of asserting truths, great or small alike, except in this
language'.[11] Science, often equated with modernity, is seen as the embodiment of the new
era, an era where old ways of thinking have no place.

Realism in Arabic fiction was largely a reflection of the scientific and technological age
where the writer saw him/herself as the rational voice interpreting reality. Thus, the novel
provided the framework for expressing the ideas of progress and change that characterise the
modern era. With the period of gloom following the 1967 Arab defeat, fiction started to offer
a fragmented vision of reality that emphasised its contradictions rather than tried to resolve
them. Like Romanticism in poetry, Realism lost its impact, and novelists started to search
for other forms of writing. They often turned to psychological experience as a way
of understanding reality. *Season of Migration to the North* (1966), by the Sudanese novelist
al-Tayyib Salih, explores the violence of the inner conflicts brought about by the confrontation between the West and the East through the theme of the relationship between a
European woman and an Arab emigrant, a theme explored by more than one writer.[12] More
critical than the previous generation of the *Nahdah* about the civilising mission of Europe,
writers like al-Tayyib turned inwards to interpret their own experience.[13]

The novel occupies an important place in the search for ways of redefining the individual's
relation to the past. New perceptions of reality as well as influences from other literatures,
particularly from Latin American writers, have led Arabic fiction away from Realism.
Writers, such as the Egyptian novelist Yusuf Idris, have also found in the short story a way
of portraying the fragmentation of today's world.

The development of North African writing in Arabic reflects the need to go beyond the
duality between the old and the new, the East and the West, in order to create an authentic
language. As it has been suggested, this 'new language' was born of a reappraisal of the
Arabic classical tradition and the introduction of new forms of writing borrowed from other
literatures and adapted to the North African context. In the French-speaking former colonies
of North Africa, a similar process can be observed. Francophone Maghrebian writers deal
with the contradictions and dualities of modern Arab societies by adapting the French
language to their own world view.

Writing in French

North African literature in French has a relatively short history. In the period following the
Second World War, writers from the North African French colonies (namely Morocco,

Algeria and Tunisia) started to use fictional modes to describe their condition and their aspirations as colonised people. The collapse of the structures of precolonial society and the devalued (or non-existent) status which the Arabic language and culture occupied in this region meant that, for these writers, using the French language was the only way of making their voices heard. The French presence in the Maghreb resulted in an 'acculturation' whereby the French language was imposed at all levels of society, excluding all other languages and cultures. This was clearly reflected in the French policy of cultural *assimilation* – carried out mainly through the educational system – which meant that North Africans had to accept French culture and language as their own and deny their Arab Berber heritage. This does not mean that the indigenous traditions died out completely. The Berber culture was handed down from generation to generation through oral tradition, while the Muslim Arab tradition was kept alive, particularly by the Ulema, the religious scholars whose movement played an important role in shaping the nationalist consciousness that led to the independence of North Africa. A literature in Arabic and a literature in French, the products of different traditions, have developed side by side in the Maghreb as writers have been concerned with finding a voice of their own. In the case of the literature in French, this search has taken the form of an exploration and an alteration of the French language to make it suit the reality of North Africa.

[. . .]

Notes

1   Magali Morsy, *North Africa 1800–1900: A Survey from the Nile Valley to the Atlantic* (London, 1984), p. 15.
2   See, for example, Mouloud Mammeri, *Poèmes Kabyles Ancients* (Paris, 1980).
3   For a detailed analysis of this period, see Edward Said, *Orientalism: Western Conceptions of the Orient* (London, 1978).
4   Salma Khadra Jayyusi, *Modern Arabic Poetry* (New York, 1987), p. 99.
5   M. M. Badawi, *A Critical Introduction to Modern Arabic Poetry* (Cambridge, 1975), p. 260.
6   It is interesting to note that *The Arabian Nights*, which is believed to have originated in Egyptian folk literature, never achieved as great a success in the Arab world as it did in the West.
7   *Encyclopedia Universalis* (Paris, 1985), p. 431. Author's translation.
8   Tawfiq al-Hakim, *Hayati*, as quoted in Pierre Cachia, *An Overview of Modern Arabic Literature* (Edinburgh, 1990), p. 37.
9   Naguib Mahfuz, "En creusant sa propre réalité on Débouche sur l'universel", in *Arabies, Mensuel du Monde Arabe et de la Francophonie*, no. 24 (1988), p. 75.
10   Sasson Somekh, *The Changing Rhythm* (Leiden, 1973), p. 136.
11   As quoted in P. Cachia, *An Overview of Modern Arabic Literature*, p. 120.
12   Titles are given in English whenever a translation is available; the date in brackets, however, refers to the year of publication of the original text.
13   See also writers such as Tawfiq al-Hakim and Yusuf Idris.

Chapter 6

A Continent and its Literatures in French

Jonathan Ngate

Writing about African literature in French in the Afrocentric journal *Peuples Noirs-Peuples Africains*, Midiohouan was insistent in reminding his readers that this literature has been, from the beginning, the site of an ideological battle the importance of which seems to have been unrecognized or downplayed in critical works, works such as Lilyan Kesteloot's seminal *Les Ecrivains noirs de langue française* (Midiohouan, 1982: 119–26). The sense of urgency Midiohouan brings to bear on the issue is best understood by keeping in mind that the term *littérature africaine* itself is ambiguous in French. Before the 1930s, the decade now generally considered to have witnessed the beginning of francophone African literature, there had been indeed a flourishing African literature produced by Frenchmen living in Africa, for the most part. It was part of the colonial literature which came to the fore with and especially after the creation of a French colonial empire, from the time of the 1884–5 Berlin Conference to the first decade of this century, that is. The colonial literature that emerged sought to distinguish itself from the exotic literature that had preceded it.

Dismissed as being too subjective and superficial, exoticism was rejected in favor of the colonial literature which laid claim to being more accurate. "L'exotisme désuet – forme de nos ignorances et de nos étonnements – fait place à un exotisme nouveau, dépouillé d'artifice, expression d'un plus grand effort de pénétration sincère. Les auteurs veulent acquérir une connaissance vraie des choses africaines" ("The old-fashioned exoticism – a form of our ignorance and sense of wonder – is making way for a new, unadorned exoticism that is the expression of a much greater effort at sincere penetration. The authors wish to gain a much more accurate knowledge of things African") (Lebel, 1925: 118). In speaking of a "grand effort de pénétration sincère" (in Conrad's *Heart of Darkness*, it becomes a "fantastic invasion"), Lebel was obviously trying to encourage a sympathetic reading of French colonial literature; coincidentally, the military and sexual connotations of the vocabulary used cannot be overlooked in their ironic and doubtless involuntary aptness.

First published in *Francophone African Fiction: Reading a Literary Tradition*, pp. 19–27. Trenton: Africa World Press, 1988.

The literature was labelled African because it dealt with Africa and was quite clearly the product of the perceptual encounter with Africa by a specific group of people, colonizers, who felt that theirs was the duty to reveal to a metropolitan French public a "true" image of the colonies and an epic understanding of the historical necessity of the colonizing enterprise.[1] Witness the glowing review Lebel gave of Paul Adam's book on French West Africa with the not so surprising title, *Notre Carthage (Our Carthage)*: "un des plus beaux ouvrages qui aient été écrits pour la meilleure connaissance et pour la glorification de notre colonie. Paul Adam est un 'colonial,' un 'africain' de longue date. Déjà, dans quelques articles, il avait laissé percer sa sympathie et son admiration pour notre entreprise africaine" ("one of the most beautiful books ever written to make possible a better knowledge of our colony and to glorify it. Paul Adam is a 'colonist,' an 'African' of long-standing. He had already shown his liking and his admiration for our African enterprise in a few articles") (Lebel, 1925: 93).

What the theoretical battle of the 1920s between proponents of colonial literature and those of its antecedent, exotic, literature revealed was that colonial literature was supposed to be the result of a quasi-scientific endeavor: "le vrai touriste africain, c'est l'enquêteur qui [...] va se documenter sur place en vue d'une action commerciale à engager, d'une entreprise à faire connaître, d'un enseignement à répandre. Ces voyages supposent certaines connaissances, et aussi le don de voir" ("the true African tourist is the investigator who [...] informs himself on the spot with an eye toward engaging in trade, making a company better known or spreading knowledge. These travels presuppose certain kinds of knowledge and a keen sense of observation") (Lebel, 1925: 117). Two conclusions can be drawn from these observations: first, that for those involved in colonial literature the will to knowledge was a very strong point, and second, as a corollary, they had no reservations about their support for the colonial enterprise of their country. And the reception of this literature in France itself was rather good if one is to believe Lebel (1925: *vii*). He seems to have no doubt that there was a readership in France for the colonial literature his book goes on to analyse in detail. What all this means, of course, is that by the time francophone Africans came on the scene and started producing their own literature, theirs was, chronologically, only the second African literature in French, which is also a way of pointing out that the general context of francophone African literature is not just Africa itself but also, and primarily, the long French tradition of literary and other discourses on Africa and Africans.

Perhaps the most elaborate formulation of what is involved here is to be found in Edward Said's *Orientalism* (1978) and warrants full citation:

> I have begun with the assumption that the Orient is not an inert fact of nature. It is not merely *there*, just as the Occident itself is not just *there* either. We must take seriously Vico's great observation that men make their own history, that what they can know is what they have made, and extend it to geography: as both geographical and cultural entities – to say nothing of historical entities – such locales, regions, geographical sectors as "Orient" and "Occident" are man-made. Therefore as much as the West itself, the Orient is an idea that has a history and a tradition of thought, imagery, and vocabulary that have given it reality and presence in and for the West. The two geographical entities thus support and to an extent reflect each other. [...] One ought never to assume that the structure of lies and of myths which, were the truth about them to be told, would simply blow away. I myself believe that Orientalism is more particularly valuable as a sign of European-Atlantic power over the Orient than it is as a veridic discourse about the Orient (which is what, in its academic and scholarly form, it claims to be). [...] Orientalism is never far from what Denys Hay has called the idea of Europe, a collective notion

associating "us" Europeans as against all "those" non-Europeans, and indeed it can be argued
that the major component in European culture is precisely what made that culture hegemonic
both in and outside Europe: the idea of European identity as a superior one in comparison with
all the non-European peoples and cultures. There is in addition the hegemony of European ideas
about the Orient, themselves reiterating European superiority over Oriental backwardness,
usually overriding the possibility that a more independent, or more skeptical, thinker might
have had different views on the matter. (1979: 4–5, 6, 7; emphases in the text)

Unlike, say, Bambara or Xhosa literature then, francophone African literature is not an
Afrocentric given. It is best appreciated as being the site of intersections between different
traditions. The importance of its place in the network of relations that bind it to the colonial
literature of France thus becomes more evident. Focus on such a network seems to be what
Fanoudh-Siefer had in mind when he complained, as early as 1968, that not enough was
being said about the conditions under which the literature started:

> si on accorde tant d'attention actuellement à la littérature négro-africaine, c'est presque toujours
> pour mettre en relief son aspect engagé et révolté, pour dire – ce qui est vrai, du reste – que c'est
> une littérature de protestation, de revendication née de la colonisation. Mais on ne dit pas assez
> contre quoi les écrivains noirs s'insurgeaient, on suppose connues les tares du système colonial;
> or ce système étant plus ou moins aboli désormais, les générations à venir risquent à brève
> échéance de ne plus se retrouver au coeur de cette littérature passionnée et à divers égards
> passionnante. (Fanoudh-Siefer, 1968: 15–16)

> (if so much attention is now being paid to Black African literature, it is almost always in order to
> highlight its being a committed literature of revolt, to say – and this, incidentally, is true – that it
> is a literature of protest and of demands born of colonization. But not enough is said about that
> against which the Black writers were rebelling; it is assumed that all the blemishes of the
> colonial system are known. The fact, however, is that since this system is now more or less
> abolished, future generations run the risk of soon finding themselves out of touch with this
> impassioned and in many ways, thrilling literature.)

Fanoudh-Siefer[2] thus insists, and correctly so, on the importance of what Makouta-M'boukou (1973a: 9) will later call the "ecological sources" of the literature that concerns us here,
on the need to look closely and critically at the conditions of possibility and of the birth of
francophone African literature.

A good starting point would therefore be a restatement of the obvious fact that this
literature was born in a colonial context, one in which the African writer found himself not
only using the language of the colonizer, but also a language that has a long tradition of
producing discourses (literary or otherwise) on Africa and Africans. For example, Martine
Astier-Loutfi's *Littérature et colonialisme* (1971) and Gérard Leclerc's *Anthropologie et colonialisme* (1972) have shown that there was essentially no difference between French ethnological
discourses and the literary imaging of Africa and Africans at the time francophone African
literature was taking shape. The implications of these and other "ecological sources" for the
development of francophone African literature are what I shall be concerning myself with.
And that is why Nara's and Landu's paradigmatic crises as they search for the word with
which to speak or write themselves are relevant and instructive: Africa was neither "vierge"
("virgin") nor "sans archives reconnues" ("without recognised archives") (Mudimbe, 1978:
66) during the colonial era which gave birth to francophone African literature.

Exoticism in French literature, as it applied to Africa, had had as its masterpiece Pierre Loti's *Roman d'un spahi*, published in 1881, a work that seems to have helped crystallize some of the most negative images of Africa. Writing about Loti in *Le Mythe du nègre et de l'Afrique noire dans la littérature française* (1968), Léon Fanoudh-Siefer states that in this Frenchman's Africa,

> tout [. . .] est triste, malsain, présageant la mort et le mauvais sort; tout y est mystérieux, bizarre, étrange, illogique et impur. Ce névropathe a rassemblé toutes les bribes de mythe qui traînaient sur l'Afrique avant lui, et il y a ajouté ses mythes personnels. Dès l'époque de Loti, le mythe de l'Afrique est déjà done structuré dans ses grandes lignes. (109)

> (everything is sad, unhealthy, a harbinger of death and bad luck; everything there is mysterious, bizarre, strange, illogical and impure. This neurotic man assembled all the bits of myth about Africa available to him and added to them some of his own. In Loti's time, the myth of Africa was already established, in its broad outlines.)

It is against this kind of literary discourse that French proponents of colonial literature chose to react. Lebel observes, for instance, that "Pierre Loti, comme Chateaubriand, exprime des sensations, des désirs, des regrets, des nostalgies; ce ne sont que ses propres états de sensibilité" ("Pierre Loti, like Chateaubriand, gives expression to his own feelings, his desires, his regrets and nostalgia; we are dealing here only with his sensibility") before adding that "un mouvement de réaction contre *le facile et le faux exotisme* des passants s'est manifesté, depuis 1900 surtout, dans la littérature coloniale" ("a reaction against this *easy and false exoticism* of people who know no better has been in evidence in colonial literature especially since 1900") (1925: 227, 228). Lebel is thus quite emphatic in stating that colonial literature had its origins, or impetus, in the reaction against an *easy and false exoticism*.

And wishing to further point out the distinguishing traits of the "educated" sensibility and techniques of colonial literature, he writes:

> Les écrivains coloniaux, observateurs avertis, curieux du fond réel, des moeurs et du caractère des noirs, conféreront à leurs livres *une valeur de documentation* qui, sans nuire à leur charme, en accroîtra l'intérêt. Ce ne seront plus des passants se livrant à de brillantes compositions, capable de séduire les ignorants, mais des fonctionnaires, des commerçants, vivant habituellement à la colonie, s'y plaisant, parlant les langues indigènes, s'étant assimilés par une lente pénétration à l'objet qu'ils ont mission d'exprimer, et ne considérant plus cet objet comme un monde extérieur à eux mais comme un milieu familier, comme leur milieu naturel. La littérature coloniale se distinguera de la littérature exotique. (Lebel, 228–9; emphasis added)

> (Colonial writers, as informed observers who are curious about the true nature of the Blacks, about their ways and character, will give their books *the quality of documents* which will add to their value without eliminating their charm. We are here no longer dealing with passers-by involved in brilliant composition exercises that would only seduce the ignorant. We are talking about civil servants and traders who have been living in the colonies which they like. They speak the natives' languages and have gained a thorough knowledge of the things they are writing about. They write not as outsiders but as people for whom the colonies are a familiar and natural milieu. This accounts for the difference between colonial and exotic literature.) (emphasis added)

The emphasis on the "valeur de documentation" of this literature is not accidental. If we keep in mind that implicit in Lebel's praise of the author of *Notre Carthage* is the critic's belief that Africa is to conquering France what Carthage had been to Rome, we would understand what gives colonial French literary discourse its redemptive value, even epic anchorage, for a French reader of the period.[3]

The fact remains that what we have here is indeed a new exoticism (Lebel, 118). This time, however, it is the product of the colonizer's justifying view of the way things are in the colony. For if there is anything we can be sure of now, with the benefit of hindsight, it is that the colonizers had no trouble at all making the colonized invisible, erasing them as subjects of any kind of meaningful discourses. The effect can be sometimes curious: in *Philoxène ou de la littérature coloniale* (1931), Eugène Pujamiscle seems, in a contradictory way, to be dismissing the colonies themselves as foreign areas to *really be discovered*; they are after all only so many versions of France herself: "Les colonies ne sont pas l'étranger. Une colonie française c'est la France encore, la France d'Asie, d'Afrique, d'Amérique ou d'Océanie" ("The colonies are not foreign. A French colony is still France, the France of Asia, Africa, America or Oceania") (15). The colonizers' confidence in thus thinking of themselves as "writing not as outsiders but as people for whom the colonies are a familiar and natural milieu" is not only obvious, it is also tellingly misguided, and accounts ultimately for the kind of Africa they succeeded in creating in their books.

The example of Albert Camus, who, though born in Algeria, could not help but write about that country and its people from a "foreign" (which is to say French and Metropolitan) perspective should be sobering for anyone wishing to talk about relations between colonial settlers and the colonized, relations which cannot but be implicitly or explicitly violent. Comparing Camus' views on French and Arabs in Algeria and Fanon's on the colonizer and the colonized in *The Wretched of the Earth*, Conor Cruise O'Brien is insightful in concluding that the image that emerges of Camus is one, it must be granted, of a "colonist who refuses" to consciously accept and play his role as colonist. However, in his celebrated novel, *L'Etranger*, Camus is shown to have been written, as it were, by his role as a member of the colonizing French population; it is a role that makes it easy, ultimately, to kill off the native who is ever the "blank and alien being," the being who is *"sans archives reconnues"* ("without recognized archives"):

> I have long wondered why so many commentators on *L'Etranger* – including Camus himself – are so ready to canonize Meursault, granted the nature of his dealings with the Arab woman and her brother. A part of the answer certainly lies in the fact that we feel him to be really tried for the failure to mourn his mother. Everyone – Meursault himself, the court, and the author – treats the actual killing and the sordid transactions which prepare the way for it as irrelevant. But it is not easy to make the killing of a man seem irrelevant; in fact it can hardly be done unless one is led in some way to regard the man as not quite a man. And this is what happens. The Europeans in the book have names – Meursault, Raymond Sintes, Marie, Salamano, and other minor characters. The man who is shot has no name, and his relation to the narrator and his friends is not that of one human being to another. He looks at them as if they were "blocks of stone or dead trees." When the narrator shoots down this blank and alien being and fires "four shots more into the inert body, on which they left no visible trace," the reader does not quite feel that Meursault has killed a man. He has killed an Arab. Both Camus and many of his readers would have been likely to reject that implication with genuine indignation, yet the relative substantiality of Arabs and Europeans in the text carries its own message. (1970: 25–6)

If a "colonist who refuses" is thus "written" by the colonizing text, what could be said of those colonists who eagerly accepted and played their role properly in "Notre Carthage"?

Given the blindness and insight in the colonialist view O'Brien extrapolates from his reading of Camus, it is not surprising that texts like *L'Etranger* (1942) should be strangely prophetic and curiously oblivious of certain colonial propensities and realities – such, for example, as what happened, starting on VE-Day, May 8, 1945, in Setif, Algeria:

> For a whole week repression fell on the Algerian population. Troops and civilians alike happily massacred, shot on sight, killed by the dozen peasants and villagers, people who had not even heard of the demonstration. The Foreign Legion, and according to some reports, even Italian PoW's were involved. Villages were bombed by aeroplanes, and a cruiser anchored in the nearby bay of Bougie (today's Bejaia) shelled indiscriminately the hills around Setif.
>
> The results were appalling. Entire populations of some villages vanished. Paupers graves were discovered with countless corpses. (Tissas, 1985: 1648)

It is, however, just as understandable that the Setif massacre should engender a "renegade" author with a distinctive way of "archiving" what might have been for Meursault-Camus essentially blank and alien: "As the great Algerian writer Kateb Yacine put it: 'I have never forgotten the shock which I felt at the ruthless slaughter. There (in Setif) my nationalism was consolidated. I was 16 years old'" (loc. cit).[4]

One can fully agree with Fanoudh-Siefer when he states that the image of Africa put forward by the "new exoticism" of colonial literature is that of "un pays préhistorique et désolé pour les uns, un pays de soleil et de mort pour les autres; elle enchante quelques-uns, rebute la plupart. D'autres veulent y soupçonner des mystères infinis et impénétrables qu'ils se gardent bien de percer" ("a prehistoric and desolate country for some, a land of sun and death for others. It enchants a few but repels most people. Others suspect deep and impenetrable mysteries that they carefully avoid bringing to light") (1968: 146). Through it all, when he was seen at all, the colonized African came across as essentially a devil, gargoyle or buffoon (Johnson, 1971). From here to portraying the colonized as a child to be taken in charge by the colonial father, there was only a small step that the French did not hesitate to take.[5] In short, it is often not easy to tell the new from the old exoticism, given the nature of the former's prior text on Africa and Africans and the acknowledged desire of the latter to justify or facilitate the colonial enterprise. As far as colonial literature itself is concerned, Pujarniscle is forthright enough on the nexus of literary image and political enterprise:

> la sécurité, la tranquillité, la prospérité de nos possessions coloniales dépendent, en partie, de la façon dont en parlent les écrivains. [. . .] Or, de toutes les propagandes, la plus efficace est la propagande par les arts, et, plus spécialement, par la littérature. (1931: 5, 6)
>
> (the security, the tranquility, the prosperity of our colonial possessions depend, in part, on the way in which writers talk about them. [. . .] It's clear that of all forms of propaganda, the most efficacious is propaganda through the arts, and particularly, through literature.)

It goes without saying that the effect of such a *propagande par les arts* ("propaganda through the arts") on *l'autre face du royaume* ("the other side of the kingdom") is, naturally, *l'odeur du père* ("the scent of the father"), against and within which the Naras and Pierre Landus define themselves. Which, incidentally, is why I find Marthe Robert persuasive when she states that

> à tout prendre, le nouveau en littérature n'a jamais que deux façons de se manifester: ou bien il déclare l'ancien périmé et se substitue à lui sans autre forme de procès; ou bien il le maintient d'abord solidement en s'inspirant de ses thèmes et de ses procédés, non pour en confirmer une fois de plus l'immuabilité, mais au contraire pour les forcer à produire au grand jour ce qu'ils ont de faux et de caduc sous leurs airs d'éternité. (1977: 120–1)

> (all things being equal, what is new in literature has only two ways of making its presence felt: it can proclaim the old out-dated and substitute itself for it without fanfare or it can keep it [the old] solidly in place at first by taking some inspiration from its themes and procedures, not in order to confirm its immutability once and for all but instead, to force it to reveal openly what is false and obsolescent about them beneath their airs of eternity.)

It should then be easy to see why the relations that have obtained between francophone African literature and French colonial literature have been not only multiple but also contradictory. If one thinks of the colonial literary discourse as a voice, a sentence, one could reasonably be tempted to say, with apologies to the Foucault of *L'Ordre du discours*, that it is as if, from the beginning, the francophone African writer could not help but perceive a French colonial voice, long preceding him, leaving him merely to enmesh himself in it, taking up its cadence, and lodging himself, when no one was looking, in its interstices. For the francophone African writer, there can be, in this reading of "ecological sources," no *intransitive* beginnings (Edward Said) as such. Instead, literary speech would have proceeded from the African writer, only while and because he stood in its path – a slender gap – the point of the francophone text's possible disappearance, and re-appearance.

Given such an "intimate" link between the colonial French and the francophone African voices, their relation "cannot be grasped as an *interval between polar opposites* but rather as an irreducible dislocation of the subject in which the other inhabits the self as its condition of possibility" (Weber, 1982: 32–3). That much I have already tried to illustrate in the paradigms that leave Pierre Landu immured in a monkish and hagiographic discourse and Nara driven to a psychiatrist's couch by dislocations that leave him trapped between Isabelle and Aminata. Multiple voices and texts in the "ecological sources" are thus revealed in twentieth-century francophone African literature.[6] And their significance is as relevant for the autobiographical or nearly autobiographical novels of Camara Laye (1953) and Cheikh Hamidou Kane (1961), for the anticolonial novels of Ferdinand Oyono (1956) or Mongo Béti (1957; 1958), as it is for three transitional and subversive novels by Camara Laye again (1966), Ahmadou Kourouma (1968) and Yambo Ouologuem (1968). The self-confidence displayed by a Bamboté (1972), a Mudimbe (1976)[7] or a Labou Tansi (beginning in 1979) is in turn understood in the evolutionary light of the "ecological sources." Dorothy Blair (1976) has provided an insightful critical overview of francophone African literature and Francis Joppa (1982) a useful thematic analysis of the francophone African novel. My own concern here, on the basis of the paradigms presented, is with periodization and "ecology" in francophone African fiction. The approach should help provide a useful answer to an old question: for whom is that literature written and to what purpose?

Notes

1　As General Duboc makes clear in the title of one of his books, *L'Epopée coloniale en Afrique Occidentale Française* (Paris: Editions Edgar Malfère, 1938), there was no doubt about the epic dimension of the colonial enterprise.

2　Mohamadou Kane will also draw attention to the lack of emphasis on the link between French colonial literature and francophone African literature in 1978, in his thesis for the "doctorat d'état": *Romans africains et traditions*, Lille: Université de Lille III (U.E.R. de Linguistique française et Sciences des littératures). It has since been published in book form by the Nouvelles Editions Africaines (1982).

3　It should perhaps be noted that after more than 2,000 years, the war between Rome and Carthage, now a suburb of Tunis, was finally brought to an end early in 1985 when the mayors of the two cities signed a peace treaty in Carthage itself. See *Jeune Afrique*, no. 1259 (20 février 1985), p. 49.

4　Less than a year earlier, on December 1, 1944, colonialism had shown how little it cared for the "blank and alien" colonized when Black African soldiers who had fought against fascism in Europe and had just been demobilized following Allies victories in Europe, were massacred by the colonial authorities in the village of Thiaroye, just outside Dakar, Senegal. See Mamadou Traore Diop's "Colonial Spasms: The Martyrs of Thiaroye" in *West Africa* (12 August 1985), p. 1647.

5　In this context, Dr Schweitzer, while in Gabon, would only have been playing his role of the elder brother who knows better.

6　For a recent interesting, but incomplete, study along the same line, see János Riesz's "The First African Novels: A Problem of Authenticity," in *Towards African Authenticity: Language and Literary Forms*, Bayreuth African Studies Series 2, eds. Eckhard Breitinger and Reinhard Sander (Bayreuth: German Research Council and the University of Bayreuth, 1985).

7　The dates given here are the first dates of publication of the texts involved. In this study, I will be quoting at times from later editions of the same texts.

Chapter 7

African Literature and the Colonial Factor

Simon Gikandi

Modern African literature was produced in the crucible of colonialism. What this means, among other things, is that the men and women who founded the tradition of what we now call modern African writing, both in European and indigenous languages, were, without exception, products of the institutions that colonialism had introduced and developed in the continent, especially in the period beginning with the Berlin Conference of 1884–5 and decolonization in the late 1950s and early 1960s. African literature had, of course, been produced outside the institutions of colonialism: the existence of oral literature in all African languages and precolonial writing in Arabic, Amharic, Swahili, and other African languages is ample evidence of a thriving literary tradition in precolonial Africa. But what is now considered to be the heart of literary scholarship on the continent could not have acquired its current identity or function if the traumatic encounter between Africa and Europe had not taken place. Not only were the founders of modern African literature colonial subjects, but colonialism was also to be the most important and enduring theme in their works. From the eighteenth century onwards, the colonial situation shaped what it meant to be an African writer, shaped the language of African writing, and overdetermined the culture of letters in Africa.

In 1955, Georges Balandier began his influential theoretical study of the colonial situation by observing that despite the changes that had occurred in the era of decolonization, "the colonial problem remains one of the main issues with which specialists in the social sciences have to deal. Indeed, the pressures of a new nationalism and the reactions resulting from decolonization give this problem an immediacy and a topicality that cannot be treated with indifference" (1970: 21). The point Balandier made about the relationship between colonialism and the social sciences can be said about the conjunction between African literature and the colonial situation. Colonialism, especially in its radical transformation of African societies, remains one of the central problems with which writers and intellectuals in Africa

First published in *The Cambridge History of African and Caribbean Literature*, vol. 1, ed. Abiola Irele and Simon Gikandi, pp. 379–85. Cambridge: Cambridge University Press, 2004.

have to deal; the tradition of African writing that has produced Nobel Prize laureates was built and consolidated when African writers began to take stock of the colonial situation and its impact on the African psyche. Even the African writing that emerged in the postcolonial era, a literature shaped by the pressures of "arrested decolonization" and the "pitfalls of national consciousness," can be said to have been driven by the same imperative as writing under colonialism – the desire to understand the consequences of the colonial moment (see Jeyifo 1990: 33–46; and Fanon 1968: 148–205). The purpose of this chapter, then, is to explore the paradigmatic and practical value of the colonial moment in the history of African literature. Our starting point is that the key to the development of modern African literature can be found in a number of institutions – the Christian mission, the colonial school, and the university – that were crucial to the emergence, nature, and function of African literature.

Colonial culture and African literature: an overview

A discussion of the relationship between colonialism and African literature should perhaps begin with a simple question: why has colonialism been the main subject of African literature and why do colonial institutions seem to be such a central component of a literature which was expressively produced as a critique of European domination? The most obvious answer, as we shall see in our discussion of several colonial institutions, is that the political and cultural force of colonialism in Africa was so enduring that writers concerned with the nature of African society could not avoid the trauma and drama that accompanied the imposition of European rule on the continent. As early as the end of the eighteenth century, Africans writing in European languages, most notably Olaudah Equiano, had appropriated dominant literary conventions to oppose slavery and to validate an African identity; but others, such as Johannes Capitein, had produced treatises arguing that slavery was not necessarily an affront to morality and Christianity. While the political interests of these early writers might now appear radically divergent, it is important to keep in mind that their writing was generated by a common desire to deploy writing both as the mark of the African's humanity and as a point of entry into the culture of modernity (see Gates 1985: 9–10).

If the late colonial period (1880–1935) seems to preoccupy the imagination even of writers who were born in the age of decolonization and after, it is because it is considered to be a period unlike any other in African history. Adu Boahen has remarked: "Never in the history of Africa did so many changes occur and with such speed as they did between 1880 and 1935 . . . The pace of this drama was truly astonishing, for as late as 1880 only very limited areas of Africa had come under the direct rule of Europeans" (1985a: 1). For almost four centuries Africans had endured traumas induced by the foreign encounter, most notably the transatlantic slave trade, but the European element had remained localized at the coast and no significant political entities had lost their sovereignty until the late colonial period. After the Conference of Berlin, however, the whole continent was divided among the major European powers and the nature of African society was rapidly transformed under the tutelage of foreign powers. And while the process of colonial rule might have appeared to the European powers to be a matter of military strategy and commercial interests, for many African societies it was tantamount to what F. Abbas has called "a veritable revolution, overthrowing a whole ancient world of beliefs and ideas and an immemorial way of life"; European conquest confronted local societies with the difficult choice "to adapt or perish" (quoted in Boahen 1985a: 3). Either way, what was at issue in the colonial encounter was the question of African autonomy, a major subject in early writing from the continent.

It is easy to underestimate the centrality of the ideology of sovereignty and the idea of autonomy to African debates on colonialism and decolonization and the literary texts they inspired. And yet, as Chinua Achebe was to note in an influential essay published in the early 1960s, one of the key motivations for producing an African literature was to restore the moral integrity and cultural autonomy of the African in the age of decolonization. The fundamental theme of African writing, noted Achebe, was that "African people did not hear of culture for the first time from Europeans; that their societies were not mindless but frequently had a philosophy of great depth and value and beauty, that they had poetry and, above all, they had dignity. It is this dignity that many African people all but lost during the colonial period and it is this they must regain now" (1973: 8). For many African writers in the age of decolonization, then, the loss of sovereignty was not simply the process by which older cultures and institutions were deprived of their authority under colonialism; it was also conceived, especially by members of the African elite, as the ultimate loss of agency and free will. Thus the narrative of colonialism came to be conceived as the unwilled evacuation of African subjects from the movement of time; for many African intellectuals in the nineteenth century and early twentieth century, to be colonized, as Walter Rodney noted aptly, was "to be removed from history" (1972: 245–56).

But the process of colonial rule was to appeal to African writers for something more than its drama and impact: for writers born between the cusp of European rule and decolonization, especially in the period between 1900 and 1945, colonialism was more than a period of loss and temporal dislocation; it also represented the challenges and opportunities of modernity. It is these opportunities that the authors of the Pan-African Conference held in London in 1900 had in mind when they reminded "the modern world" that colonized people, "by reason of sheer numbers and physical contact," were bound to have an immense effect upon the world: "If now the world of culture bends itself towards giving Negroes and other dark men the largest and broadest opportunity for education and self-development, then this contact and influence is bound to have a beneficial effect upon the world and hasten human progress" (see Langley 1979: 738). For the colonized African elite, colonialism was a challenge because its impact was evident throughout Africa and it had bound the destiny of the continent with other worlds.

At the same time, however, the colonial process presented an interpretative enigma: colonial culture had transformed many African societies through voluntary and enforced modernization, but as many observers of the African scene were quick to note, this process did not seem to penetrate too deeply into the fabric of local communities. Ostensibly, colonialism touched every aspect of social and political life on the continent, but its impact also seemed to be superficial because, in spite of the predominance and preponderance of colonial modernity, so-called traditional society seemed to function as if the colonial event was a mere interruption in the *longue durée* of African history. For the men and women who came to produce modern African literature, the subjects who were most affected by the colonial process, the simultaneous existence of a modern and traditional world could only be negotiated through works of the imagination. It is not accidental that the foundational texts of modern African literature in the European languages were concerned with the dialectic of modernity and tradition as it was played out on the continent under colonialism.

Nevertheless, this turn to writing as a way of accounting for the existence of the modern within what appeared to be traditional societies was the source of an important paradox: in order to oppose colonialism, and thus to assert indigenous interests and rights, African leaders and intellectuals had to turn to a recently discovered European language of tradition, nation, and race. This new language, which sought a synthesis between modernization and African autonomy, is evident in declarations by leaders such as Makombe Hanga, chief of the Barue, as he confronted the Portuguese in Central Mozambique in 1895: "I see how you white men advance more and more in Africa . . . My country will also have to take up these reforms and I am quite prepared to open it up . . . I should also like to have good roads and railways . . . But I will remain the Makombe my fathers have been" (quoted in Ranger 1985: 49). In his confrontation with the Germans in Namibia, the great Nama leader Hendrik Wittboi easily resorted to the language of the *Volksgeist* popularized by his European adversaries: "The Lord has established various kingdoms in the world. Therefore I know and believe that it is no sin or crime that I should wish to remain the independent chief of my land and people" (quoted in Ranger 1985: 49).

The emergence of African literatures in European language needs to be located within the crucial claim that colonized subjects had set out to use the instruments and grammar given to them by the colonizer to oppose foreign domination and assert their sovereignty. It should not hence come as a surprise that the pioneers of African literature and African cultural nationalism, writers like Sol Plaatje in South Africa or Caseley Hayford in West Africa, identified very closely with colonial culture and its institutions, even as they opposed the destructive practices of imperial rule and fought for African political rights. Indeed, a key axiom of African literary history is that the founders of African literature were the most Europeanized. What this meant was that African literature was not initially intended to provide a radical critique of European rule; rather, it was a discursive mode through which Africans could try to represent and mediate their location both inside and outside colonial culture.

But why did literature become one of the most important weapons of cultural resistance against European intervention in Africa in the late nineteenth century? Literature came to occupy a central place in colonial culture for three closely related reasons. First, one of the most attractive aspects of colonial culture, from the perspective of the colonized, was what came to be universally conceived as the gift of literacy. Even though many African subjects may have been ambivalent about many aspects of colonial modernity, they seemed unanimous about the power and enchantment of literacy and the culture of print that enabled it: "Literacy was for many African peoples a new magic, and was sought after as such and at all costs since it appeared to open the treasure house of the modern world. To know the amount of power, authority and influence which the first generation of African clerks, interpreters and teachers exercised is to have some idea of the spell which literacy cast over many African peoples" (Afigbo 1985: 496).

The literary history of Africa has often been written from the perspective of university-educated writers and intellectuals (see Wauthier 1979 and July 1968), but we need to foreground the significance of the first generation of literate Africans, many of them clerks, interpreters, and teachers with only a few years of education, in the establishment of an

African tradition of letters. Out of this class came not only the writers who produced the earlier works in European languages (Plaatje and Tutuola, for example), but even more influential writers working in African languages, including Thomas Mofolo (Sotho), H. I. E. Dlomo (Zulu), D. O. Fagunwa (Yoruba), and Shabaan Robert (Swahili). These writers were the great mediators between colonial culture and the newly literate African masses. Indeed, the subject, language, and form used in the most influential works of these writers was intended to simultaneously represent the bourgeois public sphere that colonialism had instituted and satisfy the reading desires of the newly literate African.

But there was a second reason why literature came to occupy such an important role in the mediation of the colonial relationship: in both the popular imagination and the annals of Africanism or Orientalism (see Miller 1985 and Said 1979), the process of colonization existed as both an unprecedented historical episode and a monumental literary event. While it is true that colonial conquest and rule were effected through violent military methods, aggressive diplomacy, and blatant economic exploitation, these processes ultimately came to acquire their authority and totality when they were represented in powerful narratives of conquest. Napoleon's invasion of Egypt (1789), to cite one of the most prominent examples, came to have a presence, a voice, and rationale when it was represented in *Description de l'Egypte*, the massive twenty-four volume account of the expedition. In this account, as Edward Said has noted, a diachronic and contested event was transformed into a synchronic narrative of European conquest and rule; Orientalism acquired its intellectual power through textualization, which brought together 'a family of ideas and a unifying set of values proven in various ways to be effective' (1979: 41–2). Nevertheless, against the texts of European power produced during the process of conquest, there emerged powerful African texts produced in response; works written as a counterpoint to the Napoleonic narrative (the most famous example is "'Abd al-Rahman al-Jabarti's" *Ajaib al-Athar*) contested the terrain of culture as vigorously as the literature of conquest. Indeed, most of the African writing produced in the nineteenth century by writers as diverse as al-Jarbati and Edward Blyden simultaneously sought to take stock of the colonial situation and to challenge its philosophical and cultural assumptions on the nature of the colonized, their culture, and community.

The third reason why colonialism and literary culture came to be so closely associated in the history of African literature is one that has become central in postcolonial studies: this is the recognition that the idea of culture itself lay at the heart of the colonial project of conquest and rule. Colonial writers understood not only the obvious fact that culture and knowledge were used as instruments of control, but that the process of colonization produced new cultural formations and configurations, what Nicholas Dirks has described as "the allied network of processes" that spawned new subjects and nations (1992: 3). As Dirks has noted, the idea of culture, as an object and mode of knowledge, was formed out of colonial histories and spawned specific cultural forms; these cultural forms, he concludes, "became fundamental to the development of resistance against colonialism, most notably in the nationalist movements that used Western notions of national integrity and self-determination to justify claims for independence" (1992: 4). It was at this point – the point where western notions about nation, culture, and self were turned against the project of colonialism – that the largest body of work by African writers was produced.

[...]

References

Achebe, Chinua. 1973. "The Role of the Writer in a New Nation." In *African Writers on African Writing*. Ed. G. D. Killam. London: Heinemann: 7–13.

Afigbo, A. E. 1985. "The Social Repercussions of Colonial Rule: the New Social Structures." In *The UNESCO General History of Africa*, vol. vii: *Africa under Colonial Domination 1880–1935*. Ed. A. Adu Boahen. Berkeley: University of California Press: 487–507.

Balandier, Georges. [1955] 1970. *The Sociology of Black Africa: Social Dynamics in Central Africa*. Trans. Douglas Garman. New York: Praeger.

Boahen, A. Adu. 1985a. "Africa and the Colonial Challenge." In *The UNESCO General History of Africa*, vol. vii: *Africa under Colonial Domination 1880–1935*. Ed. A. Adu Boahen. Berkeley: University of California Press: 1–18.

Dirks, Nicholas B. "Introduction: Colonialism and Culture." In *Colonialism and Culture*. Ann Arbor: University of Michigan Press: 1–26.

Fanon, Frantz. [1963] 1968. *The Wretched of the Earth*. Trans. Constance Farrington. New York: Grove.

Gates, Jr., Henry Louis. 1985. "Editor's Introduction: Writing 'Race' and the Difference It Makes." *Critical Inquiry* 12. 1: 1–20.

Jeyifo, Biodun. 1990. "The Nature of Things: Arrested Decolonization and Critical Theory." *Research in African Literature* 21. 1: 33–46.

Johnson, Lemuel. 1997. *Shakespeare in Africa*. Trenton: Africa World.

July, Robert William. 1968. *The Origins of Modern African Thought: Its Development in West Africa during the Nineteenth and Twentieth Centuries*. London: Faber and Faber.

Langley, J. Ayo. 1979. *Ideologies of Liberation in Black Africa 1856–1970: Documents on Modern Political Thought from Colonial Times to the Present*. London: Rex Collings.

Miller, Christopher. 1985. *Blank Darkness: Africanist Discourse in French*. Chicago: University of Chicago Press.

Ranger, T. O. 1985. "African Initiative and Resistance in the Face of Partition and Conquest." In *The UNESCO General History of Africa*, vol. vii: *Africa under Colonial Domination 1880–1935*. Ed. A. Adu Boahen. Berkeley: University of California Press: 45–62.

Rodney, Walter. 1972. *How Europe Underdeveloped Africa*. Dar es Salaam: Tanzania Publishing House.

Said, Edward W. 1979. *Orientalism*. New York: Vintage.

Wauthier, Claude. 1979. *The Literature and Thought of Modern Africa*. 2nd English edn. Washington, DC: Three Continents Press.

Chapter 8

African Literature:
Myth or Reality?

V. Y. Mudimbe

Numerous books and hundreds of articles have been written to analyze African literature. They describe what is now commonly accepted as a young literature in African or European languages and the traditional oral experience of Black Africans. Thus, when we speak of African literature we refer to both a body of texts whose authors are known and to anonymous discourses which carry on successive deposits of supposedly unknown imaginations. This is already a problem, and I am afraid it has, so far, not been addressed in a convincing way by specialists of African studies. It is, indeed, the view of these existing bodies – written texts and oral discourses – that accounts for much of the intellectual generosity of those who believe in Africa as well as for the purely aesthetic activity of those who simply use these texts as objects for exotic curiosity or literary and ideological demands. One could think that African literary criticism grew up not so much as a necessity, nor as an original project within the framework of a scholarly tradition, which interrogates the massiveness of discourses, but rather as a consequence of a process of inventing and organising African literature.

My intervention represents both an hypothesis and a wish. On the one hand, I would like to indicate under which conditions African literature is possible and, on the other, formulate in terms of possible undertakings the perspectives from which commentaries on and analyses of African discourses could become means of understanding African experiences from a more productive viewpoint.

Could we arrive at any explicative norms as to the real nature of African literature which will put it into some sort of relation with other literatures and not give us this uncomfortable feeling that it is somehow an indigenized imitation of something else, or an adapted reproduction of psychological confusions imported from the West? New perspectives might answer this question. For, so far, traditional literary criticism, structuralism, deconstructionism, and even ideological interpretation of discourses from an Afrocentric perspective, have

First published in *African Literature Studies: The Present State/L'etat present*, ed. Stephen Arnold, pp. 7–11. Washington, DC: Three Continents Press, 1985.

not, I believe, brought about the contributions that their premises imply. Yet one may say that it is precisely in this impotence that lie the signs of new possible interpretations about African literature and discourses (See Chinweizu et al. 1983).

African literature as a commodity is a recent invention, and authors as well as critics tend to resist this fact. They seem more interested in this literature, not for what it is as discourse and what in the variety of its events it could mean in a larger context of other local and regional discourses, but rather for its significance as a mirror of something else, say, or instance, Africa's political struggle, processes of cultural disalienation, or human rights objectives. This orientation is accounted for by the fact that the world of literature is sustained by and reflects the real universe, particularly the social relationships of production and the silent impact of ideological signalisations. Thus, one would add, the literary world could well be a mythical space, yet it unveils the concrete experience of human communities. For example, Lilyan Kesteloot's book on the genesis of Negritude literature (1963) and J. Wagner's study on Black literature in the US are both valid as socio-historical and literary criticisms. In the same vein, J. Jahn's considerations on neo-African literature (1961) are witness to the symbolic currency as well as the intellectual and sociological rationality of Black cultures.

I agree. Yet, what these monuments prove most clearly from my viewpoint are, on the one hand, processes of promoting constructs and, on the other, procedures of limiting the meaning and the multiplicity of discourses. Thanks to these monuments, the art and significance of African discourses are commented upon, celebrated and bought on the basis of their value as indications of functional rules of creativity. But these rules are not the efficient references that we think found the scholarly validity of Kesteloot's or Jahn's enterprises. They are fundamentally signs of the conditions of the possibility of African literature, an "invention" that Jahn, Kesteloot, Wagner, and most of us – literary critics and authors – can work on and live upon.

Doubtless M. Foucault's students have already understood where I am leading. In his *The Discourse on Language*, the late professor of the history of systems of thought at the "Collège France" distinguishes three major types of rules of exclusion (Foucault, 1982: 215–27):

1. External procedures such as *prohibiton* ("covering objects, ritual with its surrounding circumstances, the privileged or exclusive right to speak of a particular subject." Foucault, 1982: 216), the *division of reason and madness* and the *will to truth* which integrates the others.

2. Internal procedures of controlling discourses which are directly concerned with "principles of classification, ordering and distribution": that is the *commentary* which signifies philology in terms of reconstruction and reading primary texts but also literary criticism as an intellectual exercise on given documents; second, the *author* as a center of coherence, locus of reference and theme of unity of his/her works; finally, the *organisation of disciplines* whose prescription is, as M. Foucault put it, that "what is supposed at the point of departure is not some meaning which must be rediscovered, nor an identity to be reiterated; it is that which is required for the constructions of new statements" (Foucault, 1982: 223).

3. The third type of procedure of exclusion includes systems of rarefaction of discourses such as *ritual* which "defines the qualifications required of the speaker" (Foucault, 1982: 225); the *fellowships of discourse*, about which in order to get an illuminating illustration

one could think of Journals of African Studies and their policies in terms of promoting articles, researches, and names. Finally, *the social appropriation of discourse* about which Mr. Foucault exemplifies education as "the instrument whereby every individual, in a society like our own, can gain accesss to any kind of discourse" (Foucault, 1982: 227).

It is clear that this table of systems of exclusion can serve as an order for new intellectual initiatives which would simultaneously test M. Foucault's insights and interrogate the standardization and uniformity of the so-called African literature vis-à-vis the disorder of African discourses in general. As a matter of fact, a few examples could illustrate what I mean.

1.   Aimé Césaire's work might be understood in its significance as a creation against the procedures of prohibition(s) and division of reason. Its resources of terror and violence witness more to these procedures than to the vitalistic and genitalistic dimensions noted by Sartre. Thus rather than being symbols of a "Black Orpheus" they could signify a way of questioning a will to truth.
2.   It has been suggested that there are two main sociological explanations for the genesis of African literature in European languages. First, that it is a direct consequence of colonization; second, that it has been made possible by the Western system of school- ing. In other words, these explanations imply that African literary works as well as commentaries on them depend on, and at the same time can be accounted for, by the norms of social appropriation of discourse. Thus this literature, if it makes sense, would do so only insofar as its external conditions of possibility determine it as literature.
3.   One could say that the mere existence of this African literature proceeds from the extension to Africa of Western fellowships of discourse. Therefore, despite all the invitations for an Afrocentric perspective that have been made during this conference, our meeting as well as the language of our agreements and disagreements are funda- mentally marked by a surprising coherence.

What is interesting about interrogating such hypotheses? In terms of theoretical perspec- tives, it is obvious that such hypotheses would confirm or invalidate Foucault's proposition: "I am supposing that in every society the production of discourse is at once controlled, selected, organised and redistributed according to a certain number of procedures, whose role is to avert its powers and its dangers, to cope with chance events, to evade its ponderous, awesome materiality" (Foucault, 1982: 216). On the other side, it might be useful, using this hypothesis, to find out for sure whether or not similar processes of taming discourses function in Africa, and under which conditions.

My own hypothesis is that two major rules of exclusion have, in a radical manner, provided the steps for the "invention" and organisation of African literature: the notions of commentary and author as used by the charter myth of Western Africanism since the eighteenth century. Buffon, Spencer, Tylor, or Lévy-Bruhl limit their inquiries to the question of evolution. As a consequence, they resolve their intellectual and scientific interests in the reading of non-Western experiences as fragmentary discourses and strange, anonymous bodies. Anthropological texts arose in the nineteenth century as commentaries on silent and irrational organisations, emphasizing two main issues: the ideological back- ground of the theorists and, second, the relative anonymity of the objects of the studies. In the first case, the commentary describes the history of humankind from the exteriority of a silent and exotic African history. For instance, let us rapidly look at two paradoxical cases of *Einfühlung*. Frobenius, at the beginning of this century, could wander throughout Black Africa reading Pigafetta and Portuguese travellers' reports instead of seriously listening to Africans. As to the second case, in the 1920s–30s, W. Schmidt in Austria, after his numerous Germanophone predecessors, contributed to anthropology on the assumption of an absolute inexistence of clear signed writings in African societies.

Nevertheless, it was within the violence of these commentaries on exoticism that, by means of what was ideologically signified by the dialectical reasoning on civilisation and primitiveness, the new reality of an African "author" in the Western sense appeared. In the 1940s, for example, whereas M. Griaule (1948), in a kind of revelation, recognized Ogotommeli as subject of a knowledge that he had received and was obviously interpreting in his own discourse, P. Tempels (1949) was still favoring the classical opposition and exploiting the so-called break existing between the anonymous wisdom of traditional Bantus and the moral corruption of "évolués," those bad copies of European individualism.

The break indicates the foundation of what, after J. Goody (1977), may be called the "grand dichotomy," for it determines in present-day scholarship, types of economic structures and social situations, as well as our familiar fields of African literature. In binary oppositions, we would note the following gaps: at the economic level, the agrarian society dominated by economic structures of subsistence versus the highly sophisticated division of work of urban civilization and international markets. At the sociocultural level, the oral and customary setting qualified as mono-cultural, versus the complex pluricultural contexts of big cities. At the level of religious superstructures, societies characterized by an integration of existence and beliefs versus societies functioning on the principle of a distinction between the sacred and the profane. I do not exaggerate if I affirm that, rather than analyzing the complexity of African discourses, most of our textbooks and monographs are still essentially preoccupied with this dichotomy and its signs. Let us look at the best of them and we will find the basic assumptions of the dichotomy. First: the forms and the content of oral literature witness and translate a mono-cultural experience which, I think, up to now is still called a "primitive" civilization in anthropology. Second: with the westernization and Christianization processes under colonial rule, two new types of expression – written literature in African and European languages – appeared which describe the contradictions and the problems implied by the metamorphosis signified by the colonization. Third: this metamorphosis has promoted authored texts which, although fundamentally different from those of the past, do not constitute a hiatus in terms of vital African experiences. Fourth: the notion of neo-African literature marks an internal historical and sociological dimension but it does not and cannot mean that its possibility could be elsewhere than on the exteriority of this very literature.

We have learned how to live with these contradictory assumptions. In fact, they are norms and systems since they are simultaneously the paradoxical references of our professional activities and the events which make thinkable our literary praxes. Moreover, depending on our state of mind, these norms allow us all the liberties we wish. From them we can today decide that Chinua Achebe's and E. Mphahlele's works are internal parts of English literature; Senghor's, Rabemananjara's or Camara Laye's of the French. And, tomorrow, with the same conviction we could demonstrate exactly the contrary and celebrate our authors as mirrors of African authenticity. Pessimistically, I remember that N. Frye once wrote: "literature, like other subjects, has a theory and a practice: poems and plays and novels form the practical side, and the centre of criticism is the theory of literature" (In *Critical Inquiry,* 1975, 2, p. 206). What serious theory could support the fantastic liberties of our investigations in African literature, if, at least, on the one hand we do not agree on the urgency of analyzing the conditions of existence of this literature; and on the other we do not accept the hypothesis that present-day African criticism might not be an African practice at all?

References

Chinweizu, Jemie, Madubuike. 1983. *Toward the Decolonization of African Literature.* Washington, DC: Howard University Press.

Foucault, M. 1982. *The Archaeology of Knowledge and the Discourse on Language.* New York: Pantheon.

Frye, N. 1975. "Expanding Eyes," in *Critical Inquiry,* 2, 2.

Goody, J. 1977. *The Domestication of the Savage Mind.* Cambridge: Cambridge University Press.

Griaule, M. 1948. *Dieu d'eau. Entretiens avec Ogotemmêli.* Paris: Chêne.

Jahn, J. 1961. *Muntu. An Outline of the New African Culture.* New York: Grove Press.

Kesteloot, L. 1965. *Les Ecrivains noirs de langue français: naissance d'une littérature.* Bruxelles: Institut de Sociologie.

Mudimbe, V. Y. 1973. *L'Autre face du royaume.* Lausanne: L'Age d'Homme.

——. 1982. *L'Odeur du Père.* Paris: Présence Africaine.

Tempels, Pl. 1949. *La Philosphie Bantoue.* Paris: Présence Africaine.

Vansina, J. 1961. *De la Tradition orale. Essai de méthode historique.* Tervuren: MRAC.

Wagner, J. 1963. *Les Poètes noirs des Etats-Unis.* Paris: Librairie Istra.

Part II

Orality, Literacy, and the Interface

The scholarly study of oral creative expression in Africa predates and is much more robust than that of the written literature. This is to be expected, given the late arrival of substantial written literature. In many ways, oral genres such as storytelling, proverbs, epics, incantations, panegyrics, occasion-specific poetries (funeral, wedding, investiture, rite of passage, etc.), and dramatic performances have served as veritable resource pools for writers to borrow from and transform in their written works. Isidore Okpewho in his essay here systematically explores the many ways in which writers have engaged in the transfer of styles from the oral tradition to the written text. The degree of success in that venture varies according to the skill of the particular writer, but there appears to be a general acceptance by the writers that with the concession to writing in European languages, one major way to retain any semblance of immersion in their African cultural contexts is to turn to the oral genres for inspiration or example. Indeed, much of the acknowledged stylistic difference of African literature in European languages from the European literature in those languages is precisely its indebtedness to the oral tradition. But even within Africa itself, as Abiola Irele has pointedly argued, the same difference could be seen between black and white writers. While white South African writers "do not display the sense of a connection to an informing spirit of imaginative expression rooted in an African tradition" and in a "formal sense their works are bound just as much to the European literary tradition as are those of metropolitan writers," the same could not be said of "some Portuguese-born writers such as Castro Soromenho and Luandino Vieyra, who express an engagement with Africa not simply in terms of external allusion to forms of life but as a real, formal identification with local modes of expression, that is, not merely as thematic reference but also as touchstone of form" (*African Imagination* 15, 15–16). The writings we have assembled in this section explore African orality as a composite, multidimensional milieu of the written literature.

Reference

Irele, Abiola. *The African Imagination: Literature in Africa and the Black Diaspora*. New York: Oxford University Press, 2001.

Chapter 9

Africa and Orality

Liz Gunner

The continent of Africa can be viewed as a site of enormous, long, and ongoing creativity in relation to orality as a vector for the production of social life, religious beliefs, and the constant constituting and reconstituting of society, ideology, and aesthetics. If it is language which has a crucial role in the production and reproduction of society, then in the case of orality it is often language combined with the performativity of the body, and enacted in both the public and the private space. If it is justifiable to call the African continent "the oral continent par excellence" we need to ask why this is so. What precisely might it mean and what conclusions could flow therefrom? Orality needs to be seen in the African context as the means by which societies of varying complexity regulated themselves, organized their present and their pasts, made formal spaces for philosophical reflections, pronounced on power, questioned and in some cases contested power, and generally paid homage to "the word," language, as the means by which humanity was made and constantly refashioned. Orality was the means by which Africa made its existence, its history long before the colonial and imperial presence of the west manifested itself. In this sense, orality needs to be seen not simply as "the absence of literacy" but as something self-constitutive, *sui generis*. The accepting of this proposition has consequences for an understanding of world culture: namely, it is neither possible nor accurate to take one model that valorizes the written word as the blueprint for how the human race has developed.

What we can learn from the African model is that orality, manifested as types of formal speech communication, in some circumstances coexisting with music in the form of song, or with instruments, and dance, generated an almost unimaginable range of genres that enabled and empowered social, political, and spiritual existence. In some instances a specific mode of orality encoded a state's history; this was the case with the form of *ubwwiiru*, the nineteenth-century Rwandan dynastic ritual code that the historians Joseph Rwabukumba and Alexis Kagame have turned into a written record and made part of a broader historical narrative (Feierman 1994; Rwabukumba and Mudandagizi 1974; Kagame 1975). In the west, the *oriki* (praise poetry) of the Yoruba interwove personal and public history and provided a

First published in *The Cambridge History of African and Caribbean Literature*, vol. 1, ed. Abiola Irele and Simon Gikandi, pp. 1–5, 12–13. Cambridge: Cambridge University Press, 2004.

poetic vehicle for the powerful as well as the ordinary citizen (Barber 1991; Babalola 1966; Yai 1994). Forms such as *oriki* recreated the past in the present; they made and, in the present, still "make possible the crossing from the world of the dead to the world of the living, making the past present again" (Barber 1991: 76). Thus they demonstrate the different kinds of historicity that an oral form can generate with very different conventions of interactivity from those governing a conventional historical printed text (Farias 1992; Vansina 1985; Opland 1974, 1987). History was often encapsulated in the elaborate dynastic poetry of a kingdom, composed and reproduced by specially trained bards and presenting a legitim- izing, heroic view of past and present to the people at large. This was the case with the court poets of Rwanda. Alexis Kagame has meticulously documented this "specialized and learned artistic tradition" (Finnegan 1970: 87; Kagame 1951; Coupez and Kamanzi 1970), outlining the privileged position of the association of royal poets who were split between those who performed the works of others and those who composed new work. A "long and rigorous period of apprenticeship" by young members of the families of poets ensured mastery of existing poems and of the "vocabulary, imagery and subject-matter which formed the traditional basis of any future composition" (Finnegan 1970: 89). This genre of court poetry, plus the secret ritual texts, the *ubwwiiru*, and other genres from Rwanda are among the best documented on the continent and provide an indication of how orality could operate at the heart of the state. Poetry was, in a way, the heartbeat of royalty. As the increasingly beleaguered kings of the nineteenth-century kingdom of Rwanda fended off their hostile neighbors, and then had to contend with the incoming colonial powers of Germany and Belgium, the royal poetic tradition was also affected, and shifted, taking on first the patina of the colonial overlords' voice and then reflecting also the counterviews of a dissident group of poets who sought out "antidynastic histories in their own past" (Hertefelt 1964; Feierman 1994: 60).

I have mentioned the Rwandan case in some detail to demonstrate firstly a formidable example of poetry, politics, and power operating in a particular historical context in Africa, without the mediation of the written or printed word. What the Rwandan example also shows is that the set of cultural practices that the poetry embodied was not static. Rather it was dynamic, changing in response to the historical pressures of the time. There is no evidence that the genres of the Rwandan court have survived into the modern era (the monarchy was abolished in 1959) and only the meticulous scholarship of Rwandan and non-Rwandan scholars provides an archive from which we can attempt to reconfigure, in the interests of the history of both world and African culture, the vibrant voices of a past poetic tradition.

Some forms of orality now exist only in written, audio or visual archives, although brief, remembered snatches may remain, tantalizingly, in living discourse, encapsulating meto-nymically a vast unreachable hinterland of cultural knowledge. Like the Central African drums, two of them Kuba, and one Lele, described by the historian Jan Vansina, such fragments "impress onto their own society a silent discourse, and simultaneously, as loci of memory, recite silently their own past and that of the society that made them possible" (Mudimbe 1994; 68; Vansina 1984: 47). There are, however, oral genres that exist vigorously in the contemporary era, either as part of a new global culture, as part of the local, or as what the musicologist Thomas Turino in his study of Zimbabwean music has called the indigenous, namely, a line of culture that may be closer to performance genres not significantly altered by modernity (Turino 2000: 17–18). Part of this chapter will demonstrate the ways in which orality has been extended into various configurations of modernity, thus belying the argument for a purist orality that is beyond the grasp of the modern. Nor should we see orality in Africa in the new millennium as a residual state, battered by forms of modernity: songs, chants, a dance, a gesture with a fly whisk or a spear, used simply as a nostalgic resource by politicians seeking to evoke a distant idyllic past and so link themselves to it; rather we can see it as a mode of communicative action that has in the past been finely honed to fit a myriad of different social, ideological, and aesthetic needs in many different societies on the continent. In the present, forms of orality have in some cases powered the new technologies of mass communication by influencing their direction. The extensive presence of live performances and recordings of tied and freelance singers, and poets on Hausa television and radio stations in northern Nigeria is one example of this (Furniss 1996: 126–7). Literacy has impacted in various ways on oral modes of communication and has often produced brilliant hybrid forms (touched on below), but the book itself, in terms of written literature from the continent, has been profoundly influenced by orality. It could be argued that the directions taken by contemporary written African literature, have largely been shaped by the presence of a substantial and established body of rhetoric holding deep knowledge with which writers have often felt compelled to engage, even when moving from the African language/s in which the poetry or narrative is expressed, to writing in English, French, or Portuguese.

As the example of the Rwandan school of specialist poets demonstrates, one of the roles of oral forms in many parts of the continent has been to give verbal expression to the ordering of societies through the public recitation of genealogies and praises of rulers, often by highly skilled and specialist poets. In the Rwandan case the often esoteric poetry, full of archaisms and elaborate prosody, was not accessible to the majority of the kingdom's subjects even though they all (Tutsi, Hutu, and Twa) shared the same language, Kinyar-wanda.[1] In other comparable forms of poetry, there was often a shared knowledge of the poetic skills, so that it was, in important ways, a more widely accessible form. Praise poetry in Shona and Zulu exemplify this more horizontal proliferation of both linked genres and poetic skills. Certainly the vast areas across which the form of praise poetry has been used, testify to the importance placed on the making of meaning and the place of dense, rich poetic language as carriers of public social values and ideologies.

The need for societies to have memory banks that act as mirrors and as a form of working archive led in many instances to the extensive use of oral poetry to formalize memory of the past, and to make the past comprehensible and accessible. Praise poetry, differently named, often with elaborate yet flexible prosodies, and existing in each instance in a particular hierarchy of genres, has its place in a number of very differently constituted societies covering a range of language groups across the continent. It is one of the most widespread forms of oral poetry that engaged with the attempt to provide public, active memorials through performance. It can be found in many sub-Saharan African societies and in some instances it has found a niche as an ongoing cultural practice in contemporary communities or in the modern state. A number of south and southern African societies still have considerable cultural capital held in praise poetry. In South Africa, Xhosa praise poets who supported figures opposed to the apartheid Nationalist government were on more than one occasion persecuted by the apartheid police (Opland 1998: 278–81) and in the postapartheid state former President Mandela is frequently accompanied on official business by his praise poet, Zolani Mkiva, who has also released a number of compact discs of his work, with musical backing. The praise poet has license to critique the object of his praise, but this is usually done sparingly. Praise poetry has often been constituted as history from above, for instance the *lithoko* of the Basotho (Damane and Saunders 1974; Kunene 1971), the court poetry of the old kingdom of Rwanda (Kagame 1951), Hausa praise poetry and song (Smith 1957, 1978; Gidley 1975; Muhammad 1979; Furniss 1996), and the royal and chiefly *izibongo* of the Zulu (Nyembezi 1958; Cope 1968; Gunner and Gwala 1991). Even here, the history of rulers is often rich with ambiguities and frequently contains the resistant voices of those groups that have been defeated, and the dissident voices of critics (Brown 1998: 94–5; Hamilton 1998). It is the ability of praise poetry to absorb and reflect changes within the society it enunciates (Vail and White 1991) and also to provide a sense of the past in the present (Barber 1989: 20) that are among its most compelling qualities and ensure its place as one of the great genres of the continent. Nevertheless its continued existence is uncertain. Among the Basotho in the nineteenth century, the elaborate *lithoko* with their heroic ethos and elaborate imagery captured the exploits of King Mshweshwe and his sons as they battled to maintain their mountain kingdom against Boer attacks but the poetry also allowed for moments of reflexivity and for the inclusion of close observation of the natural world and of place which frequently became absorbed into the praise names themselves (Kunene 1971). This official poetry still flourishes on state occasions but now lacks the pervasive influence it once had, and it has been argued that a new genre "of the people," *lifela*, is more representative of modern Basotho national and transnational identity than the older *lithoko* (Coplan 1994).

[. . .]

In an era of globalization, orality has not disappeared but has often adapted itself in its many different forms to become a vehicle for the expression of the fears and hopes of new generations of Africans. Thus, while it is true that, in some instances, genres of poetry or song and of narrative have not endured the erosion of the social base that sustained their performances and their producers, other genres have survived or grown. In two interesting instances from South Africa the social and economic pressures of the migrant labor system in the apartheid era have led to the emergence of new genres that retain a loose connection to their parent genre but maintain a certain independence as well. These can be seen in a double sense as "migrant" genres; thus the Sotho genre of *lifela*, fashioned by men moving between Lesotho and the mines of Johannesburg, grew both from young men's initiation songs and from the praise poetry of Basotho royalty and chiefs known as *lithoko* (Coplan 1994; Damane and Sanders 1974; Kunene 1971). Migrant or rebellious Basotho women, existing largely on the fringes of their male compatriots' social spaces, the border bars of Lesotho, and the shebeens of Johannesburg, made their own distinctive version of the genre and by so doing were able to create an identity for themselves as bold yet suffering women, enunciating a new version of what it meant to be a migrant (Coplan 1994). In another South African instance, women moving between the rural areas of the north and Johannesburg worked first within a men's song and dance genre used in the hostels (*kiba*) and then moved the form into a more exclusively female domain. The name of the genre remained the same but it took on an additional and specifically female form and became a crucial vector for the making of modern identities for migrant women, one that embraced both modernity and a sense of rural belonging (James 1994; 1997; 1999).

In many cases the electronic media, namely, television and radio, have played an important role in enabling new genres to emerge, or adaptations of old genres to continue; the audiocassette has also been a key instrument of transmission (Fardon and Furniss 2000). The use of the audiocassette as well as the radio in the spread of Somali oral poetry has been particularly remarkable and in one memorable instance a certain popular poem, *Leexo*, sung over the airwaves while a key parliamentary debate was in progress in the capital, Mogadishu, toppled a government (Johnson 1995: 115–17). In general, the evidence from contemporary studies shows that many oral genres are resilient and adaptable to the intense changes that have accompanied modern technology, urban living, and often difficult and oppressive industrial conditions. Oral genres have provided a means of formalizing new experiences and in a number of societies, for instance in the case of the Somali genres of the *balwo* and *heello* mentioned above, and in the urban genre of *isicathamiya* in South Africa, they have provided powerful new cultural texts for people's lives (Johnson 1974; Andrzejewski and Lewis 1964; Erlmann 1991; 1996; Johnson 2001).

[. . .]

Note

1   See Hintjens 2001 for a chilling and finely argued account of early colonial complicity in the construction of ethnic rivalries in Rwanda and the state planning of the ethnic genocide in 1994.

References

Andrzejewski, B. W., and Sheila Andrzejewski, trans. 1993. *An Anthology of Somali Poetry.* Bloomington: Indiana University Press.

Andrzejewski, B. W., and I. M. Lewis. 1964. *Somali Poetry: An Introduction.* Oxford: Clarendon Press.

Babalola, Adeboye. 1966. *The Content and Form of Yoruba "Ijala."* Oxford: Clarendon Press.

Barber, Karin. 1989. "Interpreting Oriki as History and as Literature." In *Discourse and its Disguises: The Interpretation of African Oral Texts.* Ed. K. Barber and P. de F. Moraes Farias. Birmingham: Centre of West African Studies, University of Birmingham: 13–23.

—— 1991. *I Could Speak until Tomorrow: "Oriki," Women and the Past in a Yoruba Town.* Edinburgh and Washington, DC: Edinburgh University Press and Smithsonian Institute Press for the International Africa Institute.

Brown, Duncan, 1998. *Voicing the Text: South African Oral Poetry and Performance.* Cape Town: Oxford University Press.

Cope, Trevor. 1968. *Izibongo: Zulu Praise Poems.* Oxford: Clarendon Press.

Coplan, David. 1994. *In the Time of Cannibals: The Word Music of South Africa's Basotho Migrants.* Chicago: University of Chicago Press.

Coupez, A., and Kamanzi, Th. 1970. *Littérature de cour au Rwanda.* Oxford: Clarendon Press.

Damane, M. and P. B. Sanders, eds. 1974. *Lithoko: Sotho Praise Poems.* Oxford: Clarendon Press.

Erlmann, Veit. 1991. *African Stars: Studies in Black South African Performance.* Chicago: University of Chicago Press.

—— 1996. *Nightsong: Performance, Power and Practice in South Africa.* Chicago: University of Chicago Press.

Fardon, Richard, and Graham Furniss, eds. 2000. *African Broadcast Cultures. Radio in Transition.* Oxford: James Currey.

Farias, P. de Moraes. 1992. "History and Consolation: Royal Yoruba Bards Comment on Their Craft." *History in Africa* 19: 263–97.

Feierman, Steven. 1994. "Africa in History. The End of Universal Narratives." In *Imperial Histories and Postcolonial Displacements*. Ed. Gyan Prakash. Princeton: Princeton University Press: 40–65.

Finnegan, Ruth. 1970. *Oral Literature in Africa*. Oxford: Clarendon Press.

—— 1977. *Oral Poetry: Its Nature, Significance and Social Context*. Cambridge: Cambridge University Press.

—— 1996. *Poetry, Prose and Popular Culture in Hausa*. Edinburgh: Edinburgh University Press for the International Africa Institute, London.

Gidley, C. G. B. 1975. "'Roko': A Hausa Praise Crier's Account of his Craft." *African Language Studies* 16: 93–115.

Gunner, Liz, and Mafika Gwala, eds. and trans. 1991. *"Musho!" Zulu Popular Praises*. East Lansing, Michigan: Michigan State University Press:

Hamilton, Carolyn. 1998. *Terrific Majesty: The Powers of Shaka Zulu and the Limits of Historical Invention*. Cambridge, MA: Harvard University Press.

Hertefelt, Marcel d', and A. Coupez. 1964. *La royauté sacrée de l'ancien Rwanda*. Tervuren: Musée royal de l'Afrique centrale.

Hintjens, Helen M. 2001. "When Identity Becomes a Knife: Reflecting on the Genocide in Rwanda." *Ethnicities* 1.1: 25–55.

James, Deborah. 1994. "Basadi ba Baeng: Female Migrant Performance from the Northern Transvaal." In *Politics and Performance in Southern African Theatre, Poetry and Song*. Ed. Liz Gunner. Johannesburg: Witwatersrand University Press: 81–110.

—— 1997. "'Music of Origin': Class, Social Category and the Performers and Audience of *Kiba*, a South African Genre." *Africa* 67.3: 454–75.

—— 1999. *Songs of the Women Migrants: Performance and Identity in South Africa*. Johannesburg: Witwatersrand University Press in association with The International African Institute, London.

Johnson, John W., Thomas A. Hale, and Stephen Belcher, eds. 1997. *Oral Epics from Africa: Vibrant Voices from a Vast Continent*. Bloomington: Indiana University Press.

Johnson, Simone L. 2001. "Defining the Migrant Experience: An Analysis of the Poetry and Performance of a South African Migrant Genre." MA diss. University of Natal, Pietermaritzburg.

Kagame, Alexis. 1951. "La poésie dynastique au Rwanda." Brussels: Institut Colonial Belge. 1975. *Un Abrégé de l'ethno-histoire du Rwanda*, vol. II. Butare: Editions Universitaires du Rwanda.

Kunene, D. P. 1971. *Heroic Poetry of the Basotho*. Oxford: Clarendon Press.

Morris, Henry F. 1964. *The Heroic Recitations of the Bahima of Ankole*. Oxford: Clarendon Press.

Mudimbe, V. Y. 1994. *The Idea of Africa*. Bloomington: Indiana University Press.

Muhammad, Dalhatu. 1979. "Interaction between the Oral and the Literate Traditions of Hausa Poetry." *Harsunan Nijeriya* 9: 85–90.

Nyembezi, C. L. S. 1948. "The Historical Background to the *Izibongo* of the Zulu Military Age." *African Studies* 7: 110–25 and 157–74.

—— 1958. *Izibongo Zamakhosi*. Pietermaritzburg: Shuter and Shooter.

Okpewho, Isidore. 1979. *The Epic in Africa*. New York: Columbia University Press.

—— 1992. *African Oral Literature: Backgrounds, Character and Continuity*. Bloomington: Indiana University Press.

Opland, Jeff. 1974. "Praise Poems as Historical Sources." In *Beyond the Cape Frontier: Studies in the History of the Transkei and the Ciskei*. Ed. Christopher Saunders and Robin Derricourt. London: Longman: 1–37.

—— 1987. "The Bones of Mafanta: A Xhosa Oral Poet's Response to Context in South Africa." *Research in African Literatures* 18.1: 36–50.

—— 1998. *Xhosa Poets and Poetry*. Cape Town: David Philip.

Pongweni, Alec. 1982. *Songs That Won the Liberation War*. Harare: The College Press.

—— 1997. "The Chimurenga Songs of the Zimbabwean War of Liberation." In *Readings in African Popular Culture*. Ed. Karin Barber. Oxford: James Currey in association with the African International Institute: 63–72.

Rwabukumba, Joseph and Vincent Mudandagizi. 1974. "Les formes historiques de la dépendance personelle dans l'état rwandais." *Cahiers d'Etudes Africaines* 14.1.

Smith, M. G. 1957. "The Social Functions and Meaning of Hausa Praise-Singing." *Africa* 27.1: 26–43.

—— 1978. *The Affairs of Daura: History and Change in a Hausa State 1800–1958*. Berkeley and Los Angeles: University of California Press.

Suso, Bamba, and Banna Kanute. 1999. *The Epic of Sunjata*. Trans. Gordon Innes with Bokari Sidibe, ed. and introd. Graham Furniss and Lucy Duran. London: Penguin.

Torino, Thomas. 2000. *Nationalists, Cosmopolitans and Popular Music in Zimbabwe*. Chicago: University of Chicago Press.

Vail, Leroy, and Landeg White. 1991. *Power and the Praise Poem. Voices in Southern African History*. Oxford: James Currey.

Vansina, Jan. 1984. *Art History in Africa*. London: Longman.

—— 1985. *Oral Tradition as History*. Oxford: James Currey.

Yai, Olabiyi. 1994. "In Praise of Metonymy: The Concepts of 'Tradition' and 'Creativity' in the Transmission of Yoruba Artistry over Time and Space." In *The Yoruba Artist: New Theoretical Perspectives on African Arts*. Ed. Rowland Abiodun, Henry F. Drewal, and John Pemberton III. Washington, DC: Smithsonian: 107–15.

Chapter 10

Orality, Literacy, and African Literature

Abiola Irele

Oho! Congo oho! Pour rythmer ton nom grand sur les eaux sur les fleuves sur toute mémoire
Que j'émeuve la voix des koras Koyaté! L'encre du scribe est sans mémoire.

Léopold Sédar Senghor, "Congo"

There seems little doubt that the attention devoted to the oral tradition in Africa in recent times has contributed in no small way to the renewed scholarly interest in the question of orality and its relation to literacy. It is of course true that the study of African oral forms has itself benefited from a preexisting climate of scholarly endeavor so that such research could be undertaken with seriousness. In this respect, it is worth mentioning two specific factors that were conducive to such a climate and thus facilitated the extensive consideration of African orality as a cultural phenomenon. First, the development of structural linguistics, in both its Saussurian formulation and its North American variant associated with Leonard Bloomfield, drew attention to the oral basis of language and all but made this fact into an orthodox precept of linguistic investigation. As is well known, the influence of structuralism extended beyond linguistics to stimulate in particular a renewal of literary theory, especially in the work of the Russian formalists, much of which, as is evident in the case of Vladimir Propp, was based on the examination of folk and oral material.

The second factor involves the work of Milman Parry, Albert Lord, and the Chadwicks and the way they encouraged a view of orality as a primary modality of literary expression. The direct impact of their work on traditional Western scholarship in its most venerated domain – the study of the European classical heritage – had the consequence of giving prominence to the question of orality in relation to literary expression and was ultimately helpful in promoting a revaluation of oral cultures and even, as in the case of Marshall McLuhan, prompting a reassessment of the literate tradition of Western civilization itself.

These developments favored a broadened awareness of literature and thus created the conditions for a scholarly investigation of African orality not merely in a purely linguistic framework, as in the early phase of Africanist studies, but also from a literary and artistic perspective. At the same time, the dominance of orality in the cultural environment of

First published in *Semper Aliquid Novi: Papers in Honour of Albert Gérard*, ed. Janos Riesz and Alain Ricard, pp. 251–63, Tübingen: Gunter Narr Verlag, 1989; and subsequently in *The African Imagination: Literature in African and the Black Diaspora*, pp. 3–38. New York: Oxford University Press, 2001.

African expression seemed to offer possibilities for validating the endeavor to state the relevance of orality not only to a general understanding of the processes involved in human communication but also, and in particular, to formulate an all-encompassing idea of imaginative expression, one that would point toward a universal concept of literature.

But while this seems to be the prospect opened up by the close attention to oral forms that developments in scholarship in the earlier part of the twentieth century encouraged, the relation between orality and literacy has of late been perceived more often in terms of an opposition than a complementarity. There is now abroad, it seems, an effort to reverse the Saussurian order of precedence in which writing serves as a secondary medium lending material support to oral speech and to affirm rather the effective primacy of writing for communicative and cognitive functions. Thus, the values of orality are being more and more discounted, when they are not being actively deprecated, in favor of what is held to be the superiority of literacy, its greater adequacy in organizing human experience.

This bias in favor of literacy is perhaps most pronounced in the work of Jack Goody (1977, 1987), who virtually identifies literacy with the reflective consciousness. For him, orality represents an incapacity to handle logical processes and amounts to a less assured mode of manipulating the world; literacy thus provides the sole basis for any kind of sustained development of civilized life. A similar orientation emerges from the work of Walter Ong, whose position, though less categorical than that of Goody, proceeds from the same premise, for the term *noetics*, which he has proposed for the comparative study of differentiated mental dispositions as conditioned by orality and literacy, presupposes that the structure of the human mind is affected and even determined by the technology of linguistic expression and human communication available to the members of a society and of a culture at a particular point in their collective development. (Ong, 1982). In both cases, an inherent evolutionism pervades the treatment of the question. I have singled out these two scholars for mention, because the influence of their work has determined the prevailing trend in discussions of the question, which has led to the setting up of a sharp dichotomy between orality and literacy. These two notions are perceived as related to two modes of human communication through language, modes that are represented as indicators not only of two types of social and cultural organization but also, and more radically, of two modes of thought and even of existence. The following extract, which bears the stamp of Ong's ideas, sums up this point of view in an unequivocal way:

> To put it simply, orality is characterized by short memory, homeostasis in memory, speaker and listener sharing a site, hence shared tribalism, transience of texuality, poorer transmission, intimacy, direct social control, paratactic and non-cumulative narrativity, adjectival description, types as narrative personae. Literacy, on the other hand, is marked by physical textual permanence, longer memory, spatial freedom in textual transmission, isolation and alienation, individualist liberalism, syntactic and cumulative narrativity, introspective analysis. (Miyoshi, 1989, 33)

Insofar as the distinction being made here applies to the productions of the imagination, it is evident that the conventional Western novel is presented as a normative reference for all forms of literary creation and experience. More generally, the passage makes clear the value judgment implied in the dichotomy between orality and literacy, in which the former is associated with the communicative and expressive schemes of so-called simple societies, while the latter is deemed to provide the basis for the conceptual procedures and moral stances that have ensured the triumph of Western civilization. Thus, the notions of orality and literacy take their place as one more pair in the scheme of contrasted principles that serve, as Ruth Finnegan has remarked, to establish a kind of "great divide" between two spheres of human consciousness and achievement (Finnegan, 1973). This effort to create theoretical boundaries between peoples and cultures is a familiar feature of Western scholarship, which has bedeviled the discipline of anthropology in particular; as such, it raises issues that go well beyond the scope of my present subject. But I have felt compelled to show the way it operates and to suggest its direction in current discussions of the question of the relationship between orality and literacy in order to point up what I consider to be the simplifications that these discussions involve, especially the incomplete understanding of the true nature of orality that they display.

It seems to me therefore that a reappraisal of the question is required, and such an endeavor must start with a recognition of the differing contexts of the situations in which the two notions can be considered to be relevant. There is certainly no difficulty about conceding the obvious truth that, in certain important respects having to do especially with positive science, a literate culture has an overwhelming advantage over one that conducts its life through a purely oral mode of expression and that it enjoys its considerable advantages by reason of its prodigious capacity for the conservation and transmission of knowledge and the tremendous potential for the organization and transformation of experience that accrues to it as a result. It cannot be doubted that, until now,[1] writing has proved the most convenient means of processing information about the external world and has for this reason given a powerful impulse to the scientific and technological development we generally associate with Western civilization. Literacy has thus become a necessary condition for any conception of modern life. It can even be affirmed that books do not merely represent a convenient and serviceable format for the representation of discourse and the expression of ideas but comprise as well a comprehensive medium of human dialogue across time and space. Although this is manifestly an idealized conception of the function that books fulfill within a literate culture, it points to a sense in which literacy can be said to serve, at least in principle, the ideals of a humanistic liberalism.

The obverse of this relates to the real limitations, spatial and temporal, from which linguistic communication suffers in cultures that are either purely or predominantly oral. But it is possible to make too much of these limitations, for it cannot be said, as it is being constantly suggested, that oral cultures are so crippled by them as to be prevented from developing expressive schemes as complex as those of literate cultures. It is well to observe in this regard that many oral cultures have developed various strategies within the complex framework of their semiotic systems for overcoming the limitations of oral communication. In the African context one might mention the constant recourse to surrogates (the use of drum language is a notable example) and to other nonlinguistic symbolic schemes, which serve both to give spatial resonance to human speech as well as to extend the expressive potential of language. The temporal limitation involved in orality is also met by the mobilization of the entire culture – the incorporation of professionals of the word and intensive development of memory techniques are crucial elements – toward keeping alive in oral form those documents of the collective life to which a particular value has been assigned, a point to which we shall return presently.

Given these considerations, the theoretical assumptions that govern the prevailing distinction between orality and literacy need to be seriously modified and the value judgments that lurk within them directly challenged. What is involved in these judgments is an extreme valorization of writing, of its imagined autonomy as a spatial category of language. But this view can only be sustained by neglecting the fact that, whatever its capacity for the elaboration of language, writing remains a secondary form, a *representation*, at a remove from the vital immediacy of spoken language itself.

This point has a direct bearing on certain important aspects of the literary experience that I shall have occasion later to evoke; meanwhile, let me state that, when one considers the African situation, it is possible to affirm that, in the area of imaginative expression, the advantage may not be altogether on the side of literacy. It needs to be appreciated that orality has preeminent virtues as an expressive modality within the symbolic universe that all forms of social participation require for their full and proper mobilization. And as far as the African situation is concerned, if it illustrates anything, it is the impossibility of isolating language from the total field of social and cultural experience that orality conditions. Indeed, it is in this area that I am inclined to look for what may well constitute the distinctive contribution of African orality to the experience of literature: the reminder it provides that the use of language for imaginative purposes represents a fundamental component of the symbolic structures by which the individual relates to society and by which society itself relates to its universe of existence. My contention then is that it is truly rewarding to ponder the nature of orality for a more rounded view of literary expression as a dimension of experience.

This observation leads to a major issue at the heart of African expression, one that must count in any consideration of orality in relation to African literature: faith in the primacy of language as a vector of experience upon which all this expression rests. It happens to be the case that this is a faith that needs to be reaffirmed at this time in the face of a modern skepticism that animates certain currents of contemporary thought in the Western world. This new skepticism seeks to deny the capacity of language to disseminate values that are other than purely textual and formal, to generate meanings that reflect the dense texture of experience. This effort to dissociate language from the sense of a human world raises important issues in critical theory that I need not go into here, except to say that it proposes an impersonal conception of language that proceeds directly from habits of mind induced by writing, a conception therefore with which those of us with a background of an oral culture cannot possibly identify.

It is therefore in the firm and clear perspective of an intimate relationship between language and consciousness, between expression and experience, that I intend to consider the status of orality within the corpus of African literature. I start then with the presupposition that texts, whether written or oral (and we shall examine the question of what constitutes a text later), are embodiments of language, that they are products of human awareness and maintain a profound complicity with the consciousness through which such an awareness is mediated. Although it is recognized in many African societies that language has a reality all its own and even a certain potency intrinsic to it as a natural phenomenon (Zahan, 1963 Calame-Griaule, 1965), it is ultimately inconceivable without the expression that it enables and sustains. We may restate this view of language by observing that, however elusive and refractive words may be, they collaborate to vivify the abstract system of language and in so doing empower our efforts to create meanings, which are nothing other than the expression of our will to order experience.

These reflections should, I imagine, begin to make clear what I consider to be the possibilities of orality for the revaluation of literature in relation to experience and as a form of mediation between life and the imaginative consciousness. The African case seems to me especially instructive in this regard, and I shall now endeavor to develop this point with specific reference to the present literary situation in Africa, marked as it is by the complex relationship between orality and literacy, a situation reflective of the dichotomy that obtains in our dual experience of tradition and modernity.

Although it is only in recent times that African literature has been attended to by the rest of the world, literary expression is not by any means a recent development in Africa. This statement, for all its banality, is dictated here by the need to direct attention to the oral tradition, which has for ages served on the continent as an institutional channel for the intense involvement with language that we recognize as the foundation of literary form. More recently, with the introduction of writing, a new dimension has been given to imaginative expression on the continent; indeed, it can be said that, given the circumstances of this transition, literature has more recently come to acquire in its status as a social institution and as a form of cultural production a new prominence and urgency. From being a natural manifestation of the processes, structures, and dispositions of the various societies and cultures that made up our precolonial, traditional world, it has more recently developed into a mode for the articulation of a new, modern experience. Literature in Africa has thus become the area of an active and focused self-consciousness that extends in its implications into both a sustained interrogation of history and a determined engagement with language.

A significant part of this process of the revaluation of literature in Africa is the preoccupation with the nature, possibilities, and formal modes of literary expression itself. To put this another way, in trying to formulate the state of disjunction between an old order of being and a new mode of existence, literary artists in modern Africa have been forced to a reconsideration of their expressive medium, of their means of address. In the quest for a grounded authenticity of expression and vision, the best among our modern African writers have had to undertake a resourcing of their material and their modes of expression in the traditional culture. Because the traditional culture has been able to maintain itself as a contemporary reality and thus to offer itself as a living resource, the modern literature strives to establish and strengthen its connection with a legacy that, though associated with the past, remains available as a constant reference for the African imagination. The oral tradition has thus come to be implicated in the process of transformation of the function of literature and in the preoccupation with the formal means of giving voice to the African assertion.

These remarks, which apply primarily to the relationship between the oral tradition and the new literature in the European languages, can be further amplified by reference to the steady development of written literature in the indigenous languages, which represents, in many instances, a direct outgrowth from the oral tradition. The complexity of the literary situation in Africa can thus be appreciated when we present the full picture of imaginative production on the continent. We have a line of progression that can be said to have begun with the oral literature whose forms and functions still operate over a wide range of social and cultural activities in the traditional context and to a considerable extent in the modern world as well. This primary domain of literary expression is extended by a body of written literature in the African languages, which maintains a natural linguistic and formal relationship with the oral tradition but is already dissociated, as a result of writing, from the immediate insertion into collective life that orality entails. The emergence of a modern expression in the European languages has resulted in the creation of a third domain of

African literature whose connection with the other two consists in the process in which it is engaged for the recuperation of the values – aesthetic, moral, and social – associated with orality.

I shall presently be considering the oral literature in its salient features and as a fundamental reference for the experience of literature in the African context. But as a preliminary, let me make a further observation in order to clarify the relationship that obtains between orality and literacy within the comprehensive field of African literature. The interest of the written literature in the African languages in this regard is obvious, since it demonstrates the direct connection between orality and literacy. In the specific case of the literature in Yoruba with which I am familiar, there is a sense indeed in which much of this literature relies for its effects on this connection and thus exists primarily as a form of "secondary orality."[2] We need to distinguish within the corpus of written literature in the African languages two distinct categories: the classical literature, represented principally by the extant works in Ki-Swahili in the so-called Afro-Arab tradition but including as well other works outside that tradition, such as those in Geez or Amharic in Ethiopia, and a second category, made up of the more recent productions in other African languages, which have resulted from the introduction of literacy from the West. To this latter category belongs the considerable body of established works in such languages as Yoruba, in which the development of a new written literature was pioneered by the novels of D. O. Fagunwa, and in Sotho, which has given us a modern classic, Thomas Mofolo's epic novel, *Chaka*. It is especially in this category that the process of direct transfer of the modes of oral expression into that of writing is clear. I should add that although the works I have cited are representative examples, they do not cover the entire range of present developments, for the spread of literacy is propelling the emergence of new African language literatures all over the continent. (Gérard, 1971, 1981).

The literature in the European languages is now generally recognized, in its formal significance, as an effort to approximate to the oral model, albeit within a literate tradition taken from the West; it is this feature that marks the most important African writing of contemporary times. The point that emerges here is that, through these two channels, the oral tradition continues to function as a fundamental reference of African expression, as the matrix of the African imagination.

This brings us to a direct consideration of the oral literature itself. There is an obvious sense in which it can be considered as the "true" literature of Africa. It is the literature that is still the most widespread and with which the vast majority of Africans, even today, are in constant touch, and it represents that form of expression to which African sensibilities are most readily attuned. The reason for this is not far to seek, for despite the impact of literacy, orality is still the dominant mode of communication on the continent, and it determines a particular disposition of the imagination of a different order from that conditioned by literacy.

We might consider at this juncture a question that arises immediately at the outset of any discussion of the phenomenon of orality in relation to imaginative expression: the levels of articulation that distinguish ordinary communication from what may be considered the literary uses of language. I have suggested elsewhere the three levels at which we might envisage the articulation of language in African orality and I will recall these and develop them further here in an effort to provide a clearer understanding of the distinctive features of oral literature, at least in the African context, as well as what I shall be proposing in due course as their comprehensive significance.

To begin with, there is, as in all cultures, an elementary level of ordinary, everyday communication, which is largely restricted to the denotative sphere of language; about this level, nothing more needs to be said. In African orality, we are plunged at once into the connotative sphere with the second level, signaled by the presence of those figurative and rhetorical forms of language that, as anyone who is familiar with African habits of speech is aware, occur as a frequent element of linguistic interaction on the continent. The culture itself offers prescribed forms of discourse, which define what one might call a "formulaic" framework for the activity of speech and even for the process of thought. To this rhetorical level of linguistic usage belong the proverbs and the aphorisms, which have a special value in practically every African community, a fact that accounts for their widespread development as fixed forms, culturally prescribed. What is more, the proverb can be considered as practically a genre in itself, and it enters as a device into almost all kinds of speech activity and is regularly made to serve a formal function in the extended forms of oral literature. When Achebe writes, adapting an Igbo proverb into English, that proverbs are "the palm oil with which words are eaten," he is drawing attention to the central position that the form occupies in African speech. He is also indicating the relish in words that has been cultivated in nearly every African society as a matter of cultural conditioning, a sensitivity to language that orality encourages, and the aesthetic function of the proverb which this cultural factor promotes.

But the consciousness of the role that the proverb fulfills in speech is not confined to the aesthetic appreciation indicated in the Igbo saying but involves as well as recognition of its possibilities for mental processes and even for cognitive orientation. For the proverb represents a compaction of reflected experience and functions as a kind of minimalism of thought. It is this awareness of the intellectual value of the proverb that is summed up in the Yoruba metaproverb: *Owe l'esin oro; ti oro ba sonu, owe l'a fi nwa* (Proverbs are the horses of thought; when thoughts get lost, we send proverbs to find them). As genre, the proverb provides a link between what I have called the rhetorical level of language and the third level, that at which, in African orality, the imagination finds its proper manifestation as *organized text* and even, in many societies, as a body of *consecrated texts*. I am aware that the notion of text as applied to oral expression can be ambiguous, but I believe it is just as relevant to orality as it is to literacy.

A variant of the opposition between orality and literacy is the distinction that has been proposed between text and utterance, a distinction that further affects the view of conditions under which instances of language are produced. In this view, an *utterance* connotes anonymity, a collective voice, whereas a *text* implies individual authorship, a singular consciousness. A little reflection should make clear however that this implication involves a restriction that is peculiar to literate cultures and that the distinction it rests upon is ultimately untenable. At best, it is merely a formal one that bears upon the modality of expression rather than on the substance. It is enough to consider the role of register in all forms of linguistic usage to understand that what is at issue here is the degree of elaboration in speech, which brings into view the character, level, and context of the speech act itself, whether it is oral or written. This seems to me to compel a more inclusive notion of text than is afforded by the sole reference to literacy.

From this perspective, we can define a text quite simply as an organized series of enunciations that combine to form a coherent discourse. In literary expression, the element of coherence is supplied by the imaginative path of the discourse and by the deployment of form in a stylized mode of language. Literary texts exist in this fundamental sense; indeed, what I have said of the proverb indicates that it is in fact a text in this sense but in a highly compacted form. It has now been established that in many African societies, extended texts based on the definition I have proposed can be identified quite frequently; they exist as autonomous and isolated works each of which is highly organized as a full and independent imaginative statement. What is more, in certain cases, these oral texts can be so rigidly fixed as to attain what can only be called canonical status; they represent "monuments," in Paul Zumthor's phrase, of the particular cultures in which they occur (Zumthor, 1983, 39).

The examples that come to mind in this latter respect are highly instructive of the relationship between literature and society in an oral culture, of the social applications of imaginative discourse in a situation in which language as embodiment of experience has become highly valorized. The case of the Ifa corpus in Yoruba culture comes immediately to mind. It is obvious that the sacred function of this corpus (linked as it is to the ritual of divination and associated with the hermetic character of the poems that comprise the corpus) has everything to do with the conservative textual requirement of the form (Bascom, 1969; Abimbola, 1977). In another case, the dynastic poems of the kingdom of Rwanda, the ideological factor is the predominant one, for the poems combine historical narration with eulogies of the ruling family in such as way as to identify the monarchy with the material and spiritual well-being of the state. It is of special interest to note that in this case, the textual integrity of the corpus is anchored in an elaborate metrical system; the social valorization of the genre exerts the pressure toward textual preservation in this form (Coupez and Kamanzi, 1970).

These two examples demonstrate that an oral culture is perfectly able to sustain literature in a strictly textual form. However, the reality of the African situation is that oral literature operates on a more flexible principle of textuality than is suggested by these examples. By its very nature, orality implies, if not absolute impermanence of text, at least a built-in principle of instability. But what may seem, from the point of view of literate culture, a disabling inconvenience has been transformed into a virtue in African orality, for although the textual elements cannot be disregarded in the forms of our imaginative expression, they are more often experienced as the outline of a verbal structure and as reference points for the development of ideas and images, as suggestive signposts in the narrative or prosodic movement of a discourse that is still in the future. This outline is simply held in the mind and expanded by the performer into a fully worked-out discourse when the occasion arises for its actualization. The point is that an oral text is almost never fully determined beforehand, given once and for all, as in the case of written literature, which strives to endow the text with the permanence of a material object. An oral text is actualized in oral performance and is thus open and mobile; what can be abstracted as the verbal content of a given work is perpetually recreated, modified as the occasion demands, and given new accents from one instance of its realization to another.

[. . .]

Notes

1   I say "until now" because, as Marshall McLuhan foresaw, the electronic revolution seems destined to create a new order of language for the representation of reality.

2   I am using this expression here in a sense slightly different from Walter Ong's usage.

References

Abimbola, Wande, ed. and trans. *Ifá Divination Poetry.* New York: NOK, 1977.

Bascom, William Russell. *Ifá Divination: Communication between Gods and Men in West Africa.* Bloomington. Indiana University Press, 1969.

Calame-Griaule, Geneviève. *Ethnologie et langage.* Paris: Gallimard, 1965.

Coupez, A., and Th. Kamanzi, eds. *Littérature de cour au Rwanda.* Oxford: Clarendon, 1970.

Finnegan, Ruth. "Literacy versus Non Literacy: The Great Divide?" in *Modes of Thought,* ed. Robert Horton and Ruth Finnegan, 112–14. London: Faber and Faber, 1973.

Gérard, Albert. *Four African Literatures.* Berkeley: University of California Press, 1971.

——. *African Language Literature.* Washington, DC: Three Continents, 1981.

Goody, Jack. *The Domestication of the Savage Mind.* Cambridge: Cambridge University Press, 1977.

——. *The Interface between the Oral and the Written.* Cambridge, Cambridge University Press, 1987.

Miyoshi, Masao. "Thinking Aloud in Japan." *Raritan* 9, no. 2 (Fall 1989): 29–45.

Ong, Walter J. *Orality and Literacy: The Technologizing of the Word.* London: Methuen, 1982.

Zahan, Dominique. *La dialectique du verbe chez les Bambara.* Paris: Mouton, 1963.

Zumthor, Paul. *Introductuon à la poésie orale.* Paris: Seuil, 1983. Trans. Kathryn Murphy-Judy as *Oral Poetry: An Introduction.* Minneapolis: University of Minnesota Press, 1990.

Chapter 11

Oral Literature and Modern African Literature

Isidore Okpewho

[...]

There has [...] been an increasing tendency on the part of modern African writers to identify with the literary traditions of their people in terms both of content and of technique. The reason is not far to seek. For a long time before African nations won political independence from their European colonizers, African culture was mis-understood and misrepresented. Words such as *savage* and *primitive* were used in describing it and [...] the literary or artistic quality of the oral literature was underplayed and undermined by foreign scholars who had little or no feeling for the languages and the attitudes in which that literature was expressed. It was only inevitable that, when these African nations won their independence from foreign domination, they undertook to reexamine and overhaul not only the institutions by which they had been governed but also the image of their culture that had long been advertised by outsiders. The aim was to demonstrate that Africa has had, since time immemorial, traditions that should be respected and a culture to be proud of.

As far as the creative writers are concerned, the main offshoots of this program have been to collect and publish texts of the oral literature of their people as practiced by them over time and to use that literature as a basis for writing original works that reflect, from a more or less modern perspective, some of the major concerns of today so as to demonstrate that traditional African culture is not obsolete but relevant for the articulation of contemporary needs and goals. In this essay, we shall examine the various ways in which modern African writers have made their contribution toward this vindication of traditional African culture.

First published in *African Oral Literature: Backgrounds, Character, and Continuity,* pp. 293–6, 301–3, 314–16. Bloomington, IN: Indiana University Press, 1992.

Translation

As we have often stressed, many Europeans who studied African oral literature and culture from the mid-nineteenth to the mid-twentieth century were laboring under a prejudice as well as a misconception. Often, this is reflected in the rather cavalier ways in which they translated the pieces of oral literature or sought to give them a respectability which, it was thought, they lacked. Burton reported one of the old prejudices about African oral literature prevalent in his time: "Poetry there is none.... There is no meter, no rhyme, nothing that interests or soothes the feelings, or arrests the passions" (1865: xii). The result of this was that some European collectors, in their translation of the songs that they encountered in African communities, tried to force them into schemes of versification that made music to European ears but were characteristically un-African.

When African writers and scholars started doing their own translations, they saw it as their primary duty to dress African oral literature in a European language in such a way as to bring out the poetic quality, the charm, of the original. Unfortunately, some of them tried to be so "fashionable" that in the end their translations sounded just as un-African as the ones the Europeans did. Although the following rendition by the Ghanaian poet G. Adali-Mortty of a traditional Ewe dirge endeavors to capture the depth of sentiment of the original, his recourse to the idiom of Eliza-bethan poetry leads us to question the authenticity of the translation.

> Methinks it's been a dream:
> But the dream has come to life!
> Atangba's son, Drofenu, says:
>   Believe them not:
>   A dream's a dream.
>   No more!
> Truly, had dreams been real,
> Death, I'd have fathomed death. (Adali-Mortty 1979: 4)

In defending his technique, Adali-Mortty makes a claim which many translators have frequently advanced in support of the liberties they have taken, that in African poetry "the thoughts are condensed in terse language, making their translation into English a hazardous venture!" This is certainly true, and I do not mean to trivialize or underestimate the depth of sentiment in much traditional African poetry. But the point is that it is not necessary to try to capture this depth by straining after archaic idioms and techniques that have an all too foreign flavor. One of the characteristic qualities of traditional African song is repetition, either of single lines or groups of lines. It is significant that in the original Ewe version of this dirge, Adali-Mortty indicates in parenthesis that the first two lines of the song are sung twice – "(bis)" – but omits that indication from the English version, as if to suggest that such a repetition has no place in the English poetic sensibility. This may well be so. But the song being translated is an African song, and the repetition does help to invest a piece of oral performance with an intensity or depth by way of emphasis.

Those African writers who appreciate this fact have consequently aimed to strike a compromise between a due regard for the European idiom and a firm loyalty to the peculiarly African character of the material at their disposal. In this dirge translated from the Acoli, Okot p'Bitek does not tamper with the repetitive structure and diction of the original, and the result is poetry that captures the vibrancy and sauciness of the oral performance and yet manages to affirm, by the sheer force of the repetition, the tragic fate of the poor.

> Ee, my aunt,
> The death of the poor is sudden;
> My aunt, was she strangled?
> What death has killed my aunt?
> The poor woman died on the roadside;
> The poor thing died suddenly;
> Who has strangled my aunt?
> The death of the poor is sudden.
>
> Oh, mother,
> I heard her by her smell oh,
> The death of the poor is sudden;
> I heard her by her smell on the roadside;
> What snake bit my aunt?
> The poor woman died on the roadside;
> The poor thing died suddenly;
> Was she killed by a lion?
> The death of the poor is sudden.
>
> Ee, harlot;
> The death of the poor is sudden;
> Ee, harlot, somebody slept with her,
> Perhaps a bull syphilis killed my aunt?
> My aunt has died a foolish death;
> The poor thing died suddenly;
> Who killed her?
> The death of the poor is sudden. (p Bitek 1974: 137)

Here, truly, is an African writer who has a feeling for the peculiar lyricism of his people's poetic traditions, and I do not think the lucidity of the English compromises the poetic intensity of the original.

There has been an equally large number of translations of African oral narratives. The first known "translation" of African tales was the Frenchman J-F. ("Le Bon") Roger's *Fables Senegalaises recueillies dans l'Ouolof* (1828), which is really a retelling or recapitulation. In the later nineteenth and much of this century, in fact, there have been volumes of translations of uneven quality. Some of them are little more than summaries of tales collected by anthropologists interested more in the ideas (of culture and social life) than in the literary merits of the tales.

African writers and scholars have, however, sought to correct the picture and to demonstrate that their narrative traditions can boast as much charm as anything found in modern narrative. One of the most notable nationalist ideologies of this century has been the philosophy of negritude, especially as propagated by the Senegalese Leopold Sedar Senghor in his poetry and essays. The aim of negritude was to project everything African – the color black, the physical features of the African and his environment, the humane quality of

African culture, etc. – as beautiful and salutary. This movement, designed to put Africa in a good light at a time (in the 1940s and 1950s) when African nations were agitating for independence from European powers, was advertised mostly in the verse of the period – by Francophone African poets such as Senghor, Birago Diop, David Diop, and Bernard Dadie as well as the Caribbean poets Leon Damas and Aime Cesaire – but there were also works of prose narrative.

One of the most outstanding of these prose works is the historian Djibril T. Niane's edition of the legend of Sunjata, the thirteenth-century Malian king and emperor, under the title *Soundjata ou l'épopée mandingue* (1960), translated into English by G. D. Pickett as *Sundiata: An Epic of Old Mali* (1965). In this evocation of the great historical tradition of the Mandinka, Niane was obviously influenced by Thomas Mofolo's narration of the life and career of the legendary Zulu leader Chaka. Although the story of Chaka's exploits has traditionally been told by *imbongi* (bards) who render their subject in highly metaphorical praise chants, Mofolo – then working on the staff of a missionary publishing house – chose to render his *Chaka* as a historical novel presented "as a study of human passion, of an uncontrolled and then uncontrollable ambition leading to the moral destruction of the character and the inevitable punishment."[1] Niane also casts his own story of Sunjata as a historical novel, although it is traditionally told in poetic chants by *griots* (bards) to the accompaniment of a chordophone called *kora*. However, in place of Mofolo's moral didacticism, Niane retains the element of glorification by portraying Sunjata as an insuperable champion of a just cause and the architect of an eternal imperial glory.
[. . .]

Adaptation

It must be emphasized [. . .] that translation is by no means an easy task. Indeed, we shall go further and say that there is hardly any translation that does not show some element of stylization, however close the translator may have tried to stay to the original text. The reason for this is not hard to understand. However deeply attached the translator is to the proud heritage of a people, he or she is equally aware that some of the outlook revealed by the text no longer prevails. Things have changed somewhat, and although there is a continuing need to translate the old classic tales and songs so as to save them from extinction, it is equally inevitable that they will be presented in ways that reflect the changed styles of living and perception in contemporary society.

Translating the old texts in stylized language and techniques is one way of adapting to the changed outlook; finding new subjects and new contexts for the old forms is another good example of this form of adaptation is the Sotho writer B. M. Khaketla's description of a train (Kunene 1970: 150–1). The author's closeness to the traditions of his people may be seen in the fact that he has chosen the language of praise (as in the *lithoko*) to describe this object, especially in reflecting the beastly fierceness of the train's movement. Take the opening lines of the poem:

> *Tjbutjbumakgala,*[2] beautiful thing of the White man,
> There's a steel rope tethering this black bovine,
> As for a woven rope, he would break it!

It is, indeed, the mother-of-smoke-that-trails behind,
A Madman, Wearer-of-a-*towane*-grass-hat,
Creator-of-fog even while the skies are clear,
Churner-of-clouds even while the winds are still,
Leaving us covered with blackness;
Smoke billows up, and sparks fly,
As when a bonfire is fed with dry reeds.

Like the praise poet of the oral tradition, Khaketla tries to mix this heroic portrait of the train with a tone of subtle protest or disclaimer:

The train is spiteful, Little-Black-One,
It took away my brother and he was lost forever,
My heart was sore, tears welled in my eyes,
And flowed like rivers down my cheeks,
And there I stood crying aloud with grief!

The significant thing here, however, is the treatment of an object of modern technology – the train. Although Khaketla writes in his own native tongue (Sotho) and remains attached to the Sotho tradition of poetic eulogy, he has chosen to treat a modern subject as a way of demonstrating the adaptability and the continuing relevance of that tradition.

A similar achievement has been recorded by the Ugandan poet Okot p'Bitek in his songs, most notably the *Song of Lawino*. To his death in 1982, Okot remained a staunch believer in the vitality of the oral traditions. When some of his colleagues, including Taban lo Liyong, complained that compared with West Africa, East Africa was a kind of "literary desert," Okot replied that critics like Taban were suffering from some form of "literary deafness" (p'Bitek 1974: v). Although he went to some of the best universities in Britain (Bristol, Oxford, etc.), he had a firm attachment to the traditions of his native Acoli, devoting himself to a study of its indigenous belief systems and translation of the oral literature. Even when he wrote his own poetry in English he tried to stay as close as possible to the forms of his native Acoli, mainly to demonstrate that there were enough resources in his indigenous traditions for him to use in the treatment of any topic whatsoever.

Song of Lawino was the first such effort that Okot made. Like Khaketla perhaps, Okot had written the poem in Acoli under the title *Wer pa Lawino;* but he soon translated it into English to give it larger circulation.[3] The poem, a work of social criticism, follows closely on the Acoli tradition of the poetry of abuse. A young woman (Lawino), aggrieved that her educated husband (Ocol) has ignored her in favor of a sophisticated urban mistress (Clementina), pours complaint and abuse not only on her husband and his mistress but also on the ways of Western civilization which have drawn him away from the traditions in which he was raised. Although the English translation of this poem fails to capture much of the lyrical appeal of the Acoli original, as Heron has shown (1984: 6), Okot manages to stay as close as possible to the tone and imagery of the tradition. Notice, for instance, the sauciness and contempt with which Lawino describes the act of kissing between Ocol and Clementina.

You kiss her on the cheek
As white people do,
You kiss her open-sore lips

As white people do
You suck the slimy saliva
From each other's mouths
As white people do. (p'Bitek 1984: 44)

We can see here the repetitive structure of the traditional African song. Heron has pointed
out (1984: 7) how closely the poem borrows from the imagery of specific Acoli traditional
songs. For example, take this image of a spear from one of the traditional songs recorded by
Okot in his collection *Horn of My Love*:

The spear with the hard point
Let it split the granite rock
The spear that I trust
Let it split the granite rock
The hunter has slept in the wilderness
I am dying, oh. (p'Bitek 1974: 69)

It reoccurs in *Song of Lawino*, with rather strong echoes, toward the end of the poem where
Lawino urges her husband to be reconciled with the sustaining forces of his native traditions.

Beg forgiveness from them
And ask them to give you
A new spear
A new spear with a sharp and hard point
A spear that will crack the rock
Ask for a spear that you will trust. (1984: 119)

As a protest against the shortcomings of contemporary African society, Lawino's complaint is just as notable for the images of Western civilization that it derides as for those of
the tradition that it upholds. The satirical tone is very effective; Okot has convincingly
demonstrated that the local idiom is up to the task of representing the new ideas and habits
from the chosen perspective of the protagonist.
[. . .]

Exploitation

The line between adaptation and exploitation of the oral literary tradition is not a sharp one,
but it is nevertheless noteworthy. In adaptation, both the matter and the manner of the
tradition are quite recognizable. For instance, the fantasy world of Tutuola's works appears
much as it is in the tales of the oral tradition. In *The Marriage of Anansewa* the trickster is still
called Ananse, and the occasional introduction of the spider's web into the setting serves to
enhance the theme of entanglement by his cunning. In exploitation, however, the modern
writer makes only a selective use of elements of the oral tradition. The form of presentation
bears a limited relationship to the oral tradition, and even when familiar characters are used,
they are deployed in an unfamiliar setting and in a somewhat altered order of relationships.
What appeals to the writer in his or her recourse to the oral tradition is not so much the

physical factors of performance as the essential concepts and ideas contained in it which are seen as having an enduring relevance.

Naturally, there are various levels of subtlety in African writers' exploitation of the material of the oral tradition. One level may be seen in the fiction of Chinua Achebe. Although his novels deal with the realistic world largely of Igbo society (whether past or present) and although there is no noticeable effort on his part to structure them on any known folktale pattern, he nevertheless sprinkles them with elements of content and technique taken from the oral literary tradition. One of these is proverbs. In *Things Fall Apart* Achebe tells us: "Among the Ibo the art of conversation is regarded very highly, and proverbs are the palm-oil with which words are eaten" (1962: 6). Consequently, when characters (especially adult males) converse in Achebe's Igbo-set novels, they season (or oil) their speech quite liberally with these well-chosen witticisms.

The art of conversation or public speaking is marked not only by the copious use of proverbs but also by the selective use of stories. Stories and songs are found once in a while in Achebe's *Arrow of God*, especially in interludes of relaxation when women and children sit in the yard in the evenings to amuse themselves; such moments bring needed relief to the tragic tension in the story of the confrontation between the traditional culture and the European presence. In the following passage Ezeulu harangues two bellicosé clansmen with both proverbs and a story told, in a manner characteristic of the explanatory tale, to drive home a moral lesson about the fate of a headstrong son of the clan.

> Ezeulu did not speak until the last. He saluted Umuaro quietly and with great sadness.
> "Umuaro kwenu!"
> "Hem!"
> "Umuaro obodonesi kwenu!"
> "Hem!"
> "Kwezuenu!"
> "Hem!"
> "The reed we were blowing is now crushed. When I spoke two markets ago in this very place I used one proverb. I said that when an adult is in the house the she-goat is not left to bear its young from the tether. I was then talking to Ogbuefi Egonwanne who was the adult in the house. I told him that he should have spoken up against what we were planning, instead of which he put a piece of live coal into a child's palm and asked him to carry it with care. We have all seen with what care he carried it. I was not then talking to Egonwanne alone but to all the elders here who left what they should have done and did another. They were in the house and yet the she-goat suffered in her parturition.
> "Once there was a great wrestler whose back had never known the ground. He wrestled from village to village until he had thrown every man in the world. Then he decided that he must go and wrestle in the land of spirits, and become champion there as well. He went, and beat every spirit that came forward. Some had seven heads, some ten; but he beat them all. His companion who sang his praise on the flute begged him to come away, but he would not. He pleaded with him but his ear was nailed up. Rather than go home he gave a challenge to the spirits to bring out their best and strongest wrestler. So they sent him his personal god, a little, wiry spirit who seized him with one hand and smashed him on the stony earth.
> "Men of Umuaro, why do you think our fathers told us this story? They told us because they wanted to tell us that no matter how strong or great a man was he should never challenge his *chi*. This is what our kinsman did – he challenged his *chi*. We were his flute player, but we did not plead with him to come away from death. Where is he today? The fly that has no one to

advise it follows the corpse into the grave. But let us leave Akukalia aside; he has gone the way his *chi* ordained. . . . " (pp. 31–2)

Although Achebe makes a selective use of resources from his people's oral literary art, as the above example demonstrates, we can still see the physical factors of performance exactly as they appear in the tradition from which he has borrowed. On a more subtle level of exploitation, however, these factors are not so readily evident. In fact, the basis of exploitation of the oral literary tradition by modern African writers lies in the understanding that times have changed. Although they are driven by cultural pride to identify with the legacies of their people, the painful facts of contemporary life require that they reorder these cultural legacies in a way that represents sometimes a slight, sometimes a radical, departure from the tradition, especially if the tradition itself presents an outlook with which the writer does not necessarily agree. At any rate, at this level the oral tradition is turned to metaphorical or symbolic use rather than slavishly mirrored.

Something of this radical exploitation of the oral tradition may be seen in the works of the writers Sembene Ousmane, Wole Soyinka, and Ayi Kwei Armah. Ousmane is a committed writer of a Marxist-socialist persuasion, a novelist who in his works portrays and exposes the indignities suffered by the underprivileged classes of citizens at the hands of the corrupt and ruthless middle and upper classes who manipulate the system to their own advantage. A good example of Ousmane's radical use of the oral tradition is revealed in his short novel *The Money Order* (1977).

[. . .]

The exploitation of the African oral literary tradition attains perhaps its most intense and skillful level in the work of Wole Soyinka. In a number of his plays and in some of his poems, and definitely in both his novels, he has borrowed heavily from traditional mythology for the construction of characters and situations. He is principally indebted to Yoruba mythology, especially that aspect of it that narrates the relationships between the divinities and so contains for Soyinka the basic elements of the Yoruba outlook on life.

Notes

1   Mofolo's *Chaka* was published first in the Sesotho language in 1925, then in an English translation by F. H. Dutton (1930). A more authoritative translation by fellow Sotho Daniel Kunene was published in 1981.
2   This is an ideophone for the chug-chug movement (or choo-choo sound) of the train.
3   We also learn from Heron, in his introduction to the *Songs* (p'Bitek 1984: 3), that Okot had written a novel in Acoli in 1953.

References

Achebe, C. 1962. *Things Fall Apart*. London: Heinemann (1959).

Adali-Mortty, G. 1979. Ewe Poetry. In *Introduction to African Literature*, ed. U. Beier. London: Longman.

p'Bitek, O. 1974. *Horn of My Love*. London: Heinemann.

——. 1984. *Song of Lawino and Song of Ocol*, ed. G. Heron. London: Heinemann (1966, 1967).

Burton, R. F. 1865. *Wit and Wisdom from West Africa*. London: Tinsley Brothers.

Heron, G. 1984. Introduction to p'Bitek 1984.

Johnson, J. W. 1986. *The Epic of Son-Jara: A West African Tradition*. Bloomington: Indiana University Press.

Kunene, D. P. 1970. *Heroic Poetry of the Basotho*. Oxford: Clarendon Press.

Niane, D. T. 1965. *Sundiata: An Epic of Old Mali*, trans. G. D. Pickett. London: Longman.

Chapter 12

Women's Oral Genres

Mary E. Modupe Kolawole

In problematizing women's space in a modern African setting, orature is a domain of visibility and audibility, as scholars such as Carole Boyce-Davis and Molara Ogundipe–Leslie have remarked. In recent studies, scholars are highlighting areas of positive women's location. Contrary to some existing myths and theories, creativity in traditional African setting is not an exclusively male affair. Obioma Nnaemeka, Helen Nabatusa Mugabe, Grace Okereke, Chinyere Okafor, and Akosua Ayidoho have confirmed this. Even male scholars like Kofi Agovi, Ropo Sekoni, and Thomas Hale are unfolding oral genres that are tools of women's self-enhancement in African orature.

As in several spheres of life, role sharing is vivid in African orature. Many genres are women's genres but in certain places this is undermined or subverted. Ode Ogede makes this revelation with regard to the stifling and subversion of women's voices in the Igede area of Nigeria:

> My primary interest is to explore some Igede female voices that persist in the face of opposition. One of the injustices in the experiences of the women in contemporary Igede society is the fact that many of the oral forms with which some Igede male artists are now associated were, in fact, first invented by women but strangely enough, Igede religious and social precepts no longer allow or have marginalised the participation of members of the female sex in many of those cultural practices.[1]

In many other places, however, women's voices remain audible, as we see in satirical songs and poetry which are women's domain. Egungun satirical songs among the Yoruba, Hausa women's court poetry, Nzema Maiden songs in Ghana, Impongo solo among the Ila and Tonga of Zambia, Akan dirges and Nnwonkoro in Ghana, Galla lampoons, Kamba grinding (work) songs, are specific female oral genres. A plethora of female genres exists among the Yorubas. These include Obitun Songs, Olori songs, Aremo songs, Ago-Oka, Gelede, Olele, and Alamo songs. The Fulani Bori songs in northern Nigeria consist of overt modes of self-expression and self-assertion for the women in this esoteric religious group. Other genres

First published in *Womanism and African Consciousness*, pp. 73–9. Trenton: Africa World Press, 1997.

specifically dominated by women include Hausa women's court poetry, Igbo birthsongs, Ogori Ewere, many panegyric poems, and folktales, among others.

In addition to the historical evidence of African women's active impact on their society, traditional oral literature confirms their immense contributions. Contrary to some existing myths and theories also, African women have an immeasurable creative force. Many oral genres were and still are exclusively women's domains. The central role of women in sustaining and transmitting African culture in the diaspora during the slave trade has been a focal point of my on-going research (Kolawole, 1994). They are deconstructing old and existing myths to recreate new ones that reflect women's positive self-esteem.

Ali Mazrui believes that African indigenous culture has been endangered (Mazrui, 1991). But certain aspects of this culture have also been engendered, as we have seen, in the way myths have been manipulated to create disadvantages in women's social space. The documentation of matriachates in African history past and present raises important points about women's empowerment as well as the historic actions. Myths, legends, and history confirm the visibility of the African woman. Among several groups such as the Dogan, Ondo and Ewe people, women cannot be said to be effaced. The variables of power and cultural creativity in such societies reveal unique value structures. Other sources of women's empowerment and leadership come from diverse crafts (Afonja, 1986). African women's oral literature as a source of empowerment needs to be re-inscribed because several women writers derive inspiration from this.

Oral Genres as a Source of Women's Self-Expression

Their roles in cultural creativity have been undermined in the usual male/positive, female/ negative attitude. In spite of extensive research into this region's orature, basic misconceptions remain. Certain critics maintain that African women are not artists; at best, they parrot communal oral pieces. As usual, women have been consigned to a secondary status in an attempt to overlook the diversity of creative role and their pragmatic functions. Many critics, including well-meaning ones, have adopted an essentialist perspective. Ruth Finnegan's *magnum opus, Oral Literature in Africa*, has made a profound contribution to the documentation of African oral genres. Yet, her attitude is sometimes ambivalent:

> Certain kinds of poetry are typically delivered or sung by women (particularly dirges, lullabies, mocking verses and songs to accompany women's ceremonies or work), and each culture is likely to have certain genres considered specially suitable for women. However, references to men seem to occur even more often and, with a few striking exceptions, men rather than women tend to be the bearers of the poetic tradition. (Finnegan, 1976: 98)

There are many instances of oral poetry by women all over Africa and Finnegan's observation reveals the basic problem of an outsider researching into African culture from a Western perspective. With the best of intentions, there are usually conspicuous absences.

One needs to go beyond glossing over the predominantly female genres that exist all over the continent. It is relevant to reiterate that Africa is not one small cultural entity. The study of African culture is at once the study of a part and a whole. Cultural identity does not necessarily imply homogeneity. So much remains to be discovered about African female oral genres and their creative worth. Critics who contend that African women are no artists but ululators or parroters are either only partially informed or else wholly *mis*informed about the dynamic, complex, and varied scope of this region's orature. A Yoruba proverb is relevant to this issue, *Agbongbo tan ede, ija ni da* – 'Incomplete understanding or partial knowledge generates conflicts.'

A keen appraisal of selected female genres of African orature reveals the wealth of original creativity. From Hausa Bori songs to women's court poetry, this creative impulse is visible. These oral genres are manifestations of collective women's voices, dynamic group consciousness and a tool of eliciting positive influence on the society. They are not passive texts. From Akan dirges to Nzema satirical songs, the women are not simply parroting communal texts. Among the Yorubas, dirges, wedding chants, *rara*, satirical songs, and story-telling are areas in which women excel in creativity, adaptation and manipulation of existing or new texts into contemporaneous situations.

Women's oral genres are a rich repertoire of literariness and the exposition of semantic and linguistic innovation. In some parts of the continent, orature is not a passive pastime. Women's voices are effectively women's outcry as June Goodwin observes in *Cry Amandla*. If these women's oral pieces were mere parroting, there would be no sustained interest. The diversity of genres illustrates their prevalent roles. Among the Yorubas alone, women's genres include: Obitun songs (Ondo), Olori songs (Igede), wedding chants (Igbomina and Oyo), Aremo songs, Ago, (Oka-Akoko), Gelede songs (Egbado), Olele (Ijesa), Alamo songs (Ekiti) as well as panegyrics.

In spontaneous performances such as Igbo birth songs or solo performance as in the case of impango of the Tonga of Zambia, creativity and originality are inevitable. What is often overlooked is the functional womanist purpose of African orature which necessitates relevance and instant adaptations of texts to the occasion. Oral genres are strong weapons of self-assertion and Micere Mugo confirms this:

> Within the world of orature the woman had a lot of power. She spoke the word. She created the word. She was instrumental to defining the ethics and aesthetics around which the world operated . . . [2]

The African woman as a transmitter and vector of cultural, spiritual, social and moral values implies the process of original creativity.

Among the Ogori people of Nigeria, some measure of primary orality is still maintained in spite of the impact of literacy. Orature still underlines much of the values of society and women play a cardinal role. *Ewere* is a predominantly female genre. Although this genre is largely composite (Kolawole, 1984), some scholars consider the poetic trait of Ewere as the most noticeable (Olabayo, 1989). Ewere is only an instance of the individual talent, methodology and originality that women oral artists put into their performance. It is a vivid example of the way women use oral genres for self-expression, social castigation and rejection of oppressive laws. In many parts of Africa, folktales are dominated by women (Ojo, 1991). Akan story-telling with the famous intricate weaving of Anansi's web of stories is elderly women's domain. In addition, queen mothers interpret the rich poetry encapsulated in drum language. Women move from the original communal structure by adapting the oral genre to women's needs. Women use oral literature and exclusive female genres to condemn social problems, immorality, unfaithfulness, and idleness – and to make demands. Nzema maiden songs in Ghana are a good example of this. These values are expressed in rich poetic forms. Other aims of women's oral art include moral mediation and legalistic intervention as well as confrontation of and resistance to negative change and acculturation, as we see in Nzema satirical songs (Agovi, 1992). These texts reveal women's collective consciousness, composite voice, female bonding, unity, identity and positive eliciting and reassessment of womanhood and femininity. They act as a metaphor and a repository for the predicament, problems, hopes, aspirations, burdens, and ideals of womanhood:

> Nzema women appropriate a profound awareness of changes in the environment as a form of empowerment to undermine fixed perceptions of women and their seeming marginality in the social process.[3]

In many other parts of Africa, women use satirical songs to resist oppression and call for gender justice. All these are channels for enunciating women's self-healing and self-assertion. In Southern Sudan, Nuba women enjoy a level of equality that is exceptional, as they participate in all levels of activities except hunting. Here and in many parts of the Sudan, folktale is also women's genre. Indeed, in Central Sudan, the role of grandmothers in story-telling is so dominant that grandmothers, *Habboba*, are an institution. Satirical wedding songs or '*Aghani Al-Banat*' are a strong avenue of girls' self-expression too. They castigate men for suppressing women. Through this genre, girls also condemn social ills, negative values, and the move towards materialism while reinforcing positive values. Women folk poets are also common in the Sudan and praise songs as well as eulogies are dominated by women. Another popular genre is *hija*, a traditional defamatory Arabic poetic form that satirises people's moral laxity. *Hija* is exclusively a women's genre in northern Sudan. (Although this is not an exclusively female genre in the south; it is equally used by both women and men for self-expression. It is considered more serious, however, if women use *hija* to ridicule or castigate a man than if he is so satirized by a 'fellow' man.)

African women's contribution to cultural creativity and their ability to use oral art for gender retrieval poses an important challenge to modern writers. Women writers are facing the challenge posed by traditional women who saw oral literary genres as avenues for self-enhancement. The role of literature and orature in fostering African women's relocation is vital to the womanist philosophy (Kolawole, 1992). Many female genres are sources of positive self-evaluation, society's well-being and positive self-retrieval. Abu Abari cites Birom women (Jos, Nigeria) as another group that manipulates oral literature to elicit its plight and fate as socially constructed, so as to transcend the same. Afam Ebeogu also highlights the vital role of Igbo birth songs:

> These birthsongs are an extremely convenient avenue for Igbo women to express their under-standing of the norms and values of the Igbo society, and to comment on some of these norms and values.[4]

If through proverbs and other areas of folklore, the African woman has been demonised, female oral artists are still attempting self-retrieval and repositioning of their gender's social status and self-image. Through oral creative master-pieces, women writers as their gender mouthpieces are underscoring women as the source of virtue. They are analyzing myths, proverbs, folktales, and history and are recreating new myths and archetypes that strengthen positive images of women too. This is true of legends, myths, and folktales as well.

Notes

1   Ode S. Ogede, "Counters to Male Domination: Images of Pain in Igede Women's Songs," *Research in African Literature*, Vol. 25, No. 4 (Winter 94).
2   Micere Mugo, in James, p. 93.
3   Kofi Agovi, "Women's discourse in Social Change in Nzema (Ghanaian) Maiden Songs," a paper presented at the African Studies Association Conference, St Louis, Missouri, December, 1991.
4   Afam Abaogu, "Igbo Birthsongs," an unpublished seminar paper at the Folklore Society of Nigeria annual conference, Obafemi Awolowo University, Ile-Ife, Nigeria, 1984.

References

Afonja, S & Bisi Aina. *Women in Social Change in Nigeria* Ife: Obafemi Awolowo University Press, 1994.
Agovi, Kofi. "Women's discourse in Social Change in Nzema (Ghanaian) Maiden Songs," a paper presented at the African Studies Association Conference, St Louis, Missouri, December, 1991.
Finnegan, Ruth. *Oral Literature in Africa*. Nairobi: Oxford University Press, 1976.
James, Adeola. *In Their Own Voices*. London: Heinemann, 1990.
Kolawole, Mary E. Modupe. "An African View of Transatlantic Slavery and the Role of Oral Testimony in Creating a New Legacy" in *Transatlantic Slavery: Against Human Dignity*, ed. Anthony Tibbles. London: HMSO/National Museum and Gallery, 1994.
——. "Gender and Changing Social Vision in the Nigerian Novel." In *Women in Social Changein Nigeria*. Mt. Saint Vincent University and Women's Studies Group, Obafemi Awolowo University Press, 1993.
Mazrui, Ali. *Cultural Forces in World Politics*. Portsmouth, NH: Heinemann, 1990.

Chapter 13

The Oral Artist's Script

Harold Schenb

> Insights of all kinds are welcome; but no wisdom will substitute for an instinct for action and pattern, and a perhaps savage wish to hold, through your voice, another soul in thrall.
>
> John Updike, interviewed in *Writers at Work*

"Kwathi ke kaloku ngantsomi . . ." "And now for a story. . ." The storyteller pronounces these familiar formulaic words, and moves her audience into the bounteous riches of the cultural past, into a world charged with fantasy and festooned with delights and the bijoux of the storyteller's art. But in the process, members of the audience never leave the tangible, perceptible world: the storyteller moves them into antiquity, scrupulously making the connections between past and present, and in that magical nexus shapes their experience of the present.

Story occurs within the mesmerizing, unreal realm of performance – it is a world unto itself, with its own set of laws. Patterning involves the repetition of fantasy images and their satellite contemporary images. It involves the aesthetics of performance: the body of the performer, the music of her voice, and the complex relationship between her and her audience. The storyteller breaks through the force of the linear movement of the story to move the audience to deeper and more complex experiences. She does this to a great extent by juxtaposing unlike images, then revealing, with the full emotional participation of the members of the audience, the connections between them that render them analogous. In this way are past and present blended: ideas are thereby generated, forming our conception of the world that we inhabit.

Performance gives the images their context, and gives the members of the audience a ritual experience that bridges past and present, shaping their contemporary lives. A performer of oral narratives utilizes the materials of her culture much as a painter uses color. The audience must therefore not mistake the cultural elements found in such narratives for direct reflections of the culture itself. There are few one-to-one relationships between the events in the performances and the artist's society. It is this poetic truth that South African storytellers underscored for me again and again in discussions regarding their stories. If the narrative tradition does mirror nature, it does so only in intricate, aesthetically perceived forms, which ultimately have the same effect on an audience as visual art, dance, and music do.

First published in *The Poem in the Story: Music, Poetry and Narrative*, pp. 16–20. Madison: University of Wisconsin Press, 2002.

Performance is the ritualistic organizing of mythic images: the audience is ceremonially moved into the center of the story, to the poem in the story. This ritual is composed of and accompanied by the music of the story, the melodic line and the rhythmic undercurrent of that line, with meaning as the result. This combination of music, mythic image, contemporary image, and ritual results in metaphor. The poetics of storytelling involves all of these, but most especially metaphor and the music that constructs it as the poem at the center of the story. So meaning in story is essentially a complex combination of varied feelings elicited by words and images, which are then worked into form. It is the formal containment of the emotional experiences of the members of the audience that generates the meaning, or message, of the story. In the poetics of storytelling, the story begins with a mythic image; that image is organized in linear form with other more contemporary images. The combination of mythic image and other imagery is worked into a melodic line or theme that may be combined with other themes occurring within the context of other images that reflect upon, reinforce, and otherwise color the theme or themes. When there is more than one theme, they are contrapuntal. The poetics of storytelling deals with meaning, with emotion, form, repetition, and myth. It has to do with music and the consequent metaphor; and with performer and audience, with ritual and performance.

This is the oral artist's script. His materials include ancient images, his body and voice, his imagination, and an audience. Within a broad thematic framework, he is free to deal with the images as he chooses, and he is praised by the audience for the originality with which he weaves them. Little is memorized, so the artist must depend on his imagination and on the controlled cooperation of the members of the audience to develop the skeletal mythic image that he has drawn from a repertory of remembered images inherited from a venerable artistic tradition.

The development of the linear plot is not always the most important achievement in a performance. The performers are storytellers, intellectuals as well as artists, a role that has been defined for them for generations. They are craftsmen who can use the narrative surface as a tool to be utilized to state a theme, to create an argument, or to elicit some emotional or intellectual response from the audience. The image that is externalized has never before been produced in just that fashion, and will never again be created that way. The narrative surface can be manipulated by the artist, and made to project a certain idea at one time, a special emotion when it is produced the next time, a solution to a problem plaguing the society the next, as well as communication of the artist's own preoccupation. But most important are the emotions called forth by the mythic images and then made rhythmical. This plotting of images is really the special language of all humans: communication happens not through words but by images created with the assistance of nonverbal as well as verbal techniques.

In the creation, combination, and manipulation of images, ideas, values, arguments, and the affirmation of social institutions will emerge. These are stated and developed in a manner that is logical and rational within the context of the oral traditions. The linear narrative plots are constructed of mythic images, that part of the special language of the tradition that is transmitted through the generations. These easily remembered mythic images contain implicitly the conflict and resolution that will become evident only when the artist develops them in a performance, giving the mythic images life with his words, with his body, with the rhythm of the language. As the artist urges the images forward in a linear development, underlying structures simultaneously guide the imaginations of the members of the audience in a circular fashion, so that the surface narrative becomes a means of commenting upon itself. It is through this commentary that metaphor emerges. What critics often dismiss as a simple fascination with a world of fantasy is really a metaphorical language, sophisticated and useful, that is transmitted through the ages.

As the performer projects the remembered mythic image, he is constantly in need of the assistance of the audience, and if he is a talented and confident artist, he makes use of the many potentially disruptive tensions that exist between him and the members of the audience. That audience has the same repertory of mythic images as the artist, and it therefore fills in gaps left by a performer who, in his concentration on some special aspect of the image, may neglect other aspects, perhaps even leaving out certain parts of the narrative. This is not an aesthetic problem as far as the audience is concerned. Artistic proportion is a concern of members of storytelling societies, but this typically goes beyond the linear plot itself: members of the audience become involved in the complex logic and interweaving of the imaged language itself. What initially appears a simple matter of verbal equivalence is actually a unique metaphorical language.

This relationship between artist and audience becomes further complicated when one considers its nonverbal quality. The performer expects that the members of the audience will physically and vocally assist him in the development of his images. It is necessary to the success of his production that he wholly involve the audience in the work of art, and to do so he utilizes several devices. These devices are used most obviously to externalize the images, to clarify the plotting of those, and to take it to its climax. The participation of the audience in these verbal and nonverbal aspects of production assists in this process. But at the same time that the audience, always under the control of the artist, is helping to create and sustain the images, it is simultaneously being integrated into the images. The audience is a part of the work of art in two ways: it helps to build the images, and it is emotionally caught up in the images. The linear plot is the most apparent of these narrative devices. The conflict develops and slowly moves toward a resolution; with a deft alteration of mythic images, the artist can change it to suit his own designs. The opening images of the performance are often filled with realistic details drawn from the immediate environment of the audience as the artist seeks to make the transition into his world of metaphor as smooth as possible. The demand for realism goes beyond this, of course. In fact the entire performance is realistic, the fantastic and magical elements being the metaphorical extensions of reality. The artist will exploit the rhythmic possibilities of the language, with its sounds constantly ready to dissolve in song. He will move his body, arms, face, and shoulders rhythmically; at times he is dancing in place, all that rhythmic movement ready to dissolve into pure dance. These musical characteristics of the performance have their own beauty, but they are also used to bring the members of the audience into a fuller participation in the developing images. They move their bodies in harmony with that of the performer; they clap, sing, express their approval, and are in physical and emotional accord with the artist and his creation. The audience knows the hackneyed plots, for its members have witnessed their production countless times. But there is a freshness about the work that is not evident on the surface. Moreover, the artistic delight in the performance goes deep, and the rhythms set in motion by the performer sustain images that are very complex.

The society is somehow affirmed every time the mythic images are elicited with serious intent and the members of the audience are wholly caught up in that narrative. They are totally involved in the images being paralleled metaphorically in the performance. At the moment of creation, the entire society is woven into the artistic image. The audience learns not by means of analytical investigation, but by emotional involvement in the artistic logic of the imagistic structures that the artist is manipulating. All of the aesthetic tensions in the production, the repeated images, the surface plot, the song, the dance, are calculated to attract and involve the audience in the developing image. The entire aesthetic system has developed as an integral part of this compelling system of communication and communion, existing both for mnemonic and communicative purposes. Form and content are indivisible, for the aesthetic allows for no separation; to attempt to isolate one from the other is to miss the point of the performance. During the production, the members of the audience are immersed in their culture as it is ideally visualized by the artist-philosopher, involved in its structure, and emotionally caught up in its values and aspirations. The externalized image brings the members of the community together, ties them rhythmically into the developing performance, imbues them with the ideals of the society in an aesthetic system that is never openly didactic. It allows no direct moralizing and preaching, but instead communicates values by means of a language of images.

When he reaches the climax of one mythic image, the performer may choose to incorporate yet another into the production, one that may not have any apparent connection with the previous image. Through his artistic genius, he introduces it into the production, skillfully linking it to the image that is being created, and giving the whole an illusion of unity. He can bring as many such mythic images into the performance as he chooses, using a complex mental cuing and scanning process to call up from his repertory those images that can be made relevant to the developing work of art. There are many mythic images in his repertory, and the possible combinations are endless.

The mythic image is repeated a number of times in the development of a performance, and in its repetition the linear image plotting is steadily moved from conflict to resolution with allied and supporting details connecting the repeated images. These repeated images move characters and events forward toward resolution, but an alteration must usually occur in that repetition if the resolution is to be attained. In the final repetition of the mythic image, a slight change may take place, the perfect pattern of repeated images with the mythic image at their center is broken, and it is in that change that the images are brought to resolution.

Part III

Writer, Writing, and Function

If the only literary and critical tradition one is familiar with is the African, one could be forgiven for thinking that writers and critics of African literature invented the idea that literature has a function, and that that function is to serve society. Nearly all writers, old and young, male and female, subscribe to the idea even if in varying degrees. Critics too – and indeed, many of the continent's accomplished writers are also some of its finest critics – have helped produce and reproduce a solid critical consensus on the matter. The fact, of course, is that reflections on the function of literature – or art generally – in society is as old as the existence of recorded commentaries on art, and no doubt well before, since we cannot assume that oral societies do not ruminate on their art in relation to their social circumstance. Ancient Greek philosophers such as Plato, Aristotle, Horace, and Longinus, to name the most commonly taught from that era, all had much to say about it. Since the emergence of formal African literature and criticism in the last century, the dominant conception of literature is as a pathfinder for society, a deconstructive searchlight of truth against all the dark burdens that circumscribe the ability of the community to achieve its best and realize its finest aspirations. There are two major explanations for the dominance of this idea of African literature. The first is that the literature emerged largely as a counter-discourse to European racism during colonial rule, and is therefore extremely sensitive to the uses of imaginative fiction. One of the classic earliest articulations of this idea is Achebe's 'The Novelist as Teacher.' The second explanation is the understanding, broadcast most memorably by Wole Soyinka in one of his early essays, that it has always been the task of African art and artists to be critical prods and guides of their societies: 'The artist has always functioned in African society as the record of the mores and experience of his society *and* as the voice of vision in his own time' (1967: 20). Whatever the explanation, the idea has become dominant. Two other well-known elaborations not included in the excellent selections here are Ngugi wa Thiong'O's *Writers in Politics* and Niyi Osundare's *The Writer as Righter*.

References

Ngugi wa Thiong'O. *Writers in Politics: Essays*. London: Heinemann, 1981.

Ngugi wa Thiong'O. *Writers in Politics: A Re-Engagement with Issues of Literature and Society*. Revsd and enlarged edn Oxford: James Currey, 1997.

Osundare, Niyi. *The Writer as Righter*. Ife Monographs on Literature and Criticism, 4th Series, No 5. Ife: Department of Literature in English, University of Ife, 1986.

Soyinka, Wole. "The Writer in a Modern African State," in *Art, Dialogue and Outrage: Essays on Literature and Culture*. Ibadan: New Horn, 1988, 15–20.

Part II

Status, Warfare and Religion

Chapter 14

The Novelist as Teacher

Chinua Achebe

Writing of the kind I do is relatively new in my part of the world and it is too soon to try and describe in detail the complex of relationships between us and our readers. However, I think I can safely deal with one aspect of these relationships which is rarely mentioned. Because of our largely European education our writers may be pardoned if they begin by thinking that the relationship between European writers and their audience will automatically reproduce itself in Africa. We have learnt from Europe that a writer or an artist lives on the fringe of society – wearing a beard and a peculiar dress and generally behaving in a strange, unpredictable way. He is in revolt against society, which in turn looks on him with suspicion if not hostility. The last thing society would dream of doing is to put him in charge of anything.

All that is well-known, which is why some of us seem too eager for our society to treat us with the same hostility or even behave as though it already does. But I am not interested now in what writers expect of society; that is generally contained in their books, or should be. What is not so well documented is what society expects of its writers.

I am assuming, of course, that our writer and his society live in the same place. I realise that a lot has been made of the allegation that African writers have to write for European and American readers because African readers where they exist at all are only interested in reading textbooks. I don't know if African writers always have a foreign audience in mind. What I do know is that they don't have to. At least I know that I don't have to. Last year the pattern of sales of *Things Fall Apart* in the cheap paperback edition was as follows: about 800 copies in Britain; 20,000 in Nigeria; and about 2,500 in all other places. The same pattern was true also of *No Longer at Ease*.

Most of my readers are young. They are either in school or college or have only recently left. And many of them look to me as a kind of teacher. Only the other day I received this letter from Northern Nigeria:

First published in the *New Statesman* (London: January 29, 1965); and subsequently in *Morning Yet on Creation Day: Essays*, pp. 42–5. London: Heinemann, 1975.

Dear C. Achebe,

I do not usually write to authors, no matter how interesting their work is, but I feel I must tell
you how much I enjoyed your editions of *Things Fall Apart* and *No Longer at Ease*. I look forward
to reading your new edition *Arrow of God*. Your novels serve as advice to us young. I trust that
you will continue to produce as many of this type of books. With friendly greetings and best
wishes.

Yours sincerely,
I. Buba Yero Mafindi

It is quite clear what this particular reader expects of me. Nor is there much doubt about
another reader in Ghana who wrote me a rather pathetic letter to say that I had neglected to
include questions and answers at the end of *Things Fall Apart* and could I make these
available to him to ensure his success at next year's school certificate examination. This is
what I would call in Nigerian pidgin 'a how-for-do' reader and I hope there are not very
many like him. But also in Ghana I met a young woman teacher who immediately took me
to task for not making the hero of my *No Longer at Ease* marry the girl he is in love with. I
made the kind of vague noises I usually make whenever a wise critic comes along to tell me
I should have written a different book to the one I wrote. But my woman teacher was not
going to be shaken off so easily. She was in deadly earnest. Did I know, she said, that there
were many women in the kind of situation I had described and that I could have served them
well if I had shown that it was possible to find one man with enough guts to go against
custom?

   I don't agree, of course. But this young woman spoke with so much feeling that I couldn't
help being a little uneasy at the accusation (for it was indeed a serious accusation) that I had
squandered a rare opportunity for education on a whimsical and frivolous exercise. It is
important to say at this point that no self-respecting writer will take dictation from his
audience. He must remain free to disagree with his society and go into rebellion against it if
need be. But I am for choosing my cause very carefully. Why should I start waging war as a
Nigerian newspaper editor was doing the other day on the 'soulless efficiency' of Europe's
industrial and technological civilisation when the very thing my society needs may well be a
little technical efficiency?

   My thinking on the peculiar needs of different societies was sharpened when not long ago I
heard an English pop song which I think was entitled *I Ain't Gonna Wash for a Week*. At first I
wondered why it should occur to anyone to take such a vow when there were so many much
more worth-while resolutions to make. But later it dawned on me that this singer belonged to
the same culture which in an earlier age of self-satisfaction had blasphemed and said that
cleanliness was next to godliness. So I saw him in a new light – as a kind of divine administrator
of vengeance. I make bold to say, however, that his particular offices would not be required in
my society because we did not commit the sin of turning hygiene into a god.

   Needless to say, we do have our own sins and blasphemies recorded against our name. If I
were God I would regard as the very worst our acceptance – for whatever reason – of racial
inferiority. It is too late in the day to get worked up about it or to blame others, much as they
may deserve such blame and condemnation. What we need to do is to look back and try and
find out where we went wrong, where the rain began to beat us.

   Let me give one or two examples of the result of the disaster brought upon the African
psyche in the period of subjection to alien races. I remember the shock felt by Christians of

my father's generation in my village in the early forties when for the first time the local girls' school performed Nigerian dances at the anniversary of the coming of the gospel. Hitherto they had always put on something Christian and civilised which I believe was called the Maypole dance. In those days – when I was growing up – I also remember that it was only the poor benighted heathen who had any use for our local handicraft, e.g. our pottery. Christians and the well-to-do (and they were usually the same people) displayed their tins and other metal-ware. We never carried water pots to the stream. I had a small cylindrical biscuit-tin suitable to my years while the older members of our household carried four-gallon kerosene tins.

Today things have changed a lot, but it would be foolish to pretend that we have fully recovered from the traumatic effects of our first confrontation with Europe. Three or four weeks ago my wife, who teaches English in a boys' school, asked a pupil why he wrote about winter when he meant the harmattan. He said the other boys would call him a bushman if he did such a thing! Now, you wouldn't have thought, would you, that there was something shameful in your weather? But apparently we do. How can this great blasphemy be purged? I think it is part of my business as a write to teach that boy that there is nothing disgraceful about the African wearher, that the palm-tree is a fit subject for poetry.

Here then is an adequate revolution for me to espouse – tot help my society regain belief in itself and put away the complexes of the years of denigration and self-abasement. And it is essentially a question of education, in the best sense of that word. Here, I think, my aims and the deepest aspirations of my society meet. For no thinking African can escape the pain of the wound in our soul. You have all heard of the African Personality; of African democracy, of the African way to socialism, of negritude, and so on. They are all props we have fashioned at different times to help us get on our feet again. Once we are up we shan't need any of them any more. But for the moment it is in the nature of things that we may need to counter racism with what Jean-Paul Sartre has called an anti-racist racism, to announce not just that we are as good as the next man but that we are much better.

The writer cannot expect to be excused from the task of re-education and regeneration that must be done. In fact he should march right in front. For he is after all – as Ezekiel Mphahlele says in his *African Image* – the sensitive point of his community. The Ghanaian professor of philosophy, William Abraham, puts it this way:

> Just as African scientists undertake to solve some of the scientific problems of Africa, African historians go into the history of Africa, African political scientists concern themselves with the politics of Africa; why should African literary creators be exempted from the services that they themselves recognize as genuine?

I for one would not wish to be excused. I would be quite satisfied if my novels (especially the ones I set in the past) did no more than teach my readers that their past – with all its imperfections – was not one long night of savagery from which the first Europeans acting on God's behalf delivered them. Perhaps what I write is applied art as distinct from pure. But who cares? Art is important but so is education of the kind I have in mind. And I don't see that the two need be mutually exclusive. In a recent anthology a Hausa folk-tale, having recounted the usual fabulous incidents, ends with these words:

They all came and they lived happily together. He had several sons and daughters who grew up and helped in raising the standard of education of the country.[1]

As I said elsewhere, if you consider this ending a naive anti-climax then you cannot know very much about Africa.

Note

1   W. H. Whiteley (ed.), *A Selection of African Prose*, Oxford, 1964.

Chapter 15

The Truth of Fiction

Chinua Achebe

Picasso once pronounced that all art was false. Since the West gave him credit for something like 90 per cent of its twentieth-century artistic achievement, Picasso no doubt felt free to say whatever he liked on the matter! Even so, I believe he was merely drawing attention in the exaggerated manner of seers and prophets to the important but simple fact that art cannot be a carbon copy of life; and thus, in that specific sense, cannot be 'true'. And if not true, it must therefore be false!

But if art may dispense with the constraining exactitude of literal truth, it does acquire in return incalculable powers of persuasion in the imagination. Which was why a single canvas, *Guernica*, by Picasso himself could so frighten the state machinery of Spanish fascism. For how could a mere painting on canvas exercise such awe unless in some way it accorded with, or had a disquieting relationship to, recognizable reality? Unless, in other words, it spoke a kind of truth?

In his 'Memorial Verses', Matthew Arnold put these words into the mouth of the poet and philosopher Goethe:

> The end is everywhere
> Art still has truth, take refuge there.[1]

Placed in that grand, apocalyptic setting, art and whatever truth is claimed for it are bound to become unduly remote.

Actually art is man's constant effort to create for himself a different order of reality from that which is given to him; an aspiration to provide himself with a second handle on existence *through his imagination*. For practical considerations, I shall limit myself to just one of the forms he has fashioned out of his experience with language – the art of fiction.

In his brilliant essay, *The Sense of an Ending*, Frank Kermode defines fiction simply as 'something we know does not exist but which helps us to make sense of, and move in, the world'.[2] Defining it in this practical way does prepare us not for one but for many varieties of fiction. Kermode himself draws attention to some of them, for example the mathematical

First printed by The Caxton Press (West Africa) Limited, Ibadan; and subsequently published in *Hopes & Impediments: Selected Essays*, pp. 95–105. London: Heinemann, 1988.

fiction of 'infinity plus one' which does not exist and yet facilitates the solution of certain problems in pure mathematics; or the legal fiction in certain legal systems which holds that when a man and his wife die at the same time the law, in pursuit of equity, will pretend that the woman dies before her husband, so that excessive hardship may not be brought upon their estate.

In other words we invent different fictions to help us out of particular problems we encounter in living. But of course these problems are not always as specific and clear-cut, or indeed as consciously perceived, as the lawyer's or the mathematician's formulations. When two very young children say to each other, 'Let us pretend . . .' and begin to act such roles as father and mother they are obviously creating a fiction for a less definite, more spontaneous and, I dare say, more profound purpose.

What is the nature of this purpose? I don't think anyone can say for certain. All that we do know is that judging from the evidence of man's fiction-making in all places and at all times he must surely have an inescapable need for that activity. No one has yet come upon the slightest evidence that any human group now or in the past managed to dispense with the need to make fictions.

Given the great gulf between being and knowing, between his essence and existence, man has no choice really but to make and believe in some fiction or other. Perhaps the ultimate judgement on a man is not whether he acquiesces to a fiction but rather what *kind* of fiction will persuade him into that acquiescence, that willing suspension of disbelief which Coleridge spoke about or that 'experimental submission', to quote I. A. Richards.

However, we must not overlook the carefulness displayed by both Coleridge and Richards in their choice of words; and for a very good reason. Coleridge's disbelief is only *suspended*, not abolished, and will presumably return at the appropriate moment; and Richards's submission is experimental, not definitive or permanent.

It is important to stress this point because man makes not only fictions to which he gives guarded or temporary acquiescence like the pretending games of healthy children; he has the capacity also to create fictions that demand and indeed impose upon him absolute and unconditional obedience. I will shortly return to this, but first of all let me extend what I have said about man's desire for fictions to include the question of his capacity. Man's desire for fictions goes with his ability for making them, just as his need for language is inseparable from his capacity for speech. If man only had the need to speak but lacked his peculiar speech organs, he could not have invented language. For all we know, other animals in the jungle might be in just as much need to talk to one another as man ever was and might have become just as eloquent had they been endowed with the elaborate apparatus for giving expression to that need. And certainly no one would suggest that the mute is silent because he has no need to speak or nothing to say. If we apply the same reasoning to man's propensity for fictions we can see that his need to create them would not adequately explain their existence; there must also be an effective apparatus.

This equipment, I suggest, is man's imagination. For just as man is a tool-making animal and has recreated his natural world with his tools, so is he a fiction-making animal and refashions his imaginative landscape with his fictions.

All attempts to define man neatly must fail because of his complexity. Man is a rational animal; man is a political animal; man is a tool-making animal, man is etc., etc. If you ask me I will add that man is a questioning animal, a highly curious animal. Given his mental and imaginative capacities this curiosity is only to be expected. Man finds himself caught, as it were, in a tiny glow-worm of consciousness. Behind him is the impenetrable darkness of his origin, and before him is another deep obscurity into which he seems headed. What is shrouded by those darknesses? What is the meaning of this tiny, intervening spot of light which is his earthly existence? In the face of these mysteries man's capacities are at once immense and severely circumscribed. His knowledge though impressive and expanding will never in all likelihood match what he needs to know. Not even the accumulated knowledge and wisdom of all his species will suffice. The ultimate questions will in all probability remain.

In the 1950s a Nigerian microbiologist, Dr Sanya Onabamiro, published a book which he entitled, with great perspicacity, *Why Our Children Die*, echoing what must have been one of the most poignant and heart-rending questions asked by our ancestors down the millennia. Why do our children die? Being a modern scientist Dr Onabamiro gave appropriate twentieth-century answers: disease, undernourishment and ignorance. Every reasonable person will accept that this 'scientific' answer is more satisfactory than answers we might be given from other quarters. For example a witch-doctor might tell us that our children die because they are bewitched; because someone else in the family has offended a god or, in some other secret way, erred. Some years ago I watched the pitiful spectacle of an emaciated little child brought out and sat on a mat in the midst of the desperate *habitués* of a prayer-house while the prophetess with maniacal authority pronounced it possessed by the devil and ordered its parents to fast for seven days.

The point of these examples is to suggest two things: first, the richness, the sheer prodigality, of man's inventiveness in creating aetiological fictions; second, that not all his fictions are equally useful or desirable.

But first of all I must explain my temerity in thus appearing to lump together under the general rubric of fictions the cool, methodical and altogether marvellous procedures of modern medicine with the erratic 'visions' of a religious psychopath. In all truth, the two ought never to be mentioned in the same breath. And yet they share, however remotely it may seem, the same need of man to explain and alleviate his intolerable condition. And they both make use of theories of disease – the germ theory, on the one hand, and the theory of diabolical possession, on the other. And theories are no more than fictions which help us to make sense of experience and which are subject to disconfirmation when their explanations are no longer adequate. There is no doubt, for instance, that scientists in the twenty-first and later centuries will look at some of the most cherished scientific notions of our day with the same amused indulgence that we show towards the fumblings of past generations.

And yet we can say, indeed we must say, that the insights given by Dr Onabamiro into the problem of high infant mortality, however incomplete future generations may find them, are infinitely more helpful to us than the diagnosis of a half-mad religious fanatic. In conclusion, there are fictions that help and fictions that hinder. For simplicity, let us call them beneficent and malignant fictions.

What is it then about fictions – good or bad – that makes them so appealing? Why does man have to take leave of reality in order to ease his passage through the real world? What lies behind this apparent paradox? Why is the imagination so powerful that it lures us so constantly away from the animal existence that our physical senses will impose on us?

Let me frame these questions somewhat differently so that we may not fly off at a tangent and get lost altogether in the heady clouds of abstraction.

Why does Amos Tutuola's *The Palm-Wine Drinkard* offer us a better, stronger and more memorable insight into the problem of excess than all the sermons and editorials we have heard and read, or will hear and read, on the same subject?

The reason is that while editorials and other preachments may tell us all about excess, Tutuola performs the miracle of transforming us into active participants in a powerful drama of the imagination in which excess in all its guises takes on flesh and blood. Afterwards we can no longer act as hearers only of the word; we are initiates; we have made our visit; we have encountered ourselves in the Drinkard in much the same way as the Drinkard has encountered himself in the course of a corrective quest – albeit unknowingly – in that preposterous clump of unpleasantness that is his own son, the half-bodied baby. The encounter like much else in the novel is made unforgettable for us because of Tutuola's inventiveness not only in revealing the variety of human faces that excess may wear, but also in his deft exploration of the moral and philosophical consequences of breaching, through greed, the law of reciprocity which informs like a gravitational force the seemingly aberratic motions of his bizarre, fictive universe.

This self-encounter which I consider the major source of the potency and success of beneficent fictions may be defined also as imaginative identification. Things are then not merely happening, *before* us; they are happening, by the power and force of imaginative identification, *to* us. We not only see; we *suffer* alongside the hero and are branded with the same mark of 'punishment and poverty', to use Tutuola's familiar phrase.

Thus without having to undergo personally the ordeals which the Drinkard has to suffer in atonement for his idleness and lack of self-control we become, through an act of our imagination, beneficiaries of his regenerative adventure. That we are able to do this is one of the greatest boons to our reflective humanity – the capacity to experience *directly* the highway on which we are embarked and also, *vicariously*, 'the road not taken', as Robert Frost might say.

Given our questioning nature the end of which is discovery, and given our existential limitations especially the vastness of our ignorance, one can begin to appreciate the immeasurable blessing that our imagination could confer on us. It is a truism and a cliché that experience is the best teacher; it is even arguable whether we can truly *know* anything which we have not personally experienced. But our imagination can narrow the existential gap by giving us in a wide range of human situations the closest approximation to experience that we are ever likely to get, and sometimes the safest too, as anyone who has travelled on Nigerian roads can tell you! For it is hardly desirable to be run over by a car in order to *know* that automobiles are dangerous. We can learn from that battered corpse by the roadside; not simply by observing it but by creating the chastening fiction *that we are it*, that the corpse of another man is *not*, as an Igbo proverb would have it, a log of wood, but ourselves. (Except that on further reflection that proverb is not in fact the outrageous thing I have just said. Another man's corpse *seems to us* like a log of wood, is what it says – a rather different matter and a very sad reflection on our impaired imagination, on our malfunctioning powers of identification with the plight of our fellows.)

Life is short and art is long, said the ancients. We can mitigate the brevity of the one with the longevity of the other. This is why human societies have always attempted to sustain their cultural values by carefully preserved oral or written literatures which provide for them and their posterity a short cut now and again to the benefits of actual experience. What about history, you might ask, does it not vouchsafe the same enlightenment? The lessons of history are important, of course. But think how many aeons of history will be needed to distil the wisdom of Shakespeare's *King Lear*. And in any case what great solace can many of us recent colonials derive from an effective history which is so nasty, British and short?

For a society to function smoothly and effectively its members must share certain basic tenets of belief and norms of behaviour. There must be a reasonable degree of consensus on what is meant by virtue and vice; there must be some agreement on the attributes of a hero, on what constitutes the heroic act. Different societies will not hold identical ideas on these questions in every part of the world or at every time in history. And yet, in spite of local and historical variations, we do not know of any society which has survived and flourished on totally arbitrary notions of good and evil, or of the heroic and the cowardly. Our very humanity seems to be committed to a distinction between these pairs however fuzzy the line may sometimes appear. But a society, like an individual, can sicken or become unhinged mentally, as in the phenomenon of mass hysteria which is well known. There are, of course, quieter and less dramatic symptoms of social pathology. Vulgar ostentation, callousness, disorderliness, filth and shoddiness are clear signs of disease. What is the cure? More exhortations? I think not.

The great virtue of literary fiction is that it is able by engaging our imagination to lead us 'to discovery and recognition by an unexpected and instructive route',[3] in the words of Kermode. It helps us locate again the line between the heroic and the cowardly when it seems most shadowy and elusive, and it does this by forcing us to encounter the heroic and the cowardly in our own psyche.

How often do we hear people say, 'Oh I don't have the time to read novels', implying that fiction is frivolous? They would generally add – lest you consider them illiterate – that they read histories or biographies, which they presume to be more appropriate to serious-minded adults. Such people are to be pitied; they are like a six-cylinder car which says: Oh, I can manage all right on three sparking-plugs, thank you very much. Well, it can manage somehow but it will sound like an asthmatic motor cycle!

The life of the imagination is a vital element of our total nature. If we starve it or pollute it the quality of our life is depressed or soiled.

We must not, however, celebrate the beauties of imagination and the beneficent fictions that are spun in its golden looms without mentioning the terrible danger to which it can be exposed.

Belief in superior and inferior races; belief that some people who live across our frontiers or speak a different language from ourselves are the cause of all the trouble in the world, or that our own particular group or class or caste has a right to certain things which are denied to others; the belief that men are superior to women, and so on – all are fictions generated by the imagination. What then makes them different from the beneficent fiction for which I am making rather large claims? One might reply: By their fruits, ye shall know them. Logically that may be a good answer, but strategically it is inadequate. For it might imply that Hitler should first commit genocide before we can conclude that racism is a horrendous evil, or that South Africa should go up in flames to confirm it. So we must find a criterion with an alarm system that screams red whenever we begin to spin virulent fictions.

Such an early-warning system is ready to hand and really quite simple. You remember the example of the children at play, how they preface their little drama by saying, 'Let us pretend'. What distinguishes beneficent fiction from such malignant cousins as racism is that the first never forgets that it is fiction and the other never knows that it is. Literary fiction does not ask us to believe, for instance, that the Palm-Wine Drinkard actually drank one hundred and fifty kegs of palm-wine every morning and seventy-five kegs in the evening, that he underwent the adventure so vividly described in the novel or indeed that he even existed. And yet reading the novel explains so much to us and affects radically the way we perceive the world thereafter.

Malignant fictions like racial superiority, on the other hand, never say, 'Let us pretend'. They assert their fictions as a proven fact and a way of life. Holders of such fictions are really like lunatics, for while a sane person might act a play now and again, a madman lives it permanently. Some people would describe malignant fictions as myths, but I find no justification for soiling the reputation of myths in that way. I would prefer to call malignant fictions by their proper name, which is superstitions. But whatever we call them, it is essential to draw a clear distinction between beneficent fiction and any arbitrary nonsense emanating from a sick imagination. Watching a magician and marvelling at his sleight of hand and management of optical tricks is something quite different from seeing him and *believing* that his powers derive from midnight visits to cemeteries or from reading the Sixth and Seventh Books of Moses. Beneficent fiction operates within the bounds of imagination; superstition breaks the bounds and ravages the real world.

We are totally wrong when we imagine that self-centredness is smart. It is actually very stupid, an indication that we lack enough imagination to recreate in ourselves the thoughts that must go on in the minds of others, especially those we dispossess. A person who is insensitive to the suffering of his fellows is that way because he lacks the imaginative power to get under the skin of another human being and see the world through eyes other than his own. History and fiction are replete with instances of correlation between indifference and lack of imagination. Think of the aristocratic lady who was driving home to her estate one winter evening and saw through the shutterless windows of a wretched hut a boy shivering in rags.

Moved to pity, she said to her coachman, 'Remark that hut, for as soon as I get home I must send warm things to that poor boy.'

When she got home and sat in front of a huge, crackling fire her coachman came to her and said, 'Madam, about the poor boy...'

'Oh, but it's nice and warm again,' she replied.

Think of the Queen of France before the French Revolution who was told that the people had no bread to eat and she said, 'Well, let them eat cake.' It is generally thought that she was a heartless monster. More likely she was only a pathetic, stupid woman who genuinely believed that if people were out of bread they should be able to manage with cake until they could stock up again.

Privilege, you see, is one of the great adversaries of the imagination; it spreads a thick layer of adipose tissue over our sensitivity.

We see the same deadening of consciousness all around us today at all levels – personal, communal, national and international. Not so long ago I saw a startling sight right under a multi-million-*naira* flyover in Lagos. A beggar was crouching in the middle of the road scooping something into a bowl while furious cars dodged him on all sides. As we got close I realized that the brownish-white stuff he was collecting was not pure sand but a mixture of sand and salt. A salt bag must have fallen out of a van and broken there and he had come on the scene rather late. The friend driving me said, 'This is one Nigerian whom the oil boom missed.' I could not get over the gigantic, almost crude, irony of that scene: the multi-million modern bridge overhead, a beggar defying instant death to scoop sand into a bowl for his soup. I recalled a poem I had just received for the *Okike* magazine, 'The Romance of Beggars':

> We want risk capital
> Not beggars
> Social overhead capital
> Not a begging bowl
> Don't rattle it
> Don't rattle your begging bowl in
> this economy.

Later, in another sequence of the same poem, a hot-blooded beggar, living as many do in Lagos, prehistorically in concrete caves below modern bridges, gives out this invitation:

> Come here into the hollow of my conscience
> I will show you a thing or two
> I will show you the heat of my love.
> You know what?
> I can give you babies too
> Real leaders of tomorrow
> Right here under the bridge
> I can give you real leaders of thought.

I don't think that elegant Miss Nigeria will have the imagination or conscience to explore the possibilities of that encounter. She will dodge the rude beggar and speed away in her expensive car to a sterile assignation with her bloated Mr Overhead Capital.

No, indifference to suffering is not clever at all. The late Hannah Arendt showed real perceptiveness when she called her study of the psychology of totalitarianism *The Banality of Evil*.

Imaginative identification is the opposite of indifference; it is human connectedness at its most intimate. It is one step better than the golden rule: Do unto others . . . Our sense of that link is the great social cement that really holds, and it will manifest itself in fellow-feeling, justice and fair play. My theory of the uses of fiction is that beneficent fiction calls into full life our total range of imaginative faculties and gives us a heightened sense of our personal, social and human reality. One thing that worries one above all else in the frenetic materialism that pervades our contemporary life is that as a species we may be losing the Open Sesame to the *mundo* of fiction – that ability to say 'Let us pretend' like grace before our act; and to say 'Our revels now are ended' like a benediction when we have finished – and *yet* to draw from this insubstantial pageant essential insights and wisdoms for making our way in the real world. The supple articulation of our imagination seems, alas, to be hardening rapidly into the sclerotic rigidity of literal-mindedness and material concerns.

An English friend, a marvellous raconteur at dinner, had just told a group of us of an anxious flight he and his wife recently made from the Far East when it occurred to his wife to ask him, by the way, if he had taken out flight insurance on that trip. 'Oh yes,' he replied blithely, 'if the plane had crashed we would have been the richest couple in the cemetery.' A few days later I repeated the joke to a doctor friend, who retorted promptly and unsmilingly that the money would have been paid to their next of kin. I thought: Oh my God, what a fate to befall the descendants of those incomparable fabulists who made our great oral traditions!

And I began to think of that other and far more serious experience which I had. I wrote a social satire called *A Man of the People*, which was published in January 1966, as fate would have it, two days after Nigeria's first military coup. Because the novel ends also with a military coup a certain degree of surprise and conjecture and, I might add, admiration was inevitable among my readers. What was not inevitable, however, was the theory which grew apparently during the civil war in certain quarters that because I wrote the novel I must have been one of the planners of the military coup. Long after the civil war I was questioned rather closely on this matter after I had given a lecture in one of our universities. Rather annoyed, I asked my questioner if he had read the book and he said vaguely yes. Did he remember, I asked him then, that before the coup in my story there was first a blatant rigging of an election, civil commotion in the land, murder and arson, which happened to be paralleled also by similar events in Nigeria before the January coup. Was he suggesting that I too planned those upheavals in Ibadan and elsewhere? Did he remember that my story specifically mentions a counter-coup, a prophecy which, alas, was also fulfilled in Nigeria in July 1966. Was he suggesting that I sat in on the planning of that as well? In general, did he think that a group of dissident army officers planning to overthrow their government would invite a novelist to sit in on their plot, go back to their barracks and wait for two years while the novelist wrote up the book, had it edited and produced by his publishers, and only then spring into action and effect their coup to coincide with the book's publication? Such a theory might have been excusable in 1966 for the armed soldiers who had gone in search of me first to my office and then, fortunately, to a house I had already vacated. How could they know that the offending book had taken two years to write and publish? But a university teacher in 1977!

This lengthy personal anecdote would not be necessary if it did not show more clearly than almost anything I have direct experience of how easy it is for us to short-circuit the power of our imagination by our own act of will. For when a desperate man wishes to believe something however bizarre or stupid nobody can stop him. He will discover in his imagination a willing and enthusiastic accomplice. Together they will weave the necessary fiction which will then bind him securely to his cherished intention.

The fiction which imaginative literature offers us is not like that. It does not enslave; it liberates the mind of man. Its truth is not like the canons of an orthodoxy or the irrationality of prejudice and superstition. It begins as an adventure in self-discovery and ends in wisdom and humane conscience.

Notes

1   Matthew Arnold, "Memorial Verses," *The Works of Matthew Arnold*, vol. I, New York: AMS Press, 1970, p. 251.
2   Frank Kermode, *The Sense of an Ending*, New York: Oxford University Press, 1967.
3   Ibid.

Chapter 16

Three in a Bed:
Fiction, Morals, and Politics

Nadine Gordimer

Three in a bed: it's a kinky cultural affair. I had better identify the partners.

Politics and morals, as concepts, need no introduction, although their relationship is shadily ambiguous. But fiction has defining responsibilities that I shall be questioning all through what I have to say, so I shall begin right away with the basic, dictionary definition of what fiction is supposed to be.

Fiction, says the *Oxford English Dictionary*, is 'the action of feigning or inventing imaginary existences, events, states of things...prose novels and stories collectively'. So poetry, according to the OED, is not fiction. The more I ponder this, the more it amazes me; the more I challenge it. Does the poet not invent imaginary existences, events, states of things?

If I should ask any erudite and literary gathering to give examples of the powers of the poets' invention of imaginary existences, events, the poets' matchless evocation of 'states of things', all drawn, just as the prose writers' is, from life – the fact of life – as the genie is smoked from the bottle, I could fill pages with quotations. If fiction is the suprareal spirit of the imagination, then poetry is the ultimate fiction. In speaking of fiction, I should be understood to be including poetry.

What is politics doing in bed with fiction? Morals have bedded with story-telling since the magic of the imaginative capacity developed in the human brain – and in my ignorance of a scientific explanation of changes in the cerebrum or whatever, to account for this faculty, I believe it was the inkling development that here was somewhere where the truth about being alive might lie. The harsh lessons of daily existence, coexistence between human and human, with animals and nature, could be made sense of in the ordering of properties by the transforming imagination, working upon the 'states of things'. With this faculty fully developed, great art in fiction can evolve in imaginative revelation to fit the crises of an age that comes after its own, undreamt of when it was written. *Moby-Dick* can now be seen as an allegory of environmental tragedy. 'The whale is the agent of cosmic retribution':

First published in *Living in Hope and History: Notes from our Century*, pp. 3–15. New York: Farrar, Strauss & Giroux, 1999.

we have sought to destroy the splendid creature that is nature, believing we could survive only by 'winning' a battle against nature; now we see our death in the death of nature, brought about by ourselves.

But the first result of the faculty of the imagination was, of course, religion. And from the gods (what a supreme feat of the imagination they were!), establishing a divine order out of the unseen, came the secular, down-to-soil-and-toil order of morals, so that humans could somehow live together, and in balance with other creatures.

Morals are the husband/wife of fiction. And politics? Politics somehow followed morals in, picking the lock and immobilizing the alarm system. At first it was in the dark, perhaps, and fiction thought the embrace of politics was that of morals, didn't know the difference ...And this is understandable. Morals and politics have a family connection. Politics' ancestry is morality – way back, and generally accepted as forgotten. The resemblance is faded. In the light of morning, if fiction accepts the third presence within the sheets it is soon in full cognisance of who and what politics is.

Let me not carry my allegory too far. Just one generation further. From this kinky situation came two offspring, Conformity and Commitment. And you will know who fathered whom.

Until 1988 I would have said that the pressures to write fiction that would conform to a specific *morality*, whether secular or religious, long had been, could be, and were, safely ignored by writers in modern times. The Vatican still has its list of proscribed works, but in most countries one assumed there was freedom of expression – so far as religion was concerned. (The exception was perhaps in certain North American schools...)

Blasphemy? A quaint taboo, outdated, like the dashes which used to appear between the first and last letters of four-letter words. Where censorship was rigidly practised, in Eastern Europe, the Soviet Union, and South Africa, for example, the censors were concerned with what was considered politically subversive in literature, not with what might offend or subvert religious sensibilities. (In the Soviet Union these were not recognized, anyway.) This was true even in South Africa, where the Dutch Reformed Church with a particular form of Calvinistic prudery had twisted religion to the service of racism and identified the church with the security of the state, including its sexual morality based on the supposed "purity" of one race. A decade ago, in 1988, an actor in South Africa could not get away with exclaiming "My God!" in a secular context on the stage, and *Jesus Christ Superstar* was banned; by 1989, savage satire of the church and its morality was ignored. As for sexual permissiveness, full frontal nudity in films was not snipped by the censor's scissors.

But in holding this illusion about freedom of expression in terms of religious and sexual morality, I was falling into the ignorance Islam finds reprehensible in the Judeo-Christian-atheist world (more strange bedfellows) – that world's ignorance of the absolute conformity to religious taboos that is sacred to Islam. And here Islam was right; I should have known that this kind of censorship was not evolving into tolerance, least of the rights of non-Muslim countries to grant their citizens the freedom of disbelief, but was instead becoming an international gale force of growing religious fanaticism. Then came the holy war against *The Satanic Verses*, in which the enemy was a single fiction, a single writer, and the might and money of the Islamic world were deployed in the *fatwa*: death to Salman Rushdie.

Now I, and other writers, were stunned to know that situations were back with us where religious persecution – the denial of people's right to follow their faith in freedom – is turned on its head, and religion *persecutes* freedom – not alone freedom of expression but a writer's freedom of movement, finally a writer's *right to life itself*. Now in a new decade, with freedoms rising, we see that while a writer becomes president in one country, another writer is being hounded to death throughout the world. We see how a religion has the power to terrorize, through its followers, across all frontiers. Political refugees from repressive regimes may seek asylum elsewhere; Salman Rushdie has nowhere to go. Islam's edict of death takes terrorist jurisdiction everywhere, contemptuous of the laws of any country.

Pre-Freudian hypocrisy, puritan prudery may be forgotten. The horror of what has happened to Rushdie is a hand fallen heavily on the shoulder of fiction: pressures to write in conformity with a specific morality still can arrive, and pursue with incredible vindictiveness, even if this is unlikely to happen to most writers.

Am I positing that morals should be divorced from fiction? That fiction is free of any moral obligation? No. Fiction's morality lies in taking the freedom to explore and examine contemporary morals, including moral systems such as religions, with unafraid honesty.

This has not been an easy relationship, whether in the ghastly extreme of Salman Rushdie's experience or, say, that of Gustave Flaubert, who, commenting on the indecency case against *Madame Bovary* after he won it in 1857, wrote of the establishment of spurious literary values and the devaluation of real literary values such a case implies for fiction. 'My book is going to sell unusually well ... But I am infuriated when I think of the trial; it has deflected attention from the novel's artistic success ... to such a point that all this row disquiets me profoundly ... I long to ... publish nothing; never to be talked of again.'

The relationship of fiction with politics has not had the kind of husband/fatherly authoritarian sanction that morals, with their religious origins, lingeringly have. No literary critic I know of suggests that *moralizing* as opposed to 'immorality' has no place in fiction, whereas many works of fiction are declared 'spoiled' by the writer's recognition of politics as as great a motivation of character as sex or religion. Of course, this lack of sanction is charactistic of an affair, a wild love affair in which great tensions arise, embraces and repulsions succeed one another, distress and celebration are confused, loyalty and betrayal change place, accusations fly. And whether the fiction writer gets involved with politics initially through his/her convictions as a citizen pushing, within, against the necessary detachment of the writer, or whether the involvement comes about through the pressure of seduction from without, the same problems in the relationship occur and have to be dealt with *in the fiction* as well as in the life.

For when have writers not lived in time of political conflict? Whose Golden Age, whose Belle Epoch, whose Roaring Twenties were these so-named lovely times?

The time of slave and peasant misery, while sculptors sought perfect proportions of the human torso? The time of revolutionaries in Czar Alexander's prisons, while Grand Dukes built mansions in Nice? The time of the hungry and unemployed, offered the salvation of growing Fascism while playboys and girls danced balancing glasses of pink champagne?

When, overtly or implicitly, could writers evade politics? Even those writers who have seen fiction as the pure exploration of language, as music is the exploration of sound, the babbling of Dada and the page-shuffling of Burroughs have been in reaction to what each revolted against in the politically-imposed spirit of their respective times; theirs were literary movements that were an act – however far-out – of acknowledgement of a relationship between politics and fiction.

It seems there is no getting away from the relationship. On the one hand, we live in what Seamus Heaney calls a world where the 'undirected play of the imagination is regarded at best as luxury or licentiousness, at worst as heresy or treason. In ideal republics...it is a common expectation that the writer will sign over his or her venturesome and potentially disruptive activity into the keeping of official doctrine, traditional system, a party line, whatever...' Gerard Manley Hopkins felt obliged to abandon poetry when he entered the Jesuits 'as not having to do with my vocation'; a submission of the imagination to religious orthodoxy exactly comparable to that demanded of writers, in many instances in our time, by political orthodoxies.

We are shocked by such clear cases of creativity outlawed. But things are not always so drastically simple. Not every fiction writer entering a relation with politics trades imagination for the hair shirt of the party hack. There is also the case of the writer whose imaginative powers are genuinely roused by and involved with the spirit of politics as he or she personally experiences it. And it may not be the free choice of a Byron. It can be virtually inescapable in times and places of socially seismic upheaval. Society shakes, the walls of entities fall; the writer has known the evil, indifference, or cupidity of the old order, and the spirit of creativity naturally pushes towards new growth. The writer is moved to fashion an expression of a new order, accepted on trust as an advance in human freedom that therefore also will be the release of a greater creativity.

'Russia became a garden of nightingales. Poets sprang up as never before. People barely had the strength to live but they were all singing' – so wrote Andrey Bely in the early days of the Russian Revolution. And one of Pasternak's biographers, Peter Levi, notes that Pasternak – popularly known to the West, on the evidence of his disillusioned *Dr Zhivago*, as *the* Russian anti-Communist writer – in his young days contributed manifestos to the 'infighting of the day'. In his poem to Stalin he sang:

> We want the glorious. We want the good.
> We want to see things free from fear.
> Unlike some fancy fop, the spendthrift
> of his bright, brief span, we yearn
> for labour shared by everyone,
> for the common discipline of law.

This yearning is addressed by writers in different ways, as fiction seeks a proper relation with politics. In the Soviet Union of Pasternak's day, some fell into what the Italian contemporary writer Claudio Magris, in a different context, calls with devastating cynicism, 'A sincere but perverted passion for freedom, which led...into mechanical servitude, as is the way with sin.' The noble passion deteriorated to the tragically shabby, as in the 1930s the Writers Union turned on itself to beat out all but mediocrity-mouthing platitudes, driving Mayakovsky to suicide and turning down Pasternak's plea to be granted a place where he would have somewhere other than a freezing partitioned slice of a room in which to write and live. Yet Pasternak had not abandoned belief – never did – in the original noble purpose of revolution. When Trotsky asked why he had begun to abstain from social themes, Pasternak wrote to a friend, 'I told him *My Sister, Life* [his then recent book] was revolutionary in the best sense of the word. That the phase of the revolution closest to the heart...the *morning* of the revolution, and its outburst when it returns man to the *nature* of man and looks at the state with the eyes of *natural* right'. But for Pasternak the writing of this period had become, by the edicts of the state and the Writers Union, 'a train derailed and lying at the bottom of an embankment'. And in this choice of an image there is a kind of desperate subconscious assertion of the creativity so threatened in himself and his fellow writers, since trains, in his era perhaps symbolic of the pace at which passes, fleetingly, the meaning of life the writer must catch, recur so often in his work.

Yeats's 'terrible beauty' of the historic moments when people seek a new order to 'return man to the nature of man, a state of natural right', does not always make politics the murderer of fiction. The Brechts and Nerudas survive, keeping that vision. But the relation, like all vital ones, always implies some danger. The first dismaying discovery for the writer is once again best expressed by Magris's cynicism: 'The lie is quite as real as the truth, it works upon the world, transforms it'; whereas the fiction writer, in pursuit of truth beyond the guise of reasoning, has believed that truth, however elusive, is the only reality. Yet we have seen the lie transforming; we have had Goebbels. And his international descendents, practising that transformation on the people of a number of countries, including the white people of my own country, who accepted the lie that apartheid was both divinely decreed and secularly just, and created a society on its precepts.

To be aware that the lie also can transform the world places an enormous responsibility on art to counter this with its own transformations; the knowledge that the writer's searching and intuition gain instinctively contradicts the lie.

> We page through each other's faces
> We read each looking eye . . .
> It has taken lives to be able to do so

– writes the South African poet Mongane Wally Serote. We may refuse to write according to any orthodoxy, we may refuse to toe any party line, even that drawn by the cause we know to be just, and our own, but we cannot refuse the responsibility of what we know. What we know beyond surface reality has to become what – again in Serote's words – 'We want the world to know'; we must in this, our inescapable relation with politics, 'page for wisdom through the stubborn night'.

At its crudest and most easily identifiable, the stubborn night is politically-inspired censorship, and yet, in some countries where no writer is locked up or his writings banned, and censorship is minimal and open to challenge by the law, fiction remains threatened by the power of the lie. Orwell alerted us to the insidious destruction of truth in the distortion of what words mean; but 1984 passed years ago, and he is remembered more for the cute cartoon movie of an *Animal Farm* than for a prophetic warning about the abuse of language. Harold Pinter spoke recently of 'a disease at the very centre of language, so that language becomes a permanent masquerade, a tapestry of lies. The ruthless and cynical mutilation and degradation of human beings, both in spirit and body . . . these actions are justified by rhetorical gambits, sterile terminology and concepts of power which stink. Are we ever going to look at the language we use, I wonder? Is it within our capabilities to do so? . . . Does reality essentially remain outside language, separate, obdurate, alien, not susceptible to description? Is an accurate and vital correspondence between what is and our perception of it impossible? Or is it that we are obliged to use language only in order to obscure and distort reality – to distort what *is* – to distort what *happens* – because we fear it?...I believe it's because of the way we use language that we have got ourselves into this terrible trap, where words like freedom, democracy and Christian values are still used to justify barbaric and shameful policies and acts.'

The writer has no reason to be if, for him or her, reality remains outside language. An accurate and vital correspondence between what is and the perception of the writer is what the fiction writer has to seek, finding the real meaning of words to express 'the states of things', shedding the ready-made concepts smuggled into language by politics.

All very fine in theory, yes – but how would you refer, in a novel, to the term 'final solution', coined by the Nazis; the term 'Bantustans', coined by a South African government in the sixties to disguise the dispossession of blacks of their citizenship rights and land; the term 'constructive engagement' coined by the government of the USA in the seventies in its foreign policy that evaded outright rejection of apartheid – how would you do this without paragraphs of explanation (which have no place in a novel) of what their counterfeits of reality actually were?

The false currency of meaning jingles conveniently in our vocabularies; but it is no small change. It becomes accepted values, for which writers bear responsibility. Every fiction writer has to struggle to expose them by discarding them, for the reader, in favour of the reality of the 'states of things', since generally journalism – supposed to be 'fact' as opposed to 'fiction' – won't. Here, on the primal level of language itself, by which we became the first self-questioning animals, able to assess our own behaviour, is where fiction finds its footing in relation to politics.

My own country, South Africa, provides what can be cited as the paradigm of problems of the full development of the relationship: the wild affair between fiction and politics, with its embraces and repulsions, distress and celebration, loyalty and betrayal. Perhaps echoes of the debate at present in progress over what post-apartheid fiction will be, ought to be, have relevance for the outside world. Of course, the very term 'post-apartheid' fiction reveals the acceptance that there has been such an orthodoxy as 'apartheid' or, more accurately, 'anti-apartheid' fiction. In the long struggle against apartheid, it has been recognized that an oppressed people need the confidence of cultural backing. Literature, fiction including plays and poetry, became what is known as 'a weapon of struggle'. The current debate among us now is between those who, perceiving that the cost was the constraint of the writer's imaginative powers within what was seen narrowly as relevant to the political struggle, think the time has come for writers to release themselves if they are to be imaginatively equal to the fullness of human life predicated for the future, and others who believe literature still must be perceived as a weapon in the hands and under the direction of the liberation movement come to power in a future democracy.

The revolutionary and writer Albie Sachs, with the undeniable authority of one who lost an arm and the sight of one eye in that struggle, has gone so far as to call, if half-seriously (not even the car-bomb was able to damage his lively humour), for a five-year ban on the slogan 'culture is a weapon of struggle'. But, of course, there are some writers who have been – I adapt Seamus Heaney's definition to my own context – 'guerrillas of the imagin-ation': in their fiction serving the struggle for freedom by refusing any imposed orthodoxy of subject and treatment, but attempting to take unfettered creative grasp of the complex 'states of things' in which, all through people's lives, directly and indirectly, in dark places and neon light, that struggle has taken place.

Since I am bound to be taken to account about this in relation to my own fiction, I had better answer for myself now. As a citizen, a South African actively opposed to racism all my life, and a supporter and now member of the African National Congress, in my *conduct* and my *actions* I have submitted voluntarily and with self-respect to the discipline of the liberation movement.

For my *fiction* I have claimed and practised my integrity to the free transformation of reality, in whatever forms and modes of expression I need. There, my commitment has been and is to make sense of life as I know it and observe it and experience it. In my ventures into non-fiction, my occasional political essays, my political partisanship has no doubt shown bias, perhaps a selectivity of facts. But then, as I have said before, and stand by: nothing I write in such factual pieces will be as true as my fiction.

So if my fiction and that of other writers has served legitimately the politics I believe in, it has been because the imaginative transformations of fiction, in the words of the Swedish writer Per Wästberg, 'help people understand their own natures and know they are not powerless . . . '

'Every work of art is liberating,' he asserts, speaking for all of us who write. That should be the understanding on which our fiction enters into any relationship with politics, however passionate the involvement may be. The transformation of the imagination must never 'belong' to any establishment, however just, fought-for, and longed-for. Pasternak's words should be our credo:

> When seats are assigned to passion and vision
> on the day of the great assembly
> Do not reserve a poet's position:
> It is dangerous, if not empty.

Chapter 17

Nobel Lecture

Naguib Mahfouz

Ladies and Gentlemen,

To begin with I would like to thank the Swedish Academy and its Nobel committee for taking notice of my long and perseverant endeavours, and I would like you to accept my talk with tolerance. For it comes in a language unknown to many of you. But it is the real winner of the prize. It is, therefore, meant that its melodies should float for the first time into your oasis of culture and civilization. I have great hopes that this will not be the last time either, and that literary writers of my nation will have the pleasure to sit with full merit amongst your international writers who have spread the fragrance of joy and wisdom in this grief-ridden world of ours.

I was told by a foreign correspondent in Cairo that the moment my name was mentioned in connection with the prize silence fell, and many wondered who I was. Permit me, then, to present myself in as objective a manner as is humanly possible. I am the son of two civilizations that at a certain age in history have formed a happy marriage. The first of these, seven thousand years old, is the Pharaonic civilization; the second, one thousand four hundred years old, is the Islamic one. I am perhaps in no need to introduce to any of you either of the two, you being the elite, the learned ones. But there is no harm, in our present situation of acquaintance and communion, in a mere reminder.

As for Pharaonic civilization I will not talk of the conquests and the building of empires. This has become a worn out pride the mention of which modern conscience, thank God, feels uneasy about. Nor will I talk about how it was guided for the first time to the existence of God and its ushering in the dawn of human conscience. This is a long history and there is not one of you who is not acquainted with the prophet-king Akhenaton. I will not even speak of this civilization's achievements in art and literature, and its renowned miracles: the Pyramids and the Sphinx and Karnak. For he who has not had the chance to see these monuments has read about them and pondered over their forms.

Nobel Lecture December 8, 1988. Read at the Swedish Academy by Mr Mohammed Salmawy (first in Arabic, then in English). Translated by Mohammed Salmawy. First published in *Nobel Lectures, Literature 1981–1990*. Copyright © 2001 The Nobel Foundation.

Let me, then, introduce Pharaonic civilization with what seems like a story since my personal circumstances have ordained that I become a storyteller. Hear, then, this recorded historical incident: Old papyri relate that Pharaoh had learned of the existence of a sinful relation between some women of the harem and men of his court. It was expected that he should finish them off in accordance with the spirit of his time. But he, instead, called to his presence the choice men of law and asked them to investigate what he has come to learn. He told them that he wanted the Truth so that he could pass his sentence with Justice.

This conduct, in my opinion, is greater than founding an empire or building the Pyramids. It is more telling of the superiority of that civilization than any riches or splendour. Gone now is that civilization – a mere story of the past. One day the great Pyramid will disappear too. But Truth and Justice will remain for as long as Mankind has a ruminative mind and a living conscience.

As for Islamic civilization I will not talk about its call for the establishment of a union between all Mankind under the guardianship of the Creator, based on freedom, equality and forgiveness. Nor will I talk about the greatness of its prophet. For among your thinkers there are those who regard him the greatest man in history. I will not talk of its conquests which have planted thousands of minarets calling for worship, devoutness and good throughout great expanses of land from the environs of India and China to the boundaries of France. Nor will I talk of the fraternity between religions and races that has been achieved in its embrace in a spirit of tolerance unknown to Mankind neither before nor since.

I will, instead, introduce that civilization in a moving dramatic situation summarizing one of its most conspicuous traits: In one victorious battle against Byzantium it has given back its prisoners of war in return for a number of books of the ancient Greek heritage in philosophy, medicine and mathematics. This is a testimony of value for the human spirit in its demand for knowledge, even though the demander was a believer in God and the demanded a fruit of a pagan civilization.

It was my fate, ladies and gentlemen, to be born in the lap of these two civilizations, and to absorb their milk, to feed on their literature and art. Then I drank the nectar of your rich and fascinating culture. From the inspiration of all this – as well as my own anxieties – words bedewed from me. These words had the fortune to merit the appreciation of your revered Academy which has crowned my endeavour with the great Nobel Prize. Thanks be to it in my name and in the name of those great departed builders who have founded the two civilizations.

Ladies and Gentlemen,

You may be wondering: This man coming from the third world, how did he find the peace of mind to write stories? You are perfectly right. I come from a world labouring under the burden of debts whose paying back exposes it to starvation or very close to it. Some of its people perish in Asia from floods, others do so in Africa from famine. In South Africa millions have been undone with rejection and with deprivation of all human rights in the age of human rights, as though they were not counted among humans. In the West Bank and Gaza there are people who are lost in spite of the fact that they are living on their own land; land of their fathers, grandfathers and great grandfathers. They have risen to demand the first right secured by primitive Man; namely, that they should have their proper place recognized by others as their own. They were paid back for their brave and noble move – men, women, youths and children alike – by the breaking of bones, killing with bullets, destroying of houses and torture in prisons and camps. Surrounding them are 150 million Arabs following what is happening in anger and grief. This threatens the area with a disaster if it is not saved by the wisdom of those desirous of a just and comprehensive peace.

Yes, how did the man coming from the Third World find the peace of mind to write stories? Fortunately, art is generous and sympathetic. In the same way that it dwells with the happy ones it does not desert the wretched. It offers both alike the convenient means for expressing what swells up in their bosom.

In this decisive moment in the history of civilization it is inconceivable and unacceptable that the moans of Mankind should die out in the void. There is no doubt that Mankind has at last come of age, and our era carries the expectations of *entente* between the Super Powers. The human mind now assumes the task of eliminating all causes of destruction and annihilation. And just as scientists exert themselves to cleanse the environment of industrial pollution, intellectuals ought to exert themselves to cleanse humanity of moral pollution. It is both our right and duty to demand of the big leaders in the countries of civilization as well as their economists to affect a real leap that would place them into the focus of the age.

In the olden times every leader worked for the good of his own nation alone. The others were considered adversaries, or subjects of exploitation. There was no regard to any value but that of superiority and personal glory. For the sake of this, many morals, ideals and values were wasted; many unethical means were justified; many uncounted souls were made to perish. Lies, deceit, treachery, cruelty reigned as the signs of sagacity and the proof of greatness. Today, this view needs to be changed from its very source. Today, the greatness of a civilized leader ought to be measured by the universality of his vision and his sense of responsibility towards all humankind. The developed world and the Third World are but one family. Each human being bears responsibility towards it by the degree of what he has obtained of knowledge, wisdom, and civilization. I would not be exceeding the limits of my duty if I told them in the name of the Third World: Be not spectators to our miseries. You have to play therein a noble role befitting your status. From your position of superiority you are responsible for any misdirection of animal, or plant, to say nothing of Man, in any of the four corners of the world. We have had enough of words. Now is the time for action. It is time to end the age of brigands and usurers. We are in the age of leaders responsible for the whole globe. Save the enslaved in the African south! Save the famished in Africa! Save the Palestinians from the bullets and the torture! Nay, save the Israelis from profaning their great spiritual heritage! Save the ones in debt from the rigid laws of economy! Draw their attention to the fact that their responsibility to Mankind should precede their commitment to the laws of a science that Time has perhaps overtaken.

I beg your pardon, ladies and gentlemen, I feel I may have somewhat troubled your calm. But what do you expect from one coming from the Third World? Is not every vessel coloured by what it contains? Besides, where can the moans of Mankind find a place to resound if not in your oasis of civilization planted by its great founder for the service of science, literature and sublime human values? And as he did one day by consecrating his riches to the service of good, in the hope of obtaining forgiveness, we, children of the Third World, demand of the able ones, the civilized ones, to follow his example, to imbibe his conduct, to meditate upon his vision.

Ladies and Gentlemen,

In spite of all what goes on around us I am committed to optimism until the end. I do not say with Kant that Good will be victorious in the other world. Good is achieving victory every day. It may even be that Evil is weaker than we imagine. In front of us is an indelible proof: were it not for the fact that victory is always on the side of Good, hordes of wandering humans would not have been able in the face of beasts and insects, natural disasters, fear and egotism, to grow and multiply. They would not have been able to form nations, to excel in creativeness and invention, to conquer outer space, and to declare Human Rights. The truth of the matter is that Evil is a loud and boisterous debaucherer, and that Man remembers what hurts more than what pleases. Our great poet Abul-'Alaa' Al-Ma'ari was right when he said:

> A grief at the hour of death
> Is more than a hundred-fold
> Joy at the hour of birth.

I finally reiterate my thanks and ask your forgiveness.

Chapter 18

Redefining Relevance

Njabulo S. Ndebele

Recently, I have suggested that what has been called protest literature may have run its course in South Africa.[1] It is my intention here to probe further into this evaluation by attempting to bring out clearly its theoretical foundations. Basically, the problem is that 'protest literature' appears to have lost its objective basis. The fact that much of the writing produced in the townships of South Africa since 1976 still reproduced this protest tradition, with little modification, reveals what seems to me to be the characteristics of a socially entrenched manner of thinking about the South African reality; a manner of thinking which, over the years, has gathered its own momentum and now reproduces itself uncritically. It is like a train the driver of which has lost control, and it runs dangerously on its fixed rails, passing, with great speed, even where it is supposed to stop. The difference might be that in the case of the train, its driver will know almost immediately that he or she is in trouble. He or she is, after all, not the train. In the case of the writer of 'protest literature', on the other hand, it may not be so easy for him or her to separate himself momentarily from his mind.

[...]

[T]he greatest challenge of the South African revolution is in the search for ways of thinking, ways of perception, that will help to break down the closed epistemological structures of South African oppression, structures which can severely compromise resistance by dominating thinking itself. The challenge is to free the entire social imagination of the oppressed from the laws of perception that have characterised apartheid society. For writers this means freeing the creative process itself from those very laws. It means extending the writer's perception of what can be written about, and the means and methods of writing.

It seems to me that a redemptive approach can begin to be formulated when South African writers ask the question: where is the struggle in South Africa at the moment? Many recent events in the country have led inevitably to that question. For example, the prolonged school boycott that began in 1976, and still continues today, has finally led to similar questions with regard to education: where do we go from here? What kind of education do we want for the future? Beyond that, questions have been asked in relation to other

First published in *South African Literature and Culture: Rediscovery of the Ordinary,* pp. 60, 66–74. Manchester: Manchester University Press, 1994.

aspects of society: what legal system do we envisage for a new South Africa? What system of public health will adequately cater for the health needs of all citizens? What kind of cultural policy are we going to evolve? What are we going to do with ethnicity? All these questions, and more, have been prompted by the momentum of current events in which the state has been found to be increasingly unable to manage society without recourse to more repressive measures even as it speaks of reform: a situation that reflects a near total bankruptcy of vision on the part of the ruling Nationalist Party.

Significantly, the act of asking such questions already suggests that the closed structures of thought under the culture of apartheid oppression are cracking. A vast new world is opening up, for the possible answers to the questions are as infinite as the immensity of the questions themselves.

It seems to me that these are the most important questions that have ever been asked by our people in recent times, and they are questions that can only be answered fully from as complete an understanding as possible of the position from which they have been asked. For example, as far as education is conceded, the oppressed have reached a position at which an aspect of the structure of domination has, through their own actions, been rendered largely inoperative. The question is: what next? A point has been reached, therefore, at which the oppressed have to ask themselves some fundamental questions about the future of education and its contribution towards a new and free society. What is at issue now is no longer the moral condemnation of Bantu education; rather, it is the creation of a new kind of education. This change in understanding is reflected in the fact that initially, the political act of challenging the legitimacy of education under apartheid was carried out under the slogan of 'liberation first, education later'. However, following further reflection on developments, this slogan was rejected. It was replaced by one which recognised the need for education even during the process of struggle: 'people's education for people's power'.

The overall significance of these questions is that they indicate the beginning of the freeing of the oppressed social imagination from the constraints of attempting to envisage the future under the limitations of oppression. The future, at this point, is perceived as being possible only with the contribution of the oppressed themselves as decision makers. That attitude of the oppressed brings with it heavy responsibilities for them. It suggests the appearance of challenging yet daunting tasks, amenable to no easy solutions, for in it are springs of a new society. One of the central tasks of an alternative ideology, in this situation, is to provide, among other things, new ways of thinking about the future of the country.

The starting point is the need and demand of the oppressed for liberation. The political imperatives of that demand are the positing of an alternative future followed by the seizure of state power. For the political activist, the task seems clear. For the producer of cultural artefacts, on the other hand, the situation may not be so clear because his or her role as well as that of his or her work, has not been as clearly defined. The South African writer, in particular, has not begun to ask some fundamental questions about his or her role, as well as that of his or her artistic practice. By and large, he or she appears to have handed over this task to the political activist, who may not him or herself have articulated a comprehensively analytical position on the role of the arts in the struggle. This situation, it seems to me, has been responsible for the rather slow growth of South African literature.

The problem has been that questions about art and society have been easily settled after a general consensus about commitment. This has led to the prescription of solutions even before all the problems have been discovered and analysed. The writer, as a result, has tended to plunge into the task of writing without fully grappling with the theoretical demands of that task in all its dimensions. Armed with notions of artistic commitment still constrained by outmoded protest bound perceptions of the role of art and of what constitutes political relevance in art, he set about reproducing a deadend. Consequently, the limited range of explorable experience characteristic of writing under the protest ethos has continued to plague much of South African writing. We can perhaps begin to edge away from that situation by addressing the issue of the nature of art as well as the question of what constitutes relevance under a situation of radical flux such as obtains in South Africa today.

One accusation that has often been levelled at writers, particularly in those countries hungry for radical change, is that many of them have not offered solutions to the problems they may have graphically revealed. It seems to me that this accusation has been based on a set of premises by which the nature of the relationship between art and society could never be adequately disclosed. More often than not, the accusation has been premised on the demand that artists produce works that will incite people to political action, something which, most people will agree, is strictly speaking the task of the professional propagandist. The propagandist generally aims at immediate action. His intentions are entirely practical.

The artist, on the other hand, although desiring action, often with as much passion as the propagandist, can never be entirely free from the rules of irony. Irony is the literary manifestation of the principle of contradiction. Its fundamental law, for the literary arts in particular, is that everything involving human society is in a constant state of flux; that the dialectic between appearance and reality in the conduct of human affairs is always operative and constantly problematic, and that consequently, in the representation of human reality, nothing can be taken for granted. If the writer has an ideological goal, and he always has, he has to reach that goal through a serious and inevitable confrontation with irony, and must earn his conclusions through the resulting sweat. And when he has won that battle, he will most likely leave us, the readers, more committed, but only on the necessary condition that we have been made to reflect deeply on the nature and implications of our commitment in the context of the compelling human drama presented before us.

The relationship between politics and art is by definition always mediated by reflection. With this understanding, we distinguish only between immediate action, on the one hand, and delayed action, on the other. But this distinction does not necessarily enable us to make a mechanical choice between politics and art: rather, it enables us to participate in the dialectic between the two. To understand this is to understand the creative possibilities of both.

The way seems clear now for us to deal with the question of 'relevance'. The more limited understanding of the relationship between politics and art would define as relevant any subject or act that is perceived to contribute dramatically to the struggle for liberation. The operative word here is 'dramatic'. What is dramatic is often defined according to the imperatives of *realpolitik*. According to this definition, the dramatic can easily be determined: strike action, demonstrations; alternatively, the brutality of the oppressive system in a variety of ways.

It should not be difficult to realise that from the point of view of the South African writer today the range of what is traditionally regarded as relevant is tragically limited in comparison to the complex structure of the oppression itself. The system does not only send tanks into the townships. It does a lot more as its strategies for domination have diversified to take advantage of a complex industrial society. It works at subtle co-option; it tries to produce a middle class; it sets off a series of diplomatic initiatives, overt and covert; it seeks to create normality by insidiously spreading a hegemony that the oppressed are designed to absorb without being conscious of actually doing so through film, radio, television and a range of publications. It may even permit a controlled 'experimental' opening up of white private schools to African children where the latter can absorb a wide range of largely liberal hegemonic practices that may ultimately not be in their own interests. Central to all these sophisticated strategies of containment is the rampant growth and promotion of consumerism ranging from fashion through cars right up to houses. In other words, the system mobilises its own range of extra-governmental institutions in an attempt to impose and propagate its hegemony. In this sense, it responds as a total system.

Clearly, if it is the entire society that has to be recreated, then no aspect of that society can be deemed irrelevant to the progress of liberation. Clearly, the broader the focus, the more inclusive, then the more manifold and more complex the attack. In this context, relevance, for the post-protest South African writer, begins, as it should, with the need for the seizure of state power. For the writer, this need also fragments into a concern with an infinite number of specific social details which are the very objects of artistic reflection; and it is such social details which constitute the primary reason why the struggle occurs in the first place.

Most paradoxically, for the writer, the *immediate* problem, just at the point at which he sits down to write his novel, is not the seizure of power. Far from it. His immediate aim is a radically contemplative state of mind in which the objects of contemplation are that range of social conditions which are the major ingredients of social consciousness. Exclusion of any on the grounds that they do not easily lend themselves to dramatic political statement will limit the possibilities of any literary revolution, by severely limiting the social range on which to exercise its imagination.

What are the practical implications of all this? We have already seen how the structural status of the oppressed within South African society has altered radically. The implications of this newly found power are the writer's starting point. That power is clearly aware of itself, and that self-consciousness is destined to grow. But, judging from the fundamental questions being asked, as shown above, that power is still not fully aware of what it can actually achieve. Details still have to be worked out. And this is where the writer's role becomes crucial. It is his or her task to contribute effectively to the consolidation of that power, by consolidating consciousness of it at all levels of society. He or she can do so in a number of ways.

First of all, there must be a freeing of the imagination in which what constitutes the field of relevance is extended considerably. What is relevant is the entire community of the oppressed. For example, politics is not confined only to the seizure of state power; it can also be the decision by members of a township women's burial society to replace a corrupt leader with a new one. The significance of the moral and ethical issues that may be involved in this matter together with whatever insightful revelations may be made about the interplay of human motives, ought not to be underestimated. They have a direct bearing on the quality of social awareness.

This whole issue is so important that a few more examples are in order. Firstly, for a highly industrialised society such as South Africa, there is a tragic paucity of imaginative recreations of the confrontation between the oppressed and the tools of science. Supposing a character wants to study science: what goes on in his mind when he makes that decision? What is his vision of the social role of the scientific endeavour? Turgenev, for example, in

Fathers and Sons, provides a compelling view of the impact of the scientific method on human behaviour in the context of nineteenth-century Russia. Alternatively, what kind of relationships are created between a worker in a factory and his machine? The answer to this question is not necessarily obvious. Will he necessarily feel oppressed and alienated, as traditional radical wisdom would suggest? There is much to suggest that this confrontation is much more problematic than is often assumed.

Secondly, we have, for better or for worse, a group of politicians in the so-called independent states of South Africa. Stooges, no doubt, in the total scheme of things. But what are the intricacies of their flawed diplomatic practice? We have no literature of diplomacy which can reveal the human dimension of this barren politics. The artist should help the reader condemn a stooge while understanding something of his motivations. That way the reader reads something about the psychology of the co-opted. The aesthetics of protest would be content to kill off the man, thus enacting what might be necessary, from the point of view of natural justice, but leaving us with no knowledge.

Thirdly, the pressures of modern life on the family have been immense. We know some of the causes: migrant labour, influx control laws, and political exile, for example. Protest literature, commendably, has kept these causes in our minds. But what, really, has happened to the family itself? Currently, a most painful clash of generations has emerged in the townships between parents and children. It appears in the main to result from the perception by the youth that their parents did not do enough to combat their oppression. This situation has momentarily catapulted the youth into the forefront of the liberation struggle with some agonising consequences for the structure of authority not only in the community at large, but also in the family itself. Many values that have governed family relationships have been changed. What happened to those values, and how have new emergent ones helped to bring about either relief or more misery to families and the community?

Fourthly, the energetic and creative world of sport and fashion has seldom been treated beyond the sensationalism of the popular press. Consequently, we have no body of imaginative fiction that explores how popular culture in the hands of the state and big business can compromise severely a revolutionary consciousness. Sport and fashion as subjects of serious fiction have been dismissed too easily as irrelevant to politics. Indeed, since Mphahlele's 'Grieg on a Stolen Piano',[2] that particular theme has not received much imaginative attention.

Lastly, I have commented in the past on the lack of compelling imaginative recreations of rural life in our literature.[3] All we know about are dejected peasants, suffering pathetically under a tyrannical Boer farmer. Alternatively, the peasants are the focus of Christian evangelism. Clearly, rural culture as a serious fictional theme needs to be revisited.

Beyond these five examples, the settings as well as the themes that can be imaginatively explored are infinite.

One other way by which the South African writer can move effectively into the post-protest era is by working towards a radical displacement of the white oppressor as an active, dominant player in the imagination of the oppressed. This tactical absence will mean that the writer can consolidate the sense of a viable, psychologically self-sufficient community among the oppressed. This attitude can only work, though, if the writer genuinely believes in the oppressed, in the first instance, as makers of the future. This implies a radical rearrangement of the dialectical poles. Where the thesis was the oppressor, it is now the oppressed confidently introducing new definitions of the future to which the oppressor will have of necessity to respond. The latter, no longer having the intellectual and imaginative capability to initiate redemptive action, has to be relegated to the reactive pole of the dialectic. He is no longer in possession of the initiative.

Finally, there must be an accompanying change of discourse from the rhetoric of oppression to that of process and exploration. This would imply an openhandedness in the use of language, a search for originality of expression and a sensitivity to dialogue. The complexity of the daily problems of living in fact coincides with the demands of the creative act. As the writer begins to work on that story, he may not know where it is heading, and how it is going work towards its conclusion; but he has to find a way. That means a search for appropriate form and technique, which would enable him to grasp the complexity and render it understandable. Here, the question of technique does not mean a rarefied, formal, and disembodied attempt at innovation for its own sake. On the contrary, technique implies the attempt to find the best possible ways of extending social perception through appropriateness of form. Technique, then, is inseparable from the exploration of human perception.

Earlier, in my discussion of the mine dispute, I made reference to the fact that at least 100,000 people were dismissed by the mine management. It is towards the silent 100,000 that our writers must now turn their attention. I mean this analogically, of course. The operative principle of composition in post-protest literature is that it should probe beyond the observable facts, to reveal new worlds where it was previously thought they did not exist, and to reveal process and movement where they were hidden. In this way, the social imagination of the oppressed can be extended considerably and made ready in concrete terms to deal with the demands of a complex future. The aim is to extend the range of personal and social experience as far as possible in order to contribute to bringing about a highly conscious, sensitive new person in a new society. This, it seems to me, is the function of art in, and its contribution to, the ongoing revolution in South Africa.

These observations, it should be stated, are put forward not as laws, but as possible guidelines by which our writers can conduct a debate and bring to bear further analysis on the tasks of writers and the role of their art in the unfolding revolution in South Africa. The tasks themselves are immense and challenging; I believe a vigorous discussion of them will, in itself, be a significant act of freedom.

Notes

1   See N. S. Ndebele, 'The Rediscovery of the Ordinary: Some New Writings in South Africa', *Journal of Southern African Studies*, Vol. 12, No. 2. 1986.

2   Ezekiel Mphahlele, 'Grieg on a Stolen Piano', in *In Corner B*, (Nairobi: East African Publishing House, 1967), pp. 37–61.

3   Njabulo S. Ndebele, 'Turkish Tales and Some Thoughts on South African Literature'. *Staffrider*, Vol.6, No.1, 1984.

Chapter 19

Preparing Ourselves for Freedom

Albie Sachs

We all know where South Africa is, but we do not yet know what it is. Ours is the privileged generation that will make that discovery, if the apertures in our eyes are wide enough. The problem is whether we have sufficient cultural imagination to grasp the rich texture of the free and united South Africa that we have done so much to bring about.

For decades now we have possessed a political programme for the future – the Freedom Charter. More recently the National Executive of the ANC has issued a set of Constitutional Guidelines which has laid down a basic constitutional approach to a united South Africa with a free and equal citizenry. What we have to ask ourselves now is whether we have an artistic and cultural vision that corresponds to this current phase in which a new South African nation is emerging. Can we say that we have begun to grasp the full dimensions of the new country and new people that is struggling to give birth to itself, or are we still trapped in the multiple ghettoes of the apartheid imagination?

For the sake of livening the debate on these questions, this paper will make a number of controversial observations.

The first proposition I make, and I do so fully aware of the fact that we are totally against censorship and for free speech, is that our members should be banned from saying that culture is a weapon of struggle. I suggest a period of, say, five years.

Allow me, as someone who has for many years been arguing precisely that art should be seen as an instrument of struggle, to explain why suddenly this affirmation seems not only banal and devoid of real content, but actually wrong and potentially harmful.

In the first place, it results in an impoverishment of our art. Instead of getting real criticism, we get solidarity criticism. Our artists are not pushed to improve the quality of their work, it is enough that it be politically correct. The more fists and spears and guns, the better. The range of themes is narrowed down so much that all that is funny or curious or genuinely tragic in the world is extruded. Ambiguity and contradiction are completely shut out, and the only conflict permitted is that between the old and the new, as if there were only bad in the past and only good in the future. If we had the imagination of Sholokhov,

First published in *Spring is Rebellious: Arguments about Cultural Freedom*, pp. 19–29. Cape Town: Buchu Books, 1990.

and one of us wrote: And Quiet Flows the Tugela, the central figure would not be a member of UDF or Cosatu, but would be aligned to Inkatha, resisting change, yet feeling oppression, thrown this way and that by conflicting emotions, and through his or her struggles and torments and moments of joy, the reader would be thrust into the whole drama of the struggle for a new South Africa. Instead, whether in poetry or painting or on the stage, we line up our good people on the one side and the bad ones on the other, occasionally permitting someone to pass from one column to the other, but never acknowledging that there is bad in the good, and, even more difficult, that there can be elements of good in the bad; you can tell who the good ones are, because in addition to being handsome of appearance, they can all recite sections of the Freedom Charter or passages of Strategy and Tactics at the drop of a beret.

In the case of a real instrument of struggle, there is no room for ambiguity: a gun is a gun is a gun, and if it were full of contradictions, it would fire in all sorts of directions and be useless for its purpose. But the power of art lies precisely in its capacity to expose contradictions and reveal hidden tensions – hence the danger of viewing it as if it were just another kind of missile-firing apparatus.

And what about love? We have published so many anthologies and journals and occasional poems and stories, and the number that deal with love do not make the fingers of a hand. Can it be that once we join the ANC we do not make love any more, that when the comrades go to bed they discuss the role of the white working class? Surely even those comrades whose tasks deny them the opportunity and direct possibilities of love, remember past love and dream of love to come. What are we fighting for, if not the right to express our humanity in all its forms, including our sense of fun and capacity for love and tenderness and our appreciation of the beauty of the world? There is nothing that the apartheid rulers would like more than to convince us that because apartheid is ugly, the world is ugly. ANC members are full of fun and romanticism and dreams, we enjoy and wonder at the beauties of nature and the marvels of human creation, yet if you look at most of our art and literature you would think we were living in the greyest and most sombre of all worlds, completely shut in by apartheid. It is as though our rulers stalk every page and haunt every picture; everything is obsessed by the oppressors and the trauma they have imposed, nothing is about us and the new consciousness we are developing. Listen in contrast to the music of Hugh Masekela, of Abdullah Ibrahim, of Jonas Gwanga, of Miriam Makeba, and you are in a universe of wit and grace and vitality and intimacy, there is invention and modulation of mood, ecstasy and sadness; this is a cop-free world in which the emergent personality of our people manifests itself. Pick up a book of poems, or look at a woodcut or painting, and the solemnity is overwhelming. No one told Hugh or Abdullah to write their music in this or that way, to be progressive or committed, to introduce humour or gaiety or a strong beat so as to be optimistic. Their music conveys genuine confidence because it springs from inside the personality and experience of each of them, from popular tradition and the sounds of contemporary life; we respond to it because it tells us something lovely and vivacious about ourselves, not because the lyrics are about how to win a strike or blow up a petrol dump. It bypasses, overwhelms, ignores apartheid, establishes its own space. So it could be with our writers and painters, if only they could shake off the gravity of their anguish and break free from the solemn formulas of commitment that people (like myself) have tried for so many years to impose upon them. Dumile, perhaps the greatest of our visual artists, was once asked why he did not draw scenes like one that was taking place in front of him: a crocodile of men being marched under arrest for not having their passes in order. At that moment a hearse drove slowly past and the men stood still and raised their hats. "That's what I want to draw," he said.

Yet damaging as a purely instrumental and non-dialectical view of culture is to artistic creation, far more serious is the way such a narrow view impoverishes the struggle itself. Culture is not something separate from the general struggle, an artifact that is brought in from time to time to mobilise the people or else to prove to the world that after all we are civilised. Culture is us, it is who we are, how we see ourselves and the vision we have of the world. In the course of participating in the culture of liberation, we constantly re-make ourselves. It is not just a question of the discipline and interaction between members that any organisation has; our movement has developed a style of its own, a way of doing things and of expressing itself, a specific ANC personality. And what a rich mix it is . . . African tradition, church tradition, Ghandian tradition, revolutionary socialist tradition, liberal tradition, all the languages and ways and styles of all the many communities in our country; we have black consciousness, and elements of red consciousness (some would say pink consciousness these days), even green consciousness (long before the Greens existed, we had green in our flag, representing the land). Now, with the dispersal of our members through-out the world, we also bring in aspects of the cultures of all humanity, our comrades speak Swahili and Arabic and Spanish and Portuguese and Russian and Swedish and French and German and Chinese, not because of Bantu Education, but through ANC Education, we are even learning Japanese. Our culture, the ANC culture, is not a picturesque collection of separate ethnic and political cultures lined up side by side, or mixed in certain proportions, it has a real character and dynamic of its own. When we sing our anthem, a religious invocation, with our clenched fists upraised, it is not a question of fifty-fifty, but an expression of an evolving and integrative interaction, an affirmation that we sing when we struggle and we struggle when we sing. This must be one of the greatest cultural achievements of the ANC, that it has made South Africans of the most diverse origins feel comfortable in its ranks. To say this is not to deny that cultural tensions and dilemmas automatically cease once one joins the organisation: on the contrary, we bring in with us all our complexes and ways of seeing the world, our jealousies and preconceptions. What matters, however, is that we have created a context of struggle, of goals and comradeship within which these tensions can be dealt with. One can recall debates over such diverse questions as to whether non-Africans should be allowed on to the NEC, whether corporal punishment should be applied at SOMAFCO, or whether married women should do high kicks on the stage. Indeed, the whole issue of women's liberation, for so long treated in an abstract way, is finally forcing itself on to the agenda of action and thought, a profound question of cultural transformation. The fact is that the cultural question is central to our identity as a movement: if culture were merely an instrument to be hauled on to the stage on ceremonial or fund-raising occasions, or to liven up a meeting, we would ourselves be empty of personality in the interval. Happily, this is not the case – culture is us, and we are people, not things waiting to be put into motion from time to time.

This brings me to my second challenging proposition, namely, that the Constitutional Guidelines should not be applied to the sphere of culture. What?! you may declare, a member of the Department of Legal and Constitutional Affairs saying that the Guidelines should not be applied to culture. Precisely. It should be the other way round. Culture must make its input to the Guidelines. The whole point of the massive consultations that are taking place around the Guidelines is that the membership, the people at large, should engage in constructive and concrete debate about the foundations of government in a post-apartheid South Africa. The Guidelines are more than a work-in-progress document, they set out well-deliberated views of the NEC as enriched by an in-house seminar, but they are not presented as a final, cut-and-dried product, certainly not as a blueprint to be learnt off by heart and defended to the last mis-print. Thus, the reasoning should not be: the Guidelines lay down the following for culture, therefore we must line up behind the guidelines and become a transmission belt for their implementation. On the contrary, what we need to do is to analyse the Guidelines, see what implications they have for culture, and then say whether we agree and make whatever suggestions we have for their improvement. In part, we can say that the method is the message; the open debate the NEC wants on the Guidelines corresponds to the open society the guidelines speak about. Apartheid has closed our society, stifled its voice, prevented the people from speaking, and it is the historic mission of our organisation to be the harbingers of freedom of conscience, debate and opinion.

In my view there are three aspects of the Guidelines that bear directly on the sphere of culture.

The first is the emphasis put on building national unity and encouraging the development of a common patriotism, while fully recognising the linguistic and cultural diversity of the country. Once the question of basic political rights is resolved in a democratic way, the cultural and linguistic rights of our diverse communities can be attended to on their merits. In other words, language, religion and so-called ways of life cease to be confused with race and sever their bondage to apartheid, becoming part of the positive cultural values of the society.

It is important to distinguish between unity and uniformity. We are strongly for national unity, for seeing our country as a whole, not just in its geographic extension but in its human extension. We want full equal rights for every South African, without reference to race, language, ethnic origin or creed. We believe in a single South Africa with a single set of governmental institutions, and we work towards a common loyalty and patriotism. Yet this is not to call for a homogenised South Africa made up of identikit citizens. South Africa is now said to be a bilingual country: we envisage it as a multi-lingual country. It will be multi-faith and multi-cultural as well. The objective is not to create a model culture into which everyone has to assimilate, but to acknowledge and take pride in the cultural variety of our people. In the past, attempts were made to force everyone into the mould of the English gentleman, projected as the epitome of civilisation, so that it was even an honour to be oppressed by the English. Apartheid philosophy, on the other hand, denied any common humanity, and insisted that people be compartmentalised into groups forcibly kept apart. In rejecting apartheid, we do not envisage a return to a modified form of the British Imperialist notion, we do not plan to build a non-racial yuppie-dom which people may enter only by shedding and suppressing the cultural heritage of their specific community. We will have Zulu South Africans, and Afrikaner South Africans and Indian South Africans and Jewish South Africans and Venda South Africans and Cape Moslem South Africans (I do not refer to the question of terminology – basically people will determine this for themselves). Each cultural tributary contributes towards and increases the majesty of the river of South African-ness. While each one of us has a particularly intimate relationship with one or other cultural matrix, this does not mean that we are locked into a series of cultural 'own affairs' ghettoes.

On the contrary, the grandchildren of white immigrants can join in the toyi toyi – even if slightly out of step – or recite the poems of Wally Serote, just as the grandchildren of Dinizulu can read with pride the writings of Olive Schreiner. The dance, the cuisine, the poetry, the dress, the songs and riddles and folk-tales, belong to each group, but also belong to all of us. I remember the pride I felt as a South African when some years ago I saw the production known as the Zulu Macbeth bring the house down in the World Theatre season in London, the intensely theatrical wedding and funeral dances of our people, performed by cooks and messengers and chauffeurs conquering the critics and audiences in what was then possibly the most elite theatre in the world. This was Zulu culture, but it was also our culture, my culture.

Each culture has its strengths, but there is no culture that is worth more than any other. We cannot say that because there are more Xhosa speakers than Tsonga, their culture is better, or because those who hold power today are Afrikaans-speakers, Afrikaans is better or worse than any other language.

Every culture has its positive and negative aspects. Sometimes the same cultural past is used in diametrically opposite ways, as we can see with the manner in which the traditions of Shaka and Ceteswayo are used on the one hand to inspire people to fight selflessly for an all-embracing liberation of our country, and on the other to cultivate a sanguinary tribal chauvinism. Sometimes cultural practices that were appropriate to certain forms of social organisation become a barrier to change when the society itself has become transformed – we can think of forms of family organisation, for example, that corresponded to the social and economic modes of pre-conquest societies that are out of keeping with the demands of contemporary life. African society, like all societies, develops and has the right to transform itself. What has been lacking since colonial domination began, is the right of the people themselves to determine how they wish to live.

If we look at Afrikaans culture, the paradoxes are even stronger. At one level it was the popular creole language of the Western Cape, referred to in a derogatory way as kitchen Dutch, spoken by slaves and indigenous peoples who taught it to their masters and mistresses. Later it was the language of resistance to British imperialism; the best MK story to appear in South Africa to date was written (in English) by a Boer – On Commando, by Denys Reitz, a beautiful account of his three years as a guerilla involved in actions of armed propaganda against the British occupying army. Afrikaans literature evolved around suffering and patriotism. Many of the early books, written to find a space in nature to make up for lack of social space, have since become classics of world ecological literature. At another level, the language has been hijacked by proponents of racial domination to support systems of white supremacy, and as such been projected as the language of the baas. In principle, there is no reason at all why Afrikaans should not once more become the language of liberty, but this time liberty for all, not just liberty for a few coupled with the right to oppress the majority.

At this point I would like to make a statement that I am sure will jolt the reader or listener: white is beautiful. In case anyone feels that the bomb has affected my head, I will repeat the affirmation, surely the first time it has been made at an ANC conference: white is beautiful. Allow me to explain. I first heard this formulation from a Mozambican poet and former guerilla, whose grandmother was African and grandfather Portuguese. Asked to explain Frelimo's view on the slogan: Black is beautiful, he replied – Black is beautiful, Brown is beautiful, White is beautiful. I think that affirmation is beautiful. One may add that when white started saying black was ugly it made itself ugly. Shorn of its arrogance, the cultural input from the white communities can be rich and valuable. This is not to say that we need a WCM in South Africa – in the context of colonial domination, white conscious-ness means oppression, whereas black consciousness means resistance to oppression. But it does establish the basis on which whites participate in the struggle to eradicate apartheid. Whites are not in the struggle to help the blacks win their rights, they (we) are fighting for their own rights, the rights to be free citizens of a free country, and to enjoy and take pride in the culture of the whole country. They are neither liberators of others, nor can their goal be to end up as a despised and despising protected minority. They seek to be ordinary citizens of an ordinary country, proud to be part of South Africa, proud to be part of Africa, proud to be part of the world. Only in certain monastic orders is self-flagellation the means to achieve liberation. For the rest of humankind, there is no successful struggle without a sense of pride and self-affirmation.

The second aspect of the Guidelines with major implications for culture is the proposal for a Bill of Rights that guarantees freedom of expression and what is sometimes referred to as political pluralism. South Africa today is characterised by States of Emergency, banning orders, censorship and massive State-organised disinformation. Subject only to restrictions on racist propaganda and on ethnic exclusiveness such as are to be found in the laws of most countries in the world, the people in the South Africa envisaged by the Guidelines will be free to set up such organisations as they please, to vote for whom they please, and to say what they want.

This highlights a distinction that sometimes gets forgotten, namely the difference between leadership and control. We are for ANC leadership; our organisation's central position in South Africa has been hard won and the dream of the founders of the organisation is slowly being realised. Without doubt, the ANC will continue to be the principal architect of national unity after the foundations of apartheid have been destroyed and the foundations of democracy laid. Yet this does not mean that the ANC is the only voice in the anti-apartheid struggle, or that it will be the only voice in post-apartheid South Africa.

We want to give leadership to the people, not exercise control over them. This has significant implications for our cultural work not just in the future, but now. We think we are the best (and we are), that is why we are in the ANC. We work hard to persuade the people of our country that we are the best (and we are succeeding). But this does not require us to force our views down the throats of others. On the contrary, we exercise true leadership by being non-hegemonic, by selflessly trying to create the widest unity of the oppressed and to encourage all forces for change, by showing the people that we are fighting not to impose a view upon them but to give them the right to choose the kind of society they want and the kind of government they want. We are not afraid of the ballot box, of open debate, of opposition. One fine day we will even have our Ian Smith equivalents protesting and grumbling about every change being made and looking back with nostalgia to the good old days of apartheid, but we will take them on at the hustings. In conditions of freedom, we have no doubt who will win, and if we should forfeit the trust of the people, then we deserve to lose.

All this has obvious implications for the way in which we conduct ourselves in the sphere of culture. We should lead by example, by the manifest correctness of our policies, and not rely on our prestige or numbers to push our positions through. We need to accept broad parameters rather than narrow ones: the criterion being pro- or anti-apartheid. In my opinion, we should be big enough to encompass the view that the anti-apart-heid forces and individuals come in every shape and size, especially if they belong to the artistic community. This is not to give a special status to artists, but to recognise that they have certain special characteristics and traditions. Certainly, it ill behoves us to set ourselves up as the new censors of art and literature, or to impose our own internal states of emergency in areas where we are well organised. Rather, let us write better poems and make better films and compose better music, and let us get the voluntary adherence of the people to our banner ("it is not enough that our cause be pure and just; justice and purity must exist inside ourselves" – war poem from Mozambique).

Finally, the Guidelines couple the guarantees of individual rights with the necessity to embark upon programmes of affirmative action. This too has clear implications for the sphere of culture. The South Africa in which individuals and groups can operate freely, will be a South Africa in the process of transformation. A constitutional duty will be imposed upon the state, local authorities and public and private institutions to take active steps to remove the massive inequalities created by centuries of colonial and racist domination. This gives concrete meaning to the statement that the doors of learning and culture shall be opened. We can envisage massive programmes of adult education and literacy, and extensive use of the media to facilitate access by all to the cultural riches of our country and of the world. The challenge to our cultural workers is obvious.

Part IV

Creativity in/and Adversarial Contexts

Poetry – or literature, in general – may be the "spontaneous overflow of powerful feelings," to invoke the still widely popular theory of literature by the British Romantic poet William Wordsworth, but, for African writers, its origin is certainly far from being "emotion recollected in tranquility." Born and having had to survive in the flaming kilns of history marked by colonialism and then unresponsive and tyrannical post-independent states, postcolonial pathologies of all kinds including religious fundamentalism, and an ever-widening inequality between Africa and the world, African literature and literary studies propose another theory, much more valid for many parts of the world today, of the complex intersection of adversarial contexts and the flowering of the creative muse. The selections in this part robustly capture the many dimensions and effects of that intersection in terms not just of thematic preoccupations, formal predilections, influence of colonial literary traditions and languages, but also of the more practical existential matter of the survival of the culture producer whether in his or her native land or in exile. One dirty little secret of the African literary tradition is the flourishing of the form of writing we could call "writers' prison diaries," that is, poems, fictional and non-fictional prose, and dramatic works by writers about their experience in the jail of the postcolonial state as political prisoners. When we realize that only those who survive jail can live to tell about it in a "prison diary," we can only be even more attentive to the substantive critical explorations gathered here of the reciprocal impacts of taxing, unsupportive contexts and African literary creativity.

Chapter 20

A Voice That Would Not Be Silenced

Wole Soyinka

This voice from the grave urges itself on our hearing. For let no one be in any doubt – the life-and-death discourse of the twenty-first century is unambiguously the discourse of fanaticism and intolerance. We can subsume this however we will under other concerns – economy, globalization, hegemonism, the arms race, AIDS, even environmental challenges; some of these rightly dominate the attention of the world. Ultimately, however, we come face to face with one overweening actuality: the proliferation of a mind-set that feeds on a compulsion to destroy other beings who do not share, not even the same beliefs, but specific subcategories of such beliefs. It is a mind-set that destroys the creative or adventurous of any community. It continues to prove efficient at fueling devastating conflicts all over the world, often in places that are remote from the accustomed circuits of global attention.

Attempts are made throughout history to plumb the depths of this singular mind-set, one that appears to find fertile ground most readily in ideology and religion. The findings of such inquiries – and have we not all, at some time or the other, encountered walking repositories of such convictions? – can be frightening. For we soon come to a realization that such minds are unreachable, permanently in the dark ages, in the darkest ages of superstition, the home of phantoms, of a terror of the unknown, the phobia for every new or alien experience, a phobia of such all-consuming intensity that, for survival, it must eliminate all doubters. It is the setting of the mind, not on questions, but on the mantra "I am right, you are wrong," whose ultimate goal of unreason is "I am right; you are dead!"

But is it all about ideology or religion? Or has it to do just as much with power and domination? Conformism is an elementary conditioning of society that is essential for the exercise of power, be the route one of the imposition of a secular or a theocratic ideology. The history of censorship is an old one, censorship not merely of the written word, but of the spoken, censorship in dress codes, human relationships, dietary choices, lifestyles, and even thought. The culture of the taboo appears to have evolved with the earliest human

First published as Foreword to Tahar Djaout, *The Last Summer of Reason*, trans. Marjolijn de Jager, pp. ix–xvi. St Paul, MN: Ruminator Books, 2001.

cohabitation, its origins – often traceable to strategies for combating shortages and ensuring communal survival – now dissipated in the mists of antiquity. What remains of the taboo is its opportunistic mechanism of control – that is, the enthronement of the monopoly of power – by a class, usually a religious elite, through mystification. No matter how elaborate the scriptures that now sanctify the original taboos, or the veneration that time has accorded such scriptures, they remain nothing but jealously guarded mechanisms of power by a few over the many. What once translated as "taste not of the fruits of this tree" has not changed in character. The fruits of the forbidden tree remain knowledge and inquiry – ironically, the original authors of the fable of the Garden of Eden were far more honest than their successors and heirs.

We know that no one is born with such mind closure; it must be carefully inseminated and nurtured, often with a single-minded ruthlessness. But why, in the past century, has this tendency appeared to have gained in such murdeous intensity? Are we confronted here perhaps with a parallel phenomenon of the deliberate cultivation of unawareness, an attitude of hoping, silently, that the menace will eat itself up, collapse inwards from its own untenable doctrines, that it will vanish if it is simply ignored? The strategy of evasion sometimes involves attributing far-reaching causes to this phenomenon, thus becoming a willing tool in the accommodation of the culture of intolerance. An example: highlighting the slights of history that have been inflicted by external forces, accompanied usually by imposition of hostile values and alien customs. History is thus used to justify both a hostility to and a rejection of new ideas, conveniently dubbed alien. Following, as a matter of course, is the internal repression of those who are themselves part of the terrain of external aggression, but refuse to remain eternal prisoners of the resented history. Indeed, the latter are considered far more potent enemies than the external agents of that history. They are traitors from within, who must be forcibly weaned from their delusions or simply eliminated. We are thus faced with a category of permanent victims, victims of the murderous arrogance of their own kind, victims of a messianic zeal that parades itself as divine consciousness for the redress of history. At the forefront of such victims are the creative minds, the writers, artists and visionaries of society.

Conveniently designated purveyors of alien values, they become disposable. Never mind the fact that they quarry inwards into their own society and culture, query its own internal contradictions, and attempt to highlight antecedent cultural values that have become dislodged from popular consciousness by the obscurantism of the new gospelers. Have they dared propose a preexistent right of women to dignity, insist on their place as equal members of the human race? Or simply observed that conformism is actually a retrogressive face of evolution, and that the authentic life instinct is toward originality and variety? What matters is that they are identified as subversives who reveal alternatives to a simplistic understanding and ordering of society. If writers, they possess an armory of unholy words with which to rephrase or reinterpret, for the purposes of demystification, even passages from those same scriptures that seemingly encrypt the doctrine of conformism or female subservience. They embrace a morality that compels them to challenge the authority of the fatal interpreter of the divine word. But it is not the writers alone who find themselves gravely at risk. Other clerics whose reading of the holy book lacks the desired homicidal zeal are equally marked for elimination. And then, of course, the suspected carriers of this new contamination, the consumers.

It is thus essential that we take note that Tahar Djaout bears witness from within his own society, from within his own milieu, and in defense of his assailed humanity. But let no one be tempted to narrow the bane of bigotry and intolerance to just one milieu from which this powerful testimony has emerged. Lucid and poignant, it is an exploration of the very phenomenon of intolerance, and its application is universal, as in the best allegories that are grounded in reality. At the same time, however, we dare not take refuge in universalisms when the victims are specific and immediate. It is not a universal principle that gets stabbed, shot, and even mutilated. It is a very specific voice, one that has made a conscious choice and died in defense of that choice. And it is only by recognizing that individuality that we are enabled to recollect, and respond to the fate of other individuals, to the fate of hundreds like Djaout, and the fate of hundreds of thousands on behalf of whom that voice has been raised, against whom the hand of atavism is also constantly raised, aiming ever more boldly for a body count that will pave the way of killers to a paradise of their imagining.

The most ambitious enemies of humanity are the absolutist interpreters of the Divine Will, be they Sikhs, Hindus, Jews, Christians, Muslims, born-agains of every religious calling. In the United States, after nearly three years on the run, a self-appointed "sword of God," raised against the upholders of the right to abortion, was finally arrested. From arson attacks on abortion clinics, he had graduated to righteous executions of doctors in their homes. His coreligionists openly cheered him, several protected him. Let such examples serve to remind us that the phenomenon of fanaticism is not always contingent on environment and history but is a teaching, nurturing, indoctrinating occupation. That certain social conditions provide congenial breeding grounds for susceptible human material is not in dispute, especially when the indoctrinating process can be linked, as already remarked, to real or imagined social or historical injustices. Nonetheless, the fanatic, intolerant mind, to be effectively countered, must first be addressed as a willfully manipulated, proliferating phenomenon. It is a contagion like any other known transmissible disease. The accommodative language of "political correctness," so fashionable in some of the world's largest democracies, must be recognized as a language of complicity with the league of darkness and intolerance in the life-and-death struggle of enlightenment and creativity. It comforts the proponents of terror and dehumanizes the victims even further, for it subsumes their trauma under a doctrine of relativity that denigrates their fundamental and universal right to life and freedom. The arrogant elimination of the Djaouts of our world must nerve us to pursue our own combative doctrine, namely: that peaceful cohabitation on this planet demands that while the upholders of any creed are free to adopt their own existential absolutes, the right of others to do the same is thereby rendered implicit and sacrosant. Thus the creed of inquiry, of knowledge and exchange of ideas, must be upheld as an absolute, as ancient and eternal as any other.

This posthumous allegory bequeathed to the world by Tahar Djaout is a literary gem that gleams from beyond the grave. It is also, surely, a humanistic testament, beamed at the complacent conscience of the world.

Chapter 21

Exile and Creativity:
A Prolonged Writer's Block

Micere Githae Mugo

Stage Directions

The subtitle of the following drama is: How the pangs of exile caused my prolonged writer's block – a reflective autobiographical narrative, not an apologia. *Read on.*

When I originally agreed to make a presentation on the above subject, the task had seemed straightforward. I had planned to conduct some library research focusing on any work that explored the exile experience, analyze the emerging perspectives through contrast and comparison, revamp my findings with some personal illustrations, draw up lessons to be learned, and thus neatly conclude my assignment. On sitting down to attack my agenda, however, I found the task to be more demanding than I had anticipated. In the first place, the undertaking refused to be just another academic exercise. The notion of referencing, footnoting, and abstracting an experience that insisted on being narrated from the heart began to register as another form of intellectual posturing. I was in a dilemma as to how to go about my task.

Finally, amid my agonizing and introspection, I was seized by a compelling urge to address my audience simply and directly in a personal, conversational manner. The experience of a woman writer, also a single parent, faced with the challenges of exile under unique circumstances, demanded that this story be told through empowering discourse. A big load dropped off my shoulders. I was ready to run. But then another problem emerged.

Having developed such intimacy with the subject matter – under exploration since 1982, the year I left Kenya to go into exile – my effort to distance myself from deeply felt experiences proved to be another futile academic endeavor. This time, defiance against the kind of theorizing that equates involvement with irrationality and noninvolvement with objectivity took fast care of that problem. After all, what is so objective or rational about the unfeeling composure of the cold murderer who puts a knife through a victim's throat

First published in *The Word Behind Bars and the Paradox of Exile*, ed. Kofi Anyidoho, pp. 80–7. Evanston: Northwestern University Press, 1997.

without wincing? That is the scientific style in which the A-bomb was dropped on Hiroshima and Nagasaki, no? Calculated, callous, precise objectivity. On the other hand, what is irrational about telling a tragic story with feeling and even tears? Does being human mean surrendering intellectual capacity? That particular problem was also thus solved.

But there was yet another problem to wrestle with. In demonstrating how harrowing, draining, eroding, and imaginatively vacuuming the exile experience can be and has been, I might be perceived as writing an apologia for my creative barrenness during the initial period of this nightmare. After all, many writers, including the famous Karl Marx, have not only written volumes while in exile but actually composed great literature on toilet paper smuggled out of prison cells. All that is needed is discipline – period. Well, as might be put in extended, reversed, hackneyed terms: not all birds are made of the same feather. Apologia or protest, the compelling story must be told.

But who was going to assume the narrative voice? I considered trying a first-person narrator all through to provide the needed immediacy and dramatic embodiment, but the story sounded individualistic, if not actually egocentric. I tried a distanced analytical tone, through the eyes of an omniscient narrator, but the intended distancing injected awkwardness and fictitiousness into unyielding hard facts. A factual, descriptive essay then suggested itself – an attractive option, but its immanent trimness would require maneuvering and contriving to contain zigzagging ends. This might in turn transform the whole discourse into an abstraction of life and pain.

The harder I tried to imaginatively capture the voice of an omniscient narrator, the more it failed to breathe life into the living person of the real woman at the heart of the story – a story rejecting fictionalization, for the narrative was, has been, and is a part of one's continuing history. It is one's tomorrow.

Ultimately, the story chose to unfold itself at the crossroads of collective narrative, dramatized dialogue, true anecdote, generalized observations, and autobiographical discourse. It begins with reflection on the conditions that led to exile, showing the move as an imposed course of action and not an open, voluntary choice. The exile experience is indeed depicted as a rough journey which is exacting not just for the key traveler but also for the traveler's immediate family and for the children in particular. Illustrations, anecdotes, and firsthand testimony are frequently brought in for authentication of the experiences explored, providing a personal touch to the narrative. The primary objective of the piece is to draw attention to the unique and adverse ways in which exile affects the creativity of some writers – in this case, a professional woman, political activist, and single head of a household. The obstacles outlined, the story closes with a celebration of the triumph of the human will over forces of oppression, as those exiled for their opposition to the abuse of human rights relentlessly struggle on for justice and freedom.

Let us begin with the question of what leads to exile while posing another related one: whether or not going into exile can be considered a voluntary choice. These questions cannot be addressed in isolation from a larger concern, that of the writer's role in society, including duty to the homeland. This, then, constitutes our point of departure.

First, a classification regarding writers: in the African context, writers tend to be members of the privileged elite, the products of a colonial education which, in most cases, trained them to view themselves as a unique breed of people, occupying an elevated presence in relation to the rest of the colonized population. Lured by the image of the Bohemian artist of the Western liberal tradition, African writers came to view themselves as even more special than the group of specials that their colonial masters had created of them. Okello Oculi, the Ugandan poet and political scientist, once referred to them as "spoilt children." The neocolonial state plays upon this spoiled-child syndrome, offering privileges here and there, volunteering assured patronage, in an attempt to coerce the recipients into collaboration. Those accepting the bribes have a good life, taking appointments as cabinet ministers by the patronizing neocolonial regimes or by accepting lucrative directorships where they can make a quick buck, and so the alluring offers roll on. Those who reject the blackmail are severely punished for daring to prohibit the violation of their consciences. Others try to abstain from casting the decisive ballot, lying low, and either remain mute or speak in paradoxes: this way they save their necks while not quite throwing conscience to the wind, like the collaborators. We will come back to these groups momentarily.

At this juncture, it is important to underline the fact that these initial observations point to the fact that writers cannot be lumped together as a cohesive group of people. Indeed, it is mandatory that we further scrutinize the above broad categorizations, using a class analysis in order to accurately place writers within the general production process.

As members of the intelligentsia, writers represent three main strands: conservatives, liberals, and revolutionaries. Given that under neocolonialism members of the ruling elite (whether military or civilian) essentially represent the interests of imperialism at the expense of the economically deprived masses, the above ideological positions assume telling significance. In sanctioning and servicing proimperialist neocolonial states, reactionary writers ultimately become promoters of antipeople practices, reinforcing the oppressive systems and structures at the root of the people's dehumanization. Often these writers reduce their writing into apologia for the systems of injustice that they live under. Indeed, in many cases, such writers have not only raised the volume of the choruses of state praise-singers and parroting chanters but also joined the ruling parties of the oppressive regimes, often operating as their active agents. A number have even been known to write treatises on state philosophies, unfounded as some of these philosophies are, no more than mere footsteps on sinking sand.

Liberal writers assume a middle position, choosing to be neither hot nor cold (as the Bible would say). They are more anxious to make it in their personal careers than to struggle for the collective emancipation of their societies. Hiding behind compromise and pragmatism, they run away from decisive action by refusing to use writing as intervention to change the oppressive reality around them. In the final analysis, they end up chasing the proverbial rat (of Chinua Achebe's Ibo proverbial evocation) even as the house is perishing in flames of consuming fire. Another tactic used by these writers is to engage in either mysticism or enigmatism, thus keeping their readers mesmerized and confused by what they write. This way they free themselves from the responsibility of conscientizing their audience in preparation for transforming the suffocating reality around them.

The third major category of writers within the neocolonial state is represented by the revolutionary artist. This artist's creative energies are devoted to affirming human dignity and creating a world in which each and every human being finds possibilities for utmost self-realization within a nurturing, validating collective environment. Revolutionary or progressive writers take sides with individuals and groups who are denied a voice in naming themselves and the world around them by the violation or suffocation of their imagination, as well as through exclusion from the production process. Using their writing as a vehicle for the affirmation of humanity and life in general, such writers are dedicated to creating the visions of hope and limitless possibility to which human beings can and will reach out, if given the opportunity.

All three types of writers exist side by side in African neocolonial states. However, the ranks of the third category have yielded the most would-be victims of imprisonment and torture, even though in some of the most repressive regimes a writer does not have to engage in any serious revolutionary activity to be targeted for harassment. The simple act of speaking out and breaking the terror of silence imposed by such states is enough of a "crime." Indeed, most writers under neocolonial dictatorships find their creativity censored, stifled, and targeted for vicious attack by the system. Through the use of terror, the offending systems go all out to impose silence in yet another effort to close another channel for raising the consciousness of the people. This is particularly so when the artistic works reach the oppressed as their primary audience.

Thus a lot of writers have landed in detention, in prison (usually on trumped-up charges), or have been subjected to police harassment or army brutality – or all of these and more – for denouncing the gross abuse of rights and individual liberties that is characteristic of our neocolonial existence. Where writers have not actually been locked up, they have been kept under the kind of censorship and surveillance that makes "freedom" under oppressive environments a farce. These writers have remained "inmates" in the larger prison of society, metaphorically living behind bars and inside the barbed wire of suffocating repressive institutions that seek to fetter their imagination and lock up their creativity.

In a situation like that of neocolonial Kenya, from which this writer departed to go into exile, the symbolism of this larger prison is real, painful, and torturous. Writers have either been detained without trial or served prison terms on planted evidence, and walked out into "freedom" (usually following a lot of local and international pressure) only to find themselves joining the armies of the unemployed for years – this, in spite of their badly needed professional skills which no African country can afford to waste. Beyond this, constant surveillance of the writers, their families, and friends by state security forces and their agents is such that, hyperbolically speaking, the aggressors know when their victims turn in bed at night or even go to the toilet in the assumed privacy of their own homes. Deliberate attempts are made to create a sense of fear all around, to permeate the air with suspicion, while enforcing abandonment and alienation from the communities in which the writers live, including circles of loved ones. Obviously, all these measures are aimed at breaking the victims and turning them into neurotic psychological wrecks who are so intimidated by their insecurity that they are pressured to surrender their consciences, agreeing to become parrots for the repressive regime.

It is to the credit of these writers that they have resisted such persecution, refused to be silenced, and continued not just to denounce injustice but to reaffirm, through activism, their commitment to the people's struggle for human dignity. However, in some cases the tyrannical practices outlined above have caused untold suffering to the targeted writers and their families. They have at times succeeded in destroying the lives of the individuals affected, breaking circles of friendship and even rupturing cemented family relationships. When immediate families are targeted the experience has been extremely painful. The violation of children's psyches is particularly frightening as the oppressive police-states try to criminalize the parent. I remember my elder daughter, then about three years of age, viciously attacking the security officers who had come to arrest me. She tried to bite them when they pushed me around, treating me like a criminal. That image still tears a mother's heart. Other children have, of course, witnessed much worse.

Given the foregoing, it becomes clear that for the writer under the siege of state terror, going into exile is not a voluntary choice. The term "self-imposed" exile is not only a contradiction in terms but a perversion of reality. Why impose exile on oneself? It is as illogical as suggesting that an innocent human being would opt for a prison sentence and then check into a jail, just for the fun of it. No normal human beings have ever been known to engage in this kind of crazy behavior. However, when conditions such as those described above are imposed on a writer, living at home translates into a more acute form of exile, and one has no option other than to leave. In the first place, remaining at home is a risk to one's life. Second, it is a sadistic version of self-supervised extended arrest. Third, it is psychological self-deportation, even as one is seen to be living among other free people.

On the question of self-exile, I experience some of the most agonizing moments in my own exile when I am subjected to sermons, usually from collaborators of neocolonial Kenya's repressive regime, blaming me for having left the country. Some of them would even go to the extreme of accusing me of imagined persecution, vouching that nothing would really have happened had I stayed. The very thought that a woman – who holds one of the highest jobs in the academic world, has a comfortable home, and is the mother (and custodial parent) of two young girls aged seven and five – would suddenly wake up, pack a few bags, abandon her home and job, and flee into exile is more than ludicrous; it is an act of insanity. Yet, of all the problems and ailments I might have suffered, insanity has never been one of them.

Another time, a woman who visited me in exile and who knew where and how I lived at home simply burst into tears when she walked into my flat. I could not tell whether it was the sight of the bare, faded, aged furnishings of my simple university flat that touched a soft part of her heart, but she just broke down on me. You see, official government propaganda spreads false tales of how those who go into exile do so in order to live in luxury in foreign countries. The propaganda even mischievously implies that the exiles are in the paid employ of "foreign masters," usually imaginary "communists." But let us return to what I have termed "psychological deportation" or "mental exile."

The targeted writer can be subjected to this whether at home or in exile. For instance, propaganda in government-controlled media disseminates thuggish-looking photographs of those under attack, enforcing images of criminalization and brutalization. Someone once sent me one such photograph from Kenya and it was truly dramatic: in it my mouth was wide open, as if I were either madly screaming at someone or getting ready to cannibalize a victim. In yet another, my eyes were sleepy and drooping as if I were high on drugs or as though I had hit the bottle rather hard. No wonder someone who had never met me before – who had only seen photographs of me in government-controlled media – stared at me open-mouthed upon being introduced to me. He was truly in shock and all he could ask was: "Are you really *the* Micere Mugo?" This man obviously expected to meet some creature with horns! This subtle criminalization is yet another form of dehumanization. It has a profoundly negative effect on a public who have access to little, if anything, outside government-controlled media. Indeed, some of the photographs of exiled colleagues are so scary that, if the individuals depicted were not known personally, a casual glimpse would have provoked the urge to turn around and run in the opposite direction! The terror of repressive media registers with sobering impact.

The argument, then, is that exile is not a normal choice; rather, it is a step in the victim's refusal to become a martyr or an adventurer in a situation where state terror is the rule of law. It is a dignified attempt to retain control of one's imagination as it is threatened with invasion and silencing: a determination not to have one's conscience buried under persecution and terror. It is a refusal to allow the human being in oneself to die under the treachery of negative silence. Above all, it is a calculated retreat from a bombarded war zone and surrounded battlefront, not a permanent withdrawal from, or abandonment of, a continuing struggle. Indeed, the progressive exiled writer uses displacement to create new networks of resistance away from home, joining with other internationalist struggles against injustice, oppression, and dehumanization.

[. . .]

Chapter 22

Containing Cockroaches
(Memories of Incarceration Reconstructed in Exile)

Jack Mapanje

The limelight:

The fundamental transgression of our despotic times is to be in the limelight; and to think or do anything on your own terms is its perfect embodiment. When I returned home after about four years of my studies in London, I expected to be arrested. I had not committed any crime against anybody or against my country. You did not need to commit a crime to be arrested. Being in the limelight was sufficient. I had been dangerously in the limelight. I therefore expected to be arrested and detained on April 1, 1983, at Chileka Airport in Blantyre upon my arrival from London. Not because I was guilty. You did not have to be guilty to be arrested and detained. In these hopeless times even laughing at the blank space might land you in prison. "Why is he laughing so loudly? Who is he laughing at?" These loaded questions, implicating that you were laughing at the system or someone in authority, were common. Everything was a statement, a punishable statement. Your very presence was a statement.

Publishing a book of poems outside the country is worse. It only needed someone in some authority to consider your poem, your book, your thoughts and ideas subversive, rebellious, or merely radical, for you to be in trouble. And everyone was incredibly generous. Warmth emanated from every corner. They warned you when you were going below the belt. But my return home was just another Fool's Day. Nothing happened. No arrest. No detention or imprisonment, despite the stories I had been told when I was in London about how subversive my poems had been.

I had had some inkling of the extraordinary influence my slim volume of poems, *Of Chameleons and Gods*, published in London in 1981, was having particularly among the civil

First published in *The Word Behind Bars and the Paradox of Exile*, ed. Kofi Anyidoho, pp. 47–50, 53–6, 65–7. Evanston: Northwestern University Press, 1997.

servants in Capital Hill offices in Lilongwe. Some who had clearly not read the poems invented their own quotations and made me responsible for their origin. Others linked up lines of one poem to the lines of another to exercise their faculties of interpretation of the contemporary politics of Malawi. The result was blamed on me. I could do nothing to stop them. At any rate, I realized that their faculties of deduction and interpretation, which had been paralyzed for so long, needed exercise. I had come to understand the truth I had always feared: the interpretation of an artifact after its publication was outside the artist's control. I suspected that my poems might have been causing some stir among some authorities. Unexpected questions, like "So, what's this we hear that you are into good books then?" came far too frequently not to unnerve. I knew that my book of verse was waiting for its time to be banned or withdrawn from circulation. I knew I would be arrested. I did not know when. "They wait for you to hatch then they take you in, you know, like chickens!" everybody said intimately. And like everybody I could have left the country. They encouraged you to go into exile. I did not want exile. I was already living in exile in my own country as it was! Why look for another? I wanted to die and be buried at home. I did not see anything wrong with being that romantic. Our ancestors started it. And by what right could some people lay a more legitimate claim to citizenship than yours, especially when you too were born there? Some of these cockroaches were not even born in Malawi!

The censorship board was cautious about banning my book outright. They refused to ban it. It would have made me an instant hero. They did not want other heroes here. One hero was enough: His Excellency the Life President of the Republic of Malawi, the Ngwazi Dr. Hastings Kamuzu Banda, the lion of Malawi, the father and founder of the nation. No other person mattered. But perhaps for the first time, and I gather on recommendation of the principal of Chancellor College, the censorship board had invited academics to read and report on my book. "We'll get his colleagues, his friends, and his ex-students to ban him," someone apparently said cynically. The list of readers included one British professor of English teaching in the university, several Malawian lecturers, and the university's alumni working throughout the country. These readers had promptly sent their reports to the censors. Luckily, a colleague, brother, and friend had stumbled on the reports. He photocopied and sent them to me in London so I could sample the type of official response I was likely to encounter. One report summed up how the officials were going to react: "These poems poke at the raw wounds of the nation." They decided neither to ban nor not to ban the book. Keeping the book on a shelf in one's living room was neither acceptable nor unacceptable. That was more painful than banning. Meanwhile, the fifty or so copies still held by the university bookshop in Zomba were bought off by the Special Branch, only to be thrown into a pit latrine, as I was later to learn. Those that were in the central bookshop in Blantyre were either impounded, ordered to be returned to the United Kingdom publishers, or merely withdrawn from the shelves.

Instead of being daunted, however, I wrote a letter to the chief censoring officer to explain why the poems were only another batch that would not destabilize the "peace and calm and law and order" prevailing in Malawi! There was nothing rebellious about them. And having been largely influenced by our oral traditions, as she would discover after reading them, the pieces tried to preserve something of our culture, however unsuccessful the exercise might have been. What did she, in her considered opinion, think? "Should I bring copies of the book when I return to the university?" In reply she asked why I had not sent the poems in manuscript to the censorship board in Malawi first, before giving them to Heinemann in

London to publish. I laughed. I wondered why nobody had warned me about that. Months later, the managing director of Dzuka Publishing Company, Malawi's de facto official publishing house, wrote to ask if I could give them permission to buy the rights to publish the bulk of the volume. He wanted a Malawian version of my poems, he said. He was sure that I would appreciate that Malawian readers deserved to enjoy my work. He did not indicate which poems he would exclude. It was patent, however, that the book had increased my conspicuousness.

In addition, I had coedited with Angus Calder and Cosmo Pieterse an anthology of contemporary African poems that was published by Heinemann UK before I returned home. This was based on the 1981 BBC Poetry Competition for Africa, for which we were judges. Part of our duties as judges of the competition was to explain for listeners of the BBC World Service for Africa what type of poems we chose and why. These programs were heard by ordinary Malawian listeners as well as by government informers. They were probably recorded in Special Branch files. I had also coauthored with Landeg White an anthology of oral poetry from Africa which was published by Longmans in the United Kingdom. "This is too much," said one friend when I showed him the three books I had had published in the United Kingdom while I was doing my doctorate degree. My fears were encapsulated by the loaded question I was asked by an unknown police officer at Chileka Airport on my return: "Have you decided to come back, then? What happened to the BBC jobs we used to hear about?" I expected to be arrested.

Everybody expected to be arrested, everybody who was in the limelight. If you did not anticipate arrest, you were one of them or you lied to yourself or you were a foreigner. If you were a foreigner, you expected to be deported. And no special qualities were needed. Whether you were an adventurer, worked for yourself, or worked for others, you were in the limelight. No village or town, however remote, no profession or trade was safe from the limelight. You did not have to perform any feats to be in the limelight for your arrest or deportation. And when an expatriate was deported or a local decided to go into exile or was detained without charge or trial, nobody asked why. Everybody either knew or could speculate why. The late James Stuart, professor and head of the Department of English, used to cite Russian experiences, particularly Akhmatova's cry quoted in Nadezhda Mandel-stam's *Hope against Hope*: "It's time you understood that people were arrested *for nothing!*"

[...]

The arrest,

when it came, felt like some stupid ancestral saying come true. An idle fragment of colonial superstition, probably invented by the British, says "when Friday falls on payday or payday falls on Friday, the world grinds to a halt and begins to spin in the opposite direction!" The locals held on to this belief long after the colonials had left the political arena, although nobody really believed such incredulities ever happened. Today is Friday. Payday. Anthony Nazombe and I have just had fish and chips for lunch at Gymkhana Club, Zomba. We are washing it down with our respective Sheffield and London pub experiences and joking about the papier-mâché Queen Victoria, who used to arbitrate over the golf, tennis, and football trophies in the bars of Gymkhana Clubs once upon a time. Where has she been moved to? Who dared move that precious symbol?

We are rudely interrupted.

"Is there a person by the name of Dr Mapanje here?"

We look at each other. Silence. The man is in civilian clothes. He is wearing a dark blue blazer. He had walked quietly towards our table. Having checked in vain for whatever he wanted in the other bars of the club, the man comes back to survey our bar over-looking the ex-colonial cricket pitch, now occasionally used for independence celebrations football. Except for the two of us, the barman, and one soldier drinking in the corner, this bar is also empty. The man comes our way again, repeats his question more loudly. Perhaps he is chagrined by our silence. We are amused. Still silence. He walks towards the Golfers' Bar next door.

My children at home are waiting for me for lunch. I do not know why I was so irresponsible as to have been persuaded to come here for fish and chips with Anthony, a poet, friend, and colleague, when my lunch was waiting for me at home. Why did I not tell the children they should not wait for me? I hope they had a lovely time at the lake at Uncle Cuthbert's. They had brought my favorite fish, Judith had said on the phone. How thoughtful of them. The man comes back and more anxiously interrupts us again.

"Mapanje here?"

"Don't you know him?"

I decide to spare him more breath.

"Are you Dr Mapanje, the head of the Department of English, Chancellor College, University of Malawi?" he resolutely says.

"Supposing I was?"

"Well, there's a man in the Golfers' Bar next door. He would like to see you."

"Man, down here, it is the monkey that follows the mountain, not the other way round. What about where you have come from?" I answer with ease.

He snaps back, "My friend, this is no time for proverbs. You must see the man waiting for you there!"

He points where I have to go. He is clearly hurt. But where has he come from? His face is new in these parts. Another one of the Special Branch to scare us into submission, perhaps? We won't be cowed. We get up.

My heart jumps when I see in the Golfers' Bar the Eastern Division commissioner of police. Everybody recognizes him. Few know his name. He is spruced up in full commissioner gear. The bar is desolate; the high stools around it and the wooden chairs that have lost their cushions since goodness-knows-when are forlorn, scattered all over, as if there had been a chair-throwing fight the previous night; the stench of stale beer hangs uncomfortably in the air; the dart board is firmly shut. Why is nobody here today? No drunk on payday at lunch hour in the Golfers' Bar? I wonder. . . . The commissioner suggests we step outside. Anthony nervously follows behind us, stops at the club's gate, and watches me hobble toward the car park. Only my car and the police Pajero brood in the dusty car park. The commissioner stops near his Pajero and asks another question.

"Are you Dr Mapanje, head of the English Department at Chancellor College, University of Malawi?"

"Yes."

"We have been directed by His Excellency the Life President to arrest you."

"But His Excellency does not know me, and I do not know him except as the chancellor of the university and the Life President!"

The police commissioner is obviously not listening to my protestations.

"Have you got the handcuffs?"

"Yes, sir!" the junior constable quickly answers, shrugging to attention. He takes the handcuffs from the right-hand pocket of his dark blue blazer. I should have known. His hands feel scabrous as the iron of his handcuffs clumps tightly around my wrists. He forcefully elbows me into the Pajero, which dispatches down the university road at a speed reminiscent of British colonial armed vehicles during the 1959 emergency in the country's fight for independence. My car is still parked at the Gymkhana Club. They have taken my car keys. I am glad I have finished paying the loan for the car. When we reach the university, I am turgidly nudged up the stairs to my office. I feel like an escaped criminal rearrested. When you are still handcuffed, limping up any steps is not easy. And whoever invented handcuffs had a contorted mind. Did they hang him for this massive crime against humanity?

The office of the head of the Department of English is full of new books which have just been donated by Ntchima Trust (one of the organizations which first started growing tea here) based in York, England and the British Council office in London. There is a crisis at hand: these books are intended to beat IMF directives that have imposed fees on university students. Our courses in English literature and literature in English are in danger of not being taken by students because they have no money to buy the texts. (The government has patently found an impeccable excuse for killing the literature section of the department: IMF structural readjustment directives. When did literature departments begin to be regarded as subversive?) So I thought I should appeal for assistance from friends. This is the result. But such gestures are not appreciated here. And when the search begins, the Special Branch belligerently throw the fresh-smelling books all over the floor, deliberately trampling the delicate pages with their boots. The commissioner shouts.

"What type of office is this? How do you work in here? Where does one put his feet? How can you clutter the floor with books, books, nothing but books? Is this the office of the head of the department? What do you head in such a place?" The commissioner nearly chokes in the barrage of his own rhetorical questions.

Out of the blue, I hear myself saying:

"If you've heard that there's a head of the Department of English and you are looking for his office, this is it! Tell me what you are looking for amid this sumptuous confusion of fresh books, and I will get it for you."

Silence.

The search continues.

[...]

The interrogation

is farcical. At 7.30 p.m., it is getting late even for the officers who must have better business at hand on a Friday. I have to be hurriedly ushered into the large bare room where the imposing oval-shaped mahogany table is flanked by eight commissioners of police with their inspector general at the head. All is quiet. I bite my teeth. I don't like it. When did they arrive here? There must have been some brisk business in town. If it's about me, it must be very serious indeed. Perhaps these are the people we were waiting for. How did they travel here in a country where the airplane is reserved for only the Life President? The ubiquitous portrait of His Excellency the Life President above the inspector general's chair ominously mediates the grim proceedings. Despite the agony of waiting for more than four hours in a dismal waiting room, it is a relief to see some movement at last, however macabre its direction was eventually going to be. If I must go, it had better be now. Let's get it over with.

The ammunition which the Special Branch had abducted from my bedroom are the passports and a banned novel. If there is justice, I will easily handle this court of commissioners, the tradition of no provision of defense lawyers notwithstanding. Alas, the vindication which I had been carefully preparing since my arrest at 1.35 this Friday afternoon does not materialize. Anything planned on your own terms here is always repulsed. Endeavoring to frustrate whatever imaginative schemes you might hoard is the policy they vigorously pursue. I had expected the interrogation to be a more protracted and tortuous affair. But, technically, there is no inquisition. It's too brief, too abrupt. I cannot even begin to defend myself!

The inspector general of police starts.

"I went to see His Excellency the Life President at 11.30 this morning. H. E. has directed me to arrest you and detain you. Since it is a directive from above, we must tell you that we cannot investigate your case. It would be questioning the wisdom of the Life President. I have called upon these commissioners, therefore, to find out if there is anything in our files about you. There is nothing. They all say they do not know you. So we thought we should ask you to tell us why we should detain you. Who are you? Why should we detain you? What have you done to each other at the university?"

I am flabbergasted. I have not misheard. What have we done to each other at the university? My mind is blank. I am nervous. First, who is going to believe that I am really a nobody when matters have reached this far? Second, someone at the university has reported me to the Life President. Although anyone could have done it, the options must narrow down from the country's population of ten million to the handful who have easy access to the state house. In the context of the university, these must whittle down to a nephew and his uncle. These officers genuinely want the tale from me. But watch. How could H. E.'s commissioners not know? How could H. E.'s and the country's eyes and ears instantaneously not see and not hear? Pray. I look again at H. E.'s portrait on the wall and notice the rebuke on the octogenarian's youthful face. An uncomfortable silence reigns. I not only refuse to talk but I cannot see on what I should waste my breath. Silence.

The inspector general does not like silence. He continues.

"Tell us where you come from and where you grew up, that is, where you went to school."

That's better. All the commissioners suddenly look at me at once. I choose to dwell on the innocent parts of the "rebel" district where I was born. The East Bank, as the locals call that part of Mangochi district where I was born, is as explosive as the Middle East after which it was named. There are no more desperadoes left there. The first son of the land who would have toppled this tyrannical police state, if his foolish exiled friends in Mbwani had not betrayed him, had been mysteriously killed by "CIA's sugar disease" in the exile of California, as everyone claimed. The other two dissidents were publicly hanged. The nation only "sobbed in its stomach," as some people said, unable to protest in any substantive way, for years having been terrified into abandonment and resignation. The list of victims in the East Bank alone – those accidentalized by crocodiles, lions, cars, even by timid hyenas, largely from police cells and Young Pioneer bases – runs into the thousands.

A friend told me the story of a well-known retired assistant commissioner of police (who now boasts the most successful tobacco farm in the district, second only to the farms run by the Greeks who decided to settle here goodness-knows-since-when): the retired police officer apparently shoots dead the rebellious village men, women, and children in the name of the party and government; he loads them on the back of his small truck, covers them with canvas, and does his drinking rounds from bar to bar. When fights cunningly instigated by him break out in the drinking bars, as reconciliation he invites the combatants to come out and take a fish each from his catch at the back of his truck. When they see the reeking bodies, they run for their lives, never to enter the bars again. Besides, it is a well-known story that after the abortive rebellion led by Masauko Chipembere, the little population of more than three hundred men, women, and children of CheMoto village was severely trounced for surreptitiously supporting the revolt. Except for a woman who was too old to travel, everybody in the village was rounded up, packed into police and army vans, and thrown into Maula Prison some three hundred miles away. Most of them died there. Their houses and grain stores were burned down or confiscated by the Congress Party's invincible Young Pioneer paramilitary.

The open secrets that helped to subjugate the whole district and sustain the heinous tyrant are abundant. Would I have had the nerve to want to become another martyr, at this late hour? No way. I must mention Mangochi as my home of birth without too much enthusiasm. I decide to answer the commissioners' sudden effrontery by emphasizing Chikwawa District as the home where I grew up. There are very few well-known dissidents who have fought this government there. It is a trick we have all learned to invoke in time of trouble. Cowardice, really. But what the hell!

[...]

Chapter 23

Writing Against Neo-Colonialism

Ngugi wa Thiong'O

The African writer who emerged after the Second World War has gone through three decisive decades which also mark three modal stages in his growth. He has gone, as it were, through three ages within only the last thirty years or so: the age of the anti-colonial struggle; the age of independence; and the age of neo-colonialism.

First was the fifties, the decade of the high noon of the African people's anti-colonial struggles for full independence. The decade was heralded, internationally, by the triumph of the Chinese Revolution in 1949 and by the independence of India about the same time. It was the decade of the Korean revolution; the Vietnamese defeat of the French at Dien Bien Phu; the Cuban people's ouster of Batista; the stirrings of heroic independence and liberation movements in Asia, the Caribbean and Latin America. In Africa the decade saw the Nasserite national assertion in Egypt, culminating in the triumphant nationalization of the Suez Canal; armed struggles by the Kenya Land and Freedom Army, Mau Mau, against British colonialism and by the FLN against French colonialism in Algeria; intensified resistance against the South African Apartheid regime, a resistance it responded to with the Sharpeville massacre; and what marks the decade in the popular imagination, the independence of Ghana in 1957 and of Nigeria in 1960 with the promise of more to follow. In Europe, the immediate postwar decades, particularly the fifties, saw a consolidation of socialist gains in Eastern Europe; and important social-democratic gains in the west; in USA, the fifties saw an upsurge of civil rights struggles spearheaded by the Afro-American people.

It was, in other words, the decade of tremendous anti-imperialist and anti-colonial revolutionary upheavals occasioned by the forcible intervention of the masses in history. It was a decade of hope, the people looking forward to a bright morrow in a new Africa finally freed from colonialism. Kwame Nkrumah was the single most important theoretician and spokesman of this decade. *Towards Colonial Freedom*: that was in fact the title of the book Kwame Nkrumah had published at the beginning of the fifties. How sweet it must have sounded in the ears of all those who dreamt about a new tomorrow! His Ghana became the revolutionary Mecca of the entire anti-colonial movement in Africa. Hutchison, a South

First published in *Criticism and Ideology: Second African Writers' Conference, Stockholm, 1986*, ed. Kirsten H. Petersen, pp. 92–103. Uppsala: Scandinavian Institute of African Studies, 1988.

African nationalist captured Ghana's centrality to the era when he called his book – itself an account of his life and his escape from South Africa – simply, *Road to Ghana*. All the continent's nationalist roads of the fifties led to Kwame Nkrumah's Ghana. Everywhere on the continent, the former colonial slave was breaking his chains, and singing songs of hope for a more egalitarian society in its economic, political and cultural life and Nkrumah's Ghana seemed to hold the torch to that life!

The African writer we are talking about was born on the crest of this anti-colonial upheaval and world-wide revolutionary ferment. The anti-imperialist energy and optimism of the masses found its way into the writing of the period. The very fact of his birth was itself, whether in poetry, drama or fiction, even where it was explanatory in intention, was assertive in tone. It was Africa explaining itself, speaking for itself, and interpreting its past. It was an African rejecting the images of its past as drawn by the artists of imperialism. The writer even flaunted his right to use the language of the former colonial master anyway he liked. No apologies. No begging. The Caliban of the colonial world had been given European languages and he was going to use them even to subvert the master.

There is a kind of self-assuredness, a confidence, if you like, in the scope and mastery of material in some of the best and most representative products of the period: Chinua Achebe's *Things Fall Apart*, Wole Soyinka's *A Dance of the Forests*, Camara Laye's *The African Child*, and Sembene Ousmane's *God's Bits of Wood*. The decade, in politics and in literature, was however best summed up in the very title of Peter Abraham's autobiography, *Tell Freedom*, while the optimism is all there in David Diop's poem 'Africa'. After evoking an Africa of freedom lost as well as the Africa of the current colonialism, he looks to the future with unqualified, total confidence:

> Africa tell me Africa
> Is this you this back that is bent
> This back that breaks under the weight of humiliation
> This back trembling with red scars
> And saying yes to the whip under the midday sun
> But a grave voice answers me
> Impetuous son that tree young and strong
> That tree there
> In splendid loneliness amidst white and faded flowers
> That is Africa your Africa
> That grows again patiently obstinately
> And its fruit gradually acquires
> The bitter taste of liberty.

Here the writer and his work were part of the African revolution. Both the writer and his work were products of the revolution even as the writer and the literature tried to understand, reflect, and interpret that revolution. The promptings of his imagination sprung from the fountain of the African anti-imperialist, anti-colonial movement of the forties and fifties. From every tongue came the same tune: Tell Freedom.

But very often the writer who sang Tell Freedom in tune and in time with the deepest aspirations of his society did not always understand the true dimensions of those aspirations, or rather he did not always adequately evaluate the real enemy of these aspirations. Imperialism was far too easily seen in terms of the skin pigmentation of the colonizer.

It is not surprising of course that such an equation should have been made since racism and the tight caste system in colonialism had ensured that social rewards and punishments were carefully structured on the mystique of colour. *Labour* was not just *labour* but *black labour: capital* was not just *capital* but *white-owned capital*. Exploitation and its necessary consequence, oppression, were black. The vocabulary by which the conflict between colonial labour and imperialist capital was perceived and ideologically fought out consisted of white and black images, sometimes freely interchangeable with the terms "European" and "African". The sentence or phrase was "*...when the whiteman came to Africa...*" and not "*...when the imperialist, or the colonialist, came to Africa...*", or "*...one day these whites will go...*" and not "*...one day imperialism, or these imperialists, will go...*"! Except in a few cases, what was being celebrated in the writing was the departure of the whiteman with the implied hope that the incoming blackman by virtue of his blackness would right the wrongs and heal the wounds of centuries of slavery and colonialism. Were there classes in Africa? No! cried the nationalist politician, and the writer seemed to echo him. The writer could not see the class forces born but stunted in a racially demarcated Africa.

As a result of this reductionism to the polarities of colour and race, the struggle of African people against European colonialism was seen in terms of a conflict of values between the African and the European ways of perceiving and reacting to reality. But which African values? Which European values? Which Black values? Which White values? The values of the European proletariat and of the African proletariat? Of the European imperialist bourgeoisie and of the collaborationist African petty bourgeoisie? The values of the African peasant and those of the European peasant? An undifferentiated uniformity of European, or white, values was posited against an equally undifferentiated uniformity of African, or black, values.

The uniformity of African values was often captured in the realm of political parlance by the grandiloquent phrase, African socialism. Socialism (and therefore its opposite, imperialist capitalism) was reduced to a matter of beliefs, moral absolutes, and not that of a historically changing economic, political and cultural practice. Values without the economic, political and cultural practice that gives rise to them even as they in turn reflect that practice were seen as racially inherent in a people.

In short the writer and the literature he produced did not often take, and hence treat, imperialism and the class forces it generated as an integrated economic, political and cultural system of its opposite: national independence, democracy and socialism.

And so the writer, armed with an inadequate grasp of the extent, the nature and the power of the enemy and of all the class forces at work could only be shocked by the broken promises as his society entered the second decade.

The Age of Independence

The beginning of the sixties saw an acceleration of the independence movements. Tanzania, Uganda, Zaire, Kenya, Zambia, Malawi, Congo (Brazzaville), Senegal, Ivory Coast, Mali: country after country won the right to fly a national flag and to sing a national anthem. At the end of the sixties only a few smudges on the map represented old colonies. The OAU was the symbol of the new age, or rather it was the promise of greater unity to come. But if the sixties was the decade of African independence, it was also the decade when old style imperialism tried to halt the momentum of the anti-colonial struggles and the successes of the fifties. Old style imperialism tried to make a last stand. Thus Portuguese colonialism clung tenaciously to Angola, Guinea-Bissau and Mozambique. In Zimbabwe Ian Smith and his Rhodesian Front, with the active covert and overt encouragement of the big imperialist bourgeoisie, tried to create a second South Africa by means of an American sounding Unilateral Declaration of Independence (UDI). Internationally – that is, outside of Africa – this last stand of old style imperialism was represented by the USA in South Vietnam. But US domination of South Vietnam also represented new style imperialism – that is US-led imperialism ruling through puppet regimes. Thus in Vietnam lay a clue as to what was happening to the Africa of the sixties, happening that is, to its independence from classical colonialism. New style imperialism was dependent on the 'maturing' of a class of natives, already conceived and born by colonialism, whose positions and aspirations as a group were not in any fundamental conflict with the money juggling classes, the financial gnomes of the real centres of power like Zurich, the City of London and Wall Street. There is a Kikuyu word, *Nyabaara*, which means an overseer which adequately describes these mediators between the imperialist bourgeoisie and the mass of workers and peasants in the former colonies.

To the majority of African people in the new states, independence did not bring about fundamental changes. It was independence with the ruler holding a begging bowl and the ruled holding a shrinking belly. It was independence with a question mark. The age of independence had produced a new class and a new leadership that often was not very different from the old one. Black skins, white masks? White skins, black masks? Black skins concealing colonial settlers' hearts? In each of the African languages there was an attempt to explain the new phenomenon in terms of the 'White' and 'Black' symbols by which colonialism had been seen and fought out. But really, this was a new company, a company of African profiteers firmly deriving their character, power and inspiration from their guardianship of imperialist interests.

The new regimes in the independent states increasingly came under pressure from external and internal sources. The external pressure emanated from the West who wanted these states to maintain their independence and non-alignment firmly on the side of Western economic and political interests. Where a regime showed a consistent desire to break away from the Western orbit, destabilization through economic sabotage and political intrigue was set in motion. The US role in bringing down Lumumba and installing the Mobutu military regime in Zaire at the very beginning of the decade was a sign of things to come.

The internal pressure came from the people who soon saw that independence had brought no alleviation to their poverty and certainly no end to political repression. People saw in most of the new regimes a dependence on foreigners, grand mismanagement and well-maintained police boots.

Some military intervened either at the promptings of the West or in response to what they genuinely saw and felt as the moral decay. But they too did not know what else to do with the state except to run the status quo with the gun held at the ready – not against imperialism – but against the very people the army had ostensibly stepped in to save.

Thus the sixties, the age of independence, became the era of coup-d'états whether Western-backed or in patriotic response to internal pressures. Zaire in 1960 and 1965; Nigeria and Ghana in 1966; Sierra Leone, Sudan, Mali, Uganda: all these and more fell to the armies and by 1970 virtually every independent state had experienced a measure of military coups, attempted coups or threats of coups. The result was often intraclass fratricide as in the case of Zaire and Nigeria but one that dragged the masses into meaningless deaths, starvation and stagnation. Wars initiated by Nyabaaras! The era of coups d'états also threw up two hideous monstrosities: Bokassa and Idi Amin, two initial darlings of the West, who were to make a total mockery of the notion of independence, but who also, in those very actions, made a truthful expression of that kind of independence. Hideous as they were, they were only symbols of all the broken promises of independence.

What was wrong with Africa? What had gone wrong? The mood of disillusionment engulfed the writer and the literature of the period. It was Chinua Achebe in *A Man of the People* who correctly reflected the conditions that bred coups and rumours of coups.

A Man of the People, coming out at about the same time as the first Nigerian military coup, had shown that a writer could be a prophet. But other writings – particularly Ayi Kwei Armah's *The Beautyful Ones Are Not Yet Born*, and Okot p'Bitek's *Song of Lawino* – were equally incisive in their horror at the moral decay in the new states. The writer responded to the decay by appealing to the conscience of the new class. If only they would listen! If only they would see the error of their ways! He pleaded, lamented, threatened, painted the picture of the disaster ahead, talked of a fire next time. He tried the corrective antidote of contemptuous laughter, ridicule, direct abuse with images of shit and urine, every filth imaginable. The writer often fell back upon the kind of revenge Marx once saw the progressive elements among the feudal aristocracy taking against the new bourgeoisie that was becoming the dominant class in 19th century Europe. They, the aristocracy, 'took their revenge by singing lampoon on their new master, and whispering in his ears sinister prophecies of coming catastrophe.'

> In this way arose feudal socialism; half lamentation, half lampoon; half echo of the past, half menace of the future; at times, by its bitter, witty and incisive criticism, striking the bourgeoisie to the very heart's core but always ludicrous in its effect, through total incapacity to comprehend the march of history (The Communist Manifesto)

Thus the writer in this period was still limited by his inadequate grasp of the full dimension of what was really happening in the sixties: the international and national realignment of class forces and class alliances. What the writer often reacted to was the visible lack of moral fibre in the new leadership and not necessarily the structural basis of that lack of a national moral fibre. Sometimes the writer blamed the people – the recipients of crimes – as well as the perpetrators of the crimes against the people. At times the moral horror was couched in terms perilously close to blaming it all on the biological character of the people. Thus although the literature produced was incisive in its observation, it was nevertheless characterized by a sense of despair. The writer in this period often retreated into individualism, cynicism, or into empty moral appeals for a change of heart.

The Age of Neo-colonialism

It was the third period, the seventies, that was to reveal what really had been happening in the sixties: the transition of imperialism from the colonial to the neo-colonial stage. On the international level, the US-engineered overthrow of the Allende regime in Chile showed the face of victorious neo-colonialism. The decade saw the clear ascendancy of US-dominated transnational financial and industrial monopolies in most of Asia, Africa and Latin America. This ascendancy was to be symbolized by the dominance of the IMF and the World Bank in the determination of the economy and hence the politics and culture of the affected countries in Asia, Africa and Latin America. The era saw the USA surround Africa with military bases or with some kind of direct US military presence all the way from Morocco via Diego Garcia to Kenya, Egypt and of course the Mediterranean Sea. The aims of the Rapid Deployment Forces, formed in the same decade, were unashamedly stated as interventionist in Third World affairs – i.e. in affairs of the neo-colonies. Indeed, the decade saw an increasing readiness of former colonial powers to militarily enter Africa without even a trace of shame. The increasingly open, naked financial, industrial (e.g. Free Trade Zones etc), military and political interference of Western interests in the affairs of African countries with the active cooperation of the ruling regimes in the same countries, showed quite clearly that the so-called independence had only opened each of the African countries to wider imperialist interests. Dependence abroad, repression at home, became the national motto.

But if the seventies revealed more clearly the neo-colonial character of many of the African countries, the seventies also saw very important and eye-opening gains by the anti-imperialist struggles. Internationally (outside Africa), the single most important event was the defeat of the USA in Vietnam. But there were other shattering blows against neo-colonialism: Nicaragua and Iran, for instance.

In Africa, the seventies saw a victorious resurgence of anti-imperialism. The armed struggles in Angola, Mozambique, Guinea-Bissau and Zimbabwe had clearly gained from errors of the earlier anti-colonial movements in the fifties. They could see the enemy much more clearly and they could clearly analyze their struggles in terms that went beyond just the question of colour and race. Their enemy was imperialism. Within the independent African countries, coup d'états began to take on a more anti-imperialist and anti-neo-colonial character.

Although occurring in 1981 and 1983 respectively the Rawling's coup in Ghana and Sankara's in Burkina Faso (previously Upper Volta) are the better examples of this tendency. But a more telling symbol was the emergence in the seventies of a people-based guerilla movement fighting for a second independence. The armed liberation guerilla movements in places like Uganda, Sudan and Zaire may well come to stand to neo-colonialism what the Kenya Land and Freedom Army and the FLN in Algeria stood to colonialism in the fifties. The phenomenon of university educated youth and secondary school graduates opting to join workers and peasants in the bush to fight on a clear programme of a national democratic revolution as a first and necessary stage for a socialist transformation is something new in the Africa of the seventies. Whatever their ultimate destiny, these post-colonial guerrilla movements certainly symbolize the convergence of the worker's hammer and the peasant's machete or jembe with the pen and gun.

The awakening to the realities of imperialism was reflected in some very important theoretical political breakthroughs in the works of Amilcar Cabral, Walter Rodney, Samir Amin, Dan Nabudere, Bala Mohamed, Nzongola-Ntalaja and in many papers emanating from university centres in many parts of the continent. Imperialism was becoming a subject of serious and even passionate academic debate and scholarly dissertations. The Dar es Salaam debate, now published as a book by Tanzania Publishing House under the title *Debate on Class, State & Imperialism*, stands out. But other places like Ahmadu Bello

University and the Obafemi Owolowo University of Ife in Nigeria; Nairobi University in Kenya; and the Universities of Cape Coast and Ghana were emerging as centres of progressive thought. But even outside the University campuses, progressive debate was raging and it is not an accident that the *Journal of African Marxists* should emerge during the seventies.

Once again this new anti-imperialist resurgence was reflected in literature. For the writer from Mozambique, Angola, Guinea Bissau, his content and imagery were clearly derived from the active struggles of the people. Even in the countries that became independent in the fifties and the sixties, the writer started taking a more and more critical stand against the anti-national, anti-democratic, neo-colonial character of the ruling regimes. He began to connect these ills not just to the moral failings or otherwise of this or that ruler, but to the perpetuation of imperialist domination through the comprador ruling classes in Africa.

The writer in the seventies gradually began to take imperialism seriously. He was also against the internal classes, those new companies of profiteers that allied with imperialism. But the writer tried to go beyond just explanation and condemnation. One can sense in some of the writing of this period an edging towards the people and a search for new directions. The writer in the seventies was coming face to face with neo-colonialism. He was really a writer in a neo-colonial state. Further he was beginning to take sides with the people in the class struggle in Africa.

The writer who edged towards the people was caught in various contradictions. Where, for instance, did he stand in relation to the neo-colonial state in which he was a citizen, and within which he was trying to function?

A neo-colonial regime is, by its very character, a repressive machine. Its very being, in its refusal to break with the international and national structures of exploitation, inequality and oppression, gradually isolates it from the people. Its real power base resides not in the people but in imperialism and in the police and the army. To maintain itself it shuts off all venues of democratic expression. It, for instance, resorts to one-party rule, and since in effect the party is just a bureaucratic shell, this means resorting to one man rule, despotism a la Marquez's novel, *The Autumn of the Patriarch*! All democratic organizations are outlawed or else brought under the ruler, in which case they are emptied of any democratic life. Why then should the regime allow any democracy in the area of culture? Any democratic expression in the area of culture becomes a threat to such a regime's very peculiar brand of culture: the culture of silence and fear, run and directed from police cells and torture chambers.

[. . .]

The Writer in the Eighties

In the world, the struggle between democratic and socialist forces for life and human progress on the one hand, and the imperialist forces for reaction and death on the other is still going on and it is bound to become more fierce. Imperialism is still the enemy of human kind and any blow against imperialism whether in the Philippines, El Salvador, Chile, South Korea is clearly a blow for democracy and change. In Africa, the struggle of Namibian people and of South African/Azanian people will intensify. And as the Zimbabwean, Angolan, and Mozambican struggles took the African revolution a stage further than where it had been left by the FLN and the Kenya Land and Freedom Army in the fifties, in the same way the successful outcome of the Namibian and South African peoples' struggle will push the entire continent on to a new stage. In a special way, the liberation of South Africa is the key to the liberation of the entire continent from neo-colonialism.

With the neo-colonial states, the anti-imperialist alliance of democratic forces will intensify the struggle against the rule of the alliance of the comprador classes and imperialism. There will be more and more anti-imperialist coups in the Rawlings and Sankara type. There will be an increase in the Uganda type anti-neo-colonial guerrilla movements. There will be a greater and greater call and demand for a Pan-Africanism of the proletariat and the peasantry through their progressive democratic organizations. Each new stage in the struggle for real independence, democracy and socialism will have learnt from the errors of the previous attempts, successes and even failures. The main thing is that the eighties and the nineties will see the heightening of the war against neo-colonialism. For as in the days of colonialism, so now in the days of neo-colonialism, the African people are still struggling for a world in which they can control that which their collective sweat produces, a world in which they will control the economy, politics, and culture to make their lives accord with where they want to go and who they want to be.

But as the struggle continues and intensifies, the lot of the writer in a neo-colonial state will become harder and not easier. His choice? It seems to me that the African writer of the eighties, the one who opts for becoming an integral part of the African revolution, has no choice but that of aligning himself with the people: their economic, political and cultural struggle for survival. In that situation, he will have to confront the languages spoken by the people in whose service he has put his pen. Such a writer will have to *rediscover* the *real* language of struggle in the actions and speeches of his people, learn from their great heritage of orature, and above all, learn from their great optimism and faith in the capacity of human beings to remake their world and renew themselves. He must be part of the song the people sing as once again they take up arms to smash the neo-colonial state to complete the anti-imperialist national democratic revolution they had started in the fifties, and even earlier. A people united can never be defeated and the writer must be part and parcel of that revolutionary unity for democracy, socialism and the liberation of the human spirit to become even more human.

Author's note: The terms 'he' and 'his' as used above are not meant to denote the 'maleness' of the person. It should be read to indicate an individual person, whether male or female.

Chapter 24

The Writer and Responsibility

Breyten Breytenbach

I am particularly grateful for the chance to address the Dutch PEN Centre. You are probably aware of the fact that one of the purposes of imprisonment in South Africa is to isolate the prisoner from the outside world. (This, by the way, is largely true for all prisoners and detainees, including the so-called 'common criminals'.) In the case of a political prisoner everything is done to destabilize him, to keep him off balance: for instance, not only is any expression of outside support kept from him, but the authorities try hard to create the impression that he is forgotten, rejected even, by his friends, colleagues or comrades.

But prison is never a watertight world; it cannot be so. Even behind those walls life manifests itself, sometimes taking on strange shapes. And rumours of 'real' life in the 'real', 'outside' world do penetrate. Thus I learned at various times, in bits and snippets at least, of actions undertaken on my behalf by the PEN Club of several countries. I know that PEN International sent a delegate to South Africa in an attempt to intervene with the authorities.

Such manifestations of solidarity are indeed terrific morale boosters for the incarcerated people. It is a confirmation of other realities, other values, other commitments existing beyond the frontiers of the penal universe. Life does continue!

For what you did and what you attempted to do I wish to thank you. And for your ongoing concern for authors in difficulty, in whatever country they may be, I'd like to congratulate you. Permit me to remark that it is with this type of intervention, concerning specific people and within the framework of our communal craft and concerns as writers, that you have the most effect and obtain the best results.

I'd like to say a few words on the theme, a very extensive one of course, of 'The Writer, and Responsibility'; and then more specifically on the writer's responsibility within a given social and cultural context, and perhaps a little also on the writer's stance when it comes to international issues such as, for instance, censorship and the oppression of free thought, economic and cultural imperialism, genocide even, and Apartheid particularly. Obviously the writer's basic commitment is to the integrity of his own work; he acts first of all through

First published in *End Papers: Essays, Letters, Articles of Faith, Workbook Notes*, pp. 98–106. New York: Farrar, Straus & Giroux, 1986.

his work – it is his means of exploring himself, the network of his relationships, the objective world. I'm not ignoring this initial dimension; in fact, I think the writer's public actions form an extension of his private honesty or lack thereof.

You must forgive me if what I have to say at times sounds inevitably like a confession of faith. At this stage I'm not particularly interested in the cerebral debating of arguments. What's more, I cannot pretend to speak for anyone, I don't represent any group or school of thinking. I'm sure a few writers in South Africa, or even among you here, agree with some of my statements while fiercely disagreeing with others. And that is as it should be. All I'd like to do is to sketch my own position at this place and time.

A first conclusion obviously imposes itself: moral or political evaluations can never be used as literary criteria. We all know that 'good' writing can come out of profound dishonesty, decadence, treachery.

A second conclusion: a writer, any writer, to my mind has at least two tasks, sometimes overlapping; he is the questioner and the implacable critic of the mores and attitudes and myths of his society, but he is also the exponent of the aspirations of his people.

In the poor and colonized countries the writer plays a more visible role: faced with acute social and economic iniquities he is called upon to articulate the dreams and the demands of his people. From these contradictory responsibilities come the dichotomies of the writer's existence giving rise to so much tension and ambiguity. And from this flows the impossibility of the writer ever fitting in completely with any orthodoxy. Sooner or later he is going to be in disaccord with the politicians. He can be at times the expression of politics, even directly so, but the demands of his freedom and integrity may isolate him at other moments, may make him marginal. Call it the impotence and the glory of the writer if you wish!

And this holds true also for those societies and cultures where the writer is considered a 'cultural worker'. The highest and most difficult state of the writer is to be totally aware and self-questioning while contributing to the endless struggle for greater justice and more liberty. Yevgeny Zamyatin already claimed that writers should be heretics. 'Heretics', he wrote, 'are the only (bitter) remedy against the entropy of human thought . . . The world is kept alive only by heretics: the heretic Christ, the heretic Copernicus, the heretic Tolstoy. . .'

Yes, I too would want to wish with a Jan Campert 'that I could erect barricades between myself and the world' but I know that it is impossible.

There is in fact no Truth. We are too fragile and volatile for that; we work with too many uncertainties. There is rather the continual shaping of something resembling, poorly, provisionally, 'truth'.

I must try to situate myself more clearly. You are aware of the context within which any South African writer works, be he in the country or in exile. I am referring of course to Apartheid. But what does it mean to me personally?

Sometimes one is more impatient with one's friends than with one's enemies. We all agree that Apartheid is Evil. We often take the short cut. We oversimplify, we condemn out of hand. And perhaps sometimes we do it more out of consideration for the good of our own souls and not necessarily because we reject in a reasoned way the socio-political and economic (and cultural) exploitation, discrimination and humiliation of the history and the system that, inadequately, we call Apartheid. It is not so easy to wriggle out from under our responsibilities. Absolutism doesn't always imply absolution. In our simplicity we expose ourselves to the White masters – and to some Black lackeys too. Also, in our generalization we make it possible for some so-called 'allies' to oppose Apartheid while strengthening the foundations of the system. It is, as Mao might have said, like waving the red flag to combat the revolution.

Let me explain. You will find in the very cabinet of South African ministers people who claim to oppose Apartheid. And correctly so. In their prime objective to retain power they will abolish racial segregation. All they ask for is some 'understanding', the time to effect the necessary changes in an orderly fashion. Which foreign capitalist investor would disagree with them?

Many false impressions are created along the way of trying to improve their image and thus their respectability and thus their defendability. What we witness taking shape down there is in reality a controlled experiment in co-opting a number of non-Black politicians to bolster the present power structures against the Black majority. The real scenario is a militarist one; the strategy – against the so-called Total Onslaught (of Communism) – worked out by non-elected security 'experts'; the real power already in the hands of the military and of the political police. Meanwhile we shall hear more about South Africa being an outpost of Western culture, a bulwark against subversion, the strategic treasure house of the democratic powers, the economic turbine of the subcontinent. As the misery and the unrest elsewhere in the impoverished world deepen, more and more 'realists' will lend out their ears to this hogwash. Already American investment in South Africa had risen by 13.3 per cent in 1981 to 2.63 billion dollars and it is estimated that it had risen to 2.8 billion dollars in 1982. (These figures come from the US Department of Commerce.)

We should nevertheless have no illusions. Some of the structural changes being effected down there, such as the creation of the Bantustans, have already altered the landscape to the extent that any future solution of South Africa's problems will have to accommodate the changed and contaminated situation.

Yes, Apartheid remains a barbarity. But what I personally am more interested in is a feel of the grittiness, of the texture of everyday life. Here are a few recent examples.

It was revealed in the South African Parliament on 29 March this year that 722 'Coloureds' had been reclassified as 'Whites' between July 1981 and July 1982. That means, if they are employed by the state, that their salaries and pensions will now increase by 20 to 30 per cent. Seven Chinese were similarly 'upgraded'. They may now live in White zones, drink in any bar, send their children to the best schools. Fifteen 'Whites' were declared 'Indian' and three 'Coloured' – losing all the above privileges of course. Thirty-nine 'Coloureds' were changed to 'Indians'. One hundred and nine 'Blacks' were 'promoted' to 'Coloured', now no longer needing passbooks. Last year 135 people were caught and sentenced for 'immorality', that is mixed-race sex.

In the Transvaal the little village of Driefontein has been declared a 'black' spot; in terms of the government's resettlement policy all 5,000 inhabitants are to be displaced to a distant 'homeland'. (The village had been bought legally by a group of Africans in 1912.) On Saturday, 2 April, the village leader, Saul Mkhize, tried through his bullhorn to exhort a meeting of his people to remain calm, telling them that non-violence was the only solution. Two policemen arrested him for holding an 'illegal meeting'. In the ensuing confusion they shot and killed the old man.

It was announced in Parliament that 1,259 people have been killed by the police since 1976. These figures do not include people who died during the riots, nor those executed by the state. On an average 1,500 people per year are wounded by the officers of law and order during shooting incidents.

I cite these few examples to give you an indication of the tenor of everyday life in that bastion of democracy.

It is seen against this background that I, as a writer, growing through my own experiences, must take personal responsibility for my actions, all the while pursuing my journey on the two legs of theory and practice.

I subscribe to the cause of liberation and of majority rule in South Africa. At this juncture I believe I can best support that cause through my writing – and in not attempting to pull the wool over anyone's eyes. This is not an abstract idea I pursue (although I am committed ideologically to the transformation of the South African society) but the total sense of my life. I should like to see, through the pain and the hopes and the mistakes even of our struggle, the tempering of a truly *South African* culture, drawing its richness from the diversity of its origins – and I think it is gradually happening. The common roots are there: they need to be valorized. Even the common denominator, Apartheid, is there.

But I dispute the right of any orthodoxy or pressure group to tell me what and how I must write. My loyalty can be true only in my freedom to remain an agnostic.

I write mostly in Afrikaans. Now that I am relatively free to make my own choices I shall attempt to see to it that my work is handled by publishers who are not dominated by or in the pay of the Afrikaner Establishment. I cannot compromise on censorship in any way. If I cannot publish legally in South Africa, I shall try to explore other means of doing so.

I do not consider myself an Afrikaner; the definition, whichever way you turn it, has a political content with which I cannot identify. Even culturally I can't claim to be an Afrikaner. (I'm not particularly concerned about being a South African either; in fact I'm just a *bandiet*!). The Afrikaans language doesn't belong to the Afrikaners. I have no anguished feelings either way about its survival or its disappearance or its mutation. I recognize that it is fatally tainted and classified as the voice of the Master; I also know that it is a means of awareness and expression of astonishing beauty. But people will sing in whatever language they happen to dip their tongues into.

If I have any contribution to make to the changing of that tormented society it will have to be as a non-Black exile. My effectiveness inside South Africa, however tenuous, can be only within the White community. But I am isolated there. Although many White writers are against Apartheid, or rather the effects thereof, in varying degrees of disgust and anxiety, I do not know of any identifying with the Liberation Movement. (Admittedly, it would be suicidal to do so inside the country and it is completely unfair of us to expect them to be martyrs.)

The gulf created by Apartheid exists. The problems, although springing from one and the same source, are translated differently by the various population groups. If I were to deny this reality it would be a crass denial of class analysis.

The White writer is either a traitor or a hostage or a sell-out. In the deeply polarized South African environment he will be out of touch with some sector of the population wherever he may stand. In trying to heal yourself, in trying to recuperate some human dignity by spewing out Apartheid, you will find that it is a lonely business. But ultimately it is the only way to self-integration and possible brotherhood. Life is shitty enough as it is.

You, here in Holland, have been called upon to support the Cultural Boycott against South Africa. I should like to raise a few questions pertaining to that subject.

What can a Dutch writer do? What can PEN do? What exactly is the aim of a boycott? Who benefits from it? Who is touched by it? What is its effectiveness?

Let me say immediately that I support entirely the cancelling of all cultural links and exchanges between Holland and any official or officious or South African government-tolerated bodies. This is not something you can go back on, however much paper may be used by South African cultural organizations trying to cover the cracks in the ugly face of racist reality. You will have to be vigilant though. When they find it convenient the South African agents will break your ranks with the corrupting lure of money (big money too, as they have shown themselves capable of when buying sportsmen or journalists) or the equally tempting illusion of importance accorded to mediocre writers.

But the Dutch Cultural Boycott doesn't really make the headlines in South Africa. W. F. Hermans going there, for example, is locally perhaps a hotly disputed event – which may be what he intended to achieve – but nobody outside the restrained Afrikaner academic community cared or even knew about it. I doubt whether the authorities there saw his visit as an endorsement of their policies. Nevertheless, the man going there, fully aware of the implications of his visit as seen from this end, and Hermans is certainly not stupid, must be interpreted at the least as tolerating the set-up.

And apart from literature and some art collectors and museums down there acquiring the works of Dutch artists, what cultural exchanges have there really been?

I take it for granted that as concerned and informed Dutch writers you would want to express, through your positions and actions, abhorrence of racial discrimination. You would also want to show some form of support and solidarity with the oppressed majority, perhaps even an identification with the hunt for freedom led by the liberation organizations. Some of you may want, in the process of supporting action against the South African power élite, also to come to a clearer delineation of your own role and responsibilities as writers, not only with reference to South Africa, but in your own environment.

One must be clear about your motives and your means. In this equation cultural or collective guilt feelings have no place, I believe any support for the liberating of the South African people – in all the multiple devolutions and expressions it must have – implies the responsibility of at least knowing exactly what one is about.

Responsibility implies the freedom to be critical. Few positions are as demeaning as that of the 'fellow-traveller'. Too often the intellectual is a sheep, one of the bourgeoisie who, as Lenin pointed out, will make the revolution for us. All too often also the intellectual, ill at ease because of the contradictions of his condition, is hood-winked by the promise of 'playing an important role'.

The cause is a good one, the issues at stake and the implications (worldwide even) are momentous, encompassing our emotions as well as our reasoning and our interests; but we are dealing with political organizations employing political means for political goals. I repeat – the cause is noble: be entirely aware in your support however of both the ends and the means employed to attain those ends. Not so that you may be paternalistic in any way, but as responsible writers knowing the scope and the limitations of your actions.

I must insist that I find it totally unacceptable that any organization, however representative it may be, should decide what writing is to be allowed and diffused and what not. If you agree to that you must also accept potentially at least the tragedy of a Mandelstam or a Pasternak or a Solzhenitsyn. What do you do about Céline or a latterday Hemingway? What about a poet with the stature of Roy Campbell who ended up supporting Franco? And, closer to home, what about Mazisi Kunene who, as far as I know, is not at present in favour with the ANC?

The difficult balance to achieve is clarity of principle and purpose while refusing any oversimplification of the options. To insist on a blanket boycott of all literary work produced inside South Africa is politically stupid. It denotes a blindness to the reality of the situation there with all its cracks and interstices of freedom; it is furthermore a running away from your own responsibilities, taking the easy way out. You are denying to yourself the means of political action and of moral manoeuvre.

Athol Fugard's *Master Harold and the Boys* is at present being staged in Johannesburg. In a review, published internationally, I read:

> When the lights dimmed on the powerful last scene, in which the two Black waiters affirm their self-respect in the embrace of a slow, heart-rending foxtrot, roughly half the audience rose to give the play's three actors a standing ovation. The rest had yet to emerge from the private world of grief and loss into which the play appeared to have plunged them. Many, Blacks and Whites, were crying.

So what are the alternatives? It seems as if we are all waiting for the Apocalypse down there. I too am frustrated by the monolithic nature of the South African set-up, the fact that nothing seems to have any effect on the smooth surface of repression – at least not anything one may be able to do from here. But although you may not always realize it, some things have happened here. It may take years for an idea to come to fruition. I remember that we discussed, years ago already, with some Dutch friends present here, the need to get South African authors and artists, both in exile and inside the country, to meet and get to know one another. Well, we weren't the only ones thinking along those lines – I still have some correspondence pertaining to the matter – and eventually the meeting did take place. I also remember how particular attention was paid in Rotterdam, years ago too, to Zulu poetry. Over the years quite a few poets have participated there – Kunene, Pieterse, Kgotsitsile, Brutus, Serote. I remember discussing with Dutch students of Afrikaans the need to dissociate Dutch from Afrikaans, to see Afrikaans as just one African language among others – Swahili too was shaped by a non-African language, Arabic – and to shift the accent to *South African* literary studies. This concept, I believe, is no longer as foreign as it may have sounded then.

In South Africa I know of at least one university where a similar healthy development has taken place: Dutch is taught there as a totally separate foreign tongue, not only as the prehistory of Afrikaans.

I believe, in the question of a Cultural Boycott, that alternative links should be forged strengthening and amplifying the real voices of resistance in the country – always keeping in mind that these are the people being smothered either by censorship or other ways of harassment and suffocation.

I am not suggesting a dialogue with any official body, neither am I advocating the idea of keeping communication lines open in the hope of influencing the minds and hearts of the racists.

Of course, as far as selling books through official channels or exchanging lecturers, etc., are concerned – that should be totally out. But always remember that there are some brave people there who need your support, a few Dutch expatriates even; I'm thinking of one, for instance, who is instrumental in having most of the Black poetry inside published. They must be helped to survive.

Why not try to be more adventurous? Why not, for example, try to get good quality Dutch works to prisoners in South Africa? You may not succeed but at least you would have made a point. Protest actions, standpoints decided upon here, should be brought to the individual attention of the South African authors themselves. The crux of the matter is that as far as the Whites are concerned you can really influence only those writers and academics who look nostalgically to Holland for approval – rather in the way the Calvinists there are sensitive to the authority and the influence of the Calvinists here. Why not attempt to have books against Apartheid published there? You should in any event try to assure that critical works printed there, and most likely banned, are translated and made available outside. It is also a form of protection for the dissident writers.

It is even more important to help create the possibilities of printing here in the original languages publications banned there, and to find ways of getting these back into South Africa.

You see, there is no easy solution to the dilemma South Africa poses, neither for me as a non-Black exile, nor for you as sympathetic Dutch writers.

Chapter 25

Dissidence and Creativity

Nawal El Saadawi

What Is Dissidence?

I have tried to find the Arab word for dissidence. In Arabic we say protest (*al-ihtijaj*), or opposition (*al-mu'arada*), or disputation/litigation (*al-mukhasama*), or to rebel (*yatamarradu*), or to revolt (*yathuru*). But each of these words has a different meaning according to the context in which the dissidence or struggle takes place. For me the word *struggle* in Arabic (*alnidal*) sheds most light on the meaning of dissidence. The *dissident* in Arabic (*al-munadil*) means the fighter who cooperates with others to struggle against oppression and exploitation, whether personal or political.

I believe there is no dissidence without struggle. We cannot understand dissidence except in a situation of struggle and in its location in place and time. Without this, dissidence becomes a word devoid of responsibility, devoid of meaning.

Demystifying Words

Can I be dissident without being creative? Can I have the passion and knowledge required to change the powerful oppressive system of family and government without being creative? What do we mean by creativity? Can we be creative if we obey others or follow the tradition of our ancestors? Can we be creative if we submit to the rules forced upon us under different names: father, God, husband, family, nation, security, stability, protection, peace, democracy, family planning, development, human rights, modernism, or postmodernism?

These fifteen terms are used globally and locally by both the oppressors and the oppressed. I chose them because we read or hear them all the time, whether we live in Egypt, the United States, Brazil, or India. They constitute a large part of the language of imperialism and oppression. But they are often used by the oppressed in a different meaning, in the fight against imperialism and oppression.

First published in *The Dissident Word: The Oxford Amnesty Lectures 1995*, ed. Chris Miller, pp. 151–60, 163–4. New York: Basic Books, 1996.

For example the word *protection* seems a very positive word. British colonialism in Egypt was inaugurated by a military occupation in 1882.[1] It hindered our economic and cultural development for more than seventy years. Instead of having the freedom to develop our agriculture to satisfy our needs, we were obliged to produce cotton for the needs of British industry. The result was increasing poverty in Egypt and increasing wealth in Britain. This was done in the name of protection, not of colonialism or exploitation. The British used military power and terrorism to achieve these ends. The rulers of Egypt, the khedives, submitted to British power.[2] The royal family and the ruling class collaborated with the colonizers to protect their joint interests. Egyptians who challenged the government or the British were labelled dissidents, communists, or nationalists, and were killed, imprisoned, dismissed from their work, or forced to live in exile or starvation.

Today the neocolonizers do not use the word protection anymore. The colonized people in Egypt, Africa, India, and elsewhere have seen through it. The word protection was demystified through people's living experience; protection to us in Egypt now means colonialism. Another word therefore had to be used by the neocolonizers. It had to be just as positive and innocent, but more progressive. So the word *development* came into use in the early seventies. Many people in Egypt and other so-called developing countries were deceived by this word, but the results of development proved to be even more pernicious than the results of protection.

Much more money traveled from the developing countries (or third world) to the first world than in the opposite direction. The gap between the rich and poor increased both locally and globally. Even the United Nations Organization could not hide these facts. They appeared in statistics and in UN reports written by field workers in Africa, Asia, and Latin America.

In 1979 I was one of the UN field workers in Ethiopia. I worked with the UN for two years, then I left. I discovered that development projects promoted by the UN and Western corporations and agencies hindered development in Egypt and Africa. They were a disguised form of economic genocide, more pernicious than military genocide because they killed more people but were not as visible as blood shed in war.

When the word development was demystified the neocolonizers shifted their terms. The new term is *structural adjustment*, now being promoted by the World Bank. Few people understand this word. But when structural adjustment is implemented in Africa and other parts of the so-called South, the effect is no different from that of protection or development. The result is even greater poverty in the poor South, and greater riches for the rich North. To name just one example: from 1984 to 1990 Structural Adjustment Policies (SAPs) led to the transfer of US$178 billion from the South to the commercial banks in the North.

Another neocolonial word is *aid*. It is another myth that is becoming demystified. Many countries in the South have started to raise the slogan: Fair Trade Not Aid. Here is one example from Egypt: between 1975 (when American aid to Egypt began) and 1986, Egypt imported commodities and services from the US to a total of US$30 billion. During the same period Egypt exported to the US commodities worth only US$5 billion.

Egyptians who stand up and challenge the global neocolonialist powers and their collaborators in local governments are labelled dissident, communist, nationalist, or feminist. They are punished according to the effectiveness of their dissidence; this ranges from losing their job and censorship of their writings, to prison and even death.

In Egypt, under Sadat, we had to demystify some of the words and slogans he used. One of his slogans was The Open Door Policy. It proved to be no more than opening the doors to a neocolonial assault on the economy of Egypt and its culture. American products (Coca Cola, cigarettes, nylon clothes, McDonald's, makeup, TV programs, films, and so on) invaded Egypt, destroying local production. Sadat inaugurated his rule with what he described as a "corrective revolution." The corrective revolution in fact was no more than a correction in the flow of money to ensure that it ended up in the pockets of the ruling groups that came to power after Nasser's death in 1970.

Mutual Responsibility

Our struggles are becoming more and more difficult. They need more and more creativity. There are always new words emerging that we have to demystify, words such as: peace, democracy, human rights, privatization, globalization, multiculturalism, diversity, civil society, nongovernmental organizations (NGOs), cultural difference, liberation theology, religious fundamentalism, postmodernism, and others. We need to discover new ways of exposing the paradoxes or double meanings in the many new and old words that are endlessly repeated. This needs greater knowledge and more understanding of modern and postmodern techniques of oppression and exploitation.

We cannot acquire this knowledge through books, through formal education or the mass media. All of them are controlled by the global and local powers of domination and exploitation, and they help to veil our brains with one myth after another. We have to acquire this knowledge by ourselves, from our own experience in the daily struggle against those powers globally, locally, and in the family. This is creativity. It is inspired and stimulated by our living our own lives and not by copying theories of struggle from books.

Every struggle has its own unique theory inseparable from action. Creativity means uniqueness: innovation. Discovering new ways of thinking and acting, of creating a system based on more and more justice, freedom, love, and compassion. If you are creative, you must be dissident. You discover what others have not yet discovered. You may be alone at the beginning, but somehow you feel responsible toward yourself and others; toward those who are not yet aware of this discovery, who share your struggle with the system; toward those who have lost hope and have submitted.

Can there be any struggle or dissidence without responsibility toward oneself and others? Is there any human who does not struggle against oppression? We are all born dissidents to a greater or a lesser degree. But during the last two years I have ceased to consider myself a dissident. I have been a dissident since childhood. My name was put on the Egyptian government's black list in 1962. I had to face censorship. I lost my job in 1972, our health association and magazine were banned in 1973. In 1981, I was put in jail and in 1991 our women's association, AWSA (Arab Women's Solidarity Association), and magazine *Noon* were banned. In 1992, my life was threatened and security guards were placed around my house.

Now I am a visiting professor in Duke University in the United States. I teach creativity and dissidence to students. But can you really teach these things? All you can do is to open up closed doors; undo what education did; encourage students to discover their own dissidence in their own lives.

Dissidence and Distance

I watch what is happening in Egypt from a distance. In November 1994, floods in upper Egypt left thousands of people homeless. I received a letter from a young woman student, who lives in Cairo. Her family lives in a village in Luxor (one of the places hit by the floods). She said:

I went to visit my family and my village when I heard about the floods. Thank God my father and mother survived but they were left with no home, no shelter. The authorities were busy with a big tourist show, busy preparing to mount the opera *Aida*, in front of the Temple of Hatshepsut. Priority was given to satisfying the needs of American tourists and not the homeless thousands. Each tourist sat on a blanket to warm his seat while he was watching the show. My family received no blankets to sleep in the cold nights. They lost their cane sugar farm because the local authorities took it over together with other farms to build roads and bridges for tourists, so that they could reach Hatshepsut's Temple easily. Four hundred acres of cane sugar were taken by force from homeless people. Other farms were taken from people to secure a space around the open *Aida* stadium (a security belt to protect the tourists from the so-called fundamentalists). The average yield of each acre is 50 tons, the price of each ton is 90 pounds constituting a loss of about 2 million pounds to the people. Two other bridges were built on Asjun canal for tourists to cross on their way to the show, and more farms were taken from people. This will result in an acute drop in the local production of cane sugar. An American company called Orascom built the bridges and the stadium in collaboration with Onsy Saweeris who opened a McDonald's eating place as well. The waters of the flood were quickly pumped out of the graves and temples of the dead pharaohs. The local authorities were boasting to the tourists that the waters did not spend one night in Siti the First Temple in Korana, or rather, that Siti the First did not sleep one night in the waters. But thousands of homeless people were left to the floods with no shelter. In front of the Karnak temple there was another big tourist show. One thousand five hundred girls and boys danced for one month and half. Each one of them received ten pounds. The police were everywhere to protect the tourists and the dancers. The fundamentalists are against music shows and dances. The tourists call them terrorists. But the tourists are terrorists too. They frightened everybody, even the local authorities, who were so afraid of the fundamentalists that they destroyed hundreds of cane sugar farms.

They said that the fundamentalists used these cane sugar farms as hiding places. My father and mother are among these people. I do not know how I can help them. I have to go to Cairo and let a friend of mine who is a journalist in *Ruz al-yusif* magazine write about it. Our government does not help anybody unless the journalists write about them, or the TV or CNN broadcast something about their story. During the population conference in Cairo last September, the CNN showed something about female circumcision. After that everybody in the government and in the media was speaking about female circumcision. Even the Mufti, the highest Islamic authority in Egypt, wrote in *Ruz al-Yusif* opposing this operation. The Sheik of Al-Azhar also wrote in the same magazine, but he supported the operation and said that it is an Islamic duty. I will send you a copy of this issue. It was published on 17 October 1994. I hope that the government listens to the Mufti and prohibits the circumcision of girls, but the government is afraid of the fundamentalists, who force the people to circumcise their girls and to veil them.

After the show of *Aida* people caught an old tourist with a girl dancer hiding in Karnak temple. The girl was veiled. The tourist was very drunk and he told the people that he is more excited by the veil than by belly dancing.

The fundamentalists are becoming more and more harsh on girls and women. They prevent them from going out even to school. They tell the girls that they are protecting them from being raped by tourists.

In the Cairo International Population Conference I met a young woman in the AWSA workshop. I was glad to know from her that you have started an AWSA branch in North America. Her name is Amina Ayad. She read the paper you prepared on AWSA. It made me aware of the fact that increasing poverty in Egypt is due to the development forced on us by the West rather than the high fertility of Egyptian women.

I used to come to the AWSA weekly seminars and to read *Noon* magazine. I met you many times. You may remember my face but you do not know my name. I was not a member of AWSA but I was very sad when the government banned it in Egypt in 1991. I read in *Al-ahali* that you have taken the government to court. But the court is part of the government. I have no hope in this government. Nobody is helping my father and mother. I have to leave them and go back to my school in Cairo. I took your address in America from Amina Ayad. She told me that she met you in the University of Washington. You may know someone in the CNN who can broadcast something about my family in Luxor. If this happens the government will hurry up and build them a home or a shelter or at least give them blankets. It is very cold at night in Luxor, more cold than Cairo. I am crying while writing to you.

In Durham, I am ten thousand miles from Egypt and from women and men whose struggles I have shared: against British colonialism, Egyptian governments, neocolonialism, fanatical religious and political groups, the oppressive family code, and other forms of oppression in our private and public lives. In Durham I look at my country from a distance. Sometimes I lose hope. But we cannot be dissidents without hope. We cannot be dissidents from a distance or if we are not in the struggle. When we struggle we do not lose hope. We feel responsible toward ourselves and the others.

[. . .]

Dissidence and Heroism

The creative dissident is not a hero or heroine. He or she should be the first to be killed in the battle. The concept of heroism or leadership differs from that of dissidence. In battles the leader is often the last to be killed, while unknown soldiers are shot at the front. The dissident is not a hero or leader. The hero is worshipped as a demigod, but the dissident is punished and cursed like Satan (*Iblis* in Arabic). The devil is responsible for what is called evil. Since the evolution of monotheism, Satan has become the symbol of dissidence, of disruption of the existing order.

The devil is responsible for disasters, defeat, and misery. But the devil has no power relative to God. Though God has all the power, he is not responsible for any disaster, defeat, or misery. The split between power and responsibility has lain at the core of oppression and exploitation from the advent of slavery to this day. Dissidence is the antithesis of power divorced from responsibility for the misery of people. Responsibility does not mean aid or charity; it means trying to eradicate the causes of poverty and oppression. The concept of charity or aid is as pernicious to others as the concept of replacing the other's language or mind.

For creative dissidence does not believe in the dichotomy "god-devil" or "self-other." Both are to be challenged and criticized equally. This means directing a critical gaze at the self as well as at the other.

If we wanted to translate these ideas into postmodern language, we might say that the deheroization of self and other is at the core of real dissidence: of radical ethics, an aesthetics of creativity, or a critical ontology of self and other. Real dissidence avoids lapsing into the reverse essentialism of a cult of self or the other. It also avoids one-way reflexive self-monitoring by including the other in this process. It is thus that the analytical links between ourselves and our social context are maintained.

[. . .]

Notes

1   Egypt was declared a "protectorate" in 1914, when Britain went to war with Turkey; it had been under English "administration" since the 1882 invasion, the pretext for which had been anti-European demonstrations. – *Ed.*
2   The title "khedive" was that of viceroy under Ottoman suzerainty. – *Ed.*

Chapter 26

Culture Beyond Color?
A South African Dilemma

Zoë Wicomb

In Bessie Head's novel *A Question of Power*, there is a rare moment of hilarity when a Danish development worker in Botswana proudly makes the following comment about Denmark: "In our country culture has become so complex, this complexity is reflected in our literature. It takes a certain level of education to understand our novelists. The ordinary man cannot understand them.... There's a whole lot of novelists no one can understand." South Africa, too, is extremely complex, but then we do not produce much by way of literature, and when we do our writing-from-the-roots movement recommends that everyone understand it, including the illiterate. The draft document of the new Federation of South African Cultural Organizations (FOSACO), after numerous references to common nationhood and national pride, insists that cultural workers, including oral storytellers, have a central role to play in the reconstruction of the country and demands that the constitution guarantee cultural rights. The protection of the arts in the New South Africa will not then protect works from being understood but aims for broad cultural development and conservation of our cultural heritage. Respect for our tradition, which the New South Africa, frightened by its own newness, invokes almost as often as it does the imagined community of nation, will ensure that our oral and written literature stays alive.

Given this central role in the New South Africa, writers, also known for their knowledge of the future, are often asked what its writing will be like. In a sense the answer is already inscribed in a description of writing from the old South Africa, to which the exciting new writing would be diametrically opposed: there will be no protest writing, no stereotypes of idle madams lounging at swimming pools and attended by flagging servants, no missionary English, no patronizing publishers or critics waxing lyrical about our least attempts, and much experimentation with new forms. But I fear that we will be disappointed. What my list does not make explicit is that it speaks of black writing. It cannot speak of an interracial culture; the New South Africa is too much like the old and is therefore necessarily a racial affair.

First published in *Transition* 60 (1993): 27–32

Our new society remains umbilically linked to the matrix of apartheid so that parturition is a slow affair. Since we are shaped by race-specific conditions, the protracted and bewildering weaning from the old is radically different for different racial groups. Moreover, we have all become rather perversely attached to apartheid. How will black people, long accustomed to dispossession and deprivation, adjust to a new condition of not being racial victims? Our chant of we-the-oppressed-black-majority with its moral upper hand has at times a curious ring of comfort, since it absolves us from taking responsibility for our own condition, precisely because our more assertive cries have never had any perlocutionary effect. How will we transform that chant, invent a new language for reconstructing ourselves to replace the fixed syntagmas of the discourse of oppression? And will our writing be about these kinds of painful psychological adjustments? I have no idea, and there seems little point in describing that which hasn't happened. What does seem clear is that an interracial culture is a long way off – that to think of an achromatic writing is simply premature, if not altogether a mistake.

My experience recently of attempting to judge the interracial Bessie Head/Alex la Guma Fiction Award says something, I think, about the politics of culture. These anonymous manuscripts were not only easily identified in terms of race, they were all about race, and our criteria in a context of reconstruction cannot ignore race. To imagine our society as achromatic, as an interracial competition would suggest, seems a serious anachronism that can do little more than perpetuate inequities. After years of underdevelopment by apartheid there can surely be no such thing, since white writers with their cultural and linguistic capital will necessarily walk off with the prizes, and to award them to less competent black writers for trying hard is no solution. The response that one should recognize and reward potential, that natural ability, genius, and talent will shine through, is of course misguided. Linguistic research has shown that there is no such thing as a literary language that certain people somehow have access to; there is only language which a writer will comfortably use and abuse to her own advantage. In our situation, where apartheid conditions have militated against the linguistic development of black people, both in the imposition of European languages and the neglect of education, the function of the literary prize becomes obvious. Not only is it inappropriate or inadequate as a means of encouraging writing, but it actively perpetuates inequity by rewarding those who have been privileged.

To speak of the politics of a culture is to speak of the ways in which the culture represents itself, the structures that privilege certain forms of representation and the means by which such forms are legitimated. The National Arts Policy Plenary (NAPP), a cultural Convention for a Democratic South Africa (CODESA), is currently bringing together politically diverse cultural groups to formulate recommendations for arts policies, structures, and funding mechanisms, and it will no doubt play a significant part in establishing the cultural politics of the New South Africa. The NAPP's draft document does not explicitly address our official resistance culture, with its conservative appeal to tradition and its privileging of the documentary; its broad endorsements of freedom of expression cannot, however, guarantee the covert replacement of ANC resistance culture with another set of prescriptions or, at best, predilections of those in control. In many ways it does not matter that structures exercise pressure on individual production: culture, which can be tautologically defined as that which already is, ensures a growing gap between what is actually produced and what legislative bodies imagine it ought to produce.

What does matter and what literary arbiters so often forget is that writing is made of the common mundane material of language. Far more basic than Virginia Woolf's room of her own and so many pounds per year as a necessary condition for writing is the question of literacy and education, and the material conditions of production predict a dismal future for writing in South Africa. Where illiteracy is high and educational opportunities narrow, people simply will not, cannot write. The divided system of apartheid is still in place when schooling for black children, administered by the segregated Department of Education and Training, is a brutalizing experience of fighting for space in overcrowded buildings with impossible teacher-pupil ratios. Attempts made by frustrated pupils, who are being taught outdoors or in a "platoon system" of shifts, to occupy empty school buildings in white areas have been met with police defense of this property of the white Department of Education and Schooling. The government continues with its "rationalization" program, by which it means closing down schools and making teachers redundant. There are no jobs for black teachers who graduate at the end of this year.

It is no accident that the most vibrant cultural production among black people is in the visual arts, where poorly educated artists produce works that have more in common with Western postmodernism than with that mythical referent we so fondly think of as traditional Africa. I am thinking of Derek Nxumalo or illiterate artists like Chickenman Mkhize and Tito Zungu, who engage directly with writing and with language as social semiotic. Their images have in common an interest in issues of communication and their orthographic inscription in the geo-social terrain: Nxumalo's roads, railways, road signs, and place names constitute the physical planes of a curious rural-urban landscape, the world(s) inhabited by the black work force. The role of language in the culture is encoded in the socio-semantic exchange between linguistic and visual information where, for example, toponymy and topography are linked in bold signs of mountain names that visually replace the referent. Mkhize roughly copies "found" language in both Zulu and English in a typically illiterate hand and with no regard for word breaks onto placards balanced on a crude circle of wire. These three-dimensional objects consisting of triangle with rudimentary image above a rectangle of text resemble road signs that not only explore writing as visual information but invite us to make meaning at the intersection of image and text. Zungu started making art by decorating letters that his migrant workmates would send home to the Bantustans. His images of airplanes, ocean liners, trains, and cityscapes communicate to rural people the language of the metropolis. As an act of communication, the images covering the private letters become tropes of desire that speak loudly of access and exclusion. Included in the meticulous detail of Zungu's drawings are the linguistic signs of industrial enterprise such as "PTY LTD."

Concern with literacy and the symbolic power of language can be visually articulated in challenging works by artists in a way that cannot be explored in writing, which relies on linguistic competence. So it seems strange to be talking about literary production when to learn to read and write involves jostling and struggling within an educational system that offers no alternative to the brutal conditions of the township. If we think more broadly of culture, the way in which people behave, then it may be more appropriate to talk about our ravaged culture of violence. Where other countries speak hopefully about the dominant culture being regenerated from below, from the marginalized everyday culture of the people, we can only remain silent. Our corrupt and sterile official culture of apartheid has nothing to offer; our everyday culture has in turn been brutalized by it. In order to discuss the polite subject of literature, we may first have to speak about the unspeakable, and I have in mind the Afrikaner cultural activity of the *braaivleis*, the bonhomie of the barbecue, translated into township necklacing, the burning of human beings who are *impimpis* or traitors to the state.

Rian Malan in *My Traitor's Heart* describes his investigation of a *braaivleis*, a "profound cultural ritual," where drunken jolly-japing by the side of the swimming pool includes the torture of a black man. Malan describes

> That quintessentially South African tableau of braaivleis, rugby, sunny skies, and torture. It was all so fucking, heartbreakingly traditional. Dennis Moshweshwe died a completely traditional South African death. There is even a traditional word for it in the Afrikaans language: he died of a kafferpak, meaning a "kaffir hiding", a brutal beating of the sort whites have been administering to blacks since the day we set foot on this continent.

Malan's narrative is partly framed as an act of translation. The story of Moshweshwe's death is told by his girlfriend to a black journalist, Eugene, who translates it into English. Malan's account of the actual torture is told in a stilted language in which is embedded its history of actual speech, translation, and the author's repetition/translation into writing. This discursive rewording in its successive forms raises issues of what George Steiner calls "the topology of culture," by which he means that cultural expression is characterized by metamorphic repetitions. We do not have access to the necessary transformations through which Malan's story has passed, but the translation can be seen as a model for the "rewording" of *braaivleis* as necklacing, where a number of invariants underpin these cultural activities.

The most obvious recursive feature is the act of burning as a communal activity; necklacing, like the *braaivleis*, is never a private affair. Both activities are marked by the iconography of postindustrial culture: the swimming pool (itself a wry transformation from the veld) is topologically rewritten as the waste from another coveted marker of bourgeois culture, the motor car, the discarded tire that is placed around the victim's neck. Both originate in the need to survive: Boers trekking from British domination relied on shooting buck and eating the roasted meat in the open veld; necklacing eliminates those who endanger the community by spying for the government. Necklacing then is about displacing Boer culture both physically and symbolically. It is about positioning: placing the victim as other within an isolating circle of fire and outside of the community; replacing the decorative necklace with the destructive tire, a symbolic reminder to victims of where they have placed themselves as they embraced the enemy with its lure of lucre; and positioning the necklacers above such treachery.

Amid hunger and homelessness, even the piffling amount offered to individuals by the South African Police is hard to resist, and the hungry, homeless, and outraged communities respond with acts that challenge our liberal humanist assumptions. Necklacing does not tell us about communities pitted against each other, but about cohesion within communities who take collective responsibility for such a death and who honor the dead with sympathetic ululations as if it were a natural one. The barbarism of such cultural activity speaks of a topological process, a generative transformation in the barbarism of official white culture. Necklacing responds to the countless deaths in the townships recorded as unrest-related and therefore not worthy of investigation, deaths caused by the agents of government who use *impimpis* to destabilize black communities. The "official" status of necklacing was confirmed in a recent news report of its use in Maputo, where the community used burning tires as punishment for theft, yet another transmutation of our export culture.

The question of what kind of literature such a culture will produce cannot take priority. Legislation on the arts, the well-meaning documents produced by our cultural organizations, will only lead to shrewd investments by those who already have cultural capital, unless we address the question of literacy, the raw material for producing poetry. And how can a literary culture be interracial if it conducts its business in a minority language and its minority dialect of standard English that few have access to? Without a decent, compulsory, multilingual system of education for all, we cannot move toward the national interracial culture of which our policy documents or euphonic conference titles speak. We need a radical pedagogy, a level of literacy that will allow our children to read works of literature that will politicize them into an awareness not only of power, but of the equivocal, the ambiguous, and the ironic which is always embedded in power. We need a radical pedagogy that will sensitize those whose privilege has blinded them to the ironies of power. Only then can we speak of an interracial culture of readers and writers who are not passive consumers of culture, but rather who interrogate received views, who interrogate the magisterial discourse of the New South Africa and its cultural institutions, and who above all interrogate the fixed positions that we have allowed ourselves to adopt and assign to others in our practice of necklacing. And with competent readers, who knows, we may even develop a way of reading, which is to say disambiguating, those complex and incomprehensible Danish works.

Chapter 27

In Praise of Exile

Nuruddin Farah

When I was younger and of a more romantic cast of mind, I had a love affair with the Somali language, whose orthography was then no older than an infant with teething troubles. Alas, the affair didn't last long. I had been in the Soviet Union, touring that enormous country as a guest of the Writers' Union, while my novel was being published in weekly installments by the daily newspaper in Mogadiscio. The paper's editor received a telephone call from a member of the censorship board, who told him to discontinue publication. When I was informed of this turn of events by an official of the Somali Embassy in Moscow, the news didn't disturb me. Rather, I was pleased, although at the time I had no idea why.

Infused with unprecedented calm and self-confidence, I made a number of unnecessary stopovers, like those of the mythical chameleon in the African story of creation. I gave myself a week in Budapest, another in Cairo. When I flew into Somalia, I was pregnant with ideas for the novel which was to become, in Somalia, my most well-known work – *Sweet & Sour Milk*.

I should mention that by then I had published a number of short stories, plays, a novella, and *From a Crooked Rib* (in English). I had just completed my second novel, *A Naked Needle*, and posted it to my publishers in London. The result of all this was that I told friends and acquaintances that my novel in Somali was of no relevance to the political changes taking place in the country (a statement with which the pro- and anti-Siyad Barre factions agreed). Abandoning it altogether, I got down to *Sweet & Sour Milk*.

Except for *A Naked Needle* (which, I am pleased to say, is out of print), all my major writing has taken place outside Somalia, beginning with *From a Crooked Rib*, which I wrote when I was a second-year student at a university in India. For me, distance distills; ideas become clearer and better worth pursuing. I like to place an intellectual and a physical distance between myself and what I am writing. By writing several drafts of a novel, and not publishing it directly, I have sought to achieve the distance which I so badly need. With-drawals from the humdrum of everyday obsessions, anthropological reality, and self-isolations enable me to extract from life's mundanities the essence of a graphic narrative.

First published in *Literature in Exile*, ed. John Glad, pp. 64–7. Durham and London: Duke University Press, 1990.

Indeed, I did my first published effort, a novella, while hospitalized in 1965, recovering from an operation I thought I wouldn't survive. Alone in a private ward and away from home, I felt grown-up, a man endowed with a voice seeking articulation.

We Somalis are a loving lot and we are a physical people; we touch noisily, and we talk a great deal. Myself, I have a morbid dislike of crowds and loathe coming into bodily contact with more than one person at a time. My attention span, when someone else is speaking, is of a brief duration. In the years I lived in Somalia, I remember agonizing over my privacy and avoiding friends and relations who wished to talk and talk and talk.

While writing *A Naked Needle* and doing occasional pieces for the newspapers, I had no place of my own – not even a room in the family home. I discovered that you couldn't plot the overthrow of a tyrannical regime from your mother's home – a home crowded with elder brothers and younger sisters.

One of the pleasures of living away from home is that you become the master of your destiny, you avoid the constraints and limitations of your past and, if need be, create an alternative life for yourself. That way everybody else becomes *the other*, and you the center of the universe. You are a community when you are away from home – the communal mind, remembering. Memory is active when you are in exile, and it calls at the most awkward hour, like a baby waking its parents at the crack of dawn.

Before my ninth year, I was conscious of a gulf existing between myself and my parents, a gulf as wide as the distance separating the oral and written traditions, the one theirs, the other mine. For my parents the written word had a magic relevance on a par with the Holy Scriptures. And so, when the proofs of *Crooked Rib* arrived and I showed them to my mother, there was a dubious mixture of excessive delight and sadness in her eyes. One of my sisters narrated to my mother Ebla's story, translating it into Somali. My mother's reaction was: "But this happens every day, and Ebla's life is as common as sandstorms in Mogadiscio." In retrospect, I can only conclude that to her the ordinary was of no subliminal significance. The person from an oral tradition turns to the written tradition to gain access to an exalted feeling of awareness, similar to the ecstasy of a dervish chanting the Almighty's names of praise. In other words, there was no mileage in the ordinary, no magic. A writer depicting humdrum realities is comparable to a prophet incapable of performing miracles in which mountains are dislodged and rivers are turned into roads. This leads us to the notion of exile in the *Koran*.

The notion of exile is central to many faiths. In almost all of them, the prophet bearing God's message starts from a position of exile, of isolation, temptation, and meditation. The Muslim era, Hijrah, begins with the Prophet Mohammed's date of departure from Mecca. Adam's ejection, together with Eve, from paradisiac delight is where it all begins. My novels are about states of exile: about women shivering in a cruel, cold world ruled by men; about the commoner denied justice; about a torturer tortured by guilt, his own conscience; about a traitor betrayed.

However, in this prophetless age, in the Africa of inefficient dictatorships, something extraordinary, in Somali terms, occurred: I published *Sweet & Sour Milk*, a novel which made clearer, in a magical-realistic metaphor, a phenomenon known but not written about. Somalis – both those belonging to the oral and those belonging to the written traditions – began taking my works seriously, and my novel became the most talked about and read book in the country.

But I could not have written it in Somalia. For in the early days of Siyad Barre's rule, there was a great deal of applause, a noisier-than-thou clapping of hands; there was also a pronounced sense of self-adulation and self-congratulation. Since I suffer from agoraphobia, I was never part of these crowds. I spent my spare time writing. I wrote in longhand at night, only to type the same at two in the afternoon, when Mogadiscio was having its siesta. I worked in my mother's living room, tucked away from curious neighbors and the National Security paranoia.

Worried about my safety, my London publishers wouldn't release *A Naked Needle*, which I wanted published while I was still living in Somalia. In the meantime, friends, makeshift ministers in Siyad Barre's cabinet, and foreign diplomats whom I met at cocktail parties all wondered if I was writing about the "revolution." The then minister of higher education and culture (now in detention) suggested that I record the nation's historical turning point in the glowing words of a truly inspired work of fiction. I recall saying that I hadn't the time, that I had been deafened by the loudness of the applause and blinded by the dust the marchers had stirred. The minister then made an oblique reference to my novel, the publication of which had been canceled by the censors. I think he described it as "irrelevant" – to the political happenings in the country.

To "write a truly inspired work of fiction" about Somalia, I had to leave the country. If I hadn't, in all probability I would have spent many years in detention centers (prison being another form of exile). Maybe I would have been supplied with plenty of time to plot my novels, but no pens and no opportunity for publication. Maybe I wouldn't have written much; definitely my manner would not have been as confident and detached. Being away from home has provided me with the time to pursue my profession, that of a writer.

Chapter 28

The African Writer's Experience of European Literature

D. Marechera

My first contact with English Literature was at school, and later at university. I enjoyed it but detested having to work at it. The choice of texts – ranging from Chaucer to D. H. Lawrence and James Joyce – was unimaginative, especially to a student who was inclined to disagree with everything and everybody. I would, with Jorge Louis Borges, have written a dissertation on the refutation of Time itself. I wrote my essays and tried to insult (privately) English Literature by crossing the Channel on a translation ferry to continental Europe.

Translators have served me well. I refer to such as Christopher Middleton who did a good translation of Hölderlin; to Kenneth Northcott who translated Gotthold Lessing's *Von Barnhelm*; to P. K. Stone who rendered Laclos into English; to H. Sloman who did Guy de Maupassant; to J. M. Cohen who did Rabelais; to Stephen Heath at Cambridge who has done singular service to Roland Barthes. This is to name only a few of those translators I have had to depend on. Though I was taught French and Latin at school, I have been anglicized enough to stubbornly insist that a foreigner is somebody who does not know English and whose language is not worth knowing.

From early in my life I have viewed literature as a unique universe that has no internal divisions. I do not pigeon-hole it by race or language or nation. It is an ideal cosmos co-existing with this crude one. I had a rather grim upbringing in the ghetto and have ever since tried to deny the painful reality of concrete history. If, as it is said, we all have something to hide, then my whole life has been an attempt to make myself the skeleton in my own cupboard. If brightness can fall from the air, then, as with Heinrich Heine, poetry is the art of making invisibility visible. Translating the literary imagination into fact may perhaps make writers acknowledged legislators. It becomes a question of perspective, almost of optics. If I am looking at something, and I am conscious of myself looking, does that affect what I see? Can I learn to experience the world from that quality in us which is the source of dreams?

First published in *Zambezia* 14.2 (1987): 99–105.

It is Pirandello whose plays torture out of us the shadowline between illusion and reality, in particular his *Henry IV* and *Six Characters in Search of an Author*. Eugene Ionesco, especially in his play *Rhinoceros*, sets himself the same task. He goes beyond Pirandello in that for him internal corruption leads to actual physical transformation. Here we are in Ovid's territory of "metamorphosis", which centuries later Franz Kafka was to depict as a literal fact. Such transformations occur again and again in the work of the Nigerian, Amos Tutuola, whose *Palmwine Drinkard* the Welsh poet, Dylan Thomas, quite justly acclaimed as a masterpiece. To *see* takes time; and within time are countless transmutations. Therefore, the evidence of our own eyes is always provisional; therefore, the element of fantasy, in terms of metamorphosis, becomes the only fact we are truly capable of. To know that one can be anything at any instant is to liberate oneself. Motive no longer matters; the only thing is to be or not to be. Hamlet's dilemma becomes existential. It leads to Albert Camus's rediscovery of Sisyphus, to Samuel Becket's two tramps waiting for Godot. But in the meantime something has changed metamorphosis as myth into metamorphosis as a historical nightmare. We are caught in the very act of changing into some other form; we are frozen in that monstrous midway, as in the film *The Fly*, when an experiment goes wrong and the scientist is changed into a grotesque shape that is neither fly nor human being but something in between. The Nigerian writer, Wole Soyinka, tackles this theme in his novel *The Interpreters*. Albert Camus, very conscious of the drastic transformation of Europe under the Nazi machine, had attempted such a task in his novel *The Plague*. Ngugi wa Thiongo, in his *A Grain of Wheat*, struggles with the same beast. Though the heat may differ in temperature, the heat is everywhere the same. The degree of pain may differ but the torturer's technique is the same. We are not at the beginning, we are not at the end – we are at the mid-point of the scream, the eye of the storm. That, for me, is the unifying factor in the scenario of contemporary literature in Europe and in Africa.

There is a healthy interchange of technique and themes. That Europe had, to say the least, a head start in written literature is an advantage for the African writer: he does not have to solve many problems of structure – they have already been solved. I do not consider influences pernicious: they are a type of apprenticeship. When I started writing, D. H. Lawrence was the skeleton in my cupboard. After that it was James Joyce, Kurt Vonnegut, Jack Kerouac, Allen Ginsberg, Charles Bukowsky, etc., until I began to doubt the existence of any originality in myself. This naturally switched me off writers; I turned to Dr Freud and his counterpart Dr Jung. Some would say the expansion of psychology has had a disastrous effect on twentieth-century literature. I disagree. That part of the European novel which is descended from Petronius's *Satyricon*, Boccaccio's *Decameron*, Rabelais's *Gargantua and Pantagruel*, has in fact gained in depth, especially in the novels of John Fowles, Anthony Burgess, and Günter Grass. John Fowles's *The Magus* and Günter Grass's *The Tin Drum* are formidable works whose expanse is covered with psychology and the anatomy of violence. Because of the numerous and incredible conflicts of the twentieth century, a knowledge of animal aggression is indispensable. It is in this area that I find African literature rather shallow. How can Africa write as if that Black Frenchman, Frantz Fanon, never existed – I refer to the Fanon of *Black Skin, White Mask*.

The critic and lecturer Neil McEwan, in his book *Africa and Novel*, argues that, far from imitating the practice of past generations of European writers, African novelists have extended the possibilities and uses of fiction. He notes that the Soviet critic Mikhail Bakhtin has offered a category of narrative whose unifying factor is a 'carnival' attitude to the world. This category includes writers from different backgrounds. They range from Aristophanes, Lucian and Apuleius (the first African novelist, perhaps) to Dostoevsky by way of Rabelais and Dean Swift. I add John Fowles and Günter Grass, and the Nigerian, Wole Soyinka, in *The Interpreters*. *Don Quixote* is quite at home. The world of such novels, says McEwan, is complex, unstable, comic, satirical, fantastic, poetical and committed to the pursuit of truth. The hero can travel anywhere in this world and beyond. Fantasy and symbolism are combined with low-life naturalism. Odd vantage points offer changes of scale. Heaven and hell are close and may be visited. Madness, dreams and day-dreams, abnormal states of mind and all kinds of erratic inclinations are explored. Scandalous and eccentric behaviour disrupts 'the seemly course of human affairs' and provides a new view of 'the integrity of the world'. Society is unpredictable; roles can quickly change. Current affairs are treated with a satirical, journalistic interest. Genres are mixed. Stories, speeches, dramatic sketches, poetry and parody exist side by side. This category of novel is called the menippean. It is no longer necessary to speak of the African novel or the European novel: there is only the menippean novel. At this point I wish to pay my respect (or silence) to the latest addition to those writers of the menippean novel: John Kennedy Toole, a young United States' citizen who, after obtaining his Master's degree at Columbia University, committed suicide because he could not find a publisher for his only novel, *A Confederacy of Dunces*. He wrote this book in the early 1960s, the time of 'flower power', the era of psychedelic mysteries, an implosion of brain into soul. But his novel is anything but effete: it is a gigantic 'NO' to everything the twentieth century stands for.

I do not like this century. I do not like any other century, past or future. I do not like to live under the backside of a medieval god or a nuclear bomb, which amounts to the same thing. I am no mystic, yet no materialist either. I believe in nature but refuse to live with it in the same room. What Thoreau and Walt Whitman did for letters in the United States – a stubborn individual sensibility which by its excessiveness actually mirrored a national dilemma – had actually begun much earlier with the German philosopher-writer, Goethe, in his portrayal of what Colin Wilson calls the 'Romantic Outsider' in the *Sorrows of Young Werther*. What Sir John Suckling had earlier derided:

> Will, when looking well can't move her,
> Looking ill prevail?

was transformed into the type of the high, idealistic young poet, pale, but manly. Schiller's *Robbers* and *Don Carlos* followed. Other writers within this particular tradition are Novalis, Coleridge (in his translation of Schiller), Byron (in 'Childe Harold's Pilgrimage') and Shelley. More recently we have Thomas Mann's *Tonio Kröger*, Sartre's *Roquentin* and Albert Camus's *Meursault*. I have been an outsider in my own biography, in my country's history, in the world's terrifying possibilities. It is, therefore, quite natural for me to respond with the pleasure of familiar horror to that section of European literature which reflects this. The inquisitor who resides in the human heart and refuses to believe in God on humanitarian grounds is familiar to all who have experienced warfare.

To quote Albert Camus from his book, *The Rebel*: 'On the day when crime puts on the apparel of innocence, through a curious reversal peculiar to our age, it is innocence that is called on to justify itself.' In Holland, the novelist Harry Mulisch in his recent book, *The Assault*, tears off post-war scar tissue protecting his society: the story begins with the assassination of a Nazi collaborator in 1945. In Holland, also, there was recently discovered *The Diaries of Etty Hillesum, 1941–43*; a young Jewish woman whose resilience, until she is taken to Auschwitz, shines because of her 'thinking heart'. The concept of the thinking heart is close to T. S. Eliot's idea of thought at the tips of the senses. It is not a giant step from these writers to the world of another writer in Holland, Cees Nooteboom, in his novel *Rituals* where he explores different styles of living in today's world surrounded by the loose trapdoors of the hideous past. We are refugees fleeing from the excesses of our parents. I have no respect for those who presume to be parents. Tradition, on closer examination, always reveals secrets we prefer to flush down the toilet. As taxpayers to the imagination, we expect the City Council to quietly get rid of the shit. In this sense, the German novelist Heinrich Böll psychoanalyses the sanity out of the insanity of the Nazi and post-Nazi era. We have become ruthless enough to judge while cynically knowing that judgement is useless, beside the point. The judge and the accused know that both of them are guilty and the trial a farce. This is the world not of Simone de Beauvoir, but of Celini and Jean Genet.

With Genet, I find myself next door to the *House of Hunger*, my *doppelgänger*, in fact the ghost which, until the Kenyan novelist Meja Mwangi arrived, African literature had refused to greet: the life of blind poverty, blind impulse. It is not far from the material of the Argentinian novelist, Marta Traba – she was killed at Madrid airport in 1983 – in her book *Mothers and Shadows*, on the plight of people who are now called 'the disappeared'. This is the realm in which the South African novelist Alex La Guma takes *A Walk in the Night*. He died on 11 October 1985, in Havana, Cuba. The inquisitor in the mind controls the sources of the imagination: the imagination is seated within a body which an assassin can destroy at any moment. In other words, eternity contained within the finite, the permanent within the temporal. We are provisional yet have the seeds of limitlessness. Which is more glorious: to live in minute detail, or to live within a timeless design? The Booker Prize winner, Thomas Keneally, in his book *Schindler's Ark*, provides us with perhaps an answer. Human life may be just a minor detail, but it is all we have, and therefore all means are permissible to save it. His book is about a German industrialist who used cunning, deceit and bribery to save the lives of thousands of Jews during the Nazi era.

Typically, the English have failed to produce a great novel based on the events of the Second World War. But let's touch on the Norwegian novelist, Knut Hamsun: his books, especially *Hunger*, are remarkable. The commitment to nature as opposed to sophistication is abundantly clear, disturbing, mindboggling, especially in *Hunger* where he explores the connection between extreme physical starvation and reverie. Like the American, Ezra Pound, Knut Hamsun was a Nazi collaborator and his own country still does not know what to do with him. He is at one with Celini. The behaviour of writers in times of conflict will always be dubious.

This was the case with the Nigerian poet, Christopher Okigbo, who fought and died for secessionist Biafra. Okigbo's poetry is unique in African literature. What the Soviet writer Andrei Sinyavsky said of Yevtushenko, I think applies to Okigbo:

> For all his proneness to self display, he lacks the stamp of an exclusive personality, the idea of a vocation, or of a great and terrible fate which would allow him to develop his own biography like a legend, in which personal life is raised to the level of a unique saga, half real, half invented, and created day by day before an astonished public.

This is part of the Russian tradition, the nineteenth-century greats like Nikolai Gogol, Turgenev, Pushkin, Goncharov, Lermontov, Dostoevsky and Tolstoy, and those of this century like Mayakovsky, Yesenin and Tsvetaeva.

Beneath reality, there is always fantasy: the writer's task is to reveal it, to open it out, to feel it, to experience it. La Guma's walk into the night becomes a jump into the unknown. Sinyavsky, forced into exile by his own need to write, exclaims: 'A writer's life is a journey, it *has* to be a journey, it has a fate.' The writer is no longer a person: he has to die in order to become a writer. People never find their appearance quite convincing – they are constantly amazed at their own ghastly reflection in the mirror. For the writer, looking at himself in the mirror, the most important thing is his writing; he looks down from above at his own person and despises it. His whole life is lived in the expectation of what is going to be written. The writer is a vampire, drinking blood – his own blood – a winged creature who flies by night, writing his books. The writer has no duty, no responsibilities, other than to his art. Art is higher than reality.

In spite of the moralizing in Gogol, Leo Tolstoy and Pasternak, Russia had one writer – Pushkin – who was completely outside this framework. His work is art, not sermons. Speaking of his technique of 'fantastic realism', Sinyavsky says:

> I don't think of modernism as some kind of device. It is no more so than realism which is itself a convention, an artificial form. Realism pretends to be able to say the truth about life. I'm not against truth, but it can be sought by different routes. In the nineteenth century realism was very productive as a form, but in this century – it's impossible.
>
> What happened in Russia was that at the beginning of this century poetry was highly developed, while prose somehow lagged behind – with some exceptions: Bely, Bulgakov, Babel. My task as a writer was to take the veins of modernism, symbolism, futurism that had developed in poetry and transfer them to the language of prose.

I find myself in the same position as Sinyavsky. In that quotation he was replying to the question why he saw himself as a modernist – the same accusation directed at me by the censorship board when they banned *Black Sunlight*. Sinyavsky is now dying in the environs of Paris – an exile, like I was. It takes only an instant to become a person without titles, without a label, to become the raw person, the point at which low-life naturalism meets its *doppelgänger*, the existentialist. Tragedy peers over everyone's shoulder. There are those who write while working in the service of the State, or some religion or ideology. There are writers who can only write while they are free to develop their own personality, to be true to themselves. What is the answer? Sinyavsky replies:

> A writer who is a fanatic can be a great writer. There are many examples of fine writers who have written within the framework of a state ideology or religion – Derzhavin, Mayakovsky, for example. But their greatness comes not from the fact that they served an ideology but from the fact that they believed in it. If a writer has lost that faith, then he will not be able to produce real art by trying to adapt himself in the service of the state. That is where freedom becomes absolutely essential. But then, people still argue about whether genuine art requires absolute political freedom. For instance, the poet Brodsky defended censorship on the grounds that it helped to develop metaphorical language, yet it was censorship that killed Brodsky's fellow poets, especially Mandelshtam. I will never give my blessing to censorship on those grounds – any more than I would to war, or prison, or, for that matter, death.

It is not unworthy to now mention the so-called absurdist writers of Leningrad. These are Dmitry Prigov, Kharms, Vvedensky and Zabolotsky. Prigov is still alive. His poems have a disarming lightness, his characteristic tone of mild grievance and bewilderment, which is underlined by a nihilistic view of a world in which modest and inoffensive souls find themselves inexplicably thwarted, inexplicably guilty, and unable to make sense of the grand notions – conscience, freedom, dignity – whose names nevertheless invade their day-to-day vocabulary. I quote:

> You've put four walls around yourself
> And hung a ceiling overhead
> Locked yourself inside your room
> To do shameful things alone
>
> And do not see, and do not hear
> That you are visible in there
> As if they'd lifted off the roof
> And fixed their gaze upon your shame
>
> You raise your eyes – and Oh, just Lord!
> Either the criminal must run
> Or do his trousers up at least
> Or at least remove the corpse.

The Czechoslovak novelist, exiled, of course, Jan Pelc, in his first novel *It's Gonna Get Worse* – he is only 29 years old – follows this absurdism or fantastic realism, or menippean manner, to produce a work which is still making heads shake among emigré Czech communities and the readers of samizdat literature. It is in fact the ugly twin to John Kennedy Toole's *A Confederacy of Dunces*. This is the same territory as that of the English Liverpool Poets, their articulate chagrin against the pigs, the fascists, social injustice and English racism. But these were rather a late reflection of the American Beat Generation with its gurus like Allen Ginsberg, Allan Watts, Gary Snyder and Jack Kerouac. Ginsberg's words, 'I saw the best minds of my generation destroyed by madness, starving hysterical naked dragging themselves through the negro streets at dawn looking for an angry fix', were echoing in my ears when I was writing *The House of Hunger*.

Part V

On Nativism and the Quest for Indigenous Aesthetics: Negritude and Traditionalism

Nativism, referring in this specific context to cultural nativism, is the proposition that one's world-view and all its many components be anchored in and determined or guided by fidelity to the dictates of one's culture. It is an affirmation of the autochthonous self against pressing outside forces. Philosophically, nativism assumes that the mind needs no sources external to its culture in the production of ideas. But there is a problem: nativism speaks in the name of Africa, but Africa is composed not of one but many cultures. This reveals that though nativism speaks in the name of "culture," it is actually racialist or based on race, yet culture and race are hardly collapsible. The primary argument of nativism is that colonization and its attendant cultural Westernization (through Christianity, Western-style education, bureaucracy, and forms of governance) of Africa have produced an abnormal situation in which "authentic" African ideas and ways of doing things have been displaced or corrupted by foreign ones. The urgent solution then is to recover and return to paths and directions suggested by truly indigenous African traditions. In both content and form, how does an African writer write in fidelity to "authentic" African traditions? What do those traditions say of "realism," "modernism," and indeed of the use of non-African languages in both the literature and the criticism of the literature? And, since it had not been so difficult for cultural nativism to morph into political policy during certain regimes, what are the much wider implications of this philosophical outlook? Negritude may have waned in esteem but it was the first widely popular nativist theory of African literature, and the strand led by Chinweizu has been the most vociferous. The selections in this part both eloquently make the case for and critically respond to the many challenges of nativism in African literary and culture studies.

Chapter 29

Negritude:
A Humanism of the Twentieth Century

Léopold Sédar Senghor

During the last thirty or so years that we have been proclaiming negritude, it has become customary, especially among English-speaking critics, to accuse us of *racialism*. This is probably because the word is not of English origin. But, in the language of Shakespeare, is it not in good company with the words humanism and socialism? Mphahleles[1] have been sent about the world saying: "Negritude is an inferiority complex"; but the same word cannot mean both "racialism" and "inferiority complex" without contradiction. The most recent attack comes from Ghana, where the government has commissioned a poem entitled "I Hate Negritude" – as if one could hate oneself, hate one's being, without ceasing to be.

No, negritude is none of these things. It is neither racialism nor self-negation. Yet it is not just affirmation; it is rooting oneself in oneself, and self-confirmation: confirmation of one's *being*. Negritude is nothing more or less than what some English-speaking Africans have called the *African personality*. It is no different from the "black personality" discovered and proclaimed by the American New Negro movement. As the American Negro poet, Langston Hughes, wrote after the first world war: "We, the creators of the new generation, want to give expression to our *black personality* without shame or fear . . . We know we are handsome. Ugly as well. The drums weep and the drums laugh." Perhaps our only originality, since it was the West Indian poet, Aimé Césaire, who coined the word negritude, is to have attempted to define the concept a little more closely; to have developed it as a weapon, as an instrument of liberation and as a contribution to the humanism of the twentieth century.

But, once again, what is negritude? Ethnologists and sociologists today speak of "different civilizations." It is obvious that peoples differ in their ideas and their languages, in their philosophies and their religions, in their customs and their institutions, in their literature and their art. Who would deny that Africans, too, have a certain way of conceiving life and of living it? A certain way of speaking, singing, and dancing; of painting and sculpturing, and

First published in *The Africa Reader: Independent Africa*, ed. Martin Kilson and Wilfred Cartey, pp. 179–92. New York: Random House, 1970.

even of laughing and crying? Nobody, probably; for otherwise we would not have been talking about "Negro art" for the last sixty years and Africa would be the only continent today without its ethnologists and sociologists. What, then, is negritude? It is – as you can guess from what precedes – *the sum of the cultural values of the black world*; that is, a certain active presence in the world, or better, in the universe. It is, as John Reed and Clive Wake call it, a certain "way of relating oneself to the world and to others."[2] Yes, it is essentially relations with others, an opening out to the world, contact and participation with others. Because of what it is, negritude is necessary in the world today: it is a humanism of the twentieth century.

"The Revolution of 1889"

But let us go back to 1885 and the morrow of the Berlin Conference. The European nations had just finished, with Africa, their division of the planet. Including the United States of America, they were five or six at the height of their power who dominated the world. Without any complexes, they were proud of their material strength; prouder even of their science, and paradoxically, of their *race*. It is true that at that time this was not a paradox. Gobineau, the nineteenth-century philosopher of racial supremacy, had, by a process of osmosis, even influenced Marx, and Disraeli was the great theoretician of that *"English race, proud, tenacious, confident in itself, that no climate, no change can undermine."* (The italics are mine.) Leo Frobenius, the German ethnologist, one of the first to apprehend the rich complexity of African culture, writes in *The Destiny of Civilizations*: "Each of the great nations that considers itself personally responsible for the 'destiny of the world' believes it possesses the key to the understanding of the whole and the other nations. It is an attitude raised from the past."

In fact, this attitude "raised from the past" had begun to be discredited toward the end of the nineteenth century by books like Bergson's *Time and Free Will*, which was published in 1889. Since the Renaissance, the values of European civilization had rested essentially on discursive reason and facts, on logic and matter. Bergson, with an eminently dialectical subtlety, answered the expectation of a public weary of scientism and naturalism. He showed that facts and matter, which are the objects of discursive reason, were only the outer surface that had to be transcended by *intuition* in order to achieve a *vision in depth* of reality.

But the "Revolution of 1889" – as we shall call it – did not only affect art and literature, it completely upset the sciences. In 1880, only a year before the invention of the word electron, a distinction was still being drawn between matter and energy. The former was inert and unchangeable, the latter was not. But what characterized both of them was their permanence and their continuity. They were both subject to a strict mechanical determinism. Matter and energy had, so to speak, existed from the beginning of time; they could change their shape, but not their substance. All we lacked in order to know them objectively in space and time were sufficiently accurate instruments of investigation and measurement.

Well, in less than fifty years, all these principles were to be outmoded and even rejected. Thirty years ago already, the new discoveries of science – quanta, relativity, wave mechanics, the uncertainty principle, electron spin – had upset the nineteenth-century notion of determinism, which denied man's free will, along with the concepts of matter and energy. The French physicist, Broglie, revealed to us the duality of matter and energy, or the wave-particle principle that underlies things; the German physicist, Heisenberg, showed us that objectivity was an illusion and that we could not observe facts without modifying them; others showed that, on the scale of the infinitely small as on that of the immensely great, particles act on one another. Since then, the physico-chemical laws, like matter itself, could no longer appear unchangeable. Even in the field, and on the scale, where they were valid, they were only rough approximations, no more than probabilities. It was enough to scrape the surface of things and of facts to realize just how much instability there is, defying our measuring instruments, probably because they are only mechanical: *material*.

It was on the basis of these discoveries, through a combination of logical coherence and amazing intuition, of scientific experiment and inner experience, that Pierre Teilhard de Chardin was able to transcend the traditional dichotomies with a new dialectic, to reveal to us the living, throbbing unity of the universe. On the basis, then, of the new scientific discoveries, Teilhard de Chardin transcends the old dualism of the philosophers and the scientists, which Marx and Engels had perpetuated by giving matter precedence over the spirit. He advanced the theory that the stuff of the universe is not composed of two realities, but of a single reality in the shape of two phenomena; that there is not matter and energy, not even matter and spirit, but spirit-matter, just as there is space-time. Matter and spirit become a "network of relations," as the French philosopher, Bachelard, called it: energy, defined as a network of forces. In matter-spirit there is, therefore, only one energy, which has two aspects. The first, *tangential energy*, which is external, is material and quantitative. It links together the corpuscles, or particles, that make up matter. The other, *radial energy*, which is internal, is psychic and qualitative. It is centripetal force. It organizes into a complex the center-to-center relations of the internal particles of a corpuscle. Since energy is force, it follows that radial energy is the creative force, the "primary stuff of things," and tangential energy is only a residual product "caused by the interreactions of the elementary 'centers' of the consciousness, imperceptible where life has not yet occurred, but clearly apprehensible by our experience at a sufficiently advanced stage in the development of matter" (Teilhard de Chardin). It follows that where life has not yet occurred the physico-chemical laws remain valid within the limitations we have defined above, while in the living world, as we rise from plant to animal and from animal to Man, the psyche increases in consciousness until it makes and expresses itself in freedom. "Makes itself": that is, *realizes* itself, by means of – yet by transcending – material well-being through an increase of spiritual life. "Realizes itself": by that I mean it develops in harmonious fashion the two complementary elements of the soul: the heart and the mind.

The Philosophy of Being

The paradox is only apparent when I say that negritude, by its ontology (that is, its philosophy of being), its moral law and its aesthetic, is a response to the modern humanism that European philosophers and scientists have been preparing since the end of the nineteenth century, and as Teilhard de Chardin and the writers and artists of the mid-twentieth century present it.

Firstly, African ontology. Far back as one may go into his past, from the northern Sudanese to the southern Bantu, the African has always and everywhere presented a concept of the world which is diametrically opposed to the traditional philosophy of Europe. The latter is essentially *static, objective, dichotomic*; it is, in fact, dualistic, in that it makes an absolute distinction between body and soul, matter and spirit. It is founded on separation and opposition: on analysis and conflict. The African, on the other hand, conceives the world, beyond the diversity of its forms, as a fundamentally mobile, yet unique, reality that seeks synthesis. This needs development.

It is significant that in Wolof, the main language of Senegal, there are at least three words to translate the word "spirit": *xel, sago,* or *degal,* whereas images have to be used for the word "matter": *lef* (thing) or *yaram* (body). The African is, of course, sensitive to the external world, to the material aspect of beings and things. It is precisely because he is more so than the white European, because he is sensitive to the tangible qualities of things – shape, color, smell, weight, etc. – that the African considers these things merely as signs that have to be interpreted and transcended in order to reach the reality of human beings. Like others, more than others, he distinguishes the pebble from the plant, the plant from the animal, the animal from Man; but, once again, the accidents and appearances that differentiate these kingdoms only illustrate different aspects of the same reality. This reality is *being* in the ontological sense of the word, and it is life force. For the African, matter in the sense the Europeans understand it, is only a system of signs which translates the single reality of the universe: being, which is spirit, which is life force. Thus, the whole universe appears as an infinitely small, and at the same time an infinitely large, network of life forces which emanate from God and end in God, who is the source of all life forces. It is He who vitalizes and devitalizes all other beings, all the other life forces.

I have not wandered as far as might be thought from modern ontology. European ethnologists, Africanists and artists use the same words and the same expressions to designate the ultimate reality of the universe they are trying to know and to express: "spider's web," "network of forces," "communicating vessels," "system of canals," etc. This is not very different, either, from what the scientists and chemists say. As far as African ontology is concerned, too, there is no such thing as dead matter: every being, every thing – be it only a grain of sand – radiates a life force, a sort of wave-particle; and sages, priests, kings, doctors, and artists all use it to help bring the universe to its fulfilment.

For the African, contrary to popular belief, is not passive in face of the order – or disorder – of the world. His attitude is fundamentally ethical. If the moral law of the African has remained unknown for so long, it is because it derives, naturally, from his conception of the world: from his ontology – so naturally, that both have remained unknown, denied even, by Europeans, because they have not been brought to their attention by being re-examined by each new generation of Africans.

So God tired of all the possibilities that remained confined within Him, unexpressed, dormant, and as if dead. And God opened His mouth, and he spoke at length a word that was harmonious and rhythmical. All these possibilities expressed by the mouth of God *existed* and had the vocation *to live*: to express God in their turn, by establishing the link with God and all the forces deriving from Him.

In order to explain this *morality in action* of negritude, I must go back a little. Each of the identifiable life forces of the universe – from the grain of sand to the ancestor[3] – is, itself and in its turn, a network of life forces – as modern physical chemistry confirms: a network of elements that are contradictory in appearance but really *complementary*. Thus, for the African, Man is composed, of course, of matter and spirit, of body and soul; but at the same time he is also composed of a virile and a feminine element: indeed of several "souls."

Man is therefore a composition of mobile life forces which interlock: a world of solidarities that seek to knit themselves together. Because he exists, he is at once end and beginning: end of the three orders of the mineral, the vegetable, and the animal, but beginning of the human order.

Let us ignore for the moment the first three orders and examine the human order. Above Man and based on him, lies this fourth world of concentric circles, bigger and bigger, higher and higher, until they reach God along with the whole of the universe. Each circle – family, village, province, nation, humanity – is, in the image of Man and by vocation, a close-knit society.

So, for the African, living according to the moral law means living according to his nature, composed as it is of contradictory elements but complementary life forces. Thus he gives stuff to the stuff of the universe and tightens the threads of the tissue of life. Thus he transcends the contradictions of the elements and works toward making the life forces complementary to one another: in himself first of all, as Man, but also in the whole of human society. It is by bringing the complementary life forces together in this way that Man reinforces them in their movement towards God and, in reinforcing them, he reinforces himself; that is, he passes from *existing* to *being*. He cannot reach the highest form of being, for in fact only God has this quality; and He has it all the more fully as creation, and all that exists, fulfil themselves and express themselves in Him.

Dialogue

Ethnologists have often praised the unity, the balance, and the harmony of African civilization, of black society, which was based both on the *community* and on the *person*, and in which, because it was founded on dialogue and reciprocity, the group had priority over the individual without crushing him, but allowing him to blossom as a person. I would like to emphasize at this point how much these characteristics of negritude enable it to find its place in contemporary humanism, thereby permitting black Africa to make its contribution to the "Civilization of the Universal" which is so necessary in our divided but interdependent world of the second half of the twentieth century. A contribution, first of all, to international cooperation, which must be and which shall be the cornerstone of that civilization. It is through these virtues of negritude that decolonization has been accomplished without too much bloodshed or hatred and that a positive form of cooperation based on "dialogue and reciprocity" has been established between former colonizers and colonized. It is through these virtues that there has been a new spirit at the United Nations, where the "no" and the bang of the fist on the table are no longer signs of strength. It is through these virtues that peace through cooperation could extend to South Africa, Rhodesia, and the Portuguese colonies, if only the dualistic spirit of the whites would open itself to dialogue.

In fact, the contribution of negritude to the "Civilization of the Universal" is not of recent origin. In the fields of literature and art, it is contemporary with the "Revolution of 1889." The French poet, Arthur Rimbaud (1854–91), had already associated himself with negritude. But in this article I want to concentrate on the "Negro revolution" – the expression belongs to Emmanuel Berl – which helped to stir European plastic art at the beginning of this century.

Art, like literature, is always the expression of a certain conception of the world and of life; the expression of a certain philosophy and, above all, of a certain ontology. Corresponding to the philosophical and scientific movement of 1889 there was not only a literary evolution – symbolism then surrealism – but another revolution, or rather revolutions, in art, which were called, taking only the plastic arts, nabism, expressionism, fauvism, and cubism. A world of life forces that have to be *tamed* is substituted for a closed world of permanent and continuous substances that have to be *reproduced*.

Since the Greek *kouroi* (the term used for the statues of young men in classical Greek sculpture), the art of the European West had always been based on realism; the work of art had always been an imitation of the object: a *physeôs mimêsis*, to use Aristotle's expression: a corrected imitation, "improved," "idealized" by the requirements of rationality, but imitation all the same. The interlude of the Christian Middle Ages is significant insofar as Christianity is itself of Asian origin and strongly influenced by the African, St Augustine. To what will the artist then give expression? No longer to purely objective matter, but to his spiritual self: that is, to his inner self, his spirituality, and beyond himself to the spirituality of his age and of mankind. No longer by means of perspective, relief, and chiaroscuro, but, as the French painter, Bazaine, writes, "by the most hidden workings of instinct and the sensibility." Another French painter, André Masson, makes it more explicit when he writes: "By a simple interplay of shapes and colors legibly ordered." This interplay of shapes and colors is that of the life forces and which has been illustrated in particular by a painter like Soulages.

"Interplay of life forces": and so we come back to – negritude. As the French painter, Soulages, in fact, once told me, the African aesthetic is "that of contemporary art." I find indirect proof of this in the fact that, while the consecration and spread of the new aesthetic revolution have occurred in France, the majority of its promoters were of Slav and Germanic origin; people who, like the Africans, belong to the mystical civilizations of the senses. Of course, without the discovery of African art, the revolution would still have taken place, but probably without such vigor and assurance and such a deepening of the knowledge of Man. The fact that an art of the subject and of the spirit should have germinated outside Europe, in Africa – to which ethnologists had not yet given its true place in world culture – was proof of the human value of the message of the new European art.

Over and above its aesthetic lesson – to which we shall return later – what Picasso, Braque and the other artists and early explorers of African art were seeking was, in the first place, just this: its human value. For in black Africa art is not a separate activity, in itself or for itself: it is a social activity, a technique of living, a handicraft in fact. But it is a major activity that brings all other activities to their fulfilment, like prayer in the Christian Middle Ages: birth and education, marriage and death, sport, even war. All human activities down to the least daily act must be integrated into the subtle interplay of life forces – family, tribal, national, world, and universal forces. This harmonious interplay of life forces must be helped by *subordinating* the lower forces – mineral, vegetable, and animal – to their relations with Man, and the forces of human society to its relations with the Divine Being through the intermediary of the Ancestral Beings.

A year or two ago I attended, on the cliffs of Bandiagara in the Mali Republic, an entertainment which was microcosm of Dogon art.[4] Even though it was but a pale reflection of the splendors of the past, this "play-concert" was an extremely significant expression of the Dogon vision of the universe. It was declaimed, sung, and danced; sculptured and presented in costume. The whole of the Dogon universe was portrayed in this symbiosis of the arts, as is the custom in black Africa. The universe – heaven and earth – was therefore *represented* through the intermediary of Man, whose ideogram is the same as that of the universe. Then the world was *re-presented* by means of masks, each of which portrayed, at one and the same time, a totemic animal, an ancestor and a spirit. Others portrayed the foreign peoples: nomadic Fulani[5] and white Europeans. The aim of the entertainment was, by means of the symbiosis of the arts – poetry, song, dance, sculpture, and painting, used as techniques of integration – to *re-create* the universe and the contemporary world, but in a more harmonious way by making use of African humor, which corrects distortions at the expense of the foreign Fulani and the white conquerors. But this ontological vision was an entertainment – that is, an artistic demonstration – as well: a joy for the soul because a joy for the eyes and ears.

It was perhaps – indeed, it was certainly – this last aspect of the African aesthetic lesson that first attracted Picasso and Braque when, toward 1906, they discovered African art and were inspired by it. For my part, what struck me from the start of the Dogon "play-concert," even before I tried to understand its meaning, was the harmony of form and movement, of color and rhythm, that characterized it. It is this harmony by which, as a spectator, I was moved; which, in the re-creation of reality, acts on the invisible forces whose appearances are only signs, subordinates them in a complementary fashion to one another and establishes the link between them and God through the intermediary of Man. By appearances I mean the attributes of matter that strike our senses: shape and color, timbre and tone, movement and rhythm.

I have said that these appearances are signs. They are more than that: they are meaningful signs, the "lines of force" of the life forces, insofar as they are used in their pure state, with only their characteristics of shape, color, sound, movement, and rhythm. Recently M. Lods, who teaches at the National School of Art of Senegal, was showing me the pictures his students intend exhibiting at the projected Festival of African Arts. I was immediately struck by the noble and elegant interplay of shape and color. When I discovered that the pictures were not completely abstract, that they portrayed ladies, princes, and noble animals, I was almost disappointed. There was no need for me to be: the very interplay of colored shapes perfectly expressed that elegant nobility that characterizes the art of the northern Sudan.

This, then, is Africa's lesson in aesthetics: art does not consist in photographing nature but in taming it, like the hunter when he reproduces the call of the hunted animal, like a separated couple, or two lovers, calling to each other in their desire to be reunited. The call is not the simple reproduction of the cry of the Other; it is a call of complementarity, a *song*: a call of harmony to the harmony of union that enriches by increasing *Being*. We call it pure harmony. Once more, Africa teaches that art is not photography; if there are images they are rhythmical. I can suggest or create anything – a man, a moon, a fruit, a smile, a tear – simply by assembling shapes and colors (painting/sculpture), shapes and movement (dance), timbre and tones (music), provided that this assembling is not an aggregation, but that it is ordered and, in short, rhythmical. For it is rhythm – the main virtue, in fact, of negritude – that gives the work of art its beauty. Rhythm is simply the movement of attraction or repulsion that expresses the life of the cosmic forces; symmetry and asymmetry, repetition or opposition: in short, the lines of force that link the meaningful signs that shapes and colors, timbre and tones, are.

Before concluding, I should like to pause for a moment on the apparent contradiction that must have been noticed between contemporary European art (which places the emphasis on the subject) and African art (which places it on the object). This is because the "Revolution of 1889" began by reacting, of necessity, against the superstition of the *object*; and the existentialist ontology of the African, while it it is based on the being-subject, has God as its pole-object; God who is the fullness of Being. What was noticed, then, was simply a nuance. For the contemporary European, and the African, the work of art, like the act of knowing, expresses the confrontation, the embrace, of subject and object: "That penetration," wrote Bazaine, "that great common structure, that deep resemblance between Man and the world, without which there is no living form."

We have seen what constitutes for the African the "deep resemblance between Man and the world." For him, then, the act of restoring the order of the world by re-creating it through art is the reinforcement of the life forces in the universe and, consequently, of God, the source of all life forces – or, in other words, the Being of the universe. In this way, we reinforce ourselves at the same time, both as interdependent forces and as beings whose being consists in revitalizing ourselves in the re-creation of art.

Notes

1   The South African writer, Ezekiel Mphahlele, author, among other books, of *The African Image*, strongly disagrees with the concept of negritude.

2   *Léopold Sédar Senghor: Selected Poems*, introduced and translated by John Reed and Clive Wake. See also: *Léopold Sédar Senghor: Prose and Poetry*, by the same authors.

3   In African religion, the ancestors are the essential link between the living and God. This is why they are surrounded by a complex ritual so as to ensure the maintenance of this link.

4   The Dogon are a West African tribe among whom wood sculpture has achieved a very remarkable degree of excellence.

5   The Fulani are a nomadic pastoral people found throughout West Africa.

Chapter 30

What is Négritude?

Abiola Irele

The term 'Négritude' has acquired, in the way it has been used by different writers, a multiplicity of meanings covering so wide a range that it is often difficult to form a precise idea of its particular reference at any one time or in any one usage. The difficulty stems from the fact that, as a movement and as a concept, Négritude found its origin and received a development in a historical and sociological context whose implications for those whom it affected were indeed wide-ranging, and which ultimately provoked in them a multitude of responses that were often contradictory, though always significant. In its immediate reference, Négritude refers to the literary and ideological movement of French-speaking black intellectuals, which took form as a distinctive and significant aspect of the comprehensive reaction of the black man to the colonial situation, a situation that was felt and perceived by black people in Africa and in the New World as a state of global subjection to the political, social and moral domination of the West.

The term has thus been used in a broad and general sense to denote the black world in its historical being, in opposition to the West, and in this way resumes the total consciousness of belonging to the black race,[1] as well as an awareness of the objective historical and sociological implications of that fact. It is perhaps not without significance that Aimé Césaire, who originally coined the term and was the first to use it in his long poem, *Cahier d'un retour au pays natal*[2] should have given the kind of general definition which not only indicates the scope of the black consciousness embraced by the term in its relation to history, but also its extension beyond this contingent factor:

> Négritude is the simple recognition of the fact of being black, and the acceptance of this fact, of our destiny as black people, of our history, and our culture.[3]

In this broad perspective, Négritude can be taken to correspond to a certain form of Pan-Negro feeling and awareness, and as a movement, to represent the equivalent on the French-speaking side of what has come to be known as Pan-Africanism.[4] It thus forms a distinctive

First published as "Négritude – the Philosophy of African Being," in *Nigeria Magazine* 122–3 (Lagos: 1977), special number, World Festival of Black and African Arts; and subsequently in *The African Experience in Literature and Ideology*, pp. 67–89, 74–9. Ibadan: Heinemann, 1981.

current of a larger movement of black nationalism, inasmuch as the French-speaking black intellectuals involved in the movement faced special problems in their relationship to French colonial rule, which gave a particular dimension and quality to their reaction. The French-speaking black writers and intellectuals tended therefore to develop a distinctive style and language which, by giving a specific coloration to a general sentiment, and a distinctive orientation to a common preoccupation, came to mark off their reaction to the colonial situation from the form this reaction took among their English-speaking counterparts.

It is with respect to this formal expression of the black nationalist consciousness – or to be more precise, of black cultural nationalism – that a second and closer sense of the term Négritude can be defined. It can be taken here to describe the writings of the French-speaking black intellectuals in their affirmation of a black personality, and to designate the complex of ideas associated with their effort to define a new set of references for the collective experience and awareness of black people. In this sense, Négritude has come to mean the ideology which was either implicit in the production of the literary school associated with the French-speaking black intellectuals or came expressly to be formulated for it.

The body of imaginative and ideological writings produced by the French-speaking black intellectuals represents an extensive exploration of the black condition in both its historical setting and in its direction towards an ultimate significance. The constancy and intensity of this exploration have come to establish in the literature of Négritude a number of characteristic themes and a particularity of tone which give it a certain distinction. In this literature, the preoccupation with the black experience which has provided a common ground base for the imaginative expression of black writers develops into a passionate exaltation of the black race, associated with a romantic myth of Africa.

The immediate polemical significance of this revaluation of Africa merges itself into a quest for new values, for a new spiritual orientation, such that, in the most expressive parts of the literature, the cultivation of Africa formulates itself as an intense imaginative celebration of primal values. It is clear that beyond their immediate preoccupation with the historical experience of the black man as expressed in the leading themes that have emerged in their writings, the French-speaking black writers have been concerned in a fundamental way with seeing through the facts of history as it affected the black man, to the essential relation between the race and African civilization as a more positive determination of its destiny. A distinctive vision of Africa and the black man, and of his relation to the world, thus stands at the very heart of the literature of Négritude and informs it in a fundamental way, provides what can be said to constitute the 'mental structure'[5] that underlies the imaginative expression of the French-speaking black writers, and which emerges with a sharp clarity in the ideological writings. The rehabilitation of Africa which stands out as the central project of Négritude thus represents a movement towards the recovery of a certain sense of spiritual integrity by the black man, as the definition of a black collective identity, as well as of a new world view, derived from a new feeling for the African heritage of values and of experience.

[...]

Senghor has singled out, as the dominant trait of this consciousness, its emotive disposition. He presents the African as being, in his physical constitution, a being of emotion, or as he puts it, 'one of the worms created on the Third Day...a pure sensory being'.[6] The African's response to the external world in Senghor's conception is an upsurge of the sensibility, at the level of the nervous system, an intense, engulfing experience in which the whole organic being of the self is involved. Senghor establishes an association between the material and the psychic, an association that he holds to be particularly acute and intimate in the make-up of the African. 'Our psychology is the expression of our physiology, even though the former, in turn, conditions the latter and transcends it,'[7] he has remarked, and he explains the extreme sensibility of the African by the action of the hot and humid climate of his tropical milieu upon his nervous system which has resulted in a 'Negro temperament'.[8] He thus postulates a total coincidence of the African's nervous reactions with his psychic operations to explain his affective mode of apprehension. The psycho-physiological constitution of the African determines his immediate response to external reality, his total absorption of the object into the innermost recesses of his subjectivity: 'By the very fact of his physiology,' writes Senghor, 'the Negro has reactions which are more *lived*, in the sense that they are more direct and concrete expressions of the sensation and of the stimulus, and so of the object itself, with all its original qualities and power.'[9] It is this disposition, stemming from his physiological equipment, that one observes in the African's highly developed sense of rhythm – in Senghor's words, 'organic sense of rhythm'. However, notwithstanding the profound association between his constitution and his emotivity, the African's response to reality is not a mere instinctive reaction, but is an expression of an intention. Senghor explains the process as follows: 'But the movement of excitement, provoked by the object, is not a mechanical movement nor indeed a physio-logical movement. *It is the subject who is moved.* He reacts to the object, but with his own particular orientation and rhythm: his own subjective style, which he imposes upon the object.'[10] In other words, the emotive response of the African is an act of cognition, in which the subject and the object enter into an organic and dynamic relationship, and in which intense perception through the senses culminates in the conscious apprehension of reality. Thus, as Senghor says, 'the African's spirituality is rooted in his sensuous nature: in his physiology'.[11] His mode of apprehension involves a warm, living dialectic of consciousness and reality. Emotion then is the accession to a higher state of reality.[12]

As can be seen, Senghor derives from his exposition of the distinctive psychology of the Negro-African, what one might call a theory of knowledge implicit in the African's attitude to the world, a black epistemology. The African's apprehension amounts to 'living the object' in the depth of his soul, penetrating through sensuous perception to its essence: 'Knowledge then is not the superficial creation of discursive reason, cast over reality, but discovery through emotion: less discovery than re-discovery. Knowledge coincides, here, with the *being* of the object in its discontinuous and indeterminate reality'.[13] And it is this sensuous grasp of reality that Senghor refers to as 'intuition'.

It is not surprising that Senghor's theory of the African's method of knowledge and his aesthetic theory should be intimately related, and even coincide. It is certainly not a matter of chance that his philosophy of Négritude is a spiritualist one, and that the terms he uses are far from being the precise, positive and sharply defined ones that one would expect in an analytical exposition: for even in his theorizing, Senghor remains the poet. The significant factor here is that, in his theory, Senghor associates knowledge with the imaginative faculty. The African's attitude to the world precludes objective intellection, so that his mind works less by abstraction than by intuitive understanding. Thus, as Senghor says, he is 'sensitive to the spiritual and not the intellectual qualities of ideas'[14] – hence the privileged role of image and symbol in the expressive schemes of African civilization. Senghor has provided a striking illustration of what he means by this observation:

The African is moved not so much by the outward appearance of the object as by its profound reality, less by the *sign* than by its *sense*. What moves him in a dancing mask, through the medium of the image and the rhythm, is a new vision of the 'god'. What moves him in water is not that it flows, is liquid and blue, but that it washes and purifies. The physical appearance, however intensely perceived in all its particulars by the neuro-sensory organs, indeed, through the very intensity of such perception, is no more than the sign of the object's real significance.[15]

Artistic expression thus becomes the prime mediator of the African consciousness. It is singularly in artistic creation that he participates most fully with the world of creation and it is through the emotion engendered by the symbolic content of artistic form that he seizes upon the ultimate significance of reality. Thus artistic expression has for him a metaphysical import. This is the point of Senghor's essay, 'L'esthétique négro-africaine' in which he describes the place of rhythm (taken as a paradigm of African artistic feeling) in the world-view of African civilization in these terms:

Rhythm is the architecture of being, the internal dynamics which gives it form, the system of waves which it sends out towards *Others*. It expresses itself through the most material, the most sensuous means: lines, surfaces, colours, volumes in architecture, sculpture and painting; accents in poetry and music, movements in dance. But in doing so, it guides all this concrete reality towards the light of the spirit. For the Negro-African, it is in the same measure that rhythm is embodied in the senses that it illuminates the spirit.[16]

Moreover artistic expression and religious feeling are inseparably linked, in so far as art is conceived primarily as an epiphany of the sacred, of the cosmic energy with which the visible world is permeated. Art is the imaginative restitution of the fundamental network of relationships which exist between the various manifestations of this cosmic energy. This is the foundation of the African's mystical participation in the universe. Senghor has written:

The Black man had succeeded in perceiving the harmonious order of nature. Then, thanks to his sense and to his intuitive intelligence, to his hands and to his techniques, he had integrated himself into it. To perceive the harmonious order of Nature, that is to grasp the correspond-ences which bind one to the other, the cosmic forces which underlie the universe, but at the same time, those which bind nature to man: the exterior, physical universe to the moral, interior universe. *It is the expression of these correspondences that constitutes the analogical image: the symbol.*[17]

The essential idea in Senghor's aesthetic theory is that the African arrives at a profound knowledge of the world by feeling the material world to the cosmic mind of which it is an emanation, to the transcendental reality underlying it – what Senghor calls, in a modifica-tion of Breton's term, *'la sous-réalité'*. The role of emotion in the theory of Négritude culminates in Senghor's enunciation of a hypothetic Negro-African *cogito*, which he explicitly opposes to the traditional enunciation handed down to the West by Descartes. Senghor's text runs thus:

'I think, therefore I am', wrote Descartes, the European *par excellence*. 'I feel, I dance the other' the Negro-African would say. He does not need, like Descartes, a 'tool-word' as my old master Ferdinand Brunot used to term it, a conjunction, in order to realize his *being*, but an *object complement*. He does not need to think but to live the other by dancing him.[18]

But Senghor maintains that the African's experience is a reflective and conscious act and therefore merits the name of reason: the creative reason of imaginative intuition. It is different in kind from the logical intelligence of the European, because it does not follow the canons of thought which regulate the latter. The distinction between Europe and Africa is drawn by Senghor in terms of the cultural form that, traditionally, mental operations have taken in their respective civilizations, and of their opposed directions, hence his well-known formula: 'Classical European reason is analytical and makes use of the object. African reason is intuitive and participates in the object.'[19]

It is in the light of this spiritualist conception of the African mode of consciousness that Senghor interprets the cosmologies and social institutions of traditional Africa. The spirit of African civilization is resumed in a Negro-African ontology, which identifies *being* with life, with 'vital force'.[20] This vitalist philosophy which Senghor attributes to Africa explains the traditional forms of religious experience and expression on the continent. By his emotive and mystical disposition, and by the very fact of his intimate insertion into an organic milieu, the African is naturally a religious being, in whom the sense of the sacred is acutely alive.

He communes directly with nature and with the elements, and through these, with the absolute fountain-head of vital force, God himself. African animism and totemism, and their elaboration in myth, represent the objectified forms of emotive participation in the cosmos. This is how Senghor has more lately put the matter: 'There are three realities in presence: man, visible nature – animals, plants, minerals – and the invisible cosmic forces expressed by the sentient forms of nature. "African" mysticism is thus the impulse towards union with the cosmic forces, and beyond, with the force of forces, *God* . . . The privileged mode, the most adequate mode of this union is myth.'[21]

African society is in turn structured on the basis of this mystical world view. Society is a complex network of individualized incarnations of vital force, and social participation is at bottom a complex of relationships between these. The family, which is the focal unit of society, is primarily a religious, mystical union, and extends into the clan, 'the sum of all persons, living and dead, who acknowledge a common ancestor'.[22] The larger society as such is constituted by a polycentric (as opposed to serial) network of families and clans; African society is thus, essentially, not so much a community of persons, as 'a communion of souls'. All social relationships and activities, down to economic life, are informed in greater or lesser measure by this religious vision. 'Among Africans,' writes Senghor, 'man is bound to the object of collective ownership by the legal bonds of custom and tradition; over and above all by a mystical bond.'[23]

The line that runs through Senghor's exposition of African values to his doctrine of African socialism passes through this interpretation of the traditional system of social organization in Africa. The theory of Négritude that forms the basis of the doctrine can be resumed at this point as a comprehensive interpretation of a distinctive African approach to the universe, and of the way of life founded upon it.

Our examination of Senghor's theory of Négritude cannot be complete without some mention of his doctrine of African socialism which is its social expression and which is intended to give it practical significance. The doctrine of African socialism itself is conceived by Senghor as an updating of the traditional African world view, a translation of Négritude into the modern conditions of the technological age on one hand, and on the other, of the nation-state, the modern unit of political association. It is not however so much a practical programme of action as a mental projection into the future, the necessary preliminary reflection upon the conditions of meaningful collective action.

The example of European socialism inspires Senghor to elaborate a parallel system of social philosophy which is African in its references. Marxism in particular offers a convenient jumping-off ground from which to review African realities in the effort to rethink them and to determine the role of the values of the past in the modern world.

There is a certain paradox in the fact that Senghor's application of the Marxist method to African realities engenders in him the dissatisfaction that he has described in these terms:

> What embarrassed us in Marxism was, along with its atheism, a certain disdain for spiritual values: this discursive reason pushed to its outermost limits, turned into a materialism without warmth, into a blind determinism.[24]

Despite this dissatisfaction, Senghor's *critique* of Marxism does not imply a total rejection, for he recognizes that it provides a dynamic vision of man in his relationship to nature, and as a consequence, a liberating view of social relationships in which the primary concern is the fulfilment of human virtualities. He believes however that Marxism is a theory that needs to be completed in the light of new developments since it was propounded, especially in the sciences, and modified to suit the African situation.

In reality, however, Senghor's African socialism marks a break with Marxist theory, turning rather to the philosophy of Pierre Teilhard de Chardin for its inspirational ground-work. The exact connection between socialism and Teilhard de Chardin's philosophy is not easy to grasp, but its fascination for Senghor can be explained on three closely related counts. First, it offers a prospective ideal almost as impressive as Marxism, with the added advantage of being grounded in an appealing scientific theory. Secondly, Teilhard de Chardin's theory of convergence – the progressive development of a higher form of consciousness from all forms of life and experience – offers scope for the participation of African values in a universal civilization. Thirdly, Teilhard de Chardin restores in his vision of man, the spiritual dimension which Senghor considered lacking in Marxist philosophy. His reconciliation of science with religion, which was felt as a liberating influence by Catholic intellectuals, may also have appealed to Senghor, who is himself a Catholic. But he experienced this influence less as a Catholic than as the theoretician of Négritude, the advocate of a spiritualist outlook on the world, as is shown by this comment he makes of Teilhard de Chardin's ideas: 'Beyond material well-being, the spiritual maximum-being – the flowering of the soul, of the intelligence and of the heart – is confirmed as the ultimate goal of human activity.'[25] The specific contribution of Teilhard de Chardin's philosophy to Senghor's African socialism is more explicitly indicated in another passage: 'Teilhard's *socialization*, our socialism is nothing but the technical and spiritual organization of human society by the intelligence and the heart.'[26] In other words, African socialism is an ideal in which the spiritual values of traditional Africa are integrated into the process of modernization through new forms of social and political organization and technological progress: a synthesis of Négritude and Western socialism.

However, Senghor's African socialism does not offer more than the idea of social and political action. His socialism does not have the concrete quality of parallel ideas evolved in English-speaking Africa. It lacks the pragmatic edge of Nkrumah's pronouncements or the urgent conviction of Nyerere's manifestoes. Nonetheless, taken as an extension of his theory of Négritude and in the historical context in which Senghor's work and thinking are situated, it is not without a certain relevance and significance.

Notes and References

1 For a presentation of the full range of meanings evoked by the term 'Négritude', see Janheinz Jahn, *History of Neo-African Literature* (London: Faber and Faber, 1968), and also Albert Memmi, 'Négritude et Judéité', in *L'Homme dominé* (Paris: Gallimard, 1969).
2 Translated into English under the title *Return to My Native Land* (Harmondsworth: Penguin, 1969).
3 Quoted by Lilyan Kesteloot in 'La Négritude et son expression littéraire', in *Négritude africaine, négritude caraibe* (Paris: 1973).
4 Cf. Philippe Decraene, *Le Panafricanisme* (Paris: Press Universitaires de France, 1959), and Colin Legum, *Pan-Africanism* (London: Pall Mall Press, 1962).
5 The expression is used by Karl Mannheim in his essay 'Conservative Thought', in Paul Kecskemeti (ed.) *Essays on Sociology & Social Psychology* (London: Oxford University Press, 1953).
6 'Psychologie du négro-africain', *Diogène*, No. 37 (Paris: 1962); English quotation from John Reed and Clive Wake, *L. S. Senghor: Prose and Poetry* (London: Heinemann Educational Books, 1976), p. 30.
7 *Liberté I*, p. 257.
8 Ibid., p. 255.
9 *Diogène*, No. 37, p. 5.
10 *Fondements*, p. 54; italics in the original.
11 *Diogène*, No. 37, p. 7.
12 *Prose and Poetry*, p. 35.
13 *Diogène*, No. 37, p. 11.
14 *Liberté I*, p. 23.
15 *Prose and Poetry*, pp. 34–5.
16 *Liberté I*, pp. 212–15.
17 *Fondements*, p. 64; italics in the original.
18 *Diogène*, No. 37, p. 7.
19 *Prose and Poetry*, p. 34.
20 *Liberté I*, p. 264. For an extensive discussion of this aspect of Senghor's theory, see Sylvia Washington Ba, *The Concept of Négritude in the Poetry of Léopold Sédar Senghor* (Princeton: Princeton University Press, 1973), pp. 44–73.
21 *Fondements*, p. 69.
22 *Prose and Poetry*, p. 43.
23 *Liberté I*, p. 30.
24 *Pierre Teilhard de Chardin et la politique africaine* (Paris: Cahiers Pierre Teilhard de Chardin No. 3, 1962), p. 22.
25 *On African Socialism* (London: Pall Mall Press and New York: Praeger, 1965), p. 154.
26 Ibid., p. 146.

Chapter 31

Negritude and a New Africa:
An Update

Peter S. Thompson

In this attempt to outline the present reputation of Negritude we will at times remark that the movement is held in low esteem. It is vital to be clear: what seems like a low reputation is simply the contrast with past eras when feelings about Negritude were more generally positive. There is now a lack of consensus about the movement. Inevitably, an age-old lack of agreement over the definition of Negritude plays a part in this discussion. It is time to try to clarify the multiplicity of views about Negritude, and to give some reasons for the complexity of critical opinions on the subject. The goal here is to be sufficiently precise about the latter to be of use to specialists, while also helping generalists who may have been surprised to read that there are not uniformly positive views of the movement. The question arises – and as yet remains impossible to answer: can the Negritude movement still serve as an inspiration to writers and leaders in black cultures, as a step towards "the creation of a meaningful perspective of collective life and action for the African people in the modern world" (86)?

A status report of the present kind follows, in part, a simple chronology, from the conception of the movement in the late thirties by Léopold Sédar Senghor and Aimé Césaire, through its changes and voluminous defenses (chiefly by Senghor) into the seventies. Three strains of thought, which grow more insistent in the seventies and eighties, add interest to the chronological approach: accusations of a neocolonialist (economic) presence in Africa; the "language problem" and African languages in literature; and the demand for multiculturalism in school curricula. All three of these are reflected, subtly and paradoxically, in both the tenets of Negritude and some of the attacks it has suffered. More than any chronological development, however, the very diversity of these attacks gives insight into a large sense of dissatisfaction. The first criticisms were some of the strongest – for example, an essay by Gabriel d'Arboussier in 1949. Since the late forties Negritude has suffered incrementally, a kind of decline from a thousand cuts. These disparate reactions should be examined, as they provide more insight into African writing than does the search for any

First published in *Research in African Literatures* 33.4 (Winter 2002): 143–53.

unifying trend that might gradually have pushed the Negritude movement outside of consensus. Let us look at some of the severest criticisms, while conceding that their very complexity makes an assessment of Negritude's status shift constantly in and out of focus. Emotion, prejudice, and ideology grip almost all speakers on the subject, and what can be said without arousing the rhetoric of riposte becomes as problematic as what can be known by non-Africans. We can be sure, at least, that two great poets – Senghor and Césaire – are remnants of this movement, along with René Maran and the earliest Africa-centered prose writers. And prominent critics – among them Ezekiel Mphahlele and Abiola Irele – continue to give Negritude its due as an important historical stage.

In Africa[1] one often hears that the goals of Negritude, both political and literary, have been by-passed. In the Caribbean, Boukman, speaking in the sixties, offered the same:

> It is no service to African culture to cling like an oyster to notions overtaken by history. The concept of Negritude which was revolutionary in the forties and fifties is today only fit for the museum of literature. (qtd. in Irele 84)

This notion, with its chronological frame of reference, is worth exploring before setting forth the many specific quarrels. The assertion that Negritude is dead gives us the pause necessary to reexamine its earliest definitions, and to see how these were often misinterpreted. Senghor's best known definition is that Negritude is "l'ensemble de valeurs de civilisation du monde noir" 'the totality of civilization and its values within the black world' (Vaillant 244). Sylvia Bâ summarizes much of Senghor's vast writing on biology and ethnography in asserting that "[o]ne of the cornerstones of Senghorian Négritude is the affirmation of a specific psychophysiology proper to the black man, traces of which persist regardless of his environment or degree of acculturation" (49). The emphasis on what it is to be black, and on the essence of African culture, helped build the platform of Senghor's political life: "He believed that the strengthening of the unique aspects of African culture was a precondition of any truly independent development" (Vaillant 289). Césaire's definition also mentions history and culture: "La Négritude est la simple reconnaissance du fait d'être noir, et l'acceptation de ce fait, de notre destin de noir, de notre histoire et de notre culture" 'Negritude is the simple recognition of the fact of being black, and the acceptance of this fact, of our destiny as blacks, of our history and of our culture' (Vaillant 244). The attempts to define Africanness, to find the roots of African culture in the precolonial period and to preserve this period of history and culture in positive terms have often been summed up as the "objective" definition of Negritude. It is this relatively simple project that has drawn the harshest attacks. Less commented on are the *engagement* and the efforts of both Senghor and Césaire toward a "subjective Negritude. This includes their militancy, their reaction (especially Césaire's plays) to colonialism and slavery, their definitions (especially Senghor's *métissage culturel*, or "cultural cross-breeding") of a new role for Africans in a multiracial world. "La Négritude, c'est une certaine manière d'être homme, surtout de vivre en homme" 'Negritude is a certain way of being human, above all of living as a human' (Senghor 139).

Most criticisms of Negritude also fail to reckon with its evolution over four decades. It has been a little easy to proclaim the movement dead when picking as a target the earliest ("objective") definitions from the forties. Senghor, meanwhile, in the sixties and seventies, used the word *Négritude* less and *Africanité* more, stressing brotherhood with Arabs on the continent, and evolving away from what has been called a "nostalgic" vision of tribal life before the arrival of whites. He later borrowed heavily from Teilhard de Chardin, in speaking of a "civilisation de l'universel" and of a world role for the specific African talents in a new "humanism" to which all cutures could accede. As Janet Vaillant points out, he had broached this humanism even in 1935 (113); this gives an idea of the simplifying tendency of many of his critics. Césaire, meanwhile, has said much less on the whole subject. Even reticence has been overinterpreted: "Le silence de Césaire parle" 'Césaire's silence speaks [volumes]' (Tidjani-Serpos 100). Yet the complexity of Césaire's views – at least in political life – can be seen in his resignation from the Communist Party and in his steering Martinique toward a political bond with France, rather than away from it. These events, in 1956 and 1946, respectively, enraged many of his allies.

An aside, of interest to academics in America, is that even a well-meaning multicultural-ism gets an uneven grip on Negritude. Multiculturalism (from the American point of view) is enacted by inserting discrete and distinctly non-American cultures into the curriculum. This can give offense to Africans by making of African life and African sentiments a kind of *exotisme*. Senghor himself spoke out against this *exotisme*, as did the first prose writers who made Africa the center of their stories, rather than an ornament. Senghor's critics, especially his most vocal opponents in anglophone Africa, have objected as well, while criticizing Negritude at the same time. They object to the facile gloss of things African, feeling that there is no African unity and that it is fallacious to lump all blacks or all Africans together as one culture. The possibility of a Pan-Africanism and the "African personality" has, of course, been a debate unto itself since Nkrumah and the independence of the first African states. In any case, there is in Senghor's *métissage culturel* and elsewhere the desire for an Africa-centered multiculturalism:

> But though Négritude was a legitimate reaction, it is probably true that today our need is less to press our claim, however justified, to an original difference, than to begin to restate our common involvement with the rest of humanity. It is precisely in this perspective that our modern literature will derive its enduriong interest – in the way it throws a vivid light upon an area of human life and experience which, though circumscribed in its immediate reference, has nonetheless a fundamental correspondence to other areas, in other climes and other times. (Irele 3)

The point is that a multicultural emrace of Negritude, like any other perspective of it, is embarrassed by the interplay of two tenets that represent an evolution, not a contradiction. First, that there is an essence of Africanness, and that it should be isolated and extolled. Second, that the destiny and self-definition of Africa is open, and that Africans should assimilate whatever is helpful form other cultures. As Senghor said in an address in 1975 at the Université Gaston Berger, "Chacun doit être métis à sa façon" 'We all should be mixed-race in our own ways.'

Writers, critics, politicians, and the voting public in such places as Senegal and Martinique have always seen in Negritude what they wanted. There is in the elasticity of its definitions something for everyone – supporter or opponent. This makes lively reading of the following inventory of the objections by various groups and ideologies. It is helpful to organize most of these objections under two headings. There is, first, the overadherence of most objectors to the romanticism of Senghor's earliest definition of Negritude, his vision of a primitive society and of "le royaume d'enfance" 'the kingdom of childhood.' Second, there are irritations deriving from his defensive and intellectualizing personality, along with his accommodation of French influence and his affinity with French literature and civilization.

One objection that spans decades is that Negritude is racist, or that it is uncomfortably close to the themes of racism. Sartre, in his important preface to Senghor's anthology of black writers, spoke of a "racisme anti-raciste." There is certainly anti-white, anti-Western, anti-European language in the speeches, plays, poems, novels, and these of this group. "Blanc" becomes a negative image in Césaire's poetry, for example. Kwaku Asante-Darko describes this hostility in a recent essay on the various "negritudes" (153). Graziano Benelli sees this as part of a radical stage: "Per un certo tempo la Negritudine si radicalizza, diventa intollerante come solo sa esserlo l'intransigenza adolescenziale" 'For a while Negritude became radical and intolerant as only adolescent intransigence can be' (25). As he says, these themes reached an "obsessive" level even when focused on the color black (11). Sékou Touré has objected that "[t]he color of one's skin can't justify anything" (Michael xv), yet blackness or Africanness was made to justify everything about Negritude – not only its *raison d'être* but all the themes of its opposition to the West. Further, a broad range of critics are unhappy with Senghor's uncomfortable adoption of the early qualifications of Africans made by ethnographers, among them Gobineau and Lévy-Bruhl. Aside from the natural dislike of these descriptions because they came from Europe, there is the objection that the essence of being African is as difficult to describe as any human style. Senghor tried at enormous length to describe an African style, especially in the areas of thinking and feeling. It is possible to find this offensive on the grounds that there can be no unity of style among the world's blacks. These same objectors – somewhat at odds with the Pan-Africanist movement – resist any portrait of continental unity in biological, psychological, economic, or cultural terms. A related, and more passionate, dissension has been that all these assumptions of racial or continental unity, and the glorification of Africanness of which they are a premise, are simply reactions to the degrading views of whites (Asante-Darko 153). Negritude loses prestige because it appears an obligated or dictated response to Europe. This view first crystallized as a reaction to Sartre's statement that Negritude was the minor term in a kind of dialectic with Europeanness, destined to phase itself out in the synthesis (like Senghor's *métissage*) of a future universalism. Clearly, this offends on two counts: that blackness only exists in opposition to whiteness, and that Africanness – to whatever extent it exists – will have a common destiny with Europe. Implicit in Senghor's early writings along this line, and in Sartre's endorsement of them, is the abdication of logic and analytical thinking to Europe, while sentiment and analogical "apprehension" of truth are assigned to Africa. One may object that this is not only inaccurate but abject.

The range of controversy among contemporary critics and writers is even greater than these arguments suggest. There are those who feel that the Senghorian view of Africa (to which some Caribbean writers were attracted as well) is a nostalgic falsehood. It is rightly asserted that Senghor never knew the idyllic setting and tribal community he evokes, any more than did the Caribbeans Damas and Césaire, or even Maran who lived in Africa and whose novel *Batouala* was precursor of Negritude in 1921. Kofi Awoonor (of Ghana), not among the youngest generation of African writers, has dismissed this vision as "Senghorian myth."[2] Even if some elements of the "royaume d'enfance" exist today, they will have disappeared, it is argued, when industrialization is complete. Thus, even those who do not accuse Negritude of mythologizing find it irrelevant on the grounds that its vision is static (Asante-Darko 157).

Demography helps explain some other distinct groups of objections. There has always been some antipathy for Senghor's ideology and politics outside of urban West Africa, because he is a Catholic. There is anti-Catholic feeling, of course, both because the religion is alien and because its imposition was organized and powerful. Some feel that the simple appeal that Negritude claims to have for all Africans is hypocritical, since its authors do not even write in African languages.[3] Senghor does not mitigate this by scattering Sere (his father's language) words in the poetry; most of Senegal speaks Wolof. Some of the strongest attacks have come from anglophone Africa. Although it is acknowledged that "anglophone Africa" and "francophone Africa" are misnomers, it is commonly suggested that the "indirect" or nonassimilationist style of British colonial rule may have softened the reaction that produced Negritude in French-controlled areas. Protestant missionaries were more likely than Catholics to learn native languages and to translate the Bible into them. French administrators, as an outcome of the ideals of 1789, were more likely to make Africans French citizens, or at least to assert an equality under the law. The concomitant assumption was that the citizens were becoming completely French without a backward glance at the culture that was being lost. The less assimilated English-speakers, then, have been alienated by the strident independence of Negritude's reactionary thesis, and by the paradoxical strains of Cartesian logic and Bergsonian philosophy in its formulation. This leads to Wole Soyinka's famous questioning of the need for Negritude, when he says that a tiger does not need to go around asserting his tigritude. The Nobel laureate feels that Negritude was too directly a reaction to Europe, and yet "stayed within a pre-set system of Eurocentric intellectual analysis both of man and society and tried to re-define the African and his society in those externalised terms" (136). As with Abanda-Ndengue's sentiment in his "Négrisme," Soyinka is less attached to anti-colonial themes, and more receptive to diverse cultural influences. Ofr course, the later Negritude essays (Senghor, *Liberté III: Négritude et la civilisation de l'universel*) strike a similar note, with the themes of *métissage* and universalism. An analogy is the embrace of Arab cultures in Senghor's later writings and his shift to the term *Africanité*, which followed objections by Arabs that Negritude – by excluding them – did not promote Africanness or African unity (Melady 28).

In an overtly political arena the Marxists have also criticized Negritude. The anti-spiritual bias of Marxism is antithetical to the apparent "mysticism" of some of Senghor's remarks. Contemporary Marxists like Chidi Amuta tend to feel that Negritude, by emphasizing culture, isolates the question of decolonialization from the real struggle, which is social and economic. This contemporary view also surfaced as early as the late forties, when some of the first attackers proclaimed Negritude a nonrational and mystifying diversion from the class struggle. The fact that Senghor was one of the inventors of African socialism, and that Césaire was a communist until 1956, only increases the Marxists' disgust with the impurity of their efforts. Another recent political objection has arisen to the universalism of Senghor's later essays. Even his theme of *métissage*, while sounding realistic to some, has angered others. This is because it is taken as an accommodation of Western encroachments. In the context of neocolonialism it is seen as a concession of some kind, and, like very different concessions that Negritude made in its early days, this theme is seen as offering too much to please Europeans and Americans. Perhaps René Depestre is a link between this view and that of the Marxists when he says, "Loin d'armer leur conscience contre les violences du sous-développement, la négritude dissout *ses nègres* et *ses négro-africains* dans un existentia-lisme parfaitement inoffensif pour le système qui dépossède les hommes et les feemes de leur identité" 'Far from arming them with awareness against the violence of under development, Negritude dissolves *its Negroes* and *its black Africans* in an existentialism that is perfectly harmless to the system that robs men and women of their identity' (82). Yet another distinct difficulty exists for French-speaking blacks outside of Africa, like Césaire himself. Some object to the very Africanness at the heart of Negritude, feeling that they do not want to lose what sense of identity and of country they have in an endless yearning for Africa (Corzani 4: 47). As Zadi Zaourou points out, there has always been the complication of this duality for Césaire (248), and it has probably shaped not only his poetry but also his vision of the political future of Martinique.

The foregoing inventory gives an idea of the variety and proliferation of objections to Negritude, along with the elements of its intrinsic appeal. A chronological look at the generations of Africans writers will help organize some of the objections – not, as one might suspect, according to the evolution of Negritude itself, but according to other trends in African political and intellectual life. At a recent conference, Biyi Bandele-Thomas outlined four generations.[4] The first is that of the "explorers" – Césaire, Senghor, Cheik Hamidou Kane, Camara Laye, Birago Diop, and others writing in French, and Gladys Caseley-Hayford, Denis Osadebay, R. J. Armattoe, and others in English. Among this group the francophone writers were generally in sympathy with Negritude, even in its emphasis on the past and early cultural roots. Even among the anglophone writers, "there is the same element of racial feeling and the same compulsion to the glorification of the African past and things African" (Irele 110). The different perspective of those in English colonies has been mentioned, and it is also possible that they felt overshadowed by the success in Europe of Césaire and Senghor, and by the *succès de scandale* and Prix Goncourt of Maran's earlier *Batouala*. Still, there was a common idealism in this period that presaged independence from Europe – "realism was clearly impossible, for it was on the innocence of Africa that it was important to insist" (Irele 112). Realism, meaning a depiction of independent Africa with all its problems, came with the next generation, which includes Kofi Awoonor, J. P. Clark, Soyinka, and Chinua Achebe. This group includes some of the sharpest critics of Negritude and has portrayed itself as more forward-looking and less afraid to appear Westernized. Soyinka, particularly, as a writer of prose and drama, has been able to add humor and irony to his realism and to give an existential sense of Africa in transition, rather than to cherish an essential African past as counterpoint to Europe: "Today this goes beyond the standard anti-colonial purge of learning and education and embraces the apprehension of a culture whose reference points are taken from within the culture itself" (Soyinka viii).

It is fair to note that Soyinka's starting point – "reference points" – is the same as Senghor's end point, and that the two are never as far apart as Soyinka makes it seem. Further, over the years he has ignored the Senghorian appeal to "universalism" and has reacted to Negritude as if it had remained static and narcissistic. Soyinka's position appears to the non-partisan eye fairly close to the later conciliation and *métissage* of Senghor, and it "by no means implies a complete denial of the past, but rather a new integration which situates the past and the traditional culture within a moral perspective" (Irele 112). Analysts like Irele have reconciled Negritude with many of its enemies, finding, for example, "no better fulfilment of the idea of Négritude in modern literature than in the work of Soyinka himself" (112). He makes a similar analysis of the political leader Nkrumah, an avowed opponent of Negritude at the time of his *Consciencism* (1964). One can see in Nkrumah's interest in the Pan-Negro and Pan-Africa movements a "fulfilment of the idea of Negritude"; to do so only requires a clearer sense of the elasticity of Negritude than its critics have generally shown.[5]

The seventies produced a generation, according to Bandele-Thomas, that was over-shadowed by the great Nigerians – rudderless, without great individual successes, and profoundly affected by the promise and collapse of the oil boom in Nigeria. The realism of their writing reflected disappointment with the progress of independence, and increasing awareness of neocolonialism. Anti-Western feeling grew along with the feeling of entrap-ment in the industrialized world's sytem of banking, trade, and commodities markets. Of this generation the most important note is that they were the first – not just in anglophone Africa – to be silent on Negritude, increasingly finding it irrelevant. It was no longer the pivotal African statement on which everyone had a position. Césaire was preoccupied with politics, and Senghor was losing political popularity, while writing more theory and less poetry. When this group has spoken, they, like the new "fourth" generation, have had a harsh reaction to what they see (as did many in the forties) as its racism. The generation just beginning to publish now, which includes Tsitsi Dangarembga (Zimbabwe) and Mbulelo Mzamane (South Africa), seems especially intolerant of the racial and biological elements of Negritude: "La jeunesse africaine est heureusement composée en majorité de ces Nègres marrons excommuniés par Senghor parce qu'ils refusèrent de bannir leurs préoccupations des idées pensées par des Jaunes ou des Blancs". 'African youth is luckily composed mostly of those blacks broken free, who are excommunicated by Senghor because they refuse to rid themselves of ideas thought by yellows and whites' (Tidjani-Serpos 99). Nouréini Tidjani-Serpos, seeking to present a unified approach on behalf of young Africans, combines several angles. The young object (and they are not the first, as has been noted here) to Senghor's having borrowed the racial notions of the early ethnographers. As a correlative, they sense that he puts a "brake" or limit on the potential of blacks (98). In addition, they raise the old objection that there is no unanimity of outlook or sentiment among blacks – an objection that is currently heard in the context of multiculturalism in America. The young, according to Tidjani-Serpos, also object that Segnhor's idealized Africa hides certain "aspects négatifs" of the precolonial era (99). This scholar's contemporary (and rather extreme) gloss is that "[a]u nom de la Négritude les tontons macoutes et le régime duvalliériste ont conduit Haïti vers un sombre destin" 'it was in the name of Negritude that the tonton macoutes and the Duvallier regime led Haiti to its dark fate' (99). More intriguing, however, is the unsup-ported inference from Césaire's "silence" that he no longer agrees with the early principles of Negritude. Césaire has recently said little on the theory in general, and, like Senghor, now has a much lower political profile. Yet his silence is probably misjudged by Tidjani-Serpos, just as Soyinka judges this silence and the many new developments of Senghor's thought to be "tactical withdrawals" (126).

Then there is the "language question." The call is louder than ever for an African literature written in African languages. Ngugi wa Thiong'o, in *Decolonising the Mind* (1986), is adamant and makes the book his farewell to English. Césaire is often seen as someone who did violence to the colonizer's language, twisting French style and syntax while exploiting its vocabulary. Senghor, however, is often condemned for sounding like Claudel – even while some give him credit for reproducing the patterns of African oral literature. Achebe's many remarks about the stimulative value of his divided position, between languages and literatures, can be seen as rationalizing. It is the last two generations of writers, again, who see Negritude – embodied in the explorer generation – as irrelevant in this complex debate whose terms are still being defined. The newest generation of literary critics in Africa are also generally indifferent to the Negritude corpus, at least where *nouvelle critique*, formalism, and deconstructionism are concerned. This is because of the emphasis on the referent in Negritude writing, the constant reference to the root experience of African life from which the works draw. Outside the text some new critical approaches are also stymied by the ongoing invocation of African unity, and beyond even that there is the constant, implied reference to the alien colonizers. At the same time, though, some African critics are ambivalent about French criticism and other formalist approaches. They are ambivalent about the need to keep up with what is happening in the West, even while making repeated calls for more discipline and science in African literary criticism.[6]

What the present seems to allow, then, in terms of Negritude's prestige, is an acceptance – sometimes difficult, sometimes condescending – of its place in history: "Yet the necessity of a Senghor *as* and *when* he sang his 'sweet songs,' cannot be discountenanced considering the context of the psychological damage done to the Negro by colonialist mythology" (Amuta 178). The word "damage" seems to lessen the positive and independent imapct of the Negritude poems and novels. A somewhat older group seems a little more comfortable with the lasting value of the movement: "Who is so stupid as to deny the historical fact of Négritude as both a protest and a positive assertion of African cultural values?" (Mphahlele 282). Moreover, as Irele says, Negritude's principles of African unity help "to define as it were a founding myth as the basis of our action and collective existence in modern times. Herein lies what constitutes, in my opinion, the continuing relevance of concepts such as Négritude and African personality" (113). Others imply a debt to Negritude with suggested modifications; Abanda Ndengue's "Négrisme," Y. E. Dogbe's "Neo-Negritude," Adotévi's "Melanism." For still others, critics and academics working outside Africa, there is little awareness of the twists and turns in the fate of Negritude that this essay has attempted to bring up to date. Many Americans, for example, are aware that the Harlem Renaissance helped inspire Negritude and assume that the latter has enjoyed the uncomplicated and positive fortunes of the former. In fact, Western interest in Negritude has often contributed to lowering its prestige in Africa. Irving Markovitz says (of the pre-independence days, however), "It 'worked' because it contained a moral appeal to the French intelligentsia couched in terms of their own culture and tradition" (42). As has been seen, opponents have been very specific about the elements that appealed to the West. Non-Africans see only with difficulty how these elements have weakened the appeal of Negritude in modern Africa. The question of vogue arises, then, and is especially refractory in the midst of our fashionable concerns for multiculturalism. We are most attracted to those voices that express the pride and independence of a distinct culture, and that seem – to the outsider and student – most clearly to define it.

Notes

1   For this observation I cite writers generally whom I heard while I worked in Africa, along with students and academics there, and writers who have spoken while traveling in the US. I also cite Tidjani-Serpos, whose remarks (later in the paper) bear specifically on contemporary Africa.

2   Festival of African Writing, Brown University, 6 Nov. 1991.

3   Ngugi's *Decolonising the Mind* is indispensable on the language question and will be discussed later
    in the paper. Also see the citations for his article in *RAL* 31.1 (2000) and the article on him by Simon
    Gikandi in *RAL* 31.2.

4   Colloquium on "Gender and Generation," Festival of African Writing, Brown University, 8 Nov.
    1991. Bandele-Thomas's remarks concerned only "generation."

5   Asante-Darko, cited earlier, is especially helpful on the subject of the elasticity of Negritude's
    definition.

6   This point was made in passing by several African writers, on both the opening and the closing days
    of the Festival of African Writing, Brown University, Nov. 1991.

References

Adotévi, Stanislas. *Négritude et négrologues*. Paris: UGE, 1972.

Amuta, Chidi. *The Theory of African Literature*. Atlantic Highlands, NJ: Zed, 1989.

Asante-Darko, Kwaku. "The Co-Centrality of Racial Conciliation in Negritude Literature." *Research in
    African Literatures* 31.2 (2000): 151–62.

Bâ, Sylvia. *The Concept of Negritude in the Poetry of Léopold Sédar Senghor*. Princeton: Princeton UP, 1973.

Benelli, Graziano. *La Necessità della Parola: Léopold Sédar Senghor*. Ravenna: Longo, 1982.

Corzani, Jack. *La littérature des Antilles-Guyane françaises*. Vols. 4–6. Fort-de-France: Désormeaux, 1978.

d'Arboussier, Gabriel. "Une dangereuse mystification de la théorie de la Négritude." *La Nouvelle
    Critique* (1949): 52–60.

Depestre, René. *Bonjour et adieu à la Négritude*. Paris: Seghers, 1980.

Dogbe, Y. E. *Le divin amour*. Paris: P.J. Oswald, 1976.

Gikandi, Simon. "Traveling Theory: Ngugi's Return to English." *Research in African Literatures* 31.2
    (2000): 194–209.

Irele, Abiola. *The African Experience in Literature and Ideology*. Bloomington: Indiana UP, 1990.

Markovitz, Irving. *Léopold Sédar Senghor and the Politics of Négritude*. New York: Atheneum, 1969.

Melady, Margaret. *Léopold Sédar Senghor: Rhythm and Reconciliation*. South Orange: Seton Hall UP, 1971.

Michael, Colette. *Négritude: An Annotated Bibliography*. West Cornwall, CT: Locust Hill, 1988.

Mphahlele, Ezekiel. "Remarks on Négritude." *Léopold Sédar Senghor: An Intellectual Biography*. Ed.
    J. L. Hymans. Edinburgh: Edinburgh UP, 1971. 280–301.

Ndengue, Abanda. *De la Négritude au négrisme*. Yaoundé: CLE, 1970.

Ngugi wa Thiong'O. *Decolonising the Mind: The Politics of Language in African Literature*. London: James
    Currey, 1986.

Sartre, Jean-Paul. "Orphée noir." Preface to *Anthologie de la nouvelle poésie nègre et malgache de langue
    française*. Paris: Presses Universitaires de France, 1969. ix–xliv.

Senghor, L. S. *Ce que je crois*. Paris: Grasset, 1988.

Soyinka, Wole. *Myth, Literature and the African World*. Cambridge: Cambridge UP, 1976.

Tidjani-Serpos, Nouréini. *Aspects de la critique africaine*. Paris: Silex, 1987.

Vaillant, Janet. *Black, French, and African: A Life of Léopold Sédar Senghor*. Cambridge: Harvard UP, 1991.

Zaourou, Zadi. *Césaire entre deux cultures*. Dakar: Nouvelles Editions Africaines, 1978.

Chapter 32

Prodigals, Come Home!

Chinweizu

Consider the following questions: should we have Modern Art in Africa or Modern African Art? Modern Poetry in Africa or Modern African Poetry? Should we import Modernity into Africa, or create an African Modernity? Are we committed to the erection of Modern Culture in Africa or to the Modernization of African Culture? If one should ask: "But what is the distinction? Isn't this merely a semantic exercise?" one would be confessing to unawareness of this widespread danger of cultural servitude masquerading as cultural development; this danger of cultural death wearing the mask of "civilization"; this danger from which we all are already half dead. But how do we make clear this distinction loaded with consequences of life and death for African Culture?

Beier and Moore have, correctly, given the title "Modern Poetry from Africa" to their anthology of poetry written in European languages by contemporary Africans. One thing this anthology is not: it is not an anthology of poetry written, spoken or sung by Africans working today on extended seams of the African poetic tradition, tuning their voices to echoes from our tradition in order to sing of our world of now and here. And that they are written in European languages is not even the point! For their forms, as well as the sensibilities and the attitudes that inform their treatment, remain, for the most part, outside the African tradition. For exemplars of Modern African Poetry, poetry written today in styles informed by traditional African poetics, for poetry written today that continues and develops the African tradition we must look to Ahmad Nassir's *Gnomic Verses* (Swahili), to p'Bitek's *Song of Lawino* (Acoli and English) and to Okigbo's "Path of Thunder" poems (English). No matter in what language they are written, these poems stand as prototypes of what a Modern African Poetry might be like.

Unlike Modern Poems from Africa, these Modern African Poems, even when they are written in English, are within the poetic traditions of indigenous African cultures. Though Modern Poetry from Africa is poetry written by Africans, it is poetry dominated by modern European sensibility. Modern African Poetry, on the other hand, is poetry written by Africans, and, above all else, dominated by a sensibility derived from the African tradition. And to get a flavor of that tradition we might consult Beier's *Yoruba Poetry*, his *African Poetry*, and Andrezjewski and Lewis's

First published in *Okike: An African Journal of New Writing* 4 (1973): 1–12.

Somali Poetry. In them we find translations of traditional African poetry. These traditional works, whether handed down from antiquity or written and collected in the past century, distinctly convey the traditional African voice. And even these English translations cannot but convince us that the mark of un-Africanness is not simply language, but rather the form, the attitude and the sensibility that go into the treatment of a poem.

Lest the language or the sheer talent of the poet confuse this issue of sensibility, I shall use poems written in English by one distinguished African poet to illustrate the vast distance between Modern Poetry in Africa and Modern African Poetry. Okigbo's poem "Water-maid," a section of his five-part "Heavensgate," begins as follows:

> Eyes open on the sea,
> eyes open, of the prodigal;
> upward to heaven shoot
> where stars will fall from.

But by the time Okigbo gets to his "Path of Thunder" poems, the anemic modernity of his early "Heavensgate" is abandoned. One result is his "Elegy for Slit-drum." And it begins:

> Condolences . . . from our swollen lips laden with condolences:
>
> The mythmaker accompanies us
> The rattles are here with us
>
> Condolences from our split-tongue of the slit drum condolences
>
> one tongue full of fire
> one tongue full of stone –
>
> condolences from the twin-lips of our drum parted in condolences

The tired syntactic jugglery of "Watermaid" is gone. Vanished! And in its place? Stirring sequences of rhythmic lament; the towncrier's clear and unambiguous declaratives, each short line a complete and telling expression, firm in tone, ending on a highlighting stress; each stanza of short lines followed by one long line, an echoing variation anchored on the rhythms of *condolences*. And to anyone familiar with the recurring chorus lines of African folk tales, children's stories and songs of lamentation, familiar with the rhythmic phrasings of *Ikoro* drumming, the basic African influences on "Elegy" are not mysterious. (To determine the tradition to which "Elegy" partly belongs one should re-examine various popular recordings of the fifties and early sixties in which deceased notables were lamented. *Onwu Nwapa* and *Odoemezina* are two Igbo laments that come to my mind right away. The declarative lines, the one-or-more-line refrains are all there in these Igbo songs of lamenta-tion). One could use Okigbo's "Elegy" at a wake, the short declarative lines going to a lead singer, the long "Condolences" lines going to the assembled mourners! Here is a powerful use of traditional form in a non-traditional poem in English; an enrichment as well as an extention of African poetry in English by elements from the African traditional.

In considering Okigbo's "Hurrah for Thunder," another poem in his "Path of Thunder" sequence, the juvenescent influence is even more readily presentable. From "Hurrah for Thunder" we have:

Whatever happened to the elephant –
Hurrah for thunder –

The elephant, tetrarch of the jungle:
With a wave of the hand
He could pull four trees to the ground;
His four mortar legs pounded the earth:
Wherever they treaded,
The grass was forbidden to be there.

Now compare that with the following lines from the Yoruba oriki "Erin":

Elephant, a spirit in the bush.
With his single hand
He can pull two palm trees to the ground.
If he had two hands
He would tear the heavens like an old rag.
. . . .
With his four mortar legs
He tramples down the grass.
Wherever he walks,
The grass is forbidden to stand up again.

Tr. by Ulli Beier & Gbadamosi
Taken from *300 Years of Black Poetry*
Edited by Lomax and Abdul, Fawcett

The blurb on the back cover of the Africana edition of *Labyrinths* says that Okigbo's "Path of Thunder" sequence of poems "shows a new fierceness which held the promise of remarkable development." That is an unavoidable impression. I have pointed out some of the African sources of this outbreak of new poetic power. This triumphant juvenescence is not a mere matter of rhythms. (It is that too!) It is not a mere matter of formal imitations and direct borrowings and close adaptations. It is far more a matter of his having abandoned what Leroi Jones called the "meta-language and shallow ornament of contemporary academic British poetry," (Leroi Jones, in *Home*). Okigbo abandons it for a language of African particulars; he accepts an African poetic landscape with its flora and fauna – a landscape of elephants, beggars, calabashes, serpents, pumpkins, baskets, towncriers, iron bells, slit drums, iron masks, hares, snakes, squirrels; a landscape that is no longer used as an exoticism for background effect, no longer used for exotic references sprinkled among anemic images, but a landscape which has been moved to the dramatic centre of his poetry; a landscape portrayed with native eyes to which aeroplanes naturally appear as iron birds; a landscape in which the animals behave as they might behave in African folk-lore, of animals presented through native African eyes. And "native" is not a pejorative! And this juvenescence is clearly a result of his consciously working within African traditions and of his bringing to his work valuable lessons he had learned from other traditions, Western Modernism not excluded. Whereas in "Heavensgate" we find . . . a Modern European poem made exotic, and find in "Hurrah . . ." an apprentice poem whose traditional models show too clearly through gaps in the stitches, in "Elegy..." we find a poem which, though written in English, owes nothing to modern European sensibility; a poem at the third transmuted corner of a cultural triangle at whose other corners stand the African Traditional and the Modern European sensibilities; but still a poem whose African lineage is beyond dispute.

This distinction between Modern African Poetry and Modern Poetry in Africa, based as it is on continuities or discontinuities with the poetic traditions of Africa's indigenous cultures, is a paradigm of the distinction between African Modernity and Modernity in Africa, (i.e. Western Bourgeois Modernity in Africa). A Modern African Culture, whatever else it is, must be a continuation of Old African Culture. Whatever else it includes, it must include seminal and controlling elements from the Old African tradition, elements that determine its tone, hold it together and give it a stamp of distinctiveness. The problem of an African Modernity is the obverse side of the problem of African traditions. Those who deny to African traditions – and traditional Africa – a controlling place in their consciousness have no alternative but to formulate African Modernity in Western Bourgeois terms.

Echeruo's discussion of Nigerian poetry is a case worth considering. He is a modern-minded Nigerian, a poet as well as a critic. He discussed the problems of Nigerian poetry in a paper he read at the University of Nigeria, Nsukka, in 1966; a paper which was published in *Nigeria Magazine#89* and has been acclaimed in African and Africanist literary circles. In this paper "Traditional and Borrowed Elements in Nigerian Poetry," he contends that

> one of the problems facing the Nigerian writer today in transferring from indigenous to modern poetry is that of suppressing the over-explicit nature of traditional reflective poetry, and of encouraging a more subtle complicating of narration, reflection and resolution.

Echeruo also contends that both modern European and modern Nigerian poetry shun explicit moral tags, "preferring for the most part to fuse setting and reflecting into one single poetic moment." Let me point out, right away, that he misses the real problem of the contemporary Nigerian writer, be he modernist or traditionalist. The traditionalist – such as the late Fagunwa who wrote in Yoruba, and Tutuola who writes captivatingly in English without abandoning his traditionalist imagination – is content to work in his tradition, and is not transferring to anything, let alone to "modern poetry" if he is a poet. He cannot therefore be said to be faced with Echeruo's problem. The modern Nigerian writer – such as Okigbo at the end of his career – is transferring from "modern poetry" to the tradition of indigenous poetry (i.e. if he is a poet). His problems are those of journeying in the opposite direction from that claimed for him by Echeruo. Whose problems then is Echeruo con-cerned with? They are precisely those of any Nigerian writer who seeks to abandon the indigenous tradition and write modern European poetry. In other words, the problems of a would-be "modern poet," i.e. the would-be modern European poet, who happens to have been brought up in the African tradition and must overcome that "handicap"; the problems of the writer of African extraction who wants to abandon his tradition; the problems of the "de-tribalizing" African writer.

Echeruo's usage of the expressions "modern European poetry" and "modern Nigerian poetry" is cause for alarm! These terms are wielded as if they denoted two animals, different and coequal. But what really is this "modern Nigerian poetry" of his but modern European poetry, alias modern poetry, written by Europeanized sensibilities in Nigerian skin? Poetry written by Nigerians who are disciples of modernist European poetry? But from the way Echeruo denotes them one could get the impression that they shun the same things because both are modern, though independent and different. Which is not the case. In actual fact one, the Nigerian, shuns whatever it is said to shun, not because it is "modern" in some culturally neutral way, but just because the other, the European mentor, shuns those things. The impression that they are two different but equal things, two things which by virtue of some common modernity share some common attitudes – that impression vanishes! The derivativeness and dependency of the Nigerian imitation now stands out to be dealt with. And once we have stripped modernity of its cultural commitment to the West, once modernity ceases to be an alias for Western Modernity, it becomes much easier to attack the substantive issue raised by Echeruo's claims.

Is there anything modern, in a culturally neutral non-Western sense, about a "subtle complicating of narration, reflection and resolution?" But first, let us detour and understand what Western Modernity is all about. A good reference for that would be *The Idea of the Modern in Literature and the Arts*, edited by Irving Howe. In his introduction to this anthology – an anthology in which outstanding Western critics and writers tell us what Modernity (or Modernism) is in the literature and arts of the West – Howe lists some of the attributes of modernism. Now Howe, writing as he is for members of his Western culture, does not bother to say: the idea of the Modern in the Literature and the Arts *of the West*. But any non-Westerner who wants to keep his own cultural perspectives straight must supply for himself the appropriate modifiers. And in my recapitulation of what he has to say I shall supply such modifiers whenever necessary.

Among the reasons why modernism emerged are:

1. The Avant-Garde came into being as a special caste in Western society, a caste at its margins, a caste alienated from it and its traditions.
2. This Avant-Garde criticised the classical Western idea of esthetic order and either abandoned or radically modified it. In the process naturalism was out and
3. Nature ceased to be a central subject and setting for Western literature. Also,
4. in contradistinction to the classical western hero, a whole new sense of character, structure and the role of the protagonist or hero appeared in the Western novel.

And foremost among the literary attitudes and values which emerged triumphant from all this are:

5. Perversity – which is to say: surprise, excitement, shock, terror, affront
6. Primitivism – which is to say: a fascination with what in Western tradition has been considered primal, decadent or atavistic (e.g. Negro art!)
7. Nihilism – which is to say: a breakdown and accepted loss of belief in traditional values as guide to conduct, together with a feeling that human existence is meaningless.

These became dominant motifs and central preoccupations of modern Western literature. And the kind of literature that these attitudes brought into being, the modern or modernist literature of the West, is almost always difficult to comprehend. "That is a sign of its modernity," Howe assures us.

That a literature of this kind should become dominant in the West at the time when it did can be accounted for by looking closely into Western literary and social history. There was a specific burden of tradition that Western modernism reacted against in its revolt. But however familiar we may be with all that; however familiar we may be with that tradition or with the various modernist revolts against it (Symbolism, Dadaism, Surrealism, Futurism, etc.) they are not part of *our* history. They do not belong to *our* past. The individual African writer may school himself into all that knowledge (just like his Western contemporary), but the fact remains that (quite unlike his Western contemporary) none of that revolt affected and went directly into the constitution of our culture. But which culture? The African or the European? And this raises the question: who do our writers work for? Who are their audience, their listeners, the responding part of their cultural community? The Europeans – and the Europeanized – or the Africans? Which community and tradition do they elect to function in? Are they Africans or Europeans? Or more exactly, are they Africans influenced by Europe, or are they Black Europeans influenced by Africa? Which do they prefer to be? We must stop thinking that the past trajectory of Western history, literary or otherwise, is our own. We may have been hit over the head by the West; but that does not make us Westerners – at least not yet.

It should be obvious by now that the attributes Echeruo considers "modern" are merely attributes of "modern Western literature"; are culturally determined by the history of the Western tradition, and cannot be regarded as modern in any culturally neutral non-Western sense. Since their taste was cultivated on that modern Western tradition, our Nigerian "modernists" derive their attitude to explicitness and complex obscurantism wholly from the West. By becoming "modern" in the way of the West, any Nigerian or African writer would be inheriting the distinctly Western, as against the distinctly African, tradition. Since African society is far different today from Western society in its hallmarks, attitudes, and crises, in its sense of problems and fulfilments; since our crisis of values consists in our having to make hasty choices while reeling from confusing blows from the West, blows that are dislodging us from the equilibrium of our traditions, would our communicators of values not be avoiding their responsibility to *our* community if they, rather than be clear and accessible, preferred to emulate the Western fashion and be perversely difficult and irrelevant? Let us assume (and is that an unwarranted assumption?) that these African poets are writing primarily for us Africans. Then, as regards most of the works of those "Western modernist" poets who happen to be African, I must join Ama Ata Aidoo in saying:

> We are waiting around for answers and praying that those who can see things will sometimes speak in accents which the few of us who read English can understand. For we are tired of betrayals, broken promises and forever remaining in the dark.

Ama Ata Aidoo entered this plea while reviewing Wole Soyinka's *Idanre* in *West Africa* #2641. But that plea could have been, and still could be, entered with equal aptness in reviews of the many more Western modernist poets among us.

Another reviewer of *Idanre* remarks in *Nigeria Magazine* that Soyinka is in that work "at once snobbishly detached from and convulsively involved with the goings on around him" – as perhaps befits any disciple of Western modernism. He says the work is difficult, obscure and (perhaps therefore?) a work of genius! – a remark that might be expected from a reviewer unsure of his African responsibilities when faced with the glamour of Western modernist attitudes. (Which is not to say that Soyinka does not have genius – whatever that is. Look at his drama! Excellent and compelling. Look at his early poetry before he abandoned the transparency and humor of "Telephone Conversation" and chose to wallow in dense obscurities! It is just that "genius" is not a word I like to use. It is too damned up-cloud elitist for me. It sticks in my teeth. Art for me is craft, not a romantic wet-dream!) Whereas explicitness is a hallmark of African poetry, the obscurity we find in many of our poets, the obscurity they impose upon their poems out of that creed that demands a "subtle complicating of narration, reflection and resolution," this obscurity is a badge of Western modernism.

[...]

If the careers of Nassir and p'Bitek have nothing to teach our cultural exiles, Okigbo's certainly does. For he had been one of them; had been foremost among them; yet he found a way home to his cradle. But if it is already too late for them to wander back home, let our prodigals stop masquerading. Let them declare themselves for what they are – modernists of the West, not modernists of Africa. Let them acknowledge what they are and cease and desist from influencing and advising us and our posterity in the wrong directions. If and when, like Okigbo, they return home, we shall gladly celebrate their homecoming. For we cannot reject our prodigals if they come home.

Chapter 33

Neo-Tarzanism:
The Poetics of Pseudo-Tradition

Wole Soyinka

Pretenders to the crown of *Pontifex Maximus* of African poetics must learn to mind the thorns. For a start, especially when their credentials are declared to be a love and espousal of the virtues of traditional African poetry, they must penetrate into what constitutes poetry in traditional art or be contradicted by their own limitations and superficial understanding of this activity of the imagination. Traditional African poetry is not merely those verses which, being easiest to translate, have found their way into anthologies and school texts; it is not merely those lyrics which because they are favourites at Festivals of the Arts haunted by ethnologists with tape-recorders, supply the readiest source-material for uprooted academics; nor is it restricted solely to the praises of yams and gods, invocations of blessings and evocations of the pristine. Traditional poetry is all of this; it is however also to be found in the very *technique* of riddles, in the pharmacology of healers, in the utterance of the possessed medium, in the enigmas of diviners, in the liturgy of divine and cultic Mysteries (in addition to the language of their public address systems), in the unique temper of world comprehension that permeates language for the truly immersed – from the Ifa priest to the haggler in the market, inspired perhaps by economic frustration! The critic who would arrogate to himself the task of formulating an African poetics – a typical pre-occupation of the European critical tradition, by the way – had better understand this from the start or confine himself to extolling the virtues of European nursery rhymes – a field which appears more suited to the analytical capacity of our critical troika.

An earlier published essay by Chinweizu ("Prodigals, Come Home," *Okike* No. 4) defines the troika's concept of the African poetic landscape with its flora and fauna – "a landscape of elephants, beggars, calabashes, serpents, pumpkins, baskets, towncriers, iron bells, slit drums, iron masks, hares, snakes, squirrels…*a landscape protrayed with native eyes to which aeroplanes naturally appear as iron birds*; a landscape in which the animals behave as they might behave in Africa of folk-lore, animals presented through native African eyes" (my

First published in *Transition* 48 (Kampala: 1975): 38–44; and subsequently in *Art Dialogue and Outrage: Essays on Literature and Culture*, pp. 315–21, 327–9. Ibadan: New Horn Press, 1988.

italics). We must add in fairness that Chinweizu rejects the use of such a landscape as "an exoticism for background effect"; nevertheless it is one which must be moved to "the dramatic centre of poetry". I am not at all certain how this proves more acceptable than the traditional Hollywood image of the pop-eyed African in the jungle – "Bwana, bwana me see big iron bird". My African world is a little more intricate and embraces precision machinery, oil rigs, hydro-electricity, my typewriter, railway trains (not iron snakes!), machine guns, bronze sculpture, etc., plus an ontological relationship with the universe including the above listed pumpkins and iron bells. This may result in a subtle complication in the "narration, reflection and resolution" of these phenomena but emphatically denies the deliberate complicating of them. Echeruo, alas, chose his wording most unwisely and Chinweizu & Co., can hardly be blamed for seizing that big stick to hit their unfavourable poets over the head. The trouble is that, being rather unsure critics and superficial traditionalists, they have wielded that stick with a destructive opportunism rather than with an intelligent concern for poetry. Their case is worse than over-stated; it is mis-stated. And it is not only modern poetry by Africans which has been maligned in the process but the very traditional poetry whose virtues they present as examplar. When critics are weaned on, or have chosen to limit knowledge of their own heritage to one-dimensional verses on cassava and yam – not that this form of poetry is in any way belittled, the gods forbid! – and evade even one example of the mildly extra dimensional, such as, for example, the following lines from Ifa's "Irete Meji", can they really claim true knowledge of the poetic experience of the modern African writer?

> Slender as a needle
> Grimy and frayed as clothesline
> Shiny as fool's gold
>
>> Full purse clinks to the ground
>> Encumbered net slumps down, tightening the noose
>> Two cocks young: tease and tag
>> Two cocks old: bedraggle themselves along
>> Bony buttocks fall with a dry thud
>
> Made Ifa for My-thoughts
> waterbuck, bush cow
> blocked up riverrun
>
>> who worshipped Our Mother of the Waters at Ido
>> on the day he was using the tears in his eyes to
>> hunt for the good things of life
>
> Can he prosper when everything seems to elude him?[1]

Of course, Ifa did not claim to be engaged in the art of poetry when he uttered this gnomic prelude to the full body of response to a supplication. But then, neither did the anonymous author of "Humpty-Dumpty" who lampooned a public figure in English history in the words of that rhyme. The lines later passed into the nursery-ryhme repertoire of Britain – a fact which our troika may not know. What the rightful inheritors of these delightful lines dared not do, our troika have more than dared – raised "Humpty Dumpty" to the level of "great poetry" and equated it not only with William Blake's "Tiger" but with Langston Hughes' "Harlem"! Fools rush in . . .

Is this a joke? Or are our critical troika indulging in that mystification of which they accuse other critics and poets?

As a writer, given a choice between the model of "Humpty Dumpty" and the Ifa lines I have quoted, my creative sensibility opts naturally and effortlessly for the latter. As a critic I find my receptivity more rewardingly engaged, stimulated – even aggravated, yes – but ultimately more enriched by the analytical exercise of sharing my discoveries with my readers: this incidentally is one of the functions of the critic, one which Messrs Chinweizu, Jemie and Madubuike preach – No. 2 on their list of a critic's functions – but resolutely refuse to practice where some extra intellectual effort is required.

"Irete Meji" disobeys the major canons laid down by the troika – except perhaps one: it is full of similes, a poetic device that must win their approval, being straightfoward and demanding little of mental effort –

> Slender as a needle
> Grimy and frayed as clothesline
> etc., etc.,

But does it all "read well"? Is it "smooth"? Has it "music"? Is it "pleasurable" or at least "pleasurable nonsense"?

> Two cocks young: tease and tag
> Two cocks old: bedraggle themselves along
> Bony buttocks fall with a dry thud
> Made Ifa for My-thoughts
> waterbuck, bush cow
> blocked up riverrun

I rather suspect it is "heavy", "tongue-twisting", "difficult to articulate". And the only reason why it is necessary to bring up this melody aspect of a mere translation is that this is the operational mode of the troika, blithely moving from original composition to translations of traditional poetry and adjudicating these without the least note being taken of the inapplicability of all critical criteria to both categories of composition, musicality most notably of all. This level of criticism lacks acquaintance with the very rudiments of its occupation, requires perhaps a little more practice with nursery rhymes. But what is the pronouncement, musically, on traditional poetry? Is it all mellifluous? Do we never encounter passages of great internal cohesion yet "difficult to articulate"? How, in any case, does the troika define "musicality"? Our critics appear to belong to that school of ethno-musicologists who, until two or three decades ago, brainwashed the European world (including its Africans) into believing that African musical tradition was nothing but a cacophony of sounds, that the polyrhythmic tradition was the original sound of bedlam and choral dirges a wail of jackals in the night. The smooth musicality which the troika wish to foist on modern poetry by Africans as its passport to authenticity is nothing but an alienated sensibility which stems from this curtailed musical education. Yes, poetry is an "auditory" medium[2] and instead of pronunciamentos of ignorance from the wilderness, it would profit would-be champions of tradition to actually immerse themselves in recitals of traditional poetry. There is no need to go back to the village to do it. The libraries of Europe and America are full these days of recordings and even attempted notations. The musicality of poetic recitations of the Yoruba people, for example, is *not* the bland mono-rhythmic smoothness advocated by our critics; it is often staccato and deliberately so. Themes are abandoned, recovered, merged with a new arbitary inclusion under the deft, inspired guidance of both reciter and accompanist. The stark linear simplicity of translations should never be permitted to obscure the allusive, the elliptical, the multi-textured fullness of what constitutes traditional poetry, especially *in recital*. And those who read the original lines in cold print do *hear* it, and in the generous intricacy of rhythm and structure. The most faithful expression of this counterplay in the New World is Modern Jazz – the music, not often the lyric.

> Wó ni, alóló alòlò.
> Àtiròrun àkàlà.
> Ojú ro wón tòki
> Ló difá fún olómitútù
> Ti nsobirin Àgbonirègún.
> Èdidi àlò.
> Ifa ò ni polómitútù kó pupa.
> E è ni ba won kúkú òwówò lailai.

"Sprung rhythm", if I may risk faulting for borrowing the terminology of a British poet, is probably the handiest expression to describe the internal rhythm of these lines. I suggest the troika obtain the services of a good Yoruba reciter and listen to the above Ifa utterance from an egungun chant. They might then in wisdom apply their own adage to themselves – "that I am a man, and older than you are, does not mean I am your father" – and make the discovery that Gerard Manley Hopkins did not invent "sprung rhythm", nor is its exploit-ation forbidden to modern Africans who use his language because he so uniquely made it his tool. They might even commence to listen to their own poetic tradition with a new ear, eschewing the simplistic insults under which they ironically persist in burying it. Is the following really the hallmark of traditionalism by which the modern poet is to regulate himself?

> In our little village
> When elders are around
> Boys must not look at girls
> And girls must not look at boys
> Because the elders say
> That is not good.
>
> Even when night comes
> Boys must play separately
> Girls must play separately
> But humanity is weak
> So boys and girls meet
>
> The boys play hide and seek
> And the girls play hide and seek
> The boys know where the girls hide

> And the girls know where the boys hide
> So in their hide and seek
> Boys seek girls,
> Girls seek boys,
> And each to each sing
> Songs of love.

This trite, prosaic, coy, kindergarten drivel which my seven-year-old daughter would be ashamed to write is extolled by the troika critics. "Markwei's poem(!) is simple and vivid. It conveys the experience of moonlight play, whereas Wonodi's *Moonlight play* is dark and dense". I hold no brief for Wonodi's poem about which I have indeed grave objections. But to hold up Markwei's jejune prosification as the ideal can only arouse suspicions that our critics have deliberately chosen to scrape the bottom of the barrel and subvert, for reasons of their own, the entire future of African poetry. "Humpty Dumpty" is at least witty; it stretches the imagination a little, though it is not the "great poetry" claimed for it by the troika. In what line do Markwei's verses achive a moment of "vividness"? Do Messrs Chinweizu & Co. understand the word? Where does it engage the imagination? Or is this attribute of poetry no longer applicable to poems written by Africans? Looking through the window of my study as I type this, I observe and "reflect":

> Over my neighbour's fence
> A boy
> Throws a rubber ball to a girl
> The girl
> Throws a rubber ball to a boy
> Over my neighbour's fence
> The games and laughter
> Recall the bygone days beneath
> The moonlight in our village square
> When boys must play separately
> Girls must play separately
> The ball separates boy from girl . . .

Balls! There is a limit to self-abasement in the service of uncreative empathy. Also to one's patience with critics who find no room in their kingdom of poetry for both Egudu's "The First Yam of the Year" and the Yoruba traditional "New Yam". What kind of perverse, mental castration is this! Two contrasting approaches, both highly successful. Only an enemy of poetry would seek to exclude one or the other or indulge in evaluative comparison such as leads to this astounding assessment: that Romanus Egudu's poem fails to convey "tenderness or exaltation or bite" or, merely celebrates emotions "in the abstract".

> I have dug it fresh,
> this boneless flesh
> of air, earth, warmth
> and water, this
> life out of the heart
> of death . . .

Restraint is very difficult when one encounters such destructive and inaccurate criticism. I suggest that these critics wash out their ears (and eyes) and listen again. The above lines not only convey tenderness but extend that emotion. They call this poem "privatist, sterile", a "laboured and lifeless attempt at nostalgic revivalism". This is the language of borrowed pedagoguery, barren and meaningless; it bears no relation to and no knowledge of the material it engages. I suggest that these critics read the poem again from the point of view of the involved participant, one who is however not afraid to utilise language that truly reflects the numinous essence of the experience, the social symbolism of the new yam and the metaphysical context both of its celebration, its seeding and maturation from decay. The Yoruba poem is witty; Egudu does not attempt wit. Egudu's poem is visceral and sensuous; unless our critics, with their noted reductionist tendency find the last line in the traditional poem sensuous, the Yoruba poem attempts to be neither visceral nor sensuous. It plucks its images from the domestic relations (and relationships) of the new yam, it is joyously hyperbolic, irreverent; indeed it fills the mouth with the good satisfying feelings of a morsel of yam. These however are not the only attibutes or evocative potential of yam and Romanus Egudu explores some of the other, attempting to enter the deeper and essential association, including the cosmic. He extends the significance of the yam into a parable of the human condition. It appears now that this is a crime and a disservice to African literature and the African heritage. And it earns his poem what can only be best described as a malicious, untruthful analysis.

[. . .]

The central issue of their [the troika] contention – wilful obscurity and private esoterism – is one which does plague a good proportion of the modern poetry of Africans, and some of the examples they provide are justified. But just as critics like Anozie do not help by clogging up understanding further by undue fascination with structuralist faddism, nor a Paul Theroux by abdicating critical judgement as premature, the Simple Simons of criticism as represented by Chinweizu & Co. subvert the principle of imaginative challenge which is one of the functions of poetry. And the denigration and misunderstanding of traditional forms of African art should now stop. The sculpture of Africa alone is visual evidence of a dynamism that eschews superficial and surface meanings. Sculpture, the dance, music, the integration of various media of expression in any given public performance have all gone into the moulding of the sensibility which tries today to carve new forms out of alien words, expressing not only the itemised experience, but reflecting the unified conceptualisation of the experience. And poetry, let it be remembered, is not the single work of one man but the totality and variety of this activity. Within this rich, constant expression of society, individual aberrations pale into insignificance and are deservedly ignored, their championing by masochist critics notwithstanding.

It is time also that critics and social commentators alike recognised that the more-committed-than-thou breast-thumping, in all its various forms, has become boring and suspect. Social commitment is a citizen's commitment and embraces equally the carpenter, the mason, the banker, the farmer, the customs officer etc., etc., not forgetting the critic. Yet none of these thousand and one categories of contributors to social progress spends twenty-four hours a day being "socially committed". That non-stop mandate is miraculously reserved for the artist alone. It does not matter that the bulk of his total work, his life is devoted to urgent social issues; every posturing critic is privileged to haul out one "uncommitted" work, wave it aloft, mount the rostrum and bleat: "What is this doing here? How dare this artist define one moment of private reflection?" Nothing for it but they must out-Trotsky Trotsky who was sufficiently confident in his own revolutionary vision to concede that:

> Culture is the organic sum of knowledge and capacity which characterises the entire society. It embraces and penetrates all fields of human work and unifies them into a system. Individual achievements rise above this level and elevate it gradually.

No, for many critics, the concept of individual experimentation – which contributes to what may be judged as a social achievement – is anathema. Some have even gone so far as to declare, solemnly and categorically, that the concept of the individual performer or creativity is alien to African tradition. This, for a culture whose poetry constantly celebrates outstanding creative talents in every art-form, whose oral history of art records most faithfully the achievements of carvers and griots, whose art criticism, alive till today, disinguishes between the technique and refinements of one smelter and another, between one father and a son in the same line of profession! The new school of art criticism will prove yet that the art of oriki-chanting (including the self-extolling interjections) by professionals is paradoxically an antithesis of that bourgeois and decadent individualism that supposedly affects modern introspective poetry by Africans. It will be asserted that while the Mbari-house sculptor who isolates himself for a period of intense self-communion, awaits divine inspiration, a visionary flash to be translated into mud figures, is working overtime at social commitment, his modern (educated) compatriot is not, even though the latter puts down his pen and ink and perishes fighting for a cause in which he passionately believes. The latter is damned because he has larded his poems with christian and private mythology though, "luckily for him, just before his death" he was saved by events which gave him a public voice. We hope that our three-headed *Pontifex Maximus Simplicissimus* will not keep poor Christopher Okigbo burning too long in Purgatory.

The error is really a simple one: the equation of the "immediate" with "commitment". The Mbari-house sculptor who shuts himself away from day-to-day contact undertakes this period of purgation and reflection on behalf of his society. The resulting mud figures are never given the same interpretation by any two individuals yet the presence of this isolated grouping – placed usually away from the frequented parts of the village and left to crumble and decay with time – is experienced by the community as contributing to the spiritual well-being of the village in its homage to earth. The most obscure result of private reflection is a homage to life. Those to whom it communicates anything at all may be no more than the entire beneficiaries of one Mbari group of sculptures, maybe less. Both products of the spirit will perish with time, but that is no proof of their irrelevance or uselessness. I freely admit that the works of a number of African poets do absolutely nothing for me; I do not respond to them in any way. But in spite of frequent groans of irritation at the flaunting derivations of Okigbo's poetry, its frequent relapses into private biography, hagiography, geography and jokes, it performs a similar function for me as the sculptural aesthetics of several African societies. Not being possessed of that instant-tradition perceptiveness of Chinweizu and Co., I cannot claim *a transparency* of communication even from the sculpture, music and poetry of my own people the Yoruba, but the aesthetic matrix is the fount of my own creative inspiration; it influences my critical response to the creation of other cultures and validates selective eclecticism as the right of every productive being, scientist or artist. Sango is today's god of electricity, not of white-man magic-light. Ogun is today's god of precision technology, oil rigs and space rockets, not a benighted rustic cowering at the "iron bird".

Notes

1   Free translation by Judith Gleason: *A Recitation of Ifa*.
2   The naïvety of any literary critic who actually believes that the visual actuality of print can or should have no formative effect on poetry requies of course no commentary whatever. The phenomenonlogy of the printed word is too vast a subject to be tackled here however; it is sufficient to invite formulators of poetics to direct a small part of their energies to a comparative analysis of written contemporary poetry in the vernacular languages and oral poetry in the same languages. Even radio, which is an oral medium exerts formative influences on poetic texts as can be testified by anyone with an experience of radio programmes in the vernacular. They acquire traits which are absent from poetry of a purely oral genesis, and lose others. To suggest that the printed (visual) medium will result in identical products of the imagination as the oral, transient form is simply unintelligent.

Chapter 34

My Signifier is More Native than Yours:
Issues in Making a Literature African

Adéléké Adééko

Since 1962, the year of the now famous Makerere African Writers' conference and also the year Heinemann Educational Books created its very influential African Writers Series, anglophone African literary criticism has been preoccupied with devising strategies for indigenizing the substance and language of its governing principles. All leading African writers and critics have participated in formulating the parameters for devising a meta-language and a hermeneutic predisposition that will place indigenous forms at the center of the definition, classification, and appreciation protocols of culture, especially literature. Advocates of deliberately nativized material instruments of knowing propose that any genuinely *African* cultural practice must seek organic origins in the pre-colonial, oral, and folk forms. According to Obianjuwa Wali, for example, the colonial powers would have succeeded far beyond their own designs if post-independence African culture should surrender to the dominance of European *forms*. If African literature and its criticism are not conducted in African languages, scholars would be "pursuing a dead end" (14). Less idealistic others hold, like the writers who met at Makerere, that the pre-colonial traditions have served their historical purpose argue that the precolonial traditions and languages have served their historical purposes and the supposed certainties buried in them supported old orders that have succumbed to newer formations. There can be no doubt that historical developments have *nationalized* and Africanized the originally European languages and forms. These not-quite-not African *national* forms and languages will make trans-ethnic communication possible and political and cultural stability feasible.

In what has grown to be a very influential article, Kwame Anthony Appiah summarizes as *nativism* the visceral rhetoric often used in the "nationalist" theses of the side that favors

First published in *Proverbs, Textuality, and Nativism in African Literature*, pp. 1–27. Gainesville, FL: University Press of Florida, 1998.

founding an African cultural and intellectual identity on the advancement of the oral and pre-colonial traditions. Appiah says,

> Both the complaints against defilement by alien traditions in alien tongue and the defenses of them as a practical necessity...seem often to reduce to a dispute between a sentimental Herderian conception of Africa's languages and traditions as expressive of the collective essence of a pristine traditional community, on the one hand, and, on the other, a positivistic conception of European languages and disciplines as mere tools; tools that can be cleansed of the accompanying imperialist – and more specifically, racist – modes of thought.
>
> The former view is often at the heart of what we can call "nativism:" the claim that true African independence requires a literature of one's own. Echoing the debate in 19th century Russia between "Westerners" and "Slavophiles," the debate in Africa presents itself as an opposition between "universalism" and "particularism," the latter defining itself, above all else, by its opposition of the former. But there are only two players in this game: us, inside; them, outside. That is all there is to it. ("Topologies of Nativism," 56)

This summary, of course, caricatures the sincere altercations involved in the ciphering of a most effective scheme for cultural and intellectual discourse in Africa after colonization. It excludes the "moderate" middle occupied by a great number of writers and critics, including the very influential African Marxist community. The "nationalist" or "traditionalist" voices, the promoters of the folk, the oral, and the rural, did not dictate the governing assumptions of how best to privilege the native perspective, as Appiah's statement suggests.

In an essay published about a decade before Appiah's, Emmanuel Obiechina argued that the adversarial (anti-colonial) context in which the humanities developed in Africa is largely responsible for both the activist orientation of the dominant thinking and the nativist orientation of the language. According to Obiechina,

> Cultural nativism, or that aspect of it called literary nationalism, is so fundamentally universal a phenomenon in unequal social situations such as that engendered by colonialism that its inevitability hardly deserves an argument....Whether this nativism or cultural affirmation finds expression in psycho-political terms such as the African Personality or in the literary ideology of Négritude its cultural implications are obvious. There is a fundamental assumption that the African has had a civilization which is distinct from all other civilizations and which distinguishes him from all other human beings." ("Cultural Nationalism," 26)

For Obiechina, the *intellectual rhetoric of indigenization* with which various Africans branded their visions of an independent society is a generative category because it has enabled the development of diverse models of cultural and intellectual reconstruction for post-colonial Africa.

The articulation of nativism – including the nationalists' – involve predominantly secular registers that include but are not limited to sociolinguistics, historical and cultural materialism, classificatory biology, development economics, and sociology. The nativization polarities are also present in the social sciences where the character and the relevance of the informal to the formal, the unorganized to the organized, and the rural to the urban sectors remain important questions. Even the "natural" sciences – ethno-botany[1] and ethnopharmacology, for instance – sometimes get involved in the kind of questions Wali's essay provoked. Gender studies have also not been able to avoid the fray. For example,

Ifi Amadiume's approach to African feminism in *Male Daughters* seems to be driven by the nativist impulse. She says that while she was planning the research for her book she "decided it was best to go home and, with the help of Nnobi people themselves, write *our own* social history, especially from the women's point of view." In Nnobi, her "right to ask questions, act as a spokeswoman and make recommendations for change and improvement" is assured (9–10; emphasis added).[2]

In literary criticism alone, the methods of charting the discovery of the native ways of knowing had been conceptualized in so many ways that grouping them under three headings as I do below only begins to reflect their intricacies. The first group, that which I call thematic or classical nativism, calls for the foregrounding of *local* and *public* subject matter, the rejection of tendentious universalism in critical standards, and the development of an aesthetic that privileges translucent communication. Classical nativism claims inspiration from an Africanized aesthetic theory of "use" and "relevance." The second group, which I name structuralist or speculative nativism, proposes idealistic interpretations of the formal dimensions of "traditional" theater, fiction, and poetry upon which contemporary practices ought to be based. Unlike the thematists, the structuralists do not use "tradition" to disavow dense and solipsistic arts. The third group, the one I call linguistic or artifact nativism, demands a radical translation of all arts that aspire to be called African into indigenous languages and cultural conventions. Decolonized African culture, according to the linguistic nativists, must free itself from European languages and cultivate the native tongues in order for liberating educational and pedagogic theories to flower fully. None of the three groups deviates significantly from a functionalist aesthetics. Even the linguists and the structuralists, who both settle definition parameters around language and form, affirm that an African aesthetic must bear direct relevance to the everyday.

Classical nativists from nationalists to dialecticians teach that "usefulness" is the fundamental African aesthetic principle. They argue that pre-colonial African poets, story-tellers, and ritual actors who constitute the African "classical" tradition, did not sing solely for sheer excitation but also for conducting practical affairs like counseling, night-time entertainment, and official record-keeping. Liturgies, divination chants, and ritual conventions are all expressed in poetically intense forms. The pre-colonial traditions show amply, as the Yorùbá proverb, "*ìwà lewà* (character [being] is beauty)," implies that effective stylization anticipates usefulness.[3]

Classical nativism finds its most vocal expression in *Toward the Decolonization of African Literature*. In the name of African cultural essence, the book prescribes lyrical speech, musical rhythm, mellifluousness, and other voice dependent styles and recommends the cultivation of intense emotions, sweeping vision, and concrete imagery. The book ignores orature coded in dense, esoteric, and elusive idioms, speaks against the use of "muddy" language, and *de-Africanizes* writers who prefer such language regardless of the thematic relevance of their work to contemporary questions. In the peculiar reading of pre-colonial (oral) traditions proposed by Chinweizu, Jemie, and Madubuike, the truly *African* writer cannot "preoccupy himself with his puny ego" (252). Their *African* writer cannot indulge in self-conscious figuration.

The name which the authors of *Toward the Decolonization* give their envisaged school of criticism reveals the contradictions and problems faced in converting the broad principles of classical nativism into a positive rhetoric. In an obviously proud imitation of the behaviors of the operators of a class of mass transit buses in urban southwestern Nigeria, the critics style themselves *bolekájà* (come down and let us fight), or the outraged touts of the "passenger lorries of African literature." In Lagos, the touts are actually called *"omo ìta,"* literally "the outside child," or "the homeless fellow," and not *"bolekájà,"* which is the name given to the trucks and buses. Both terms imply *"untraditional"* effrontery enabled by urban alienation and anonymity. The authors' substitution of *bolekájà* for the more correct *omo ìta* gives away what I believe to be the militant classical nativist's dilemma. The militant nativist admires the brash bravery and the outspokenness of the urban tout but his interest is only the speech style. As two well-known characters in African fiction demonstrate, one cannot at once be like the youthful and traditional Okonkwo in Achebe's *Things Fall Apart* and the foul mouthed bus conductor in Armah's *The Beautyful Ones Are Not Yet Born*. The two men live in different worlds. Modern critics live in a world that is even more different from the ones occupied by the characters. Rare is the nativist trained in divination arts, priestly roles, and even public spectacular poetry. Rarer still is the nativist scholar who consumes these arts directly. All that a self-aware nativist critic can do, as Achebe's literary criticism indicates, is to devise general principles based on an interpretation of second order information. The incontrovertible truths of classical nativism that African cultures did not begin with European contacts, and that modern writers should locate their inspiration in their traditional predecessors, sound less anxious whenever the theorist states explicitly that the arts of the diviners, the hunters' guilds, and the priesthood, are *forms* that are being appropriated for a localist foundation of the emergent post-independence culture.

Where classical nativism focuses on the clear expression of public themes, structuralist nativists Africanize the expression of public themes in forms that need not be clear. As discussed above, classical nativism doubts the *African-ness* of any work that exhibits self-conscious artistry. To contest the very effective strategy with which classical nativism indigenizes its preferred stylistic of clarity, structuralist nativists reject the narrow interpretation given the traditional "back cloth" of contemporary written cultures and treats as philosophical matters much of what the others regard as phenomenal peculiarities. The structuralists search for the identity markers of modern African writing in the structural and hermeneutic *principles* that are derivable from traditional high arts such as rituals, divination chants, esoteric lyric, and the secular narratives of the Sahelian griot. Wole Soyinka, for example, derives his theory of African tragedy and willful social action from his Nietzschean reading of Yoruba rituals. He shows in his speculative interpretation of rituals that the duty of a "serious" African literature is to inflect the cosmic overview that organizes traditional performances. A proper appreciation of Ògún's ritual will enable the formation of a theory of knowledge: all "engineering," like Ògún's steel cutlass, must serve communal good. Such understanding will also enable a theory of acting: choral performance, like Ògún's wail, must aid the strengthening of a will to invent. Also, knowing the essence of the rituals will lead to a theory of tragedy which requires that the hero's will, like Ògún's, must not succumb to destructive forces.[4]

The central quests of linguist nativism are inventing effective pedagogies for national development and creating instruments of rapid growth for literate artifacts in the indigenous languages. These tasks are always expressed as imperative defenses against imminent *cultural death*. This most controversial variety of nativisms returned to the critical center stage in 1977 when Ngũgĩ wa Thiong'O condemned as *un-African* all writing, his own included, done in European languages. The prominent historical materialist broke ranks with his Marxist colleagues when he declared publicly that material languages, *in themselves*, carry significant ideological connotations. In his manifesto statement, "Return to the Roots," which he expanded later into the book-length essay *Decolonising the Mind*, Ngũgĩ ruffled African Marxist activism with the claim that the language selected by a writer from the menu available in a stratified, multilingual, and ex-colonial society cannot but be of ideological significance. He premised this proposition on the belief that national languages in multilingual ex-colonies are not neutral communication instruments but partisan tools in the unending skirmishes between liberating and colonizing forces. For Ngũgĩ, material languages are depositories of both ethnic and national histories. Narrative forms, vocabulary range, rhetorical apparatuses, sociolinguistic patterns, and even syntax, are shaped by the history of the community to which they are specific.

I find at the core of all nativisms certain common questions on the cultural character of the post-independence nation, the symbolic significance of material language, and the extent to which independent nations can reshape colonial legacies. The pragmatic classical and structuralist nativists want to create in local accents an African literature that can use any of its historical languages and forms. They believe that languages and cultural conventions are instruments that do not on their own define cultures, literatures, or nations. When different geographical and political entities share a common language in the articulation of their literatures, the expressed *cultural, ethnic*, and *national* differences establish their individual identities. For the pragmatists, code switching, characters individuated by native speech patterns, elaborate world views, fictionalized local response to history, and other markers of culturally specific narrative, poetic, and dramatic protocols are more important for the creation of a distinctly nationalist culture than the raw verbal materials. Literatures, for them, are *not* languages but linguistic embodiments of cultural patterns.[5] Achebe, ever a realist, once pondered aloud in a rebuttal of linguistic nativism that

> Some of my colleagues . . . have tried to rewrite their history into a straightforward case of oppression by presenting a happy monolingual African childhood brusquely disrupted by the imposition of a domineering foreign language. This historical fantasy demands that we throw out the English language in order to restore linguistic justice and self respect to ourselves.
>
> My position is that anyone who feels unable to write in English should follow their desires. But they must not take liberties with our history. It is not simply true that the English forced us to learn their language. . . . We chose English not because the English desired it, but because having tacitly accepted the new nationalities into which colonialism had grouped us, we needed its language to transact our business, including the business of overthrowing colonialism itself . . . For me, it is not *either* English or Igbo, it is both. ("Song" 32)

This evidently pragmatic statement suggests that history has created multi-ethnic, multi-lingual, and culturally pluralistic African nations. History has also imposed on the various creations a homogenizing language.

The linguistic nativists respond that history is not "tamper" proof: it is intended to be rewritten and reconstituted constantly. They agree with the pragmatists that languages, for understandable reasons, shed off their national(istic) and cultural origins when they cross boundaries, and are sometimes used in creating forms unrecognizable to the initial users. They add, however, that those tongues do not migrate on their own. The languages find and make homes in strange lands usually after bloody conquests. Decolonized people cannot, after having freed themselves again, be less anxious about the languages and conventions of their cultures. History teaches that linguistic and other cultural variables usually correlate with a hierarchy propped by educational, sociological, economic, and cultural privileges. In post-independence Africa, the language and cultural forms introduced during the colonial era remain dominant because the hegemonic structures that were devised for maintaining conquest have not been dismantled. If the post-independent culture must fulfill its promise adequately, it has to pay greater attention to the native conventions of signification.

A reader who encounters the globalist explanations of the place of African literature in world cultures without a knowledge of the fratricidal divisions among Africanists might not be able to reckon with the unacknowledged indebtedness of those theories to nativist in-fighting. In particular, the rhetoric of difference and liberal multi-culturalism used in contemporary criticism to comment on what is broadly called the post-colony are inspired by nativist discourses of self-assertion.

We may consider the methodologically innovative Christopher Miller's "Theories of Africans." That exploratory essay, later expanded into the lead chapter in his book of the same title, balances two contradictory tasks. It heeds the nativist demand for an analytical differentiation that respects local initiatives and also fulfills the homogenizing conditions of contemporary theory. Miller proposes an interdisciplinary criticism that will study indigenous ideas on representation for the purpose of understanding how chosen cultures order and *rhetoricize* facts. The method which he calls a literary anthropology explores the discourses of "man" in a way that adapts localist (native) theoretical perspectives for practical literary and cultural criticism. Such a study will make use of both "ethnic" insights and cosmopolitan theory, it will correct both the blind spots of globalism (especially its purported mastery of regional differences) and the unjustifiable "theoretical" shyness of nativism. Such meta-figural studies will expose the *differences* between "European" ideas of representation and the African "native" perception of the same. Miller thinks that a literary anthropological criticism of African literature will be ethical in that it will overcome the implicit arrogance of "What's the difference?" (as in Paul de Man's famous reading of an Archie Bunker episode), and then set out "What's different!" Miller's literary anthropology theorizes the native's signifier and also signifies the native's theory. Miller tells the non-native investigator that in regard to literary theory, "the most fruitful path for the western critic of African literature is not to play it safe and 'stay home,' nor to 'leave home without it,' and pretend to approach African literature with a virgin mind, but to balance one against the other, by reconsidering the applicability of all our critical terms and by looking to traditional African cultures for terms they might offer" (139).

Although Miller confesses that a literary anthropology will not make the scholar a native, that "outsider" humility, to my mind, is merely a professional disclaimer and a pre-empting of passionate nativist critics who might accuse the self-confessed Western critic of a surreptitious entry. Henry Louis Gates, Jr, whose choice of personal pronoun indicates that he considers himself a native, once advised virtually the same direction for the African Literature Association: "we must first, demand that the major theorist of Western literature be accountable for African literary theory; and we must, second, turn into our vernacular traditions to define indigenous systems of interpretation that arise from within African cultures themselves ("On the Rhetoric," 16). Both the native and the self-confessed non-native critic repudiate, from what I call a *neo-nativist* platform, the classical nativist notion that dense theoretical speculation is by nature imperialistic and Western. Like the structuralist nativists that came before them, they refuse to dismiss "theory," in itself, as alien. Instead, they attempt an understanding of the native's theories.

Of course, Miller and Gates benefit from advances in theories of identities which the older nativists did not have. Popular academic axioms now say that ethnography is implicated in imperialism, that theory is very ethnocentric, and that ethnicity itself is a theoretically produced identity. We also know that in the contemporary late capitalist academe, the most eminent criticisms ask theories to stake rigor against rigor, and not the emotions of intimate belongingness against an imperial "outsider." The native scholar, we also know now, is not always an "insider." As Miller will say, for instance, "the fact of being biologically or culturally African neither guarantees nor necessarily permits any sort of purely 'African' reading, in a relation of total oneness with its text or with Africa itself" (121). So, whenever in the contemporary late capitalist environment anyone of Miller, Appiah, Gates, Chinweizu and his collaborators invokes a personal pronoun in respect of a culture to which he claims (or does not claim) belongingness, that person talks primarily to a *professional intellectual* community. The immediate addressees of the theories are other theorists whose non-intellectual ethnic identities might not be too critical for a sufficient comprehension of their propositions. The referential import of Miller's "our critical terms" and Gates's "our own vernacular traditions" can at best be figures of speech for discursively constituted groups. "Ethical" commitment in that context is an intellectual claim and differs profoundly from the direct political engagement that inspired the earlier nativisms like Achebe's "earnest" fiction.

Still, I interpret the contemporary advances (and critiques) in Miller and Gates as the most flattering homage, even when not explicitly acknowledged, to the foresight of the earlier nativisms. The first generation of African post-independence intellectuals not only success-fully opposed the domineering "universalism" that granted their cultures no generative subjective status, they were also able to dictate the terms of future debates. Achebe refused literary high modernism with "indigenist" aesthetics, Soyinka reinterpreted Yorùbá myths with a Nietzschean model in order to give a native philosophical depth to his drama. Chinweizu, Madubuike, and Jemie experienced the Black Arts phenomenon in the United States and were provoked enough to smash back at home a few critical and cultural icons they viewed as betrayals of an African outlook. Ngugi constantly moves his global materialist concept of cultural activism toward the indigenous languages. However, partly because of the sociology of contemporary intellectual traffic, the devastation of post-independence economies, and the ideological compromises that result from migration, some critics of African literature want to believe that those earlier defenses of "local knowledge" are wrong headed and claustrophobic: it is a matter of "us" against "them," Appiah says. As the preceding discussions of the major currents in African literary criticism show, African nativists responded to global encroachments and they, in turn, influenced cosmopolitan views of the world. The important lesson of nativist formulations for the history of literary criticism is not whether or not they offer profoundly original theories of art, whether or not they propose a thoroughly new poetics of culture, whether or not the exclusivist and specificist language of some of the nativists is self-defeating. Countless non-nativist cultural theories can be so criticized. The philosophical challenge of nativism for criticism lies, I believe, in devising the means with which to measure how well an identitarian discourse like African literature can fulfill its classical role of persuasion at the same time that it says conspicuous figuration is immaterial.

Notes

1 See, for example, Omotoye Olorode, "Aspects of Plant Naming and Classification among the Yoruba." *Odu* 27 (1985): 80–95.

2 Ifi Amadiume, *Male Daughters, Female Husbands: Gender and Sex in an African Society.* London: Zed Books, 1987.

3 Babatunde Lawal, "Some Aspects of Yoruba Aesthetics." *British Journal of Aesthetics* 14:3 (Summer 1974): 239–49.

4 Wole Soyinka, *Myth, Literature, and the African World.* Cambridge: Cambridge University Press, 1976.

5 See al-Amin Mazrui, "Relativism, Universalism, and the Language of African Literature." *Research in African Literatures* 23:2 (Spring 1995): 65–72; Simon Gikandi, "Ngugi's Conversion: Writing and the Politics of Language." *Research in African Literatures* 23:1 (Spring 1992): 131–44; and Akinwumi Isola, "The African Writer's Tongue." *Research in African Literatures* 23:1 (Spring 1992): 17–26.

References

Achebe, Chinua. "The Song of Ourselves." *New Statesman and Society,* 9 Feb. 1990: 30–2.

Appiah, Anthony Kwame. *In My Father's House: Africa in the Philosophy of Culture.* New York: Oxford University Press, 1992.

Chinweizu, Ihechukwu Madubuike, and Onwuchekwa Jemie. *Toward the Decolonization of African Literature.* Enugu: Fourth Dimension, 1980.

Gates, Henry Louis, Jr. "On the Rhetoric of Racism in the Profession." *African Literature Association Bulletin* 15, no. 1 (Winter 1989): 11–21.

Miller, Christopher. "Theories of Africans: The Question of Literary Anthropology." *Critical Inquiry* 13, no. 1 (Autumn 1986): 20–39.

Obiechina, Emmanuel. "Cultural Nationalism in Modern African Creative Literature." *African Literature Today* 1 (1968): 24–35.

Wali, Obiajunwa. "The Dead End of African Literature." *Transition* 10 (1963): 13–15.

Chapter 35

Out of Africa:
Topologies of Nativism

Kwame Anthony Appiah

[…]

Consider, then, that now classic manifesto of African cultural nationalism, *Toward the Decolonization of African Literature*. This much-discussed book is the work of three Nigerian authors – Chinweizu, Onwuchekwa Jemie, and Ihechukwu Madubuike – all of them encumbered with extensive Western university educations. Dr Chinweizu, a widely published poet and quondam editor of the Nigerian literary magazine *Okike*, was an undergraduate at MIT and holds a doctorate from SUNY Buffalo; and he has emerged (from a career that included time on the faculty at MIT and at San Jose State) as one of the leading figures in contemporary Nigerian journalism, writing a highly influential column in *The Guardian* of Lagos. Dr Jemie holds a PhD from Columbia University in English and Comparative Literature, is also a distinguished poet, and has published an introduction to the poetry of Langston Hughes. And Dr Ihechukwu Madubuike – who has been Nigeria's Minister of Education – studied at Laval in Canada, the Sorbonne, and SUNY Buffalo. All of these critics have taught in Black Studies programs in the United States – in their preface they thank the Department of Afro-American Studies at the University of Minnesota and the Black Studies Department at Ohio State University for "supportive clerical help." If their rhetoric strikes responsive chords in the American ear, we shall not find it too surprising.

Not that their language fails to incorporate Nigerian elements. The term *bolekaja* – which means "Come down, let's fight" – is used in western Nigeria to refer to the "mammy-wagons," the main means of popular transportation; and it reflects "the outrageous behaviour of their touts." In their preface, Chinweizu, Jemie and Madubuike call themselves "*bolekaja* critics, outraged touts for the passenger lorries of African literature."

> There comes a time, we believe, in the affairs of men and of nations, when it becomes necessary for them to engage in *bolekaja* criticism, for them to drag the stiflers of their life down to earth for a corrective tussle. A little wrestle in the sands never killed a sturdy youth.[1]

First published in *Yale Journal of Criticism* 2.1 (1988): 157–61, 169–76.

But clearly it is not really the "sturdy youth" of African criticism that they take to be at risk; for the work of the succeeding chapters is to wrestle the critical ethnocentrism of their eurocentric opponents to the ground in the name of an afrocentric particularism. If this is to be a struggle to the death, Chinweizu and his compatriots expect to be the survivors. They assert, for example, that

> [m]ost of the objections to thematic and ideological matters in the African novel sound like admonitions from imperialist motherhens to their wayward or outright rebellious captive chickens. They cluck: "Be Universal! Be Universal!"[2]

The authors condemn as well

> [t]he modernist retreat of our poets into privatist universalism [which] makes it quite easy for them to shed whatever African nationalist consciousness they have before they cross the threshold into the sanctum of "poetry in the clouds." And that suits the English literary establishment just fine, since they would much prefer it if an African nationalist consciousness, inevitably anti-British, was not promoted or cultivated, through literature, in the young African elite.[3]

Thus, when the British critic, Adrian Roscoe, urges African poets to view themselves as "inheritors of a universal tradition of art and letters and not just as the recipients of an indigenous legacy," he reaps the nationalists' scorn.[4] For their central insistence is that "African literature *is* an autonomous entity separate and apart from all other literature. It has its own traditions, models and norms."[5]

Now we should recognize from the start that such polemics can be a salutary corrective to a great deal of nonsense that has been written about African literature, by critics for whom literary merit is gauged by whether a work can be inserted into a Great White Tradition of masterpieces. It is hard not to be irritated by highhanded pronouncements from critics for whom detailed description of locale amounts to mere travelogue, unless, say, the locale is "Wessex" and the author is Thomas Hardy; for whom the evocation of local custom amounts to mere ethnography, unless, say, they are the customs of a North English mining town and the author is D. H. Lawrence; and for whom the recounting of historical event amounts to mere journalism, unless the event is the Spanish Civil War and the author is Hemingway.

In other words, Chinweizu and his colleagues object to the posture that conceals its privileging of one national (or racial) tradition against others in false talk of the Human Condition. It is not surprising, then, that Chinweizu and his colleagues also endorse T. S. Eliot's view that "although it is only too easy for a writer to be local without being universal, I doubt whether a poet or novelist can be universal without being local too."[6] And here, plainly, "universal" is hardly a term of derogation. For characteristically those who pose as anti-universalists use the term "universalism" interchangeably with "pseudo-universalism"; and in fact their complaint is not with universalism at all. They truly object – and who would not? – to eurocentric hegemony *posing* as universalism. Thus, while the debate is couched in terms of the competing claims of particularism and universalism, the actual ideology of universalism – and if "pseudo-universalism" receives the brunt of our polemics, we must have in reserve a conception of universalism *simpliciter* – is never interrogated; and, indeed, is even tacitly accepted.

The appeal of this nativist rhetoric is most easily understood in the context of the subcontinent's politico-linguistic geography. We should begin with the fact that more than half of the population of black Africa lives in countries where English is an official language and almost all the rest of Africa is governed in French or Arabic or Portuguese. Both francophone and anglophone elites not only use the colonial languages as the medium of government, but know and often admire the literature of their excolonizers, and have chosen to make a modern African literature in European languages. Even after a brutal colonial history and nearly two decades of sustained armed resistance, the decolonization in the mid-seventies of Portuguese Africa left a lusophone elite writing African laws and literature in Portuguese.

Yet, at the same time – with few exceptions outside the Arabic-speaking countries of North Africa – the language of government is still the first language of a very few and is securely possessed by only a small proportion of the population; and in most of the anglophone states even the educated elites learned at least one of the hundreds of indigen-ous languages as well as – and almost always before – English. In francophone Africa there are now elites that speak French better than any other language, and whose French is particularly close in grammar, if not always in accent, to the language of metropolitan France. But even here French is not confidently possessed by anything close to a majority.

Precisely this combination of a europhone elite and a noneurophone populace makes for the appeal of nativism. That the European languages – and, in particular, the dialects of them in which elite writing goes on – are far from being the confident possession of the populace does not, of course, distinguish Third World literature – the writings that are taught – from the bulk of contemporary European or American taught writings. But the fact that contemporary African literature operates in a sphere of language that is so readily identifiable as the product of schooling – and schooling fully available only to an elite – invites the nativist assimilation of formal literature to the alien. The recognition that there is, in Africa as in the West, a body of distinctive cultural production – over the whole range of popular culture – that *does* have a more immediate access to the citizen with less formal education reinforces this association.

So, for example, there are certainly strong living practices of oral culture – religious, mythological, poetic and narrative – in most of the thousand and more languages of sub-Saharan Africa; and there is no doubt as to the importance of the few languages that were already (as we say) reduced to writing before the colonial era. But we must not fall for the sentimental notion that the "people" have held on to an indigenous national tradition, that only the educated bourgeoisie are "children of two worlds." At the level of popular culture, too, the currency is not a holdover from an unbroken stream of tradition; indeed, it is like most popular culture in the age of mass production, hardly national at all. Popular culture in Africa encompasses (the Americans) Michael Jackson and – have you heard of him? – Jim Reeves; and when it picks up cultural production whose sources are geographically African, what it picks up is not usually in any plausible sense traditional. Highlife music is both recognizably West African and distinctly not precolonial; and the sounds of Fela Kuti would have astonished the musicians of the last generation of court musicians in Yorubaland. As they have developed new forms of music, drawing on instrumental repertoires and musical ideas with a dazzling eclecticism, Africa's musicians have also done astonishing things with a language that used to be English. But it is *as* English that that language is accessible to millions around the continent (and around the world).

[...]

But what exactly – in the postcolonial context – is the content of the nativist's injunction to read literature by means of a theory drawn from the text's own cultural or intellectual inheritance? Initially it would seem that to accept this principle would have wide-ranging consequences for the way we read all literature. For it seems to accord to African literature a deference that we do not accord the high-canonical works of Western literature. Most of us are inclined to think that our insights into (say) the cultural production of genre and gender are not to be kept for our own age and region; we do *not* think that a feminist or marxian reading of Milton is merely an exercise in cultural imperialism (a temporal *imperium* corresponding to the geographical). The book that is widely regarded as having revitalized modern Wordsworth criticism (I refer to Hartman's 1964 study) draws extensively on the categories of Jung and of the German phenomenologists – not because anyone supposed these were part of Wordsworth's intellectual climate, but because it was thought they might help explicate the nature of Wordsworth's poetic achievements.

Then again, we could indeed replace such a pluralism of critical perspectives with a criticism grounded on the text's (or its author's) own cultural or intellectual foundations; but there would be nothing recherché about that attempt either. J. R. Caldwell's classic *John Keats's Fancy* (the examples are taken almost entirely at random) reads Keats in terms of the categories of associationism, categories that featured large in Keats's own literary and intellectual inheritance and were part of the general intellectual and literary legacy of the eighteenth century. Tony Nuttall has read Wordsworth in terms of Lockean psychology – again, something indigenous to the poet's own intellectual climate; something, so to speak, from the inside.

One trouble with *this* rationale for nativism, though, is precisely that it ignores the multiplicity of the heritage of the modern African writer. To insist on nativism on these grounds would be to ignore plain facts: to ignore the undeniable datum that Soyinka's references to Euripides are as real as his appeal to Ogun (and also to Brazilian syncretisms of Yoruba and Christian religions); or the certainty that, whatever their ethical or legal relations, Ouologuem's *Le devoir de violence*, is intimately bound up with Graham Greene's *It's a Battlefield*;[7] or Achebe's report, apropos of his reading as a child, that "the main things were the Bible and the Book of Common Prayer and the [English] Hymn Book."[8]

No one should contest the point that an adequate understanding of a work of literature will involve an understanding of its cultural presuppositions. Does it matter to *Madame Bovary* how adultery matters in the France of her day? Then it matters to Soyinka's *Death and the King's Horseman* that the death of the title is a death whose meaning the King's horseman accepts, a death he has chosen. But the history of the reception of African literature in the West suggests that this hasn't been the problem: on the contrary, people have been all too eager to attend to the ethnographic dimension of African literature. (Significantly, when, in my own undergraduate days there, Cambridge University appointed Wole Soyinka as a lecturer, it was through the department of anthropology.) And, as I have suggested, it would be another thing altogether to hold that a critical perspective that simulates the authorial will vouchsafe a reading more adequate to the text. Dr Johnson had undoubted advantages as a reader of his contemporaries, and we benefit from his insights, but that doesn't mean that we will – or that we should – afford him the last word on the subject.

There is, at all events, a fundamental reason why nativism in theory is unlikely to lead us away from where we already are. Time and time again, cultural nationalism has followed the route of alternate genealogizing. We end up always in the same place; the achievement is to have invented a different past for it. In the fervor of cultural reassertion, as Immanuel Wallerstein has observed, "the antecedents of scientificity were rediscovered under many different names";[9] today certain African intellectuals are doing the same for literary theory. If we start with a conception of hermeneutics borrowed from the Western academy, we may well succeed in producing an "elegant variation," inserting the odd metaphor from indigenous oracle-interpretation, say. But the whole exercise puts me in mind of a certain disreputable trading concern I once visited in Harare – a product of the frankly desultory attempts at sanctions against the Republic of South Africa. Their specialty was stamping "Made in Zimbabwe" onto merchandise imported, more or less legally, from the South. Perhaps a few are really fooled: but the overall effect of the procedure is only to provide a thin skin of legitimacy to stretch over existing practices.

For all our gestures of piety toward the household gods cannot disguise that fact that the "intellectual" is the product of a particular social formation – that, as Gayatri Spivak has taught me (and, no doubt, many others) to see, there is a sense in which the "Third World intellectual" is a contradiction in terms; precisely because, as I said at the start, intellectuals from the Third World are a product of the historical encounter with the West. And the problematic from which the theoretical discourse about literature arises is not a universal one – not, at least, until it is *made* universal. Literary theory is not only an intellectual project, it is also a genre; and genres have histories, which is to say times and places. Here again, the covert universalism within the rhetoric of particularism rears its head: for it is surely eurocentric presumption to insist on a correspondence within African culture to the institutional discourses of the West.

But there is another difficulty with this nativism in theory: namely, that (in keeping with the rhetoric of contemporary theory generally) it grounds a politics of reading on a spurious epistemology of reading. And the talk of theoretical adequacy – which is both the carrot and the stick – is seriously misleading.

In place of this, I think we shall be better off in our choice of theory if we give up the search for Mr Right; and speak, more modestly, of *productive modes of reading*. Here, especially in approaching these texts for which we lack well-developed *traditions* of reading, we have the opportunity to rethink the whole activity of reflection on writing. So that before I turn, finally, to some of the particulars of African literary production, I want to say a little about an alternative to the epistemology of reading that informs much of our current rhetoric.

Focus on the issue of whether a reading is *correct* invites the question, "What should a reading give a correct account *of*?" The quick answer – one that, as we shall immediately see, tells us less than it pretends to – is, of course, "the text." But the text exists as linguistic, as historical, as commercial, as political event; and while each of these ways of conceiving the very same object provides opportunities for pedagogy, they all provide different opportunities: opportunities between which we must choose. We are inclined at the moment to talk about this choice as if the purposes by which it is guided were, in some sense, given. But were that true, we would have long agreed on the nature of a literary reading: and there is surely little doubt that the concept of a "literary reading," like the concept of "literature," is what W. B. Gallic used to call an "essentially contested concept." To understand what a reading is, is to understand that what counts as a reading is always up for grabs.

By what purposes, then, should we judge our readings? To offer an answer to this question is not to rise above the contest, but to engage in it: to take a stand and to argue for it. And I think it will be clear enough why – at this point, at least – the overwhelming differences between the sociopolitical situations of teachers of literature in Africa, on the one hand, and the West, on the other, may very well suggest different stands, different arguments, and, thus, different conceptions of reading.

Consider, then, these differences: the African teacher of literature teaches students who are, overwhelmingly, the products of an educational system that enforces a system of values that ensures that, in the realm of cultural production, the West in which they do not live is *the* term of value; the American teacher of literature, by contrast, has students for whom the very same West is the term of value, but for whom that West is, of course, fully conceived of as their own. While American students have largely internalized a system of values that prohibits them from seeing the cultures of Africa as a source of value for them – despite ritualized celebrations of the richness of the life of savages – they have also acquired a relativist rhetoric, in which this "for them," allows them, at least in theory, to grant that "for the Other" his or her world is a source of value. American students would thus expect African students to value African cultural production, *because it is African*; while African students, raised without relativism, expect Americans to value their own cultural products because they are, by some objective standard, superior.

These sociological facts, reflexes of asymmetries of cultural power, have profound consequences for reading. If one believes that the kinds of cultural inferiority complexes represented in the attitudes of many African students need to be exorcised, then the teaching of literature in the westernized academy in Africa will require an approach that does three crucial things: first, identify accurately the situation of the modern African text as a product of the colonial encounter (and neither as the simple continuation of an indigenous tradition nor as a mere intrusion from the metropole); second, stress that the continuities between precolonial forms of cultural production and contemporary ones are nevertheless genuine (and thus provide a modality through which students can value and incorporate the African past); third, challenge directly the assumption of the cultural superiority of the West, both by undermining the aestheticized conceptions of value that it presupposes, and by distinguishing sharply between a domain of technological skill in which – once goals are granted – comparisons of efficiency are possible, and a domain of value in which such comparisons are by no means so unproblematic. This final challenge – to the assumption of Western cultural superiority – requires us, in the last analysis, to expose the ways in which the systematic character of literary (and, more broadly, aesthetic) judgments of value is the product of certain institutional practices and not something that exists independently of those practices and institutions.

In the American academy, on the other hand, the reading of African writing seems to me to need to be directed by other purposes: by the urge to continue the repudiation of racism; by the need to extend the American imagination – and imagination that regulates much of the world system economically and politically – beyond the narrow scope of the United States; by the desire to develop views of the world elsewhere that respect more deeply the autonomy of the Other; views that are not generated by the local political needs of America's multiple diasporas.

To stress such purposes in reading is to argue that, from the standpoint of an analysis of the current cultural situation – an analysis that is frankly political – certain purposes are productively served by the literary institutions of the academy.

But having made these distinctions, it may be well to insist that some of our critical materials can be put to use on both sides of the Atlantic. Thus, for example, there are distinctive formal features that arise, as has often been pointed out, from the particular closeness of African readers and writers to living traditions of oral narration. Addressing the incorporation of orality in writing allows us both to meet the need to connect modern African students with their geographical situations, and the concern to expand the American student's imagination of the world.

And – to provide another less familiar example – African writing raises a set of difficulties that stem from one of the characteristics of the cultural situation of African writers in the colonial languages: namely, the fact that they conceive of themselves always as addressing a readership that encompasses communities wider than any "traditional" culture. To address these issues productively is to allow students to explore the space of cultural politics: to allow students both African and Western to learn to resist facile reductions of modern African cultural production; and so it will be well to exemplify my claims in this specific area.

The most often-discussed consequences of the situation I have just outlined appear at the thematic level. When authors write in English or French about lives in their own countries in all their specificity, they necessarily find themselves accounting for features of those lives which derive from that specificity. This entails the use of particular concepts of, for example, kinship and family, marriage and status. As we have seen, the presentation of such details has often been read, especially by people outside Africa, as anthropologizing. We are told that Achebe's *Arrow of God*, for example, fails, in part, because it cannot take its setting for granted; that Achebe is always telling us what we need to know, acknowledging the reader's distance from Igbo traditions, and thus, allegedly, identifying the intended reader as a foreigner. I have heard the same point made about Soyinka's dramas, and I confess to finding it difficult to accept. For there are reasons, reasons highly specific to the situation of black African writing in metropolitan languages, why this is a mistake.

There is one trivial reason. Achebe and Soyinka are very consciously writing for Nigerian – and not just Igbo or Yoruba – audiences. The fact that a certain amount of detail is introduced in order to specify a thick description of the cultural milieu simply does not imply a foreign – if that means a non-African – reader. That is the first point.

But it *is*, essentially, trivial because of a second point. To make that point I should begin with a not-to-be-neglected fact: Achebe and Soyinka are popular writers at home. If the presence of these accumulations of allegedly ethnographic detail were indeed a way of identifying an alien reader, why do Nigerian (and more specifically Yoruba or Igbo) readers not find them alienating? The fact is that the accumulation of detail is a device not of alienation but of incorporation. The provision, in traditional narrations, of information already known to the hearer does not reflect a view of the hearer as alien. Otherwise oral narrations would not consist of twice-told tales. The function of a rehearsal of the familiar in narration often depends precisely on our pleasure in recognizing in a tale what we already know.

The centrality of this issue – of the inscription of the social world out of which one writes – is only an example, of course, of the sort of circumstance we need to be aware of if we are to write intelligently about modern African writing. And it depends essentially upon seeing the writer, the reader and the work in a cultural – and thus a historical, a political and a social – setting.

So let me end with an observation that derives from just such a contextualizing grasp, one that identifies the dual sources of the situation of the modern African text. Chinua Achebe once remarked,

> I'm an Igbo writer, because this is my basic culture; Nigerian, African and a writer . . . no, black first, then a writer. Each of these identities does call for a certain kind of commitment on my part. I must see what it is to be black – and this means being sufficiently intelligent to know how the world is moving and how the black people fare in the world. This is what it means to be black. Or an African – the same: what does Africa mean to the world? When you see an African what does it mean to a white man?[10]

Notice the presupposition of Achebe's question – "When you see an African what does it mean to a white man?": the recognition that a specifically African identity began as the product of a European gaze.

Anthropologizing modes of reading would stress the sources of Achebe's "social vision" in an African setting.[11] It seems to me, by contrast, essential to insist that the nationalist dimensions of public history that are central to so much modern African writing are not mere reflexes of the epic mode of oral history and myth; they grow out of the world situation of the African writer and not out of a purely local eccentricity. Achebe is a fine example of someone who draws on the reserves of his native orature; but we misunderstand those uses if we do not see them in their multiple contexts.

We need to transcend the banalities of nativism – its images of purgation, its declarations, in the face of international capital, of a specious "autonomy," its facile topologies. The language of empire – of center and periphery, identity and difference, the sovereign subject and her colonies – continues to structure the criticism and reception of African literature *in* Africa as elsewhere. And this makes the achievement of critical balance especially difficult to maintain. On the one hand, we find theorists who emphasize the processes of demonization and subjection, the ways in which the margin is produced by the cultural dominant; Europe defining her sovereignty by insisting on the otherness of her colonies. On the other (Other?) hand, talk about the production of marginality by the cultural dominant is wholly inadequate by itself. For it ignores the reciprocal nature of power relations; it neglects the multiform varieties of individual and collective agency available to the African subject; and it diminishes both the achievements and the possibilities of African writing.

The point to be borne in mind here is not that ideologies, like cultures, exist antagonistically, but that they *only* exist antagonistically. In the ferment of present-day African literary debate, we do well to remember that the very meaning of postcolonial discourse subsists on these conflictual relations. Indeed, they are *the* topos of contemporary African literature.

Yet I, at least, worry about our entrancement with the polarities of identity and difference; partly because the rhetoric of alterity has too often meant the evacuation of specificity; partly because too many African intellectuals, captivated by this Western thematic, seek to fashion themselves as the (image of the) Other. We run the risk of an ersatz exoticism, like the tourist trinkets in the Gifte Shoppes of Lagos and Nairobi.

Nativism invites us to conceive of the nation as an organic community, bound together by the *Sprachgeist*, by the shared norms that are the legacy of tradition, struggling to throw off the shackles of alien modes of life and thought. "Here I am," Senghor once wrote, "trying to forget Europe in the pastoral heart of Sine."[12] But for us to forget Europe is to suppress the agon of history. And surely that has always been the task of the organicist aesthetic: to conceal the startling violence that sustains the dominion of culture.

Notes

1   Chinweizu, Onwuchekwa Jemie, and Ihechukwu Madubuike, *Toward the Decolonization of African Literature* (Enugu: Fourth Dimension Publishing Co., 1980), xiv, text and footnote.
2   Ibid., 89.
3   Ibid., 151.
4   Ibid., 147.
5   Ibid., 4.
6   Eliot is cited on page 106. When Chinweizu et al. assert, typically, that "there was in precolonial Africa an abundance of oral narratives which are in no way inferior to European novels," they presuppose the universalist view that there is some (universal) value-metric by which the relative excellence of the two can be gauged; ibid., 27.
7   For an illuminating discussion of the charges that Ouologuem was guilty of "plagiarism" of Greene's work, see Christopher Miller's *Blank Darkness: Africanist Discourse in French* (Chicago: University of Chicago Press, 1985), 219–28.
8   "Interview with Achebe," by Anthony Appiah, John Ryle and D. A. N. Jones, *Times Literary Supplement*, February 26, 1982.
9   Immanuel Wallerstein, *Historical Capitalism* (London: Verso, 1983), 88.
10 "Interview with Achebe."
11 Soyinka, of course, uses the expression "social vision" to other more complex purposes in Wole Soyinka, *Myth, Literature and the African World* (Cambridge: Cambridge University Press, 1976). For further discussion of these issues see my "Soyinka and the Philosophy of Culture," in *Philosophy in Africa: Trends and Perspectives*, ed. P. O. Bodunrin (Ile-Ife: University of Ife Press, 1985).
12 Leopold Senghor, "Tout le long du jour," in *Chants d'ombre* (Paris: Editions du Seuil, 1964).

Chapter 36

On National Culture

Frantz Fanon

To take part in the African revolution it is not enough to write a revolutionary song; you must fashion the revolution with the people. And if you fashion it with the people, the songs will come by themselves, and of themselves.

In order to achieve real action, you must yourself be a living part of Africa and of her thought; you must be an element of that popular energy which is entirely called forth for the freeing, the progress, and the happiness of Africa. There is no place outside that fight for the artist or for the intellectual who is not himself concerned with and completely at one with the people in the great battle of Africa and of suffering humanity.

Sékou Touré[1]

Each generation must out of relative obscurity discover its mission, fulfill it, or betray it. In underdeveloped countries the preceding generations have both resisted the work or erosion carried by colonialism and also helped on the maturing of the struggles of today. We must rid ourselves of the habit, now that we are in the thick of the fight, of minimizing the action of our fathers or of feigning incomprehension when considering their silence and passivity. They fought as well as they could, with the arms that they possessed then; and if the echoes of their struggle have not resounded in the international arena, we must realize that the reason for this silence lies less in their lack of heroism than in the fundamentally different international situation of our time. It needed more than one native to say "We've had enough"; more than one peasant rising crushed, more than one demonstration put down before we could today hold our own, certain in our victory. As for we who have decided to break the back of colonialism, our historic mission is to sanction all revolts, all desperate actions, all those abortive attempts drowned in rivers of blood.

In this chapter we shall analyze the problem, which is felt to be fundamental, of the legitimacy of the claims of a nation. It must be recognized that the political party which mobilizes the people hardly touches on this problem of legitimacy. The political parties start from living reality and it is in the name of this reality, in the name of the stark facts which weigh down the present and the future of men and women, that they fix their line of action. The political party may well speak in moving terms of the nation, but what it is concerned with is that the people who are listening understand the need to take part in the fight if, quite simply, they wish to continue to exist.

Today we know that in the first phase of the national struggle colonialism tries to disarm national demands by putting forward economic doctrines. As soon as the first demands are set out, colonialism pretends to consider them, recognizing with ostentatious humility that

First published in *The Wretched of the Earth*, trans. C. Farrington, pp. 206–27. New York: Grove Press, 1963.

the territory is suffering from serious underdevelopment which necessitates a great economic and social effort. And, in fact, it so happens that certain spectacular measures (centers
of work for the unemployed which are opened here and there, for example) delay the
crystallization of national consciousness for a few years. But, sooner or later, colonialism
sees that it is not within its powers to put into practice a project of economic and social
reforms which will satisfy the aspirations of the colonized people. Even where food supplies
are concerned, colonialism gives proof of its inherent incapability. The colonialist state
quickly discovers that if it wishes to disarm the nationalist parties on strictly economic
questions then it will have to do in the colonies exactly what it has refused to do in its own
country. It is not mere chance that almost everywhere today there flourishes the doctrine of
Cartierism.

The disillusioned bitterness we find in Cartier when up against the obstinate determination of France to link to herself peoples which she must feed while so many French people
live in want shows up the impossible situation in which colonialism finds itself when the
colonial system is called upon to transform itself into an unselfish program of aid and
assistance. It is why, once again, there is no use in wasting time repeating that hunger with
dignity is preferable to bread eaten in slavery. On the contrary, we must become convinced
that colonialism is incapable of procuring for the colonized peoples the material conditions
which might make them forget their concern for dignity. Once colonialism has realized
where its tactics of social reform are leading, we see it falling back on its old reflexes,
reinforcing police effectives, bringing up troops, and setting a reign of terror which is better
adapted to its interests and its psychology.

Inside the political parties, and most often in offshoots from these parties, cultured
individuals of the colonized race make their appearance. For these individuals, the demand
for a national culture and the affirmation of the existence of such a culture represent a special
battlefield. While the politicians situate their action in actual present-day events, men
of culture take their stand in the field of history. Confronted with the native intellectual
who decides to make an aggressive response to the colonialist theory of pre-colonial
barbarism, colonialism will react only slightly, and still less because the ideas developed by
the young colonized intelligentsia are widely professed by specialists in the mother country.
It is in fact a common-place to state that for several decades large numbers of research
workers have, in the main, rehabilitated the African, Mexican, and Peruvian civilizations.
The passion with which native intellectuals defend the existence of their national culture
may be a source of amazement; but those who condemn this exaggerated passion are
strangely apt to forget that their own psyche and their own selves are conveniently sheltered
behind a French or German culture which has given full proof of its existence and which is
uncontested.

I am ready to concede that on the plane of factual being the past existence of an Aztec
civilization does not change anything very much in the diet of the Mexican peasant of today.
I admit that all the proofs of a wonderful Songhai civilization will not change the fact that
today the Songhais are underfed and illiterate, thrown between sky and water with empty
heads and empty eyes. But it has been remarked several times that this passionate search for
a national culture which existed before the colonial era finds its legitimate reason in the
anxiety shared by native intellectuals to shrink away from that Western culture in which they
all risk being swamped. Because they realize they are in danger of losing their lives and thus
becoming lost to their people, these men, hotheaded and with anger in their hearts,

relentlessly determine to renew contact once more with the oldest and most pre-colonial springs of life of their people.

Let us go further. Perhaps this passionate research and this anger are kept up or at least directed by the secret hope of discovering beyond the misery of today, beyond self-contempt, resignation, and abjuration, some very beautiful and splendid era whose existence rehabilitates us both in regard to ourselves and in regard to others. I have said that I have decided to go further. Perhaps unconsciously, the native intellectuals, since they could not stand wonderstruck before the history of today's barbarity, decided to back further and to delve deeper down; and, let us make no mistake, it was with the greatest delight that they discovered that there was nothing to be ashamed of in the past, but rather dignity, glory, and solemnity. The claim to a national culture in the past does not only rehabilitate that nation and serve as a justification for the hope of a future national culture. In the sphere of psycho-affective equilibrium it is responsible for an important change in the native. Perhaps we have not sufficiently demonstrated that colonialism is not simply content to impose its rule upon the present and the future of a dominated country. Colonialism is not satisfied merely with holding a people in its grip and emptying the native's brain of all form and content. By a kind of perverted logic, it turns to the past of the oppressed people, and distorts, disfigures, and destroys it. This work of devaluing pre-colonial history takes on a dialectical significance today.

When we consider the efforts made to carry out the cultural estrangement so characteristic of the colonial epoch, we realize that nothing has been left to chance and that the total result looked for by colonial domination was indeed to convince the natives that colonialism came to lighten their darkness. The effect consciously sought by colonialism was to drive into the natives' heads the idea that if the settlers were to leave, they would at once fall back into barbarism, degradation, and bestiality.

On the unconscious plane, colonialism therefore did not seek to be considered by the native as a gentle, loving mother who protects her child from a hostile environment, but rather as a mother who unceasingly restrains her fundamentally perverse offspring from managing to commit suicide and from giving free rein to its evil instincts. The colonial mother protects her child from itself, from its ego, and from its physiology, its biology, and its own unhappiness which is its very essence.

In such a situation the claims of the native intellectual are not a luxury but a necessity in any coherent program. The native intellectual who takes up arms to defend his nation's legitimacy and who wants to bring proofs to bear out that legitimacy, who is willing to strip himself naked to study the history of his body, is obliged to dissect the heart of his people.

Such an examination is not specifically national. The native intellectual who decides to give battle to colonial lies fights on the field of the whole continent. The past is given back its value. Culture, extracted from the past to be displayed in all its splendor, is not necessarily that of his own country. Colonialism, which has not bothered to put too fine a point on its efforts, has never ceased to maintain that the Nergo is a savage; and for the colonist, the Negro was neither an Angolan nor a Nigerian, for he simply spoke of "the Negro." For colonialism, this vast continent was the haunt of savages, a country riddled with superstitions and fanaticism, destined for contempt, weighed down by the curse of God, a country of cannibals – in short, the Negro's country. Colonialism's condemnation is continental in its scope. The contention by colonialism that the darkest night of humanity lay over pre-colonial history concerns the whole of the African continent. The efforts of the native to rehabilitate himself and to escape from the claws of colonialism are logically inscribed from the same point of view as that of colonialism. The native intellectual who has gone far beyond the domains of Western culture and who has got it into his head to proclaim the existence of another culture never does so in the name of Angola or of Dahomey. The culture which is affirmed is African culture. The Negro, never so much a Negro as since he has been dominated by the whites, when he decides to prove that he has a culture and to behave like a cultured person, comes to realize that history points out a well-defined path to him: he must demonstrate that a Negro culture exists.

And it is only too true that those who are most responsible for this racialization of thought, or at least for the first movement toward that thought, are and remain those Europeans who have never ceased to set up white culture to fill the gap left by the absence of other cultures. Colonialism did not dream of wasting its time in denying the existence of one national culture after another. Therefore the reply of the colonized peoples will be straight away continental in its breadth. In Africa, the native literature of the last twenty years is not a national literature but a Negro literature. The concept of negritude, for example, was the emotional if not the logical antithesis of that insult which the white man flung at humanity. This rush of negritude against the white man's contempt showed itself in certain spheres to be the one idea capable of lifting interdictions and anathemas. Because the New Guinean or Kenyan intellectuals found themselves above all up against a general ostracism and delivered to the combined contempt of their overlords, their reaction was to sing praises in admiration of each other. The unconditional affirmation of African culture has succeeded the uncon-ditional affirmation of European culture. On the whole, the poets of negritude oppose the idea of an old Europe to a young Africa, tiresome reasoning to lyricism, oppressive logic to high-stepping nature, and on one side stiffness, ceremony, etiquette, and scepticism, while on the other frankness, liveliness, liberty, and – why not? – luxuriance: but also irresponsibility.

The poets of negritude will not stop at the limits of the continent. From America, black voices will take up the hymn with fuller unison. The "black world" will see the light and Busia from Ghana, Birago Diop from Senegal, Hampaté Ba from the Soudan, and Saint-Clair Drake from Chicago will not hesitate to assert the existence of common ties and a motive power that is identical.

The example of the Arab world might equally well be quoted here. We know that the majority of Arab territories have been under colonial domination. Colonialism has made the same effort in these regions to plant deep in the minds of the native population the idea that before the advent of colonialism their history was one which was dominated by barbarism. The struggle for national liberty has been accompanied by a cultural phenomenon known by the name of the awakening of Islam. The passion with which contemporary Arab writers remind their people of the great pages of their history is a reply to the lies told by the occupying power. The great names of Arabic literature and the great past of Arab civilization have been brandished about with the same ardor as those of the African civilizations. The Arab leaders have tried to return to the famous Dar El Islam which shone so brightly from the twelfth to the fourteenth century.

Today, in the political sphere, the Arab League is giving palpable form to this will to take up again the heritage of the past and to bring it to culmination. Today, Arab doctors and Arab poets speak to each other across the frontiers, and strive to create a new Arab culture and a new Arab civilization. It is in the name of Arabism that these men join together, and that they try to think together. Everywhere, however, in the Arab world, national feeling has preserved even under colonial domination a liveliness that we fail to find in Africa. At the same time that spontaneous communion of each with all, present in the African movement, is not to be found in the Arab League. On the contrary, paradoxically, everyone tries to sing the praises of the achievements of his nation. The cultural process is freed from the indifferentiation which characterized it in the African world, but the Arabs do not always manage to stand aside in order to achieve their aims. The living culture is not national but Arab. The problem is not as yet to secure a national culture, not as yet to lay hold of a movement differentiated by nations, but to assume an African or Arabic culture when confronted by the all-embracing condemnation pronounced by the dominating power. In the African world, as in the Arab, we see that the claims of the man of culture in a colonized country are all-embracing, continental, and in the case of the Arabs, worldwide.

This historical necessity in which the men of African culture find themselves to racialize their claims and to speak more of African culture than of national culture will tend to lead them up a blind alley. Let us take for example the case of the African Cultural Society. This society had been created by African intellectuals who wished to get to know each other and to compare their experiences and the results of their respective research work. The aim of this society was therefore to affirm the existence of an African culture, to evaluate this culture on the plane of distinct nations, and to reveal the internal motive forces of each of their national cultures. But at the same time this society fulfilled another need: the need to exist side by side with the European Cultural Society, which threatened to transform itself into a Universal Cultural Society. There was therefore at the bottom of this decision the anxiety to be present at the universal trysting place fully armed, with a culture springing from the very heart of the African continent. Now, this Society will very quickly show its inability to shoulder these different tasks, and will limit itself to exhibitionist demonstrations, while the habitual behavior of the members of this Society will be confined to showing Europeans that such a thing as African culture exists, and opposing their ideas to those of ostentatious and narcissistic Europeans. We have shown that such an attitude is normal and draws its legitimacy from the lies propagated by men of Western culture, but the degradation of the aims of this Society will become more marked with the elaboration of the concept of negritude. The African Society will become the cultural society of the black world and will come to include the Negro dispersion, that is to say the tens of thousands of black people spread over the American continents.

The Negroes who live in the United States and in Central or Latin America in fact experience the need to attach themselves to a cultural matrix. Their problem is not fundamentally different from that of the Africans. The whites of America did not mete out to them any different treatment from that of the whites who ruled over the Africans. We have seen that the whites were used to putting all Negroes in the same bag. During the first congress of the African Cultural Society which was held in Paris in 1956, the American Negroes of their own accord considered their problems from the same standpoint as those of their African brothers. Cultured Africans, speaking of African civilizations, decreed that there should be a reasonable status within the state for those who had formerly been slaves. But little by little the American Negroes realized that the essential problems confronting them were not the same as those that confronted the African Negroes. The Negroes of Chicago only resemble the Nigerians or the Tanganyikans in so far as they were all defined in relation to the whites. But once the first comparisons had been made and subjective feelings were assuaged, the American Negroes realized that the objective problems were fundamentally heterogeneous. The test cases of civil liberty whereby both whites and blacks in America try to drive back racial discrimination have very little in common in their principles and objectives with the heroic fight of the Angolan people against the detestable Portuguese colonialism. Thus, during the second congress of the African Cultural Society the American Negroes decided to create an American society for people of black cultures.

Negritude therefore finds its first limitation in the phenomena which take account of the formation of the historical character of men. Negro and African-Negro culture broke up into different entities because the men who wished to incarnate these cultures realized that every culture is first and foremost national, and that the problems which kept Richard Wright or Langston Hughes on the alert were fundamentally different from those which might confront Leopold Senghor or Jomo Kenyatta. In the same way certain Arab states, though they had chanted the marvelous hymn of Arab renaissance, had nevertheless to realize that their geographical position and the economic ties of their region were stronger even than the past that they wished to revive. Thus we find today the Arab states organically linked once more with societies which are Mediterranean in their culture. The fact is that these states are submitted to modern pressure and to new channels of trade while the network of trade relations which was dominant during the great period of Arab history has disappeared. But above all there is the fact that the political regimes of certain Arab states are so different, and so far away from each other in their conceptions, that even a cultural meeting between these states is meaningless.

Thus we see that the cultural problem as it sometimes exists in colonized countries runs the risk of giving rise to serious ambiguities. The lack of culture of the Negroes, as proclaimed by colonialism, and the inherent barbarity of the Arabs ought logically to lead to the exaltation of cultural manifestations which are not simply national but continental, and extremely racial. In Africa, the movement of men of culture is a movement toward the Negro-African culture or the Arab-Moslem culture. It is not specifically toward a national culture. Culture is becoming more and more cut off from the events of today. It finds its refuge beside a hearth that glows with passionate emotion, and from there makes its way by realistic paths which are the only means by which it may be made fruitful, homogeneous, and consistent.

If the action of the native intellectual is limited historically, there remains nevertheless the fact that it contributes greatly to upholding and justifying the action of politicians. It is true that the attitude of the native intellectual sometimes takes on the aspect of a cult or of a religion. But if we really wish to analyze this attitude correctly we will come to see that it is symptomatic of the intellectual's realization of the danger that he is running in cutting his last moorings and of breaking adrift from his people. This stated belief in a national culture is in fact an ardent, despairing turning toward anything that will afford him secure anchorage. In order to ensure his salvation and to escape from the supremacy of the white man's culture the native feels the need to turn backward toward his unknown roots and to lose himself at whatever cost in his own barbarous people. Because he feels he is becoming estranged, that is to say because he feels that he is the living haunt of contradictions which run the risk of becoming insurmountable, the native tears himself away from the swamp that may suck him down and accepts everything, decides to take all for granted and confirms everything even though he may lose body and soul. The native finds that he is expected to answer for everything, and to all comers. He not only turns himself into the defender of his people's past; he is willing to be counted as one of them, and henceforward he is even capable of laughing at his past cowardice.

This tearing away, painful and difficult though it may be, is however necessary. If it is not accomplished there will be serious psycho-affective injuries and the result will be individuals without an anchor, without a horizon, colorless, stateless, rootless – a race of angels. It will be also quite normal to hear certain natives declare, "I speak as a Senegalese and as a Frenchman..." "I speak as an Algerian and as a Frenchman..." The intellectual who is Arab and French, or Nigerian and English, when he comes up against the need to take on two nationalities, chooses, if he wants to remain true to himself, the negation of one of these determinations. But most often, since they cannot or will not make a choice, such intellectuals gather together all the historical determining factors which have conditioned them and take up a fundamentally "universal standpoint."

This is because the native intellectual has thrown himself greedily upon Western culture. Like adopted children who only stop investigating the new family framework at the moment when a minimum nucleus of security crystallizes in their psyche, the native intellectual will try to make European culture his own. He will not be content to get to know Rabelais and Diderot, Shakespeare and Edgar Allen Poe; he will bind them to his intelligence as closely as possible:

> La dame n'était pas seule
> Elle avait un mari
> Un mari très comme il faut
> Qui citait Racine et Corneille
> Et Voltaire et Rousseau
> Et le Père Hugo et le jeune Musset
> Et Gide et Valéry
> Et tant d'autres encore.[2]

But at the moment when the nationalist parties are mobilizing the people in the name of national independence, the native intellectual sometimes spurns these acquisitions which he suddenly feels make him a stranger in his own land. It is always easier to proclaim rejection than actually to reject. The intellectual who through the medium of culture has filtered into Western civilization, who has managed to become part of the body of European culture – in other words who has exchanged his own culture for another – will come to realize that the cultural matrix, which now he wishes to assume since he is anxious to appear original, can hardly supply any figureheads which will bear comparison with those, so many in number and so great in prestige, of the occupying power's civilization. History, of course, though nevertheless written by the Westerners and to serve their purposes, will be able to evaluate from time to time certain periods of the African past. But, standing face to face with his country at the present time, and observing clearly and objectively the events of today throughout the continent which he wants to make his own, the intellectual is terrified by the void, the degradation, and the savagery he sees there. Now he feels that he must get away from the white culture. He must seek his culture elsewhere, anywhere at all; and if he fails to find the substance of culture of the same grandeur and scope as displayed by the ruling power, the native intellectual will very often fall back upon emotional attitudes and will develop a psychology which is dominated by exceptional sensitivity and susceptibility.

This withdrawal, which is due in the first instance to a begging of the question in his internal behavior mechanism and his own character, brings out, above all, a reflex and contradiction which is muscular.

This is sufficient explanation of the style of those native intellectuals who decide to give expression to this phase of consciousness which is in the process of being liberated. It is a harsh style, full of images, for the image is the drawbridge which allows unconscious energies to be scattered on the surrounding meadows. It is a vigorous style, alive with rhythms, struck through and through with bursting life; it is full of color, too, bronzed, sunbaked, and violent. This style, which in its time astonished the peoples of the West, has nothing racial about it, in spite of frequent statements to the contrary; it expresses above all a hand-to-hand struggle and it reveals the need that man has to liberate himself from a part of his being which already contained the seeds of decay. Whether the fight is painful, quick, or inevitable, muscular action must substitute itself for concepts.

If in the world of poetry this movement reaches unaccustomed heights, the fact remains that in the real world the intellectual often follows up a blind alley. When at the height of his intercourse with his people, whatever they were or whatever they are, the intellectual decides to come down into the common paths of real life, he only brings back from his adventuring formulas which are sterile in the extreme. He sets a high value on the customs, traditions, and the appearances of his people; but his inevitable, painful experience only seems to be a banal search for exoticism. The sari becomes sacred, and shoes that come from Paris or Italy are left off in favor of pampooties, while suddenly the language of the ruling power is felt to burn your lips. Finding your fellow countrymen sometimes means in this phase to will to be a nigger, not a nigger like all other niggers but a real nigger, a Negro cur, just the sort of nigger that the white man wants you to be. Going back to your own people means to become a dirty wog, to go native as much as you can, to become unrecognizable, and to cut off those wings that before you had allowed to grow.

The native intellectual decides to make an inventory of the bad habits drawn from the colonial world, and hastens to remind everyone of the good old customs of the people, that people which he has decided contains all truth and goodness. The scandalized attitude with which the settlers who live in the colonial territory greet this new departure only serves to strengthen the native's decision. When the colonialists, who had tasted the sweets of their victory over these assimilated people, realize that these men whom they considered as saved souls are beginning to fall back into the ways of niggers, the whole system totters. Every native won over, every native who had taken the pledge not only marks a failure for the colonial structure when he decides to lose himself and to go back to his own side, but also stands as a symbol for the uselessness and the shallowness of all the work that has been accomplished. Each native who goes back over the line is a radical condemnation of the methods and of the regime; and the native intellectual finds in the scandal he gives rise to a justification and an encouragement to persevere in the path he has chosen.

If we wanted to trace in the works of native writers the different phases which characterize this evolution we would find spread out before us a panorama on three levels. In the first phase, the native intellectual gives proof that he has assimilated the culture of the occupying power. His writings correspond point by point with those of his opposite numbers in the mother country. His inspiration is European and we can easily link up these works with definite trends in the literature of the mother country. This is the period of unqualified assimilation. We find in this literature coming from the colonies the Parnassians, the Symbolists, and the Surrealists.

In the second phase we find the native is disturbed; he decides to remember what he is. This period of creative work approximately corresponds to that immersion which we have just described. But since the native is not a part of his people, since he only has exterior relations with his people, he is content to recall their life only. Past happenings of the byegone days of his chlidhood will be brought up out of the depths of his memory; old legends will be reinterpreted in the light of a borrowed estheticism and of a conception of the world which was discovered under other skies.

Sometimes this literature of just-before-the-battle is dominated by humor and by allegory; but often too it is symptomatic of a period of distress and difficulty, where death is experienced, and disgust too. We spew ourselves up; but already underneath laughter can be heard.

Finally in the third phase, which is called the fighting phase, the native, after having tried to lose himself in the people and with the people, will on the contrary shake the people. Instead of according the people's lethargy an honored place in his esteem, he turns himself into an awakener of the people; hence comes a fighting literature, a revolutionary literature, and a national literature. During this phase a great many men and women who up till then would never have thought of producing a literary work, now that they find themselves in exceptional circumstances – in prison, with the Maquis, or on the eve of their execution – feel the need to speak to their nation, to compose the sentence which expresses the heart of the people, and to become the mouthpiece of a new reality in action.

The native intellectual nevertheless sooner or later will realize that you do not show proof of your nation from its culture but that you substantiate its existence in the fight which the people wage against the forces of occupation. No colonial system draws its justification from the fact that the territories it dominates are culturally non-existent. You will never make colonialism blush for shame by spreading out little-known cultural treasures under its eyes. At the very moment when the native intellectual is anxiously trying to create a cultural work he fails to realize that he is utilizing techniques and language which are borrowed from the stranger in his country. He contents himself with stamping these instruments with a hallmark which he wishes to be national, but which is strangely reminiscent of exoticism. The native intellectual who comes back to his people by way of cultural achievements behaves in fact like a foreigner. Sometimes he has no hesitation in using a dialect in order to show his will to be as near as possible to the people; but the ideas that he expresses and the preoccupations he is taken up with have no common yardstick to measure the real situation which the men and the women of his country know. The culture that the intellectual leans toward is often no more than a stock of particularisms. He wishes to attach himself to the people; but instead he only catches hold of their outer garments. And these outer garments are merely the reflection of a hidden life, teeming and perpetually in motion. That extremely obvious objectivity which seems to characterize a people is in fact only the inert, already forsaken result of frequent, and not always very coherent, adaptations of a much more fundamental substance which itself is continually being renewed. The man of culture, instead of setting out to find this substance, will let himself be hypnotized by these mummified fragments which because they are static are in fact symbols of negation and outworn contrivances. Culture has never the translucidity of custom; it abhors all simplifi-cation. In its essence it is opposed to custom, for custom is always the deterioration of culture. The desire to attach oneself to tradition or bring abandoned traditions to life again does not only mean going against the current of history but also opposing one's own people. When a people undertakes an armed struggle or even a political struggle against a relentless colonialism, the significance of tradition changes. All that has made up the technique of passive resistance in the past may, during this phase, be radically condemned. In an underdeveloped country during the period of struggle traditions are fundamentally unstable and are shot through by centrifugal tendencies. This is why the intellectual often runs the risk of being out of date. The peoples who have carried on the struggle are more and more impervious to demagogy; and those who wish to follow them reveal themselves as nothing more than common opportunists, in other words, latecomers.

In the sphere of plastic arts, for example, the native artist who wishes at whatever cost to create a national work of art shuts himself up in a stereotyped reproduction of details. These artists who have nevertheless thoroughly studied modern techniques and who have taken part in the main trends of contemporary painting and architecture, turn their backs on foreign culture, deny it, and set out to look for a true national culture, setting great store on what they consider to be the constant principles of national art. But these people forget that the forms of thought and what it feeds on, together with modern techniques of information, language, and dress have dialectically reorganized the people's intelligences and that the constant principles which acted as safeguards during the colonial period are now undergoing extremely radical changes.

The artist who has decided to illustrate the truths of the nation turns paradoxically toward the past and away from actual events. What he ultimately intends to embrace are in fact the castoffs of thought, its shells and corpses, a knowledge which has been stabilized once and for all. But the native intellectual who wishes to create an authentic work of art must realize that the truths of a nation are in the first place its realities. He must go on until he has found the seething pot out of which the learning of the future will emerge.

Before independence, the native painter was insensible to the national scene. He set a high value on non-figurative art, or more often specialized in still lifes. After independence his anxiety to rejoin his people will confine him to the most detailed representation of reality. This is representative art which has no internal rhythms, an art which is serene and immobile, evocative not of life but of death. Enlightened circles are in ecstasies when confronted with this "inner truth" which is so well expressed; but we have the right to ask if this truth is in fact a reality, and if it is not already outworn and denied, called in question by the epoch through which the people are treading out their path toward history.

In the realm of poetry we may establish the same facts. After the period of assimilation characterized by rhyming poetry, the poetic tom-tom's rhythms break through. This is a poetry of revolt; but it is also descriptive and analytical poetry. The poet ought however to understand that nothing can replace the reasoned, irrevocable taking up of arms on the people's side. Let us quote Depestre once more:

> The lady was not alone;
> She had a husband,
> A husband who knew everything,
> But to tell the truth knew nothing,
> For you can't have culture without making concessions.
> You concede your flesh and blood to it,

You concede your own self to others;
By conceding you gain
Classicism and Romanticism,
And all that our souls are steeped in.[3]

The native poet who is preoccupied with creating a national work of art and who is determined to describe his people fails in his aim, for he is not yet ready to make that fundamental concession that Depestre speaks of. The French poet René Char shows his understanding of the difficulty when he reminds us that "the poem emerges out of a subjective imposition and an objective choice. A poem is the assembling and moving together of determining original values, in contemporary relation with someone that these circumstances bring to the front."[4]

Yes, the first duty of the native poet is to see clearly the people he has chosen as the subject of his work of art. He cannot go forward resolutely unless he first realizes the extent of his estrangement from them. We have taken everything from the other side; and the other side gives us nothing unless by a thousand detours we swing finally round in their direction, unless by ten thousand wiles and a hundred thousand tricks they manage to draw us toward them, to seduce us, and to imprison us. Taking means in nearly every case being taken: thus it is not enough to try to free oneself by repeating proclamations and denials. It is not enough to try to get back to the people in that past out of which they have already emerged; rather we must join them in that fluctuating movement which they are just giving a shape to, and which, as soon as it has started, will be the signal for everything to be called in question. Let there be no mistake about it; it is to this zone of occult instability where the people dwell that we must come; and it is there that our souls are crystallized and that our perceptions and our lives are transfused with light.

[. . .]

Notes

1   "The political leader as the representative of a culture." Address to the second Congress of Black Writers and Artists, Rome, 1959.
2   The lady was not alone; she had a most respectable husband, who knew how to quote Racine and Corneille, Voltaire and Rousseau, Victor Hugo and Musset, Gide, Valéry and as many more again. (René Depestre: "Face à la Nuit.")
3   René Depestre: "Face à la Nuit."
4   René Char, *Partage Formel.*

Chapter 37

True and False Pluralism

Paulin Hountondji

'Cultural pluralism' generally means three things: (1) the *fact* of cultural plurality, under-stood as the coexistence of cultures belonging, at least in principle, to different geographical areas; (2) the *recognition* of this fact; (3) the *advocacy* of this plurality and the *will* to make use of it in one way or another, either by preserving these cultures from mutual contamination or by organizing a peaceful dialogue among them for their mutual enrichment.

In this now classic form cultural pluralism is a reaction against the cultural exclusivism of the West, and it is important to note that this reaction itself came from the West. The Europe that produced Lévy-Bruhl also produced Lévi-Strauss. The Europe that produced Gobineau also produced Jean-Paul Sartre. The Europe that produced Hitler had previously produced Marx – a sign that European culture is itself pluralistic, a criss-cross of the most diverse tendencies, so that, when we speak of Western civilization we may not be clear what we are talking about, and there is a danger that we will confuse currents that are opposed and irreconcilable.

But whether imaginary or real, this 'Western civilization' has been created as a unitary civilization and has become the yardstick by which the civilizations of other continents are deprecated and devalued. The cultural achievements of other societies have been destroyed for its sake. This attitude bears a name: ethnocentrism. It has had its day of glory – the second half of the nineteenth century and the beginning of our own; and today nobody would seriously dispute that it was linked historically to colonization. It has also had its professional ideologues, one of the most illustrious of them being Lévy-Bruhl (who, by the way, has the distinction of being 'entirely francophone').

From 'progressive' ethnologists to the Third World 'nationalists'

It was as a reaction against this cultural imperialism that it began to be asserted at least fifty years ago,[1] and continues to be today, that European civilization is only one of a number of

First published in the *Acta*:53–65, and in *Diogène* 84 (October–December 1973); and subsequently in *African Philosophy: Myth and Reality*, trans. Henri Evans, 2nd edn, pp. 156–69. Bloomington: Indiana University Press, 1996.

ways of organizing people's relations to each other and to nature. Thus was recognized the
plurality of cultures. Thus was rejected, at least in principle, the myth of Western superiority
as a result of a new awareness that the technical and economic advancement of a society did
not automatically produce social or moral superiority. Some even went so far as simply to
invert the scale of imperialistic values and to valorize the non-technicity of 'exotic' societies
by interpreting their lesser technological development as a condition of greater 'authenticity', i.e. of a greater transparency in human relations. As early as 1930 Malinowski wrote:

> Many of us...see a menace to all real spiritual and artistic values in the aimless advance of
> modern mechanization.
>   One of the refuges from this mechanical prison of culture is the study of primitive forms of
> human life as they still exist in remote parts of our globe. Anthropology, to me at least, was a
> romantic escape from our over-standardized culture.[2]

Closer to our own time, Lévi-Strauss has adopted the same Rousseauist tone, arguing that
'primitive' societies are more 'authentic' than 'civilized' societies because they are free from
exploitation, because their human relations are less anonymous and more personal, because
they are small enough for everyone to know everyone else and to enjoy perfect unanimity on
all the most important problems.[3]

So we are now witnessing the valorization of a cultural plurality, the very existence of
which was inconceivable to imperial ethnology. The evolutionism of Tylor or Morgan and
the brash and reactionary ethnocentrism of Lévy-Bruhl could not accept the idea that non-
European cultures might actually exist. They could not conceive of the cultural life of
'primitive' societies except as representing the early stages in a single cultural process of
which Europe represented for them the most advanced stage. Today, however, Western
anthropology accepts the existence of other cultures; and, more than that, it sees them as
representing the possible salvation of a Western civilization suffering from an excess of
technology and standardization and yearning for what Bergson called a 'heightening of the
soul'.

It is remarkable how quickly the nationalists of the 'Third World' began to follow in the
footsteps of the ethnologists of the new school. Césaire was one of them. Many African
intellectuals of my generation read with fervour and delighted in those admirable stanzas
from his *Cahier d'un retour au pays natal*, and my nostalgia for past enthusiasms forces me to
quote them at length:

> Those who did not invent gunpowder or the compass
> Those who never knew how to tame steam or electricity
> Those who have explored neither the seas nor the sky
> But those without whom the earth would not be the earth
> A hump of greater bounty on earth-forsaking earth
> A silo to preserve and ripen the earthmost in earth,
> My negritude is not a stone to rush unhearing at screaming daylight
> My negritude is not a film of dead water on the dead eye of the earth
> My negritude is neither a tower nor a cathedral
> It dips in the red flesh of the earth
> It dips in the burning flesh of the sky
> It pricks the blank torpor of its direct patience

Eia for the royal mahogany!
Eia for those who have never invented anything
For those who have never explored anything
For those who have never tamed anything
But they yield, possessed, to the essence of all things
Blind to surfaces but possessed of the motion of all things
Careless to tame but gamesters of the world
Truly the elder sons of the world
Porous to all the world's breathing
Drainless bed for the world's waters
Spark from the world's sacred fire
Flesh of the flesh of the world pulsating with the world's self-motion![4]

These lines are remarkable for their poetic sweep, capable of moving the most frigid temperament; but they are also of great historical interest, since they include what I think is the first occurrence of the now famous neologism: 'negritude'[5] in a context capable of bringing out its significance.

But even more remarkable is the fact that they display a black poet spontaneously employing a mode of argument originally devised in white society to express his revolt against white racism. The *Cahier d'un retour au pays natal* was published in 1939.[6] At that time functionalism was no novelty, since Malinowski's classic work *The Argonauts of the Western Pacific* had appeared in 1922. So Césaire was not being original when he claimed that the non-technicity of blacks was not a defect but a virtue, that it is the obverse of an essential responsiveness unknown to Europe, that the West has nothing to teach the rest of the world in the essential human qualities of brotherhood, openness to experience, and rootedness.

Césaire himself was perfectly aware of this. Like his friend Senghor, he was almost as happy to invoke the authority of Malinowski, Herskovits and other functionalists as that of Frobenius. It is therefore true to say that nationalism in the colonies has never involved a total rejection of the colonizer's culture; rather, it has always consisted in choosing from the many currents of that culture those which are most favourable to the Third World. An initial stage of spontaneous revolt and unreflective self-assertion has been followed by a second stage, involving the discovery of favourable currents in violent contrast to colonial practice as it was experienced.

Thus there has arisen what can truly be called a complicity between Third World nationalists and 'progressive' Western anthropologists. For years they will assist each other, the former using the latter in support of their cultural claims, the latter using the former to buttress their pluralistic theses.

Culture and politics: culturalist ideology

The hypertrophy of the cultural

I have cited Césaire as an exponent of nationalism. I could just as well have cited Senghor who, of course, has done much more than Césaire, its inventor, to popularize the word 'negritude' and whose endless dissertations have woven around it a whole negro ideology.

This garrulous negrism has a very simple explanation: whereas for Césaire the exaltation of black cultures functions merely as a supporting argument in favour of political liberation, in Senghor it works as an alibi for evading the political problem of national liberation. Hypertrophy of cultural nationalism generally serves to compensate for the hypotrophy of political nationalism. This is probably why Césaire spoke so soberly about culture and never mentioned it without explicitly subordinating it to the more fundamental problem of political liberation. This also explains why, in works like *Liberté I*, Senghor, as a good Catholic and disciple of Teilhard de Chardin, emphasizes rather artificial cultural problems, elaborating lengthy definitions of the unique black mode of being and of being-in-the-world, and systematically evades the problem of the struggle against imperialism.

The above-mentioned complicity between the nationalist and the ethnologist is therefore particularly disastrous in the case of the cultural nationalist – that is to say, the nationalist who is inclined to emphasize only the cultural aspect of foreign domination at the expense of other aspects, the economic and political in particular. For want of a more adequate term, we can call this attitude 'culturalism' (by analogy with 'economism' and without reference to the anthropological current usually so named). The characteristic of culturalism in this sense is to distort the political and economic problems, neatly side-stepping them in favour of exclusively cultural problems. Worse still, these cultural problems are themselves strangely simplified as culture is reduced to folklore, its most obvious superficial and flashy aspect. Its deeper life and internal contradictions, the fruitful tensions by which it is animated are all neglected, along with its history, development and revolutions. Culture is petrified in a synchronic picture, flat and strangely simple and univocal, and is then contrasted with other cultures which are also trimmed and schematized for the sake of the comparison.

A deceptive singular

In this way we speak of African civilization as 'traditional' in contrast to Western civilization, as if there could be African civilization, Western civilization, in the singular, and as if civilization were not, by nature, a permanent clash of contradictory cultural forms.

I am not saying, of course, that the use of the word 'civilization' in the singular should be proscribed for ever, but simply that this singularity must be reinterpreted: it should refer not to the imaginary unity of a system of values but to the real empirical unity of a specific geographical area. European civilization is not a closed system of values but a set of irreducible cultural products which have appeared on the European continent; or, at a deeper level, it is the set of these products and of the creative tensions which underlie them, the necessary infinite act of these products and tensions, in the forms they have assumed in the past and in the as yet unpredictable forms they will assume tomorrow in that little strip of the world called Europe. Nor is African civilization a closed system in which we may imprison ourselves (or allow ourselves to be imprisoned). It is the unfinished history of a similar contradictory debate as it has proceeded, and will continue to proceed, in that fraction of the world called Africa. Only in this sense – as an external label rather than an impossible inner description – can we speak of African civilization in the singular, the only real unity being here that of a continent.

However, while the use of the word 'civilization' in the singular may in the last resort be acceptable, the adjective 'traditional', in the phrase 'traditional African civilization', must be banished once and for all because it favours a pernicious misconception. In practice the phrase is used to mean 'pre-colonial African civilization', and there is no real objection to the idea of 'pre-colonial African civilization', but again only in the sense of a purely conventional historical division. But when, instead of this neutral phrase, we use the more vivid phrase 'traditional African civilization', we add a value connotation, and pre-colonial civilization as a whole is being contrasted with so-called 'modern' civilization (that is to say, colonial and post-colonial civilization, with the connotation 'highly Westernized'), as if they were two essentially distinct systems of values. The pre-colonial history of Africa is condensed into a single synchronic picture, whose points exist simultaneously and are uniformly opposed to the points in a different synchronic chart, symmetrical with the first, the two being distinguished in terms of what is taken to be the only important division in the history of the continent, the moment of colonization. We ignore, or pretend to ignore, the fact that African traditions are no more homogeneous than those of any other continent, that cultural traditions are always a complex heritage, contradictory and heterogeneous, an open set of options, some of which will be actualized by any given generation, which by adopting one choice sacrifices all the others. We ignore, or pretend to ignore the fact that cultural traditions can remain alive only if they are exploited anew, under one of their aspects at the expense of all the others, and that the choice of this privileged aspect is itself a matter for struggle today, for an endlessly restless debate whose ever uncertain outcome spells the destiny of society. Above all, we ignore or pretend to ignore the fact that African cultural traditions are not closed, that they did not stop when colonization started but embrace colonial and post-colonial cultural life. So-called modern Africa is just as 'traditional' as pre-colonial Africa in the only acceptable sense of the word 'traditional' – tradition does not exclude but necessarily implies a system of discontinuities.

The culturalist system

All these flaws, real or imaginary, are present in culturalism. They are even organized into a vast ideological (i.e. indirectly political) system. I do say *indirectly political*, for ideology is camouflaged politics. Culturalism is an ideological system because it produces an indirect political effect. It eclipses, first, the problem of effective national liberation and, second, the problem of class struggle.

In the first moment culturalism, in the guise of an exclusively cultural nationalism, drastically simplifies the national culture, schematizes and flattens it in order to contrast it with the colonizer's culture, and then gives this imaginary opposition *precedence* over real political and economic conflicts.

In independent countries culturalism takes the form of a backward-looking cultural nationalism, flattening the national culture and denying its internal pluralism and historical depth, in order to divert the attention of the exploited classes from the real political and economic conflicts which divide them from the ruling classes under the fallacious pretext of their common participation in 'the' national culture.

Césaire is therefore not the typical cultural nationalist because for him culture has always been subordinate to politics. He merely invented the word 'negritude' and crystallized the arguments for revolt around it; but unfortunately these were subsequently taken over by others and degraded into a mystifying ideology.

However, negritude is not the only form of cultural nationalism. There are other phrases –
for instance, 'authenticity' or 'the repersonalization of the African', which it has seized upon.
The diversity of labels and the importance of local variations should not be allowed to conceal
the unity of the structure. The dominant feature of this structure is always what is commonly
called traditionalism, understood as the exclusive valorization of a simplified, superficial
and imaginary blueprint of cultural tradition.

It is this structure for which I use a very general term, 'culturalism'. I say 'culturalism' and
not merely 'cultural nationalism', because this structure is characteristic of Third World
nationalists and Western ethnologists: it is the locus of their objective complicity.

Ethnologists too tend to isolate the cultural aspects of society and to stress it at the
expense of the economic and political aspects. Even when dealing with politics, ethnologists
will generally be concerned with the traditional kind, arbitrarily reduced to its pre-colonial
dimension, petrified, ossified and emptied of its internal tensions, discontinuities and
confrontations. The political problem of colonial or neo-colonial domination is never
posed. Anthropology presents itself as apolitical, even when it specializes in the study of
political structures. The numerous works devoted to 'political anthropology' have always
attempted to evade the problem of the national liberation of the peoples under study. In
some cases, it is true, they felt compelled to describe what they abstractly called the 'colonial
situation' (cf. Balandier), thus translating what was in fact a (political) *conflict* into terms of
(cultural) *ambiguity*. But in the large majority of cases political anthropologists do not even
go as far as this: they prefer to ignore the present political life of dominated peoples and
interest themselves exclusively in their so-called traditional (i.e., in fact, pre-colonial) political
organization.

Thus the flight from politics permeates even so-called political anthropology. Different
anthropologists at various times have always either affirmed the supremacy of the West,
presenting it as possessing the only mature civilization while other societies are at best at the
early stages of a process which the West has already completed (Lévy-Bruhl and the classical
evolutionists), or, conversely, in a gesture of repentance which is still motivated by the same
comparative problematic, they have tried to show that European civilization is not unique
but that there are others, equally valid. But, of course, these other civilizations are now in
contact with Europe and as a result of colonization have been subjected to an involuntary
process of Westernization; pluralist anthropologists refuse to consider their present condition, but prefer to try and reconstruct their pre-colonial existence. Moreover, when they
investigate this pre-colonial past, they refuse to see the evolution, revolutions and discontinuities that may have affected it, and the precarious balance which has made these
civilizations temporarily what they are today. Anthropologists need to play with simple
units, univocal cultural totalities without cracks or dissonances. They need dead cultures,
petrified cultures, always identical to themselves in the homogeneous space of an eternal
present.

Such are the main features of the culturalist mode of thought, in which the complicity of
ethnologists and nationalists takes shape. Such is the all-embracing structure which accommodates the otherwise differing activities of 'progressive' anthropology (functionalist, structuralist, dynamic, etc.) and cultural nationalism. This is the universal structure which has
given rise to the common thesis of 'progressive' ethnologist and nationalist: the plurality of
cultures. For both groups this thesis functions as a refuge: it enables Western anthropologists
to escape from the boredom of their own society and third-world nationalists to escape from

the psychological and political rape perpetrated upon them by Western imperialism, by plunging back into their (imaginary) cultural origins.

True pluralism

The false problem of acculturation

Thus a theoretical affirmation of the plurality of cultures invariably serves as a pretext for a conservative cultural practice. Neither the anthropologist nor the nationalist can today be unaware of the fact that the 'exotic' cultures no longer exist in their pure state: that they no longer offer the nostalgic European or the rebellious nationalist an absolute alternative. If they ever did represent *the* difference as such, they can certainly no longer do so, owing to the growth of cultural interpenetration. Both ethnologist and nationalist readily recognize that we are more and more witnessing the irreversible advent of a world civilization. But instead of grasping this phenomenon in all its complexity, they simplify and trivialize it, emptying it of all real content by calling it 'acculturation'.

A young (and 'entirely francophone') anthropologist, Gérard Leclerc, has recently shown in an admirable book how field anthropologists, faced with the impossibility of sweeping the facts of colonialism under the carpet, have introduced it surreptitiously into their discussions under the name of 'acculturation'.[7] Between 1930 and 1950 an enormous literature was devoted to this theme, but learned discussions of the 'changing native', 'culture clash' and 'culture contact' or 'social change', etc., were all founded on the same pervasive ideological assumption: in a non-Western culture, change can only come from outside.

Gérard Leclerc draws attention to the mechanistic vocabulary that is invariably used in all these analyses. But what he fails to point out (and has possibly not noticed)[8] is that this vocabulary, far from 'driving out speculation and ideology', actually expresses the ideological conception that non-Western cultures are dead, petrified, reified, eternally self-replicating and lacking any internal capacity for negation or transcendence. But Gérard Leclerc has not sustained his critique to the point of finally abandoning the (epistemologically indefensible) ideological prejudice which makes anthropology an autonomous discipline and has chosen instead to try to resurrect ethnology in the form of a 'critical anthropology', and this is why he fails to make the all-important point that we must stress: that a culture is always active and creative; it is a contradictory debate between people chained to the same destiny and anxious to make the best of it. What we must understand is that never in any society does everyone agree with everyone else. One of the most perverse myths invented by ethnology, whose effects in return contribute to the survival of ethnology itself, is the myth of primitive unanimity, the myth that non-Western societies are 'simple' and homogeneous at every level, including the level of ideology and belief. What we must recognize today is that pluralism does not come to any society from outside but is inherent in every society. The alleged acculturation, the alleged 'encounter' of African civilization with European civilization, is really just another mutation produced from within African civilizations, the successor to many earlier ones about which our knowledge is very incomplete, and, no doubt, the precursor of many future mutations, which may be more radical still. The decisive encounter is not between Africa as a whole and Europe as a whole: it is the continuing encounter between Africa and itself. Pluralism in the true sense did not stem from the intrusion of

Western civilization into our continent; it did not come from outside to a previously unanimous civilization. It is an internal pluralism, born of perpetual confrontations and occasional conflicts between Africans themselves.

A dangerous polarization

Far from having come to Africa with colonization, it is highly probable that cultural pluralism was checked and impoverished by its advent, which artificially reduced it to a confrontation between two poles, one dominant and the other dominated. All the profit that might have accrued to our cultures from free exchange with European cultures, and the extraordinary enrichment our internal debate might have known if it had been able to supplement its own terms through the assimilation of terms derived from abroad (as European art, for instance, was able to broaden its range by adopting a style known as 'African art'), all these fine hopes were betrayed and dashed because no genuine exchange has ever been possible in a climate of violence. Colonialism has thus arrested African cultures by reducing their internal pluralism, diminishing the discords and weakening the tensions from which they derived their vitality, leaving Africans with an artificial choice between cultural 'alienation' (which is supposedly connected with political betrayal) and cultural nationalism (the obverse of political nationalism and often a pathetic substitute for it).

What we must now realize is that this polarization has been disastrous and that its destruction is one of the first and most important conditions of our cultural renaissance. African culture must return to itself, to its internal pluralism and to its essential openness. We must therefore, as individuals, liberate ourselves psychologically and develop a free relationship both with African cultural tradition and with the cultural traditions of other continents. This will not be a process either of Westernization or of acculturation: it will simply be creative freedom, enriching the African tradition itself as an open system of options.

[. . .]

Notes

1   I am adopting the conventional landmark of the publication of Malinowski's classic work *Argonauts of the Western Pacific* in London in 1922. But in fact the idea of a plurality of cultures is really much older than this, and was widely debated, for instance, in 1911 at the first Universal Congress of Races in London (cf. Gérard Leclerc, *Anthropologie et colonialisme*, Paris 1972, p. 83).

2   Bronislaw Malinowski, 'The rationalization of anthropology and administration', *Africa* (journal of the International Institute of African Languages and Culture), vol. 3, no. 4 (1930), pp. 405–30. The quotation is on pp. 405–6.

3   See in particular G. Charbonnier, *Entretiens avec Lévi-Strauss* (Paris 1961), pp. 51–65.

4   Aimé Césaire, *Cahier d'un retour au pays natal* (Paris: Présence Africaine 1956), pp. 71–2.

5   It is common to credit Senghor with the invention of the word 'negritude'. But he himself is ready to deny it. Cf. the Introduction of *Liberté I. Négritude et humanisme* (Paris: Seuil 1964): 'We merely studied it [negro-African civilization] and gave it the name of negritude. I say "we", but I must not forget to render unto Césaire that which is Césaire's. It was he who invented the word in the years 1932–1934' (p. 8).

The stanza quoted is in fact the second place where the word 'negritude' occurs in the *Cahier*. However, the earlier use of the word is not very enlightening. It is in a stanza in which, in the course of summarizing his historical heritage, Césaire mentions 'Haiti where negritude stood on its own feet for the first time' (p. 44). The word seems to be used simply to denote the black race, without any evaluative overtones. However, in the long stanza I have quoted, it is clearly used to designate a set of virtues connected with blacks.

6   The poem was first published in the twentieth and last number of a review entitled *Volontés*, Paris (August 1939). It later appeared in a bilingual edition, with a Spanish translation, in Cuba in 1944. It was prefaced by André Breton ('Martinique, charmeuse de serpents') in a new edition by Bordas (Paris 1947), and reissued by Editions Présence Africaine.

7   Leclerc, *Anthropologie et colonialisme*.

8   Leclerc attempts a sort of defence of this 'mechanistic vocabulary which may perhaps be a mockery of rigour and "science", but which was at least intended to reduce speculation and ideology' (p. 89).

Chapter 38

"An Open Letter to Africans" c/o The Punic One-Party State

Sony Labou Tansi

Thinking, selling and buying have made a mockery of geographical boundaries. Even if from a philosophical point of view buying and selling are trivial pursuits whereas they are all important in the realm of economics, it is obvious that thinking is the irreplaceable means of creating an impact on the future. In the present situation, our tragedy is that Africa does little thinking, trades badly, and is even worse at buying. To crown it all we use a simple and poetic expression to describe this tragedy: afro-pessimism, a terrible word used to conceal the greatest mess of all time. We accept, smiling, that history (which, incidentally has cuckolded us more than once) makes of us the victims of a shameful chill: the North-induced chill in the prices of raw materials that dooms us to construct and build garbage economies in the depths of the most cruel, unbearable, and inhuman form of indignity that humans can swallow without as much as a retch.

Africa in this respect is unrivalled in the art of self-deception. In fooling themselves on the subject of development, none of our states can be found wanting. We deluded ourselves into believing that the single party was sufficiently revolutionary to become the manufacturing site of national unities, and we contemptuously disregarded all the historical misunderstanding generated by those who badmouthed History in Berlin. How childish to have sought to resolve the problem of national unity by the simple and shameful negation of our differences. Unity, until further proof, is harmony voluntarily built from a field of differences. It is in this sense a site of transcendence and not of degeneracy. It is the painstaking elaboration of a consensus of similarities from a terrain of specificities. In the notion that unity can be forged through uniformisation, lay the same methods and ingredients that contributed to the negation of Inca, Maya, and Black cultures in the historical genocide that resulted from civilizing expeditions to the lands of peoples deemed inferior. What a disgrace to listen to fellow Africans continuing to propagate ideas articulated yesteryear by slavers and other prophets of the inferiority of so-called primitive peoples. What a shame for Africa to hear

First published in *Jeune Afrique Economie* 136 (1990): 8–9. Trans. John Conteh–Morgan.

one of her worthy sons, Kaunda,[1] declare publicly that to disagree with him on the running of the country is tantamount to being "a rabid dog."

The walls of the last thirty years of our history are unbearably decorated not with trophies of unity but of national exclusions. Unity does not necessarily lead to the refusal of the other, unless of course one is a past master at fooling oneself. From the Republic of South Africa to the uppermost reaches of the North, our continent is an immense warehouse of national exclusions draped in the colors of stability and unity. Everywhere, in an Africa given to indignity and bereft of a soul, wonderful constitutions studded with fundamental rights and liberties groan in pain under the buckshot that has been fired at the four corners of democracy. A deathly, leaden silence, a silence of terror, reigns. On the green lawns of this cramped peace, the most outrageous theories are advanced – in the streets as well as in colloquia halls: theories that Africa is inhabited by hordes of tribes and primitive peoples possessed of every demon of disunity, and who therefore need to be kept in check by strong doses of tear gas, police batons, purges, squadrons of the political police, and troops of national armies shamefully reduced to opening fire on tax payers; theories that in Africa exist vast and wild lands where to disagree is a crime against the Hernia-State which alone knows what and where reason is, and where the future, unity, prosperity, and the life of each citizen are. According to some dignitaries, those primitive peoples need time to learn the exercise of liberty. Be it said in passing that even animals know how to use liberty. Of course, all nations have their own ways of savoring liberty, except those that are denied it. Every nation knows how to respond in the face of the confiscation of its rights and freedoms. The defenders of the Party-Nation or the Party-State think that Africans need a few more decades to acquire the art of exercising their rights and freedoms. Can one hide a camel in a pin? Is it reasonable and serious to link the recognition of plural opinions and sensibilities to time alone? And which time? That of dictatorial regimes and political traditions where the person that exercises power is accountable to no one, not even to his conscience, given the vagueness of the elements of the social contract and the absence of any clear rules of the game? What sort of national unity can one get from an overkill of refusal of all contradiction? We know that differences are unavoidable, even in politics.

To push the depressing logic of the defenders of Punic one-party states to its conclusion – a racist and *racisant* logic – I see myself obliged to give advice to the divinely-sanctioned monarchies of an Africa adjudged not mature enough for republican status, the Republic being in essence the political site of delegated and representative power, controlled by a sovereign people, and which, according to the defenders of Single-Party-Nation-States, is inappropriate for Africa, given its current state of backwardness. So, let us then examine absolute monarchy – that salutary piece of self-deception designed not to create stability, (no form of national exclusion can ever lead to lasting stability), but to the reinforcement, pure and simple, of racist arguments that Africans are overgrown children, second-class human beings suffering damnation from heaven and hell. Let's for a moment play the role of a people consumed by overpowering cannibal instincts; let's pretend to forget, intellectually, the existence of local councils and elective royalties in pre-Portuguese Africa; let's forget about the existence of pre-Independence multi-ethnic organizations (MNC, PPC, UDDIA . . .); let's forget about Lumumba, Nkrumah, Matswa, Simon Kimbangu,[2] etc; let's endure the customary insult to the Negro defeated in all areas of modernism (I understand by modernism the advent of a culture of the human). The die would then have been cast for a new enslavement of Negroes, colonization by bread and the stomach.

I think, myself, that the refusal of difference and contradiction has become Africa's greatest tragedy, its most terrible weakness. The absence of a clear social contract between the people and its leaders dooms the latter to infantilization. It is only through the exercise of responsibility that one is human. The refusal to entrust the people with responsibility condemns our continent to bring up the rear on the chessboard of the future.

The primacy of the law remains and will remain the foundation stone in the building and consolidation of African nations. It is the crucial condition of our independence and development; the only means, in any case, to bring to bear the greatest reality of tomorrow's world, namely interdependence in the mutual respect of cultures and stakes. There is no state or strong nation that is not subject to the all-mighty rule of law. The countries of South America are stagnating from 150 to 200 years of successive dictatorships – time is their cruel ally: time only becomes what we make of it and how we conceive it.

Thirty years of monopoly of political power must have been of enormous good to Africans. That good, alas, remains less visible than the corruption, waste, and shootings of high school children and taxpayers. What remains noticeable and remarkable, at any rate, are the exclusions of all sorts and not the national unities secreted during the rule of the Party-State. Sycophancy has everywhere been bought more expensively than competence. Economic and social stagnation for the most part remain attributable to the injustice done to competence by complicity. The sycophancy of opinions and the devout abdication to the miraculous founding father of the nation, (of the single party), were the only form of competence that, up to now, could guarantee and buy everything, playing both the role of the law and justifying all kinds of irregularities. Let it be said that the word "founding father" carried with it a magical halo that tragically suggested the idea of a shameless founding father endowed with patriotic, national, and procreative powers; powers that in turn carry a hint of the notion of the fatherland as the product of an act of birthing, in some infamous tower, cut off from reality, as if nations can emerge from a baker's oven.

The birth of the nation-state proceeds by many acts of give-and-take, negotiations with time and geography, histories and cultures, peoples and spaces. The idea of a supreme insemination of the fatherland by the sole father of the nation is beyond ridiculous. How much longer, fellow men and brothers of Africa, shall we cover ourselves in such infamy?

Editors' Notes

1   Kenneth Kaunda (b. 1924), nationalist leader and first President of Zambia (1964–91).

2   MNC, Mouvement National Congolais (Congo-Kinshasa); PPC, Parti Progressiste Congolais (Congolese Progressive Party, Congo-Brazzaville); UDDIA, Union Démocratique pour la Défense d'Intérêts Africains (Democratic Union for the Defence of African Interests, Congo-Brazzaville), all independence-era political parties. Patrice Lumumba (1925–61), nationalist leader and first Prime Minister of the Democratic Republic of the Congo (1960) (Congo-Kinshasa); Kwame Nkrumah (1909–72), nationalist leader and first President of Ghana (1957–66); André Matswa (1899–1942), staunch anticolonial religious and political leader and trade unionist from the Congo-Brazzaville; Simon Kimbangu (1889–1951), born in the Congo Free State, which became Democratic Republic of the Congo, he was a Baptist convert who subsequently became a famous religious leader known among his followers as Ngunza or the "prophet."

Chapter 39

Resistance Theory / Theorizing Resistance or Two Cheers for Nativism

Benita Parry

[. . .]

When we consider the narratives of decolonization, we encounter rhetorics in which 'nativism' in one form or another is evident. Instead of disciplining these, theoretical whip in hand, as a catalogue of epistemological errors, of essentialist mystifications, as a masculinist appropriation of dissent, as no more than an anti-racist racism, etc., I want to consider what is to be gained from an unsententious interrogation of such articulations which, if often driven by negative passion, cannot be reduced to a mere inveighing against iniquities or a repetition of the canonical terms of imperialism's conceptual framework. This of course means affirming the power of the reverse-discourses[1] by arguing that anti-colonialist writings did challenge, subvert and undermine the ruling ideologies, and nowhere more so than in overthrowing the hierarchy of colonizer/colonized, the speech and stance of the colonized refusing a position of subjugation and dispensing with the terms of the colonizer's definitions.

The weak and strong forms of oppositional discursive practices have been designated as re/citation and de/citation by Terdiman and counter-identification and disidentification by Michel Pêcheux. For Pêcheux a 'discourse-against' is that in which the subject of enunciation takes up a position of separation 'with respect to what 'the universal subject' gives him to think . . . (distantiation, doubt, interrogation, challenge, revolt) . . . a struggle against ideological evidentness on the terrain of that evidentness, an evidentness with a negative sign, reversed on its own terrain'. Disidentification however 'constitutes a working (transformation-displacement) of the subject-form and not just its abolition'.[2] In Terdiman's terms, the technique of re/citation seeks 'to surround the [ir] antagonist and neutralize or explode it'; whereas

First published in *Colonial Discourse/Postcolonial Theory*, ed. F. Barker, P. Hulme, and M. Iversen, Manchester: Manchester University Press, 1994; and subsequently in *Postcolonial Studies: A Materialist Critique*, pp. 40–3. London: Routledge, 2004.

de/citation, a total withdrawal from the orbit of the dominant, strives 'to exclude it totally, to expunge it' (*Discourse/Counter Discourse*, pp. 68, 70). Neither writes off the force of the counter-discursive, and Terdiman, who concedes that reverse-discourses are always interlocked with and parasitic on the dominant they contest – working as opposition without effacing the antagonist, inhabiting and struggling with the dominant which inhabits them – maintains that they function to survey the limits and weaknesses of the dominant by mapping the internal incoherences: 'From this dialectic of discursive struggle, truths about the social formation – its characteristic modes of reproduction and its previously hidden vulnerabilities – inevitably emerge' (p. 66).

A recent discussion of nativism condenses many of the current censures of cultural nationalism for its complicity with the terms of colonialism's discourse, with its claims to ancestral purity and inscriptions of monolithic notions of identity cited as evidence of the failure to divest itself of the specific institutional determinations of the west. Although allowing the profound political significance of the decolonized writing themselves as subjects of a literature of their own, Anthony Appiah's critique, which is principally directed against its current forms, extends to older (all?) articulations. In exposing the operation of a 'nativist topology' – inside/outside, indigene/alien, western/traditional – it installs a topology of its own, where the colonizer is dynamic donor and the colonized is docile recipient, where the west initiates and the native imitates. Thus while the reciprocity of the colonial relationship is stressed, all power remains with western discourse. For example: 'the overdetermined course of cultural nationalism in Africa has been to make real the imaginary identities to which Europe has subjected us'; the rhetoric of 'intact indigenous traditions' and the very conception of an African personality and an African past are European inventions; the Third World intellectual is europhone, immersed in the language and literature of the colonial countries.[3] These statements could be modulated without underplaying or obscuring a necessary registration of western discursive power: Europe's fabrications of 'Africa' were deflected and subverted by African, Caribbean and African-American literary discourses; 'African identity' is the product of refusing Europe's gaze and returning its own anti-colonialist look; europhone colonials transgress their immersion in European languages and literatures, seizing and diverting vocabularies, metaphors and literary traditions.

The occasion for Appiah's case against nativism is *Toward the Decolonization of African Literature*. The authors, Chinweizu, Jemie and Madubuike, invite censure for taking an unqualified position on cultural autonomy, but their object is a critique of cultural nationalism's entrapment in a reverse-discourse:

> Railing against the cultural hegemony of the West, the nativists are of its party without knowing it. Indeed the very arguments, the rhetoric of defiance, that our nationalists muster are . . . canonical, time tested . . . in their ideological inscription, the cultural nationalists remain in a position of counteridentification . . . which is to continue to participate in an institutional configuration – to be subjected to cultural identities they ostensibly decry . . . Time and time again, cultural nationalism followed the route of alternate genealogizing. We end up always in the same place; the achievement is to have invented a different past for it.
>
> ('Out of Africa', pp. 162, 170)

The effect of this argument is to homogenize the varieties of nationalisms and to deny both originality and effectivity to its reverse-discourses. Such a contention is disputed by Partha Chatterjee's study; for despite a subtitle (a derivative discourse) encouraging selective citation in the interest of relegating nationalist thought as mimetic, and while recognizing the inherent contradiction of its reasoning within a framework serving a structure of power it seeks to repudiate, the book is concerned to establish its difference: 'Its politics impel it to open up that framework of knowledge that presumes to dominate it, to displace that framework, to subvert its authority, to challenge its morality'.[4]

Some of the implications of arguments according a totalizing power to colonialist discourses emerge in Rosalind O'Hanlon's discussion of current research concerned to emphasize the British 'invention' of nineteenth-century caste as a challenge to 'the notion of an ageless caste-bound social order', but which maximizes the effectivity of 'colonial conjuring', and by occluding the 'complex and contradictory engagements with colonialist categories . . . often produces a picture of Indian actors who are helpless to do anything but reproduce the structures of their own subordination'.[5] In this connection Ranajit Guha's eloquent inventory establishing the presence of an 'Indian idiom of politics' discernible in the many languages of the subcontinent, demonstrates that the modes of subaltern colonial resistance, far from being determined by forms and vocabularies borrowed from the dominant culture, were rearticulations of pre-colonial traditions of protest.[6]

Mindful of Robert Young's caution that the search for a nativist alternative may simply represent 'the narcissistic desire to find an other that will reflect western assumptions of selfhood' (White Mythologies, p. 165), I will argue that something quite different animates those modes of postcolonial critique concerned to reconstruct a story from tales, legends and idioms which are themselves transcriptions and improvisations of dissent that was never formally narrativized, and to produce an uncensorious but critical interrogation of colonial resistance when they were. It will be evident that the interest of such readings is to retain in the discussion that realm of imaginary freedom which these histories prefigured or config-ured, as well as to register decolonizing struggles as an emancipatory project despite the egregious failures these brought in their wake. Although the assumption here is that the discourses or discursive retracings of past dissidence come to us already encoded with the elements of a counter-narrative (which diminishes the critics' claim to be performing the insurgent act), it is we who by appropriating it to our theoretical purposes alter the material, in the process making visible its erasures, suppressions and marginalizations, evident for example in the foregrounding of male figures of praxis and authority.

Elleke Boehmer's discussion of narratives of nationalist recuperation, identity reconstruc-tion and nation formation shows how images of the female body were used to embody ideals of the wholeness of subjectivity, history and the state. Thus, while reversing colonialist iconography figuring penetration, pillage and dismemberment – 'repression upon the objectified, enslaved, colonised body' – such invocations of the female body 'rest upon the assumption of predominantly masculine authority and historical agency', nationalism's core concepts nesting in the metaphor of the maternal body. Because, Boehmer argues, post-colonial discourses of self-determination 'have a considerable investment in nationalist concepts of "selving" and of retrieving history, the gender specifics of nationalist iconog-raphy are accepted, or borne with, or overlooked', the deconstructions of such configur-ations only now being effected in postcolonial literatures.[7] In a related register, Ella Shohat writes that 'Anti-colonial intellectuals, though not particularly preoccupied with gender issues, have . . . used gender tropes to discuss colonialism', Césaire and Fanon implicitly subverting representations of rape by violent dark men and cultures, and fantasies of rescuing virginal white and at times dark women, 'while at the same time using gendered discourse to articulate oppositional struggle'.[8] Where Shohat seems to be overstating her case is in suggesting that stories of sexual violence against Third World women are 'relatively privileged' over those of violence towards Third World men.

Such attention to the retention of patriarchal positions in anti-colonialist discourses points up the inadvisability of using the sources to write an optimistic narrative of liberation struggles as 'ideologically correct'. But in order to do justice to their histories – to borrow a phrase from Jonathan Dollimore[9] – it is surely necessary to refrain from a sanctimonious reproof of modes of writing resistance which do not conform to contemporary theoretical rules about discursive radicalism. Instead I would argue that the task is to address the empowering effects of constructing a coherent identity or of cherishing and defending against calumniation altered and mutable indigenous forms, which is not the same as the hopeless attempt to locate and revive pristine and intact pre-colonial cultures.[10] It is an unwillingness to abstract resistance from its moment of performance that informs my discussion of Césaire and Fanon as authors of liberation theories which today could stand accused of an essentialist politics. For, as I read them, both affirm the invention of an insurgent, unified black self, acknowledge the revolutionary energies released by valorizing the cultures denigrated by colonialism and, rather than construing the colonialist relationship in terms of negotiations with the structures of imperialism, privilege coercion over hegemony to project it as a struggle between implacably opposed forces – an irony made all too obvious in enunciations inflected, indeed made possible, by these very negotiations.
[. . .]

Notes

1   A case for the power of the reverse-discourse which uses the same categories and vocabulary as the texts of social control it contests is made by Jonathan Dollimore, citing Foucault's argument in *History of Sexuality*, vol. 1: 'Deviancy returns from abjection by deploying just those terms which relegated it to that state in the first place – including "nature" and "essence" . . . A complex and revealing dialectic between the dominant and the deviant emerges from histories of homosexual representation, especially from the homosexual (later gay) appropriations of nature and essence'; *Sexual Dissidence: Literatures, Histories, Theories* (Oxford: Oxford University Press, 1991), pp. 95–6.

2   Michel Pêcheux, *Language, Semantics and Ideology* (London: Macmillan, 1982), pp. 157, 159.

3   Anthony Appiah, 'Out of Africa: Topologies of Nativism', *Yale Journal of Criticism*, vol. 1/2 (1988), pp. 153–78, p. 164.

4   Partha Chatterjee, *Nationalist Thought and the Colonial World: a Derivative Discourse?* (London: Zed Books, 1986), p. 42.

5   Rosalind O'Hanlon, 'Cultures of Rule, Communities of Resistance: Gender, Discourse and Tradition in Recent South Asian Historiographies', *Modern Asian Studies*, vol. 22 (1989), pp. 95–114, pp. 98, 100, 104.

6   See Ranajit Guha: 'peasant uprisings variously called *hool, dhing, bidroha, hangama, fituri*, etc. . . . *hizrat* or desertion *en masse* of peasants or other labouring people . . . *dharma* or protest sitting down in the offender's presence with the pledge not to move until the redress of grievance . . . *hartal* or the general suspension of public activity . . . *dharmaghat* or withdrawal of labour . . . *jat mara*, or measures to destroy the offender's caste by refusal to render such specialist services as are required to insure him and his kin against pollution . . . *danga* or sectarian, ethnic, caste and class violence involving large bodies of the subaltern population'; 'Dominance without Hegemony', p. 267.

7   Elleke Boehmer, 'Transfiguring the Colonial Body into Narrative', *Novel*, vol. 26 (1993), pp. 268–77.

8   Ella Shohat, 'Imagining Terra Incognita: the Disciplinary Gaze of Empire', *Public Culture*, vol. 3 (1991), pp. 41–70, pp. 56–7.

9   See Dollimore, who argues for avoiding a 'theoreticist' writing-off of the histories of 'essentialist politics'; *Sexual Dissidence*, pp. 44–5.

10 But nor should the cost of the 'hybridity' effected by colonialism's invasions be uncounted. Glossing Edward Brathwaite's definition of creolization as 'one's adaptation to a new environment through the loss of parts of oneself and the gain of parts of the Other', Manthia Diawara adds that one must be aware of the fact that in fusing whiteness with the seductiveness of hybridization, one is also sacrificing not only a part of blackness, but certain black people; 'The Nature of Mother in *Dreaming River*', *Third Text*, vol. 13 (1990/1991), p. 82. These certain black people, inhabiting extant although neither static or intact autochthonous cultures, emerge in Caroline Rooney's reading of a story by Ama Ata Aidoo where she draws attention to a narration which legitimates 'a culture that predates and is not erased by colonial founding fathers who are not then an originating point of reference', and criticizes the amnesia of those who, having embraced the metropolitan culture, renounce their natal communities. See 'Are We in the Company of Feminists?: a Preface for Bessie Head and Ama Ata Aidoo', in *Diverse Voices: Essays in Twentieth Century Women Writers*, ed. Harriet Devine Jump (London: Harvester Wheatsheaf, 1991), pp. 214–46, p. 222.

Part VI

The Language of African Literature

"Is it right that a man should abandon his mother-tongue for someone else's? It looks like a dreadful betrayal and produces a guilty feeling." So ruminated Chinua Achebe in the early 1960s ("African Writer" 62). Grave as this soul-searching was, Achebe then was optimistic that he could arrive at both a practical and psychological balance between being a born-and-bred Igbo African writer and writing in English: "I feel that the English language will be able to carry the weight of my African experience. But it will have to be a new English, still in full communion with its ancestral home but altered to suit its new African surroundings" (62). Several accomplished novels in English later and a solid worldwide fame for his mastery and distinctive use of the language, Achebe issued, just a decade after the earlier statement, not a triumphalist self-celebration but a heart-rending lament: "[T]he fatalistic logic of the unassailable position of English in our literature leaves me more cold now than it did when I first spoke about it . . . And yet I am unable to see a significantly different or a more emotionally comfortable resolution of that problem" ("Preface" xiv). If Achebe's experience is any guide, the point here is that in spite of the great achievements so far of African writers in the European languages, it is still the case that the continued dominance of those languages in African literary creativity constitutes a composite adversarial context. A tamed and tropicalized English, Achebe discovered, is still no less English. Ngugi wa Thiong'O, after a distinguished career of several novels and plays in English, switched to writing in his Kenyan Gikuyu language, the point being that translation ought to be the egalitarian mode of interaction between and among languages. Most of the theoretical discussion of the language issue has focused more on writers, but it is time that theorists and critics of the literature be queried too about the language of their enterprise. Beyond literary studies, the bigger issue is the dominance of the European languages in the educational, commercial, political and bureaucratic lives of Africans. The essays in this section leave no stone unturned in considering the problematic of languages, European or African, in African literature and literary studies.

References

Achebe, Chinua. "The African Writer and the English Language." *Morning yet on Creation Day: Essays*. London: Heinemann, 1975. 55–62.
——. "Preface." *Morning yet on Creation Day: Essays*. xiii–xiv.

Chapter 40

The Dead End of African Literature?

Obiajunwa Wali

PERHAPS THE MOST IMPORTANT ACHIEVEMENT of the last Conference of African Writers of English Expression held in Makerere College, Kampala, in June 1962, is that African literature as now defined and understood, leads nowhere.

The Conference itself marked the final climax of the attack on the Negritude school of Léopold Senghor and Aimé Césaire. For some time now, African writers of English expression like Ezekiel Mphahlele, Wole Soyinka, and Christopher Okigbo, have treated this kind of literature which expresses sterile concepts such as "negritude" or the "African personality"[1] with the utmost derision. One would say that negritude is now dead, judging from the confident tones of the remarks and decisions made at the Makerere conference.

Another significant event in the conference, is the tacit omission of Amos Tutuola. Not only was Tutuola, who undoubtedly is one of the most significant writers in Africa today, not present in the conference, but there was a careful exclusion of his works in the discussions of the conference. In fact, according to the Conference report, Tutuola's publishers protested at the implied questioning of their integrity in publishing this writer's works. One can guess that Tutuola received this kind of treatment partly because influential critics like Janheinz Jahn have repeatedly grouped him in the negritude school, and partly because he has gone out of line winning acclaim overseas for using that kind of English expression that is non-Ibadan, and non-Makerere.

With the now seeming defeat of the Negritude and Tutuola schools of African writing, what now represents African literature can be seen from these examples from some of the writings of the artists and critics who now dominate our literature. Una Maclean, reviewing J. P. Clark's play, *Song of A Goat*, opens in the following fashion: "The author of this poetic melodrama possibly perceives himself as some sort of Tennessee Williams of the Tropics. Suddenly the sultry symbolism of the sex war seeps through the swamps, to hang like a horrid miasma upon the polluted air... It is a simple and familiar tale, impotent man, ardent

First published in *Transition* 10 (1963): 13–15.

woman. But this cat on a hot tin roof had once known better times, for her partner had once given palpable token of his potency in siring a son."[2]

Christopher Okigbo in his acknowledgement prefixed to his poem, *Silences*, makes the following observations: "the author wishes to acknowledge his debt to those composers whose themes he has used or varied in certain parts of the present work. The INTROIT is a variation on a theme in Raja Ratnam's *At Eight-fifteen in the Morning*; the first three passages of the first movement are variations on a theme by Malcolm Cowley; "Sand banks sprinkled with memories" in the 4th passage of the same movement is a variation on Stephane Mallarme's "Au bosquet arrose d'accords" in his *L'Apres-midi d'un Faune*; the 6th passage of the same movement is a variation on a theme in Rabindranath Tagore's *Stray Birds*."[3]

Ulli Beier, in his paper read to the Makerere conference, discussing the poetry of J. P. Clark, remarks, "John Pepper Clark is a very different poet. His background is similar to that of Okigbo ... He studied English, and what Ezra Pound is to Okigbo, Eliot and Hopkins are to Clark. As the case of Okigbo, one finds it occasionally disturbing to recognise the 'ready made' language."[4]

What these examples clearly show is that African literature as now understood and practised, is merely a minor appendage in the main stream of European literature. Both creative writers and literary critics, read and devour European literature and critical methods. The new drama of J. P. Clark is seen in terms not only of the classical past of Aristotle and the Greeks, but in the current present of Tennessee Williams, and the Absurds, leading to such crudities as Una Maclean's comparison of the simple and child-hungry Ebiere, to the sexual complications of Big Daddy's American family. In this kind of literary analysis, one just goes back to parrot Aristotle, and the current clichés of the English and American new critics.

The consequence of this kind of literature is that it lacks any blood and stamina, and has no means of self-enrichment. It is severely limited to the European-oriented, few college graduates in the new Universities of Africa, steeped as they are in European literature and culture. The ordinary local audience, with little or no education in the conventional European manner, and who constitute an overwhelming majority, has no chance of participating in this kind of literature. Less than one per cent of the Nigerian people have had access to, or ability to understand Wole Soyinka's *Dance of the Forest*. Yet, this was the play staged to celebrate their national independence, tagged on to the idiom and traditions of a foreign culture. It is no wonder, that a poet like Christopher Okigbo, so readily resorts to Mallarmé's idea of an aristocratic and limited poetic community, for his impertinent remark, "I don't read my poetry to non-poets" is Mallarmé in paraphrase.

The purpose of this article is not to discredit these writers who have achieved much in their individual rights within an extremely difficult and illogical situation. It is to point out that the whole uncritical acceptance of English and French as the inevitable medium for educated African writing, is misdirected, and has no chance of advancing African literature and culture. In other words, until these writers and their western midwives accept the fact that any true African literature must be written in African languages, they would be merely pursuing a dead end, which can only lead to sterility, uncreativity, and frustration.

The conference itself, faced with the fundamental question of defining African literature, and the problems involved for an African writing in a language that is not native to him, came very near the truth: "It was generally agreed that it is better for an African writer to think and feel in his own language and then look for an English transliteration approximating the original."[5] This very conclusion, as naive and as misguided as it is, expresses the problem concisely and accurately, and it is from that we shall find a new direction for African literature, if we are really serious and sincere in what we are doing.

An African writer who thinks and feels in his own language *must* write in that language. The question of transliteration, whatever that means, is unwise as it is unacceptable, for the 'original' which is spoken of here, is the real stuff of literature and the imagination, and must not be discarded in favour of a *copy*, which, as the passage admits, is merely an approximation.

Of course all the old facile arguments would arise again – the multiplicity of African languages, the limitation of the audience to small patches of tribal groups, questions of orthography, and all the rest of them. Yes, but why not? I believe that every language has a right to be developed as literature. There is no part of the world where a false literary unity has been attempted in the way that we are doing today in Africa, not even in Europe. The problem has always been met by the technique of translating outstanding literary achievements into other languages, especially the more widespread and influential languages of the world.

One wonders what would have happened to English literature for instance, if writers like Spenser, Shakespeare, Donne, and Milton, had neglected English, and written in Latin and Greek simply because these classical languages were the cosmopolitan languages of their times. Even though a man like Milton could write even more easily in Latin and Greek, he did his major works in his own mother tongue without playing to the gallery of international fame.

Literature after all, is the exploitation of the possibilities of language. It is the African languages that are in crying need of this kind of development, not the overworked French and English. There is, for instance, a good deal of scholarly work being done in the linguistic structure of several African languages, but there is practically no use being made of these in creative writing, simply because we are all busy fighting over the commonplaces of European literature. If linguistic science devotes so much energy and attention to African languages in spite of their tribal and limited scope, why should imaginative literature which in fact has more chances of enriching the people's culture, consider it impossible to adventure in this direction?

The criticism being done today in African writing in English and French, sounds so dull, drab, and flippant, mainly because there is no opportunity for original thinking. It is the same clichés over and over again – romantic and classic, realism, sentimentality, Victorianism, surrealism, and so on. There is no need for creative thinking in order to become a 'leading, critic or authority' in African literature. Fraser, Freud, Darwin, and Marx, are, as in European literature, the necessary reading for the acquisition of fundamental critical tools.

What I am advocating here is not easy, for it entails a good deal of hard work and hard thinking, and what is more, a necessary casting overboard of hardened debris of the overblown ego. It would force some "leading" critics to go in for the hard school of African linguistic studies, a knowledge of some of the important African languages, before generalising and formulating all kinds of philosophical and literary theories. Literature in Africa would then become the serious business that all literature truly is, reaching out to the people for whom it is meant, and creating a true culture of the African peoples that would not rely on slogans and propaganda, nor on patronage of doubtful intentions.

The basic distinction between French and German literature for instance, is that one is written in French, and the other in German. All the other distinctions, whatever they be, are based on this fundamental fact. What therefore is now described as African literature in English and French, is a clear contradiction, and a false proposition, just as "Italian literature in Hausa" would be.

What one would like future conferences on African literature to devote time to, is the all-important problem of African writing in African languages, and all its implications for the development of a truly African sensibility. In fact, the secondary place which African languages now occupy in our educational system would be reversed if our writers would devote their tremendous gifts and ability to their own languages. Attempts have recently been made to include the study of African languages in the curriculum of some of the new African universities. This programme would certainly have no future, for all that is available even at the university level is the usual string of proverbs, a few short stories on the tortoise and the tiger, and a number of inadequate grammar books written by untrained linguists. The student of Yoruba for instance, has no play available to him in that language, for Wole Soyinka, the most gifted Nigerian playwright at the moment, does not consider Yoruba suitable for *The Lion and the Jewel* or *The Dance of the Forest*.

The main reason for the study of a language is that it contains great literature or some form of literature. This was what led scholars like Eliot and Pound to the study of oriental languages in their poetic experiments early in this century. There is little doubt that African languages would face inevitable extinction, if they do not embody some kind of intelligent literature, and the only way to hasten this, is by continuing in our present illusion that we can produce African literature in English and French.

The last junketing at Makerere was good as far as it went, but it is a little scandalous to admit that its only concrete achievement is that it gave African writers and their patrons, the opportunity to get to know one another!

Notes

1   Ezekiel Mphahlele *Press Report*, Conference of African Writers of English Expression, MAK/V(2), Makerere, 1962.
2   Una Maclean, "Song of A Goat," *Ibadan*, October, 1962, p. 28.
3   Christopher Okigbo, "Silences", *Transition* 8, March, 1963, p. 13.
4   Ulli Beier, "Contemporary African Poetry in English, Conference of African Writers Report, MAK/II(4), Makerere, 1962.
5   Ezekiel Mphahlele, *Press Report*, Conference of African Writers, MAK/V(2), Makerere, 1962.

Chapter 41

The Language of African Literature

Ngugi wa Thiong'O

I

The language of African literature cannot be discussed meaningfully outside the context of those social forces which have made it both an issue demanding our attention and a problem calling for a resolution.

On the one hand is imperialism in its colonial and neo-colonial phases continuously press-ganging the African hand to the plough to turn the soil over, and putting blinkers on him to make him view the path ahead only as determined for him by the master armed with the bible and the sword. In other words, imperialism continues to control the economy, politics, and cultures of Africa. But on the other, and pitted against it, are the ceaseless struggles of African people to liberate their economy, politics and culture from that Euro-American-based stranglehold to usher a new era of true communal self-regulation and self-determination. It is an ever-continuing struggle to seize back their creative initiative in history through a real control of all the means of communal self-definition in time and space. The choice of language and the use to which language is put is central to a people's definition of themselves in relation to their natural and social environment, indeed in relation to the entire universe. Hence language has always been at the heart of the two contending social forces in the Africa of the twentieth century.

The contention started a hundred years ago when in 1884 the capitalist powers of Europe sat in Berlin and carved an entire continent with a multiplicity of peoples, cultures, and languages into different colonies. It seems it is the fate of Africa to have her destiny always decided around conference tables in the metropolises of the western world: her submergence from self-governing communities into colonies was decided in Berlin; her more recent transition into neo-colonies along the same boundaries was negotiated around the same

First published in *Decolonising the Mind: The Politics of Language in African Literature*, pp. 4–33. London: James Currey, 1986.

tables in London, Paris, Brussels and Lisbon. The Berlin-drawn division under which Africa is still living was obviously economic and political, despite the claims of Bible-wielding diplomats, but it was also cultural. Berlin in 1884 saw the division of Africa into the different languages of the European powers. African countries, as colonies and even today as neo-colonies, came to be defined and to define themselves in terms of the languages of Europe: English-speaking, French-speaking or Portuguese-speaking African countries.[1]

Unfortunately writers who should have been mapping paths out of that linguistic encirclement of their continent also came to be defined and to define themselves in terms of the languages of imperialist imposition. Even at their most radical and pro-African position in their sentiments and articulation of problems they still took it as axiomatic that the renaissance of African cultures lay in the languages of Europe.

I should know!

II

In 1962 I was invited to that historic meeting of African writers at Makerere University College, Kampala, Uganda. The list of participants contained most of the names which have now become the subject of scholarly dissertations in universities all over the world. The title? 'A Conference of *African Writers of English Expression*'.[2]

I was then a student of *English* at Makerere, an overseas college of the University of London. The main attraction for me was the certain possibility of meeting Chinua Achebe. I had with me a rough typescript of a novel in progress, *Weep Not, Child*, and I wanted him to read it. In the previous year, 1961, I had completed *The River Between*, my first-ever attempt at a novel, and entered it for a writing competition organised by the East African Literature Bureau. I was keeping in step with the tradition of Peter Abrahams with his output of novels and autobiographies from *Path of Thunder* to *Tell Freedom* and followed by Chinua Achebe with his publication of *Things Fall Apart* in 1959. Or there were their counterparts in French colonies, the generation of Sédar Senghor and David Diop included in the 1947/48 Paris edition of *Anthologie de la nouvelle poésie nègre et malgache de langue française*. They all wrote in European languages as was the case with all the participants in that momentous encounter on Makerere hill in Kampala in 1962.

The title, 'A Conference of African Writers of English Expression', automatically excluded those who wrote in African languages. Now on looking back from the self-questioning heights of 1986, I can see this contained absurd anomalies. I, a student, could qualify for the meeting on the basis of only two published short stories, 'The Fig Tree (Mũgumo)' in a student journal, *Penpoint*, and 'The Return' in a new journal, *Transition*. But neither Shabaan Robert, then the greatest living East African poet with several works of poetry and prose to his credit in Kiswahili, nor Chief Fagunwa, the great Nigerian writer with several published titles in Yoruba, could possibly qualify.

The discussions on the novel, the short story, poetry, and drama were based on extracts from works in English and hence they excluded the main body of work in Swahili, Zulu, Yoruba, Arabic, Amharic and other African languages. Yet, despite this exclusion of writers and literature in African languages, no sooner were the introductory preliminaries over than this Conference of 'African Writers of English Expression' sat down to the first item on the agenda:. 'What is African Literature?'

The debate which followed was animated: Was it literature about Africa or about the African experience? Was it literature written by Africans? What about a non-African who wrote about Africa: did his work qualify as African literature? What if an African set his work in Greenland: did that qualify as African literature? Or were African languages the criteria? OK: what about Arabic, was it not foreign to Africa? What about French and English, which had become African languages? What if an European wrote about Europe in an African language? If…if…if…this or that, except the issue: the domination of our languages and cultures by those of imperialist Europe: in any case there was no Fagunwa or Shabaan Robert or any writer in African languages to bring the conference down from the realms of evasive abstractions. The question was never seriously asked: did what we wrote qualify as African literature? The whole area of literature and audience, and hence of language as a determinant of both the national and class audience, did not really figure: the debate was more about the subject matter and the racial origins and geographical habitation of the writer.

English, like French and Portuguese, was assumed to be the natural language of literary and even political mediation between African people in the same nation and between nations in Africa and other continents. In some instances these European languages were seen as having a capacity to unite African peoples against divisive tendencies inherent in the multiplicity of African languages within the same geographic state. Thus Ezekiel Mphahlele later could write, in a letter to *Transition* number 11, that English and French have become the common language with which to present a nationalist front against white oppressors, and even 'where the whiteman has already retreated, as in the independent states, these two languages are still a unifying force'.[3] In the literary sphere they were often seen as coming to save African languages against themselves. Writing a foreword to Birago Diop's book *Contes d'Amadou Koumba* Sédar Senghor commends him for using French to rescue the spirit and style of old African fables and tales. 'However while rendering them into French he renews them with an art which, while it respects the genius of the French language, that language of gentleness and honesty, preserves at the same time all the virtues of the negro-african languages.'[4] English, French and Portuguese had come to our rescue and we accepted the unsolicited gift with gratitude. Thus in 1964, Chinua Achebe, in a speech entitled 'The African Writer and the English Language', said:

> Is it right that a man should abandon his mother tongue for someone else's? It looks like a dreadful betrayal and produces a guilty feeling. But for me there is no other choice. I have been given the language and I intend to use it.[5]

See the paradox: the possibility of using mother-tongues provokes a tone of levity in phrases like 'a dreadful betrayal' and 'a guilty feeling'; but that of foreign languages produces a categorical positive embrace, what Achebe himself, ten years later, was to describe as this "fatalistic logic of the unassailable position of English in our literature".[6]

The fact is that all of us who opted for European languages – the conference participants and the generation that followed them – accepted that fatalistic logic to a greater or lesser degree. We were guided by it and the only question which preoccupied us was how best to make the borrowed tongues carry the weight of our African experience by, for instance, making them 'prey' on African proverbs and other pecularities of African speech and folklore. For this task, Achebe (*Things Fall Apart; Arrow of God*), Amos Tutuola

(*The Palm-wine Drinkard; My life in the Bush of Ghosts*), and Gabriel Okara (*The Voice*) were often held as providing the three alternative models. The lengths to which we were prepared to go in our mission of enriching foreign languages by injecting Senghorian 'black blood' into their rusty joints, is best exemplified by Gabriel Okara in an article reprinted in *Transition*:

> As a writer who believes in the utilization of African ideas, African philosophy and African folklore and imagery to the fullest extent possible, I am of the opinion the only way to use them effectively is to translate them almost literally from the African language native to the writer into whatever European language he is using as medium of expression. I have endeavoured in my words to keep as close as possible to the vernacular expressions. For, from a word, a group of words, a sentence and even a name in any African language, one can glean the social norms, attitudes and values of a people.
>
> In order to capture the vivid images of African speech, I had to eschew the habit of expressing my thoughts first in English. It was difficult at first, but I had to learn. I had to study each Ijaw expression I used and to discover the probable situation in which it was used in order to bring out the nearest meaning in English. I found it a fascinating exercise.[7]

Why, we may ask, should an African writer, or any writer, become so obsessed by taking from his mother-tongue to enrich other tongues? Why should he see it as his particular mission? We never asked ourselves: how can we enrich our languages? How can we 'prey' on the rich humanist and democratic heritage in the struggles of other peoples in other times and other places to enrich our own? Why not have Balzac, Tolstoy, Sholokov, Brecht, Lu Hsun, Pablo Neruda, H. C. Anderson, Kim Chi Ha, Marx, Lenin, Albert Einstein, Galileo, Aeschylus, Aristotle and Plato in African languages? And why not create literary monuments in our own languages? Why in other words should Okara not sweat it out to create in Ijaw, which he acknowledges to have depths of philosophy and a wide range of ideas and experiences? What was our responsibility to the struggles of African peoples? No, these questions were not asked. What seemed to worry us more was this: after all the literary gymnastics of preying on our languages to add life and vigour to English and other foreign languages, would the result be accepted as good English or good French? Will the owner of the language criticise our usage? Here we were more assertive of our rights! Chinua Achebe wrote:

> I feel that the English language will be able to carry the weight of my African experience. But it will have to be a new English, still in full communion with its ancestral home but altered to suit new African surroundings.[8]

Gabriel Okara's position on this was representative of our generation:

> Some may regard this way of writing English as a desecration of the language. This is of course not true. Living languages grow like living things, and English is far from a dead language. There are American, West Indian, Australian, Canadian and New Zealand versions of English. All of them add life and vigour to the language while reflecting their own respective cultures. Why shouldn't there be a Nigerian or West African English which we can use to express our own ideas, thinking and philosophy in our own way?[9]

How did we arrive at this acceptance of 'the fatalistic logic of the unassailable position of English in our literature', in our culture and in our politics? What was the route from the Berlin of 1884 via the Makerere of 1962 to what is still the prevailing and dominant logic a hundred years later? How did we, as African writers, come to be so feeble towards the claims of our languages on us and so aggressive in our claims on other languages, particularly the languages of our colonization?

Berlin of 1884 was effected through the sword and the bullet. But the night of the sword and the bullet was followed by the morning of the chalk and the blackboard. The physical violence of the battlefield was followed by the psychological violence of the classroom. But where the former was visibly brutal, the latter was visibly gentle, a process best described in Cheikh Hamidou Kane's novel *Ambiguous Adventure* where he talks of the methods of the colonial phase of imperialism as consisting of knowing how to kill with efficiency and to heal with the same art.

> On the Black Continent, one began to understand that their real power resided not at all in the cannons of the first morning but in what followed the cannons. Therefore behind the cannons was the new school. The new school had the nature of both the cannon and the magnet. From the cannon it took the efficiency of a fighting weapon. But better than the cannon it made the conquest permanent. The cannon forces the body and the school fascinates the soul.[10]

In my view language was the most important vehicle through which that power fascinated and held the soul prisoner. The bullet was the means of the physical subjugation. Language was the means of the spiritual subjugation. Let me illustrate this by drawing upon experiences in my own education, particularly in language and literature.

III

I was born into a large peasant family: father, four wives and about twenty-eight children. I also belonged, as we all did in those days, to a wider extended family and to the community as a whole.

We spoke Gĩkũyũ as we worked in the fields. We spoke Gĩkũyũ in and outside the home. I can vividly recall those evenings of story-telling around the fireside. It was mostly the grown-ups telling the children but everybody was interested and involved. We children would re-tell the stories the following day to other children who worked in the fields picking the pyrethrum flowers, tea-leaves or coffee beans of our European and African landlords.

The stories, with mostly animals as the main characters, were all told in Gĩkũyũ. Hare, being small, weak but full of innovative wit and cunning, was our hero. We identified with him as he struggled against the brutes of prey like lion, leopard, hyena. His victories were our victories and we learnt that the apparently weak can outwit the strong. We followed the animals in their struggle against hostile nature – drought, rain, sun, wind – a confrontation often forcing them to search for forms of co-operation. But we were also interested in their struggles amongst themselves, and particularly between the beasts and the victims of prey. These twin struggles, against nature and other animals, reflected real-life struggles in the human world.

Not that we neglected stories with human beings as the main characters. There were two types of characters in such human-centred narratives: the species of truly human beings with qualities of courage, kindness, mercy, hatred of evil, concern for others; and a man-eat-man two-mouthed species with qualities of greed, selfishness, individualism and hatred of what was good for the larger co-operative community. Co-operation as the ultimate good in a community was a constant theme. It could unite human beings with animals against ogres and beasts of prey, as in the story of how dove, after being fed with castor-oil seeds, was sent to fetch a smith working far away from home and whose pregnant wife was being threatened by these man-eating two-mouthed ogres.

There were good and bad story-tellers. A good one could tell the same story over and over again, and it would always be fresh to us, the listeners. He or she could tell a story told by someone else and make it more alive and dramatic. The differences really were in the use of words and images and the inflexion of voices to effect different tones.

We therefore learnt to value words for their meaning and nuances. Language was not a mere string of words. It had a suggestive power well beyond the immediate and lexical meaning. Our appreciation of the suggestive magical power of language was reinforced by the games we played with words through riddles, proverbs, transpositions of syllables, or through nonsensical but musically arranged words.[11] So we learnt the music of our language on top of the content. The language, through images and symbols, gave us a view of the world, but it had a beauty of its own. The home and the field were then our pre-primary school but what is important, for this discussion, is that the language of our evening teach-ins, and the language of our immediate and wider community, and the language of our work in the fields were one.

And then I went to school, a colonial school, and this harmony was broken. The language of my education was no longer the language of my culture. I first went to Kamaandura, missionary run, and then to another called Maanguuū run by nationalists grouped around the Gīkūyū Independent and Karinga Schools Association. Our language of education was still Gīkūyū. The very first time I was ever given an ovation for my writing was over a composition in Gīkūyū. So for my first four years there was still harmony between the language of my formal education and that of the Limuru peasant community.

It was after the declaration of a state of emergency over Kenya in 1952 that all the schools run by patriotic nationalists were taken over by the colonial regime and were placed under District Education Boards chaired by Englishmen. English became the language of my formal education. In Kenya, English became more than a language: it was *the* language, and all the others had to bow before it in deference.

Thus one of the most humiliating experiences was to be caught speaking Gīkūyū in the vicinity of the school. The culprit was given corporal punishment – three to five strokes of the cane on bare buttocks – or was made to carry a metal plate around the neck with inscriptions such as I AM STUPID or I AM A DONKEY. Sometimes the culprits were fined money they could hardly afford. And how did the teachers catch the culprits? A button was initially given to one pupil who was supposed to hand it over to whoever was caught speaking his mother tongue. Whoever had the button at the end of the day would sing who had given it to him and the ensuing process would bring out all the culprits of the day. Thus children were turned into witch-hunters and in the process were being taught the lucrative value of being a traitor to one's immediate community.

The attitude to English was the exact opposite: any achievement in spoken or written English was highly rewarded; prizes, prestige, applause; the ticket to higher realms. English became the measure of intelligence and ability in the arts, the sciences, and all the other branches of learning. English became *the* main determinant of a child's progress up the ladder of formal education.

As you may know, the colonial system of education in addition to its apartheid racial demarcation had the structure of a pyramid: a broad primary base, a narrowing secondary middle, and an even narrower university apex. Selections from primary into secondary were through an examination, in my time called Kenya African Preliminary Examination, in which one had to pass six subjects ranging from Maths to Nature Study and Kiswahili. All the papers were written in English. Nobody could pass the exam who failed the English language paper no matter how brilliantly he had done in the other subjects. I remember one boy in my class of 1954 who had distinctions in all subjects except English, which he had failed. He was made to fail the entire exam. He went on to become a turn boy in a bus company. I who had only passes but a credit in English got a place at the Alliance High School, one of the most elitist institutions for Africans in colonial Kenya. The requirements for a place at the University, Makerere University College, were broadly the same: nobody could go on to wear the undergraduate red gown, no matter how brilliantly they had performed in all the other subjects unless they had a credit – not even a simple pass! – in English. Thus the most coveted place in the pyramid and in the system was only available to the holder of an English language credit card. English was the official vehicle and the magic formula to colonial elitedom.

Literary education was now determined by the dominant language while also reinforcing that dominance. Orature (oral literature) in Kenyan languages stopped. In primary school I now read simplified Dickens and Stevenson alongside Rider Haggard. Jim Hawkins, Oliver Twist, Tom Brown – not Hare, Leopard and Lion – were now my daily companions in the world of imagination. In secondary school, Scott and G. B. Shaw vied with more Rider Haggard, John Buchan, Alan Paton, Captain W. E. Johns. At Makerere I read English: from Chaucer to T. S. Eliot with a touch of Graham Greene.

Thus language and literature were taking us further and further from ourselves to other selves, from our world to other worlds.

What was the colonial system doing to us Kenyan children? What were the consequences of, on the one hand, this systematic suppression of our languages and the literature they carried, and on the other the elevation of English and the literature it carried? To answer those questions, let me first examine the relationship of language to human experience, human culture, and the human perception of reality.

IV

Language, any language, has a dual character: it is both a means of communication and a carrier of culture. Take English. It is spoken in Britain and in Sweden and Denmark. But for Swedish and Danish people English is only a means of communication with non-Scandinavians. It is not a carrier of their culture. For the British, and particularly the English, it is additionally, and inseparably from its use as a tool of communication, a carrier of their culture and history. Or take Swahili in East and Central Africa. It is widely used as a means of communication across many nationalities. But it is not the carrier of a culture and history of many of those nationalities. However in parts of Kenya and Tanzania, and particularly in

Zanzibar, Swahili is inseparably both a means of communication and a carrier of the culture of those people to whom it is a mother-tongue.

Language as communication has three aspects or elements. There is first what Karl Marx once called the language of real life,[12] the element basic to the whole notion of language, its origins and development: that is, the relations people enter into with one another in the labour process, the links they necessarily establish among themselves in the act of a people, a community of human beings, producing wealth or means of life like food, clothing, houses. A human community really starts its historical being as a community of co-operation in production through the division of labour; the simplest is between man, woman and child within a household; the more complex divisions are between branches of production such as those who are sole hunters, sole gatherers of fruits or sole workers in metal. Then there are the most complex divisions such as those in modern factories where a single product, say a shirt or a shoe, is the result of many hands and minds. Production is co-operation, is communication, is language, is expression of a relation between human beings and it is specifically human.

The second aspect of language as communication is speech and it imitates the language of real life, that is communication in production. The verbal signposts both reflect and aid communication or the relations established between human beings in the production of their means of life. Language as a system of verbal signposts makes that production possible. The spoken word is to relations between human beings what the hand is to the relations between human beings and nature. The hand through tools mediates between human beings and nature and forms the language of real life: spoken words mediate between human beings and form the language of speech.

The third aspect is the written signs. The written word imitates the spoken. Where the first two aspects of language as communication through the hand and the spoken word historically evolved more or less simultaneously, the written aspect is a much later historical development. Writing is representation of sounds with visual symbols, from the simplest knot among shepherds to tell the number in a herd or the hieroglyphics among the Agĩkũyũ gicaandi singers and poets of Kenya, to the most complicated and different letter and picture writing systems of the world today.

In most societies the written and the spoken languages are the same, in that they represent each other: what is on paper can be read to another person and be received as that language which the recipient has grown up speaking. In such a society there is broad harmony for a child between the three aspects of language as communication. His inter-action with nature and with other men is expressed in written and spoken symbols or signs which are both a result of that double interaction and a reflection of it. The association of the child's sensibility is with the language of his experience of life.

But there is more to it: communication between human beings is also the basis and process of evolving culture. In doing similar kinds of things and actions over and over again under similar circumstances, similar even in their mutability, certain patterns, moves, rhythms, habits, attitudes, experiences and knowledge emerge. Those experiences are handed over to the next generation and become the inherited basis for their further actions on nature and on themselves. There is a gradual accumulation of values which in time become almost self-evident truths governing their conception of what is right and wrong, good and bad, beautiful and ugly, courageous and cowardly, generous and mean in their internal and external relations. Over a time this becomes a way of life distinguishable from other ways of life. They develop a distinctive culture and history. Culture embodies those moral, ethical and aesthetic values, the set of spiritual eyeglasses, through which they come to view themselves and their place in the universe. Values are the basis of a people's identity, their sense of particularity as members of the human race. All this is carried by language. Language as culture is the collective memory bank of a people's experience in history. Culture is almost indistinguishable from the language that makes possible its genesis, growth, banking, articulation and indeed its transmission from one generation to the next.

Language as culture also has three important aspects. Culture is a product of the history which it in turn reflects. Culture in other words is a product and a reflection of human beings communicating with one another in the very struggle to create wealth and to control it. But culture does not merely reflect that history, or rather it does so by actually forming images or pictures of the world of nature and nurture. Thus the second aspect of language as culture is as an image-forming agent in the mind of a child. Our whole conception of ourselves as a people, individually and collectively, is based on those pictures and images which may or may not correctly correspond to the actual reality of the struggles with nature and nurture which produced them in the first place. But our capacity to confront the world creatively is dependent on how those images correspond or not to that reality, how they distort or clarify the reality of our struggles. Language as culture is thus mediating between me and my own self; between my own self and other selves; between me and nature. Language is mediating in my very being. And this brings us to the third aspect of language as culture. Culture transmits or imparts those images of the world and reality through the spoken and the written language, that is through a specific language. In other words, the capacity to speak, the capacity to order sounds in a manner that makes for mutual comprehension between human beings is universal. This is the universality of language, a quality specific to human beings. It corresponds to the universality of the struggle against nature and that between human beings. But the particularity of the sounds, the words, the word order into phrases and sentences, and the specific manner, or laws, of their ordering is what distinguishes one language from another. Thus a specific culture is not transmitted through language in its universality but in its particularity as the language of a specific community with a specific history. Written literature and orature are the main means by which a particular language transmits the images of the world contained in the culture it carries.

Language as communication and as culture are then products of each other. Communication creates culture: culture is a means of communication. Language carries culture, and culture carries, particularly through orature and literature, the entire body of values by which we come to perceive ourselves and our place in the world. How people perceive themselves affects how they look at their culture, at their politics and at the social production of wealth, at their entire relationship to nature and to other beings. Language is thus inseparable from ourselves as a community of human beings with a specific form and character, a specific history, a specific relationship to the world.

V

So what was the colonialist imposition of a foreign language doing to us children?

The real aim of colonialism was to control the people's wealth: what they produced, how they produced it, and how it was distributed; to control, in other words, the entire realm of the language of real life. Colonialism imposed its control of the social production of wealth through military conquest and subsequent political dictatorship. But its most important area of domination was the mental universe of the colonised, the control, through culture, of how people perceived themselves and their relationship to the world. Economic and political control can never be complete or effective without mental control. To control a people's culture is to control their tools of self-definition in relationship to others.

For colonialism this involved two aspects of the same process: the destruction or the deliberate undervaluing of a people's culture, their art, dances, religions, history, geography, education, orature and literature, and the conscious elevation of the language of the coloniser. The domination of a people's language by the languages of the colonising nations was crucial to the domination of the mental universe of the colonised.

Take language as communication. Imposing a foreign language, and suppressing the native languages as spoken and written, were already breaking the harmony previously existing between the African child and the three aspects of language. Since the new language as a means of communication was a product of and was reflecting the 'real language of life' elsewhere, it could never as spoken or written properly reflect or imitate the real life of that community. This may in part explain why technology always appears to us as slightly external, *their* product and not *ours*. The word 'missile' used to hold an alien far-away sound until I recently learnt its equivalent in Gĩkũyũ, *ngurukuhĩ*, and it made me apprehend it differently. Learning, for a colonial child, became a cerebral activity and not an emotionally felt experience.

But since the new, imposed languages could never completely break the native languages as spoken, their most effective area of domination was the third aspect of language as communication, the written. The language of an African child's formal education was foreign. The language of the books he read was foreign. The language of his conceptualisation was foreign. Thought, in him, took the visible form of a foreign language. So the written language of a child's upbringing in the school (even his spoken language within the school compound) became divorced from his spoken language at home. There was often not the slightest relationship between the child's written world, which was also the language of his schooling, and the world of his immediate environment in the family and the community. For a colonial child, the harmony existing between the three aspects of language as communication was irrevocably broken. This resulted in the disassociation of the sensibility of that child from his natural and social environment, what we might call colonial alienation. The alienation became reinforced in the teaching of history, geography, music, where bourgeois Europe was always the centre of the universe.

This disassociation, divorce, or alienation from the immediate environment becomes clearer when you look at colonial language as a carrier of culture.

Since culture is a product of the history of a people which it in turn reflects, the child was now being exposed exclusively to a culture that was a product of a world external to himself. He was being made to stand outside himself to look at himself. *Catching Them Young* is the title of a book on racism, class, sex, and politics in children's literature by Bob Dixon. 'Catching them young' as an aim was even more true of a colonial child. The images of this world and his place in it implanted in a child take years to eradicate, if they ever can be.

Since culture does not just reflect the world in images but actually, through those very images, conditions a child to see that world in a certain way, the colonial child was made to see the world and where he stands in it as seen and defined by or reflected in the culture of the language of imposition.

And since those images are mostly passed on through orature and literature it meant the child would now only see the world as seen in the literature of his language of adoption. From the point of view of alienation, that is of seeing oneself from outside oneself as if one was another self, it does not matter that the imported literature carried the great humanist tradition of the best in Shakespeare, Goethe, Balzac, Tolstoy, Gorky, Brecht, Sholokhov, Dickens. The location of this great mirror of imagination was necessarily Europe and its history and culture and the rest of the universe was seen from that centre.

But obviously it was worse when the colonial child was exposed to images of his world as mirrored in the written languages of his coloniser. Where his own native languages were associated in his impressionable mind with low status, humiliation, corporal punishment, slow-footed intelligence and ability or downright stupidity, non-intelligibility and barbarism, this was reinforced by the world he met in the works of such geniuses of racism as a Rider Haggard or a Nicholas Monsarrat; not to mention the pronouncement of some of the giants of western intellectual and political establishment, such as Hume ('... the negro is naturally inferior to the whites ...'),[13] Thomas Jefferson ('... the blacks ... are inferior to the whites on the endowments of both body and mind ...'),[14] or Hegel with his Africa comparable to a land of childhood still enveloped in the dark mantle of the night as far as the development of self-conscious history was concerned. Hegel's statement that there was nothing harmonious with humanity to be found in the African character is representative of the racist images of Africans and Africa such a colonial child was bound to encounter in the literature of the colonial languages.[15] The results could be disastrous.

In her paper read to the conference on the teaching of African literature in schools held in Nairobi in 1973, entitled 'Written Literature and Black Images',[16] the Kenyan writer and scholar Professor Mĩcere Mũgo related how a reading of the description of Gagool as an old African woman in Rider Haggard's *King Solomon's Mines* had for a long time made her feel mortal terror whenever she encountered old African women. In his autobiography *This Life* Sydney Poitier describes how, as a result of the literature he had read, he had come to associate Africa with snakes. So on arrival in Africa and being put up in a modern hotel in a modern city, he could not sleep because he kept on looking for snakes everywhere, even under the bed. These two have been able to pinpoint the origins of their fears. But for most others the negative image becomes internalised and it affects their cultural and even political choices in ordinary living.

Thus Léopold Sédar Senghor has said very clearly that although the colonial language had been forced upon him, if he had been given the choice he would still have opted for French. He becomes lyrical in his subservience to French:

> We express ourselves in French since French has a universal vocation and since our message is also addressed to French people and others. In our languages [i.e. African languages] the halo that surrounds the words is by nature merely that of sap and blood; French words send out thousands of rays like diamonds.[17]

Senghor has now been rewarded by being anointed to an honoured place in the French Academy – that institution for safe-guarding the purity of the French language.

In Malawi, Banda has erected his own monument by way of an institution, The Kamuzu Academy, designed to aid the brightest pupils of Malawi in their mastery of English.

> It is a grammar school designed to produce boys and girls who will be sent to universities like Harvard, Chicago, Oxford, Cambridge and Edinburgh and be able to compete on equal terms with others elsewhere.
>
> The President has instructed that Latin should occupy a central place in the curriculum. All teachers must have had at least some Latin in their academic background. Dr Banda has often said that no one can fully master English without knowledge of languages such as Latin and French . . . [18]

For good measure no Malawian is allowed to teach at the academy – none is good enough – and all the teaching staff has been recruited from Britain. A Malawian might lower the standards, or rather, the purity of the English language. Can you get a more telling example of hatred of what is national, and a servile worship of what is foreign even though dead?

In history books and popular commentaries on Africa, too much has been made of the supposed differences in the policies of the various colonial powers, the British indirect rule (or the pragmatism of the British in their lack of a cultural programme!) and the French and Portuguese conscious programme of cultural assimilation. These are a matter of detail and emphasis. The final effect was the same: Senghor's embrace of French as this language with a universal vocation is not so different from Chinua Achebe's gratitude in 1964 to English – "those of us who have inherited the English language may not be in a position to appreciate the value of the inheritance".[19] The assumptions behind the practice of those of us who have abandoned our mother-tongues and adopted European ones as the creative vehicles of our imagination, are not different either.

Thus the 1962 conference of "African Writers of English expression" was only recognising, with approval and pride of course, what through all the years of selective education and rigorous tutelage, we had already been led to accept: the "fatalistic logic of the unassailable position of English in our literature". The logic was embodied deep in imperialism; and it was imperialism and its effects that we did not examine at Makerere. It is the final triumph of a system of domination when the dominated start singing its virtues.

VI

The twenty years that followed the Makerere conference gave the world a unique literature – novels, stories, poems, plays written by Africans in European languages – which soon consolidated itself into a tradition with companion studies and a scholarly industry.

Right from its conception it was the literature of the petty-bourgeoisie born of the colonial schools and universities. It could not be otherwise, given the linguistic medium of its message. Its rise and development reflected the gradual accession of this class to political and even economic dominance. But the petty-bourgeoisie in Africa was a large class with different strands in it. It ranged from that section which looked forward to a permanent alliance with imperialism in which it played the role of an intermediary between the bourgeoisie of the western metropolis and the people of the colonies – the section which in my book *Detained: A Writer's Prison Diary* I have described as the comprador bourgeoisie – to that section which saw the future in terms of a vigorous independent national economy in African capitalism or in some kind of socialism, what I shall here call the nationalistic or patriotic bourgeoisie. This literature by Africans in European languages was specifically that of the nationalistic bourgeoisie in its creators, its thematic concerns and its consumption.[20]

Internationally the literature helped this class, which in politics, business, and education, was assuming leadership of the countries newly emergent from colonialism, or of those struggling to so emerge, to explain Africa to the world: Africa had a past and a culture of dignity and human complexity.

Internally the literature gave this class a cohesive tradition and a common literary frame of references, which it otherwise lacked with its uneasy roots in the culture of the peasantry and in the culture of the metropolitan bourgeoisie. The literature added confidence to the class: the petty-bourgeoisie now had a past, a culture and a literature with which to confront the racist bigotry of Europe. This confidence – manifested in the tone of the writing, its sharp critique of European bourgeois civilisation, its implications, particularly in its negritude mould, that Africa had something new to give to the world – reflects the political ascendancy of the patriotic nationalistic section of the petty-bourgeoisie before and immediately after independence.

So initially this literature – in the post-war world of national democratic revolutionary and anti-colonial liberation in China and India, armed uprisings in Kenya and Algeria, the independence of Ghana and Nigeria with others impending – was part of that great anti-colonial and anti-imperialist upheaval in Asia, Africa, Latin America and Caribbean islands. It was inspired by the general political awakening; it drew its stamina and even form from the peasantry: their proverbs, fables, stories, riddles, and wise sayings. It was shot through and through with optimism. But later, when the comprador section assumed political ascendancy and strengthened rather than weakened the economic links with imperialism in what was clearly a neo-colonial arrangement, this literature became more and more critical, cynical, disillusioned, bitter and denunciatory in tone. It was almost unanimous in its portrayal, with varying degrees of detail, emphasis, and clarity of vision, of the post-independence betrayal of hope. But to whom was it directing its list of mistakes made, crimes and wrongs committed, complaints unheeded, or its call for a change of moral direction? The imperialist bourgeoisie? The petty-bourgeoisie in power? The military, itself part and parcel of that class? It sought another audience, principally the peasantry and the working class or what was generally conceived as the people. The search for new audience and new directions was reflected in the quest for simpler forms, in the adoption of a more direct tone, and often in a direct call for action. It was also reflected in the content. Instead of seeing Africa as one undifferentiated mass of historically wronged blackness, it now attempted some sort of class analysis and evaluation of neo-colonial societies. But this search was still within the confines of the languages of Europe whose use it now defended with less vigour and confidence. So its quest was hampered by the very language choice, and in its movement toward the people, it could only go up to that section of the petty-bourgeoisie – the students, teachers, secretaries for instance – still in closest touch with the people. It settled there, marking time, caged within the linguistic fence of its colonial inheritance.

Its greatest weakness still lay where it has always been, in the audience – the petty-bourgeoisie readership automatically assumed by the very choice of language. Because of its indeterminate economic position between the many contending classes, the petty-bourgeoisie develops a vacillating psychological make-up. Like a chameleon it takes on the colour of the main class with which it is in the closest touch and sympathy. It can be swept to activity by the masses at a time of revolutionary tide; or be driven to silence, fear, cynicism, withdrawal into self-contemplation, existential anguish, or to collaboration with the powers-that-be at times of reactionary tides. In African this class has always oscillated between the imperialist bourgeoisie and its comprador neo-colonial ruling elements on the one hand, and the peasantry and the working class (the masses) on the other. This very lack of identity in its social and psychological make-up as a class, was reflected in the very literature it produced: the crisis of identity was assumed in that very preoccupation with definition at the Makerere conference. In literature as in politics it spoke as if its identity or the crisis of its own identity was that of society as a whole. The literature it produced in European languages was given the identity of African literature as if there had never been literature in African languages. Yet by avoiding a real confrontation with the language issue, it was clearly wearing false robes of identity: it was a pretender to the throne of the mainstream of African literature. The practitioner of what Janheinz Jahn called neo-African literature tried to get out of the dilemma by over-insisting that European languages were really African languages or by trying to Africanise English or French usage while making sure it was still recognisable as English or French or Portuguese.

In the process this literature created, falsely and even absurdly, an English-speaking (or French or Portuguese) African peasantry and working class, a clear negation or falsification of the historical process and reality. This European-language-speaking peasantry and work-ing class, existing only in novels and dramas, was at times invested with the vacillating mentality, the evasive self-contemplation, the existential anguished human condition, or the man-torn-between-two-worlds-facedness of the petty-bourgeoisie.

In fact, if it had been left entirely to this class, African languages would have ceased to exist – with independence!

VII

But African languages refused to die. They would not simply go the way of Latin to become the fossils for linguistic archaeology to dig up, classify, and argue about the international conferences.

These languages, these national heritages of Africa, were kept alive by the peasantry. The peasantry saw no contradiction between speaking their own mother-tongues and belonging to a larger national or continental geography. They saw no necessary antagonistic contra-diction between belonging to their immediate nationality, to their multinational state along the Berlin-drawn boundaries, and to Africa as a whole. These people happily spoke Wolof, Hausa, Yoruba, Ibo, Arabic, Amharic, Kiswahili, Gĩkũyũ, Luo, Luhya, Shona, Ndebele, Kimbundu, Zulu or Lingala without this fact tearing the multinational states apart. During the anti-colonial struggle they showed an unlimited capacity to unite around whatever leader or party best and most consistently articulated an anti-imperialist position. If anything it was the petty-bourgeoisie, particularly the compradors, with their French and English and Portuguese, with their petty rivalries, their ethnic chauvinism, which encouraged these vertical divisions to the point of war at times. No, the peasantry had no complexes about their languages and the cultures they carried!

In fact when the peasantry and the working class were compelled by necessity or history to adopt the language of the master, they Africanised it without any of the respect for its ancestry shown by Senghor and Achebe, so totally as to have created new African languages, like Krio in Sierra Leone or Pidgin in Nigeria, that owed their identities to the syntax and rhythms of African languages. All these languages were kept alive in the daily speech, in the ceremonies, in political struggles, above all in the rich store of orature – proverbs, stories, poems, and riddles.

The peasantry and the urban working class threw up singers. These sang the old songs or composed new ones incorporating the new experiences in industries and urban life and in working-class struggle and organisations. These singers pushed the languages to new limits, renewing and reinvigorating them by coining new words and new expressions, and in generally expanding their capacity to incorporate new happenings in Africa and the world.

The peasantry and the working class threw up their own writers, or attracted to their ranks and concern intellectuals from among the petty-bourgeoisie, who all wrote in African languages. It is these writers like Heruy Wäldä Sellassie, Germacäw Takla Hawaryat, Shabaan Robert, Abdullatif Abdalla, Ebrahim Hussein, Euphrase Kezilahabi, B. W. Vilakazi, Okot p'Bitek, A. C. Jordan, P. Mboya, D. O. Fagunwa, Mazisi Kunene and many others rightly celebrated in Albert Gérard's pioneering survey of literature in African languages from the tenth century to the present, called *African Language Literatures* (1981), who have given our languages a written literature. Thus the immortality of our languages in print has been ensured despite the internal and external pressures for their extinction. In Kenya I would like to single out Gakaara wa Wanjaũ, who was jailed by the British for the ten years between 1952 and 1962 because of his writing in Gĩkũyũ. His book, *Mwandĩki wa Mau Mau Ithaamĩrioinĩ*, a diary he secretly kept while in political detention, was published by Heinemann Kenya and won the 1984 Noma Award. It is a powerful work, extending the range of the Gĩkũyũ language prose, and it is a crowning achievement to the work he started in 1946. He has worked in poverty, in the hardships of prison, in post-independence isolation when the English language held sway in Kenya's schools from nursery to University and in every walk of the national printed world, but he never broke his faith in the possibilities of Kenya's national languages. His inspiration came from the mass anti-colonial movement of Kenyan people, particularly the militant wing grouped around Mau Mau or the Kenya Land and Freedom Army, which in 1952 ushered in the era of modern guerrilla warfare in Africa. He is the clearest example of those writers thrown up by the mass political movements of an awakened peasantry and working class.

And finally from among the European-language-speaking African petty-bourgeoisie, there emerged a few who refused to join the chorus of those who had accepted the 'fatalistic logic' of the position of European languages in our literary being. It was one of these, Obi Wali, who pulled the carpet from under the literary feet of those who gathered at Makerere in 1962 by declaring in an article published in *Transition* (10, September 1963), 'that the whole uncritical acceptance of English and French as the inevitable medium for educated African writing is misdirected, and has no chance of advancing African literature and culture', and that until African writers accepted that any true African literature must be written in African languages, they would merely be pursuing a dead end.

What we would like future conferences on African literature to devote time to, is the all-important problem of African writing in African languages, and all its implications for the development of a truly African sensibility.

Obi Wali had his predecessors. Indeed people like David Diop of Senegal had put the case against this use of colonial languages even more strongly.

> The African creator, deprived of the use of his language and cut off from his people, might turn out to be only the representative of a literary trend (and that not necessarily the least gratuitous) of the conquering nation. His works, having become a perfect illustration of the assimilationist policy through imagination and style, will doubtless rouse the warm applause of a certain group of critics. In fact, these praises will go mostly to colonialism which, when it can no longer keep its subjects in slavery, transforms them into docile intellectuals patterned after Western literary fashions which besides, is another more subtle form of bastardization.[21]

David Diop quite correctly saw that the use of English and French was a matter of temporary historical necessity.

> Surely in an Africa freed from oppression it will not occur to any writer to express, otherwise than in his rediscovered language, his feelings and the feelings of his people.[22]

The importance of Obi Wali's intervention was in tone and timing: it was published soon after the 1962 Makerere conference of African writers of English expression; it was polemical and aggressive, poured ridicule and scorn on the choice of English and French, while being unapologetic in its call for the use of African languages. Not surprisingly it was met with hostility and then silence. But twenty years of uninterrupted dominance of literature in European languages, the reactionary turn that political and economic events in Africa have taken, and the search for a revolutionary break with the neo-colonial status quo, all compel soul-searching among writers, raising once again the entire question of the language of African literature.

VIII

The question is this: we as African writers have always complained about the neo-colonial economic and political relationship to Euro-America. Right. But by our continuing to write in foreign languages, paying homage to them, are we not on the cultural level continuing that neo-colonial slavish and cringing spirit? What is the difference between a politician who says Africa cannot do without imperialism and the writer who says Africa cannot do without European languages?

While we were busy haranguing the ruling circles in a language which automatically excluded the participation of the peasantry and the working class in the debate, imperialist culture and African reactionary forces had a field day: the Christian bible is available in unlimited quantities in even the tiniest African language. The comprador ruling cliques are also quite happy to have the peasantry and the working class all to themselves: distortions, dictatorial directives, decrees, museum-type fossils paraded as African culture, feudalistic ideologies, superstitions, lies, all these backward elements and more are communicated to the African masses in their own languages without any challenges from those with alternative visions of tomorrow who have deliberately cocooned themselves in English, French, and Portuguese. It is ironic that the most reactionary African politician, the one who believes in selling Africa to Europe, is often a master of African languages; that the most zealous of European missionaries who believed in rescuing Africa from itself, even from the paganism of its languages, were nevertheless masters of African languages, which they often reduced to writing. The European missionary believed too much in his mission of conquest not to communicate it in the languages most readily available to the people: the African writer believes too much in 'African literature' to write it in those ethnic, divisive and under-developed languages of the peasantry!

The added irony is that what they have produced, despite any claims to the contrary, is not African literature. The editors of the Pelican Guides to English literature in their latest volume were right to include a discussion of this literature as part of twentieth-century English literature, just as the French Academy was right to honour Senghor for his genuine and talented contribution to French literature and language. What we have created is another hybrid tradition, a tradition in transition, a minority tradition that can only be termed as Afro-European literature; that is, the literature written by Africans in European languages.[23] It has produced many writers and works of genuine talent: Chinua Achebe, Wole Soyinka, Ayi Kwei Armah, Sembene Ousmane, Agostino Neto, Sédar Senghor and many others. Who can deny their talent? The light in the products of their fertile imaginations has certainly illuminated important aspects of the African being in its continuous struggle against the political and economic consequences of Berlin and after. However we cannot have our cake and eat it! Their work belongs to an Afro-European literary tradition which is likely to last for as long as Africa is under this rule of European capital in a neo-colonial set-up. So Afro-European literature can be defined as literature written by Africans in European languages in the era of imperialism.

But some are coming round to the inescapable conclusion articulated by Obi Wali with such polemical vigour twenty years ago: African literature can only be written in African languages, that is, the languages of the African peasantry and working class, the major alliance of classes in each of our nationalities and the agency for the coming inevitable revolutionary break with neo-colonialism.

IX

I started writing in Gĩkũyũ language in 1977 after seventeen years of involvement in Afro-European literature, in my case Afro-English literature. It was then that I collaborated with Ngũgĩ wa Mĩriĩ in the drafting of the playscript, *Ngaahika Ndeenda* (the English translation was *I Will Marry When I Want*). I have since published a novel in Gĩkũyũ, *Caitaani Mũtharabainĩ* (English translation: *Devil on the Cross*) and completed a musical drama, *Maitũ Njugĩra*, (English translation: *Mother Sing for Me*); three books for children, *Njamba Nene na Mbaathi i Mathagu, Bathitoora ya Njamba Nene, Njamba Nene na Cibũ Kĩng'ang'i*, as well as another novel manuscript: *Matigari Ma Njirũũngi*. Wherever I have gone, particularly in Europe, I have been confronted with the question: why are you now writing in Gĩkũyũ? Why do you now write in an African language? In some academic quarters I have been confronted with the rebuke, 'Why have you abandoned us?' It was almost as if, in choosing to write in Gĩkũyũ, I was doing something abnormal. But Gĩkũyũ is my mother tongue! The very fact that what common sense dictates in the literary practice of other cultures is being questioned in an African writer is a measure of how far imperialism has distorted the view of

African realities. It has turned reality upside down: the abnormal is viewed as normal and the normal is viewed as abnormal. Africa actually enriches Europe: but Africa is made to believe that it needs Europe to rescue it from poverty. Africa's natural and human resources continue to develop Europe and America: but Africa is made to feel grateful for aid from the same quarters that still sit on the back of the continent. Africa even produces intellectuals who now rationalise this upside-down way of looking at Africa.

I believe that my writing in Gĩkũyũ language, a Kenyan language, an African language, is part and parcel of the anti-imperialist struggles of Kenyan and African peoples. In schools and universities our Kenyan languages – that is the languages of the many nationalities which make up Kenya – were associated with negative qualities of backwardness, underdevelopment, humiliation and punishment. We who went through that school system were meant to graduate with a hatred of the people and the culture and the values of the language of our daily humiliation and punishment. I do not want to see Kenyan children growing up in that imperialist-imposed tradition of contempt for the tools of communication developed by their communities and their history. I want them to transcend colonial alienation.

Colonial alienation takes two interlinked forms: an active (or passive) distancing of oneself from the reality around; and an active (or passive) identification with that which is most external to one's environment. It starts with a deliberate disassociation of the language of conceptualisation, of thinking, of formal education, of mental development, from the language of daily interaction in the home and in the community. It is like separating the mind from the body so that they are occupying two unrelated linguistic spheres in the same person. On a larger social scale it is like producing a society of bodiless heads and headless bodies.

So I would like to contribute towards the restoration of the harmony between all the aspects and divisions of language so as to restore the Kenyan child to his environment, understand it fully so as to be in a position to change it for his collective good. I would like to see Kenya peoples' mother-tongues (our national languages!) carry a literature reflecting not only the rhythms of a child's spoken expression, but also his struggle with nature and his social nature. With that harmony between himself, his language and his environment as his starting point, he can learn other languages and even enjoy the positive humanistic, democratic and revolutionary elements in other people's literatures and cultures without any complexes about his own language, his own self, his environment. The all-Kenya national language (i.e. Kiswahili); the other national languages (i.e. the languages of the nationalities like Luo, Gĩkũyũ, Maasai, Luhya, Kallenjin, Kamba, Mijikenda, Somali, Galla, Turkana, Arabic-speaking people, etc.); other African languages like Hausa, Wolof, Yoruba, Ibo, Zulu, Nyanja, Lingala, Kimbundu; and foreign languages – that is foreign to Africa – like English, French, German, Russian, Chinese, Japanese, Portuguese, Spanish will fall into their proper perspective in the lives of Kenyan children.

Chinua Achebe once decried the tendency of African intellectuals to escape into abstract universalism in the words that apply even more to the issue of the language of African literature:

> Africa has had such a fate in the world that the very adjective *African* can call up hideous fears of rejection. Better then to cut all the links with this homeland, this liability, and become in one giant leap the universal man. Indeed I understand this anxiety. *But running away from oneself seems to me a very inadequate way of dealing with an anxiety* [italics mine]. And if writers should opt for such escapism, who is to meet the challenge?[24]

Who indeed?

We African writers are bound by our calling to do for our languages what Spencer, Milton and Shakespeare did for English; what Pushkin and Tolstoy did for Russian; indeed what all writers in world history have done for their languages by meeting the challenge of creating a literature in them, which process later opens the languages for philosophy, science, technology and all the other areas of human creative endeavours.

But writing in our languages per se – although a necessary first step in the correct direction – will not itself bring about the renaissance in African cultures if that literature does not carry the content of our people's anti-imperialist struggles to liberate their productive forces from foreign control; the content of the need for unity among the workers and peasants of all the nationalities in their struggle to control the wealth they produce and to free it from internal and external parasites.

In other words writers in African languages should reconnect themselves to the revolutionary traditions of an organised peasantry and working class in Africa in their struggle to defeat imperialism and create a higher system of democracy and socialism in alliance with all the other peoples of the world. Unity in that struggle would ensure unity in our multilingual diversity. It would also reveal the real links that bind the people of Africa to the peoples of Asia, South America, Europe, Australia and New Zealand, Canada and the USA.

But it is precisely when writers open out African languages to the real links in the struggles of peasants and workers that they will meet their biggest challenge. For to the comprador-ruling regimes, their real enemy is an awakened peasantry and working class. A writer who tries to communicate the message of revolutionary unity and hope in the languages of the people becomes a subversive character. It is then that writing in African languages becomes a subversive or treasonable offence with such a writer facing possibilities of prison, exile or even death. For him there are no 'national' accolades, no new year honours, only abuse and slander and innumerable lies from the mouths of the armed power of a ruling minority – ruling, that is, on behalf of US-led imperialism – and who see in democracy a real threat. A democratic participation of the people in the shaping of their own lives or in discussing their own lives in languages that allow for mutual comprehension is seen as being dangerous to the good government of a country and its institutions. African languages addressing themselves to the lives of the people become the enemy of a neo-colonial state.

Notes

1   'European languages became so important to the Africans that they defined their own identities partly by reference to those languages. Africans began to describe each other in terms of being either Francophone or English-speaking Africans. The continent itself was thought of in terms of French-speaking states, English-speaking states and Arabic-speaking states.' (Ali A. Mazrui, *Africa's International Relations*, London: 1977, p. 92.)

Arabic does not quite fall into that category. Instead of Arabic-speaking states as an example, Mazrui should have put Portuguese-speaking states. Arabic is now an African language unless we want to write off all the indigenous populations of North Africa, Egypt, Sudan as not being Africans.

And as usual with Mazrui his often apt and insightful descriptions, observations, and comparisons of the contemporary African realities as affected by Europe are, unfortunately, often tinged with approval or a sense of irreversible inevitability.

2   The conference was organized by the anti-Communist Paris-based but American-inspired and financed Society for Cultural Freedom which was later discovered actually to have been financed by CIA. It shows how certain directions in our cultural, political, and economic choices can be masterminded from the metropolitan centres of imperialism.

3   This is an argument often espoused by colonial spokesmen. Compare Mphahlele's comment with that of Geoffrey Moorhouse in *Manchester Guardian Weekly*, 15 July 1964, as quoted by Ali A. Mazrui and Michael Tidy in their work *Nationalism and New States in Africa*, London: 1984.

    'On both sides of Africa, moreover, in Ghana and Nigeria, in Uganda and in Kenya, the spread of education has led to an increased demand for English at primary level. *The remarkable thing is that English has not been rejected as a symbol of Colonialism; it has rather been adopted as a politically neutral language beyond the reproaches of tribalism.* It is also a more attractive proposition in Africa than in either India or Malaysia because comparatively few Africans are completely literate in the vernacular tongues and even in the languages of regional communication, Hausa and Swahili, which are spoken by millions, and only read and written by thousands.' (My italics)

    Is Moorehouse telling us that the English language is politically neutral vis-à-vis Africa's confrontation with neo-colonialism? Is he telling us that by 1964 there were more Africans literate in European languages than in African languages? That Africans could not, even if that was the case, be literate in their own national languages or in the regional languages? Really is Mr Moorehouse tongue-tying the African?

4   The English title is *Tales of Amadou Koumba*, published by Oxford University Press. The translation of this particular passage from the *Présence Africaine*, Paris edition of the book was done for me by Dr Bachir Diagne in Bayreuth.

5   The paper is now in Achebe's collection of essays *Morning Yet on Creation Day*, London: 1975.

6   In the introduction to *Morning Yet on Creation Day* Achebe obviously takes a slightly more critical stance from his 1964 position. The phrase is apt for a whole generation of us African writers.

7   *Transition* No. 10, September 1963, reprinted from *Dialogue*, Paris.

8   Chinua Achebe 'The African Writer and the English Language', in *Morning Yet on Creation Day*.

9   Gabriel Okara, *Transition* No. 10, September 1963.

10 Cheikh Hamidou Kane *L'aventure Ambiguë*. (English translation: *Ambiguous Adventure*). This passage was translated for me by Bachir Diagne.

11 Example from a tongue twister: 'Kaana ka Nikoora koona koora koora: na ko koora koona kaana ka Nikoora koora koora.' I'm indebted to Wangui wa Goro for this example. 'Nichola's child saw a baby frog and ran away: and when the baby frog saw Nichola's child it also ran away.' A Gĩkũyũ speaking child has to get the correct tone and length of vowel and pauses to get it right. Otherwise it becomes a jumble of *k*'s and *r*'s and *na*'s.

12 'The production of ideas, of conceptions, of consciousness, is at first directly interwoven with the material activity and the material intercourse of men, the language of real life. Conceiving, thinking, the mental intercourse of men, appear at this stage as the direct efflux of their material behaviour. The same applies to mental production as expressed in the language of politics, laws, morality, religion, metaphysics, etc., of a people. Men are the producers of their conceptions, ideas etc. – real, active men, as they are conditioned by a definite development of their productive forces and of the intercourse corresponding to these, up to its furthest form.' Marx and Engels, German Ideology, the first part published under the title, *Feuerbach: Opposition of the Materialist and Idealist Outlooks*, London: 1973, p. 8.

13 Quoted in Eric Williams *A History of the People of Trinidad and Tobago*, London 1964, p. 32.

14 Eric Williams, ibid., p. 31.

15 In references to Africa in the introduction to his lectures in *The Philosophy of History*, Hegel gives historical, philosophical, rational expression and legitimacy to every conceivable European racist myth about Africa. Africa is even denied her own geography where it does not correspond to the

myth. Thus Egypt is not part of Africa; and North Africa is part of Europe. Africa proper is the especial home of ravenous beasts, snakes of all kinds. The African is not part of humanity. Only slavery to Europe can raise him, possibly, to the lower ranks of humanity. Slavery is good for the African. 'Slavery is in and for itself *injustice*, for the essence of humanity is *freedom*; but for this man must be matured. The gradual abolition of slavery is therefore wiser and more equitable than its sudden removal.' (Hegel, *The Philosophy of History*, Dover edition, New York: 1956, pp. 91–9.) Hegel clearly reveals himself as the nineteenth-century Hitler of the intellect.

16   The paper is now in Akivaga and Gachukiah's *The Teaching of African Literature in Schools*, published by Kenya Literature Bureau.

17   Senghor, Introduction to his poems, 'Éthiopiques, le 24 Septembre 1954', in answering the question: 'Pourquoi, dès lors, écrivez-vous en français?' Here is the whole passage in French. See how lyrical Senghor becomes as he talks of his encounter with French language and French literature.

Mais on me posera la question: 'Pourquoi, dès lors, écrivez-vous en français?' parce que nous sommes des métis culturels, parce que, si nous sentons en nègres, nous nous exprimons en français, parce que le français est une langue à vocation universelle, que notre message s'adresse *aussi* aux Français de France et aux autres hommes, parce que le français est une langue 'de gentillesse et d'honnêteté'. Qui a dit que c'était une langue grise et atone d'ingénieurs et de diplomates? Bien sûr, moi aussi, je l'ai dit un jour, pour les besoins de ma thèse. On me le pardonnera. Car je sais ses ressources pour l'avoir goûté, mâché, enseigné, et qu'il est la langue des dieux. Ecoutez donc Corneille, Lautréamont, Rimbaud, Péguy et Claudel. Écoutez le grand Hugo. Le français, ce sont les grandes orgues qui se prêtent à tous les timbres, à tous les effets, des douceurs les plus suaves aux fulgurances de l'orage. Il est, tour à tour ou en même temps, flûte, hautbois, trompette, tamtam et même canon. Et puis le français nous a fait don de ses mots abstraits – si rares dans nos langues maternelles – où les larmes se font pierres précieuses. Chez nous, les mots sont naturellement nimbés d'un halo de sève et de sang; les mots du français rayonnent de mille feux, comme des diamants. Des fusées qui éclairent notre nuit.

See also Senghor's reply to a question on language in an interview by Armand Guiber and published in *Présence Africaine* 1962 under the title, Léopold Sédar Senghor:

Il est vrai que le français n'est pas ma langue maternelle. J'ai commencé de l'apprendre à sept ans, par des mots comme 'confitures' et 'chocolat'. Aujourd' – hui, je pense naturellement en Français, et je comprend le Français – faut-il en avoir honte? Mieux qu'aucune autre langue. C'est dire que le Français n'est plus pour moi un 'véhicule étranger' mais la forme d'expression naturelle de ma pensée.
   Ce qui m'est étrange dans le français, c'est peut-être son style:
   Son architecture classique. Je suis naturellement porté à gonfler d'image son cadre étroit, sans la poussée de la chaleur émotionelle.

18   *Zimbabwe Herald* August 1981.

19   Chinua Achebe 'The African Writer and the English Language' in *Morning Yet on Creation Day* p. 59.

20   Most of the writers were from universities. The readership was mainly the product of schools and colleges. As for the underlying theme of much of that literature, Achebe's statement in his paper, 'The Novelist as a Teacher', is instructive:
   'If I were God I would regard as the very worst our acceptance – for whatever reason – of racial inferiority. It is too late in the day to get worked up about it or to blame others, much as they may

deserve such blame and condemnation. What we need to do is to look back and try and find out where we went wrong, where the rain began to beat us.

'Here then is an adequate revolution for me to espouse – to help my society regain belief in itself and put away the complexes of the years of denigration and self-abasement.' *Morning Yet on Creation Day,* p. 44.

Since the peasant and the worker had never really had any doubts about their Africanness, the reference could only have been to the 'educated' or the petty-bourgeois African. In fact if one substitutes the words 'the petty-bourgeois' for the word 'our' and 'the petty-bourgeois class' for 'my society' the statement is apt, accurate, and describes well the assumed audience. Of course, an ideological revolution in this class would affect the whole society.

21   David Diop 'Contribution to the Debate on National Poetry', *Présence Africaine* 6, 1956.

22   David Diop, ibid.

23   The term 'Afro-European Literature' may seem to put too much weight on the Europeanness of the literature. Euro-African literature? Probably, the English, French, and Portuguese components would then be 'Anglo-African literature', 'Franco-African literature' or 'Luso-African literature'. What is important is that this minority literature forms a distinct tradition that needs a different term to distinguish it from *African Literature,* instead of usurping the title *African Literature* as is the current practice in literary scholarship. There have even been arrogant claims by some literary scholars who talk as if the literature written in European languages is necessarily closer to the Africanness of its inspiration than similar works in African languages, the languages of the majority. So thoroughly has the minority 'Afro-European Literature' (Euro-African literature?) usurped the name 'African literature' in the current scholarship that literature by Africans in African languages is the one that needs qualification. Albert Gérard's otherwise timely book is titled *African Language Literatures.*

24   Chinua Achebe 'Africa and her Writers' in *Morning Yet on Creation Day,* p. 27.

Chapter 42

Anamnesis in the Language of Writing

Assia Djebar

I

To write, to return to the body, or, at the very least, to the hand in motion. First, a detour via the mother: to turn away from those beauties asleep, from those so melancholy in their silences, from those who watch the threshold in vain. To forget the closed-in gardens, the subdued voices, the courtyards without windows to the outside, opening onto a still and stubborn sky. Once, only once, but for a moment that lasts, to betray the faraway gaze of she who waits: the gaze of another woman, or of the same one; of another who thought she had passed you, and then stopped, still.

Anamnesis? No, first of all, a surge forward and, as the hand begins to race across the page, the feet stir, the body takes flight.... And the eyes, the eyes especially, the eyes fix themselves on the horizon, a horizon searched for, then found, sliding far away, sinking close at hand.... Nothing counts but the first glimmer, nothing but the light, nothing but the sun, persisting deep into the heart of the night.

To write, or to run? To write in order to run; indeed, to remember, in spite of oneself: not the past, but pre-memory, before the rising of the first dawn, before the night of nights, before....

II

This would be writing in flight, let us say, writing as riding (but what mount could carry my tireless fever, and my doubt?): to write to the beat of my breath, exhaling, inhaling, pausing....

First published in *Studies in Twentieth Century Literature* 23.1 (1999), 179–89. Translated by Anne Donadey, with Christi Merrill, University of Iowa. Thanks go to Michel Laronde for his close reading of and suggestions about this translation. All notes are translator's notes.

To write – why not – eyes closed, fast advancing, with sure step, like a sightless person navigating through the crowd. Eyes closed, to perceive the iridescent movement inside oneself, twirling and gliding. Above all, not to immerse oneself in memory: rather, to touch nothing but its silkiness, or its slow tearing away. Rather, to imagine the air to be released, the space to be freed, navigating neither wildly nor recklessly, but with a steady hand.

Writing in order to flee, not in order to survive. Next fall, when I go to Oklahoma City, I shall begin to write, for myself, what will become a long poem, a poem set to the rhythm of walking, as though I were carried along by some slow caravan from the past; as though I were setting out to join the fenced-in Indian tribes of the last century who, most surely, wait for me; as though I were going to encounter the phantoms of the past – mine, certainly, as well as theirs....[1]

I shall thus begin, next fall:
To write close to, or rather, alongside the abyss.

"Alongside" is certainly as important as the last word, "abyss," if not more. "Alongside": since this will be, as it already is, a motionless race, simply an inner journey, a ceaseless wandering, without delay, with neither pause nor respite, a sometimes slow, sometimes precipitous advance, always forging ahead (if I should wake in the middle of the night, my sleepy voice softly sings, "Faraway friends are falling, oh, my poor heart!"). And then, as soon as I begin to assess the situation by outlining the theme of anamnesis, as soon as this desire surges within me, already a contrary project presents and imposes itself on me.

III

Anamnesis...

A year ago, I was just finishing *Vaste est la prison*....[2]
But have I really left it behind? A prison whose walls keep widening, whose sentence keeps lengthening, like the effects of time on Saharan frescoes as they appear, then disappear, little by little, on prehistoric cave walls – were they dreamed of, or truly encountered? Women hunters on the cave walls, striding somewhere, among ostriches and buffalo, on the lookout for some way out, seen only in a flash....
Vaste est la prison: the novel barely written, gaps begin to appear, widening under the substance of the text, memory gaps.
A wind suddenly sweeps through them now – is it a tornado, or a slight, subtle breeze? Unexpected memory gaps: for example, during the grandmother's early adolescence, what I never knew, what the mother (that is, her daughter) never told me, what the mother most likely never heard put into words, but somehow guessed at, was an occluded transmission. And yet, some seventy-five, no, ninety years later (for if my grandmother were alive today she would be a centenarian), what my grandmother overshadowed and sealed up (she and the women around her and with her at the time) was the tragic death of her own mother – a death from jealousy and powerlessness, a death from the incurable wound of an unthinking husband's blatant cruelty. The very thing that should have been

obvious to all the women, enough to keep them from living, from laughing, bearing children, hoping – facing all of them was this savage grief coming from one of them, causing all to slowly begin to putrefy. That is what should have happened and yet never did, not even with the grandmother!

As a fourteen-year-old girl, ready to enter into early matrimony, or perhaps married just recently, she suddenly wanted to obliterate the mother and her defeat, the stricken mother, taken away and so quickly buried. The grandmother, on this occasion, hardened herself, armed herself with virile energy, but also with a voracious silence and with the mud of forgetfulness.

At the price of forgetting, or pretending to forget, the mother's defeat, she, the grandmother, was able to live, with a strength first only glimpsed fleetingly, then recovered gradually, thanks to constant struggle. She turned her back on memory – with its ridges, its rough spots, its desert, and its sterility.

In the end, she presented herself to me as a virile foremother, unwilling to communicate to me the price she had to pay, initially and then again each day, silently. In a way, opening an abyss behind her, inverting her sexual role from that point on, she nevertheless wanted to become for me – me, the little girl of yesteryear sitting at evening gatherings by the glowing embers – the transmitter, the storyteller of heroic ways and deeds.

Deeds of men of old, of their battles, and of their glories, even in defeat.

Thus memory inverts itself. The guardian, my grandmother, masked herself for me; night after night, she would faithfully recount the history of the tribe for me – the palms of her hands, reddened by henna, holding mine together in their warmth. At last, she softened into the role of storyteller, taking up the golden thread.

The thread of life, to be sure, the trace of battles. In front of the seated storyteller, the little girl is listening, crouching at her knee. Behind this screen of reconstituted glory, a woman nevertheless keeps on falling, in the mortal faint of a defeated wife, defeated till death.

Fifty years later, it is the daughter of the deceased who recounts memories of...her second husband to me, the little girl crouching at her knee. In turn, fifty years later, I seize her voice for my writing in French. I intercept the foremother's Arabic sound. She had extinguished a woman's originary grief (her mother swallowed in forget-fulness) in order to rekindle the fiery fervor of her noble husband: was that a slippage, an inversion, a betrayal of women, or an obscure strategy erected on the summit of her craggy memory that allowed her to continue, to survive, to hope against all odds?

Thus have I reached this strange denial of the mother of yester-year, of the felled woman, who felled herself. The adolescent daughter, who was probably ready to take her own marital vows, became frightened. And wanted to forget everything at once.

To disavow the mother, the immolated one.

Anamnesis?

IV

Memory gaps, as I said, resurface in my search for *Vaste est la prison*. But there is also the loss of voice: first, my mother's aphasia, as a little girl, a loss that lasted an entire year.

And suddenly I am reminded of the Iranian poet who died a young woman, at age thirty-two, on a street in Teheran in 1967:

> The voice, the voice, the voice,
> Only the voice remains –
> Why should I stop?

This was to be one of her last poems. This poet "of another birth," Forugh Farrokhzad, has been haunting me for so long now.[3]

"Only the voice remains." Now the mother, a six- year-old girl who remained mute for a year, and then tried to forget, the mother – my mother –kept silent for all that time ("a cold season" that stretched into a year), wanting to follow the wake of her disappeared sister Cherifa. To leave as if following her; her voice evaporated at the hour of the funeral, as if preceding her, pulling her far away, beyond the Lethe....[4]

For an entire year in this white tunnel of silence, she must have staggered, teetered, on the brink of the abyss. Days of vertigo, all those months without words, prayers, or sighs....Only her eyes faced the others, staring beyond them, searching for a voice that would not return, like the flight of a lark frozen in a steel sky! The city by the sea, with its ancient harbor and its lighthouse, immutable over two millennia, the city waited its turn....

And what if it were always this way, at least in my country today? All violence, turmoil, and stifled rumblings....Yes, what if it were always this way, even today: to know that for each disappeared girl (for Cherifa who died yesterday of typhoid fever, how many young girls and grown women of Algeria have fallen, murdered, today? The count for just one year has reached at least sixty!), for each of these, for each contemporary Algerian Iphigeneia, or for each Antigone with no fiancé to accompany her to the grave, alive, to await her death (yes, thanks to the mother – my own mother – and to this desire for anamnesis that her ancient sorrow imposed upon me), I know now, I am sure that for each woman who must die in the light of day, for each sacrificed woman, for the loss of each immolated woman, a young girl, a single one, in the neighborhood close by, loses her voice, for weeks or for months, or longer still, sometimes forever.

The face of the child-witness is suddenly left with only her gaze, her waiting eyes to face us.

Ordinarily, young girls do not haunt tragedies. They remain in the shadows, standing behind the curtain, or at most, in the wings (it is most likely at the moment in which the blood of their nubile bodies begins to flow that they are supposed to arrive on the dangerous, even fatal, stage!).

But what of my land where nearly all women, young or old, have been fenced in, packed in, confined together in enclosed spaces (gardens, shacks, or patios) in order to prevent their hymns, their cries, their showers of song from ever reaching a potential audience?

There only remain streets, empty, or full of men and young boys, which amounts to the same thing.

No, there is no theater for this world; the people I come from do not have the right to witness the ritual of a tragedy unfolding before them, because the same tenacious division of the sexes keeps reappearing at the very center of social life, of the city, of its two-pronged history.

What if there were, precisely, a theater for mute women, a theater of the blank stare, unfolding in all its mystery and invisibility? Then, could the voices of the young girls who must have looked death in the face and seen its grimace have fled toward such a ritual, such a liturgy? Such a necessary purification rite?

In the context of such a draining of voice, such an entombment of the past, where can the trajectories of our memories carry us today? Where does the archaeology of our reclaimed female genealogy lead us? As much towards loss and vertigo as towards a possible renewal?

V

Long ago, perhaps close to twenty years ago already, I believed that to navigate the night of women (at least, of Islamic women) would help me to recover the strength, the energy, the faith of the steadfast foremothers. I dreamed that if only I could attempt to swim against the current, to confront the violent ebb and flow of dispersal through orality, they would be able to pass their survival secrets on to me . . . I believed.

I approached this undertaking in a naive way. I was deluding myself, of course: these old women with their weather-beaten, wrinkled skin, their tattooed cheeks, brightly colored headdress, and their ancient talk laced with religious formulas like brasswork glittering on a breastplate, these foremothers had silenced their originary voices, had swallowed the sounds of their youthful hopes from the beginning. And when it was their daughters – such as my mother – who stood up, vulnerable, petrified, then the matrons quickly resorted to magic, poetry, and trances: quick, quick, let the voice return!

> Only the voice remains –
> Why should I stop?

still sighs the ghost of the 1960s poet in Tehran.

These rural and city women of yesteryear, Berber and pious Arabicized women from my Maghreb, these women so far from Forugh Farrokhzad, could nevertheless have taken up for themselves the refined lament of the mortally wounded poet.

My very mother – to return to the novel *Vaste est la prison* – could not have known that it was, in fact, thanks to this long year of aphasia that she was able, so many years later, to carry out her escapes and her passages. Her crossings.

At the beginning of her womanhood, my mother grafted all her strength onto this initial loss of voice, a loss that one could view as the price paid for sisterhood, briefly glimpsed then erased. She found the strength, as a child, to turn her back on the Berber language, the language of a father who never was to return; as a young woman, to fall in love with the suitor who came to her, French books in hand; to then risk forfeiting some of her status of cherished city-dweller while initiating a dialogue, in French, with European women in her neighborhood.

Then the mother turned into a traveler, for the sake of her son, incarcerated in faraway French prisons. She went there by boat, by train, by plane – awkward and elegant, with her proper spoken French and a secret in Arabic hidden in her poise and stiff pride.

Loss of yesterday's voice: it is in this shattering, in this stretch of time without memory, almost without a trace (except for the echo of my search, brought back by chance), that my mother's victorious mobility – her rebirth – inscribes itself. For she must have ardently desired to continue walking along the edge of the shadows. Innocent shadows dissolving into sunlight.

I have said it before and say it again now: today, in my country, so many other young girls must brave the same vertigo: to let their voices, their hearts, or their memories, accompany their sacrificed female relatives, to shroud themselves in silence at the risk of never returning.

Only time will tell, one day, what unexpected strength these countless mute women will discover in themselves. Armed again, but for what purpose if not to sketch the voice and seal it firm, to fix it indelibly on the page, in stone, or on the wind, in other words, for writing, painting, sculpting, music. Yes, indeed, for all types of writing.

VI

I will conclude with Luce Irigaray's urgings:

> we must not once more kill the mother who was sacrificed to the origins of our culture. We must give her new life, new life to that mother, to our mother within us and between us.... We must give her the right to pleasure, to *jouissance*, to passion, restore her right to speech, and sometimes to cries and anger.

She then adds the following, on the same topic of the "bodily encounter with the mother" (and indeed, what signification could any anamnesis have if it did not take that bodily encounter as its starting point?):

> We have to discover a language [*langage*] which does not replace the bodily encounter, as paternal language [*langue*] attempts to do, but which can go along with it, words which do not bar the corporeal, but which speak corporeal.[5]

Thus, these quotations allow me to finally return to the "language [*langue*] of writing" announced in my title, this language that I could have called my "paternal language" (as the first volume of my novelistic quartet, *Fantasia*, made quite explicit in 1985).

To return from my crossing into a female memory, a memory that spans nearly a century (my mother, my grandmother, and her own mother, the very first sacrificed woman), and to bring back a new kind of viaticum, strength and nourishment for the road ahead – not goatskins of holy water, but the ebb and flow of biographies that risk being frozen, obscured, suddenly turned into gold or lead, but not, alas, into a mother's fluid, a father's seed, or reviving spirits where all that matters is the strength of the alcohol.

In other words, must so many narratives – rearing up like wild mares, rushing forward, or fleeing in retreat – must all this chaotic movement, incessantly searching for a way out, freeze up under my fingers the moment I write them in French? Turn to stone, motionless, petrified, as if striking an aesthetic pose, listening to others who also turned to stone?

Must any paternal language, the moment it is put into use, lead us on, almost in spite of itself, to the ultimate instant, swiftly bringing death, in the hands of a female narrator of the "maternal bodily encounter"?

Because I write and speak in the Others' language, the language of the mediating father as well, do I not, in turn, compromise myself in some way through an objective alliance with the murderers of the first mother?

Am I not an accomplice to the first blood, to the first sacrificing father, to some obscure Maghrebian Agamemnon who would have departed, like the other, to conquer some illusory Troy?

"Words which speak corporeal," Irigaray writes. How may I conclude, if not through a last allusion to *Vaste est la prison*, a novel that I henceforth question from the outside and now call into question? It is I think not by chance that my crossing over into my female genealogy (titled "A silent desire" in Part III of that same novel) is next to and confronts the erasure of the Berber alphabet.

The re-reading – the end of the illegibility – of the earliest writing (I would almost call it the mother-writing), only occurs thanks to the intervention of the many foreigners (travelers, former slaves, archaeologists) who came in search of mystery for mystery's sake, or, on the contrary, for a very concrete gain.

For me, as well, the language of writing that was, throughout my childhood, the language of the father ("a little Arab girl going to school for the first time, walking hand in hand with her father"), that language is, first and foremost, for me, as an Algerian woman, the language of the previous century's invaders, the language of battle and virile bodily encounters – in other words, the language of blood.[6] Perhaps, after all, that is why the first sacrifice of my genealogy – the great-grandmother's sudden death, as if by suffocation, as if her boiling emotions had poisoned her blood – could only resurface in my memory through (or thanks to) that adverse language . . . "Adverse language" used to tell about adversity, including that suffered by women and swallowed for so long.

It is not by chance, either, that in *Vaste est la prison* – which I will call the book not only "of the mother" but "of the mothers" – a throng of dead others rises up (and most certainly not in the mother's tongue), those who perished by the thousands in the fall of Carthage. . . . The books rescued, the fire consuming the bodies, the disaster and its relentless rhythm, the whole scene is resurrected thanks to the Greek historian Polybius: a third type of writing, then, neither mine (the French) nor the Berber on the Dougga stele, but the Greek, encircles my female genealogy – passing, as it did, from Arabic and Berber to the French inscription – in a ring of fire. This backdrop of disaster glows red in History's infinite spiral.

VII

What can I say about "my" French language, however, in this game of opposites, in this bodily encounter with so many mothers? It seems to me sometimes that my French is cracking, shattering, that its marble surface breaks into pieces. The muzzled sounds of oral languages behind my French, muted languages on its margins, placed outside the realm of writing since my early childhood, their music, their movement, the overflow of their hidden life resurface within my French and stir up an effervescence under its very flesh.

I write in a language deemed clear (the language of Descartes), but against a backdrop of fire, surrounded by danger and sometimes, these days, by terror. I attempt to communicate I'm not sure quite what, in a language, at any rate, whose main criterion seems to be clarity.

Yet, in spite of myself, in spite of my respect for this language, whose deep rhythms, whose very breath move me, in spite of being aware of its "dignity" (isn't the "dignity" of a language simply its soul?), in my sentences, or in the structure of my verbal constructions (of which I conceive as an alliance between my need for architecture and my aspiration for musical fervor), in spite, then, of this language that became the father's, the movement animating my characters – the people of my genealogy as well as their shadows who, in a sense, are looking at me, challenging me, expecting me to pull them, to make them enter, in spite of myself, in spite of themselves, into the house of this foreign language – this movement becomes my principal thrust, the central core of my novelistic form.

Thus, I see myself riding with so many shadows, but also with the voices of invisible, illiterate women; indeed, riding a language that must be guided and sometimes coaxed like a wild mare. A language of movement, my movement that invents and recharges itself in the very writing of the novel.... Step by step, the slow rhythm gains momentum, and I no longer know if it is the others that I carry (the mothers, sisters, foremothers) who pull the language and I, its rider, along, or if it is the language of writing, neither dominated nor driven wild, simply inhabited and thus transformed, that sweeps us along and carries us away. Us? Myself and the other women, of course, who all populate my crowded memory.

Thus goes the ride, for the length of a novel, a narrative, or a short story.

To write, or to run. To write in order to run. To run, and to remember. Forward, or back, what's the difference?

Notes

1   This essay was written in April 1996. In the fall of 1996, Djebar was awarded the prestigious Neustadt International Prize for Literature in Oklahoma. See the special issue of *World Literature Today* dedicated to her works.

2   The 1995 novel, which is the third volume of a novelistic quartet begun with *L'Amour, la fantasia* and *Ombre sultane*, has not yet been translated into English. The other two were translated by Dorothy S. Blair under the titles *Fantasia: An Algerian Cavalcade* and *A Sister to Scheherazade*.

3   *Another Birth* is the title of Farrokhzad's most famous collection of poems.

4   In Greek mythology, the Lethe is the Underworld river of forgetfulness. The dead descending to the Underworld drank from its waters and forgot about their lives on earth.

5   Luce Irigaray, "The Bodily Encounter with the Mother" 43. This text was first published in French, in 1981, as *Le Corps à corps avec la mère*.

6   The quotation is from the sentence that opens the autobiographical novel *Fantasia*.

References

Djebar, Assia. *A Sister to Scheherazade*, Trans. Dorothy S. Blair. Portsmouth, NH: Heinemann, 1993.

——. *Fantasia: An Algerian Cavalcade*. Trans. Dorothy S. Blair. Portsmouth, NH: Heinemann, 1993.

——. *L'Amour, la fantasia*. Paris: J. C. Lattès, 1985.

——. *Ombre sultane*. Paris: J. C. Lattès, 1987.

——. *Vaste est la prison*. Paris: Albin Michel, 1995.

Irigaray, Luce. *Le Corps à corps avec la mère*. Montreal: Editions de la pleine lune, 1981.

——. "The Bodily Encounter with the Mother." Trans. David Macey. *The Irigaray Reader*. Ed. Margaret Whitford. Oxford, UK: Basil Blackwell, 1991. 34–46.

World Literature Today 70.4 (1996). Special issue on Assia Djebar.

Chapter 43

African-Language Literature:
Tragedy and Hope

Daniel P. Kunene

Since language is the *sine qua non* of literary activity, it is at the very heart of my concerns in this article. Language is the means by which the writer reveals his soul, and, by the same token, the writer's language is the vehicle whereby the reader or critic attempts to fathom the depth of feeling he or she conveys. We can only begin to comprehend, in a small way, the identity of the writer – his/her religious beliefs, folklore, myths, proverbs, superstitions, humor, attitude towards life and death (in other words the totality of his/her world view) – if we know his/her language. Story is the universal means by which these facets of a human being are revealed. That is why psychoanalysts encourage their patients to tell them stories. And that is why many novels by Africans who have experienced, and, in some cases, continue to experience, oppression and exploitation by foreign powers are autobiographical. It is with this in mind that we should approach the question of language in Africa as a means of creating literature.

Africa is not a country, but a continent. Obviously, therefore, there is no language called "African," any more than there is a language called "European." And this is the beginning of our woes as both writers of "African" literature and its critics. It is no fault of ours. We have, somehow, been painted into a corner by history, and the peculiar circumstances under which the African writer writes and the African literary critic critiques remind us daily of the tragedy of Europe's violation of the integrity of African societies. The Berlin Conference both carved us up into islands and then, with the help of anthropologists and Africanists of other persuasions, glued the pieces together rather crudely into an artificial "homogeneity." One's first gripe, therefore, is that somehow someone came up with the label "African" to characterize a whole host of activities and concepts, including "African" literature. The origin of this term is no mystery. "African" literature is a relatively new concept, not because there was no literature in Africa before the missionaries and other white people "brought it," but because those who performed it in their indigenous languages did not perceive what

First published in *Research in African Literatures* 23.1 (1992): 7–15.

they were doing as an "African" activity. For them, it was an activity relevant to their own languages and cultures. When She-karisi Candi Rureke narrates the Nyanga epic of Mwindo in twelve days of "singing, narrating, dancing, miming" (Biebuyck and Mateene vi), he is affirming Nyanga culture as surely as the Djeli (i.e., Griot) Mamadou Kouyate affirms Mandinke culture in his narrative of the Sundiata epic. Neither Rureke nor Kouyate would consider themselves "African," even though they would no doubt recognize any linguistic and/or cultural continuities spreading out from where they are.

Albert Gérard warns that "it is a matter of ascertained scientific fact that various African societies have elaborated various civilizations that are all the more diversified, as they grew without any intimate or prolonged contacts with one another," and further that "each of these civilizations has its specific features that are reflected in its literary folk tradition and are likely to echo further in its written art" (*Four African Literatures* 13).

Other scholars have made similar observations. For example, B. W. Andrzejewski and his colleagues have remarked that "African literatures do not seem to form a distinct group which could be contrasted, as a whole, with all the other literatures of the world oral or written," a diversity they attribute to "linguistic fragmentation of the African continent" (26). They go further and state that "[t]he differences between members of separate language groups, for example between Zulu (Bantu), Luo (Nilotic) or Oromo (Cushitic), are so great that it would be difficult to find any recognizable common features; as far as the possibility of communication is concerned, the differences between them are comparable to those between English, Hungarian and Basque" (26).

There ought to be no separation of language and literature either in the minds of "African" literature scholars and teachers, or in the institutions in which such research and teaching take place. It is ironic that, in the United States, for example, "African" literatures are often taught in English departments! Instead of this aberration, any genuine interest in African literatures should be reflected in a serious attempt to combine literature studies with compatible language studies. Given the will, this should not be difficult. A study of the literature of a given area should be accompanied by a concurrent study of at least one of the languages of that area. For example, Zimbabwean literature should be studied together with Shona and Ndebele regardless of whether that literature is written in English or in any of the Shona-group languages or in Ndebele (a Nguni-group language). Similar kinds of language-literature compatibilities could be worked out for other areas, so that, for example, the study of southern African literatures would coincide with a concurrent study of one Nguni-group language (Zulu, Xhosa, Ndebele, Swati, etc.) and one Sotho-group language (Sesotho, Sepedi, Setswana, etc.). Again, this would be done regardless of whether the literature studied is written in one of the above languages or in English by an African.

Needless to say that this linguistic dilemma, found throughout the African continent, is a consequence of the conquest and subjugation of most of Africa by European powers which had, as one of its consequences, the introduction of their respective languages, especially English, French, and Portuguese. The few blacks who obtained education from schools set up by these powers and their missionary adjuncts, acquired their languages and became an educated élite. A significant number of them even went to the metropolitan centers of their colonizers to obtain higher education. Varying degrees of alienation took place, including the habitual use of the new languages, both for ordinary communication and for the creation of literature. Yet, despite the languages they were written in, these emerging literatures were not considered to be English or French or Portuguese literatures, and thus was born the idea of "African" literature. Referring to the period from the mid-1950s to the early 1960s, Gerald Moore states that, "[a]t that time, the concept of African literature was for many readers a new one" (7). He might have added that it was an idea that was then being formulated by white critics who, for the first time, had a small glimpse into what the African was thinking, especially about his state of disenfranchisement by the colonial powers. The phenomenon of colonialism and its attendant evils was spread throughout much of the continent. The beginning of the Africans' articulation of their discontent with their situation, while not simultaneous in all the colonies and settler areas, was nonetheless a sweeping, snowballing movement that was soon to be observed as an African, rather than a disarticulated country-by-country or region-by-region phenomenon. It gathered greater impetus following the end of World War II. Harold Macmillan, then Prime Minister of England, nicknamed it "the winds of change sweeping down the African continent" in his early 1960s address to the South African Parliament in Cape Town.

He was referring to a primarily political movement with a powerful cultural adjunct. The Africans' self-emancipation was both physical and psychological. It was a realization that one cannot entirely, or even significantly, free the body from its chains unless one first frees the mind of its enslavement. There was a search for roots, a new pride in being black and African, a new kind of literature and poetry and art that expressed the struggle to free oneself. A new identity was being born. Paradoxically, the poetry and literature articulating these new ideas were being written in the languages of the oppressors. One of the reasons for this was that the Africans, having conquered their fear of their master's wrath, had decided to confront him directly in his own language. One should not forget also that there was a strong sense of pan-Africanism, a sense that the continent shared the same destiny, and that bridges were being built between and among the élites of the different African cultural and linguistic groups.

Concurrently with this movement, and often overshadowed by it in the new-found euphoria accompanying the "discovery" of "African" literature, creators of literatures in the languages of Africa continued to ply their trade, largely ignoring, if not totally unaware of, it. For them, verbal art in whatever their language might be – Kikuyu, Acoli, Nyanga, Sesotho, Setswana, Zulu, Amharic, Fante, etc. – continued as it had before the "Great Event." Anchored in the souls of the people, this literature not only refused to be silenced or to be swept into the general excitement of the new "African" literature, but indeed allowed it to grow and maybe one day spend its own momentum and then "come back home," as has been so well demonstrated by Ngũgĩ wa Thiong'O in his decision to go back to Kikuyu in order to reach the souls of his people.

The effect of the above-summarized movement was that there were thenceforth two streams of literature: the new-found "African" literature written in the European languages, and the much-older grassroots literatures, composed in the languages of Africa, which remained autonomous even while being aware of their immediate neighbors, the very antithesis of "African" literature. However, bits and pieces of the African-language-based literatures were syphoned into the stream of "African" literature through translation. Thomas Mofolo's *Chaka* has long enjoyed an unprecedented lavishment of attention throughout Europe and the United States, as well as in many parts of Africa, since it was first translated into English by F. H. Dutton in 1931. A. C. Jordan's Xhosa classic, *Ingqumbo Yeminyanya*, first published in 1940, has recently (1980) been published in English translation, and one can predict that it will find its way into other languages as well. Mostly, however,

African-language literatures have received attention from European and Eurocentric critics who pieced together scraps of information obtained from reviews and other commentaries by scholars who knew the languages or worked in close collaboration with those who did. As an example, G. H. Franz's good, long, and well-documented article, "The Literature of Lesotho" (1930), has found its way, too often without acknowledgement, into many "African" literature articles. Inevitably, much charlatanism relied on this secondary information, often after it passed through many other hands, to claim "authoritative" knowledge of the subject. But from time to time something reflecting deep, serious scholarship resulted. An excellent example of this is Albert S. Gérard in his two major works, *Four African Literatures: Xhosa, Sotho, Zulu, Amharic* and the more recent *African-Language Literatures: An Introduction to the Literary History of Sub-Saharan Africa.* Despite his lack of knowledge of the languages he was writing about, Gérard's meticulous scholarship contributed significantly to the historical study of literatures in the languages of Africa. It is also to his credit that Gérard admits that "cogent critical comment on the works that have been written in their own languages" can only be made by "African scholars, for they alone are both able and entitled to offer" such comment (*African Language Literatures* X).

What I have been leading up to is the conclusion that the concept "African," especially as applied to literature, is first, foremost, and last a political one imposed on us by history. Like our fellow human-beings universally, we, as Africans, are products of history, and history, as everyone knows, has the nasty habit of refusing to erase itself. Yet, while we cannot change history, we can certainly use it to critique our current modes of thought and behavior. As inheritors of the bitter fruits of partition and colonization, we are burdened with the task of living a myth and trying to make it work. This myth is reinforced by the modern "Africanist" scholar from Europe and America who, in the majority of cases, is an extension of his/her country's foreign policy, with all that that implies. It is the myth that Africa is one undifferentiated mass of inferior human beings who, in the eyes of Europe and America, are united in their need to be studied, to be exploited economically under the guise of "aid," to be destabilized for the benefit of international imperialism. And we, as Africans, are co-opted to perpetuate that myth.

I am not denying that Africa needs unity as underscored by scholars, philosophers, and dreamers of the caliber of Kwame Nkrumah (Pan-Africanism) and Léopold Sédar Senghor (Négritude). But this is a political, not an artistic, necessity.

I accept, as a given, that there are two streams of literature on the African continent, namely literatures in the European languages ("African" literature), and literatures created in several hundred African languages spread throughout the continent. This means that some African writers have written, are now writing, and will in the future continue to write, in languages other than their mother tongues, specifically in European languages. By the same token, however, there are, as stated above, African writers who have written, are now writing, and will in the future continue to write, in their own mother-tongues. Also, and most importantly, African storytellers have told, are now telling, and will in future continue to tell their stories, their legends, their myths, and their epics in their own individual African languages. African literature scholarship cannot afford to pay exclusive attention to literatures written in European languages, while ignoring those written in African languages. A commitment has to be made – a commitment which, as indicated above, would require a knowledge of at least one African language on the part of the specialist. But, more than that, it would have to be accepted that no one could claim to be a specialist in "African" literature without being familiar with the individual cultures relevant to the geographical areas of their speciality.

There is no question but that the demands of such scholarship are rigorous. The combination of skills required for such studies includes thorough linguistic proficiency, a knowledge of the customs, mores and world view of the people, and a keen sense of the possibilities the languages offer to a skillful writer. The latter would open up hitherto unsuspected possibilities for new critical criteria and methodologies best suited to individual languages or groups of related languages. While it is entirely possible (though rare) that individual scholars with all these skills do exist, in most cases teamwork would be the answer. This has been proved to be possible, with excellent results. For example, the skills of Daniel Biebuyck and Kahombo Mateene have given considerable impetus to the study of Nyanga culture and literature. One need only read the elaborate introduction and copious footnotes accompanying *The Mwindo Epic* to realize the remarkable skills of these two scholars and their contribution to the understanding of Nyanga culture and literature. Thus, the much-maligned anthropologist can often boast a much more rigorous scholarship in the area of African-language literatures than can the modern African literature specialist. In the same vein, many missionaries have engaged in research that has provided valuable insights into specific cultures. The name of Bishop Henry Callaway immediately comes to mind. His *Nursery Tales, Traditions and Histories of the Zulus* is a monumental work in which many Zulu tales, legends, and traditions have been preserved. In addition, the missionaries, through their translations of the Bible, indirectly contributed to the beginnings of written literatures, to say nothing about their introduction of literacy, thus opening up a whole new world for the specific groups among whom they worked. In the words of Professor C. L. S. Nyembezi, "An examination of the contribution by missionaries in the nineteenth century reveals that the emphasis was on translation of the scriptures, preparation of grammars and compilation of dictionaries" (2).

The moral of such references to African literature studies by anthropologists, missionaries, and, in some cases indeed by colonial civil servants, is that, despite all the acknowledged evils of colonialism, the deculturating influence of christianization, and the arrogant, paternalistic attitude of the bearers of "Western" civilization in general, some studies made by the agents of these processes have a value that is essential to the study of the literatures of various African societies; what they began ought to be carried forward (if anything with even greater rigor) by modern "African" literature scholars.

It should be obvious to the reader, by now, that I am deliberately steering clear of the controversy over whether African writers should, or should not, write in non-African languages. This is an extremely important issue; it is being debated right now, and there is so much to be said on both sides that no resolution seems to be in sight. This question arises, needless to say, because it is implicitly assumed that African writers know at least one African language, have acquired at least one colonial or settler language, and therefore have a choice. In a thorough and informative survey, Lee Nichols interviewed eighty-three African writers on many aspects of their writing, including their choice of language. The writers came from different parts of the African continent. Some wrote in European languages, some in their native languages. Some who wrote in African languages translated their own writings into a European language, notably English; some preferred to have someone else translate their works; and some saw no point in translation. It all boiled down to audience, and to the purpose of one's writing: Was it to draw the attention of the world at large to internal problems in the writer's country? Or was it to involve one's own people in resolving their own conflicts? Or was it the less noble motive of easy fame and fortune? It is instructive to read the two publications in which Nichols engages in lively discussions with African writers, some of whom are, and have been, committed to writing in African languages from the start—Penina Mlama (Swahili), Akinwumi Isola (Yoruba), Ntseliseng M. Khaketla (Sesotho), and Tsegae Gabre-Medhin (Amharic) to mention just a few. Ngũgĩ wa Thiong'o is the best known example of the few who have switched from writing in a European language to writing in their mother-tongues. Ngũgĩ's choice of Kikuyu was dictated by a redefinition of his target audience for sociopolitical reasons. As a result, he shook the Kenyan establishment to its foundations and suffered imprisonment, termination from his university teaching post, and other forms of harassment.

The question of language choice is one that is addressed by many contributors to this special issue of *Research in African Literatures*. It is a question that I consider enormously important. But I have, over the years, found myself almost exclusively attracted to an equally important, but rather different, question. It seems to me that African scholars should, as suggested by Gérard, take the leadership in these matters and set the pace by revisiting literary compositions in their mother tongues (be they oral or written) and by establishing their authority in the same way that English critics and scholars have established themselves as the foremost authorities in the scholarship of English literature. We need to pause and confront these issues, and we need to come up with answers demanded by the logic of our situation, however unpalatable these may be to some of us. Failing this, we will, deservedly, remain irrelevant to those practitioners of African literatures, both written and oral, who live in Africa and create and perform in their mother-tongues with, and for, African audiences.

Equally tragically, if African critics fail to rise to this challenge, they will, *deservedly*, continue to be the targets of paternalism from non-African critics whose very tone defines them as talking not only from outside in relation to the African cultures they are critiquing, but from above, with pontifical authority. While, for example, one acknowledges the important contributions that Albert Gérard has made to the study of African literatures in African languages, one cannot help being irked by some blatant reminders that he is often "talking from above." For example, after stating that the novel is "the outcome of a particular form of civilization, the premises of which are entirely at variance with those of indigenous African cultures," and that it is "the favorite medium of an individualistic society," and further yet, that "African cultures are based on values that are primarily societal," Gérard comes to the conclusion that:

> This is why so many African novelists and playwrights have been unable – as has often been observed *and deplored* – to achieve convincing individual characterization. In many cases, they continue the folktale tradition of emphasis on anecdotal incidents or on allegorical morality. The absence of any native tradition in those genres also accounts for *clumsiness in plot management and in the depiction of personal emotions: constant resorting to implausible coincidences and awkward handling of the love theme are illustrative of the difficulties that they will have to overcome. (Four African Literatures* 379; emphasis added)

Steve Biko has responded to this kind of paternalistic attitude on the part of liberal do-gooders by stating:

I am against the superior-inferior white-black stratification that makes the white a perpetual teacher and the black a perpetual pupil (and a poor one at that). I am against the intellectual arrogance of white people that makes them believe that white leadership is a *sine qua non* in this country and that whites are the divinely appointed pace-setters in progress. (24)

Regarding the African writer's exposure of the negative effects of urbanization, especially in so far as they destroy the moral fiber of African youth, Gérard declares that:

> This concentration on the negative aspects of modernization is akin to the *shrill anticolonialism* and the *négritude cult* in the French literature of West Africa, and it largely reflects an *immature tendency to let others shoulder all responsibility for Africa's present troubles*. It is a token of the *swift maturation of the African mind* that a number of younger writers in the newly independent countries should resolutely turn to self-criticism of a highly pertinent, and often pungent kind. (*Four African Literatures* 381–2; emphasis added)

Concerning this statement, I have commented, in *Thomas Mofolo and the Emergence of Written Sesotho Prose*, that "Gérard's message seems to be 'Blame the victim' or, which is even worse, 'Browbeat the victim into blaming himself'" (244n).

Speaking of "the African mind," Gérard goes on to state that "vernacular writing is certainly a most important potential source for *our knowledge and understanding of the African mind* in the present phase of acculturation" (*Four African Literatures*, 386; emphasis added). The tell-tale our in "our knowledge and understanding of the African mind" says it all. One can, therefore, understand Gérard's insensitivity in casually using terminology, (e.g., "Bushmen," "Hottentots," and "Kaffir wars"), that has long been rejected as insulting.

And I say, we, as Africans, deserve it all if we fail to rise to the occasion, to the challenge, and take the lead in affairs that affect us the most, and of which we have the most intimate knowledge: *We've got to get inside those languages and listen to what they say!* – OR PERISH! In this regard, the pioneering work of A. C. Jordan, *Towards an African Literature: The Emergence of Literary Form in Xhosa* is an example that ought to be emulated by African scholars. [...]

Appendix: A Case in Point

"Imbila yaswel' umsila ngokuyalezela" [The rock-rabbit lacked a tail through sending someone else to get one for him] is a Zulu proverb that is also found in most other southern African languages. It is based on the following aetiological tale, which I am retelling in my own words:

> In the beginning, the Maker made animals, but without giving them tails. When he looked at them moving around the earth, he saw that they were ugly. He felt sorry for them and decided that he was going to give them tails.

> A Great Call was made: "All ye animals, come back to the Place of Creation to obtain tails!" When they heard the Call, the animals went in large numbers back to the Place of Creation, where huge piles of tails awaited them. But the rock-rabbit alone did not go. He was so fond of basking in the sun that he decided he could not spend the time needed to go and get a tail.

So the rock-rabbit asked one of the other animals to bring him a tail. When this animal got there, there was so much excitement with all the animals fitting on tails, that he totally forgot about the rock-rabbit.

To this day, therefore, the rock-rabbit has no tail, for he failed to go and get one for himself.

References

Andrzejewski, B. W., S. Pilaszwicz, and W. Tyloch, eds. *Literatures in African Languages: Theoretica Issues and Sample Surveys*. Warsaw: Wiedza Powszechna, 1985.

Biebuyck, Daniel and Mateene, Kahombo C., eds. and trans. *The Mwindo Epic – From the Banyanga (Congo Republic)*. Berkeley: University of California Press, 1971.

Biko, Steve (Posthumous). *I Write What I Like – A Selection of His Writings*. Edited, with a personal memoir, by Aelred Stubbs, C.R. San Francisco: Harper and Row, 1978.

Callaway, Henry. *Nursery Tales, Traditions and Histories of the Zulus*. 1868. Springdale, Natal, London: J. A. Blair; Trubner, 1970.

Franz, G. H. "The Literature of Lesotho." *Bantu Studies* 4 (1930): 145–80.

Gérard, Albert S. *Four African Literatures – Xhosa, Sotho, Zulu, Amharic*. Berkeley: University of California Press, 1971.

——. *African Language Literatures: An Introduction to the Literary History of Sub-Saharan Africa*. Washington, DC: Three Continents Press, 1981.

Jordan, A. C. (Posthumous). *Towards an African Literature: The Emergence of Literary Form in Xhosa*. Berkeley: University of California Press, 1973.

Kunene, Daniel P. *Thomas Mofolo and the Emergence of Written Sesotho Prose*. Johannesburg: Ravan, 1989.

Moore, Gerald. *Twelve African Writers*. Bloomington: Indiana University Press, 1980.

Nichols, Lee. *Conversations with African Writers*. Washington, DC: Voice of America, 1981.

——. *African Writers at the Microphone*. Washington, DC: Three Continents Press, 1984.

Nyembezi, C. L. S. A *Review of Zulu Literature*. Pietermaritzburg: University of Natal Press, 1961.

Part VII

On Genres

One of the most basic features of genre – and therefore its implications for genre theorizing – is the intimate relationship among genre, writer, and audience, all living in historical time. At the moment, African writers are publishing more prose (and this genre is therefore the most popular) than drama or poetry collections. Let us consider this a "fact." There are two cogent issues to be raised here. First, what does the "fact" mean in terms of the basic feature of genre just stated? And, second, what has been the impact of the "fact" on genre studies? To answer the first question is to assume that given the structural, aesthetic and historical relationship among genre, writer and audience, the novel, being the most published genre, is the one with the widest readership and therefore also the one with the deepest indigenous resonance. After all, as Wellek and Warren argued in the 1940s in their classic *Theory of Literature*, "Every 'culture' has its genres" (234). We invoke Wellek and Warren particularly because their descriptive, functional (that is, culturally bound) and therefore relativist theory of genre is in support of Africans who a generation later would battle heroically against a Eurocentric discourse that inferiorized Africans for not having, for instance, "drama" that looked like European drama. But "audience" in African literary studies is more complicated than it seems, for we are talking about a minority, those Africans who are literate and literate in the European languages in which the literature and criticism are written. So the novel may be the most popular in Africa but that is merely among the literate minority. And, what is more, it is the genre with the shallowest indigenous provenance. The irony is that it is more popular among the literate than drama and performance and poetry, which have far deeper anchors in African cultures. In the oral context, drama and poetry are the arts of the majority and many of their styles have proven scribally transformable in the hands of skillful writers. As to the second question, again, an irony: more novels are being published but the more innovative and adventurous genre theorizing are to be found in drama and poetry studies, and no doubt part of the reason is because written drama and poetry are more easily discussed in relation to oral drama and poetry than the novel is to indigenous storytelling. The novel, it appears, is undetachable from its perceived Western origin and garb in spite of its extensive Africanization in structure, imagery, and language use.

Reference

Wellek, Rene and Warren, Austin. *Theory of Literature*. New York: Harcourt, Brace & World, 1942.

Chapter 44

Background to the West African Novel

Emmanuel N. Obiechina

> The process of modernization powerfully transforms individual lifeways. The move from the familiar and deeply personal life of a family farm in an isolated village to the strange impersonality of a "job" in a busy city crowded with unknown persons is one such transformation.
>
> Daniel Lerner in *The Passing of Traditional Society*

The relationship between literature and society has long been recognized; but it has not always been fully appreciated how far a particular society both influences the themes and subject matter of its representative literary types and also profoundly affects their formal development. Though most commentators on West African fiction are quick to point out its main peculiarities, they sometimes fail to see that these are clearly determined by the West African cultural tradition and environment. The result is that such commentators tend to expect West African writers to write like writers with different cultural and environmental compulsions.

This study is an attempt to establish the determining background factors of the West African novel. It relates the writing to their cultural and environmental situation; it aims to show that the changing cultural and social situation in West Africa both gave rise to the novel there, and in far-reaching and crucial ways conditioned the West African novels' content, themes and texture.

Literacy and the broadening of consciousness

The most important single factor is the introduction of literacy into West Africa where, before, the dominant cultural tradition had been based on the spoken word.[1] Literacy is crucial to the emergence of the novel, because the novel is meant to be read by the individual in quiet isolation, and complex narrative is more easily sustained and followed by reading it than by hearing it.[2] Moreover the achievement of literacy produces psychological and social capacities in the individual which facilitate the growth of the novel.

First published in *Culture, Tradition and Society in the West African Novel*, pp. 3–12. Cambridge: Cambridge University Press, 1975.

The spread of literacy has been, obviously, a major source of change in human life and society. Richard Hoggart's *The Uses of Literacy* describes how the establishment of mass literacy introduced far-reaching changes in the culture and social habits of the British working class. The introduction of literacy into the predominantly non-literate West African societies brought about an even more profound social change. And this, in turn, registers unmistakably in the history and content of the novel in West Africa.

The novel demands both from the novelist and from the reader a gift of empathy, the ability to slip imaginatively into circumstances and conditions of life beyond their immediate milieu. Writing or reading a novel implies this widening of the imaginative capability of writer and audience, so that the one can manage a faithful portrayal of social reality and the other an adequate reception of the vicarious experience. The situation implies a fundamental rapport between novelist and reader. Literacy mediates between the novelist and the reader and makes the rapport possible.

Both the novelist and reader are themselves products of a literary tradition which gives the capacity and training that the mind requires to absorb facts, realities and experiences which may not be part of the immediate milieu. Literacy increases the mobility of the individual mind by widening the individual's experience and his imaginative capacity to enter into new situations, or at least to envisage them with a fair degree of certainty. The introduction of literacy into West Africa therefore necessarily involved a profound change both in the traditional mode of acculturation and in the psychological outlook of the people. As David Riesman observed in *The Lonely Crowd*, literacy and written literature are potent factors in the shift from tradition-direction to inner-direction in the education of the individual...and in the shaping of individual attitudes and values.[3] Literacy increases individual awareness of separateness from the collectivity and increases the power to enter imaginatively into other individualities in a way not possible within the oral culture.

Before the introduction of Western literary education, African children were inducted into the traditional way of life in two ways: by formal teaching in initiation ceremonies, and by informal teaching in seeing and following the examples of grown-ups – through "watching and imitating" as Phoebe and Simon Ottenberg have called it. By participating in the everyday life of the community they came to know the rights and duties of the individual, the values, beliefs and mores of the community, the sanctions and etiquette of social behaviour; and in the same way they acquired a knowledge of the material repertoire of the culture. Cultural content and cultural behaviour were transmitted to the individual by contact and deliberate induction. Experience outside the immediate cultural environment was beyond individual apprehension because it was inaccessible to the individual through traditional education. The individual therefore tended to see the world in terms of his own circumscribed milieu, and to apprehend only those experiences which had been culturally determined for him. The chief effect of the introduction of Western education was to break the psychic insularity of traditional education and limited physical mobility, and to substitute for it a cosmopolitan and mobile psyche.

Through the introduction of literacy, the corpus of Western, indeed world civilization, its institutions and values, arts and sciences, philosophies and theology, its aesthetic values, and the artefacts of its material culture were made available to people in West Africa and, as James Coleman says, "awakened new aspirations, quickened the urge toward new emulation and provided the notions". Moreover, the use of a cosmopolitan language like English as a medium of instruction provides a vital link for West African peoples who speak different mother-tongues: this encourages greater physical mobility and consequently the broadening of their social as well as psychological outlook.

The introduction of Western education, the creation of Westernized urban settlements (as distinct from traditional urban settlements), and the establishment of a cash economy and modern industries opened new opportunities to the individual, and drew together people from different ethnic areas into urban aggregations. To fit into the economic scheme the individual had to acquire literacy, and through literacy some specialized skill or profession. The result was that he removed himself from a community where status and social hierarchy had determined the individual's place in society and where the individual counted in terms of the group to which he belonged, and entered a situation in which he was free to assert, if only in a limited way, his individuality. He thus predisposed himself to play a range of roles which did not exist in the traditional setting – roles depending on his level of education and professional training.

More important still, especially from the point of view of the novel, was that while following one skill or vocation the individual's broadened contact and multifarious attachments to others in different walks of life made him capable of envisaging himself imaginatively in any of the roles attached to the other professions and vocations. The school-teacher who can imagine himself as a daring leader of the underworld can, if he turns his mind to novel-writing and if he has the gifts of the novelist, be expected to explore the life of his hero with a reasonable degree of conviction; and his readers can be expected, if he has done his job competently and if they are sufficiently imaginative, to enter into the life and circumstances of the hero.

The significance of the development of greater physical and imaginative mobility for the emergence of the novel in West Africa can be seen by reference to the novelists themselves. We can take Achebe as an example. His first three novels deal with the impact of Western civilization on the traditional culture of Africa, seen in the life of two essentially traditional characters, Okonkwo (in *Things Fall Apart*) and Ezeulu (in *Arrow of God*), and the disintegrative forces of tradition and modernism on the character of a Western-educated Nigerian (*No Longer at Ease*). For all his middle-class educational background and upper-middle-class job, Achebe is able to enter imaginatively into the lives of his traditional characters and to explore the strains to which they are exposed as a result of the disruptive effect of a foreign culture on the relatively stable and self-sufficient culture they grew up in. His rural upbringing is an advantage in developing his peculiarly lucid insight into the predicament of his traditional characters, but he has never himself experienced the actual circumstances of Okonkwo or Ezeulu. His ability to portray them and their predicament convincingly shows his capability, extended by his literary education, which equips him to imagine people and circumstances in a historic setting, though the outline of that setting remains still visible. His Obi Okonkwo, though a graduate like himself, and a man of his own generation, is no self-portrait. Almost every point in Obi's life differs from Achebe's; that both of them have teacher–evangelist fathers is a coincidence. In the fourth novel, *A Man of the People*, we find a complex picture in which the point of view shifts rapidly between identification and dissociation, between the author's seeing things through the eye of the major character-narrator and standing aside to take a critical look at the narrator, a feat made possible by the author's imaginative nimbleness in moving between moral positions. For that reason the novel is a tribute to the kind of imaginative awareness which is the point and product of literary education. It follows the course of events so doggedly and intelligently in accordance with the truths of human and social behaviour that its fictional world and the world of conventional reality merge; the military *coup d'état* predicted in the novel actually happened while the novel was with the printers.

The multiplicity of imaginative detail, the social variety of the characters involved, the complexity and variety of personality involved, and the numerous hiatuses that have to be imaginatively overleaped between what is available in immediate experience and what must be anticipated, assumed or made up by the author, all these would have been too much to demand from the traditional imagination subsisting largely on the limited powers of the unaided memory and conditioned as it was by the orally transmitted knowledge of the group.

The spread of mass media

The broadening of empathetic power is also a function of mass communication. The media – newspapers, radio, television, cinema – also advance the process of modernization.

Through them the West African is made aware of "an infinite vicarious universe",[4] of diversity of peoples, climates and costumes, customs and manners, morals and values; diversity in all the things which compose a way of life. These media affect people in different ways according to the mode of appeal of each.

The function of the press in moulding opinion is too obvious to require comment. Access to the content of newspapers requires literacy. Apart from specialized articles, most of the content of newspapers is available to literate West Africans who have completed primary education. For those not literate in English there are vernacular newspapers. So the acquisition of literacy opens up for the individual this new way of absorbing ideas and of broadening his mind. He is exposed to a battery of fresh ideas through leading articles, readers' opinions and editorial comment. He is called upon to balance points of view, to sift evidence, to accept or reject opinions – in short to train his imagination to cope with situations within and sometimes outside his milieu, and to be involved in the lives and situations of other people. He is also introduced directly through advertising to the material repertoire of world industrial civilization.

The cinema, radio and, in recent times, television are accessible both to the literate and to the illiterate. Through suggestion they tend to affect the life-ways of traditional people and broaden their experience by introducing them to other ways of life. In West Africa, the mass media have disrupted the old social order and accelerated social change. They have rapidly expanded their audiences, and so their capacity for spreading new cultural influences is growing. Millions of people read English-language and vernacular newspapers, go to cinemas, listen to the radio and watch television; this is in stark contrast with the hundreds or the few thousands who once listened to the harangue of the "crier", or the smaller numbers in the country areas who spread "information" face to face. By extending cultural influence, especially by familiarizing the individual with different situations of life, by increasing his store of knowledge of material culture through their pictorial representation and by acquainting him with changes in the society in which he lives and the world outside it, the mass media have increased the individual's perceptive power, and could be said to have prepared the ground for the emergence of the novel.

The actual relationship between people working in the mass media and their audiences is not often direct or physical, but obviously the first group, by the very nature of their calling, must be interested in the lives and situations of their audience and are sometimes over-whelmingly tempted to explore them in a more intimate way through the medium of the novel. It is no coincidence that nearly all the West African novelists have at some time been involved in mass communications. Achebe was in broadcasting between 1954 and 1966, Ekwensi moved from broadcasting to the information service, Nwankwo was in *Drum* magazine before taking up radio work and later turned to newspaper work, Nzekwu was first a teacher and then went over to journalism, Gabriel Okara has been in the information service for the greater part of his working life, and Ayi Kwei Armah spent some time as a scriptwriter on Ghana Television.

The movement from mass communications to novel-writing is a natural one. The journalist, radio scriptwriter or announcer, film or television producer, in addition to his other functions, is an agent of change in the social system and in the personalities of his audience. As novelist he would be expected to explore characters in relation to social life. Having helped to direct change through the mass media and having an interest in human beings and social situations, the media man may find the novel suitable for a more direct and personal imaginative effort.

Ian Watt observes of Defoe and Richardson and their connection with the mass media of their time: "By virtue of their multifarious contacts with printing, bookselling and journal-ism,...they were in very direct contact with the new interests of the reading public."[5] Equally, the development of mass media in West Africa has helped to produce the kind of society in which the novel can subsist, and it had also provided the first group of West Africans whose contact with contemporary culture and people of different walks of life has qualified them to engage their creative energies in the exploration of character and society. Even novelists not directly concerned with mass communications are in touch with a cross-section of society or involved in the modernization process, and so they can feel the pulse of social and cultural movements among the population. Soyinka's work in the theatre and Amadi's and Conton's school-teaching gave them insight into cultural and human disposi-tions in the unfolding West African scene. In that regard, they are also exposed to the impulses that find creative outlet in the novel.

The literate middle class and the rise of the novel

Given the effect of literacy and the mass media in preparing the ground, psychologically and socially, for the emergence of the novel, it remains that the actual writing of novels tends to be confined to those who add a fairly high level of education to the basic intellectual sophistication needed to be able to cope with its technical demands. Just as the oral story-telling technique is acquired by constant attendance at story-telling sessions, that of the novel is likely to be achieved by a wide reading of novels and an understanding of the intricacies of characterization, plot, language, and social and psychological insight. The serious reading of novels in West Africa does not begin before the grammar school, so it follows that exposure to the novel takes place at that level of education, as is clearly borne out by the educational backgrounds of the novelists. Of the ten novelists whose works are studied here, all but two are university graduates, and those two have had full grammar school education or its equivalent. It is also no coincidence that all but one of the novelists were educated in the government colleges of Ibadan, Umuahia and Ughelli in Nigeria and Achimota in Ghana and at Fourah Bay College in Sierra Leone. These were the best secondary schools in English-speaking West Africa and provided the best education. They offered the best opportunities to the talented among them, preparing them for higher education and for their subsequent careers as writers. In other words the novelists belong to the cream of the modern educated West African middle class, the class that pioneered the novel in the other parts of the world. The story of the training of the literate middle class in West Africa can only be touched on here; but a few sentences are necessary to show the educational background and social circumstances which gave rise to the novel in West Africa.

Formal literary education was introduced in West Africa by the Christian missionaries, and was an offshoot of the evangelical and pietistic movement of late eighteenth- and early nineteenth-century Protestant Britain. The English philanthropists and abolitionists who between 1787 and 1800 encouraged the establishment of Freetown for freed African slaves also made sure that education and evangelization were focal points of the policy of those who ran the new settlement. From the first decade of the nineteenth century, elementary and grammar schools were set up in Freetown by various missionary bodies, and from the mid-nineteenth century elementary and grammar schools were established in such main coastal towns as Bathurst, Cape Coast, Accra and Lagos, as well as in Freetown. Wealthy education-conscious Africans in these coastal towns sent their children to school both locally and overseas, and these towns became centres of a small educated African elite of wealthy businessmen, lawyers, doctors, teachers, ministers of religion, architects and so on. Fourah Bay College, established in 1827, played an important role in the development of education both in Sierra Leone and all over West Africa.[6]

Education was utilitarian from the beginning. The spread of the Christian religion, the introduction of modern institutions and the running of modern government required a cadre of literate men and women. Education was therefore geared towards producing clerks, teachers, evangelists and artisans – personnel for the lower ranks of the civil service and commercial enterprises and for teaching and missionary work. The Sierra Leoneans and the Ghanaians, because they had an early start over the Nigerians, were recruited into Nigeria and became known as "native foreigners". Some of them rose to prominent posts in the colonial administration.

West African education was based on the educational system in English schools. Especially in Sierra Leone, where the Creoles were distinctly affected by the evangelical Christianity of their Methodist and Church Missionary Society emancipators and teachers, it was old-fashioned, classical and theological rather than practical and scientific. The Victorian partiality for black-coated callings – clerkships and teaching – and the professions dominated the aspirations of the early middle-class coastal elite. (They were called "Black Victorians" and "Black Englishmen" by West Africans of later generations.)

Between the second half of the nineteenth century and the 1930s, the literate middle class grew gradually and was constantly being reinforced by immigrants from the West Indies and Brazil. Its members formed a sub-cultural group who entertained one another in newspapers and in journals, pamphlets and public addresses couched in elaborate Victorian prose. They also staged operas and plays which they reviewed by stringent European standards. Evidence from the journals and newspapers shows that the Black Victorians, like their counterparts in the metropolis, were interested in culture as the expression of the people's historical and contemporary experience and as a scale for the evaluation of human achieve-ment, an unfortunate extension of scientific Darwinism into human institutions and cultures. Influenced by the climate of the time, some of the Black Victorians felt their traditional culture was of a lower order than the European culture and so strove to uphold the European and to show hostility towards the traditional culture. Others stood for African "authenticity" and preached the rehabilitation of African traditional culture in education and in creative art and literature.

Prominent among the supporters of the traditional culture were Dr Edward Wilmot Blyden, author of *Christianity, Islam and the Negro Race* (1888) and other polemical treatises against the anti-Negro philosophers of the nineteenth century, Dr Africanus Horton of Sierra Leone, an MD of Edinburgh University, who wrote *West African Countries and Peoples* (1868) and John Casely Hayford of Ghana who wrote *Gold Coast Native Institutions* and *Ethiopia Unbound: Studies in Race Emancipation* (1911). These were the pioneers of West Africa's cultural nationalism who spent their learning and intellectual energies in defence of the native heritage.

Below the highly educated gentlemen were the masses of less well-educated teachers, clerks and artisans, who could not share their elite culture and even satirized their Victorian tendencies by setting up anti-theatres like the Lagos "Melo Dramatic Society" which staged such plays as *Don't Use Big Words*. This was obviously a retaliation against the antitraditional snobbery of the elite, some of whose members referred to vernacular plays as "low forms of heathenism",[7] and to national costume as "a recurrence of primitive quasi-nudity".[8]

Some West Africans in the latter group began, with the active collaboration of the missionaries, to record local history and the customs of their peoples, to write grammars and dictionaries of the indigenous languages, and to record the oral tradition, sometimes in the vernacular and sometimes in English. The missionaries, as in Europe after the fall of the Roman Empire, had earlier converted the vernaculars into writing. There is a parallel between the entry of European literary forms into West Africa and the introduction of Graeco-Roman models into Anglo-Saxon Britain by Augustine and his missionaries fourteen centuries before.

It is natural to ask why the novel did not develop in West Africa until the mid-twentieth century, even though there had been this educated middle-class elite from the mid-nineteenth century. There may be many reasons: the most important only need be mentioned here. First, despite their knowledge of Tennyson, Milton and Aristotle (they quoted from them in their essays and polemics), the coastal intellectual elite were essentially cultural parasites, despised by the British, whose culture they were assiduously cultivating; in their turn they despised African culture, which they regarded as uncivilized. "Couriferism" – an uncritical imitation of Western customs[9] – was not conducive to creative confidence. Status-consciousness, another aspect of their Victorian outlook, also inhibited literary creativity. The Black Victorians were keenly attached to the sedate and "respectable" professions, such as medicine, law and the Christian ministry; so far as literary interests were concerned, they shared the puritan suspicion of fiction as ineffectual, frivolous, even morally subversive. They never went beyond genteel literary activities such as writing journals, newspapers, diaries, polemical pamphlets and amateur anthropological mono-graphs. At the lower level, "passing my Cantab" and the pressure to work for a certificate, a necessary passport to good employment, narrowed the scope of reading too much to allow for adequate cultivation of a distinct literary taste, one obvious prerequisite for the cultivation of the creative habit. Finally, the educated middle class was too small to offer a would-be novelist a large enough potential audience. All in all, the social, psychological, cultural and educational conditions for the novel did not exist until the 1950s, but events were beginning to move towards it in the thirties.

[. . .]

Notes and References

1   E. N. Obiechina, "Growth of Written Literature in English-Speaking West Africa", *Présence Africaine* (Paris, 1968), pp. 58–78.

2   E. M. Forster, *Aspects of the Novel*, p. 9; H. I. Chaytor, *From Script to Print*, p. 4.

3   See especially pp. 87–94.

4   Daniel Lerner, *The Passing of Traditional Society*, pp. 52–3.

5   *The Rise of the Novel*, p. 59.

6   See Helen Kitchen (ed.), *The Educated African*; A. I. Porter, "The Formation of Elites in West Africa" in W. von Fröhlich (ed.), *Africa im Wandel seiner Gesellschaftsformen*; J. F. A. Ajayi, *Christian Missions in Nigeria*; Sir Eric Ashby, *African Universities and Western Tradition* and Nduka Okafor, *The Development of Universities in Nigeria*.

7   *The Lagos Observer*, 18 January 1883.

8   *The Lagos Observer*, 22 June 1889.

9   "Mr. Courifer", a short story by Adelaide Casely Hayford, in Langston Hughes (ed.), *An African Treasury*, p. 135.

Chapter 45

Languages of the Novel:
A Lover's Reflections

André Brink

[...]

2

When on the threshold of our century the Age of Realism drew to a close and Modernism was born, mankind, as Santayana phrased it, "started dreaming in a different key." And the key to that dreaming meant, for the arts, a widespread discovery – or, in some cases, rediscovery – of the medium as the message. From Cézanne onwards, painting turns its back on a long tradition of "truth to nature" as it begins to focus on the materiality of paint on canvas. The theater renounces its earlier attempts to create the perfect illusion and in the plays of Pirandello and his contemporaries embraces the space of the stage as stage (which to Shakespeare would have been nothing new). In Stravinsky, and even more so in Schönberg, music is no longer to be enjoyed simply as a melodic system but turns its attention to the very processes which *produce* melody.

Likewise, literature also begins to foreground its own medium, language, first in the poetry of Mallarmé and Rimbaud, and the fiction of Flaubert and Henry James. Soon, from their ranks, rose the definitive figure of James Joyce. And what Joyce is concerned with, most particularly in *Ulysses* and *Finnegans Wake*, is "not with representing experience through language but with experiencing language through a destruction of representation" (Mac-Cabe 1978:4). Not that one should ever underestimate the "story" level in these novels: purely in terms of an old-fashioned "plot" they are among the richest texts in the genre. But ultimately all these various stories collapse, like old stars into a black hole, within the language in which they are told. Language becomes its own greatest story.

But is this really as new as it sounds?

First published in *New England Review* 19.3 (Summer 1998), 5–17.

3

Our response may borrow from the experience of painters and their public in the second half of the nineteenth century when the rise of photography caused great turmoil in the field of art: there were painters who renounced their métier because photography appeared to have taken over what many artists, for a very long time, had come to regard as the prerogative of *their* art: the faithful visual representation of nature (or of history; or of dreams, or whatever). But there were others to whom the experience was truly liberating, as they discovered – or rediscovered – that the primary business of painting had *never* been visual representation as such but, instead, the exploitation of all the possibilities available in the process of bringing paint and canvas together. From the passionate immersion of the Impressionists in the here-and-now of the fleeting instant which they attempted to translate into brush-strokes and daubs of paint, arose the acknowledgment that even in the most "realistic" periods of painting the artist's true vocation had always been an involvement with his/her material. This had been as true of Corot as of Rembrandt; as true of Jan Steen as of Bosch, or in fact of Zeuxis (whose painting of grapes, it is said, was so true to life that birds came to peck at it).

This does not mean that these artists as individuals were necessarily conscious of it: but *painting* was aware of it, as it pursued the never-ending dialogue between pigments of different kinds on surfaces of different kinds. The final confirmation of the discovery, if confirmation was still required, came with the shock provided by artists like Mondrian, Malevitch, and Kandinsky in their "abstract art" – which was arguably the most "concrete" form of painting the world had seen up to that point, confronting the viewer with the unmediated reality of paint as paint, the whole of paint, and nothing but paint.

And it is my argument that the same may be said of language and the novel. It is in narrative language, I believe, that one should look for the key to the full experience of engaging with the genre. One is reminded of Magritte's famous painting of a pipe bearing the title *Ceci n'est pas une pipe – This is not a pipe*, which is, of course, strictly true: what we have before us is not a pipe but a painting of a pipe. This can be confirmed, in the domain of literature, by any reader who takes up a book to make the simple but immensely significant discovery that there are no people or houses or trees or dog shit between the pages but, as Hamlet would have said, only words, words, words. And not just words but written – *printed* – words.

Unlike "a piece of clay [which] on its own *has no meaning*," as Bakhtin explains (in Shukman 1983:94) language uses a unique signifying system, which imposes a peculiar interaction between *what* is said and *how* it is said, between medium and message. More than has ever been the case in oral literature, language in the novel exists "neither before the fact nor after the fact but in the fact" (Ashcroft etc. 1989:44). It does not only tell a story, but reflects on itself in the act of telling.

If this is true of those great fanfares and fun-fairs of novels written by Rabelais, Cervantes, or Sterne, finally to erupt in Joyce and his successors, it is my argument that this is *no less true* of even the most "classical" or "traditional" or "realistic" of novels, whether by Defoe, or Marivaux, or Jane Austen, or Stendhal, or Manzoni, or Zola.

4

The remarkable shifts in language theory in the twentieth century made it possible for the novel to dramatize and exploit its relationship with language much more self-consciously than ever before. After all, postmodernism in literature is as much the outcome of developments within literature as within our perception of language – and this goes back to the early years of the century, when the traditional view of language as "re-presenting" reality (whatever "reality" might have meant in any given context) was first problematized.

Heidegger still remains quite close to the more traditional view of language, but at the same time he destabilizes the received wisdom by introducing a separation between word and world:

> When we go to the well, when we go through the woods, we are always already going through the word "well," through the word "woods," even if we do not speak the words and do not think of anything relating to language. (Heidegger 1971:52)

With Ferdinand de Saussure we cross the threshold into the domain of language as part of a social and cultural contract by approaching it, not as a metaphysical truth but as a system of signs based on notions of *difference* rather than *correspondence*. These signs, as we all know by now, do not function by virtue of the "presence" of a meaning trapped in them, but merely the absence of other meanings: cat "means" "cat" only because in a given linguistic situation it is *not* a hat or a mat, or a plucked green chicken.

Wittgenstein extends these perceptions to the quite radical view that reality itself, and our whole experience of it, is shaped and determined by the language in which we conceive it. It is summarized in perhaps the most famous statement of his *Tractatus* (1983:151): "The limits of the language [. . .] mean the limits of *my* world." In such a view the traditional notion of "referentiality" falls away entirely: language can no longer refer to something "out there" but, at most, only to itself.

The most radical innovator, and of pervasive importance for the discussion to follow, has undoubtedly been Jacques Derrida. In his view of the endless intertextuality of our world an extreme in our twentieth century's perception of language is reached. What we encounter here is the exuberant subversion of a logocentric world, replacing the authority, the presence and the hierarchies of speech with the absences and *traces* of writing, floating signifiers within a boundless process of dissemination, pointing towards endlessly displaced, deferred, and different meanings and supplements to meaning, a palimpsest in which earlier or alternative meanings are never completely obliterated.

These deep-seated suspicions about language also permeate, in quite different ways, the thinking of Lacan and Foucault. In Lacan the marker of unreliability in language is its inherent "otherness," the fact that it is by definition the language of *others*, primarily of the oppressive Father and his Symbolic Order – a language always already shopsoiled in the mouths of others. It reverberates with Rimbaud's famous utterance: "*Je est un autre* – I is another."

For Foucault, too, a point of departure is the awareness that "the relation of the sign to its content is not guaranteed by the order of things in themselves" (Foucault 1970:63). Taken to an extreme, he arrives at a view of literature as a manifestation of a language which has no other law than that of affirming – in opposition to all other forms of discourse – its own precipitous existence and so there is nothing for it to do but to curve back in a perpetual return upon itself [. . . .] (Foucault 1970:330)

To place it in a slightly different context: Hofstadter (1980:30) quotes a Zen koan concerning two monks arguing about a flag fluttering in the wind. The first insists that the flag is moving, the other that it is the wind. Finally a patriarch arrives and says, "Not the wind, not the flag; mind is moving." In our reading of novels the conclusive remark would be, "Not the flag, not the wind; language is moving."

5

It is in the novel, more acutely than in any other genre, that we are confronted with "the major and crucial fates of literature and language." These are Bakhtin's words (1981:8), and I admit happily that more than any other writer he has influenced my perception of the dialogic nature of language, and the heteroglossia, "the multi-tongued consciousness" (ibid: 11), at work in the novel. His concept of languages in the novel is not quite identical, however, with my use of the term. Bakhtin has in mind the actual plurality of language forms activated in any novel: "territorial dialects, social and professional dialects and jargons, literary language, generic languages within literary language, epochs in language and so forth" (ibid:12) – whereas my own interest is more the *notion* or *concept* of language as a system, as a phenomenon, as a practice, as a process, in every novel we read. My premise is not so much the materiality of the languages at work in a text as *the way in which a particular view and concept of language is demonstrated implicitly or explicitly in the text*. What makes this so fascinating is that it seems to me to hold true, not only of postmodernist texts where self-consciousness has become an accepted part of the package, but even of the most "trad-itionalist" or "realist" novels, as I shall try to show. And this, it seems to me, may open up new dimensions to our enjoyment of the text.
[. . .]

8

At this point, if I may, I'd like to offer a few observations about developments associated with the colonial and postcolonial novel. In Conrad's *Heart of Darkness*, perhaps the most controversial colonial novel ever written, many critics have deplored the writer's inability to resolve ambiguity and come to terms with the indescribable. But surely, not the *nature* of the indescribable, but the futile and doomed "attempts" to describe it, are the focus of Conrad's entire narrative enterprise.

Conrad's text becomes a dramatic demonstration of the *limits* of conventional (imperial) language when faced with the Unknown or the (colonial) Other. Most specifically it concerns the language of his narrator, Marlow: the language of a worldly-wise and world-weary sailor, a male, a cynical and opportunistic agent in the imperial system. By extension it may become the language of this system, of the European mind at the end of the nineteenth century. By further extension, read at the end of the twentieth century, it may involve the entire logocentric mentality faced with an experience that lies beyond its customary horizon.

The African continent is described as a system of empty signifiers still to be filled:

> There it is before you – smiling, frowning, inviting, grand, mean, insipid, or savage, and always mute with an air of whispering. Come and find out. This one was almost featureless, as if still in the making. (p. 39)

This is Marlow's first attempt to say the unsayable, and very obviously he is proposing *his* terminology as an explicitly futile attempt to fill the blank/silence of the signifiers of the Other. There is, at most, an intimation of whispering: that is, of what Barthes would call *le bruissement de la langue*, the "rustle" or the "hum" of language. It suggests a key to that most urgent problematic of postcolonial writing: "the question of how the third-world subject is represented within Western discourse" (Spivak 1988:271), the confusion of "Them as Us," the difficulties and dangers of "taming the subject" raised by the question, "Can the Subaltern Speak?" (Spivak 1988:306).

In the heart of the heart of darkness lurks Kurtz. And it is evidence of Conrad's consummate insight that at the very moment when the reader is brought to the threshold of a confrontation with Kurtz himself, not only the story, but grammar itself, breaks down:

> I was cut to the quick at the idea of having lost the inestimable privilege of listening to the gifted Kurtz. Of course I was wrong. The privilege was waiting for me. Oh, yes, I heard more than enough. And I was right too. A voice. He was very little more than a voice. And I heard – him – it – this voice – other voices – all of them were so little more than voices – and the memory of that time itself lingers around me, impalpable, like a dying vibration of one immense jabber, silly, atrocious, sordid, savage, or simply mean, without any kind of sense. Voices, voices – even the girl herself – now. (p. 84)

The grand rhetorical gesture ("inestimable privilege," "impalpable," "dying vibration") falters as the narrator resorts desperately to one inadequate adjective after the other ("silly," "atrocious," "sordid," "savage," "mean"); the syntax becomes disjointed and the semantic load of the sentence grows unmanageable. And in the incoherent jabbering of the last words we encounter a wholly unexpected figure who has not yet surfaced in the text but who is to become both "the heart of the matter" and "the end of the affair": "the girl herself." There is, sadly, no time to explore this further: enough to say that the dimension of femininity, evoked by "the girl," in the heart of the male imperial world, radically changes the tenor of the whole story; and that it is the breakdown of male language which creates the opening for suppressed femininity to assert itself, is a stroke of genius.

It is significant that in one of her most important postcolonial novels, *July's People*, Nadine Gordimer also represents the breakdown of white and male language when, as refugees with the black man who used to be their house servant, Maureen Smales and her family discover that "they [are] blocked by an old vocabulary" (p. 127) and that the whole complicated terror contained in the oppression of apartheid is encapsulated in unresolved collisions of "language" (in the widest possible sense of the term). And here, too, there is a pointer towards the language of femininity as the starting point of possible renewal.

In Margaret Atwood's remarkable postcolonial novel *Surfacing* this is restated with a variety of new facets as the (significantly nameless) narrator, doubly colonized as woman and as Canadian, finds herself between the states of the Imaginary Order and the Symbolic Order of the Father, agonizing about language which is always, inevitably, the language of others, which means that her very identity is threatened from the moment she says, "I am." The problem this poses for the novel is to say in language what, per definition, language cannot say. What makes it a tour de force is that her pyrrhic victory encompasses both the affirmation and the denial of human language.

9

Language thus embodies all the great moral and gender and philosophical and, in fact, physical issues humanity has been grappling with throughout its history. But what makes the novel such an amazingly versatile form is its capacity to undertake such explorations in a ludic mode, as Kundera would have it. And in the modernist and postmodernist novel this dimension is highlighted more explicitly than ever before (which is one reason, apart from time constraints, why I do not propose to explore it here): ranging from the presentation of language as a room without a view in Kafka's *The Trial* to language as a gap through which reality escapes in Robbe-Grillet's *Le Voyeur*; or from cyclic language as a process of "making and unmaking" in Marquez's *One Hundred Years of Solitude*, to language as seduction and disillusionment in Nabokov's *Lolita*, to language as quest in Calvino's *If on a Winter's Night a Traveller*, there is a sense of carnivalesque enjoyment in the pyrotechnical properties of language-as-narrative. This is perhaps best expressed in a delightful passage from Elizondo's *The Graphographer* which Mario Vargas Llosa uses as his epigraph in *Aunt Julia and the Scriptwriter*, with which I conclude:

> I write. I write that I am writing. Mentally I see myself writing that I am writing and I can also see myself seeing that I am writing. I remember writing and also seeing myself writing. And I see myself remembering that I see myself writing and I remember seeing myself remembering that I was writing and I write seeing myself write that I remember having seen myself write that I saw myself writing that I was writing and that I was writing that I was writing that I was writing. I can also imagine myself writing that I had already written that I would imagine myself writing that I had written that I was imagining myself writing that I see myself writing that I am writing.

Ceci n'est vraiment pas une pipe.

References

Ashcroft, Bill, Griffiths, Gareth and Tiffin, Helen 1989: *The Empire Writes Back*. London and New York: Routledge.

Atwood, Margaret 1995 (1972): *Surfacing*. London: Virago.

Bakhtin, M. M. (ed. Michael Holquist) 1981. *The Dialogic Imagination*. Austin: University of Texas Press.

Barthes, Roland (trans. Richard Miller) 1975 (1970): *S/Z*. London: Jonathan Cape.

Cervantes de Saavedra, Miguel de (trans. J. M. Cohen) 1950 (1605, 1615): *The Adventures of Don Quixote de la Mancha*. Harmondsworth: Penguin.

Conrad, Joseph 1985 (1902): *Heart of Darkness*. Harmondsworth: Penguin.

Flaubert, Gustave 1951 (1957): *Madame Bovary.* In: *Ocuvres* (ed. A. Thibaudet and R. Dumesnil). Paris: Collection de la Pléiade, Gallimard.

Foucault, Michel 1970 (1966): *The Order of Things*. London: Tavistock Publications.

Foucault, Michel 1985 (1965): *Madness and Civilisation*. London: Tavistock.

Fuentes, Carlos 1990 (1988): *Myself With Others*. New York: Noonday Press (Farrar, Strauss & Giroux).

Gordimer, Nadine 1980: *July's People*. London: Jonathan Cape.

Heidegger, Martin (trans. Hofstadter, Albert) 1971: *Poetry, Language, Thought*. New York: Harper & Row.

Hofstadter, Douglas R. 1980: *Gödel, Escher, Bach: An Eternal Golden Braid*. London etc.: Penguin.

Llosa, Mario Vargas 1982 (1977): *Aunt Julia and the Scriptwriter*. London and Boston: Faber & Faber.

Shukman, Ann (ed.) 1983: *Bakhtin School Papers. Russian Poetics in Translation No. 10*. Oxford: of Essex/ Holdan Books.

Spivak, Gayatri Chakravorty 1988: Can the Subaltern Speak? In: Nelson, Cary and Grossberg, Lawrence (eds.) *Marxism and the Interpretation of Culture*. London: Macmillan.

Todorov, Tzvetan 1977: *The Poetics of Prose*. Oxford, Blackwell.

Chapter 46

Realism and Naturalism
in African Fiction

Neil Lazarus

[. . .]

In radical African literary theory, as in its orthodox counterpart (although for different reasons), the apparently natural priority of realism is very largely taken for granted.[1] A good example of this privileging in operation is to be found in a recent article, "The Rediscovery of the Ordinary," by the South African writer and critic Njabulo Ndebele.[2] Despite its lavish use of Roland Barthes' *Mythologies*, Ndebele's essay is profoundly un-Barthesian in its retrieval and valorization of the critical ethic of realism. Setting out to discuss recent tendencies in black South African fiction, it builds its argument upon a primary distinction between two narrative modes: a first, that "merely reflect[s] the situation of oppression . . . merely document[s] it"; and a second, that "offers methods for [this situation's] redemptive transformation."[3] The former mode, which Ndebele labels "the spectacular," tends to convey the impression that circumstances are bleak and unalterable. It depicts the powerless in their powerlessness, as believing that "their situation seems hopeless."[4] The cardinal registers of "the spectacular" are, accordingly, moralism and self-pity. The second mode, by contrast, "the ordinary," is dynamic and disclosive. It goes "beyond spectacle in order to reveal the necessary knowledge of actual reality so that we can purposefully deal with it."[5] It is an analytical mode, not a documentary one, concerned to portray and not merely to report.

We may not recognize the terms "spectacular" and "ordinary," but we certainly recognize their dimensions and effectivities. In "The Rediscovery of the Ordinary," Ndebele has "rediscovered," not the ordinary, but Georg Lukacs' classic distinction between realism and naturalism. Basing himself on Engels' celebrated characterization of realism as implying, "beside truth of detail, the truth in reproduction of typical characters under typical circumstances,"[6] Lukacs, it will be recalled, had moved to define realism as the progressive avatar of truth in post-feudal (capitalist and socialist) art – an aesthetic mode uniquely sensitive to and expressive of the movement of history. Realism, in these terms, was to be

First published in *Critical Exchange* 22 (Spring 1987), 55–62.

distinguished from naturalism, which, in its concern to replicate the look – the "spectacle" – of everyday life, fetishized it, mistaking its surface for its deep meaning. Lukacs was far from being dismissive of the ideological aspirations of naturalism, which he saw as stemming from the oppositionality of a sector of the petit-bourgeoisie. Oppositional writers from this class fraction, "who stood in greater or lesser proximity to the workers' movement"[7] attempted to express their radicalism in their work through objective representation of "the most crying abuses and grievances"[8] within capitalist society. As such, Lukacs argued, naturalism was to be faulted less for its intentions than for its execution of them. For in representing the blunt facts of social life, the naturalists lost sight of the social meaning of these facts. Their failure, accordingly, was a failure to render society in its totality, as a contradictory unity. In naturalism, Lukacs wrote, there was a "weakening of the relation between ideological principle and individual fact.... Bourgeois naturalism expressed the bourgeois writers' bafflement, his inability to discover a rational pattern in the multiplicity of facts."[9] The most significant narrative consequences of this inability were a determinate incapacity to grasp what Lukacs termed "the 'slyness' of reality,"[10] its overdetermined potentiality, on the one hand, and a tendency to represent society, as constituted, in its violence and enormity, as unalterable, on the other. Thus it is that we find Lukacs drawing attention, time and again, to the *defeatism* of naturalism, a defeatism whose ideological symptomaticity is not only, in the final analysis, reactionary, but also profoundly different from that disclosed in realist art. In his famous essay, "Reportage or Portrayal," for example, Lukacs addressed the question of naturalism's defeatism in these terms:

> [In naturalism] the exposure of the bourgeoisie's repressive apparatus, which is made with good revolutionary intent, is given a false emphasis politically. It appears all-powerful and invincible. What is missing is the struggle and resistance of the working class. The proletariat is depicted as the impotent object of the judicial system. Indeed, in most cases what we see are not the genuine representatives of the class, but rather characters who have already been worn down and had the life beaten out of them, people incapable of resistance who have fallen into the lumpen-proletariat.[11]

To turn from this formulation to the field of African literature is immediately, one might suppose, to be able to discriminate between a novel like Ngugi's *Petals of Blood* and another Kenyan work, *Going Down River Road*, by Meja Mwangi. And indeed, such Lukacsian discriminations have often been made. In them, predictably, *Petals of Blood* is celebrated as an example of socialist realism and *Going Down River Road* is castigated for its objectivism, which is read as politically retrograde. The question here, however, is whether this sort of reading is adequate to its object: can the discourse of naturalism in African literature be theorized in Lukacsian terms as a degraded form, one whose effective politicality emerges as contrary to its radical intent?[12]

At first glance, and looking at *Petals of Blood* and *Going Down River Road*, it might seem that it can. Certainly, the conclusions of the two novels can be taken to support a Lukacsian reading. *Petals of Blood*, the realist text, ends with an explicit evocation of the vigor and purpose of working-class militancy as Karega, its protagonist, a trade union activist, looks forward to the day when "it would be the workers and the peasants leading the struggle and seizing power to overturn the system ... bringing to an end the reign of the few over the many... Then, only then, would the kingdom of man and woman really begin, they joying and loving in creative labour."[13] Possessed of this happy vision, he glories in the political awareness that "he was no longer alone."[14] *Going Down River Road*, by contrast, ends much as it had begun, in the squalor of a Nairobi slum. It is true that there is here, too, a coming together of sorts, but it is a coming together of Ben and Ocholla, two isolated and dissolute slum-dwellers, and it bespeaks nothing more than a mutual desire on each of their parts for comradeship in the face of overwhelming deprivation. Also seeming to substantiate the Lukacsian categorization is the fact that while Ngugi's narrative never ceases to remind us of the transformability of existing conditions, Mwangi's seems to place these conditions as irremediable, as when he speaks of the march of laborers to work every morning as "the endless routine trudge, the tramp of the damned at the Persian wheel."[15]

Yet to appropriate *Going Down River Road* as a naturalist text in the Lukacsian sense would be to misrepresent it fundamentally. It is not only that Mwangi's novel is altogether free of the moralism that Lukacs and, following him, Ndebele, claimed to be able to discern in all naturalist work. The truth is, rather, that in its defiant embrace of a naturalistic code that is not fatalistic, Mwangi's text is subversive of the totalizing, rationalistic progressivism upon which the discourse of realism as Lukacs theorizes it and Ngugi practises it ultimately rests. What is evoked for us in *Going Down River Road* is the prospect of an oppositional politics whose content, unspecifiable in advance, will yet not be reducible to the centering categories, chiefly of class and nation, that inform a work like *Petals of Blood*. It is the indeterminacy of the political action to which it points – an indeterminacy of "how" and "when" and "where," though not of "if" – that makes for the radicalism of Mwangi's novel. In this ideological respect – though not in respect of form – it closely resembles Ayi Kwei Armah's *The Beautyful Ones Are Not Yet Born*. The spectral promise of insurrection haunts the margins of *Going Down River Road*. "*If you hold down one thing you hold down the adjoining*" Salman Rushdie observes in his novel, *Shame*. "In the end, though, it all blows up in your face."[16] In these terms, Mwangi's achievement may be said to consist in showing us characters being held down by the scamless web of oppression. The future explosion is then latent in his figuration of a resilience that is negative, contentless, illustrative only of sheer resistance:

> [Ocholla] leads Ben into an alleyway, past a heap of excrement, Ben wonders who squats here and when. They emerge in a dark back street that smells of dust though it is wet. This leads into another lane that in turn vomits them into River Road. The place is crowded with its usual mass of haunted, hungry faces, poverty-hypnotised faces, hateful faces, and fragrant stink of un-washed bodies and burst sewers. Though most shops are closed down, the ghostly wanderers are still here. This is one place where there will still be people left after doomsday. They have survived repeated police clean ups. They can take anything.[17]

Two points of emphasis need to be drawn here, in conclusion. The first of these is negative, the second positive. Negatively, then, it seems to me that we must insist that the new naturalism in African fiction – represented by such writers as Mwangi, Dambudzo Marechera, and Mongane Serote – cannot adequately be addressed through a critical lens that has been tuned, through frequent usage over the years, to see in a naturalist narrative only a localistic welter of abstract facts straining towards but failing to reach their social truth. The short stories that Bessie Head writes in the naturalist idiom, for instance, in their implicit utopianism, their pragmatism, and their sensitivity to the materiality of everyday existence in the rural villages of Botswana that constitute their field of action, simply render inapplicable the conventional radical commentary on naturalism.

The mention of Bessie Head here enables us, moreover, to turn to the second of our two points of emphasis – the positive one. For Head's work does not simply retrieve the cogency of *naturalism* as a narrative idiom, it also actively throws into question the acceptability of *realism*. On the level of form, it does so through its problematization of the transparency of representation, a strategy whose significance those of us who have taken the thrust of post-structuralism's critiques of realism can readily appreciate. Yet it is on the level of content, through its disavowal of the progressivist ideologies that sustain realism as a discourse, that the radicalism of Head's challenge to the credentials of realism becomes full apparent. In "Critical Realism and Socialist Realism," Lukacs had argued that "the great works of realist art are a main factor in creating the intellectual and spiritual climate which gives human personality its specifically national character."[18] Of great interest here is the contention that the discourses of realism and nationalism cannot be separated, either historically or aesthetically. The contention might be extended still further: realism is necessarily aligned, not only with nationalism, but with all the other totalizing collectivities implicated in and by capitalist social existence. Among these latter, as Jean Baudrillard has so outrageously suggested, would have to be included Marxism: not without cause did Engels observe, in a famous utterance, that the German workers' movement was the heir to classical bourgeois philosophy. The significance of Head's work, in these terms – and the significance, I would argue, of naturalist writing in Africa today in general – is that, although it refuses to relinquish its radicalism, its commitment to a transindividual utopia, it is resolutely opposed to the totalizing collectivities affirmed by realism, viewing these as dominative, as alternative hegemonies rather than counter-hegemonies, to use Raymond Williams' valuable distinction.[19] In rejecting these progressivistic discourses, naturalism rejects also the master narrative of realism, which renders them. In this respect, it rejoins the critique of realism articulated in other Third World literatures. From quite different directions, thus, the project of Bessie Head's fiction may ultimately be said to emerge as consonant with that of writers like Gabriel Garcia Marquez and Salman Rushdie.

Neil Lazarus

Notes

1 One of the very few critical reflections on realism as a narrative mode in African fiction is to be found in Gerald Moore's *Twelve African Writers* (Bloomington: Indiana University Press, 1980), pp. 12–15.

2 Njabulo Ndebele, "The Rediscovery of the Ordinary: Some New Writings in South Africa," *Journal of Southern African Studies*, 12, (April 1986), 143–57.

3 Ibid., 151.

4 Ibid., 152.

5 Ibid.

6 Engels, quoted in Georg Lukacs, "Roportage or Portrayal," in *Essays on Realism*, trans. David Fernbach (Cambridge: The MIT Press, 1981), p. 52.

7 Ibid., p. 48.

8 Ibid.

9   Georg Lukacs, "Critical Realism and Socialist Realism," in *The Meaning of Contemporary Realism*, trans. John and Necke Mander (London: Merlin Press, 1977), p. 119.

10 Ibid., p. 125.

11 "Reportage or Portrayal," p. 54.

12 A cautionary note on terminology might be in order here. Lukacs defines naturalism negatively, in opposition to his prior categorization of realism. The opposition is thus formal and diacritically derived. In following Lukacs here, I am not suggesting that we blind ourselves to the problems that attend his conceptualizations of realism and naturalism. On the contrary, the rationalism and expressivism of these conceptualizations plainly stand in need of critique. In the present context, however, I am more concerned with the consequences of a direct transposition of Lukacs' ideological reading of naturalism to the universe of African literature than with the admittedly more fundamental question of the philosophical cogency of his theory.

13 Ngugi wa Thiong'O, *Petals of Blood* (London: Heinemann Educational Books, 1977), p. 344.

14 Ibid., p. 345.

15 Meja Mwangi, *Going Down River Road* (London: Heinemann Educational Books, 1980), p. 6.

16 Salman Rushdie, *Sharne* (New York: Alfred A. Knopf, 1983), p. 189.

17 *Going Down River Road*, p. 57.

18 "Critical Realism and Socialist Realism," p. 103.

19 Raymond Williams, *Marxism and Literature* (Oxford: Oxford University Press, 1977), pp. 12–13. The ideological status of nationalism in the Third World is currently the subject of considerable debate. In his recent article, "Third-World Literature in the Era of Multinational Capitalism," Fredric Jameson attempts to weigh the implications of this debate. His resolution, however, seems to me insufficiently motivated. Jameson is sensitive to the charge that nationalism might represent an alternative hegemonic as distinct from a counter-hegemonic tendency: "one cannot," he observes, "acknowledge the justice of the general poststructuralist assault on the so-called 'centered subject,' the old unified ego of bourgeois individualism, and then resuscitate this same ideological mirage of psychic unification on the collective level in the form of a doctrine of collective identity" ("Third-World Literature in the Era of Mulinational Capitalism," *Social Text*, 15, (Fall 1986), 78). Yet in his article Jameson moves to define all Third-World texts as, necessarily, "national allegories." It is not only that the texts he refers to (and there are very few of them) constitute a suspiciously selective sample. Rather, he provides no reasons for overruling his own caution, besides the less-than-convincing suggestion that since "a certain nationalism is fundamental in the third world," it becomes "legitimate to ask whether it is all that bad in the end" (65).

Chapter 47

"Who Am I?":
Fact and Fiction in African First-Person Narrative

Mineke Schipper

[...]

My specific intention here is to discuss the first-person narrative form, its main genres and various techniques, as they are used in African literature. Not all the genres I am dealing with are fictional: the autobiography for instance is not, or at least is supposed not, to be fictional.

If we look first of all at the oral tradition, we could say that all oral literature is told in the first person, since, inevitably, the narrator himself is presenting his story to the audience which is on the spot. It is important to distinguish clearly between the *real author* who presents the "text" orally or in print, and the *narrator* who belongs to the text as a narrative transaction. At the other end of the communication line there are the *narratee* and the *real reader*. The narratee "is the agent which is at the very least implicitly addressed by the narrator. A narratee of this kind is always implied, even when the narrator becomes his own narratee".[1] An example of the latter is the diary novel. This may be schematized as follows:

TEXT

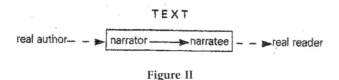

Figure II

We can even go a step further and say that the real author is always a first-person "agent", whether announcing orally "I am going to tell you ..." or, silently, in the written form, transmitting his text in book form as a gesture of "I am herewith presenting you my

First published in *Research in African Literatures* 16.1 (Spring 1985): 53–79; and subsequently in *Beyond the Boundaries: African Literature and Literary Theory*, pp. 102–14. London: W. H. Allen & Co., 1989.

story...". In both cases the text (the "message") can be presented either in the first or in the third person or, although that is much less common, in the second person. I propose that we leave the oral or written "I am going to present you my story" outside the literary texts we are to study here.[2]

The "frontiers" of the oral text are often marked by means of special formulas or expressions which emphasize the real beginning of the narrative: "Here comes my story"; "Once, long ago"; "How did it happen?"; and so forth. The same is true of the end: "This was the story of hare and leopard" or "This is the end, not of me but of my story".[3]

The first-person presentation by the author is normally lacking in written narrative because the beginning and end of the printed texts make themselves clear without further notice. Thus the written text starts, hierarchically speaking, on the next level, the textual narrative level. The author's explicit "here comes my story" is felt as superfluous and is therefore omitted, but formally the I of the author lies behind every text. A distinction should be made between this "I" and the introduction of "the author" as a literary device *within* the text by writers, as for instance Fagunwa does when he presents his stories in *The Forest of a Thousand Daemons*. He starts his first chapter under the heading: "The Author Meets Akara-Ogun". The latter is presented as the narrator-hero of the story, who dictates it to "the Author":

> When he had spoken thus I hurried to fetch my writing things, brought them over to my table, settled myself in comfort, and let the stranger know that I was now prepared for his tale. And he began in the words that follow to tell me the story of his life.[4]

In the text itself, the real author should not be confused with the narrator, although they may be synonymous and coincide with the main character, as in the case of autobiographical writing. In the terms of Gérard Genette, one could say that a narrator who is "above" or superior to the story he tells, should be called an "extradiegetic" narrator (*diegesis* meaning the story) if he belongs only to the narrative level and does not participate in the story as a character. He is to be called an "intradiegetic" narrator if he also participates in the presented story as a character.[5] This is the case with "the Author" in Fagunwa's *Forest of a Thousand Daemons*: the narrator-character tells how he starts writing down Akara-Ogun's adventures. These adventures are told to him by Akara-Ogun who is himself the hero on the next level. Thus we find a narrator-character's presentation of a whole series of embedded stories in which the second narrator is the main character. At the end of each chapter the

Fagunwa writes:	I First narrative level: "the Author" tells about meeting Akara-Ogun eho introduces ll	ll sec. narraative level: Akara-Ogun's (= hero's)[1] adventures	I First narrative level: "the Author" becomes narrator again: back to the "embedding" first level

Figure III

narrator of the first level "takes over" again and switches back to the frame of the first level narrative (see fig. III):

There are different types of narrators. The narrator is a device, a construction which is there to serve the specific needs of narration in a particular text. The first-person narrative can be presented in such different forms as a letter, an epistolary novel, a real or a fictional diary, an autobiography and many mixed or in-between forms. The narrator is an agent of the text which can be identical with the real author (as in the autobiography, for instance) or fictional.

The hierarchy of narrative levels can be used by the author in various ways. In the case of Fagunwa, it is clear that the use of the first narrator serves as a narrative framework only to present the character who is going to tell another (= the main) story consisting of the series of adventures. The latter is an inner narrative which is subordinate to the first-level narrative in which it is embedded. The function of the embedded narrative in this case is a *function of action*.

The embedded narrative may also have other functions, for example *an explicative function*, like in Achebe's *Things Fall Apart* (p. 72), answering a question of the first level by telling a second story on a "lower" level ("hypodiegetic") embedded by the first one: Okonkwo suffers from mosquitoes whining around his ears and he suddenly remembers the story his mother once told him about why Mosquito always attacks Ear.[6] In the beginning of *Aké*, Wole Soyinka described the parsonage and the Canon's square white building as:

> a bulwark against the menace and the siege of the wood spirits. Its rear wall demarcated their territory, stopped them from taking liberties with the world of humans.[7]

This is followed by further allusions to spirits, ghosts and gommids together with references to the Bible. He then fits in his mother's experiences with spirits and daemons by means of an embedded, explicative narrative, in which Wild Christian is the narrator and the young Wole and his sister are the audience. It is an explicative, inserted story about the mixture of Christian and African beliefs in his mother's faith.

The third function an embedded narrative can have is *thematic*: "the relations established between the hypodiegetic and the diegetic level are those of analogy, i.e. similarity and contrast".[8] A good example of the thematic use of embedded narrative is to be found in Mariama Bâ's *Une si longue lettre*. In the main narrative level of this epistolary novel, another story is embedded, also in the form of a letter. Besides this formal analogy (and many thematic analogical elements), there is also a contrasting point vis-à-vis the main theme: the friend, Aïssatou, to whom the heroine addresses her long letter, divorced when her husband took a second wife, while the main character, Ramatoulaye, has swallowed her disappointment and accepted her husband's second marriage and his subsequent behaviour. The narrator-heroine quotes the whole letter in which her friend tells her husband she wants to leave him. The thematic analogy gives an extra dimension to the main (Ramatoulaye's) story. The latter, who is the first narrator in the book, in this passage yields the act of narration to a character (i.e. her friend Aïssatou) who presents, on the hypodiegetic level, her narrative to another addressee (= the narratee): Mawdo her husband. The thematic parallel – the effects on a first wife of a husband's taking a second wife – in this "mirror story" is reversed by an opposite reaction: divorce in the embedded story versus acceptance in the main narrative.[9] Of course the transition from one level to the other is not always as clearly indicated as in the above examples.

"Who speaks?" and "Who sees?"

First-person narrators can take different positions with regard to the narrated events: First, they can tell a story in which they are or have been the hero/heroine; second, they can tell a story in which they mainly figure as observers; or third, they can tell a story which has been transmitted to them by somebody else in an oral or written form and which they are merely "presenting literally" on paper now.

In the first case, the "I" has a central position on the first level, as a narrator, and also on the second level, the level of the story itself where the "I" acts and is presented as the main character. In this case first-person narrators tell and observe; they express themselves and recall their past experiences, as in Tutuola's *Palm-wine Drinkard* or his *Feather Woman of the Jungle*.[10] An example of the second category is *The Poor Christ of Bomba*: in his diary Denis observes the Reverend Father Dumont, who is the main character in this diary novel, although we also get to know Denis himself as an important character through his comments and reflections. One example of the third category is Fagunwa's afore-mentioned book; a second example could be Ferdinand Oyono's *Houseboy*. In Fagunwa's case, the main story has been transmitted orally to the first narrator on the extradiegetic level, while in the second case the first narrator functions as the translator and "editor" of the received manuscript.[11]

In the field of narratology, it is useful to raise two questions concerning the relation between narrator and character, namely Who speaks? and Who sees? In terms of concepts, a distinction is to be made between *narration* and *focalization*. The narrator tells the story but at the same time the events and situations are presented from a specific perspective, a point of view, which is not always necessarily the narrator's. For instance, in the scene in which Denis tells about the Father's quarrel with the chief whom he wants to forbid to dance, the focalization shifts from the Chief to the Father, while the narrator remains the same, i.e. Denis in his diary:

> The chief himself was still glaring murderously at the Father, but they gripped him tight. The Father looked back at the chief with a sort of amused pity, quite free of dislike. (p. 55)

In most studies about perspective or point of view,[12] narration and focalization have often been used confusingly, as is demonstrated convincingly, by Shlomith Rimmon (who uses the word "agent" instead of "character"):

> Obviously, a person (and, by analogy, a narrative agent) is capable of both speaking and seeing and even of doing things at the same time – a state of affairs which facilitates the confusion between the two activities. Moreover, it is almost impossible to speak without betraying some personal "point of view", if only through the very language used. But a person (and, by analogy, a narrative agent) is also capable of undertaking to tell what another person sees or has seen. Thus, speaking and seeing, narration and focalization, may, but need not, be attributed to the same agent. The distinction between the two activities is a theoretical necessity, and only on its basis can the interrelations between them be studied with precision.[13]

The focalization can shift from one character to another and is therefore an important device in its contribution to the effect a character may have on the reader. If we are not aware of it, we are easily manipulated in our opinions, as Eleanor Wachtel stresses with regard to contemporary Kenyan autobiographical novels:

> As in nearly all third-world countries, most of the Kenyan novelists are men. Their central characters are preponderantly males. Further, the male viewpoint is underlined not only by the many characterizations of young men, but by the literary device of the first person protago-nist...This is quite natural to the relatively inexperienced author who would tend to be somewhat autobiographical anyway. At the same time, however, it is also more intimate, personal, and hence, more explicitly male in outlook and tone...This device creates a rapport between author and reader and enlists the latter's sympathy. It does not allow for another point of view...Women are necessarily "the other". In Kenya, this male-focused lens on life is an accurate reflection of society. It is consistent with a society where men are the primary decision-makers.[14]

Although narration and focalization can coincide in first-person narrative, they can also be separate, as they often clearly are in first-person retrospective narratives. I give an example of both. In Mariama Bâ's novel, the following quotation shows how narration and focalization coincide (attributed to the same "agent", to use Rimmon's term):

> Modou Fall is indeed dead, Aissatou. The uninterrupted procession of men and women who have "learned" of it, the wails and tears all around me, confirm his death. This condition of extreme tension sharpens my sufferings and continues till the following day, the day of interment (p. 3).

In *Aké*, the difference between narrator and character-focalizer is clear in the following lines:

> I lay on the mat pretending to be still asleep. It had become a morning pastime, watching him exercise by the window. A chart was pinned to the wall, next to the mirror. Essay did his best to imitate the white gymnast...There was a precise fusslessness even in the most strenuous movements. In...Out...In...Out...breathing deeply. He bent over, touched his toes, slewed from one side to the other, rotated his body on its axis. He opened his hands and clenched them, raising one arm after the other as if invisible weights were suspended from them. Sweat prickles emerged in agreed order, joined together in disciplined rivulets. Finally, he picked up the towel – the session was over. (p. 77)

In *Aké*, it is the (author-)narrator, the older Wole, who tells, but the (author-)character, the younger Wole, who sees, who focalizes his father's actions. Focalization has a subject and an object: the focalizer is the agent whose perception leads the presentation; the focalized object is (the selection of) what the focalizer perceives.[15] Focalization is not purely perceptive as in the *Aké* example; it is also psychological (cognitive and emotive) and ideological. All these aspects may harmonize or belong to different focalizers. An example of the psychological aspect is to be found in the following quotation from *Aké*, where the reactions the young Wole felt after his little sister's death are recounted by the narrator so many years later:

> Suddenly, it all broke up within me. A force from nowhere pressed me against the bed and I howled. As I was picked up I struggled against my father's soothing voice, tears all over me. I was sucked into a place of loss whose cause or definition remained elusive. I did not compre-hend it yet. (p. 98)

The ideological facet of the focalization, or the norms of the text, consists in the evaluation of events and characters. It can be presented "through a single dominant perspective, that of the narrator-focalizer". The latter's ideology is then considered as "authoritative". In the first-person retrospective narrative, one often finds the latter's view as superior to the narrator-character's earlier views recalled by the older I, many years afterwards. If other norm systems are presented as well, they are generally evaluated in comparison with the narrator-focalizer's ideological authority.[16] In the following example several ideological viewpoints are presented, but the main perspective throughout the text is the narrator's, who imposes himself at the end:

> After dinner the Father set to work with the catechist. I followed the interrogation as long as I could, then went to bed. Zacharia exasperated me again with his uninvited interventions. For instance, the Father asked the catechist this question: "Why is it, do you think, that so many backslide from the true religion? Why did they come to Mass in the first place?" The catechist answered: "My Father, at that time we were poor. Well, doesn't the Kingdom of Heaven belong to the poor? So there's nothing surprising in many of them running then to the true God. But nowadays, as you know yourself, Father, they are making pots of money by selling their cocoa to the Greeks; they are all rich. Now, isn't it easier for a camel to pass through a needle's eye than for a rich man to enter the Kingdom of...?" But just then Zacharia blurted out, interrupting the wise words of the catechist: "Get away with you! That's not the truth of the matter at all. I tell you just how it is, Father. The first of us who ran to your religion, came to it as a sort of...revelation. Yes, that's it, a revelation; a school where they could learn your secret, the secret of your power, of your aeroplanes and railways...in a word, the secret of your mystery. Instead of that, you began talking to them of God, of the soul, of eternal life, and so forth. Do you really suppose they didn't know those things already, long before you came? So of course, they decided that you were hiding something. Later, they saw that if they had money they could get plenty of things for themselves – gramophones and cars, and perhaps even aeroplanes one day. Well, then! They are turning from religion and running elsewhere, after money, no less. That's the truth of it, Father. As for the rest, it's all make-believe..." And speaking in this fashion, he put on an important air. I was boiling with indignation when I heard this illiterate gabble, this "bla-bla-bla"...I was hot with anger. I would gladly have slapped his silly face. But the Father listened to him with great attention. (pp. 29–30)

Thanks to the irony of the author this assertive ideological main perspective is, after all, effectively undermined. The norms of the text may be presented through statements by the narrator and or one or more characters; norms can also be implicitly given with events and behaviour as they are narrated and perceived by narrator or characters. The device of shifting the focalization among the different characters or from narrator to character always affects the meaning of a text. When the focalization shifts regularly in the text, we may get a rather broad idea of the various aspects of a conflict or problem. This technique may produce the suggestion of the narrator's neutrality vis-à-vis the various characters and their relations: this is often the case in the realistic novel (subject of the next chapter). The way the focalization is handled definitely contributes to the effect a character (and in fact the whole text) has on the reader, e.g. we are more inclined to share views or to sympathize with a character when the story is presented mainly from his or her particular view, feeling, ideology. The fact that in *The Poor Christ of Bomba* the missionary's servant Denis is the first-person narrator as well as the main focalizer in the text results in a specific view and coloured information.

Different first-person genres

Without pretending to give a complete and detailed inventory of the various first-person narrative forms to be found in African prose, I will try to present a brief description of the main genres as they are mentioned in figure IV.

FIRST-PERSON NARRATIVE

FACTUAL	FICTIONAL
a. Diary	a. Diary novel
b. Letters	b. Epistolary novel
c. Autobiography	c. First person memoir novel

Figure IV

In African literature, many first-person narratives are presented as autobiographical. The construction is often that of the older I who looks back to his/her earlier life and who, usually years later, narrates what he/she remembers from the past. Many texts of this kind deal with the theme of colonialism, e.g. in *Cette Afrique-là*, the old Mômha tells his experiences which, in a foreword, the author, Ikellé-Matiba, authenticates as "real events". Mômha was born before the colonial occupation of his country, Cameroon, by the Germans and in this book he presents his life and "cette Afrique-là que nous ne verrons plus".[17]

Before giving a brief description and some examples of the above-mentioned genres, I should like to look more closely at the opposition between "facts" and "fiction" as it has been used here. This point always raises more questions than can be answered. Sometimes authors pretend to speak the truth while in fact they are telling lies or producing phantasies. Others pretend to be writing fiction while they are telling the story of their own life. Of course, some of the facts are verifiable, notably when the author refers to concrete places and well-known events. However, thoughts, dreams, feeling and beliefs are never controllable. Some scholars have pointed out that an autobiography may contain only historical, biographical material about the author, while others claim that the autobiographer should have the right to see and express himself as subjectively as he pleases. In all this confusion, the real autobiographical narrative must meet one overall minimum requirement, i.e. the *autobiographical pact* as it has been defined by Philippe Lejeune: in his view the autobiography is a retrospective narrative in prose told by an existing person about his or her own existence, when his/her personal life is emphasized and particularly the story of his/her own personality. From that definition we may deduce the following:

1. the form is a prose narrative
2. the subject is the life story (the growth of the personality)
3. author and narrator are identical
4. author and main character are identical and the story is retrospectively told.[18]

The "pact" is realized when the reader gets the guarantee from the text that the author, narrator and main character are one and the same person. This is a formal, verifiable criterion on the basis of which one can determine whether a given text is autobiographical or not. For the rest, it is seldom possible to establish exactly to what degree invented or untrue elements have been introduced in the autobiographical text.

[...]

Notes

1　Shlomith Rimmon-Kenan, *Narrative Fiction. Contemporary Poetics*, London/New York, Methuen (Series New Accents), 1983, pp. 8–9. See also: Mieke Bal, *Narratology, Introduction to the Theory of Narrative*, Toronto, University of Toronto Press, 1985.

2　More research needs to be done with regard to the comparison of differences in presentation of oral and written texts. Still I agree with Rimmon-Kenan (op. cit. p. 89) that "the empirical process of communication between author and reader is less relevant to the poetics of narrative fiction than its counterpart in the text".

3　Cf. Roland Colin, *Les contes de l'Ouest Africain*, Paris, *Présence Africaine*, 1957, p. 84; Ruth Finnegan, *Oral Literature in Africa*, Oxford, At the Clarendon Press, 1970, pp. 380–1.

4　D. O. Fagunwa, *The Forest of a Thousand Daemons*, translated by Wole Soyinka, London, Nelson, (1968) 1982, pp. 8–9.

5　Gérard Genette, *Figures III*, Paris, Seuil, 1972. In English translation: *Narrative Discourse*, Ithaca/New York, Cornell University Press, 1980. Genette combines theory and description in his analysis of possible narrative systems with the application of his theoretical considerations to Proust's *A la recherche du temps perdu*. Rimmon (op. cit.) gives a practical and clear introduction to the new approaches of narrative fiction, in which she also discusses Genette's theories.

6　Chinua Achebe, *Things Fall Apart*, Greenwich, Conn., Fawcett Publications, 1959, p. 72.

7　Wole Soyinka, *Aké. The Years of Childhood*, London, Rex Collings, 1981, p. 2.

8　Cf. Rimmon-Kenan, op. cit., p. 91ff.

9　Mariama Bâ, *Une si longue lettre*, Dakar, Nouvelles Editions Africaines, 1979. The English translation (by Modupé Bodé-Thomas) *So Long a Letter*, London, Heinemann, 1981, has been used here.

10　Amos Tutuola, *The Palm-Wine Drinkard and His Dead Palm-Wine Tapster in the Deads' Town*, London, Faber and Faber, 1952; idem, *Feather Woman of the Jungle*, London, Faber and Faber, 1962. See also my "Perspective narrative et récit africain à la première personne" in the collection of papers I edited for the African Studies Centre in Leiden: *Text and Context. Methodological Explorations in the Field of African Literatures*, 1977, pp. 113–34.

11　Mongo Beti, *Le pauvre Christ de Bomba*, Paris, Laffont, 1956. The English translation (by Gerald Moore): *The Poor Christ of Bomba*, London, Heinemann, 1971, has been used here; Ferdinand Oyono, *Une vie de boy*, Paris, Juilliard, 1956. The English translation (by John Reed), London, Heinemann, 1966, has been used here.

12　Norman Friedman, "Point of View in Fiction: the Development of a Critical Concept", in: PMLA, 70, pp. 1160–84, 1955. Wayne C. Booth, *The Rhetoric of Fiction*, Chicago, The University of Chicago Press, 1961; Bertil Romberg, *Studies in the Narrative Technique of the First-Person Novel*, Stockholm, Almqvist and Wiksell, 1962 among others have not seen the difference between narration and focalization, as Genette observed in his *Figures III* (cf. note 13) for the first time.

13　Rimmon, op. cit., p. 72.

14　Eleanor Wachtel, "The Mother and the Whore: Image and Stereotype of African Women", in: *Umoja*, 1 (2), p. 42.

15　Cf. Rimmon, op. cit., p. 74 and Mieke Bal, *Narratologie. Essais sur la signification narrative dans quatre romans modernes*, Paris, Klincksieck, 1977, p. 33ff.

16　Cf. Rimmon, op. cit., p. 82.

17　Jean Ikellé-Matiba, *Cette Afrique-là*, Présence Africaine, Paris, 1963, p. 13.

18　Philippe Lejeune, *Le pacte autobiographique*, Paris, Seuil, 1975, pp. 13–46.

Chapter 48

Festivals, Ritual, and Drama in Africa

Tejumola Olaniyan

African performance traditions entered the orbit of European discourse – which, by virtue of language, supplies the operative terms "festival," "ritual," and "drama" – primarily as negative examples. As a result, the origins of that entrance were marked in the main by condemnation, inferiorization, and general disregard. It was asserted or implied that blacks either had no traditions of drama indigenous to them, or had traditions that, in comparison with Europe and Asia, were merely "proto-dramatic" or "quasi-dramatic," cretinous forms in a state of developmental arrest in terms of style, esthetic canons, formalization of technique, and mode of historical transmission. Wherever "properly dramatic" traditions were found, they were marked off as but products of the African encounter with Europe – a way of claiming that the "properly dramatic" traditions are nothing less than derivatives of western forms and traditions (Jeyifo 1990: 242–3). There is a larger context, of course, to these deeply ethnocentric claims. They were part and parcel of the implacable inferiorization of African corporeality and cultural forms that matured in Europe in the eighteenth century and remains a major constituent of Eurocentrism. In the operations of the discourse, the inferiorization of a cultural practice becomes a shorthand to the inferiorization of the bearers of that culture and practice.

This is not the appropriate space exhaustively to engage the Eurocentric archive in all its details and dimensions. I will, instead, exemplify the discourse with the work of the distinguished contemporary scholar Ruth Finnegan. The chapter titled "Drama" in her influential work *Oral Literature in Africa*, published in 1970, still remains for many the canonical survey. Her opening lines alone reveal her restrictive methodology:

> How far one can speak of indigenous drama in Africa is not an easy question. In this it differs from previous topics [treated in the book] like, say, panegyric, political poetry, or prose narratives, for there it was easy to discover African analogies to the familiar European forms.

First published in *The Cambridge History of African and Caribbean Literature,* vol. 1, ed. Abiola Irele and Simon Gikandi, pp. 35–48. Cambridge: Cambridge University Press, 2004.

When concepts describing cultural practices or forms cross cultural borders without some form of domestication before speaking the realities of their new abode, some excess, misrepresentation, or violence, is produced. For Finnegan, it is only if Africa could supply indigenous "analogies to the familiar European forms" that it would be established as a continent with drama. There is no other way. So she keeps looking for European drama on the African continent: "what . . . *we* normally regard as drama" (500); what "*we* are accustomed [to]" (516). The "definition" of drama she proposes, in all its pedantry and formal rigorism, is designed to achieve little else if not failure:

> It is clearly necessary to reach at least some rough agreement about what is to count as "drama". Rather than produce a verbal definition, it seems better to point to the various elements which tend to come together in what, in the wide sense, we normally regard as drama. Most important is the idea of enactment, of representation through actors who imitate persons and events. This is also usually associated with other elements, appearing to a greater or lesser degree at different times or places: linguistic content; plot; the represented interaction of several characters; specialized scenery, etc.; often music; and – of particular importance in most African performances – dance. Now it is very seldom in Africa that all these elements of drama come together in a single performance.
>
> (501)

Her – undeniably productive – failure prepares and authorizes her thesis, even against acknowledged contrary evidence: "Though some writers have very positively affirmed the existence of native African drama, it would perhaps be truer to say that in Africa, in contrast to western Europe and Asia, drama is not typically a wide-spread or a developed form" (500).

It is important to understand Finnegan's concept of difference, given her insistence that Africans in Africa produce European drama. To the extent that we are all the same, her work becomes unnecessary. If it is difference that enables her project, then her insistence on its erasure becomes paradoxical. But we must not assume that this illogicality lacks any logic, or that it thus self-destructs in the realm of power. Difference here is not erased but whipped into conformity and *hierarchized* (see also Graham-White 1974; Havemeyer 1966). It is interesting then to note that Ibadan, where Finnegan stayed for a time while working on her book, and where she signed the preface, is one of the main centers of the still vibrant Yoruba traveling theater movement, with a recorded tradition going back to the late 1590s. Apparently, this theater refused to provide Finnegan with "analogies to the familiar European forms."

If, today, such ethnocentric demands have ceased being made on Africa, it is because of the gargantuan effort of a host of African scholars such as Joel Adedeji, Wole Soyinka, Oyin Ogunba, Bakary Traore, Ebun Clark, Biodun Jeyifo, Penina Mlama, and others, who gave voice to the varieties of dramatic traditions in Africa while also redefining "drama" away from its received, Aristotle-centered conception, to the great profit of world theater history scholarship.

Africa is home to several traditions of theater, conceived as an ensemble of culturally marked and consciously staged practices in space and time and before an audience. Many of these traditions are of ancient origin, while others emerged with formal European colonization of the continent in the nineteenth century and the subsequent imposition of western education, religion, and culture. The older traditions are mostly nonscripted, improvisatory, and performed in indigenous African languages. Their conceptions of theater space is fluid, and stage-audience relations are not governed by inflexible rules: any space can be turned into a performance stage, while the audience, within acknowledged boundaries, is free to interact with the performers and performance in a variety of ways and even move in and out of the theater space during performance. The performance is often public and the audience non-fee-paying, though performers could be rewarded in cash or kind for their artistry. On the other hand, many of the newer theater traditions are text-based, written in European languages or indigenous African languages of European alphabet. The plays are designed to be performed in more or less formal theater buildings with fixed relations between performers and audience. The audience is usually fee-paying though the theater may not be expressly commercial. In all cases, as indeed in all societies, the functions of the theater traditions are broadly similar in their mixing of the pleasing and the pedagogical: their representations provide the audience with pleasurable entertainments while simultaneously channeling its passions and sentiments in certain directions.

Theater in Africa could be categorized into four distinct traditions: festival theater, popular theater, development theater, and art theater.

Festival theater and ritual

In many African communities, the foremost indigenous cultural and artistic institution is the festival. Organized around certain deities or spirits, or to mark generational transitions or the passage of the seasons whether of climate or agricultural production, festivals are sprawling multimedia occasions – that is, incorporating diverse forms such as singing, chanting, drama, drumming, masking, miming, costuming, puppetry, with episodes of theatrical enactments ranging from the sacred and secretive to the secular and public. Festivals could last for a few hours to several days, weeks or months. Each festival dramatizes a story or myth – or related sets of stories or myths – connecting the particular subject of the festival, be it a deity or the season of the harvest, to significant events in the life of the community and to its place in sustaining communal harmony, plenty, and stability. Artistically, the performances also serve to showcase the community's new artistic forms and talents as well as advancements and mutations in existing ones.

Festival theater is performed in an open space in the town square or a similarly appointed location. The audience sits or stands in rings of circles around the performers, and is able to drift in and out of the performance. The audience closes in or fans out depending on perceptions of the volume of space needed by the performers at particular moments of the action. There is a close relationship between the performers and the audience, with the latter even serving as chorus, but there are also distinctions, and it is treasured cultural knowledge to know when to and when not to interject in the performance. Esthetically, the performance is most often nonillusionistic, with acting or dancing occurring in the full range from realism to surrealism and spirit possession. This is partly why an empty space, with few prop or theatrical fripperies, is all that is needed for the communion between performer and audience on one hand, and the performance and society on the other.

There are two ways in which scholars have tried to understand African festivals. Some scholars label the festival as "pre-drama" or "traditional ritual" or "ritual drama," because of its expansive multimedia format, its firm integration of the dramatic amidst the other arts, and the presence of both religious and secular re-enactments (Echeruo 1981).

The assumption of the scholars, whether acknowledged or not, is often that the twentieth-century western theater, with its packaged three hours, strict compartmentalization of the arts, and the virtual absence of the sacred, constitutes the norm of "theater." Other scholars have argued that the festival is full-fledged theater that is dynamic, spectacular, and inventive, and that the contemporary western theater could in fact be seen as nothing more than severely abbreviated festival. The argument of Wole Soyinka, Africa's leading dramatist and winner of the Nobel Prize in Literature, best exemplifies this view. He insists that festivals be seen as constituting "in themselves *pure theatre* at its most prodigal and resourceful . . . the most stirring expressions of man's instinct and need for drama at its most comprehensive and community-involving" (1988: 194). In one sweeping move, he turns a colonialist interpretation of the festival on its head: "instead of considering festivals from one point of view only – that of providing, in a primitive form, the ingredients of drama – we may even begin examining the opposite point of view: that contemporary drama, as we experience it today, is a contraction of drama, necessitated by the productive order of society in other directions" (195).

Even the sacred core of many festivals – much maligned as "ritual" or "pre-drama" – do have consciously staged performances in space and time, though before a more restricted audience, and in language that may be more arcane, composed of incantations and elliptic proverbs. In many instances, such performances could be produced with very elaborate plots and costuming, indicating that even within the sacred, the more secular concerns of the artistic and pleasurable are never short-changed. A few useful studies of festival theater and ritual in Africa include works by scholars such as Oyin Ogunba (1978), Ossie Enekwe (1987), and Nnabuenyi Ugonna (1983).

Popular theater

"Popular" is a much-debated concept in African theater studies. It is important therefore to begin with a working definition. "Popular" as used here refers to those theater forms that have large followings at the point of reception. This mass – and indeed, massive – audience cuts across class or status boundaries. One reason for such wide appeal is that the theater is most often performed in the indigenous languages, or hybrids of them designed to be understood across linguistic borders. Increasingly, many subtraditions are being produced in simplified forms of the European languages that came with colonization, or in "pidgin" – a distinctive mixture of one such foreign language and an indigenous language. The last two – simplified European languages and pidgin – constitute much of the language of urban Africa today.

Early dramatic forms that have their roots in sacred ceremonies and involve elaborate masking, such as the Alarinjo and Apidan theaters of Nigeria, are composed mainly of male performers. With the famous exception of the Ghanaian Concert Party, it is generally the case that more recent forms – such as the Yoruba Popular Travelling Theatre, the Chikwakwa Theatre of Zambia, and the South African Township Theatre – are composed of both male and female performers.

The recurring themes in African popular drama are those with broad appeal, and are intimately linked with genre. Particularly common in comedies and melodramas are themes such as unrequited love, marital infidelity, unemployment, pretensions to wealth, status, or sophistication, the conundrums of modern city life, dreams of travel abroad, and so on. Satires predominate and have targeted egotistical chiefs, the rich but miserly, the strange manners of Europeans (explorers, missionaries, or colonial administrators and their spouses), corrupt politicians, overly westernized African men and women, prostitutes, the rural village teacher, and so on. Matters of fate and predestination, and the mythological lives of deities, legends, and powerful historical figures have been explored in tragedies and other serious dramas.

Most popular theater forms are not scripted but based on improvisations, giving the performers much leeway but also demanding an unusual dexterity in speech, movement, and gesture. Partly for economic reasons (size of troupe) and partly for artistic preferences (most popular plays are multimedia performances), performers are often skilled in many aspects of the enterprise such as acting, singing, costuming, playing a musical instrument or two, set designing, and business management. The performers are in most cases organized as traveling troupes, performing in a variety of available spaces: open squares, enclosed courtyards of kings and chiefs, school classrooms, concert or cinema halls, bars or night-clubs, and well-equipped theaters. Troupes are either kin- or lineage-based, or composed of close friends or understanding partners and acquaintances. The performers are generally professionals and the troupes run as commercial enterprises. It is not infrequent, though, that performers hold other jobs such as clerks, traders, crafts makers, and sedentary herbalists during lulls or off seasons.

The economic fortunes of the troupes ebb and flow with the sociopolitical and economic health of their societies. In Nigeria with the largest number of professional popular theater troupes, the boom decades were the 1970s and 1980s. Figures such as Hubert Ogunde, Moses Olaiya, Isola Ogunsola, Ade Love, Lere Paimo, and others became very successful entrepreneurs and even went into filmmaking as a result, making their most popular plays even more widely available on celluloid. Those who survived the harsh economic climate of the late 1980s and through the 1990s have branched into video production as a cheaper and low-tech alternative to crosscountry road shows (with no guarantee of sizeable audience) and capital-intensive filmmaking. In South Africa, Gibson Kente reigned supreme from 1966 until his detention by the apartheid government in 1976. Popular culture in Africa is generally understudied, but African popular theater has been the subject of valuable attention by scholars such as Robert Kavanagh (1977), Biodun Jeyifo (1984), Kwabena Bame (1985), David Kerr (1995), Karin Barber (2001), and Catherine Cole (2001), among others.

Development theater

In certain radical or leftist traditions of African theater scholarship, "development theater" is also known as popular theater, but the conception of the "popular" in this case is vastly different from that in the preceding section. While in popular theater the "popular" is measured at the point of consumption or reception, in development theater, the "popular" is marked at the point of production; the theater need not be popular at all in terms of reaching a wide audience. In other words, "popular" here means produced by an alliance of discriminating and ideologically astute intellectuals, workers, and peasants and expressly constructed to advance the interests of the underprivileged classes in society. Because the underprivileged classes constitute the majority of the people in the society, the theater is also known more polemically as "people's theater."

The conception of the "popular" operative in development theater is inspired by the radical Marxist German dramatist Bertolt Brecht, who writes:

> "Popular" means intelligible to the broad masses, taking over their own forms of expression and enriching them/adopting and consolidating their standpoint/representing the most progressive section of the people in such a way that it can take over the leadership: thus intelligible to other sections too/linking with tradition and carrying it further/handing on the achievements of the section now leading to the section of the people that is struggling to lead.
>
> (1964: 108)

This form of theater is geared toward raising the consciousness of the exploited classes so they can recognize their interests, band together against their common enemies, and struggle for liberation. To liberate themselves, in the Marxist understanding, is also to liberate the productive forces of the society from private appropriation and so ensure genuine development – a development in which there is no private appropriation of public wealth. It is in this sense that this tradition of theater is called "development theatre." In addition to Brecht, other significant conceptual supports for development theater come from Latin America: Augusto Boal, whose theater experiments are documented in his book *Theatre of the Oppressed* (1979), and Paulo Freire, adult educator and author of the famous *Pedagogy of the Oppressed* (1970).

A minor form of development theater practice is the "guerrilla theater," in which committed activist groups emerge unannounced at carefully chosen public locations and stage provocative performances, usually against particular government policies, and disappear before the agents of law and order appear. For a time in the early 1980s, the Obafemi Awolowo University Drama Department had a famous Guerrilla Theatre unit, under the direction of Wole Soyinka. However, not all forms of development theater are obviously ideologically charged. Many are designed as adult education programs to teach literacy, explain the political process to bridge the gap between the rulers and the ruled so people can better know their rights and responsibilities, communicate better agricultural techniques, teach new and improved ways of treating or preventing certain diseases, and encourage community mobilization for self-help projects and general rural development. In many instances where this is the case, the designation is the populist and less polemical "community theater." Workshops are held regularly by development theater practitioners to teach the people how to organize themselves to use the theater both as an expression of culture and as a tool for fostering social, political, and economic development.

Development theater practitioners are mostly professional intellectuals, often affiliated with a university, or educated individuals affiliated with a development agency or nongovernmental organization. They work with a variety of groups in mostly rural areas – areas that are in much of Africa the least recipients of the "benefits" of "modernity" and therefore the target of development schemes by states, nongovernmental organizations, as well as World Bank and United Nations agencies. Indeed, most – though not all – development theater practices in Africa receive funding from such institutions. The theater is noncommercial and most of those involved have regular occupations or are funded by grants. Given the direct, instrumentalist goal of the theater, the performances are often didactic and exhortatory, though the more skilled adult educators go to great lengths to emphasize esthetics and even incorporate popular forms from the people's indigenous performance traditions.

An important example of development theater practice is the Laedza Batanani of Botswana in the mid-1970s, which subsequently served as model and inspiration for similar experiments in Lesotho, Zambia, Malawi, Sierra Leone, and especially the well-known practice at Ahmadu Bello University in Nigeria. Perhaps the most oppositional of the experiments was the Kamiriithu Education and Cultural Center, led by Ngugi wa Thiong'O, the leading Kenyan writer. The center was so successful in mobilizing the community to explore critically their history and culture and contemporary situation through theater that Ngugi was imprisoned for a year without trial in 1977. By 1982, the Kenyan government had razed the center and banned all theater activities in the area. Scholars such as Robert Mshengu Kavanagh (1977), Michael Etherton (1982), Ingrid Bjorkman (1989), Penina Mlama (1991), David Kerr (1995), Jane Plastow (1996) have produced illuminating work on development theater tradition in Africa.

Art theater

Art theater is the tradition of African theater most familiar to the outside world through the published works of the continent's notable playwrights such as Wole Soyinka, Athol Fugard, Femi Osofisan, Ama Ata Aidoo, Zulu Sofola, Efua Sutherland, Ola Rotimi, J. P. Clark-Bekederemo, Sony Labou Tansi, Guillaume Oyono-Mbia, Werewere Liking, and Tess Onwueme, among others. Art theater in Africa is of colonial origin; it emerged with the training of Africans in European languages and literatures and dramatic traditions, and it is most often written in the European colonial languages. The label "art theater" signifies the tradition's relationship to, and investment in, notions of "high art" or "great works" characteristic of western bourgeois cultural discourse since the nineteenth century.

The practitioners of art theater are usually professional intellectuals affiliated with universities or other institutions of higher education. Although the best dramas of this tradition borrow richly from indigenous performance forms, the overall "mold" of drama into which those borrowings are poured, as well as the languages in which they are written and performed, are European and greatly circumscribe their popularity with the majority of Africans who are not schooled in those esthetics or languages. After a successful career writing in English, Ngugi wa Thiong'o switched to his native Gikuyu language in the 1980s. The Nigerian dramatist J. P. Clark once considered the matter and observed that, in comparing the Yoruba Popular Travelling Theatre with the art theater, "Some would say that the latter has its head deep in the wings of American and European theatre! The works of Mr. Wole Soyinka, Dr. Ene Henshaw, and my own plays, I am told, clearly bear this badge, but whether of merit or infamy it is a matter still in some obscurity" (1970: 85). Clark hints here at a charge sometimes leveled against African art theater: whether it could really be original and authentically African as long as it borrows esthetic structures from and speaks the language of Europe. Such a charge and its subtending purist conceptions of transcultural relations and of its vehicle, cultural translation, has never represented much of a handicap for the truly creative minds of African art theater. They continue to confront the colonial inheritance and revise it from a variety of perspectives, without any surrender of initiative.

For them, the centuries of African unequal contact with Europe are undeniable, and cultural purism, absolutism or insularity are not necessarily worthy coordinates of "originality." The Mexican writer Octavio Paz speaks for the writers of the ex-colonial world, from Africa to Asia and Latin America, when he argues that "The special position of our literatures, when compared to those of England, Spain, Portugal, and France, derives precisely from this fundamental fact: they are literatures written in transplanted tongues," but that they "did not passively accept the changing fortunes of their transplanted languages: they participated in the process and even accelerated it. Soon they ceased to be mere transatlantic reflections. At times they have been the negation of the literatures of Europe; more often, they have been a reply" (1990: 4–5).

The hub of art theater activity in Africa is mostly the urban areas, cities, and universities. This is also where most of the audience, those schooled in western languages, is located. Performance takes place in formal theater buildings, frequently with the proscenium stage that is hegemonic in Europe and America. Art theater is primarily state-subsidized and rarely self-sustaining as a commercial enterprise. Indeed, art theater is consumed more as dramatic literature – read widely in schools and colleges – than as theater.

Many practitioners of art theater have attempted to ameliorate the obvious elitism of the tradition by establishing community theaters or traveling theaters run by university resident professionals or drama students. These efforts, in less formal surroundings, make art theater performances – sometimes of plays in translations or in pidgin, or of text-based improvisations – available to audiences that would otherwise not have access to them. These projects designed to take the art theater to the masses of the people are often very expensive and have existed only intermittently. Some of the famous examples are the University of Ibadan Travelling Theatre (Nigeria, in the 1960s), the Makerere Free Travelling Theatre (Uganda, 1960s and 1970s), the University of Malawi Travelling Theatre (1970s), and the University of Zambia Chikwakwa Theatre (1970s and 1980s). There is the particularly unique case of the South African Athol Fugard, who broke for some time from his normal routine of formal playwriting in the 1970s to collaborate with the actors Winston Ntshona and John Kani. Their improvisations led to many well-received plays against the apartheid state and inaugurated a genre of popular theater labeled South African Protest theater. The most performed of such plays is *Sizwe Bansi Is Dead* (1973).

Although the four traditions of African dramatic performance described above exist simultaneously and often share, or overlap at the level of, deep formal structures, it is nevertheless the case that the social relations among them is hierarchical. Festival performances are still going on, though the scale has obviously been affected by the continent's economic downturn since the mid-1980s. More significantly, festivals no longer occupy a central position in civil society and are therefore no longer a preeminent instrument of sociopolitical and cultural socialization of the young. Since the last half century, that position has been taken over by cultural forms of westernization such as western-style schools and religious institutions and their myriad offshoots. The point is this: festival performance, the most widespread and truly mass African cultural form, no longer has the cultural capital it used to have, mainly because the cultural knowledge festivals impart no longer has much value in a person's quest for social mobility. Development theater is by no means widespread, and depends too much on institutional sponsorship, whether of a government or nongovernmental agency. In some instances, the charge that development theater is no more than elitist condescension to rural folks, a kind of "planning from above" to bring "modernity" to the "uncivilized," is not entirely unjustified. With the participation of a large number of western nongovernmental organizations in the last decade, including religious ones, it is also not out of place to query the level of agency rural Africans have in the development theater process. Because popular theater is basically commercial, it has to be close to urban centers where most of its clientele who can afford the price of tickets reside. Its thematic and esthetic choices are determined to a large extent by the preferences of its audience; and while many of its performances may have profound cultural significance for the collective, popular theater is not often catalyzed by any grand and well articulated idea of a cultural direction to which to steer the audience. Like all businesses, it does what it has to do to survive.

By far the most prestigious of the traditions is the art theater. Art theater tradition – scripted plays written in European languages or African languages of European alphabet, and made widely available by large and often multinational publishing houses – is the tradition by which Africa is known globally, and the primary bridge by which nationals of different African countries come into contact with one another's dramatic traditions. The practitioners of art theater are nearly exclusively the internationally well-known "African dramatists." Hubert Ogunde may be the father of modern Nigerian theater tradition, but it is Wole Soyinka who is known globally, the one whose works are easily available and weightily read as classic representations of Yoruba African culture to the world and in the world marketplace of cultural transactions. Because this tradition shares similar origins with the contemporary African state, and its bureaucracy and system of education – it is westernized and speaks a European language – it occupies a significant space in the ruling, dominant civil society. Although many of the distinguished art theater practitioners are employees of one institution of higher learning or the other and few to none have lived solely on the proceeds of their writings, it is nevertheless the case that competence in this tradition is a sure means of social mobility in the larger society, and in the world. This, then, is the fundamental reason for the tradition's prestige.

We come to a profound irony, one that, after more than four decades, is only now being substantively addressed by the practitioners. Art theater may hold all the cultural capital according to the logic of what constitutes that resource in contemporary Africa, but it is the case that this would-be representative tradition speaks, by virtue of its predominant European language of expression, to only the small percentage of Africans who are literate in that language. The irony is made more poignant by the fact that art theater is the main tradition that most directly and persistently confronts the issue of colonial cultural deracination of African societies and the need for vigorous African cultural self-reclamation. It has performed that task by plumbing the depths of indigenous African performance traditions and both critically and creatively anchoring itself simultaneously in autochthonous forms as well as those borrowed from Europe. The tradition's deployment of the colonial languages goes beyond mimicry to contribute in very original ways to those languages. As early in Soyinka's career as 1965, a British reviewer of *The Road* wrote of the dramatist's use of English: "Every decade or so, it seems to fall to a non-English dramatist to belt new energy into the English tongue. The last time was when Brendan Behan's 'The Quare Fellow' opened at Theatre Workshop. Nine years later, in the reign of Stage Sixty at the same loved Victorian building at Stratford East, a Nigerian called Wole Soyinka has done for our napping language what brigand dramatists from Ireland have done for centuries: booted it awake, rifled it pockets and scattered the loot into the middle of next week" (Gilliatt 1965: 25).

But to return to the irony, the majority of Africans simply can not read or speak European languages. Art theater practitioners themselves have endlessly debated the issue (for a review of the question, see Ngugi 1986), suggesting solutions such as infusing the European languages with African imagery, writing in a mixture of African and European languages, translating between African and European languages, and writing in African languages. The more practical solution that is becoming widespread today is cross translation, as leading dramatists such as Soyinka and Osofisan have encouraged the translation of their classics from English to Yoruba. If this trend continues apace and becomes widespread, the art theater tradition will have done a lot to justify its throne of prestige among African theater traditions.

References

Adedeji, Joel A. 1969. "The Alarinjo Theatre: The Study of a Yoruba Theatrical Art Form from Its Earliest Beginnings to the Present Time." PhD diss. University of Ibadan.

Bame, Kwabena N. 1985. *Come to Laugh: African Traditional Theatre in Ghana*. New York: Lilian Barber.

Banham, Martin, Errol Hill, and George Woodyard, eds. 1994. *The Cambridge Guide to African and Caribbean Theatre*. Cambridge: Cambridge University Press.

Barber, Karin. 2001. *The Generation of Plays: Yoruba Popular Life in Theatre*. Bloomington: Indiana University Press.

Barber, Karin, John Collins, and Alain Ricard. 1997. *West African Popular Theatre*. Bloomington: Indiana University Press.

Barber, Karin, and Bayo Ogundijo, transcribed, trans., and ed. 1994. *West African Popular Theatre: Three Plays by the Oyin Adejobi Company*. USA: ASA Press.

Bjorkman, Ingrid. 1989. *Mother, Sing for Me: People's Theatre in Kenya*. London: Zed.

Brecht, Bertolt. 1964. *Brecht on Theatre: The Development of an Aesthetic*. Ed. and trans. John Willet. New York: Hill and Wang.

Clark, Ebun. 1980. *Hubert Ogunde: The Making of Nigerian Theatre*. Oxford: Oxford University Press.

Clark, J. P. 1970. *The Example of Shakespeare*. London: Longman.

Cole, Catherine. 2001. *Ghana's Concert Party Theatre*. Bloomington: Indiana University Press.

Conteh-Morgan, John. 1994. *Theatre and Drama in Francophone Africa: A Critical Introduction*. Cambridge: Cambridge University Press.

De Graft, J. C. 1976. "Roots in African Drama and Theatre." *African Literature Today* 8: 1–25.

Echeruo, Michael J. C. 1981. "The Dramatic Limits of Igbo Ritual." In *Drama and Theatre in Nigeria: A Critical Sourcebook*. Ed. Yemi Ogunbiyi. Lagos: Nigeria Magazine: 136–48.

Enekwe, Ossie. 1987. *Igbo Masks: The Oneness of Ritual and Theatre*. Lagos: Nigeria Magazine.

Etherton, Michael. 1982. *The Development of African Drama*. London: Hutchinson.

Finnegan, Ruth. 1970. *Oral Literature in Africa*. Nairobi: Oxford University Press.

Gilliatt, Penelope. 1965. "A Nigerian Original." *The Observer* 19 Sept.: 25. Cited in *Critical Perspectives on Wole Soyinka*. Ed. James Gibbs. Washington, DC: Three Continents Press: 106.

Gotrick, Kacke. 1984. *Apidan Theatre and Modern Drama*. Stockholm: Almqvist and Wiskell.

Graham-White, Anthony. 1974. *The Drama of Black Africa*. New York: Samuel French.

Havemeyer, Loomis. [1916] 1966. *The Drama of Savage Peoples*. New York: Haskell House.

Jeyifo, Biodun. 1984. *The Yoruba Popular Travelling Theatre of Nigeria*. Lagos: Nigeria Magazine.

—— 1990. "The Reinvention of Theatrical Tradition: Critical Discourses on Interculturalism in the African Theatre." In *The Dramatic Touch of Difference: Theatre, Own and Foreign*. Ed. Erika Fischer-Lichte, J. Riley, and M. Gissenwehrer. Tübingen: Gunter Narr: 239–51.

Kavanagh, Robert Mshengu. 1977. *Making People's Theatre*. Johannesburg: Witwatersrand University Press.

—— 1985. *Theatre and Cultural Struggle in South Africa*. London: Zed.

Kerr, David. 1995. *African Popular Theatre*. London: Heinemann.

Kidd, Ross. 1982. *The Popular Performing Arts, Non-Formal Education and Social Change in the Third World: A Bibliography and Review Essay*. The Hague: Centre for the Study of Education in Developing Countries.

Kirby, E. T. 1974. "Indigenous African Theatre." *Theatre Drama Review* 18. 4 (Dec.): 22–35.

Mlama, Penina M. 1991. *Culture and Development: The Popular Theatre Approach in Africa*. Uppsala: Scandinavian Institute of African Studies.

Ngugi wa Thiong' O. 1986. *Decolonising the Mind: The Politics of Language in African Literature*. Oxford: James Currey.

Obafemi, Olu. 1996. *Contemporary Nigerian Theatre: Cultural Heritage and Social Vision*. Bayreuth: Eckhard Breitinger.

Ogunba, Oyin. 1978. "Traditional African Festival Drama." In *Theatre in Africa*. Ed. O. Ogunba and A. Irele. Ibadan: Ibadan University Press: 3–26.

Ogunbiyi, Yemi, ed. 1981. *Drama and Theatre in Nigeria: A Critical Sourcebook*. Lagos: Nigeria Magazine.

Olaniyan, Tejumola. 1995. *Scars of Conquest/Masks of Resistance: The Invention of Cultural Identities in African, African-American, and Caribbean Drama*. New York: Oxford University Press.

—— 1999. "African Theatre." In *Microsoft Encarta Africana*. Ed. Henry L. Gates and Kwame A. Appiah. CD-ROM.

Paz, Octavio. 1990. *In Search of the Present*. 1990 Nobel Lecture. New York: Harcourt Brace Jovanovich.

Plastow, Jane. 1996. *African Theatre and Politics: The Evolution of Theatre in Ethiopia, Tanzania and Zimbabwe: A Comparative Study*. Amsterdam: Rodopi.

Schipper, Mineke. 1982. *Theatre and Society in Africa*. Johannesburg: Ravan.

Soyinka, Wole. 1988. *Art, Dialogue and Outrage: Essays on Literature and Culture*. Ibadan: New Horn.

Traore, Bakary. 1972. *Black African Theatre and its Social Functions*. Ibadan: Ibadan University Press.

Ugonna, Nnabuenyi. 1983. *Mmonwu: A Dramatic Tradition of the Igbo*. Lagos: Lagos University Press.

Wertheim, Albert. 2000. *The Dramatic Art of Athol Fugard: From South Africa to the World*. Bloomington: Indiana University Press.

Chapter 49

The Fourth Stage:
(Through the Mysteries of Ogun[1] to the Origin of Yoruba Tragedy)

Wole Soyinka

The persistent search for the meaning of tragedy, for a re-definition in terms of cultural or private experience is, at the least, man's recognition of certain areas of depth-experience which are not satisfactorily explained by general aesthetic theories; and, of all the subjective unease that is aroused by man's creative insights, that wrench within the human psyche which we vaguely define as 'tragedy' is the most insistent voice that bids us return to our own sources. There, illusively, hovers the key to the human paradox, to man's experience of being and non-being, his dubiousness as essence and matter, intimations of transience and eternity, and the harrowing drives between uniqueness and Oneness.

Our course to the heart of the Yoruba Mysteries leads by its own ironic truths through the light of Nietzsche[2] and the Phrygian deity; but there are the inevitable, key departures. 'Blessed Greeks!' sings our mad votary in his recessional rapture, 'how great must be your Dionysos, if the Delic god thinks such enchantments necessary to cure you of your Dithyrambic madness.' Such is Apollo's resemblance to the serene art of Obatala[3] the pure unsullied one, to the 'essence' idiom of his rituals, that it is tempting to place him at the end of a creative axis with Ogun, in a parallel evolutionary relationship to Nietzsche's Dionysos–Apollo brotherhood. But Obatala the sculptural god is not the artist of Apollonian illusion but of inner essence. The idealist bronze and terra-cotta of Ife which may tempt the comparison implicit in 'Apollonian' died at some now forgotten period, evidence only of the universal surface culture of courts and never again resurrected. It is alien to the Obatala spirit of Yoruba 'essential' art. Obatala finds expression, not in Nietzsche's Apollonian 'mirror of enchantment' but as a statement of world resolution. The mutual tempering of illusion and will, necessary to an understanding of the Hellenic spirit, may mislead us, when we are faced with Yoruba art, for much of it has a similarity in its aesthetic serenity to the plastic arts of

First published in *The Morality of Art: Essays Presented to G. Wilson Knight*, ed. D. W. Jeffers, pp. 140–60, London: Cambridge University Press, 1973; and subsequently in *Myth, Literature and the African World*, pp. 140–60. Cambridge: Cambridge University Press, 1976.

the Hellenic. Yoruba traditional art is not ideational however, but 'essential'. It is not the idea
(in religious arts) that is transmitted into wood or interpreted in music or movement, but a
quintessence of inner being, a symbolic interaction of the many aspects of revelations
(within a universal context) with their moral apprehension.

Ogun, for his part, is best understood in Hellenic values as a totality of the Dionysian,
Apollonian and Promethean virtues. Nor is that all. Transcending, even today, the distorted
myths of his terrorist reputation, traditional poetry records him as 'protector of orphans',
'roof over the homeless', 'terrible guardian of the sacred oath'; Ogun stands for a transcendental, humane but rigidly restorative justice. (Unlike Sango, who is primarily retributive.)
The first artist and technician of the forge, he evokes like Nietzsche's Apollonian spirit, a
'massive impact of image, concept, ethical doctrine and sympathy'. Obatala is the placid
essence of creation; Ogun the creative urge and instinct, the essence of creativity.

> Rich-laden is his home, yet decked in palm fronds
> He ventures forth, refuge of the down-trodden,
> To rescue slaves he unleashed the judgment of war
> Because of the blind, plunged into forests
> Of curative herbs, Bountiful One
> Who stands bulwark to offsprings of the dead of heaven
> Salutations, O lone being, who swims in rivers of blood.

Such virtues place Ogun apart from the distorted dances to which Nietzsche's Dionysiac
frenzy led him in his search for a selective 'Aryan' soul, yet do not detract from Ogun's
revolutionary grandeur. Ironically, it is the depth-illumination of Nietzsche's intuition into
basic universal impulses which negates his race exclusivist conclusions on the nature of art
and tragedy. In our journey to the heart of Yoruba tragic art which indeed belongs in the
Mysteries of Ogun and the choric ecstasy of revellers, we do not find that the Yoruba, as the
Greek did, 'built for his chorus the scaffolding of a fictive chthonic realm and placed thereon
fictive nature spirits . . .' on which foundation, claims Nietzsche, Greek tragedy developed: in
short, the principle of illusion.

Yoruba tragedy plunges straight into the 'chthonic realm', the seething cauldron of the
dark world will and psyche, the transitional yet inchoate matrix of death and becoming. Into
this universal womb once plunged and emerged Ogun, the first actor, disintegrating within
the abyss. His spiritual re-assemblage does not require a 'copying of actuality' in the ritual
re-enactment of his devotees, any more than Obatala does in plastic representation, in the
art of Obatala. The actors in Ogun Mysteries are the communicant chorus, containing
within their collective being the essence of that transitional abyss. But only as essence, held,
contained and mystically expressed. Within the mystic summons of the chasm the protagonist actor (and every god-suffused choric individual) resists, like Ogun before him, the final
step towards complete annihilation. From this alone steps forward the eternal actor of the
tragic rites, first as the unresisting mouthpiece of the god, uttering visions symbolic of the
transitional gulf, interpreting the dread power within whose essence he is immersed as agent
of the choric will. Only later, in the evenness of release from the tragic climax, does the
serene self-awareness of Obatala reassert its creative control. He, the actor, emerges still
as the mediant voice of the god, but stands now as it were beside himself, observant,
understanding, creating. At this stage is known to him the sublime *aesthetic* joy, not within

Nietzsche's heart of original oneness but in the distanced celebration of the cosmic struggle. This resolved aesthetic serenity is the link between Ogun's tragic art and Obatala's plastic beauty. The unblemished god, Obatala, is the serene womb of chthonic reflections (or memory), a passive strength awaiting and celebrating each act of vicarious restoration of his primordial being. (We shall come later to the story of that first severance.) His beauty is enigmatic, expressive only of the resolution of plastic healing through the wisdom of acceptance. Obatala's patient suffering is the well-known aesthetics of the saint.

For the Yoruba, the gods are the final measure of eternity, as humans are of earthly transience. To think, because of this, that the Yoruba mind reaches intuitively towards absorption in godlike essence is to misunderstand the principle of religious rites, and to misread, as many have done, the significance of religious possession. Past, present and future being so pertinently conceived and woven into the Yoruba world view, the element of eternity which is the gods' prerogative does not have the same quality of remoteness or exclusiveness which it has in Christian or Buddhist culture. The belief of the Yoruba in the contemporaneous existence within his daily experience of these aspects of time has long been recognised but again misinterpreted. It is no abstraction. The Yoruba is not, like European man, concerned with the purely conceptual aspects of time; they are too concretely realised in his own life, religion, sensitivity, to be mere tags for explaining the metaphysical order of his world. If we may put the same thing in fleshed-out cognitions, life, present life, contains within it manifestations of the ancestral, the living and the unborn. All are vitally within the intimations and affectiveness of life, beyond mere abstract conceptualisation.

And yet the Yoruba does not for that reason fail to distinguish between himself and the deities, between himself and the ancestors, between the unborn and his reality, or discard his awareness of the essential gulf that lies between one area of existence and another. This gulf is what must be constantly diminished by the sacrifices, the rituals, the ceremonies of appeasement to those cosmic powers which lie guardian to the gulf. Spiritually, the primordial disquiet of the Yoruba psyche may be expressed as the existence in collective memory of a primal severance in transitional ether,[4] whose first effective defiance is symbolised in the myth of the gods' descent to earth and the battle with immense chaotic growth which had sealed off reunion with man. For they were coming down, not simply to be acknowledged but to be re-united with human essence, to reassume that portion of re-creative transient awareness which the first deity Orisa-nla possessed and expressed through his continuous activation of man images – brief reflections of divine facets – just as man is grieved by a consciousness of the loss of the eternal essence of his being and must indulge in symbolic transactions to recover his totality of being.

Tragedy, in Yoruba traditional drama, is the anguish of this severance, the fragmentation of essence from self. Its music is the stricken cry of man's blind soul as he flounders in the void and crashes through a deep abyss of a-spirituality and cosmic rejection. Tragic music is an echo from that void; the celebrant speaks, sings and dances in authentic archetypal images from within the abyss. All understand and respond, for it is the language of the world.

It is necessary to emphasise that the gods were coming down to be reunited with man, for this tragedy could not be, the anguish of severance would not attain such tragic proportions, if the gods' position on earth (i.e. in man's conception) was to be one of divine remoteness. This is again testified to by the form of worship, which is marked by camaraderie and irreverence just as departure to ancestorhood is marked by bawdiness in the midst of grief. The anthropomorphic origin of uncountable deities is one more leveller of divine class-consciousness but, finally, it is the innate humanity of the gods themselves, their bond with man through a common animist relation with nature and phenomena. Continuity for the Yoruba operates both through the cyclic concept of time and the animist interfusion of all matter and consciousness.

The first actor – for he led the others – was Ogun, first suffering deity, first creative energy, the first challenger, and conqueror of transition. And his, the first art, was tragic art, for the complementary drama of the syncretic successor to Orisa-nla, Obatala's 'Passion' play, is only the plastic resolution of Ogun's tragic engagement. The Yoruba metaphysics of accommodation and resolution could only come after the passage of the gods through the transitional gulf, after the demonic test of the self-will of Ogun the explorer-god in the creative cauldron of cosmic powers. Only after such testing could the harmonious Yoruba world be born, a harmonious will which accommodates every alien material or abstract phenomenon within its infinitely stressed spirituality. The artifact of Ogun's conquest of separation, the 'fetish', was iron ore, symbol of earth's womb-energies, cleaver and welder of life. Ogun, through his redemptive action became the first symbol of the alliance of disparities when, from earth itself, he extracted elements for the subjugation of chthonic chaos. In tragic consciousness the votary's psyche reaches out beyond the realm of noth-ingness (or spiritual chaos) which is potentially destructive of human awareness, through areas of terror and blind energies into a ritual empathy with the gods, the eternal presence, who once preceded him in parallel awareness of their own incompletion. Ritual anguish is therefore experienced as that primal transmission of the god's despair – vast, numinous, always incomprehensible. In vain we seek to capture it in words; there is only for the protagonist the certainty of the experience of this abyss – the tragic victim plunges into it in spite of ritualistic earthing and is redeemed only by action. Without acting, and yet in spite of it he is forever lost in the maul of tragic tyranny.

Acting is therefore a contradiction of the tragic spirit, yet it is also its natural complement. To act, the Promethean instinct of rebellion, channels anguish into a creative purpose which releases man from a totally destructive despair, releasing from within him the most energetic, deeply combative inventions which, without usurping the territory of the infernal gulf, bridges it with visionary hopes. Only the battle of the will is thus primally creative; from its spiritual stress springs the soul's despairing cry which proves its own solace, which alone reverberating within the cosmic vaults usurps (at least, and however briefly) the powers of the abyss. At the charged climactic moments of the tragic rites we understand how music came to be the sole art form which can contain tragic reality. The votary is led by no other guide into the pristine heart of tragedy. Music as the embodiment of the tragic spirit has been more than perceptively exhausted in the philosophy of Europe; there is little to add, much to qualify. And the function and nature of music in Yoruba tragedy is peculiarly revealing of the shortcomings of long accepted conclusions of European intuition.

The European concept of music does not fully illuminate the relationship of music to ritual and drama among the Yoruba. We are inhibited even by recognition of a universality of concepts in the European intuitive grasp of the emotions of the will. First, it is 'unmusical' to separate Yoruba musical form from myth and poetry. The nature of Yoruba music is intensively the nature of its language and poetry, highly charged, symbolic, myth-embryonic.

We acknowledge quite readily the technical lip-service paid to the correspondence of African music to the tonal patterns (meaning and allusion) of the language, but the aesthetic and emotional significance of this relationship has not been truly absorbed, one which springs from the primal simultaneity of art-forms in a culture of total awareness and phenomenal involvement. Language therefore is not a barrier to the profound universality of music but a cohesive dimension and clarification of that wilfully independent art-form which we label music. Language reverts in religious rites to its pristine existence, eschewing the sterile limits of particularisation. In cult funerals, the circle of initiate mourners, an ageless swaying grove of dark pines, raises a chant around a mortar of fire, and words are taken back to their roots, to their original poetic sources when fusion was total and the movement of words was the very passage of music and the dance of images. Language is still the embryo of thought and music where myth is daily companion, for there language is constantly mythopoeic.

Language in Yoruba tragic music therefore undergoes transformation through myth into a secret (masonic) correspondence with the symbolism of tragedy, a symbolic medium of spiritual emotions within the heart of the choric union. It transcends particularisation (of meaning) to tap the tragic source whence spring the familiar weird disruptive melodies. This masonic union of sign and melody, the true tragic music, unearths cosmic uncertainties which pervade human existence, reveals the magnitude and power of creation, but above all creates a harrowing sense of omni-directional vastness where the creative Intelligence resides and prompts the soul to futile exploration. The senses do not at such moments interpret myth in their particular concretions; we are left only with the emotional and spiritual values, the essential experience of cosmic reality. The forms of music are not correspondences at such moments to the physical world, not at this nor at any other moment. The singer is a mouthpiece of the chthonic forces of the matrix and his somnabulist 'improvisations' – a simultaneity of musical and poetic forms – are not representations of the ancestor, recognitions of the living or unborn, but of the no man's land of transition between and around these temporal definitions of experience. The past is the ancestors', the present belongs to the living, and the future to the unborn. The deities stand in the same situation to the living as do the ancestors and the unborn, obeying the same laws, suffering the same agonies and uncertainties, employing the same masonic intelligence of rituals for the perilous plunge into the fourth area of experience, the immeasurable gulf of transition. Its dialogue is liturgy, its music takes form from man's uncomprehending immersion in this area of existence, buried wholly from rational recognition. The source of the possessed lyricist, chanting hitherto unknown mythopoeic strains whose antiphonal refrain is, however, instantly caught and thrust with all its terror and awesomeness into the night by swaying votaries, this source is residual in the numinous area of transition.

This is the fourth stage, the vortex of archetypes and home of the tragic spirit.

It is necessary to recall again that the past is not a mystery and that although the future (the unborn) is yet unknown, it is not a mystery to the Yoruba but co-existent in present consciousness. Tragic terror exists therefore neither in the evocation of the past nor of the future. The stage of transition is, however, the metaphysical abyss both of god and man, and if we agree that, in the European sense, music is the 'direct copy or the direct expression of the will', it is only because nothing rescues man (ancestral, living or unborn) from loss of self within this abyss but a titanic resolution of the will whose ritual summons, response, and expression is the strange alien sound to which we give the name of music. On the arena of the living, when man is stripped of excrescences, when disasters and conflicts (the material of drama) have crushed and robbed him of self-consciousness and pretensions, he stands in present reality at the spiritual edge of this gulf, he has nothing left in physical existence which successfully impresses upon his spiritual or psychic perception. It is at such moments that transitional memory takes over and intimations rack him of that intense parallel of his progress through the gulf of transition, of the dissolution of his self and his struggle and triumph over subsumation through the agency of will. It is this experience that the modern tragic dramatist recreates through the medium of physical contemporary action, reflecting emotions of the first active battle of the will through the abyss of dissolution.[5] Ogun is the first actor in that battle, and Yoruba tragic drama is the re-enactment of the cosmic conflict.

To recognize why Ogun was elected for his role (and the penalty of horror which he had to pay for his challenge) is to penetrate the symbolism of Ogun both as essence of anguish and as combative will within the cosmic embrace of the transitional gulf. We have said that nothing but the will (for that alone is left untouched) rescues being from annihilation within the abyss. Ogun is embodiment of Will, and the Will is the paradoxical truth of destructiveness and creativeness in acting man. Only one who has himself undergone the experience of disintegration, whose spirit has been tested and whose psychic resources laid under stress by the forces most inimical to individual assertion, only he can understand and be the force of fusion between the two contradictions. The resulting sensibility is also the sensibility of the artist, and he is a profound artist only to the degree to which he comprehends and expresses this principle of destruction and re-creation.

We must not lose sight of the fact that Ogun is the artistic spirit, and not in the sentimental sense in which rhapsodists of negritude would have us conceive the negro as pure artistic intuition. The significant creative truth of Ogun is affirmation of the re-creative intelligence; this is irreconcilable with naive intuition. The symbolic artifact of his victory is metallic ore, at once a technical medium as it is symbolic of deep earth energies, a fusion of elemental energies, a binding force between disparate bodies and properties. Thus Ogun, tragic actor, primordial voice of creative man is also, without a contradiction of essences, the forerunner and ancestor of palaeotechnic man. The principle of creativity when limited to pastoral idyllism, as negritude has attempted to limit it, shuts us off from the deeper, fundamental resolutions of experience and cognition. The tragic actor for the future age (already the present for Europe) is that neo-technic ancestor Sango,[6] god of electricity, whose tragedy stems similarly from the principle of a preliminary self-destruction, represented (as in a later penalty of Ogun) in the blind ignorant destruction of his own flesh and blood. What, for Ogun, was a destructive penalty leading to a secondary drama of 'Passion' was in Sango the very core of his tragedy. The historic process of dilution in tragic challenge is manifested in the relationship of these two myths. Sango is an anthropomorphic deity; his history revolved around petty tyranny; his self-destruction was the violent, central explosion from ego-inflation. Where Ogun's human alienation was the postscript error, an exaction for his basic victory over the transitional guardians of the gulf, Sango's was 'in character', a wild vengeful slaughter upon menials who had dared to defy his authority. But the 'terror and pity' of Sango is undeniable, only it is the 'terror and pity' of human disavowal for that new disciple standing on the edge of the sublimating abyss already subdued by Ogun. We will not find the roots of tragedy in the Mysteries of Sango.

Yoruba myth is a recurrent exercise in the experience of disintegration, and this is significant for the seeming distancing of will among a people whose mores, culture and metaphysics are based on apparent resignation and acceptance but which are, experienced in depth, a statement of man's penetrating insight into the final resolution of things and the constant evidence of harmony. What moral values do we encounter in the drama of Obatala, representative though it also is of the first disintegration experienced by godhead? We are further back in Origin, not now engaged in the transitional battle of Ogun, but in the fragmentation of Orisa-nla, the primal deity, from whom the entire Yoruba pantheon was born. Myth informs us that a jealous slave rolled a stone down the back of the first and only deity and shattered him in a thousand and one fragments. From this first act of revolution was born the Yoruba pantheon.

The drama which stems from this is not the drama of acting man but that of suffering spirit, the drama of Obatala. Yoruba myth syncretises Obatala, god of purity, god also of creation (but not of creativity!), with the first deity Orisa-nla. And the ritual of Obatala is a play of form, a moving celebration whose nearest equivalent in the European idiom is the Passion play. The drama is all essence: captivity, suffering and redemption. Obatala is symbolically captured, confined and ransomed. At every stage he is the embodiment of the suffering spirit of man, uncomplaining, agonised, full of the redemptive qualities of endurance and martyrdom. The music that accompanies the rites of Obatala is all clear tone and winnowed lyric, of order and harmony, stately and saintly. Significantly, the motif is white for transparency of heart and mind; there is a rejection of mystery; tones of vesture and music combine to banish mystery and terror; the poetry of the song is litanic, the dramatic idiom is the processional or ceremonial. It is a drama in which the values of conflict or the revolutionary spirit are excluded, attesting in their place the adequacy and certainty of a harmonious resolution which belongs in time and human faith. It is antithetical to the tragic challenge of Ogun in man.

Proportion in tragedy is governed by an element of the unknown in the forces of opposition or by a miscalculation by the tragic victim of such powers. The drama of Obatala dispenses with the effect of the unknown, and his agony is an evocation of the loneliness of the first deity, for this drama is, as we have stated, all pathos. And the essence is the emotional prelude to the creation of man, the limited, serene aesthetics of moulding man, not to be compared to the cosmic eruption within consciousness brought about by the re-creation of the self. The sympathetic need to be redeemed by evidence of love and human contact, by extension of the self into recognisable entities and other units of potential consciousness – this is the province of Obatala, the delicate shell of the original fullness. The profounder aspect of self-recreation, the anguish of the Will, is the portion of original restoration which has been left to the peculiar talents of Ogun, and the statement of Yoruba tragic rites is the complements of his Will to the essence of anguish. The latter by itself is crystallised in the Passion play. The drama of Obatala is prelude, suffering and aftermath. It symbolises firstly the god's unbearable loneliness and next, the memory of his incomplete-ness, the missing essence. And so it is also with the other gods who did not avail themselves, as did Ogun, of the chance for a redemptive combat where each might recreate each by submission to a disintegrating process within the matrix of cosmic creativity, whence the Will performs the final reassemblage. The weightiest burden of severance is that of each from self, not of godhead from mankind, and the most perilous aspect of the god's journey is that in which the deity must truly undergo the experience of transition. It is a look into the very heart of the phenomena. To fashion a bridge across it was not only Ogun's task but his very nature, and he had first to experience, to surrender his individuation once again (the first time, as a part of the original Orisa-nla Oneness) to the fragmenting process; to be resorbed within universal Oneness, the Unconscious, the deep black whirlpool of mythopoeic forces, to immerse himself thoroughly within it, understand its nature and yet by the combative value of the will to rescue and re-assemble himself and emerge wiser, powerful from the draught of cosmic secrets, organising the mystic and the technical forces of earth and cosmos to forge a bridge for his companions to follow.

It is true that to understand, to understand profoundly, is to be unnerved, deprived of the will to act. For is not human reality dwarfed by the awe and wonder, the inevitability of this cosmic gulf? It must be remembered that within this abyss are the activities of birth, death and resorption in phenomena (for the abyss is the transition between the various stages of existence). Life, the paltry reflection of the forces of the matrix, becomes suddenly inadequate, patronising and undignified when the source of creative and destructive energies is glimpsed. Suffering cancels the opaque pleasure of human existence; suffering, the truly overwhelming suffering of Sango, of Lear, of Oedipus, this suffering hones the psyche to a finely self-annihilating perceptiveness and renders further action futile and, above all, lacking in dignity. And what has the struggle of the tragic hero been, after all, but an effort to maintain that innate concept of dignity which impels to action only to that degree in which the hero possesses a true nobility of spirit? At such moments he is close to the acceptance and wisdom of Obatala in which faith is rested, not on the self, but on a universal selfhood to which individual contributions are fundamentally meaningless. It is the faith of 'knowing', the enigmatic wisdom of spiritual serenity. It is this which is often narrowly interpreted as the philosophy of the African. But philosophies are the result of primal growth and formative experience; the oracular wisdom of a race based on and continually acted upon by the collective experience of the past, present and unborn (prognostic) realities, complements the intuitive glimpse and memory of the heart of transitional being.

Yoruba 'classical' art is mostly an expression of the Obatala resolution and human beneficence, utterly devoid, on the surface, of conflict and irruption. The masks alone occasionally suggest a correspondence to the chthonic realm and hint at the archetypes of transition, yet even the majority of them flee the full power of cosmic vision, take refuge in deliberately grotesque and comic attitudes. Such distortions are easily recognised as the technique of evasion from the fullness of numinous powers. Terror is both contained by art in tragic form and released by art through comic presentation and sexual ambience. The tragic mask, however, also functions from the same source as its music – from the archetypal essences whose language derives not from the plane of physical reality or ancestral memory (the ancestor is no more than agent or medium), but from the numinous territory of transition into which the artist obtains fleeting glimpses by ritual, sacrifice and a patient submission of rational awareness to the moment when fingers and voice relate the symbolic language of the cosmos. The deft, luminous peace of Yoruba religious art blinds us therefore to the darker powers of the tragic art into which only the participant can truly enter. The grotesquerie of the terror cults misleads the unwary into equating fabricated fears with the exploration of the Yoruba mind into the mystery of his individual will and the intimations of divine suffering to which artistic man is prone. Ifa's cycle of masonic poetry – curative, prognostic, aesthetic and omniscient – expresses a philosophy of optimism in its oracular adaptiveness and unassailable resolution of all phenomena; the gods are accommodating and embrace within their eternal presences manifestations which are seemingly foreign or contradictory. It is no wonder therefore that the overt optimistic nature of the total culture is the quality attributed to the Yoruba himself, one which has began to affect his accommodation towards the modern world, a spiritual complacency with which he encounters threats to his human and unique validation. Alas, in spite of himself, from time to time, the raw urgent question beats in the blood of his temples demanding, what is the will of Ogun? For the hammering of the Yoruba will was done at Ogun's forge, and any threat of disjunction is, as with the gods, a memory code for the resurrection of the tragic myth.

Yoruba morality has also contributed to the mistaken exclusion of tragic myth from present consciousness; for, as always, the placid surface of the process of healing for spiritual or social rupture is mistaken for the absence of the principles of psychic experience that went into the restoration. Morality for the Yoruba is that which creates harmony in the cosmos, and reparation for disjunction within the individual psyche cannot be seen as compensation for the individual accident to that personality. Thus good and evil are not measured in terms of offences against the individual or even the physical community, for there is knowledge from within the corpus of Ifa oracular wisdoms that a rupture is often simply one aspect of the destructive–creative unity, that offences even against nature may be part of the exaction by deeper nature from humanity of acts which alone can open up the deeper springs of man and bring about a constant rejuvenation of the human spirit. Nature in turn benefits by such broken taboos, just as the cosmos does by demands made upon its will by man's cosmic affronts. Such acts of hubris compel the cosmos to delve deeper into its essence to meet the human challenge. Penance and retribution are not therefore aspects of punishment for crime but the first acts of a resumed awareness, an invocation of the principle of cosmic adjustment. Tragic fate is the repetitive cycle of the taboo in nature, the karmic act of hubris witting or unwitting, into which the demonic will within man constantly compels him. Powerful tragic drama follows upon the act of hubris, and myth exacts this attendant penalty from the hero where he has actually emerged victor of a conflict. Sango's taboo is based on an elementary form of hubris. Over-reaching even beyond the generous toleration due to a monarch, he fell victim to a compulsion for petty intriguing which finally led to his downfall. A final, desperate invocation of unnatural strength gave him temporary ascendancy and he routed his disloyal men. Then came the desecration of nature in which he spilt the blood of his kin. Ogun not only dared to look into transitional essence but triumphantly bridged it with knowledge, with art, with vision and the mystic creativity of science – a total and profound hubristic assertiveness that is beyond any parallel in Yoruba experience. The penalty came later when, as a reward and acknowledgement of his leadership of the divinities, gods and humans joined to offer him a crown. At first he declined but later he consented to the throne of Ire. At the first battle the same demonic energies were aroused but this was no world womb, no chthonic lair, no playground of cosmic monsters, nor could the divisions between man and man, between I and you, friend and foe, be perceived by the erstwhile hero of the transitional abyss. Enemy and subjects fell alike until Ogun alone was left, sole survivor of the narrowness of human separation. The battle is symbolic of tragic hindsight common alike to god and man. In the Ogun Mysteries this drama is a 'Passion' of a different kind, released into quietist wisdom, a ritual exorcism of demonic energies. There is no elation, not even at the end of purgation, nothing like the beatified elation of Obatala after his redemption, only a world-weariness on the rock-shelf of Promethean shoulders, a profound sorrow in the chanting of the god's recessional.[7]

Once we recognise, to revert to his Hellenic equation, the Dionysian–Apollonian–Promethean essence of Ogun, the element of hubris is seen as innate to his tragic being, requiring definition in Yoruba terms, taking it to its cyclic resolution of man's metaphysical situation. Of the profound anguish of Dionysos, the mythic disintegration of his origin is the now familiar cause, and the process of the will, no less, is what rescues the ecstatic god from being, literally, scattered to the cosmic winds. The will of Zeus is as conceptually identifiable with that of Dionysos as the elemental fragmentation of Orisa-nla can be recognised as the recurrent consciousness within Ogun (and other gods) of this kernel of terror of a previous rendering. Ripped in pieces at the hands of the titans for the (by him) unwilled acts of hubris, a divine birth, Dionysos–Zagreus commences divine existence by this experience of the destruction of the self, the transitional horror. For it is an act of hubris not only to dare the gulf of transition but to mingle essences for extra measure. We approach, it seems, the ultimate pessimism of existence as pronounced by Nietzsche's sage Silenus: it is an act of hubris to be born. It is a challenge to the jealous chthonic powers, to *be*. The answer of the Yoruba to this is just as clear: it is no less an act of hubris to *die*. And the whirlpool of transition requires both hubristic complements as catalyst to its continuous regeneration. This is the serene wisdom and essential art of Obatala. All acts are subordinate to these ultimates of the human condition and recreative will. To dare transition is the ultimate test of the human spirit, and Ogun is the first protagonist of the abyss.

The Phrygian god and his twin Ogun exercise irresistible fascination. Dionysos' thyrsus is physically and functionally paralleled by the *opa Ogun* borne by the male devotees of Ogun. But the thyrsus of Dionysos is brighter; it is all light and running wine, Ogun's stave is more symbolic of his labours through the night of transition. A long willowy pole, it is topped by a frond-bound lump of ore which strains the pole in wilful curves and keeps it vibrant. The bearers, who can only be men, are compelled to move about among the revellers as the effort to keep the ore-head from toppling over keeps them perpetually on the move. Through town and village, up the mountain to the grove of Ogun this dance of the straining phallus-heads pocks the air above men and women revellers who are decked in palm fronds and bear palm branches in their hands. A dog is slaughtered in sacrifice, and the mock-struggle of the head priest and his acolytes for the carcass, during which it is literally torn limb from limb, inevitably brings to mind the dismemberment of Zagreus, son of Zeus. Most significant of all is the brotherhood of the palm and the ivy. The mystery of the wine of palm, bled straight from the tree and potent without further ministration, is a miracle of nature acquiring symbolic significance in the Mysteries of Ogun. For it was instrumental in the tragic error of the god and his sequent Passion. Like Obatala also, the gods commit their error after an excess of the potent draught. Ogun was full of wine before his battle at the head of the Ire army. After his dark deed, the wine fog slowly lifted and he was left with nothing but dread truth. Obatala, moulder of men, fell also to the fumes of wine; his craftsman's fingers lost their control and he moulded cripples, albinos, the blind and other deformed. Obatala the eternal penitent therefore forbids wine to his worshippers in or out of his seasonal rites while Ogun, in proud acceptance of the need to create a challenge for the constant exercise of will and control, enjoins the liberal joy of wine. The palm fronds are a symbol of his wilful, ecstatic being.

And how else may the inhibiting bonds of man be dissolved when he goes to meet his god, how else may he quickly enter into the god's creative being, or his inner ear and eye respond to the fleeting presences which guard the abode of gods, how else partake in the psychic revelry of the world when it celebrates a crossing of the abyss of non-being?

The sculpted rites of the worship of Obatala are rapturous also, but lacking in ecstasy. It is a dance of amelioration to tyrannic powers, not a celebration of the infinite will of the Promethean spirit. The one is withdrawal, the other an explosion of the forces of darkness and joy, explosion of the sun's kernel, an eruption of fire which is the wombfruit of pristine mountains, for no less, no different were the energies within Ogun whose ordering and control through the will brought him safely through the tragic gulf. Even through the medium of this ecstasy, a glimpse is obtained of the vastness of the abyss; the true devotee knows, understands and penetrates the god's anguish. In the centre of the swaying, milling, ecstatic horde where his individuation is routed and he submits to a union of joy, the inner being encounters the precipice. Poised on the heights of the physical mountain-home of Ogun he experiences a yawning gulf within him, a menacing maul of chthonic strength yawning ever wider to annihilate his being; he is saved only by channelling the dark torrent into the plastic light of poetry and dance; not, however, as a reflection or illusion of reality, but as the celebrative aspects of the resolved crisis of his god.

Notes

1 Ogun: God of creativity, guardian of the road, god of metallic lore and artistry. Explorer, hunter, god of war, Custodian of the sacred oath.
2 Nietzsche, *The Birth of Tragedy.*
3 Obatala: God of creation (by syncretist tradition with Orisa-nla), essence of the serene arts. Obatala moulds the forms but the breath of life is administered by Edumare the Supreme deity. The art of Obatala is thus essentially plastic and formal.
4 I would render this more cogently today in terms of race origination, uprooting, wandering and settling. This group experience is less remote, and parallels the mythology of primordial chaos, as well as the rites of transition (birth, death etc.). See reference to Sango's drama in chapter 2.
5 Or again the collective memory of dispersion and re-assemblage in racial coming-into-being. All these, and of course the recurring experience of birth and death, are psycho-historic motifs for the tragic experience: the essence of transition.
6 Sango: God of lightning and electricity. A tyrant of Oyo, he was forced to commit suicide by factions, through his own over-reaching. His followers thereupon deified him and he assumed the agency of lightning.
7 In contemporary (public) festivals of Ogun the usual intermingling of idioms has occurred – the ritual dismembering of a surrogate dog, enactment of the massacre at Ire, the dispute between Sango and Ogun, Ogun's battle triumphs etc. The note is summatively festive.

Chapter 50

Introduction to *King Oedipus*

Tawfiq Al-Hakim

[...]

If only a literary figure had risen among us during the last century or two to cry out questioningly: "O Arabic literature, from ancient times there have been between you and Greek thought close ties and bonds. You have reflected on it and taken the sciences and philosophy from it. You have, however, turned your face away from the poetry it has. How far will this rupture go? When will a truce be concluded between you and Greek poetry? Consider it a bit. Allow it to be translated and researched. Perhaps you will find in it something to reinforce your inheritance and to augment your bequest to future generations."

This voice was not raised during the past centuries. Therefore, the rupture continued to exist between Arabic literature and Greek literature. The persistence of this rupture has made it difficult for the theater to stand on a solid foundation and to find a place among us within the colonnades of literature, thought, and culture.

There must be a truce then between the two literatures, if we wish to have established within the deep-rooted history of Arabic literature this dramatic genre, whether in poetry or prose, in a valuable and lasting way. But how is the truce to come about? We must first of all learn the reasons for the estrangement so that we can work successfully afterwards and take the measures necessary for a covenant.

Before anything else, we must ask ourselves whose responsibility it was that Greek poetry was not translated into Arabic. This question leads us to study the way the Greek legacy was translated and the causes and reasons for that.

It is known that following Alexander's conquests the Greek spirit penetrated Asia. Syria and the area of Mesopotamia, between the Tigris and Euphrates rivers, were among the most important regions which were subject to the influence of Greek civilization. There, in the cells of the Syrian ascetics throughout those areas, for a period of centuries an extensive movement of translation was energetically carried out for scientific and philosophic works

First published in *Plays, Prefaces, and Postscripts, vol. 1: Theatre of the Mind*, trans. William M. Hutchins, pp. 274–80. Washington, DC: Three Continents Press, 1981. Copyright © 1981 by Lynne Rienner Publishers, Inc. Reprinted with permission of the publisher.

from Greek to Syriac. It was from these Syriac translations that the Arabs later drew inspiration and made translations.

If this account is correct, the Arabs can say that they translated what they found. Poetry was not something those monks cared about...but what happened was that many Arabs afterwards learned Greek and were able to translate from it directly.

Among the works translated into Arabic was the book of poetry or *Poetics* of Aristotle, containing his definitions of tragedy and comedy and their characteristics as parts of dramatic poetry. Ibn Rushd came and showed us with his famous commentary on the *Poetics* that the Arabs did not intentionally close their minds to knowledge of the art of poetry among the Greeks. How was it then that curiosity did not impel them thereafter to translate some of the representative tragedies or comedies into Arabic?

It is understandable that they would refrain from translating lyric poetry like that of Pindar or Anacreon, for in pre-Islamic or 'Abbasid Arabic poetry there are comparable works of that type. But why did they – since they were, as we know, eager to learn – fail to translate the tragedies of the Greek poets?

For us to answer that we must know first what tragedy is? How did it arise in Greece? There is no longer any doubt today that tragedy originated from the worship of Bacchus, the wine god known to the Greeks under the name of Dionysus. Every spring, religious celebrations were held for this god. There was boisterous drunkenness with an outpouring of gaiety. People danced and sang at these times around a statue of the wine god. They were decked out in goat skins and leaves. This dancing and singing was at first improvised. After that, with the passing of time, the performance was refined. The people prepared them according to patterns with set elements. That singing was soon mixed with a type of praise for the deeds of that god in the form of a narrative recital of praise for his triumphs, his adventures, and his amazing journeys. Then the matter of the troupe of dancers developed till they began to vary their costumes and portray different characters – not just goats and animals. The narrative also developed and began to take on different ideas unrelated to the life of the god whose festivals they were celebrating. This led reactionary and conservative elders to make a row about this innovation. They said, "There is nothing about Bacchus in this." This phrase later became proverbial in the Greek language.

But from this innovation which aroused criticism and anger came the dramatic art. It was not long before a man appeared, called Thespis, whose reflection led him to compose what the chorus would have to recite and the words of a dialogue for one actor to hold with the chorus. He gave this actor different masks and costumes. He was able in that way to take on a number of characters by himself.

In this fashion, the matter passed from the stage of narrative recital to that of dialogue and action. Drama was born and tragedy came into existence. After Thespis there came a poet named Phrynichos who took this art another step. It was said that he was the first to introduce women characters into the performance. He divided the chorus into two sections. One of them could address the actor in a tone of approval of his actions. Meanwhile the other addressed him in a tone of displeasure and criticism. It was as though the chorus with its two parts were the people in society, including those who support the deeds they see and those who oppose them. History also mentions to us that two of the poet's contemporaries, Choirlos and Pratinas, each played a part in improving this form of art. All of these prepared the way for the appearance of the great masters of tragedy: Aeschylus, Sophocles, and Euripides.

That is a quick look at the genesis of dramatic poetry in Greece. From it we see that worship of Bacchus was the mother of tragedy. This art then poured out to us like wine...from the jug of religion. In this way, the great poets of tragedy proceeded to weave their immortal works from their religious legends, from mythology. They imbued them with a spirit of the struggle between man and divine powers. Do you suppose it was this religious character which discouraged the Arabs from embracing this art?

This is the opinion of a group of scholars. They assert that Islam stood in the way of the acceptance of this pagan art. I do not share this opinion. Islam has never been an obstacle for an art form. It permitted the translation of many works produced by heathens. There was *Kalila and Dimna* which Ibn al-Muqaffa' translated from Pahlavi. There was Ferdowsi's *Shahnameh* which al-Bundari translated from the Persian. It is about their pagan age. Similarly, Islam did not prevent the circulation of the wine poetry of Abu Nuwas, the carving of statues for the palaces of the caliphs, or the expert portraiture of Persian miniatures. Likewise, it did not prevent the translation of many Greek works which mentioned pagan customs. No, it was not the pagan quality as such which turned the Arabs away from dramatic poetry. What did hold them back then? Do you suppose it was the difficulty of understanding a story in poetry which revolves entirely around legends which could only be understood after a long explanation spoiling the pleasure of the person trying to understand them and ending the enjoyment of someone desiring to sample them? Perhaps there is some truth to this explanation, for I was astonished by the comment of the critic Francisque Sarcey counselling the spectators when "Oedipus Tyrannus" was presented on the stage of the Comédie-Française in 1881 AD. I consider it, of the Greek tragedies, the one least immersed in religious mythology, the clearest and purest of them, and the one closest to the soul's naked humanity.

The critic said: "I advise the audience – in particular the ladies among them – to open a book or dictionary of Greek mythology and to read in it before seeing the play performed, a summary of the Oedipus legend. This will spare them the boredom of losing the thread and wandering through the obscurities of the first act."[1]

To whom was this advice directed? To the public of a nation whose culture was based on the Greek legacy...a public most of whom had been to school where they were taught – and there is no doubt about what they were taught – Greek literature with its tragedies and comedies. If a public like that, in that modern age, still needed a summary or dictionary to follow the tragedy of Oedipus, what are we to think of the Arab reader in the 'Abbasid or Fatimid eras?

But, despite the validity of this explanation, I do not believe that it, either, would have prevented translation of some examples of this art. For Plato's *Republic* was translated into Arabic, and I have no doubt that it contains ideas concerning that ideal city which would be difficult for the Islamic mentality to digest. Yet that did not prevent its translation. Indeed it was precisely this difficulty that moved al-Farabi to take Plato's *Republic*, wrap it in a gown of his thoughts, and pour it into the mold of his philosophic and Islamic mentality.

Something similar could have happened for Greek tragedy. It would have been possible for a tragedy like "Oedipus" to have been translated and then afterwards taken up by a poet or prose author. He would have removed from it the hard-to-understand mythological references and stripped it of the obscure pagan beliefs. He would have presented it, clear and unambiguous, in its bare human structure. Or, he might have thrown over it a diaphanous gown of Islamic belief or Arab thought.

Why did not that take place? Because there was another reason, no doubt, which turned the Arabs away from adopting Greek theater. Perhaps the reason was that the Greek tragedies were not considered at that time to be literature meant to be read. At that time, they may have been something that would not be independently read the way Plato's *Republic* was. They were written not to be read but to be performed. The author knew that his work would be presented to the people in performance on a stage. He would therefore leave his texts and his dialogue free of explanations, observations, or information necessary to grasp the story's atmosphere. He could rely on the spectator's perceiving it visually, realized and portrayed, when it was produced. In truth, the Greek theater reached a precision and complexity in its machines and instruments that excites astonishment. It had machines that moved and rotated as well as theatrical tricks and devices sufficient to allow those people to produce "Prometheus Bound" by the poet Aeschylus which contains sea nymphs which appear out of the clouds and the sea. Prometheus comes in mounted on the back of that fabulous animal with the head of an eagle and the body of a stallion.

Perhaps this is what made the Arab translator stop perplexed before tragedy. He would cast his eyes over the silent texts trying to see them in his mind throbbing and moving with their characters, atmosphere, locations, and times. But that mind would not comply with his wishes. For he had never seen this art acted in his land. The chorus among the Greeks created acting. It was the actor Thespis who created the play. The play did not create the theater. The theater was the creator of the play. So long as the Arab translator was certain that he had before him a work not made to be read, for what purpose would he translate it then?

Perhaps this is the reason that Greek dramatic poetry was not translated into Arabic. The activity of translation of Greek works was designed to be useful. It was not merely for the love of discovery or just from curiosity. In this case, the benefit from the ideas and thoughts of the tragedies was lost, because they could not be grasped or attained solely by reading. In order to make them clear, there had to be a means for presenting them. That was not something that was available or known. The question, however, which must then be posed is why there was no acting in Arab culture. Why wasn't it known?

The Arabs too had their pagan age. Among their poets of that age were those said to have travelled to "Caesar's land," like Imru' al-Qays. There he no doubt saw the Roman theaters looming tall. They had inherited this art from the Greeks. Could not the sight of the theater have inspired the pagan Arab poet with the idea of importing, transmitting, or adapting it?

Where would he have taken it? Here is the problem. The homeland to which the pagan Arab poet would have transmitted this art, had he wanted to, was nothing other than a desert vast as the sea. Through it hastened camels like ships, roaming from island to island. These were scattered oases which would gush with water one day and be green with plants. On the morrow the water supply would dwindle away and the green growth would wither. It was a homeland moving on the backs of caravans, running here and there in pursuit of a drop from the clouds. It was a homeland continuously rocked atop camels in a rhythmic, harmonic way encouraging the riders to sing. From this, Arabic poetry was born. It originated with the camel chant, as the person holding the reins of the first camel raised his voice to chant to the beat of that faint, hidden music coming from the camels' hoof beats on the sand.

Everything, then, in the moving homeland separated it from the theater. The first thing the theater requires is stability. The Arabs lacked a settled feeling. That is, in my opinion, the true reason for their neglect of dramatic poetry which requires a theater. The theater of Bacchus, the ruins of which have been uncovered by archaeological work in modern times, was a solid building with a massive foundation. It was an establishment belonging to the state. Anyone who becomes acquainted, from the ruins or from drawings, with that enormous structure and its capacity for thousands of spectators will judge at once that this is something which must have been the product of a settled community and of a concentrated and united social life. A researcher would have the right to object that the Arabs under the Umayyad and 'Abbasid dynasties and thereafter experienced that sedentary community and united and concentrated society. Why did the Arabs in those eras refrain from erecting a theater when they were capable of it? We see that they surveyed different cultures and adopted from their architecture elements they used to establish a stunning architecture bearing their new stamp.

There is a simple answer to that. The Arabs under the Umayyad dynasty and later continued to consider the Bedouin and desert poetry the finest example to be imitated. They looked to pre-Islamic poetry as the most perfect model to be followed. They sensed their lack of architecture, but they never felt a shortcoming in poetry. When they wished to borrow and sample from others, they went in every direction and looked at every art – except the art of poetry. They believed that they had reached the ultimate in it long before. Thus we find ourselves turning round a complex group of reasons each of which could have discouraged the Arabs from becoming interested in drama.

However, was it necessary for Arab literature to produce tragedies? Is tragedy a genre necessary for the development of Arabic literature to complete its personality?

Anyone who reads the famous preface to *Cromwell* by Victor Hugo finds a partial answer. He divides the history of mankind into three ages. The primitive age in his opinion is the age of lyric poetry. Of it he says that in the primitive age man chants as though breathing. He is in the age of chivalrous youth, of breaking into song, etc. Then comes the antique age, the age of the epic. The tribe has developed and become a nation. The societal urge has replaced the urge to travel. Nations have been formed and become important. One of them rubs against another. They clash and engage in battle. Here poetry arises to narrate the events that have taken place, to tell the story of what happened to the peoples and what befell the empires. Finally comes the modern age which is the age of drama. In his opinion, it is the complete poetry, because it includes within it all the varieties. It contains some of the lyric and some of the epic.

Let us listen to him summarize his thought: "Human society progresses and matures while singing of its dreams. Afterwards it begins to narrate its deeds. Then it finally undertakes to portray its thoughts."[2]

Hugo invites us to test his doctrine on each literature individually. He assures us that we will find that each bears out this division. According to him, the lyric poets always precede the epic poets, and the epic poets precede the dramatic poets.

Do you suppose this doctrine can be applied to Arabic literature? In my opinion it can be, if we disregard the genres and confine our investigation to the objectives. There is no doubt that Arabic poetry did sing of dreams, describe wars, and portray ideas. It did not change its method, leave its genre, or deviate from its principles. On its way, it followed the same order that Hugo set forth. In the 'Abbasid era alone we find al-Buhturi (d. 897 AD) is before al-Mutanabbi (d. 965 AD) and al-Mutanabbi before Abu al-'Ala' (d. 1057 AD). Had these poets been planted in the Greek soil, al-Buhturi, the Arab cymbal player, would have been Pindar.

Al-Mutanabbi who makes our ears resound across the generations with the ring of swords would have been Homer. Abu al-'Ala' who portrayed for us thought about man and his destiny and the heavenly hosts would have been Aeschylus. The development, then, in terms of content was completed. But the development with respect to form was hindered by those circumstances which attended the growth of the Arab state. The circumstances, which as we have seen did not limit the Arabs' mentality or restrain their artistic nature, were able in any case, against their will, to keep them away from this one of the literary arts at that stage of their history.

There is then no inherent animosity between the Arabic language and dramatic literature. It is a question rather of a temporary estrangement, resulting from a lack of the instrument. The matter for the Arabs here is like that when they knew no riding animals other than the camel. Had circumstances conspired to deny them the horse, they would have continued to the present day without knowing how to ride it. But no sooner had the horse entered the desert than the Arabs became horsemen. They mastered the arts of rearing it and of describing it. What is there to say today anywhere in the world about the original horse before the Arabian? If a splendid description of the traits of the horse is sought, where is it but in Arabic poetry?

The whole question then is one of instrument. It is as though the Arabs in the age of camels were saying: "Give us the horse; we will ride it." They might similarly have said: "Give us the theater and we will write for it."

There is no doubt that the world has changed today. Theater in the broad sense of the word has become one of the necessities of contemporary life. It is not restricted to any one class. It is the daily nourishment for the minds of the people. Its richness varies according to their cultural level. In the final analysis it is the instrument of art which spreads through the Eastern and Western lands of the earth. By 'theater' I mean here every art which sets out to portray things, persons, and thoughts on a stage, screen, page or over the air in such manner that they appear alive, conversing and debating, displaying their secrets and thought before a viewer, hearer, or reader.

There is no longer any way to ignore this worldwide style of presenting ideas in a living way in dramatic form. Wherever we go today in the Arab world we find high, lofty, ornamented buildings, the most luxurious in our cities. These are the theaters!

Thus we have the theater, that is, the instrument. For our Arab way of life, it has become one of the necessities like bread and water. Every day the field of operation for this instrument called acting has expanded until it has become – with the spread of broadcasting – daily nourishment entering every home. All of this ought to have reached the ears of the deep-rooted Arabic literature and prompted it to pay attention to this art and lay foundations for it within its own procedures and categories. It is my guess that Arabic literature yearns to do that, for it is not a dead literature nor ossified.

But how can this be done? It cannot be expected to open a door into its noble frame and set within it an art with no foundations. For it is not a frivolous or spurious literature. These are the people who have preserved the lineages of human beings and horses. We must not give them cause for distress over their long-established literature at this late date. We must then create the missing link of the lineage and return to it so that it can firmly bond Arabic literature with dramatic art. This link can only be Greek literature.

For all these reasons, there must a truce between the two long-established literatures. Here we approach the great question: how can this reconciliation be achieved? Is it sufficient to be, with care and concern, devoted to Greek dramatic literature, transmitting all of it to our Arabic language? This matter is obviously necessary, and most of that has been accomplished. Indeed, *Oedipus the King* by Sophocles was presented for all to see on the Arab stage more than a third of a century ago.

But the mere transmission of Greek dramatic literature to the Arabic language does not achieve for us the establishment of a dramatic literature in Arabic. Similarly, the mere transmission of Greek philosophy did not create an Arab or Islamic philosophy. Translation is only a tool which must carry us to a farther goal.

This goal is to ladle water from the spring, then to swallow it, digest it, and assimilate it, so that we can bring it forth to the people once again dyed with the color of our thought and imprinted with the stamp of our beliefs. This was the way the Arab philosophers proceeded when they took the works of Plato and Aristotle. We must proceed in that same way with Greek tragedy. We must dedicate ourselves to its study with patience and endurance and then look at it afterwards with Arab eyes.

[...]

Notes

1   Francisque Sarcey, *Quarante ans de théâtre* (Paris: Bibliothèque des Annales, 1900–1902), III, 312.
2   Victor Hugo, *Oeuvres complètes: Cromwell* ([n, pl.]: Editions Rencontre, 1967), p. 26.

Chapter 51

Poetry as Dramatic Performance

Kofi Anyidoho

> The preliminary postulate here is that modern African Literature (writing) is produced in a cultural environment where the dominant mode of communication is oral. But African Literature as writing is produced and consumed by people who have acquired the technology of literacy. What connection is there between this isolated coterie and the larger body of oral communicators to warrant the introduction of issues of orality in African Literature?
>
> (Biakolo 6)

The above postulate raises a fundamental issue that has been at the core of much recent critical debate on African Literature. Elsewhere in Biakolo's paper, he suggests that, as "a more enduring theoretical engagement" with this issue, we need "to problematise African Literature as the confluence of two alternative media: oral and written communication." Such a view, he argues, shifts critical attention from a consideration of "authors and themes and styles to one of medium."

My main task in this paper is to take up one important implication of producing African Literature within an environment where the dominant mode of communication is oral. But my concern is more of a practical rather than a theoretical nature. This paper seeks to examine the essential features, forms, inspirations, and implications of a phenomenon that has become quite established on the poetic scene in Ghana: the dramatization of written poetry for stage presentation to live audiences. In an earlier paper, "Mythmaker and Myth-breaker: The Oral Poet as Earwitness," I urged our writers to "attempt to explore the possibilities of using the technology of sound as the primary medium of poetic dialogue ... [since] many of our people do not have eyes to witness the poetry of print but do have ears for the power of the sound and sense of words" (13). My recent experiences with the poetic scene in Ghana have brought me to a slightly different kind of awareness, and a firm conviction that new developments in poetic practice have radical implications for the impact of written poetry in Africa. The *re*-presentation of written poetry through the multiple media of African performance tradition holds great potential for overcoming the communication gap that has forced the poet, as a writer, into an often celebrated but clearly marginalized position as a contemporary artist.

Against the background of a lack of avenues for the printed publication of poetry and an inadequate audience for the printed word, and in consonance with the traditional African practice of "publishing" poetry through live performances, the current generation of

First published in *Research in African Literatures* 22.2 (Summer 1991): 41–8, 53–5.

Ghanaian poets have turned to dramatized presentations of their work. The gains so far recorded by this change in artistic practice, as well as some of its associated problems and limitations, are worth examining in some detail.

Essential Components of African Performance Tradition

The concept and practice of performance are central to artistic expression and experience in African tradition. As a rule, however, the validity of this rule may not be obvious partly because we often encounter difficulty in finding precise non-African equivalents for the various terms that an African people uses in defining its art forms. Try finding a precise equivalent for, say, *poetry* or *poet*. Among the Ewe, the terms you are given, *ha* or *hɛno*, suggest that poetry and music generally occur as a combined art form; almost invariably the poet is also a composer and/or singer. In the actual public performance of his role, the picture becomes even more complex, for the poet-singer performs as part of an ensemble of drummers, dancers, and singers. Indeed, the Ewe word *w̃ufofo* (drumming) is a composite of almost all the performing arts:

> Poetry among the Ewe comes to life around the drums. In the mood and the cadences of the drums, and in the structure of songs, we come face to face with the form and content of original poetry. (Awoonor 17)

The Ewe example is by no means unique. Mazisi Kunene explains that "Zulu poetry being communal, requires a special method of presentation. The poet does not just recite his poetry but acts it, uses variation of pitch, and aims at communicating his poem through the simulation of all the senses. He produces at one level a symphonic chant, at another, drama, and still another, music" (12).

To fully appreciate this tendency towards the fusion of artistic forms we need to look at *the festival*. Oyin Ogunba refers to the festival as "the prime artistic institution of traditional Africa," arguing that it is "the only institution which has the framework which can coordinate virtually all the art forms of a community" (5). And K. E. Agovi identifies "the interplay of at least three important factors that may influence role-fulfilment in festival drama": the composite nature of the dramatic performance; the presence of an active audience; the actor's conception of what is expected of him; and his understanding and skills of his performance (148). The clear picture that emerges is *the integrative nature of the tradition of the performing arts in Africa*. African artistic tradition seeks to integrate the various art forms. It also inevitably integrates artist, audience, and artistic forms into one unified and unifying experience (Kunene; Scheub).

The Nature of Performance

In defining the performance of verbal art and its relevance to the subject of poetry as a dramatic experience, we must envision various levels of performance. Richard Bauman's *Verbal Art as Performance* (1977) provides a brief but classic insight into a concept of performance that has become central to oral literature studies. His short chapter on "the nature of performance" offers a useful critique of earlier, essentially text-oriented approaches to performance. He then advocates a more theoretically and analytically useful approach to performance as "a species of situated human communication." In evaluating this sort of performance, he argues, special attention should be paid to the implications of the performer's "assumption of responsibility to an audience for display of communicative competence" (11). Of particular relevance to our subject matter is Bauman's further observation that:

> Additionally, [performance] is marked as available for the enhancement of experience, through present enjoyment of the intrinsic qualities of the act of expression itself. Performance thus calls forth special attention to and heightened awareness of the act of expression and gives licence to the audience to regard the act of expression and the performance with special intensity. (11)

The crucial role this framework assigns to the audience is especially relevant to artistic performance in Africa. The members of a typical audience in Africa will probably not applaud a bad performance out of politeness and then walk away mumbling their disgust to themselves. They expect a high display of competence, and they would insist on it. A tedious performer may suddenly receive a loud burst of applause, which is really a warning signal: "Give us a good show or cut it off!" Student audiences in Ghana, for instance, would interrupt with a well-known song: "All we are saying.../Don't waste our time." It is not uncommon for bad performers to be booed off stage. And there have been instances of demands for refunds of gate fees. Performers have even been assaulted and their instruments or props damaged.

In the light of this potentially unpleasant side of an African audience's response, performance might be regarded as an exercise in risk-taking (Nabasuta 46–7; Yankah). Against the dangers of this risk-taking, however, we must always balance the potential pleasures of a satisfying performance. The audience is not necessarily a threat to the performer. On the contrary, the audience is more likely to be an ally, a prompter, and an inspirer to excellence, than an obstacle to a satisfying experience. After all, the audience is anxious to be offered the pleasures of performance, just as the performer experiences a sense of personal satisfaction over a successful performance.

In order to meet the rather severe expectations of the audience, poets who decide on performance rather than the print medium for the transmission of their work have a number of options which may be identified in terms of various levels of performance:

Level One Performance – Dramatic Reading

At this level, the poet and the poem are still somewhat bound to the written or printed text. But by the dramatic use of body language, voice, pause, tempo, gesture, and other paralinguistic techniques, the poetry is lifted from the cold print on a page and energized into a warm and living experience, an experience with which the audience spontaneously identifies and which it may enhance through various degrees of participation and through encouraging applause or comment.

A number of writers have drawn attention to the popularization of poetry in Ghana, especially since the 1970s, through the medium of public recitals as well as radio and television programs wholly or partly devoted to poetry in English and in Ghanaian

languages (Apronti, "Ghanaian Poetry" 31; Anyidoho "Atukwei Okai" and "They Sing";
Fraser 313–14). Indeed, Apronti considers that:

> The most important development that these new poets have introduced into Ghanaian society
> in the 1970s has been the institutionalisation of the poetry recital as a popular event, an occasion
> that attracts people from all walks of life. The recitals have thus reinstated poetry as a public
> event in the African tradition. . . . (31)

It has often been suggested that the rise of this phenomenon has much to do with a lack of
avenues for the publication of poetry. Fraser, for example, argues that such recitals are
regarded "as preliminary to the definitive act of publication" (313). Naturally, the new poets
involved in this exercise hope for the eventual publication of their work. However, one of my
basic contentions in this essay is that, given the reality of poetry written in "a cultural
environment where the dominant mode of communication is oral," the printed word may
not necessarily be "the definitive act of publication."

We need to revise our understanding of the concept of "publication" to include the act of
public poetry performance. Otherwise, how do we account for the fact that even poets
whose work is already in print nevertheless insist on publicizing their poetry through
continued public performance? In fact, a whole generation of Ghanaian poets who enjoy
national recognition include many who have never published a single poem. The Entertainment Critics and Reviewers Association of Ghana (ECRAG) has, over the past few years,
awarded their annual "Poet of the Year" prize to more of these "unprinted" poets than to
the more established and internationally recognized ones. As far as ECRAG is concerned,
the poetic voices of Kwabena Asiedu Aboagye and Abeiku Sagoe are more accessible to the
public eye and ear than the widely acclaimed works of, say, Kofi Awoonor or Kwesi Brew.

Until recently the central figure in this phenomenon of poetry presentation in performance was Atukwei Okai, and he has been given due credit for helping popularize poetry
performance as a legitimate mode of artistic expression (Apronti "Ghanaian Poetry"; Anyidoho "Atukwei Okai" and "They Sing"). Apronti describes him as "the most picturesque
Ghanaian poet of the 1970s, the man who turned the poetry recital into a public event" (42).
The dominant presence of Okai has much to do with his unique performance style, a style
that appropriately captures and transmits what has been described as "the torrential swell of
his verse" (Apronti, "Ghanaian Poetry" 43).

A particularly impressive example of the dramatic reading of poetry as a public performance was introduced into the poetic scene in Ghana in early 1987 by the Afro-Caribbean
poet-historian Edward Kamau Brathwaite, who had earlier lived and worked in the country
for about eight years. Brathwaite was back in Ghana as a special guest of the W.E.B. DuBois
Memorial Centre for Pan African Culture. His visit took him on a poetry reading-lecture
tour that had as one of its high points an Open Lecture at the University of Ghana titled
"Atumpan: The Making of an African-Caribbean Poetry." Referring to his presentation as a
"lecture" would be a clear case of misrepresentation. More appropriately, it was a unique
performance, re-enacting the many new ways in which his creative career has been shaped
by the experience of his earlier stay in Ghana, a land he acknowledges in his presentation as
having provided him with "an abiding sense of metaphor" and a sense of appropriate
rhythms in which he has been able to reconstruct the catastrophic history of African peoples
in the Caribbean.

Julien Pearn celebrates Brathwaite as "one of the most innovative poets of our period [a poet whose] poetry has also reached a wide, often 'non-literary' audience, and has paved the way for a genuinely popular interest in poetic performance throughout the Commonwealth Caribbean." And Zagba Oyortey talks of Brathwaite's unique contribution to the British Poetry Society's attempt, "after more than seventy years of closeted activity... to popularise poetry and return it to its communal roots" (62). Of all the invited poets who participated in this event, Oyortey seems to have been most impressed by Brathwaite, mainly on account of the dramatic quality of his performance:

> Brathwaite offered the audience a rare insight into the nature of oral performance as it obtains in Africa and the Caribbean. He used a combination of percurssive African words, "Dam... Damirifa... Due" [an Akan dirgechant], as a spring board from which he sprung to bring out the history of the Caribbean through reggae and dub rhythms seen as typifying the socially responsive and communicative role of art [or poetry in this case], which reaches beyond its individual voice to encapsulate and amplify popular aspirations. (62–3)

All these qualities about Brathwaite's poetry and his impressive performance style were amply displayed in the climactic event of his Ghana homecoming on February 4, 1987. At the Ghana Drama Studio, the DuBois Centre presented a special program significantly entitled "Drums & Voices: A Performance Dialogue." There were two main dimensions to the dialogue. First, there was dialogue between the African-heritage Caribbean poetry of Brathwaite and the African-rooted poetry of his Ghanaian counterparts, represented by the purely oral poet Okyeame Kwasi Akuffo as well as by the writer-performers Kwabena Asiedu Aboagye, Kobena Eyi Acquah, Kofi Anyidoho, and Kofi Awoonor. More importantly, there was a dialogue between the poets as writers and the drummers as poets.

The program opened with a drum prelude performed by the Ghana Dance Ensemble from the University of Ghana and continued with a Libation performance by Okyeame Akuffo. The Dance Ensemble then played a *fontomfrom* drum suite, followed by drum poetry that was performed, recited, and translated by Okyeame Akuffo. And when the Dance Ensemble ushered Brathwaite onto the stage with a *fontomfrom* herald, he immediately seized and fascinated the audience with an impressive rendition of his poem "Negus," a piece marked by the artistry with which the poet worked polyrhythmic percussive beats into its performance structure. At this point each of the Ghanaian poets was in turn ushered into his performance by appropriate and often poetically meaningful drum rhythms. The program ended with a final dramatic reading by Brathwaite followed by a drum volley. When it was all over, the audience was left with only one regret, the recognition they had experienced a unique event, probably never to be recaptured – a well-known limitation of any oral performance. Fortunately, the DuBois Centre video-taped the occasion, so it is possible to relive something of the intensity of the original experience.

Level Two Performance – Fusion of Poetry, Music, Action

The event just described takes us beyond the level one performance where the writer continues to hold on to a written or printed text. At the second level of poetic performance, the dramatic impact is frequently intensified by an ever greater liberation from the text as cold print. Indeed, such performance is frequently marked by a situation in which, even though the poet may still be holding the text, he performs with little or no reference to it. The ideal situation occurs when the text has been memorized, or rather assimilated into an artistic design that makes for spontaneity of performance reinforced by a more elaborate use of body language and paralinguistic devices.

Another usual element of performance at this level is the use of music and/or simultaneous mimed enactments of the situations depicted in the unfolding poetic text. The music may, in fact, be incorporated into the text of the poem, as we often find in the works of writers such as Atukwei Okai, Asiedu Aboagye, and Kobena Acquah. More often, however, the music is performed as prelude, background, refrain, or epilogue.

The use of all these devices tends to draw the audience into the performance. When a particular piece of music is a familiar one, the audience may join in, even without direct invitation from the poet-performer. Drawing on the popular African tradition of call-and-response, the performer may even establish a pattern that makes allowances for audience participation. One of the most important implications of this orientation towards a poetry meant for performance is the manner in which the actual process of writing may be influenced by the awareness of a potential audience presence and participation. In my poem "Fertility Game," for example, provision is made for coopting the audience into the performance with the line "Come back home, Agbenoxevi, come back home." This phrase is to be repeated at carefully marked intervals sometimes signaled by an appropriate gesture or some special voice indicator (Anyidoho, *Harvest 19–22; Earthchild 1–3*).

This level of performance may be regarded as an intermediary one in which the focus on the text as written or printed material is minimized but not totally eliminated. Developments in Ghanaian poetry during the last few years have gone even further in this direction, for the written text has increasingly been reduced to the status of a *pre*-text or a script that is transformed and fused into a full-scale dramatic production for stage presentation.

Level Three Performance – Total Art

At this final level, poetry is no longer a textual art bound to the written/printed page. It is fully liberated from the distancing effect of print technology. In this process, poetry is no longer a privately, silently produced and enjoyed experience. It becomes subject to all the laws and principles that govern the communal art form. And within such a communal framework, fundamental transformations take place:

a. The transformation of the poem as written/printed text into a full-scale stage production or drama means that the poet's initial, often lonely act of creation is reinforced and enriched by the complementary creative skills of other artists and technical resource persons – directors, actors/actresses, dancers, singers, drummers, producers, etc. – and by such material accoutrements as costumes, props, lighting, and sound effects.

b. Congruent with a common aesthetic norm in much of African performance tradition, this poetry is often fused with music, dance, mime, and gesture to form the integrated whole. The essential structure of this drama, or *total art*, is the building of bridges to reconnect an otherwise fragmented artistic universe (Kubayanda; Anyidoho "Divine Drummer").

c. The involvement and relevance of the audience becomes crucial in these performances. Such involvement contrasts sharply with the situation of the reader as audience. The complete elimination of the usual spatial and temporal gap between writer and reader allows for a face-to-face interaction.

[. . .]

Social and Artistic Implications of Poetry as Dramatic Performance

One of the most important consequences of this development has been identified by Dekutsey in his review of "Earthchild and Other Poems":

> Dramatization will undoubtedly affect the very writing of poetry; the poet, during those silent moments as he creates . . . will have his audience very much in mind; the poetic voice will tend to be more social rather than private. (619)

For a society that is predominantly oral and nonliterate, poetry as written/printed text clearly has limited possibilities for making any serious impact on the general public. With this new development, the written/printed text is effectively reduced to little more than a *pre*-text, waiting to be brought to its full realization in a face-to-face dramatic encounter with a live audience through the enriched form and meaning helped by director and performers. The audience, and the process of dramatization influence the final form of "total art" as well as certain details of the written poetic text.

In the course of the two productions that I have supervised, I was compelled to rework various details of the original texts in order to meet the peculiar demands of dramatization. With "Earthchild . . . ," a major addition to the original script was made in response to a demand by one member of the Abibigromma cast. Originally, the poem "In the High Court of Cosmic Justice" featured only one female voice as a witness at the trial of Dr Kwame Nkrumah. I tried to persuade Dzifa Glikpoe, one of the key female performers in the cast, to assume the role of a male character. She objected, pointing out that, given the dominant role women played in Nkrumah's political career, it was a serious historical blunder to have no more than one female witness at his trial. She insisted that I write a special piece for her as a partial redress of this imbalance. Her insistence prompted me to compose "Lolita Jones," the final piece in the dramatized version of the poem – a piece that was of course, missing from the original version published in *Earthchild with Brain Surgery* (1985).

The impact of dramatized poetry on its audience is another measure of its significance. In this form, the poetry has the capacity to make a great impact on a wide cross-section of the community in any typically African population with diverse social and educational back-grounds. On the basis of my own experience, I am convinced that the dramatized poem is more deeply appreciated than the printed poem, and by a surprisingly wide cross-section of the population. In fact, it reaches many who would never have been exposed to these poems in their printed form. One of my greatest satisfactions as an artist occurred when the poet Atukwei Okai recounted something that had happened at the Ghana Drama Studio as he sat watching the premiere of "Earthchild." Suddenly, he heard clapping and a small voice exclaiming in Ga: *"Amee bo mode. Amee bo mode"* (They have done really well). He looked around and discovered to his surprise that the commentator was none other than his four-year-old daughter. After watching these various productions, others have also confessed that, even though they are not great lovers of poetry, they found enjoyment and meaning in the performances.

Some people might object that dramatizing poetry into total art performance requires too large an investment. Each of the productions discussed above was made possible only through substantial individual and institutional patronage in the form of financial and/or material support. Others might argue that, in spite of this considerable expense, each production or performance is a unique experience not easily captured in permanent form such as that offered by the printed word. However, modern technology enables audio-visual recordings of performances to be made; in fact each of the productions mentioned in this paper is already at least partially available as a relatively permanent document on video-tape. As Dekutsey says, "if we weigh these disadvantages against obvious advantages to be gained by way of enriched meaning...the experiment is worth the effort [and] one is almost persuaded to shout encouragement to [this] experimentation with new forms" (619). An investment that has clearly managed "to take poetry out of the books and bring it to the people, alive and fresh," is hardly excessive if our goal is the promotion of a healthy artistic tradition.

References

Acquah, Kobena Eyi. *The Man Who Died*. Accra: Asempa, 1984.

——. *Music for a Dream Dance*. Accra: Asempa, 1989.

Agovi, J. Kofi. "Of Actors, Performers and Audience in Traditional African Drama." *Présence Africaine* 116.4 (1980): 141–58.

Anyidoho, Kofi. "Atukwei Okai and His Poetic Territory." *New West African Literature*. Ed. Kolawole Ogungbesan. London: Heinemann, 1979. 45–59.

——. "A Communal Celebration of Individual Poetic Talent: The *Haikotu* Dance Club of Wheta." *Cross Rhythms: Occasional Papers in African Folklore*. Eds. Kofi Anyidoho et al. Bloomington: Trickster Press, 1983. 172–92.

——. "Divine Drummer: Drum Poetics in Brathwaite and Okai." *Black Culture and Black Consciousness in Literature*. Ed. E. N. Emenyonu. Ibadan: Heinemann, 1987. 197–210.

——. *Earthchild*. Accra: Woeli, 1985.

——. *A Harvest of Our Dreams*. London: Heinemann, 1984.

——. "Mythmaker and Mythbreaker: The Oral Poet as Earwitness." *African Literature in its Social and Political Dimensions*. Eds. Eileen Julien et al. Washington, DC: Three Continents Press, 1986. 5–14.

Apronti, Jawa. "Ghanaian Poetry in the 1970s." *New West African Literature*. Ed. Kolawole Ogumgbesan. London: Heinemann, 1979. 31–44.

——. "John Atukwei Okai: The Growth of a Poet." *Universitas* (Legon) 2.1 New Series (1972): 117–29.

Awoonor, Kofi. *Guardians of the Sacred Word: Ewe Poetry*. New York: Nok, 1974.

Bauman, Richard. *Verbal Art as Performance*. Rowley, MA: Newbury House, 1977.

Biakolo, E. A. "Orality and the Criticism of African Literature: A Critique." Paper presented at the 8th Ibadan Annual African Literature Conference, 1989.

Brathwaite, Edward Kamau. "*Atumpan*: The Making of an African Caribbean Poetry." An Open Lecture. University of Ghana, Legon. January 11, 1987.

Dekutsey, Atsu. "Poetry as Theatre." *West Africa* 3577 (March 24, 1986): 618–19.

Fraser, Robert. *West African Poetry: A Critical History.* Cambridge: The University Press, 1986.

Kubayanda, J. Bekunuru. "Polyrhythmics and African Print Poetics: Césaire, and Atukwei Okai." *Interdisciplinary Dimensions of African Literature.* Ed. Kofi Anyidoho et al. Washington, DC: Three Continents Press, 1985. 155–62.

Kunene, Daniel. In *ALA Newsletter* 2.4 (1976). Also quoted in *Artist and Audience: African Literature as a Shared Experience.* Ed. R. Priebe and T. Hale. Washington, DC: Three Continents Press (1979). iii–iv.

Nabasuta, Helen. "The Dynamics of the Storytelling Experience: Kiganda Prose Narratives." *Cross Rhythms.* Ed. Kofi Anyidoho et al. Bloomington: Trickster Press, 1983. 43–67.

Ogunba, Oyin. "Traditional African Festival Drama." *Theatre in Africa.* Eds. Oyin Ogunba and Abiola Irele. Ibadan: Ibadan UP, 1978. 3–26.

Oyortey, Zagba. "Poetic Concerns and Styles." *Africa Events* 3/6 (June 1967): 62–3.

Pearn, Julien. In *Art Links* 20.

Scheub, Harold. "Body and Image in Oral Narrative Performance." *New Literary History* 8.3 (1977): 345–67.

Yankah, Kwesi. "Risks in Verbal Art Performance." *Journal of Folklore Research* 22.2–3 (1985): 133–53.

Chapter 52

"Azikwelwa" (We Will Not Ride): Politics and Value in Black South African Poetry

Anne McClintock

In the colonial context the settler only ends his work of breaking in the native when the latter admits loudly and intelligibly the supremacy of the white man's values. In the period of decolonization, the colonized masses mock at these very values, insult them and vomit them up.

Frantz Fanon, The Wretched of the Earth

On the winter morning of 16 June 1976, fifteen thousand black children marched on Orlando Stadium in Soweto, carrying slogans dashed on the backs of exercise books. The children were stopped by armed police who opened fire, and thirteen-year-old Hector Peterson became the first of hundreds of schoolchildren to be shot down by police in the months that followed. If, a decade later, the meaning of Soweto's "year of fire" is still contested,[1] it began in this way with a symbolic display of contempt for the unpalatable values of Bantu education, a public rejection of the 'culture of malnutrition' with which blacks had been fed.[2] The local provocation for the Orlando march was a ruling that black children be taught arithmetic and social studies in Afrikaans – the language of the white cabinet minister, soldier, and pass official, prison guard, and policeman. But the Soweto march sprang from deeper grievances than instruction in Afrikaans, and the calamitous year that passed not only gave rise to a rekindling of black political resistance but visibly illuminated the cultural aspects of coercion and revolt.

The children's defacement of exercise books and the breaking of school ranks presaged a nationwide rebellion of uncommon proportion. The revolt spread across the country from community to community, in strikes, boycotts, and street barricades. It represented in part the climax of a long struggle *between* the British and Afrikaans interlopers for control over an unwilling black populace and was at the same time a flagrant sign of the contestation of culture, an open declaration by blacks that cultural value, far from shimmering out of reach in the transcendent beyond, would now be fought for with barricades of tires, empty classrooms, and precocious organization.

First published in *Critical Inquiry* 13 (Spring 1987): 597–600, 610–13, 614–16, 619–23.
"Azikwelwa," we will not ride, is a slogan expressing the people's refusal to ride on state transport during the bus and train boycotts.

After Soweto, new forms of artistic creation appeared across the country. Poetry groups burgeoned in the black townships, creating poetic forms which by received standards were 'unliterary' and incendiary, written in 'murdered' English, formally inelegant and politically indiscreet. Yet, as it turned out, the poetry reached a far wider audience in South Africa than ever before, posing an unsettling threat to the legitimacy of white settler aesthetics on South African soil and giving rise to an unusually intense debate on the nature of aesthetic value and its relation to what might broadly be termed politics.

The most visible sign of the new Soweto poetry was the launching of *Staffrider* magazine in 1978 by Ravan Press. A 'staffrider' is the township name for one who – in mimicry of railway staff – boards at the last minute the dangerous trains hurtling workers to the white city, snatching free rides by clambering onto the roofs of the overcrowded coaches or by hanging from the sides. A staffrider poet, as the editorial of the first issue explained, is thus a "*skelm* of sorts," a miscreant hanging at an acute angle to official law and convention.[3] Tenacious and precarious, at odds with state decree, a black poet becomes a "mobile, disreputable bearer of tidings."[4] More than anything else, the *Staffrider* poet is figured as part of a group in motion, destined to arrive suddenly in the midst of white urban centers.

From the outset, *Staffrider* flouted almost every decorum of sacerdotal authority. A fierce rebuttal of white poetic standards, the magazine paraded an aesthetics of calculated defiance and collectivity. Not only did its literary contents and format – a generic mosaic of poems, photography, articles, graphics, oral history, and short stories – effectively challenge the prestige of the "literary," but its methods of creation and distribution revolutionized periodical publishing in South Africa.

Staffrider was literature in a hurry. Partly because of the nervous post-Soweto climate of surveillance and bannings, it named no editors and placed responsibility for speedy distribution in the hands of township groups and small shops. *Staffrider* had to be a magazine "that would move very quickly without drawing too much attention to itself...a contradiction in normal publishing terms."[5] Carefully egalitarian from the outset, the magazine was intended to air the growing number of poets around the country who were writing collectively, and to do so in a way that allowed the art groups themselves to choose the poems to be published. In other words, editorial policy and content lay very much in the hands of readers and writers beyond the publishing house. As Mike Kirkwood, director of Ravan Press, explained, "Nobody wanted the kind of editorial policy that comes from the top: 'We've got a policy. We've got standards. If you fit in with this policy, come up to these standards, we'll publish you.'"[6]

Not surprisingly, the state took immediate umbrage, and the first issue was banned – the Publications Directorate justifying its actions on the grounds that some of the poems undermined "the authority and image of the police."[7] Nor was the state alone in its displeasure. Members of the white literary establishment were piqued by the appearance of a magazine which could brazenly announce: "Standards are not golden or quintessential: they are made according to the demands different societies make on writers, and according to the responses writers make to those demands."[8] Soweto poetry became as a result the locus of a fierce debate over the value of black culture and the politics of black aesthetics, not only in the white academy and white publishing houses but also in black classrooms and universities, community halls, poetry groups, and private homes. At stake was whether aesthetic value could any longer credibly be seen to emanate from the text itself, a transcendental immanence somehow detached from the squalor of politics and "the shame of the ideological." In South Africa, as elsewhere, though perhaps more flagrantly, the question of value became entangled with the history of state and institutional power; the history of publishing houses and journals; the private and public histories of the black and white intellectuals, teachers, writers, and evangelists; and the changing relation between this black intermediate class and the worker and oral poets – the Xhosa *iimbongi*, or the migrant Sotho *likheleke*, "the people of eloquence."[9] Questions of education, constituency, and audience were evoked and therewith the possibility that value is not an essential property of a text but a social relation between a work and its audience, constituted rather than revealed, and endorsed or outstripped by successive orders of power.

[. . .]

Soweto poetry was born in the cradle of Black Consciousness and has to be seen within this milieu. Black Consciousness began largely as a black campus movement in 1968 and spanned almost a decade until the banning, after Soweto, of all Black Consciousness organizations in October 1977. Mobilizing black students around the rallying cry of color and the slogan, "Blackman, you are on your own," Black Consciousness was at this stage, however, the dream of the elite black urban petite bourgeoisie, a movement of students, professionals, intellectuals, artists, and a few clergy.[10] In 1972 the South African Student Organization (SASO) tried to breach the gulf between the intellectual elite and the people of the ordinary black community and in 1972 formed the Black People's Convention in an effort to give Black Consciousness nationwide clout. But the appeal to the community was uncertain and contradictory, and, partly because the tendrils it extended to organized workers were always slender, it never grew into a mass organization.

The question of cultural values took center stage as literacy campaigns, black theater, and poetry readings were fostered in the belief that cultural nationalism was the road to political nationalism. Since shedding canonized white norms and values was imperative, whites had to be barred and all white values challenged and replaced. As Steve Biko put it, "Black culture . . . implies freedom on our part to innovate without recourse to white values."[11] Politically, early Black Consciousness was reformist rather than radical, a blend of moderates, Christian anticommunists, liberals, and black entrepreneurs. It was chronically masculine in orientation (calling for "the restoration of black manhood"), without an analysis of class or gender, and strongly anti-Marxist: "We are not a movement of confrontation but a movement of introspection."[12]

The Black Consciousness movement has as a result been rebuked for being politically naive and theoretically inconsistent, for placing its faith in a timeless black soul and the personal growth of the individual. But at the same time, as the poet Mafika Gwala put it: "Everywhere it was surveillance. It seemed that reading and cultural topics were the only things to sustain one."[13] At a time when so many political organizations and people were being scotched, black poetry helped revive and sustain resistance to white culture. "The brooding was replaced by an understanding of hope" ("CW," p. 40). Moreover, as the Nationalists drove wedge after wedge between the so-called different ethnic groups, Black Consciousness and the resurgence of black cultural values embraced all embattled groups, Coloreds, Indians, and Asians, within the term "black." For all its undoubted political shortcomings, which became most telling and costly during the Soweto revolt, Black Consciousness provided a rallying cry, a powerful and necessary incitement. As the writer Essop Patel put it, "Black Consciousness provided the initial impetus in the rejection of art as an aesthetic indulgence. Once the black poet freed himself from Eurocentric literary conventions, then he was *free* to create within the context of a national consciousness. The black poet's starting point was the articulation of the black experience."[14]

> and when I'm supposed to sing
> I croak curses.
>
> Zinjiva Winston Nkondo

Black poetry flourished at this time, becoming what Gwala called a "jaunt in search of identity" ("CW," p. 38). Not surprisingly, the first Soweto poetry shared many of the dilemmas of the Black Consciousness movement. Not the least of its problems was that it was written, even though in protest, in English, with a privileged white audience in mind, and thus bore the subtle onus of having to curtail itself for the liberal press.

The English literary establishment was beginning to listen to black poets with half an ear. White poets had trickled back from their lonely jaunts into the veld looking for roots and were now writing a little uneasily about black men honing their pangas in the woodshed. In 1971 Lionel Abrahams took a publishing gamble and printed Oswald Mtshali's phenomenally successful *Sounds of a Cowhide Drum*, sparking at the same time an agitated debate on the value of black poetry and provoking a number of white critics to fits of discriminating judgment bordering on incivility.[15]

Until the seventies, the white and almost exclusively male British canon was troubled only by mild internal differences over value in the English-speaking universities, remaining squarely within an imported Leavisite tradition. In 1959 the Oxford University Press could publish *A Book of South African Verse* that featured thirty-two white male and four white female poets, yet not one black writer of either sex. Until the seventies, the presiding liberal aesthetic faith – in individual creativity, imminent and "universal" literary values, unity of vision, wholeness of experience, complexity of form, refined moral discrimination untainted by political platitude, irony, taste, cultivated sensibility, and the formal completion of the work of art – had for the most part been artificially cordoned off from black experience by segregated education, severe censorship of texts, bannings of writers, and blocking of distribution.

From the seventies onward, however, white liberals began to court black poets while simultaneously having for the first time to defend the presiding liberal tenets within the English-speaking universities at the level of ideology, in an unprecedented flurry of reviews, debates, articles, conferences, and so on. In other words, if some black poetry was to be selectively ushered into the canon, it was only if it could be shown to exhibit at the door certain requisite values which, in turn, had to be vociferously announced without betraying the selective and interested nature of these values. The first phase of reforming the canon thus began with its circumspect expansion to include some black texts previously ignored but now revealed to exhibit certain features shared with the already existing white tradition. [...]

In a period of record unemployment and a steady barrage of work stoppages, there began a spate of cultural forums and conferences – the Theatre Council of Natal (TECON), the SASO conference on Creativity and Black Development (1972), the Black Renaissance Convention at Hammanskraal (1974). A flurry of black poetry collections appeared, and most were summarily banned: Kunene's *Zulu Poems* (1970), Keorapetse Kgositsile's *My Name Is Afrika* (1971), *Seven South African Poets* (1971), James Matthews' and Gladys Thomas' *Cry*

Rage (1972), Mongane Serote's *Yakhal'inkomo* (1972), and *To Whom It May Concern: An Anthology of Black South African Poetry* (1973). Hostile, impassioned, and well beyond the pale of accepted aesthetic standards, the new Soweto poetry was an intemperate, jangling, often hallucinatory depiction of "the terrible canopy of nightmares" that shadowed ghetto life:

> They stole the baritone
> Wifey eats her own head-bone
> She squeezes a stony brow into the spoon
> Children may nibble the pap-like moon . . . [16]

Most significantly, as the new poetry poached liberally on jazz and jive rhythms, black Americanisms, township vernacular, and the gestural, musical, and performative aspects of oral traditions, notions such as the integrity of the text and the test of time came to be rendered increasingly irrelevant. Much of this transitional poetry was still written for print but was beginning to evince signs of an imminent abandonment and destruction of the text:

> I leave in stealth
>   and return in Black anger
> O—m! Ohhhhmmmm! O-hhhhhhmmmmmmmm!!![17]

and:

> You've trapped me whitey! Meem wanna ge aot Fuc
> Pschwee e ep boobooduboooboodu blllll
> Black books,
>   Flesh blood words shitrrr Haai,
>   Amen.[18]

The Soweto poets' refusal to see poetry in the Coleridgean sense as that which contains "within itself" the reason why it is so and not otherwise was, moreover, resonant with the powerful, if embattled, traditions of oral poetry within black culture.[19] In African oral poetry the

> focus is on the performance in its social context, on the function of the performance in society, almost to the exclusion of transmission of the text over time.
>
> The poet serves as a mediator between the ruler and the ruled, as an inciter, a molder of opinion, a social critic. He is not only concerned to chronicle the deeds and qualities of the ancestors of his contemporaries, he also responds poetically to the social and political circumstances confronting him at the time of his performance.[20]

Not only did the yardsticks of imminent value brandished by white critics bear scant resemblance to the traditions of the Xhosa *izibongo* and *Ntsomi*, the Sotho *lithoko*, and *sefela*, but white critics' failure to recognize the presence within contemporary poetry of such oral infusions left them ill-equipped to pass judgment either on the poems themselves or on their social roles and contexts.[21] Ignorant of the intricate traditions of repetition and parallelism that hold in oral poetry, white critics disparaged black poetry on more than one occasion for falling into cliché and repetitious image. Moreover, as Ursula Barnett and others have shown, "often we find in the imagery of black poetry a complicated system of symbols which works on several levels and requires a knowledge of history, myth and legend."[22] Drawing on powerful oral traditions of communality of theme and performance, energetic audience participation, conceptions of the poet as lyric historian and political commentator, black poetry was making the case, as Tony Emmett has put it, for its study "on its own terms, and it is in the light of the oral, political and communal facets of black poetry that the most penetrating criticism is likely to be made."[23]

[. . .]

> Let them cough their dry little academic coughs.
>   Richard Rive

When James Matthews and Gladys Thomas brought out *Cry Rage*, "critics hyena-howled. It was not poetry, they exclaimed."[24] The profusion of black poetry could not, however, be ignored; neither could it any longer be pinched and squeezed to meet canonical requirements. It began to pose a discomforting threat not only to some of the most cherished values of the established aesthetic but also to the very idea of the canon itself. Critics became more vocal in their complaints: black poets were trampling on every propriety of the English language, sacrificing formal decorum for the "red haze of revenge lust"[25] and the " 'rat-tat-tat' of machine guns" of protest ("PM," p. 160). As Alan Paton would have it, "a writer is, more often than not, a private creature,"[26] whereas black writers, seduced by "the portentously-conceived category 'Black,' " tended chronically to "group-thinking."[27] Livingstone felt that blacks would face considerable difficulty surviving "the harsh glacier of time" and would have trouble qualifying for "the toughest definition of a poet . . . a man who has been dead for 100 years, and one of his works is still read" ("PM," p. 157), a tough definition indeed for black female poets. These were the four general charges leveled against black writing in the seventies: sacrifice of the intrinsic rules of the craft for political ends, formal ineptitude, loss of individual expression and originality, and hence sacrifice of longevity.

In return Gwala asked, "Questions crop up. Questions such as: what moral right does the academic have to judge my style of writing? What guidelines outside the culture of domination has he applied?" ("CW," p. 48). Unwilling to give ground in the struggle for "command" over the English language, white critics peppered their reviews of black poetry with quibbles over formal lapses, "bad" grammar, and decline of standards. Black poets rejoined that "there has never been such a thing as pure language" ("CW," p. 43), and Sepamla urged, "If the situation requires broken or 'murdered' English, then for God's sake one must do just that."[28] The critical skirmishes over grammatical niceties concealed in this way the much more serious question of who had the right to police township culture. Black poetry was in fact a very conscious flouting of received notions of formal elegance: poets were forging their own precepts out of forms of township speech unfamiliar, and therefore unnerving, to white critics. Black poetry was often a hybrid medley of English, *tsotsitaal*,[29] and black Americanisms, with blends of black South African languages:

> Once upon a bundu-era
> there was *mlungu* discrimination
> as a result of separate *masemba* . . . [30]

The language of white officialdom was mocked, insulted, and inverted: "Your dompas is dom to pass you / Your X-mas gift: 72 hours . . ."[31]

Black poets were equally suspicious of Paton's claim that politics destroyed the sovereignty of the intrinsic "rules of the craft."[32] Frankie Ntsu kaDitshego/Dube's poem "The Ghettoes" argues figuratively that the apolitical stance is itself a political act:

> Those who claim to be non-smokers are wrong
> The place is polluted with smoke from
>> Chimneys
>> Trucks
>> Hippos
>> Gun-excited camouflage
>> dagga-smokers
>> and burning tyres
> Non-smokers are smokers too![33]

In more ways than one, black poetry posed a serious challenge to notions of the poem as a freestanding creation, judged excellent if obedient to immanent rules radiating from within the craft. For black poets, the canon as the patrimony of excellence, bequeathed from generation to generation by the finest of minds and borne unscathed through history, was rendered indefensible by the very circumstances in which they were living. In his poem "The Marble Eye" Mtshali parodied the formal completion of the work of art housed in tradition's mausoleum:

> The marble eye
> is an ornament
> coldly carved by a craftsman
> to fill an empty socket
> as a corpse fills a coffin.
>
> [*S*, p. 71]

Given the conditions of township life, the poem could no longer pretend to mimic the burnished completion of a well-wrought urn or the jeweled finish of an icon. Gwala for one called for "an art of the unattractive,"[34] and N. Chabani Manganyi argued that the "unified image" sanctioned by literary tradition was an unforgivable indulgence.[35] Against Paton's commonplace claim that protest would damage the fine formal filigree of the artwork, these poets charged that the paramount value of their poetry was neither ontological nor formal but strategic. Strategic change rather than the test of time became the reiterated principle. "In our ghetto language there can be no fixity. The words we use belong to certain periods of our history. They come, they assume new meanings, they step aside" ("CW," p. 48). Gwala was equally unimpressed by the lure of immortality. Publication was not the sole aim: "What mattered would be the spoken word. Whether it lay hidden under mats or got eaten by the rats would be a different story" ("CW," p. 37).

Most significantly, the performative, gestural, and dramatic traces in much of the poetry evinced its gradual transformation from a printed "literary" phenomenon to a social performance, from text to event, replete with theatrical, gestural, and oral traces:

> Soon they are back again
> Arriving as bigger black battalions
>   with brows biceps brains
>   trudging the 'white' soil: phara-phara-phara!
> And the kwela-kwela cop:
> 'These Bantus are like cheeky flies:
>   You ffr-ffr-ffrrr with Doom!'
> And see them again![36]

In this way, much of the new Soweto poetry bore witness to what Raymond Williams has described as "the true crisis in cultural theory" in our time, that is, the conflict "between [the] view of the work of art as object and the alternative view of art as a practice."[37] For most black poets, and there *are* exceptions, aesthetic value is neither immanent nor genetic but rather what Terry Eagleton has called "transitive," that is, "value for somebody in a particular situation.... It is always culturally and historically specific."[38] Supporting, albeit independently, many of the theoretical arguments on value in the work of Western critics such as Eagleton, Catherine Belsey, Tony Bennett, Stuart Hall, Paul Lauter, Francis Mulhern, Barbara Herrnstein Smith, and Jane Tompkins,[39] the Soweto poets claimed that the literary canon is less a mausoleum of enduring truths, less a *thing*, than it is an uneven, somersaulting social practice scored by contestation, dissension, and the interests of power.

Beset by censorship, by strictly curtailed access to commercial publishing channels, by the dangers of identification and subsequent harassment, and inheriting to boot powerful traditions of communal performance, black Soweto poetry began to evince the calculated destruction of the text.[40] More and more, black poetry is composed for a black listening audience rather than an overseas readership in ways that create poetic forms less vulnerable to censorship and easier to memorize, the spoken word spreading more quickly, more widely, and more elusively than printed texts. Poetry has taken flight from the literary magazines and has been performed increasingly at mass readings, United Democratic Front rallies, funerals, memorial services, garage parties, community meetings, and musical concerts, sometimes to the accompaniment of flutes and drums, drawing on oral traditions and miming customs.

Mbulelo Mzamane points out that many black poets, while quite unknown to white South Africans, have vast followings in Soweto, Tembisa, Kwa-Thema.[41] Flouting the prestige of the "literary," this "poetry turned theater," transient, immediate, and strategic, beloved and popular, overturns the essentialist question of "what constitutes good literature" and insists that it be recast in terms of what is good for whom, and when it is good, and why. Tenacious in the face of great distress, wary of some of the more moderate demands of early Black Consciousness, politically more radical in its demands yet relentlessly plagued by problems of gender, engaging at every moment the difficulties and bounty of its multiple traditions, this transitional black South African poetry faces considerable formal and social challenges. Black poets are no longer solely intent on desecrating those Western norms they feel to be invalid, vomiting them up and insulting them; they are now also engaged in the necessarily more difficult yet more positive endeavor of fashioning poetic values defensible in terms *other* than those simply of opposition and resistance to white values. Forcing poetry and criticism to step outside the magic circle of immanent value, into history and politics where criteria of judgment remain perpetually to be resolved, black poets are no longer content to snatch impudent rides on the dangerous trains of white tradition. Instead they are expressing increasingly a collective refusal to ride at all until the trains are theirs: "azikwelwa," we will not ride.

Notes

1   At least three general analyses of the Soweto uprising have emerged: deeper African National Congress involvement in the community; strains on the educational system, unemployment and recession, with greater industrial militancy stemming from the strikes in the early seventies; and the emergence of Black Consciousness ideology. See Tom Lodge, *Black Politics in South Africa Since 1945* (Johannesburg, 1983), pp. 321–62.

2   See M. K. Malefane, "'The Sun Will Rise': Review of the Allahpoets at the Market Theatre, Johannesburg," *Staffrider* (June/July 1980); reprinted in *Soweto Poetry,* ed. Michael Chapman, South African Literature Series, no. 2 (Johannesburg, 1982), p. 91. *Soweto Poetry* will hereafter be cited as *SP.*

3   "About Staffrider" (editorial), *Staffrider* 1 (May/June 1978); reprinted in *SP,* p. 125.

4   Michael Kirkwood, quoted in Ursula A. Barnett, *A Vision of Order: A Study of Black South African Literature in English, 1914–1980* (Amherst, Mass., 1983), p. 37.

5   Nick Visser, "'*Staffrider*: An Informal Discussion': Interview with Michael Kirkwood," *English in Africa* 7 (Sept. 1980); reprinted in *SP,* p. 129. *Staffrider* was conceived in 1977 during discussions with groups such as the Mpumulanga Arts Group. One of the best known of these groups, the Medupe Writers, with a membership of over two hundred, had taken poetry readings to the schools and communities, and was promptly banned in October 1977, along with the South African Students' Organization, the Black People's Convention, and other Black Consciousness organizations.

6   Ibid.

7   *Staffrider* (May/June 1978); quoted in Barnett, *A Vision of Order,* p. 38.

8   *Staffrider* (July/Aug. 1978); quoted ibid.

9   See David B. Coplan, *In Township Tonight: South Africa's Black City Music and Theatre* (London, 1985), and "Interpretive Consciousness: The Reintegration of Self and Society in Sotho Oral Poetry," *American Ethnologist,* forthcoming.

10 See Hirson, *Year of Fire,* pp. 60–114; Lodge, *Black Politics,* pp. 321–62.

11 Steve Biko, "Black Consciousness and the Quest for a True Humanity," in *Black Theology: The South African Voice,* ed. Basil Moore (London, 1973), p. 45. See also his *I Write What I Like,* ed. Aelred Stubbs (New York, 1978), and "White Racism and Black Consciousness," in *Student Perspectives on South Africa,* ed. Hendrik W. van der Merwe and David Welsh (Cape Town, 1972), pp. 190–202.

12 Drake Koka, quoted in "Inside South Africa: A New Black Movement Is Formed," *Sechaba* 7 (March 1973): 5.

13 Mafika Gwala, "Writing as a Cultural Weapon," in *Momentum,* p. 37; all further references to this article, abbreviated "CW," will be included in the text.

14 Patel, "Towards Revolutionary Poetry," in *Momentum,* p. 85.

15 Some of the reasons for the cultural shift and for the success of Mtshali's book – the first book of poems by anyone, black or white, ever to make a commercial profit – lay in the external interest

taken in Africa as one African nation after another won independence. But it is one of the stubborn quirks of decolonization that as Europe decamped from African soil, the literary scramble for Africa began – with Western publishing houses vying for black writers. Inside South Africa, some white liberals, increasingly inched into inconsequence, also saw fit to throw in their lot with black protest.

16   Anonymous, "They Took Him Away," *Staffrider* (Mar. 1978).

17   Gwala, *Jol'iinkomo* (Johannesburg, 1977), p. 68.

18   Mongane Serote, "Black Bells," *Yakhal'inkomo* (Johannesburg, 1972), p. 52.

19   See S. T. Coleridge, *Biographia Literaria* (New York, 1834), chap. 14.

20   Jeff Opland, "The Isolation of the Xhosa Oral Poet," in *Literature and Society in South Africa*, ed. Landeg White and Couzens (New York, 1984), pp. 175, 176–7.

21   See Ruth Finnegan, *Oral Literature in Africa* (Oxford, 1970); Harold Scheub, *The Xhosa Ntsomi* (Oxford, 1975); Elizabeth Gunner, "Songs of Innocence and Experience: Women as Composers and Performers of *Izibongo*, Zulu Praise Poetry," *Research in African Literatures* 10 (Fall 1979): 239–67; Mbulelo Mzamane, "The Uses of Traditional Oral Forms in Black South African Literature," in *Literature and Society in South Africa*, pp. 147–60; Coplan, *In Township Tonight* and "Interpretive Consciousness."

22   Barnett, *A Vision of Order*, p. 43.

23   Tony Emmett, "Oral, Political and Communal Aspects of Township Poetry in the Mid-Seventies," *English in Africa* 6 (Mar. 1979); reprinted in *SP*, p. 183.

24   James Matthews, in *Momentum*, p. 73.

25   Lionel Abrahams, "Political Vision of a Poet," *Rand Daily Mail*, 17 June 1974; reprinted in *SP*, p. 74.

26   Alan Paton, in *Momentum*, p. 90.

27   Abrahams, "Black Experience into English Verse: A Survey of Local African Poetry, 1960–70," *New Nation* 3 (Feb. 1970); reprinted in *SP*, pp. 138–9.

28   Sepamla, "The Black Writer," p. 117.

29   *Tsotsitaal* is an urban African dialect spoken by all African proletarians, especially by young members of street gangs or possible criminals. Coplan argues that *tsotsi* is a corruption of the American term "zoot suit" (see *In Township Tonight*, p. 271).

30   Mothobi Mutloatse, "Bundu Bulldozers," quoted in *SP*, p. 170. *Mlungu* means "white man"; *masemba* means "shit."

31   Anonymous, "It's Paati to Be Black," *Staffrider* (Mar. 1978). *Dompas* refers to the hated passes; *dom* is Afrikaans for "stupid."

32   Paton, in *Momentum*, p. 89.

33   Frankie Ntsu kaDitshego/Dube, "The Ghettoes," *Staffrider* (July/Aug. 1979).

34   Gwala, "Towards a National Theatre," *South African Outlook* (Aug. 1973); quoted in Chapman, intro., *SP*, p. 21.

35   See Chapman, intro., *SP*, p. 21.

36   Anonymous, "It's Paati to Be Black." *Kwela-kwela* is the township name for the large police pickup vans. See Coplan, *In Township Tonight*, pp. 157–60, for the origins of the term. *Doom* is a spray insecticide.

37   Raymond Williams, *Problems in Materialism and Culture* (London, 1980), pp. 47–8.

38   Terry Eagleton and Peter Fuller, "The Question of Value: A Discussion," *New Left Review* 142 (Nov./Dec. 1983): 77.

39   See, for instance, Eagleton, "Aesthetics and Politics," *New Left Review* 107 (Jan./Feb. 1978): 21–34; *Criticism and Ideology: A Study in Marxist Literary Theory* (London, 1978); and "Criticism and Politics: The Work of Raymond Williams," *New Left Review* 95 (Jan./Feb. 1976): 3–23; Catherine Belsey, *Critical Practice* (London 1980); Tony Bennett, *Formalism and Marxism* (London, 1979), and "Marxism and Popular Fiction," *Literature and Popular History* 7 (Fall 1981): 138–65; Stuart Hall,

"Cultural Studies: Two Paradigms," in *Culture, Ideology and Social Process: A Reader*, ed. Bennett et al. (London, 1981), pp. 19–37; Barbara Herrnstein Smith, "Contingencies of Value," *Critical Inquiry* 10 (Sept. 1983): 1–36, and "Fixed Marks and Variable Constancies: A Parable of Literary Value," *Poetics Today* 1 (Autumn 1979): 7–31; Paul Lauter, "History and the Canorr," *Social Text* 12 (Fall 1985): 94–101; Francis Mulhern, "Marxism in Literary Criticism," *New Left Review* 108 (Mar./Apr. 1979): 77–87; Jane Tompkins, *Sensational Designs: The Cultural Work of American Fiction, 1790–1860* (New York, 1985); Peter Widdowson, " 'Literary Value' and the Reconstruction of Criticism," *Literature and History* 6 (Fall 1980): 139–50.

40   The performative and popular aspects of this poetry mark it off from the Western modernist destruction of the text.

41   See Mbulelo Mzamane, "Literature and Politics among Blacks in South Africa," *New Classic* 5 (1978); reprinted in *SP*, p. 156.

Chapter 53

Revolutionary Practice and Style in Lusophone Liberation Poetry

Emmanuel Ngara

Introduction

The poetry produced before the fighting phase in Angola, Mozambique and Guinea Bissau shares some common characteristics in both content and form with Negritude poetry. Like that of David Diop much of the Lusophone poetry of the period was characterized by realism. But, however practical and committed they were to the fight for justice, some of the poets were bound to engage, at least to some degree, in theoretical abstractions. This is certainly true of Noémia de Sousa, who declares in the poem 'Black Blood':

> Oh my mother Africa
> Great pagan, sensual slave
> mystic, charmed
> to your transgressing daughter
> Give forgiveness![1]

Even Agostinho Neto in 'The Blood and the Seed', a very down-to-earth poem, refers abstrusely to 'cries', 'voices' and 'hymns':

> Our cries
> are drums heralding desire
> in the tumultuous voices, music of nations,
> our cries are hymns of love that hearts
> might flourish on the earth like seeds in the sun
> the cries of Africa
> cries of mornings when the dead grew from the seas
> chained

First published in *Ideology and Forum in African Poetry: Implications for Communication*, pp. 103–9. London: James Currey, 1990.

the blood and the seed
For the future – here are our eyes
for peace – our voices
for peace – our hands

from Africa, united in love.

These are poems by members of the intellectual elite using revolutionary language that is divorced from practice. Very often the resistance to Portuguese oppression was 'passive' resistance, consisting of theorizing without concrete action. All that was to change in the 1960s after the launching of the armed liberation struggle by the People's Movement for the Liberation of Angola (MPLA), the Independence Party for Guinea Bissau and Cape Verde (PAIGC) and the Front for the Liberation of Mozambique (FRELIMO).

The fighting phase gave birth to a new category of poetry. In Mozambique and Angola the poetry of this period is completely free of mystification and subjective idealism. It is a poetry that reflects the concrete reality of a people fighting for freedom, independence and social justice. Although written in Portuguese, the poetry reflects the concerns and wishes of a whole society in which class barriers have been broken down, as the people's sense of unity and purpose grows in their determination to defeat colonialism and build a new and just society.

The poetry of this phase is characterized by the unity of theory and practice. In other words, the philosophy that the poetry articulates is not based on abstractions, but is the result of participation in an actual struggle. One indication of this is the pattern of imagery that runs through Part 2 of Margaret Dickinson's collection, *When Bullets Begin to Flower*. Contrary to the earlier period when the poet used the protest language of 'voices', 'songs', 'drums', 'hope' and 'progress', suggesting a purely theoretical involvement in the struggle,[2] now there is a new set of images which signify a concrete liberation struggle. The images can be put in the following major categories: images of blood and pain; images of cultivation and planting; and images of fertility – flowering, water and rain. In addition, there are constant references to struggle, revolution, unity and hope. Hope is now for something achievable, based on the observable progress of the struggle and not on speculation and wishful thinking, as in the previous phase.

Imagery and Language

Images of blood and pain run through such poems as Agostinho Neto's 'February', Sampadjudo's 'Our Sure Road' and Helder Neto's 'We shall not Mourn the Dead', to name but a few. In these and other poems the necessity for suffering, for shedding blood for the sake of freedom, is accepted without regret. There is now a firm realization that independence cannot be given on a platter; it calls for suffering, endurance and sacrifice. To Sampadjudo pain and blood are the prelude to the joy of freedom:

Pain and blood
Pain and blood is the road,
the ticket we must buy
to reach our independence along the endless path of our work and our joy
Our sure road is pain and blood

> straight road to the sun
> to the sun of our freedom.

These words are echoed by Helder Neto, who repeats again and again in 'We shall not Mourn the Dead':

> The liberation of our country calls for
> blood
> The blood of her best sons.

These images of blood and suffering bespeak a concrete revolution, a people's real struggle and the poet's participation in it. That the war is a people's war, a collective war waged by the masses, is evident in the constant reference to 'we' and 'the people', as in Antonio Jacinto's 'The People Went to War' and Marcelino dos Santos's 'To Point a Moral to a Comrade'. In the latter poem the individual, the 'You' or 'I', is consciously and openly subordinated to the collective:

> What matters is not what I want
> or YOU want
> but what WE want

And again:

> Each of us
> has a private wish
>
> but what WE want
> is not what I want or you want
> but what WE want

It is in this collective spirit that we see the people of Angola and Mozambique 'planting' the revolution, making it grow. Images of planting, cultivating, creating and building take various forms. Marcelino dos Santos adopts the image of planting as the heading of one of his poems, 'We Must Plant', where the new tree of independence is to be planted everywhere:

> everywhere
> we must plant
> the certainty
> of tomorrow's good
> in the endearments of your heart
> where every child's eyes
> renew their hope
>
> Yes, mother
> We must plant,
> We must plant
> Along the road of freedom
> the new tree
> of National Independence.

In Helder Neto the liberation of the country is associated not only with blood but also with rain which enables the wild grass to grow 'as high as the savannah'. In dos Santos's 'To Point a Moral to a Comrade' the guerrillas:

> Create hospitals
> Create schools
>
> Their task is to
> dig the basic soil of Revolution
> and make a strong people grow

The protagonist points out time and time again:

> We must cultivate
> the shamba of the Revolution
> a hard future
> of sweat, of toil, of blood

And the poem closes with these words in block capitals to make the message loud and clear:

> WE ARE FRELIMO SOLDIERS
> ACCOMPLISHING THE PARTY'S TASK
> DIGGING THE BASIC SOIL OF REVOLUTION
> FOR AN END OF EXPLOITATION MAN BY MAN
> TO BUILD COMPLETE NATIONAL
> INDEPENDENCE

Images of planting are naturally associated with those of flowering, indicating the fruitfulness of the revolution. Hence, as the Frelimo soldiers 'dig the basic soil of Revolution', they see 'the first young shoots proclaimed / in Cabo Delgado and Niassa Province'. And rightly so because

> To expect rice
> without sowing it
> is not the history of man.

It is through labour and the armed struggle that planters and fighters can make flowers grow, as Sampadjudo tells us in 'Our Sure Road':

> Listen Caboverdian,
> the siren of the future must sing
> in the factories of our land
> Look, Caboverdian
> how the flower of the future opens all things
> in the garden of our land.

There is a clear philosophy behind these images of cultivation and building. First, they are concrete images which bespeak a materialist non-metaphysical conception of life and social struggle. Secondly, through these images the poets proclaim the Marxist philosophy of the dignity of labour, the centrality of work in any endeavour to wage a revolution or to embark on a programme of development. That is why in the poem 'To Point a Moral to a Comrade' which is packed with ideological content Marcelino dos Santos proclaims:

> TODAY
>
> We must cultivate
> the shamba of the Revolution,
> a hard future in the bush
>
> wearing out our hands and eyes
> in the great sustained effort.

It is through labour that struggling people will eventually see themselves 'gathering the first fruits' of freedom. It is by carrying guns that fighters will see their revolution flower into independence and sovereignty.

An important feature of the poetry of the liberation phase in Angola, Mozambique and Guinea Bissau is simplicity. There is neither complicated stylization nor artificial adornments; the poets make no show of intellectual erudition. The poems are simply written, so as to be accessible to all classes of people. They depict the people's struggles and their sufferings, achievements and hopes. Margaret Dickinson's collection appropriately ends with Jorge Rebelo's 'Poem', of which the final words are a fitting epilogue:

> Come tell me these dreams become war,
> the birth of heroes
> land reconquered,
> Mothers who, fearless
> send their sons to fight.
>
> Come, tell me all this, my brother.
>
> And later I will forge simple words
> which even the children can understand
> Words which will enter every house
> like the wind
> and fall like red hot embers
> on our people's souls
>
> In our land
> Bullets are beginning to flower.

Lusophone Poetry and Frantz Fanon's Categories

In *The Wretched of the Earth* Frantz Fanon sees the literature of colonized nations developing as part of national consciousness. In the first stage of its literary activity, the intelligentsia seeks to appeal to or denounce the colonial master. Later, the writer turns to and addresses his or her own people, and finally engages in a literature of combat which calls on the people to fight for their existence as a nation:

The continued cohesion of the people constitutes for the intellectual an invitation to go farther than his cry of protest. The lament first makes the indictment; then it makes an appeal. In the period that follows, the words of command are heard. The crystallization of the national consciousness will both disrupt literary styles and themes, and also create a completely new public. While at the beginning the native intellectual used to produce his work to be read exclusively by the oppressor, whether with the intention of charming him or of denouncing him through ethnical or subjectivist means now the native writer progressively takes on the habit of addressing his own people.[3]

While it is true to say that Frantz Fanon developed these categories at a particular juncture of history, they nevertheless have a certain generality which illuminates our understanding of the development of poetry in Portuguese-speaking Africa. In our analysis we have identified two distinct phases. First, there is the phase (the second in Fanon's categories) when the poet writes about the people, highlighting how they have been affected by slavery, colonialism or segregation. This poetry is marked by a degree of objective realism, by an appeal to the history, sufferings and struggles of the people. Many of the poems of Agostinho Neto, Viriato da Cruz, Noémia de Sousa and others belong to this precombat phase which is characterized by much theorizing about the struggle against colonialism, and sometimes by language that is highly charged with emotion, as in Noémia de Sousa. Then there is the poetry of combat, written under the influence of the armed liberation struggle, when the writer has advanced ideologically through theory and practice. This poetry is frequently sad and moving, but it is almost free of feelings of hatred, presenting facts objectively. In this poetry the focus is no longer on the oppressor, but on the prosecution of the armed liberation struggle, and on the people who have now become the subject of history.

Simplicity of Style and Artistic Value – Conclusion

As already indicated, much of the poetry of the fighting phase is written in a simple and direct style. In the case of Mozambican poetry, the simplicity is sometimes overdone, as in Marcelino dos Santos's 'We Must Plant'. If we accept the view that 'good' poetry should stand the test of time and remain effective even after the war has been fought and won, then the extreme simplicity of style in dos Santos and others would appear to militate against this. We have to remember, however, that liberation poetry, like liberation songs, is meant to have popular appeal and make an immediate impact on the listener or reader. Putting aside the fact that it was written in Portuguese, which many of the masses could not understand, Mozambican and Angolan liberation poetry is otherwise an example of this kind of popular poetry.

Notes

1   This poem and all the poems cited in this chapter are quoted in Margaret Dickinson (ed) *When Bullets Begin to Flower*, Nairobi, East African Publishing House, 1972 (reprinted 1980).
2   See ibid., pp. 28–9.
3   Frantz Fanon, *The Wretched of the Earth*, Harmondsworth, Penguin edition, 1967 (reprinted 1980), p. 193.

Part VIII

Theorizing the Criticism of African Literature

The questions that are dealt with in this section have to do with the nature and character of the critical traditions that have been applied to the study of African literature. Early criticism of African literature came from the Western tradition, often though not exclusively promoted by Western scholars. This early tendency was marked by the assumption that African writing was an extension of "English" literature, and thus to be judged by the values defined for that literature. At times this tendency produced a species of what might be called geneticist criticism, in which evidence of the influence of European writers was traced in order to show the at least partial derivativeness of African writing. To counter this now disputed tendency, the quest for critical tradition that would be properly attuned to the task of evaluating African literature has gone through a number of articulations. Some have argued for a strictly formalist approach that would be sensitive to the intertextual relations among texts and the processes of defamiliarization that help to delimit African literary writing from the non-literary sphere as such. Others have pointed out the need for introducing a gender corrective to what appears to be an objective mode of criticism but which is inherently tilted towards canonizing male writers. And yet others have focused on the question of who has the right to write about African literature, and with what cultural sensitivity and local knowledge. Each of these positions is represented in the essays in this section.

Chapter 54

Academic Problems and Critical Techniques

Eldred D. Jones

English literature as a subject is due for a redefinition which will bring into its scope all literature in English. In the traditional syllabuses of English universities, this need has not been fully accepted and perhaps this reluctance is understandable. But even in non-British English-speaking areas the old and narrower definition of English literature as the literature of England still largely prevails. In this University College we have introduced some African writing in English in the syllabuses of the early years of the degree courses and are contemplating giving it a more significant place. This is inevitable if the vital connection between literature and life is to be preserved. Because literature has for so long meant for us the study of works set in an alien background and arising out of a different pattern of life, it has an air of artificiality and irrelevance to real life – at least it does for a large number of students. They wrestle so long and hard with the environment and the convention that often the essential content is lost. I do not speak here of the very good student but of the average student in our universities. More study of a literature which arises out a familiar environment and familiar circumstances of life will establish a vital connection which would otherwise be lost. Nothing in this approach denies the universality of great literature and the relevance of non-African literature to the university syllabuses of Africa.

As soon as we start thinking about African literature in English, or French for that matter, we soon realise that the readership is not mainly African. The publishers who decide what shall or shall not be published mostly live and work outside the environment which produced the literature. The majority of the critics also live outside the home of these works. Thus the standing of African writers has largely been determined outside Africa. This had led to assessments which almost frighten many intelligent African readers, among whom the standing of Tutuola, for instance, must be rather lower than the excessive praise heaped on him outside Africa would seem to indicate.

First published in *African Literature and the Universities,* ed. G. Moore, pp. 89–91. Ibadan: Ibadan University Press, 1965.

Of course, non-Africans are fully entitled to participate in the criticism of literature of Africa, and they should and will make their views known. But when the main critical voices are non-African there is a danger that the writers may come to emphasise the values which they think their foreign readership demands. This could lead to an expatriate literature produced by Africans, and to false artistic values.

It is the task of African universities to stimulate a discerning readership for African literature. This is only partly met by including works by African writers in specialist syllabuses. Our engineers and chemists, economists and divines and their children should be the backbone of the general critical public. Various parts of the university syllabus recognize the need for guiding students to participate in reading outside their particular fields. In any curriculum reform, the writing which treats in an imaginative way the consequences of the African way of life should be brought to the attention of all African students. Through the extra-mural departments and the departments of education, universities can also stimulate a greater interest in African writing outside the universities.

The specialist students of literature have the additional task of applying their minds in a special way to the critical examination of African literature in order to reveal the qualities of individual works and to help to establish general critical standards. Many of the techniques used in judging non-African works will apply in this task but I believe that we ought to be aware of the particular state of African writing.

We are dealing with a young literature which has, however, deep roots in the past. This young literature is coming out straight into competition with the well-established literature of other lands against which it will be judged. When we talk of English poetry we have a large and well-established body of work on which critical minds have played for a very long time. African literature is much more difficult to view as a whole.

Let us look at the poetry. The most accessible body of African poetry is to be found in anthologies like Bassir's *Anthology of West African Verse*, Langston Hughes' *African Treasury* and Peggy Ruther-foord's *Darkness and Light*. The selections have been made by personal contact or through an elaborate grapevine. This does not give the reader a chance to assess the work of individual writers, and it gives a false picture of the state of African poetry. What Africa needs is a large number of slim volumes of the works of individual writers whose work can then be viewed as a whole. It is from these that the anthologies should be compiled. I realise that the anthology approach has been useful in creating an outlet for some poets and for this we should be grateful. Mbari publications are now beginning to give us these much needed publications of individual poets. The anthologies should really come later. Whatever the university presses can do to provide editions of single poets would be a great contribution to African literature. This is the material on which critics will work.

Because we are dealing with a young literature with promise rather than fulfilment, criticism should be judicious, and without being patronising, should be at pains to reveal whatever promise the work has, rather than to destroy it by unsympathetic criticism. This might offend the sensibilities of many scholars, but let me try to make my meaning clear. I shall illustrate with the example of Nigeria.

Some of the best writing in Africa today comes from Nigeria. I think that there is a direct connection between Nigeria's leadership in African literature and the fact that the country also supports a large market in cheap pamphlets. I am told that in the market in Onitsha on any one day it is possible to count up to sixty different pamphlets on sale, on all topics. Mr K. A. B. Jones-Quartey, who is now working on a biography of Dr Azikiwe, told me recently about the large number of pamphlets written on the Governor-General alone. This is apart from the large mass of writing in Nigerian languages. All this may or may not be of a high literary quality, but if this kind of writing is discouraged, then good writing may die with it. Good writing needs manure as plants need muck. Nothing in this mass of cheap pamphlets should be beneath the notice of the scholar, and his notice should be tinged with sympathy. This kind of literature makes the passage of the literary writer smoother. It overcomes the inhibition which writing frequently imposes both on the reader and the writer. The least the scholar can do is to keep in touch with writing at any level and try to bring out what is good in it. We tend to be too occupied in our study with material within hard covers while we ignore the cheap broadsheet. *All I am advocating is a balance.*

I see something of this balance in the operation of the drama studio in Accra which Mrs Sutherland founded. In the building up of a national theatre, the studio puts on work of varying quality. Nothing with any good in it is rejected. This attitude is vital in dealing with a young literature. Criticism should be tolerant, and publication permissive.

But of course, we can also kill good literature by overpraising bad. We tend to be rather loose with our superlatives in our pride in the work of our own people. Our criticism should always be controlled.

Chapter 55

African Literature, Western Critics

Rand Bishop

When modern African literature began blossoming in the late 1940s and early 1950s, it was primarily for European consumption. An essay by a leading European intellectual ("Orphée noir" by Jean-Paul Sartre) and the establishing of an African-run journal and publishing house, Présence africaine, in Paris and Dakar, under the patronage of a group of Western intellectuals whose names read like a Who's Who of the period, were two early developments that helped bring about this peculiar writer-audience relationship. Certainly the paucity of a literate and literature-reading audience and a lack of publishers in Africa also contributed to this state of affairs. Thus it was inevitable, perhaps, if not desirable, that Westerners became involved very early on in the criticism of this new body of literature.

The Western critic was also filling a vacuum of sorts, a cultural lag growing in the wake of the literature due to the lack of a written critical tradition. Oral criticism is no doubt as old as oral literature, though we know little about it and await eagerly a definitive study of it. But it seems clear that the carry-over from oral to written criticism is more complex and less obvious than the carry-over from oral to written literature. And the bulk of written literature to this time would hardly have warranted a critical tradition. A chronological analysis of Jahn and Dressler's *Bibliography of Creative African Writing* (1971) reveals that the number of items published for the years 1965–6 equaled the entire publication record prior to 1950. Thus B. W. Vilakazi could say in 1942 that Zulu literature had "no governing body which could decide on any classic in our Bantu languages in South Africa today. We have no critical opinions of men of taste and knowledge, whose qualifications today enable them to judge a work by certain positive standards" (274).

Vilakazi's comment is interesting from another standpoint as well. He lamented a lack of critics rather than "certain positive standards," but his standards were very likely those of white South Africa, if not of the entire Western literary tradition. The problematical nature

First published in *African Literature, African Critics: The Forming of Critical Standards, 1947–1966*, pp. 59–67, 68–9. New York: Greenwood Press, 1988.

of the relationship of African literature to this tradition was to be raised later and is treated at some length below. The relationship became problematical because of the nature of this early Western criticism, which must be understood if one is to appreciate the importance of the reaction to it in establishing an African literary criticism.

The most unfortunate aspect of this early Western criticism was that very few of the Westerners knew much about Africa (the state of affairs that had led to the choosing of "Présence africaine" as a title). Sartre's own essay indicated little specific knowledge of African culture; it was, rather, a brilliant psychological study of the colonizer and the colonized, even if stated in Marxist terms that today seem a little stilted. One could make much, perhaps, of the fact that Sartre chose *not* to become a major Western critic of African literature.

Undaunted, less timid minds forged ahead into the field, until it became apparent to increasing numbers of Africans that something was drastically wrong: the criticism of the literature was being based on the assumption that, because it employed European languages, African literature in French and English were therefore, respectively, branches of French and English literature, and that one need only apply the underlying principles of Western literary criticism in assessing the new literature. Thus Chinua Achebe found himself the grand-nephew of Joseph Conrad, and the mark of T. S. Eliot and Gerard Manley Hopkins was ferreted out in many African poets. Judgments by comparison to Western writers and values became common practice, which allowed Westerners to "locate" African writers in terms they understood – in terms, that is, of the Western literary tradition. But the practice was predicated on the false premise – an old Western failing where Africa was concerned – that, beyond the mastering of a few anthropological details, there was little about the literature or the culture it sprang from that demanded serious study. And so, as in so many other areas of twentieth-century life, Africa's literary situation – or rather the understanding of it by non-Africans – came to be compared to a seemingly similar institution in the West. More often than not, Africa's institutions, because they did not correspond exactly to their Western counterparts, were thought to be "underdeveloped," if not inferior or nonexistent. Thus the oral tradition was seen merely as a precursor to writing, as it was in medieval Europe – the implication being that since written literature was relatively new to Africa, it had a lot to learn before one could speak of an African literary tradition and, worse, that the African tradition, when it did develop, would perforce develop along the lines of the Western tradition since it was clearly "behind" in its "evolution."

Faced with this cultural hegemony, African critics began to question the inevitabilities voiced by Westerners and soon experienced a *prise de conscience* that led to a reexamination of the relationship of Africa's newly written literature to the traditions of the West. It is this reexamination that I here wish to explore, as well as to show that, not only was the relationship reexamined, but became itself a standard by which critics judged individual works of the literature.

The criticism indicates three major stances by Africans vis-à-vis the Western literary tradition: reliance upon it, avoidance of it, and a synthesis of Western and African elements. That there was not total agreement on the question need not surprise us any more than the variances on other questions have not. It was, rather, an indication of the complexity and importance of the issue in the critics' minds.

Although African literature increased dramatically in volume, particularly after the publication of Senghor's *Chants d'ombre* in 1945 and the advent of *Présence africaine* in 1947, it was inevitable that Western critics, armed with their ready-made literary tradition, had a head start in the criticism of the new literature. Neither should their political (colonial) advantage be underestimated. Senghor wrote in 1950,

> Europe has developed the critical spirit in us, which is more method than invention. Levy-Bruhl considers "invention" an essential virtue of the "primitive." Thus the critical spirit is, above all, perception, objective comprehension of all aspects of a problem. But for the European there is more, there is this glow, this warmth, that underlies the method and brings about a solution. ("L'Afrique s'interroge," 438)

Yet a few years later, Senghor himself opened the attack on Western criticism of African literature. Writing in 1956 of a Westerner's critique of the poetry of Aimé Césaire, he said, "To criticize Césaire and others for their rhythm, their 'monotony,' in a word their style, is to criticize them for being born 'Negroes,' West Indians or Africans and not 'French' or Christian; it is to criticize them for having remained themselves, totally sincere" ("Comme les lamantins," 118*).

The attack was taken up in earnest a few years later by two Nigerian writers, J. P. Clark and Chinua Achebe, in *Nigeria Magazine*. And the attack became general in tone. Writing in 1962, Clark delineated three types of "non-link" Western critics. The first were those who "go for what to them is exotic and unspoilt," such as the critic who doted on Tutuola,

> lisping and lapping the poor fellow out of breath until he got out of step with the flow of *The Palm Wine Drinkard* that had brought them upon him. "Oh, the man has begun taking lecture notes from Wolsey Hall," they complained and swept aside *The Brave African Huntress* and all the old master's later efforts. ("Our Literary Critics," 79–80)

The second was the type who "goes for anthropology," who sees no difference in quality in the works of Cyprian Ekwensi, Chinua Achebe, or Onuora Nzekwu, and who "has conveniently tacked all three together as explorers of the theme of cultural conflict" (80). The third type was those who went "the Paul Gauguin way" (80), and who, "because they need a guide, ... would swallow everything a so-called expert tells them" (81).

Three months later Achebe took up the question and, speaking for his fellow Africans, said, "We are not opposed to criticism but we are getting a little weary of all the special types of criticism which have been designed for us by people whose knowledge of us is very limited" ("Where Angels," 61). Achebe also arranged the Westerners into three categories, though somewhat different from those of Clark: "the peevishly hostile, what-do-they-think-they-are Honor Tracy breed. These are angry with the new-fangled idea of colonial freedom and its gross ingratitude for colonial benefits" (61); those who "are amazed that we should be able to write at all" (61); and a group "which is fully conscious of the folly of the other two and is bent on restoring a sense of balance to the argument," of whom Achebe said, "This is the group with which we could hold a dialogue, with frankness on either side," but he added also that "this group annoys us by their increasing dogmatism" (61).

About this same time, several Africans (Achebe and Clark among them) were gathered at a Conference of English-Speaking African Writers at Makerere University in Kampala, where an attitude toward Western critics seems to have crystallized. Reporting on the conference, Bernard Fonlon said that "strong disapproval was expressed from the very start, at the attitude of some Europeans who, considering themselves as experts in Negro literature, lay down canons on what this literature should be, and dismiss as not African any work by an African that does not conform to their dogma" ("African Writers," 42). And while attending the conference African Literature and the Universities in Freetown a few months later, John Akar, a Sierra Leone critic, gave a particularly vexing example of this dogmatism. He told of a friend's sending a novel to several publishing houses and that "one in particular wrote and said 'Very interesting novel, but it did not sound African enough'. ... Now who is to say that it does not sound African enough – the publishing house? An African is writing about his own personal experience" ("General Discussion," 130).

Some years later Joseph Okpaku, in the initial editorial in his *Journal of the New African Literature and the Arts*, made a similar comment:

> Much of African literature has been severely restricted to what the Western world would like to classify as purely African or authentically African. The result of this limitation which essentially has been an imposition on the African writer by those who prefer to preserve what they claim is the characteristic eroticism and exoticism of African culture, is that African literature has been frozen in this anachronistic mode and thereby deprived of the opportunity to grow and develop along with the growth and development of the African society. ("The Philosophy," 1–2)

In more concrete terms, Robert Serumaga summarized the responses of the British critics to a London production of Wole Soyinka's *The Road* and was critical of a remark by Gerard Fay in *The Guardian*, which was that "when [Soyinka] knows, or perhaps more accurately when he can make us others know what he is trying to say, he will be going places" (ii). Serumaga replied, "But it may at least equally forcibly be argued that the shoe is on the other foot. When Mr. Fay can understand at once what a play set in a different culture is all about, he will be going places. On the evidence of the review he may not even be trying" (ii). Serumaga preferred the *Daily Mail* critic, who, he said, "struck a note that augers well for a continued dialogue between cultures: 'I do not myself pretend to have understood half of Soyinka's play. I am sure for one thing that I have got the plot all wrong. But throughout the evening I was thrilled enough to want to understand'" (i).

Lewis Nkosi, as well as others, described a different danger in Western criticism: while it may be accurate, it may also be patronizing. He said, "What is threatening to ruin most of us [African writers], including some writers of genuine promise, is over-exposure and over-praise. The reputations of some writers have simply been 'manufactured' by busy-body students of African affairs determined to find something exciting and new to study and write home about" ("Where Does," 8). George Otieno echoed this sentiment upon reviewing some of J. P. Clark's poems: "Most foreign critics and publishers are still reluctant to judge our writers purely on merits; they must judge them as African writers, and this tendency sometimes leads to an unhealthy patronisation which can only kill the creative impulse" (43).

Mohamadou Kane summed up the position perhaps as well as anyone else. He spoke of the "misunderstanding" caused by European criticism, which had been able to hold sway because

> between the African public and itself there is no established African opinion to intervene with the same persuasion. Its sympathy towards Africa in general and towards our literature in particular is undeniable. Its good intentions are those which pave the way to the worst hells for,

finally, such criticism leads to imposing its views or to the total falsification of the meaning of a work. ("African Writer," 20)

Kane's positive suggestion was that

> the only attitude this [Western] criticism could take which would help in promoting our writing would be in maintaining a stronger conviction that the future of our writing will become concrete in the continent itself. African literature, expressed in any form whatever, cannot, for innumerable reasons, be considered as the common property of Europe and Africa but must be appreciated for itself as an element of cultural solidarity. (23)

African Literature and the Western Literary Tradition: A Critical Standard

The comments by Africans on Western criticism are legion. Of more interest is the discussion, not of the Westerners themselves, but of the tradition that lay behind them. What was the relationship between African literature and the Western literary tradition? What should it be? These questions provoked serious discussion among Africans and became, finally, a criterion used in the evaluation of individual works of African literature. Let us consider first the critics who recognized the influence of the Western literary tradition on African literature and who considered such influence as good, in and of itself.

Pro-Western Critics

The earliest of these comments came from a South African, D. D. T. Jabavu, who wrote a small book on the subject, *The Influence of English on Bantu Literature* (1948), based on a speech made in 1943. In it, he said of B. W. Vilakazi's poetry, *Inkondlo kaZulu* (1935), that it was

> the one great book of poetry in Zulu that attains to the rank of a classic. It is English influence *in excelsis*, by reason of its outright imitation of English modes (metres long, short and common; all varieties of stanzas, elegaics, sonnets, rhymes, and even the heroic couplet, reminiscent of Pope and Dryden) all punctiliously observed. Even the titles remind one of Keats in disguising their subject, ensuring that *ars artem celare est*. (11)

Jabavu concluded his study saying, of A. C. Jordan's novel, *IngQumbo yemiNyanya* (1940), "If the influence of English on Bantu literature will inspire further classics of this calibre, then its continuation is worthwhile" (26).

Another large problem was recognized at the First International Congress of Black Writers and Artists, held in Paris in 1956. Senghor had spoken of African rhythm, which prompted the following statement from N. Damz:

> I would like to ask Mr. Senghor one thing: if we listened – for example – to the African griots, who compose this music, which delights us, and which is the basic element of the art they compose, I think we would perceive that their aesthetic nuances are governed by European aesthetic nuances.... I mean that, in general, all the problems we face here are affected by our European education, that is, by the stamp of our European education upon us. ("Débats," 83)

The impact of European education on African thinking and aesthetic feeling is much too complex a question to be dealt with here. It is clear, however, that the problem Damz posed was discussed at this important conference.

Less problematic – but perhaps more dogmatic – was the comment some years later by Paulin Joachim, who favored the Western tradition by implication when he criticized Charles Nokan's *Le Soleil noir point* (1962) for not conforming to any "traditional" (read Western) literary genre. He said, "This is neither a novel nor a tale nor a short story, but a little of each, a formless, incoherent mixture. But why this penchant for innovation and for looking for ways to express oneself in forms so far removed from the traditional ones? Is this the only way to express one's originality?" ("Le Soleil noir point," 58–9).

Pro-Synthesis Critics

More reasoned, perhaps, were the comments by critics who argued for a syncretic relationship with the West. One of the earliest expressions of this view seems to have been made in 1956 by Antoine-Roger Bolamba, a Zairian critic, who said of the Malgache poet that "the great achievement of Flavien Ranaivo is that he remains true to the genius of his race while respecting French thought and technique" ("Flavien Ranaivo," 119). Joseph Miezan Bognini of the Ivory Coast was another critic who accepted a syncretic relationship with the Western tradition. Reviewing Bernard Dadié's novel, *Un Nègre à Paris* (1959), he said,

> I do not think this book seeks to transplant Western development – a part of whose culture we have acquired – into Africa. The issue is one involving her individual evolution confronted with Western culture, because it must be said that she can only evolve in terms of what she has received. This does not mean a mere copying but a synthesizing of her own in order to acquire her own individuality. (156)

Joachim, modifying somewhat his earlier position on Nokan's work, applied a similar standard when he quoted comments on a Senegalese writer: "[Abdoulaye] Sadji was the extreme, the product of the shock of the two civilizations. The Senegalese found him too Europeanized and the French a little too casual about the requirements of assimilated life. But Sadji was a cultured man. He had roots in the soil, his head and heart open to the winds of Europe" ("Trois livres," 39).

Bernard Fonlon noted in 1966 two trends of African literature, one largely a protest literature influenced by European education, which "arouses little or no interest among the African literate public and remains largely unread" ("A Word," 10), and the other that "looks for approval not from foreign critics who judge according to the canons established by the European literary tradition, but from the African readers who are better qualified to pronounce on its authenticity" (11). He went on to say that a more powerful African literature will come about when these two trends merge, and he then applied the idea as a critical standard when he said, "Already the merger of these two tendencies is being effected by some writers. The novel of the Western Nigerian writer, T.M. Aluko, *One Man, One Matchet*, is a skillful blend of both" (12).

In his PhD dissertation, Romanus Egudu sanctioned the mixing of Western and African elements when he concluded of the poetry of Christopher Okigbo, J. P. Clark, George Awoonor-Williams, and Lenrie Peters that "these poets seem to believe (and this author agrees) that while making use of their indigenous poetry (vernacular and colonial) and experiences for creating works of art, they can still tap foreign sources of experiences, which are made accessible to them by their acquisition of a second language" (269).

Anti-Western Critics

Such statements, however, were clearly outnumbered by those directed against the Western literary tradition, by those who saw it as a danger and threat to the ultimate integrity of African literature. Perhaps the first of such comments was by Ben Obumselu, a Nigerian critic, who, upon reviewing Achebe's *Things Fall Apart* in 1959, was at least mildly reproachful because he said Achebe had overlooked "implications in our music, sculpture and folklore which the West African novelist cannot neglect if he wishes to do more than merely imitate a European fashion" (Review, 38).

Another critic, using the same standard, implied a different evaluation of Achebe. Christina Aidoo commented on Gerald Moore's early critical work, *Seven African Writers* (1962), asking rhetorically, "How far should one go with Moore in viewing the work of Chinua Achebe as an African development of the English literary tradition that includes Conrad?" (46).

And once again, the Benin critic, Paulin Joachim, could be found using this standard, albeit in some contrast to those instances already cited. He compared the first two novels of Guinean writer Camara Laye and thought that *L'Enfant noir* was superior to *Le Regard du roi* because the latter "is less interesting, principally because its form is no longer original or African and it approaches too closely current European writing" ("Contemporary," 298). He concluded his review by saying, "The African novel will begin an authoritative existence the day its writers abandon a sterile imitation of Western forms of expression and return to their native land to search for originality and a specifically African style" (300).

The novel was not the only genre to draw out the critics in this regard. The drama also led Africans to warn against the encroachment of Western tradition. Viewing two Soyinka plays in 1959 in Ibadan, Phebean Ogundipe had the following misgivings: "I was afraid that they might be just another of those pseudo-original pieces of literature where the English framework on which they are built is only too painfully obvious, and that they might turn out to be a re-hash of Shakespeare or Rattigan, thinly clothed with Nigerian names and settings" (29).

[...]

Commenting on the poetry of Christopher Okigbo, Ezekiel Mphahlele raised the same standard and was bothered by the same influences, asking, "Should African writers not be a little more choosy about the models they adopt in English writing? For instance, one of the first and most obvious things that strikes me in Okigbo's poetry is how close he is to Pound" ("Postscript," 83).

It is impossible to arrive at any final certainty regarding the African view of the Western literary tradition. Literary criticism – like literature itself – is in a constant state of flux. One can speak of tendencies during limited periods of time, by smaller or larger groups of critics – being aware that, even then, one is dealing subjectively with a very complex phenomenon. That need not detain us, however, nor cause those of us in the humanities to apologize (as we are prone to do). It is surely of importance, to both Africans and non-Africans, to understand that during the 1950s and 1960s, African critics were extremely aware of Western criticism and the Western literary tradition as they bore on African literature. The richness of the dialogue they engaged in ensures that, whatever position is eventually taken, it will have been arrived at with care. From the earliest discussions, however, one can conclude that African critics were aware of the problematic nature of the relationship of their literature to the West and that it often became a standard of their criticism.

References

Abraham, W. E. *The Mind of Africa*. Chicago: University of Chicago Press, 1962.

Achebe, Chinua. "Where Angels Fear to Tread." *Nigeria Magazine* 75 (1962): 61–2.

Aidoo, Christina. *The Dilemma of a Ghost*. Acrra, Ikeja: Longmans, 1965.

Bognini, Joseph Miezan. Review of *Un Nègre a Paris* by Bernard Dadié. *Présence africaine* 36 (Eng. ed. vol. 8) (1961): 156–7.

Bolamba, A[ntoine]. R[oger]. "Flavien Ranaivo." *La Voix du congolais* 119 (1956): 118–19.

Clark, John Pepper. "Our Literary Critics." *Nigeria Magazine* 74 (1962): 79–82.

"Débats, ler Congrès international des écrivains et des artistes noirs." *Présence africaine* n.s. 8–9–10 (1956): 66–83.

Egudu, Romanus Nnagbo. "Criticism of Modern African Literature: The Question of Evaluation." *World Literature Written in English* 21, no. 1 (1982): 54–67.

Fonlon, Bernard. "African Writers Meet in Uganda." *Abbia* 1 (1963): 39–53.

——. "A Word of Introduction." *Abbia* 14–15 (1966): 5–13.

"General Discussion on Publishing African Literature." In *African Literature and the Universities*, 130–2. Ed. Gerald Moore. Ibadan: Ibadan University Press, 1965.

Jabavu, Davidson Den Tengo. *The Influence of English on Bantu Literature*. Lovedale: Lovedale Press, 1948.

Joachim, Paulin. "Le Soleil noir point par Charles Nokan." *Bingo* 123 (1963): 58–9.

——. "Trois livres d'Abdoulaye Sadji." Reviews of *Maimouna, Nini*, and *Tounka* by Abdoulaye Sadji. *Bingo* 153 (1965): 39.

——. "Contemporary African Poetry and Prose. 3. French-Speaking Africa's Poètes-Militants." In *A Handbook of African Affairs*, 296–300. Ed. Helen Kitchen. New York: Praeger, 1964.

Kane, Mohamadou. "The African Writer and His Public." *Présence africaine* 58 (Eng. ed. vol. 30) (1966): 10–32.

Mphahlele, Ezekiel. "Postscript on Dakar." In *African Literature and the Universities*, 80–2. Ed. Gerald Moore. Ibadan: Ibadan University Press, 1965.

Nkosi, Lewis. "Where Does African Literature Go from Here?" *Africa Report* 9, no. 9 (December 1966): 7–11.

Obumselu, Ben. "The Background of Modern African Literature." *Ibadan* 22 (1966): 46–59.

Ogundipe, Phebean. "Three Views of 'The Swamp-Dwellers': For What Audience?" *Ibadan* 6 (1959): 29–30.

Okpaku, Joseph O. "The Philosophy of the New African Literature." Editorial. *Journal of the New African Literature and the Arts* 1 (1966): 1–2.

Otieno, George. "African Writers' Break Through." Review of *A Reed in the Tide* by J.P. Clark. *East Africa Journal* (December 1966): 43.

Sartre, Jean-Paul. "Orphée noir." In *Anthologie de la nouvelle poésie nègre et malgache d'expression française*, ix–xliv. Ed. Léopold Sédar Senghor. Paris: Presses universitaires de France, 1948.

Senghor, Léopold Sédar. "L'Afrique s'interroge: Subir ou choisir?" *Présence africaine* 8–9–10 (1950): 437–43. Also in his *Liberté I*.

——. "Comme les lamantins vont boire à la source." In his *Ethiopiques*, 103–23. Paris: Editions du Seuil, 1956. Also in his *Liberté I*.

Vilakazi, B. W. "Some Aspects of Zulu Literature." *African Studies* 1 (1942): 270–4.

Chapter 56

A Formal Approach to African Literature

Kenneth W. Harrow

Introduction

African literary criticism has been plagued by a disregard for intrinsically African literary qualities as well as by a general failure to recognize both its broad development into a literary tradition of its own and the way in which the process of change took place. This failure has generated a preoccupation with extra-literary qualities, substituting cultural motivations/explanations and historical-social changes for literary choices and effects. Formalism restores the text to its proper place by defining its relationship to other texts as the primary constituents of the discourse to which it belongs, rather than to a society or a reality which exists in some fashion apart from the text, or which gives authenticity to the text. If "texts" and intertexuality can no longer be neatly differentiated in such clearly oppositional terms, this does not erase the major role played by prior literary texts in locating a given text within a literary system. The sense of an evolving tradition is what legitimizes this approach, as well as what poses various problems for us.

What problematizes this issue is precisely the determination of which work constitutes a prior text. As for African literature, it is apparent that chronological priority has nothing to do with the kind of relationship which locates a text within a tradition. Rather, it is the commentary of one text upon another, or even more, the sense that one of them has outgrown its predecessor, that gives a tradition its continuity. A close study of the relationship between Camara Laye's *L'Enfant noir* and Ferdinand Oyono's *Une Vie de boy* reveals the mechanisms by which change within African literature has occured. The Formal approach supplies us with the conceptual frame for those mechanisms.

First published in *Research in African Literatures* 29.3 (1997): 79–84.

Defamiliarization

The first key idea of Formalism, elaborated initially by Victor Shklovskij in 1914, is defamiliarization (ostranenie), which is opposed to automization. Shklovskij uses the term in reference to the devices of poetic language whose literariness, or visibly literary qualities, set literature off from non-literature or ordinary life (*byt*), and especially ordinary speech. Ordinary speech becomes invisible to us by virtue of our having become accustomed to it; literary devices, such as inversion, parallelism, the structuring of plot, or poetic meter, rhyme, or figures of speech, render the ordinary communication visible. Shklovskij's first concern, then, is language, which is why he distinguishes poetic language from prose. Since prose is by definition not imbued with the literary devices which would render it visible or unaccustomed, it must resort to non-linguistic means to achieve this goal. These means, for Shklovskij, have to do with the inhabitual way objects or events are described, as in the well-known example of Tolstoy's story "Kholstomer," which is narrated from a horse's point of view, or the reference, in *War and Peace*, to the setting in an opera performance as "pieces of painted cardboard" (Erlich 177).

These definitions of defamiliarization have been much contested and repudiated, especially in Bakhtin's study, *The Formal Method in Literary Scholarship*. However, what appeals to me in this theory is not the distinction between poetry and prose, or literary language and ordinary speech as initially defined by the Formalists and later by their heirs, the Structuralists, but the broader notions of automization and defamiliarization.

Legitimization

All texts become automatized with time. If the actor has to work up the inspiration to bring a part to life every night, the audience at least is not required to attend as frequently. Yet, even though one reads a text only once, views a film or play on a unique occasion, or hears the sole recitation of a poem, eventually an accumulation of similar works, themes, approaches, and techniques pall. All facets of culture grow, inspire or catch hold, achieve full fruition, and then, with satiation, cloy and fade. Whatever gives the audience its final measure of tedium also acts in the process of artistic inspiration, demanding renewal with time.

The concept of defamiliarization was marred at the outset when Shklovskij sought to define it universally. Rather, it should always be taken relatively. For African literature, defamiliarization might be considered in two historical circumstances. The first applies to the literature characteristic of the colonial period. Works like *Force bonté* (or other Senegalese fiction written before World War II), and the early South African works of didactic Christian persuasion drew inspiration from European models. From the 19th century, travel literature and the literature of the exotic characterized European writings about Africa. As African writers acquired literacy in European languages in the 1920s–30s, they often embraced the ideal of progress by creating portraits of success. Figures like Ousmane Socé's Karim pursued, with whatever contradictions this might entail, the European model of modernity. This was a literature that never seemed to emerge into its own because the novelists, unlike the poet-fathers of the Negritude movement, never attained a level of defamiliarization that would separate them from European premises and their hostility to traditional African culture.

Yet this literature served as a springboard because the generation of Laye, Sheikh Hamidou Kane, Birago Diop, Bernard Dadié, Chinua Achebe, and Ousmane Sembène embarked by forging a literature of testimony, of bearing witness, which seemed to be in response to the earlier generation of sycophantic writings. The key model or type which emerged for the generation of the fifties was the autobiography – a story of success defined not by the processes of acculturation and self-abnegation but by cultural affirmation or, eventually, by the rejection of the European cultural model.

The works of the writers of the early colonial period perpetuated the automatized values implicitly grounded in the colonial enterprise. Nonetheless, as these works purported to portray the Africans, they provided a point of departure for subsequent models of positive cultural validation.

Once the patterns of the discourse had established themselves, they continued. The first stage of testimonial literature was followed by one of revolt: Mongo Beti, Oyono, Ahmadou Kourouma, Gabriel Okara, Yambo Ouologuem, the later Ngugi and Sembène became the stalwarts of ironic, anti-colonial or revolutionary fiction. The story of success could no longer be perpetuated; its negation constituted the new form, a reaction grounded again in the dialectical negation of the old, but now automatized idealizations of African culture, history, or society, or of Negritude itself. The new generation of interpreters, rebels, cynics, agnostics, but most of all strugglers, once again sought a new order. Their act of negation rested upon defamiliarization, not on creation *ex nihilo*.

The process continues now, vis-a-vis that generation of the sixties or late fifties. If our period is not monolithic, no literary stage ever was. But its general tendencies resist fragmentation, and continue to achieve the effect of unity through the on-going processes of defamiliarization.

This is precisely the conclusion at which Shklovskij arrived when he affirmed Formalist doctrine, asserting that literary development is totally immanent: "New works come about to change our perception not of *byt* (ordinary reality) but of the artistic form itself, which has become automatized through our acquaintance with older works. The work of art is perceived against the background of and though association with other works of art. Its form is determined by its relation to other forms that existed prior to it. . . . A new form appears not to express a new content but to replace an old form that has lost its artistic quality" (Steiner 56). We can take this affirmation as the first step in understanding how change is defined within a literary discourse.

Periodicity

The major problem which this approach poses is in the definition of a period or stage of literature. "Stage" implies development or progress – a Western bias one associates with past apologists for colonialism, like Count Gobineau. "Period" implies a temporal distinction, one which has nothing to do with the process of defamiliarization. Other terms would seem to be disguised versions of these.

These terms imply a monolithic formation. The problem is not that a multitude of works cannot be reduced to one form, but that a general tendency can only be elucidated if it is seen as dominant. Without this, no tradition can be viewed as emergent or changing or developing. If there is a generation of the 1950s – of Laye's *L'Enfant noir* or Feraoun's *Le fils du pauvre* – what other works are to be included, and on what basis? This problem was first addressed by Sklovskij in his most problematic formulation, the notion of canonized as opposed to non-canonized texts. "In every literary period," he writes, "not one but several literary schools may be found. They coexist; one of them is the canonized apex and the others are a noncanonized [lower stratum]. . . . While the forms of the older art become as little perceptible as grammatical forms in language . . . the new forms of art that substitute for the older ones are produced in the lower stratum. A younger school bursts into the place of an older one" (Steiner 56). Without having to resort to dialectical models, one can use these concepts of strata and periodicity in assessing the relationship between any accepted works of major significance – blocks of the "canonized apex."

Shklovskij's words were written some sixty years before the notions of canon were called into question by recent critics, but even then they pointed to an unavoidable problem. If a tradition is to be described, some works must be isolated. And those that define a period or stage must function better according to that definition than others. Thus, we would include in our elaboration of *littérature de témoignage* not only the first novels of Laye or Feraoun, but also *Les Contes d'Amadou Koumba*, *L'Aventure ambiguë*, and *Things Fall Apart*. Although there are reasons to read *The Palm-Wine Drinkard* as part of this stage, the absence of any apparent intention to revalidate African culture would seem to marginalze it when compared to the others. According to Shklovskij's definitions, such works would be non-canonical. In terms of defamiliarization it might be difficult to see how to fit Tutuola into any periodic schemata: his proximity to the oral tradition, his choice of modified pidgin, his use of the episodic and the fantastic bear little relationship to the automatized works of the previous period. *Drinkard* certainly burst into place, though not, perhaps, in place of older forms.

Systemization

The problems encountered when one considers an individual work in terms of defamiliarization may be overcome by considering its function in terms of the larger system, an approach better explored by Tynjanov. His view, close to that of Bloom, is that "all literary texts are directed towards other works. The identity of a work in respect to genre, style, or school, indeed its very identity as literature, is based on its relations to other literary works *through the underlying literary system*" (Steiner 120, my emphasis). A work becomes "perceptible" not just because it utilizes literary devices, but because it renders the literary devices of the previous dominant works outdated. In other words, literary change is relative as well as dialectical. Initially this dialectic was defined by the Formalists as entirely immanent with respect to art. But Tynjanov expands the systems to which the work of art belongs to include three levels: the level of the single work; literature in its totality; and the whole national culture of a given time (Steiner 114–15). The smaller systems were subordinated to the larger, so that whereas a single text can function as a system unto itself, it becomes a variable in the larger system of literature to which it belongs. And the system of literature itself becomes such a variable for culture as a whole.

Change within the system, at any level, is a function of the struggle for competing parts, in which some feature emerges as dominant. "Art lives through this interplay, the struggle. Without the sensation of subordination, the deformation of all the factors by the factor fulfilling the constructive role, there would be no fact of art. . . . If the sensation of the interplay of factors (necessarily presupposing the presence of two elements – the dominating and the subordinated) vanishes, the fact of art is obliterated; it becomes automatized"

(Steiner 106). Eventually Tynjanov elaborated a more pluralistic definition of art in which "several new principles of construction different from the dominant emerge and struggle for control," wherein those features of dominance that emerge as victorious "converge with the developmental tendencies of the overall cultural system" (Steiner 112). This development is based on the most felicitous Formalist view, the notion that the measure of a literary system, on all levels, is defined by a relatively autonomous process. The dominant feature or features that define the single work may respond to earlier texts, but are not determined solely or rigidly by the automatized aspects of the older works; they escape subordination to the process through the struggle for control and domination in which competing elements participate.

Tynjanov's formulation displaces the problem of distinguishing canonical from noncanonical texts, but at the cost of erecting the distinction between dominant versus subordinated principles of construction. Nonetheless, his insistence on the larger systemic point of view, and on the relative autonomy of the text and its principles of construction, would seem to answer the objection that the attempt to discern an African literary tradition presupposes a hegemonical or authoritarian tendency. Most importantly, relative autonomy is grounded in the notion of the struggle for dominant constructive principles within the text, as well as that of the struggle between new works which defamiliarize and old works which perpetrate automatized forms.

In contrast to those who are content to fall back on facile sociological explanations for change – explanations that ignore defamiliarization within the literary system itself – formalism restores to literature its integrity as a system, while at the same time obeying the logic which would hold that the most natural target for change in the systems of art are other works of art themselves, and only secondarily the larger social system. In other words, art defamiliarizes art, and the impulse to move beyond the automatized is grounded most naturally within the system of art.

[...]

References

Bakhtin, M. M., and P. N. Medvedev. *The Formal Method in Literary Scholarship* (Cambridge: Harvard University Press, 1985).

Erlich, Victor. *Russian Formalism.* (New Haven: Yale University Press, 1981).

Laye, Camara. *L'Enfant noir.* (Paris: Plon, 1953).

Oyono, Ferdinand. *Une Vie de boy.* (Paris: Julliard, 1956).

Steiner, Peter. *Russian Formalism: A Metapoetics.* (Ithaca: Cornell University Press, 1984).

Chapter 57

African Absence, a Literature without a Voice

Ambroise Kom

[...]

[L]et us not forget: literary criticism is above all the affair of professionals, academics. [...]

[I]n the aftermath of the independences, we have seen the birth of university institutions, like mushrooms, a bit everywhere on the continent. Each State claimed it wanted to establish as quickly as possible its administrative staff. And it is in the bosom of the aforementioned institutions that African literary criticism has made its voice heard and has traced out its paths. From the heights of Ngoa-Ekele, the perch of the University of Yaoundé, Thomas Melone paraded the world's scholars and initiated numerous studies. He published, among other works, *Mongo Beti, l'homine et le destin* (1972) as well as *Chinua Achebe et la tragédie de l'histoire* (1973), two works that unleash an avalanche of critical works on the two writers in question. Beyond his numerous articles printed in *Présence Africaine* and elsewhere, Mohamadou Kane, firmly installed with the Faculty of Letters at the University of Dakar, positioned himself as the indisputable exegete of Birago Diop (*Les contes d'Amadou Coumba; du conte traditionnel au conte moderne d'expression française*, 1968, 1981; *Birago Diop, l'homme et l'oeuore*, 1971) before delivering to us his monumental *Roman africain et traditions* (1982).

From Ibadan, Abiola Irele enriched the list of achievements through numerous studies that he later collected under the title *The African Experience in Literature and Ideology* (1981). And before becoming a novelist, the Kenyan Ngũgĩ wa Thiong'o was first a teacher and literary critic who offered instructive points of view on problems of language (*Decolonising the Mind: The Politics of Language in African Literature*, 1986). As for Bernard Fonlon, the Cameroonian Socrates, he invigorated the literary and cultural life of his country by means of *Abbia*, the review he founded. But how can we forget Pius Ngandu, Georges Ngal, Barthélemy Kotchy, Adrien Huannou, all of whom contributed in writing the first pages of African literary criticism?

First published in *Research in African Literatures* 29.3 (1997): 152–7. Translated by R. H. Mitsch.

One constant stands out, however. Of the first generation of African critics, the majority of those who remained on the continent have now departed us. And few of the structures that they created or that existed in their time have survived. Such is the case with Bernard Fonlon's *Abbia* or Thomas Melone's Equipe de Recherche en Littérature Africaine Comparée (Research group in comparative African literature). All the other channels for the popularization of literature have likewise disappeared. Born in Kampala, *Transition* first emigrated to Accra with Wole Soyinka before finally choosing a home in the USA. *The Journal of African and Comparative Literature* from Ibadan never produced more than a single issue. *The Horn* enjoyed a longer life, but also ceased operation. And if *African Literature Today* – which was supposed to be the review of Sierra Leone's Fourah Bay – has survived, it is because it is based in London.

In the years 1960–70, the continent's francophone universities published annals quite regularly. Kadima Nzuji observed that the annals of the Faculty of Letters in Dakar were even published and distributed by the Presses Universitaires de France. Today, however, not a single one of the francophone universities puts out a publication at regular intervals. Independent reviews are episodic, to say the least. The same may be said of *Ethiopiques*, whose number 59 (second trimester 1997), devoted to Senghor's ninetieth birthday, appeared after several years of inactivity.

Following the example of *Présence Africaine*, other initiatives from the continent have seen daylight in France. But these initiatives have not been able to withstand for long periods the centrifugal forces that are paralyzing Africa. After a few issues, *Nouvelles du Sud*, a literary and cultural review, ceased publication to give its name to a new publishing house that succeeded Silex. *Peuples Noirs-Peuples Africains* hung in for about ten years, but the publishers seem to have definitively closed the books on this enterprise.

Even at the level of scientific meetings, by all appearances it would seem that no colloquium of significance has taken place on the continent since the conference in Yaoundé in 1973 on "L'écrivain africain et son peuple comme producteur de civilisation" (The African writer and his/her people as producer of civilization). In fact, there have been two colloquia of the African Literature Association, one in Dakar in 1989 and the other in Ghana in 1992. But were these African initiatives? There is room for doubt and some are given to understand that the ALA was searching to fill a void. One could also point to the colloquium on Frantz Fanon held in Brazzaville in 1984; the colloquium in Lagos in 1987 celebrating the Nobel Prize awarded in 1986 to Wole Soyinka; or, to a lesser degree, the meetings in Yaoundé in 1985 on oral literature, in Abidjan in 1991 on myth, or even in Brazzaville in 1996 on Sony Labou Tansi. But here we are speaking about periodic events that are not written into any institutional framework such as the annual colloquia of the Association Pour l'Etude des Littératures Africaines (APELA – Association for the study of African literatures), the African Literature Association (ALA), or the Association for the Study of Caribbean and African Literature in French (ASCALF).

In the absence of professional channels and institutions, African criticism could have found expression through local media: national newspapers and magazines, radio, television, etc. But how can we forget that in Africa, the only media that can be certain of their durability are controlled by the State and, in a lesser measure, the churches? We know the case of *Congo/Zaire/Afrique* and of *Semaine Africaine* in Brazzaville, which publish literary and cultural chronicles but whose specific missions are something quite different, promoting the religion that they incarnate.

As for the public service media, they are for the most part the servants of the standing regimes, with the notion of public service considered a myth in the majority of our countries. The State's journalists act as specialists on all issues and do not hesitate to treat literature as they would any other social or political event. What is important is what the regime they serve can get from them. Thus the only voices worthy of transmission over the airwaves, screens, or columns of the governmental press are the prince's scribes or, in a pinch, texts that the regime does not find offensive. In short, in post-independence Africa, the critical function of the scholar is fundamentally challenged.

That is what justifies the censorships and the repressions that are inflicted upon the writers and a number of African critics who are the least bit contestatory. Ngũgĩ's brush with the Kenyan regime forced his departure and he now lives in the USA. Mongo Beti experienced 32 years of exile, and since his return to the country in 1991, he has scarcely been sheltered from harassment of all kinds. Wole Soyinka, Nobel Prize winner in literature, is a fugitive. Bernard Nanga is dead, probably for having written *Les chauves-souris* (1981). Even Sony Labou Tansi did not find shelter from harassment. What can we say about Williams Sassine, who died the victim of the precariousness imposed on him by his native Guinea? Guy Ossito Midiouhouan almost disappeared within the jails of Bongo because of a text posted for publication in *Peuples Noirs-Peuples Africains* (see PNPA 20 (Apr.–May 1981)).

Sad to say, but literary criticism, we recognize, only knew its hours of glory in the immediate postcolonial era, in the framework of the embryos of universities set in place by the colonial power. Everything takes place as if the colonizer had planned to create institutions in Africa modeled after the metropolitan model, with all the accompanying apparatus: endowed centers of research; frameworks for publication and distribution; research teams; a search for excellence. Paradoxically, the political project of post-colonial regimes ran counter to the development of the critical function, the erection of the university as a place of inventiveness, creativity, as well as the emergence of an intellectual power endowed with freedom of thought.

[. . .]

Progressively, scholars have been solicited, enticed to become organic intellectuals in order to legitimize monocracies, thereby sapping the embryos of colonial-model universities of their initial objectives or of their intrinsic substance – for which reason few scholars of the second and third generations have benefited from the support of local structures. It is in the columns of publications controlled by powers outside Africa – *Présence Francophone, Matatu, Etudes Francophones, Research in African Literatures, L'Afrique Littéraire, Notre Librairie, Journal of African Studies*, etc. – that African literary criticism has developed, thereby evading the African public, whose modest means do not permit them to purchase or subscribe to periodicals published elsewhere. And above all let us not forget: it is a new form of the interruption of history that is now threatening our horizon. To the degree that initiatives escape us, the Other recuperates and appropriates these.

African literature thus finds itself left an orphan by endogenous criticism. What is more, this literature is increasingly published solely on the banks of the Seine or the Thames and it is even being written there in greater and greater numbers these days. Publishing houses located on the continent know a vegetative rhythm, and productions coming from the interior are derisory when set against the arrival of a young diaspora on the scene, of whom we can sometimes regret the limits of their native experience.

It is quite understandable. The continent's countries cannot permit themselves, indefinitely, to go without a true struggle for liberation and the implementation of a strategy to appropriate culture. For, as Edward Said writes quite correctly, "Imperialism did not end, did not suddenly become 'past,' once decolonization had set in motion the dismantling of the classical empires" (341). It cannot be repeated enough: in the majority of cases, independence was only a trap, and not always because of yesterday's colonizer, but even because of the ex-colonized. Borrowing the dialectic of Prospero and Caliban, Said explains thus:

> The basic form of the debate is best immediately translated into a set of alternatives that we can derive from the Ariel-Caliban choice.... One choice is to do it as Ariel does, that is, as a willing servant of Prospero; Ariel does what he is told obligingly, and, when he gains his freedom he returns to his native element, a sort of bourgeois native untroubled by his collaboration with Prospero. A second choice is to do it like Caliban, aware of and accepting his mongrel past but not disabled for future development. A third choice is to be a Caliban who sheds his current servitude and physical disfigurements in the process of discovering his essential, pre-colonial self. (257–8)

The stakes seem clear. Most African leaders are engaged in post-independence in following Ariel's tracks. They have been content to be smug aristocrats, not hesitating to sow about intellectual misery. The intellectual, writes a group of Cameroonian scholars,

> inspire de la pitié parce que sa vocation trangresse les normes d'une société pour laquelle les études supérieures ne sont rien d'autre qu'un marchepied vers le pouvoir bureaucratique et économique. Se placer en dehors de cette norme est considéré comme une condamnation à l'échec. Travailler pour l'enrichissement de la Connaissance est propre à inspirer la pitié de la Société. Aux yeux de celle-ci, l'activité intellectuelle est un bouche-trou institutionnel, et ceux qui l'exercent méritent quelque compassion quand ce n'est pas le mépris.

> inspires pity because his/her calling transgresses the norms of a society for which higher learning is nothing more than a stepping stone to bureaucratic and economic power. Placing oneself outside this norm is considered condemning oneself to failure. Working for the enrichment of Knowledge is enough to inspire the pity of Society, in whose eyes intellectual activity is an institutional stopgap, and those who work for it deserve a bit of compassion if not disdain. (Forum des Universitaires Chrétiens 15)

Anglophone Africa has fared no better. To echo slightly the analysis by the Cameroonians, we can read in a recent report coming out of Kenya:

> What some see as a crisis of confidence among intellectuals is closely linked to the sad state of higher education in many countries. Across Africa, crumbling public universities are barometers of intellectual malaise. Relentless financial crises – as poor governments cannot or will not support higher education – have led to declines in research funds, teaching facilities, and ultimately, intellectual resources.
>   According to three African academics, the most serious casualty of the years of austerity has been staff morale. Without access to books, professional journals, or electronic networks, and unable to attend conferences, take sabbaticals, or even find chalk for their blackboards, many African academics lose professional self-esteem. Eventually, they seek refuge in cynicism... truancy... and opportunism. (Useem A47–8)

In fact, it is an endeavor that must be undertaken since it is so difficult to isolate African literary criticism from the whole of the ills threatening our countries. Wole Soyinka, for his part, recalls that we cannot deny "la responsabilité du continent africain dans ses malheurs ... et nos bibliothèques sont pleines des accusations incessantes que nos écrivains et intellectuels profèrent depuis des décennies, notamment contre nos classes dirigeantes" "the responsibility of the African continent in its problems ... and our librairies are full of the ceaseless accusations that our writers and intellectuals have proffered for decades, especially against the managerial classes" (Serageldin et al. 241).

The subject, we recognize, has many implications and here we must be content to signal a few courses. Africanist literary criticism – that which is written in the four corners of the earth – is not at issue here, and one could hardly accuse the scholars of that sector of failing in their duty! Africanist literary research is indeed in full bloom. But whereas in the 1960–70s, there were the Melones, the Kanes, the Soyinkas, the Ngũgĩs, and other Abiolas who, installed in African universities, set the pace, it is clear that since then, African and Africanist literary criticism is taking place essentially in institutions situated outside the continent.

References

Eboussi Boulaga, Fabien. "L'identité négro-africaine," *Présence Africaine* 99/100 (1976): 3–8.

Fanon, Frantz. *Les damnés de la terre*. Paris: Maspero, 1961.

Forum des Universitaires Chrétiens. *La misère intellectuelle au Cameroun*. Yaoundé: CCU, 1997.

Hountondji, Paulin. "Recapturing." *The Surreptitious Speech: Présence Africaine and the Politics of Otherness 1947–1987*. Ed. V.-Y. Mudimbe. Chicago: University of Chicago Press, 1992.

Irele, Abiola. *The African Experience in Literature and Ideology*. London: Heinemann, 1981.

Kane, Mohamadou. "L'actualité de la littérature africaine d'expression française." *Présence Africaine* 1971: 218.

——. *Birago Diop, l'homme et l'oeuvre*. Paris: Présence Africaine, 1971.

——. "L'écrivain africain et son public." *Présence Africaine* 58 (1966): 13.

——. *Essai sur les contes d'Amadou Coumba: du conte traditionnel au conte moderne d'expression française*. 1968. Abidjan: Nouvelles Editions Africaines, 1981.

——. "Réflexions sur la première décennie des indépendances en Afrique noire." *Présence Africaine* 3rd trim. 1971: 218.

——. *Roman africain et traditions*. Dakar: Nouvelles Editions Africaines, 1982.

Kom, Ambroise. "Une nécrologie, la critique littéraire au Cameroun." *Notre Libraine* 100 (1990): 30–4.

Melone, Thomas. *Mongo Beti, l'homme et le destin*. Paris: Présence Africaine, 1972.

——. *Chinua Achebe et la tragédie de l'histoire*. Paris: Présence Africaine, 1973.

Mouralis, Bernard. "*Présence Africaine* Geography of an 'Ideology.' *The Surreptitious Speech: Présence Africaine and the Politics of Otherness 1947–1987*. Ed. V.-Y. Mudimbe. Chicago: University of Chicago Press, 1992. 3–13.

Ngũgĩ wa Thiong'O. *Decolonising the Mind: The Politics of Language in African Literature*. London: Currey; Portsmouth: Heinemann, 1986.

Nzuji, Mukala Kadima. "Bilan de la recherche sur la francophonie littéraire." *Présence Africaine* 155 (1997): 150–63.

Said, Edward. *Culture and Imperialism*. 1993, London: Vintage, 1994.

Soyinka, Wole. "Culture, mémoire et développement." *Culture et développement en Afrique*. Ed. Ismail Serageldin, June Taboroff, et al. Washington, DC: BIRD/BM, 1994. 241.

Useem, Andrea. "An Era of Painful Self-Examination for Many Intellectuals in Africa." *The Chronicle of Higher Education* 44.7 (10 Oct. 1997): A47–8.

Chapter 58

The Nature of Things:
Arrested Decolonization and Critical Theory

Biodun Jeyifo

Olofi created the earth and all the things in it. He created beautiful things and ugly
things. He created Truth and he created Falsehood. He made Truth big and powerful, but
he made Falsehood skinny and weak. And he made them enemies. He gave Falsehood a
cutlass, unbeknownst to Truth. One day, the two met and started fighting. Truth, being
so big and powerful felt confident, and also very complacent since he didn't know that
Falsehood had a cutlass. So Falsehood cunningly cut off Truth's head. This jolted and
enraged Truth and he started scrambling around for his head. He stumbled on Falsehood
and, knocking him down, Truth felt the head of Falsehood which he took to be his own.
His strength being truly awesome, a mere pull from Truth yanked off the head of
Falsehood and this Truth placed on his own neck. And from that day what we have
had is this grotesque and confusing mismatch: the body of Truth; the head of Falsehood.

an Afro-Cuban myth

The messenger pointed in his direction and the other man followed with his eye and saw
Ezeulu. But he only nodded and continued to write in his big book. When he finished
what he was writing he opened a connecting door and disappeared into another room.
He did not stay long there; when he came out again he beckoned at Ezeulu, and showed
him into the white man's presence. He too was writing, but with his left hand. The first
thought that came to Ezeulu on seeing him was to wonder whether any black could ever
achieve the same mastery over book as to write it with the left hand.

Chinua Achebe, Arrow of God

The Nature of Things

There can hardly be a greater affirmation for literary criticism than the view offered by
Frank Kermode in his book, *Forms of Attention*, to the effect that critical discourse (which
Kermode blithely calls "conversations") is the primary medium in which literature survives.
What Kermode calls "perpetual modernity" is achieved by a literary work, or a writer, only
to the extent that they continue not only to be read but also to be talked and written about.

First published in *Research in African Literatures* 21.1 (Spring 1990): 33–48.

His contention might of course seem like saying the obvious in a more fanciful, sophisticated critical idiom, Shakespeare being always a ready instantiation of his point. But part of the facination of Kermode's ruminations in this monograph – as canonically orthodox as his arguments are – is that he concedes that "mere" opinion often weighs as much, if not even more, than solid "knowledge" in securing lasting reputation or "perpetual modernity" for a work or an author. As we shall see, the vexed distinction between "opinion" and "know-ledge" is a crucial factor in the instability of critical discourse as the medium in which literature survives, merely subsists, or suffers total oblivion. But first, a few qualifications on Kermode's conception of critical discourse are necessary in approaching the subject of this essay: scholarly critical discourse and the fate of African literature[s].[1]

First of all, critical discourse not only assures the survival of literature, it also determines the condition in which it survives and the uses to which it will be put. For it to play such a role, it must accede to a position of power relative to other discourses, both within and beyond the domains of literature and the Humanities, a point central to much of contem-porary post-modern critical theory (Macdowell).[2] Some of these parallel or competing discourses are either incorporated into the "dominant" discourse or neutralized, marginal-ized. At this level where one discourse achieves relative dominance over other discourses, we are beyond the power of individual scholars, critics or theorists to serve as arbiters of opinion, knowledge, or value, no matter how gifted or influential they might be. What gives a particular critical discourse its decisive effectivity under these circumstances is the combination of historical, institutional and ideological factors that make the discourse a "master" discourse which translates the avowed will-to-truth of all discourse into a consum-mated, if secret, will-to-power. In other words, this "master" discourse becomes the discourse of the "master," in its effects and consequences at least, if not in its conscious intentions. Once we recognize this discourse and the privileged subject position(s) out of which it speaks, once we identify the "natural" magisterial register of its accents, we can recognize how its avowed will-to-truth masks the will-to-power which pervades all dis-course, especially when we recognize discourse as epistemic behaviour. Such observations imply that, at a fundamental level, all discourse is agonistic particulary when, as in the present case, we are in a social and historical context which is massively overdetermined.

The foregoing discussion is especially relevant to current debates over the pertinence of theory to African literature where "theory" almost always implies "their" theory in relation to "our" literature, Western or "eurocentric" evaluative norms and criteria in relation to non-Western traditions of writing (Gates, Showalter). If these objections are valid, the traditions of critical discourse on African literature that we have "inherited" – traditions whose premises, frames of intelligibility, and conditions of possibility have been yoked to foreign, historically imperialist perspectives and institutions of discursive power – raise serious problems with regard to the survival and vitality of its object, African literature. Thus, the question of an African critical discourse which is self-constituted and self-constituting in line with the forces acting on the production of African literature is intimately connected with the fate of that literature.

But what exactly is a self-constituted and self-constituting African critical discourse? Does it exist? If it does not (yet) exist, is there a need for its existence, or an aspiration for its constitution? What established positions have emerged in the debates that have taken place during the last two decades on these questions? Since these are large questions which we cannot hope to adequately explore in one essay, I would like to focus on one single, but crucial aspect of these debates: the emergence of African literature as an academic discipline. As I hope to demonstrate, this is one area of critical discourse on African literature in which "theory" can play a decisive role in clearing up the confusion and sterile acrimony that have characterized many attempts to define a role for the scholar of African literature and to stake a claim of validity and legitimacy for the "discipline" of African literary studies. With few exceptions, these debates have been under-theorized or characterized by the assumption that it is an untheorizable discursive space ontologically charged with the mysteries that supposedly lie at the heart of the nature of things.

Nothing better reveals the troubled state of critical discourse on African literature than the problematic accession of the literature to the status of an object of study in Africa and, perhaps more crucially, in Europe and North America. The historical emergence of this phenomenon, if not its historicity, has been the subject of many international conferences and seminars, many essays and books (Moore, Heywood, Hale and Priebe, Lindfors 1984, Littératures, Arnold 1985a). The diverse expressions of this phenomenon need not concern us here, especially the early exchanges on the definition of African literature or the delimitation of its constitutive elements. What stands at the center of these debates and what concerns us in this essay, is the clearly emergent subsumption of *all* criticism and scholarship on African literature into two basic, supposedly distinct, polarized camps: first, the foreign, white, European or North American critic or scholar and second, the native, black African "counterpart." It is impossible to underestimate the hypostasis that presides over the representations which govern debates over this presumed dichotomy.[3] Clearly what is called for is, first, the careful identification of this hypostasis and, second, its demythologization by a theoretical critique that presents it with its secret, repressed conditions of possibility – the structured conditions and relationships of its being-in-the-world, to use the Heideggerian formulation.

Two early observations of Soyinka and Achebe draw attention to the exceptionally problematic nature of the conventional dichotomy between "foreign" and "local", external and homegrown in the constituted publics of modern African literature. In "And After the Narcissist?", (Soyinka 1966) an early essay which perhaps marks Soyinka's emergence as a "strong" presence in the then newly emergent field of African literature, he makes the following observation:

> In any culture, the cycle of rediscovery – Negritude or Renaissance enlightment or pre-Raphaelite—must, before the wonder palls, breed its own body of the literature of self-worship. African writing has suffered from an additional infliction: apart from his own discovery the African writer has experienced rediscovery by the external eye. It is doubtful if the effect of this has any parallel in European literature. (56)

As elaborated in this essay, the "effect" without parallel in European literary history is the inculcation and promotion in African writing of themes and attitudes deleterious to the health and vitality of the nascent literary tradition by an exoticizing, paternalistic foreign commentary. Soyinka's indictments are specific: "quaintness mongers", "exoticists," and "primitivists" are the designations he applies to these foreign critics. The following sentence captures the tone of Soyinka's umbrage at the promotion by the "external eye" of themes, trends, and a particular *type* of African writer: "The average published writer in the first few years of the post-colonial era was the most celebrated skin of incompetence to obscure the true flesh of the African dilemma" (1988, 17). This questioning of a dislocated foreign commentary on African literature is given a slightly different inflection by Achebe in "The Novelist as Teacher", an essay which has come to be regarded as his manifesto:

> I am assuming, of course, that our writer and his society live in the same place. I realize that a lot has been made of the allegation that African writers have to write for European and American readers because African readers, where they exist at all, are only interested in reading text-books. I don't know if African writers will always have a foreign audience in mind. What I do know is that they don't have to. (42)

The point of these two observations is that both writers perceive an abnormal mutation, in what is normally regarded as the rather normal existence (or co-existence) of local and foreign readerships for *any* literature. Although neither author goes deeply into the historical and ideological roots of the epistemological consequences of the situation, their objections are not based on the mere fact that such scholars and critics are "foreign", "non-African", "alien" rather than being "native", "African", an "indigene." Both Soyinka and Achebe argue in a rational way and refuse to base their contentions on the "nature of things."

We are in an entirely different order of critical discourse when we engage a vast array of African critics and scholars for whom African literature is "our own literature" and non-African critics and scholars for whom the literature is "theirs." For them, it "belongs" to Africans, even when they themselves defend the usefulness and relevance of *their* participation in the criticism of African literature. This view concerns the staking and conceding of "natural" proprietary rights in the criticism of African literature, and it is one of the few consensual positions between virtually all critics and scholars of African literature. Such a phenomenon is neither surprising nor particularly problematic: who would deny that Chinese literature "belongs" to the Chinese, Japanese literature to the Japanese, and Russian literature to the Russians? What is anomalous, and problematic is that this point, which in most other cases is taken for granted and silently passed over in the criticism of specific works or authors, becomes, in this instance, a grounding, foundational critical rubric, a norm of evaluation and commentary. Pushed to the limits of its expression, it becomes a veritable *ontologization* of the critical enterprise: only Africans must criticize or evaluate African literature, or slightly rephrased, only Africans can give a "true" evaluation of African literary works. Of course nobody expresses this ontologization and racialization of this "truth" quite so blatantly, but the tone, the inflections, the nuances are often not too far from it. Among the most clamorous advocates of this viewpoint, Chinweizu is exemplary in his constant deployment of the collective, proprietary pronoun "we", which he invariably uses in a supremely untroubled fashion as if he were absolutely certain of its axiomatic representativeness:

> Of course, Americans or Europeans or Chinese may choose to study African literature and interpret it for American, Russian audiences. There we Africans have no say. It is their business entirely what they do with it, or tell their people about it; we cannot tell them what to say. . . . We don't say that others should not do what they want with African literature. But we do say that, if what they say has consequences in Africa, either through their journals and books which we read in Africa, or through the students whom we send them to educate, then they should be conscious of the fact that they are no longer interpreting African literature for British or Americans exclusively, but are doing so for Africans too. (16–17)

Being "African" as a criterion of participating in the critical discourse is always, of course, refracted through other somewhat less hypostatized mediations. There is, first, the refraction through *culturalism*, which either implies sharing ethnic identity with an author, or speaking the same "native" language, or *living* the culture and thus being rooted in its customs, mores and codes. There is also the refraction of the "Africanness" of the critic through the appeal to "experience," which excludes all those alien to an ethnic-communal or racial-continental experience. In the famous controversy between Ernest Emenyonu and Bernth Lindfors over Cyprian Ekwensi, Emenyonu's espousal of his privileged "Africanness" in correcting Lindfors' "alien" evaluation of Ekwensi embraces all these expressions: ontology, culturalism, and facile experiential empiricism (Emenyonu, Lindfors 1975). Lindfors' rebuttals of Emenyonu from the standpoint of an *Africanist* critical fortress is not without its occlusions of crucial epistemological and ideological issues in the politics of interpretation; moreover, his halting, carping tone in this debate is fairly representative of the discomfiture most *foreign* Africanist critics and scholars experience when confronted with the full charge of the proprietorial espousals of the "native" critic:

> The native critic, it has been argued, is better equiped than anyone else to appreciate the creative genius of his own culture. He is able to achieve this . . . partly because his upbringing has endowed him with superior insight into the workings of his society, the ground upon which this truth stands. Yet it would seem that . . . if all interpretation were left to native critics, truth might be sought principally on a local level, its universal dimensions all but forgotten. Common sense just does not allow a single tribe of critics to claim a monopoly of clear vision. Every individual will have his blind spots, and some critics – native as well as foreign – will be much blinder than others. (The Blind Men and the Elephant, 53–4)

Negritude writers have of course been the most prominent advocates of the nativist position. Its influence went beyond its immediate historical context, transcending its institutional and practical consolidation in *Présence Africaine*. However, by pushing the ontological rubric too far, by hypostatizing an hypostasis and reifying a reification, Negritude effectively argued itself out of relevance in the debate over who has proprietory rights to the turf of African critical discourse. Who could stake a claim to serious critical, *evaluative* rights on the basis of Senghor's famous slogan: Emotion is Negro as Reason is Greek? Even to "native" critics eager to assert "natural" territorial rights to a virgin field, some of Senghor's Negritudist excesses could not but be a great embarrassment. Criticism is, after all, an eminently *rational* activity, whereas "emotion", "feeling", "intuition", "rhythm," and some of the other "keywords" of Negritude are characteristically relegated to the margin of the critical enterprise. As shocking as the following passage from Senghor may be to Reason, innumerable others can easily be culled from Senghor's theoretical musings on the supposed ontology of black African aesthetics:

> The African is as it were shut up inside his black skin. He lives in primordial night. He does not begin by distinguishing himself from the object, the tree or stone, the man or animal or social event. He does not keep it at a distance. He does not analyze it. Once he has come under its influence, he takes it like a blind man, still living, into his hands. He does not fix it or kill it. He turns it over and over in his supple hands, he fingers it, he feels it. The African is one of the worms created on the Third Day . . . a pure sensory field. Subjectively, at the end of his antennae, like an insect, he discovers the other. He is moved to his bowels, going out in a centrifugal movement from the subject to the object on the waves sent out from the Other. (Reed and Wake, 29–30)

Behind the claims and counter-claims the "foreign" scholar-critics and "native" claimants of "natural" proprietory rights to critical insight lies a vastly displaced play of unequal power relations between the two camps. The fact of this displacement accounts for some of the bizzare self-representations and the occlusions of the social production of meaning by individual scholars and critics from either camp. Unfortunately few critics or scholars have paid close, scrupulous, critical attention to this issue. Only rarely, as in the following observations by Steven Arnold, does the Africanist scholar acknowledge the vastly unequal relations of power and privilege between African and non-African scholars and critics of African literature:

> If expatriates have won the right to take part in African literature unmolested – unless their work merits abuse – their role in assisting to broaden the margin of freedom of African literature, as part of a larger struggle, has not been acknowledged. International consciousness and pressure have been a definite fertilizing factor in the growth of our discipline and the object it studies. Nevertheless a very serious imbalance exists in the funding of research on African literatures. Non-Africans can get money to do what Africans often could do better, yet the Africans must sit and watch it get done. Justice, as well as intellectual probity in our discipline, demands that bodies such as UNESCO be pressured to back more basic research in the humanities so that the patronage and political pressure of state and bilateral government sponsorship of research can be minimized. (60)

Although such observations admit a privileged access to research funding by European or American scholars relative to their African counterparts, Arnold remains silent about the possibility that this situation may involve impersonal structural power relationships on an international, global scale. Most non-African scholars of African literature would strenuously repudiate the suggestion that they exercise power over their African colleagues. For isn't the business of criticism and scholarship a matter of the individual scholar's conscience, integrity, and competence? To confront the evasions behind such assumptions, which are not by themselves invalid, we must confront the historical dialectic of the professionalization of African literary study and the attendant crystallization of scholars and critics into the Nationalist and Africanist schools.[4] By doing so we can engage the great paradox, surrounding the study of African literature today: historic de-colonization having initially enabled the curricular legitimation of African literary study in African universities and schools, the equally historic arrest of de-colonization has swung the center of gravity of African literary study away from Africa to Europe and America.

One could hardly find better exemplifications of the basic tensions in the Africanist school of African literary discourse than in two essays of Albert Gérard, "The Study of African Literature: Birth and Early Growth of a New Learning" (1980) and "Is Anything Wrong with African Literary Studies?" (1985). Beyond the zealous wish expressed in both essays for the attainment of a rigorous scientificity in African literary studies, a deep tension marks the spirit that animates both essays.

The earlier essay, "The Study of African Literature", is an authoritative, learned, and informative historical account of the study of African literature. Many in the discipline would be surprised to learn from this essay how far back the study of African literatures goes; moreover, the humbling realization that the present generation of scholars did not initiate the discipline but have much learn from hitherto unrecognized precursors cannot but be salutary. All told, Gérard's essay makes a powerful case for the collaborative comparatist nature of what needs to be done in shoring up the scholarly foundations of the discipline.

The latter essay, "Is Anything Wrong with African Literary Studies?", has a more limited purview; its purpose is more ideologically inspired, its tone marked by deep anxiety, the anxiety that the discipline has not yet attained the standards required by the leading professional associations and journals in the developed, industrialized countries. Nothing reveals how this anxiety generates tension than Gérard's vascillations in his views about the complementary but distinct roles of Africans and non-Africans in the new, fledgeling discipline of African literary studies. We can perceive how this tension emerges in the juxtaposition of two passages, one from each essay, on the adequacy of the "scientific" training of the "native" literary scholar:

> In francophone and lusophone countries, both colonial and post-colonial authorities have hitherto managed effectively to prevent any significant development of vernacular writing. The situation is different in the former British empire, even though very little official help or even encouragement has been forthcoming from the postcolonial leadership. All the more reason for literary scholars to do what they can within the limits of their competence. Clearly, only native speakers of the languages involved are truly competent. *The problem is that they have seldom been properly initiated into the mysteries of modern literary scholarship* (my emphasis). ("Is Anything Wrong," 22–3)

This thaumatological representation of the "scientificity" of literary scholarship is hardly different from the famous passage from Achebe's *Arrow of God*. It is cited as the second epigraph to this essay, and in it Ezeulu observes the "white man's" "mastery over book as to write it with the left hand." Does that gap still exist? Does the "native" scholar come into "modern literary scholarship" through such mystified encrustations, or does she come to "it" through the adequacy of the institutional apparatus of literary study and its socio-economic environment? Gérard's views in the *earlier* essay is a remarkable departure from the mystagogy of literary scholarship that the latter essay, the essay of "anxiety of (profes-sional) rejection" purveys:

> The enormous rise in the quality as well as quantity of contributions by African scholars was of two fold significance: not only did it testify to the seriousness of the training dispensed in the increasingly numerous universities of black Africa but also to the scholars' growing awareness of the social environment at a time – the late sixties – when creative artists were becoming more and more vocally critical of the newly "established" societies. ("The Study of African Litera-ture," 75–6)

I have focussed on Gérard's essays for two reasons. First, Gérard is probably the most prolific Africanist in the discipline today, followed closely by Bernth Lindfors. Second, and more importantly, these two essays, and others like them, establish the two main planks on which Africanist literary scholarship rests: the claim of historical depth and the demand for a rigorous, conscientious scientificity. Although linked, these criteria are clearly separate. The historical priority of "Africanist" literary scholarship over the "Nationalist" variety consists of the fact that, according to Gérard, European Africanist interest in the continent's languages and literatures dates from the Enlightenment (Gérard, 1980), whereas

"Nationalist" literary scholarship emerged only after, and *because* of political decolonization in the late twentieth century. Only a European with a rigorous philological education could thus have been an Africanist in the early days of the profession. The single-minded collection of documents, materials, artefacts, and archives on Africa had begun and it was often not even necessary for Africanists to have actually been to Africa.

Anthropology was the central intellectual model in early Africanist studies, and a concern once expressed by Evans-Pritchard with regard to the study of Amerindians is also applicable to Africa: "with the exception of Morgan's study of the Iroquois (1851)," he acknowledged, "not a single anthropologist conducted field studies till the end of the nineteenth century." (Fabian 175). This approach to the study of African literature can be found as recent as 1974 when Graham-White boasted about the circumstances under which he wrote his book, *The Drama of Black Africa*: "How did an Englishman living in the United States, who has never visited Africa, come to write a book on African drama?" (viii). A special mode of the production of knowledge is involved here – a mode that privileges the axiological exteriority and distance of a sovereign cognitive subject from the object of that knowledge. In this case, the object of this knowledge is Africa, its cultural production, its human sciences, its historical encounter with itself and other peoples, other societies and cultures. "Science" both demands and validates that exteriority and distance, that positivist "science" which, as Foucault has shown, had its roots in the Enlightenment separation of Reason and Madness. The historic divisions which constitute positivist science are thus regarded as forming the basis of *any* discipline that aspires to professionalism and "scientificity." These are the divisions that separate truth from error, knowledge from opinion, rigor from shoddiness, expertise from dilletantism, objectivity from bias, application from laziness. In strict compliance with these distinctions, Lindfors and Gérard *magisterially* castigate the simplifications, prolixities, triteness, over-generalizations, and bombast that, according to them, suffuse much of African critical discourse. The frames of intelligibility (which, for instance, permits Graham-White to declare that "tragedy" does not exist in pre-colonial African performance traditions, even though he had never set foot on the continent) (Jeyifo "The Reinvention of Theatrical Traditions"), and the techniques of evaluation which approximate most closely this regime of "truth" derive from varieties of formalist, New Critical, and aestheticist approaches to the analysis and evaluation of African literary works. Among African Africanist literary scholars, Solomon Iyasere, Eldred Jones and Daniel Izevbaye have been crusading spirits for this broad paradigm. Their eternal despair is that the discipline has not been won away, and *cannot* perhaps be won away, from non-literary, extra-literary, or "impure" critical concerns.

These "extra-literary" and "non-literary" concerns are precisely what the advocates of a Nationalist literary scholarship emphasize. One of the founding texts of this school is the famous passage from Fanon's *The Wretched of the Earth* where Fanon delineates three phases in the emergence of modern African literature: an "apprentice" stage of derivativeness and imitativeness of European traditions; a phase of protest, romanticism, and idyllic nostalgia; and a revolutionary phase of "a fighting literature" (178–9). This brilliant, heuristic schema of Fanon's has inspired applications, misapplications and counter-positions in African literary criticism (Booth, Jahn 277–83). I would also draw attention to the "Report of the Commission on Literature" of the Second Congress of Negro Writers and Artists in Rome, 1959 as another major document of this school (423–8). Agostinho Neto's little-known "On Literature and National Culture", a conflation of several short addresses given by the late poet and statesman to the Angolan Writers' Union between 1977 and 1978 also qualifies as an important document of Nationalist literary discourse in the way it connects freedom of artistic expression, experimentation, and innovation with commitment to the tasks of constructing a socialist democracy in the conditions of underdevelopment (*Ufahamu*, 1981–2).

But strictly in terms of laying the principles and foundations of a *curricular* and *disciplinary* consolidation for the use of African literature in the schools and universities of independent Africa, the document produced by Ngugi wa Thiong'o and his colleagues at the University of Nairobi in 1968 is incontrovertibly the most important document of all (145–50). Apart from its specific views and positions, this document put a definitive stamp on a historic fact that has all but receded into a zone of amnesia in accounts of the intellectual and cultural history of postcolonial Africa – the fact that the constitution of African literary study as a legitimate academic discipline with certified degrees and professional specialization began in Africa, not in Europe or America. The Nairobi document boldly took the nationalist logic of the tentative deliberations at earlier conferences on the topic (Kampala, Dakar and Free-town) to its logical conclusion. However, the vague impulse of these earlier conferences to "indigenize" some aspects of the literature curriculum became in this document a manifest nationalist programme only by abandoning the "Africanist" scruples of Eldred Jones and others, who espoused an "objective" literary scholarship based on truly "aesthetic", formal criteria of evaluation. In this way, the Nationalist scholarly and critical rubric instituted its own occlusion, which is repeated by Ngugi who proclaimed the necessity for the scholar to be committed to the truth and then moved on to a list of ideological and political factors which *always* condition the scholar's commitment to truth. In the process, Ngugi makes it clear that *his* ideal scholar would place "truth" in the service of national liberation and the construction of a social order that favors the mass of urban workers and rural producers at the base of the socio-economic pyramid in neo-colonial Africa. Such a regime of "truth" and "knowledge" involves an underspecification of those scholarly criteria emphasized by Africanists: "objectivity", "rigour", formalism, "literary" norms of evaluation, the structure of the "text" and the economy of its effects on readers. Conversely, there is an over-specification of the extra-literary criteria decried by Africanists: the literary scholar's ideological commitment to the cause of the oppressed and against Africa's continued dependency, tyrannical misrule, and what Ngugi has termed the "culture of silence." This dual movement of under-specification of *intrinsic*, formalist criteria and over-specification of *extrinsic*, "political" criteria affords us a means of overcoming the seemingly unbridgeable breach between the two camps.

Two considerations patently reduce the seeming breach between the narrowly professional scholar-critics of African literature and their ideologically motivated adversaries. First, the dichotomy does not hold true for most scholars in either camp; most non-African Africanists tend to be politically liberal, while their African fellow travellers tend to be politically conservative, although not openly or militantly anti-nationalist. In light of these factors, a rather vague, but sincere, well-meaning liberalism informs most "Africanist" literary criti-cism, although sometimes the naivety about the structure and direction of global politics and its impingement on African literature and critical discourse is truly awesome. Second, "Nationalist" scholars and critics are not always indifferent to questions of form, artistic design, or intrinsic criteria of evaluation: some of Ngugi's critical essays, some of Abiola

Irele's articles and monographs, and Ngara's book on the African novel evince sensitive, informed explorations of these "intrinsic" questions.

The real danger in a dichotomization of the two camps is located elsewhere: in recent times, "Africanists" have come to hold sway over the discipline in an especially problematic manner, and their narrowly formulated agenda increasingly dominates perceptions of "what is to be done" at the present time in the field. This agenda consists primarily of winning respectability and legitimacy for the discipline of African literary study *in the developed countries*. Bernth Lindfors, whose influence has been felt during his long and able tenure as editor of *Research in African Literature*, perhaps the dominant scholarly journal in the field, has even written a statement entitled "On Disciplining Students in a Nondiscipline," essentially a manifesto for such an agenda (Hale and Priebe 41–7). On account of this agenda and its uncritical acceptance by a large segment of the profession, the extensive, ground-breaking syntheses in contemporary Western literary theory (on knowledge and power relations, on the politics of interpretation, on the always agonistic, always *constructed* nature of representation and signification) has washed over the "Africanist" critical establishment without leaving significant traces. In the deafening silence on the connection between demands for critical fidelity or rigorous analytical techniques and the positions of entrenched power and privilege (or lack of them) from which any scholar or critic evaluates or theorizes, only feminist critics, and to a lesser extent, Marxists, have systematically drawn attention to the political grounding or *situatedness* of critical discourse.

The "Africanist" fetishization of professionalism and the "Nationalist" occlusion of technical, formalistic concerns, in the abstract, idealist constructions of these schools, could be corrected by drawing upon the work of literary scholars in other societies, other periods, other discursive spaces, scholars who have brilliantly synthesized attributes separated in the false binarism that keeps the best features of "Africanist" and "Nationalist" schools apart – scholars like Samuel Johnson, Mathew Arnold, Eric Auerbach, Ernst Fischer, Walter Benjamin, Raymond Williams. The very fact that we *need* to insist on this reminder, this re-memory of a powerful motive force in all intellectual history, including the history of Western literary criticism, is itself the product of a willed *lacuna* with regard to the understanding of our present historic context: arrested de-colonization world-wide and the fluid, uncertain conjuncture initiated by Gorbachev's call for "de-ideologization" of international relations between states. This "historic space" defines and consecrates the shift away from the African continent, away from African universities where the center of gravity of serious, engaged study and teaching of African literature was initially located. However in apprehending this phenomenon, we enter into a seemingly endless chain of determinations and effects, for this shift itself results from a combination of other factors impacting on all African countries today: heavy external debt burdens, economic stagnation conjoined with rampant inflation (what some radical economists have given the arresting neologism of "stagflation"), drastic scarcity of books and journals, the lack of spending power to purchase them even when they are available, the material impoverishment of the educational infrastructure, the massive demoralization of teachers, etc., etc. From this perspective we can see that African literary study today is truly "over-determined" in the full Althusserian sense of the term.

This over-determination defines the relevance of the first epigraph to this essay, the Afro-Cuban myth that gives powerful figural articulation to the aporia under which we all, singly or collectively, work today. Whatever genuine "truths" our studies and readings generate, there is always the uncomfortable, compromising "falsehood" of its massive displacement from its true center of gravity on the African continent, there is always the harrowing "falsehood" involved in the production and reproduction of Africa's marginalization from the centers of economic and discursive power in an inequitable capitalist world system.

Notes

1   I am bracketting the pluralization of African literature here because, while most scholars now accept the diverse currents and traditions of written and oral literatures in Africa, I shall be using the collective unpluralized designation in this essay. This is based on my belief that my observations in the essay are pertinent to critical discourse on any of the currents and traditions of African Literature.

2   I am using the term "post-modern critical theory" loosely here to both indicate the broad range of contemporary theoretical schools and approaches which have problematized the conventional certitudes about the nature, content and methodologies of literary study and artistic representation, and the more focussed theorectical work on the nature of critical discourse and power – work which has drawn substantially on the publications of Althusser, Foucault, and others.

3   The "classic" Marxist text on *hypostasis* is of course Marx's "The German Ideology," where, using the image of inversion ("camera obscura"), Marx analyses hypostasis as a form of ideological self-mystification and as a false consciousness of the "real" conditions of social relations of production. I have retained this conception here but infused some aspects of the Althussenian notion of ideology as a structured, produced, and necessary "imaginary" of the real.

4   It is necessary to emphasize that by these terms I intend a typology which has a *polemical*, rather than a theoretically rigorous or "scientific" status of validity. Thus the "Africanist" rubric implies professional specialism rendered as a sort of Weberian ideal type, and the "Nationalist" rubric connotes a heuristic-polemical rendering of critical positions which span a spectrum involving, among others, cultural-nationalist, Marxist or "Fanonist", feminist and even "nativist" views and discourses on African literature. I hope the elaboration of this particular deployment of "Nationalism" in the essay makes it clear that the conflation of so many diverse views and positions is sufficiently self-aware and non-essentialist. For recent important discussions of African and Third-world literatures and nationalism as a political, ideological, and discursive formation, see Fredric Jameson, "Third-World Literature in the Era of Multinational Capital", *Social Text* 15 (1986): 65–88 and Aijaz Ahmad, "Jamesons's Rhetoric of Otherness and the 'National' Allegory", *Social Text* 17 (1987): 3–12.

References

Achebe, Chinua. "The Novelist as Teacher" in *Morning Yet on Creation Day.* Garden City NY: Anchor Press, 1975.

Arnold, Stephen, ed. *African Literature Studies: The Present State/L'Etat Présent*. Washington, DC: Three Continents Press, 1985.

——. "African Literary Studies: The Emergence of a New Discipline." in *African Literature Studies: The Present State/L'Etat présent* 47–70.

Booth, James. *Writers and Politics in Nigeria*. New York: Africana Publishers, 1980.

Chinweizu. "The Responsibilities of Scholars of African Literature." *Research Priorities in African Literatures*. 13–19.

Emenyonu, Ernest. "African Literature: What does it take to be its critic?" *African Literature Today.* 5 (1971): 1–11.

Fabian, Johannes. *Time and the Other: How Anthropology Makes its Object.* New York: Columbia University Press, 1983.

Fanon, Frantz. *The Wretched of the Earth.* New York: Grove Press, 1963.

Foucault, Michel. *Madness and Civilization: A History of Insanity in the Age of Reason.* New York: Vintage Books, 1973.

Gates, Henry Louis. "Authority (White), Power, and the (Black) Critic; or it's all Greek to me." *The Future of Literary Theory,* Ed. Ralph Cohen. New York: Routledge, 1989.

Gérard, Albert. "The Study of African Literature: Birth and Early Growth of a New Branch of Learning." *Canadian Review of Comparative Literature.* Winter (1980): 67–98.

——. "Is Anything Wrong with African Literary Studies?" in *African Literature Studies: The Present State/L'Etat présent.* Ed. Steven Arnold. 17–26.

Graham-White, Anthony. *The Drama of Black Africa.* New York: Samuel French 1974.

Hale, Thomas and Priebe, Richard, eds. *The Teaching of African Literature: selected working papers from the African Literature Association.* Austin, Texas: University of Texas Press, 1977.

Heywood, Christopher, ed. *Perspectives on African Literature: selections from the proceedings,* New York: African Publishing Corp., 1971.

Irele, Abiola. *The African Experience in Literature and Ideology.* London: Heinemann, 1981.

Jahn, Janheinz. *A History of Neo-African Literature.* Trans. Oliver Coburn and Ursula Lehbruger, London: Faber, 1968.

Jeyifo, Biodun. "The Reinvention of Theatrical Traditions: Critical Discourses on Interculturalism in the African Theatre." *Proceedings of an International Conference on Interculturalism in World Theatre.* Bad Homburg, West Germany (forthcoming).

Kermode, Frank. *Forms of Attention.* Chicago and London: The University of Chicago Press, 1985.

Lindfors, Bernth, ed. *Research Priorities in African Literatures,* New York: Hans Zell Publishers, 1984.

——. "The Blind Men and the Elephant." *African Literature Today.* 7 (1975): 53–64.

——. "Some New Year's Resolutions." *ALA Bulletin.* 13.1 Winter (1987): 35–6.

——. "On Disciplining Students in a Nondiscipline." in *The Teaching of African Literature.* Eds. Thomas Hale and Richard Priebe. 41–7.

Littératures africaines et enseignement: actes du colloque de Bordeaux. Talence: Presses Universitaires de Bordeaux, 1985.

Macdowell, Diane. *Theories of Discourse.* New York: Basil Blackwell, 1986.

Moore, Gerald, ed. *African Literature and the University.* Ibaden: Ibaden University Press, 1965.

Ngara, Emmanuel. *Art and Ideology in the African Novel.* London: Heinemann, 1985.

Ngugi wa Thiong'O. *Homecoming: Essays on African and Caribbean Literature, Culture and Politics,* New York: Heinemann, 1972.

Reed, John and Wake, Clive, eds. *Prose and Poetry: Léopold Sédar Senghor.* London: Heinemann, 1976.

Second Congress of Negro Writers and Artists. "Resolution on Literature." *Présence Africaine,* Feb–May, 24–5 (1959).

Showalter, Elaine. "A Criticism of Our Own: Autonomy and Assimilation on Afro-American and Feminist Literary Theory." *The Future of Literary Theory* Ed. Ralph Cohen. London: Routledge, 1989.

Soyinka, Wole. "And After the Narcissist?" *African Forum.* 1.4 (1966): 53–64.

——. "The Writer in a Modern African State." *Art, Dialogue and Outrage: Essays on Literature and Culture.* Ibaden: New Horn Press, 1988.

Ufahamu. 11,2 (Fall 1981–Winter 1982): 7–18.

Chapter 59

Reading through Western Eyes

Christopher L. Miller

Une caravane traverse l'étendue infinie et morne de ces plaines, caravane de négriers, le plus souvent poussant devant eux de lamentables théories d'hommes, de femmes, d'enfants couverts d'ulcères, étranglés par le car-can, mains ensanglantées par les liens.

A caravan traversed those dismal and endless plains: slave traders driving wretched files ["theories"] of men, women, and children, covered with open sores, choked in iron collars, their wrists shackled and bleeding.

Yambo Ouologuem, Le Devoir de violence

At the moment when this study was first conceived, American literary criticism was beginning to open its doors once again to the outside world. Edward Said wrote in 1983 that "contemporary critical discourse is worldless;"[1] today, it is somewhat less so. For the reader of black African literature in French, the dethroning of rigid theoretical criticism and the questioning of the Western canon (which was the material base of that criticism), have come none too soon. The approach to a reading of Camara Laye, Ahmadou Kourouma, or Mariama Bâ should never have been the program prescribed for Rousseau, Wordsworth, or Blanchot. If one is willing to read a literature that might not be a rewriting of Hegel (or even of Kant), and if the negative knowledge of recent theoretical criticism is questioned in the universality of its applications, then what options are really open to a Western reader of non-Western literature? Claiming a break with his/her own culture and critical upbringing, can he/she read the other, the African, as if from an authentically African point of view, interpreting Africa in African terms, perceiving rather than projecting?

A consideration of the Western reading of African literature should begin with what African critics have written on the subject. Their comments are sobering. J. P. Makouta-M'Boukou, a francophone critic and novelist, rightly scolds Western critics who refuse to take into account the distance between themselves and African culture, and who read African literature only in function of their own cultural context.[2] The Nobel laureate Wole Soyinka, more forbiddingly, complains : "We black Africans have been blandly invited to submit ourselves to a second epoch of colonisation – this time by a universal-humanoid abstraction defined and conducted by individuals whose theories and prescriptions are derived from the apprehension of *their* world and *their* history, *their* social neuroses and *their* value systems." Elsewhere, Soyinka refers to Westerners hovering over African literature like vultures.[3] Chinua Achebe denounces Western critics who arrogantly claim to

First published in *Theories of Africans: Francophone Literature and Anthropology in Africa*, pp. 1–6. Chicago: University of Chicago Press, 1990.

understand Africa better than African writers do, and he invites Westerners to adopt a new humility "appropriate to [their] limited experience of the African world;" he also urges that "the word *universal* [be] banned altogether from discussions of African literature until such time as people cease to use it as a synonym for the narrow, self-serving parochialism of Europe."[4] (For all practical purposes, the United States may be considered part of "Europe" here; in francophone Africa, Americans are included among *Européens*.)

The most powerful analysis of the system that gives rise to these complaints comes from the francophone African philosopher Paulin Hountondji. In a critique of the market dynamics that control the relation between Western academies and the African world, Hountondji shows how the division of labor has been unequal, with the highly valued role of *theorizer* belonging almost exclusively to Westerners, while Africans are confined to the gathering of raw information. Africa provides materials (like palm oil or literary texts), which European institutes process into finished commodities (like Palmolive soap or works of criticism of African literature). The "brain drain" of intellectuals from the South into the academies of the North is just a symptom of a large centripetal machine which sweeps "all intellectual and scientific expertise . . . toward the center," that is, toward Europe and the United States.[5] According to Hountondji's analysis, no individual can escape from this system (but I take him to mean that everyone must try). For an American scholar, positioned at the extreme margin in relation to Africa, yet living and working in the country that Hountondji calls the very "center of the center" of the knowledge industry, the contradiction could not be greater.[6]

This series of quotations from African critics would appear to leave little hope of a positive role for the Western critic. The most salutary contribution might be to fall silent and wait for the balance of power to change. In my opinion, however, the change is already taking place, and the solutions to European hegemony are implicit in the critiques I have cited. Hountondji's work – to which I will return later in this chapter – already constitutes a step toward altering the system he describes. Along with V. Y. Mudimbe, Hountondji makes it possible for readers to conceptualize Africa and its cultures using models that are proposed by Africans; these scholars are breaking down the wall between "theory" as exclusively Western and "information" as all that Africa can provide. So the intellectual landscape is already different from the one lamented by Makouta-M'Boukou, Soyinka, and Achebe, or at least *it should be*. In order for anything to change, the Western reader must now contextualize African texts within an increasingly African framework. All of the disciplines of the humanities are in the process of decolonization, and as the process moves forward, it becomes both possible and imperative for readers to supplant Eurocentrism with Afrocentrism, while remaining attentive to *eccentric* strategies that operate in new, overdetermined spaces. Thus, for example, the publication of UNESCO's multivolume history of Africa has made it possible to see history written from the point of view of the colonized and to end the monopoly of history told from the European perspective; thus the publication of Mudimbe's *The Invention of Africa* makes manifest a sea change in African discourse: as Mudimbe puts it, the African "subject-object" now has "the freedom of thinking of himself or herself as the starting point of an absolute discourse."[7]

In the wake and in the midst of these changes, African literature can no longer be seen as the passive client of Western readership and criticism; Africa can no longer be treated (and never should have been treated) as a "void" or a "blank." Responsible critics will no longer be able to ignore the mediation and authority of African commentaries, critiques, and theoretical models, no more than in the past they seemed able to ignore the so-called universal standards of Western judgment. Only in *dialogue* with these new voices can Western reading and criticism of African literature continue with any claim to legitimacy. The spirit and practice of dialogue thus provide a temporary answer to the initial question of how Western reading might dare to proceed in the wake of colonial history. But dialogism is itself a problem that will warrant further consideration, in a later movement of this chapter.

Thinking programmatically about Western approaches to African literature leads me to one major hypothesis, around which the rest of this book will turn: that a fair Western reading of African literatures demands engagement with, and even dependence on, anthropology. The demonstration of this point begins from the premise that good reading does not result from ignorance and that Westerners simply do not know enough about Africa. Much of what I will be arguing here grows out of my basic belief that no responsible Western reading of African literature can take place in the vacuum of a "direct" and unmediated relationship with the text. What the literary text says is necessary but not sufficient; other texts must be brought into the dialogical exercise of a good reading. Taken at face value, my hypothesis means simply that any non-African reader (or even an African reader from a different cultural area) seeking to cross the information gap between himself or herself and an African text will very probably be obliged to look in books that are classified as anthropology. The history of the academic separation of disciplines has made this a fact. But it is a fact that is both surrounded by controversy (due to the colonial history of anthropology) and largely ignored: critics have pored over numerous African texts, texts that deal with culturally encoded and culture-specific issues, without bothering to look at the ethnographic works that form an implicit dialogue with their literary counterparts.[8] In this study, I will therefore be trying to fill a gap, to perform an obvious task that has mostly been neglected. The task is to seek a better understanding of francophone African literature by placing it within its historical, political, but especially anthropological context. This is not intended to place anthropology in a position of dominance or to let it block out other concerns, which I hope will find adequate attention here. Rather my desire is to blend disciplines together in a hybrid approach befitting the complexity of cultural questions in Africa and their translation into Western understanding.[9]

If the task has been neglected, it is perhaps due to the controversy surrounding the very mention of "anthropology" in Africa, with its imperialist connotations and its threat to "tact."[10] To make use of anthropology is to borrow trouble, for reasons that I will explore. But while still on the threshold, I would like to outline the basic links between francophone African literature and anthropology, those ties that cannot be ignored. The first link is a matter of history: the French-language literature of sub-Saharan Africa emerged at the same time as the new body of ethnography on Africa; the two bodies of writing produced versions of Africa in tandem, and, as we will see, they were inextricably interwoven. This is connected to a more general point made by Jonathan Ngate: that "francophone African literature has been, in effect, a continuous attempt at fleeing from its Western models."[11] Particularly in the early, pre-Independence years, from 1920 to 1960, francophone African discourse was one part of a larger phenomenon, colonial discourse as a whole; and in the politics of the time, anthropology was the most powerful mode of colonial discourse.

The second link between anthropology and this literature is a matter of rhetoric. If the term "anthropological rhetoric" can be used as a description of the devices by which cultures are represented to each other – through modes of address to a reader who is presumed to be alien to the culture in the text – then francophone African literature has always practiced some form of anthropological rhetoric. From its first through its most recent text, this literature continually uses devices such as footnotes, parentheses, and character-to-character explanations in order to provide the reader with necessary cultural information. Due to the conditions in which this literature arises – notably the limited literacy and knowledge of French throughout "francophone" Africa – readers of a francophone text cannot be presumed to be local. Every time an author uses a phrase like "here in Africa," a *non-Africa* is revealed to be at play in the writing and reading process. A degree of "otherness" is inscribed in any text which addresses itself to a world that is construed as outside. This means that the controversial "otherness" associated with anthropology is not wholly absent from the literature in question here, and that the relationship between the two bodies of texts must be approached with an open mind.

[...]

Notes

1   Edward W. Said, *The World, the Text and the Critic* (Cambridge: Harvard University Press, 1983): 151.

2   *Introduction à l'étude du roman négro-africain de langue française* (Abidjan: Les Nouvelles Editions Africaines, 1980): 9.

3   *Myth, Literature and the African World* (Cambridge: Cambridge University Press, 1976): x; on vultures, quoted in Omafume F. Onoge, "The Crisis of Consciousness in Modern African Literature," in Georg M. Gugelberger, ed., *Marxism and African Literature* (Trenton, NJ: Africa World Press, 1985): 41.

4   Chinua Achebe, "Colonialist Criticism," in *Morning Yet on Creation Day* (London: Heinemann, 1975): 6, 9. See also D. Ibe Nwoga, "The Limitations of Universal Critical Criteria," in Rowland Smith, ed., *Exile and Tradition: Studies in African and Caribbean Literature* (New York: African Publishing Co., 1976): 8–30.

5   Paulin Hountondji, "Reprendre," in V. Y. Mudimbe, ed., *The Surreptitious Speech: "Présence Africaine" and the Politics of Otherness 1947–1987*, forthcoming. For historical perspective on the division of labor in African studies, see Robert Thornton, "Narrative Ethnography in Africa, 1850–1920: The Creation and Capture of an Appropriate Domain for Anthropology," *Man* n.s. 18, no. 3 (September 1983): "There is a clear division of labor between the producers of information and the theory-smiths of the universities in Europe, Britain and America" (516); see also Michael Crowder, " 'Us' and 'Them': The International African Institute and the Current Crisis of Identity in African Studies," *Africa* 57, no. 1 (1987): 109–22. For a radical critique of the American African-Studies establishment, motivated by anti-Vietnam war sentiments, see Africa Research Group, "Les études africaines en Amérique: la famille étendue," in Jean Copans, ed., *Anthropologie et impérialisme* (Paris: Maspero, 1975): 155–212.

6   Portions of this paragraph are taken from my essay, "Alioune Diop and the Unfinished Temple of Knowledge," in *The Surreptitious Speech*, ed. V. Y. Mudimbe (Chicago: University of Chicago Press, 1992): 427–34.

7   V. Y. Mudimbe, *The Invention of Africa: Gnosis, Philosophy and the Order of Knowledge* (Bloomington: Indiana University Press, 1988): 200.

8   There are exceptions to this rule, such as Jacques Bourgeacq's *"L'Enfant noir" de Camara Laye: Sous le signe de l'éternel retour* (Sherbrooke, Québec: Naaman, 1984), and Robert Philipson's article "Literature and Ethnography: Two Views of Manding Initiation Rites," in Kofi Anyidoho, ed., *Interdisciplinary Dimensions of African Literature*, Annual Selected Papers of the African Literature

Association, no. 8 (1982): 171–82; I will refer to both of these works in chapter 4. See also Bernard Mouralis's discussion of anthropology in *Littérature et développement: Essai sur le statut, la fonction et la représentation de la littérature négro-africaine d'expression française* (Paris: Silex/ACCT, 1984): 44–57. The practice of a self-reflexive Western reading is not totally without precedent: Daniel Delas, in his *Léopold Sédar Senghor: Lecture blanche d'un texte noir ("L'Absente")* (Paris: Temps Actuels, 1982), stages a deliberately "unauthorized" reading. He consciously *applies* Western methods (8), while remaining attentive to their limitations, and he concludes that there is a fundamental "conflict" between "white reading" and "black reading" (113).

9   I have been influenced in this undertaking by James Clifford's "On Ethnographic Authority," *Representations* 1, No. 2 (Spring 1983), 118–46 (reprinted in his *The Predicament of Culture: Twentieth-Century Ethnography, Literature, and Art* (Cambridge: Harvard University Press, 1988): 21–54), by V. Y. Mudimbe's *L'Odeur du père: Essai sur les limites de la science et de la vie en Afrique noire* (Paris: Présence Africaine, 1982), and by Michèle Duchet's *Anthropologie et histoire au siècle des lumières* (Paris: Maspero, 1971). One of the most important precursors to this study is Sunday O. Anozie's *Structural Models and African Poetics: Towards a Pragmatic Theory of Literature* (London: Routledge & Kegan Paul, 1981), which the author describes as an attempt to impose "a more rigorous ordering of sense" within the criticism of African literature (viii). Anozie takes as given the universalism of structuralism and its focus on the "immanence of language." His analysis of Negritude thus addresses questions of grammar and semiology rather than, for example, politics. The role Anozie accords to Western theory is exemplified in the following statement: "It is therefore hard to vizualize the constitution of a viable African theory of poetics outside the framework of semiology" (159–60). Anozie nonetheless struggles, within the frame provided by Lévi-Strauss, Jakobson, and Barthes, toward a description of African difference. *Structural Models and African Poetics* stands as a sign of its times – at the high water mark of "theory" – and as a brilliant exercise in applied theory. For a harsh critique, see Anthony Appiah, "Strictures on Structures: The Prospects for a Structuralist Poetics of African Fiction," in Henry Louis Gates, Jr., ed., *Black Literature and Literary Theory* (New York: Methuen, 1984): 127–50. Other works relevant to the present context include: Dan Sperber, *Le Savoir des anthropologues* (Paris: Hermann, 1982), Clifford Geertz, *The Interpretation of Cultures* (New York: Basic Books, 1973), and Paul Désalmand, *Sciences humaines et philosophie en Afrique: la différence culturelle* (Paris: Hatier, 1978).

10   See Kwame Anthony Appiah, "Out of Africa: Topologies of Nativism," *Yale Journal of Criticism* 2, no. 1 (Fall 1988): 165.

11   Jonathan Ngate, *Francophone African Literature: Reading a Literary Tradition* (Trenton, NJ: Africa World Press, 1988): 18. In this useful study, Ngate explores modes of engagement and resistance to such Western models.

Chapter 60

Inherited Mandates in African Literary Criticism:
The Intrinsic Paradigm

Olakunle George

The history I construct is partial and strategic: partial because I focus only on a particular conjuncture in the adventure of Anglophone African literary criticism, strategic because my construction is driven by a metacritical purpose. My account is not an institutional history of African literary criticism, neither does it claim to exhaust its diverse strands and ideological positions. Rather, my analysis is intended to be illustrative of a sociopolitical and intellectual problematic that can roughly be dated from the late 1950s to the early 1980s. What I want to do is to isolate two principal literary-critical approaches that enabled the struggle for self-representation and self-understanding in Anglophone Africa, namely, "intrinsic" criticism and its "extrinsic" antithesis.

[...]

In Anglophone African literature, Chinua Achebe is generally credited with inaugurating black Africa's self-representation in fiction. Less than a decade after *Things Fall Apart* (1958), the novel that launched a thousand ships if ever one did, Achebe is already called upon to reflect on his role and his readership. In an essay entitled "The Novelist as Teacher," first published in 1965, Achebe begins with characteristic clear-sightedness: "Writing of the kind I do is relatively new in my part of the world and it is too soon to try and describe in detail the complex of relationships between us and our readers" (40). At the high point of this essay, Achebe writes: "I would be quite satisfied if my novels (especially the ones I set in the past) did no more than teach my readers that their past – with all its imperfections – was not one long night of savagery from which the first Europeans acting on God's behalf delivered them" (45). Somber, almost brooding, this essay has come to be seen as Achebe's artistic manifesto. Let us note the deliberate modesty inherent to Achebe's formulation, the self-circumscription evoked by the phrases "quite satisfied" and "no more than." A little,

First published in *Relocating Agency: Modernity and African Letters*, pp. 85–91. Albany: SUNY Press, 2003.

Achebe is very pointedly announcing, goes a long way. And yet, that modesty is accompanied by some defiance. For in the next sentence after the one just quoted, Achebe adds the following rider: "perhaps what I write is applied art as distinct from pure. But who cares" (45).

This circumscription of purview and defiance towards the conventional definition of "pure art" raises an issue of theoretical interest. What Achebe demonstrates here is at once an acceptance of a modern Western apprehension of the role of literature in society, and a rejection of part of it. Achebe reveals a traditional (reflectionist) attitude to literary representation even as he rejects another traditional (aestheticist, "art-for-art's sake") view. The presupposition underwriting the reflectionist view of literature is that adequate representation of an idea, an object, or a constellation of values is possible. Related to this is the assumption that literary texts encode, or can be made so to do, the reality of cultures or peoples. If this view characterizes some versions of traditional Eurocentric criticism, the anti-utilitarian view is not entirely compatible. If indeed the literary "artifact" rewards us purely in our contemplation of its formal beauty, it really does not matter what literature encodes. In fact, to encode anything other than its own intrinsic-formal worth might detract from its purity as aesthetic achievement. What Achebe does is to claim that his novels reflect the "real Africa" and therefore, cannot be "pure art." In this way, he opens up an immanent tension between two equally conventional attitudes to the interaction of form and content in literature.

In Achebe's essay we see a writer thinking through his craft. But what about the academic critic(s) contemplating what writers do? It is often said that Anglophone African fiction emerged in the late 1950s and 1960s, precisely at the point of the publication of Achebe's *Things Fall Apart*. According to this view, Achebe's novel demonstrates sophisticated literary craftsmanship and portrays precolonial Ibo society and the colonial encounter adequately. By contrast, African writing in the first half of the twentieth century is said to be important but immature, almost subliterary, because (i) the writers lacked the sophisticated craftsmanship associated with "great" literature, and (ii) their vision bought into Western ideology and is therefore not sufficiently decolonized.

Eustace Palmer opens his *The Growth of African Literature* by identifying the moment at which he is writing in these terms: "A quarter of a century after the publication of the first African novels worth the name a substantial body of criticism has emerged which in its range and erudition indisputably matches the volume and importance of the new literature" (*Growth*, 1). And Albert Gérard's *European-Language Writing in Sub-Saharan Africa* attributes the importance of *Things Fall Apart* to the fact that it came to fill a literary vacuum: "the mediocre poetry of Osadebey had attracted little attention and did not deserve more; although the originality of Tutuola was recognized everywhere, his *Palmwine Drinkard* was regarded as a freak of the literary imagination and became for that reason the object of a heated controversy; Ekwensi's *People of the City* had awakened considerable interest, but chiefly as a social document and a sample of popular writing devoid of any high aesthetic ambition or value" (689). Talk of novels "worth the name," of a novel being "devoid of high aesthetic ambition or value" because the interest it arouses is "chiefly as a social document," should recall Matthew Arnold, T. S. Eliot and F. R. Leavis. For them, as for the New Critical regime they inspired, criticism has a crucial job to do (in the face, need we add, of a deadening of sensibility occasioned by the real world of guns and industrial smoke). That job involves demarcating a realm of "great" art, a tradition, that would capture and radiate the spirit of a milieu, thereby disseminating cultural value.

We may cite Eliot's early essay, "Tradition and the Individual Talent," which famously defines literary tradition as an overarching repertoire of literary production generated by and in a given culture. Of course, Eliot has in mind the literary productions that have come out (and will come out) of Europe, and he states this explicitly, characterizing it as "our civilization." In his reading of the so-called metaphysical poets in an essay of the same title, Eliot endorses the "recondite" poetry of the metaphysicals, historicizing it as a testimony to the nature of sixteenth-century English civilization in contrast to that of the Victorians. For Eliot, the difference between Herbert's poetry and Tennyson's "is not a simple difference of degree between poets. It is something which had happened to the mind of England between the time of Donne or Lord Herbert of Cherbury and the time of Tennyson and Browning; it is the difference between the intellectual poet and the reflective poet" (307). This difference resides in the "dissociation of sensibility" which, according to Eliot, occurs in the seventeenth century. Due to this dissociation, poets became "reflective," rather than "intellectual." Thus, earlier poets like Donne could "feel their thought as immediately as the odour of a rose" (307). They could amalgamate disparate experiences, assume an analytical posture in relation to these experiences, and then synthesize them into new wholes, new wholes that thereafter acquire their objective correlative in poetic rendition.

The assumption in this account is that the poem has an internal dynamic that connotes its value as an artistic achievement and a carrier of the temper of its milieu. Value is taken as self-evident, and the burden of Eliot's analysis is to identify the divergent exemplifications of that value in the metaphysicals on the one hand, and on the other, from the mid-seventeenth century onwards. Eliot can then read the poetry of both periods to be symbolic – documentary – of the difference between the mind of England in the sixteenth century, and the mind of England by the nineteenth century. Contemporary cultural criticism has shown that the passion of figures like Eliot or Leavis is impelled by a sense of past cultural plenitude that needs to be rescued from a "contaminating" present. The transposition of this to the United States in the form of the New Criticism inherits this logic and reinforces it with the aspiration to "objectivity."

I bring up the old story of Leavisite criticism and new-critical "objectivity" because the criticism of African literature in Anglophone Africa owes much to both. We need not spend time on the demystification of new-critical orthodoxy that has effectively been accomplished with the emergence of theory and cultural studies.[1] In the New Criticism, there is a basic contradiction whereby texts are said to represent "our tradition" while at the same time representing the best of pure art, pure because it refers most powerfully to its own form and beauty. Despite its constitutive Eurocentric underlay, the New Criticism found an attentive audience in Anglophone Africa, and it is crucial to see why. In "Literature and History in Africa," Landeg White complains about what he perceived in the criticism of African Literature as inadequate attention to the material conditions of the literary work. As a result of this tendency, he argues, "critics [of African literature] set themselves no larger task than simple exposition – a mixture of plot summary and praise" (539). "Part of the trouble," he observes, "seems to lie in the state of literary criticism in England and America in the late fifties when studies of African Literature began to proliferate. The emphasis of the 'new criticism,' of the 'well wrought urn' and 'the verbal icon,' when critics like Ransom and Empson and Wimsatt stressed the benefits of close study of the text as artefact, led too easily to the assumption that there was some special virtue in isolating the text from its social and historical setting" (539). White has legitimate grounds for his observations, but I think he overstates his case. He identifies the surface contours of the critical scene that infuriates him, but he does not adequately identify its structural determinations. Discussing the prevailing tendencies in critical analyses of African Literature, he writes:

> It became part of critical strategy to apologise for the assumed anthropological orientation of African novels of the 1950s and 1960s, and to set up such status claiming parallels as that Soyinka uses language like Joyce, that Laye is Kafkaesque, that Armah shares Swift's "excremental vision," that Tutuola's novels are, like *Wuthering Heights*, a "kind of sport." Forced by the very nature of the literature to look a little further, critics have been content to take their image of Africa from the literature itself and then praise the literature for its "truth," operating within such simple concepts as the "traditional African way of life," the clash between African and Western culture, and the corruption following independence – concepts which must seem strangely innocent to the historian or to the social or political scientist. Only recently, with the emphasis on stylistic analysis or on commitment have there been attempts to transcend a criticism based on personal impressions backed up by appeals to a Leavis-type "tradition." (539)

The diagnosis that African literature was ever isolated from its historical setting by critics seems to me inaccurate. I suggest, in fact, that the reverse is the case. From its beginnings, African literature has always been seen as a function of the history of colonialism. The writer's vocation has always been formulated as that of enabling the decolonization of Africa, and authors have been evaluated on the basis of how well they achieve this task. However, although the criticism has always been centrally activated by a political awareness (and prescriptiveness) of the tasks of African literature, critics part ways on the question of method. The divergence in critical method (or, in White's terms, the "improvement" from formalist-aestheticist to "committed" ways of reading) is not a temporal – i.e., "recent" – phenomenon but one that has always accompanied Africanist literary criticism. In this vein, the temporal dichotomy White installs between formalist and so-called committed critical strategies is flawed. Both formalists and nonformalist have always been "committed": committed to the project of contesting the distortions of colonial representations.

Nonetheless, White touches on an important point in remarking a derivativeness in the criticism of African literature, a dependence on Euro-American categories that makes critics fall back on "status claiming parallels" between Soyinka and Joyce, or Laye and Kafka. How then can he be right and not-quite-right at the same time? To answer this question, one needs to historicize both the formalist and nonformalist positions that governed the critical landscape in Anglophone Africa. On the one hand, you have critics for whom the concern with decolonization is expressed via an exclusively aestheticist conception of literature, an aestheticism inherited from Leavis and the New Criticism. But this aestheticism is then appropriated, not simply as a means to the refinement and acculturation of the reader, but rather as a strategic tool for the political cause of decolonization. For example, Abiola Irele suggests in "Studying African Literature" that, although Leavisite criticism is "really not 'sociological' in any methodological or technical sense, [it] implies a strong awareness of the social implications of literature" (*Ideology*, 23). Indeed, argues Irele, Leavis's work "is based on a strongly articulated social theory – of an élite in touch through the best literature with a vital current of feeling and of values, and having responsibility for maintaining, in the practice of criticism, the moral health of the society" (23). Irele finds this pastoralist element "highly questionable"; but, "the basic idea is to my thinking, not: it is a position which has the eminent merit of making us take literature seriously enough to commit one's total intelligence to making explicit what in it takes the forms of nuance and symbol, in other words, of applying its insights to the actual business of living" (23).

In a similar way, Chidi Maduka undertakes a reconciliation of the New Criticism with the political impetus of African literary criticism. He rejects three assumptions he associates with the New Criticism: (i) the idea of "self-containment" in the literary text, (ii) the tendency to "turn literature into a discipline of extreme specialization for *competent readers*," and (iii) the claim of "uniqueness" in true works of art. But he yet maintains that the new-critical rubric "can help in sharpening the critic's sensitivity to the mechanics of language (and structure)." "Consequently," he concludes, "if modified to recognize the importance of seeing form as an instrument of revealing meaning, it [formalism] can contribute to the current search for the essence of African aesthetics" (198–9).

The Africanist formalists inherited their categories from the literary-critical tradition of the Anglo-Saxon world in the middle of the twentieth century, but with the political awareness that these categories have historically been used to ground Western claims of cultural superiority. They therefore took key new-critical categories (e.g., value as an intrinsic quality that gives great art its greatness, and value as an ethical/cultural category that art encodes, and that the critic's objective labor recovers and disseminates), with some unease at its high-cultural leanings, but with a basic adoption of its substantive premises. Their project was to bring these categories to bear on African writing. They simply did for African literature what Leavis sought to do for English literature. In so doing, the Africanist formalists bring their Leavisite/new-critical inheritance down to earth by concretely (that is, in their use of it) deconstructing its self-reification.

A journal like *African Literature Today* served as a launching pad for the institutionalization of African literature. The journal was significant to the reproduction of a new-critical and academicist ideology. The editorial statement of the first issue is an interesting document. Its second paragraph reads in part: "Publishers publish what they decide to publish for a variety of reasons, not least among them the reason that they are in business to make money. Readers also read books with a variety of expectations, not the least being their wish to be entertained. It is the critic's business to read discerningly and demonstrate the qualities of a work and thus (a) to make it accessible to a larger readership than the absence of criticism might have opened to it, and (b) by an accumulation of such examinations to help establish literary standards."[2] What is worth noting in this passage is its recognition of the logics of exchange value in academic scholarship and publishing, a recognition that is immediately followed by a more conventional invocation of aesthetic pleasure and putatively objective establishment of "standards."

There were those who rejected an exclusive concern with the intrinsic dimensions of literature. These critics, who generally tend to be more strongly nationalist than the aestheticists, stress the extrinsic dimensions of literature, claiming that only a sociological approach can ensure effective mobilization of African literature toward the ideal of decolonization. One can delineate within this group the Marxist critics, as against non-Marxist, but patently nationalist ones. The latter operate with a nationalist commitment that may take various forms. *Toward the Decolonization of African Literature*, authored by three Nigerian critics – Chinweizu, Onwuchekwa Jemie, and Ihechukwu Madubuike – is a highly polemical instance of this kind of reflectionist and nativist criticism.

[...]

Notes

1   On the complex social and epistemological underpinnings of Leavisite criticism in Britain and the New Criticism in the United States, see Francis Mulhern, John Guillory 134–75, and Mary Poovey. Both Guillory and Poovey show that the significant transformations that current theory has brought onto literary studies should not blind us to the fact that the teaching of literature in the United States as we begin a new century remains indebted to the New Criticism in many ways. After the advent of theory, cultural studies, and now postcolonial theory, the new-critical regime of ordering knowledge in matters of literature remains hard to throw out the window. Perhaps this is because one cannot (except in theory) "throw" cultural formations "out the window": one can only reorganize and reorient them in preferable directions. In our terms, this would be agency in motion.

2   Peter Benson's Black Orpheus, Transition, *and Modern Cultural Awakening in Africa* (1986) provides an account of the temper of the ferment I am indicating by tracing the history of *Black Orpheus* and *Transition*, two other magazines that, as he puts it, "were at the center of much that happened intellectually and culturally in anglophone black Africa during the period from the late fifties to the late seventies" (ix).

References

Achebe, Chinua. *Hopes and Impediments: Selected Essays.* New York: Doubleday, 1989.

Eliot, T. S. "Tradition and the Individual Talent" 302–11 in *English Critical Texts: 16th Century to 20th Century.* Eds. D. J. Enright and Ernst De Chickera. London: Oxford University Press, 1962.

Gerard, Albert, ed. *European-Language Writing in Sub-Saharan Africa.* (2 vols.) Budapest: Akademiai Kiado, 1986.

Irele, Abiola. *The African Experience in Literature and Ideology.* 1981. Bloomington: Indiana University Press, 1990.

Maduka, Chidi. "Formalism and the Criticism of African Literature: The Case of Anglo-American New Criticism." *The Literary Criterion* 23.1–2 (1988): 185–200.

Palmer, Eustace. *The Growth of the African Novel.* London: Heinemann, 1979.

White, Landeg. "Literature and History in Africa." *Journal of African History* 21 (1980): 537–46.

Chapter 61

Exclusionary Practices in African Literary Criticism

Florence Stratton

[...]

In characterizing African literature, critics have ignored gender as a social and analytic category. Such characterizations operate to exclude women's literary expression as part of African literature. Hence what they define is the male literary tradition. When African literary discourse is considered from the perspective of gender, it becomes evident that dialogic interaction between men's and women's writing is one of the defining features of the contemporary African literary tradition. Such a redefinition has important implications for both critical and pedagogical practices. What it indicates is that neither men's nor women's writing can be fully appreciated in isolation from the other.

This study also has two secondary aims: to supplement current definitions of the male literary tradition and to define the features of the emerging female tradition in African fiction. I will begin, however, by examining some of the ways in which women writers have been written out of the African literary tradition.

African women writers and their works have been rendered invisible in literary criticism. General surveys have neglected them as have more theoretical works such as Abdul R. JanMohamed's *Manichean Aesthetics*. The first book-length treatment of African fiction, Eustace Palmer's *An Introduction to the African Novel*, refers only once to a woman writer – a reference to Flora Nwapa that labels her 'an inferior novelist' (61). Women authors are also notably absent from Palmer's *The Growth of the African Novel*, as they are from other standard surveys such as David Cook's *African Literature: A Critical View* and Gerald Moore's *Twelve African Writers*. In his introduction, Moore goes so far as to plead with critics 'to step beyond what have already become the "safe" writers' and then expresses regret that space does not permit him to include in his own study 'such new writers' as Nuruddin Farah, Ebrahim Hussein, Kole Omotoso, and Femi Osofisan (8). In light of this list of men writers, it is worth

First published in *Contemporary African Literature and the Politics of Gender*, pp. 1–7. New York: Routledge, 1994.

noting that by the late 1970s there were several women writers who could no longer be described as 'new' – writers such as Bessie Head and Flora Nwapa, each of whom had three novels and a collection of short stories to her credit. But Moore shows not the slightest compunction about excluding them from his study.

Similarly, the African authors JanMohamed treats are all men: Chinua Achebe, Ngũgĩ wa Thiong'o, and Alex La Guma. So too are the writers Ngũgĩ refers to in 'Writing against neo-colonialism', an essay in which he outlines the development of African literature since the Second World War. This same practice is evident among critics who theorize 'third-world' or 'post-colonial' literatures, although they do refer to African men authors. Thus Fredric Jameson, in elaborating his 'theory of the cognitive aesthetics of third-world literature' ('Third-world literature' 88), cites only men writers (two of whom are African). In *The Empire Writes Back*, Bill Ashcroft, Gareth Griffiths, and Helen Tiffin do at least make passing reference to two women writers – Jean Rhys and Doris Lessing – and they also discuss in some detail one novel by the New Zealand writer, Janet Frame. But this is in the course of an extended treatment of a large number of men (including African men) writers.

African women writers have fared no better in critical journals. To take just one example, *African Literature Today* did not publish a full-length article on a woman writer until its seventh volume (1975). It published its second in its eighth volume (1976) and did not include another until its twelfth volume (1982). Recently, the trend has been toward 'special issues' – issues devoted mainly to women writers, like the fifteenth volume of *African Literature Today: Women in African Literature Today* (1987). Considering the content of succeeding volumes, such issues are open to the charge of tokenism. For the established pattern of issues, which, although they are not labelled 'special', are devoted exclusively to men writers, tends to reassert itself, as is the case with the sixteenth (1989) and seventeenth (1991) volumes of *African Literature Today*. Special issues also raise the question of ghettoiza-tion, as Ama Ata Aidoo indicates when she asks: 'why a special issue on the work of women writers especially as these supposed special issues never come out at all, or once in a half decade?' (162). This same kind of question can be raised in relation to the two book-length studies of women writers which have been published – Lloyd W. Brown's insightful *Women Writers in Black Africa* and Oladele Taiwo's trite and ill-informed *Female Novelists of Modern Africa*:[1] Why are the titles of these books marked for feminine gender? Or conversely: Why is Gerald Moore's book not entitled 'Twelve African men writers'?

Palmer justifies his selection of texts for inclusion in *An Introduction to the African Novel* by claiming that he has 'concentrated . . . on the dozen or so novels which seem to be of some importance, and which are gradually finding their way into school and university syllabuses' (xv). But texts become important and find their way into syllabuses – are, in short, admitted to the literary canon – when they are written about. This is the point Bernth Lindfors emphasizes in presenting the results of one of the tests he has devised for measuring the literary stature of Anglophone African writers:

> The unexamined literary career is not worth much in a noisy marketplace of ideas. To be famous, to be reputable, to be deemed worthy of serious and sustained consideration, an author needs as much criticism as possible, year after year after year. Only those who pass this test of time – the test of persistent published interest in their art – will stand a chance of earning literary immortality.
>
> ('Famous authors' ' 143)

Considering their invisibility in the dominant critical tradition, it is not surprising that women writers have not gained admission to the literary canon. Lindfors analyses two types of data in order to establish a writer's canonical status: the frequency with which, between 1936 and 1986, an author was discussed by literary critics ('Famous authors' reputation test'); and the frequency with which in 1986 an author was included in the literature syllabuses of Anglophone African universities ('Teaching of African literatures'). The result in each case is an all-male canon. Achebe, Ngũgĩ, and Soyinka (not necessarily in that order) are the three top-ranking authors, while the next seven positions on the combined-ranking scale are occupied by Ayi Kwei Armah, John Pepper Clark, Okot p'Bitek, Christopher Okigbo, Peter Abrahams, Alex La Guma, and Dennis Brutus. Ranking fifteenth and eighteenth respectively, Aidoo and Head are the only women who come close to acquiring canonical status ('Teaching' 54). Thus Soyinka is speaking from a privileged position – from within as well as on behalf of the dominant literary tradition – when he complains in a paper he presented at the 1986 Stockholm African Writers' Conference that African literature has been subjected to too much criticism:

> The amount of criticism of African literature, which is now probably about a thousand fold of the actual [literary] material being put out, really constitutes a barrier, not only to the literature itself, but in fact to the very personalities of the producers of literature.
>
> ('Ethics' 26)

Speaking at the same conference, but from quite a different position – from the margins of the canon and on behalf of women writers – Ama Ata Aidoo, by contrast, is bitter about the literary establishment's neglect of women writers. Making a plea not for less but for more criticism, she claims that what most distinguishes African women from African men writers is the vast difference in the amount of critical attention paid to them:

> [I]t is especially pathetic to keep on writing without having any consistent, active, critical intelligence that is interested in you as an artist.... Therefore, it is precisely from this point that African writing women's reality begins to differ somewhat from that of the male African writer. Once we have faced the basic fact of the oppression and marginality that is almost endemic in the lives of... Africans, we also begin to admit that at least, some people are interested in the male African writer. These include African, non-African, male and female literary critics, different categories of publishers, editors, anthologists, translators, librarians, sundry academic analysts, and all other zealous collectors of treasures! ('To be' 158)

Lindfors clearly subscribes to the conventional formalist view of the canon as the corpus of texts that defines excellence – classic texts produced by great writers. Thus, for example, he labels authors who score badly on his tests as 'second-rate talents' ('Famous authors'' 133). Recently critics concerned with marginalized literatures have challenged this view and insisted that literary canons, rather than reflecting objective judgements of literary merit, are artificial constructs that are imposed by an elite and that operate to reproduce and reinforce existing power relations. What these critics argue is that biases are embedded in the prevailing critical paradigms and that these work to marginalize or discredit certain perspectives. As Arnold Krupat puts it in his discussion of Native American literature: 'there are unmistakable connections between critical paradigms and canon formation'

(91).[2] What I hope to show in the pages that follow is that sexism has operated as a bias of exclusion in African literary criticism.

As Biodun Jeyifo indicates, New Critical formalism has been the reigning point of view in African literary studies since the 1960s, its proponents, who include both western critics like Lindfors and Cook, and African ones like Eustace Palmer, Eldred Jones, and Daniel Izevbaye, advocating 'an "objective" literary scholarship based on truly "aesthetic", formal criteria of evaluation' (43). The main charge that has been levelled against this mode of criticism from within African literary studies is that of Eurocentrism, the most influential formulation of this accusation being that of Chinweizu, Onwuchekwa Jemie, and Ihechukwu Madubuike who argue that the universal values New Criticism purports to embody are, in fact, 'provincial, time-and-place bound *European preferences*' (4); and that to judge African litera-ture by these criteria is therefore to define it 'as an appendage of European literature' (10). Ashcroft and his colleagues make a similar point. New Criticism's false claim to objectivity, they state, facilitated the 'assimilation of post-colonial writers into a "metropolitan" trad-ition' which retarded the development of indigenous theories, as works were not considered 'within an appropriate cultural context' (160–1).

In its claims to objectivity and universality, New Criticism has also been challenged by western feminists. Rejecting 'universal' values as masking male preferences, they have confronted New Criticism with its andro- or phallocentrism. This same male bias is apparent in New Criticism's reading of African literature. Most evidently, the texts it privileges – the titles that make up the all-male canon – encode a reactionary gender ideology. Revealing this hidden ideology – making explicit the gender codes of canonical texts – is the main undertaking of my first two chapters. What can be noted here is that it is not only New Criticism that fails to mention this reactionary ideology. Other modes also suppress it which suggests that there is a coincidence between this ideology and that of a variety of non-feminist critical positions.

New Criticism's method of evaluating texts is also revealing. As Chinweizu and his colleagues indicate, it betrays its Eurocentrism by only endorsing texts which conform to western standards. But there is also a tendency within the New Critical paradigm to assess works written by women differently from those written by men. For whereas the general practice has been to compare the latter to canonical (usually male-authored) European texts, the former have tended to be compared to valorized male-authored African ones. In the second case, that comparison, in my reading, is always derogatory. This is not surprising given the fact that women's texts are being assessed on the basis of standards established first by western and then by African men writers, and it illustrates the extent to which African women writers have been alienated from the African literary tradition. New Criticism's exclusionary methods will be considered in more detail in later chapters where, as part of a discussion of women writers' critical reception, a number of reviews written in the New Critical mode will be examined. As we shall see, works by women writers have been trivialized, distorted, and maligned as a result of their non-conformity to standards that are both Euro- and androcentric.

Lindfors considers the African literary canon to be 'still in a state of creative gestation' with only Achebe, Ngũgĩ, and Soyinka being quite secure in their standing ('Teaching' 55). If the tradition of New Criticism can be seen to have led to the exclusion of women writers from the canon, as Lindfors's data (which are current to 1986) represent it, what is the likelihood of their gaining admission as the canon changes?

It is evident that New Criticism is finally giving way to other paradigms and it is to a consideration of some of those that are gaining currency that I will turn in addressing this question. These include a number of models which are subsumable under the rubric of historicist or cultural criticism – JanMohamed's, Ngũgĩ's, Jameson's, and that of Ashcroft and his colleagues, all of which theorize African / 'post-colonial' / 'third-world' literature as having been shaped by a particular set of socio-political conditions. As we have already seen, these critics do not treat any African women writers in their discussions. The question is, then, do their models preclude such a treatment? Do they manifest an underlying bias of exclusion?

Like New Criticism, this historicist criticism represents itself as universal, although only in terms of gender. Thus the critics use generic terms such as 'the African writer' and ' "post-colonial" / "third-world" writing'. Thus, too, none of these critics treats gender as a socio-political category. Ashcroft and Jameson's sole category of analysis is coloniality, while Ngũgĩ privileges class and JanMohamed race. Moreover, the only socio-political conditions they consider in relation to the literary structures produced by African / 'post-colonial' / 'third-world' writers are the conditions of colonialism or neo-colonialism, and these they represent as being universal as to gender. Thus JanMohamed, drawing on Fanon's insight into the structure of colonial society, posits 'a manichean allegory of white and black, good and evil, salvation and damnation, civilization and savagery, superiority and inferiority, intelligence and emotion, self and other, subject and object' (4) as the source of 'such a powerful socio-political-ideological force field that neither colonial nor African literature is able to escape or transcend it':

> [Writers] may decry or simply depict its existence and effects, they may try to subvert it or overcome its consequences, or they may valorize it; but regardless of the overt thematic content of their writing, they cannot ignore it. (277)

In criticizing JanMohamed for ignoring gender, Susan Z. Andrade observes that while his 'allegorical model is useful in deciphering race relations', it 'seems capable of addressing only one category of analysis at a time, which requires that marginalized categories be assimilated into, rather than accommodated by, the model, which remains fixed' (93). It is, however, perhaps more a failure to insert other categories that is the problem.
[…]

Notes

1   For a critique of Taiwo's book, see Ama Ata Aidoo, 'To be an African woman writer – an overview and a detail', in Kirsten Holst Petersen (ed.) *Criticism and Ideology: Second African Writers' Conference, Stockholm 1986*, Uppsala, Scandinavian Institute of African Studies, 1988: 155–72. Aidoo aptly characterizes Taiwo's book as 'patronizing', 'self-righteous', and 'insensitive'. She also exposes his androcentrism and his careless reading of women's novels.

2   In their concern with (white) western women writers' exclusion from the canon, Nina Bahm, 'Melodramas of beset manhood: how theories of American fiction exclude women authors', in Elaine Showalter (ed.) *The New Feminist Criticism: Essays on Women, Literature, and Theory*, London, Virago, 1986, 63–80; and Lillian S. Robinson, 'Treason our text: feminist challenges to the literary canon', in Showalter, op. cit.: 105–21, make the same point as Krupat.

References

Aidoo, Ama Ata, 'To be an African woman writer – an overview and a detail', in Kirsten Holst Peterson (ed.), *Criticism and Ideology: Second African Writers' Conference, Stockholm*, 1986, Uppsala, Scandinavian Institute of African Studies: 1988, 155–72.

Andrade, Susan Z., 'Rewriting history, motherhood, and rebellion: naming an African women's literary tradition', *Research in African Literatures*, 1990, 21.1: 91–110.

Ashcroft, Bill, Gareth Griffiths, and Helen Tiffin, *The Empire Writes Back: Theory and Practice in Post-Colonial Literatures*, London, Routledge, 1989.

Brown, Lloyd, *Women Writers in Black Africa*, Westport, Connecticut, Greenwood Press, 1981.

Chinweizu, Onwuchekwa Jemie, and Ihechuwu Madubuike, *Toward the Decolonization of African Literature*, vol. 1, Enugu, Fourth Dimension, 1980.

Cook, David, *African Literature: A Critical View*, London, Longman, 1977.

Jameson, Fredric, 'Third-world literature in the era of multinational capitalism', *Social Text*, 1986, 15: 65–88.

JanMohamed, Abdul R., *Manichean Aesthetics: The Politics of Literature in Colonial Africa*, Amherst, University of Massachusetts Press, 1983.

Jeyifo, Biodun, 'The nature of things: arrested decolonization and critical theory', *Research in African Literatures*, 1990, 21.1: 33–48.

Krupat, Arnold, *The Voice in the Margin: Native American Literature and the Canon*, Berkeley, University of California Press, 1989.

Lindfors, Bernth, 'The famous authors' reputation test: an update to 1986', in János Riesz and Alain Ricard (eds), *Semper Aliquid Novi: Litérature compare et litterature d'Afrique: Mélanges Albert Gérard*, Tübingen, Gunter Narr Verlag, 1990: 131–43.

——. 'The teaching of African literatures in Anglophone African universities: an instructive canon', *Matatu*, 1990, 7: 41–55.

Moore, Gerald, Review of *The Promised Land* by Grace Ogot, *Mawazo*, 1967, 1.2: 94–5.

Ngũgĩa wa Thiong'O, 'Writing against neo-colonialism', in Kirsten Holst Peterson (ed.), *Criticism and Ideology: Second African Writers' Conference, Stockholm*, 1986, Uppsala, Scandinavian Institute of African Studies, 1988: 92–103.

Palmer, Eustace, *The Growth of the African Novel*, London, Heinemann, 1979.

——. *An Introduction to the African Novel*, London, Heinemann, 1972.

Soyinka, Wole, 'Ethics, ideology and the critic', in Kirsten Holst (ed.), *Criticism and Ideology: Second African Writers' Conference, Stockholm* 1986, Uppsala, Scandinavian Institute of African Studies, 1988: 26–51.

Taiwo, Oladele, *Female Novelists of Modern Africa*, London, Macmillan, 1984.

Part IX

Marxism

Central to Marxist criticism of African literature has been the definition of literature as essentially a vehicle of class struggle. But 'class' has been seen in a variety of ways by the critics in this section. Apart from its default interpretation as pertaining to social relations within specific national entities, the term has also been interpreted within the larger scope of decolonization and cross-cultural contact. Significant in this purview has been the call for freeing of the mind of the African from the shackles of Western ideas that are ultimately aimed at distorting his or her self-image. Thus Marxist criticism in African letters has gone well beyond the criticism of African literature itself. Its purview has included state–citizen relations, the relation between hegemonic knowledges that percolate through the agency of local elites, and the dialectical interplay between society-as-context and literature-as-product. Also significant in this area have been explications of the role of the African writer as the vanguard in the revolutionary effort towards a better society. Despite the overall strongly approving character of the essays in this section it has to be noted that the internal consistency of Marxism has not escaped critique. Most trenchant in this regard is Ayi Kwei Armah's essay in this section, which sets out to show how much Marxism is part of a larger Western hegemonic project. That his critique deploys a scrupulous dialectical method that would earn the admiration of most Marxists must not divert attention from the fact that Marxism has not had an entirely uncritical reception in African literary-critical circles.

Chapter 62

Towards a Marxist Sociology of African Literature

Omafume F. Onoge

Colonial Politics and African Culture

In the world today all culture, all literature and art belong to definite classes and are geared to definite political lines. There is in fact no such thing as art for art's sake, art that stands above classes or art that is detached from or independent of politics[1]

Mao Tse-Tung, *Talks at the Yenan Forum*

Political interests have been the crucial factors in the appraisal of African culture since the colonial period. At no time was the domain of African culture conceived of as a neutral field for the unfettered play of objective study. The only significant division has always been one of 'whose political interest?' The politics of oppression versus the politics of liberation. This political partisanship which is now obscured in 'post-independence' African culture and literary studies was boldly visible in the cultural policies of colonial regimes.

As is now common knowledge, the colonizer did not stop at the conquest of the pre-capitalist relations of production. The cultural superstructure was also a major target of assault in order to bring about a new collective consciousness and individual psychological habits favourable to the advance of the violent installation of the capitalist economy. This cultural assault is what today is summed up by the expression, 'cultural imperialism'. In the days of colonial self- assurance, the process of cultural imperialism often entailed a ban on traditional productions and performances of sculpture, dances and songs on the ostensible grounds that they were pagan pollutions in the christian colonial theocracies. 'Coming- out' ceremonies of age-groups – important occasions for dramatic performances of democratic transfer of political power from one generation to another – were banned in societies such as Banyakyusa and the Agikuyu, because of the fear that they could escalate into

First published in *Marxism and African Literature*, ed. Georg M. Gugelberger, pp. 50–63. Trenton, NJ: Africa World Press, 1985.

realistic dramas of anti-colonial politics. The cultural imperialist process went beyond mere acts of vandalism. The vandalism, we must always remember, had as its goal the creation of a personality type, whose essential attribute would be the lack of self-affirmation. A personality that would define *itself* by an ascribed 'constitutional depravity' and thus accept the new world of the King Léopolds as an essential passage to salvation. Fanon, as always, grasped this subtle process of consciousness-transformation in these words:

> Native society in not simply described as a society lacking in values. It is not enough for the colonist to affirm that those values have disappeared from, or still better never existed in, the colonial world. The native is declared insensible to ethics; he represents not only the absence of values but also the negation of values. *He is . . . the enemy of values, . . .* the absolute evil.[2]

And as Fanon noted, the christian missionary and his religion functioned as the special ideological DDT to destroy the 'native parasites'.

This violent psychological conversion was not without its successes. Until fairly recently, the new personality with its negative consciousness affected the educated African's relationship to the traditional arts. There was a time when many educated Africans required a major act of intellectualization to ascribe aesthetic value to our traditional arts. I recall the dismay of an American professor of art history who complained, in the early sixties, that his African students recoiled from his exhibitions of African masks with a 'missionary complex.' This negative response to the traditional arts has also been featured in recent African fiction. In Chinua Achebe's *No Longer at Ease*, for example, there is a scene where Obi's father reacts strongly against the performance of traditional welcome songs on the grounds of their 'heathenist' content.

The emergence of African literature written in the colonizer's tongue did not escape this encounter with colonial politics. In Southern Africa, Thomas Mofolo's first novel was refused publication by the Morija press until he turned to themes reflecting the official manicheism of colonial society. That is, only works in which Mofolo created characters whose moments of insight and maturity coincided with their recognition of the 'superiority' of Christian ethics, were published. René Maran, we were told, was placed in considerable difficulties with colonial officials and French literary critics, because of his naturalistic depiction of the material deprivation which French colonialism visited on Africans, in his novel, *Batouala*. Indeed, 'by their mere presence', African writers in the middle period of colonialism, 'created a scandal'. Let us reproduce Aimé Césaire more fully:

> Under a colonial society there is not merely a hierarchy of *master and servant*. There is also, implicit, a hierarchy of *creator and consumer*.
>
>   The creator of cultural values, under good colonization, is the colonizer. And the consumer is the colonized. And everything goes well so long as nothing happens to disturb the hierarchy. There is one law of comfort in every colonization. 'Si prega di non disturbare.' Please do not disturb.[3]

This situation is still very much with us today in parts of the continent. Today, as we in Nigeria dance away our temporary oil harvest in Festac, there are many African writers who still constitute a scandal in South Africa by their presence. Their works exist under an automatic ban. In fact, for some of them, the simple physical act of transferring thought to paper, is defined as veritable treason.

In light of the above, the current boom in African literature is traceable, in its broad aspects, to the concrete gains of anti-colonial struggles and changes in the international political scene. The new literature, not only suffered political obstacles at its birth, but was also conditioned by this very politics. As we have argued elsewhere,[4] the general thrust of the new petty-bourgeois African literature has been anti-imperialist because African writers saw their motivation in anti-colonial political terms. The forerunners of the Negritude movement in Paris conceived of their literary journal, *Légitime défense*, as a vehicle for a literature using the 'weapons of words' against colonialism. And three decades later in West Africa, Chinua Achebe restated this political motivation in his conception of the novelist as teacher:

> I would be quite satisfied if my novels (especially the ones I set in the past) did no more than teach my readers that their past – with all its imperfections – was not one long night of savagery from which the first Europeans acting on God's behalf delivered them. Perhaps what I write is applied art as distinct from pure. But who cares? Art is important but so is education of the kind I have in mind. And I don't see that the two need be mutually exclusive.[5]

Achebe's statement will serve as our point of departure for a more direct confrontation with the subject of this paper. Consider the statement once more. Its apologetic tone is unmistakeable. In one of our earlier submissions on this subject, we argued that this 'apologetic tone in Achebe's justification of the applied or functional purpose of his works is a reflection of the unsettled nature of the criteria by which modern African literature should be appraised'.[6] We have not revised our judgement. The dominant mode of academic criticism of contemporary African literature and culture is unable to judge the literature in any satisfactory way. The dominant mode is bourgeois. Most of its errors and inconsistencies stem from both theoretical handicaps of a bourgeois outlook and its lack of fidelity to the *political* circumstances of the evolution of African literature. Our purpose in subsequent sections is to indicate the nature of this confusion in current bourgeois African literary studies and why a Marxist sociological criticism is advocated.

This bourgeois domination of the field does not imply a consensus of approach within the ranks. The empirical situation is one of sharp controversy. A recent issue of *African Literature Today* devoted specially to *criticism*, shows that the language of the polemics has been quite robust and often intemperate. The considerable output of this school shows many different nuances. It is by a process of analysis that we have arrived at the conclusion that their differences are mere variations within a single bourgeois conception of literature and society.

The central issue around which bourgeois critics have polemicized with one another concerns the status of sociological factors in the evaluation of African literature. In the theoretical pronouncements there is a noisy division between those who insist on a formalist appraisal of literary techniques and those who emphasise the sociological understanding of the idea – content of literature. Given the marked socio-political content of the literary works themselves, the polarization reduces ultimately to *a-political* versus *political* criticism. The advocates of a non-sociological criticism actually are the African variety of the familiar theorists of the disembodied conception of 'art-for-art's sake'.

Art for art's sake critics

It is the intervention of this kind of criticism that forced Achebe into his self-doubt. 'Perhaps what I write is applied art as distinct from pure.' The Nigerian critic Dan S. Izevbaye is the most sophisticated advocate of art for art's sake criticism. In 1971, he acknowledged without apparent regret the sociological conditioning of the colonial milieu which informed the birth of literature, but hoped that a literature with a 'suppressed social reference' would develop, so that non-sociological criticism could in fact advance:

> With this new emphasis in criticism, that is the suppression of the social reference of literature as a significant influence in criticism, it may be easier for critics to pay greater attention to the literary work itself. But the influence of the referential element on African criticism has not really been an intrusion. The social factor was important only because the literature itself was largely sociological. As the literature becomes less preoccupied with the social or national problems and more concerned with the problems of men as individuals in an African society, the critical reference will be human beings rather than society, and the considerations which influence critical judgement will be human and literary rather than social ones.[7]

In his most recent survey of "The State of Criticism in African Literature" (1975) there is a stronger tone of lament that the suppression of the social reference has still not dominated literary scholarship. In the process his earlier theoretical errors of a false counterposing of abstract 'human beings' against society, remain intact. The immaculate conception of a transcendent literature remains unrevised. Instead of seeing the predominance of socio-logical criticism of African literature as a signal of the intrinsic *sociality* of literature, he blames this critical tendency on the 'present intellectual climate which encourages the critical faculty' towards the 'sociological imagination'.[8] And in a further ambiguous sen-tence, which is nonetheless ideologically revealing, he states that 'the political option implied in this preference for sociological significance over moral values may be related to the precedence which political liberation takes over religious piety in Africa'.[9] Thus, Izevbaye's art-for- art's sake advocacy is really for a depoliticized literary universe inhabited by abstract human beings with the abstract moral values of an abstract religious pietism. A literary universe which, our prosaic logic compels us to add, must be created by astral writers and equally astral critics!

If with Izevbaye, we end up with an astral animism, with Eustace Palmer, the search for the ideal literature of pure form, leads us to a fundamental linguistic perversion. For a critic who never tires of searching for 'signs of technical competence' in his recent book-length study of African novels, he displays remarkable linguistic incompetence. Consider the following usage of 'decolonization' in this passage:

> The decolonization of African literature is already in progress. Novelists are becoming less preoccupied with cultural and sociological matters, and more concerned about exposing the corruption and incompetence which are so wide-spread in African political and government circles.[10]

In this search for 'decolonized' literature in which the ordinary meaning of 'sociological matters' is newly restricted to social issues of an anti-colonial salience, Eustace Palmer virtually *misreads* all the novels he has considered in his book. To take a ready example, his enthusiasm for Western civilization, makes him transform the content of Mongo Beti's *Mission to Kala*, into its very opposite:

> *Mission to Kala* is neither an attack on education nor on Western civilization; rather, it is a brilliant satire directed against all those half-baked young men who feel that a partial exposure to Western ways makes them superior to their countrymen who still live the tribal life. Mongo Beti subjects Jean Marie's personal weaknesses – his condescension, arrogance, and stupidity – to rigorous criticism by means of his comic act.[11]

The foregoing excerpts, brief as they are, sufficiently indicate the ideological motivation of the art for art's sake advocates. Their true concern is to proscribe literature of an anti-imperialist content. It is this preoccupation that leads them to misconceptions about the meaning of the term 'sociological.' In their practical criticism, of course, they are unable to concentrate solely on technical stylistic matters. In fact, with a critic like Palmer, the much-vaunted formalistic criticism does not go beyond the labelling of an author's style as 'ironic' or 'satirical.'

Criticism of this type very often consists of documenting the technical affinity between an African writer and a writer in Euro-America. However, this documentation, this tracing of an author's artistic ancestry, is not pursued with the knowledge that artistic forms are themselves historical products. The fact that Euro-American models, which are often held as the atemporal, immutable yardsticks with which the African writer's achievement is judged, were usually consequences of conscious literary manifestos by writers consciously reacting to the political issues of their times is ignored. For example, when the symbolism or surrealism of this or that writer is praised, there is no awareness of the ideological purposes for which these literary movements were created in the milieu of capitalist-industrial Europe. Whether or not such ideological purposes are at cross-purposes with contemporary African reality is never broached.

Interlude

> The bourgeoisie has stripped of its halo every occupation hitherto honoured and looked up to with reverent awe. It has converted the physician, the lawyer, the priest, the poet, the man of science, into its paid wage labourers.
>
> Marx and Engels, *The Communist Manifesto*

Bourgeois sociological criticism

In light of the foregoing, it is not surprising that most bourgeois criticism of African literature is predominantly of the sociological kind. But even here the theoretical premise does not rise above the *obvious truth* that 'literature deals with life'. Thus, whereas we encounter abstract 'human beings' without political and cultural vitality among the purists, here we are faced with the conception of a literature that flows from an undifferentiated life. It derives from a conception of society that is undifferentiated by class. If the 'mellifluous universalism' (Kwame Nkrumah's phrase) of art for art's sake is tempered by a recognition of concrete particularity, then it is only the particularity of culture. Within each culture there are no class cleavages. All is consensus. The favoured image of a society or culture is the organismic one.

The theory of art and literature implicit in this sociological criticism is naturally the rigid mimetic one. Art and literature reflect the whole cultural organism – the 'collective mind' of the whole society. Literature does not struggle against society. Its reflective attribute is invested always with the integrative flavour characteristic of the homeostatic functions which functionalist social anthropology ascribed to any and all institutions. In fact, in their contest with the art for art's sake theorists, they cite the findings of social anthropologists of the functionality of traditional African arts for the sustenance of religious values, socialization, social control and the like.

In recent debates with art for art's sake advocates, protagonists of the sociological school frequently cited, for support, Abiola Irele's 1971 justification of the sociological approach as:

> . . . attempts to correlate the work to the social background to see how the author's intention and attitude issue out of the wider social context of his art in the first place and, more important still, to get to an understanding of the way each writer or each group of writers captures a moment of the historical consciousness of the society. The intimate progression of the collective mind, its working, its shapes, its temper, these – and more – are determinants to which a writer's mind and sensibilities are subject, to which they are responding all the time and which, at a superficial or profound level, his work will reflect in its moods and structures.[12]

This rather undialectical conception of literature and society has led to various kinds of bourgeois sociological criticism. Bourgeois sociology of African literature is variegated: each variety has its special nuances and conclusions. However, all versions of this sociological criticism thus far, have seized on 'culture', rather than 'society' as its operational concept. This operational focus has enhanced the tendency of veering away from social-relational dynamics in the analysis of the interaction between literature and society. Culture, with its more immediate mentalistic connotations, was a sure path to various forms of literary idealism. The current in African political parlance has been to see African culture or 'tradition', not as a specific ideological rationalization of the ways our forebears at specific historical periods tackled their problem of survival, but as the eternally valid source of wisdom by which African behavior, a-temporally conceived, must be judged. This is an endemic habit of bourgeois sociological criticism. Terry Eagleton has recently shown how a progressive sociological critic of English literature, Raymond Williams, was often led to idealist conclusions, in spite of his personal radical commitment, because of the operational centrality of the concepts of culture and tradition in his early works.[13]

In the hands of the less progressive sociological critics of African material, the upshot of these fundamental concepts – African culture and African tradition – has been the institutionalization of what we may call a Festac anthropology. A 'Festac' anthropological thrust which has transmuted 'African extended family', 'African religion', 'African rhythm', 'African time' into eternal base categories for the analysis of contemporary literature. The difficulties which currently plague the new literary movement among African critics in quest of indigenous black/African aesthetics stem from this idealistic Festac anthropology. It is not surprising, that beyond the hortatory language of advocacy, the findings of the movement to date have not advanced beyond the metaphysical sensibilities of animism, spontaneous *Gemeinschaft*, rhythm, balance, and vital force, attributed to the African by the Senghorean variant of Negritude.[14]

We might add in passing, that this idealistic distortion of the African and his society is also on the rise in the new dramatic literature issuing from Nigeria. The representation of the African as being exclusively interested in 'ontological questions rather than on the "prosaic" issues of economy and politics', as well as his abdication of politics before his feudal king – negritude's 'custodian of African tradition' – has been the dominant theme of enthusiastic Nigerian petty-bourgeois theatre in the neo-fascist era of Gowon.[15]

Another kind of bourgeois sociological criticism has been the preoccupation with what we might call cultural archaeology. By this we refer to the attempt to excavate the literary texts for traditionalia, in terms of which the text is then explained. While for some this is the critical procedure, others (usually non-Africans) have absolutized the procedure into a normative requirement for good African literature. Thus the injunction that the writer should describe his 'cultural anxiety' about issues such as the 'abuses of the dowry system or of polygamy'. The writer should probe the 'telluric' sentiment of the black continent for 'an authentic exoticism'.[16] However, be it a critical procedure or normative prescription, we can do no better than quote Biodun Jeyifo, the Nigerian Marxist critic of theatre, who passed this sharp judgement on this form of petty-bourgeois sociological perspective:

> ...(it) enthrones 'culture' and cultural facts as inexhaustible reservoirs of sociological capital. These 'natural' cultural facts are made to give either ethnic-racial-civilizational values as the determinants of the destinies of conflicted individual heroes...or give the use of ethno-cultural lore, idioms and motifs for the sensuous material surface of dramatic action as an undialectical validation of the social attitudes and relations which these cultural facts and traditionalia initially sustained...[17]

The recourse to functionalist sociology and the cultural anthropology of cultural relativity also trap critical works that seek to examine a particular corpus of African literature in dynamic perspective. The problems which beset the emphasis of bourgeois academic sociology on 'role-players', rather than role-authors, 'culture-bearers', rather than culture-creators, in the handling of structure-breaking change, exist in the literary critical tradition predicated on this sociology. The theoretical preference for *gradualist* reformist dynamics, the distortion of the colonial situation as 'culture-contact', the diagnosis of the Third World's agenda as that of 'modernization', and the projection of advanced capitalist culture as the final aspiration of true man, all of which bourgeois sociology has propagandized, are typical features of this type of criticism.

It is this essentially mellifluous utopian cultural diffusionist trajectory that informs Charles R. Larson's study of the 'emergence' of African fiction. For him the African writer's passage has been to play the 'historian of his continent's increasingly widened outlook on life, moving from a limited, virtually closed-off societal view of the village and the clan to an ever-widening world view'.[18] Since Larson never strays from within the rigid parameters of undialectical cultural anthropology, the individual-character dominated novel of this specific epoch of the bourgeois West, inadvertently becomes the true novelistic form (inadvertent because of his initial premise of cultural relativity in the determination of literature) to which the African novel is emerging.[19].

The power of a false theoretical perspective to vitiate the insights of a serious sociological critic whose personal progressive temper is not in doubt, is nowhere better revealed than in Emmanuel Obiechina's massive study *Culture, Tradition and Society in the West African Novel*.

The book opens with an approving quotation of Daniel Lerner's saccharine formulation of the Third World agenda in *The Passing of Traditional Society*. Not surprisingly, the book ends with a consideration of 'culture contact and culture conflict'. This sublimination of the revolutionary project as psycho-cultural modernization, prevents Obiechina from offering a critique of the artist's apprehension of the colonial situation which produced the culture-contact in the first place. As with Larson, unfactored notions such as 'urbanization,' 'adjustment to modern social change' are used to paper over a specific critic of the writer's consciousness. Instead, Obiechina postpones the task:

> The latter themes (e.g. politics) are in themselves important and constitute a vast, promising area of their own, but it seems sound sense, first and foremost, to survey the terrain, to observe the physical features, locate the signposts and generally create an outline map as aid to more realistic purposeful exploration of the literature.[20]

But it is a postponement largely based on the false theoretical premise that indigenous cultural categories constitute the dynamic basis of life in the violent manicheism of colonial society.

The Festac Consciousness

> If we truly seek a rebirth from the culture of colonialism to the collectivist anti-imperialist culture of the African masses, the masses must first have sovereignty in the decisions that affect the political and economic future of the nation.
>
> The Nigerian Academy of Arts, Sciences & Technology, *The Nigerian Peoples Manifesto, Political Programme*, Ibadan, 1974.

The Festac metaphor which we have already invoked at several junctures, is an appropriate one for summing up the consciousness of bourgeois approaches to the study of African literature. All variants of bourgeois criticism, nationalist variants included, are implicated in this consciousness. Like the Festac revisionisms which have become as prominent as military coups and pseudo-economic indigenization projects, bourgeois sociological criticism creates the illusion of a classless, cultural consensus in contemporary African societies.

Secondly, bourgeois criticism shares with Festac activists a fundamental misunderstanding of the true purpose of colonial cultural imperialism. Bourgeois cultural scholars imagine that cultural aggression was not necessary to colonial domination. The attempt by the colonizer to transplant his own values is seen in the result of the colonizer's ignorance or the Christian missionary's proselytizing zeal. They fail to realize that the new capitalist economy which the colonizer introduced, logically required the institutionalization of a bourgeois consciousness in order to facilitate the advance of the economy. In fact, bourgeois critics as well as many of our Festac statesmen, restrict the definition of the colonial trauma to the loss of political sovereignty and cultural initiative. They maintain amnesia over the decisive character of the colonial experience – which is the coerced incorporation of African societies into the exploiting capitalist social system. It is this amnesia, which is self-serving, that makes Festac statesmen imagine that the periodic revival of 'traditional' dances in the urban sports stadia of our African capitalist societies, would stem the erosion of our pre-colonial heritage. When bourgeois literary critics devalue anti-colonial literature a priori, they are in the throes of this amnesia.

Since this literary criticism is even more backward than the actual literature which it 'criticizes', it is unable to evaluate literary content in any rigorous manner. Confronted with two novels inspired by the same social theme, bourgeois literary criticism is unable to tell us in any scientific way, which treatment is more valid. If we may invoke Plekhanov, this criticism has been largely unable to discriminate between false and true ideas.[21] Instead, criticism of content stagnates on the mere descriptive reproduction of manifest material.

In so far as criticism is held to have an impact on the development of literature, the effect of bourgeois criticism of African literature can only impede, rather than inspire it towards revolutionary heights. The defects of bourgeois criticism are not solely a question of the handicaps of theoretical outlook in every instance. In a world where the NLF, PAIGC, FRELIMO and MPLA exist as concrete realities, the persistence of a bourgeois outlook must stem also from the material class interest of the literary critic. The 'educational' role which bourgeois critics have ascribed to their activity has, in several instances, become a mask for a self-promoting careerist industry. For example, when in a study of Soyinka's plays, a Nigerian critic can talk of 'alleged corruption', 'alleged election rigging' during the blatantly obvious man-of-the-people politics of pre-war Nigeria, we are forced to agree with Biodun Jeyifo's conclusions that criticism has become a 'parasitic, opportunistic vocation of salaried, petty-bourgeois intellectual hustlers.'[22]

Interlude

> Revolutionary literature and art should create a variety of characters out of real life and help the masses to propel history forward. For example, there is suffering from hunger, cold and oppression on the one hand, and exploitation and oppression of man by man on the other. These facts exist everywhere and people look upon them as commonplace. Writers and artists concentrate such everyday phenomena, typify the contradictions and struggles within them and produce works which awaken the masses, fire them with enthusiasm and impel them to unite and struggle to transform their environment.
>
> Mao Tse-Tung, *Talks at the Yenan Forum*

Marxism and African Literature, a Prospectus

Unlike bourgeois criticism, Marxist criticism has never involved itself in any internal conundrums about the admissibility of sociological factors in the consideration of art and literature. Marxist criticism is necessarily sociological. This sociological nature, as Lunacharsky[23] once argued, is what immediately distinguishes it from all other types of literary criticism. However, its sociology is rooted in the materialist understanding of cultural consciousness given by Marx:

> The mode of production of the material means of life determines, in general, the social, political and intellectual processes of life. It is not the consciousness of human beings which determines their existence, it is their social existence which determines their consciousness.[24]

Marxist critics have always insisted that in class societies, this contingent relationship of intellectual production and consciousness on material economic relationships is mediated by the class structure, by way of class interests and class psychology. In class societies, culture, art and literature take on a class character. Literature in such circumstances is fully implicated in the class struggle. It can either evince a consciousness that seems to conserve the society in behalf of privileged interests or exude a revolutionary consciousness congruent with the objective interests of the oppressed class which is engaged in the struggle to change the social status quo.

The charge by bourgeois critics (often heard at conferences on African literature) that Marxist critics devalue art and literature is, of course, unfounded. A host of Marxist critics, Plekhanov, Hauser, Caudwell, Fischer and Thomson, to name a few, have in fact demonstrated the importance of art in the very evolution of human culture. *The Necessity of Art* is indeed the revealing title of Fischer's contribution. It is bourgeois critics who, having concocted a variety of non-historical pagan muses as the sources of literature and art, have in fact robbed artistic productions of any vitality in the activities of *real* men to liberate themselves from social exploitation and prostration before nature.

Given this revolutionary understanding of the dialectical relationship between literature and social struggle, Marxist critics do not conceive of literary criticism as an abstract academic activity with abstract justifications. Marxist critics are necessarily class partisan. They do not camouflage this partisanship. Marxist critics also recognize that the very analytical categories which constitute the vocabulary of literary scholarship are themselves historical products. These vocabularies and theories, like their counterparts in other domains of scholarship, must at all times be subjected to a radical sociology of knowledge – a sociology of knowledge which includes an assessment of the objective material interests of the class creators of the ideas. Marxist critics are always concerned, in the final analysis, with the assessment of artistic visions in terms of their practical relevance to the struggle for ever more democratic forms of social existence.

Consequently, Marxist criticism also goes beyond a formal and content analysis of artistic works, to a consideration of the very institutional processes of art creation and art-criticism. Marxist critics are concerned to struggle for a democratization of the structures of artistic production and criticism. They are concerned to free the artistic process from structural fetters. This has become very pressing in our late capitalist period where art and literature have value, only as commodities. The Marxist critics' dream is for a community where all can be artists and art-appreciators.

Finally, we must repeat (because of the state of decadence of contemporary African sociology) that a Marxist sociological perspective is not to be confused with the bourgeois sociology or anthropology which sees men as passive 'role-players' and 'norm-bearers'. For a Marxist sociology, men are not just stage performers, they are also fundamentally playwrights and authors. Roles and norms are not scripted by a *deus ex machina*. On the contrary, it is always within the possibility of *real* men living in *real* societies to alter the scripts.

The achievements of Marxist critics such as Lukács and Goldmann in the field of European scholarship are no longer contested. Therefore, my final remarks will be devoted to a prospectus of the possibilities of a Marxist criticism of African literature. Perhaps we should begin by drawing attention to what the emergent Marxist mode of African literary criticism has in fact achieved.

African Marxist criticism has thus far concentrated on the ideological critique of the literature. This critique of the social-world outlook of African writers as represented in their concrete texts, is founded on a firm sociology of the exploiting capitalist essence of the colonial social order. This critique of the history of the new literature reveals that it is the colonial social order that constituted its concrete parameters. Marxist criticism is therefore predicated on the practical necessity of anti-colonial revolution which is anti-imperialist and prospectively socialist. The class constituency of this criticism is unabashedly the proletarian-peasant. From this standpoint, Marxist critics have been able to indicate whether or not the conceptual representations and evocative images which infuse the social universe imagined in a writer's poem, story or play, are progressive, reactionary or reformist. They do not, like bourgeois critics, reach these judgements by an abstract a- historical universalism. On the contrary, their materialist premise and their dialectical method has led Marxist critics to show that African literary movements such as Negritude were in the historical situation of their emergence, progressive tendencies. Today, the development of classes and class struggle within Africa in the context of the international imperialist order has qualitatively transformed the effects of these literary ideologies into their opposite. Negritude today has an attractive reactionary purpose for many ruling circles in African states.

The problem of universalism that has plagued bourgeois criticism has generally been solved by reference to proletarian internationalism. This, for example, is one of the thrusts of the theoretical essays of Ngugi wa Thiong'o in *Homecoming*. Bourgeois African criticism lays emphasis on the analysis of 'form' as its special province of distinction in African literary studies. Yet its analysis of *form* (which is only vaguely defined) does not go beyond the itemization of technique, the tracing of Euro-American parallels and, in novelistic and dramatic literature, the judging of the appropriateness of the language of a character. But Marxist critics have also attended to this issue of formal structures. Characterization, which is crucial to literature, has been an especial focus. The Marxist concern for characterization goes beyond a mere descriptive reproduction of the surface material into a critique of the class representations. Marxist critics have not seen the *imagined* characters simply as free-floating individuals. On the contrary, the characters who populate a writer's fictional universe also belong to social classes. And it was a Marxist-oriented critic, Ngugi, who first drew attention to the fact that one of the problems of Soyinka's literature, was the unreal face-lessness of his working-class characters. Since Marxists hold that the working masses are the true makers of history, the images of the masses contained in literature are crucial signals of a writer's political standpoint.

Thus, in a work like Achebe's *A Man of the People*, Nigerian critics have often pointed out the significance of the writer's silence on the 1964 General Strike of the workers. Instead, workers and peasants are represented as clowns steeped in the bourgeois culture of corruption, although in real Nigerian life, they have no structural opportunities to receive bribes. These are some of the real structural weaknesses of the book. It is these, rather than its supposed 'journalism', which vitiate the artistic achievement.

However, criticism of African literature, bourgeois and Marxist, has not investigated some of the other issues which bourgeois sociological criticism elsewhere has normally thrived on. I refer here to what Terry Eagleton, in a negative context, has described as the 'means of literary production, distribution and exchange in a particular society – how books are published, the social composition of their authors and audiences, levels of literacy, the social determinants of "taste"'.[25]

In our view, these topics are important for rigorous study in Africa. First, the very sociality of literature requires that criticism go beyond the literary text to include the very structures of its manufacture. Secondly, in the special circumstances of Africa, where the entire institutional fabric of book publishing, film and record manufacture, is dominated by neo-colonial agencies, studies of their impact on what currently passes for African arts, are urgent. The reactionary ideological impact of this domination which Nkrumah pointed out long ago in his book *Neocolonialism*, was recently borne out by a letter to the Tanzanian *Daily News* during a controversy on films. This particular letter wondered why 'Kung-Fu' films, etc., popular with the Dar es Salaam audiences, were being condemned.

This kind of situation shows that when Marxist sociologists study the media and the audiences, their studies must go beyond mere empiricist fact-finding. They must be guided by the necessity to create alternative democratic structures where the masses can become creators rather than passive consumers of art. Post-Cultural Revolution China has shown this to be a practical possibility in the arts. And if African examples were needed, the traditions of *communal* artistic creation and criticism of pre-colonial and pre-class oral literatures show us what was achieved by our forebears before 'the rain began to beat' *the masses*.

Notes

1   Mao Tse-Tung 'Talks at the Yenan Forum on Literature and Art,' May, 1942, in Mao Tse-Tung *On Literature and Art*, Foreign Language Press, Peking, 1967, p. 25.
2   Frantz Fanon, *The Wretched of the Earth*, Grove Press, Inc., New York, 1968, p. 41.
3   Aimé Césaire, 'The Man of Culture and His Responsibilities', *Présence Africaine*, Nos 24–5, February–May 1959, p. 127.
4   See Omafume F. Onoge, 'The Crisis of Consciousness In Modern African Literature: A Survey', in *Canadian Journal of African Studies*, Vol. VIII, No. 2, 1974, pp. 385–410. This essay has been reprinted in this book.
5   Chinua Achebe, 'The Novelist as Teacher', in Chinua Achebe's *Morning Yet On Creation Day*, Heinemann, London, 1974.
6   Omafume F. Onoge, 'The Possibilities of a Radical Sociology of African Literature: Tentative Notes', in Donatus Nwoga, ed., *Literature and Modern West African Culture*, Ethiope Publishing Corporation, Benin, 1978, pp. 90–6.
7   Dan Izevbaye, 'Criticism and Literature in Africa', in Christopher Heywood, ed., *Perspectives on African Literature*, Heinemann, London, 1971, p. 30.
8   Dan Izevbaye, 'The State of Criticism in African Literature', in *African Literature Today* (No. 7, Focus on Criticism), 1975, p. 16.
9   Ibid., p. 16.
10 Eustace Palmer, *An Introduction to the African Novel*, Heinemann, London, 1972, p. 129.
11 Ibid., p. 154.
12 Abiola Irele, in C. Heywood, ed., op. cit., p. 16.
13 See Terry Eagleton, 'Criticism and Politics: The Work of Raymond Williams', *New Left Review*, No. 95, January–February 1976, pp. 3–23.
14 See for example, Pio Zirimu and Andrew Gurr, eds., *The Black Aesthetic*, East African Literature Bureau, Nairobi, 1973. Several papers in this conference collection confirm this point. Indeed, Grant Kamenju's paper which politicized the topic along Fanonian lines remains isolated in this volume of idealist reification. The journal, *Okike*, edited by Chinua Achebe, has carried several essays seeking an African aesthetic. The Afro-American world of letters has also been involved in this search. Unfortunately, most of their efforts to seek African roots have been marked by a

reliance on the categories of Festac anthropology. For example, Reverend John Mbiti's idealist *African Religions and Philosophy* is very popular in certain Afro-American circles.

15 For a preliminary radical critique of this theatre see, Omafume F. Onoge and G. G. Darah, 'The Retrospective Stage: Some Reflections on the Mythopoeic Tradition at Ibadan', in CH'INDABA, Vol. 3, No. 1, October/December 1977, pp. 52–7.

16 The quoted injunctions are from Lilyan Lagneau-Kesteloot and Dorothy Blair, respectively. A contextual discussion of them is contained in my 'Crisis of Consciousness In Modern African Literature: A Survey', *op. citl.*, pp. 396–7.

17 Biodun Jeyifo, 'Toward A Sociology of African Drama', (mimeo), Dept of English Staff Seminar Paper, University of Ibadan, April 27, 1976.

18 Charles R. Larson, *The Emergence of African Fiction*, Indiana University Press, Bloomington, 1972 (revised edition), p. 280.

19 Larson, of course, in the last paragraph of his book declaims that it would be 'impossible to expect that there could be only one direction for African fiction', p. 282. However, we insist that the general thrust of his text contradicts this caveat. Throughout the work his conception of the Western novel – which, incidently is a-historical – is the contrasting yardstick for the evaluation of the African novel. The evolutionary forms of the Western novel in the hands of bourgeois and anti-bourgeois writers are ignored. (No consideration is given to the fact that Chinese literary history speaks of the novel form at least two centuries before the emergence of the 'Western' novel.)

20 Emmanuel Obiechina, *Culture, Tradition and Society in the West African Novel*, Cambridge University Press, 1975, pp. 265–6.

21 G. Plekhanov, *Unaddressed Letters, Art and Social Life*, Foreign Languages Publishing House, Moscow, 1957 (translated from the Russian by A. Fineberg).
Note: This is a crucial point for Plekhanov in the sections of the book which deal with 'Art and Social Life'. Here is one of his remarks:

I have already said that there is no such thing as a work of art which is entirely devoid of ideas. And I added that not every idea can serve as the foundation of a work of art. An artist can be really inspired only by what is capable of facilitating intercourse among men. The possible limits of such intercourse are not determined by the artist, but by the level of culture attained by the social entity to which he belongs. But in a society divided into classes, they are also determined by the mutual relations of these classes and, moreover, by the phase of development in which each of them happens to be at the time. (p. 187)

22 Biodun Jeyifo, 'Literalism and Reductionism In African Literary Criticism: Further Notes on Literature and Ideology', unpublished manuscript.

23 Anatoly Lunacharsky, *On Literature and Art*, Progress Publishers, Moscow, 1973 (second revised edition).

24 Karl Marx, *Introduction To the Critique of Political Economy.*

25 Terry Eagleton, *Marxism and Literary Criticism*, Methuen & Co. Ltd., London, 1976, p. 2.

Chapter 63

Writers in Politics:
The Power of Words and the Words of Power

Ngugi wa Thiong'O

We cannot pose the problem of native culture without at the same time posing the problem of colonialism for all native cultures today are developing under the peculiar influence of the colonial, semi-colonial and para-colonial situations.

Aimé Césaire

There is a dramatic poem of Léopold Sédar Senghor in which a white man is so overwhelmed by Chaka's power and mastery over language that he exclaims: 'my word, Chaka . . . you are a poet . . . a politician.'

The poet and the politician have certainly many things in common. Both trade in words. Both are created by the same reality of the world around them. Their activity and concern have the same subject and object: human relationships. Imaginative literature, dealing with a people's consciousness, and politics, with the operation of power in society, are reflected in one another and they act on one another.

There is no area of our lives including the very boundaries of our imagination which is not affected by the way that society is organized, by the whole operation and machinery of power: how and by whom that power has been achieved; which class controls and maintains it; and the ends to which power is put. The class in power, for instance, controls not only the productive forces in the community but cultural development as well. The means of life, and how they are produced, exchanged and shared out, and the social institutions that the whole process gives rise to do move men, do profoundly affect the very quality of their lives: how they eat, laugh, play, woo and even make love. They constitute a universe of moral significance, of values and determine the quality of human life and are what imaginative literature is about. The universe is itself simultaneously a product of and a reflection on the material process of living. Its method may entail a refraction of the material process in order to reveal its inner vitality. Thus literature and politics are about living humans, that is to say, actual men and women and children, breathing, eating, crying, laughing, creating, dying, growing, struggling, organizing, people in history of which they are its products, its producers and its analysts.

First published in *Writers in Politics: A Re–Engagement with Issues of Literature and Society*, pp. 67–77. Oxford: James Currey, 1997.

The way power in society is organized can affect writers and their writing in several ways. The writer as a human being is a product of history, of time and space. As a member of society, he belongs to a certain class and he is inevitably a participant in the class struggle of his times. As a writer in a given society, it does make a difference whether he is allowed to write or not; whether what he writes is controlled or not; and whether he is espousing this or that class outlook.

A writer's subject matter is history: the process of a people acting on nature, changing it, and in so doing, acting on and changing themselves. The changing relations of production including power relations is a whole territory of concern to a writer. Politics is hence part and parcel of this literary territory.

The product of a writer's imaginative involvement – what Shakespeare called mirror unto nature – becomes a reflection of society: its economic structure, its class formations, conflicts, contradictions, political and cultural struggles, and its structure of values – particularly the conflict and tensions arising from the antagonism between those which are dying and those which are pointing to the future. Hence literature has often given us more and sharper insights into the moving spirit of an era than all the historical and political documents treating the same moment. The novel in particular, especially in its critical realist tradition, is important in that respect: it pulls apart and it puts together; it is both analytic and synthetic.

The relationship between the poet and politician, or between writers and politics, is particularly important in our situation where our cultures – our literature, music, songs, dances – are developing under the strangulating embrace of western industrial and finance capital and the fierce struggles of our people merely to breathe. The embrace of Western imperialism is total (economic, political, cultural): and of necessity our struggles against it must be total. Literature and writers cannot be exempted from the battlefield.

In Africa the relationship has taken various forms. Often the writer and the politician have been the same person. In the very process of articulating a people's collective consciousness, the writer is led into active political struggles. Léopold Sédar Senghor is a case in point: he was a writer, he is still a writer, who went into active politics, ending up as the President of Senegal. Or the politician steeped in active political struggle takes up the pen as a necessary and a most important adjunct to his involvement. Agostinho Neto[1] is an outstanding poet and politician. For him the gun, the pen and the platform have served the same ends: the total liberation of Angola. But whether actively involved in political struggle or not, many African writers have often found that the very subject matter of their poems and stories has placed them on the wrong side of the ruling cliques. Most South African writers – Dennis Brutus, Ezekiel Mphahlele, Bloke Modisane, Alex la Guma, Mazisi Kunene, Lewis Nkosi – are now in exile, while those who remained, like Can Themba, were slowly strangled to death by the racist atmosphere and system of violent repression. Their books, need I say, have all been banned, and this is not surprising in a nervous fascist outpost of Western imperialism and monopoly capital that once banned *Black Beauty*, the story of a horse, because it might carry the implication of black being beautiful.

Even where the writer has not ordinarily been actively immersed in politics, i.e. in a situation where the writer does not consciously see himself in terms of open political activism either as an individual citizen or in the subject matter of his literary concern, he may well find himself suddenly involved in the hot political power struggles of the day. Christopher Okigbo, who once remarked that he wrote his poems for poets only and that anyway he would rather have lived fully than write, died for the Biafran secessionist cause. The others such as Chinua Achebe, Gabriel Okara, Cyprian Ekwensi, who in an earlier decade of optimism had put Anglophone African literature on the world map, were all active in Biafran politics. The involvement was what prompted Achebe to write thus in 1969:

> It is clear to me that an African creative writer who tries to avoid the big social and political issues of the contemporary Africa will end up being completely irrelevant like that absurd man in the proverb who leaves his house burning to pursue a rat fleeing from the flames[2]

Without minimizing the pertinence of Chinua Achebe's image, there is a sense in which no writer of imaginative literature from the very best to the moderately significant can really avoid the big issues of the day, for literature, to the extent that it is a mirror unto man's nature, must reflect social reality or certain aspects of social reality. How beautifully we get from Shakespeare, Marlowe, Jonson, Rabelais, a feel of sixteenth- and seventeenth-century English and French societies: the emerging empirical spirit, the bourgeois individualism, the mercantilist capitalist spirit struggling against feudalism for the freedom to move and conquer the seas, to colonize and christianize the natives, crying in the same breath: my God, my Gold! Unforgettable too is the frenzy 'the trembling rage' of characters in nineteenth-century Russian fiction reflecting the volcanic rumblings of the peasants' and the workers' struggle against tsarist feudalism and capitalism that later ushered in a new socialist order in the world. On the other hand Jane Austen is often criticized and accused of insulating herself from the big upheavals of her day – but even she unwittingly gives a wonderful picture of a leisurely parasitic landed middle class in early nineteenth-century England. Or Emily Brontë isolating herself in the Yorkshire moors, setting her novel *Wuthering Heights* in the same moors, amidst the local howling wind and rainstorms, but giving us a most incisive examination of the limiting repressive and oppressive ethical values of an industrial bourgeois class with all its suffocating comforts derived from the exploitation of the working class and the people of the colonies.

What is important is not only the writer's honesty and faithfulness in capturing and reflecting the struggles around him, but also his attitude to those big social and political issues. It is not simply a matter of a writer's heroic stand as a social individual – though this is crucial and significant – but the attitudes and the world view embodied in his work and with which he is persuading us to identify vis-à-vis the historical drama his community is undergoing. What we are talking about is whether or not a writer's imaginative leap to grasp reality is aimed at helping, or hindering, the community's struggle for a certain quality of life free from all parasitic exploitative relations. We are talking about the relevance of literature in our daily struggle for the right and security to bread, shelter, clothes and song, the right of a people to the products of their sweat. The extent to which the writer can and will help in not only explaining the world but in changing it will depend on his appreciation of the classes and values that are struggling for a new order, a new society, a more human future, and which classes and values are hindering the birth of the new and the hopeful. And of course it depends on which side he is in these class struggles of his times.

There are, however, two types of writers defined by their attitudes to society. There are those who assume that a society is basically static and stable either because they live in a period when society is generally assumed to be stable or, because cocooned in their class or being prisoners of the propaganda of the dominant class, they become insensitive to basic structural conflicts. Some nineteenth-century English novelists assume such a stability of the basic static structure. Their world is vast, the issues they are dealing with are wide, but the intellectual and moral conflicts do not arise out of an awareness of a changing world – a world constantly in motion, always in the process of transforming itself from one form to another, and hence giving rise to new class alignments and possibilities of new social orders. What interests such writers is just the moral conduct of their characters whatever their class, race or religious origins. Such writers have often the ideal of human conduct to which the different characters approximate with differing degrees of success and failure. At their best, these writers can and do produce a literature of sharp social criticism. But such an attitude to society, such abstraction of human types and moral ideals from their basis in the class structure and class struggle, often gives rise to a literature distinguished for its shallow dive into society and only redeemed from oblivion by those of our critics who have no other critical tools apart from such worn and meaningless phrases as 'human compassion', 'timeless and universal,' etc. Haven't we heard critics who demand of African writers that they stop writing about colonialism, race, colour, exploitation, and simply write about human beings? Such an attitude to society is often the basis of some European writers' mania for man without history – solitary and free – with unexplainable despair and anguish and death as the ultimate truth about the human condition.

But other writers, either because of the nature of the period in which they live, or because of their instinctive or conscious dialectical approach to life and society, do not assume a static stability. The very conduct of their characters is firmly rooted in history and changing social conditions. Being aware of a changing world, great writers like Aeschylus, Shakespeare, Tolstoy, Conrad, Sholokhov, Sembene and Chinua Achebe, place conflicts between peoples in differing classes with differing and often antagonistic conceptions of world order; of who holds, and who should hold power, the ends toward which that power is put, and of the possibilities of a new social order from the womb of the old. The tragic dilemma of Okonkwo and Ezeulu is so profound and encompassing because at the basis of their conduct and decisions are two world orders in irreconcilable conflict: Okonkwo's world of emergent feudalism based on family and partly slave labour and that of European colonial capitalism and imperialism based on racism and ruthless exploitation of African labour. The old classes and social, economic and political order – its entire value structure – are challenged by new classes and a new structure of values. In Joseph Conrad's novel *Nostromo*, set in a fictional Latin American republic the issues are not the simplistic ones of a Christian morality and that of America's Wild West – absolute good (God) versus absolute evil (Satan). Here in this Latin American republic, where British and American mining interests hold power, there is not a universal-once-for-all-time ideal of conduct to which people conform or fail to conform. Here morality, religion, ethics are rooted in class: we can only adequately evaluate the characters' conduct and alienation by recognizing the historical, economic, class and racial basis of conflicting moralities and outlooks. Here, as in Sembene's Africa, is no metaphysical evil versus metaphysical good. Imperialism and the exploitation of the labour power and the natural resources of the colonized peoples by international monopoly capital is at the root of the problems. Hence Conrad's images of coal, ivory, silver that abounds in his novels.

The African writer and Joseph Conrad share the same world and that is why Conrad's world is so familiar. Both have lived in a world dominated by imperialism. They have known Hola camps, My Lai, Algiers, Sharpeville, the Arab mother and child driven from Palestine.

They have seen the bowels of pregnant mothers ripped open; they have witnessed the artistic finesse of the colonial mercenary hewing the bodies of struggling peasants and workers as carcasses fit for the God of profit. They have seen the workings of justice in a social system whose base is capitalism so well described by Shakespeare in King Lear:

> ... Plate sin with gold,
> And the strong lance of justice hurtless breaks;
> Arm it in rags, a pigmy's straw does pierce it.

They have witnessed mercenaries, coups, and they know that Macbeth's bloody dagger is not a figment of imagination from the heated brains of starry-eyed idealists. Have they not seen imperialist dogs of war and oppression bathe in the blood of the people in neo-colonial regimes and cry out in glee:

> How many ages hence
> Shall this our lofty scene be acted over,
> In states unborn and accents yet unknown.

Theirs is a world in which societies are demonstrably changing much of the time, with the proletariat and the poor peasants with a section of the petty bourgeoisie struggling against a combination of local big business and foreign business interests and against the political and cultural system protecting the status quo. The social energy – heat and light – from the economic, political and cultural struggle between the various classes finds itself transmitted into the writers' work. The situation, especially in the colonial era, compelled many writers into a progressive ideological stance: they were swept off their feet as it were by the dynamic force and vision of a total national liberation. Hence much of African literature was anti-colonialist and anti-imperialist.

A substantial amount of this writing, then, was against a background of hope for better and more egalitarian black organized states. But like Conrad – whose bourgeois position limited his vision making him, for instance, unable to condemn British imperialism or rid himself of the very racism he correctly saw as inherent in colonialism – the African writer's petty-bourgeois position could not allow him to see the nature of imperialism and the need for a continuous class struggle against it and its local comprador allies. I myself can remember writing in 1962 how I looked forward to the day when all the preoccupation of African writers with colonial problems and politics would be over and we would all sit back and poke sophisticated irony at one another and laugh at ourselves, whatever that was supposed to mean: we would then indulge in the luxury of comedies of social manners (what a philistine hollow bourgeois ideal!) or explore the anguished world of lonely individuals abstracted from time and actual circumstances.

Often we never moved beyond blackness, beyond the racial aspect of the struggle for national liberation from colonial rule, to see what was basic to colonial oppression: the fact that we were part and parcel of a world-wide system of production called capitalism; the fact that the colonial, political and cultural invasion was to make the conquest in the economic sphere more entrenched and permanent; and therefore the African people's anti-colonial struggle was more than a racial struggle. It was also, and more fundamentally, a struggle against that system that for four hundred years had devastated a continent. It was

Africa that fed capitalism from its beginnings in slavery, through the colonial phase to the current phase of neo-colonialism with all the intricate tubes leading from Africa to the metropolis of the Western world.

Even today the African writer has often refused to see that values, cultures, politics, and economics are all tied up together, that we cannot call for meaningful African values without joining in the struggle against all the classes that feed on a system that continues to distort those very values. We must join the proletarian and the poor peasant struggles against the parasitism of the comprador bourgeois, the landlords and chiefs, the big business African classes that at the same time act in unison and concert with foreign interests.

The fundamental opposition in Africa today is between imperialism and capitalism, on the one hand, and national liberation and socialism, on the other: between a small class of native 'haves', which is tied to international capital, and the masses of the people. Within that fundamental antagonistic contradiction is the opposition between the urban and the rural, between relatively highly developed pockets of the country and others close to the stone ages. The cut-throat competition between the emergent native bourgeoisie of the various nationalities who try to identify their interests as the interests of the whole ethnic group (nationality) can often blind us to these more real, more basic contradictions which link us to the class struggles in Asia, Latin America, Europe and America.

Faced with these contradictions, the African writer can often retreat into individualism, mysticism and formalism: such an African writer, who often can see the shortcomings of the neo-colonial economies, the consequent distortion of values, the fascism in so many neo-colonial ruling classes, is at the same time scared of encountering socialism as an alternative social system. He is scared of the possibility of the working class and the peasantry controlling the productive forces and consequently of their seizure and exercise of political power as the only route to that control of the means of production. To avoid the two alternatives – the continuation of a neo-colonial status quo and the violent overturning of that status quo by the masses – he makes a cult of Africanness, of Blackism, of the dignity of the African past, of the African approach to problems; or he simply becomes cynical and laughs at everything equally; at capitalism and its exploitative and oppressive social system and at the struggles of the people for total liberation; or he may condemn every effort and everything – gains and losses in the struggle – in the name of abstract humanism and abstract universalism, without seeing that free, unfettered human intercourse is impossible within capitalistic structures and imperialism; that true humanism is not possible without the subjection of the economy, of the means of production (land, industries, the banks, etc.) to the total ownership and control by the people; that for as long as there are classes – classes defined by where or how the various people stand in relation to the production process – a truly human contact in love, joy, laughter and creative fulfillment in labour, will never be possible. We can only talk meaningfully of class love, class joy, class marriage, class families, class culture, class values.

What the African writer is called upon to do is not easy: it is demanded of him that he recognize the global character of imperialism and the global character and dimension of the forces struggling against it to build a new world. He must reject, repudiate, and negate his roots in the native bourgeoisie and its spokesmen, and find his true creative links with the pan-African masses over the earth in alliance with all the socialistic forces of the world. He must of course be very particular, very involved in a grain of sand, but must also see the world past, present, and future in that grain. He must write with all the vibrations and tremors of the struggles of all the working people in Africa, America, Asia and Europe behind him. Yes, he must actively support and in his writing reflect the struggle of the African working class and its class allies for the total liberation of their labour power. Yes, his work must show commitment, not to abstract notions of justice and peace, but the actual struggle of the African peoples to seize power and hence be in a position to control all the forces of production to lay the only correct basis for real peace and real justice.

In conclusion, I would like to single out one African writer who exemplifies the kind of commitment that I have been talking about. He is Sembene Ousmane, a Senegalese, who gave us *God's Bits of Wood*. Read it – an account of West African workers' struggle in 1948 – and you'll see how he analyses and then synthesizes: how he is involved in one particular without losing sight of the links to other particulars. One feels that he is with the people, that it is their fate and their eventual triumph in which he is interested. He also wrote a poem called 'Fingers' and it illustrates the kind of vision informing his work:

> Fingers, skilful at sculpture
> At modelling figures on marble
> At translation of thoughts
> Fingers that would impress,
> Fingers of artists.
> Fingers, thick and heavy
> That dig and plough the soil
> And open it up for sowing,
> And move us,
> Fingers of land tillers.
> A finger holding a trigger
> An eye intent on a target finger
> Men at the very brink
> Of their lives, at the mercy of their finger
> The finger that destroys life.
> The finger of a soldier.
> Across the rivers and languages
> Of Europe and Asia
> Of China and Africa,
> Of India and the Oceans,
> Let us join our fingers to take away
> All the power of their finger
> Which keeps humanity in mourning[3]

Unless we as African writers embrace such a vision – a vision anchored in the struggles of the people – we shall succumb to self-despair, cynicism and individualism, or else we will become mesmerized by superficial bourgeois progress which, in the words of Karl Marx, has never been possible without dragging individuals and peoples through blood and dirt, through misery and degradation. To borrow words from the same author, bourgeois progress resembles that hideous pagan idol who would drink nectar but from the skulls of the slain.

The reign of that pagan idol in Africa is doomed. African writers must be with the people in burying the imperialist idol and his band of white and black angels, for ever.

Notes

1   In 1976 the President of the People's Republic of Angola.
2   Chinua Achebe, 'The African Writer and the Biafran Cause', *Morning Yet on Creation Day* (Heine-
     mann, London, 1975), p. 78.
3   Sembene Ousmane, 'Fingers' quoted in Lotus Awards 1971, published by the Permanent Bureau of
     Afro-Asian Writers.

Chapter 64

National Liberation and Culture

Amilcar Cabral

[. . .]

When Goebbels, the brain behind Nazi propaganda, heard the word 'culture', he reached for his pistol. This shows that the Nazis – who were and are the most tragic expression of imperialism and of its thirst for domination – even if they were all degenerates like Hitler, had a clear idea of the value of culture as a factor of resistance to foreign domination.

History teaches us that, in certain circumstances, it is very easy for the foreigner to impose his domination on a people. But it likewise teaches us that, whatever the material aspects of this domination, it can be maintained only by the permanent and organized repression of the cultural life of the people concerned. Implantation of domination can be ensured definitively only by physical elimination of a significant part of the dominated population.

In fact, to take up arms to dominate a people is, above all, to take up arms to destroy, or at least to neutralize and to paralyse their cultural life. For as long as part of that people can have a cultural life, foreign domination cannot be sure of its perpetuation. At a given moment, depending on internal and external factors determining the evolution of the society in question, cultural resistance (indestructible) may take on new (political, economic and armed) forms, in order fully to contest foreign domination.

The ideal for foreign domination, whether imperialist or not, lies in this alternative: either to eliminate practically all the population of the dominated country, thereby excluding the possibilities of a cultural resistance; or to succeed in imposing itself without damage to the culture of the dominated people, that is, to harmonize economic and political domination of these people with their cultural personality.

The first hypothesis implies genocide of the indigenous population and creates a void which empties foreign domination of its content and its object: the dominated people. The second hypothesis has not, until now, been confirmed by history. The broad experience of mankind enables us to postulate that it has no practical viability: it is not possible to

First published in *Unity and Struggle: Speeches and Writings*, trans. Michael Wolfers, pp. 139–47 and 149–50. London: Heinemann, 1980.

harmonize the economic and political domination of a people, whatever the degree of their social development, with the preservation of their cultural personality.

In order to escape this alternative – which might be called the *dilemma of cultural resistance* – imperialist colonial domination has tried to create theories which, in fact, are only crude formulations of racism, and which, in practice, are translated into a permanent state of siege for the aboriginal populations, on the basis of racist dictatorship (or democracy).

This, for example, is the case with the supposed theory of progressive *assimilation* of native populations, which is no more than a more or less violent attempt to deny the culture of the people in question. The unmistakable failure of this 'theory', put into practice by several colonial powers, including Portugal, is the most evident proof of its non-viability, if not of its inhuman character. It reaches the highest degree of absurdity in the Portuguese case, where Salazar asserts that *Africa does not exist*.

This is likewise the case with the supposed theory of *apartheid*, created, applied and developed on the basis of the economic and political domination of the people of southern Africa by a racist minority, with all the crimes against humanity that this entails. The practice of *apartheid* takes the form of unrestrained exploitation of the labour force of the African masses, incarcerated and cynically repressed in the largest concentration camp mankind has ever known.

National liberation, an act of culture

These examples give a measure of the drama of foreign domination in the face of the cultural reality of the dominated people. They also show the close, dependent and reciprocal connexion existing between the *cultural factor* and the *economic* (and political) *factor* in the behaviour of human societies. In fact, at every moment of the life of a society (open or closed), culture is the result, with more or less awakened consciousness, of economic and political activities, the more or less dynamic expression of the type of relations prevailing within that society, on the one hand between man (considered individually or collectively) and nature, and, on the other hand, among individuals, groups of individuals, social strata or classes.

The value of culture as an element of resistance to foreign domination lies in the fact that culture is the vigorous manifestation, on the ideological or idealist level, of the material and historical reality of the society that is dominated or to be dominated. Culture is simultaneously the fruit of a people's history and a determinant of history, by the positive or negative influence it exerts on the evolution of relations between man and his environment and among men or human groups within a society, as well as between different societies. Ignorance of this fact might explain the failure of several attempts at foreign domination as well as the failure of some national liberation movements.

Let us examine what *national liberation* is. We shall consider this phenomenon of history in its contemporary context, that is national liberation in the face of imperialist domination. The latter is, as we know, distinct both in form and content from preceding types of foreign domination (tribal, military-aristocratic, feudal and capitalist domination in the age of free competition).

The principal characteristic, common to every kind of imperialist domination, is the denial of the historical process of the dominated people by means of violent usurpation of the freedom of the process of development of the productive forces. Now, in a given society, the level of development of the productive forces and the system of social utilization of these forces (system of ownership) determine the *mode of production*. In our view, the mode of production, whose contradictions are manifested with more or less intensity through class struggle, is the principal factor in the history of any human whole, and the level of productive forces is the true and permanent motive force of history.

For every society, for every human group considered as a dynamic whole, the level of the productive forces indicates the status reached by the society and each of its components in the face of nature, its capacity to act or react consciously in relation to nature. It indicates and conditions the type of material relations (expressed objectively or subjectively) existing between man and his environment.

The mode of production, which at every stage of history represents the result of the ceaseless search for a dynamic equilibrium between the level of productive forces and the system of social utilization of these forces, indicates the status reached by a given society and each of its components before itself and before history. In addition, it indicates and conditions the type of material relations (expressed objectively or subjectively) existing between the various elements or groups which constitute the society in question: relations and types of relations between man and nature, between man and his environment; relations and types of relations between the individual or collective components of a society. To speak about this is to speak of history but it is likewise to speak of culture.

Culture, whatever the ideological or idealist characteristics of its expression, is thus an essential element of the history of a people. Culture is, perhaps, the resultant of this history just as the flower is the resultant of a plant. Like history, or because it is history, culture has as its material base the level of the productive forces and the mode of production. Culture plunges its roots into the humus of the material reality of the environment in which it develops, and it reflects the organic nature of the society, which may be more or less influenced by external factors. History enables us to know the nature and extent of the imbalances and the conflicts (economic, political and social) that characterize the evolution of a society. Culture enables us to know what dynamic syntheses have been formed and set by social awareness in order to resolve these conflicts at each stage of evolution of that society, in the search for survival and progress.

Just as occurs with the flower in a plant, the capacity (or responsibility) for forming and fertilizing the germ which ensures the continuity of history lies in culture, and the germ simultaneously ensures the prospects for evolution and progress of the society in question. Thus it is understood that imperialist domination, denying to the dominated people their own historical process, necessarily denies their cultural process. It is further understood why the exercise of imperialist domination, like all other foreign domination, for its own security requires cultural oppression and the attempt at direct or indirect destruction of the essential elements of the culture of the dominated people.

Study of the history of liberation struggles shows that they have generally been preceded by an upsurge of cultural manifestations, which progressively harden into an attempt, successful or not, to assert the cultural personality of the dominated people by an act of denial of the culture of the oppressor. Whatever the conditions of subjection of a people to foreign domination and the influence of economic, political and social factors in the exercise of this domination, it is generally within the cultural factor that we find the germ of challenge which leads to the structuring and development of the liberation movement.

In our view, the foundation of national liberation lies in the inalienable right of every people to have their own history, whatever the formulations adopted in international law. The aim of national liberation is therefore to regain this right, usurped by imperialist domination, namely: the liberation of the process of development of the national productive forces. So national liberation exists when, and only when the national productive forces have been completely freed from all kinds of foreign domination. The liberation of productive forces and consequently of the ability freely to determine the mode of production most appropriate to the evolution of the liberated people, necessarily opens up new prospects for the cultural process of the society in question, by returning to it all its capacity to create progress.

A people who free themselves from foreign domination will not be culturally free unless, without underestimating the importance of positive contributions from the oppressor's culture and other cultures, they return to the upwards paths of their own culture. The latter is nourished by the living reality of the environment and rejects harmful influences as much as any kind of subjection to foreign cultures. We see therefore that, if imperialist domination has the vital need to practise cultural oppression, national liberation is necessarily an *act of culture*.

The class character of culture

On the basis of what has just been said, we may regard the liberation movement as the organized political expression of the struggling people's culture. Thus the leadership of that movement must have a clear notion of the value of culture in the framework of struggle and a profound knowledge of the culture of their people, whatever the level of economic development.

Nowadays, it has become a commonplace to assert that every people has its culture. The time is past when, in an attempt to perpetuate the domination of peoples, culture was regarded as an attribute of privileged peoples or nations and when, out of ignorance of bad faith, culture was confused with technical skill, if not with the colour of one's skin or the shape of one's eyes. The liberation movement, as representative and defender of the culture of the people, must be conscious of the fact that, whatever the material conditions of the society it represents, the society is the bearer and the creator of culture. The liberation movement must in addition understand the mass character, the popular character of culture, which is not and could not be an attribute of one sector or of some sectors of society.

In the thorough analysis of social structure which every liberation movement must be able to make, by virtue of the imperatives of struggle, the cultural characteristics of each social category have a place of prime importance. For, while culture has a mass character, it is not uniform, it is not evenly developed in all sectors of society. The attitude of each social category towards the struggle is dictated by its economic interests, but is also profoundly influenced by its culture. We may even admit that the differences in cultural levels explain the differing behaviour towards the liberation movement of individuals within the same socio-economic category. It is at this point that culture reaches its full significance for each individual: understanding and integration in his environment, identification with the fundamental problems and aspirations of society, acceptance of the possibility of change in the direction of progress.

In the specific conditions of our country – and we should say of Africa – the horizontal and vertical distribution of levels of culture is somewhat complex. In fact, from the villages to the towns, from one ethnic group to another, from the peasant to the artisan or to the more or less assimilated indigenous intellectual, from one social class to another, and even, as we have said, from individual to individual within the same social category, there are significant variations in the quantitative and qualitative level of culture. It is a question of prime importance for the liberation movement to take these facts into consideration.

In the societies with a horizontal structure, like the Balanta society, for example, the distribution of cultural levels is more or less uniform, variations being linked solely to individual characteristics and to age groups. In the societies with a vertical structure, like that of the Fula for example, there are important variations from the top to the bottom of the social pyramid. This shows once more the close connexion between the cultural factor and the economic factor, and also explains the differences in the overall or sectoral behaviour of these two ethnic groups towards the liberation movement.

It is true that the multiplicity of social and ethnic categories somewhat complicates the determining of the role of culture in the liberation movement. But it is vital not to lose sight of the decisive significance of the *class character* of culture in development of the liberation struggle, even in the case when a category is or appears to be still embryonic.

The experience of colonial domination shows that, in an attempt to perpetuate exploitation, the colonizer not only creates a whole system of repression of the cultural life of the colonized people, but also provokes and develops the cultural alienation of a part of the population, either by supposed assimilation of indigenous persons, or by the creation of a social gulf between the aboriginal elites and the mass of the people. As a result of this process of division or of deepening the divisions within the society, it follows that a considerable part of the population notably the urban or peasant 'petty bourgeoisie', assimilates the colonizer's mentality, and regards itself as culturally superior to the people to which it belongs and whose cultural values it ignores or despises. This situation, characteristic of the majority of colonized intellectuals, is crystallized to the extent that the social privileges of the assimilated or alienated group are increased with direct implications for the behaviour towards the liberation movement by individuals in this group. A spiritual reconversion – of mentalities – is thus seen to be vital for their true integration in the liberation movement. Such reconversion – *re-Africanization* in our case – may take place before the struggle, but is completed only during the course of the struggle, through daily contact with the mass of the people and the communion of sacrifices which the struggle demands.

We must, however, take into consideration the fact that, faced with the prospect of political independence, the ambition and opportunism from which the liberation movement generally suffers may draw into the struggle individuals who have not been reconverted. The latter, on the basis of their level of education, their scientific or technical knowledge, and without losing any of their class cultural prejudices, may attain the highest positions in the liberation movement. On the cultural as well as the political level vigilance is therefore vital. For in the specific and highly complex circumstances of the process of the phenomenon of the liberation movements, all that glitters is not necessarily gold: political leaders – even the most famous – may be culturally alienated.

But the class character of culture is still more noticeable in the behaviour of privileged groups in the rural environment, notably where ethnic groups with a vertical social structure are concerned, where nevertheless the influences of assimilation or cultural alienation are nil or virtually nil. This is the case of the Fula ruling class, for example. Under colonial domination, the political authority of this class (traditional chiefs, noble families, religious leaders) is purely nominal, and the mass of the people are aware of the fact that the real authority lies with and is wielded by the colonial administrators. However, the ruling class retains in essence its cultural authority over the mass of the people in the group, with very important political implications.

Knowing this reality, colonialism, which represses or inhibits significant cultural expression at the grass roots on the part of the mass of the people, supports and protects the prestige and cultural influence of the ruling class at the summit. It installs chiefs whom it trusts and who are more or less accepted by the population, gives them various material privileges including education for their eldest children, creates chiefdoms where they did not exist, establishes and develops cordial relations with religious leaders, builds mosques, organizes journeys to Mecca, etc. Above all, by means of the repressive organs of colonial administration, it ensures the economic and social privileges of the ruling class in relation to the mass of the people. All this does not remove the possibility that, among these ruling classes, there may be individuals or groups of individuals who join the liberation movement, although less frequently than in the case of the assimilated 'petty bourgeoisie'. Several traditional and religious leaders join the struggle from the start or in the course of its unfolding, making an enthusiastic contribution to the cause of liberation. But there again vigilance is vital: holding strongly onto their class cultural prejudices, individuals in this category generally see in the liberation movement the only valid means for using the sacrifices of the mass of the people to eliminate colonial oppression of their own class and hence to re-establish their complete cultural and political domination over the people.

In the general framework of challenge to imperialist colonial domination and in the specific circumstances to which we are referring, it can be seen that among the oppressor's most faithful allies are found some senior civil servants and assimilated intellectuals from the liberal professions, and a significant number of representatives of the ruling class in the rural areas. This fact gives some measure (negative or positive) of the influence of culture and of cultural prejudices on the question of the political option towards the liberation movement. It likewise shows the limits of this influence and the supremacy of the class factor in behaviour of the various social categories. The senior civil servant or the assimilated intellectual, characterized by total cultural alienation, identifies in the political option with the traditional or religious leader, who has experienced no significant foreign cultural influence. For these two categories set above all factors or demands of a cultural nature – and against the aspirations of the people – their own economic and social privileges, their *class interests*. That is a truth which the liberation movement cannot ignore, on pain of betraying the economic, political, social and cultural aims of the struggle.

Towards a definition of national culture

As on the political level and without minimizing the positive contribution which privileged classes or strata may make to the struggle, the liberation movement must, on the cultural level, base its action on popular culture, whatever the diversity of cultural levels in the country. The cultural challenge to colonial domination – the primary phase of the liberation movement – can be effectively envisaged only on the basis of the culture of the mass of workers in the countryside and the towns, including the (revolutionary) nationalist 'petty bourgeoisie', which has been re-Africanized or is disposed towards a cultural reconversion. Whatever the complexity of this cultural panorama at the base, the liberation movement must be capable of distinguishing within it the essential from the secondary, the positive from the negative, the progressive from the reactionary in order to characterize the key line of progressive definition of *national culture*.

For culture to play the important role which falls to it in the framework of development of the liberation movement, the movement must be able to conserve the positive cultural values of every well-defined social group, of every category, and to achieve the *confluence* of these values into the stream of struggle, giving them a new dimension – the *national dimension*. Faced with such a necessity, the liberation struggle is, above all, a struggle as much for the conservation and survival of the cultural values of the people as for the harmonizing and development of these values within a national framework.

The political and moral unity of the liberation movement and of the people it represents and leads implies the achievement of the cultural unity of the decisive social categories for the struggle. This unity take the form on the one hand of total indentification of the movement with the environmental reality and with the problems and fundamental aspirations of the people and on the other hand of progressive cultural identification of the various social categories which take part in the struggle. The latter process must harmonize divergent interests, resolve contradictions and define common aims in the search for liberty and progress. If broad strata of the population become aware of these aims and this is shown in determination in the face of all the difficulties and all the sacrifices, it is a great political and moral victory. The same result is likewise a decisive cultural achievement for the further development and success of the liberation movement.

[. . .]

The dynamic of culture

Obviously, this reality constitutes a motive for pride and stimulus for those who struggle for the freedom and progress of African peoples. But it is important not to lose sight of the fact that no culture is a perfect, finished whole. Culture, like history, is necessarily an expanding and developing phenomenon. Even more important, we must bear in mind that the fundamental characteristic of culture is its close, dependent and reciprocal connexion with the economic and social reality of the environment, with the level of productive forces and the mode of production of the society which created it.

Culture, as the fruit of history, reflects at all times the material and spiritual reality of the society, of man-the- individual and man-the social-being, faced with conflicts which set them against nature and the imperatives of life in common. It follows from this that any culture contains essential and secondary elements, strengths and weaknesses, virtues, defects, positive and negative aspects, factors for progress and stagnation or for regression. It follows likewise that culture – a creation of the society and a synthesis of the checks and balances society devises to resolve the conflicts that characterize it at each stage of history – is a social reality independent of men's will, the colour of their skin or the shape of their eyes.

A profound analysis of cultural reality removes the supposition that there can be continental or racial cultures. This is because, as with history, culture develops in an uneven process, at the level of a continent, a 'race' or even a society. The co-ordinates of culture like those of any developing phenomenon, vary in space and time, whether they be material (physical) or human (biological and social). The fact of recognizing the existence of common and special traits in the cultures of African peoples, independently of the colour of their skin, does not necessarily imply that one and only one culture exists on the continent. In the same way that from the economic and political point of view one can note the existence of various Africas, so there are also various African cultures.

Without any doubt, underestimation of the cultural values of African peoples, based upon racist feelings and the intention of perpetuating exploitation by the foreigner, has done much harm to Africa. But in the face of the vital need for progress, the following factors or behaviour would be no less harmful to her: unselective praise; systematic exaltation of virtues without condemning defects; blind acceptance of the values of the culture without considering what is actually or potentially negative, reactionary or regressive; confusion between what is the expression of an objective and historical material reality and what appears to be a spiritual creation or the result of a special nature; absurd connexion of artistic creations, whether valid or not, to supposed racial characteristics; and finally non-scientific or a scientific critical appreciation of the cultural phenomenon.

The important thing is not to waste time in more or less hair-splitting debates on the specificity or non-specificity of African cultural values, but to look upon these values as a conquest by a part of mankind for the common heritage of all mankind, achieved in one or several phases of its evolution. The important thing is to proceed to critical analysis of African cultures in the light of the liberation movement and the demands of progress – in the light of this new stage in the history of Africa. We may be aware of its value in the framework of universal civilization, but to compare its value with that of other cultures, not in order to decide its superiority or its inferiority, but to determine, within the general framework of the struggle for progress, what contribution African culture has made and must make and contributions it can or must receive.

The liberation movement must, as we have said, base its action on thorough knowledge of the culture of the people and be able to assess the elements of this culture at their true worth, as well as the different levels it reaches in each social category. It must likewise be able to distinguish within the totality of the people's cultural values the essential and secondary, the positive and negative, the progressive and reactionary, the strengths and weaknesses. This is necessary by virtue of the demands of the struggle and in order to be able to centre its action on the essential without forgetting the secondary, to instigate development of positive and progressive elements and to fight, with subtlety but strictness, negative and reactionary elements; finally so that it can make effective use of strengths and remove weaknesses, or transform them into strengths.

[. . .]

Chapter 65

Concerning National Culture

Agostinho Neto

Text of a speech by Comrade Agostinho Neto, President of the MPLA – Workers Party and of the People's Republic of Angola, and President of the Board of the General Assembly of the Angolan Writers Union. The address was delivered on January 8, 1979 on the occasion of the investiture of the governing body of the Angolan Writers' Union for the biennium 1979/1980.

Comrades and Dear Colleagues

Today brings to an end one more process in the life of the Angolan Writers' Union, an action which, after duly held elections, culminates with the installation of the new governing bodies.

A period of activities is about to begin for all writers with the installation of officers elected on December 29, 1978. And I hope that in March of 1981[1] we will be able to take very positive account of this period which promises to be one of great prospects and production.

The directorship of our Union has made every effort to dynamize literary production at a time when there still exists some confusion in content about an Angolan, African, and universal future for literature and the political necessity of nationalism, or about the future of the writer's political activities and politics itself.

Thus, the task that lies before the new officers will not be merely one of administrative responsibilities, but also one of analysis and criticism. It will not be an easy task. I believe that we will soon open debate to the assessment of our work within the true context of the Angolan Nation or, better yet, of the Angolan People.

Therefore, in the name of the Board of the General Assembly it gives me great pleasure to congratulate the elected executive body of the present directorship, which has before it a grand task to perform in the dynamization of Angolan culture. May their work go well.

I think it necessary to talk about culture in general before dealing with literature in particular. Let us take advantage of this excellent opportunity to examine some essential aspects of our culture.

First published in *Ideologies and Literature* II. 10 (Sept.–Oct. 1979): 12–15.

Fortunately, among Angolan intellectuals some hesitation and doubts have already been raised as to whether Portuguese culture, which did serve some Angolans who were detached from their own people, is or is not that which should be presented as the cultural emanation of the Angolan people. Doubts lead to affirmation.

Obviously, culture cannot be inscribed in chauvinism, nor can it avoid the dynamism of life. Culture evolves with material conditions and at each stage it corresponds to a form of expression and of concretization of cultural acts. Culture results from the material situation and from the state of social development.

In the Angolan context cultural expression results, if not from imitation, at least, for the time being, from the effects of centuries of acculturation. This acculturation has claimed to reflect the material evolution of the people who, after being independent, became submissive and completely dependent, and then became independent again under new conditions.

We must turn to our own reality, without chauvinism and without denying our universalist calling. Cultural chauvinism is as detrimental as was the concept of *proletkult* which emerged right after the Revolution of October and which Lenin so vigorously opposed. Lenin insisted that the Soviet nation, for the elaboration of a new socialist culture aimed at the masses, should necessarily find fulfillment in and take advantage of its cultural heritage. Later on, of course, the concept of *socialist realism* also proved to be detrimental.

Today, the culture of the Angolan people is composed of fragments that extend from the assimilated urban areas to rural areas where European assimilation had only superficial effects. And because capital cities like ours,[2] overgrown with bureaucracy, exert a magic influence on the rest of the Country, there is a tendency to imitate. This tendency to imitate is readily apparent in the cultural realm. Thus, the Angolan Writers Union has a special responsibility. Both the responsibility and the task are enormous. Where to begin? Or, how to continue?

If my esteemed comrades and colleagues will permit me, I will say that we should not fall into fixed patterns or stereotypes like those of the *socialist realist* theorists. On a par with our nationalist capacities, we have to intervene in such a way as to join with the rest of the world even as we go about laying claim to our national reality.

In our initial phase, and from the cultural point of view, it is necessary to analyze and not indulge in mechanical adaptations. It is necessary to analyze reality profoundly and to utilize the benefits of outside techniques only when we are in possession of an Angolan cultural heritage.

To develop our culture does not mean to subject it to other cultures.

We have not yet reached a level of material production that will permit us to dedicate ourselves intensively to spiritual production. We need more time. But, Comrade Writers, that time cannot be taken up with accomodations to imported themes and forms.

Angolan culture is African; above all, it is Angolan. Thus, we have always been offended by the way our people were treated by Portuguese intellectuals.

If it is not yet within our capacity to transform the writer into a professional of literature or cultural research, we are headed in that direction. And some proposals put forth by the Secretariat may be able to be honored during vacation periods or active weekends.

I believe that shortly artists and writers will just be artists and writers, able to devote themselves to problems that I merely touch on now, at the end of this Assembly.

To my way of thinking, however, it will be necessary to go deeply into issues that have to do with the culture of the several Angolan nations, today united into one, and with the effects of acculturation resulting from contacts with European culture. There is likewise a need to reach an agreement on the utilization of agents of culture from the people and to bring about a single comprehensive current of this culture in Angola.

Not unlike the botanist or the zoologist, the scientist or the philosopher, let us bring together all elements. Let us analyze these elements, and let us do it scientifically, and within two years let us present our results. And I am sure that we shall arrive at the conclusion that Angola has its own characteristic culture, one that has resulted from its history, or from its histories.

It would be a good thing (but if it's not possible, we won't cry over it) if during the next Party Congress we could count on the opinions of the Angolan Writers' Union on these matters.

As for other agents of culture, like painters and sculptors and even those who, under present conditions, are charged with the dissemination of information among the casses of the people, I think it only normal procedure for the Angolan Writers Union to assume responsibility in orienting and transmitting ideas. This function is one that the party organisms can only define through texts, and one which the State organism can dynamize by becoming itself the vehicle for the results to be obtained by those engaged in formulating ideas.

I think it necessary that we have the broadest possible debate on ideas, the most extensive efforts in research dynamization, and public presentation of all forms of culture existing in this Country. And we should do this without any preconceived notions of an artistic or linguistic nature.

We need to make it so that the artists of the people can create!

We would need a lot more time to emphasize the fact that in order to speak for the Angolan people it is necessary to be part of the Angolan people. It is not a question of language, but one of national quality.

Dear Colleagues and Comrades,

If we persist in attitudes which are inattentive to our people, we will not be capable of interpreting the ≪spirit≫ of the people as it emerges from study and from lived experience.

To narrate the political experience of the moment is easy, but to arrive at the essence of thought of the several ex-nations is not so easy.

Thus, let us free artists from the incumbrances of the past in order that they gain a broad and comprehensive attitude toward all of our processes of cultural reconstruction.

Once again, we should remind ourselves of the necessity of our commitment to the artists of the people, not for reasons of interpreting folklore, but in order to understand and to interpret culture, and in order for us to be capable of reproducing folklore and culture.

The repetition of the imported aspects of culture is certainly an act of which no one approves. And since I have been called on to express an opinion, I would wish that all that which is directed to our people by the most capable agents of Angolan culture be representative of the people's aspirations and forms of expression.

All of this must be accomplished as it was with respect to independence, as it is with respect to the adoption of the Party's political line, as it is with respect to the forms of carrying out this political line, and, on the other hand, as it is, and will be, with respect to the People's spiritual activity.

May I recommend to my esteemed comrades and colleagues that they take every advantage of those conditions that will permit our writers to work and produce and to observe every nook and cranny of our national geographic sphere as they live the life of the people. Material conditions will always be created to the extent that it is possible, until such time as we can turn writers and artists in general into authentic professionals of culture, linked to socio-political realities.

By the same token, I would hope that by bringing about these conditions we will aid in the formation of an Angolan literature that encompasses political circumstances and, especially, the very life of the People.

Once again, I wish to direct my most sincere congratulations to all those who take office today.

The struggle continues!

Victory is certain!

Notes

1   The next General Assembly of the Angolan Writers Union was scheduled for this date (trans. note).
2   The reference is to Luanda, capital of the People's Republic of Angola (trans. note).

Chapter 66

Masks and Marx:
The Marxist Ethos vis-à-vis African Revolutionary Theory and Praxis

Ayi Kwei Armah

[. . .]

A Global Perspective on Revolution and Communism

The informing motif of this article is the understanding that revolution and communism are phenomena and concepts of universal occurence. They have been known and experienced in different parts of the world during different periods of history. The world's oldest literature speaks of revolutionary changes in social, economic and political structures in a language that is as unambiguous as, though more refinedly poetic than, Marx's explosively alliterative 'expropriation of the expropriators'. Listen to Neferti:

> *I show you the land in turmoil,*
> *What should not be has come to pass.*
> *Men will seize weapons of warfare,*
> *The land will live in uproar.*
> *Men will make arrows of copper,*
> *Will crave blood for bread,*
> *Will laugh aloud at distress.*
> *None will weep over death,*
> *None will wake fasting for death,*
> *Each man's heart is for himself.*
> *Mourning is not done today,*
> *Hearts have quite abandoned it.*

First published in *Présence Africaine* 131 (1985): 37–49.

A man sits with his back turned,
While one slays another.
I show you the son as enemy, the brother as foe,
A man slaying his father (. . .)[1]

[. . .]

The sample could be multiplied indefinitely because there have been numerous revolutionary movements and countless insurrections in history, whether this be the history of Africa, Asia or the Western continents. Maji Maji, Hau Hau, Mau Mau are only the garbled names uncomprehending observers have given to some of Africa's recent insurrectionary movements. Such movements, wherever in the world they occur, tend to become communistic when the revolutionary momentum they generate is married to the ideal of universal justice. Phenomenon and ideal, revolution and communism are both of ancient lineage and the thinking about them in the past was not always chaotic, primitive, unsystematic, unscientific. Nineteenth-century European claims of having discovered or pioneered scientific thinking about revolution and communism deserve to be received with humor, as charming instances of *chutzpah*. It is the same kind of naïve nerve that enabled nineteenth-century European adventurers to claim to be the discoverers of rivers, mountains, waterfalls etc., to all of which these self-styled discoverers had literally to be led by people to whom the discoveries were old, everyday realities and commonplaces. It should not be difficult to recognize in the Western attempt to place a stamp of proprietorship on revolution and communism as just one more expression of the familiar nineteenth-century Western imperialist ethos, this time disguised in intellectual, leftist phrases.

Is there an alternative? Of course. An intelligent – and honest – approach would acknowledge that communism and revolution are universal value-systems and phenomena, universal not in the obtuse liberal sense of something Westerners dream of imposing on the world, but in the sharp common sense of something any unprejudiced searcher may find throughout the world among different peoples.

Let a water image illustrate the point: give communism the image of a central sea of ideas. Into this common sea run tributary rivers from all the world's continents, all the peoples of the world. Call the African rivers Africa's contribution to communism; call the Asian rivers Asia's contribution to communism and call the European rivers Europe's contribution to communism. But do not impose the identity and the name of one continent on the common sea. Worse still, do not impose the identity of one individual from one continent first on all that continent's streams, then on the common sea of human values. To do that would simply be to place obstacles in the way of a rational, universel theory of revolution and communism.

Such a rational, universal theory is desirable for several reasons. From the perspective of Africans, Asians and anyone else not yoked to Eurocentric values, the alternative to communism – capitalism (also known as the Western way of life) – has had roughly five hundred years in which to prove itself. In that time it has demonstrated mainly that it is inherently unjust, anti-human, inefficient, wasteful and destructive. The existing experiments in communist social organization, principally in the USSR, China, Korea and Vietnam, though still relatively young and raw, and though still exhibiting numerous structural faults and stresses, have already achieved convincing results and demonstrated superior potential and performance in comparison with the Western way of life.

Naturally, then, the need for accurate information about revolution and communism is world-wide, genuine and intense. But there are problems blocking the way to a rational, unprejudiced, universal theory. Of these problems some are particularly germane from the point of view of African revolutionary theory and praxis.

Problem 1: Western hegemonism. In principle, Western hegemonism is the tendency of Westerners to minimize or to annihilate the value of non-Western factors, while maximizing or universalizing the value of Western factors. In colonial Africa, this tendency took protean forms: in historiography, for example, Western hegemonism created the fashion according to which the only genuine history was the history of Westerners in Africa; the West was supposed to have brought Africans into the stream of history by colonizing Africa. In religion, African religious practices and beliefs were given negative value as superstitions while Western religious practices and beliefs were defined as the true religion.

Marxism, in its approach to non-Western societies and values, is decidedly colonialist, Western, Eurocentric and hegemonist. Marxists do not present their philosophy as a Western variant of communist theory – which would be the accurate, intelligent and honest thing to do. Marxists in Africa exhibit a desire to institutionalize Western communist hypotheses as the only correct philosophy. Some of the most enthusiastic believers go so far as to pretend to think that Marxism is not just a philosophy but a science, the only correct science of liberation.

Problem 2: The Manichaean stigmatization of non-Western peoples and values. This, when one comes down to it, is just a fancy intellectual way of saying 'white racism'. White, Eurocentric racism is Manichaean in that it splits the world along racial lines, then assigns a negative, lower value to the world's majority of non-Western peoples and a positive, superior value to the Western white minority. The Manichaean assumption here is that the world is generally primitive, savage and barbarian and that, against the world, the West is civilized. This stigmatization is not based on knowledge, on a systematic study of the world's peoples: it is based on ignorance strengthened by dishonest denial. It has nothing to do with science; its source is racial prejudice.

Marxism, in its approach to the non-Western majority of the world's peoples, is demonstrably racist – racist in a prejudiced, determined, dishonest and unintelligent fashion. Western racists hold that Western art is art, but African art is primitive art. Western racists believe that Western poetry is modern poetry when it respects organic units of sense and form, but African poetry, fused with that respect from birth, is only primitive poetry. It makes no difference to the Western racist mind if Western artists imitate African forms and techniques. Because what makes Western art civilized and modern is that it originates in the West; what makes African art primitive is that it originates in Africa. Racism is luxuriously illogical.

That is partly why, for Marx and Engels, communism is modern, civilized and serious when it appears in Europe (even if it has only a spectral form). The same communist phenomenon, when it manifests itself in the non-Western world, is dismissed as primitive communism, even though it appears there not as a fuzzy liberal specter but in human form – vigorous, pushing toward birth in societies familiar for ages with communism as a lost tradition and a real hope, often aborted, sometimes fleetingly realized.

Problem 3: The linear philosophy of history. As a rule, Westerners, whether they are historians or lathe operators, are indoctrinated to think of history as a linear progression with Western society at the head of the line. This linear philosophy is not the result of a scientific, empirical study of the world's history: it is one of the rationalized forms of Western self-esteem, one of the intellectual supports of Western racism.

The Marxist schematization of history conforms to this linear philosophy. It arranges history in such a way that societies move in stages and, of course, it happens that Western societies are at the top. Not only are they at the top of the line: Western societies are destined to stay there and, by the force of their example, to integrate the lower, non-Western societies progressively into their high Western civilization. It bears repeating that this linear Marxist schema is not grounded in empirical evidence gathered from a study of the world's history: it is erected on a flimsy foundation of inadequate data of poor quality, liberally supplemented with the fanciful notions of assorted unsavory collectors – missionaries, anthropologists, imperialist officials, soldiers and mercenaries.

Problem 4: The dogma of autotelic technology. The phrase is hyperbolic but essentially true. The problem arises from the Marxist tendency to give excessive weight to material factors in the processes of history. Such a tendency assumes that materially powerful societies are superior to materially dispossessed societies. The notion that the rich are better than the poor is sacred to devoted domestic servants, but outside ancillary circles it is silly even when disguised in heavy intellectual jargon.

Problem 5: The doctrine of abundance as a precondition for communism. The assumption underlying this doctrine is that only a materially wealthy society can reach that level of economic, social and political democracy that is communism. In part, it was this assumption that misled Marx and Engels to rush down the unwise path of revolutionary prophecy. Marxists in nineteenth-century Europe were sure that the socialist revolution was just around the corner and that it would begin in Western Europe, because Western European societies were richer, more materially developed than non-Western ones. The actual evidence of history contradicts the Marxist prediction. Neither history nor logic supports the prophecy because it is based on an unexamined assumption. Stripped of mystifying jargon, that unexamined assumption is that only rich people can institutionalize democratic sharing as a way of life and that people cannot presume to share power and wealth with others unless they first take care to accumulate overflowing piles of both.

Problem 6: The notion of proletarian rationality. Marxist doctrine makes industrial proletarians the bringers of revolution not only because they are real workers (unlike peasants who are presumably the playboys of the Western world) but also because the nature of the proletarian work process supposedly refines out of their systems such archaic feelings and beliefs as egotism, nationalism and theism, while rationalizing their thinking processes and habits, making them truly modern human beings. That high status once achieved, proletarians are then supposed to recognize their occupational identities as primary and powerful enough to override secondary and tertiary identities. That chain of assumptions leads to the hope that Western proletarians will be mature enough to respond positively to the disingenuous slogan «*Workers of the world, unite: you have nothing to lose but your chains*». So far, the verdict of history is that Western proletarians know they are not workers of the world but workers of Britain, France, Germany and America – Westerners riding on top of the world. If they are chained, they see their chains as golden chains: so far from aspiring to lose them, they want more. The doctrine is a good example of liberal fuzz, and Marx misread the psychology of the Western industrial proletariat just as seriously as he undervalued the importance of cultural, non-material factors in the shaping of history.

Problem 7: The dogma of peasant stupidity. This is a corollary of Problem 6. Marx and Engels were convinced that peasants were stupid. There is no evidence that they knew enough peasants at first hand to reach such a conclusion from scientific observation. What the evidence indicates is that they simply agreed with the prejudices current in their society at that time. Those prejudices were demonstrably unscientific and anti-human. The root of the problem is that peasants as a class, and peasant-based civilizations in their generality, have worldviews distinctly different from those of industrially-based civilizations. In some respects, peasant values may be more democratic and human-centered than their urban counterparts. An instructive difference in outlook, for instance, is that between the patient, protracted and stoically democratic *cultivation of power* characteristic of revolutions made from peasant bases and the hurried, relatively swift, practically putschist *seizure of power* characteristic of urbanized revolutions. To turn these differences into valuations of superiority and inferiority, intelligence and stupidity, we would require a clear scale of purposive values. In the absence of such a scale, the Marxist notion of peasant stupidity is absurd.

Problem 8: The fable of Oriental stagnation and negativity. This is a child of Problems 2 and 7. Marx and Engels persistently characterize Oriental society and civilization as stagnant and essentially negative. This is partly because they see the Orient as the opposite of the West and they have no doubt that the West represents positive values. An additional reason is their perception of Oriental civilizations as peasant-based. Marx and Engels write in the style of experts, but evidential probing reveals that neither had reliable knowledge or experience, direct or vicarious, of the subject. A systematic study of Chinese civilization may have been feasible, though difficult, for Marx. The fact remains that he did not undertake such a projet. In the absence or real knowledge, he and Engels accepted and used the conventional stereotypes of that branch of Western academic charlatanism popularly known as ≪Orientalism≫. The result is racist prejudice, not science.

Problem 9: The absence of Africa. In practical terms, Africa as a human habitat has no true presence in Marxist literature. The absence is intentional and premeditated. It is based on the blunt assumption that Africans had no human history but had to wait to be introduced into its stream by Western conquest. That Marx and Engels made no attempt to study African history is axiomatic. One does not set out to study something if one is convinced before one starts that it cannot exist. To the extent that African reality before Western penetration could be taken into account at all, it would presumably fit into the Oriental category under the classification of 'savagery'.

Problem 10: The academic fallacy. This results from the assumption that library and liberal research can reveal laws suitable for the making of future social revolutions.

The synecdochic misnomer. This is the most engagingly humorous fallacy of them all. By birth it is really just a figurative flower-child of Problem 1. The joke is this: grown-up people (thinking ones at that) take the trouble to build up a body of ideas diametrically opposed to individualism. At the end of their labors, they cast around for a fitting name for this monument to anti-individualist values. Naturally, they choose to name the whole thing after an individual. It does not make sense, but it is fun. Who cares if the synecdoche is not scientific? It is artistic and the anecdotal disclaimer attributed to Karl Marx – *'I am not a Marxist'* – may well be a Western analogue of the tail-end of a Zen *koan*.

Solutions: The intellectual solution to the problem of Western hegemonism is an accurate, integral view of the world. For Westerners, and those brought up with Eurocentric worldviews, this means intellectual growth to a recognition of the fact that the world is not

coterminous with the West, any more than civilization is; that in all human terms Westerners are a minority among the peoples of the world; that Western contributions in all areas
are a particular part of the human whole; that in the area of technology the West has led the
world in innovations for about the last five hundred years, pirating other people's resources
to help do it but that, before then, other cultural centers were leaders; that present trends
indicate future shifts in power and leadership away from the West; that in the area of human
values and teleology the Western world has established no basis for hegemony, not even a
basis for respect, because the Western record in the non-Western majority societies of the
world over the last five hundred years or so has been a series of lessons in how *not* to be
human; that to this moment the prime use of Western power outside the West is to fight
against democracy in other peoples' countries.

As for the stigmatization of non-Western societies as primitive, barbarous, savage, etc., the
intellectual solution (for those interested in a solution) is a systematic study of the history,
philosophy, culture, science and technology of all societies prior to the pronouncement of
judgements. That solution would necessitate the redesigning of all curricula on a comparative and comprehensive basis. Looked at purely as an issue in curriculum design, this is not
even a problem; it is a highly desirable challenge for intellectuals. If real problems arise, they
are likely to come from political and cultural imperatives such as the Western need to
maintain Problem 1. Racist stigmatization works on a basis of ignorance, reinforced with a
determination not to seek accurate information when it is not on tap and to deny it even
when it is available.

The linear philosophy of history may be intellectually justifiable when restricted to the
history of Western people and the modern period may, for them, be the best of all, hitherto
unsurpassed. That is something for Western historians to determine. When this linear
philosophy is imposed on the world, however, it becomes simply dogma. The evidence
just does not support it. Many of the world's peoples have had greater periods of extended
ascendancy, well-being, amelioration of living conditions and civilizations in the past than
they do now. Such histories require for their comprenhension philosophical frameworks in
which multiple processes (not necessarily lined up obediently like so many Prussian soldiers)
interact in varied patterns – decline, resurgence, brilliant flowering, decay, morbidity and
even extinction. The historiographic traditions of the world contain many different, useable
designs and new designs will of course be developed from future study. What is clear is that
it is unintelligent to impose a linear design on the history of the world without prior ground-
work inseparable from a global study of history – something no institution has attempted to
date and that no individual can accomplish.

The solution to the fallacy of autotelic technology is the empirical study of the relationship between teleology and technology as opposed to the uninformed legislation of a
pre-judged relationship. This means a willingness to see such relationships as processes
characterized by change – inverse, random, direct and other connections being possible at
different times and from different perspectives.

The root of the error in the dogma of abundance as a precondition for communism is
faulty logic. The precise location of the mistake is in the assumption that human beings
are capable of sharing the fruits of abundance but incapable of sharing the sacrifices
made necessary by scarcity. There really is no reason why abundance should make human
sharing any easier than scarcity does. If anything, the threat to human survival posed by
conditions of scarcity reinforces the human capacity to share in a disciplined manner with

an environmentally imposed necessity to share or disintegrate. At the source of the assumption of human incapacity to share the responsibilities, the sacrifices and the substance of scarcity is the psychologizing hypothesis that the basic human unit is the individual person. That hypothesis is shaky, far less reasonable than the hypothesis that humanity is, by definition, a social and socializing enterprise. Atomic fission in social terms has to do with the destruction of human civilizations, not their creation. Outside the Western world, a more prevalent assessment of human psychology is that the individual may be basic in a restricted, purely animal sense (even that is highly arguable) but that, on the human plane, the basic unit is necessarily and fundamentally social, larger than the isolated individual; that, by extension, the more human a society aims to be, the more socialist it has to plan to become[2] and that in human affairs the rise of individualist perspectives is a symptom of dehumanization, not an index of any amelioration in the human condition. The element of choice is therefore crucial. A social system chooses whether to reinforce individualist or socialist psychology and that is why there is no escaping the ethical dimension of communist philosophy. It is a philosophy built on the principle of justice, an unambiguous principle which entails a commitment to share scarcity and sacrifices democratically; to plan and execute improvements in the material and cultural environment democratically and to share resultant increased margins of freedom and wealth, even abundance – again democratically. This is not an easy program under any circumstances but, taken as a logical propositon, communism is not so much about ease or hardship as it is about justice.

The supposition that the European industrial workers' involvement with the machine process would rationalize their thinking processes, turning them into suitable harbingers of socialist rationality, is an error springing from a misreading of the machine process, a misreading of the psychology of European industrial workers and a misreading of the connection between machine and worker. Historically, the rôle of the industrial worker has been not to get involved with the machine process but to adjust to it or, to put it less kindly, to serve it. Such a rôle is not calculated to make the industrial worker's thinking processes more rational; it might make his reflexes more automatic on the job. The social result of the factory *régime* is a kind of regimentation which is neither a revolutionary characteristic nor a trait that prepares anyone to initiate communist organizational structures.

Superficially, the regimentation of the industrial worker and the marked collective discipline of the communist revolutionary *cadre* may strike the callow mind as identical. That is the problem of the callow mind. Under the surface, the difference is enormous. The worker submits to a mechanical discipline imposed on him by the external needs of the machine production process. The *cadre* participates voluntarily in a disciplined movement whose political imperative are his own aspirations. Teleologically, the discipline of the machine process tends to cretinize the Western factory worker. The result is that the Western proletariat has no history of achievement where revolution and communism are concerned. What the Western proletariat does have is a history of betrayal of the ideal of international justice. The record is different when we turn to fascism. The Western proletariat does have a spectacular history of fascist activity and achievement, notably in Nazi Germany and Italy. If we look closely at the record, it is more inclined toward fascism than toward communism.

The notion of peasant stupidity is so inhuman and so ill-informed that the temptation is to treat it as an instance of psychological projection on the part of Marx and Engels. It seems clear that neither had the kind of living contact with peasants which might have generated real knowledge of that class. Marxist stereotypes of the peasant class are based partly on bookish misinformation and partly on bourgeois prejudice. The antidote to this type of prejudice is the combination of integrity and intelligence in practical study. The same antidote applies to the dogma of oriental stagnancy and negativity.

The solution to the problem of the absence of Africa in Marxist or any other type of historiography is the study of African history. For the benefit of the dormant and the dead it needs to be pointed out that African history is the history of the African people, not the history of Europeans or Arabs in Africa.

As for the problem of the synecdochic fallacy, there may be a case for leaving it delibertely unsolved, even though the solution is clear enough – the accurate naming of phenomena, processes and concepts. The paradox is not only a source of comic relief; it may also serve as a mnemonic mistake, a monumental reminder of the great usefulness of bovine faeces in the fertilization of academic intellects.

[. . .]

Notes

1   Miriam Lichtheim: *Ancient Egyptian Literature: A Book of Readings, Vol. I: The Old and Middle Kingdoms* (University of California Press, 1973), 142.
2   Amilcar Cabral: *Return To The Source* (New York, Monthly Review, 1973) 65.1.1.

Chapter 67

Marxist Aesthetics:
An Open-Ended Legacy

Chidi Amuta

> Marxism is the symbolism of dialectical conflict, of drama, of the unity of opposites, of revolutionary change, of matter and man in motion, constantly transcending the moment, pointing into the future. **Maynard Solomon**[1]

> When I...used to write plays and novels that were only critical of the racism in the colonial system, I was praised. I was awarded prizes, and my novels were in the syllabus. But when toward the seventies I started writing in a language understood by peasants, and in an idiom understood by them and I started questioning the very foundations of imperialism and of foreign domination of Kenya economy and culture, I was sent to Kamiti Maximum Security Prison. **Ngugi Wa Thiong'O**[2]

To seek to transcend the limitations of the various formations of bourgeois criticism of African literature is to quest for a politically engaged, ideologically progressive and dialectical theory of that literature. In this quest, Marxism has been palpably and critically implicated not only because it represents the finest crystallization of dialectical thought into a social and political proposition but also because it encapsulates an ideological proposition in the context of which progressive forces in Africa are engaged in the struggle for negating the legacy of neo-colonialism and frustrating the designs of imperialism. Somewhat paradoxically, however, the Marxist theory of literature or the body of postulations that have come to be consecrated into a Marxist aesthetics is an area fraught with conflicting and often contradictory positions. Part of the problem arises from the familiar fact that Marx and Engels never had enough time to develop their aesthetic perceptions and observations into a coherent aesthetic. This was a task which Marx in particular continued to procrastinate on until his death, as evidenced in his numerous correspondences on the matter. In a letter to Engels in July, 1865, he wrote:

> As for my work, I want to tell you the unvarnished truth. Three chapters have still to be written to finish the theoretical part ... Then the fourth book, the historical and literary part, remains to be written.[3]

Consequently, what successive generations of Marxist theoreticians have come to consecrate into Marxist aesthetics is derived largely from a combination of the random jottings/

First published in *The Theory of African Literature: Implications for Practical Criticism*, pp. 52–6 and 72–6. London: Zed Books, 1989.

observations of Marx and Engels on specific aspects of artistic creativity and extrapolations of thoughts from their key philosophical writings into matters of literature and art.

It is important to note, however, that even if Marx/Engels were able to devote a volume to matters of aesthetics, such a work would have borne the marks of inconclusiveness and open-endedness which inhere in the very essence of dialectical thinking itself. In effect, Marxist aesthetics could not and can never be a closed system in the sense of Aristotle's *Poetics* for instance, for Marx's work was essentially a rebellion against the constrictive systematization of knowledge implicit in most idealist philosophies before him. Observes Maynard Solomon:

> Marx's work arose in part as a reaction against the grandiose attempts at the systematization of knowledge by his metaphysical predecessors. His intellectual labours can be regarded as a perpetual tension between the desire to enclose knowledge in form and the equally powerful desire to reveal the explosive form-destroying power of knowledge.[4]

On the strength of this rather sensitive observation, Solomon concludes further that Marx's writings on aesthetic and artistic matters "are aphorisms pregnant with an aesthetics – an unsystematized aesthetics open to endless analogical and metaphorical development".[5]

To make this vital admission, however, is not to imply that Marxist aesthetics cannot be identified in terms of certain determinate tasks, goals and assumptions which mark it out from bourgeois aesthetics in general. To the extent that Marx recognized artistic production as a form of labour and the work of art as an embodiment of cognitions and values which could be deployed in the service of freedom, he also saw the artist as a vital agent (among other collaborating agents in the social totality) in the shaping of social consciousness through the creation of artifacts which reveal the dynamics of social life and shatter the veils and complacencies of false consciousness. The elaboration of this central perception yields the following broad features as the primary characteristics of Marxist aesthetics:

a.   a definite relationship (even if ambiguous) between literature/art and the material base defined in terms of the totality of the relations of production;
b.   the class basis of art and the progressive nature of proletarian art;
c.   a dialectical relationship between content and form;
d.   a glorification of realism as the most progressive form of artistic representation.

In turn, specific problems in the sociology of literature and art arise from the application of Marxist dialectics to literature and art. Some of these include

a.   the relationship between literature and history,
b.   the nature of creativity,
c.   the dialectics of form itself,
d.   the nature of the aesthetic experience,
e.   the etiology of art forms,
f.   the evolving relationship between the writer and his audience.

Most of these areas, it needs to be pointed out, have as yet remained relatively unexplored by successive generations of Marxist literary theoreticians and critics.

From Plekhanov to Adorno and Althusser, from Trotsky and Mao to Eagleton, Ngugi and Gramsci, the precise manner and relative prominence which individual theoreticians have given to the above features and problems has been historically determined. As with Marxism itself, Marxist aesthetics and its applications to literary criticism contains what Raymond Williams calls a "variety of selective and alternative traditions within it" which are defined in terms of differing national and epochal imperatives.[6] This historical variability of Marxist aesthetics is in turn conditioned by the stage in the evolution of historical and productive forces in a given society which in turn define the conflicts and contradictions of social life which art, through mediation, seeks to resolve. Consequently, while for instance, contemporary Western Marxist literary theory as articulated by Fredric Jameson, Terry Eagleton and others has been concerned mainly with defining the precise relationship between advanced capitalism and art in the form of post-modernism,[7] radical Marxist literary theory in Africa and parts of the Third World is preoccupied with the responsibility of literature and art in the task of national liberation, anti-imperialism and the redressing of social inequities within individual national societies.

To a certain extent, it can further be argued that the great diversity of perspectives and approaches in Marxist aesthetics and criticism is contingent on the nature of art itself. A true work of art presents a dialectical image, at once specific and universal, immediate and transcendental, tangible and intangible, structured and yet exploding all attempts at rigid structuration; even defying at times the original formative intention. "Art has both a *here* and *now* and a certain universality. This is what enables specific works of art to survive beyond the particular eras that generated them".[8] When, therefore, the dialectical essence of art is matched with the very historical nature of dialectical thinking itself, Marxist aesthetics emerges as an internally differentiated open system, defying a monolithic perspective of both art and reality. Adolfo Vazquez summarizes this point with characteristic pungency:

> Art is a phenomenon that constantly defies vacuous and hasty generalizations that result from a one-dimensional point of view. Within the Marxist camp today we can see profound differences in the emphasis given a particular aspect or function of artistic creation. These emphases derive from a shared conception of humanity and society and should not be considered exclusive as long as no one of them walls itself in and closes its door to a different basic approach to art.[9]

To restate the above fact is to call into question the very credentials of mechanical materialists whose insistence on a one-to-one correspondence between art and ideology has given Marxist aesthetics the reputation of unrelieved dogmatism. Both Marx/Engels and Lenin recognized the relative autonomy of literature and art and relentlessly emphasized the problematic relationship between literature and art on one hand and ideological and historical development on the other.[10] Obviously angered by the excesses of those of his "disciples" who tended to constrict and subvert the *spirit* of his own thoughts, Marx protested: "I am not a Marxist". Trotsky was later to react in the same vein by somewhat overstating the autonomy of art in *Literature and Revolution*. No better resolution can be found for the danger posed by the mechanical materialist usurpation of Marxist aesthetics than to restate that art is one (only one) of the spheres in which social men and women wage the historical struggle for the positive alteration of their circumstances and themselves. As a sphere of practical and constitutive social activity, literature and art possess an autonomy in the form of internal laws of performance and evaluation which are nevertheless subject to socio-historical conditioning. Again, Vazquez has the last word on this matter: "Art is an autonomous sphere, but its autonomy exists only *by, in* and *through* its social condition-ing."[11] Given the rather young history of Marxist theorizing in Africa, the fledgling tradition of Marxist criticism of African literature (whose manifestations we shall presently discuss) can be protected against the pitfalls of the earlier Marxists, especially the neo-Hegelians. Such protection is best offered in the form of disclaimers emphasizing what Marxist theory of literature *is not*. Briefly, these warnings are as follows

1. Literature and art cannot be mechanically equated with ideology: ("class ideologies come and go, but true art persists").
2. There is no parallel relationship between class interest and artistic/literary expression although literary works cannot but bear the stamp of their class origins and orientation.
3. Literary/artistic achievement does not stand in direct relationship with social develop-ment but literature appropriates and testifies to its socio-historical determination.
4. The social and historical conditioning of literature and art is not reducible to economic determinism but economic factors cannot be ignored in the production and under-standing of literature.

Again, these disclaimers do not amount to an acquiescence to the indeterminancy and absolute relativism which are the hallmarks of liberal bourgeois poetics. On the contrary, they amount to an admission that within Marxist literary theory and criticism, there are gradations in terms of level of approximation to the dialectical paradigm. But the crucial discrimination which needs to be made within literary theory in general is between Marxist and non-Marxist positions.

Marxist aesthetics, therefore, is ultimately an open-ended legacy, a fact which inheres in its dialectical heritage. In the African context, we can identify specific challenges which have provided the locus for the engagement of Marxism in literary creativity, theory and criticism. Prominent among these is the centrality of politics and ideology in African literature, the implication of literature in the struggle for national liberation and definition and the use of literature and culture to objectify and illuminate the national and class contradictions within individual African national societies to date.

[...]

Beyond Orthodox Marxism: The Framework for a Post-Marxist Theory of African Literature and Culture

There are certain features of contemporary African society which suggest possibilities far too trying for the categories of orthodox Marxist social historical theory. Much as the major conjunctural tragedies of present day Africa can be traced ultimately to Western imperial-ism, itself an aspect of the deformation of capitalism, this contact has unleashed a plethora of socio-historical manifestations which the largely linear logic of Marxism may not quite have anticipated. In Africa today isolated urban-based pockets of industrial capital coexist with stubborn survivals of decadent feudalism often in the same urban setting. There is also an identity of material circumstances between the urban poor and the rural peasantry which cannot yet be said to have galvanized into a class consciousness and a recent high incidence of maniacal dictators (Mobutu, Nguema, Bokassa, Idi Amin etc.) whose psychological make-up would have baffled Marx's most imaginative application of the theory of class struggle. Similarly in today's Africa, the attempts at revolutionary transformation of society have been carried out mainly by military regimes (Ethiopia, Burkina Faso, Libya, Ghana) rebelling against the legacy of colonialist military traditions while the vanguards of the African revolution have been drawn, not from an industrial working class but from an odd mixture of peasants, students, women's groups and the urban poor, with workers in industry often constituting an incoherent minority. These features, which are also manifest in other parts of the world, have tended to problematize human history in a manner that has compelled a reassessment of Marxism and the socialist project.

While the contradictions in question have tempted bourgeois intellectuals to celebrate the apocalypse of Marxism, Marxist and progressive intellectuals have been challenged to undertake a more thorough and rigorous understanding of what Marx really *said* about the course of human history and the socio-cultural consequences of the process of history.

Among Western Marxists, the main sources of doubt have come from such developments as the welfare state, the cold war, nuclearism, ethnic-racial conflicts, nationalism and feminism within post-industrial Western societies, developments which tend to dull the centrality of the class struggle almost to extinction. The extent of this crisis is so deep that the New Left in Europe has of recent years been forced (from its academic and polemical exchanges on the matter) to admit that like capitalism, Marxism, and in fact the leftist alternative is caught in a deep crisis. Part of the editorial of the silver jubilee issue of *New Left Review* ran thus:

> Today the political scenery of the 80's is a much harsher one than anything the left has known since the 30's. A new imperialist cycle of the Cold War is pushing the nuclear arms race beyond the limits of the earth itself. A global recession is steadily increasing unemployment in the upper side of the capitalist world, and spreading debt and famine in its underside. The world communist movement has passed away: the post-revolutionary states of the East which once formed its magnetic pole have lost their force of attraction. The labour movement in the West has been unable to resist the consolidation of regimes of the Anglo-American Right, or the emulation of their policies by governments of the Eurosocialist Left.[12]

The most far-reaching implication of this admission resounds fundamentally at the level of Marxism as the theoretical bedrock of the left itself. Writes Ronald Aronson:

> In spite of its sheer appeal as a system and in spite of its claims to be comprehensive, Marxism becomes increasingly reductive and sterile in trying to account for [the] decisive concerns of our world.[13]

The sources of these increasing reservations are contained in the theoretical limitations of Marxism itself. The principal limitation is in the implication of the linear emphasis of Marxist philosophy of history, which does not seem to have sufficient elasticity to accommodate the dizzying developments in today's world. Allied to this is the fact that the development of productive forces in world societies has tended to challenge the predictive validity of Marx's philosophy of history.

On the part of committed African intellectuals, the source of worry about the appropriateness of Marxism as a theoretical framework for prosecuting the African revolution inheres in the very limitations imposed by the historical determination of Marxism itself and which are manifest in its very world view and conceptual categories. Marxism developed as a philosophical response to capitalism and the liberal idealism of the bourgeoisie. Its theoretical inspiration and conceptual categories were formulated in the context of industrial capitalism in its infant stages. This historical determination and theoretical orientation renders Marxism impotent when it comes to the elaboration of societies, cultural manifestations and historical developments that did not form part of the cognitive universe of Marx and Engels. Consequently, the works of Hegel and Marx/Engels after him contain blatant ignorances and even outright uncomplimentary remarks about Africans and other non-Western peoples. Ayi Kwei Armah has provided the most rigorous and "Afrocentric" articulation of these aberrations. These include Marxism's patronizing and Eurocentric silence about Africa, its implicit belief in the stupidity of the peasantry and the wisdom of the industrial proletariat, the notion of autotelic technology as well as the linear conception of history which places Western man at the helm and forefront of human history and progress.[14]

Given these limitations and to the extent that African literature is essentially an artistic mediation of the main features of contemporary African society, a progressive anti-imperialist theory of that literature, in order to approach a *total* picture of its historical conditioning, must of necessity transcend the limitations of orthodox Marxism. For the progressive African intelligentsia enamoured of the revolutionary potential of Marxism and yet sufficiently alert to its contextual limitations and theoretical blindspots, the way out seems to lie in a recourse to the philosophical breakthrough which Marxism represents, namely, historical materialism. As the application of the principles of dialectical materialist thought to the understanding of human societies and their process of development, historical materialism transcends Marxism and embodies a certain general theoretical *elasticity* that could salvage Marxism from its present crisis and imminent obsolescence. Ronald Aronson illuminates this option further:

> If Marxism as we know it is inadequate, . . . historical materialism provides a path out of the crisis.

> I am distinguishing historical materialism *from* Marxism: it alone allows us to pursue a layered analysis of the complex evolution of bourgeois society, following its displacements and repressions of original conflict *and* its generation of new conflicts, to the point it has reached today. . . [15]

The revolutionary implication of historical materialism inheres in the fact that it makes possible "a radical, structured, layered analysis of contemporary society" in general. In its dialectical sweep, therefore, historical materialism can incorporate "classical Marxism and the systemic changes since its heyday". The new vista of revolutionary change that emerges is essentially a collaborative one, what Aronson calls a *radical pluralism* in which workers as a *conscious* minority align with other groups *created* by capitalism in its negating logic. In Africa, the alliance would include the urban proletariat, urban poor students, progressive intellectuals, the peasantry, progressive army cadres, progressive women's organizations etc. Taken together, this group constitutes, in a demographic and political sense, the "vital majority" who are carrying the burden of imperialist hegemony and capitalist exploitation in Africa.

The challenge of this proposition for literary theory inheres in a totalizing, dialectical (in place of a metaphysical) perspective anchored on the specific experiences in the context of which literary creativity is taking place and which also provide the subject of and social necessity of literature.

Notes

1   Maynard Solomon (ed.), *Marxism and Art: Essays Classic and Contemporary* (New York: Vintage Books, 1973) p. 17.
2   Ngugi Wa Thiong'o, *Barrel of a Pen* (London/Port of Spain: New Beacon, 1985) p. 65.
3   Karl Marx and Friedrich Engels, *On Literature and Art* (Moscow: Progress Publishers, 1976) p. 111.
4   Solomon, *Marxism and Art*, p. 8.
5   Ibid., p. 9.
6   Raymond Williams, *Marxism and Literature* (Oxford: Oxford University Press, 1977) p. 3.
7   See, for instance, the following recent essays: Fredric Jameson, "Post Modernism, or the Cultural Logic of Late Capitalism", *New Left Review*, no. 146, 1985, pp. 53–92; Terry Eagleton, "Capitalism, Modernism and Post-Modernism", *New Left Review*, no. 152, 1985, pp. 60–73.
8   Adolfo Sanchez Vazquez, *Art and Society: Essays in Marxist Aesthetics* (New York: Monthly Review Press, 1973) p. 25.
9   Ibid., p. 23.
10 See Marx and Engels: *On Literature and Art*, p. 88. This refers specifically to Engels' letter to Minna Kautsky, 26 November 1885.
11 Vazquez, *Art and Society*, p. 98.
12 *New Left Review*, no. 150, 1985, p. 1.
13 Ronald Aronson, "Historical Materialism, Answer to Marxism's Crisis", *New Left Review*, no. 152, 1985, p. 87.
14 Armah, "Marx and Masks" p. 54 ff.
15 Aronson, "Historical Materialism" p. 88.

Part X

Feminism

One distinctive feature of the essays on feminism in this section is that most of them are by women writers themselves, as opposed to critics of their work. Thus there is a heavy emphasis on the processes by which they came to the consciousness of being writers and the choices that they exercised in deciding on the content and themes of their work. In all instances these choices were influenced by the blatant oppression that women suffered in both traditional and modern African society. Yet more important than the implications of these writerly choices is the fact that identifying a project of liberation cannot subsist on an unexamined generalization about what is to be liberated. It is clear that male writers and critics think of the oppressed in quite different ways from how women think of them; the variegated and often discrepant oppressions that are manifest on the continent are assimilated by male critics to a particular order of urgency. The temptation to read the essays here as sociological correctives to the absence of positive female images in African literature has to be avoided. What is more pertinent is the fact that the perspective from which a work is read has major implications for what is to emerge as of literary value or otherwise. Thus the restored (absent) detail of womanhood in all its range – sex, maternality, domestic labor, the bearing of cultural knowledge – serves to secure a different kind of critical enterprise from that which ignores these vectors of feminist identity.

Chapter 68

To Be an African Woman Writer – an Overview and a Detail

Ama Ata Aidoo

[. . .]

We experience some sadness – though mixed with some more positive emotions – at the mere confrontation with the notion of African women and writing. Nothing really tragic, and nothing really worthy of jubilation either. Certainly however, there is no denying the pathos and the wonder in being an African (and a woman) with sensibilities that are struggling ceaselessly to give expression to themselves in a language that is not just alien but was part of the colonizers' weaponry . . . There is pathos in writing about people, the majority of whom will never be in a position to enjoy you or judge you. And there is some wonder in not letting that or anything else stop you from writing. Indeed, it is almost a miracle, in trying and succeeding somewhat to create in an aesthetic vacuum. For, from the little we learnt of one another's backgrounds, none of us writers in our formative years was involved in any formal process, through which we could have *systematically* absorbed from our environment, the aesthetics that govern artistic production in general, and writing in particular. Some of us were lucky enough to have had mothers and grandmothers who could sing traditional lyrics. Some of us grew up around griots and other traditional poets. But those are few and in any case, even they could not have had that much. Because after primary or early primary school, we all left the village, the urban slum or township through the medium of some scholarship, and went to some exclusive school. And in those places, further development of the child, artistic or otherwise, depended on the communicative talents of a teacher and the skill with which she or he conveyed the aesthetics of good European literature and other dynamics of Western civilization . . . or at least, a version of it which was well-pruned to suit the colonial or neo-colonial environment.

"Do you write only in French?" asked the interviewer of Mariama Bâ. "I do not know any other written language, only French", answered Mariama Bâ, of *So Long a Letter*.[1]

First published in *Criticism and Ideology: Second African Writers' Conference, Stockholm 1986*, ed. Kirsten H. Petersen, pp. 157–65. Uppsala: Scandinavian Institute of African Studies, 1988.

That indeed is the pathos underlying much of 'modern African literature' and that too is the wonder of it.

If anyone protested than none of this was any different from what male African writers had to confront, my response to that would be: 'But of course not'. There could not be any earth-shaking differences. Indeed, if we thought that anyone was providing us with a platform from which to prove that African women writers were different in any way from their male counterparts, or that they faced some fundamental problems which male African writers did not face, some of us would not really want to use such a platform. How could there be? Did we not all suffer the varied wickedness of colonialism, apartheid, neo-colonialism and global imperialists and fascism together? What we are saying though, is that it is especially pathetic to keep on writing without having any consistent, active, critical intelligence that is interested in you as an artist (or creator). Therefore, it is precisely from this point that the African writing women's reality begins to differ somewhat from that of the male African writer. Once we have faced the basic fact of the oppression and marginality that is almost endemic in the lives of the peoples of the so-called Third World, and especially those of Africans, we also begin to admit that at least, some people are interested in the male African writer. These include African, non-African, male and female literary critics, different categories of publishers, editors, anthologists, translators, librarians, sundry academic analysts, and all other zealous collectors of treasures! (My apologies to Bessie Head – A. A. A.)

Am I jealous? But of course. In March of 1985, Professor Dieter Riemenschneider came to Harare to give a lecture on some regional approach to African literature.[2] The lecture lasted at least two hours. In all that time, Professor Riemenschneider did not find it possible to mention a single African woman writer. When this was pointed out to him later, he said he was sorry, but it had been 'so natural'. I could have died. It had been natural to forget that quite a bit of modern African literature was produced by women? Why should it be 'natural' to forget that some African women had been writing and publishing for as long as some African men writers? Efua Sutherland of Ghana must have begun to write in the late 1950s because her plays, *Foriwa* and *Edufa* were produced in 1962. These were subsequently published. Since then, she has also published, among others, *The Marriage of Anansewa*, a hilariously modern portrayal of the folk villain, Ananse, the Spiderman. How can it be natural to forget the existence of Bessie Head, who between 1971 and 1974 published two of the most powerful novels to have come out of Africa? I speak of *Maru* and *A Question of Power*. In relation to Bessie Head, we have not even thrown in *When Rain Clouds Gather* (1969) or *The Collector of Treasures* (1977) which, according to Hans Zell, is a 'carefully sequenced collection of short stories in which she has refashioned myths, examined the problems of Christianity and traditional religions', besides being an 'exploration of the women in Africa'.[3] How could Riemenschneider not remember that Flora Nwapa published *Efuru* in 1966, *Idu* in 1969, *Never Again* in 1976 and since then both *Wives at War* and *Other Stories* and *Once is Enough* in 1981? Micere Mugo is formidably uncompromising, both in terms of the aesthetic criteria and the political relevance against which she judges the achievement of the few African women writers whose works she has analysed. In her hands, quite a number of the fictional characters from the group virtually come tumbling down, but even she hails Efuru, her warmth, her love, her enterprise:

> Efuru truly symbolises the struggles that face millions of female workers and peasants all over
> the African continent [who] daily wage heroic struggles against the shackles of the negative

tradition, muffling religions, overwhelmingly hostile natural forces and exploitative econo-political systems that seek to silence them all together.[4]

Furthermore, whereas one might just wonder how anybody can forget the existence of *The Dilemma of a Ghost* (1965), *Anowa* (1970), and *No Sweetness Here* (1970), the question is how anybody dares to seriously discuss the so-called contemporary African literature and not mention *Our Sister Killjoy or Reflections from Black-eyed Squint* (1977)?[5]

Maybe, Mariama Bâ and her brilliant novel did not feature in Riemenschneider's lecture because she came from the Francophone zone and his lecture was on Anglophone writing? But then, doesn't one remember him saying something about *Houseboy* by Oyono of the Camer-oun, a book whose original title was *La Vie de Boy*? In any case, linguistic and any other such basis cannot continue to be valid for discussing African literature, if it would mean the exclusion of the first winner of the Noma Award for publishing in Africa, and to date, the most movingly intimate picture of what Lauretta Ngcobo describes as 'the educated, urban, middle-class women of Africa'. Ngcobo goes on: 'Rarely is this class acknowledged in print in African writing, let alone its fears and pains explored.'[6] If we agree with the critic, and therefore, Ramatoulaye becomes a symbol of such women, then frankly, their utter spineless-ness is frightening to behold. Except that, it also takes a great book to bring that out, doesn't it?

Actually, it is not only the good German professor who forgets African women and their books. He is only nice enough to admit it. It is standard practice. In a volume whose purpose was 'to offer an account of the best work of African novelists since 1950 in the context of a discussion of the competing claims made on literature and on all of us by the idea of "the modern"', Neil McEwan does not mention a single novel written by an African woman. Then to literally add pain to injury he has the temerity, under *Select Bibliography Suggesting Further Reading*, to say that 'the novels of the exiled South African Bessie Head are the most glaring omission from the present study'.[7] So why the omission if it was so glaring? The fact that McEwan then goes on to mention other omitted African female and male novelists does nothing to lessen the outrage. For after all, within the pages of this book on *Africa and the Novel*, he finds a solid raison d'être to discuss works by Nadine Gordimer and Laurens van der Post, presumably as 'some novels by outsiders inspired by experience of Africa', as he declares with some vague determination in his introduction.

However, McEwan too is a relative newcomer to the 'if-we-are talking-about-African-writers-who-are-those-female-scribblers-anyway?' game. All analysts in the field do it.[8] Do you remember Gerald Moore and his *Seven African Writers*? That was 1962. So long ago, and so few writers? No one had the courage to ask questions of the honourable pundit then. So now, are we expected to take notice or not, that the booklet, updated and expanded to cover the work of *Twelve African Writers* and published in 1980 still does not look at the work of a single woman writer? Yet, Hans Zell says of it that it is a 'critical introduction to . . . Africa's most significant and well-established . . . authors whose work represent Anglophone and Francophone writing and draws from West, East, and Southern Africa', as well as the 'richness and the range of the continent's writing'[9] and on and on and on!

Maybe it is time one even confessed that precisely because of one's own nationalism, one feels most bewildered by such slights when they are administered by other Africans, that is, African critics. And they do it all the time. According to Lloyd Brown, African women writers are: 'the voices unheard, rarely discussed and seldom accorded space in the repetitive anthologies and predictably male-oriented studies in the field'.[10]

Jane Bryce (who quotes Brown in her review of Oladele Taiwo's *Female Novelists of Modern Africa*) goes even further. She names names:

> One only has to skim the contents page of the manifold publications with weighty titles like *The Emergence of African Fiction*, or *The Growth of the African Novel* to verify this. For on each occasion women's writing is conspicuously absent. Even a radical text like *Toward the Decolonisation of African Literature* by Chinweizu, Jemie and Madubuike omits to mention a single woman writer.[11]

Actually, in *Toward the Decolonisation of African Literature* the authors mention Ama Ata Aidoo and Flora Nwapa; but very much *en passant*, as an afterthought; and frankly, it is not clear whether that hurts even more. What is clear is that there is a truly shocking and everlengthening list of African commentators on African literature who manage to convey – solidly – to the interested world community, an impression that either there are no African women writers around at all, or if there are, then their work is not deserving of serious critical attention. Have you heard of *Art and Ideology in the African Novel*, published by Heinemann as recently as 1985? Quite clearly Emmanuel Ngara did not mention a single African woman writer even in passing because he did not think anything African women are writing is of any relevance to the ideological debate. Unless of course, we learn to accept that a study of Nadine Gordimer (again!) answers all such queries.

We have heard of editors of some well-known journals on African literature who routinely refuse good studies on the work of women writers on the pretext that they 'are not ready with our special issue on women writers'. Of course, the question again is: why a special issue on the work of women writers, especially as these supposed special issues never come out at all, or once in a half-decade? Maybe it is time we confessed that precisely because of our own unashamed commitment to African nationalism, we feel most bewildered by such slights when they are administered by other Africans.

In fact, the whole question of what attention has been paid or not paid to African writing women is so tragic, sometimes one wonders what desperation keeps us writing. Because for sure, no one cares. To have blundered our way into this one more exclusively male sphere of activity can be forgiven. After all, clumsiness is a human failing. We all make mistakes.

What is almost pathetic is to have persisted in staying there in the face of such resistance and sometimes resentment. Some of us believe that for writers and other creative persons any critical attention is better than none at all. Therefore it is also obvious that one factor that has definitely damaged the career of so many women writers is the absence of attention from the critical world. There never was a question of African woman writers wanting to be considered better than African male writers. We were not asking to be hailed as geniuses, it was simply that some African women have written books that have been as good as some of the books written by some of the African male writers, and sometimes better. We wanted to be noticed. For not only is is true, at least part of the time – that 'literature (is) an occupation in which you have to prove your talent to people who have none',[12] but the fact that we wrote at all in the face of the greatest odds should be enough: 'whether that is literature or whether that is not literature we will not presume to say'. What we dare say though, in agreement with Virginia Woolf, is that 'what so many women write explains much and tells much and that is certain'.[13] Consider Lauretta Ngcobo's *Cross of Gold*: are there any more vivid portrayals of how an individual could be hounded into a realization of what it is to be black in South Africa? The need to struggle against powerlessness and dehumanization? Or Miriam Tlali's *Muriel at the Metropolitan*: its loving albeit tongue-in-cheek concern with which Tlali has demonstrated that there could be no black petit-bourgeoisie in apartheid South Africa? That is assuming that anyone was unashamed enough to sympathize with that selfish class and the efforts it makes to survive, no matter what the cost might be.

We are not saying that either Ngcobo or Tlali with one book apiece are in the class of Alex La Guma. But then, how many other writers with one book can be in the class of La Guma? What we are asserting though is that Bessie Head is in anybody's first class, that wherever the African novel is discussed, depending on the scope of the discussion or its bearing on life within South Africa or of South Africans in exile, the novels of Bessie Head, Alex La Guma and others must be discussed.

Certainly, the issue can be viewed from several angles. For instance, if we did not talk about the class positions of writers or the political contents of their writings, and therefore allowed ourselves to enjoy Elechi Amadi's *The Concubine* as a tender love story with a dash of the mystique, then could we not talk of Rebeka Njau's *Ripples in the Pool* as a look at the tragedy of loving with a dash of the mystique?

The stuff we write deserves to be looked at and judged, seriously, like those by our male counterparts, because the very act of creating has cost us too much. Nor should this be strange, or hard to believe, since every artist/writer suffers to produce. After all, 'all art is subsidised by artists with their lives'. The lost lives and loves, the atrophied careers and the need to give up more lucrative alternatives inevitably results in the sheer poverty of existence for all of us, except a few very highly successful ones. And throughout our lives, some questions that we can never answer but which keep nagging at us:

> Was it worth it?
> Has it been worth it?
> Is it worth it?

All writers are plagued by fears, real and imaginary, by all sorts of uncertainties and some very solid problems. After all, we are also human. The truth though, is that some of us suffer a little more, simply because we are women, and our positions are nearly hopeless because we are African women.

Naturally, we would have to admit that the realities of our lives are nowhere as harsh as those of our sisters, who, with the most meagre formal education or none at all, have to struggle out their lives in deprived rural environments and oppressive urban slums. Yet in relative terms – of what could be possible for us even as the few whom circumstances of birth and environment colluded to rescue – our situations are unenviable enough. Consider the fact of just about everybody around us feeling abandoned, because we have to abandon if we are to write. How silly, how ridiculous, that when our loved ones are jealous, they are not jealous of other humans they suspect we love and who could, perhaps, return the affection, but of the pieces of paper which it seems to them we give so much time to, which claim so much of our attention. The unpolished poems, the half-written plays, the never-finished short stories, the novels that are forever 'in progress'.

And of all the pain, the hardest to bear is that which results from the writer/mother situation. That one is very real and very hard. According to one Western woman writer, her 'grandmother who wrote and sold short stories before raising six children used to claim with some bitterness that bearing and raising children drained a woman's creativity'. Sally Bingham then continues: 'I don't believe there is a solution to this problems or at least, I don't believe there is one which recognizes the emotional complexities involved. A life without children is . . . an impoverished life for most women: yet life with children imposes demands that consume energy and imagination as well as time and that cannot all be delegated even supposing there is a delegate available'.[14]

Consider the fact that such woefully inadequate 'delegates', even when available, include the fathers that begat . . . and God knows they are often not available! In the face of such testimonies, how can anyone be unimpressed with Buchi Emecheta, who bore five children, struggled to raise them single-handed in a decidedly hostile milieu, and in the years between 1972 and 1984 managed to publish nine novels? Quality is important of course: but its presence or absence in a novel can be exposed only through a reading of that novel, and in comparison of it with others. Therefore, any reasonably lengthy discussion of the African novel that is not limited by any special sub-regional bias to my mind becomes automatically invalid, if it was done within the last decade, and did not demonstrate any awareness of the works of Emecheta. I speak of *In the Ditch* (1972), *Second-Class Citizen* (1974), *The Joys of Motherhood* (1974), and *Double Yoke* (1981), to mention only four.

Considering how we thirst for attention, what do we do, when the little that comes our way is of the wrong and damaging kind? And there can be damaging critical recognition. Listen to no less a genius than the eminent English novelist William Thackeray on no less a genius than the English novelist Charlotte Brontë:

> The poor little woman of genius! . . . [The] . . . homely-faced creature! I can read a great deal of her as I fancy her in her book [*Villette*] and see that rather than have fame . . . she wants some Tomkins or another to love her and be in love with . . . here is one genius . . . longing to mate itself [but] destined to wither away into old maidenhood with no chance to fulfil the burning desire.[15]

Nobody knows de trouble (we) see, O lawd! Nearly everybody takes women writers for a joke, or worse. That includes publishers, literary agents and any others who profit from our existence and our toil, when they can. 'There was but little feminine charm about her, and of this fact she was herself uneasily and perpetually conscious . . . I believe she would have given all her genius and all her fame to have been beautiful'.[16] Guess who said that about whom? It was said about the same Charlotte Brontë by her publisher, George Smith. Can anyone imagine anybody saying anything so scurrilous about any male writer, dead or alive? Yet Brontë's publishers could say that about her, forty- five years after her death, and just when they could begin to print and sell all they wanted of her books, and make all the money they could, without even pretending to look for which of her heirs owned the copyrights.

I bring the foregoing to our attention because, any writing woman is vulnerable to such insults and naked slander. Already in the discussion of modern African writing, even when women writers are vouchsafed any mention, it is often absent-minded at the best, and at the worst, full of veiled ridicule and resentment. When commentary on African women in literature is none of the above, it is certain to be disorganized (or rather unorganized) and choked full of condescension.

Notes

1   Mariama Bâ in *African BPR*, Vol VI, Nos 3/4, 1984, p. 213.
2   Dieter Riemenschneider, 'Regional Similarities and Differences in African Literature', Park Lane Hotel Harare, 18 March, 1985.
3   Hans Zell, ed., *A New Reader's Guide to African Literature* (London, Heinemann, 1983).
4   Micere Mugo.
5   Works by Ama Ata Aidoo.
6   Lauretta Ngcobo, 'Four African Women Writers' in *South African Outlook*, May, 1984.
7   Neil McEwan, *Africa and the Novel* (London, MacMillan, 1975) p. 175.
8   The situation is completely bad. Virtually every single commentator has been guilty, from Gerald Moore and onwards, including Charles Larson (1972), Eustace Palmer (1979), Kolewole Ogungbesan (1979), S.O. Anozie (1981), Emmanuel Ngara (1983), the list is endless and keeps on growing.
9   Hans Zell, op. cit. p. 40.
10 Lloyd W. Brown, *Women Writers in Black Africa* (Westport, Connecticut, Greenwood Press, 1981) p. 3.
11 Jane Bryce, 'The Unheard Voices', a review of *Female Novelists of Modern Africa* by Oladele Taiwo (London, *West Africa*, 28 January 1985) p. 172.
12 Jules Renhard quoted by Tillie Olsen, op. cit.
13 Virginia Woolf, *Life As We Have It, Memoirs of the Working Women's Guild*, quoted by Tillie Olsen, op. cit.
14 Sally Bingham, *The Way it is Now*, quoted by Tillie Olsen, op. cit., p. 210.
15 William Thackeray in a letter to a friend, quoted by Tillie Olsen, op. cit., p. 233.
16 George Smith, quoted by Tillie Olsen, op. cit., pp. 233–4.

Chapter 69

The Heroine in Arab Literature

Nawal El Saadawi

[. . .]

Among the male authors I have read, both in the West and in the Arab world, irrespective of the language in which they have written, or of the region from which they have come, not one has been able to free himself from this age-old image of women handed down to us from an ancient past, no matter how famous many of them have been for their passionate defence of human rights, human values and justice, and their vigorous resistance to oppression and tyranny in any form. Tolstoy, with his towering literary talent and his denunciation of the evils of feudal and bourgeois Russian society, when speaking of women found nothing better to say than: 'Woman is the instrument of the devil. In most of her states she is stupid. But Satan lends her his head when she acts under his orders.'[1]

Arab literature is littered with the image of the she-devil, possessed of many faces:

> Sometimes when you look at her, you feel as though you are in the company of a playful child opening its innocent eyes with all the simplicity, astonishment and naivete of spontaneous nature, without artifice or deceit. Then, after a while, you look at her again, maybe on the same day, only to find yourself faced by an old and cunning creature who has exhausted her life in the daily practice of conspiracy hatched against other women and men. She laughs and presents to you a face that is meant for nothing else but passion. Then she laughs once more – maybe just a few moments later – and you are in the presence of a mind imbued with humour, and an intelligence sharp with sarcasm, a mind which is that of philosophers, and wits which belong only to those who have the experience of a long embattled life.[2]

In these 'thoughts' Akkad once more contradicts his contention that women are devoid of a brain with which to think, and that men should therefore lock them up in the home between four walls for being creatures without mind or religious piety or morals, 'idolators who have never known what it is to believe.'[3]

Akkad and other contemporary men of letters in the Arab world have not travelled very far from the positions held by their ancestors hundreds of years ago, nor does the image they

First published in *The Hidden Face of Eve*, pp. 155–68. London: Zed Books, 1980.

paint of women differ much from the exotic curves of the slave women heroines in the 'classic' *A Thousand and One Nights*. Woman continues to appear on the scene as a capricious vamp, a play-ful and beautiful slave, a she-devil imbued with cunning and capable of a thousand artifices, an explosive danger versed in all the arts of deceit and conspiracy, a seductive mistress captivating in her passion. She is as positive and dynamic as Satan and his evil spirits, wherever matters of sex and love are concerned. Woman in all the aspects of the role she is made to play, whether it be that of a queen or a slave bought from the market, remains a slave. She may be the daughter of a king, fighting with courage, while her lover shivers in fear, yet she will always be made to call him master, and to serve him, just as Mariam El Zanaria placed herself at the service of Nour El Dine. In most of the stories she is bought and sold, and thus the characteristics and behaviour of the slave become a natural part of her milieu and of her apparel.[4]

A Thousand and One Nights, throbs with hundreds of these captivating women creatures who use magic and sorcery to reach their lovers. Women cast a spell on their husbands so that they cease to be obstacles blocking the path of their desires. It is interesting to note that in this book sorcery is the monopoly of these seductive beings versed in the secrets of conspiracy, intent on getting to where they wish to be, that is to their lovers' arms. Sleeping potions, drugs, anaesthetics are all used by these women to send their husbands into a deep sleep and then slip away to another man's bed. Thus the book has painted an image of women, with its own intrinsic logic and therefore its own peculiar system of rituals, that serves to maintain and reinforce the image handed down from the past. This phenomenon repeats itself throughout *A Thousand and One Nights*, right from the tale of Sultan Mahmoud, Ruler of the Black Islands, at the beginning of the first volume, through the almost endless nights to the story of Kamar El Zaman and his mistress in the fourth. Deceit, cunning and conspiracy in *A Thousand and One Nights* are invariably associated with women, love and sex.

Yet Shawahi and many of the other women mentioned in these tales in fact reflect the strong and positive Arab woman personality, who used to participate unhesitatingly in politics and war, carry her sword and put on her shield and fight in the front lines of the battle field. Such a woman was Hind Bint Rabia, mentioned earlier, who killed a number of Mahomet's followers in the Battle of Ahad. That is why in *A Thousand and One Nights* a woman who fights is not portrayed as a Muslim, but rather as an evil old witch or sorceress.

Just as some Arab women gained prominence in the fields of war, politics, and *fitna*, others became well known for their versatility, creativeness and understanding in literature, the arts and the sciences. There were free women, and also slave women, who reached a very high standing in these fields. Thus it was that El Rasheed was quite fond of marrying women who had sufficient culture and presence of mind to give a wise answer to some philosophical question, or to a problem of life that might arise, or who were sufficienctly versed in poetry to complete with grace and harmony an unfinished line or stanza, or to compose a poem which won his admiration. In the tales of *A Thousand and One Nights*, such occurrences find a place in the form of news items, stemming from literary writings.

Woman is at her best and most powerful when she takes on the form of a genie or spirit in *A Thousand and One Nights*. Men fall victims to her beauty and her spells, and go through great suffering and even torture to gain her favours.

The woman spirit or genie occupies a prominent place in these tales which indicates that the power and strength of women remained an idea and a feeling deeply ingrained in the mind and emotions of the Arab peoples, and continued to be linked with the supernatural powers of genies, devils, sorcery, *fitna* and sex. However, woman in modern Arab literature has not taken on both the form and the substance of these genies. She has discarded the form and kept the substance. She is therefore human on the outside like the others, but intrinsically she has remained a genie, imbued with the same fundamental nature that leads her to practise deceit, to betray, to conspire against others, and to seduce them into her traps. Thus she belongs much more to the world of genies and spirits than to the world of human beings. Zaki Mobarak describes what he considers as being her characteristics when he says that women have a greater power to destroy men than Satan and all his devils together. Akkad expresses the same view but attributes woman's capacity for destruction, betrayal and seduction to her innate weakness. Eve did not eat of the forbidden fruit and tempt Adam to do the same for any other reason than the fact that her nature makes her yearn for all that is not allowed. As a result of this fundamental weakness, she is given to seducing and to tempting others. For El Akkad the forbidden tree 'symbolizes and embodies all that lies within woman in the form of a desire to be subjugated, which breeds the pleasure she takes in rebellion, a capriciousness that gives birth to the pleasure of withholding herself, a suspiciousness and a tendency to doubt, a weak and inborn obstinacy, an ignorant curiosity, and an incapacity to resist and to overcome except by arousing passion, by exhibitionism and seduction.'[5]

Tewfik El Hakim has been given the title 'enemy of woman'. In this area he has contributed thoughts very similar to those of El Akkad although they might differ in points of detail. In his story *El Robat El Mokadass* (The Sacred Bond), El Hakim portrays a woman who rebels against her life. However this rebellion, according to the story, is not due to intellectual ambition, or to a desire to do something worthwhile in her life, but rather to fill the emotional vacuum with which circumstances have afflicted her. The intellectual in this story, who in fact represents the author, maintains that woman no longer has sufficient religious conviction or motives, and that his role is to awaken her conscience and to bring her to realize what is fundamentally wrong Hakim in his turn describes woman as a creature who bears no loyalty or fidelity except to her 'baser instincts' and physical desires, and who behaves very much like Akkad's heroine, Sarah, taking not the slightest account of religious, intellectual or social values.

No one can help feeling that both El Akkad and El Hakim carry within themselves a conscious or unconscious fear, or even terror, of this feminine creature, endowed as she is with exceptional powers and sexual vitality, characteristics that are contained with difficulty inside the limits of conventional religious, moral and social values. For El Hakim, woman believes that pleasure and dissipation are her right and she speaks of this fact 'in terms that are full of the confidence and challenge, born of legitimate rights'.[6]

Arab literature also reflects the concept of honour as related to virginity discussed in the first part of this book. In fact this concept has not progressed much from its earliest, most primitive and absurd forms. In his novel, *Do 'a El Karawan*, Taha Hussein describes this conventional attitude towards honour. The little girl, Hanadi, is slaughtered like a sheep by her maternal uncle, aided and abetted by the mother whom the author portrays as so weak that she is unable to protect her daughter and even participates with the uncle in the killing. The uncle goes scot free, and nowhere is he looked upon as a criminal but rather as a man worthy of respect for defending the honour of his family. (An oft repeated Arab proverb says: 'Shame can only be washed away by blood.') The young engineer who is responsible for having sullied Hanadi's honour also escapes punishment, and at the end of the novel is rewarded with the love of the victim's sister, Amna. At the beginning, the story revolves around Amna's desire to take revenge on the young man who was the cause of her sister's horrible death. In her words: 'there is now no way out of an inevitable struggle between us. The time will come sooner or later when we will know whether Hanadi's life has been taken without a price, or whether there still remains on earth somebody who is capable of avenging the blood that was spilt.'[7]

Amna does not for one moment envisage taking revenge on her uncle whose hand held the knife that ended the life of her sister. The author in his novel says of women that 'they are a stigma that should be concealed, a *horma* that needs to be protected, and an *ard*[8] that has to be kept intact.'

Taha Hussein, in this novel, sees woman as helpless once she has lost her virginity, impotent when she decides to take vengeance on those who have wronged her, and reduced to nothing the moment she falls in love.[9] She gravitates inertly within the orbit of man without weapons or power or strength or a will to do anything, even fending for herself. She is always a victim, destroyed, annihilated. She is annihilated by man, but also by a host of other things; love, hatred and vengeance, and a total subjugation to man that extends to all aspects of her life whether material, psychological, emotional or moral. On occasion Taha Hussein shows some sympathy towards woman, but his feeling is always that of the conventional Arab, the condescending mercy of the superior and powerful male who looks down from his heights on the weaker and inferior female. He describes the sexual struggle between Amna and the engineer, the male fighting with all the weapons and power at his disposal against the female who is conquered and subjugated and broken in advance, a struggle which illustrates almost to perfection all the overtones of a sado-masochistic relationship in both the hero and the heroine.

Woman in the literary works of Naguib Mahfouz, perhaps the most well-known of contemporary Egyptian writers, remains 'a woman' whether poor or rich, ignorant or cultured. Throughout, she is fundamentally the same since her honour does not go further than an intact hymen and a chaste sexual life. In most cases, her downfall and the loss of her honour are brought about by poverty. This is perhaps a step forward since, before Naguib Mahfouz, male authors always brought about the perdition of their heroines through their baser instincts, their passions (in the sense of sexual desire), their female weakness, or the fact that they lacked a mind or brain. In contrast, for Naguib Mahfouz the sins of women are attributed to economic reasons (poverty). Nevertheless, his conception of honour remains the same and its kingdom stays concentrated in the limited area of the external genital organs.

Although Naguib Mahfouz is progressive in so far as his views on social justice are concerned, his attitude and concepts in relation to woman do not differ much from those of his predecessors. He permitted her the right to education and work in support of the father or husband and as a contribution to the income of the family, on condition that she did not overstep the limits of morals and religion (morals in the sense of the patriarchal family), and the double standard prevalent in society where a man and a woman join in love or intercourse, but where it is only the woman who is considered as having fallen or been dishonoured. Mahfouz sometimes waxes enthusiastic and, in the words of one of his characters, calls for the construction of a socialist society and imagines a more humane and prosperous way of life: 'The hope of being able to fulfil what he had dreamt of in his imagination, without transgressing the precepts of religion, brought a feeling of happiness to his heart.'[10]

It was inevitable that Naguib Mahfouz should fall prey to insoluble contradictions. He allows a woman to work and earn in society, and at the same time denies her individual freedom. He permits her to love, yet stigmatizes her for being a fallen woman if she really does. He considers marriage as the only legitimate and permissible relation between a man and a woman, but when a woman thinks in terms of marriage he accuses her of conservatism, caution and an inability to love. One of his heroes, commenting on the desire of his girl to be betrothed to him, says: 'She wishes to marry me, not to love me. This is the secret of her caution and her coldness.'[11] He describes her on occasion as being an animal without brain or religious belief, and on others sees in her the source of all the power embodied in the things of this world. 'No movement emanates from a man unless behind it there stands a woman. The role played by woman in our lives is akin to that of the gravitational forces extending between the stars and the planets.'[12]

Separation between love and marriage was one of the results of a concept inherited from the distant past that glorified *el hob el ozri* or romantic love, and that considered marriage, of which sex is a part, as relatively sinful. This led to the division of women into two categories: the female characterized by seductiveness and sexual passion, and the mother pure, virtuous, virgin devoid of sex or passion.

Arab literature is threaded throughout with innumerable examples of these two opposing and contradictory categories of women. The mother symbolizes a great and noble love, whereas the female symbolizes a degraded kind of love. The sacred respect in which Arab men hold their mothers appears clearly in songs, poems, novels and culture.

Most heroines' hope in life is to legitimize their existence through marriage. The woman's world is limited to thinking of men and dreaming of a husband. After marriage, a woman is solely occupied with the art of keeping her husband. The mother trains her daughter to perfect this art and says to her: 'You must be a new woman to him every day, a woman who is challenging, tempting and seductive.'[13]

The man who marries a working woman, one with a strong personality and who is self-confident, is looked upon as being weak and dominated by his wife.[14] He is depicted as having opposed his mother who always warned him against allowing his wife to go out to work. Naguib Mahfouz describes this husband as being a failure because he is leading a life in which decisions rest with the wife who has the upper hand.

Naguib Mahfouz depicts the woman, Rabab, as bearing no real love for her husband and of nurturing a passion for another man. She betrays her husband with her lover and the author does not forgive her, but makes her die during an abortion.

For man, the feminine woman represents danger and an ancient fear, both related to sex. He therefore wishes her to be pure like his mother, in other words not a female, and as passive and weak as an angel child. At the same time he harbours a burning desire for the female. Her seductiveness and her charms captivate him, yet he is afraid of these qualities because when faced by them his resistance collapses.

Most contemporary Arab writers manifest an undisguised hatred towards bold and emancipated women. The hero of one of Abdel Hamid Gouda El Sahar's books feels disgust when he sees his beloved, Kawsar, wearing a bathing suit: 'His blood raced hotly through his head and he was seized with a feeling of impatience and disgust. She appeared to him shallow and abhorrent.'[15]

Most stories and novels depict the conservative type of man, overcome with repulsion when faced with an educated woman who mixes freely and dances with men. Yet, at the same time, he is overcome by an equal if not greater repulsion when in the presence of a woman whose face is hidden behind a veil or who comes from a poor family and is liable to be led astray because of her poverty. The educated emancipated woman, however, falls lower than any other in his eyes just because she is liberated. Tom on all sides by these conflicting forces, his defences completely collapse and he ends up in a state of confusion: 'He felt as though everything had collapsed around him, and struck out blindly on to the road, like one who was lost. Deep down inside of him was the feeling of being surrounded by a strange and alien world.'[16]

[. . .]

Notes

1   Tolstoy, *Memoirs*, 3 August 1898, or quoted in Abbas El Akkad, *Hathibi El Shagara*, p. 88.

2   Abbas Mahmoud El Akkad, *Sarah*, p. 115.

3   Ibid., p. 84.

4   Soheir El Kalamawi, *A Thousand and One Nights*, (Dar El Maaref, Egypt, 1976), p. 303.

5   Abbas Mahmoud El Akkad, *Hathihi Al Shagara*, p. 15.

6   Tewfik El Hakim, *El Robat El Mokadas*.

7   Taha Hussein, *Doa'a El Karawan*, (Dar El Maaref Publishers, Cairo), p. 135.

8   This word, *ard*, has a special sense in Arabic. It means the honour of a man as embodied in his womenfolk. His duty is to keep his honour intact by preventing anyone (apart from the husband) from having any relations with one of the women. This is especially so with regard to protection of virginity.

9   Taha Hussein, *Doa'a El Karawan*, p. 151.

10   Naguib Mahfouz, *Bidaya Wa Nihaya*, p. 302.

11   Ibid., p. 298.

12   Naguib Mahfouz, *El Sarab*, (Maktabat Misr), p. 310.

13   El Mazni, *Ibrahim El Thani*, p. 52.

14   Naguib Mahfouz, *El Sarab*, p. 249.

15   Abdel Hamid Gouda El Sahar, *Kafilat El Zaman*, (Maktabat Misr, Cairo,) p. 325.

16   Abdel Hamid Gouda El Sahar, *El Nikab* (Maktabat Misr), p. 284.

Chapter 70

Women and Creative Writing in Africa

Flora Nwapa

[. . .]

In 1980, a woman journalist with the *Guardian of London* interviewed me and came out with this headline: "Running out of Boredom." You see, I had told her truthfully in the interview that I started writing because when I was a high school teacher, I had too much time on my hands and did not know what to do with it. I am a Capricorn, restless and hard-working. So, I began to write about my school days, a period in my life I look back on with nostalgia; a happy period when I learned and shared with my school mates; a period that saw the beginning of many years of sisterhood. Young, innocent, and trusting, my fellow boarders and I found ourselves in a school where the white missionaries taught us the ethics of the Christian religion. The white missionaries and some of our teachers introduced us to the world of books. We became avid readers, reading everything we could lay our hands on. One day, I stumbled upon a book written by a Nigerian (Cyprain Ekwensi), *When Love Whispers*, the first book written by a non-white person I ever read. Hitherto, all the authors we read were white and dead. The second Nigerian author I read that made a great impression on me is Chinua Achebe, whose *Things Fall Apart* was published in 1958.

As a high school teacher, I began to write about my childhood in the boarding school. Then, one day, the story of Efuru struck me in a most dramatic way as I was driving at a speed of 80 miles per hour along Enugu-Onitsha Road. I got to my destination, borrowed an exercise book and began to write Efuru's story. I wrote chapter one ("They Saw Each Other") and I did not stop until I finished the entire novel. I gave it to Chinua Achebe, who kindly read it and sent it to his publishers, Heinemann Educational Books, London, that published it in 1966. I have become a writer. I asked myself: Do you want to be a writer? I was not sure. Before I could find answers, the critics had taken over: What was Flora Nwapa trying to do in *Efuru*? Did she succeed? The deed had already been done. I have become

First published in *Sisterhood is Global: Feminism and Power from Africa to the Diaspora*, ed. O. Nnaemeka, pp. 89–99. Trenton, NJ: Africa World Press, 1998.

a writer. I racked my brain trying to figure out what exactly I was trying to do apart from writing the story of Efuru. All my thoughts led me to the African woman.

The woman's role in Africa is crucial for the survival and progress of the race. This is, of course, true of all women across the globe, be they black or white. In my work, I try to project a more balanced image of African womanhood. Male authors understandably neglect to point out the positive side of womanhood, for very many reasons which I will not attempt to discuss in this address. Recent changes in Nigeria – the 1967–70 civil war, economic changes, and an emphasis on the education of women – have affected men's views about women. Women have started to redefine themselves; they have started to project themselves as they feel they should be presented.

More than anything else, I would like to give examples of the crucial roles that Igbo women play in their communities; for example, the powerful role of women as *Umuada* (all daughters born in a clan, married or not, and wherever they may be) in burial and title-taking ceremonies and in peace-making where they constitute the final court of appeal; the role of women as *Umunwunyeobu* (wives of the clan); women's various roles as priestesses and members of age-grades. Every member of *Umuada* knows where she belongs and what is expected of her. Members possess individual and group power but rarely act individually. No burial or title-taking ceremony is complete without the presence of *Umuada*, and woe betide any daughter who fails to show up in these ceremonies.

Peace-making is an important function of *Umuada*, *Umunwunyeobu*, and the women's age-grades. When there is a quarrel between husband and wife, parents and children, these groups of women are called upon to make peace. The role of the wives of the clan is very visible and considerable at home in terms of participating and intervening in their husbands' decision-making processes. If the women find out that their husbands are proving difficult and obstinate, they could take a far-reaching stand, the most common being the refusal to cook for or sleep with their husbands.

Priestesses feature prominently in many parts of Nigeria, especially in the riverine areas of the south. They wield tremendous power in many areas, including healing and predicting the future. As women, they mediate between the supernatural and natural worlds, between the divine (deities) and the human. Those of you who have read *Things Fall Apart* will remember Chielo, the mouthpiece of the oracle.

How do African literary texts project women? A few of them have tried to project an objective image of women, an image that actually reflects the reality of women's role in the society. Peter Abraham's *A Wreath for Udoma* and Sembène Ousmane's *God's Bits of Wood* recognize the "full and complete woman" and provide role models for the female reader-ship. There are three prominent female characters in *A Wreath for Udoma* – Lois, Selina, and Maria. All three women are portrayed, not as victims of male subjugation in a patriarchal society, but as full woman-beings who take up their rightful positions in the society. These three women are the real power behind the struggle for independence. In Adebhoy's words, Selina is: "The real power behind us, homeboy. She tells all the women in all the villages what to tell their men, and the men do what the women tell them. Without her, we wouldn't have this party." Also in Ousmane Sembène's *God's Bits of Wood*, the success of the railway workers' strike is the handiwork of the women. They scout for food and water. They fight the police. They march on to Dakar, their sheer number breaking the power of the colonialists. After the strike, the men learned a hard lesson – i.e., never to tackle or undertake any major issues or projects without first consulting the women.

However, Nigerian male writers, such as Chinua Achebe, Cyprain Ekwensi, Wole Soyinka, J. P. Clark, and Elechi Amadi, have all in their earlier works played down the powerful role of women. Unlike Peter Abraham and Ousmane Sembène, Nigerian male writers have in many instances portrayed women negatively or in their subordination to men. Ekwensi's Jagua Nana is a prostitute; Wole Soyinka's Amope is a ceaselessly nagging woman who makes life intolerable for her husband. Achebe's Miss Mark does not hesitate to put her sex appeal to work in order to attain desired objectives. J. P. Clark's Ebiere entices her husband's younger brother into a sexual relationship. The focus has always been on the physical, prurient, negative nature of woman. Woman's subordinate position is redressed (somewhat) in the name given to the heroine of Achebe's *Anthills of the Savanah*, Nwanyi-buife ("Woman is Something" – an assertion that women are a force to be reckoned with). The heroine, Beatrice Nwanyibuife, is a liberated and powerful woman, leading one to surmise that she symbolizes perhaps a sudden awakening to the importance of woman-being.

Yes, in African literature, there have been female portraits of sorts presented by men from their own point of view, leading one to conclude that there is a difference between the African male writer and his female counterpart. So what did I do in *Efuru*? In my two heroines, Efuru and Idu, I was inspired by the women around me when I was growing up. These women were not like Jagua Nana, Amope, Miss Mark, or Ebiere. They were solid and superior women who held their own in society. They were not only wives and mothers but successful traders who took care of their children and their husbands as well. They were very much aware of their leadership roles in their families as well as in the churches and local government. The models for Efuru and Idu were there – in real life – for me to exploit. In my first two novels, I tried to recreate the experiences of women in the traditional African society – their social and economic activities and above all their preoccupation with the problems of procreation, infertility, and child-rearing. Apart from exposing the pain, misery and humiliation which childless or barren women suffer in the traditional society, the two novels (I hope!) give insight into the resourcefulness and industriousness of women which often made them successful, respected, and influential people in the community. In these two novels, therefore, I tried to debunk the erroneous concept that the husband is the lord and master and that the woman is nothing but his property. I tried to debunk the notion that the woman is dependent on her husband. The woman not only holds her own, she is astonishingly *in*dependent of her husband.

So while some Nigerian male writers failed to see this power base, this strength of character, this independence, I tried in *Efuru* and *Idu* to elevate the woman to her rightful place. Unlike African male writers, I could overlook neither the safeguards with which custom surrounds the woman in her community nor the weight of women's opinions. I tried to analyze the woman's independent economic position and the power she wields by the mere fact that she controls the pestle and the cooking pots.

Efuru is the story of a beautiful, intelligent, hardworking, wealthy, and childless woman. Thus, both her stature and tragic dimension are carefully established from the very first few chapters of the novel. Yet, in spite of her handicap (childlessness), she attains a very high and respectable position in her community. No one could do anything about the luckless Efuru for she is already the chosen one of the Great Woman of the Lake; she is called late in life to be the priestess of the water goddess. By this choice, Efuru is elevated to a plane higher than that of human beings; she communicates with gods and goddesses. Similarly, in *Idu*, the protagonist, Idu, in the end does not kill herself, she simply dies preferring to join her dead husband in the spirit world.

The woman writer cannot fail to see the woman's power in her home and society. She sees her economic importance both as mother, farmer, and trader. *She writes stories that affirm the woman*, thus challenging the male writers and making them aware of woman's inherent vitality, independence of views, courage, self-confidence, and, of course, her desire for gain and high social status.

In Nigeria and other countries of Africa, there have been tremendous changes in all facets of life which contribute to the continent-wide awareness and rethinking of women's problems and roles in the society. These changes are affecting both men and women in many ways and creative writers are responding to them by recreating meaningfully women's culture and world-view in this age of female awakening and feminist consciousness. It is this new vision of women that I have striven to depict in my novels (*One is Enough, Women are Different, Never Again*) and short stories (*This is Lagos, Wives at War*, and *Cassava Song and Rice Song*). The thread that runs through these works is women's struggles for survival by whatever means as they respond to the tremendous changes in the society.

Cassava Song and Rice Song is an attempt to re-live in poetry the form and themes of English neo-classical poetry by poets such as Alexander Pope and John Dryden. Cassava is elevated to about the same height as, for example, the "lock" of Belinda, the beautiful lady in Alexander Pope's work, *Rape of the Lock*. Cassava is a staple food in Igboland. The Cassava tuber is accessible to both the rich and the poor in many parts of Nigeria and Africa. Cassava is planted by women, unlike yam, the "King of all Crops," that is planted by men. Every year in Igboland, the New Yam Festival is observed. New yam is not eaten until this festival is performed. But, is there a festival for Cassava? No. In "Cassava Song," the many uses of cassava are enumerated to show that she deserves to be celebrated and sung like the yam. In mock heroic style, "Cassava Song" opens with an invocation:

> We thank thee Almighty God
> For giving us Cassava
> We hail thee, Cassava
> The great Cassava

Cassava is personified as a Great Mother, a forgiving mother, more sinned against than sinning. Cassava is given the Divine Redeemer motif; like Christ who goes through suffering, Cassava remains obedient to fire even unto death. Cassava is enthroned above yam and cocoyam – above all other foodstuff. Cassava is woman. Yam is man.

In *Wives at War and Other Stories*, the story, "The Chief's Daughter," tells of the changing role of the woman in the society. A favorite daughter could be made by her father to remain single in order to have children to bear his name and continue the paternal lineage. The Chief's daughter, Adaeze, is about to return from the land of the white people when the story begins. The Chief is bent on not letting her get married. She rejects her father's plans and marries a man of her choice. In *This is Lagos and Other Stories*, "The Child Thief" is a story that depicts the trauma a woman faces when it dawns on her that she cannot have a child. In order to keep her marriage, she employs all kinds of deceit, and finally resorts to stealing a baby from the hospital. Amaka, the heroine of *One is Enough*, finds herself performing tasks considered to be men's jobs. She becomes a contractor and attains economic independence. Because Amaka sees men as unreliable, she charts her own path to happiness and works hard so as to be in a position to live on her own terms.

Rose, Agnes and Dora in *Women Are Different* reflect their own spirit of liberation. They explode the myth of female passivity and docility and are blazing a new trail in female consciousness. It is true that this new radicalism has come after the women have been victimized and betrayed by their men. Victim of child marriage, Agnes is made to marry a man old enough to be her father; Dora's husband abandons her and her five children; Mark jilts Rose after exploiting her. This is also the experience of Amaka *(One is Enough)*, who, after eight years of a childless marriage, moves to Lagos determined that: "She would find fulfillment. She would find pleasure, even happiness in being a single woman. The erroneous belief that without a husband a woman was nothing must be disproved." In the case of Dora *(Women Are Different)*, her husband returns after a long absence but now she has acquired the strength and economic independence to dictate the terms of their renewed relationship.

The question I would like to ask is why these women become assertive and aggressive only after they have been brutalized or betrayed by their men. Are there no women in Africa today who can hold their own without waiting to be brutalized or betrayed? Are there no women in Africa today who can say:

> To hell with men and marriage.
> I don't want to have children.
> I want to be free to do just as I please.

Perhaps the time has not yet come. Majority of the women in Africa live in the rural area. Many are uneducated, and there are not too many alternatives to being married and having children. The most natural thing for the rural woman is to marry and procreate. Even for us, the educated urbanites, the time has not come. We still have our roots in the rural areas where we were brought up. Our umbilical cord is still buried in the rural environment. We are the very few that are exposed to Western education. We have traveled in Europe and America, yet we are not Europeans and Americans. We are Africans. We have our ways of doing things; things like marriage, divorce, and motherhood. Marriage is a sacred bond that transcends a simple union between a man and a woman; it is a bond between two families. Therefore, a woman or indeed a man cannot divorce at will, but yet within this tradition, divorce is possible, though difficult when children are involved.

An educated Nigerian woman will not take her husband to court if he commits bigamy. It is true that bigamy is committed every day in Nigeria, but even the educated wife would hesitate to take action against her husband *for the sake of her children*. What would it profit the educated wife if her husband, the father of her children, were sentenced to prison on her own account? How does she explain it to her children? How would the society view her action? But it is interesting to note that the so-called rural woman, at least in my own community, has no such inhibitions. This is an area where the educated woman envies her rural sister. Is the latter more liberated in this regard? Some in-depth research is called for. So Dora *(Women Are Different)* goes out of her way to look for her wayward husband, and when he returns after many years, she throws a party to welcome him. She consoles herself with these words: "But I have the whip hand. I am not a fool. Now my children have a father. That's all that matters. . . . and I have a husband. But it is not the same again . . . What is left now is stark reality and common sense."

African women writers have been accused of dwelling too much on barrenness. They are told by male critics to write on other "more important" themes. What *are* these other important themes? One of the panelists in this conference asked women writers to "project into the future the figure of a female president; fiction may lead to fact." In addition, a panelist said yesterday in his presentation, "Women are not only Africans but also women." True, the life of a man and that of a woman are interdependent. But then the problem that a woman faces in the world is the pain of not being able to bring forth a child from her womb, a feat no man can (yet) perform. The pain is great if she is denied this function and this is why the theme of barrenness is explored by many African writers, particularly the female ones. A wife is more often than not betrayed and abandoned by her husband if she does not have a child. Therefore, the desire to be pregnant, to procreate is an overpowering one in the life of the woman. She is ready to do anything to have a child, be she single or married.

The African woman writer is urged to break new ground by projecting the future of a female president. Does the woman writer live in an environment in which this is possible? My answer is yes. Because women's issues are very much alive in Africa today and various African governments are using women as resources in nation building. And it is left to the creative writers, male and female, to explore this new awareness, this new image of women's sensibilities, possibilities, and realities, and produce works which modern African women can relate to. Having said that, I must quickly add that we must not force issues on fiction. It is true that the woman writer has found a voice, but (one may ask) what kind of voice? Are we heard? Are we not sometimes completely ignored? Here we must thank our feminist sisters at home and abroad (America and Europe) who have made it possible for African critics to notice us. Projecting a female president can be achieved, why not? But she must be there for all to see. Anowa is there, Adah is there, Efuru is out there for all to see. I must reiterate the fact that this is not exclusively the task of African women writers, but also that of the male writers.

My conclusion on this issue of barrenness is that women are what they are because they can give life, they can procreate. So in African societies, when this unique function is denied a woman, she is devastated. But should this be so, all the time, in this day and age? Does this handicap, this childlessness make a woman less woman, less human? I do not think so. Efuru finds fulfillment by becoming the priestess of the water goddess. Therefore, we *should* create characters that are fulfilled and not weighed down by the shackles of marriage and motherhood. But, of course, there are choices; there are choices in the African environment itself. There must be choices because this handicap, childlessness, does not make a woman less a woman or less human.

In my novels, I explore the theme of moral laxity, but this is treated in response to earlier novels written by men where prostitution is always associated with women. Some of the most notable prostitutes are Jagua Nana of Ekwensi's *Jagua Nana*; Simi of Soyinka's *The Interpreters*; and Wanja of Ngugi's *Petals of Blood*. But in my novels there is a reversal of roles – men are the prostitutes. In *Women Are Different*, Chris, Dora's husband, is a male prostitute, kept by a German woman. Ernest, Rose's former boyfriend, goes from one woman to another without finding satisfaction. Mark is a kept man; he lives with Rose whom he exploits by duping her of hundreds of pounds before deserting her. Olu's sexual adventures take him through numerous affairs in several cities but he always goes back to his wife after each affair. In these novels, women have the upper hand; they are more forthcoming and in control. Dora claims that she "has the whip hand" after her husband returns to her. Amaka is in control in her relationship with the Alhaji and the Reverend Fr. Maclaid. The men have lost initiative, always on the move, finding it impossible to settle down anywhere.

Again, I am asserting that a woman is also flesh and blood. She has a heart and soul and she is capable of human feelings. She can stand on her own two feet just as a man can. But I think that women should have an open mind about relationships with men. I also think that women writers should not only have an open mind but create avenues for this openness of mind. Our task should be to exploit elements of our indigenous traditions – such as democracy, tolerance, sharing, and mutual support – in order to achieve our goal. The fact that one man betrays and brutalizes you does not mean that another will do the same. There should be interdependence and some measure of understanding which blossoms to mutual respect and equality. Did I say equality? Yes, because the lives of a man and a woman are interdependent, there must be mutual understanding and respect. The African woman writer has a great responsibility now and in the future, but can she alone champion the cause? A man can portray a powerful heroine as well as a woman can if he sets his mind to it and if he does not feel that portraying a strong heroine makes him less of a man. As earlier pointed out, Peter Abraham and Ousmane Sembène, in their respective novels, gave a truer and more balanced portrayal of the African women.

The Women's Movement inside and outside Africa as well as the various Women's Studies programs in African, North American, and European universities have created awareness among our own African critics. The voice of the African woman writer is being heard, though somewhat inaudibly. A lot still needs to be done. The global recession is causing a lot of havoc in Africa. What cost us one naira to produce ten years ago, costs a hundred now. With the support of our American and European sisters and our men, we (African women) shall succeed.

References

Abrahams, Peter. *A Wreath for Udoma*. New York: Alfred Knopf, 1956.

Achebe, Chinua. *Things Fall Apart*. London: Heinemann, 1958.

——. *Anthills of the Savannah*. New York: Anchor, 1987.

Ekwensi, Cyprain. *When Love Whispers*. Onitsha: Tabansi Bookshop, 1950.

——. *Jagua Nana*. London: Hutchinson, 1961.

Nwapa, Flora. *Efuru*. London: Heinemann, 1966.

——. *Idu*. London: Heinemann, 1970.

——. *This Is Lagos and Other Stories*. Enugu: Nwankwo-Ifejika, 1971.

——. *Never Again*. Enugu: Nwamife, 1975; Trenton, NJ: Africa World Press, 1992.

——. *Wives at War and Other Stories*. Enugu: Tana Press, 1981; Trenton, NJ: Africa World Press, 1992.

——. *One Is Enough*. Enugu: Tana Press, 1981; Trenton, NJ: Africa World Press, 1992.

——. *Women Are Different*. Enugu: Tana Press, 1986; Trenton, NJ: Africa World Press, 1992.

——. *Cassava Song and Rice Song*. Enugu: Tana Press, 1986.

Pope, Alexander. *Rape of the Lock*. London: Lane, 1902.

Sembène, Ousmane. *God's Bits of Wood*, trans., Francis Price. Garden City, NY: Anchor Books, 1970.

Soyinka, Wole. *The Interpreters*. New York: Africana Publishing Corp., 1972.

wa Thiong'O, Ngugi. *Petals of Blood*. New York: Dutton, 1978.

Chapter 71

African Motherhood – Myth and Reality

Lauretta Ngcobo

African motherhood is one experience that is shrouded in layers of assumptions. At a distance these appear like billowing soft, pink clouds of a joyous, profound and an exciting experience. Ask many people about this in this audience, and they will nod their heads in concurrence. This impression is derived directly or indirectly from some of the literature that we read, written by Africans themselves, some of them in this audience. To be fair, few of them, if any have actually written that motherhood is beautiful and joyous. But what they have indicated, most of them not being mothers themselves, is that they respect motherhood and that in Africa they preserve a special place of honour for motherhood and that they love their mothers. But away from this hall of writers, into the streets and hills of Africa one will meet hordes of mothers who will smile shyly, allow you your frothing excitement and quietly qualify what motherhood, the institution, really means, for them. If you have the humility to listen you will soon realize that you do not share the same understanding. If you are a conscientious researcher you will want to know why. You might even talk to some of their happy children – African motherhood is about children. You might look through their school books. And if you can read the indigenous languages that they are written in you will soon understand, for that literature will present impressions of motherhood that are very revealing and are alive with a different reality. They come out of the seething experience of African life rather than the dreamlike recapture of an escaping tradition such as many of us write about and read from each other's books.

As elsewhere, marriage amongst Africans is mainly an institution for the control of procreation. Every woman is encouraged to marry and get children in order to express her womanhood to the full. The basis of marriage among Africans implies the transfer of a woman's fertility to the husband's family group. There is a high premium placed on children and the continuity of each lineage. To facilitate this transfer of fertility, a dowry must be paid;

First published in *Criticism and Ideology: Second African Writers' Conference, Stockholm 1986*, ed. Kirsten H. Petersen, pp. 141–51. Uppsala: Scandinavian Institute of African Studies, 1988.

not to buy the wife as missionaries have wrongly understood. The dowry not only gives exclusive sexual rights to the man, but essentially it is a means of social control over the children that the woman might bear in marriage. This becomes clearly evident where the dowry has not been paid, for no matter how long and strong a relationship may be between a man and woman, in many societies in Africa, the children they get will belong to the wife's people, taking her family name as well. And where a man dies after paying the dowry, and the wife later enters other relationships with other men, her subsequent children will continue to belong to her deceased husband, taking his name with no social reference whatsoever to their biological father or his family. That is why, in most cases, the husband's family are anxious that the young widow is taken over by her deceased husband's brother or a close relation of his in order to keep the children within the family, biologically and socially.

The reason why African families desire high fertility have to do with 'human capital' and 'social security'. This all important need for children has led to the institutionalizing of motherhood through fertility rites, taboos and beliefs and has acquired some religious significance. For a man it has become a sacred duty towards his whole lineage. Failure to immortalize the ancestors is taboo and a shame that a man cannot bear. As a result, childlessness is associated with women, for the alternative is unthinkable. Central to many African beliefs is that there are three states of human existence – the land of the unborn, the land of the living and the land of the ancestors and the dead. Belief has it that the children of any given family are always there waiting for the mothers to come and rescue them from oblivion and bring them to life in the land of the living. Failure therefore, to 'rescue' the children is a sorrowful capitulation and a betrayal. In cases of childlessness, people do not think of and share the couple's or woman's agony – rather, they hear the echoing cries of the unborn children that she (the mother) will not 'rescue' and bring to life.

Marriage is a relationship between two groups, not just two people. Sometimes even the death of one partner does not invalidate the marriage itself. If it is the wife who dies, the husband may go back to his in-laws to ask for another wife for more or less the same dowry. This makes the position of motherhood socially and cosmologically very central. In many societies, to this day, the choice of partners is exercised by the parents on behalf of their daughters and sometimes their sons as well. This emphasizes the paramount reason for marriage itself. It is not marriage; it is the children of the marriage; it is not the companionship, nor the love or friendship, nor the mutual emotional satisfaction of the couple.

A little girl child is born to fulfil this role. She is made aware of the destiny awaiting her development and is prepared from the earliest age possible for the role of motherhood that she will play elsewhere, away from her family home. She is well loved but her rights within the family are limited compared to those of her brothers. She is aware that somehow she is on her way out. It is significant that in some of the Bantu languages the word marriage is synonymous with journey. In short, from earliest childhood she is an outsider who is being prepared for the central role that she will play at her in-laws. Many young girls will be forgiven for their eager anticipation of their marriage and a place where they will finally belong. But as we shall soon see, disillusionment awaits them. This is double jeopardy, for they will never really belong anywhere.

The major weakness in this formidable role of motherhood is that women can only exercise it from the outside, for they remain marginalized at their new husband's homes. At her in-laws she does not move in to attain her independence or find her place of centrality. Instead, she is reduced to a permanent state of dependence and estrangement. She will always be an outsider among his people, always the first suspect when things go wrong. And her position of motherhood entails hard labour to provide food for the family. Nothing will change this until in old age, if she is a powerful woman or a senior wife, she will be empowered to move centrally, to exercise authority and train the younger women in the practised art of walking the tight-rope, which is exercising her immense power from the outside – the paradox of a position of centrality which is exercised from the periphery. For, let us make no mistake – motherhood as an institution is very powerful in our societies.

Right from the earliest stages of the marriage there is a conscious effort to distance the young wife from the young husband. Men and women live diverse segregated lives. In most societies they will not eat together. Men often share their food in a communal meal away from the women, while the women eat in their own houses or at best with other women. A young wife is in close touch with the other women in the home rather than with her husband, for social organization and work roles tend to keep the sexes apart in everyday life. In most societies like the Bemba of Zambia, young girls are taught that a 'good wife does not talk to her husband much'. Sometimes she is supposed to leave her husband with her co-wives as soon as she is pregnant. The rationale is that she has got what she wanted and throughout her pregnancy and lactation she will no longer need the husband. This at a time when the rigours of pregnancy may render her weak and in need of him emotionally if not physically. This distancing of the young bride will affect all aspects of her life. In some societies like the Nguni she will never be called by her own name. They might call her by her father's name – the daughter of so and so, or they may simply call her 'the bride' until she has her first child. Then she will be referred to as the mother of so and so – thus living her identity through her father or her child. The fact of losing their names distances and isolates married women emotionally and further confirms the alienation in their new home. To further confirm her alienation her position is attended by many taboos. Depending on the society, there may be complicated patterns of behaviour towards each member of the new family. She will call none of them by their names, except the very youngest; sometimes not even her husband. She might call him as the brother of so and so, referring to his youngest brother or sister. That will be his name until he has his first child when she will call him 'the father of so and so'. Nowhere that intimacy that existed before marriage. She will not only avoid calling her 'father-in-law' by name, but she will adopt a conduct of avoidance between the two of them – she will never ever bare her head in his presence. In extreme cases of the practice, she will avoid in ordinary conversation all those words that have the same sound as his name. Another area of strong taboos is food. She may not be allowed to eat certain foods. This might be milk. Among the Nguni this will mean that she brings her own cows from her father, so that where milk is a staple diet she will continue to be fed by her father years after she left his home to be a valued member of the other family.

It must be clear also that she has no property that accrues to her entirely. She has no rights of inheritance nor can she give legacies to anyone. Many studies have shown how the contribution of women to labour is underrated, especially in rural areas. The problem lies with the arbitrary demarcation between the so called 'economic' and 'non-economic' work which bears no relation to the actual physical input. Dr Evelyn Amarteifo, a Ghanaian woman, has researched extensively in this area and she confirms the common male habit of letting women do the bulk of the work in the home, as in the fields, but giving them nothing for it. Under matriarchy women have more rights than under patriarchy. Although matri-archy in itself does not imply real social power on the part of the women, they certainly have more say in the community and within the family structure. Among the Ashanti of Ghana, a woman enjoys definite inheritance and property rights and elderly women are consulted in the making of community decisions. Whereas in patrilineal society a woman cannot own land or cattle; neither can she participate in a debate or negotiation concerning property. As a 'minor' she cannot be a party to a legal action. She has always got to be represented by her father or brother or husband or son. Also, she often has limited authority even over her sons who are above a certain age. Matrilineal law is incompatible with private ownership of land. Historically we note that the transition from matriarchy to patriarchy was fraught with social struggles, with some Africans supporting private ownership of land under patriarchy and others supporting matriarchy and its communal ownership of land. It was also in the interests of the colonialists to support the patriarchal system which enabled them to acquire private ownership of land. But this option, more than anything else deprived women of their customary rights. A typical case occurred among the Tonga along the Zambezi during the building of the Kariba dam in the 1950s. Under matriarchy Tonga women have the same land rights as men upon inheritance. But when the communities were moved to be resettled, to make way for the dam, the women's rights were seriously affected. When the land was redistributed upon resettling, it was allocated to the male members only and the women lost their rights. And slowly matriarchy is becoming outdated and contradictory.

But worse than that is that our men themselves are losing out to the capitalists who exploit all the African people. Africans have yet to work out a system of social organization of their own that is not founded on the exploitation of one group by another, within the same society nor preyed on by other societies, nations or political systems from outside.

Polygamy is almost universal in Africa, although under the money-economy it is showing signs of stress. In places like South Africa it is decidedly on the way out. Relations among the co-wives are seldom wholesome. Rivalry and insecurity within the institution often result in hatred. This sort of bitterness has little outlet, for its expression is discouraged.

The indigenous literature reflects a turbulent change for the worse in the condition of women in a changing Africa. In the reality of Africa where fathers live away from home, working in the cities or are weakened by liquor in the stressful life of those cities, women often have to combine the roles of motherhood and fatherhood in bringing up the children. They themselves have to be strong to take on both roles, loving, protecting and counseling in turns. African women may not be born that way, but they do wax strong, faced with the challenges in the African context. It is not surprising that the relationship between mothers and sons, far from being harmonious and loving is often ambivalent and erratic. When the sons are young it is loving, loyal and close. In polygamous or large families, where the wider family relationships are competitive, mothers and sons can get very close, for mutual protection. This is particularly so where matters of inheritance are concerned. But in non-competitive situations mothers are depicted as strong disciplinarians, therefore admired and feared. In many books written by Africans in our languages and in English this image appears again and again. In Marechera's *The House of Hunger*, the mother is strong, fearsome and unloved. After all, she not only beats the sons up when they are mischievous, but she beats the father as well when he is drunk. She is forthright and unflinching to the point of embarrassing her sons, such as when she tells him to stop masturbating on her sheets. Sometimes the mother's manly ways can cause embarrassment and are a challenge, and mothers may be regarded as unreasonable or even mentally disturbed. In *Aftermaths* in the story 'Crossing the River' Stanley Nyamfukudza quotes the son saying of his mother 'her laughter carried so much disdain that you knew nothing you said would make any difference with her'. She dares the conductor and wins the bet. The son is proud of her courage but he has a socially determined expectation of how mothers ought to behave – so he vacillates between embarrassment at her stubborn insistence which is unwomanly and pride when she triumphs.

Sometimes mothers are seen as making unreasonable demands, full of high expectations. Mothers have to drive their sons hard and far because they themselves are driven to the ultimate in their struggle to survive. What sons see as unreasonable demands have to do with the pressing needs of today and the hopes for a better tomorrow. Where fathers are weak, absent or dead, sons often assume that the mother drove him away, if not through her shrewish ways, perhaps through her malevolent ways. Thus it is not uncommon to read of sons who accuse their mothers of witchcraft against their fathers or their wives or even their children.

The accusation involving witchcraft is a common ploy designed to cause the mother's social demotion. It will often be used against a powerful woman when the real aim is to discredit her socially or even to have her physically removed from her in-laws and sent back to her people, even after many years. Often it is levelled against women who are old and beyond child bearing age, and have therefore outlived their usefulness in the homes of their affines. In Mazibuko's *Umzenzi Kakhalelwa* Masibanda, the mother, is accused of witchcraft by her son, Mloyiswa and his wife, MaNdlovu. Several of their children have died in infancy. She is also accused of having neglected and thus caused the death of her husband, Mloyiswa's father.[1]

This is the conflict mothers often find themselves in, for the long years of separation under migratory labour often lead to years of neglect, causing strained and distant relations between wives and husbands. Children in general and sons in particular will grow unaware of these stresses and tensions, filled with their own longing for a full life with the father – he remains distant, desirable and untainted in their eyes. Unlike the mother, he manages to get away with sweet talk and token gifts, seldom having to discipline or harass them for any slackness on their part. When, in old age he comes home, ill perhaps, they sense a coldness between the parents. This they blame on the hardness that they have known in the mother, and the belief that she kept him away all those years is confirmed. As the sons get older they slowly acquire authority, as empowered by tradition. This too gradually leads to tensions, if not open conflict with a mother who will not give way to the son when the time comes. This will most likely coincide with the time of his marriage when he seeks to assert his own authority, not only as a husband but as a son as well.

Another source of conflict has to do with the mother's personal interests. In the absence of their husbands most women will develop their own interests such as a passionate belief in some religion or even a secret love affair. Almost invariably, such personal interests will lead to family conflicts and bitter accusations against the mother. It could be said in general that the greatest cause of conflict occurs when mothers pursue their own personal interests and are seen to be neglecting the welfare of the family.

The arrival of the daughter-in-law introduces an added strain and a triangular one in the relationship between the mother, the son and his wife. The mother and the wife see themselves as competing for his love and income. But underlying all this is the tug for authority between mother and son. Sons are often at a loss how to handle these conflicts between mothers and wives. On some occasions they take the wife's side and accuse the mother of malevolence. In short, this is a complex tangle of relationships. But in spite of all the conflicts there are strong ties that bind mothers to their sons on the one hand, and mothers to their daughters-in-law on the other. Often in a quarrel against her son, the mother will climb down first, for her security in her home is firmly rooted in her sons. Without the support of her sons, she is redundant, especially if she is beyond child-bearing age. The authority to keep her secure in the home and well-provided for lies with him. On the other hand the sons are aware of the earlier struggles that the mother put up to secure them a foothold and a claim in the competitive politics of an extended family. They know they owe her a lot. And between the mother and her daughter-in-law there is the ever present awareness that the two have a lot in common – that they will always be outsiders in the family lineage of their husbands. They share disadvantages and the young woman can always learn from the older woman; one serving apprenticeship, the other tutoring. The son/husband on the other hand is aware of the necessity for a healthy learning relationship between these two women for he knows that soon, in her turn, his young wife will be fighting to secure her own children's position in the family structure. The whole relationship is governed by power and intrigue more than anything else. And in all this, fathers-in-law emerge uninvolved and unscathed. It could be said they are outside the whole play for power and security. As a result, they come out well liked on all sides.

On the other hand, relationships between mothers and daughters are close and often assumptions are made that a good mother will have a good daughter, and that an evil mother will invariably influence her daughter. In a large number of books this close relationship is portrayed. Rudo Gaidwanza in her book *Images of Women* catalogues a long list of books that portray this – a domineering wife will influence her daughter to do the same: a mother of loose morals will teach her daughter to cheat her husband; a witch of a mother will impart her craft to her daughter. In many books written by male writers this collusion between mothers and daughters is given prominence, but this is not so evident in books written by women. This perhaps is a reflection of what men feel about the vices in their wives – often blaming their mothers-in-law for whatever problems they encounter in their wives. Disagreeable as this may sound, there could be some truth in it, for mothers prepare their daughters for the alienating experience of marriage in the almost hostile home of the in-laws.

Newly married daughters will often ask their mothers for advice in matters of running a household, raising children and handling a husband and difficult in-laws. Needless to say, these 'tricks of the trade' that mothers will pass on to their powerless, intimidated daughters will border on the manipulative and will of necessity be exclusive of male experience. This is threatening and intriguing to most men.

The ideal wife is defined through her relationship with her husband and her children. More so if this commitment entails the sacrifice of her own interests. Tsitsi in Chakaipa's *Garandichauya* is the ideal wife for she is loyal even when he deserts her for another woman. She goes home and waits almost a lifetime for him to return. When he finally does so, a broken man, she is happy to have him back. Vida in Kuimba's *Rurimi Inyoka* sticks to her post even when she is taunted and maltreated by her mother-in-law. She remains reasonable and amiable even under the curse of childlessness, offering to leave him if she is the culprit and to stay with him if he is the one. Mandlovu in Mazibuko's *Umzenzi Kakhalelwa* passes the test then she bears the pain of all her children dying in infancy, staying on in the home of her in-laws without her husband and her mother-in-law. This type of character constitutes the ideal wife.

A close analysis of these characters and their motives reveals characters who opt for the path of martyrdom for lack of any alternatives. But those women who fail to make it as good wives are treated very harshly – the authors are merciless against a woman character who fails to conform to traditional expectations. They commonly die for their mistakes. Jordan's *Ingqumbo YeMinyanya* is one such work.

On the whole widows are respected and get a lot of sympathy from the community. This is the case particularly where they are young and have young children. It also depends on whether they are not suspected or accused of causing the death of the husband directly or indirectly. On the surface this would seem to cater for a small percentage of women, as few would say that women would deliberately kill off their husbands. But this is a complex issue, complicated by the politics of inheritance in Africa.

In many parts of the continent the death of a man attracts a lot of attention from his relatives in relation to his property. Underlying all this is the feeling that what he owns, rightly belongs to his family group, not to the wife who remains an outsider. This is the case even when a wife has worked hard to assist in the accumulation of the family property, as many wives do. So, at his death, to salvage their conscience as they plunder his family goods, they will discredit the wife through accusations of adultery or of killing him directly or indirectly. As a result, not many widows get away with sympathy and understanding. This scene is well documented in Mariama Bâ's book *So long a Letter* when Modou dies suddenly and Ramatoulaye lies helplessly propped up on pillows and watches them ransack her home. And this, even without any specific accusation against her.

Most older widows, seeing that old age and motherhood confer power and status, are content to remain at their in-laws to assist their grown sons in anchoring a strong male dominated establishment against young wives and outsiders. In return they are well looked after by their sons and their grandchildren. It is from this vantage point that a lot of books written by male writers see the women of Africa, propped high on a pedestal of power, virtue and conformity and well loved. But younger widows face a much more difficult time of decision. Seeing marriage is primarily for procreation such women are at the mercy of circumstances. To continue her role of motherhood and also to get some economic support from the family, she may have to agree to being inherited by one of the members of the family who is to continue giving her children on behalf of her deceased husband. If she is older the question of re-marriage will not even enter the debate, for the need for companionship and sexual compatibility is not considered.

The image of divorced women in our society and our literature is negative. Only a handful may earn the understanding of the community such as in cases where the woman has a clean reputation which contrasts sharply with her husband's maltreatment of her. Only in a few cases do some women win the sympathy of the public. This is confirmed if they are seen to behave with dignity after the divorce. On the whole a wife will do everything to endure even a stressful marriage, for in a divorce she comes out the loser: Even when her husband is the offending party, society sees her as having failed to hold him in place – therefore his failure is her failure as well. The welfare of the children constitutes another consideration. Children will always belong to the husbands lineage and in a divorce the wife loses the children and leaves them behind. So the concern for the children's welfare will force even divorced women back to the in-laws to live with them.

Seen from these various points of view the plight of a woman is desperate, especially if she is left on her own. Many will hang on to the same man long after he has lost interest. This raises a crucial question for African women today – that of self-definition and self-determination. We have seen how the married woman and the widowed woman and even the divorced woman are defined by their relationship to men, a father or a husband or their sons. Thus the anguished cry that Emecheta's main character Nnu Ego makes in *The Joys of Motherhood*: 'God when will you create a woman who will be fulfilled in herself, a full human being, not anybody's appendage?' Women have been driven to this position where they may only live through men. So great is the power of tradition that no single woman in Africa, in spite of her awareness, is able to shift the power of tradition. Abandoning certain practices in tradition does nothing for the embedded attitudes of African men.

These attitudes which are enfeebling to our women, are perpetuated by our writers in our own literature. A writer observes and interprets the norms, the values and the customs of society. He or she affirms or negates those values according to his or her personal convictions. In this way he creates or destroys social values. His interpretation will depend largely on his vantage point and could sway public opinion one way or another. In most of the books we have referred to we see women punished severely, even by death, for the mistakes they have made. There are no acceptable extenuating circumstances to justify any of their crimes – adultery, promiscuity, disobedience, a domineering nature – they incur vicious and immediate condemnation and punishment. On the other hand, men guilty of adultery or desertion or cruelty, suffer no severe punishment for these. They are often accepted back by their families, chastened, wiser but forgiven. None die for their mistakes. These attitudes are inculcated into the minds of the young African readers – for these are the books that are read in our schools and which help to perpetuate unfair attitudes towards women.

If writers took time to explore the circumstances, the pressures and the deprivations that their characters suffer, this would soften the social conscience and society's scales of justice would shift towards the correct balance. Punitive literature perpetuates the oppression of women; it denies them justice. All these crimes against women stem from one fundamental principle – the social and sexual subordination of women. There is an age-old fear that the independence of the female spirit will destroy the pillars of our society. Writers have a responsibility to society, and in this instance, to women in particular. We are looking for a changed portrayal of women in our books; an accurate and a just portrayal that will recognize the labour that women put into the economy of their societies, a liberating literature that not only forgives women their mistakes but condemns men who take advantage of women and does not condone men's fallibility. Women should not have to be martyrs to win the respect of their societies. We are looking for a self-defining image of women who win respect in their own right because they are strong and achieve things in their lives and triumph, not only because they are men's wives or mothers of sons but because they are valued members of their societies, outstanding in their societies as bread winners, teachers, farmers, nurses, politicians and whatever else. These portrayals will in time focus correctly on the values that our societies should uphold and preserve.

Perhaps things will not always be the way they are for the African woman – we may not always plead for justice and fair play – under the glare of world movements like feminism and human rights, African women may have to fight for their rights. But those structures and attitudes that cripple us must be done away with, for in the context of our

African struggles for freedom – freedom from imperialism, neo-colonialism and all oppression – it makes little sense to condone such extremes of oppression as our men are prepared to put the women of Africa through.

Note

1 Rudo B Gaidzanwa, *Images of Women in Zimbabwean Literature*, The College Press, Harare, 1985.

Chapter 72

Stiwanism:
Feminism in an African Context

Molara Ogundipe-Leslie

[...]

This very appropriate title was provided by Fatima Haidara and the African students at Virginia Technical Institute, Blacksburg, USA It opens up the issue of feminism at a very problematic and controversial point in African discourse on gender. People always want to know whether feminism is relevant to Africa. In thinking of Africa, one wonders, "what is an African context?" "What can feminism be in Africa?"

A broad range of attitudes about feminism in Africa today is being expressed by different kinds of persons and groups at different levels. For example, currently in Nigeria, right-wing women, most men, and apolitical women, like to quip that African women do not need liberation or feminism because they have never been in bondage. Progressive, political, and left-wing women, however, are saying that African women suffer subordination on two levels: as women, and as members of impoverished and oppressed classes where women are in the majority. That is the official position of Women in Nigeria (WIN), the organization with which I was involved in the founding.[1] The public position of the Federation of Muslim Women of Nigeria (FOMWAN) is that the woman has been liberated for thousands of years under the Shari'a law, never mind that Islam itself, a religion which demands our respect in its own right, has not been around for thousands of years. The point that the Federation of Muslim Women makes is that feminism is influenced by Western white feminists. They say things like, "it breeds pervasive traits like lesbianism.", (I don't know what is meant by that; "pervasive traits".) " ... abstracting the individuals from all concrete and collective bonds; pitting the individuals against institutions, relativising and trivializing the family... "[2]

The point to note is that religious fundamentalisms in Africa, and fundamentalism as a worldwide movement, are issues to be looked into as they affect attitudes towards women, and the struggle for progressive conditions for women all over the world.

Frist published in *Recreating Ourselves: African Women and Critical Transformations*, pp. 214–26, 229–30. Trenton, NJ: Africa World Press, 1994.

Our title, "Feminism in an African Context," also necessitates an interrogation of itself. We could ask, "what is feminism?" and "what is it in an African context?" What is the reality for African women?

When they think of Africa, most Africans think only of Black Africa or more correctly, if they would be honest, of their own little ethnic groups. When we say, "Africa," we mean "the Yorubas," "the Ibos," "the Kikuyu," "the Luo," "the Toucoulour," "the Serer," or "the Fulani," and so forth. We generalize from the characteristics of our own ethnic groups to describe the whole of the continent.

Some social scientists like to speak of "Black Africa" or "Africa south of the Sahara," but, what does "Black" mean in relation to, say, Libyans, or Egyptians or Moroccans who are white in Africa but are as black as people designated "black" in the United States. Again, North Africans who are considered white in America are darker than some high-colored African-Americans who can pass for white but are considered black in affirmative action forms. Obviously, being "black" is a political metaphor and importantly, skin color is not a useful, necessary and sufficient way to taxonomize Africans.

In view of the history of Africa and cross-cultural links across the Sahara, the reality of cultures and acculturations in Africa, and in view of countries like Chad and North Mali, which have an expanse into the Sahara, what does "sub-Saharan" mean? The term "sub-Saharan" itself is political. To repeat, Africa cannot be taxonomized in terms of color, which extends above the Sahara. Euro-American color notions cannot be easily transferred to a global context. North Africans are Africans. Africans think North Africans are black, but they are often considered white in the United States. Racism is a messy and unhealthy subject.

We must all avoid simplistic statements about Africa's reality, in particular, the reality of her political and social complexity. Therefore, when we speak of an "African context", do we mean all the countries of the geographical continent of Africa? This is what I like to mean when I use the term "Africa". This is a large piece to take on one's analytical plate, I admit. Our question then becomes: What is feminism in the context of Africa as I have defined it? We must define specificities. Again we cannot generalize Africa. Do we mean: a Christian or a Muslim Africa; Africa with indigenous religions; the Lusophone African countries which underwent liberation struggles; South Africa still under siege; independent African countries; Arab Africans; Black or White South Africans; the right-wing Inkatha elements, or white liberals; are the white leftists in the South African Communist Party included; Africans who adhere to pre-colonial values; or westernized Africans, by which we mean Africans with syncretized values?

With regard to color, and the following fact is particularly important for Africans of the diaspora, there are no color purities in Africa; if there ever were since the beginning of time. Everything, biology and culture, has been mixed or shall we say, "dynamized", by Africa's historical movements of peoples. These movements are not only the result of Western influence, as hegemonic Euro-Americans like to think. They have been going on since the beginning of time. Africa has been open to the world since the dawn of history.

In fact, history began with her, as archaeologists are saying. Some Western historiographers and other social scientists like to think and state that indigenous Africans were isolated from each other. In fact, Africa has not been isolated but has been at the heart of human concourse and interactions in those early times when so much was going on, and from which events Europe was isolated. The interactions were between the then civilized peoples of the world: China, India, South America (the Incas, Mayans and Aztecs), Southeast Asia, the Middle East, the countries of the Mediterranean and Africa. Much later Europe emerged from her Middle Ages to learn science (e.g. mathematics), technology, and many arts from the rest of the world. Europe enriched herself from the world of people of color to have her Renaissance. Europe's triumph after the 1400s was not due to superior intellect or courage but to the capacity for acts of unbelievable cruelty and political treachery such as the world had perhaps never known before. It was Europe, not Africa, which was isolated from the world before the 1400s.

We tend to think of Egypt as being outside of Africa. Some of us have been socialized to think of Egypt as in the Middle East. That is the result of political scholarship. Egypt is within Africa and gives to and was influenced by the Sudan. Egypt is also connected to and influenced by, African countries farther South and West. From North Africa, it is only across the Sahara to West Africa. On the other hand, the world connects with, did and still does influence East Africa and South Africa from across the Indian Ocean. These are some of the currents of movements and cultures in which Africa has been the central point in both receiving and giving.

How complex it is to speak of an African context! Africa or Africans cannot be generalized. We must always be aware of specifics while we describe our criteria for taxonomies. We must acknowledge our delimitations and realize always that there are many kinds of Africans. We cannot essentialize blackness, even on the African continent itself. Race, class and gender, among other variables must mediate our discourses as they mediate our understanding of ourselves and each other. Race and class also mediate gender for the three categories intersect each other at points. Let us simplify our task by thinking of the continent of Africa, rather than our own familiar home cultures, and let us try to identify patterns on that continent. Needless to say, such a discussion will not be exhaustive. We can only identify patterns and themes, but we will be extrapolating from the whole continent.

What is my own location in this epistemological cartography? I am speaking as a middle-aged African woman of Yoruba descent; now middle-class but from traditional aristocratic origins, alas; born by Christian and of a color, "black," which is devalued. Yet I do not think of myself as "black" nor do I refer to myself as "a black woman." This is not because I do not love my color or the idea of being black, but because I was not socialized to describe myself physically and in terms of color. Africans do not suffer from "colorism," to use Alice Walker's phrase; they do not suffer from the colorism of the Western world that Gayatri Spivak calls "chromatism."[3] We do not have a mentality of animal husbandry; of classing or grading people in terms of how they look: the color of their eyes or hair as if we were running kennels.

Africans, in Africa's non-racially organized countries, that is, outside the settler territories, tend to see themselves in terms of culture; how people think and behave. You are the culture that you carry, despite your color. Hence, a black person in color could be white mentally. It is not that Africans do not recognize racial difference. They see it but they do not assume that a person is necessarily African from the way that he/she looks. They do not privilege one kind of a color over another. They do not privilege whiteness over blackness, nor do they essentialize. I am talking now of the peasant majority Africans, not middle-class Africans. Peasant Africans attribute superiority to whites in the realm of technology. They do not, however, think that the white person is inherently and essentially superior to them as a human being. They know that s/he has certain cultural things which they admire and which they want – the automobiles and airplanes, blenders, to minimize the labor of grinding, yam pounding machines – but they do not think that these gadgets make her/him intrinsically superior. The problem of accepting superiority is usually one of middle class Africans who have undergone colonial education. The middle-class African may tend to think that whites are superior. In any case, problems of identity and issues of negritude are issues of the middle-class. The level of the colonial mentality of the African will dictate the level of a sense of inferiority that he or she has. Usually, you will find that the less Westernized a person, the more self-assured that person is.

Because culture, not color, determines identity, most Africans, use many terms such as: h/she is white or Oyinbo or Mzungu or toubab or brofo, to describe a person who is physiognomically black but "white" in behavior and mentality.

In the West, I am a "woman of color." Personally, I do not know what that phrase means. It sounds like some rare bird or creature of Nature. I am Molara Ogundipe-Leslie, a middle-aged Yoruba and Nigerian woman. I have included middle- aged because among my people as among many African peoples, a woman's status is mediated and improved by age, economics, kinship roles and by the class she comes from as well as birth and her achievements in her lived experience. Therefore, it is in my interest to emphasize my middle-agedness, in fact, my oldness, and not try to compete with teenagers. In the West, however, I find that the first and constant variable for me is race: a "woman of color," a "black woman," a "brown woman," a "chocolate woman."

The subject of feminism is no less complex to define than the phrase, "an African context." The chosen title of this talk is good for another reason: that it raises very common but important controversies in Africa today, namely, "Does feminism exist in Africa?" Should it exist in Africa? What are the definitions of feminism? For us? For me? Perhaps I can reverse this definitional task by naming what feminism is not, in order to confront the notion embedded in the counter-discourses to feminism in Africa today.

In answer to the usual reactions of most African men, right-wing and apolitical women:

1. Feminism is not a cry for any one kind of sexual orientation and I am not homophobic or heterosexist. Sexual practice in Africa tends to *be* private and *considered* private. Same-sex sexuality still awaits more attention and research. Homosexuals are not persecuted by the State in West Africa.
2. Feminism is not the reversal of gender roles, "gender" being defined simply as socially constructed identities and roles. It is not only the doing of dishes or the washing of napkins as my Malawian poet friend thinks. I shall share a part of the poem which he addressed to me. I should note that we used to have many arguments and an inter-textual intellectual life in Nigeria.

The poem is called:

> *Letter to a Feminist Friend* (an excerpt)
>
> My world has been raped
> looted
> and squeezed
> by Europe and America...
> AND NOW
> the women of Europe and America

after drinking and carousing
on my sweat
rise up to castigate
and castrate
their menfolk
from the cushions of a world
I have built!

Why should they be allowed
to come between us?
You and I were slaves together
uprooted and humiliated together
Rapes and lynchings...

do your friends "in the movement"
understand these things?...

No, no, my sister,
my love,
first things first!
Too many gangsters
still stalk this continent...

When Africa
at home and across the seas
is truly free
there will be time for me
and time for you
to share the cooking
and change the nappies –
till then,
first things first![4]

I use this poem at the beginning of my essay on women in Nigeria which is published in *Sisterhood is Global* (edited by Robin Morgan), a collection of essays by women of different countries. Again, I want to draw your attention to the use of the first person in his poem. It is his world that has been raped, that endured the slave trade, colonialism, imperialism, and neo-colonialism. He is the Prometheus figure. He does not yet have time for women's rights. The world has been built by him and he must attend to those pressing issues. His position is the usual one of "divide and rule" strategists. Divide and rule the women of the world who are perhaps united around gender oppressions. Women may differ about strategies and methods, but they do not differ on basic assumptions: that women are oppressed as women and they are oppressed as the majority members of subordinate classes which are also in the majority. But his position is almost typical of most of the men of the continent.

3. Feminism is not penis envy or gender envy; wanting to be a man as they like to say to us. "Well, do you want to be a man? You can join us if you want to." Or, "Whatever you do, you can never have a penis." A car mechanic once told me that I could not fix my car because I did not have a penis.

4. Feminism is not necessarily oppositional to men. It argues, rather, that a woman's body is her inherent property,[5] "not to be owned, used, and dumped by men," as radical theology feminists are saying.
5. Feminism is not, "dividing the genders," as they say to us in Africa. It is not dividing the race or "the struggle" – whatever that overused word means.
6. It is not parrotism of Western women's rhetoric.
7. It is not opposed to African culture and heritage, but argues that culture is dynamically evolving and certainly not static; that culture should not be immobilized in time to the advantage of men as most men in Africa want it to be.
8. Feminism is not a choice between extreme patriarchy on the one hand or hateful separatism from men on the other.

What then is this feminism? I have made these rejoinders because they touch on the points that some African men make to counter our feminist discourses in Africa. We are accused of the attributes implied by their criticism. Often the argument is that feminism is not necessary in Africa because gender was balanced in an idyllic African past, which is their own creation. African feminists are said to be merely the parrots of Western women. Race and nationalism are used in bad faith to attack gender. Sometimes race, nationalism, and class are brought together to attack gender politics. Feminist concerns are said to be the predilections of Westernized women like myself or Ifi Amadiume or Filomina Steady, for example.[6] Feminist concerns are, then, not those of the great rural and faithful African women who are "the true African women" who are happy as they are and have always been. But what do research and analysis tell us about these newly discovered and glamorized creatures; "the rural women of Africa?" Certainly not that "rural," poor women are happy with the status quo and desire no change.

Feminism can be defined by its etymological roots. Femina is "woman" in Latin. Feminism, an ideology of woman; any body of social philosophy about women. This definition of feminism gives us enough leeway to encompass various types of feminisms: right-wing, left-wing, centrist, left of center, right of center, reformist, separatist, liberal, socialist, Marxist, non-aligned, Islamic, indigenous, etc. Believe me, all these feminisms exist. Nawal el Saadawi is an Islamic socialist feminist. So, one question could be, "What is feminism for you." What is your feminism? Do you, in fact, have an ideology of women in society and life? Is your feminism about the rights of women in society? What is the total conception of women as agents in human society – her conditions, roles and statuses – her recognition and acknowledgement? Generally, feminism, however, must always have a political and activist spine to its form. If we take feminism to imply all these, is the African woman on the African continent, in an African context without problems in all these areas?

For those who say that feminism is not relevant to Africa, can they truthfully say that the African woman is all right in all these areas of her being and therefore does not need an ideology that addresses her reality, hopefully and preferably, to ameliorate that reality? When they argue that feminism is foreign, are these opponents able to support the idea that African women or cultures did not have ideologies which propounded or theorized woman's being and provided avenues and channels for women's oppositions and resistance to injustice within their societies? Certainly, these channels existed. Are the opponents of feminism willing to argue that indigenous African societies did not have avenues and strategies for correcting gender imbalance and injustice? Will they argue that these aspects of social engineering could only have come from white or Euro-American women? Are they saying that African women cannot see their own situations and demand change without guidance from white women? Nationalism and race pride, I know, will make our men beat a retreat at this question and they had better beat that retreat. The issue is that there were indigenous feminisms. There were indigenous patterns within traditional African societies for addressing the oppressions and injustices to women.

So, what kind of feminism exists in an African context? In view of all I have said above, in view of all that I have argued as well as the realities of Africa, we should more correctly say: What *feminisms* exist in Africa? Indeed, there are many feminisms, depending on the center from which one is speaking or theorizing. These feminisms have to be theorized around the junctures of race, class, caste and gender; nation, culture and ethnicity; age, status, role and sexual orientation. Certainly more research is needed to discover what African women themselves, particularly, the working classes and the peasantry think about themselves as women, what ideology they possess and what agenda they have for themselves, daily and historically.

Once we agree that an ideology of women and about women is necessary and has always existed in Africa, we can proceed to ask if these existent ideologies remain relevant or need to be changed. Our opportunistic and irredentist compatriots who argue culture and heritage when it serves their interests, should consider whether our inherited cultures should be taken hook, line and sinker, or should be subjected to change where necessary. Should we, when necessary, change the notion that man is always superior to woman, hence, boys should go to school and girls should only go when they can, when there is money to "waste" and no work to be done at home or in the farms and markets? Should we apply the sexist ideas in the Bible, without criticism, with preference for Old Testament ideas and the Pauline section of the New Testament, stressing only the verses on male dominance? Should we adapt Koranic ideas to modern times or continue to beat the recalcitrant woman lightly as said in the fourth Sura of the Koran. (If your woman does not listen, first admonish her then, sexually withdraw from her and finally beat her "lightly.") How light is light? Is not the issue the proprietary right to beat her in the first place? Should culture be placed in a museum of minds or should we take authority over culture as a product of human intelligence and consciousness to be used to improve our existential conditions? Should we preach cultural fidelity only when it does not affect us negatively, which is usually the position of African men who wish to keep only those aspects of culture which keep them dominant?

For the rest of this essay, I shall try to indicate what some of the outspoken African women are saying about feminism in Africa. Some quite outstanding women like Buchi Emecheta, say they are not feminists without saying why. Others like the Nigerian writer, Flora Nwapa, say that they are not feminists, but they are "womanists". There are still other views: the great and late South African writer, Bessie Head, says in her posthumous essays collected under the title *A Woman Alone*, that in the world of the intellect where she functions as a writer and an intellectual, feminism is not necessary because the world of the intellect is neither male nor female.[7] I think she is deceived or perhaps deluded on this point by the post-romantic and Victorian patriarchal notion and myth about the world of the intellect being sexless. This, women know to be a myth, although it has been sold to all the women of the world. We know how male sexism actually functions in the world of the intellect or in the world of "the life of the mind" as they say. Bessie Head, in my view, expresses a false consciousness often expressed by successful middle-class women of all cultures (including

African women who proudly and aggressively announce that their achievement has taken place outside of their identity as women). "I am just a writer, not a woman writer," "I am a professor of physics," "an astronaut," "a prime minister, not a woman" and I wonder what is that? What is that neuter thing? But notice that only women engage in that kind of rhetoric. It speaks volumes that only women make that kind of statement. Have you ever heard a man say, "I'm just a professor, not a man." "I'm just a professor," "a mathematician," "a tycoon," "a president of the United States, but not a man, not a man at all." Perhaps we need to deconstruct that formulation elsewhere.

Let us now, however, consider the theories of some of the most visible African women who hold that feminism is relevant to the African context. A summary of their positions indicates some common denominators:

1. That feminism need not be oppositional to men. It is not about adversarial gender politics.
2. That women need not neglect their biological roles.
3. That motherhood is idealized and claimed as a strength by African women and seen as having a special manifestation in Africa. Davies has asked whether African women have specially cornered motherhood.[8]
4. That the total configuration of the conditions of women should be addressed rather than obsessing with sexual issues.
5. That certain aspects of women's reproductive rights take priority over others.
6. That women's conditions in Africa need to be addressed in the context of the total production and reproduction of their society and that scenario also involves men and children. Hence, there has always been an emphasis on economic fulfillment and independence in African feminist thinking.
7. That the ideology of women has to be cast in the context of the race and class struggles which bedevil the continent of Africa today; that is, in the context of the liberation of the total continent.

It is this generally holistic attitude of African women to feminism which often separates them from their Western sisters.

[. . .]

I have since advocated the word "Stiwanism," instead of feminism, to bypass the combative discourses that ensue whenever one raises the issue of feminism in Africa.

The creation of the new word is to deflect energies from constantly having to respond to charges of imitating Western feminism and, in this way, conserve those energies, to avoid being distracted from the real issue of the conditions of women in Africa. The new word describes what similarly minded women and myself would like to see in Africa. The word "feminism" itself seems to be a kind of red rag to the bull of African men. Some say the word is by its very nature hegemonic, or implicitly so. Others find the focus on women in themselves somehow threatening. Still others say it is limiting to their perspectives, whatever those are. Some, who are genuinely concerned with ameliorating women's lives sometimes feel embarrassed to be described as "feminist," unless they are particularly strong in character. The embarrassment springs from being described by a word which encodes women (in "femina") so directly. So effective are the years of phallocratic socialization! Be a Stiwanist. I am a Stiwanist.

"Stiwa" is my acronymn for *Social Transformation Including Women in Africa*. This new term describes my agenda for women in Africa without having to answer charges of imitativeness or having to constantly define our agenda on the African continent in relation to other feminisms, in particular, white Euro-American feminisms which are unfortunately, under siege by everyone. This new term "STIWA" allows me to discuss the needs of African women today in the tradition of the spaces and strategies provided in our indigenous cultures for the social being of women. My thesis has always been that indigenous feminisms also existed in Africa and we are busy researching them and bringing them to the fore now. "STIWA" is about the inclusion of African women in the contemporary social and political transformation of Africa. Be a "Stiwanist."

Notes

1 *Women in Nigeria Today*, ed., WIN Collective (London: Zed Press, 1985), Introduction.

2 Bilikisu Yusuf, "Hausa-Fulani Women: The State of the Struggle," *Hausa Women in the Twentieth Century*, eds. Catherine Coles and Beverly Mack (Madison: University of Wisconsin Press, 1991), 90–108. Gives a history of FOMWAM in Nigeria. See also Murad Khurram, "On the Family" *Muslim World Book Review* 5 (1984) for some Muslim positions.

3 Gayatri Spivak, *The Post-Colonial Critic: Interviews, Strategies and Dialogues* (NY and London: Routledge and Kegan Paul, 1990), 62.

4 Felix Mnthali, "Letter to a Feminist Friend," the poem will appear in an as yet unpublished volume entitled *Beyond the Echoes*.

5 See brochure of the World Council of Churches, on the Ecumenical Decade Solidarity with Women.

6 Ifi Amadiume, *Male Daughters, Female Husbands* (London: Zed Press, 1987), and Filomena Steady, *The Black Woman Cross-Culturally* (Cambridge, MA: Schenkman, 1981), see Bibliography. Steady, "African Feminism, a Worldwide Perspective," *Women in Africa and the African Diaspora*, eds., Harley, Rushing and Terbog-Penn (Washington, DC: Howard University Press, 1987).

7 Bessie Head, *A Woman Alone: Autobiographical Writings* (London: Heinemann, 1990), 95.

8 Carole Boyce Davies, "Motherhood in the Works of Male and Female Igbo Writers," *Ngambika: Studies of Women in African Literature* (Trenton, NJ: Africa World Press, 1986), 241–56. See also the introduction to the book.

Chapter 73

Feminism with a Small "f"!

Buchi Emecheta

I am just an ordinary writer, an ordinary writer who has to write, because if I didn't write I think I would have to be put in an asylum. Some people have to communicate, and I happen to be one of them. I have tried several times to take university appointments and work as a critic, but each time I have packed up and left without giving notice. I found that I could not bring myself to criticize other people's work. When my husband burned my first book, I said to him 'If you can burn my book, you can just as well burn my child, because my books are like my children, and I cannot criticize my children.' When I had my babies they were very, very ugly; they had big heads, like their father and their bodies looked like mine. But if anybody looked into the pram and said 'What an ugly baby,' I would never talk to that person again. And I know that I am not the only writer who finds it hard to accept criticism. One critic asked me 'You have so much anger in you, how can you bear it?' 'Well', I said, 'I can't bear it, so I have to let it out on paper.' I started writing in 1972, and a few weeks ago I handed in my sixteenth novel. In order to make you understand how I work I will tell you about my background.

I was born in Lagos, Nigeria, and was raised partly there and partly in my village, Ibuza, and this explains my wish to tell stories when I was a child. My parents both came from Ibuza and moved to Lagos in search of work. As both of them were partly educated they embraced the CMS (Church Missionary Society) way of life. But being of the old Ibo kingdom they made sure that my brother and myself never lost sight of home, of life in Ibuza.

We worked at home during the rains, to help on the farm and to learn our ways. If I lived in Lagos I could start to have loose morals and speak Yoruba all the time. So my parents wanted me to learn the rigorous Ibo life. You can see that even in Nigeria we still discriminate against each other.

It was at home that I came across real story tellers. I had seen some Yoruba ones telling their stories and songs and beating their drums whilst we children followed them – Pied Piper like – from street to street. But the Ibo story teller was different. She was always one's

First published in *Criticism and Ideology: Second African Writers' Conference, Stockholm 1986*, ed. Kirsten H. Petersen, pp. 173–81. Uppsala: Scandinavian Institute of African Studies, 1988.

mother. My Big Mother was my aunt. A child belonged to many mothers. Not just one's biological one. We would sit for hours at her feet mesmerized by her trance-like voice. Through such stories she could tell the heroic deeds of her ancestors, all our mores and all our customs. She used to tell them in such a way, in such a sing-song way that until I was about fourteen I used to think that these women were inspired by some spirits. It was a result of those visits to Ibuza, coupled with the enjoyment and information those stories used to give us, that I determined when I grew older that I was going to be a story teller, like my Big Mother.

I learned to my dismay at school in Lagos that if I wanted to tell stories to people from many places I would have to use a language that was not my first – neither was it my second, or third, but my fourth language. This made my stories lose a great deal of their colour, but I learned to get by. My English must have been very bad because when I first told my English teacher, who came from the Lake District, and who was crazy about Wordsworth that I was going to write like her favourite poet, she ordered me to go to the school chapel and pray for forgiveness, because she said: 'Pride goeth before a fall.' I did not go to the chapel to pray because even then I knew that God would have much more important things to do than to listen to my dreams. Dreams which for me, coming both from the exotic so-called Ibo bush culture and the historic Yoruba one, were not unattainable.

Some of these early missionaries did not really penetrate the African mind. That incident confirmed what I had always suspected as a child, that the art of communication, be it in pictures, in music, writing or in oral folklore is vital to the human.

I never learn from my experiences. My first attempt to write a book, called *The Bride Price* was resented by my husband. He too, like my English teacher, told me that 'Pride goeth before fall'. I left him and I found myself at twenty-two, husbandless with five young children. I thought I would wait to be as old as Big Mother with a string of degrees before writing. But I had to earn my living and the only thing I could do was write. Whilst looking after my fast-growing family I decided to read for a degree that would help me master the English language and help me write about my society for the rest of the world. I chose sociology and continued writing. I had enough rejection slips to paper a room. But in 1972 the *New Statesman* started serializing my work and those recollections later appeared as my first book, *In the Ditch*.

I have been writing ever since, and I am now living entirely on my writing. Those babies of mine are now beginning to leave home. One of them has started to write as well, so perhaps writing runs in the family. I am not doing anything particularly clever. I am simply doing what my Big Mother was doing for free about thirty years ago. The only difference is that she told her stories in the moonlight, while I have to bang away at a typewriter I picked up from Woolworths in London. I am not good at reading, and sometimes when I write I can't even read my writing. Writing is a very lonely profession. One is there at one's desk, thinking of ideas and reasoning them out and putting them into works of fiction or stories, and if one is not careful, one will start living the life of the characters in the book. Conferences like this one save some of us from becoming strange.

Writers are often asked 'Who are you writing for?'. How am I supposed to know who is going to pick up my works from the library shelf. I wonder sometimes if people ask painters, when they are doing their paintings, who they are painting them for. The painter can control the picture while he is still painting it, but can we expect him to foretell who is going to love looking at it? A book is akin to a child on his mother's back. The mother knows she is carrying a baby on her back but the child can use its hands to lift anything that passes by, without the mother knowing. I find this question sometimes rather patronizing. In fact it is sometimes healthier not to think of one's readers at all. Writers are communicators. We chronicle everyday happenings, weave them into novels, poetry, documentary fiction, articles etc. The writer has the freedom to control, to imagine and to chronicle. I write for everybody.

The writer also has a crucial control over the subject s/he writes about. For myself, I don't deal with great ideological issues. I write about the little happenings of everyday life. Being a woman, and African born, I see things through an African woman's eyes. I chronicle the little happenings in the lives of the African women I know. I did not know that by doing so I was going to be called a feminist. But if I am now a feminist then I am an African feminist with a small f. In my books I write about families because I still believe in families. I write about women who try very hard to hold their family together until it becomes absolutely impossible. I have no sympathy for a woman who deserts her children, neither do I have sympathy for a woman who insists on staying in a marriage with a brute of a man, simply to be respectable. I want very much to further the education of women in Africa, because I know that education really helps the women. It helps them to read and it helps them to rear a generation. It is true that if one educates a woman, one educates a community, whereas if one educates a man, one educates a man. I do occasionally write about wars and the nuclear holocaust but again in such books I turn to write about the life and experiences of women living under such conditions.

Maybe all this makes me an ordinary writer. But that is what I want to be. An ordinary writer. I will read to you two pieces from my own observations. The style is simple but that is my way. I am a simple and unsophisticated person and cultural people really make me nervous. First I want to read a short piece about polygamy. People think that polygamy is oppression, and it is in certain cases. But I realize, now that I have visited Nigeria often, that some women now make polygamy work for them. What I am about to relate happened only a few weeks ago. I was in my bedroom in Ibuza listening to a conversation. It was cool and damp and I was debating whether to get up from my bed or not. I knew it was about six in the morning. I did not have to look at the clock. I just knew because I could hear the songs of the morning, children on their way to fetch water, a cock crowing here and there. Then the penetrating voice of Nwango, the senior wife of Obike came into my thoughts. 'Go away you stinking beast. Why will you not let me sleep? I have a full day ahead of me and you come harassing me so early in the morning. You are shameless. You don't even care that the children sleep next-door. You beast. Why don't you go to your new wife.' Now the man: 'All I have from you is your loud mouth. You are never around to cook for me, and when I come to your bed, you send me away. What did I pay the bride-price for?' The voice of Obike was slow and full of righteous anger. 'Go to your wife.' 'She is pregnant', said Obike. 'So what, get another woman. I need my energy for my farm and my trading, and today is the market-day', Nwango insisted. I was sorry to miss the end of the quarrel because my mother-in-law came in and told me not to mind them. 'They are always like that, these men. They are shameless. They think we women are here just to be their partners at night. He can marry another girl. But again which girl in her right senses will take him? He is too lazy to go regularly to his farm.' My mother-in-law should know. She had thirteen children. They lived in the capital, Lagos, and her husband did not have room to bring home another wife, so she had to do everything. If they had spent their life in the village it would have been different.

I know this is a situation which our Western sisters will find difficult to understand. Sex is important to us. But we do not make it the centre of our being, as women do here. In fact most of the Nigerian women who are promiscuous are so for economic reasons. The Yorubas have a saying that a woman must never allow a man to sleep with her if, at the end of the day she is going to be in debt. Few of our women go after sex *per se*. If they are with their husbands they feel they are giving something out of duty, love, or in order to have children. A young woman might dream of romantic love, but as soon as they start having children their loyalty is very much to them, and they will do everything in their power to make life easier for them. In the villages the woman will seek the company of her age-mates, her friends, and the women in the market, and for advice she goes either to her mother or to her mother-in-law. Another woman in the family will help share the house-work, like Nwango cited earlier. The day her husband wanted her was an Eke day, a big market day. She had to be up early to be at the market. She had to contribute her twenty naira which is almost ten pounds, to the savings fund of the market women. That is the way we raise capital for our business without having to go to the bank, because most banks will not lend money to a woman. So she had to contribute her twenty naira and later on in the evening, she had to put on her otuogu and she had to be at the Agbalani group, as they were going to dance at the second burial of the grandmother of one of their members. For that dance they had to tie the otuogu with the Akangwose style; all of which took them three years to save up for. They had to wear a navy-blue head-tie and carry a navy-blue Japanese fan and wear black flat shoes or slippers. None of these items was bought by their husbands. Nwango worked on her cassava farm four days of the week – we have a five-day week – and sold the garri made from the cassava on the fifth day, Eke market day. She gave twenty naira esusu of her profit to the collector who was one of the women in her group. It is from this esusu forced saving that she is sending her son to college, and she spends the rest exactly as she likes. At the funeral dance the group will give the bereaved lady a thousand naira (about five hundred pounds), from their fund to help out. And the dance will go on till very late. At about eight p.m. one will hear these women going home, singing their heads off. They drink anything from whisky, beer, gin, brandy, you name it, and no man dares tell them not to. Cooking for the husband, fiddle sticks! Get another woman to do it. Especially if the other woman is still a young seventeen- or eighteen-year-old with her head full of romantic love. By the time she is twenty-five she will become wiser too. Nwango's husband is almost a stud. Not a nice word, but that is the way most village women feel.

Sex is part of life. It is not THE life. Listen to the Western feminists' claim about enjoying sex, they make me laugh. African feminism is free of the shackles of Western romantic illusions and tends to be much more pragmatic. We believe that we are here for many, many things, not just to cultivate ourselves, and make ourselves pretty for men. The beauty in sisterhood is when women reach the age of about forty. The women who cultivated sisters either through marriage or through the village age-group start reaping their reward. In England for example I belong to the war-babies. They call us 'the saltless babies', That means we were born in Nigeria when they didn't have salt because of the war. So in our village we were called 'the Saltless Women'. There are about sixteen of my age-mates in London, and we have our own group here too. Last year a member of our group was in hospital and she said that other patients called her the Princess of Africa. On visiting days the nurses and doctors invariably shooed us away. She was there for three weeks, and the two days I went to visit her I had to wait over fifteen minutes before it came to my turn. I live in North London, a long way from her house, but those members who lived near her made sure she had visitors every night as well as her seven children. Her husband left her over three years ago to do some business in Nigeria, but we all know that he lives with another woman over there. Did our group member care? No. She is too busy to care. If he returns, good, if not, better still. She is training to be a hairdresser, now that all her children are at school. She is converting her large house into flats so that she and her older daughter can start a bed-and-breakfast business. And when she is ready she is going to come to our group and take an interest-free loan from our funds. If her husband had been around he would probably have been a help, just by being there, since he had no job anyway, but he could also be in the way of our member's self-realization. Looking after a man for sexual rewards does take a lot of time. I assure you.

In the West many women hurry to get married again after a divorce or a bereavement. Our women are slower. And many who have children don't even bother, because a new life opens for them. A new life among other women and friends. Women are very quarrelsome and jealous. We always make it up, especially after we have had a few brandies and consumed, I don't know how many chicken legs. This is because we realize that what we gain by forgiving one another is better than what we gain by being alone in order to avoid jealousy. In my book *Joys of Motherhood* I describe a family in which the women went on strike and refused to take the housekeeping money, because they knew that the husband was drinking the greater part of his income. I also describe a life of another woman who was so busy being a good mother and wife that she didn't cultivate her women friends. She died by the wayside, hungry and alone. In the same book I describe how jealous she was, when her husband brought home a new wife. Instead of going to sleep on the first night she stayed awake listening to the noise made by her husband and the new wife in love-making. She learned only a few days later that it would be better and to their mutual advantage, if she and the new wife became friends, rather that quarrel over their shared husband. They soon became so busy in their everyday life that sexuality was pushed into the background.

In many cases polygamy can be liberating to the woman, rather than inhibiting her, especially if she is educated. The husband has no reason for stopping her from attending international conferences like this one, from going back to University and updating her career or even getting another degree. Polygamy encourages her to value herself as a person and look outside her family for friends. It gives her freedom from having to worry about her husband most of the time and each time he comes to her, he has to be sure that he is in a good mood and that he is washed, and clean and ready for the wife, because the wife has now become so sophisticated herself that she has no time for a dirty, moody husband. And this in a strange way, makes them enjoy each other.

The small son of one of our group-members in London told his teacher that he had two Mummies. 'My Mummy number one is working. Mummy number two will come and collect me.' The teacher did not understand until she realized that his solicitor father had two wives, and the little child enjoys being loved and looked after by two women, his mother and the senior wife. What a good way to start one's life. In Ibuza it is the same. Once a woman starts making money she stops having children regularly. This is because women who are lucky to find the work which they love and which they are good at derive the same kind of enjoyment from it as from sex. Many female writers, many English female writers I have spoken to claimed that they find their work, not only sexually satisfactory

but sometimes masturbatory. I certainly find my work satisfying. Sex is part of our life –
it shouldn't be THE life.

In this next section I will give you a quick overview of some issues concerning black
women. In many parts of Africa only one's enemies will go out of their way to pray for a
pregnant woman to have a girl-child. Most people want a man-child. The prayers will go:
'You will be safely delivered of a bouncing baby boy, a real man-child that we can make jolly
with whisky and beer.' The pregnant woman will not protest at this prayer because in her
heart, she too would like to have a man-child, who will not be married away, but will stay in
the family home and look after his mother when she becomes weak and old. In most African
societies the birth of a son enhances a woman's authority in the family. Male children are
very, very important. Yet, this girl-child that was not desired originally comes into her own at
a very early age. From childhood she is conditioned into thinking that being the girl she
must do all the housework, she must help her mother to cook, clean, fetch water and look
after her younger brothers and sisters. If she moans or shows signs of not wanting to do any
of this, she will be sharply reminded by her mother. 'But you are a girl! Going to be a
woman.'

It is our work to bring the next generation into the world, nurture them until they are
grown old enough to fly from the nest and then start their own life. It is hard. It could be
boring and could sometimes in some places be a thankless job. But is it a mean job? I had my
photograph taken once in my office where I do my writing. The photo-journalist was a
staunch feminist, and she was so angry that my office was in my kitchen and a package of
cereal was in the background. I was letting the woman's movement down by allowing such a
photograph to be taken, she cried. But that was where I worked. Because it was warmer and
more convenient for me to see my family while I put my typewriter to one side. I tried to tell
her in vain that in my kitchen I felt I was doing more for the peace of the world than the
nuclear scientist. In our kitchens we raise all Reagans, all Nkrumahs, all Jesuses. In our
kitchens we cook for them, we send them away from home to be grown men and women,
and in our kitchens they learn to love and to hate. What greater job is there? I asked.
A mother with a family is an economist, a nurse, a painter, a diplomat and more. And we
women do all that, and we form, we are told, over half of the world's population. And yet we
are on the lowest rung. Men did not put us there, my sisters, I think sometimes we put
ourselves there. How often do you hear colleagues say; 'Oh, I don't know anything I am only
a housewife'?

There should be more choices for women, certainly women who wish to be like
Geraldine Ferrara should be allowed to be so. We need more of her type, especially
among the black women. We need more Golda Meirs, we need more Indira Gandhis, we
even need more Margaret Thatchers. But those who wish to control and influence the future
by giving birth and nurturing the young should not be looked down upon. It is not a
degrading job. If I had my way, it would be the highest paid job in the world. We should
train our people, both men and women to do housework. A few privileged African women
are now breaking bonds. They live at home and work outside. Most of these women were
lucky enough to come from families where the girls were allowed to go to school and to stay
there long enough to acquire knowledge to equip them to live away from their families and
to rub shoulders with men. Black women are succeeding in various fields along these lines.

This we must remember is not new to the black woman, because her kind has always
worked. In the agrarian setting women do petty-trading. Usually, they have small children

with them. They trade in anything from a few loaves of bread to a few packages of matches. The lucky ones have stalls or sheds. Others not so fortunate use the front of their house as their stall. Many Nigerian women live in the cities, collect their esusu profits and bank it when they think it is big enough. I have a great number of friends who have built up their families this way. This means that the others who were trained to do the lower-middle-class jobs of, for example, teaching have invariably given up their work in order to take up trading.

Being successful in whatever we undertake is not new to the women of Africa. The Aba riot is a case in point. This was a riot that spread from Owerri in Eastern Nigeria to Calabar among women who did not even speak the same language, and it included all the towns in the area to Onitsha by the river Niger and went further across the river to include women from the Asaba area. Although the white male chroniclers called it a riot it was a real war. It was a marvel that women at that time were able to organize themselves; remember, there were no telephones, no letters, only bushtracks and dangerous rivers. The whole area was equivalent to the distance from London to Edinburgh. The actual war was organized with women from different groups wearing various headgears and all using their household utensils as weapons. The war, which took place in 1929 was in answer to British demands that women should pay taxes. The black women of that war were praised by all their menfolk. They received admiration not rebuke. And in desperation, the British adminis- trators jailed all men whose wives took an active part in the war. They could not acknow- ledge that women, especially barbaric women, could organize themselves to achieve such a feat.

Working and achieving to great heights is nothing new to the woman of Africa, but there are still many obstacles in her way. Her family still prefers to educate the boy, while she stays at home to do the important jobs called 'women's duties'. And we accept the tag, knowing full well that the boy, however clever he is, would not be where he is today without the sacrifices made by his mother, his sweetheart, his wife or even his sister. The African woman has always been a woman who achieves. This does not necessarily mean that she becomes a successful international lawyer, a writer or a doctor, although African women in these professions are doing very well, and there are quite a few of us. But for the majority of women of Africa, real achievement – as I see it – is to make her immediate environment as happy as is possible under the circumstances, by tending the crops or giving comfort. But she still will have higher aspirations and achieve more when those cleverly structured artificial barriers are removed, when education is free and available to every child, male or female, when the male-dominated media does not give exposure to a black woman simply because she is a beautiful entertainer, thereby undermining our brain power, and when we ourselves have the confidence to value our contribution to the world. It is about time we start singing about our own heroic deeds.

Chapter 74

Writing Near the Bone

Yvonne Vera

There is no essential truth about being a female writer. The best writing comes from the boundaries, the ungendered spaces between male and female. I am talking of writing itself, not the story or theme. Knowing a story is one thing, writing it quite another.

I like to think of writing in limitless terms, with no particular contract with the reader, especially that of gender. When I have discovered that unmarked and fearless territory then I am free to write, even more free to be a woman writing. Sometimes the light coming through my window has been much more important than the fact that I am a woman writing.

There must be a serious purpose to my work, that is all. I must be in touch with the earth. I can never mistake that source of inspiration and energy to be gender, it is something we all share. It is true, however, that one writes best on themes, feelings, actions and sentiments one is more closely connected with. In this regard I like to think that I am writing. I am a woman. I am writing.

The woman I am is inside the writing, embraced and freed by it. For me writing is light, a radiance that captures everything in a fine profile. This light searches and illuminates, it is a safe place from which to uncover the emotional havoc of our experience. Light is a bright warmth which heals. Writing can be this kind of light. Within it I do not hide. I travel bravely beyond that light, into the shadows that this light creates, and in that darkness it is also possible to be free, to write, to be a woman.

I like the peasant shoes which Van Gogh painted for example, their lack of light. They are a lot darker than the reprints suggest, no light at all except an almost clear patch of ground behind them and that is hardly light, really. You feel the absence of light in these pictures and that really draws your head closer and your emotion and you really want to look and you feel heavy with a new delight. You look at these shoes and wonder where they have been and who has been and what has been and did these shoes ever grow anything that held some life in it, that breathed perhaps, that threw some kind of light into the world. When I went to

First published in *Word: On Being a (Woman) Writer*, ed. Jocelyn Burrell, pp. 57–60. New York: The Feminist Press, 2004.

the gallery shop in Amsterdam I looked for a postcard with the shoes: the reproduction was so bright, I said this is terrible I will not buy this card even though I want so much to do so. I went back into the gallery and looked at the shoes again and found a large evocative canvas, thrilling in its sadness. I knew this had been written not without light but beyond light.

I found the same immaculate transcription of image and emotion with ' "The Potato Eaters." It was a lot darker than the "Peasant Shoes." There were four or five little cups and something properly muddy was being poured into them. The cups were white but free of light. And figures in the foreground, possibly a child, had her back to the viewer. It was difficult standing and watching the back of this child who somehow was a potato eater and was about to drink something so muddy from a cup that was nearly white. There was a lantern of some kind hanging above the group but its presence created shadows, not warmth or recognition. The picture was very imposing in its emotion, but beautiful, harmful.

I learnt to write when I was almost six and at the same time also discovered the magic of my own body as a writing surface, I lived with my grandmother for some years while my mother was pursuing her studies. Many other children lived with my grandmother. The house was very small and most afternoons we were kept outside where we woke with some cousins and sat on large metal garbage cans, our legs hardly long enough to touch the ground.

The skin over my legs would be dry, taut, even heavy. It carried the cold of our winter. Using the edges of my fingernails or pieces of dry grass broken from my grandmother's broom I would start to write on my legs. I would write on my small thighs but this surface was soft and the words would vanish and not stay for long, but it felt different to write there, a sharp and ticklish sensation which made us laugh and feel as though we had placed the words in a hidden place.

Our hope increased we travelled downward to the legs where the skin broke like black clay, and we wrote our names to all eternity. Here we wrote near the bone and spread the words all the way to the ankles. We wrote deep into the skin and under skin where the words could not escape. Here, the skin was thirsty, it seemed, and we liked it. The words formed light grey intermingling paths that meant something to our imagination and freed us and made us forget the missing laughters of our mothers. We felt the words in gradual bursts of pain, the first words we had written would become less felt, the pain of that scratching now faded, and the last words where we had dug too deep would be pulsating still, unable to be quiet.

We looked up and laughed and drew figures of our bodies there, and the bodies of our grandmothers which we squeezed among the letters. It was possible, when you had used a small piece dry bark for your pen, to be bleeding in small dots. Such words could never depart or be forgotten. This was bleeding, not writing. It was important to write. Then, before running indoors to my grandmother who would have been distressed at the changed shades of our bodies, we would use handfuls of saliva to wipe our bodies clean. This saliva spread a warm and calming feeling over us.

I learnt to write if not on the body then on the ground. We would spread the loamy soil into a smooth surface with the palm of our hands using loving and careful motions, then we would write with the tips of our fingers. Bending over that earth, touching it with our noses, we would learn to write large words which led us into another realm of feeling and of understanding our place in the world. Proud of our accomplishment we would then stand back to see what we had written. We had burrowed the earth like certain kinds of beetles and we were immensely satisfied. We left these letters there, on the ground, and ran off to do our chores. I always liked writing after the rains when the soil held to our naked feet and claimed us entirely. Then we drew shapes on the ground which could be seen for distances. Our bodies and our earth, the smell of rain, beetles and our noses, this was writing.

Chapter 75

Some Notes on African Feminism

Carole Boyce Davies

The social and historical realities of African women's lives must be considered in any meaningful examination of women in African literature and of writings by African women writers. A number of works have examined African women from a variety of perspectives. Several statements have come from African women themselves in recent years. The only formulation of a feminist theory for African women, however, comes from Filomina Steady who, after examining the commonalities of experience and response of African women in Africa and the diaspora, defines an African feminism. In her introduction to *The Black Woman Cross-Culturally*,[1] she posits that this African brand of feminism includes female autonomy and cooperation; an emphasis on nature over culture; the centrality of children, multiple mothering and kinship; the use of ridicule in African woman's worldview. A number of traditional rights and responsibilities of women allow her to conclude that the African woman is in practice much more a feminist than her European counterpart.

> True feminism is an abnegation of male protection and a determination to be resourceful and reliant. The majority of the black women in Africa and the diaspora have developed these characteristics, though not always by choice . . . (pp. 35–6)

Steady's position is perhaps the most appropriate start for our discussion especially since she examines the socio-economic and class factors which contribute to African woman's oppression (economic exploitation and marginalization) and her responses to this oppression (self-reliance). There are a few debatable points in the Steady definition, however. Many will argue that assuming a nature over culture posture for African women denies her participation in the shaping of human culture and renders her an inert, unintelligent "vessel", not a creative person in her own right. Additionally, the discussion too quickly glosses over certain traditional inequities which continue to subordinate African women. (While acknowledging

First published in *Ngambika: Studies of Women in African Literature*, ed. Carole Boyce Davies and Anne Adams Graves, pp. 6–14. Trenton: African World Press, 1986.

their existence, Steady devotes only a footnoted paragraph to these inequities in favor of extensive discussion of what makes black women's situation different.) Among them, lack of choice in motherhood and marriage, oppression of barren women, genital mutilation, enforced silence and a variety of other forms of oppression intrinsic to various societies which still plague African women's lives and must inevitably be at the crux of African feminist theory.

Steady's introduction, nonetheless, is still, so far, the most comprehensive detailing of the various facets of African women's experience. A closer examination of the African woman's situation vis a vis the layers of oppression that have to be torn away is offered by Molara Ogundipe-Leslie's "African Women, Culture and Another Development" which locates the condition of women in Africa within the socio-economic realities of culture and development. She makes the point (extending Mao-Tse Tung's "mountain on the back" metaphor) that African women have additional burdens bearing down on them: 1) oppression from outside (foreign intrusions, colonial domination etc.); 2) heritage of tradition (feudal, slave-based, communal, 3) her own backwardness, a product of colonization and neo-colonialism and its concomitant poverty, ignorance etc.; 4) her men, weaned on centuries of male domination who will not willingly relinquish their power and privilege; 5) her race, because the international economic order is divided along race and class lines; 6) her self. While she spends less time detailing the nature and scope of the last four "mountains" than she does on the first two, Ogundipe-Leslie makes it clear that the most important challenge to the African woman is her own self-perceptions since it is she who will have to define her own freedom:

> The sixth mountain on the woman's back – herself – is the most important. Women are shackled by their own negative self-image, by centuries of the interiorization of the ideologies of patriarchy and gender hierarchy. Her own reactions to objective problems therefore are often self-defeating and self-crippling. She reacts with fear dependency complexes and attitudes to please and cajole where more self-assertive actions are needed . . . [2]

Progressive African women see the women's struggle as even more difficult than the obvious struggles for national liberation where the enemy is easily recognized. As Gwendolyn Konie describes it:

> The struggle for equal rights between the sexes is going to prove even more difficult than that of de-colonization because in essence it is a struggle between husband and wife, brother and sister, father and mother.[3]

And Annabella Rodrigues who participated in the FRELIMO struggle for Mozambican liberation identifies polygamy, initiation rites and *lobolo*, or dowry, as the most difficult of traditions to eliminate and the most oppressive to women and says,

> It is easier to eliminate the colonial, bourgeois influences that were imposed on us and identified with the enemy than to eliminate generations of tradition from within our own society.[4]

Inevitably, the question of national reconstruction along more egalitarian lines enters and has to be hinged to women's lives in African nations. The positions of more radically feminist organizations like CAMS Internationale (La Commission Internationale Pour l'Abolition des Mutilations Sexuelles), a Dakar-based organization which includes membership from Afro-America, the Caribbean, Africa and Europe, have to be considered here. Founded in 1979, it proposes to work toward enhancing woman's status in society through the abolition of sexual mutilation, institutionalized polygamy, obligatory motherhood, the mandatory wearing of clothing of constraint and illiteracy of women. CAMS insists that Third World Women ought not wait for a revolution initiated by men to institute certain changes in women's lives. ("Nous n'avons plus à attendre une révolution introduite et toujours menée par les hommes. Nous prenons en charge notre propre lutte sans devinir, comme toujours, la section féminine de la révolution des hommes, par les hommes.")[5]

A genuine African feminism can therefore be summarized as follows. Firstly, it recognizes a common struggle with African men for the removal of the yokes of foreign domination and European/American exploitation. It is not antagonistic to African men but it challenges them to be aware of certain salient aspects of women's subjugation which differ from the generalized oppression of all African peoples.

Secondly, an African feminist consciousness recognizes that certain inequities and limitations existed/exist in traditional societies and that colonialism reinforced them and introduced others. As such, it acknowledges its affinities with international feminism, but delineates a specific African feminism with certain specific needs and goals arising out of the concrete realities of women's lives in African societies.

Thirdly, it recognizes that African societies are ancient societies, so logically, African women must have addressed the problems of women's position in society historically. In this regard there already exist, in some societies, structures which given women equality. According to van Sertima, the colonial period and immediate pre-colonial period are not the only indices by which one evaluates traditional African society.[6] Revised historical records are indicating that African women in the pre-colonial period and in antiquity were competent rulers, warriors and participants in their societies.[7] In fact the mythology of several peoples shows women in leadership positions (See Nama's discussion on the "Daughters of Moombi"[8] in Gikuyu culture in this work for example).

Fourthly, African feminism examines African societies for institutions which are of value to women and rejects those which work to their detriment and does not simply import Western women's agendas. Thus, it respects African woman's status as mother but questions obligatory motherhood and the traditional favoring of sons. It sees utility in the positive aspects of the extended family and polygamy with respect to child care and the sharing of household responsibility, traditions which are compatible with modern working women's lives and the problems of child care but which were distorted with colonialism and continue to be distorted in the urban environment. African feminist author Buchi Emecheta was soundly attacked for daring to suggest that polygamy worked in many ways to women's benefit.[9] The CAMS colloquium examined both monogamy and polygamy, soundly criticizing the latter but not totally endorsing the former. The debate lingers as within both marital systems women may be dominated. What should be attacked is the privilege that is accorded to males in marriage in general and the concomitant loss of status that is the females'. The excesses of polygamy which most offend women include the man's prerogative to be catered to by several women, the fact that *he* usually has the *choice*, the rejection of women and the competition between them which his choices generate. Omolara Ogundipe-Leslie, in discussing the Nigerian situation says, "the woman as daughter or sister has greater status and more rights in her lineage. Married, she becomes a possession, voiceless and often rightless in her husband's family, except for what accrues to her through her children."[10] There are, however, other forms of male–female relationships which work favorably in Africa and these need adequate examination. Importantly, no system should be institution-alized and mandated, and the woman's right to choose, without censure, should be respected.

Fifthly, it respects African woman's self-reliance and the penchant to cooperative work and social organization (networking) and the fact that African women are seldom financially dependent but instead accept income-generating work as a fact of life. It rejects, however the over-burdening, exploitation and relegation to "muledom" that is often her lot.

Sixthly, an African feminist approach has to look objectively at women's situation in societies which have undergone a war of national liberation and socialist reconstruction. Urdang's[11] essay on the steps taken to equalize the sexes in Guinea Bissau is of immense value. So are the essays in *Third World. Second Sex. Women's Struggles and National Liber-ation.*[12] Women who have participated fully in struggles for national liberation often find that in the national reconstruction phase, a new and more sustained struggle has to be waged with and against the men along whose sides they fought.

Finally, African feminism looks at traditional and contemporary avenues of choice for women. It is important to state here that anthropologists (largely white and male) who were the first to study African women's roles took as norm outward demeanors of submissiveness and failed to extricate other modes by which African women access power. Many of these power mechanisms surface in times of crisis. New studies by African women anthropologists and sociologists are beginning to reveal more accurate findings as these women scholars are able to enter the African women's world in ways in which the male (and white) anthropo-logists could not.[13] Above all, African women themselves are beginning to tell their own stories.[14] All of this must contribute to the development of a true African feminist theory.

The obvious connection between African and Western feminism is that both identify gender-specific issues and recognize woman's position internationally as one of second class status and "otherness" and seek to correct that. An International Feminism[15] to which various regional perspectives are contributed seems acceptable to African women while the European/American model is not. The failure of Western feminists to deal with issues that directly affect Black women and their tendency to sensationalize others create antagonisms[16] as does the fact that white women are often partners in the oppression of both African women and men (South Africa as the most overt example). The term "feminism" often has to be qualified when used by most African and other Third World women. The race class and cultural allegiances that are brought to its consideration cause the most conflict. Yet, although, the concept may not enter the daily existence of the average woman, and although much of what she understands as feminism is filtered through a media that is male-dominated and male-oriented, African women recognize the inequities and, especially within the context of struggles for national liberation, are challenging entrenched male dominance.

Theoretical African feminism understands the interconnectedness of race, class and sex oppression.[17] Consequently it realizes that there are white men and women, and definitely Black men who seek to overturn the oppressive structures of their societies. Thus, it of necessity has a socialist orientation. Kenyan writer/critic Micere Mugo's position is perhaps the best summary of this interconnectedness. In a 1976 interview she stated:

First of all, let me note that we cannot only speak of women's oppression by men. In capitalist systems, women tend to be exploited by the very nature of the society, particularly the working and peasant women, just as men are exploited. The difference is that women are hit particularly hard. Their most obvious hardship is being educationally disadvantaged. Then you have forms of abuse that cut across class lines: sexual abuse, wife-beating and the fact that men take advantage of the woman's role as child-bearer. But I won't give the impression that I foster any illusions. Sexual abuse, rape etc. do take place in socialist societies, but I believe statistics will bear me out that the degree of such abuses is less than in capitalist societies, whose conditions of maldistribution and ownership tend to breed many social problems.[18]

For this reason she projects "a system where all the oppressive institutions are dismantled – politically, socially for the sake of men and women. . . . a society which actively encourages the idea of collective responsibility." Micere Mugo's own creative work, her collaborative work with writer Ngugi wa Thiong'o and her own activism which led to her exile from Kenya demonstrates the inextricable link between an African feminist consciousness and a socialist orientation – both commited to total freedom of all people. Omolara Ogundipe-Leslie's argument as expressed in "Not Spinning on the Axis of Maleness" and "The Female Writer and Her Commitment" cited earlier (fn.9) is another articulation of this position. African men who challenge the traditional social and political dominance of patriarchy and who support women's issues are obvious partners. Among writers, Ngugi wa Thiong'o is probably the most brilliant example, seeing the woman's struggle as inextricably entertwined with the total struggle. In a 1982 interview, on his novel *Devil on the Cross* and in *Detained: A Writer's Prison Diary* Ngugi describes women as the most exploited and oppressed section of the entire working class, "exploited as workers and at home, and also by 'backward elements in the culture, remnants of feudalism.'" As a result, he says, "I would create a picture of a strong, determined woman with a will to resist and to struggle against the conditions of her present being."[19]

The very fact that it is necessary to qualify feminism or limit it with the word "African" indicates implicitly the relationship between the two. In the main, therefore, African feminism is a hybrid of sorts, which seeks to combine African concerns with feminist concerns. This is the nature of the "balancing" which has to take place.

The term "womanism" defined by Alice Walker and which comes directly out of African-American and Caribbean culture is inextricably entwined in the definition of African feminism. It too is a qualification, a search for new terminology to adequately convey Black women's feminism and a recognition of the limitation of the term "feminism" for our purposes. A womanist, she says, in part, is "a black feminist, or feminist of color . . . committed to survival and wholeness of entire people, male and female . . . [but who] loves herself. Regardless."[20] Seriousness, capability, self-reliance, love of culture, love of SELF are indicated. There may be some differences in orientation but in much the same way for African feminists, the double allegiance to woman's emancipation and African liberation becomes one.

Defining an African Feminist Critical Approach

African feminist criticism is definitely engaged criticism in much the same way as progressive African literary criticism grapples with decolonization and feminist criticism with the politics of male literary dominance. This criticism therefore is both textual and contextual criticism:

textual in that close reading of texts using the literary establishment's critical tools is indicated; contextual as it realizes that analyzing a text without some consideration of the world with which it has a material relationship is of little social value. So the dichotomy between textual and contextual criticism, the perennial argument about form and content, common in literary circles finds some resolution here.

Our task here is to identify critical approaches and standards and criteria which have been applied so far to the study of African literature from a feminist perspective and which can be utilized and built upon for further examination of women in/and African literature. In a larger sense, African literary criticism, in general, if it be unbiased in the future will have to come to grips with issues such as the treatment of women characters and the growing presence of African women writers.

The African feminist theoretical framework previously outlined, along with the work of feminist theorists, combine in a unique fashion in this approach. Again, the "balancing act" described above applies. African feminist critics must take what is of value from both mainstream feminist criticism and African literary criticism, keeping in mind that both are offshoots from traditional European literary criticism and in some cases its adversaries. The result then is not reduction but refinement geared specifically to deal with the concrete and literary realities of African women's lives.

It is important to underscore the fact that a substantial amount of literature exists on the development of a feminist aesthetic,[21] on one hand, and a Black/African aesthetic[22] on the other. The work of Black feminist critics[23] in the United States also provides an important focus especially when examining African women writers and the question of their exclusion from the literary canon(s).

For this reason, Katherine Frank's "Feminist Criticism and the African Novel",[24] the only published work known to this writer to deal directly with this subject, loses by not understanding the critical connection between feminist criticism and African literature by not taking into consideration how African-American feminists apply feminist theory to Black literature. There, the geo-cultural differences notwithstanding, lies the link – in the explorations of Deborah Mc Dowell, Barbara Christian, Mary Helen Washington, Alice Walker, Barbara Smith and others. For example, her questions about whether "gender or race is the most significant defining characteristic of a writer" is already answered. For Black/African feminists never make that distinction. It is not a question of either/or, but one of an acceptance of BOTH and the balances and conflicts that go with that twin acceptance. Frank, moreover is guilty of some gross distortions in the way in which she interprets feminism, for example her conclusion: "Feminism, by definition, is a profoundly individualistic philosophy: it values personal growth and individual fulfilment over any larger communal needs or good" (p. 45) is just the kind of conclusion that some retrograde males have made. Quite to the contrary, feminism is not individualistic but openly speaks of "sisterhood" and the need for "women" to advance in society to be on at least an equal level with men for the society's overall good. Frank also, much like Ojo-Ade in his "Female Writers, Male Critics"[25] reads feminism solely as a Western import forgetting the African-American women, like Sojourner Truth's contribution to feminism and the many African women in history whose lives and deeds can be clearly read as "feminist". Frank, nonetheless has made an important contribution to the discussion and importantly delineates the various types of feminist literary theory which can be applied. For example, she sees the need for a literary history of African women writers which would account for the "lost lives" in African literary history. Our position is that women writers are not simply seeing themselves in conflict with traditionalism but are pointing out to society where some of the inequities lie and thereby are directly involved in a struggle to reshape society.

African feminist criticism so far has engaged in a number of critical activities which can be conveniently categorized as follows: 1) Developing the canon of African women writers; 2) Examining stereotypical images of women in African literature; 3) Studying African women writers and the development of an African female aesthetic; and 4) Examining women in oral traditional literature.

[. . .]

Notes

1   (Cambridge, Mass., Schenckman Publishing Company, Inc., 1981), pp. 7–41.

2   *The Journal of African Marxists* 5(February, 1984): 89, pp. 35–6.

3   In *Sisterhood is Global*, p. 744.

4   In Miranda Davies, ed. *Third World – Second Sex. Women's Struggles and National Liberation* (London, Zed Books, 1983), pp. 131–2. Jane Ngwenya a political activist from Zimbabwe had much earlier made similar points in an interview "An African Woman Speaks", *Encore*, June 23, 1975, p. 48. Grace Akello, *Self Twice Removed*, a report on Ugandan women published by Change, an International Women's Research Organization in 1982 and reported in "Struggling Out of Traditional Strait-jackets", *New African*, January 1983.

5   Le Soleil (Dakar), 29 decembre 1982. "We no longer have to wait for a revolution introduced and always led by the men. We are taking charge of our own struggle without becming, as always, the female section of the revolution of and for men" (my translation).

6   See his *They Came Before Columbus* (New York, Random House, 1976) and *Blacks in Science: Ancient and Modern* (available through African Studies Department, Rutgers University), 1983.

7   John Henrik Clarke, "African Warrior Queens" in *Black Women in Antiquity* ed. by Ivan Van Sertima (New Brunswick, Transaction Books, 1984), pp. 123–34. Caroline Ifeka-Moller, "Female Militancy and Colonial Revolt. The Woman's War of 1929, Eastern Nigeria, in *Perceiving Women* ed. Shirley Ardener (New York, John Wiley & Sons, 1975), pp. 127–57. A paper "Slavery and Women in The Pre-Colonial Kingdom of Dahomey" by Boniface Obichere (Institute of African Studies, University of ibadan, 1976) demonstrates that women participated equally in the political, social and economic life of pre-colonial Dahomey.

8   African woman writer, Charity Waciuma also has an autobiographical work entitled *Daughter of Mumbi* (Nairobi, East African Publishing House, 1969).

9   African Studies Meeting (California) October, 1984. African women in the audience, some feminists, were appalled at Emecheta's stand on polygamy. One has to admit, however, that Emecheta, who has written several novels which show polygamy in negative light would not have come to her position casually.

10   "Not Spinning on the Axis of Maleness" in *Sisterhood is Global*, pp. 500–1.

11   Stephanie Urdang, "The Role of Women in the Revolution of Guinea-Bissau." in Steady, pp. 119–39.

12   (London, Zed Press, 1983); Essays in *Sisterhood is Global* also provide views on women in countries undergoing socialist reconstruction. Some describe it as the second struggle. Others like Jane Ngwenya, "Women and Liberation in Zimbabwe", pp. 78–83 say that suffering and fighting together erodes sexual prejudices and stereotyping. More long-term study will show if this is sustained.

13   See for example D.M. Hull's bibliography "African Women in Development: An Untapped Resource" (Moorland-Spingarn Research Center, Howard University, April, 1983) which lists a number of works by African women specifically and by women in general. Audrey Smedley, "Motherhood and Women in Patrilineal Societies" presented at the ASALH Conference, Detroit, Michigan, 1983, part of a major work being prepared on women and patriliny, holds that by assuming women have no say in the shaping of the kind of society they live in, we bring a male-oriented approach to examining African societies. African and African-American anthropologists like Bolanle Awe and Niara Sudarkasa, are providing important information on women in African societies. The essays in Steady's *The Black Woman Cross-Culturally* are additional examples.

14   African women writers are making statements on the social organization of their societies, in addition to their creative writing. A number of interviews with African women are being published.

15   *Sisterhood is Global* is subtitled "The International Women's Movement Anthology". The extent of contributions to this and other similar volumes indicates the validity of international feminism.

16   The AAWORD Statement on Genital Mutilation in *Third World-Second Sex*, pp. 217–20 is a case in point. Steady's introduction is in many ways a rebuttal to Western feminism.

17   See, for example, Lillian Robinson's *Sex, Class and Culture* (Bloomington, Indiana University Press, 1978), Angela Davis, *Women, Race and Class* (New York, Random House, 1983), Lise Vogel, *Marxism and the Oppression of Women. Toward Unitary Theory* (New Jersey, Rutgers University Press, 1983); Bonnie Thornton Dill, "Race, Class and Gender: Prospects for an All-Inclusive Sisterhood," *Feminist Studies* 9 (1983), 131–50.

18   "Dr. Micere Mugo, Kenya's outspoken Intellectual and Academic Critic, Talks to Nancy Owano," *Africa Woman* 6 (September to October, 1976), pp. 14–15.

19   Profile: "Ngugi: My Novel of Blood, Sweat and Tears." *New African* (August, 1982), p. 36. The works cited are published by Heinemann (London) African Writers Series Nos. 200 (1982) and 240 (1983) respectively.

20   The definition of "womanist" is a preface to her *In Search of Our Mothers Gardens: Womanist Prose*, op. cit., pp. xi–xii.

21   Among them are essays in Cheryl L. Brown and Karen Olson, *Feminist Criticism Essays on Theory, Poetry and Prose* (New Jersey, The Scarecrow Press, Inc., 1978). Cheri Register's Review essay, "Literary Criticism" in *Signs* (Winter, 1980) is a fairly comprehensive sampling of the issues and theorists of feminist criticism. Essays in Elizabeth Abel, ed., *Writing and Sexual Difference* (University of Chicago Press, 1982) and Elaine Showalter, *Feminist Criticism* (New York, Random House, 1985) are additional examples.

22   See Addison Gayle, *The Black Aesthetic* (New York, Doubleday, 1971); Carolyn Fowler's introduction to her *Black Arts and Black Aesthetics–A Bibliography* (Atlanta, First World Foundation, 1984); Zirimu and Gurr, *Black Aesthetics* (Nairobi, East African Publishing House, 1973); Wole Soyinka, *Myth, Literature and the African World* (London, Cambridge University Press, 1976); Chinweizu et al., *Towards the Decolonization of African Literature* (Washington, DC, Howard University Press, 1983); Johnson, Cailler, Hamilton and Hill-Lubin, *Defining the African Aesthetic* (Washington, DC, Three Continents Press, 1982).

23   Section Five of *But Some of Us Are Brave*, edited by Gloria T. Hull, Patricia Bell Scott and Barbara Smith (New York, The Feminist Press, 1982) is devoted to literature and contains Barbara Smith's "Toward a Black Feminist Criticism", pp. 157–75, which is also published separately in booklet form and distributed by The Crossing Press, 1982. Deborah McDowell, "New Directions in Black Feminist Criticism", *Black American Literature Forum* 14:4 (Winter, 1980), 153–9; Claudia Tate's *Black Women Writers at Work* (New York, Continuum, 1983), Alice Walker's essays in *In Search of Our Mothers Gardens*, Mary Helen Washington's many essays and a number of other works address this issue. Toni Cade Bambara's *The Black Woman. An Anthology* (New York, New American

Library, 1970) includes essays like Francis Beale's "Double Jeopardy: To Be Black and Female" which discuss the particular situation of Black American women. Deborah Mc Dowell is preparing an extensive manuscript on feminist criticism as applied to African-American literature. Barbara Christian, *Black Feminist Criticism. Perspectives on Black Women Writers* (New York, Pergamon Press, 1985) includes Buchi Emecheta in her study.

24 Katherine Frank, "Feminist Criticism and the African Novel," *African Literature Today* 14 (London, Heinemann, 1984), 34–48.

25 Although it has a catchy introduction and conclusion, Femi Ojo-Ade's, "Female Writers, Male Critics" does not deal with criticism but is a study of Flora Nwapa and Ama Ata Aidoo. Ojo-Ade is well recognized for an overtly belligerent, condescending-to-female-writers-and-critics language and oral style of presentation which contradicts some of the points he makes in his conclusion "Criticism, Chauvinism, Cynicism . . . Commitment". While he seems to be arguing for fairness to women here, his tone may betray his true attitude to this subject. Most Black women welcome men as fellow explorers in this field and rarely descend to the gross abuses he suggests, in his final paragraph, that are levelled against male critics. It seems instead a rehashing of some of the early stereotypical language of "women's liberation".

Chapter 76

Bringing African Women into the Classroom:
Rethinking Pedagogy and Epistemology

Obioma Nnaemeka

[...]

In 1980 Zed Press (London) published Nawal El Saadawi's *Hidden Face of Eve*. This edition's preface remains one of the best analyses of the Iranian revolution and of the relation between imperialism and Islam, outlining its effect on women in the Arab world. Saadawi categorically states in the preface that to understand and explain fully the condition of women in the Arab world, one must take into account foreign, particularly American, intervention in the region. This important preface, which establishes a connection between imperialism and the rise of Islamic fundamentalism, with the attendant repression of women, did not appear in the American edition published by Beacon Press, an omission that prompted a strong reaction from Saadawi:

> Yes, and here is a very subtle form of exploitation practiced, unfortunately, by feminists – so-called progressive feminists. Gloria Steinem of *Ms* magazine writes me a letter in Cairo and asks me for an article about clitoridectomy. So I write her an article setting forth the political, social and historical analysis, along with comments about my personal experience. She cuts the political, social and historical analysis and publishes only the personal statements, which put me in a very awkward position. People asked, how could Nawal write such a thing? She has such a global perspective on clitoridectomy, how could she write such a thing? They didn't know Steinem had cut the article. The second example is Beacon Press in Boston. I gave my book, *The Hidden Face of Eve*, to the publisher in London; he published all of the book – the preface, introduction, everything. The preface, which is a long preface, is crucial and important to the

First published in *Borderwork: Feminist Engagements with Comparative Literature*, ed. Margaret R. Higgonnet, pp. 304–9, 312–16. Ithaca: Cornell University Press, 1994.

book. Beacon Press cut it without my permission, making me feel that I have been exploited and my ideas distorted. Without the preface, it appears that I am separating the sexual from the political, which I never do. To me, women who think they are liberated but who are obsessed with sexuality are not liberated. They are living a new slavery. They are obsessed by not having men around just as they were obsessed with having them around. It is the other side of the same coin.[1]

Although *The Hidden Face of Eve* has been widely read in the United States, the American audience, reading an incomplete version, is denied this powerful book's full impact. As readers of Saadawi in North America lead their war against physical excisions made on Arab girls, they should with equal enthusiasm challenge the type of excision Saadawi claims was performed on her book. Such manipulations of information have grave implications for our theorizing and praxis.

How can we theorize difference or diversity, and what are the pitfalls in such theorizing? How do we gather information about the Other? How do we organize, order, and disseminate that information? In short, how does information management contribute to our construction of a notion of self and at the same time alienate us from the Other? These are crucial questions that we, as students and teachers, confront in varying degrees. These and other related issues have led me to explore the subject in my essay titled "Bringing African Women into the Classroom." While working on this essay, I got a call from a colleague. During our conversation I told him about my topic. "Eh! Bringing African Women into the Classroom!" he sneered. "What do you mean by 'bringing'? Can't they walk? How do you bring them?" he asked. I replied, "You bring them on a leash." Although my response was meant to be a joke, in retrospect I believe I accurately described the profound objectification of African women in classrooms in the West. And as we consider the commodification of African women in Western classrooms, we must also address the issue of tokenism. Quite often the work of an African woman writer is thrown into a course syllabus in order to take care of race, gender, ethnicity, and class issues in one fell swoop, thereby creating a "multicultural course" which will in turn produce "multicultural students."

To study a culture presupposes in some ways that one is outside it. Can we teach as outsiders? Oh, yes, we can. The pertinent question, however, remains: How do we learn and teach as outsiders? In studying and teaching another culture, the teacher finds himself or herself situated at the congruence of different and often contradictory cultural currents. This point of convergence where the teacher stands has its privileges and rewards, but it is also fraught with danger. To survive at this precarious position requires a large dose of humility. Issues involved in researching, writing, and teaching about other cultures are inextricably linked to survival. Can we cross cultural boundaries and still survive? And the notion of crossing cultural boundaries is in itself problematic. What do we mean by "crossing"? Do we mean moving from one point to another, in the process abandoning one set of realities for another? It seems to me that a cross-cultural pedagogy entails not a "crossover" but a transgression whose partial enactment denies the finality implicit in a "crossover."

As students and teachers we discover that our explorations into understanding other peoples and cultures place us in an ambiguous site where we will never accomplish a "crossover" but rather stand astride cultures: our culture and other cultures. It seems to me that crossing cultural boundaries means standing at the crossroads of cultures. In other words, we must see that we enter other cultures with our own cultural baggage. The extent to which we allow narcissism and notions of self to mediate our analysis will determine the degree of distortion in our conclusions. As we learn and teach about other cultures, two fundamental questions should be asked: (1) Why do we want to learn and teach other cultures? (2) How can we learn and teach other cultures?

The first question raises the issue of intention. Charges of concern with economic advancement and professional upward mobility have been levied against some scholars, ranging from historians and social anthropologists to feminists and cultural critics, who proclaim themselves experts on Africa in general and African women in particular.[2] The same could be said about studies of other minorities in which insiders and outsiders to the minority cultures collaborate to advance themselves economically and professionally by means of distortions they invent about the minority cultures, distortions that run against the sacred nature of these cultures. As Ward Churchill writes:

> The past 20 years have seen the birth of a new growth industry in the United States. Known as "American Indian Spiritualism," this profitable enterprise apparently began with a number of literary hoaxes undertaken by non-Indians such as Carlos Castaneda, Jay Marks (AKA "Jamake High-water," author of The Primal Mind, etc.) and Ruth Beebe Hill (of Hanta Yo notoriety). A few Indians such as Alonzo Blacksmith . . . and Hyemeyohsts Storm . . . also cashed in, writing bad distortions and outright lies about indigenous spirituality for consumption in the mass market. The authors grew rich peddling their trash, while real Indians starved to death, out of the sight and mind of America.[3]

An issue related to the methodological concerns that the second question raises is that of perspective, equally crucial to evaluating how we learn and teach other cultures. Perspective, distance, objectivity. Perspective implies possibilities, alternatives, choice. How can we choose an appropriate location to situate ourselves? How far or close should we stand vis-à-vis the subject of our analysis? In a 1961 lecture in Japan, Simone de Beauvoir affirmed that in a war situation the privileged and probably the most objective position is that of the person on the sideline, the war correspondent, who witnesses the battle but is not embroiled in the fighting.[4] Richard Wright brilliantly articulated the problematic of perspective: "Perspective is that part of a poem, novel, or play which a writer never puts directly upon paper. It is that fixed point in intellectual space where a writer stands to view the struggles, hopes and sufferings of his people. There are times when he may stand too close and the result is blurred vision. Or he may stand too far away and the result is a neglect of important things."[5] In our study and teaching of other cultures, balance and humility must mediate our choice of perspective.

Different problems arise depending on whether one teaches a culture as an insider or an outsider. As I mentioned earlier, one can teach as an outsider, but to do so requires the humility that is grounded in knowledge. Unfortunately, when teaching about Africa and African women, many outsiders prove too impatient to claim expertise. A three-week whirlwind tour of Africa does not an expert on Africa make; speed-reading two or three African novels cannot produce an expert on African literature. Sadly enough, schools in the West sustain tremendous institutional tolerance and encouragement of such expertise. As the academy provides a breeding ground for such experts on Africa and African women, it puts in place stiff requirements for the teaching of Western cultures and literatures. In such areas expertise must be proven through transcripts, graduate degrees, and teaching experience. Trivializing other cultures encourages the type of miseducation that leads to further trivializing of such cultures.

Teaching as an insider poses its own set of problems. Overidentification with one's culture leads to the type of romanticization that produces other levels of distortions. Good examples surface in some Negritude writings. The romanticization of Africa and the subsequent oversimplification of issues have led to much of the negative reaction against the Negritude movement. Furthermore, insiders can also be alienated from their own culture. A Western-educated African who teaches African culture also speaks from a position of alienation which may not necessarily be as profound as that of the outsider. Whether one teaches as an insider or an outsider, the issue of distance is crucial. It is Chinua Achebe's recognition of the interplay of identification and distance that sets him apart as one of Africa's foremost writers. With Achebe we experience a rare moment in literature where the writer balances himself or herself strategically. In spite of his Western education, Achebe remains a true son of Igboland, what the Igbos would call "a son of the soil." Immersed in his cultural and social milieu but possessing a critical eye, he simultaneously identifies with and maintains a distance from his environment. In his works Achebe narrates with charm his profound identification with and love for his environment while at the same time he recognizes its flaws, particularly those generated by foreign interventions.[6] Achebe demonstrates that a post-colonial subject can maintain a balanced view of the postcolonial condition.

The issue of balance is neglected in the one-dimensional Western constructions of the African woman – usually poor and powerless. We African women have witnessed repeatedly the activities of our overzealous foreign sisters, mostly feminists who appropriate our wars in the name of fighting the oppression of women in the so-called third world. We watch with chagrin and in painful sisterhood these avatars of the proverbial mourner who wails more than the owners of the corpse.[7] In their enthusiasm, our sisters usurp our wars and fight them badly – very badly. The arrogance that declares African women "problems" objectifies us and undercuts the agency necessary for forging true global sisterhood. African women are not problems to be solved. Like women everywhere, African women *have* problems. More important, they have provided solutions to these problems. We are the only ones who can set our priorities and agenda. Anyone who wishes to participate in our struggles must do so in the context of our agenda. In the same way, African women who wish to contribute to global struggles (and many do) should do so with a deep respect for the paradigms and strategies that people of those areas have established. In our enthusiasm to liberate others, we must not be blind to our own enslavement. Activities of women globally should be mutually liberating.

[. . .]

Not too long ago I taught a course, "Women in Developing Areas: Power, Politics, and Culture," in a small Midwestern liberal arts college. We started by reading materials written by Judith van Allen and some African women scholars, Ifi Amadiume, Bolanle Awe, and Kamene Okonjo.[8] At the end of two weeks of intense reading, one of my students informed me that she was not getting anything out of the course. Her complaint surprised me since a few other students had mentioned to me that there was too much information to absorb. After a long discussion with the student, it dawned on me that her problem lay more with the nature of the materials we were reading, which discussed primarily the powerful positions that women occupy in indigenous African social and political formations. My student was basically asking, "Where are those excised/circumcised African women in marriages arranged by families who eventually shipped them off to be victimized by heavy-handed polygynists?" I told the student to exercise patience. Circumcision, arranged marriage, and polygyny would be discussed during the seventh and eighth weeks of class; she had only five short weeks to go! Our preconceived notions can be so strong that they get in the way of our learning about cultures and other peoples whose lives and realities transcend our cultural boundaries. As teachers we can overcome this difficulty by painstakingly and judiciously selecting materials that build a balanced syllabus.

The teaching of cultural studies often focuses on exposing differences between cultures. It seems to me, however, that we could accomplish much by teaching similarities and connections as well as differences. It makes sense politically that women, as teachers, teach connections, thereby reducing the distance between the student and the foreign culture and increasing points of interaction and identification. It is the teacher's responsibility to delineate the differences and commonalities between the student's culture and the foreign culture, without unduly establishing facile universalism and untenable connections. This methodology which I call teaching connections has been helpful to me in my teaching of African women to a Western audience, especially in teaching the three most discussed issues about African women – clitoridectomy, polygyny, and arranged marriage.

The pervasive sensationalization of clitoridectomy in Western media and scholarship leads to the equally pervasive belief in the incompleteness of most African women, a belief that basically questions our humanity. From the West an intense war led by Fran Hoskens, the guru of clitoridectomy, has raged against this "barbaric act" perpetrated against helpless African and Arab women. Women within Africa and the Arab world have equally condemned the practice. There is disagreement, however, about how to wage the war.[9] Our Western sisters have seen clitoridectomy primarily as an issue of sexuality, and the fixation with sexuality in the West helps explain the intensity of their intrusion. They denounce clitoridectomy because, according to them, it prevents African women from enjoying sex. But then, wasn't clitoridectomy initiated in part precisely to prevent women from going around and enjoying sex? This unmitigated advocacy of the enjoyment of sex most often leads to a stricter imposition of certain customs on African and Arab women. Foreigners, however well-meaning they may be, must not fail to see how they contribute to the intensification of oppressive patriarchal practices in Africa and the Arab world. The upsurge of religious fundamentalism in the Middle East and other parts of the Arab world occurs as a sign of resistance to imperialism and other forms of foreign intervention. The return to the veil arises not by accident. In the name of resisting foreign interventionism, patriarchal societies resort to rigid and heavy-handed enforcement of old ways – tradition, religious fundamentalism – which often oppress women. So by fighting our wars badly, our Western sisters inadvertently collaborate in tightening the noose around our necks.

Clitoridectomy goes beyond sexuality. It raises questions with profound social, political, and economic implications.[10] Any meaningful fight against this practice must coordinate with other battles against the political, social, and economic conditions that generated and continue to perpetuate such a practice. We must consider an issue such as this in all its complexities. We must establish linkages, teach connections. Furthermore, we must acknowledge the history and global nature of circumcision and clitoridectomy in order to situate the debate where it duly belongs. As Nawal El Saadawi rightly points out, the issue is not barbaric Africa and oppressive Islam. The issue is patriarchy:

In Copenhagen, we had a lot of disagreement, we women from Africa and the Third World, with her [Fran Hoskens]. In our workshop, we argued that clitoridectomy has nothing to do with Africa or with any religion, Islam or Christianity. It is known in history that it was performed in Europe and America, Asia, and Africa. It has to do with patriarchy and monogamy. When patriarchy was established, monogamy was forced on women so that fatherhood could be known. Women's sexuality was attenuated so as to fit within the monogamous system. But she doesn't want to hear any of this.[11]

There are other aspects of teaching connections which I apply to my teaching of clitoridectomy. I teach clitoridectomy in tandem with teaching abuses of the female body in other cultures: forms of plastic surgery in the West and foot-binding in China, for example. For a Western audience I bring the issue home by comparing breast reduction surgery and clitoridectomy. We must not be distracted by the arrogance that names one procedure breast *reduction* and the other sexual *mutilation*, with all the attached connotations of barbarism. In both instances some part of the female body is excised.

Some women undergo breast reduction for some of the reasons that some young girls undergo clitoridectomy – to be more attractive, desirable, and acceptable. For the women in areas where clitoridectomy is performed, beauty is inextricably linked with chastity and motherhood. The crucial questions we must ask are: For whom are these operations undertaken? For whom must these women be desirable and acceptable? Women's inability to control their bodies is not country-specific. Abuse of the female body is global and should be studied and interpreted within the context of oppressive conditions under patriarchy. Teaching connections radically shifts the grounds for debate from racial and national particularism and idiosyncrasies to comparisons of women's oppression under patriarchy. In the American classroom I have observed that this shift interrogates and modifies the notion of self among the students, particularly the female students. They go from thinking nationality (American) to thinking simultaneously nationality sex, and gender (American women).

Polygyny has been condemned in the West as one of the worst symbols of African women's oppression without any assessment of the advantages the practice accords women: sharing child care, emotional and economic support, sisterhood, companionship, and so on. Our Western sisters who pity us for having to share our husbands with other women forget that husband-sharing was perfected and elevated to an art form in the West. Polygyny comes from two Greek words: *poly* (many) and *gyne* (woman or wife). *Polygyny* has, therefore, two possible meanings – "many women," or "many wives." The English dictionary sanctifies only one of the two possibilities, "many wives," a limitation to which no one seems to object. I remember that the first English dictionary I used in the colonial school was written by one Michael West, a man. I gather that men still write dictionaries – English dictionaries!

Polygyny as "many women" places the Western man with one wife and one or more mistresses in the same category as the African man who legitimates his relationship with more than one woman. We must not also forget the brand of polygyny euphemistically called serial monogamy in the West. The need to qualify monogamy in this instance is suspect. As a matter of fact, an African woman in a polygamous relationship seems to be a step or two ahead of her Western counterpart living under the illusion that she is not sharing her husband: the African woman knows who else her husband is with. In teaching and understanding polygyny, the issue is not uncivilized Africa but men.

Arranged marriage is another issue used to illustrate the enslavement of African women. As I teach connections, I point out practices in the West similar to the arranged marriage for which African and Asian societies have been ridiculed. One wonders if the dating services mushrooming all over the United States do not engage in some similar arranging! I have watched with amazement the facility of arrangements conducted on the television show "Love Connection." On a couple of occasions I have witnessed the triumphant return of a "connected" couple to the show: the woman walks out jubilantly with a baby in her arms, and the man, now her husband, follows a few steps behind with a conspiratorial grin on his face. A family is established before our eyes, and we applaud. Again, in the issue of arranged marriage, it seems to me that African women are better off: they do not pay for the services for which their American counterparts pay exorbitantly. My American feminist friend has argued vehemently in favor of dating services because, according to her, the issue of choice is crucial. With a dating service a woman can decide to choose or not choose a particular "allocation." Incidentally, the day my friend argued her strong case, I saw sticking out of her bookshelf a book titled *Smart Women/Foolish Choices*. She must have bought the book in a moment of doubt.

At stake in our divergent views is the issue of cultural difference. In order to teach difference, we must thoroughly examine how difference comes into being. Can we distinguish between constructed and actual difference? Ideology thrives on differences; ideology actually constructs differences, thus hiding similarities and actual differences. Concerning African women in the classroom, what we see in most classrooms in the West is not the study of *African women* but rather the study of the *African woman*, in whatever way we choose to invent the myth. Usually the invented African woman carries a heavy load on her head and a baby strapped to her back, and holds two kids, with about four more in tow. Of course she lives in a village. She is the myth. The problem with myths is not what they reveal but what they conceal. In order to understand African peoples and appreciate the rich diversity of Africa, we must put a human face on the African continent. In teaching African peoples, an observer notes, "we need to breathe life into our classroom."[12] Distortions in the study and teaching of African concerns stem from imperialism's refusal to historicize and differentiate African space and peoples. We Africans must realize that our survival depends to a large extent on our ability to reclaim our history. As bell hooks correctly notes, "Our struggle is also the struggle of memory against forgetting."[13]

[. . .]

Notes

1   Quoted in Tiffany Patterson and Angela Gillam, "Out of Egypt: A Talk With Nawal El Saadawi," *Freedomways* 23 (1983): 190–1.

2   Ifi Amadiume, preface to *Male Daughters, Female Husbands: Gender and Sex in an African Society* (London: Zed Press, 1987).

3   Ward Churchill, "Spiritual Hucksterism," *Z Magazine* (December 1990): 94.

4   Simone de Beauvoir, "Women and Creativity," in *French Feminist Thought: A Reader*, ed. Toril Moi (Oxford: Basil Blackwell, 1987), 27.

5   Richard Wright, "Blueprint for Negro Writing," in *The Black Aesthetics*, ed. Addison Gayle, Jr. (New York: Doubleday, 1971), 341.

6   See in particular Chinua Achebe, *Things Fall Apart* (London: Heinemann, 1958), and *Arrow of God* (London: Heinemann, 1960). Equally pertinent is Achebe's critique of the West in his books of essays, *Morning Yet on Creation Day* (London: Heinemann, 1977), and *Hopes and Impediments* (New York: Doubleday, 1988), as well as his critique of post-independence Africa, in particular Nigeria, in *A Man of the People* and *The Trouble with Nigeria* (Enugu: Fourth Dimension Publishers, 1985).

7   An Igbo proverb.

8   The recommended readings were: Ifi Amadiume, preface and introduction to *Male Daughters, Female Husbands*; Bolanle Awe, "The Iyalode in the Traditional Yoruba Political System," in *Sexual Stratification*, ed. Alice Schlegal (New York: Columbia University Press, 1977), 144–59; Kamene Okonjo, "The Dual-Sex Political System in Operation: Igbo Women and Community Politics in Midwestern Nigeria," in *Women in Africa*, ed. Nancy Hafkin and Edna Bay (Palo Alto: Stanford University Press, 1976), 45–58; Judith Van Allen, "'Sitting on a Man': Colonialism and the Lost Political Institutions of Igbo Women," *Canadian Journal of African Studies* 6 (1972): 165–81.

9   See AAWORD, "A Statement on Genital Mutilation," in *Third World: Second Sex*, ed. Miranda Davies (London: Zed Press, 1983), 217–20.

10 See Nawal El Saadawi, preface to the English edition of *The Hidden Face of Eve: Women in the Arab World* (London: Zed Press, 1980).

11 Quoted in Patterson and Gillam, "Out of Egypt," 90–1.

12 Donna Blacker, "On Student-Centered Education," unpublished manuscript, 11.

13 bell hooks, *Yearning: Race, Gender, and Cultural Politics* (Boston: South End Press, 1990), 148. This quote is taken from the ANC Freedom Charter.

Chapter 77

Enlightenment Epistemology and the Invention of Polygyny

Uzo Esonwanne

In "The Anthropologist's Influence: Ethnography and the Politics of Conversion," V. Y. Mudimbe contends that "missionary accounts and those of anthropologists" during the colonial period "witness to the same *episteme*," adding that, if identification of their discourses is needed, then "it must be with European intellectual signs and not with African cultures."[1] He traces the genealogy of these "intellectual signs" back to European classical texts in history, drama, geography, and poetry, and identifies Herodotus, Pliny, and Diodorus of Sicily as the founts from which modern Europeans such as John Locke derived their descriptions of Africans and African cultural practices. "At the other extreme," he continues, "nineteenth-century anthropologists depict the essential paradigm of the European invention of Africa: Us/Them," which often "express the belief that the African is a negation of all human experience, or is at least an exemplary exception in terms of evolution."[2]

With changing relations between Europe and Africa in the twentieth century, this paradigm has undergone cosmetic, largely terminological, modification, with the result that it lives on in the form of the tradition/modernity opposition still found in various discourses from modernization and culture-conflict theories to conservative nationalism. In dealing with this paradigm, we shall focus on two questions not addressed in Mudimbe's work: first, what was its structure in Enlightenment thought; and, second, in what form has it been translated into nationalist discourse in *So Long a Letter*, and with what consequences?

Answers to the first question are readily available in Johannes Fabian's *Time and the Other*. Fabian describes the epistemology by which the Enlightenment accounted for the diversity of human cultural forms and practices as Time/Space distancing.[3] This paradigm supplanted that of the Middle Ages in whose model Time/Space were conceived "in terms of a history of salvation" and "the Time of Salvation was conceived as inclusive or incorporative." With the Enlightenment a naturalized, secular Time superseded the Judeo-Christian, sacred Time, and "temporal relations" were redefined "as exclusive and expansive" (TO 26–7;

Frist published in *The Politics of (M)Othering: Womanhood, Identity, and Resistance in African Literature*, ed. Obioma Nnaemeka, pp. 88–95. New York: Routledge, 1997.

see Figure 77.1). The core of this paradigm, Now/Here, corresponds to Civilization and England. From this temporal and spatial core, "given societies of all times and places may be plotted in terms of relative distance *from* the present." "Savage" Time/Space is thus effectively removed from the anthropologist's Time/Space to a primeval past and ancient place marking the evolutionary beginnings of the human species (TO 26–7).

As for the second question, we must look closely at Bâ's handling of the tradition/ modernity paradigm. Perhaps the passage which best exemplifies this handling is Ramatoulaye's recollection of "the aims of our admirable headmistress":

> To *lift* us out of the bog of tradition, superstition and custom, to make us appreciate a multitude
> of civilizations without renouncing our own, to *raise* our vision of the world, cultivate our
> personalities, strengthen our qualities, to *make up* for our inadequacies, to *develop* universal
> moral values in us: these were the aims of our admirable headmistress. (SL 15–16; my emphasis)

In this passage we can hear echoes of Diderot and d'Alembert's *philosophe* (*Encyclopédie*, 1779), trampling "on prejudice, tradition, universal consent, authority, in a word, all that enslaves most minds."[4] Ponty-Ville was, indeed, the training ground for the African *philosophe* and her double, the national bourgeoisie. It is not improbable that at institutions like Ponty-Ville she recited, among others, the line "nos ancêtres, les Gaulois [our ancestors, the Gauls]."[5]

Ponty-Ville then is the crucible in which a new, pliable post- colonial subject, the agent of social transformation, is formed. "Lift," "raise," "make up," "develop": these are stock terms of discourses informed by the evolutionist ethos of the nineteenth century. A sense of teleological motion, of transition, pervades the verbs. Movement from "tradition, superstition and custom" to "a multitude of civilizations" is evolutionary and successive, always tending toward a European norm. "Bog" designates both the place of entrapment and temporal stasis; it is at a distance, removed from the vicinity of civil society. The Time/Space of civil society (England) is now occupied by "a multitude of civilizations" whose "moral values" are "universal"; Savage Society (Figure 77.1) in which subjects are mired in stasis, gives way to Zero Society (Figure 77.2), home of "tradition, superstition and custom."

Just as distance and exclusion make possible the production of the "other" in nineteenth-century anthropology, so would they make possible the production of polygyny in twentieth-century African nationalist discourse. But this is getting ahead of the story. For Ramatoulaye, the route from the passage quoted above to the exclusion of polygyny from the structure and ethos of the nation state passes through a phase of anti-colonialist nationalist consciousness:

> The assimilationist dream of the colonist drew into its crucible our mode of thought and way
> of life. The sun helmet worn over the natural protection of our kinky hair, smoke-filled pipe in
> the mouth, white shorts just above the calves, very short dresses displaying shapely legs: a whole
> generation suddenly became aware of the ridiculous situation festering in our midst. (SL 24)

This passage does not identify "our admirable headmistress" as one of "the colonists." In view of her admiration for her instructor, this is hardly surprising. Quite plainly she is aware that not all French subjects in the colony work as functionaries in the political and economic sectors of the colonial power. Yet it is also obvious that the headmistress is indebted to French colonialism for her mission of salvation as she is indebted to

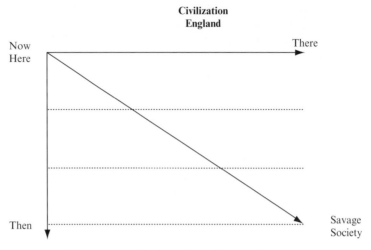

Figure 77.1   Modern Time/Space: distancing.

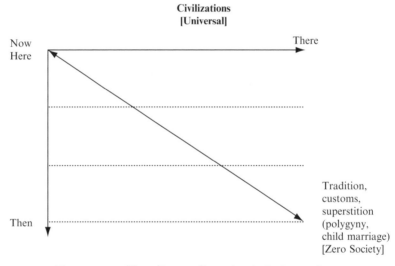

Figure 77.2   Time/Space: distancing in *So Long a Letter.*

nineteenth-century evolutionism for her instructional "aims." Her labor as a teacher, in other words, cannot be completely detached from the matrix of colonialism. In the rather paradoxical situation in which even well-meaning Europeans find themselves under colonialism, she is at once a source of inspiration and empowerment for the women and, as her "aims" reveal, a purveyor of an evolutionist view of African culture. Thus it is that she becomes the source of Ramatoulaye's disdain for "traditions" which fail to fit into the framework of the discourse of civil society and the bourgeois nation state.

The foregoing argument calls for some clarification. My contention is *not* that Ramatoulaye finds no value whatsoever in "tradition, superstition, and custom." Nor am I claiming that she maintains the tradition/modernity binary in every situation. Indeed, sometimes even her endorsement of the modern wavers. My contention is that she is selective about "tradition" and "modernity," just as a farmer would sort her seeds into viable and non-viable before planting. Aunty Nabou belongs to the latter category. She does not fit into Ramatoulaye's "imagined community" (SL 26). Neither do teenage drinking and smoking and unsupervised contacts between boys and girls, but for a different reason: they belong to the latter category because they are deleterious to "moral values" (SL 77).

As the single parent of young adults in an unstable, rapidly changing world, Ramatoulaye must find new ways of dealing with common problems. Her handling of problems such as Aïssatou's unplanned pregnancy is a case in point. Farmata expects punitive sanctions against the young woman. But realizing the agony of her daughter and reminded of bonds of filial affection between them, Ramatoulaye resolves to forgive, console, support, and assist her: "I took my daughter in my arms. Painfully, I held her tightly, with a force multiplied tenfold by pagan revolt and primitive tenderness" (SL 83). By so doing, she breaks with local expectations, here represented by the *griot* woman, Farmata: "she will never know what to expect from me. To give a sinner so much attention was beyond her" (SL 83–4). The significance of Ramatoulaye's reaction to the crisis in her family thus emerges from the contrast with local norms: wailing, threats, reprimands. As her resolve to pre-empt the recurrence of such crisis by giving her children instructions in sex education shows, her unconventional resolution of Aïssatou's crisis does not constitute an unconditional endorsement of the ethics of the emerging social order. What it does reveal is a willingness to take the measure of events in terms of contingent realities. Thus, she astutely maneuvers around the false dichotomy between modernity and tradition, those shibboleths which for most of this century have cast a long shadow over the analysis of African cultural life.[6]

Ramatoulaye's successful resolution of this domestic crisis becomes even more significant when set against the backdrop of her discussion with Daouda Dieng of the low ratio of women's representation to men's in the National Assembly. Successful as a medical practitioner and politician, grave, gentle, and considerate, Dieng cannot see any justification for Ramatoulaye's protest. He is at first dismissive, arguing that women are disorderly and disruptive. But pressed by Ramatoulaye, and forced to pay attention to her ideas, he becomes stentorian, admonishing women to become involved in national politics and condemning them for being more interested in domestic affairs and class privileges (SL 61–2). In his view, affairs of the state encompass national interests, and these are of greater importance than domestic matters which relate to individual families. Subtending this view is a distinction between the personal and the political, the family and the state, a distinction whose effect on thought is not unlike that of the tradition/modernism binary. Against the backdrop of Dieng's unimaginative response to the political crisis in the National Assembly one cannot but be impressed by Ramatoulaye's insistence on the need for increased women's representation and her creative reaction to Aïssatou's pregnancy. If her deferential yet resolute opposition to his views holds any message, it is that resistance to women's political demands is still firmly entrenched, and even in "the general economy of new African words," in "theories commenting upon the catastrophe" of colonialism and "articulating in new ways other objects of desire," that resistance is hardly diminished.[7]

In view of the foregoing observations, I hope my analysis of the representation of polygyny in *So Long a Letter* would be placed in proper perspective. Bâ is quoted as arguing that, "As women, [we] must work for our own future, [we] must overthrow the status quo which harms [us] and [we] must no longer submit to it."[8] This is certainly a desirable end. However, unless a careful analysis of the role of polygyny in the maintenance of that status quo is undertaken, unless care is taken to distinguish the exploitation of polygyny for selfish ends (Mawdo Bâ) from the supercilious and pejorative view of the practice fostered by European ethnocentrism, African women (and men) run the risk of retarding the process of cultural self-criticism implicit in Bâ's manifesto.

Bâ's deployment of Time/Space distancing (Figure 77.2) has a twofold effect: first, it facilitates the characterization of polygynous forms of reproductive association as instinctual and regressive; and, second, it contrasts these attributes with those supposedly belonging to monogamous associations – love, fidelity, individuality, lifetime commitment to one's mate. Indeed, what makes Mawdo Bâ's decision to marry Nabou odious to Aïssatou is not just the fact of his taking a second wife. Rather, it is the fact that the action betrays a prior commitment made to her during their courtship. At that time, and against his mother's wishes, he, a Toucouleur and son of a princess "from the Sine," had insisted that "Marriage is a personal thing" and "emphasized his total commitment to his choice of life partner by visiting" Aïssatou's goldsmith father (SL 17). Later, confronted by his mother's intransigent disrespect for the integrity of his marriage, he fails to stand firm by this commitment, pleading the need to preserve her life and "fulfill a duty" (SL 31). Aïssatou justifiably rejects his argument. But one of her reasons for doing so, "that there can be no union of bodies without the heart's acceptance," seems to imply that the separation of body from heart is fundamental to the functioning of polygyny. If this deduction is correct, it extends a class-specific problem beyond that class. It may well be true that in the peasantry and other classes polygyny may index inequities in relations of production and reproduction. But Mawdo is a member of both the Wolof nobility for which polygyny is permissible, and the bourgeoisie for which it is not. His failure to sustain his commitment to Aïssatou must, therefore, not be understood as revealing anything about the relationship of body to heart in polygyny as such. Rather, it discloses much about the contradictory tensions in the social and sexual life of African nobility and bourgeoisie in the post-independence era.

If this, indeed, is the case, then we are constrained to read the nationalist manifesto with which Ramatoulaye ends her letter with some skepticism:

> I remain persuaded of the inevitable and necessary complementarity of man and woman . . .
> Love, imperfect as it may be in its content and expression, remains the natural link between these two beings . . .
> The success of the family is born of a couple's harmony, as the harmony of multiple instruments creates a pleasant symphony.
> The nation is made up of all the families, rich or poor, united or separated, aware or unaware.
> The success of a nation therefore depends inevitably on the family. (SL 88–9)

In the phrase "necessary complementarity of man and woman" Ramatoulaye articulates a primordial ideal of a non-hierarchized social relations of reproduction. But if this ideal is egalitarian, it is, as the passage shows, egalitarian *because* it is monogamous: "these two beings," "each partner," "a couple's harmony." Other forms of reproductive relations are, by implication, non-egalitarian. Organic nature ("love") and musical expression ("the harmony of multiple instruments") provide her with imagery with which to legitimate this view of the ethics and politics of monogamy.

Yet implicit in Ramatoulaye's imagery is a distinction, not between nature and culture, but between harmony and disharmony, order and chaos, consonance and dissonance, *in* nature and culture. The first term in each pair – harmony, order, consonance – represents feelings and institutions whose coherence derive from being associated with the organic: love, monogamous pairs, symphonies, the nation. Here the macrocosm (nation) is the sum of microcosmic reproductive units (couples); within the larger national structure, these then become the only viable subunits. But, for this to be so, it must also be asserted, or at least implied, that other possible units (unpaired or uncoupled) are not viable as constitutive subunits of the nation state. In other words, it must be suggested that the process of national becoming is historical, that this history is diachronic, and that certain forms of reproductive association are incompatible with that process.

To put this in stark terms, it must be implied that the *difference* between the first and second set of terms is a difference in the scale of values associated with nation building, and that the value of each term is determined by *distance from* the nation. In this respect the value of romantic love in monogamous associations, and the value of the latter in nation building, derive from two things. Love is an affect subtending reproductive behavior in Ramatoulaye's Time/Space: the Now/Here of the emergent bourgeois African nation and its subjects; it is also, and maybe for that very reason, a measure of the temporal and spatial distance separating the nation and its subjects from prior forms of reproductive association and subjectification (Figure 77.2). Love, then, is that whose lack sets polygyny apart, rendering it inimical to nation building and national consciousness.

Indeed, Bâ is alleged to have declared polygyny "evil" and an instinctual behavior "innate in every man."[9] If this is correct, then it reveals the ethical scale on which she evaluates this practice. But to declare polygyny innate is counterproductive to the objectives she has outlined for the female writer. Innatism doubles as an effective apologia for that which it supposedly denigrates. After all if I cannot help myself, why hold me responsible for my actions? Neither Mawdo nor Modou are helpless victims of their sexual instincts. Mawdo's failure to keep his commitment to Aïssatou is pre-meditated. Aunty Nabou and Nabou are mere alibis. Aïssatou understands this, and so leaves him. To attribute polygyny to innatism is to surrender the struggle against "the status quo" to another status quo, namely, biologism. For women whose trust has been betrayed, and for children traumatized by conflicts arising from such betrayals, this is not a satisfactory resolution.

Those still enamored of the tradition/modernity postulate must understand that the objection to it is not that both are illusions, or that any cultural phenomenon is necessarily inferior by virtue of being associated with tradition or modernity. Rather, the objection is to conceptions and uses of each term as the antithesis of the other. Such uses have the effect of compelling us, as Paulin Hountondji argues, to choose between the two in the name of one, and to render absolute "the internal rationality of . . . traditions." Hountondji's solution to this problem is that we "try and know our traditions as they were, beyond any mythology and distortion, not merely for the purpose of self-identification or justification, but in order to help us meet the challenges and problems of today."[10]

It is not clear to me whether, and how, traditions could be known "as they were." However, it is clear that these "challenges and problems" or, as Fabian describing the origins of anthropology puts it, the "dialectic of repression and revolt" (TO 66) constitute the matrix of knowledge about African culture even today. It is this matrix that invests current evaluations of polygyny with social, economic, and political urgency. Under these circumstances, it would not do to dismiss the issue, as eighteenth-century apologetics of slavery did, as "the expression of innate lusts."[11] Nor will it do to declare it, as proper humanists might be tempted to do, a depravation of an otherwise stellar "universal human nature."[12] The problem with notions of universality is not whether or not there is such as thing. It is that whatever is universal in "human nature" (reproduction, for example) does not have a universal *expression*, and that where one is found, its morphology will disclose a repressive will-to-power rather than a transcendental truth.

Notes

1   V. Y. Mudimbe, *The Invention of Africa*, 71–7.
2   Mudimbe, *The Invention of Africa*, 71–2.
3   Johannes Fabian, *Time and the Other*, 3–4; hereafter abbreviated TO.
4   Roy Porter, *The Enlightenment*, 3–4.
5   Françoise Lionnet, *Autobiographical Voices*, 2.
6   See, especially, Paulin Hountondji, *African Philosophy*, 159–64; and Spiegel and Boonzaier, "Promoting tradition: Images of the South African past," *South African Keywords*, 40–1.
7   V. Y. Mudimbe, "Letters of Reference," *Transition* 53: 64.
8   Bâ, quoted by Christopher L. Miller, *Theories of Africans*, 271.
9   Miller, *Theories of Africans*, 280, n. 91.
10 Paulin Hountondji, "Reason and Tradition," *Philosophy and Cultures*, 137.
11 Dorothy Hammond and Alta Jablow, *The Africa That Never Was*, 23.
12 Roland Barthes, "The Great Family of Man," *Mythologies*, 101.

References

Barthes, Roland. "The Great Family of Man." *Mythologies*. Tr. Annette Lavers. London: Jonathan Cape, 1972.

Fabian, Johannes. *Time and the Other: How Anthropology Makes Its Object*. New York: Columbia University Press, 1983.

Hammond, Dorothy, and Jablow, Alta. *The Africa That Never Was: Four Centuries of British Writing about Africa*. New York: Twayne Publishers, 1970.

Hountondji, Paulin. *African Philosophy: Myth and Reality*. Tr. Henri Evans. Introduction Abiola Irele. Bloomington and Indianapolis: Indiana University Press, 1983.

——. "Reason and Tradition." *Philosophy and Cultures: Proceedings of 2nd Afro-Asian Philosophy Conference, Nairobi, October/November, 1981*. Eds. H. Odera Oruka and D. A. Masolo. Nairobi: Bookwise Limited, 1983.

Lionnet, Françoise *Autobiographical Voices: Race, Gender, Self-Portraiture*. Ithaca and London: Cornell University Press, 1989.

Miller, Christopher L. *Theories of Africans: Francophone Literature and Anthropology in Africa*. Chicago and London: University of Chicago Press, 1990.

Mudimbe, V. Y. *The Invention of Africa: Gnosis, Philosophy, and the Order of Knowledge*. Bloomington and Indianapolis: Indiana University Press, 1988.

——. "Letters of Reference." *Transition* 53: 62–78.

Porter, Roy. *The Enlightenment*. London: Macmillan, 1990.

Spiegel, Andrew, and Boonzaier, Emile. "Promoting Tradition: Images of the South African Past." *South African Keywords: The Uses & Abuses of Political Concepts*. Eds. Emile Boonzaier and John Sharp. Cape Town and Johannesburg: David Philip, 1988.

Chapter 78

Feminism, Postcolonialism and the Contradictory Orders of Modernity

Ato Quayson

Writing to Constance Webb in 1944, C. L. R. James said:

> With the increasing opportunities that modern production (and the development of ideas based upon it) gives to women, a new type of woman arises. She is called a career woman. The name is stupid but very revealing. A man is never a career man. That is his privilege. He can have his career, and the finest fruit of his successful career is wife and children. But the woman is called career woman because her 'career' in modern society demands she place herself in a subordinate position or even renounce normal life. The social dice are loaded against her; and the plain fact of the matter is that they are loaded, not only in the economic opportunities, *but in the minds of men.*
>
> (James and Grimshaw, 1992: 144)

His reference point is the American woman but the condition described is relevant to women everywhere. This condition is not to be named simply as that of the contradictory entrapment in a seeming material freedom that is nonetheless subject to prejudicial economic arrangements and the hypocritical patriarchal attitudes of men. For what James describes here to be applicable elsewhere, a different dimension of his description needs to be foregrounded. Namely, this is in the peculiar condition of women taking their rightful place in modernity but having simultaneously to renounce 'normality'. Viewed another way, this could be described as the conundrum of attaining citizenship whilst becoming alienated subjects. This conundrum that afflicts women's lives is arguably greatly aggravated in the Third World, where women's existence is strung between traditionalism and modernity in ways that make it extremely difficult for them to attain personal freedoms without severe sacrifices or compromises. The instruments of alienation have coincided with those by

First published in *Postcolonialism: Theory, Practice or Process?*, pp. 103–36, 122–6. Cambridge: Polity, 2000.

which an ostensible freedom has been attained. It is a situation which is going to be at the centre of this chapter.

Feminism has been about challenging the representations of women and arguing for better conditions for them. Representation itself has at least two meanings, both of which are relevant to post-colonialism and to feminism. The first and more political one has to do with the matter of political representation, something which even in a democracy arguably never fully satisfies the needs and aspirations of all the people for whom democratic systems are set up. For political representation to be fully representative, it has to be constantly reviewed by those it claims to serve. The second and no less significant definition lies in the area of the discursive, in the ways in which metaphors, tropes and concepts are used to project an image of some person or persons. Discursive representation has serious effects on the lived domain of everyday life and crucially sets up forms of potential agency which are offered as means of defining subject positions in the world. Both political and discursive dimensions of representation are relevant to feminism and postcolonialism, with the two frequently being conflated in general discussions so that the discursive representation of Third World women is often seen as ultimately of political consequence.

Chandra Talpade Mohanty makes the link between the political and discursive dimensions of representation explicitly in her well-known essay 'Under Western Eyes: Feminist Scholarship and Colonial Discourses', where she argues that, though the relationship between Woman and women is not a relation of 'correspondence or simple implication', some feminist writers 'discursively colonize the material and historical heterogeneities of the lives of women in the third world, thereby producing/representing a composite, singular "third-world woman"' (1994: 197). Mohanty's central contention is that this discursively created, oppressed Third World woman is nothing but a homogenized creation of Western feminist discourses whose intent is to set up an object that can be the presumed Other of the Western female culturally, materially and discursively. Even progressive Western feminists do not always escape this tendency, as Spivak shows to be the case in Julia Kristeva's *About Chinese Women* (1977). For, as Spivak points out in 'French Feminism in an International Frame' (1981), Kristeva's study has no real historical basis as the entire foundation for the speculations is library sources. The 'Chinese women' in Kristeva's account are really produced as part of structuralist debates in post-1968 France and point to the politicization of her own feminist position rather than anything directly to do with Chinese women. And so the scene is often set for a series of complex negotiations between an implied hegemonic Western feminist discourse and the heterogeneous conditions of Third World women.

In emphasizing a different dimension of this same problem, Obioma Nnaemeka (1997) argues that the homogenization of the Third World woman also extends into the media representations of traditional marital arrangements, childcare, health and so on in the Third World. Analysing the implications for discussions of polygamy in Mariama Ba's *So Long a Letter*, Nnaemeka highlights the subtle differences in media representations of polygamous relationships in America, such as those of Alex Joseph and his eight wives in Big Water, Utah, and the way in which any such polygamous set-ups in Africa might be viewed by the same media. The critical difference is seen in the manner in which the Josephs' marriages were reported in *Marie Claire*. All the groups of people involved in the relationships – Alex Joseph himself, several of his wives, and the small-town community – are given an opportunity to express their views freely on the marriages. The writers of the article, Ross Laver and Paula Kaihla (1995) describe the eight American women as 'well-adjusted', with a heavy insistence on their freedom and peace of mind. The level of objectivity displayed by the writers and their reluctance to pass judgement on what is clearly a quite unusual arrangement is what is intriguing for Nnaemeka in its contrast to how traditional African cultures are typically reported:

> This report is pertinent to the questions I raise about voice and agency primarily due to the *manner of its telling*. I have written at length on the report in order to tease out the different categories of speaking subjects – the wives spoke, Alex spoke, the neighbours spoke, and the reporters 'reported' without any noticeable insertion of the reportorial voice. The reporters did *not speak for* the Josephs. They treated with respect these 'well-adjusted' women who 'are virtually indistinguishable from typical, modern American women'; they visited the Joseph wives, saw them as reasonable adults who are capable of making personal decisions and choices, *talked with* them, and walked away convinced that the 'living arrangement works.' On the contrary, in the narration of African traditional cultures and the ways in which they are 'oppressive' for women, African women are not accorded the same respect and subjectivity as Alex Joseph's wives; African women are spoken *for, about, and against*.
>
> (Nnaemeka, 1997: 166–7; emphasis in original)

The point to note, as she argues, is the extent of the reification of traditional African practices and their interpretation as impositions on women. The homogenizing tendencies observed by Mohanty and Spivak with respect to certain emphases in Western feminism can then be seen as extensions of a larger conception of the oppressed position of the 'Other' woman common in media and popular representations as well. Though Nnaemeka and others are definitely correct in their diagnosis of the Western media's penchant for focusing on the oppression of women from other parts of the world, it would be going to the other extreme to suggest that some of this is not actually correct, or, indeed, relevant to how discussions of women's position in the Third World are to be debated. The parameters for the discussions should by no means be those set by the Western media, but the corrective to the distortions can also not be a mere debunking, or an inversion of the terms by which the Western media have set up the debates. The problem calls for more subtlety than that.

Another angle that postcolonial feminism has brought to bear on the entire field is in showing the extent to which nationalist discourses have subtly subsumed concerns about women under what turned out ultimately to be patriarchal concerns under the impetus of a nationalist agenda. Once again the discursive and political dimensions of representation are at issue. This phenomenon was evident particularly in the nationalist debates across the Third World, where women's questions were subsumed under larger nationalist ones and local women's experiences were taken as needing defence from the implications of Western feminine models. But in this arena of nationalist concerns, women became more the sites than the subjects of the debates about them, and these 'sites' were eventually construed in ways that rendered women completely alienated and absent from the experiences that were being declaimed on their behalf.

In this chapter I will be touching on these and other issues to prepare for a general discussion of questions of postcolonial women's lives. The focus will be on the degree to which women's oppression makes itself manifest through varying degrees of conjuncture between modernity and traditionalism, especially with regard to conjugal marital relationships and the pressures that are brought to bear on these by extended kinship ties. The critical move will be to historicize the conjuncture as the dialectical meeting point between residual and emergent values, and not as a reified moment of either oppression or freedom. [. . .]

The companionate nuclear marriage in Africa is itself a legacy of Christianity. According to Kristin Mann in her excellent study of the ideology and socio-economic circumstances surrounding marriage among the elite in turn-of-the-century colonial Lagos, the rules governing Christian marriage as expressed in the 1884 Marriage Ordinance not only sought to alter traditional Yoruba inheritance practices, but also gave wives and husbands rights to each other's estates and made Christian wives and their children sole inheritors of a man's property. Furthermore, it disinherited a man's siblings and any children by customary wives or concubines. The Christian form of marriage went through a series of vicissitudes and at various points men chose a dual approach combining a Christian marriage with a traditional union. Furthermore, with increasing economic hardship from the 1890s, Christian marriages were postponed, with men entering into customary unions and waiting till much later to re-establish their marriages on a Christian footing. Unlike the men, however, women as a whole were less ambivalent towards Christian marriage, and when given the choice often opted for that as against the customary one (Mann, 1985; see also Moore, 1988: 119–27). Even though the Christian marriage system is by no means the predominant one among Africans, it is nonetheless the case that an idea of a man and a woman coming together and living away from the extended family system is very popular, especially in the urban areas and among the growing educated classes.

Two key features in the nuclear family arrangement that constantly lead to tension need to be noted. Apart from the fact that spouses are supposed to have equal access to each other's property, perhaps the other key defining factor is the issue of conjugal privacy, where the spouses are supposed to build up their nuclear family together with as little interference as possible from the extended family system or, indeed, from any outside intrusion. Secondly, the Christian nuclear family arrangement is the joining of individuals in love and companionship, rather than the joining of lineages; but it is rare that the nuclear family arrangement is not entangled in other realities that constantly challenge and undermine it. The greatest strain on nuclear conjugal relationships comes from perceptions of the influence of the extended families of both spouses, with the main area of stress coming when one partner, frequently the male, is dominant in decisions about resource allocation. In her book on marriage among civil servants in Ghana, Christine Oppong (1981) states what can be taken to be a commonly shared observation among urban married couples in Ghana:

> Most of the husbands and wives were noted, either overtly or covertly, to give praise and blame to their spouses for the way in which resources were allocated and decisions taken. They also in several cases, criticized their spouses' kin and associates for their influence, either in diverting resources or loyalty elsewhere or in influencing their partners' attitudes in a way contrary to their interests. The majority of couples referred, at some point, to the marriage and family relationships of other sets of people whom they knew about, including their own parents and relatives and friends. In addition they referred to a number of ethnic stereotypes including Akan and English.
>
> (p. 142)

It is however the case that it is women who end up bearing the main brunt of the contradictions in such conjugal relationships. As I hope to show shortly, this is particularly the case with respect to spousal death, when the full force of extended family claims is brought to bear on the nuclear set-up.

Because of the nature of economic arrangements and, indeed, of the nature of lineage and family arrangements in Africa, the idea of the nuclear family is never allowed to solidify into a clear-cut category in opposition to more traditional forms. In practice there is always an area of overlap between the nuclear arrangement and the claims of extended families. Because of the difficulties in the way of childcare arrangements, especially for middle-class urban women, it is quite often the case that members of the extended family are invited to come and live within the nuclear unit. In other set-ups, the nuclear family unit takes up residence as close to other family members as possible in order to share the burden of childcare and other things. Furthermore, because of the various life-cycle rituals to do with birth, puberty, marriage and funerals in which most Africans, urban and otherwise, are encouraged to participate, there is actually the creation of a two-tiered approach to familial relations, with the nuclear and the extended family ideas acquiring different emphases depending on the contexts in which the nuclear family unit finds itself. Most middle-class marriages in Africa are the combination of two modes: the nuclear conjugal one dominates at home, while the extended family one makes itself felt during traditional family gatherings around life-cycle rituals or at important festivals. But by far the most important set of life-cycle rituals at which the status of the nuclear family faces its greatest challenge is that of rituals to do with spousal death, from the preparation of the body for burial through to the funeral and the disposal of property afterwards. The tension is most acute when the spouse dies intestate, but, as will be shown shortly, the writing of a will is no guarantee that the extended family network will not make drastic intrusions in the decisions taken by the surviving female spouse. The contradictions between modernity and traditionalism affect women most strongly at the death of their spouse, for it is then that the full force of kinship claims on the individual are brought to bear. The question of death heightens the problem immensely because of the issues of property rights which become the key focus of concern immediately after burial.

Stories abound from all across sub-Saharan Africa of the severe treatment that women face at the hands of extended family systems on the death of their spouses. Two particular examples that serve to focalize the contradictions most neatly are the accounts of what is labelled by Kenyans as the S. M. Otieno burial saga in 1987 and that of the confusion surrounding the burial of Joe Appiah in 1990, richly told by Anthony Kwame Appiah as the Epilogue to his *In My Father's House* (1992). The Otieno case is much the more complicated, partly because the misunderstanding between Wambui Waiyaki Otieno and members of her deceased husband's clan had an added political dimension since it was interpreted as a contest between the Luo and the Kikuyu. Wambui Otieno was a Kikuyu and had been deeply involved in the Mau Mau struggle against the British authorities in the period leading up to Kenyan independence. She was arrested several times, and spent a long stretch in prison before meeting her lawyer husband in the early 1960s. Her husband was a highly regarded Luo. By the time of her husband's death in 1987, the balance of power in the country was firmly in favour of the Luos because of Arap Moi's presidency. Moi took over from the Kikuyu Jomo Kenyatta in 1978, and to many observers had steadily instituted a process by which to empower the minority Luo tribe in Kenyan politics.[1] In the introduction to *Mau Mau's Daughter*, Wambui Otieno's autobiography spanning her life from Mau Mau activist, through feminist politician to the painful events surrounding her husband's burial, E. S. Atieno Odhiambo observes that one of the most important themes that has intersected with the formation of Kenyan history has been the 'deep politics of the clan, pitting insiders against outsiders, clansmen against foreigners, original landowners against sojourners' (1998: xii–xiii). In the particular case of Wambui, the events surrounding her husband's burial and her treatment at the hands of her husband's clan resonate closely with the paradigmatic insider/outsider status we noted of Medea.

The main details of the Otieno Saga are that he died intestate of a heart attack on 16 December 1987. He had said many times both to his wife and to members of his extended family that he wanted to be buried at his home in Nairobi or on one of the farms he owned on the outskirts of the city. The extended clan had different ideas and maintained that as a Luo he should be buried on the ancestral land, about 300 miles away from the city. The matter went to court. The first hearing ruled in favour of Wambui, but after a protracted judicial process this was reversed in the Appeal Court. Many witnesses, including Odera Oruka, Professor of Philosophy at the University of Nairobi, were called to explain traditional Luo customs. In Oruka's answers he sides firmly with the traditional interpretation, at a point even suggesting that a person's will might be set aside if it was thought to violate the taboos of the people. This was supported in the Appeal Court's judgement. The crucial thing in deciding whether a person's choice of burial place is sanctioned by the traditions of the tribe or not is whether a person's house has been properly blessed by parents or relatives with the necessary ceremonies. Without such blessings, the house remains a 'house' and not a 'home' in the traditional sense (Oruka, 1990: 67–83; Otieno and Presley, 1998: 188–91). The point to be noted here is not so much that there is anything wrong with getting such parental or clan blessings, but the fact that even in an urbanized setting, the clan has to sanction the house within which any conjugal relationship may be established. If, as is the case in the Otieno instance, the man has not had recourse to the blessings of his family for personal or any other reasons, his body on death is claimed by the clan irrespective of what nature of conjugal relationship he may have had with his wife. The claims of the wife are completely overruled by those of the clan. Wambui Otieno is a highly urbanized, well-travelled and politically aware woman, as can readily be gleaned from her autobiography. In marrying her husband, she enters a conjugal nuclear relationship in which man and wife are supposed to be equal. What is more important is that during his lifetime her husband was never in doubt about the pre-eminent place that his wife had in his life. There was every indication that she was his closest ally, sometimes even helping to manage his law chambers when he was travelling or ill. But on his death, we see the manifest strain that is placed on the nuclear family arrangement by the very fact of having to be blessed by the extended clan. The blessing of the house, if not sought, is ultimately a curse against the home, something which Wambui and her children discover at great emotional cost.

Note

1 For a very fascinating recent account of the complexity of ethnopolitics in Kenya, see Ndegwa (1997).

References

Appiah, Anthony. (1992). *In My Father's House: Africa in the Philosophy of Culture*. Oxford: Oxford University Press.

Bishop, Alan J. (1990). 'Western Mathematics: The Secret Weapon of Cultural Imperialism.' *Race and Class* 32.2, 51–65.

Childs, Peter and R. J. Patrick Williams. (1996). *An Introductory Guide to Post-colonial Theory.* New York: Prentice Hall.

Gandhi, Leela. (1998). *Postcolonial Theory: A Critical Introduction*. Edinburgh: Edinburgh University Press.

James, C. L. R. and Anna Grimshaw. (1992). *The C.L.R. James Reader*. Oxford: Oxford: Blackwell.

Kristeva, Julia (1977). *About Chinese Women*. Trans. Anita Barrows. London: Boyars.

Loomba, Ania. (1998). *Colonialism–Postcolonialism*. London: Routledge.

Mamdani, Mahmood. (1996). *Citizen and Subject: Contemporary Africa and the Legacy of Late Colonialism*. Princeton, NJ: Princeton University Press.

Mann, Kristin. (1985). *Marrying Well: Marriage, Status, and Social Change among the Educated Elite in Colonial Lagos*. Cambridge: Cambridge University Press.

Mintz, Sidney (1985). *Sweetness and Power: The Place of Sugar in Modern History.* New York: Penguin.

Mitchell, Timothy. (1988). *Colonising Egypt*. Cambridge: Cambridge University Press.

Mohanty, Chandra Talpade. (1994). 'Under Western Eyes: Feminist Scholarship and Colonial Discourses.' *Colonial Discourse and Post-colonial Theory.* Patrick Williams and Laura Chrisman eds. London: Harvester Wheatsheaf, 196–220.

Moore, Henrietta L. (1988). *Feminism and Anthropology.* Minneapolis: University of Minnesota Press.

Moore-Gilbert, Bart. (1997). *Postcolonial Theory: Contexts, Practices, Politics*. London: Verso.

Ndegwa, Stephen. (1997). 'Citizenship and Ethnicity: an examination of two transition moments in Kenyan politics.' *American Political Science Review,* 91:3 (Sept 1997), 599–616.

Nnaemeka, Obioma. (1997). *The Politics of (M)othering: Womanhood, Identity, and Resistance in African Literature*. London: Routledge.

Oppong, Christine. (1981). *Middle Class African Marriage: A Family Study of Ghanaian Senior Civil Servants*. Cambridge: Cambridge University Press.

Oruka, H. Odera. (1990). *Sage Philosophy: Indigenous Thinkers and Modern Debate on African Philosophy.* Leiden; New York: E. J. Brill.

Otieno, Wambui Waiyaki and Cora Ann Presley. (1998). *Mau Mau's Daughter: A Life History.* Boulder: Lynne Rienner Publishers.

Parry, Benita. (1987). 'Problems in Current Theories of Colonial Discourse.' Oxford Literary Review 9 (1 & 2). Reprinted in Ascroft et al., *The Postcolonial Studies Reader*, 36–44.

Rabinow, Paul (1989). *French Modern: Norms and Forms of the Social Environment*. Cambridge: MIT Press.

Spivak, Gayatri Chakravorty. (1981). 'French Feminism in an International Frame.' *Yale French Studies* 62, 154–84.

Wright, Gwendolyn. (1991). *The Politics of Design in French Colonial Urbanism*. Chicago: University of Chicago Press.

Young, Robert. (1990). *White Mythologies: Writing History and the West*. London: Routledge.

Part XI

Structuralism, Poststructuralism, Postcolonialism, and Postmodernism

As is well known, the "linguistic" turn in the humanities and social sciences historically produced a series of new models of reading as well as fresh epistemological crises about what constitutes literature, the nature of the world(s) that it is supposed to symbolize, and the means by which both are to be interpreted. In African literary criticism these questions have had a peculiar inflection because of the context of the colonial encounter, which was never allowed to move too far from the discussion of epistemological questions. Thus we find that even in a purely "structuralist" reading such as Sunday Anozie's in this section the effort is finally yoked to outlining a sociology of knowledge, which by implication would have to be African to make sense. Reflecting the concern with the unequal cross-cultural encounter under colonialism and the implications that arise therefrom, other critics write of the fact that colonialism is inseparable from modernity in the shaping of the world as we know it today. It is, however, in the essays on the links between postcolonialism and postmodernism that the unequal cross-cultural encounter is seen to produce different and perhaps diametrically opposed ways of understanding the processes of globalization. Thus whereas some versions of postmodernism emphasize the inherent instability and playfulness of identity, postcolonialism, even while drawing inspiration from similar sources in the early linguistic turn, refracts the crisis of globalization in terms of unequal power relations and insists on struggles for equality that are at once material and discursive. At all times the central issue in these essays is how to understand the coupling of key terms – Africa and the West, structuralism and poststructuralism, postcolonialism and postmodernism – where the conjunctive "and" masks a wide range of possible mutualities and antagonisms.

Chapter 79

Genetic Structuralism as a Critical Technique
(Notes Toward a Sociological Theory of the African Novel)

Sunday O. Anozie

[…]

Genetic Structuralism: A Sociological Method & Theory

We have already proposed in a recent work[1] a more dynamic approach to the study of West African novels by limiting our inquiry to the central characters. The question we have posed ourselves is partly thus: If a cross-section of the novels written in modern times by West Africans is examined, what can it reveal to us about the protagonists as characters in terms of their individual conflicts vis-à-vis their environments, what are their individual options and value-orientations. To vary slightly the terms of Ruth Benedict,[2] we are looking for "patterns" of fictional culture in West Africa which may also, possibly, lead to the definition of the concept of the hero in the modern West African novel. We thus conceive of our work as a study in thematic configurations.

This study is pursued in two parts. In *Part One* by deploying and utilizing ideas and concepts derived from recent works in dynamic sociology and psychology but eschewing all normative or value judgments, we attempt a general exposition of the literary and cultural dynamics of the world of the West African writer, taking into account such rubrics as the influence of nationalism, certain empirical problems, social change and social reality in West Africa. In the same section we outline a dynamic and functional concept of "determinations" in West African novels, a concept based upon the central characters. We also believe

First published in *The Conch* 3.1 (March 1971): 37–42.

that for such a study to have both depth and meaning, especially if pursued by an African conscientiously working in the field, there should be a recourse to a hypothetical paradigmatic model. In this case the background and the native experience of the research worker will be an additional advantage both in explication and comprehension of the works. This we have tried to do with the works of Igbo-speaking novelists which were classified under "tradition determination."

In *Part Two*, chiefly analytical and evaluative, we then attempt to develop the main ideas schematically proposed in the preceding sector by applying the same theoretical and empirical categories to representative West African novels in English and French and limiting ourselves, however, to those written and published within a selected period of time.

This method of approach which at first may appear to be simple becomes then gradually more complicated in the actual application. The complexity is due to the fact that the method consists essentially, or ideally, in establishing a series of genetic relationships between our two privileged levels of inquiry and analysis here: the thematic and the structural, and also in disposing each of these levels or groups of levels in correlated or homologous systems. Each system is then broken down into its several elements using the principle of an infinite set. By this principle we mean that each system together with its elements can be shown not as complete in itself but as an inclusive part of a larger and still incomplete system. In other words, one set is considered as a part of another set, and the second set considered as part of a third set etc., so that any structural modifications within one of the minor sets inevitably will affect the nature of the whole.

Genetic structuralism as envisaged here is therefore an attempt to explain in terms of natural law of growth and adaptation to milieu the causes of the dynamic changes, such as are taking place within the West African Novel, considered as an organism. As envisaged however by its chief modern exponent, the French Professor Lucien Goldmann,[3] himself also a disciple of George Lukacs,[4] genetic structuralism is much more complex: it involves the problem of epistemology or the sociology of knowledge. A few words may not be out of place here to explain the practice of Professor Goldmann and so clarify our own position.

Professor Goldmann's genetic structuralism has two fundamental hypotheses.[5] The first is the belief that every human comportment is an attempt to give a meaningful response to a particular situation and so tends to create a balance between the subject of an action and the object to which it is directed, the ambient world. The second hypothesis is that the collective character of a literary creation derives from the fact that the structures of the universe of the work are homologous to the mental structures of certain social groups, or in intelligible relationship with them, whereas on the content level, that is to say the creation of an imaginary universe governed by those structures, each writer exercises absolute liberty. The first of these beliefs tells us hardly anything profound about the essential role of a good work of art, which is to act as a form of mediation between the individual and the society in much the same way as myth is, according to Claude Levi-Strauss,[6] a form of mediation between nature and culture. Goldmann's second hypothesis raises a controversial and almost ideological issue by asserting in effect that only certain human and social groups are capable of producing certain works of art and literature. The practice of genetic structuralism is for Goldmann, therefore, identical with the attempt to establish significant relationships as homologies between the content of a given work of art and the intellectual, social, political and economic structures of the period in which it is produced. The idea is that by a series of logical approximations one can arrive – and this for Goldmann is the ideal goal of the method – at a structural hypothesis, one capable of rendering account of a perfectly coherent totality of facts.

Although we fully subscribe to Goldmann's view that a work of art has an immanent significant structure, one made intelligible by the social group within which it is elaborated, we do not see how this can be a matter of dogmatic equation or one-to-one relationship: in other words, we do not believe that comprehension can be exhausted by explication. How far, for example, does a knowledge[7] of Yoruba folklore and mythology and the interpretation of Tutuola in the light of such a knowledge exhaust comprehension of his works? However, a more important limitation in Goldmann's theory and practice of genetic structuralism comes from the fact that this method can only take into account great literary and cultural works of creation. Such a technique would be of little use if applied without some modifications to novels written in Africa, most of which are undoubtedly of very mediocre artistic standards. A unit of assessment has therefore to be found which will enable us to take into account a large variety of fictional works produced in Africa. This analytical basis we have taken to be the hero,[8] or the central character in the novel. We give below a simplified schema which illustrates this elementary structure as the unit of relationships within the West African novel:

The schema (Figure 79.1), though highly simplified, shows the system of correlations such as is envisaged as well as the levels on which they are articulated. One of the advantages of such a method of procedure is that it presents an objective picture of the internal and external growths of the West African Novel through integrating it within its socio-cultural environment. A second advantage is that by presenting such a panoramic picture of the novel it can permit of a total description of this particular literature from the outside: in other words, the West African Novel can be studied "scientifically" in itself since it embodies its own total field of discourse and is determined by its own internal laws of organic growth. A major achievement here would be the suppression of all references to external systems, that is to say other literatures or traditions, what most critics of African literature generally do when they speak of "influences." A third advantage of the methodology here advocated is that, given a set of objective criteria dynamically regulating the form and content of the literature considered, it would be fairly possible to forecast new developments, that is determine on the basis of known facts the laws of future evolution of the West African Novel.

One important disadvantage of genetic structuralism as a method of approach to the study of the African Novel, however, needs to be mentioned. This consists in the little value it accords to aesthetic considerations within the art. This omission is not deliberate but results naturally from the method itself. If anything our method is one which seeks to treat every literature, including the African, as an independent or autonomous field of discourse. Moreover it is a discourse governed like any language in the world, by its own internal laws of growth – its own system of phonemes, morphemes and syntactic structure – and therefore capable of sustaining a specific and, also in a sense, an original world view. If the description of all the objective, ascertainable elements that make up such a world view also leads, as in fact it should, to the identification of an original aesthetic system or structure, this new phenomenon will logically have confirmed our original hypothesis that, considered as a language or as a biological organism, every creative system is autonomous, within its field of reference and action, but no system is finite if it can be shown that at least in one respect it forms part of a larger and autonomous creative system.

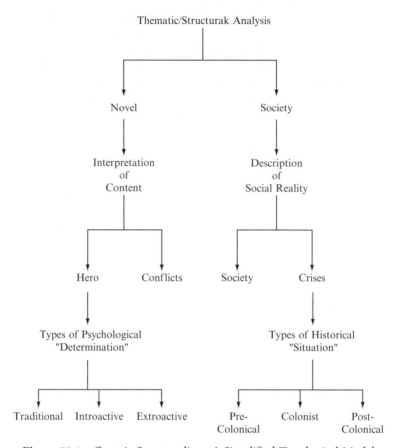

Figure 79.1   Genetic Structuralism: A Simplified Typological Model

Notes

1   S. O. Anozie, *Sociologie du Roman Africain*, Paris: Aubier, 1970.
2   Author of *Patterns of Culture* Boston, Houghton-Mufflin, 1934; reprinted New York, Pelican Books, 1946.
3   Cf. Lucien Goldmann, *Pour une Sociologie du Roman* (Paris: Gallimard), 1964.
4   Georges Lukacs, *La Théorie du Roman*, Paris: Editions Gonthier, 1963.
5   Goldmann, *op. cit.*, pp. 213, 218.
6   Claude Levi-Strauss, *Anthropologie Structurale* (Paris, Plon), 1964.
7   This question can be pertinently posed in respect of an article recently published by Robert P. Armstrong, "The Narrative and Intensive Continuity: *The Palm Wine Drinkard*" in *Research in African Literatures*, Vol. I, No. 1, 1970, pp. 9–34.
8   According to Lukacs and Goldmann, the essential hero of a novel is a problematic" or a "degraded" individual, and the internal form of a novel consists in the quest of self-discovery.

Chapter 80

In Praise of Alienation

Abiola Irele

.

The starting point of any consideration of our perception of Europe and the civilization we associate with that continent is the observed fact that it is marked by a profound ambivalence. This is a quality of emotional response that we share with other peoples who have experienced European conquest; in other words, it is a function of our historical experience. As we keep being reminded by our writers and our historians, notably by Chinweizu in his book, *The West and the Rest of Us*,[1] the circumstances of African encounter with Europe were especially brutal. The British Empire was not acquired in a fit of absent-mindedness, nor lost in a similar attitude of nonchalance; much less the French. Modern imperialism was an act of calculated aggression; as far as we in this part of the world are concerned, Obara Ikime has documented for us, in his book *The Fall of Nigeria*,[2] the violent process by which the British colonizer, and especially Lord Lugard (of venerated memory at Chatham House) subjugated the peoples and societies of the territory that now make up our modern State.

More generally still, in our historical relationship with Europe, the master–slave relationship was exemplified in a very real sense, with not merely a metaphorical but a literal significance. We played Caliban to the White man's Prospero, Man Friday to his Robinson Crusoe, as part of a historical drama of slavery, colonialism, and racism.

The consequences of this experience have been unsettling for us in all kinds of ways. The incursion of Europe disrupted traditional societies all over Africa, and in some cases this disruption was so severe as to have turned the drama of colonialism into pure tragedy. Such was the case especially in Central Africa, where the French and the Belgians, particularly those who worked for King Leopold in his Congo Free State – a name that reflects his bizarre sense of irony – wrought such devastation as to have turned the stomach of decent humanity everywhere. These facts require to be recalled, for our resentments carried over from a phase of history from which most of us have only just emerged, and into which a substantial section of the race is still locked in Southern Africa even now; these resentments remain with us extremely vivid.

First published as *In Praise of Alienation: An Inaugural Lecture*, Ibadan: New Horn Press, 1982; and subsequently in *The Surreptitious Speech: Présence Africaine and the Politics of Otherness, 1947–1987.* pp. 201–3, 214–24. Chicago: University of Chicago Press, 1992.

At the same time, we are conscious of the irreversible nature of the transformations the impact of Europe has effected in our midst and which are so extensive as to define the really significant frame of reference of our contemporary existence. The traditional precolonial culture and way of life continue to exist as a reality among us, but they constitute an order of existence that is engaged in a forced march, in a direction dictated by the requirements of a modern scientific and technological civilization. It also happens to be the case that Western civilization, at least in its contemporary manifestations and circumstance, provides the paradigm of modernity to which we aspire. Hence our mixed feelings, the troubled sense of acceptance and rejection, of a subjective disposition that is undermined by the objective facts of our life. There is something of a paradox here, for the intensity of the ambivalence we demonstrate in our response to Europe and Western civilization is in fact a measure of our emotional tribute; it is expressive, in a profound way, of the cultural hold Europe has secured upon us – of the alienation it has imposed upon us as a historical fate.

The association in our minds of Western civilization with the historical fact of colonial domination and the real discomforts of social and cultural change give to this alienation a wholly negative significance in our eyes. All our modern expression in literature and ideology has developed from a primary concern with the pathology of alienation as inscribed in our experience as a colonized people. It isn't so much the fact that our modern literature has explored the theme of culture conflict that strikes one now as that it has determined a fixation upon this pathology of alienation, and thus conditioned our emotional and intellectual reflexes to the whole subject of our relationship to Europe and Western civilization.

The classic representation of the pathology of alienation is that offered by Cheik Hamidou Kane's novel *L'aventure ambigüe* (Ambiguous adventure). The title of the novel is more than eloquent. The hero, Samba Diallo, is the archetype of the divided consciousness, of the African who suffers in his mind the effects of cultural dispossession. His agony is that of his dual nature, marked by a cleavage rather than an integration of its two frames of reference. As he says in the novel, and I quote:

> I am not a distinct country of the Diallobe facing a distinct occident, and appreciating with a cool head what I must take from it and what I must leave with it by way of a counterbalance. I have become the two. There is not a clear mind deciding between two factors of a choicé. There is a strange nature, in distress over not being two.

The very expansion of his vision upon the world becomes for him his dilemma, his existential plight. He is no longer able to relate to the world because that world is no longer coherent, no longer offers him a stable and compact order of values. His suicide at the end of the novel is thus a logical outcome of his spiritual tragedy. But it is significant that Cheik Hamidou Kane contrives an ending in which Samba Diallo's struggle with the concrete world of experience finds a resolution – he is finally integrated into the cosmos, that is, nothingness. For presented in the way in which the novelist has presented the drama of alienation, the choice is, indeed, between being and nothingness in the very perspective of Jean-Paul Sartre's brand of existentialism: between an affirmative being in the world, which confronts all its problems in order to wrest a meaning out of its contingencies, and a withdrawal into meaningless void.

[. . .]

We need a new determination, a new spirit of adventure fired by a modern imagination: a new state of mind that will enable us to come to terms with our state of alienation and to transform it from a passive condition we confusedly endure into an active collective existential project. We need to take charge of our objective alienation by assuming it as an *intention* so as to endow it with a positive significance.

It is pertinent at this point to remind ourselves that the concept of alienation, in its rigorous philosophical form (as opposed to the loose sociological application of the term with which we are more familiar) contains this positive significance. In its formulation by Hegel, from whom the concept has come down to us via Feuerbach and Marx, alienation designates the state of consciousness produced in the dialectic of mind and matter. The adventure of mind in the realm and universe of nature is for Hegel the very definition of history. From the point of view of human existence, what we commonly term "culture" is the result of man's transformation of nature, a result which stands apart from his conscious-ness but from which these transformations originally flowed. In other words, it is through the active confrontation of matter by mind that culture and thought are produced and that history itself is made possible; it sets in motion the historical process, within which mind undergoes refinement and progresses toward the ultimate perfection of the "Absolute Idea." Culture and thought are thus the objectified forms of mind within the historical process, of primal mind alienated in nature. The state of alienation is thus a condition for the fulfillment of mind, perhaps even for its self-recognition. Like the Judeo-Christian God in the Book of Genesis, the primal mind is not only moved to creation but also to the contemplation of its own work.

I have attempted this summary of Hegel's phenomenology in which the concept of alienation features because it is central to my argument. From Hegel's abstruse dialectics, we can retain the notion of alienation as the principle of all becoming or, more simply, as the moving power of the historical process. In cultural terms, it implies a willed movement out of the self and a purposive quest for new horizons of life and of experience.

In the historical context of present African development, we may now ask, Alienation for what, and in what direction? I will answer that question unequivocally: as a matter of practical necessity, we have no choice but in the direction of Western culture and civilization. If the answer is unequivocal, it is not meant to be taken unilaterally, for I am aware that my answer needs to be hedged round with all sorts of qualifications, some of which, I hope, will become apparent in my conclusion. But for the moment, let me consider one aspect of Western civilization on which there is hardly any dissent as to its importance for us, namely, science and technology. The general consensus is summed up in the expression "transfer of technology" which denotes a current obsession.

But there is a naive assumption underlying the use of this expression, that we can domesticate science and technology by a quick arrangement of rapid industrialization: we buy and install machines, train the manpower, and all will be well. I am even leaving out of account here the problems of capital and finance which come into the question and are far from negligible.

I am afraid this will not do, for there is more to science and technology than machines and their manipulation – there is the scientific spirit itself, which governs the whole functioning of the scientific and technological civilization we now wish to appropriate. It so happens that what we now recognize as the scientific spirit is the product of a whole movement of ideas by which what we now refer to as the West sought to understand man and the universe: the ground for modern science was a matter of historical fact prepared by the development of Western philosophy.

The outstanding good fortune of Western civilization was to have cultivated the deductive method which was elaborated in the philosophy of ancient Greece, and to have made it the foundation for its entire approach to the world. For all the distinction that is commonly made today between philosophy and science, modern science not only owes its existence to the fortuitous development of the deductive method, it is made possible by the application of this method to the universe of phenomena and experience. It is not only in mathematics that this observation holds true, but in all the natural sciences. The very definition of a science is that it is systematic, even systemic, that it displays order in its procedures and in its results. It is not only observation and description that make a science, but the organization of empirical data into an intelligible order. The inductive method is incompletely prosecuted without the final intervention of the deductive; the latter thus subsumes the former. The significance of this for contemporary scientific method, with its emphasis on structure and its recourse to model building, has been stressed by Popper and Kuhn. But it was recognized in the work that served as a manifesto for modern science in its infancy – Francis Bacon's *Novum Organum*, which was conceived, as its title indicates, as a restatement of Aristotle's *Organon*. It is no accident that the great biologist Linnaeus based his taxonomy on the order of concepts of formal logic.

This example will also serve to illustrate the misfortune of African civilization, the inability of our traditional world concept to break free from the prison of the mythopoetic imagination. In Yoruba *ijala* poetry, for example, there is a wealth of information about the fauna and flora of our natural environment which is truly astonishing, but all this information is fitted into an exclusively poetic mode. I understand, too, that the operation of the Ifa corpus depends upon a sophisticated calculus, but nowhere in the culture is this calculus made explicit. This second example points to the real distinction between our traditional worldview and that of Western thought. It is not, as some anthropologists have maintained – and they are well represented in the collection of readings edited by Bryan Wilson under the title *Rationality*[3] – it is not a question of the absence of a rational mode of thought in the one, and its presence in the other, but rather that of its theoretical formulation. It is not rationality as such that distinguished Western civilization but its logic of rationality.

Thus, while we have been content to celebrate the universe, Western man has been engaged in analyzing it as well. This approach bred a tough-mindedness that became a moral value in Europe, and is well expressed in the motto that Leonardo da Vinci adopted for all his activities as both artist and scientist: "ostinato rigore," which can be translated as "stubborn application." That motto was to turn out to be emblematic not only for the internal effort of development in Europe but also for the Europeans' dealings with the rest of the world. From the Renaissance onward, as Europe became increasingly conscious of its power, its civilization assumed an aggressive posture. We are only too familiar with the rest of the story – the political, economic, and human consequences of the European colonial adventure. But there is an aspect that is not sufficiently attended to and which the Italian scholar, Carlo Cipolla, has illuminated with a wealth of fine detail in his book *European Culture and Overseas Expansion*.[4] He points out that the decisive factor in the world supremacy of Europe was the stubborn application of intelligence and skill to the improvement of firearms, ocean-going vessels, and, above all, precision instruments; to the perfection of all these technical resources which finally gave the advantage to the Europeans in their onslaught upon other races, other peoples and nations, other civilizations. The terrible truth of our colonial experience, therefore, is that we were victims of the European's developed sense of method. We were overwhelmed, in fact, by the objective force of the deductive people.

Now, there is a Yoruba saying which sums up admirably the moral of the story: *Adaniloro k'oni logbon*, which can be translated into English as "One who causes you injury also teaches you wisdom." The immediate lesson of our recent past of colonial domination can be extended to our contemporary situation. We are still in a position of weakness with regard to the West. If the term "neocolonialism" sometimes has a hysterical ring, it is not meaningless, for it refers to a concrete reality of contemporary international life. I hardly need to stress the point in the present situation of Nigeria today, in which every aspect of our lives is affected by our pathetic dependence upon the West. In a situation where all the ideas and resources we require for a modern economy – for the conditions of daily existence – are still controlled from the West, all loose talk about "transfer of technology" will be of no avail. We cannot do without a through-going revolution of the mind.

It is certainly not simplistic to affirm that this revolution can be brought about by an assiduous cultivation and internalization of those values enshrined in the scientific method – organization, discipline, order, and, not least, imagination. Imagination, because the scientific culture involves projection, calls upon qualities of mental resourcefulness which translate, in social terms, into a vision of the future.

The scientific revolution in Europe did not take place in a void but in a dynamic context of political, social and cultural development, and, especially in the eighteenth century, of intense intellectual debate which Paul Hazard has described as "crisis of consciousness."[5] An intellectual like Voltaire was a passionate man: he could feel the changes taking place in his universe on his very pulse. Voltaire typifies the strengths and limitations of his age; the unbounded faith in the power of reason closed to him important avenues of the imagination and of human experience,[6] at the same time, the clarity of his moral perceptions gave meaning to his cosmopolitanism. He had a broad vision of humanity such that he was able to place the European world in the right perspective and to understand that its civilization did not have a monopoly of human achievement. Indeed, his attitude to the medieval past was much like that of the Frasers, the Tylors and the Levy-Bruhls of a later century with regard to non-Western cultures.

You may begin to wonder what all this has to do with us. I will answer directly by saying "everything"; by drawing your attention to the Nigerian constitution which came into effect in October 1979. Without the intellectual ferment of eighteenth-century Europe, without the ideas of men like Locke, Montesquieu, Voltaire, and even Kant (in his moral philosophy summed up by the phrase "man as an end in himself"), we would have had a different constitution, perhaps even no constitution at all. At any rate, these ideas are embodied in the legal document which regulates the corporate life of all of us today. Take, for example, the notion of the independence of the judiciary. That notion has come down to us via America, from the principle of the separation of powers enunciated by Montesquieu in his *L'Esprit des Lois*. Notions such as these have become commonplace today, but they were forged in the heat of political and ideological battles fought in Europe. We have entered into the intellectual inheritance of eighteenth-century Europe as regards our political culture simply because its ideas have now become the property of all mankind.

We could do, then, with a broader vision of our humanity than cultural nationalism in its present emphasis proposes to us. If we can accept that the scientific and technological civilization which has come down to us, historically, from Europe can improve the quality of our lives, if we can accept that our modern institutions should be based on political and social ideas articulated elsewhere, there is no reason why we should exclude from our acceptance other valuable areas of experience simply because of their association with Europe. There is no earthly reason why a professor at Ibadan who has mastered the mathematics of, let us say, Gauss, and enjoys the comfort of a Mercedes-Benz saloon, cannot extend the range of his satisfactions to include a Bach fugue. Between all those, there is a historical and cultural, if not a structural, connection, which can be embraced by a single sensibility. In my view, our not altogether hypothetical professor could do with a little more alienation.

Let me refer to another of our proverbs which says that one should not point the left index at one's father's house. Nothing I have said goes against the spirit of that proverb. I have not come to bury our traditional culture under a foolish scorn inspired by an alienated consciousness. Neither have I come to sing the praises of Western civilization, much less to justify its historical aggression upon us and to endorse its ideology of the civilizing mission. As Aimé Césaire has said, "From colonization to civilization, the distance is infinite."[7] Nothing I have said is meant to confirm the White man in his racial and cultural arrogance. The scientific and technological supremacy of Europe was a historical phenomenon that was both particular and contingent, marked by all the vicissitudes of human experience. European civilization did not spring forth fully formed from the brain of a providential God but was shaped over time, often under dramatic circumstances that could well have deflected its course in a direction other than the one it was eventually to pursue.

There are, indeed, interesting parallels between this development and our historical experience and present situation. Like us, the early Europeans were conquered – in their case by the Romans. They were colonized, exploited, and even enslaved. They were later Christianized; I should know something about this, for my Irish teachers did not tire of reminding me that it was St Gregory, the patron saint of the school I attended in Lagos, who sent the first Christian missionaries to England. These early Europeans were dispossessed culturally, and with time whole populations even lost their indigenous languages – you can't be alienated further than that – so that they began to speak pidgin forms of Latin which have evolved into the Romance language of today. In the all-important area of literacy, they learnt everything from the Romans as, indeed, in other areas such as civil works and architecture. When the fact is remembered that the Romans considered these people savages and barbarians, the later pretensions of European ethnocentrism and racism appear in all their hollowness: as the products of a monumental amnesia.

Some eminent European scholars and philosophers seem to have been acutely affected by this malady. For example, Max Weber, in the introduction to the final edition of his classic work, *The Protestant Ethic and the Spirit of Capitalism*, practically makes the staggering claim that all worthwhile human achievement has been the work of Europeans. The philosopher Martin Heidegger has also affirmed with a dogmatism that goes against all the principles of his discipline that philosophy is, by its very essence, a European phenomenon.[8] But we must be clear what we mean by the word "European" in this context, and whether the ancient Greeks can be considered European in the modern sense of the word. For it seems likely, from what comes through of Plato's personality in *The Republic*, that he would have recoiled from the suggestion that he should live among the ancestors of Weber and Heidegger with the classical Greek equivalent of Frazer's celebrated remark, "God Forbid!"

Joseph Conrad by the way, seems to have been affected much less than the Europeans of his time, despite appearances to the contrary. In *Heart of Darkness*, for instance, there is an evocation of the Thames estuary as it would have appeared to the Romans, this evocation placed in symbolic parallel to that of the Congo river later in the work. This double evocation of two ages of imperialism, far removed in time and place, in Conrad's short novel, makes the point I'm trying to put across here – that of the strange forgetfulness of the European racists and of the historical and moral horror it has engendered both for us and the European colonizer.

The fact remains that the civilization we now associate with Europe was originally a derivation, and as it developed it continued to assimilate elements from other world civilizations. It is surely one of the greatest ironies of history that gunpowder, which later gave Europe such immense power, was originally a Chinese invention.

The contribution of Africa itself to Western civilization is far from negligible. It is now generally accepted that ancient Egypt exercised considerable influence upon the early civilization of Greece. Moreover, African philosophers have made individual contributions to the conceptual elaboration of Western civilization all through the centuries – St Augustine of Hippo being the most eminent. In our own century, our traditional art and music have provoked a remarkable revolution in Western aesthetics, the effects of which have been more far-reaching than is generally realized. The visual landscape of Europe is still being transformed by the influence of modern art on architecture and technical design, an influence that goes right back to the impact of African sculpture on artists like Modigliani, Braque, Picasso, and Ferdinand Léger. Indeed, modern technology seems to have found in African art its most adequate mode of presentation: the very organization of volume, shapes, and lines in the manufactured objects we all handle everyday has benefited immensely from the absorption of the formal principles of African art into European aesthetics. You only have to compare nineteenth-century designs to those of the twentieth century to realize the simplifying effect of the application of these principles, and the gain in functionality it has effected. (How strange, then, that your ordinary Westernized African cannot suffer the presence of an African mask in his sitting room, side by side with his videorecorder!) We must not forget, too, that African labor and resources went into the building of the material prosperity of the West. In many ways, therefore, we have a claim upon Western civilization, as well as a considerable stake in it, as the instrument for the necessary transformation of our world. It is in our interest to make good that claim, to adopt strategies that will make our stake in that civilization pay handsome dividends. We cannot do this if we continue to be burdened by the complexes implanted in us under colonialism, and which are only intensified by cultural nationalism. If the Japanese had been deterred by the insults constantly hurled at them by the Europeans during the last century, they would not have been where they are today: as we all know, the yellow peril has become with time the yellow paradigm.

Let me conclude these reflections by going back to the essential point of my argument, which has led me to a positive evaluation of the concept of alienation. I have tried to argue with specific reference to our situation that the phenomenon of alienation in its positive aspect is the generating principle of culture, the condition of human development. There is no society, no civilization that has not experienced alienation in one form and to some degree of the other. Our present experience of alienation stems directly from our historical encounter with Europe, and from our continuing relationship with a civilization that, in its present form, was forged in that continent, and which, therefore, holds out a special interest for us. We cannot ignore the fact that the transforming values of contact with this civilization have produced the present context of our collective life, if we are to get a mental handle upon the process of transition in which we are involved. The very tensions and conditions of stress of this process would have been beneficial if they helped to concentrate our minds both wonderfully and intensely upon the nature of our alienation.

The necessary effort of understanding our alienation and coming to terms with it justifies all forms of scholarship devoted to European culture and Western civilization, considered as a totality. Indeed, we have been so involved in this civilization that to consider it as something apart from us is to set it up as an abstraction. Our ancestors may not have been the Gauls, the Saxons, the Visigoths, or what have you, but that is not because we are not descended racially from them but because we know practically nothing about what they did or thought, and it doesn't really matter for us. On the other hand, the Hellenic and Roman civilizations have a direct significance for us, as much as for any European. Indeed, in one particular respect, classical Greek civilization has a more immediate interest for us. Its philosophers were confronted with the same dualism of modes of thought in a context of social change and even of political instability that we are now confronted with, and by grappling at the level of ideas with the real problems of existence which this situation posed for their age, with the difficulties of creating a viable society such as we now experience, they made the conceptual breakthrough responsible in large part for the scientific and techno-logical civilization which defines the modern world.

This reference points to the final significance of my argument arising from my particular involvement with the discipline of modern language studies – the conviction of the universality of human experience on which it is based. To study another language is to assume that you will get to understand it, and in the perspective of modern language studies that the culture it reflects can speak to your mind and imagination in ways which may be different from those of your original culture but which can still be meaningful to you. In fact, all human history confirms this assumption: language and culture know no boundary, at least not significantly, and the reality of the contemporary world, the "global village" in the expression sent into circulation by Marshall McLuhan and now become current, has tended to reinforce our awareness of a common humanity.

Thus, it is significant that in the Humanities today the dominant trend of scholarship has been inspired by a new universalism, a direct result of contemporary historical experience. The Linguistics of Chomsky, the Structuralism of Lévi-Strauss, and the Semiology of Barthes have no other final objective than to demonstrate the proposition that different languages and different cultures are varied forms of realizations, varied modes of transformation, of a universal grammar and of a universal structure of experience. The philosophical anthropo-logy that informs contemporary scholarship in the Humanities envisages the essential unity of the human mind, no longer in terms of its rational function but from the point of view of its faculty of symbolization.

The notion of the universality of human experience does not, however, imply uniformity – quite the contrary – but it does mean that cultures maintain their dynamism only through their degree of tension between the particular and the universal. Alienation, in this view, cannot mean total loss; the fulfillment it promises resides precisely in the degree of integration it helps us to achieve. In its creative potential, alienation signifies the sensitive tension between the immediate closeness of the self and the reflected distance of the other.

Notes

1   Chinweizu, *The West and the Rest of Us* (London and Lagos: Nok Publishers, 1978).
2   Obaro Ikime, *The Fall of Nigeria* (London: Heinemann Educational Books, 1977).
3   Bryan Wilson, *Rationality* (Evanston, Ill: Harper and Row, 1970).
4   Carlo Cipolla, *European Culture and Overseas Expansion* (Hammondsworth: Penguin Books). See also J. H. Parry, *The Establishment of the European Hegemony: 1415–1715* (New York: Harper and Row, 1966).
5   Paul Hazard, *La crise de la conscience européenne* (Paris: Boivin et Cie, 1934).
6   Hence what amounts to the dismissal of Voltaire's work by Eric Auerbach in his celebrated work *Mimesis*, tr. W. R. Trask (Princeton: Princeton University Press, 1953).
7   Aimé Césaire, *Discours sur le colonialisme* (Paris: Présence Africaine, 1955), 10.
8   See Heidegger's *What is Philosophy* trans. Jean Wilde and William Kluback (New York, 1958); Paul de Man offers a critique and refutation of Heidegger's affirmation in his *Blindness and Insight*, 2d edn. (London: Methuen, 1983).

Chapter 81

In the Wake of Colonialism and Modernity

Biodun Jeyifo

[...]

This brings me to the second, perhaps more central aspect of this work-in-progress which I title "In the Wake of Colonialism and Modernity." This is the aspect which pertains to the all-encompassing cultural project of modernity, in Europe and outside Europe. As I have stated earlier in this talk, in Europe this project goes by the name of the "civilizing process"; outside Europe it generally went by the name of the loaded and fraught term of the "civilizing mission." One of my greatest surprises in my reading and research for this book project has been the failure, so far, to find any serious, sustained attempt to explore connections between these two projects. Where a link between the two is at all perceived, it is very tenuously made. My contention is that the "civilizing process" in Europe and the "civilizing mission" in the colonies are in fact fundamentally continuous and linked: one prepares the ground, the premises, for the other.

Now, what is the "civilizing process" in Europe? I must state here that my views on this topic are deeply influenced by the work of many cultural historians and philosophers, chief among who are Norbert Elias and Michel Foucault. In fact, Elias's book on this subject is titled, precisely, *The Civilizing Process*. Its English translation is published by Basil Blackwell; it is a monumental and seminal work. In my opinion, this is one of the most important books on the cultural projects of modernity; it is an absolute "must read" for anyone involved in cultural studies and cultural criticism at the present time. It meticulously describes and analyzes the "civilizing" of manners, conduct and personality which began in early modern Europe and extends into the period of the emergence of capitalism and the formation of the modern nation-state in Europe. As Elias describes and analyzes it, this "civilizing process" is a comprehensive project which pervades every facet of subjectivity and identity, from the minutest details of daily life and bodily experience such as the management of bodily effusions and the evacuation of waste, to large-scale macro-political processes like the formation of states and the monopolization of power. What this gigantic project ultimately

First published in *Anglophonia/Caliban* 7 (2000): 71–84.

entailed is the formation of a certain type of personality which would be the ideal, prototypical "civilized" modern subject. At every level, this ideal "civilized" modern subjectivity is constituted in opposition to instincts, dispositions and expressions which are considered wild, unsanitary, spontaneous and carnal. Seen from this angle, Elias's work is supplemented by the work of Michel Foucault in such books and monographs as *Madness and Civilization*, *Discipline and Punish*, *The Birth of the Clinic* and *History of Sexuality*. In sum then, the "civilizing process" entailed the separation of what is considered "civilized," rational and modern from what is deemed savage, irrational and unmodern. It dovetailed with the economic processes of class formation in Europe as the transition from late feudalism to early capitalism took place, providing the cultural sanctions for the separation of the lower social orders from the middle and upper classes. One has only to look at the discourses of the "civilizing process" as it pertained to certain groups, certain nationalities, and even certain so-called "races" in Europe itself to see that nearly all of the stereotypes and phobic projections that were later applied to "natives" in the colonies in the course of the "civilizing mission" had been formulated and given their gestation in the Europe's autotelic "civilizing process." For instance, discourses about Gypsies, about Jews, about the Irish in connection with the colonization of Ireland by the English, discourses about southern Europeans in relation to northern Europeans, and even discourses about the working poor in Europe – all of these discourses had inherent in them notions of who was "civilizable" or not, who was educable or not. Those who were not deemed educable or "civilizable" provided the stereotypes which were later applied to the "natives" in the colonies. Indeed, when I say "later applied", this has to be qualified because, at a certain historical moment, both projects – the "civilizing process" and the "civilizing mission" – became parallel and directly continuous with each other. In fact, I argue in this book project that this is the missing element in Edward Said's seminal work, *Orientalism*, because Said ignores the fact that some of the stereotypes, some of the Orientalist constructions that were applied to the East, were also applied to certain groups in Europe itself in connection with this gigantic project of the so-called "civilizing process."

A second contention that I make with regard to the overall project of the construction of cultural modernity as dialectically encompassed in the "civilizing process" and the "civilizing mission" is that while, on the whole, this project was successful in Europe, it had very limited, very partial success outside Europe. To simplify a very complex argument that I mount to prove this claim, I would say that the moral of the failure of the "civilizing mission" outside Europe is that there are more ways to being "civilized" and "modern" than the unitary, homogenized way touted by the European or Western project. This truth has in fact been demonstrated in Europe itself, which is why I said just now that the "civilizing process" in Europe was "on the whole" successful. For the fact is that there were and are large areas of successful resistance to this "civilizing process" in Europe. A book like E. P. Thompson's *The Making of the English Working Class* provides ample documentation of the creation of a distinct English working-class culture which resisted the styles, idioms and identities of the "civilizing process." But while this is true, while the process did not in every instance succeed, in Europe it did manage to consolidate a bourgeois subjectivity as the model of the properly "modern" and "civilized" subject.

Now, the opposite is true in the colonies: there the "civilizing mission" failed woefully, although again we have to acknowledge its successes in a few significant instances. One of the most widely acknowledged and discussed of these instances is that of the French colonial system of "assimilation." As is well-known, the objective of this policy was the production of the so-called "evolué" or "assimilé" who was a replication of the properly "civilized" Western modern subject. But apart from such instances of the successful formation of the so-called black and brown "sahibs" and "memsahibs" of the colonized world, I contend that the "civilizing mission" failed in the colonies.

It failed for two reasons. One reason is simple but profound: the refusal of the "natives" to be "civilized" according to the master scripts of the "civilizing mission," itself a global projection of the European "civilizing process." Many theories have been propounded to explain this refusal. One of the most powerful of these theories is that of Amilcar Cabral which places a great weight on culture in the struggle against the political and economic aspects of colonial conquest and domination. As we all know, Cabral was involved with the political and military fronts of the struggle against colonialism. But side by side with these domains of the anti-colonial struggle, Cabral formulated a theory which emphasizes the privileged role of culture in the struggle against colonialism and imperialist foreign domination. For him, culture was the domain of the last redoubt against colonial domination and hegemony, especially the hegemony inherent in the "civilizing mission" and its project of producing Westernized subjects among the colonized natives who would be replicas of the ideal "modern" bourgeois subject. I have pondered long on this theory of Cabral and I would like to share my reflections on the matter with you.

One of the most intriguing aspects of Cabral's theory of cultural resistance is the rather startling claim he makes that history does not provide a single instance of the successful integration of political and economic domination with cultural domination.

I'll repeat this: there is not a single instance in the entire history of modern colonizations where there has been a successful integration, a successful harmonization of economic and political domination with domination on the cultural plane. And according to Cabral, this is not due to lack of effort on the part of colonizers to harmonize domination on all these fronts – economic, political and cultural: all colonizers know that harmonization of political and economic domination with cultural domination would consolidate hegemonic rule and make the use of force and coercion unnecessary. But Cabral insists that there is not a single instance in the entire historical vocation of colonialism where this has been successful. I suggest that Cabral's theory has proved productive in explaining the role of cultural resistance in the anti-colonial nationalist struggles of the former colonies of Europe; I suggest that it could also be productively deployed for exploring those instances where the "civilizing process" in Europe itself met significant resistances.

Now from these two sets of discourses that I have so far reviewed in this talk, one on economic modernity and the other on cultural modernity, I argue that we need to rethink, to reconceptualize the relationship between colonialism and modernity; I argue that the two are not as distinct and separate as they are generally thought to be and are indeed enormously intimately interconnected. In order to make this contention pertinent, if not vital to current discourses about globalization and the world system, I undertake a review of widely held conceptions of the nature of the relationship between colonialism and modernity, especially those conceptions with which my own claims are in serious opposition and tension.

The contemporary commonsensical view of colonialism – which cannot be faulted on factual or historical grounds – is that colonialism pertains largely and overwhelmingly to non-Western, non-European nations and peoples. And that is a fact of history. But if you look critically at the suggestion that the so-called "civilizing process" was a form of colonization of the lower social orders whose legacy in fact later produced the actuality of colonization within Europe itself, then one can see that colonialism was both a European and extra-European phenomenon which paved the way for all of the economic and cultural projects of modernity. That is my central thesis in this book project. In other words, I am arguing for a more fundamental and more dialectical relationship between colonialism and modernity than most of the classic accounts of the relationship between the two have allowed.

This brings me to what I identified earlier in this talk as the formidable objections that I anticipate to this view of the necessary and inextricable link between colonialism and modernity. As I see it, there are two main objections to be anticipated, and part of what I am at the moment working on is the effort to finesse my arguments against these anticipated objections. This is necessary because these objections are not factually inaccurate or theoretically wrong-headed. It is rather that in the light of contemporary history and contemporary concerns world-wide, they are at this stage inadequate in meeting the challenges posed by late modernity. So I think they need to be rethought. That is my quarrel with them, not that these objections are faulty or inaccurate on factual and theoretical grounds, it is just that I think they are not adequate to engaging the challenges that we face at the present time of late capitalism or late modernity.

The first objection is one which, in my view, underspecifies and undertheorizes the relationship between colonialism and modernity. Basically, it takes the view that colonialism and modernity are like day and night, that there really is no organic or necessary relationship between the two. Now, the arguments advanced in asserting this position are, on the surface, impeccable. To sum up these arguments, it is held that if colonialism set out to modernize the colonies and produce proper "civilized," modern subjects among the natives, it did so with policies, practices and attitudes whose net effect was to subvert these projects in the colonies. In other words, because of racism, because of repression and autocracy, all of which deeply marked colonial rule and hegemony, modernization or "modernity" had to await the end of colonialism for there to be the possibility of its consummation. So colonialism and modernity, or in another formulation of the same point, colonialism and civilization, are like day and night and there are no organic, necessary connections between them. One person who has made this argument forcefully is Aimé Césaire in his mono-graph, *Discourse on Colonialism* where he asserts that colonialism worked to "de-civilize" both the colonizer and the colonized. This word, "de-civilize," is actually the very word used by Césaire in his monograph; on this account, colonialism set out with pretensions to "civilize" the colonized, but what it actually achieved was to brutalize and "de-civilize" both the colonizer and the colonized.

One other expression of this particular objection to my contention that colonialism and modernity are in fact deeply and inextricably linked is the view which holds that as a historical phenomenon, colonialism in many parts of the non-Western world was in fact a rather brief interlude in the modern history of these societies. This view is often extended to suggest that often, the consequences and legacies of colonialism on the non-Western, non-European peoples and societies are greatly exaggerated. This point is definitely often made in relation to Africa in particular; and it is definitely asserted in relation to the Japanese colonization of Korea which lasted only forty years. And it is a rather strange mix of scholars and theorists who advance this particular view. For instance, it is made by the Marxist scholar, Aijaz Ahmad in his book, *In Theory*; it is also made by Anthony Appiah in his book, *In My Father's House*; and it has been made by Wole Soyinka in many of his essays and is indeed explicitly stated in the Preface to his play, *Death and the King's Horseman*. In this Preface, Soyinka states that the colonial factor is, in his own words, a "mere catalyst" and is not fundamental to the internal dialectic of Yoruba and Nigerian culture and society that Soyinka explores in the play. Appiah for his part states that altogether, colonialism in Africa did not last more than eighty years. This argument is often extended to the contention that the general application of colonial and postcolonial studies to all of the peoples and societies of the non-Western, non-European world(s) ignores the crucial fact that many societies and nations were never in fact colonized. This includes places like Turkey, Japan, Liberia, and Ethiopia. Taken together, all of these views add up to the objection to the suggestion that an organic, necessary connection links modernity to colonialism.

The second objection which I anticipate to my central claims in this book project does in fact admit that there is a relationship between colonialism and modernity, but it asserts that it is a very fraught, very problematic relationship. One person who makes this argument is Paul Gilroy in his book, *The Black Atlantic: Modernity and Double Consciousness*. In advancing this position, Gilroy makes the following intriguing observation which indeed may be said to be symptomatic of this position: he says that the black diasporic communities in Europe and the Americas are in Western modernity but are not of it. They are in it by the sheer fact of having been transplanted to the West by the transatlantic slave trade, but on account of the legacy of racism, of slavery, of segregation and discriminatory practices, they did not, until very recently participate as full players in the projects of Western cultural and economic modernity. Hence the intriguing thesis: black diasporic communities are in Western modernity but are not of it. In effect, this view admits that a relationship does exist between colonialism or slavery and modernity, but it asserts that it is a highly fraught relationship shot through with all kinds of alienation.

This argument is also often extended to the colonized societies outside Europe to say that modernization or modernity first came to these societies via colonialism and for this reason took on the aspect of an alien, external force which produced many alienations, many negative and corrosive anti-modern ideas and attitudes. One recent book which implies this view in its central arguments is Mahmood Mamdani's *Citizen and Subject: the Legacy of Late Colonialism in Africa*. In this book, Mamdani argues that until the very last stages of colonialism in Africa, it was a fundamentally anti-democratic political regime. And for this reason, whatever colonialism brought as the "promise of modernity" was negated by the very fact that it was such a profoundly illiberal, undemocratic regime of political governance which laid the foundations of despotism and even anti-modernity in postcolonial Africa. In other words, this view admits that there is a crucial relationship between modernity and colonialism, but it must be acknowledged as deeply fractured, deeply problematic and deeply alienating.

As I have stated several times, these are all quite formidable objections which I do not hope to refute either on the basis of factual inaccuracies or even theoretical insufficiencies. My point about them is simply that they do not respond fully or even adequately to the challenges of late modernity. And here for want of time I will collapse many of these challenges into an overarching problematic of late modernity. This is the contention that one of the most important and challenging theoretical tasks of the present period is to account for the simultaneous coexistence of the worst social and economic contradictions of early capitalism with the contradictions of late capitalism. Some of the most brutal, the most degrading forms of exploitation and marginalization of entire social groups and peoples that were the specific features of early capitalism, say of the late eighteenth and early nineteenth centuries, some of these contradictions are still very much around today in three quarters of the globe. And they coexist simultaneously with new, more rarefied, more "refined" forms of exploitation and alienation. And in looking at the simultaneity of these contradictions of early and late capitalism, I would distinguish between what I would describe as the colonization of the body, of physical energies and capacities such as we find in the older modes of labor exploitation in the mines, in the migrant or seasonal labor exploited by small and large fruit and vegetable growers, and in women's and children's labor in the garment and textile industries in the United States and many parts of the world, and the colonization of the psyche in newer forms of late capitalist merchandising and advertising of products whereby what appears to be our deepest needs, our deepest desires are not really ours anymore, but obey the logic of the penetration of market forces into virtually every sphere of life. Some of these newer modes of alienation are so rarefied that at the present time, they appear only as virtualities and phantasms which we can only perceive very dimly. Examples of these are the potentialities for refashioning the human person at the very roots of conception, birth and growth that the combination of the new technologies of gene splicing and super scale computerization now makes possible. These new forms of reification are so deep and extensive that they include the determination of goals and priorities that we set ourselves as a species, both to maintain sustainable growth on our planet, and to ensure the survival and perpetuation of life – and its forms – as we know it and treasure it.

So my contention is that we have to account for the coexistence of these two forms of colonization, broadly speaking that of the body and that of the psyche. And how do we do this without revising and rethinking our discourses and conceptions of colonialism and its relationship to modernity?

I hope that it will be seen in the foregoing discussion that I have been anxious not to collapse our older and more established notions of colonization into the newer notions inscribed in the alienations and reifications of late, neoliberal capitalism. By and large, we must constantly remind ourselves that classical colonialism happened outside Europe and was perpetrated by Europe against non-European peoples. We must not lose sight of this historic fact and its legacies. However, we must revise and deepen our concept of colonization as I have tried to argue in my talk today. Doing so will enable us to perceive the equally historic fact that colonization, in its classical and neoliberal forms, applies to all parts of the globe – precisely because it is at the root of modernity and continues to be part of its enduring legacies, inside and outside Europe.

Chapter 82

Poststructuralism and Postcolonial Discourse

Simon Gikandi

I

Perhaps the most useful way to begin a discussion of the relationship between poststructuralist theory and postcolonial discourse is to call attention to the controversies and debates
that have accompanied their rise as significant intellectual movements from the late 1960s
and 1980s respectively. For one of the things these two movements have in common is
that they have always generated heated questions about their political efficacy, their location
within intellectual traditions informed by unequal relations of power, and their validity
as theoretical categories that can provide us with useful knowledge about the cultures
and literatures of previously colonized countries in Africa, Asia, and the Caribbean. These
issues often divide scholars and critiques of formerly colonized societies into two broad
groups: on one hand there are those critics who would like postcolonial theory to account
for the specific conditions in which colonialism emerged and functioned and the role of
decolonization as a specific narrative of liberation. For these critics, the pitfall of postcolonial
theory inheres in its inability to periodize and historicize the colonial experience and to
account for the role of colonized subjects as active agents in the making of culture and
history. Aijaz Ahmad, for example, argues that the primary failure of postcolonial theory is
to be found in its eagerness to foreground a set of questions – on historical agency, the
production of colonial subjects, and even the history of modernity – or to consider "the
question of cultural domination exercised by countries of advanced capital over imperialized
countries" (Ahmad 1992: 2; see also Dirlik 1994; Bartolovich and Lazarus 2002). For such
critics of postcolonial theory, its primary failure – its inability to account for the history and
process of decolonization – arises from its close affinity to poststructural theory. If poststructuralism is seen as the source of the political or epistemological failure of postcolonial

First published in *The Cambridge Companion to Postcolonial Literary Studies*, ed. Neil Lazarus, pp. 97–104.
Cambridge: Cambridge University Press, 2004.

discourse, it is because it came to privilege the act of reading over politics, or, in Ahmad's terms, posited cultural hybridity "against the categories of nation and nationalism," or even situated culture and "the literary/aesthetic realm" at "a great remove from the economy" (1992: 3).[1]

On the other hand, however, many proponents of postcolonial discourse reject the claim that theory represents the separation of culture and political economy, or that acts of reading, especially ones informed by shifting theoretical notions of hybridity and difference, necessarily negate the categories of nation and nationalism. Indeed, for leading postcolonial critics such as Homi K. Bhabha, poststructuralism (and postmodernism) provides a powerful weapon against what they see as the prison-house of European humanism and the decolonized nation as a polity that has lost legitimacy in the age of migration and globalization. For these critics, rather than being ahistorical and apolitical, detached from the concerns of postcolonial subjects, a postcolonial discourse informed by poststructuralism provides a powerful vista into the modern world system at its moment of crisis. For example, Bhabha argues that postcolonial criticism "bears witness to the unequal and uneven forces of cultural representation involved in the contest for political and social authority within the modern world order" (1994: 271).[2]

Nevertheless, both sides in this debate are united by their recognition that postcolonial discourse emerged within the larger institutions of European, especially French, theory after structuralism. In this respect, a postcolonial discourse is unthinkable without poststructuralist theory. Locating postcolonial theory within this European genealogy, however, raises another set of questions or problems: why have theoretical questions that originally developed within French theory come to dominate debates about Anglophone postcolonial identities, cultures, and literatures? Is postcolonial discourse about how French theory plays out in the institutional practices of Anglophone intellectuals rather than a theoretical reflection on what Neil Larsen calls "the realities of cultural decolonization or the international division of labor" (2002: 205), or is it a technology for understanding the postcolonial condition? A different gloss on the same problem is presented well by Bhabha in a moment of self-interrogation in *The Location of Culture*: "Is the language of theory merely another power ploy of the culturally privileged Western élite to produce a discourse of the Other that reinforces its own power-knowledge equation?" (1994: 20–1).

It is difficult to respond to all these questions without accepting the basic fact that, unlike theories of the Third World, neocolonialism, or underdevelopment that were dominant in the 1960s, postcolonial theory was not a discourse produced in the postcolonial world by postcolonial intellectuals. Postcolonial discourse was produced by émigré postcolonial writers and intellectuals based in the West. Irrespective of the validity of its claims, this is a discourse marked by its sense of dislocation from what it considers to be one of its geographical references – the postcolony. At the same time, it is not enough to dismiss postcolonial discourse as French poststructuralism traveling in the imagination of the postcolonial intellectual class. For since the 1990s, the question of what postcolonial studies was, or was not, has come to revolve around the relation between theory as a category of thought and "Third-World" practices and experiences as its object of analysis. Even when it seems to be a discourse that is more important in the metropolitan centers than in the decolonized nation, postcolonial discourse is also an attempt to come to grips with the nature and meaning of colonial modernity from the dual vantage points of decolonization and migration (Hall 1996).

Let us note, however, that the apparent European identity of postcolonial discourse has been the source of some of the most heated debates in the field. At the center of these debates is the question of whether postcolonial theory, seen as a surrogate of poststructuralism, generates any new sets of questions. The boldest dismissal of postcolonial discourse's claim to originality is the one that sees it, to quote Ahmad's words again, as "a matter of catching up with many kinds of very diverse continental developments" while at the same time "reformulating much older and recalcitrant issues . . . as regards the archive of Western knowledges and the question of cultural domination exercised by countries of advanced capital over imperialized countries" (1992: 2). On the other side of this debate are critics like Robert Young who argued that the European identity of poststructural theory conceals its fundamental connection to "Third-World" debates on decolonization and its aftermath. Young's argument, first articulated in *White Mythologies* (1990), is that the historical roots of poststructuralism are to be found not in the crisis of European culture associated with the student revolts of 1968, but in the Algerian struggle against colonialism ten years earlier. In *Postcolonialism: An Historical Introduction*, Young goes as far as to present postcolonial theory as an extension of anticolonial movements in the "Third World," arguing that poststructuralism developed as an anti-Western strategy "directed against the hierarchical cultural and racial assumptions of European thought": "Though structuralism and poststructuralism were taken up and developed in Europe both were indeed alien, and fundamentally antiwestern in strategy. Postcolonial thought has combined the radical heritage of such theory with further ideas and perspectives from tricontinental writers, together with other writers who have emigrated from decolonized tricontinental countries to the west" (2001: 67–8).

All these debates have taken place against what might best be described as an anxiety of influence: the major figures in postcolonial discourse, the symbols of its canon, are so closely identified with the dominant strands of poststructuralist theory that they have tended to be perceived as disciples of leading figures in European poststructuralist discourse. Thus, the works of Edward W. Said – especially *Orientalism* (1978), his pioneering study of the relationship between the representation of the "Orient" and Western systems of power – is indebted to Michel Foucault's work on discursive systems and power. Gayatri Chakravorty Spivak first came into prominence as the translator of Jacques Derrida's *Of Grammatology* and her work on a wide range of subjects from psychoanalysis to feminism can be considered to be a reinterpretation of Derridian deconstruction from the vantage point of colonialism and its subjects. Bhabha's work is a powerful echo of the revisionary theories of Jacques Lacan and Derrida on a set of subjects ranging from difference and split subjectivity to the indeterminate nature of meaning and representation. In the end, though, as I hope to show in this chapter, the real enigma of postcolonial discourse is not so much that it is embedded in Western theory but how a project so closely associated with European debates on questions such as representation, subjectivity, and historicism became central to the rethinking of the cultures and literatures of the postcolonial polity.

2

Still it is important to keep in mind that while the subjects who inhabit postcolonial theory and their historical experiences do originate from the colonial and postcolonial world, structuralism and poststructuralism were taken up and developed in France as responses to what were very localized moments of debate and crisis which, nevertheless, had a significant colonial dimension. These movements arose as a reaction against a European tradition of humanism whose most important proponent in the period after the Second World War was Jean-Paul Sartre. Sartre's humanism was central to the discourse of colonialism developed by anticolonial intellectuals such as Frantz Fanon, Aimé Césaire, and Léopold Sédar Senghor during this period. Because of this, the emergence of structuralism in the 1950s and 1960s as a critique of humanism could not leave the discourse of colonialism intact and unscathed. Similarly, if poststructuralism emerged as a critique of the residual humanism of structuralism, then it is important to conceive it as a critique of the central pillars of the discourse of colonialism. In this context, postcolonial discourse needs to be seen as a critique of an earlier discourse of colonialism anchored in the humanist tradition rather than as a continuation of what Young calls "tricontinental anticolonial intellectuals" (2001: 427). Rather than see postcolonial discourse as the continuation of the discourse of colonialism, we need to examine it as a radical break with this tradition, a break enabled by poststructuralist theory. However, this argument can only be clarified if we take the preceding terms or suffixes of postcolonial discourse and poststructural theory – namely, colonialism and structuralism – as key foundational terms rather than conceptual schemas that have been transcended. Indeed, postcolonial discourse and poststructural theory share an identity at a most basic level: they are haunted by their suffixes.

Thus if we are looking for a point of contact in the genealogy of post-structuralism and postcolonial discourse, the place to start is an unexpected one – in the existential phenomenology of Sartre. Here it is interesting to note that Sartre has come to be so closely associated with the discredited project of humanism, in the aftermath of poststructuralism, that critics have forgotten that in the period after the Second World War he represented the intellectual traditions against which others defined themselves. In addition, while the rejection of Sartre (in structuralism and poststructuralism) was premised on the claim that his theories of history and consciousness tended to reinforce ethnocentrism and universalism at the expense of "other" cultures and modes of knowledge, he was clearly the most important European philosopher involved in the struggle against colonialism. For this reason, his influence on the discourse of colonialism – the theoretical anticolonial project that emerged after the Second World War – cannot be underestimated. In addition to his well-known public stand and activism against French colonialism in Indochina and Algeria, Sartre's major works were preoccupied with the role of colonial violence and the colonial subject.[3] Indeed, a central goal of the Sartrean project was to overcome the gap between the European self and the colonial other by developing a theory of history – and an ethical practice – that would make the idea of a human culture *after* colonialism possible. It is in this sense that Sartre has come to be seen as the custodian of radical or syncretic humanism.[4]

It is now generally assumed that Sartre embodied the humanism which, as we will see below, structuralist and poststructuralist theorists set out to deconstruct in the 1960s and after. However, he appealed to colonized intellectuals of the 1940s and 1950s precisely *because of* his commitment to a radical form of humanism, not in spite of it. More specifically, he was the first major philosopher – perhaps the only one – to connect the colonial experience to both the limits of humanism and its utopian possibilities. Thus through Sartre's example, we can begin to understand how the critical terms that were to be discredited in poststructural and postcolonial theory because they were considered to be compromised by humanism – universalism, historicism, consciousness, and identity – were, implicitly and explicitly, cornerstones in the edifice of the discourse of anticolonialism constructed by Césaire, Fanon, and Senghor. We hence need to consider the key terms in what has come to be known as radical humanism and then see how this directly impacted the discourse of anticolonialism.

At the top of the list was the question of history and historicism. The tradition of historicism, which had dominated French thought during the Hegelian revival of the 1930s associated with Jean Hyppolite and Alexandre Kojève, invested heavily in the idea of history, or rather the philosophy of history, as the "foundation for understanding the modern world and for providing insight into how that world might be changed for the better" (Roth 1988: ix). In most of its forms, argues Michael Roth, "French Hegelianism was a vehicle for confronting the historical, for thinking about the connection between history and knowing" (2). In Sartre, this investment in the philosophy of history as the foundation of knowledge went a step further: historicism was not simply about human consciousness; rather the historical process was one in which the human subject would come to conquer nature and discover the essential truth. This view of history was to be affirmed in Sartre's most important and controversial project, *Critique of Dialectical Reason*, in which his stated goal was nothing less than the establishment of what he called "the truth of history." The goal of his project, Sartre argued, was "to establish that there is one human history, with one truth and one intelligibility – not by considering the material content of this history, but by demonstrating that a practical multiplicity, whatever it may be, must unceasingly totalise itself through interiorising its multiplicity at all levels" (1976: 69; see also Young 1990: 28–47).

Closely aligned with this view of history as a process that would lead us towards the truth was the privileging of the subject. The humanist idea of history as either spiritual progress or the quest for truth was impossible without the centering of the human subject and its consciousness in the drama of social life. In fact, in his early works on existentialism, Sartre's goal was to pose the question of freedom as, in Mark Poster's apt phrase, "the ultimate question of the human condition" (1975: 80). Sartre's phenomenological philosophy, as presented in *Being and Nothingness*, was intended to affirm the centrality of the human subject in relation to the lived world and in the process to assert the distinctiveness of consciousness in relation to this experience, to prove that "[c]onsciousness is consciousness of something" (Poster 1975: 82). Consciousness was, of course, unthinkable without a knowing subject.

The third triad in this discourse of history and consciousness was the question of the other. Here, Sartre had an important Hegelian tradition to fall back on, for as is well known, one of the factors that had attracted French intellectuals to Hegel in the 1930s had been the "master/slave dialectic," seen as a powerful counter to Kantian rationalism and its insistence on the autonomy of an identity based on reason. Roth's summary of this dialectic is worth quoting in detail:

> The story of the master/slave dialectic is fairly straightforward . . . Hegel describes the confrontation of two persons, two "consciousnesses," who have forged their identities in isolation from other people. Upon meeting, each sees the other as a threat to his or her individual existence, and, more important, each seeks to dominate the other so as to be more certain of this existence. (Hegel speaks here of "self-certainty.") The two struggle for domination, for the recognition of the strength of their respective individualities. The loser of the struggle is the one who decides that life is more important than the recognition originally sought. This person

abandons the fight and is made a slave who recognizes the sovereignty of the master. In other words, the loser allows the animal desire for self-preservation to take precedence over the human desire for recognition.

(1988: 100)

Perhaps the most important aspect of this dialectic was that, in the relation between the master and the slave, "it was the slave who moves humanity toward a higher level of self-realization ... The slave is the secret of change in history and his desire for freedom from oppression is the ground of man's becoming more human" (Poster 1975: 13). The colonial situation presented the most dramatic modern example of the master/slave dialectic. The dialectic was, in turn, to become central to the discourse of anticolonialism precisely because of the agency invested in the enslaved within the humanistic project.

In general, Sartre's major contribution to colonial discourse was his projection of what might initially have been European issues – on identity, freedom, and consciousness – into the colonial sphere. He did so, not simply in his reflections on colonial violence in the *Critique of Dialectical Reason* but more poignantly in a series of introductions or prefaces he wrote for works by a group of colonial intellectuals – Senghor, Memmi, and Fanon – who were to become crucial in the anticolonial struggle. These prefaces opened important spaces for colonized intellectuals seeking to develop an anticolonial history as a first step to what they considered to be a decolonized truth. It is in these prefaces that Sartre – and his radical humanism – have to be seen as important interventions into the (anti)colonial process. For example, while Sartre used his preface to Albert Memmi's *The Colonizer and the Colonized* to reiterate his well-known claims for the centrality of experience and transcendence – the belief that self-consciousness of an experience was not enough in itself, that it needed to be transcended to the level of the universal – he also used the occasion to represent colonialism as a system defined by a totality.

Similarly, Sartre's famous preface to Fanon's *The Wretched of the Earth* enabled him both to return to the dialectic of violence that had been part of his philosophical project since the war and to recognize the crisis of humanism that had been exposed by a dying colonialism. Sartre's argument in this preface was that when they were located at the limits of the colonial system, the colonized exemplified the unhappy consciousness of history. In responding to Fanon's challenge – the insistence on the dialectic of violence as the enabling condition of colonialism – Sartre did not entirely give up the idea of the dialectic and the process of history as stages leading to reconciliation. Indeed, he located the significance of Fanon's project in what he saw as its clarification of the historical process, as constituting "step by step, the dialectic which liberal hypocrisy hides from you and which is as much responsible for our existence as for his" (Sartre 1968: 14). At the same time, in translating the colonial experience for European readers, Sartre was forced to come to terms with the fact that the dialectic of colonial history could not lead to reconciliation, as his dialectical sense of the historical process had assumed; the contradictory nature of colonialism, a system that claimed and denied the colonial condition at the same time, was explosive; it was out of this explosion that the Europeans themselves were becoming decolonized – confronted, as they were, with "that unexpected revelation, the strip tease of our humanism" (24).

[...]

Notes

1   One of the most astute readings of postcolonial discourse as an extension of the poststructuralist project can be found in Larsen 2002.

2   However, not all postcolonial theory assumes that poststructural theory can account for the international division of labor and knowledge. For an alternative view, see Spivak 1988b.

3   Sartre's writings on colonialism are collected in Sartre 2001a. My discussion of Sartre here is indebted to Young 1990: 28–47.

4   For the influence of humanism over French intellectual life from 1945 to 1960 see Pavel 1989: 3. See also Young 1990: 21–47. According to Michael S. Roth, Sartrean existentialism would become "the guardian of a radical humanism" (Roth 1988: I).

References

Ahmad, Aijaz. *In Theory: Classes, Nations, Literatures* (London: Verson, 1992).

Bartolovich, Crystal and Neil Lazarus. *Marxism, Modernity, and Postcolonial Studies*. Cambridge: Cambridge University Press, 2002.

Bhabha, Homi. *The Location of Culture* (London/New York: Routledge, 1994).

Derrida, Jacques. *Of Grammatology*, trans. Gayatri Chakravorty Spivak (Baltimore: John Hopkins University Press, 1976).

Dirlik, Arif. "The Postcolonial Aura: Third World Criticism in the Age of Global Capitalism," in *Dangerous Liaisons: Gender, Nation, and Postcolonial Perspectives*, eds. Anne McClintock, Aamir Mufti, and Ella Shohat (Minneapolis: University of Minnesota Press, 1997).

Hall, Stuart. "What was 'the post-colonial?' Thinking at the Limit," in *The Post-Colonial Question: Common Skies, Divided Horizons*, eds. Iain Chambers and Lidia Curti (London and New York: Routledge, 1996), pp. 242–60.

Larsen, Neil. "Marxism, Poststructuralism, and *The Eighteenth Brumaire*," in Bartolovich and Lazarus, *Marxism, Modernity*, 204–20.

Pavel, Thomas G. *The Spell of Language: Poststructuralism and Speculation* (Chicago and London: University of Chicago Press, 1989).

Poster, Mark. *Existential Marxism in Postwar France: From Sartre to Althusser* (Princeton, NJ: Princeton University Press, 1975).

Roth, Michael S. *Knowing and History: Appropriations of Hegel in Twentieth-Century France* (Ithaca and London: Cornell University Press, 1988).

Said, E. W. *Orientalism* (New York: Vintage, 1979).

Sartre, J-P. *Critique of Dialectical Reason*, trans. Alan Sheridan Smith (London: New Left Books, 1976).

Sartre, J-P. "Preface" to *The Wretched of the Earth*, trans. Constance Farrington (New York: Grove, 1963).

Spivak, Gayatri Chakravorty. "Can the Subaltern Speak?" in *Marxism and the Interpretation of Culture*. Eds. Cary Nelson and Lawrence Grossberg (Urbana: University of Illinois Press, 1988), pp. 271–313.

Young, Robert. *White Mythologies: Writing History and the West* (London and New York: Routledge, 1990).

Young, Robert. *Postcolonialism: An Historical Introduction* (Cambridge: Blackwell, 2002).

Chapter 83

Subjectivity and History:
Derrida in Algeria

Robert J. C. Young

The schools were started so as to teach us how to say 'Yes' in their language.
Tayeb Salih, *Season of Migration to the North* (Salih 1969: 95)

1   *White Mythologies* Revisited

'I do not believe that anyone can detect by *reading*, if I do not myself declare it, that I am a "French Algerian"' (Derrida 1998: 46). True, for when I wrote *White Mythologies* I knew that you had been born in Algeria, in the very year that had witnessed the celebrations of the centenary of the French invasion (something for Algerians to celebrate indeed). You had once guardedly spoken of your childhood memories, your 'nostalgeria', far more briefly though than Hélène Cixous had recalled her 'Algeriance' (Derrida 1985; Cixous 1998). That was, however, my only clue, apart from when I had first seen you in 1979 and understood immediately that you were no 'français de souche'. What a relief. No blockhead, at least. All the same, even before that moment I already knew that something serious was going on. It was as plain as punch even if I found it impossible then to identify where it was coming from. What was certain was that it was somewhere else, and that it was producing a strong effect of disorientation (or rather, disoccidentation). When you visited Oxford that time, the first question we put to you was about your use of the terms 'the west' and 'western metaphysics': 'The category of the "west" and the continuity of philosophical discourse from Plato to the present remains unexplicated and unjustified in your work', we complained. You answered that there was nothing 'which would be considered the essence of the west in western philosophy', that you didn't believe in the continuity of the philosophy of the west, that the unity of 'western philosophy' was an illusion, the product of the effects of a representation, a dogma, and that in your work you were always insisting on splits, fissures, discontinuities in the corpus. 'It's a contradictory, conflictual structure which has to repress forms trying to disrupt this unity from inside and out' (Derrida 1979). Twenty years later you would still have to make the same protest (Derrida 1998: 70). In Oxford that day, you didn't comment further on 'the west' as such, but the link was easy to find:

First published in *Postcolonialism: An Historical Introduction*, pp. 411–16. Oxford: Blackwell, 2001.

> Metaphysics – the white mythology which reassembles and reflects the culture of the West: the white man takes his own mythology, Indo-European mythology, his own *logos*, that is, the *mythos* of his reason, for the universal form of that he must still wish to call Reason. Which does not go uncontested. . . . White mythology – metaphysics has erased within itself the fabulous scene that has produced it, the scene that nevertheless remains active and stirring, inscribed in white ink, an invisible design covered over in the palimpsest. (Derrida 1982: 213)

Years later, when I sent you a copy of *White Mythologies* you remarked that I had indeed detected 'a thread' that ran through your writings. That 'thread' which I followed then, with such labour, has finally become the explicit subject of some of your recent, more autobiographical work. I knew it all along, for you showed it to me in your writings from the first: whereas other philosophers would write of 'philosophy', for you it was always 'western philosophy'. Whiteness, otherness, margins, decentring: it was obvious to me what you were up to, what possibilities you were striving towards, what presuppositions you were seeking to dislodge. And this was why I gave my book a title alluding to your essay, which I have since often seen referred to as 'White Mythologies'. Permit me to recall the opening of that book:

> If so-called 'so-called poststructuralism' is the product of a single historical moment, then that moment is probably not May 1968 but rather the Algerian War of Independence – no doubt itself both a symptom and a product. In this respect, it is significant that Sartre, Althusser, Derrida and Lyotard, among others, were all either born in Algeria or personally involved with the events of the war. (Young 1990: 1)

'Poststructuralism', if I may reinvoke that curious term, as a form of epistemic violence always represented one echo of the violence of Algeria playing itself out in an insurrection against the calm philosophical and political certainties of the metropolis, a revolution initiated, as you argued, just 'at the moment when the fundamental conceptual system produced by the Greco-European adventure is in the process of taking over all of humanity' and achieving 'worldwide dominance'. An imposition, as you now put it, of 'a sovereignty whose essence is always colonial' (Derrida 1978: 82, 297; 1998: 39–40, 59). From the first, then, your target was, we would say these days, western globalization, conceptual in form but material in its effects, and the eurocentrism of western culture – 'nothing but the most original and powerful ethnocentrism in the process of imposing itself upon the world' (Derrida 1976: 3). That book of mine sought to retranslate, working from an original that I never knew, what had been predominantly regarded up to that point as deconstruction's philosophical or literary strategies into the more painful framework of colonial and postcolonial history. How to rewrite history when the very model of history was so much a product of the history that I wanted to rewrite? Your problematic exactly. It was your critique of the philosophy and concept of history, starting with Husserl, that indicated the first possibilities to me, offering 'a system of critiques' for '*shaking the entirety* of Occidental history'; your strategy of postcolonial retaliation, of overturning, cannot be disconnected from the you who when at school in Algeria in typical colonial pedagogic fashion had been taught 'History' as the history of France: 'an incredible discipline, a fable and bible, yet a doctrine of indoctrination almost uneffaceable for children of my generation' (Derrida 1978: 235; 1998: 44).

Or as Aijaz Ahmad has described it:

> Robert Young, who had until a decade ago devoted himself almost entirely to propagating
> French poststructuralism in the British Isles, with hardly a thought to spare for the erstwhile
> colonies, suddenly emerged as a leading theorist of what got called 'postcolonial criticism': even
> though he hardly uses the term in his *White Mythologies*, the book signifies his first major
> awakening to the fact of imperialism, but in a world already populated by poststructuralist
> thought. (Ahmad 1995: 8)

Ahmad's characteristic method here of reductive *ad hominem* and *ad feminam* critique
subverts his accompanying claim to Marxist objectivity – for indeed he knows as little of
the thoughts I had 'to spare' in the British Isles before writing *White Mythologies*, as I know of
his thoughts he had to spare in the USA before writing *In Theory*, where, for all the world
knew, he had 'devoted himself almost entirely to propagating' translations of Urdu poetry in
North America (and why not?) (Ahmad 1992, 1969). Behind this endearing personalism,
Ahmad's critique is predicated on the assumption that 'French poststructuralism' has
nothing to do with 'the erstwhile colonies', and that when I 'awoke' to the fact of
imperialism, Keats-like, it was, as it were, too late, for the world had already been populated
by dreaming, idealist poststructuralists. Ahmad here engages in a common anti-postcolonial
trope, the form of which repeats the assumption of cultural inferiority so searchingly
analysed by Fanon: anything that has come to be regarded as being of intellectual or political
significance in the west could have nothing to do with the (so-called) Third World, even
when it is itself a critique of the west conducted from one of the many locations and
positions of the three continents. Postcolonial theory, in other words, 'must' be European, if
it has made such an impact on the west. It is Derrida who, as Bart Moore-Gilbert observes,
'is usually the chief bogeyman in attacks on postcolonial theory's reliance on European
methodological models' (Moore-Gilbert 1997: 163, citing Ahmad 1992 and Slemon and
Tiffin 1989). Those who reject contemporary postcolonial theory in the name of the
'Third World' on the grounds of it being western, however, are themselves in doing so
negating the very input of the Third World, starting with Derrida, disavowing therefore the
very non-European work which their critique professes to advocate. A related argument sets
up an opposition between western theory and the particularity of Third World experience.
This assumes either patronizingly or deferentially that theory is itself completely western,
while the only thing that the Third World can be allowed is experience, never anything so
conceptually or politically effective as its own theory or philosophy. Such an argument
unconsciously perpetuates the relation of adult to child that lay at the heart of colonial
ideology.

Structuralism came from the east, poststructuralism from the south. Many of those who
developed the theoretical positions subsequently characterized as poststructuralism came
from Algeria or had been involved in the war of independence. Fanon, Memmi, Bourdieu,
Althusser, Lyotard, Derrida, Cixous – they were all in or from Algeria. None of them, it is
true, were Algerians proper, in the sense of coming from the indigenous Arab, Berber,
Kabyle, Chaouia or Mzabite peoples that make up the population of modern independent
Algeria (Bourdieu 1958). They were, so to speak, Algerians improper, those who did not
belong easily to either side – a condition that the subsequent history of Algeria has shown is
in its own way characteristically Algerian, for the many different kinds of Algerians 'proper'

do not belong easily to the Algerian state either. Some, such as Althusser, Derrida's mentor at the *Ecole Normale Supérieur*, were *pieds-noirs*, as was Camus, coming from the mixed communities of poor whites who had migrated from the most impoverished areas of the Mediterranean basin; Althusser's family had been deported to Algeria, along with thousands of others, as a consequence of the Franco – Prussian war, and the annexation of Alsace-Lorraine by Germany in 1871. Others such as Derrida and Cixous came from the so-called indigenous Jewish community originally expelled with the Moors from Spain by Ferdinand and Isabella in the fifteenth century, their confiscated wealth then used to finance Columbus's expedition to the new world (Laloum and Allouche 1992; Wood 1998). Strange thought: without the Derridas and Cixous's of this world, no 'Latin' America. Memmi, another Maghrebian Jew, was born in Tunis and then studied at the University of Algiers before going on to the Sorbonne. Others, such as Fanon or Lyotard, went to Algeria to work or on military service and became actively involved with the revolution (Pierre Bourdieu was also in Algeria in the 1950s doing anthropological–sociological research (Bourdieu 1958, 1979; Bourdieu and Darbel 1963; Bourdieu and Sayad 1964) and saw Derrida frequently when he had returned to Algeria to do his military service there). The poststructuralism associated with these names could better be characterized therefore as Franco-Maghrebian theory, for its theoretical interventions have been actively concerned with the task of undoing the ideological heritage of French colonialism and with rethinking the premises, assumptions and protocols of its centrist, imperial culture. In *Murder of the Other* Cixous recounts how she elaborated such thoughts out of her own experience:

> I come, biographically, from a rebellion, from a violent and anguished direct refusal to accept what is happening on the stage on whose edge I find I am placed. . . . I learned to read, to write, to scream, and to vomit in Algeria. Today I know from experience that one cannot imagine what an Algerian French girl was: you have to have been it, to have gone through it. To have seen 'Frenchmen' at the 'height' of imperialist blindness, behaving in a country that was inhabited by humans as if it were peopled by nonbeings, born-slaves. I learned everything from this first spectacle: I saw how the white (French), superior, plutocratic, civilized world founded its power on the repression of populations who had suddenly become 'invisible', like proletarians, immigrant workers, minorities who are not the right 'colour'. Women. Invisible as humans. But, of course, perceived as tools – dirty, stupid, lazy, underhanded, etc. Thanks to some annihilating dialectical magic. I saw that the great, noble, 'advanced' countries established themselves by expelling what was 'strange'; excluding it but not dismissing it; enslaving it. (Cixous and Clément 1986: 70)

'For all its potentially useful insights, poststructuralist philosophy remains the handmaiden of repression' declares the Australian critic Helen Tiffin, 'and, if I may mix metaphors, serves as District Commissioner of the 1980s, his book title now changed from *The Pacification of the Primitive Tribes of the Lower Niger* to *Enjoying the Other: or Difference Domesticated*' (cited in Moore-Gilbert 1997: 21). Things fall apart: the assumption here is that 'poststructuralist philosophy' is just another white mythology of Europe, Tiffin never apparently imagining that 'the Other' could now be writing the book him or herself. Only the white settler is allowed to use theory to write back. Woman, native, still other. As Gayatri Spivak observes of a comparable critique of her own work, 'When Benita Parry takes us [Spivak, Bhabha, Jan-Mohammed] to task for not being able to listen to the natives, or to let the natives speak, she forgets that the three of us, postcolonials, are "native" too. . . . The resistant post-colonial has become a scandal' (Spivak 1993: 60). Tiffin's comment only requires an apparently unthinkable, scandalous reversal of subject position: poststructuralism, which she characterizes as the handmaiden of repression, was in fact produced by repression, for it developed in large part out of the experience of colonialism. The structure to which it is 'post' is the colonial apparatus, the imperial machine. Its deconstruction of the idea of totality was born out of the experience of, and forms of resistance to, the totalizing regimes of the late colonial state, particularly French Algeria. That machine operated like no other, often being later redeployed, as liberals from Burke onwards always feared it would, in the metropolis. If fascism was colonial totalitarianism brought home to Europe, then totalitarianism is always colonial – externally or internally. After imperialism, after fascism, after Stalinism, after Algeria, it was time to challenge the spectacle of totality on which ideas of the state and the party had been based, and which problematically Lukács had also argued was the means by which to challenge capitalism. Sartre, the African philosopher in Mudimbe's formulation, tried hard to reformulate a Marxist theory of history which, while amounting to totality and a totalization of historical processes, would also allow for the active interventions of the agents of history. Having himself fought the Nazis as a member of the French resistance, he must have known that this theory was working against the grain, and cannot have been altogether surprised when he failed to complete its philosophical argument. His key move, which only complicated things further, and which appears at the end of the first volume of the *Critique of Dialectical Reason* as the opening that would never allow that work to be closed, was to produce the first Marxist philosophy of history in which colonialism, and the endemic violence of the colonial regime, was a central component: 'Violence, as bourgeois *exis* [the inert, stable condition opposed to *praxis*], exists in the exploitation of the proletariat as an inherited relation of the dominant class to the dominated class . . . and violence, as the *praxis* of this bourgeois generation, lay in colonization' (Sartre 1976a: 719; 1991; Young 1990: 28–47). Sartre's emphasis on the role of violence put him in solidarity with Frantz Fanon, Algeria's most famous adopted son, who argued simply that 'the development of violence among the colonized people will be proportionate to the violence exercised by the threatened colonial regime' (Fanon 1965: 69).

After 1962, more *colons, pieds-noirs* and exiles from Algeria arrived in Paris: few 'poststructuralists' have been 'françaises de souche', 'of good stock', that is, indigenous white French men or women. Althusser made the first move, starting with his theory of ideology. Althusser's primal scene of ideology, in which the subject is interpellated by a policeman shouting 'hey, you there!', is not the ideology theorized as an unconscious absorption of the values of the system, as European Marxists had conceptualized 'false consciousness'. Althusser's ideology starts with a brutal colonial address to a subject regarded as already degraded, a member of a debased cultural system who must be apprehended within an apparatus of power. Like Lyotard, Althusser had also experienced the 'relative autonomy' of the colonial apparatus in Algeria, its determination by Paris only in the last instance, and this suggested that the postcolonial state, far from existing in a passive position as an identical effect of capitalism, might share in the freeing up of the economism assumed to operate in the metropolis through the separate spheres of core, semiperiphery and periphery (Meynier 1981; Prochaska 1990). It was his critique of essentialism that provided the foundation of subsequent critiques of eurocentrism. Althusser's *Reading Capital* (1968), in the popular edition 'petite collection maspero' in which it was generally known, was part of a series, published by the Trotskyist FLN supporter Maspero, whose first thirty volumes also included works by Jomo Kenyatta, Mao Zedong, V. N. Giap, Ho Chi Minh, Che Guevara, Frantz Fanon and Malcolm X – as well as Althusser's own revolutionary pupil, Régis Debray. Derrida went further, redeploying Sartre's worried observation that 'the totalization is never achieved and that the totality exists at best only in the form of a *detotalized totality*' (Sartre 1963: 78). Totalization, Derrida argued, was in fact impossible not only empirically, but also conceptually: 'that is to say, because instead of being an inexhaustible field, as in the classical hypothesis, instead of being too large, there is something missing from it: a centre which arrests and grounds the play of substitutions' (Derrida 1978: 289). The centre cannot hold, as Yeats observed on the eve of Irish independence. Colonialism and the operation of the colonial apparatus, Derrida recognized, typically produced politically and conceptually ungoverned effects. These could then be redeployed against it. So Derrida, neither French nor Algerian, always anti-nationalist and cosmopolitan, critical of western ethnocentrism from *Of Grammatology*'s very first page, preoccupied with justice and injustice, developed deconstruction as a procedure for intellectual and cultural decolonization within the metropolis to which he had sailed on the *Ville d'Alger* in 1949, and to which he had returned after doing military service in Algeria from 1957–9 in the name of a France that expected no ambivalence from him despite having itself rejected and disowned him and then readmitted him to French citizenship. The surgical operation of deconstruction was always directed at the identity of the ontological violence that sustains the western metaphysical and ideo-logical systems with the force and actual violence that has sustained the western nations in their colonial and imperial policies, a structural relation of power that had to be teased apart if it was ever to be overturned. This preoccupation with the encounter with force and violence and their effects *on* history, politics, ethics and language, leading to their effects *in* history, politics, ethics and language, has always been fundamental to Derrida's work from the early volumes – *Of Grammatology* (1967), *Writing and Difference* (1967), and *Margins – of Philosophy* (1972) – onwards.

References

Ahmad, Aijaz. 'The Politics of Literary Postcoloniality,' *Race and Class* 36.3 (1995): 1–20.

——. *In Theory: Classes, Nations, Literatures*. London: Verso, 1992.

——. *Poems by Ghalib*, trans. Aijaz Ahmad et al., with a forenote by Aijaz Ahmad. New York: Hudson Review, 1969.

Bourdieu, Pierre. *Algeria 1960: Essays*. Trans. Richard Nice. Cambridge: Cambridge University Press, 1979.

——. *Sociologie de l'Algerie*. Paris: Presses universitaires de France, 1958.

—— and Alain Darbel. *Travail et travailleurs en Algerie*. Paris: Mouton, 1963.

—— and Abdelmalek Sayad. *Le Deracinement: la crise de l'agriculture traditionnelle en Algerie*. Paris: Editions de Minuit, 1964.

Chatterjee, Partha. *Nationalist Thought and the Colonial World: A Derivative Discourse*. London: Zed Books, 1986.

Cixous, Helene. 'My Algeriance, in other words: to depart not to arrive from Algeria,' 153–72, in *Stigmata: Escaping Texts*. London: Routledge, 1998.

—— and Catherine Clement. *The Newly Born Woman*. Trans. Betsy Wing. Manchester: Manchester University Press, 1986.

de Saussure, Leopold. *Psychologie de la colonisation française dans ses rapports avec les societes indigenes*. Paris: Felix Alcan, 1899.

de Tocqueville, Alexis. *De la Colonie en Algerie, presentation de Tzvetan Todorov*. Brussels: Editions Complexe, 1988.

Derrida, Jacques. *Monolingualism of the Other, or the Prosthesis of Origin* [1996]. Trans. Patrick Mensah. Stanford, CA: Stanford University Press, 1998.

——. 'An Interview with Derrida' ['Derrida l'insoumis,' 1983] 107–27 in *Derrida and Difference*. Ed. David Wood and R. Bernasconi. Warwick: Parousia Press, 1985.

——. *Margins – of Philosophy* [1972]. Trans. Alan Bass. Chicago: University of Chicago Press, 1982.

——. Seminar with the *Oxford Literary Review*. Unpublished transcript, 1979.

——. *Writing and Difference* [1967]. Trans. Alan Bass. London: Routledge, 1978.

——. *Of Grammatology* [1967]. Trans. Gayatri Chakravorty Spivak. Baltimore, MD: Johns Hopkins University Press, 1976.

Fanon, Frantz. *The Wretched of the Earth* [1961]. Trans. Constance Farrington. London: MacGibbon Kee, 1965.

Hargreaves, Alec G. *Immigration, 'Race' and Ethnicity in Contemporary France*. London: Routledge, 1995.

Hargreaves, Alec G. and Mark McKinney, eds. *Post-Colonial Cultures in France*. London: Routledge, 1997.

Laloum, Jean and Jean Luce Allouche. *Les Juifs d'Algerie: Images et texts*. Paris: Editions du Scribe, 1992.

Meynier, Gilbert. *L'Algérie révélée. La guerre de 1914–1918 et le premier quart du XXe siècle*. Geneva: Droz, 1981.

Moore-Gilbert, Bart. *Postcolonial Theory: Contexts, Practices, Politics*. London: Verso, 1997.

Prochaska, David. *Making Algeria French: Colonialism in Bône, 1870–1920*. Cambridge: Cambridge University Press, 1990.

Sartre, Jean-Paul. *Critique of Dialectical Reason: The Intelligibility of History* [1985], Vol. 2, ed. Arlette Elkaim Sartre, trans. Quintin Hoare. London: Verso, 1991.

——. *Critique of Dialectical Reason: Theory of Practical Ensembles* [1960], Vol. 1, trans. Alan Sheridan-Smith. London: Verso, 1976.

——. *The Problem of Method* [1960]. Trans. Hazel E. Barnes. London: Methuen, 1963.

Slemon, Stephen and Helen Tiffin, eds. *After Europe: Critical Theory and Post-Colonial Writing*. Sydney: Dangaroo Press, 1989.

Spivak, Gayatri Chakravorty. *Outside in the Teaching Machine*. London: Routlege, 1993.

Wood, Nancy. 'Remembering the Jews of Algeria,' in *Translating 'Algeria,' Parralax* 7 (1998): 169–84.

Young, Robert J. C. *White Mythologies: Writing History and the West*. London: Routledge, 1990.

Chapter 84

The Angel of Progress:
Pitfalls of the Term "Post-colonialism"

Anne McClintock

His face is turned towards the past. . . . The angel would like to stay, awaken the dead, and make whole that which has been smashed. But a storm is blowing from Paradise; it has got caught in his wings with such violence that the angel can no longer close them. This storm irresistibly propels him into the future to which his back is turned, while the pile of debris before him grows skyward. This storm is what we call progress.

Walter Benjamin

To enter the Hybrid State exhibit on Broadway, you enter The Passage. Instead of a gallery, you find a dark antechamber, where one white word invites you forward: COLONIALISM. To enter colonial space, you stoop through a low door, only to be closeted in another black space – a curatorial reminder, however fleeting, of Fanon: "The native is a being hemmed in".[1] But the way out of colonialism, it seems, is forward. A second white word, POST-COLONIALISM, invites you through a slightly larger door into the next stage of history, after which you emerge, fully erect, into the brightly lit and noisy HYBRID STATE.

I am fascinated less by the exhibit itself, than by the paradox between the idea of history that shapes "The Passage," and the quite different idea of history that shapes the "Hybrid State" exhibit itself. The exhibit celebrates "parallel history":

Parallel history points to the reality that there is no longer a mainstream view of American art culture, with several "other", lesser important cultures surrounding it. Rather there exists a parallel history which is now changing our understanding of our transcultural understanding.[2]

Yet the exhibit's commitment to "hybrid history" (multiple time) is contradicted by the linear logic of The Passage ("A Brief Route to Freedom"), which, as it turns out, rehearses one of the most tenacious tropes of colonialism. In colonial discourse, as in The Passage, space is time, and history is shaped around two, necessary movements: the "progress" forward of humanity from slouching deprivation to erect, enlightened reason. The other movement presents the reverse: regression backwards from (white, male) adulthood to a primordial, black "degeneracy" usually incarnated in women. The Passage rehearses this

First published in *Social Text* (Spring 1992): 1–15; and subsequently in *Colonial Discourse & Post–Colonial Theory: A Reader,* ed. Patrick Williams and Laura Chrisman, pp. 291–9, 302–3. New York: Columbia University Press, 1994.

temporal logic: progress through the ascending doors, from primitive pre-history, bereft of language and light, through the epic stages of colonialism, post-colonialism and enlightened hybridity. Leaving the exhibit, history is traversed backwards. As in colonial discourse, the movement forward in space is backwards in time: from erect, verbal consciousness and hybrid freedom – signified by the (not very free) white rabbit called "Free" which roams the exhibit – down through the historic stages of decreasing stature to the shambling, tongueless zone of the pre-colonial, from speech to silence, light to dark.

The paradox structuring the exhibit intrigues me, as it is a paradox, I suggest, that shapes the term "post-colonialism." I am doubly interested in the term, since the almost ritualistic ubiquity of "post-" words in current culture (post-colonialism, post-modernism, post-structuralism, post-cold war, post-marxism, post-apartheid, post-Soviet, post-Ford, post-feminism, post-national, post-historic, even post-contemporary) signals, I believe, a widespread, epochal crisis in the idea of linear, historical "progress."

In 1855, the year of the first imperial Paris Exposition, Victor Hugo announced: "Progress is the footsteps of God himself." "Post-colonial studies" has set itself against this imperial idea of linear time – the "grand idea of Progress and Perfectability", as Baudelaire called it. Yet the *term* "post-colonial," like the exhibit itself, is haunted by the very figure of linear "development" that it sets out to dismantle. Metaphorically, the term "post-colonialism" marks history as a series of stages along an epochal road from "the pre-colonial," to "the colonial," to "the post-colonial" – an unbidden, if disavowed, commitment to linear time and the idea of "development." If a theoretical tendency to envisage "Third World" literature as progressing from "protest literature," to "resistance literature," to "national literature" has been criticized as rehearsing the Enlightenment trope of sequential, "linear" progress, the term "post-colonialism" is questionable for the same reason. Metaphorically poised on the border between old and new, end and beginning, the term heralds the end of a world era, but within the same trope of linear progress that animated that era.

If "post-colonial" *theory* has sought to challenge the grand march of western historicism with its entourage of binaries (self–other, metropolis–colony, center–periphery, etc., the *term* "post-colonialism" nonetheless re-orients the globe once more around a single, binary opposition: colonial/post-colonial. Moreover, theory is thereby shifted from the binary axis of *power* (colonizer/colonized – itself inadequately nuanced, as in the case of women) to the binary axis of *time*, an axis even less productive of political nuance since it does not distinguish between the beneficiaries of colonialism (the ex-colonizers) and the casualties of colonialism (the ex-colonized). The "post-colonial scene" occurs in an entranced suspension of history, as if the definitive historical events have preceded us, and are not now in the making. If the theory promises a decentering of history in hybridity, syncreticism, multi-dimensional time, and so forth, the *singularity* of the term effects a re-centering of global history around the single rubric of European time. Colonialism returns at the moment of its disappearance.

The word "post," moreover, reduces the cultures of peoples beyond colonialism to *prepositional* time. The term confers on colonialism the prestige of history proper; colonialism is the determining marker of history. Other cultures share only a chronological, prepositional relation to a Euro-centered epoch that is over (post-), or not yet begun (pre-). In other words, the world's multitudinous cultures are marked, not positively by what distinguishes them, but by a subordinate, retrospective relation to linear, European time.

The term also signals a reluctance to surrender the privilege of seeing the world in terms of a singular and ahistorical abstraction. Rifling through the recent flurry of articles and books on "post-colonialism," I am struck by how seldom the term is used to denote *multiplicity*. The following proliferate: *"the* post-colonial condition," *"the* post-colonial scene," *"the* post-colonial intellectual," *"the* emerging disciplinary space of post-colonialism," "post-coloniality," *"the* post-colonial situation," "post-colonial space," *"the* practice of postcoloniality," "post-colonial discourse," and that most tedious, generic hold-all: *"the* post-colonial Other."

I am not convinced that one of the most important emerging areas of intellectual and political inquiry is best served by inscribing history as a single issue. Just as the singular category "Woman" has been discredited as a bogus universal for feminism, incapable of distinguishing between the varied histories and imbalances in power among women, so the singular category "post-colonial" may license too readily a panoptic tendency to view the globe within generic abstractions voided of political nuance. The arcing panorama of the horizon becomes thereby so expansive that international imbalances in power remain effectively blurred. Historically voided categories such as "the other," "the signifier," "the signified," "the subject," "the phallus," "the postcolonial," while having academic clout and professional marketability, run the risk of telescoping crucial geo-political distinctions into invisibility.

The authors of the recent book *The Empire Writes Back*, for example, defend the term "post-colonial literature" on three grounds: it "focuses on that relationship which has provided the most important creative and psychological impetus in the writing"; it expresses the "rationale of the grouping in a common past" and it "hints at the vision of a more liberated and positive future."[3] Yet the inscription of history around a single "continuity of preoccupations" and "a common past" runs the risk of a fetishistic disavowal of crucial international distinctions that are barely understood and inadequately theorized. Moreover, the authors decided, idio-syncratically to say the least, that the term "post-colonialism" should not be understood as everything that has happened *since* European colonialism, but rather everything that has happened from the very *beginning* of colonialism, which means turning back the clocks and unrolling the maps of "post-colonialism" to 1492, and earlier.[4] Whereupon, at a stroke, Henry James and Charles Brockden Brown, to name only two on their list, are awakened from their tête-à-tête with time, and ushered into "the post-colonial scene" alongside more regular members like Ngũgi wa Thiong'O and Salman Rushdie.

Most problematically, the historical rupture suggested by the preposition "post-" belies both the continuities and discontinuities of power that have shaped the legacies of the formal European and British colonial empires (not to mention the Islamic, Japanese, Chinese, and other imperial powers). Political differences *between* cultures are thereby subordinated to their temporal distance *from* European colonialism. But "post-colonialism" (like postmodernism) is unevenly developed globally. Argentina, formally independent of imperial Spain for over a century and a half, is not "post-colonial" in the same way as Hong Kong (destined to be independent of Britain only in 1997). Nor is Brazil "post-colonial" in the same way as Zimbabwe. Can most of the world's countries be said, in any meaningful or theoretically rigorous sense, to share a single "common past," or a single common "condition," called "the post-colonial condition," or "post-coloniality"? The histories of African colonization are certainly, in part, the histories of the collisions between European and Arab empires, and the myriad African lineage states and cultures. Can these countries now best be understood as shaped exclusively around the "common" experience of European colonization? Indeed, many contemporary African, Latin American, Caribbean and Asian cultures, while profoundly effected by colonization, are not necessarily *primarily* preoccupied with their erstwhile contact with Europe.

On the other hand, the term "post-colonialism" is, in many cases, prematurely celebratory. Ireland may, at a pinch, be "post-colonial," but for the inhabitants of British-occupied Northern Ireland, not to mention the Palestinian inhabitants of the Israeli Occupied Territories and the West Bank, there may be nothing "post" about colonialism at all. Is South Africa "post-colonial"? East Timor? Australia? By what fiat of historical amnesia can the United States of America, in particular, qualify as "post-colonial" – a term which can only be a monumental affront to the Native American peoples currently opposing the confetti triumphalism of 1992. One can also ask whether the emergence of Fortress Europe in 1992 may not signal the emergence of a new empire, as yet uncertain about the frontiers of its boundaries and global reach.

My misgivings, therefore, are not about the theoretical substance of "post-colonial theory", much of which I greatly admire. Rather, I wish to question the orientation of the emerging discipline and its concomitant theories and curricula changes, around a singular, monolithic term, organized around a binary axis of time rather than power, and which, in its premature celebration of the pastness of colonialism, runs the risk of obscuring the continuities and discontinuities of colonial and imperial power. Nor do I want to banish the term to some chilly, verbal Gulag; there seems no reason why it should not be used judiciously in appropriate circumstances, in the context of other terms, if in a less grandiose and global role.

One might distinguish theoretically between a variety of forms of global domination. *Colonization* involves direct territorial appropriation of another geo-political entity, combined with forthright exploitation of its resources and labor, and systematic interference in the capacity of the appropriated culture (itself not necessarily a homogeneous entity) to organize its dispensations of power. *Internal colonization* occurs where the dominant part of a country treats a group or region as it might a foreign colony. *Imperial colonization*, by extension, involves large-scale, territorial domination of the kind that gave late Victorian Britain and the European "lords of humankind" control over 85% of the earth, and the USSR totalitarian rule over Hungary, Poland and Czechoslovakia in the twentieth century.

Colonization, however, may involve only one country. Currently, China keeps its colonial grip on Tibet's throat, as does Indonesia on East Timor, Israel on the Occupied Territories and the West Bank, and Britain on Northern Ireland. Since 1915, South Africa has kept its colonial boot on Namibia's soil, first by League of Nations mandate, and then later in defiance of a UN General Assembly Resolution and a 1971 World Court Order. Only in 1990, having stripped Namibia of most of its diamond resources, was South Africa content to hand back the economically empty shell to the Namibians. Israel remains in partial occupation of Lebanon and Syria, as does Turkey of Cyprus. None of these countries can, with justice, be called "post-colonial".

Different forms of colonization have, moreover, given rise to different forms of de-colonization. Where *deep settler colonization* prevailed, as in Algeria, Kenya, Zimbabwe and Vietnam, colonial powers clung on with particular brutality.[5] Decolonization itself, moreover, has been unevenly won. In Zimbabwe, after a seven-year civil war of such ferocity that at the height of the war 500 people were killed every month and 40% of the country's budget was spent on the military, the Lancaster House Agreement choreographed by Britain in 1979 ensured that one-third of Zimbabwe's arable land (12 million hectares) was to remain in white hands, a minute fraction of the population.[6] In other words, while Zimbabwe gained formal political independence in 1980 (holding the chair of the 103-nation Non-Aligned Movement from 1986–1989) it has, economically undergone only *partial decolonization*.

Break-away settler colonies can, moreover, be distinguished by their formal independence from the founding metropolitan country, along with continued control over the appropriated colony (thus displacing colonial control from the metropolis to the colony itself). The United States, South Africa, Australia, Canada and New Zealand remain, in my view, break-away settler colonies that have not undergone decolonization, nor, with the exception of South Africa, are they likely to in the near future.

Most importantly, orienting theory around the temporal axis colonial/post colonial makes it easier *not* to see, and therefore harder to theorize, the continuities in international imbalances in *imperial* power. Since the 1940s, the United States' imperialism-without-colonies has taken a number of distinct forms (military, political, economic and cultural), some concealed, some half-concealed. The power of US finance capital and huge multi-nationals to direct the flows of capital, commodities, armaments and media information around the world can have an impact as massive as any colonial regime. It is precisely the greater subtlety, innovation and variety of these forms of imperialism that makes the historical rupture implied by the term "post-colonial" especially unwarranted.

"Post-colonial" Latin America has been invaded by the United States over a hundred times this century alone. Each time, the US has acted to install a dictatorship, prop up a puppet regime, or wreck a democracy. In the 1940s, when the climate for gunboat diplomacy chilled, United States' relations with Latin America were warmed by an economic imperial policy euphemistically dubbed "Good Neighborliness," primarily designed to make Latin America a safer backyard for the US' virile agribusiness. The giant cold-storage ships of the United Fruit Company circled the world, taking bananas from poor agrarian countries dominated by monocultures and the marines to the tables of affluent US housewives.[7] And while Latin America hand-picked bananas for the United States, the United States hand-picked dictators for Latin America. In Chile, Allende's elected, socialist government was overthrown by a US-sponsored military coup. In Africa, more covert operations such as the CIA assassination of Patrice Lumumba in Zaire had consequences as far-reaching.

In the cold war climate of the 1980s, the US, still hampered by the Vietnam syndrome, fostered the more covert military policy of "low intensity" conflicts (in El Salvador and the Philippines), spawning death squads and proxy armies (Unita in Angola, and the Contras in Nicaragua) and training and aiding totalitarian military regimes in anti-democratic, "counter-insurgency" tactics (El Salvador, Honduras, South Africa, Israel, and so forth). In Nicaragua in February 1990 the "vote of fear" of continuing, covert war with the US brought down the Sandinistas.

The US's recent fits of thuggery in Libya, Grenada and Panama, and most calamitously in Iraq, have every characteristic of a renewed military imperialism, and a renewed determination to revamp military hegemony in a world in which it is rapidly losing economic hegemony. The attacks on Libya, Grenada and Panama (where victory was assured) were practice runs for the new imperialism, testing both the USSR's will to protest, and the US public's willingness to throw off the Vietnam syndrome, permitting thereby a more blatant era of intervening in Third World affairs. At the same time, having helped stoke the first

Gulf War, the US had no intention of letting a new boy on the block assert colonial dominance in the region.

For three years before the second Gulf War, the US arms trade had been suffering a slump. After what one military industrialist gloatingly called the Gulf War's "giant commercial-in-the-sky," US arms sales have soared. Nonetheless, if the US had the political muscle to resuscitate a nearly defunct Security Council and strong-arm a consensus through the UN, and the military capacity to make short shrift of 150,000 Iraqi soldiers and an estimated 200,000 civilians in one month, it did not have the economic means to pay for the war. Saddled with its own vast debts, the US has been massively paid off in reimbursements (an estimated $50 billion) by Saudi Arabia, Kuwait, Japan and Germany, so that it now appears in fact to have profited from the war to the tune of $4–5 billion. At the same time, most of the estimated $20 billion necessary to restore Kuwait will go to western, largely US, companies. The war has thus made ever more likely a global security system based on military muscle, not political cooperation, policed by the US's high-tech, mercenary army (and perhaps NATO), moving rapidly around the world, paid for by Germany and Japan, and designed to prevent regional, Third World consensuses from emerging. Far from heralding the end of imperial intervention, the second Gulf War simply marks a new kind of interventionism. Not only is the term "post-colonial" inadequate to theorize these dynamics, it actively obscures the continuities and discontinuities of US power around the globe.

While some countries may be "post-colonial" with respect to their erstwhile European masters, they may not be "post-colonial" with respect to their new colonizing neighbours. Both Mozambique and East Timor, for example, became "post-colonial" at much the same time, when the Portuguese empire decamped in the mid-seventies, and both remain cautionary tales against the utopian promise and global sweep of the preposition "post." In East Timor, the beds of the Portuguese were scarcely cold before the Indonesians invaded, in an especially violent colonial occupation that has lasted nearly two decades. The colonial travail of the East Timoreans has gone largely unprotested by the UN – the familiar plight of countries whose pockets aren't deep, and whose voices don't carry.

In Mozambique, on the other hand, after three centuries of colonial drubbing, the Portuguese were ousted in 1975 by Frelimo, Mozambique's socialist independence movement. But across the border, white Rhodesians, resentful of Mozambique's independence and socialist promise, spawned the Mozambique National Resistance (MNR), a bandit army bent only on sowing ruin. After Zimbabwe itself became politically independent of Britain in 1980, the MNR has continued to be sponsored by South Africa. A decade of the MNR's killing-raids and South Africa's predations has subjected the country to a fatal blood-letting and displaced nearly two million people, in a war so catastrophic that Frelimo has been forced to renounce Marxism and consider shaking hands with the bandits. Now Mozambique is in every sense a country on its knees. What might have been a "post-colonial" showpiece has instead become the killing-fields of Southern Africa.

Yet neither the term "post-colonial" nor "neo-colonial" is truly adequate to account for the MNR. Neo-colonialism is not simply a repeat performance of colonialism, nor is it a slightly more complicated, Hegelian merging of "tradition" and "colonialism" into some new, historic hybrid. In recent years, the MNR has become inextricably shaped around local inter-ethnic rivalries, distinct religious beliefs, and notions of time and causality (especially ancestral intervention) which cannot be reduced to a western schema of linear time. More complex terms and analyses, of alternative times, histories and causalities, are required to deal with complexities that cannot be served under the single rubric "post-colonialism."

Singular universals such as "the post-colonial intellectual" obscure international disparities in cultural power, electronic technology and media information. The role of "Africa" in "post-colonial theory" is different from the role of "post-colonial theory" in Africa. In 1987, UNESCO calculated that Africa was spending only 0.3 percent of the world's $207 billion allocated to scientific research and development.[8] In 1975 the entire continent had only 180 daily newspapers, compared with 1,900 for the US, out of a world total of 7,970. By 1984, the number of African dailies dropped to 150, then staggered back to 180 in 1987 (the same figure as in 1955). In 1980, the annual production of films in the continent was 70. In contrast, the production of long films in Asia was 2,300 in 1965, and 2,100 in 1987.[9] The film industry in India remains the largest in the world, while Africa's share of TV receivers, radio transmitters and electronic hardware is miniscule.

The term "post-colonialism" is prematurely celebratory and obfuscatory in more ways than one. The term becomes especially unstable with respect to women. In a world where women do two-thirds of the world's work, earn 10 percent of the world's income, and own less than 1 percent of the world's property, the promise of "post-colonialism" has been a history of hopes postponed. It has generally gone unremarked that the national bourgeoisies and kleptocracies that stepped into the shoes of "post-colonial" "progress," and industrial "modernization" have been overwhelmingly and violently male. No "post-colonial" state anywhere has granted women and men equal access to the rights and resources of the nation-state. Not only have the needs of "post-colonial nations" been largely identified with male conflicts, male aspirations and male interests, but the very representation of "national" power rests on prior constructions of gender power. Thus even for Fanon, who at other moments knew better, both "colonizer" and "colonized" are unthinkingly male: "The look that the native turns on the settler is a look of lust . . . to sit at the settlers' table, to sleep in the settler's bed, with his wife, if possible. The colonized man is an envious man."[10] Despite most anti-colonial nationalisms' investment in the rhetoric of popular unity, most have served more properly to institutionalize gender power. Marital laws, in particular, have served to ensure that for women citizenship in the nation-state is mediated by the marriage relation, so that a woman's *political* relation to the nation is submerged in, and subordinated to, her *social* relation to a man through marriage.

The global militarization of masculinity and the feminization of poverty have thus ensured that women and men do not live "post-coloniality" in the same way, or share the same singular "post-colonial condition." In most countries, IMF and World Bank policy favored cash-cropping and capital surplus in the systematic interests of men, and formed a predictable pattern where men were given the training, the international aid, the machinery, the loans and cash. In Africa, women farmers produce 65–80 percent of all agricultural produce, yet do not own the land they work, and are consistently by-passed by aid programs and "development" projects.

The blame for women's continuing plight cannot be laid only at the door of colonialism, or footnoted and forgotten as a passing "neo-colonial" dilemma. The continuing weight of male economic self-interest and the varied undertows of patriarchal Christianity, Confucianism and Islamic fundamentalism continue to legitimize women's barred access to the corridors of political and economic power, their persistent educational disadvantage, the bad infinity of the domestic double day, unequal child care, gendered malnutrition, sexual violence, genital mutilation and domestic battery. The histories of these male policies, while deeply implicated in colonialism, are not reducible to colonialism, and cannot be understood without distinct theories of gender power.

Finally, bogus universals such as "the post-colonial woman" or "the post-colonial other" obscure relations not only between men and women, but among women. Relations between a French tourist and the Haitian woman who washes her bed linen are not the same as the relations between their husbands. Films like *Out Of Africa*, clothing chains like Banana Republic and perfumes like "Safari" all peddle neo-colonial nostalgia for an era when European women in brisk white shirts and safari green supposedly found freedom in empire: running coffee plantations, killing lions and zipping about the colonial skies in airplanes – an entirely misbegotten commercialization of white women's "liberation" that has not made it any easier for women of color to form alliances with white women anywhere, let alone parry criticisms by male nationalists already hostile to feminism.

How, then, does one account for the curious ubiquity of the preposition "post" in contemporary intellectual life, not only in the universities, but in newspaper columns and on the lips of media moguls? In the case of "post-colonialism," at least, part of the reason is its academic marketability. While admittedly another p-c word, "post-colonialism" is arguably more palatable and less foreign-sounding to skeptical deans than "Third World Studies." It also has a less accusatory ring than "Studies In Neo-colonialism," say, or "Fighting Two Colonialisms." It is more global, and less fuddy-duddy, than "Commonwealth Studies." The term borrows, moreover, on the dazzling marketing success of the term "post-modernism." As the organizing rubric of an emerging field of disciplinary studies and an archive of knowledge, the term "post-colonialism" makes possible the marketing of a whole new generation of panels, articles, books and courses.

The enthusiasm for "post-" words, however, ramifies beyond the corridors of the university. The recurrent, almost ritualistic incantation of the preposition "post" is a symptom, I believe, of a global crisis in ideologies of the future, particularly the ideology of "progress."
[. . .]

[. . .] there is some urgency in the need for innovative theories of history and popular memory, particularly mass-media memory. Asking what *single* term might adequately replace "post-colonialism," for example, begs the question of rethinking the global situation as a *multiplicity* of powers and histories, which cannot be marshalled obediently under the flag of a single theoretical term, be that feminism, marxism or post-colonialism. Nor does intervening in history mean lifting, again, the mantle of "progress" or the quill-pen of empiricism. "For the native," as Fanon said, "objectivity is always against him." Rather, a *proliferation* of historically nuanced theories and strategies is called for, which may enable us to engage more effectively in the politics of affiliation, and the currently calamitous dispensations of power. Without a renewed will to intervene in the unacceptable, we face being becalmed in an historically empty space in which our sole direction is found by gazing back, spellbound, at the epoch behind us, in a perpetual present marked only as "post."

Notes

1   Frantz Fanon, *The Wretched of the Earth*, Penguin: London, 1963, p. 29.
2   Gallery Brochure, "The Hybrid State Exhibit", Exit Art, 578 Broadway, New York (2 Nov.–14 Dec. 1991).
3   Bill Ashcroft, Gareth Griffiths and Helen Tiffin, *The Empire Writes Back: Theory and practice in post-colonial literatures*, Routledge: London, 1989, p. 24.
4   "We use the term 'post-colonial', however, to cover all the culture affected by the imperial process from the moment of colonization to the present day." ibid., p. 2.
5   During the Algerian war of resistance, over a million Algerians died out of a total of about 9 million.
6   Andrew Meldrum, the *Guardian*, Thursday, 25 April 1991, p. 13.
7   Cynthia Enloe, *Bananas, Beaches and Bases: Making Feminist Sense of International Politics*, University of Colorado Press: Berkeley, CA, 1989, ch. 6.
8   Davidson, op. cit., p. 670.
9   Kinfe Abraham, "The media crisis: Africa's exclusion zone", *SAPEM*, September 1990, pp. 47–9.
10 Fanon, op. cit., p. 30.

Chapter 85

Postmodernity, Postcoloniality, and African Studies

Tejumola Olaniyan

I know no African scholar – and, perhaps, very few scholars of Africa too – who would invoke the "posts" in my title without an automatic rush to qualification, if not outright dismissal. This reaction is entirely understandable. Postmodernity, a historical condition that is said to emerge out of the contradictions of over- developed modernity in Euro-America (Harvey 1990), can possibly not have much to say to societies upon whose backs that modernity was built and for whom it still remains a mirage today. We certainly have not forgotten Walter Rodney (1972) whose account of how Africa paid the exorbitant bills, both material and non-material, of European modernity, is still most perspicacious. As to "postcoloniality," whose literal meaning is time-space after colonialism, what greater evidence of its inapplicability to Africa can we find than the continent's world-historical debt peonage to its former colonizers, its chokehold by foreign-owned multinational corporations, and its invasion by ever more irresistible weapons of Euro-American cultural imperialism. Very few will disagree that all these amount to no less than colonialism in a different guise. Thus, while postmodernity clearly does not reference an African reality, postcoloniality which pretends to could only be at best a wish-fulfillment, and at worst, an easy, unjustified acquittal of Africa's guilty oppressor-colonizers, and a libelous denial of their destruction and ongoing exploitation of the continent. If postmodernity does not describe socio-historical conditions that obtain in Africa, then it is not logical for *postmodernism*, the discourses of self-constitution and self-understanding of postmodernity, to apply to the continent. By the same logic, *postcolonialism* references the discursive formations of contexts in which colonialism has ended. And that is not yet in Africa, as many scholars of Africa are wont to argue.

There are three major arguments against postmodernism from the perspective of its African critics: *its decentering of the subject, its privileging of culture,* and *its abstruse language.*

First published in *Postmodernism, Postcoloniality, and African Studies*, ed. Zine Magubane, pp. 39–53. Trenton, NJ: Africa World Press, 2003.

The subject that postmodernism decentered is the European subject, with a capital S: the subject that, for most of the last four centuries, made itself the center of reason and deified that reason. It yarned grand narratives of history and civilization, with Europe always at the center and others at the periphery. It organized the world into a hierarchical chain of being, which it then used to justify the imperialization and violent incorporation of much of the world into the orbit of the West. It is the exhaustion of the power of conviction of this Subject's self-serving account of the world that postmodernism underscores. If postmodernism is stoking the heart attack of the Western Subject, we can only expect that the African will be on the side of postmodernism by blocking all calls to the emergency ambulance. But postmodernism's deconstruction of the subject is both specific and general: not just the imperial European Subject but all putative claims to a subjecthood that would authorize or be the rallying point of knowledge or collective action or politics. This is where African critics, interested in constructing a resistant subject or identity against unending Western imperialism, part with postmodernism. One of my former teachers, who is African American, used to joke that non-Western peoples have long been attacking the master's exclusive and exclusionary privileged mansion with all sorts of weapons; when finally they succeeded in smashing down the doors – to subjectivity, to self-representation – the master, potbellied with satiation, came out, teeth-picking and belching, to claim that there was never anything of value in the mansion of the subject anyway. So, why are you guys trying to get in? The joke is meant to reveal postmodernism as no more than a hypocritical discourse, preemptively fashioned to salvage what remains of the fast fading cultural authority of the Western Story. Rejected also by the African critic are some of the ramifications of postmodernism's decentering of the subject such as a cynicism against all truth-claims, a suspicion of utopian strivings, and therefore a skepticism toward all political agendas, or, more polemically, an aversion toward politics.

The second argument against postmodernism is its exhorbitation of culture. In understanding relations of power, postmodernism emphasizes not so much actions or events, as the many meanings that are mapped upon such an action or event. And since it is in the realm of culture that meanings are produced, postmodernism focuses on the instruments used by culture to produce meanings, such as narrative, discourse, and other institutional regulators of symbolic transactions. It shows how these means of meaning-making are intrinsically tendentious. This feature of postmodernism has wrought a liberating havoc on those disciplines obsessed with epistemological realism and verifiability such as history, the social sciences, and the sciences. For postmodernism, a science experiment and its results are no more important than how the experiment is described and justified, and how the results are organized and set down for dissemination. In postmodernism, "objectivity" is not as saintly and impersonal as it used to be.

A corollary of postmodernism's privileging of culture is its concern with *subjectivity*, that is, the condition of having full consciousness of one's world and one's place/s in its many intricate networks. Postmodernism is concerned with subjectivity because it is in the context of cultural meanings that human beings develop a consciousness and sense of themselves in relation to others, immediate and remote. It holds that whoever controls the realm of cultural meanings controls the means of self-perception, and therefore, power. Now, one would expect that the postmodern "cultural turn" (Jameson 1998), with its effect of deconstructing objectivity, should please Africans who have been the victims of "objectivity" (Fanon 1968) for so long. However, many African critics see in postmodernism's cultural turn a *culturalism* which dehistoricizes culture, and demeans and sacrifices the concrete sociopolitical struggles which most African scholars believe to be where the solution to the continent's unending exploitation by the West lies. Most strands of African radical anti-imperialist thought do not consider culture to be a primary terrain of such struggle.

Finally, the abstruse language. This is the most widespread negative stereotype of postmodernism. Charges of abstruseness, and of turning theory into theoreticism, have always been the fate of self-consciously theoretical languages, and postmodernism, as the popular synonym for the current High Theory, perfectly fits the bill. The charge is to underscore postmodernism's elitist class character, and its disconnection with the lives of the masses for whom such language is nothing but another characteristic and incomprehensible indulgence on the part of university egg heads who do no real labor.

To its critics, postcolonialism is no more than appendage of postmodernism, and so shares the shortcomings of the latter. Its culpable name, which unacceptably proclaims the end of colonialism, its borrowing of obscure theoretical paradigms from postmodernism, and the fact that the Euro-American world, not the formerly colonized world, is the institutional center of its storm, are more evidence of its deserved damnation. The very concept "postcolonial" has been charged with abridging or warping time (the whole history of Empire is its purview), and squashing space (a homogenization that obliterates the historical specificities of the experience of colonization by different societies. The "post" is seen at best as tactless, or at worst, a conservative surrender to the illusory seductiveness of teleology, more condemnable given the fact of what is really not a cessation of empire, but the consolidation of what Harry Magdoff calls "informal empires" (Alavi and Shanin 1982: 25). Ngugi wa Thiong'o (1981: 25) forbiddingly describes this condition as a "more danger-ous cancer" than imperialism itself. Finally, "postcolonial" is charged with an unwitting Eurocentrism in privileging the colonial experience – and thereby the political and epistemological authority of Europe – as the master-key to reading the diverse histories and cultures of erstwhile imperialized African societies (McClintock 1992; Shohat 1992; Osundare 1993; Zeleza 1997; Sardar 1998).

The criticisms against postmodernism and postcolonialism in African studies have a logic all their own, and from that standpoint, many are unimpeachable. I suggest, however, that the originating logic, as well as many of the criticisms themselves, are faulty and need serious rethinking. If this is done, we will discover that rather than knee-jerk qualifications or out-right dismissals, we have more to simultaneously learn and unlearn from postmod-ernism and postcolonialism, and that the effects of these discursive formations on the practice of Africa's humanities have not on the whole been negative.

Take, for instance, postmodernism's deconstruction of the subject and its associated suspicion of all self-authorizing programs of knowledge or action. There are three funda-mental reasons why this is liberating for the African humanities. *First*, Africa has historically been the victim of the Western grand narrative. The long and agonizing stories of Africans' struggles to be considered "cultured" and "civilized," or to have "history" and be capable of "philosophizing," in a world in which the West colonized these concepts as descriptive of and applicable only to itself, are too well-known to be repeated here. Those struggles are centuries old, and as we all know, are sadly still ongoing. The postmodern debunking of the West as universal norm, and the authorization of multiple histories has given rise to a relativism that, while still requiring great vigilance on our part, is an advance worthy of notice. To take just one example, the struggle for the acceptance of oral tradition in the construction of African history was not finally won against a conservative history establishment until postmodernism came.

The related postmodern suspicion of all self-authorizing claims and agendas makes entrenched modes of resistance in Africa such as "anti-imperialism," "anti- neocolonialism," and the like, seriously suspect. I do not see this invitation to suspicion as a bad thing. My contention is that it is possible to reject grand narratives and still be anti- imperialist. The salutary effect of postmodernism in this regard is that it has desacralized African counter-grand narratives, such as nationalism and anti-imperialism, and shown that they can be no less repressive, politically and epistemologically, than the Western grand narratives they oppose. I have written in detail elsewhere how counter-discourses, while in many instances a decisive advance over dominant discourses, are nevertheless often still mired in the blindnesses of the hegemonic (Olaniyan 1995). The atrocities committed in the last 30 years by many African leaders in the name of the sacredness of the nation are still part of our contemporary history. What good a postmodern suspicion of truth-claims can do for us in this instance is to entrench a critical self-consciousness that is the enemy of all passions that would present themselves as unimpeachable.

In Nigeria during the mid-1980s, the really vocal and activist part of the modern civil society was constituted largely by a handful of independent press houses. By the late 1990s, there had been an explosion, literally, of all kinds of interest groups, more independent press houses, pro-democracy organizations, environmental groups, and more. This period also witnessed the explosion of non-governmental organizations (NGOs), a practice of intervention in Africa by Western governments and private organizations which attempted to bypass the unresponsive but repressive central state. Now, NGOs wholly owned and run by Africans, are very much a part of the African sociopolitical scene. Specifically in Nigeria, it was the pro-democracy groups and NGOs that were the bulwark of opposition to the late dictator General Sani Abacha. The coincidence between the percolation of postmodernism into Euro-American formal and informal foreign policy, and the explosive rise of all kinds of civil organizations with international contacts in many African countries, ought to be significant to astute watchers. Many of these civil organizations are liberal anti-imperialist, and are also against the tyranny, absolutism and utter lack of self- reflexivity of dominant African state structures. The ongoing exhaustion of the entrenched nationalist and state discourses in Africa is, on the whole, a salutary development, and part of the catalyst for that is the recent postmodern-like fracturing of the social-discursive space just described. All of this does not mean that I have forgotten that NGOs cannot in any way solve the problems of Africa, and that their thriving on the continent is more a symptom of the failure of the state than a solution. In some cases, it could even be argued that NGOs really decelerate the pace of social change by, in their typically reformist ways, offering the anodyne of scotchtape to cover huge cracks in the social system that might be more enduringly resolved through a decisive social crisis. Thus, my positive revisionary reading of the place of NGOs in the current crisis of the African state does not mean that I aim to completely overthrow the African radical image of them: representatives of the hypocrisy of western liberalism whose proboscis would suck you dry and then rub some Vaseline into the wound so that you can be available for more sucking. This reading stays until NGOs begin to seriously address the fundamental inequity that, at the global level, structures the relations between the West and Africa.

Second, and perhaps even more fundamental. The attack against postmodernism for circumscribing the emergence of an African subject, shows how very little we have been able to apprehend the fundamental philosophical tenets of the majority of our African societies. The European Enlightenment, and the grand narrative it fashioned, cannot be detached from its Christian, monotheistic context. The connection between the two is not often remembered, largely because the Enlightenment presented itself as secular. Its deep structure remained, however, deeply imbricated in a monotheistic faith and *modus operandi*, with its tyrannically absolutist and universalist claims. When postmodernism attacked the European grand narrative, it was merely striving for a metaphysic of egalitarianism, that was already the norm in our mostly polytheistic African cultures, with their non-proselytizing religions. Who is the scholar of Yoruba culture who will miss the close correlation between the hymns and odes and panegyrics and stories of Esu, the deity of the crossroads and guardian of chance, and the features that are now celebrated as "postmodern" (Ogundipe 1978; Gates 1988)? It is for its exasperatingly bewildering "postmodern" features, that the Christian missionaries translated the Christian Satan as Esu in their Yoruba version of the Bible. This was an incomparably effective rhetorical killing, as many of my generation grew up knowing Esu *first* as the Biblical Satan, and later on, with a little mental liberation from Christian missionary nonsense, reclaiming this deity of contingency. My point here is that the metaphysics of postmodernism are, in some respects, quite close to those of many African cultures.

Third, we must never forget to continually remind ourselves that the irruption of Africa that dissolved European empires in Africa, and buckled the ideologically smooth universalism of the West, is one of the main catalysts of the Western self-reexamination and self-call to epistemological humility that calls itself postmodernism. By no means has the battle been won, but increasingly, African voices are being heard in a manner and on a scale that Europe, before 1945, never imagined would ever be possible. From this perspective alone, we ought to be very actively interested in the discomfort, no matter how minor, our having a voice is causing our oppressors, so that we can know where to add more potent salt to the injury, to make it fester and become gangrenous enough to bring down the goliath.

The second argument against postmodernism is its exhorbitation of culture, the point that it is more interested in matters of discourse, meaning, interpretation, subjectivity, and understanding than in actual and concrete social and political struggles. In many regards, this is a statement that is excellent as a description, but meaningless as a reproach. As a reproach, it misses the mark and indicates an inability to properly specify the *character* of postmodernism. Postmodernism is a cultural/discursive practice, and not an economic or political discourse as such. Its primary concern is the transformation of thinking and subjectivity, meaning, and of the cultural field.

The realm of culture is, of course, linked to the economic and the political, but it is not by any means reducible to either. Several social and political theorists have underscored the crucial and irreducible significance of that realm in social struggles. Karl Marx, in the 1859 preface to *A Contribution to the Critique of Political Economy*, writes that in studying transformations wrought by a social revolution, "a distinction should always be made between the material transformation of the economic conditions of production, which can be determined with the precision of natural science, and *the legal, political, religious, aesthetic or philosophic – in short, ideological forms in which men become conscious of this conflict and fight it out*" (Kamenka 1983: 160; emphasis added). And as Gramsci (1971) has shown, it is *largely* through the organization of these "ideological forms" that a specific group or class alliance, at certain historical conjunctures, exercises that more enduring – because less obtrusive – form of authority called "hegemony" over the whole social formation. And our very own Amilcar Cabral (1980) repeatedly insisted, at the height of a war of national liberation against Portuguese colonialism, on the intensification of cultural-ideological resistance, and that success in this realm could ultimately help to reverse defeats in other areas, economic, political or military. The realm of cultural subjectivity is thus critical because it is "where the identity of individuals and groups is at stake, and where order in its broadest meaning is taking form. This is the realm in which culture and power are most closely intertwined" (Rabinow 1986: 260). This is the field, related to but *not* the economic or political *per se*, primarily occupied by postmodernism.

Having made the foregoing clarification, I should say that behind the relegation of the cultural is an implied assumption that any discourse must be fixated on the "political" to be considered as relevant in the study of Africa. This is an artificial circumscription of the multiple domains that must constitute Africa, as indeed other societies, at the level of epistemology. "Politics" or the "political" as such does not and cannot exhaust the meanings of Africa. There are other areas worthy of investigation and they need not be "obviously political" to be considered relevant. More fundamentally, the assumption that any trans-formation of culture depends solely on a basic restructuring and change in social and political relationships can no longer be taken as an absolute.

What the cultural turn has done for the African humanities is to open up the field of subjectification, that is, the field where identities are formed, to contestation and reconfig-uration. For me, to hold that meanings are multiple and every truth is questionable are not necessarily subversions of anti-imperialist humanities scholarship. On the contrary, they serve as perpetual reminders of the simple fact that all meanings and truths have interests attached to them, and the useful caution that they should never be seen as absolute. We all know how very easy it is for even radical passions and historically liberating truths to congeal quickly into crippling orthodoxies and apologia for tyranny. The cultural turn, authorizing a variety of approaches, has led to the production of all kinds of scholarship on Africa, four-fifths of which I strongly disagree with. But I would rather that there continue to be more, rather than less, scholarship on Africa. And this is not just because of Mao's famous "Let a thousand flowers bloom." It is simply that negative examples have their own real critical uses too, and that in my personal experience, I have learnt as much from good books as bad ones. I suppose this is the same for most of us, if only we listen more to our informed intuitions, after all, we often have clearer ideas of what not to do, than what to do.

As to the third and final criticism of postmodernism, that is, its elitist and abstruse language, there is very little to say. Intellectual discourse at the level of the university is always an elitist and rarefied discourse; it is by no means a discourse of or for the masses. It is simplistic, however, to argue that elitist discourse is thereby ineffective or that it contributes nothing to society. Many of us use computers, but I am certain only very few can read and understand the elementary language of software encoding. In my own language, Yoruba, there are deep, arcane forms that only those with special skills can speak or understand. I would be demeaning my own cultural tradition to mindlessly attack abstruse discourse, as if it is in only European theoretical discourses that you have that feature. There is no large and complex society in which there are no differentiated levels of discourse. The discourse of the masses is not the discourse of the elites, and this observation need not automatically carry with it a value judgment. As the reader can determine so far, I do not write abstruse language myself, but I think it is vapid romanticism to assume that transparency of discourse automatically confers relevance.

The objection to "postcolonial" as a category is a "new" crisis of naming that is all too painfully old and familiar. It is merely the latest in a long series of ill- fitting jackets, tailored to fit those Europe made into its significant victimized Others. We should perhaps start to wonder whether, epistemologically speaking, a condition of radical disjunction/incommensurability between (nomenclatural) "form" and "substance" is necessarily unhealthy for a subordinate(d) discourse, whose strategies of survival or resistance do not exclude, a priori, wile and guile. After all, even the most unforgiving critics of the term do not deny that a lot of relevant work is being done in its name. The historical fact still is that none of the terms invented for Africa has ever been acceptable across a wide spectrum of scholars. African societies were once "barbaric" or "backward" – the main ideological justification for the "colonizing/civilizing mission." With the wave (and euphoria) of decolonization after World War II, they became "emerging nations" – into Hegel's History, of course. "Underdeveloped societies" soon soured this atavistic optimism. Or appeared to. For the other rubrics that followed – "less developed societies," "developing societies" – were little different in orientation. With the crippling Cold War between the USSR and the USA, the nations became "nonaligned" or "third world," away from the two dominant grids. They were also, with increasing theoretical sophistication, "neo-colonial," "dependent," or the "periphery" of the "core." And in the heady, hopeful radical ferment of the 1970s in Africa, a reputable social scientist suggested "proletarian" countries (Ake 1978). The supposedly most radical of these representations – because it best foregrounds global structural inequalities – is "Third World," but it, too, has not escaped consistent ridicule and attack as an egregious insult, racist and demeaning, from many who live in the regions it is meant to describe.

And now on the ascendancy, "postcolonial." In conceptual fuzziness, "postcolonial" is thus positively in very good company. The crucial point, then, is this: these terms are contingent forms without any originary, essentialist content. Armed with this kind of affirmation, our unease with "post-colonial" ought to be accented differently.

Even while we insist that the term "postcolonial" account for its spatio-temporal manipulations at the expense of historical specificity, we must learn to be auto-critical about our own (investments in the) sacralization of such "specificity." Historical specificity is an identity that should be a staging, not a sacrosanct ground. There is nothing intrinsically radical or progressive about "doing" historical specificity; it is a chameleon that could also, when fetishized, take on the colors – and without necessarily dislodging our dominant positive stereotype of it – either of a coercive, ghettoizing (by the dominating), or a self-defeating, incestuous (by the dominated), relativism. And it will not do for me to simply say that it is tautological to argue that the term "postcolonial" privileges the colonial encounter and thus, European cognitive and political sway. (One wonders how the "privileging" could be different, since it is precisely the ravages and violations of that domination that are in specialized focus).

A more substantive point is that it is hardly a matter of choice for the ex-colonies, if we agree that "living," as a process in all its micro and macro details, is another name for confronting the myriad structural and institutional obstacles to that enterprise. For instance, I would not want the insurgent citizens of the "postcolonies" to give up their struggles against the characteristically tyrannical postcolonial States on the grounds that they, the insurgents, do not want to privilege European influence, since the *form* of these States remain largely Eurocentric.

I have gone this length *not* to defend postmodernism or postcolonialism, but to prod African scholars to rise up to the challenge of a discriminating, not facile, engagement with any and all strands of thought that impact/s African realities, no matter the origins of such discourses. By discriminating, I mean engagements that are not corrupted by any *apriori* conception of the relevance or otherwise of discourses because of where they come from. I mean engagements that foreground our *interests* rather than our *difference*, even if our interests ultimately include implications of our difference. There is a lot to disagree with in postmodernism, and there are absolutely no guarantees of its solidarity with our interests, outside of our constant vigilance and deliberate critical refashioning, so that what will matter in the end is not the discourse as such but the use we make of it. But then, we must grant that no discourse is homogenous in formation, and we cheapen our own intelligence when we make blanket condemnations. There is the aimless, flippant, incestuous, self-consuming practice of postmodernism which some scholars label "ludic," as well as a historically informed, socially conscious version I like to call earnest or critical postmodernism (Foster 1983). From the latter practice the study of Africa stands to gain a few insights; indeed, it is from this particular practice of postmodernism that the best of postcolonialism, in spite of ideological differences of particular articulations, has borrowed (Mudimbe 1988; Said 1993; Bhabha 1994; Jeyifo 1995; Ekpo 1995; Appiah 1992; Spivak 1999).

References

Ake, Claude. *Revolutionary Pressures in Africa*. London: Zed Press, 1978.

Alavi, Hamza and Teodor Shanin. *Introduction to the Sociology of "Developing Societies."* New York: Monthly Review Press, 1982.

Appiah, Kwame A. *In My Father's House: Africa in the Philosophy of Culture*. New York: Oxford University Press, 1992.

Bhabha, Homi. *The Location of Culture*. New York: Routledge, 1994.

Cabral, Amilcar. *Unity and Struggle: Speeches and Writings*. Translated by M. Wolfers. London: Heinemann, 1980.

Ekpo, Denis. "Towards a Post-Africanism: Contemporary African Thought and Postmodernism." *Textual Practice* 9.1 (1995): 121–35.

Fanon, Frantz. *The Wretched of the Earth*. New York: Grove Press, 1968.

Foster, Hal. *The Anti-Aesthetic: Essays on Postmodern Culture*. Port Townsend, WA: Bay Press, 1983.

Foucault, Michel. *Politics, Philosophy, Culture: Interviews and Other Writings 1977–1984*. Translated by Alan Sheridan, et al. New York: Routledge, 1988.

Gates, H. L., Jr. *The Signifying Monkey: A Theory of Afro-American Literary Criticism*. New York: Oxford University Press, 1988.

Gramsci, Antonio. *Selections from the Prison Notebooks*. Translated by. Q. Hoare and G.N. Smith. New York: International Publishers, 1971.

Harvey, David. *The Condition of Postmodernity*. Cambridge: Basil Blackwell, 1990.

Jameson, Frederic. *The Cultural Turn: Selected Writings on the Postmodern 1983–1998*. London: Verso, 1998.

Jeyifo, Biodun. "Oguntoyinbo: Modernity and the 'Rediscovery' Phase of Postcolonial Literature." *Yearbook of Comparative & General Literature* 43 (1995): 98–109.

Kamenka, Eugene, ed. *The Portable Karl Marx*. New York: Penguin, 1983.

McClintock, Anne. "The Angel of Progress: Pitfalls of the Term 'Post-Colonialism.'" *Social Text* 31/32 (1992): 84–98.

Mudimbe, V. Y. *The Invention of Africa: Gnosis, Philosophy, and the Order of Knowledge*. Bloomington: Indiana University Press, 1988.

Ngugi wa Thiong'O. *Writers in Politics*. London: Heinemann, 1981.

Ogundipe, Ayodele. "Esu Elegbara, the Yoruba God of Chance and Uncertainty: A Study in Yoruba Mythology." PhD diss., Indiana University, 1978.

Olaniyan, Tejumola. "Afrocentrism." *Social Dynamics* 21.2 (Summer 1995): 91–105.

Osundare, Niyi. *African Literature & the Crisis of Post- Structuralist Theorising*. Ibadan: Options Book and Information Services, 1993.

Rabinow, Paul. "Representations Are Social Facts: Modernity and Postmodernity in Anthropology." In *Writing Culture: The Poetics and Politics of Ethnography*, edited by J. Clifford and G. E. Marcus. Berkeley: University of California Press, 1986.

Rodney, Walter. *How Europe Underdeveloped Africa*. Washington, DC: Howard University Press, 1972.

Said, Edward W. *Culture and Imperialism*. New York: Vintage, 1993.

Shohat, Ella. "Notes on the 'Post- Colonial.'" *Social Text* 31/32 (1992): 99–113.

Spivak, Gayatri C. *A Critique of Postcolonial Reason: Toward a History of the Vanishing Present*. Cambridge: Harvard University Press, 1999.

Zeleza, Paul Tiyambe. "Fictions of the Postcolonial: A Review Article." *CODESRIA Bulletin* 2 (1997): 15–19.

Chapter 86

Postcolonialism and Postmodernism

Ato Quayson

The terms 'postcolonialism' and 'postmodernism' are both extremely elusive to classify and the attempt to bring them together might be thought only to compound the difficulties further. For some critics, any attempt to fuse the two in a common theoretical inquiry is bound to occlude serious problems of the degree to which the unfinished business of late capitalism differently affects postmodern and postcolonial conditions. More crucially, it is also argued that the postmodern is part of an ensemble of the hierarchizing impulse of Western discourses, and that even though it hints at pluralism and seems to favour an attack on hegemonic discourses, it is ultimately a-political and does not feed into larger projects of emancipation. To collocate the two, then, is somehow to disempower the postcolonial, which is conceived to be more concerned with pressing economic, political and cultural inequalities (Sangari, 1987; Tiffin, 1988). Indeed, for some commentators, such as the Nigerian Denis Ekpo, postmodernism is nothing but another stage in the West's crisis of consciousness:

> The crisis of the subject and its radical and violent deflation – the focal point of postmodern critique – are logical consequences of the absurd self-inflation that the European subjectivity had undergone in its modernist ambition to be the salt of the earth, the measure and master of all things.
>
> For cultures (such as ours) that neither absolutized, i.e. deified, human reason in the past nor saw the necessity for it in the present, the postmodern project of de-deification, de-absolutization of reason, of man, of history, etc., on the one hand, and of a return to, or a rehabilitation of, obscurity, the unknown, the non-transparent, the paralogical on the other hand, cannot at all be felt like the cultural and epistemological earthquake that it appears to be for the European man. In fact, it cannot even be seen as a problem at all ... [W]hen such a being settles for the indeterminate, the paradoxical, the strange and absurd, it is probably because he bears no more resemblance to the man as we know him, especially here in Africa; he is a post-man whose society, having overfed him and spoilt him, has delivered him over to irremediable boredom. Nothing therefore, stops the African from viewing the celebrated postmodern condition a little

First published in *Postcolonialism: Theory, Practice or Process?*, pp. 132–41. Cambridge: Polity, 2000.

sarcastically as nothing but the hypocritical self-flattering cry of the bored and spoilt children of hypercapitalism.

(Ekpo, 1995)

For Ekpo postmodernism has to be seen as the hubristic consequence of a desire to dominate the world, one that, linked to the universalizing rationality of science and anthropology, has to face its own unravelling when confronted by the loss of empire. For critics such as Hutcheon (1989) and Connor (1997: 263–8), however, there is a productive way of seeing the two as mutually reinforcing. The two may be brought together in common thematic, rhetorical and strategic concerns, especially as these are brought to bear on questions of marginality. And so an affinity of concerns and strategies has been deemed applicable on behalf of both terms, at least in the area of literary studies.

In this chapter, I take up the relation between postmodernism and postcolonialism. As in previous chapters where two seemingly opposed concepts or discourses have been at issue, my emphasis will be on exploring the conjuncture between the two and their mutual illumination of conditions in the contemporary world. After a first section in which I identify some of the main concerns of postmodernism, I move, via a brief recall of some central concepts of postcolonialism, to merge the two and to explore postcolonialism *as* postmodernism, and vice versa. To aid in the dialectical mediation of the two, I look first at questions of identity under the pressure of images of luxury under late capitalist image culture (but whose roots, I argue, can be traced back into the period of colonialism). The second site on which I try to show the relevance of the two is in the area of media representations of race and otherness that are focalized through programmes such as *The X-Files*. By linking police veridical methods to questions of otherness, normally coded as the esoteric, *The X-Files* produces a peculiar affect that has to do with law and order in the cityscape that is concomitantly related to discourses of race and class.

The Concerns of Postmodernism

Postmodernism is related to a literary and philosophical tradition of representation which could be said to have its own peculiar historical and social trajectory in Western thought. Some postmodernist critics maintain that no reality can be thought of outside the way in which it is represented, and that any attempt to do so is to ignore the implicatedness of any perspective within the very object that is being described and vice versa (see, for instance, Natoli, 1997: 5–8, 21–5). Because the desire of what passes under the rubric of postcolonial theory is frequently concerned with representational discourses, postcolonialism also regularly takes representations as the primary target of analysis, with material conditions being accessed only insofar as they can be related in varying ways to representational regimes. A simple way of viewing this similarity would be to see both theoretical terms as being the descendants of what has been called the 'linguistic turn' in the social sciences and humanities, but this approach is not always helpful as it does not take account of the different emphases the two areas place on the relation between representation and a possible praxis, something to which we shall attend more fully in the third part of this chapter.

There are other areas of perceived overlap between them. The shared prefix 'post' in postcolonialism and postmodernism aligns them both to similar problematics of temporal sequence and transcendence in relation to their second terms, colonialism and modernism. The relation of temporal or other supersession raises problems of continuity and rupture for both terms, something which has been pointed out in different directions by critics alert to the easy triumphalism inherent in such 'posts'. Alex Callinicos (1989) shows how much the definitions of postmodernism actually reproduce definitions that had been applied to high modernism, while Anne McClintock (1992) provides a stimulating critique of postcolonialism and shows how much, in its implicit temporal trajectory, it ends up reproducing elements of Enlightenment notions of progress which it seems inclined to challenge. On the other hand, the 'ism' in both indicates their shared mutuality as second-order meditations, which, even though not coalescing into clear-cut ideologies, nonetheless seek to distinguish themselves from central positions in their various fields of inquiry. Both are thought to be second-order meditations upon real (and imagined) conditions in the contemporary world, and are to be taken seriously as contributing to an understanding of the world in which we live.

A fruitful way to proceed in defining the potential conjunctures and distinctions between the two terms is to attend to their different theoretical inspirations and ultimate social referents. As a means of mapping out the theoretical terrain of postmodernism, it is perhaps best to typify it according to a number of regular concerns. These concerns get different treatment in the hands of different critics, and there are bound to be disagreements on what things are most representative of the postmodernist paradigm.

A key area of dispute is how postmodernism is to be related to modernism. Ihab Hassan, one of the earliest commentators on postmodernism, addresses the question by schematically discussing the differences between modernism and postmodernism. He sets out the differences in the form of a table (1985: 123–4), part of which is reproduced below:

Modernism	*Postmodernism*
romanticism/Symbolism	paraphysics/Dadaism
form (conjunctive, closed)	antiform (disjunctive/open)
purpose	play
design	chance
hierarchy	anarchy
mastery/logos	exhaustion/silence
art object/finished work	process/performance/happening
distance	participation
creation/totalization/synthesis	decreation/deconstruction/antithesis
presence	absence
centering	dispersal
genre/boundary	text/intertext
root/depth	rhizome/surface
interpretation/reading	against interpretation/misreading
narrative/grande histoire	anti-narrative/petite histoire
master code	idiolect
paranoia	schizophrenia
origin/cause	difference-différance/trace
determinacy	indeterminacy
God the Father	The Holy Ghost
transcendence	immanence

These are mainly stylistic oppositions and it runs the danger, as Harvey (1989) has pointed out, of reducing complex relations to simple polarizations. What Harvey shows in his discussion of this table in the context of the wider questions of definition more generally is that Hassan draws on a variety of fields as diverse as linguistics, anthropology, philosophy, rhetoric, political science and theology in setting up the distinctions (1989: 42–65). Thus, Hassan's table attempts to encompass all aspects of contemporary society and culture and to show how elements within them distinguish them from modernism and mark them out as postmodernist. These schematic polarizations, though useful as a starting point are by no means beyond dispute. In the area of architecture, for instance, there have been disputes about the ways in which contemporary buildings are either modernist or postmodernist. One such disagreement has been between Charles Jencks and Frederic Jameson on the status of John Portman's Bonaventure Hotel, with the first seeing the hotel as late modernist and the second interpreting it as postmodernist (see Jencks, 1980: 15, 70; Jameson, 1991: 38–45).

As can be seen from the debates on terminology, the discussion of what constitutes postmodernism often highlights borrowings from linguistic metaphors and their application to social and cultural discourses. Indeed, the genealogy of postmodernism has to be traced to the poststructuralism(s) that proliferated in the 1960s. For some, postmodernism is the operationalization of concepts developed initially within poststructuralism. At a rather basic level, it is the split in language between the sign and its referent, the understanding that language does not actually name an objective reality that has acted as the main import from poststructuralism into postmodernism. This split between sign and referent is then taken also to be homologous with a series of other splits, such as those between history and its narrative representation, and between the author's intention and the meaning(s) of the text.

At one level, then, postmodernism can be typified as a vigorously anti-systemic mode of understanding, with pluralism, borders and multiple perspectives being highlighted as a means of disrupting the centralizing impulse of any system. This in itself has a fascinating history in Western philosophy and has been discussed by Robert C. Holub (1995) in terms of the ways in which, from the period of German Romanticism, the maxim, the apothegm, the aphorism, the anecdote and the essay were used as a discursive means of expressing the irreducibility of human subjectivity to totalized frameworks. Holub analyses this with reference to three historical moments in Western philosophy: the elevation of the fragment into a legitimate literary and philosophical genre in the early writings of Friedrich Schlegel and Novalis; the scrupulous plurality in the thought of Friedrich Nietzsche and his attempts to take apart the fundamental categories of Western thought through various attacks on conceptions of the subject, value, representation, causality, truth-value and system; and, finally, the critique of totality expressed in poststructuralist thought. Holub comes to two important conclusions in his account. The first is that the three phases have different understandings of totality. For the Romantics he discusses, the fragment, though seeming to stand in contrast to any totalized whole, was thought to be capable of capturing the essence of totality. Thus the fragment was ultimately itself totalized and wound up being a 'religiously recuperated totality' (p. 89). In Nietzsche's work, on the other hand, it is evident that his robust attacks on totality are themselves undergirded by an implicit impulse towards totalization. This is best seen in the oppositions in the antagonistic value scales he frequently sets up in the course of his philosophizing, which he labels variously the Dionysian and the Apollonian or Socratic, the Greek and the Judaco-Christian, or describes by the oppositions good v. bad and good v. evil. Holub notes that on all such scales two common features are evident: the first term is always valorized over the second, and the second and non-favored designation or category is viewed as an 'outgrowth of sickness, deceit, deception, or an illicit attempt to gain and secure power' (p. 94). In poststructuralist thought, exemplified for Holub by the work of Lyotard, the same entanglement with a totalizing impulse is evident, particularly in Lyotard's implicit claim to oversee all historical development while tracing the factors that have led to the postmodernist loss of belief in metanarratives (p. 98). The important thing for us here is not so much whether Holub's own account fully explicates the central anti-systemic impulses behind postmodernism or not, but that historically, the anti-systemic focus on fragments and other forms of apodietic discourses has been related to specific historical and aesthetic configurations.

Jean François Lyotard in his book *The Postmodern Condition* (1984), provides another dimension to the anti-systemic disposition in postmodernism. Among other things, Lyotard argues that both scientific knowledge and ordinary anthropological knowledge are governed by narrative. However, there is a historical break from about the eighteenth century, when science suppresses forms of knowledge that depend upon narrative. The crucial distinction comes when the mode of assigning truth-value in scientific knowledge is set apart from the ways in which such assignings are achieved through narrative in everyday knowledge. For Lyotard, the central feature of the postmodern condition is an incredulity towards meta-narratives produced by science, Marxism and Enlightenment theories of progress, and one of the ways in which the postmodern is set to counter the institutions and discourses that seek to validate such metanarratives is by way of 'the atomization of the social into flexible networks of language games' (pp. 17ff). Lyotard's position might be fruitfully aligned to that of the Frankfurt School's contention that scientific universalism comes at the price of the peripheralization if not distortion of specificities. For postmodernism, it is precisely this problematic excess that is widened and rendered into the dominant epistemological truth of existence under late capitalism, with a number of strategies produced to support this key informing premise. These include a focus on indeterminacy, ambiguity and deferral; on the deliberate fragmentation and misarticulation of the text, whether this is conceived of as social or literary; on the proliferation of aporias where meaning is deliberately made unretrievable; and on a carefully parodic style that appropriates everything from tradition, history and other genres and respects nothing. There is a focus on surfaces, on play, on the dissolution of boundaries and on narrative and other jump-starts that do not necessarily lead anywhere. The key theoretical terms in postmodernism are dissemination, dispersal, indeterminacy, hyper-reality, normless pastiche, bricolage, *différance*, aporia, play and suchlike.

The third major concern of postmodernism to be highlighted in our account has to do with the way in which the contemporary condition of globalized economics and culture is interpreted. Again following on from the implications of the linguistic turn already mentioned, postmodernist thinkers have attacked economistic models of interpretation of social reality in favour of more attention to representation. Marxism was the prime candidate for critique, and the nature of the postmodernist rereading of Marx is best seen in the work of Jean Baudrillard. Classical Marxism has a three-tier interpretation of the growth of the market and its central feature, exchange-value. For Marx, the phase of industrial production is that in which things are produced primarily for exchange; use-value becomes secondary to exchange-value, unlike the case that might be thought to have pertained under feudalism, where only a small proportion of what was produced in handicrafts, agricultural products etc. was available for exchange. The third phase discussed by Marx is when abstract values such as love, virtue and knowledge, previously thought to be immune from market forces, themselves enter into the realm of exchange-value. For Baudrillard, in works like *The Mirror of Production* (1973) and *The Orders of Simulacra* (1983), it is no longer possible or desirable to separate the second from the third stage since in the 'post-industrial world' (Bell, 1973) all abstract human qualities, images and representations have become part of the economic world. Thus Baudrillard argues that a 'political economy of the sign' has come to predominate in contemporary life, to the degree that all reality, including the economic, is ultimately understandable in relation to signs. Television, the media and popular culture then become significant areas of analysis for postmodernists because it is in these areas that the economy of the sign is best seen in its varying operations.

This post-industrial scenario is thought to proliferate a number of important social and cultural features. As David Harvey puts it in *The Condition of Postmodernity*:

> Postmodernism also ought to be looked at as mimetic of social, economic, and political practices in society. But since it is mimetic of different facets of those practices it appears in very different guises. The superimposition of different worlds in many a postmodern novel, worlds between which an uncommunicative 'otherness' prevails in a space of coexistence, bears an uncanny relationship to the increasing ghettoization, disempowerment, and isolation of poverty and minority populations in the inner cities of both Britain and the United States.
>
> (1989: 113–14)

Harvey contextualizes this within a larger discussion of shifts in economic patterns. Like Baudrillard, he believes that postmodernity is due to the vast assimilation of more and more areas of life to the logic of the marketplace in place of the clear division of economic interest between labour and capital along with clear patterns of social antagonism and identification. But unlike Baudrillard, he focuses intently on the material and social referents that might be thought to undergird the economy of the sign in the first place. There is now a 'space–time' compression brought on by accelerations in travel and communications. Under these conditions, production is now organized on a global scale, with the manufacturing process being spread out across many countries and plants, with each being responsible for a minor part of the finished product. This contrasts sharply with the model he describes as exemplified in the car-maker Ford, where cars of the same make were made in the same plant and distributed to thousands of consumers all over the world. Such a form of production was centralized, dedicated to the mass production of minimally varied items, and was driven by economies of scale demanding and providing stable and continuous patterns of employment. In the post-Fordist era, economies of scale are replaced by economies of scope, where shifts in demands of taste and fashion are met by increased differentiation in the product (Harvey, 1989: 125ff). Within such contexts, and given the 'uncommunicative otherness' that reflects the ghettoization of minority populations, one then sees how multiculturalism becomes the 'praxis' by which a sense of identity is negotiated within a seemingly incomprehensible postmodern social realm.[1]

Some of the overlap between the anti-systemic concerns of postmodernism and those of postcolonialism can be gleaned from a definition of postcolonialism advanced by Homi Bhabha:

> Postcolonial criticism bears witness to the unequal and uneven forces of cultural representation involved in the contest for political and social authority within the modern world order. Postcolonial perspectives emerge from the colonial testimony of Third World countries and the discourses of 'minorities' within the geopolitical divisions of east and west, north and south. They intervene in those ideological discourses of modernity that attempt to give a hegemonic 'normality' to the uneven development and the differential, often disadvantaged, histories of nations, races, communities, peoples. They formulate their critical revisions around issues of cultural difference, social authority, and political discrimination in order to reveal the antagonistic and ambivalent moments within the 'rationalizations' of modernity. To bend Jürgen Habermas to our purposes, we could also argue that the postcolonial project, at the most general theoretical level, seeks to explore those social pathologies – 'loss of meaning, conditions of anomie' – that no longer simply cluster around class antagonism, [but] break up into widely scattered historical contingencies.
>
> (Bhabha, 1992: 437)

Lyotard's understanding of the incredulity towards metanarratives that he argues defines postmodernism is evident in Bhabha's formulation here, with the difference that Bhabha's formulation seeks to highlight the fight against perceived inequalities as central to postcolonialism.

Differences between postmodernism and postcolonialism seem pronounced when the their different social referents are disentangled from their representational domains and brought out into the open. Postmodernism references a particular socio-cultural configuration in the West and theorizes globalization from an essentially Western standpoint, generalizing about global economics and culture as they are seen from the vantage point of the Western metropolis. As has been noted earlier, postmodernity is the era of surfaces, of the flattening out of affect, of multiple and shifting subjectivities, and of the total subordination of the real under the irreality of the images generated by visual culture under capitalism. And yet, on the other hand, one of the central problems which brings the two closer is on the question of the double vision that a peripheral existence in the world engenders. This doubleness can be theorized in many ways. Du Bois provides something of a significant lead in the area of African American subjectivity when he writes in 'The Souls of Black Folk' (1997) that the African American is a product of double consciousness:

> It is a peculiar sensation, this double-consciousness, this sense of always looking at one's self through the eyes of others, of measuring one's soul by the tape of a world that looks on in amused contempt and pity. One feels his twoness, – an American, a Negro; two souls, two thoughts, two unreconciled strivings; two warring ideals in one dark body, whose dogged strength alone keeps it from being torn asunder.
>
> (1997: 615)

Coming from different theoretical and personal inspirations, writers such as Frantz Fanon in *Black Skin, White Masks* (1967) and Ngugi Wa Thiong'O in *Decolonizing the Mind* (1986) and others have also theorized the same idea in postcolonialism, both in the domain of subjectivity and in that of language more generally. In all these texts, a seeming situation of ontological crisis is ultimately traceable to material conditions. But their material conditions are mediated through images and perceptions and entangled in a series of discourses that attempt to alienate the racialized consciousness from itself and obscure the conditions that sustain the ontological split in the first place.

Note

1   For accounts of how multiculturalism has become the preferred praxis of postmodernism, but for critical accounts, see Žižek (1997); Mercer (1992); McLaren (1994).

References

Baudrillard, Jean. (1983). *The Orders of Simulacra. Simulations*. Paul Foss, Paul Patton and Philip Bleitchman, trans. New York: Semiotext(e).

Bhabha, Homi K. (1992). "Postcolonial Criticism." *Redrawing the Boundaries: The Transformation of English and American Literary Studies*, S. Greenblatt and G. Dunn, eds., Modern Languages Association of America.

Callinicos, Alex. (1989). *Against Postmodernism: A Marxist Critique*. Cambridge: Polity.

Connor, Steven. (1997). *Postmodernist Culture: An Introduction to Theories of the Contemporary*. Oxford: Blackwell.

Ekpo, Denis. (1995). "Towards a post-Africanism: contemporary African thought and postmodernism." *Textual Practice* 9.1, 121–35.

Eze, Emmanuel. (1997). "The Colour of Reason: The Idea of "Race" in Kant's Anthropology." *Postcolonial African Philosophy: A Critical Reader*, Emmanuel Eze, ed. Oxford: Blackwell, 103–40.

Fanon, Frantz. (1967). *Black Skin, White Masks*. Charles Lam Markham, trans. New York: Grove Press.

Farias, P. F. de Moraes and Karin Barber. (1990). *Self-assertion and Brokerage: Early Cultural Nationalism in West Africa*. Birmingham: Centre of West African Studies.

Harvey, David. (1989). *The Condition of Postmodernity*. Oxford: Blackwell.

Hassan, Ihab. (1985). "The Culture of Postmodernism." *Theory, Culture and Society* 2.3, 119–32.

Holub, Robert C. (1995). "Fragmentary Totalities and Totalized Fragments: On the Politics of Anti-Systemic Thought." *Postmodern Pluralism and Concepts of Totality*. J. Hermand, ed. New York: Peter Lang, pp. 83–104

Hutcheon, Linda. (1988). *A Poetics of Postmodernism: History, Theory, Fiction*. London: Routledge.

Jameson, Frederic (1991). *Postmodernism, Or, The Cultural Logic of Late Capitalism*. London: Verso.

Jencks, Charles. (1980). *Late Modern Architecture*. London: Academy Editions.

Lyotard, Jean-François. (1984). *The Postmodern Condition: A Report on Knowledge*. Manchester: Manchester University Press.

McLaren, Peter. (1994). "White Terror and Oppositional Agency: Towards a Critical Multiculturalism." *Multiculturalism: A Critical Reader*. D. T. Goldberg, ed. Oxford: Blackwell, 45–74

Mercer, Kobena. (1992). "'1968': Periodizing Postmodern Politics and Identity." In *Cultural Studies*. L. Grossberg, C. Nelson and P. Treichler, eds. London: Routledge, 424–37

Murphet, Julian. (1998). "Noir and the Racial Unconscious." *Screen* 39.1, 22–35.

Natoli, Joseph. (1997). *A Primer to Postmodernity*. Oxford: Blackwell.

Wa Thiong'O, Ngugi. (1986). *Decolonizing the Mind*. London: James Currey.

Zizek, Slavoj (1997). "Multiculturalism, or, The Cultural Logic of Multinational Capitalism." *New Left Review*, 22.5, 29–51.

Chapter 87

Is the Post- in Postmodernism the Post- in Postcolonial?

Kwame Anthony Appiah

Tu t'appelais Bimbircokak
Et tout était bien ainsi
Tu es denvenu Victor-Emile-Louis-Henri-Joseph
Ce qui
Autant qu'il m'en souvienne
Ne rappelle point ta parenté avec
Roqueffelère

Yambo Ouologuem, "A Mon Mari"

In 1987, the Center for African Art in New York organized a show entitled "Perspectives: Angles on African Art." The curator, Susan Vogel, had worked with a number of "cocurators," whom I list in order of their appearance in the table of contents of the exhibition catalogue: Ekpo Eyo, quondam director of the department of antiquities of the National Museum of Nigeria; William Rubin, director of the department of painting and sculpture at the Museum of Modern Art and organizer of its controversial exhibit, "Primitivism and Twentieth-Century Art"; Romare Bearden, African-American painter; Ivan Karp, curator of African ethnology at the Smithsonian; Nancy Graves, European-American painter, sculptor, and filmmaker; James Baldwin, who surely needs no qualifying glosses; David Rockefeller, art collector and friend of the mighty; Lela Kouakou, Baule artist and diviner from the Ivory Coast (this a delicious juxtaposition, richest and poorest, side by side); Iba N'Diaye, Senegalese sculptor; and Robert Farris Thompson, Yale professor and African and African-American art historian.[1] In her introductory essay, Vogel describes the process of selection used to pick artworks for the show. The one woman and nine men were each offered a hundred-odd photographs of "African art as varied in type and origin, and as high in quality, as we could manage" and asked to select ten for the show. Or, I should say more exactly, this is what was offered to eight of the men. For Vogel adds that "in the case of the Baule artist, a man familiar only with the art of his own people, only Baule objects were placed in the pool of photographs" (P, p. 11). At this point we are directed to a footnote to the essay, which reads:

First published in *Critical Inquiry* 17.2 (Winter 1991): 336–44, 346–50, 352–4.

Showing him the same assortment of photos the others saw would have been interesting, but confusing in terms of the reactions we sought here. Field aesthetics studies, my own and others, have shown that African informants will criticize sculptures from other ethnic groups in terms of their own traditional criteria, often assuming that such works are simply inept carvings of their own aesthetic tradition. [P, p. 17 n. 2]

I shall return to this irresistible footnote in a moment. But let me pause to quote further, this time from the words of David Rockefeller, who would surely never "criticize sculptures from other ethnic groups in terms of [his] own traditional criteria," discussing what the catalogue calls a "Fanti female figure":

I own somewhat similar things to this, and I have always liked them. This is a rather more sophisticated version than the ones that I've seen, and I thought it was quite beautiful. . . . the total composition has a very contemporary, very Western look to it. It's the kind of thing, I think, that goes very well with . . . contemporary Western things. It would look very good in a modern apartment or house. [P, p. 138]

We may suppose that Rockefeller was delighted to discover that his final judgment was consistent with the intentions of the sculpture's creators. For a footnote to the earlier checklist – the list of artworks ultimately chosen for the show – reveals that the Baltimore Museum of Art desires to "make public the fact that the authenticity of the Fante figure in its collection has been challenged." Indeed, work by Doran Ross suggests this object is almost certainly a modern piece produced in my hometown of Kumasi by the workshop of a certain Francis Akwasi, which "specializes in carvings for the international market in the style of traditional sculpture. Many of its works are now in museums throughout the West, and were published as authentic by Cole and Ross" (yes, the same Doran Ross) in their classic catalogue, *The Arts of Ghana* (P, p. 29).

But then it is hard to be *sure* what would please a man who gives as his reason for picking another piece, this time a Senufo helmet mask, "I have to say that I picked this because I own it. It was given to me by President Houphouet Boigny of the Ivory Coast" (P, p. 143); or who remarks "concerning the market in African art":

the best pieces are going for very high prices. Generally speaking, the less good pieces in terms of quality are not going up in price. And that's a fine reason for picking the good ones rather than the bad. They have a way of becoming more valuable.
I look at African art as objects I find would be appealing to use in a home or an office. . . . I don't think it goes with everything, necessarily – although the very best perhaps does. But I think it goes well with contemporary architecture. [P, p. 131]

There is something breathtakingly unpretentious in Rockefeller's easy movement between considerations of finance, aesthetics, and decor. In these responses, we have surely a microcosm of the site of the African in contemporary – which is, then, surely to say, postmodern – America.

I have quoted so much from Rockefeller not to emphasize the familiar fact that questions of what we call "aesthetic" value are crucially bound up with market value, nor even to draw attention to the fact that this is known by those who play the art market. Rather I want to keep clearly before us the fact that David Rockefeller is permitted to say *anything at all* about the arts of Africa because he is a *buyer* and because he is at the *center*, while Lela Kouakou, who merely makes art and who dwells at the margins, is a poor African whose words count only as parts of the commodification[2] – both for those of us who constitute the museum public and for collectors, like Rockefeller – of Baule art.[3] I want to remind you, in short, of how important it is that African art is a *commodity.*

But the cocurator whose choice will set us on our way is James Baldwin, the only cocurator who picked a piece that was not in the mold of the Africa of "Primitivism." The sculpture that will be my touchstone is a Yoruba piece that carries the museum label, *Man with a Bicycle* (figure 1). Here is some of what Baldwin said about it:

> This is something. This has got to be contemporary. He's really going to town! It's very jaunty, very authoritative. His errand might prove to be impossible. . . . He is challenging something – or something has challenged him. He's grounded in immediate reality by the bicycle. . . . He's apparently a very proud and silent man. He's dressed sort of polyglot. Nothing looks like it fits him too well. [*P,* p. 125]

Baldwin's reading of this piece is, of course and inevitably, "in terms of [his] own . . . criteria," a reaction contextualized only by the knowledge that bicycles are new in Africa and that this piece, anyway, does not look anything like the works he recalls seeing from his earliest childhood at the Schomburg Museum in Harlem. His response torpedoes Vogel's argument for her notion that the only "authentically traditional" African – the only one whose responses, as she says, could have been found a century ago – must be refused a choice among Africa's art cultures because he – unlike the rest of the cocurators, who are Americans and the European-educated Africans – will use his "own . . . criteria." The message is that this Baule diviner, this authentically African villager, does not know what *we*, authentic postmodernists, now know: that the first and last mistake is to judge the Other on one's own terms. And so, in the name of this relativist insight, we impose our judgment: that Lela Kouakou may not judge sculpture from beyond the Baule culture zone, because he, like all the other African "informants" we have met in the field, will read them as if they were meant to meet those Baule standards.

Worse than this, it is nonsense to explain Kouakou's responses as deriving from an ignorance of other traditions – if indeed he is, as he no doubt is supposed to be, like most "traditional" artists today, if he is, for example, like Francis Akwasi of Kumasi. Kouakou may judge other artists by his own standards (what on earth else could he, could anyone, do save make no judgment at all?), but to suppose that he is unaware that there are other standards within Africa (let alone without) is to ignore a piece of absolutely basic cultural knowledge, common to most precolonial as well as to most colonial and postcolonial cultures on the continent: the piece of cultural knowledge that explains why the people we now call "Baule" exist at all. To be Baule, for example, is, for a Baule, not to be a white person, not to be Senufo, not to be French.[4]

But Baldwin's *Man with a Bicycle* does more than give the lie to Vogel's strange footnote; it provides us with an image that can serve as a point of entry to my theme, a piece of contemporary African art that will allow us to explore the articulation of the postcolonial and the postmodern. *Man with a Bicycle* is described as follows in the exhibition catalogue:

Figure 87.1 *Man with a Bicycle*, Yoruba, Nigeria, 20th century. Wood, 35 3/4″. Collection of The Newark Museum, Purchase 1977 Wallace M. Scudder Bequest Fund and The Members' Fund. Photo: Jerry Thompson, 1986.

Man with a Bicycle
Yoruba, Nigeria 20th century
Wood and paint H. 35 3/4 in.
The Newark Museum

The influence of the Western world is revealed in the clothes and bicycle of this neo-traditional Yoruba sculpture which probably represents a merchant en route to market. [P, p. 23]

It is this word *neotraditional* – a word that is almost right – that provides, I think, the fundamental clue.

But I do not know how to explain this clue without first saying how I keep my bearings in the shark-infested waters around the semantic island of the postmodern. The task of chasing the word *postmodernism* through the pages of Jean- François Lyotard and Fredric Jameson and Jürgen Habermas, in and out of the *Village Voice* and the *TLS* and even the *New York Times Book Review* is certainly exhausting. Yet there *is*, I think, a story to tell about all these stories – or, of course, I should say, there are many, but this, for the moment, is mine – and, as I tell it, the Yoruba bicyclist will eventually come back into view.

I do not (this will come as no surprise) have a definition of the postmodern to put in the place of Jameson's or Lyotard's, but there is now a rough consensus about the structure of the modern/postmodern dichotomy in the many domains – from architecture to poetry to philosophy to rock music to the movies – in which it has been invoked. In each of these domains there is an antecedent practice that laid claim to a certain exclusivity of insight, and in each of them "postmodernism" is a name for the rejection of that claim to exclusivity, a rejection that is almost always more playful, though not necessarily less serious, than the practice it aims to replace. That this will not do as a *definition* of postmodernism follows from the fact that in each domain this rejection of exclusivity assumes a particular shape, one that reflects the specificities of its setting. To understand the various postmodernisms this way is to leave open the question of how their theories of contemporary social, cultural, and economic life relate to the actual practices that constitute that life – to leave open, then, the relations between postmodern*ism* and postmodern*ity*.[5]

It is an important question *why* this distancing of the ancestors should have become so central a feature of our cultural lives. The answer surely has to do with the sense in which art is increasingly commodified. To sell oneself and one's products as art in the marketplace, one must, above all, clear a space in which one is distinguished from other producers and products – and one does this by the construction and the marking of differences. To create a market for bottled waters, for example, it was necessary, first, to establish that subtle (even untastable) differences in mineral content and source of carbonation were essential modes of distinction.

It is this need for distinctions in the market that accounts for a certain intensification of the long-standing individualism of post-Renaissance art production: in the age of mechanical reproduction, aesthetic individualism, the characterization of the artwork as belonging to the oeuvre of an individual, and the absorption of the artist's life into the conception of the work can be seen precisely as modes of identifying objects for the market. The sculptor of the man with a bicycle, by contrast, will not be known by those who buy this object; his individual life will make no difference to the future history of his sculpture. (Indeed, he surely knows this, in the sense in which one knows anything whose negation one has never even considered.) Nevertheless, there is *something* about the object that serves to establish it for the market: the availability of Yoruba culture and of stories about Yoruba culture to surround the object and distinguish it from "folk art" from elsewhere.

Postmodern culture is the culture in which all postmodernisms operate, sometimes in synergy, sometimes in competition; and because contemporary culture is, in a certain sense to which I shall return, transnational, postmodern culture is global – though that emphatically does not mean that it is the culture of every person in the world.

If postmodernism is the project of transcending some species of modernism, which is to say some relatively self-conscious, self-privileging project of a privileged modernity, our *neotraditional* sculptor of *Man with a Bicycle* is presumably to be understood, by contrast, as premodern, that is, traditional. (I am supposing, then, that being neotraditional is a way of being traditional; what work the *neo-* does is matter for a later moment.) And the sociological and anthropological narratives of tradition through which he or she came to be so theorized is dominated, of course, by Max Weber.

Weber's characterization of traditional (and charismatic) authority *in opposition* to rational authority is in keeping with his general characterization of modernity as the rationalization of the world; and he insisted on the significance of this characteristically Western process for the rest of humankind:

> A product of modern European civilization, studying any problem of universal history, is bound to ask himself to what combination of circumstances the fact should be attributed that in Western civilization, and in Western civilization only, cultural phenomena have appeared which (as we like to think) lie in a line of development having *universal* significance and value.[6]

Now there is certainly no doubt that Western modernity now has a universal *geographical* significance. The Yoruba bicyclist – like Sting and his Amerindian chieftains of the Amazon rain forest or Paul Simon and the Mbaqanga musicians of *Graceland* – is testimony to that. But, if I may borrow someone else's borrowing, the fact is that the Empire of Signs strikes back. Weber's "as we like to think" reflects his doubts about whether the Western *imperium* over the world was as clearly of universal *value* as it was certainly of universal *significance*; and postmodernism fully endorses his resistance to this claim. The man with a bicycle enters our museums to be valued by us (Rockefeller tells us *how* it is to be valued), but just as the *presence* of the object reminds us of this fact, its *content* reminds us that the trade is two-way.

I want to argue that to understand our – our human – modernity, we must first understand why the rationalization of the world can no longer be seen as the tendency either of the West or of history, why, simply put, the modernist characterization of modernity must be challenged. To understand our world is to reject Weber's claim for the rationality of what he called rationalization and his projection of its inevitability; it is, then, to have a radically post- Weberian conception of modernity.

[...]

I do not know when *Man with a Bicycle* was made or by whom; African art has, until recently, been collected as the property of "ethnic" groups, not of individuals and work-shops, so it is not unusual that not one of the pieces in the "Perspectives" show was identified in the checklist by the name of an individual artist, even though many of them are twentieth-century works. (And no one will be surprised, by contrast, that most of them *are* kindly labeled with the names of the people who own the largely private collections where they now live.) As a result I cannot say if the piece is literally postcolonial, produced after Nigerian independence in 1960. But the piece belongs to a genre that has certainly been produced since then: the genre that is here called *neotraditional*. Simply put, what is distinctive about this genre is that it is produced for the West.

I should qualify. Of course, many of the buyers of first instance live in Africa; many of them are juridically citizens of African states. But African bourgeois consumers of neotraditional art are educated in the Western style, and, if they want African art, they would often rather have a "genuinely" traditional piece, by which I mean a piece that they believe to be made precolonially, or at least in a style and by methods that were already established precolonially. These buyers are a minority. Most of this art – *traditional* because it uses actual or supposed precolonial techniques but *neo-* (this, for what it is worth, is the explanation I promised earlier) because it has elements that are recognizably colonial or postcolonial in reference – has been made for Western tourists and other collectors.

The incorporation of these works in the West's museum culture and its art market has almost nothing, of course, to do with postmodernism. By and large, the ideology through which they are incorporated is modernist: it is the ideology that brought something called "Bali" to Antonin Artaud, something called "Africa" to Pablo Picasso, and something called "Japan" to Roland Barthes. (This incorporation as an official Other was criticized, of course, from its beginnings: hence Oscar Wilde's observation that "the whole of Japan is a pure invention. There is no such country, there are no such people.")[7] What *is* postmodernist is Vogel's muddled conviction that African art should not be judged "in terms of [someone else's] traditional criteria." For modernism, primitive art was to be judged by putatively *universal* aesthetic criteria, and by these standards it was finally found possible to value it. The sculptors and painters who found it possible were largely seeking an Archimedean point outside their own cultures for a critique of a Weberian modernity. For *post*modernisms, by contrast, these works, however they are to be understood, cannot be seen as legitimated by culture-and history-transcending standards.

The *neotraditional* object is useful as a model, despite its marginality in most African lives, because its incorporation in the museum world (as opposed to the many objects made by the same hands that live peacefully in nonbourgeois homes: stools, for example) reminds one that in Africa, by contrast, the distinction between high culture and mass culture, insofar as if it makes sense at all, corresponds, by and large, to the distinction between those with and those without Western-style formal education as cultural consumers.

The fact that the distinction is to be made this way – in most of sub-Saharan Africa, excluding the Republic of South Africa – means that the opposition between high culture and mass culture is available only in domains where there is a significant body of Western formal training. This excludes (in most places) the plastic arts and music. There are distinctions of genre and audience in African music, and for various cultural purposes there is something we call "traditional" music that we still practice and value; but village and urban dwellers alike, bourgeois and nonbourgeois, listen, through discs and, more important, on the radio, to reggae, to Michael Jackson, and to King Sunny Adé.

And this means that, by and large, the domain in which such a distinction makes the most sense is the one domain where that distinction is powerful and pervasive: namely, in African writing in Western languages. So that it is here that we find, I think, a place for consideration of the question of the *post*coloniality of contemporary African culture.

Postcoloniality is the condition of what we might ungenerously call a *comprador* intelligentsia: a relatively small, Western-style, Western-trained group of writers and thinkers, who mediate the trade in cultural commodities of world capitalism at the periphery. In the West they are known through the Africa they offer; their compatriots know them both through the West they present to Africa and through an Africa they have invented for the world, for each other, and for Africa.

All aspects of contemporary African cultural life – including music and some sculpture and painting, even some writings with which the West is largely not familiar – have been influenced, often powerfully, by the transition of African societies *through* colonialism, but they are not all in the relevant sense *post*colonial. For the *post-* in postcolonial, like the *post-* in postmodern, is the *post-* of the space-clearing gesture I characterized earlier, and many areas of contemporary African cultural life – what has come to be theorized as popular culture, in particular – are not in this way concerned with transcending, with going beyond, coloniality. Indeed, it might be said to be a mark of popular culture that its borrowings from international cultural forms are remarkably insensitive to, not so much dismissive of as blind to, the issue of neocolonialism or "cultural imperialism." This does not mean that theories of postmodernism are irrelevant to these forms of culture, for the internationalization of the market and the commodification of artworks are both central to them. But it *does* mean that these artworks are not understood by their producers or their consumers in terms of a postmodern*ism*: there is no antecedent practice whose claim to exclusivity of vision is rejected through these artworks. What is called "syncretism" here is a consequence of the international exchange of commodities, but not of a space-clearing gesture.

Postcolonial intellectuals in Africa, by contrast, are almost entirely dependent for their support on two institutions: the African university, an institution whose intellectual life is overwhelmingly constituted as Western, and the Euro-American publisher and reader. Even when these writers seek to escape the West – as Ngugi wa Thiong'o did in attempting to construct a Kikuyu peasant drama – their theories of their situation are irreducibly informed by their Euro-American formation. Ngugi's conception of the writer's potential in politics is essentially that of the avant-garde, of left modernism.

Now this double dependence on the university and the European publisher means that the first generation of modern African novels – the generation of Chinua Achebe's *Things Fall Apart* and Camara Laye's *L'Enfant noir* – were written in the context of notions of politics and culture dominant in the French and British university and publishing worlds in the 1950s and 1960s. This does not mean that they were like novels written in Western Europe at that time, for part of what was held to be obvious both by these writers and by the high culture of Europe of the day was that new literatures in new nations should be anticolonial and nationalist. In one respect, these early novels seem to belong to the world of eighteenth- and nineteenth-century literary nationalism; they are theorized as the imaginative recreation of a common cultural past that is crafted into a shared tradition by the writer. They are in the tradition of Sir Walter Scott, whose *Minstrelsy of the Scottish Border* was intended, as he said in the introduction, to "contribute somewhat to the history of my native country; the peculiar features of whose manners and character are daily melting and dissolving into those of her sister and ally."[8] The novels of this first stage are thus realist legitimations of nationalism: they authorize a "return to traditions" while at the same time recognizing the demands of a Weberian rationalized modernity.

From the later sixties on, such celebratory novels become rare.[9] For example, Achebe moves from the creation of a usable past in *Things Fall Apart* to a cynical indictment of politics in the modern sphere in *A Man of the People*. But I would like to focus on a francophone novel of the later sixties, a novel that thematizes in an extremely powerful way many of the questions I have been asking about art and modernity: I mean, of course, Yambo Ouologuem's *Le Devoir de violence*. This novel, like many of the second stage of which it is a part, represents a challenge to the novels of the first stage: it identifies the realist novel as part of the tactic of nationalist legitimation and so it is – if I may begin a catalogue of its ways-of-being-*post*-this-and-that – *postrealist*.

Now postmodernism is, of course, postrealist also. But Ouologuem's postrealism is motivated quite differently from that of such postmodern writers as, say, Thomas Pynchon. Realism naturalizes: the originary "African novel," such as Achebe's *Things Fall Apart* and Laye's *L'Enfant noir*, is "realist." Therefore, Ouologuem is against it; he rejects, indeed assaults, the conventions of realism. He seeks to delegitimate the forms of the realist African novel, in part, surely, because what it sought to naturalize was a nationalism that, by 1968, had plainly failed. The national bourgeoisie that took the baton of rationalization, industrialization, and bureaucratization in the name of nationalism, turned out to be a kleptocracy. Their enthusiasm for nativism was a rationalization of their urge to keep the national bourgeoisies of other nations, and particularly the powerful industrialized nations, out of their way. As Jonathan Ngate has observed, the world of *Le Devoir de violence* is one "in which *the efficacy* of the call to the Ancestors as well as the Ancestors themselves is seriously called into question."[10] That the novel is in this way postrealist allows its author to borrow, when he needs them, the techniques of modernism, which, as we learned from Jameson, are often also the techniques of postmodernism.

[. . .]

Because *Le Devoir de violence* is a novel that seeks to delegitimate not only the form of realism but the content of nationalism, it will to that extent seem to us, misleadingly, postmodern: misleadingly, because what we have here is not postmodern*ism* but postmo-dern*ization*; not an aesthetics but a politics, in the most literal sense of the term. After colonialism, the modernizers said, comes rationality; that is the possibility the novel rules out. Ouologuem's novel is typical of novels of this second stage in that it is not written by someone who is comfortable with and accepted by the new elite, the national bourgeoisie. Far from being a celebration of the nation, then, the novels of the second, postcolonial, stage are novels of delegitimation: they reject not only the Western *imperium* but also the nationalist project of the postcolonial national bourgeoisie. And, so it seems to me, the basis for that project of delegitimation cannot be the postmodernist one: rather, it is grounded in an appeal to an ethical universal. Indeed it is based, as intellectual responses to oppression in Africa largely are based, in an appeal to a certain simple respect for human suffering, a fundamental revolt against the endless misery of the last thirty years. Ouolo-guem is hardly likely to make common cause with a relativism that might allow that the horrifying new-old Africa of exploitation is to be understood, legitimated, in its own local terms.

Africa's postcolonial novelists, novelists anxious to escape neocolonialism, are no longer committed to the nation; in this they will seem, as I have suggested, misleadingly postmod-ern. But what they have chosen instead of the nation is not an older traditionalism but Africa – the continent and its people. This is clear enough, I think, in *Le Devoir de violence*. At the end of the novel Ouologuem writes:

> Souvent il est vrai, l'âme veut rêver l'écho sans passé du bonheur. Mais, jeté dans le monde, l'on peut s'empêcher de songer que Saïf, pleuré trois millions de fois, renaît sans cesse a l'Histoire, sous les cendres chaudes de plus de trente Républiques africaines. [*D*, p. 207][11]
>
> Often, it is true, the soul desires to dream the echo of happiness, an echo that has no past. But projected into the world, one cannot help recalling that Saif, mourned three million times, is forever reborn to history beneath the hot ashes of more than thirty African republics. [*BV*, pp. 181–2][12]

If we are to identify with anyone, it is with the "la négraille," the niggertrash, who have no nationality. For them one republic is as good (which is to say as bad) as any other. Postcoloniality has become, I think, a condition of pessimism.

Postrealist writing, postnativist politics, a *transnational* rather than a *national* solidarity – and pessimism: a kind of *post*optimism to balance the earlier enthusiasm for Ahmadou Kourouma's *Suns of Independence*. Postcoloniality is *after* all this: and its *post-*, like that of postmodernism, is also a *post-* that challenges earlier legitimating narratives. And it challenges them in the name of the suffering victims of "more than thirty African republics."

If there is a lesson in the broad shape of this circulation of cultures, it is surely that we are all already contaminated by each other, that there is no longer a fully autochthonous *echt*-African culture awaiting salvage by our artists (just as there is, of course, no American culture without African roots). And there is a clear sense in some postcolonial writing that the postulation of a unitary Africa over against a monolithic West – the binarism of Self and Other – is the last of the shibboleths of the modernizers that we must learn to live without.

[. . .]

Notes

1   *Perspectives: Angles on African Art* (exhibition catalogue, Center for African Art, New York, 1987), p. 9; hereafter abbreviated *P.*

2   I should insist now, the first time that I use this word, that I do not share the widespread negative evaluation of commodification; its merits, I believe, must be assessed case by case. Certainly critics such as Kabena Mercer (for example, in his "Black Hair/Style Politics," *New Formations 3* (Winter 1987): 33–54) have persuasively criticized any reflexive rejection of the commodity form, which so often reinstates the hoary humanist opposition between the "authentic" and the "commercial." Mercer explores the avenues by which marginalized groups have manipulated commodified artifacts in culturally novel and expressive ways.

3   Once Vogel has thus refused Kouakou a voice, it is less surprising that his comments turn out to be composite also, On closer inspection, it turns out that there is no single Lela Kouakou who was interviewed like the other cocurators. Kouakou is, in the end, quite exactly an invention, thus literalizing the sense in which "we," and more particularly "our" artists, are individuals while "they," and "theirs," are ethnic types.

4   It is absolutely crucial that Vogel does not draw her line according to racial or national categories: the Nigerian, the Senegalese, and the African-American cocurators are each allowed to be on "our" side of the great divide. The issue here is something less obvious than racism.

5   Where the practice is theory – literary or philosophical – postmodernism as a *theory* of postmodernity can be adequate only if it reflects to some extent the realities of that practice, because the practice itself is fully theoretical. But when a postmodernism addresses, say, advertising or poetry, it may be adequate as an account of them even if it conflicts with their own narratives, their theories of themselves. For, unlike philosophy and literary theory, advertising and poetry are not largely *constituted* by their articulated theories of themselves.

6   Max Weber, *The Protestant Ethic and the Spirit of Capitalism*, trans. Talcott Parsons (London, 1930), p. 13.

7   Oscar Wilde, "The Decay of Lying: An Observation," *Intentions* (London, 1909), p. 45.

8   Walter Scott, *Minstrelsy of the Scottish Border: Consisting of Historical and Romantic Ballads* (London, 1883), pp. 51–2.

9   Somewhat along these lines, Neil Lazarus's *Resistance in Postcolonial African Fiction* (New Haven, Conn., 1990), pp. 1–26, offers a useful periodization of African fiction in relation to the "great expectations" of the independence era and the "mourning after."

10 Jonathan Ngate, *Francophone African Fiction: Reading a Literary Tradition* (Trenton, NJ, 1988), p. 59; hereafter abbreviated *FAF*.

11 Yambo Ouologuem, *Le Devoir de violence* (Paris, 1968).

12 Ouologuem, *Bound to Violence*, trans. Ralph Manheim (London, 1968), p. 87.

Chapter 88

Postmodernism and Black Writing in South Africa

Lewis Nkosi

I am concerned in this chapter not with the validity or propriety of postmodernist theory and practice with regard to South African literature taken in its aggregate. That debate has been going on for some time now within the country and in my opinion remains inconclusive. My purpose is to insist that in South Africa there exists an unhealed – I will not say incurable – split between black and white writing, between on the one side an urgent need to document and to bear witness and on the other the capacity to go on furlough, to loiter, and to experiment. This split, apart from the linguistic medium, will find no ready analogy in the difference between, say, Afrikaans and English literatures, a division which is only comparable to the difference between regional literatures in the United States, especially between southern and northern, and between rural and urban writing, a difference which is largely a matter of a constellation of certain themes and preoccupations.

Though often treated as natural, sometimes as a positive sign of our cultural diversity and richness, and as such a reason for celebration rather than regret, this difference between black and white writing can also be read as a sign of social disparity and technological discrepancy. In a post-apartheid South Africa it is clearly a cause for embarrassment. It exists on the one side as a reminder of historical neglect and the impoverishment of black writing and on the other of cultural privilege and opportunity in the case of white writing. While black writing can be said to benefit by being able to draw on its rootedness in the variegated life of the majority, it is also largely impervious for the most part to cultural movements which have exercised great influence in the development of white writing. This discrepancy is particularly noticeable in the domain of theory.

My argument, then, relates first to the colonial status of black writing in South Africa. In the second part of the chapter I deal with what appears to me to be two entirely separate issues. The first of these is the argument that postmodernist theory and practice, as offshoots of poststructuralist thought, have very little to offer oppositional black writers still deeply

First published in *Writing South Africa: Literature, Apartheid, and Democracy, 1970–1995*, ed. Derek Attridge and Rosemary Jolly, pp. 75–80. Cambridge: Cambridge University Press, 1998.

preoccupied with nationalist agendas and questions of agency. This is an argument which has sometimes been offered by a few black writers sufficiently versed in postmodernist theory to discuss it. On the face of it, this is a straightforward issue of political representation, using a fictional mode. Recent and not so recent criticism of postmodernism, from critics as diverse as Christopher Norris (*What's Wrong*), Aijaz Ahmad (*In Theory*), and Charles Altieri ('What is Living'), can be presumed to lend some support, however limited, to black South African critics who, one imagines, would enthusiastically endorse Norris's attack on postmodernism as tending to sponsor a 'radicalism' which 'has now passed over into a species of disguised apologetics for the socio-political status quo, a persuasion that "reality" is constituted through and through by the meanings, values or discourses that presently compose it, so that nothing could count as effective counter-argument, much less a critique of existing institutions on valid theoretical grounds' (*What's Wrong*, 3–4).

My own ongoing reservations about black South Africans' indifference or impromptu dismissal of postmodernism is that it does not seem to have been accomplished with the necessary theoretical or critical labour, for it is rarely a question of critics who have worked through these theoretical positions and come out on the other side convinced of their hopeless inadequacy or bankruptcy. Quite the contrary; and yet even the most disaffected critics of postmodernism tend to agree that it is not a single monolithic practice. There are at least two distinguishable modes of its operation, one clearly conservative and the other drawing on what Norris describes as a 'continuing critical impulse – the enlightened or emancipatory interest' (5). Finally, is there not a disguised paternalism in the suggestion by some white South African critics that black writers do not 'need' postmodernism, or that it is not 'suitable' for them?

The other question I wish to discuss refers to indigenous African language or vernacular literatures, never even mentioned in most discussions of postmodernism, where I pause to ask whether postmodernism has any contribution to make, and if so, what form both modernism and postmodernism can take in promoting the process of modernization and technical innovation. The reasons for treating this as a somewhat different issue from the first, more technical than merely political, is my conviction that vernacular literatures, through their use of non-European languages, are rooted in or affiliated to other traditions, with different structures and modes of operation. B. W. Vilakazi's doomed experimentations with European prosody in the writing of Zulu poetry early this century provide a cautionary tale, as I shall demonstrate.

I

However, let me turn first to what I have referred to as the colonial status of black writing in South Africa. I wish to argue that its formal insufficiencies, its disappointing breadline asceticism and prim disapproval of irony, and its well-known predilection for what Lukacs called 'petty realism, the trivially detailed painting of local colour': all these naively uncouth disfigurements of which many critics, including myself, have sometimes complained, can be seen to be a result, in part, of a claustrophobia related to this internal colonialism from which, it is hoped, a post-apartheid condition will set it free. Time and again, in its gasps and stutters, in its nightmares and premonitions of a past to be endlessly repeated, black writing shows clearly its relation to this colonial history; the manner, for example, in which it discloses, at the most unexpected moments, its memory of the *sjambok*.

If my analysis is correct, it will surprise no one that black South African writers have shown no particular enthusiasm for postmodernism. Thus, although as another outgrowth of poststructuralist thought and practice, postmodernism appears to have taken some hold in South African literature, it is a movement wholly occupied, managed, and dominated by white writers, with black writers seeming either to ignore it or not even to have heard of it. In the first instance, I wish to argue that the reasons why black South Africans should know so little about these contemporary cultural movements is easy enough to explain. Much black writing, it has always seemed to me, operates in an autonomous region entirely untouched by contemporary cultural theory. In fact, what is so astonishing about Mothobi Mutloatse's introduction to the anthology *Forced Landing* (1980) is a quality of an almost defiant insouciance, an impatient refusal to countenance any discussion of theory as such beyond a succession of normative assertions.[1]

What needs to be emphasized, however, is that for many black writers this seeming indifference to matters of theory is by no means deliberate, nor is the appearance of innocence a matter of prideful or willed ignorance. Furthermore, what needs to be explained is the wide discrepancy between contemporary theory and black writing as such; but so far much of recent commentary has merely dwelled on what Graham Pechey has correctly diagnosed as a 'bifurcation' between black and white writing without bothering to explain the material conditions which can account for that bifurcation ('Post-apartheid Narratives', 165). Thus, in what at first appears to be an irreproachably nuanced description of 'South African literature', seen in process as developing in relation to the various stages of political resistance, comprising different temporalities while held together by the need to provide simultaneous anchoring to cultural identities and communities living out 'diverse times', Pechey also advances the idea of a South African writing practice which 'has never been anything other than postmodern (as a whole practice, as an institution), though not always (technically, in the sense of its internal textual relations) postmodern*ist*' (165). There is an aporia here in the proposition that parts which have nothing in common with the postmodern somehow begin to share this fate as soon as they are combined into an institutionalized whole. If nothing else, this formulation serves more as a final confirmation of the triumphant rhetoric of postmodernist discourse, rather than offering a convincing argument about an existing state of affairs. Even more suspect is the assertion that South African writing is 'the place where marginalities of *all* kinds can meet and be positively valued' (165). After all, it is black writing which is so obviously marginalized and occupies, in fact, a minority status.

However, putting aside for the moment the obfuscating language, or even the question of how to read Olive Schreiner's 1883 novel as a postmodernist text, what we are offered here is the consolation of a black writing which may be 'postmodern' without being 'postmodernist'. Equally, we are left to wonder at the characterization of black writing as having been 'wakened out of its state-inflicted amnesia' which seems to apportion the blame equally to black writing and state persecution. But what was it that black writing was forced to forget? This is never spelled out. In fact, Pechey's text is riddled with many similar equivocations and evasions which function only to paper over fissures in his line of argument. The general thrust of Pechey's 'Post-apartheid Narratives' is to misrecognize the limitations imposed upon black writing by its colonial situation, in which case it is regarded merely as a reflection of the 'rich diversity' of South African writing.

In that now notorious and much-criticized global treatment of 'third-world' texts, Jameson argued that 'a popular or socially realistic third-world novel tends to come before us, not immediately, but as though already-read' ('Third-World Literature', 65). This 'already-read' quality of much black fiction in South Africa, its tedious quality of inevitability and its inability to surprise the reader, is surely undeniable; but it is important to trace much of the backwardness of black writing to its state of internal isolation and surveillance under the apartheid regime and some of its disabilities to wounds inflicted by cultural deprivation and social neglect. In South Africa the gap between black writing practice and contemporary theory is simply too large to ignore, requiring attention in a concerted fashion, and in terms of remedial action.

Conventional wisdom has it that, until Bantu Education was imposed on an unwilling black population, missionary and provincial schools produced a 'black elite' largely divorced from the social concerns of a black proletariat. Armed with Marx and Gramsci, and writing from the comfortable chairs of 'Whites Only' university departments, these white cultural critics have sometimes managed to produce a profile of a 'black elite' which is hardly recognizable to its supposed members. But even if the charge of 'elitism' could be made to stick, it may be useful to point out here that elsewhere 'elitism' has sometimes been coupled with experimentalism and avant-gardism that have vitalized literatures in Asia and South America; the absence, by and large, of this experimentalism from black writing in South Africa has other roots and remains to be adequately explained. This cannot be done by critics who see Mtutuzeli Matshoba's *Call Me Not a Man* (1979) as an example of ground-breaking innovation.

One result of this kind of critical analysis has been to authorize a view of black writing as wilfully *sui generis* and naturally resistant to any attempts to bring it into fruitful contact with other contemporary movements in world literatures. This kind of analysis assigns a mode of writing to a racial category, then uses this essentialism to simultaneously explain and justify the limits of black realism. Such an approach overlooks the fact that black writers, apart from their isolation from the outside world, and more importantly, their isolation from the development of writing elsewhere on the African continent, until well into the seventies had no ready access to institutions of higher education where matters concerning literary theory, even in its rudimentary bourgeois form, came under discussion.

If we take the so-called *Drum* writers as representative of the fifties generation, it is surprising how few of them had any university education. When I went to work on *Drum* only Can Themba was the product of a university education; Es'kia Mphahlele was then studying for his BA by correspondence. Needless to say, writers inside and outside South Africa have produced excellent work without the benefit of a university education. There is also the added question, much in need of theoretical elaboration, whether one could be a 'postmodernist' without knowing it. In any event, where theory counts for so much – as seems to be the case with current artistic movements – it cannot be an accident that most works that are tuned into contemporary aesthetic movements are by white rather than black writers.

Above all, what the black community must reject is the insultingly patronizing attitude of some left-wing critics who, in their eagerness to privilege text that offers them a slice of black life of which they are ignorant, attempt to foist upon us something like *The Marabi Dance*. Graham Pechey asks: 'Does post-apartheid writing, then, bifurcate into a modernist or postmodernist *white* writing on the one hand and a neorealist *black* writing on the other?' ('Post-apartheid Narratives', 165; emphasis added). The question that Pechey is too embar-rassed even to pose is why this bifurcation has taken place at all; instead, he prefers to treat

South African writing as 'a rich polyphony of (its) forms and modes' which has 'tended to negotiate the heightening militancy of the struggle: either, on the black side, to thematise "fighting" in cathartic stories of recent struggles and in "battle hymns"; or, on the white side, to let violence have its effects in the formal dislocation of its texts and in its vivid imaging of a chaotic apocalypse' (164–5). Since we are here in the domain of literary production and creative skills and not, except metaphorically, in a zone of combat, given a choice on the one side of 'cathartic stories' and on the other the 'formal dislocation of texts' and 'vivid imaging', we know precisely which texts on the sides of that bifurcation will seem to yield greater aesthetic rewards; for, again to adapt Jameson to the South African situation, certain black South African texts can be read only 'for the freshness of information and a social interest that we cannot share' ('Third-World Literature', 66).

Note

1   This impatience is reflected in the modest programme which is however presented in a highly emotive language: 'We are going to pee, spit and shit on literary convention before we are through; we are going to kick and pull and push and drag literature into the form we prefer' (5).

References

Ahmad, Aijaz. *In Theory: Classes, Nations, Literatures*. London: Verso, 1992.

Altieri, Charles. 'What is Living and What is Dead in American Postmodernism?' *Critical Inquiry* 22 (1996): 764–89.

Jameson, Fredric. 'Third-World Literature in the Era of Multinational Capitalism'. *Social Text* 15 (Fall 1986): 65–88.

Norris, Christopher. *What's Wrong with Postmodernism: Critical Theory and the Ends of Philosophy.* Baltimore: Johns Hopkins University Press, 1990.

Pechey, Graham. 'Post-apartheid Narratives'. *Colonial Discourse/Postcolonial Theory.* Ed. Francis Barker, Peter Hulme, and Margaret Iversen. Manchester: Manchester University Press, 1994. 151–71.

Chapter 89

African-Language Literature and Postcolonial Criticism

Karin Barber

The "postcolonial" criticism of the 1980s and 1990s – which both continues and inverts the "Commonwealth" criticism inaugurated in the 1960s – has promoted a binarized, general-ized model of the world which has had the effect of eliminating African-language expression from view. This model has produced an impoverished and distorted picture of "the colonial experience" and the place of language in that experience. It has maintained a center-periphery polarity which both exaggerates and simplifies the effects of the colonial impos-ition of European languages. It turns the colonizing countries into unchanging monoliths, and the colonized subject into a homogenized token: "that most tedious, generic hold-all, '*the* post-colonial Other'" as Anne McClintock puts it (293) – an Other whose experience is determined so overwhelmingly by his or her relation to the metropolitan center that class, gender, and other local and historical and social pressures are elided. Despite intermittent claims to specificity, this model blocks a properly historical, localized understanding of any scene of colonial and post-Independence literary production in Africa. Instead it selects and overemphasizes one sliver of literary and cultural production – written literature in the English language – and treats this as all there is, representative of a whole culture or even a whole global "colonial experience." It thus negligently or deliberately erases all other forms of expression – written literature in African languages, oral literature in African languages, and a whole domain of cultural forms which cross the boundaries between "written" and "oral," between "foreign" and "indigenous" – making way for the "postcolonial Other" to emerge, defiant yet accessible, conveniently articulate in English and consolingly preoccu-pied with his or her relations to the center – "writing back" in a language the ex-colonizers can understand because it is a modified register of their own. Thus decontextualized, inflated, and made to bear an excessive metonymic burden, the role and significance of African literature in English can not be properly appreciated.

I am grateful to Mark Ralph-Bowman, Paulo Farias, and Keith Breckenridge for reading and comment-ing on this paper while I was revising it. Their suggestions were invaluable.

First published in *Research in African Literatures* 26.4 (Winter 1995): 3–11.

The Postcolonial Silence

Critics of African literature have always taken it for granted that African writers have to write in English. Commonwealth criticism enthusiastically celebrated oral traditional "vernacular" literatures in Africa,[1] but assumed that modern writers would naturally wish to write in English, in order to be able to make their distinctive contribution to the Great Tradition. But it also made it clear that they had little choice in the matter, if they wished to secure an audience worthy of the name (Larson 11; Roscoe 4; Povey 98; Adétugbò 173). The idiom of choice, in these discussions, is oddly blended with the idiom of compulsion: the African writer chooses to write in English because he or she has to.[2]

Postcolonial criticism, in an apparently radical reversal of the assumptions of Commonwealth criticism, represents English language and literature and indeed literacy itself as instruments of imperial domination. The genial model of Commonwealth literature, where the newcomer gladly offers contributions to a welcoming Great Tradition, is shown to mask stark power relations between the center and the periphery. Empire, to use Gayatri Chakravorty Spivak's phrase, "worlds" the rest of the world, using its discourses and texts to inscribe imperial relationships on the geography, history and social relations of the colonized country ("The Rani of Sirmur" 128). In the British colonies, the imposition of English language and English literature represented claims to the superiority of British civilization which were ultimately backed by force. Postcolonial criticism, following Fanon, argues that indigenous languages and literatures were devalued and displaced, and the colonial subject culturally and linguistically dispossessed, leading to deep loss of self-esteem and cultural confidence. In Abdul R. JanMohamed's words, the colonial subject is caught in a double bind between the "catalepsy" of total self-identification with imperial cultural values and the "petrification" of adhering to a devalued, "calcified" indigenous system "whose developmental momentum has been checked by colonisation" (5). Postcolonial criticism has political bite; it turns the searchlight back on the center and exposes the agenda underlying its claims to a universal literary humanism.

Nonetheless, postcolonial criticism shares with Commonwealth criticism its effacement of modern indigenous-language expression in colonized countries. Indeed, it goes further than Commonwealth criticism, replacing a well-meaning confusion with a definitive theoretical lock-out. If Commonwealth criticism felt that African writers had no alternative but to choose to write in English, post-colonial criticism eliminates virtually all hint of a choice: the discourses of empire were apparently all-encompassing and inescapable.

Though postcolonial criticism is a field of enquiry rather than a unified theory – and a field, moreover, within which people have taken up heterogenous and contradictory positions – it does nevertheless produce a predominant theoretical effect. We can distinguish two broad bands of postcolonial theory, which take up positions that are at one level antithetical, but which at the level that concerns us here have similar implications for the study of contemporary African culture. One strand, exemplified by the work of Edward Said and Homi Bhabha, and some of the work of Gayatri Chakravorty Spivak, is primarily concerned with a critique of colonial discourses, from a position which claims to be neither wholly inside nor entirely outside the colonial episteme. This critique produces an oblique and ambivalent allusion to indigenous discourses, an allusion that is half-effaced by a studious avoidance of "nativism" and essentialism. Thus, though Said's *Orientalism* is not about the Orient but about the invention of "the Orient" by a homogeneous and unchanging West, there are nonetheless hints in passing that there really is an Orient and an Oriental experience which is inaccessible to the Western episteme, trapped as it is within the prison-house of its own self-replicating fabrications. When Spivak asserts that "the subaltern cannot speak" ("Subaltern Studies"), the main effect is a salutary warning against the Western-formed scholar's assumption that the voice of the oppressed Other is simply there to be recuperated, already articulating a fully-constituted subjectivity that corresponds to the Western subject's own – an assumption which by-passes the whole history of Western "worlding." It is a statement about the limits of Western epistemic access, rather than the limits of subaltern articulacy. But at the same time, her critique is effective precisely because it uses the idea of alterity to provide a kind of virtual vantage point outside the Western episteme, from which to gain leverage for its deconstruction. Bhabha is preoccupied with the interface between colonizer and colonized, in which he perceives the apparently solidly-constituted subjective identity of the colonizer fragmenting and splitting in the face of mimicry, repetition and parody by the colonized – a mimicry which always has the potential for subversion. While he avoids invoking a "real," other identity which can oppose and challenge the colonial discourse (he makes clear, for instance, that his notion of "hybridity" does not mean the mixing of two different cultures: it is rather "a problematic of colonial representation"), his analysis does produce a kind of aftershadow of an alterity beyond the reach of the colonizer – he speaks, for instance, of "other, 'denied' knowledges" that "enter upon the dominant discourse and estrange the basis of its authority" (114); the dominant colonial knowledges may become "articulated with forms of 'native' knowledges" (115). He hesitates between saying that colonial inscription *produces* the simulacrum of difference and suggesting that there already *is* something different and unknown, beyond the reach of colonial assimilation. But if such discourses ever existed, he does not pretend to be very interested in them: "And what of the native discourse?" he asks, pretty rhetorically: "Who can tell?" (121).

If, then, this style of post-colonial criticism produces a counter-narrative, it is, as Robert Young observes, a narrative of how empire inscribed itself – a narrative about the imperial narrative, not about the discourses of the colonized (159). Insofar as it is invoked at all, the indigenous discourse appears only fleetingly, glimpsed out of the corner of the eye, conjured up almost inadvertently; it crosses the path of colonial discourse criticism obliquely, metaphorically, ambivalently and evasively, only to advertise its own inaccessibility. The theoretical effect is either to consign "native" discourses to the realms of the unknowable, or to imply that they were displaced, erased or absorbed by the dominant colonial discourses.

The approach of the second strand of postcolonial criticism is more direct and more optimistic. It is also much more closely related to Commonwealth criticism. It takes over Commonwealth criticism's field of inquiry – all literature written in English outside the metropolitan center – and infuses it with the table-turning critical spirit of Said, Bhabha, and Spivak. In this essay, I take as my main examples of this criticism two recent works: *The Empire Writes Back* (1989) by Bill Ashcroft, Gareth Griffiths, and Helen Tiffin, and *The African Palimpsest* (1991) by Chantal Zabus. The former is a position statement, summarizing the state of the field at the end of the eighties, which has been enormously influential; the latter is a fairly rare example of an extensive and sustained attempt to bring postcolonial analysis to bear specifically on African texts.

This style of postcolonial criticism takes the idea of the "silencing" of the native by the imposition of imperial discourses quite literally – as a statement about the native's muteness more than the colonizer's deafness. The colonial subject, it is said, was forced to learn the colonizer's language, in which he or she was (initially) trapped and constrained as by a straitjacket. According to Ashcroft et al., indigenous languages all over the British Empire were "rendered unprivileged" by the imposition of English to such an extent that they became unusable for expressive purposes and in some cases even died out. "It is this concept of silence, not any specific cultural concept of meaning, which is the active characteristic linking all post-colonial texts" (*The Empire Writes Back* 187). The postcolonial silence is pictured as having been comprehensive:

> By implication, the silencing of subaltern women [discussed by Spivak] extends to the whole of the colonial world, and to the silencing and muting of all natives, male or female. (*The Empire Writes Back* 178).

Nor is this silencing to be understood purely in terms of overt political repression. The English language silences by its sheer privileged and predominating presence: "Even those post-colonial writers with the literal freedom to speak find themselves languageless, gagged by the imposition of English on their world" (84).

However, having taken linguistic dispossession as its starting point, this style of post-colonial criticism goes on from there to celebrate a vigorous come-back by the colonized. The early stage of self-denigration and espousal of British values is succeeded by a phase of rejection of colonial culture and then its radical re-appropriation. The periphery now takes on the culture and language of the center and transforms it, breaking it, infusing it with local registers, and refashioning it so that it speaks with the voice of the marginalized. Instead of one hegemonic English we get a plurality of local englishes. Thus "the alienating process which initially served to relegate the post-colonial world to the 'margin' turned upon itself and acted to push that world through a kind of mental barrier from which all experience could be viewed as uncentred, pluralistic, multifarious. Marginality thus became an unprecedented source of creative energy" (12). The literature of the margins is thus at the frontiers of postmodern aesthetics.

In this model, then, the subaltern can and does eventually speak. In speaking, he or she asserts an identity in opposition to the identities imposed by colonisation: "Those 'Othered' by a history of European representation can only retrieve and reconstitute a postcolonized 'self' against that history" (Tiffin x). But when he or she speaks, it seems, the postcolonial subject speaks exclusively in English.

Thus in postcolonial criticism of African literature, the flowering of African literature in English, which occurred in the late 1950s and early 1960s, is interpreted as the colonial subject finally "finding a voice." It is more or less implied that until this flowering took place – showing that the colonized had mastered and subverted the colonial codes – the stunned natives literally could not articulate their responses to colonial rule.

This model brings together the literature of the whole non-metropolitan English-speaking world, including Australia, Canada, the Caribbean, and even the USA – whose existence and experience as "colonies" are boldly and provocatively conflated with those of India and Africa.[3] By defining its field in this way, *The Empire Writes Back* inevitably foregrounds what these places have in common – the problematic presence of English – and relegates to the background their utterly different political, historical, cultural, and linguistic experiences. Though distinctions are made between the "monoglossic" situation said to be characteristic of Australia, Canada, and the USA, the "diglossic" situation said to be characteristic of Africa and India, and the "polydialectical" (sic) situation said to be characteristic of the Caribbean, the generalized model of a binary world of colonizer and colonized ensures that analysis focuses on the presence of English, imbued with the values and experiences of the center, and the problem of making it speak for the margins. This automatically assigns English, and literature in English, an enormous, almost exclusive prominence even in "diglossic" cultures. The model thus inadvertently reenacts the very erasure of indigenous languages and cultures that it takes as its initial problematic. It is the relationship with English that defines the postcolonial condition, not just for the highly-educated elite or for anglophone writers but for entire populations – for "the postcolonial subject" in general: "the whole of the colonial world . . . all natives, male or female."

What Happens to African-Language Discourses?

If the African writer has to write in English, and has to transform English in order to make it bear the burden of African experience in the era of colonialism, then it seems natural to assume that writing, modernity, and the English language go together. To address present-day experience in colonial/post-independence Africa is to write; and to write is to write in English. This was the assumption made by both Commonwealth criticism and its heir, the buoyant type of post-colonial criticism. Its effect was to relegate expression in indigenous languages into a shadowy domain of "oral traditions" belonging properly to the precolonial past. The role of oral traditions/indigenous-language repertoires in this model is as a precursor, and more importantly as a pool of linguistic and thematic resources from which the anglophone writer can draw in order to refashion the English he or she is in the process of appropriating. Indigenous-language expression is consigned to the background, paradoxically by an inflation of its role as source and resource to the anglophone written tradition.

The notion of oral tradition as precursor and background, out of which modern anglophone written literature somehow emerged or grew, was established in numerous early anthologies of Commonwealth criticism of "African literature," where introductory chapters on "the oral heritage" – descriptive and celebratory in tone – would be followed by the real business of analysis and criticism in essays on Achebe, Soyinka, Ngũgĩ, and Awoonor. If "modern African literature" had its own separate origin, then it could flow into the Great Tradition from *elsewhere*, bringing renewal. But this developmental and evolutionary frame is distorting: as Eustace Palmer robustly observed, the earliest African novels in English "could not possibly be outgrowths of the oral tale" (Palmer 5). The fact that literate authors draw on thematic elements from oral as well as from written repertoires, and may achieve the *effect* of orality through specific techniques of writing, does not mean that their work "grew out of" oral traditions any more than Keats's "La Belle Dame Sans Merci" grew out of the folk ballad: the organic metaphor, with its implications of total, unwilled process, screens literary strategies and literary politics from view. The positioning of "oral tradition" as precursor suggests a view of literary history in which the oral forms had no function other than to be superseded by the "modern," "emergent" ones. Origin is there so that history can begin, and is itself outside history and outside scrutiny.

More persistent and pervasive – and more justifiable – was the view, entertained by both Commonwealth and postcolonial criticism, of indigenous languages and oral repertoires as a pool of resources for the anglophone writer to draw on. In Commonwealth criticism, it was this "influence" or "ingredient" (depending on whether the writer's role was seen as active or passive) that was held to impart to African writing in English its special Africanity, its ability to express specifically African experience in an alien tongue. This incorporation of indigenous repertoires could be conceived at the level of the linguistic code itself (e.g., "the interplay between the two languages, Yoruba and English." Afoláyan 61), at the level of "orality" as a general category (e.g., "the wholesale application of an oral narrative technique to written narrative," Moore 185), or at the level of a pool of specific textual elements (e.g., "drawing on West African folklore, traditional symbols and images, and traditional turns of speech to invest their writing with a truly West African sensibility and flavour," Obiechina, *Culture* 26). A two-layered model of language and culture is sometimes envisaged: the "traditional heritage" is what pushes up from underneath the smooth square paving stones of English english, cracking and re-forming it into unique new patterns. What began as a "problem" is converted not just into an advantage, but into a trump card: in wrestling with the "chosen tongue," the African writer enriches and transforms it. "Orality" has been singled out in much europhone criticism, as Eileen Julien has brilliantly and forcefully demonstrated, as a potent symbol of Africanity, an almost talismanic notion, guaranteeing the authenticity of the experience conveyed by the text.[4] The critical method implied by this model was invariably to start from the known, recognizable "Western" form of the work – the generic conventions of the realist novel, the standard forms of metropolitan English – and then assess to what extent and in what ways the text deviated from this norm, under the influence of something not so well known, something *outside* or *beneath* the contemporary literary tradition, something *other*: the oral heritage, the indigenous language. And in many cases, the depiction of the oral heritage was extremely vague: its presence was indicated rather than discussed, like a tapestry glowing dimly in the shadows in which no actual designs can be made out: "Africa's ancient oral traditions...the rich heritage of thought, experience, religion, custom, folklore and myth, carried down the ages in scores of African vernaculars..." (Roscoe 249). The oral tradition and its "values" and "wisdom" are often left unanalyzed: their function is simply to evoke alterity.[5] It is as if, with modernity, expression in indigenous languages has come to a full stop, and is to live on only in translated borrowings and echoes.

Buoyant-type postcolonial criticism greatly refines and extends the analysis of oral and indigenous repertoires as a pool of resources for written Europhone texts. Ashcroft et al. offer a sophisticated analysis of the use of Ijo structures and lexemes in Gabriel Okara's *The Voice*; Chantal Zabus investigates in detail the different ways that elements of indigenous linguistic repertoires can be made to speak within a range of anglophone and francophone novels. This sharper style of analysis goes with a sharper evaluation of the role of linguistic hybridization in African europhone literature: not to provide a distinctively African cocktail so much as to resist, recreate and subvert the dominant language.

But in the process, this style of criticism relegates expression in indigenous languages even further into the background. In *The Empire Writes Back*, even more strikingly than in Commonwealth criticism, the African "vernacular" (30, 42) or "tribal language" (68) comes into the discussion *only* insofar as its syntax is overlaid upon or its vocabulary co-opted into English, and African "oral tradition" only insofar as its effects are recreated in English-language written literature. Modern expression in indigenous languages is not considered to exist: as in Commonwealth criticism, African languages in this model are strongly yoked to orality and to the pre-colonial order. Black sub-Saharan Africa is credited with "extensive and highly developed oral cultures" (116), but modern, written, African-language literature is discussed only as a possibility for the future, indeed as a program of the "back to pre-colonial purity" movement whose aims are rightly dismissed. The "vernacular," "oral" culture in this model emanates from a traditional order antithetical to, and all but destroyed by, the twin irruptions of English and writing:

> the invasion of the ordered, cyclic and "paradigmatic" oral world by the unpredictable and "syntagmatic" world of the written word stands as a useful model for the beginnings of post-colonial discourse. (82)

The model is one of absolute rupture, the replacement of one world by another.[6]

Chantal Zabus is more aware of the existence of African-language writing. The preface to her book was written by Albert Gérard, the great compiler of information on African-language written literatures, and she quotes him in passing to the effect that about half of all printed works of literature emanating from Africa have been in African languages (32). At the same time her exposition denies this knowledge and buries it under a categorical assertion, from which she does not deviate:

> In West Africa, the medium of literary expression is not the writer's mother tongue but the dominant, foreign European language imposed over the indigenous African languages in the process of Euro-Christian colonisation. . . . (1)

and

> For the West African writer, the mother tongue is either a medium that has not yet been reduced to writing or is in the process of being standardised, or a written tongue he knows little of . . . the West African writer finds himself writing in a language he subsequently wished to subvert and insert in the larger project of decolonisation. (2)

In doing so, she argues, the African writer produces a literary "third code," in the "overlapping space between other tongue and mother tongue" – a palimpsest where "behind the scriptural authority of the European language, the earlier, imperfectly erased remnants of the African language can still be perceived" (3). The critic's task is to bring them to light again, to uncover the hidden traces of the indigenous, effaced by the glottophagia of the colonial language; like a chemist, the critic "makes use of critical reagents whereby s/he can 'make the effaced writing of a papyrus or a parchment visible again'" (104–5). What is almost effaced, it is implied, is the text's secret identity, its concealed capacity for resistance. The occluded indigenous repertoire, in and of itself, is held to be a site of rebellion against the all-but-victorious march of colonial linguistic domination.[7]

Zabus's acceptance of the model in which modernity currently exists only in europhone written form, superseding the oral, traditional and African-language expression which is all but erased by colonial glottophagia, leads her to some curious elisions. She describes Amos Tutuola's *The Palm-Wine Drinkard* as

> the odd and somewhat freakish "missing link" in the Yoruba literary continuum between Chief Daniel Olarunfemi (sic) Fagunwa, the master story-teller and writer of Yoruba expression, and

> Wole Soyinka, the sophisticated and syncretic interpreter of a double legacy. This outlandish "folk-novel" precariously straddles the world of orature and that of literature and bridges the two by translating the one into the other. (108)

The "missing link" image shows that here we are back in evolutionist territory. The suggestion is that ṣóyínká (anglophone, the world of literature) *evolved out of* indigenous folklore (Yorùbá, the world of orature), with Tutuọla (Yorùbá-English; oral-written) as an intermediate stage. Without actually saying so, this exposition assimilates Fágúnwà to the orature/Yorùbá language side of the divide. Why is Fágúnwà described first as "master story-teller" and only secondly as "writer," while ṣóyínká is "the sophisticated and syncretic interpreter of a double legacy"? Fágúnwà, like ṣóyínká, was first and foremost a writer. He was an extremely sophisticated literary stylist, one of whose main influences was the Yorùbá Bible. He, no less than ṣóyínká, was the interpreter of a double (or triple, or multiple) legacy: a cultural broker par excellence, a Christian convert, a cultural nationalist, who celebrated Yorùbá culture in the name of the "African race," while purveying "enlightenment" to the Yorùbá readers to whom he addressed his books. But the paradigm operated by Zabus draws Fágúnwà into the "orature" camp, putting him on the other side of a binary cultural divide from ṣóyínká. Both were writers; both drew on extensive written and oral sources for their own purposes; both dealt with the hybrid shifting world of colonial and post-independence Nigeria.[8] The exposition suggests, however, that one, because he used Yorùbá, belongs to a world of tradition and orality, while the other, because he uses English, belongs to modernity, hybridity, and literature which has superseded it. The gravitational pull of the model is such that anything in Yorùbá – whatever the facts tell us – *must* belong to the oral-traditional–precolonial camp.[9]

The contradictions and elisions in the texts of Zabus and of Ashcroft et al. suggest that the paradigm that governs their interpretation is too strong for facts to resist. This paradigm's power to distort can be attributed to the fact that it is constructed from a classic set of stereotyped pairs, which could be represented in two columns like this:

African languages	English/French/Portuguese
"traditional"	"modern"
oral	written
past-oriented	contemporary
local	international
restricted audience	wide audience
homogeneous	heterogeneous
embodiment of value	object of criticism

None of these oppositions is entirely useless in itself; but it goes wrong when, in the manner of all stereotypes, the columns get glued into permanent sets, resulting in a picture of two separate worlds of experience, one of which is in the process of superseding the other. Because the "traditional" half of the paradigm is assigned a role that is outside history and outside criticism, the absurdity of this paradigm is shielded from scrutiny. The structure of paired oppositions is never viewed as a whole; it remains below the surface of the discourse, exerting a kind of gravitational pull on it, its influence revealed in unacknowledged contradictions and in what is excluded from African literary criticism more than in what is stated.

This is not, of course, to deny that African writers, whatever language they use, do often incorporate elements of long-standing indigenous expressive registers. Nor – let me make this clear – am I taking sides in a moral debate about what language African writers *ought* to use. My point is rather that the model proposed by postcolonial criticism – the model in which colonial glottophagia silences the native until he or she masters and subverts the colonizer's language – is based on a fundamental misconception, almost a will to ignorance. By casting the indigenous as always and only outside or underneath the "mainstream" literary discourses of modern Africa, it turns a blind eye to what is in fact the actual mainstream, the cultural discourses of the majority, in most of Africa.

[...]

Notes

1   See for example the substantial representation of oral literature in critical anthologies by Ulli Beier, Bruce King, and Bernth Lindfors.

2   Povey, for instance, veers in a single paragraph from one idiom to the other: the African writer "chooses to employ his second language for his creativity and . . . recognises that for all his popular audiences in Africa he has to be published abroad and write at least partially for an international and therefore foreign readership" (98). He *chooses* to write in his second language but he *has to* be published abroad and write for a foreign readership. Larson does it even more concisely, in a single sentence: "the African writer has had little option in choosing the [English] language for his writing" (11).

3   For critiques of this conflation, see McClintock; Dirlik; Ahmad; Hutcheon. For a recent reaffirmation of common ground between two "colonies" as different as Australia and Africa, see Ashcroft.

4   Julien points out that effects of "orality" in written texts are a style of writing, selected for a purpose not genetically inherited; anyone could master them with sufficient practice, even a foreigner brought up entirely in a literate world. They demonstrate skill in writing rather than guaranteeing "authenticity" – a concept which Julien shows to be in any case useless as a measure of literary value, and which she proposes to replace with the notion of "accountability."

5   More detailed discussions of specific indigenous forms, analyzed in relation to the English-language texts they have "influenced" were occasionally offered by scholars working within the general ambit of "Commonwealth" criticism, but they are rare. One example is Robert Fraser's fine discussion of Kofi Awoonor's poetry in relation to Ewe oral poetry. Obiechina has also attempted to uncover the precise Igbo idioms and formulations that he thinks underlie Achebe's prose. At the level of linguistic code. Afolayan has provided a detailed analysis of the way Yorùbá structures have influenced Tutuola's English.

6   Ashcroft et al. do reveal a moment of hesitation about this picture. And so they should. In West Africa, four hundred years of European trade, the development of trading pidgins, and long contact with Arabic and European literacy preceded the onset of colonialism proper. Nor is it possible to picture the world of the crumbling Ọ̀yọ́ empire, the rise of military strongmen in Ìbàdàn, or the ruthless expansion of the Ashanti kingdom, in the framework of an "ordered, cyclical, and 'paradigmatic' oral world." Such a world, if it ever existed, is beyond the reach of memory. And as a destructive force, the slave trade was far more important than literacy and the English language.

7   It should be noted, however, that this is a position which Ashcroft et al. strongly reject, arguing that the meaning of "indigenous" elements is allocated by their place within the anglophone text, not imported intact from the indigenous code.

8   Fágúnwà's last novel, *Àdìùú Olódùmarè*, was published in 1961, three years before his death; Soyinka's earliest plays, including *The Lion and the Jewel* and *The Trials of Brother Jero*, were written before his return to Nigeria from England in 1960.

9 Unlike Ashcroft et al., who view a hypothetical future African-language literature with suspicion, Zabus does envisage a future renaissance of African-language literature, when "dreaming in foreign languages ... will be supplanted by a lucid vision of a new African-language writing" (7). But in her account, as in Ashcroft et al., African-language written literature is held to be, in present-day Africa, paltry to the point of complete insignificance.

References

Adetugbo. Abiodun. "Form and Style." Introduction. *Nigerian Literature*. Ed. Bruce King. Lagos and London: University of Lagos and Evans Brothers, 1971.

Afoáyan, A. "Language and Sources of Amos Tutuola." *Perspectives on African Literature*. Ed. Christopher Heywood. London/Ifè: Heinemann and Ifè University Press, 1971.

Ahmad, Aijaz. *In Theory: Classes, Nations, Literatures*. London: Verso, 1992.

Andrzejewski, B. W., et al., eds. *Literatures in African Languages: Theoretical Issues and Sample Surveys*. Cambridge: Cambridge University Press, 1985.

Ashcroft, Bill. "Africa and Australia: The Post-Colonial Connection." *Research in African Literatures* 25.3 (1994), 161–70.

Ashcroft, Bill, Gareth Griffiths, and Helen Tiffin. *The Empire Writes Back: Theory and Practice in Post-Colonial Literatures*. London: Routledge, 1989.

Babalola, Adeboye. "Yoruba literature." Andrzejewski, 157–89.

Beier, Ulli. "D. O. Fagunwa." *Introduction to African Literature: An Anthology of Critical Writing*. Ed. Ulli Beier. London: Longman, 1967, 198–209.

Bhabha, Homi K. *The Location of Culture*. London: Routledge, 1994.

Dirlik, Arif. "The Postcolonial Aura: Third World Criticism in the Age of Global Capitalism." *Critical Inquiry* 20.2 (1994), 328–56.

Doortmont. Michel. "Recapturing the Past: Samuel Johnson and the Construction of the History of the Yoruba." PhD Diss. Erasmus U [Rotterdam], 1994.

Fabian, Johannes. *Language and Colonial Power*. Berkeley: U California P, 1986.

Fafunwa, Babs. *The History of Education in Nigeria*. Ibadan: NPS Educational, 1974.

Farias, P. F. de Moraes, and Karin Barber, eds. *Self-Assertion and Brokerage: Early Cultural Nationalism in West Africa*. Birmingham: Center of West African Studies, 1990.

Fraser, Robert. *West African Poetry: a Critical History*. Cambridge: Cambridge University Press, 1986.

Hutcheon, Linda. "Circling the downspout of Empire." *Past the Last Post: Theorizing Post-Colonialism and Post-Modernism*. Ed. Ian Adam and Helen Tiffin. Hemel Hempstead: Harvester Wheatsheaf, 1991, 167–89.

Isola; Akinwumi. "Contemporary Yorba Literary Tradition." Ogunbiyi, 73–84.

——. "The African Writer's Tongue." *Research in African Literatures* 23.1 (1992), 17–26.

Julien, Eileen. *African Novels and the Question of Orality*. Bloomington: Indiana University Press, 1992.

King, Bruce, ed. *Introduction to Nigerian Literature*. London: Evans Brothers, 1971.

Knappert, Jan. *Traditional Swahili Poetry*. Leiden: E. J. Brill, 1967.

Larson, Charles R. *The Emergence of African Fiction*. Bloomington: Indiana University Press, 1972.

Lindfors, Bernth, ed. *Critical Perspectives on Nigerian Literatures*. Washington, DC: Three Continents, 1975.

McClintock, Anne. "The Angel of Progress: Pitfalls of the Term 'Post-Colonialism'." *Post-Colonial Discourse and Postcolonial Theory: A Reader*. Ed. Patrick Williams and Laura Chrisman. New York: Columbia University Press, 1994.

Moore, Gerald. "Amos Tutuola." *Introduction to African Literature*. Ed. Ulli Beier, London: Longman, 1967, 179–87.

Obiechina, Emmanuel. *Culture, Tradition and Society in the West African Novel*. Cambridge: Cambridge University Press, 1975.

Ogunbiyi, Yémi, ed. *Perspectives on Nigerian Literature: 1700 to the Present*. Vols. 1 and 2. Lagos: Guardian Books, 1988.

Palmer, Eustace. *The Growth of the African Novel*. London: Heinemann, 1979.

Pilaszewicz, Stanislaw. "Literature in the Hausa Language." Andrzejewski 190–254.

Povey, John. "The Novels of Chinua Achebe." King, 97–112.

Roscoe, Adrian A. *Mother Is Gold*. Cambridge: Cambridge University Press, 1971.

Said, Edward W. *Orientalism*. New York: Vintage, 1978.

Spivak, Gayatri Chakravorty. "The Rani of Sirmur." *Europe and Its Others*. Ed. Francis Barker et al., Essex: University of Essex Press, 1985, 128–51.

——. "Subaltern Studies: Deconstructing Historiography." *Selected Subaltern Studies*. Ed. Ranajit Guha and Gayatri Chakravorty Spivak. Oxford: Oxford University Press, 1988, 3–32.

——. "The Burden of English." *Orientalism and the Postcolonial Predicament*. Ed. Carol A. Breckenridge and Peter van der Veer. Philadelphia: University of Pennsylvania Press, 1993, 134–57.

Tiffin, Helen. "Introduction." *Past the Last Post: Theorising Post-Colonialism and Post-Modernism*. Ed. Ian Adam and Helen Tiffin. Hemel Hempstead: Harvester Wheatsheaf, 1991, vii–xvi.

Young, Robert. *White Mythologies: Writing History and the West*. London and New York: Routledge, 1990.

Zabus, Chantal. *The African Palimpsest: Indigenization of Language in the West African Europhone Novel*. Amsterdam and Atlanta, GA: Rodopi, 1991.

Part XII

Ecocriticism

Even though ecocriticism is a fairly new branch of African literary criticism, the essays in this section suggest that it is potentially one of the most vibrant areas of critical discourse. This section requires reading in one go to get a sense of the energy that has been brought to the agenda by the ecocritical perspective. From the rather skeptical viewpoint of Slaymaker to the preliminary space-clearing gestures of Nixon, and on to the attempts at applying forms of ecocriticism to African literary texts by Nfah-Abbenyi and Caminero-Santangelo, they collectively reveal how much of a rich seam is waiting to be discovered in this branch of African theory and criticism. Of pertinence also is the fact that ecocritcism helps us refocus some of the burning ideological questions that have plagued African literary criticism from its inception. These questions include the relevance for African deliberations of Western-derived models of the relationship between man and nature, the relationship between Knowledge and Power (even when posed in the guise of concern for the welfare of the earth), and the links to be made between the ecoactivism of people such as the martyred Ken Saro-Wiwa and the ways in which literary critics think about issues of equity and justice. African ecocriticism thus ultimately foregrounds the interface between theory and praxis (both local and global) in a way that that makes it as relevant to understanding today's African condition as the earlier forms of criticism to be found in this anthology.

Chapter 90

Ecoing the Other(s):
The Call of Global Green and Black African Responses

William Slaymaker

The call of the other is a call to come, and that happens only in multiple voices.
Jacques Derrida, "From Psyche: Invention of the Other" (343)

[. . .]

In the canons of literature and literary criticism issuing from sub-Saharan Africa since the 1980s, the Green Wave has made landfall, especially in the white literary establishment in South Africa, where it has had a discernible impact. Mainly, however, the African echo of global green approaches to literature and literary criticism has been faint. There is no lack of writing in Africa that might fall under the rubric of nature writing. Surveys and studies of African literary landscapes are legion. Christine Loflin's *African Horizons: The Landscapes of African Fiction* is a prime example. Loflin uses the word *environment* as a descriptor and synonym for *surroundings* in the sense of the physical landscape and ambience in which a narrative character finds acceptance or alienation. There is little in her book that relates to ecology, environmental degradation, and depredations of land and animals. Similarly, much African nature writing and criticism, especially the sort that describes or analyzes the extraordinary megafauna and megaflora of East and South African savannas and forests, do not qualify as genuine ecolit or ecocrit as Kroeber and Buell would define it. The bulk of nature writing about sub-Saharan Africa – particularly as practiced by white writers – is connected with the Euro-American academic literary traditions of thematizing landscape, space, and conservationism and with popular conservationist narratives in books and films like *Born Free, Gorillas in the Mist*, and *A Far Off Place*.

Black African critics and writers have traditionally embraced nature writing, land issues, and landscape themes that are pertinent to national and local cultural claims and that also function as pastoral reminiscences or even projections of a golden age when many of the environmental evils resulting from colonialism and the exploitation of indigenous resources have been remediated. A review of any number of bibliographies, literary histories, and anthologies of black African literature and criticism in the past several decades will bear out this intense interest in the local recapture of a violated nature. But there is no rush by African

First published in *PMLA* 116.1 (2001): 129–44.

literary and cultural critics to adopt ecocriticism or the literature of the environment as they are promulgated from many of the world's metropolitan centers. For some black African critics, ecolit and ecocrit are another attempt to "white out" black Africa by coloring it green. To some African critics and writers, who directly participated in the liberation of their nation-states from colonialism, what ecocriticism offers is not another theory of liberation like Marxism. Rather, it appears as one more hegemonic discourse from the metropolitan West. For many (but by no means all) black African writers and critics, a theory of liberation entails and espouses a liberation from Western literary theories and their domination of literary themes, images, and language.[1] Black African writers take nature seriously in their creative and academic writing, but many have resisted or neglected the paradigms that inform much of global ecocriticism. The (siren?) call of the Green Wave resounding through much of the literary world has been answered weakly by black African writers and critics.

This ecohesitation has been conditioned in part by black African suspicion of the green discourses emanating from metropolitan Western centers. Also, black African experiences of nature, it is often argued, are different and other. Indeed, there is good cause to worry that environmentalism and ecologism are new forms of dominating discourses issuing from Western or First World centers. And the suspicion that environmentalism in all its various shades of green (including red greens) is a white thing is borne out by the explosive growth of research and participation in it by white scholars in and outside Africa. This suspicion is despite the equally burgeoning Asian, particularly Japanese, interest in environmental writing. Jhan Hochman's explanation for the lack of enthusiasm for environmentalism and ecology by blacks in Africa and in the diaspora appears in his introduction to *Green Cultural Studies: Nature in Film, Novel, and Theory.* Hochman claims that "whites have more time for nature than blacks since blacks must use a great deal of energy resisting or coping with white hegemony. Whites, more than blacks, also have greater access to some semblance of nature because blacks have been forced into urban areas for jobs" (190n22). What Hochman suggests, as many others have, is that whites have more time, energy, and wealth for appreciating and aestheticizing nature and the environment. Thus, it is only natural that whites should mount a global campaign to preserve what gives them pleasure and is not tied to their daily subsistence.

For many African writers and literary critics, whose origins and interests lie in the manifold cultures south of the Sahara and north of Pretoria, Eurocentered or Eurafricanized ecodiscourses are another literary theoretical fashion emanating from the Western academic elites, something like an "art d'eco" that is culturally analogous to art deco as a decorative style created and marketed in Europe and America.[2] Art d'eco is the postmodern representation in Western literature and film of the environmental preservationist and conservationist impulses that inspire audiences wearing green-tinted glasses. There is a great deal of exotic appeal and much hype in the efforts and advertisements to save the Serengeti for megafauna and the mountain environments of Burundi and eastern Zaire for the great apes. The narratives that have promulgated these fashionable appeals for natural and environmental preservation are recognized and rewarded more often outside Africa than in.

It is also obvious to black African intellectuals, as well as to their white counterparts, that environmental justice, as a global paradigm, will be used in the world marketplace when decisions are made about production, consumption of resources, and pollution caused by modernization, industrialization, and population growth. Environmentalism and ecologism threaten to dominate global economic policies in the new world order enforced by the

World Bank and the International Monetary Fund. Westernized world financial and scientific centers will define sustainability, biodiversity, population control, and land responsibility. It is what Guy Beney calls the "globalization temptation," or the risk of a new ecotechnocratic fascism imposed by northern powers on the Third and Fourth Worlds in the name of a specious scientism (192–3).

These global economic and political power moves in the names of ecologism and environmentalism are the subject of many books and articles. Of particular relevance is an essay collection edited by Fredric Jameson and Masao Miyoshi, *The Cultures of Globalization*. An essay on African cultures by the African film and literature scholar Manthia Diawara in this volume, "Toward a Regional Imaginary in Africa," is concerned with domination of cultural markets by Eurocentrists who impose restrictions and propose fashions to the detriment of local artisans who wish to remain loyal to regional cultures and not switch allegiance to nation-states artificially created by Europeans and their African puppets. In the same collection Ioan Davies's "Negotiating African Culture: Toward a Decolonization of the Fetish" analyzes the construction and deconstruction of African images and icons by African philosophers like V. Y. Mudimbe and Kwame A. Appiah. Davies concludes that ecopreservationist schemes seen in films like *Gorillas in the Mist or Born Free* are confirmations of colonial fetishes that continue to be purveyed to a broad audience in Europe and America (141). But more important is David Harvey's essay "What's Green and Makes the Environment Go Round?" Harvey lucidly discusses the use of ecology as a social and scientific movement that provides expert "neutral" knowledge for purposes of dominating global resources.[3] These three essays point to conclusions that some black African critics and writers have already drawn: ecolit and ecocrit are imperial paradigms of cultural fetishism that misrepresent the varied landscapes of sub-Saharan Africa. These misaligned icons of the natural other are invasive and invalid and should be resisted or ignored.

Larry Lohman makes an even stronger case against the reextensions of forms of imperial and colonial domination from centers to under-developed regions. In his essay "Resisting Green Globalism" he decries the new intellectualized imperialism harbored by an environmentalist agenda that issues from Western desires for the control and containment of land and natural resources. While discrediting global environmentalism, he opts, much like Attridge, for an openness to indeterminate responsibilities in relation to the claims of the other. He argues that a more just global arrangement of relations would defend "an intercultural space which is not a language nor a system nor an attitude, but rather a readiness, such as that found in the West in literary criticism or art history, to let incommensurable points of view alone [. . .]" (167). Many black African critics and writers have followed Lohman's advice and have left ecocrit and ecolit alone. Silence creates its own space.

Because global ecologism and environmentalism as cultural prerogatives are suspect for many black and white cultural critics, it is not surprising that the movements' reception in the black African literary world has been meager. However, it is important to note the exceptions and the growing interest in ecocriticism and literature of the environment among some writers. In Bernth Lindfors's bibliographic reference *Black African Literature in English, 1987–1991*, the subject guide reveals scant attention to "ecology" (one entry), "environment" (five entries), "landscape" (eight entries), and "nature" (nine entries), while the subjects that deal with colonialism in all its incarnations, with political ideologies and personalities, and with gender have attracted substantial interest from writers and critics involved in black African literature in Africa and abroad. For example, the Nigerian poet Niyi Osundare, an avowed ecoactivist and a writer on a wide range of environmental problems, is the primary subject of fifty-two entries and secondary subject of another fifteen during the five years that the bibliography covers. But only one directly addresses Osundare's central environmental themes: "The Poet as Ecologist: Osundara's Forest of a Million Wonders" (entry 19508; 467). There are several reasons for this superficial recovery of one of Osundare's main literary themes. While he was graced with a Noma Prize in 1991, which put him into the secondary tier of the African canon,[4] he has not achieved the status and visibility of his Nobelist compatriot Wole Soyinka. And the period 1987–91 may be considered to mark only the inception of interest in ecolit and ecocrit in black African literary circles.

Osundare is the best example of a black African writer, critic, and academic whose creative energy is focused on environmental and ecological issues. Still, typical reviews of his poetry do not examine in detail his ecological or environmental themes, which are evident in his 1986 collection of poems *The Eye of the Earth* and in his later creative work. What interests critics of Osundare's nature poetry most is his critique of political corruption in Nigeria, his support of peasants and farmers and others who live on and off the land, and his thematic examinations of history and revolution. For example, Aderemi Bamikunle categorizes Osundare as a nature poet interested in both Edenic and exploited West African landscapes, but he does not go so far as to use the words *ecology* and *environment* in any of their current incarnations in the developing lexicon of ecocrit and ecolit. In an essay on the poet by J. O. J. Nwachukwu-Agbada, however, there is one direct reference to the theme of ecology: "[. . .] Osundare would like that which is worthy such as the earth's ecology to be conserved and our capitalist tradition which is retrogressive to be done away with" (79). Nwachukwu-Agbada's thesis is that Osundare's best work, *The Eye of the Earth*, connects Nigerian wisdom lore and folktales with a sympathy for all exploited peoples of the world, including the oppressed working class and especially peasant farmers in Nigeria. Accordingly, Osundare's poetic and political task is to use poetry as an instrument to communicate with and for others in language and images that are rural and traditional and not hermetic and elitist or overly affected by Eurocentered poetic discourses (84–5). Nwachukwu-Agbada only momentarily focuses on environmentalism in Osundare's poetry before moving to other themes that seem more interesting and important.

A similar review of Lindfors's bibliography for the subjects of nature, ecology, and the environment in the work of Ken Saro-Wiwa, the martyred African writer associated throughout the world with ecoactivism and bioregional resistance to multinational corporations and corrupt governments, shows that none of the 105 entries focuses on Saro-Wiwa's environmental activities. This is mainly because Saro-Wiwa's reputation as ecoactivist spread largely after 1991, the end date of Lindfors's study. But even in 1999 Saro-Wiwa's literary (not political) fame rested on novels and short stories that satirize Nigerian political corruption and not on his ecological or environmental themes. In *Basi and Company*, one of his best-known novels, which became a popular Nigerian television series, the environment is Lagos; nature is almost absent. The stories in his collection *A Forest of Flowers* are antipastorals that do not celebrate rural life in Nigeria but criticize its narrowness and superstitions. Saro-Wiwa's ecoactivism was reserved for his public political activities and finds expression in his political statements *Genocide in Nigeria: The Ogoni Tragedy* and *A Month and a Day: A Detention Diary*. Saro-Wiwa's literary works do not, as Rob Nixon has argued they do, promote an "instrumental aesthetics" whereby literary expression becomes a tool for environmental change. Nor is it accurate to claim, as Nixon does, that Saro-Wiwa "was the first African writer to articulate the literature of commitment in expressly environmental terms" (43). In a recent collection of poems and essays on Saro-Wiwa edited by Abdul-Rasheed Na'Allah, *Ogoni's Agonies: Ken Saro-Wiwa and the Crisis in Nigeria*, there are several poems by African academics, poets, and critics that express in literary form the ecological problems Saro-Wiwa and the Ogoni have faced in the oil-rich Delta region of Nigeria.[5] The overall interest in Saro-Wiwa's literary environmentalism in this collection of almost seventy poems, analyses, and tributes by prominent scholars and writers is limited, but obviously his ecoactivism, while not literary, has inspired African writers and scholars to compose and publish environmentalist poetry.

Wole Soyinka responded sharply to the political execution of Saro-Wiwa in November 1995. Soyinka's diatribe against political corruption in Nigeria, *The Open Sore of a Continent*, particularly the epilogue, titled "Death of an Activist," vents his anger not just about an unjust execution but also about the exploitation of natural resources on traditional Ogoni lands and about other misuse of land. Similar statements can be found in his later and less strident *The Burden of Memory, the Muse of Forgiveness*, where he attacks the indigenous and foreign interests responsible for fouling the Nigerian landscape. For example, he cites a tin mine near Jos, in north central Nigeria, accusing the mining company of "violating virgin spaces and wreaking ecological devastation" (140). Soyinka's expressions of concern about ecology and environmentalism in his essays have few direct equivalents in his plays, poetry, and novels. His literary work connects his love of place and his respect for culturally important natural sites around Ife, in western Nigeria, but it does not announce ecoactivist themes. However, *Many Colors Make the Thunder-King*, a recent drama by Soyinka's colleague and compatriot Femi Osofisan, makes dramatic environmentalist statements about land and forest preservation. The dramatist's notes in the play program also plead for forest preservation.[6]

Parallel to the incipient literary ecoactivism in Nigeria is the current state of ecology and environmentalism in Kenya. In the media fore-front are Green Belt activists like Wangari Maathai, who are often the focus of popular magazine articles and television documentaries in the United States and elsewhere.[7] Also, in February 1999 university students fought police in Nairobi as a part of their protests against the planned destruction of pristine forests for housing and business developments in the Nairobi metropolitan area. While these events garner considerable world attention, Kenyan literary expressions of environmental concerns have not kept pace. Ngũgĩ wa Thiong'o and Ali Mazrui are well-established Kenyan authors with international reputations who have examined land issues in their high-profile works. Mazrui's book and video series *The Africans* as well as his more academic *Cultural Forces in World Politics* take up the problems of land distribution, colonialist alienation of land, and reparations due African cultures that have been robbed of their human and natural resources. He examines ecological and environmental issues in chapter 11 of *The Africans*, where, under the heading "The Frozen Ecology of Capitalism," he refers to the "winter gap," or absence of cold weather in Africa, as a cause contributing to the lack of capital development on the continent. In essence, Mazrui makes a complex causal argument connecting acculturation and acclimatization with capitalization and explaining why Africa has too much sun, too much and too little water, no Protestant work ethic, and little money for repair of environmental damage by human beings and nature. Mazrui's unique views on environmentalism and human history are redeveloped in his essay "From Sun-Worship to

Time-Worship: Toward a Solar Theory of History," which he wrote for delivery at an important 1991 Nairobi conference on ecology. Many of the other essays from this conference make strong African ecophilosophical statements. In particular, Odera Oruka, who collected the conference papers in the volume *Philosophy, Humanity and Ecology*, makes a plea for "ecophilosophy and the parental earth ethics," which he developed from the philosophical systems of Europe, Africa, and elsewhere. Neither Mazrui's arguments nor Oruka's have had any discernible effect on Kenyan writers of literature and literary criticism.

Ngũgĩ has written a number of extremely influential essays on African literature and colonialism and postcolonialism. *Decolonising the Mind* and *Moving the Centre* have had a great impact on literary and cultural studies in and outside Africa. In these critical studies as well as in his novel *Matigari*, Ngũgĩ emphasizes the natural relations of the Agikuyu to their land. Trees and forests are important as symbols of cultural preservation for Ngũgĩ, and forests symbolize haven and security for the Mau Mau. In his more recent statement *Penpoints, Gunpoints, and Dreams*, Ngũgĩ reprises these central ideas and arguments about nature. He does not translate his constant concern with the exploitation of East African land and of Agikuyu culture into ecoactivist narratives or environmentalist essays – though even the world media report ecoactivist stories on these subjects when doing an interview with Maathai or a news spot on student riots in Nairobi. Nor does the critical industry that has grown up around Ngũgĩ and his literary and theoretical positions take up ecological or environmental themes. For instance, the criticism on Ngũgĩ that appeared in the prominent journal *Research in African Literatures* in the 1990s is most interested in his statements about European linguistic and cultural dominance of African languages and modes of thought.[8]

Ecology and environmentalism have been substantially present in white South African literature and literary criticism for almost a century. Academic essays with titles like Andrew McMurry's "Figures in a Ground: An Ecofeminist Study of Olive Schreiner's *The Story of an African Farm*" are not infrequent. Julia Martin, author of the creative essay "Long Live the Fresh Air! Long Live Environmental Culture in the New South Africa!" is perhaps the most productive ecocritic in South Africa. And Michael Cope runs a green Web site, where he posts notes relevant to the study of the environment in South Africa as well as his environmentally inspired poetry in *Scenes and Visions*, particularly his poem "Three Degree Ecosutra." His audience is obviously global and electronically immediate.

Interest in environmental topics in South Africa was not racially divided in the 1990s, but the related scholarship has often been unbalanced. There are many good collections of essays from the 1990s that deal with the environment, ecology, and literary relations in South Africa.[9] Black South African scholarship is underrepresented in such volumes, but it is growing. The editors of these collections are obviously serious about racial and ethnic inclusiveness and diversity. *Restoring the Land: Environment and Change in Post-apartheid South Africa*, edited by Mamphele Ramphele, is a good example of the racial balancing act in the past decade. Ramphele outlines in her contribution, optimistically titled "New Day Rising," the reasons for the lack of black South African interest and participation in ecological concerns and movements: the struggle for survival, lack of power, limited education on environmental problems, and focus on crisis management (7). More important, Ramphele finds greater interest now among blacks. She asserts the need to listen to black South African women, and she quotes a poem by a South African woman involved in the liberation struggle that praises the beauty of the land and expresses hope in a key line, which Ramphele adopted for her essay title: "new day rising o'er the land" (8). Nonetheless, most of the articles in Ramphele's collection are by white academics and professionals who have made careers in environmentalism. The intent to expand the spectrum of voices is obvious in the selection of papers and presenters for the Association of University English Teachers of Southern Africa conference on the theme "Literature, Nature and the Land" held at the University of Zululand in July of 1992. The resulting publication, edited by Nigel Bell and Meg Cowper-Lewis, shows diverse ecological and environmental perspectives on literature, though in the majority of the conference papers white academics mainly from South Africa deal with white European and South African authors.

The South African poet Mongane Wally Serote, now a member of Parliament for the African National Congress, is an example of Ramphele's "new day rising." While his poetry is mainly linked to urban settings – the black townships surrounding Johannesburg – and to Black Consciousness aesthetics of the 1970s, Serote continues to worry and muse about land issues, such as mining abuse and environmental destruction propelled by colonialist and apartheid policies of land use. His lecture "National Liberation Culture, Environment and Literature," presented in Harare at a book fair in 1989, announces and outlines his environmental concerns. His argument is that the lack of freedom and development among nonwhites in South Africa has created a hostile natural environment as well as a hostile political one. The land has become uninhabitable, and the natural resources are no longer available to the majority of the people who live on the land. A democratic national liberation would translate into a mass democracy where the people could determine what should become of elephant tusks and trees. Serote is not a deep ecologist but a developmentalist and anthropocentrist who, from a typical African perspective, is concerned most about human benefit through proper conservation of nature. Instrumentalizing the other, the nonhuman sentient and nonsentient being, is the humanistic survival philosophy that most African writers, like Serote, express when they write about humanity in nature. Serote brings his political and philosophical beliefs to life in his poems. The poem *Come and Hope with Me* exemplifies his environmental concerns and his progressive, hopeful approaches to land and ecological issues. This long poem also contains passages that function as atavistic pastoral visions of a South African landscape before or separate from colonial invasions and Western industrial and modernizing disturbances. The poem sets the fecundity and fertility of South African soil and of the earth in general in Edenic and arcadian forms that emphasize his plea for preservation of nature and for reconciliation between contesting cultural claims to the land and its resources.

General anthologies, reviews, and summaries of black African literary and critical practice from the late 1980s through the 1990s bear out the thesis that global ecocritical responses to what is happening to the earth have had an almost imperceptible African echo. Books that deal with black African literary criticism and literary theory rarely take up environmental or ecological topics. Chidi Amuta's *The Theory of African Literature* does not refer to any literary critical approaches that are allied to nature and the environment, nor is there any acknowledgment of the pertinence of ecocriticism in Mineke Schipper's *Beyond the Boundaries: African Literature and Literary Theory*. Nothing of relevance to ecocriticism is to be found in Eldred D. Jones's *Critical Theory and African Literature Today*. There are no references what-soever to nature, the environment, and ecology in the many critical collections that focus on black African literature and criticism. The reviews of African literature and criticism that contain chapters on "trends," such as Neil Lazarus's *Resistance in Postcolonial African Fiction* or Jones's more recent *New Trends and Generations in African Literature*, do not list ecocriticism or environmental literature as one of them. Jones's collection, though, includes his essay "Land, War, and Literature in Zimbabwe: A Sampling," which touches on related topics and is especially relevant when read in relation to Christine Ombaka's article "War and Environment in African Literature," in Patrick Murphy's valuable reference work *Literature of Nature*. And Derek Wright's current *Contemporary African Fiction* does not consider ecotopics to be contemporary. There is no discussion of ecology, the environment, or even nature in the recent publication *Mapping Intersections: African Literature and Africa's Development*, edited by Anne Adams and Janis Mayes. This collection of essays, sponsored by the African Literature Association, covers the literary topics and critical approaches that the major critics and scholars of African literature considered relevant. The contributors do not link African development to environmental or ecological problems.[10] Nothing on nature, the environment, or ecology can be found in current literary histories and journal surveys such as the issue on African literature and criticism in the *Yearbook of Comparative and General Literature* or the special issue of *Studies in Twentieth Century Literature* titled *Africa: Literature and Politics* (Dehon). An updated literary history edited by Oyekan Owomoyela, *A History of Twentieth-Century African Literatures*, has nothing to say about this topic. Most good literary histories, such as Michael Chapman's *Southern African Literatures*, and literary anthologies, such as *African Rhapsody: Short Stories of the Contemporary African Experience*, edited by Ndezhda Obradovic, do not point out, examine, or highlight environmental or ecological themes. In *African Rhapsody* no mention is made of Ken Saro-Wiwa's ecoactivism even though his short story "Africa Kills Her Sun" (1989), which is included in the anthology along with biographical information, deals with the execution of a Nigerian political activist and prophesies Saro-Wiwa's own execution in 1995.

Anthologies, reviews, and summaries of black African literature and criticism reflect the general absence of ecocriticism and literature of the environment as noteworthy and attractive topics for research and creative writing in the academic and metropolitan communities of Africanists and artists who have been active in the past two decades. There are at least two causes for this gap: few black African writers have picked up on ecocritical topics, and it was mainly in the last decade of the twentieth century that young Africanist scholars began publishing on this topic. The 1990s were *the* decade of rapid and global environmentalist literary growth, and anthologies, literary histories, and the like are notoriously behind the times. Bibliographies of black African literature that appear in the first decade of the twenty-first century will likely reflect a significant growth of interest in ecocriticism and environmental literature. The low visibility of ecolit and ecocrit in recent black African writing is temporary. The green revolution will spread to and through communities of readers and writers of African literature, "ecoing" the booming interest in other parts of the literary world. Black African ecocritics, such as Niyi Osundare, are attuned to another, or an other, voice from the land and the wild, like their counterparts in North America, Europe, Japan, and India. In the new millennium this globalized interest will perhaps be better represented in cyberspace than in harder formats. The bilingual electronic journal *Mots pluriels* (supported by and issued from the University of Western Australia) put together an issue on eco-criticsm titled *Ecologie, écocritique et littérature / Ecology, Ecocritic and Literature* in which many of the articles focus on African literature (Jaccomard). One of them, a good example of recent Afro-ecocriticism, is "The Flora and Fauna of Negritude Poetry: An Ecocritical Rereading," by Kwaku Asante-Darko, who concludes that negritude poems "embody a pedagogy of ecological awareness" and have a "positive influence on the way readers are expected to treat the environment."

Manthia Diawara has questioned the humanistic and utilitarian benefits that a global and homogenized ecolit and ecocrit can offer black Africans. He asks, "Should [Africans] be interested in [ecocriticsm] because it is a global phenomenon, or because it has a potential to enlighten them, better their lives, or give them pleasure?" (Reader's report). I think an answer to this question may be found in Diawara's book *In Search of Africa*. Much of the book, particularly chapter 7, "Africa's Art of Resistance," is devoted to outlining a genuine contemporary African aesthetics and to advocating the promotion of African art and artists in a free global marketplace as well as locally. Diawara defends free consumption and market modernity for black Africans, which he links to the liberation of the self from oppressive postcolonial and artificial nation-states in Africa. And he extols the possibilities for playful postmodern and postcolonial self-development by the African artist who is both crafty and superbly skilled at a craft and who has a sophisticated artwork to sell in the world market. This is a consumer-craftsperson model that naturally aligns itself with the global flows of ecolit and ecocrit in cultural waves. Diawara's central arguments suggest that African creative writers and literary or cultural scholars would benefit from the global environmental movement to the same extent as a contemporary Japanese nature poet or a German cultural critic. The artist or intellectual can buy and sell in the world marketplace *and* maintain local and regional identities as well as playfully develop individual interests and aesthetic abilities. Selling artworks and ideas in the world market does not necessarily entail selling out to dominating thought systems. Citing the African artists Sidime Laye and Cheri Samba, Diawara shows how the African artist can reap pecuniary and aesthetic gains from participating in local, regional, and global markets simultaneously without loss of self-esteem.

Another answer to Diawara's utilitarian questioning of global cultural and environmentalism can be found in Attridge's tentative conclusions outlined earlier in this essay. Especially appropriate is Attridge's plea that aesthetic creations and inventions of the other be accepted as resulting from a practice of the ethics of responsibility. His defense of an altruistic aesthetics of alterity is an answer to Diawara's skepticism about the global validity of environmentalism and its literary and cultural expressions. Benefits and values accrue to those who are open to other ways of seeing and doing. The critical attitudes forwarded by Wai Chee Dimock in her article "A Theory of Resonance" can be usefully appropriated here. Dimock argues that literary texts and their interpretations "resonate" across time and space with positive effects. The enrichment and democratization of literary meanings and values by means of continual temporal and spatial transformations yield, in Dimock's view, a nuanced and vibrant cacophony of literary sounds. Hearing literature against the background noises of science, peripheral disciplines, and other voices strengthens its signal and audibility. Dimock's complex transmission metaphor, which relates electronic signal-to-noise ratios to readers' receptivity and their attention to unclear and disrupting signals, is useful as a model for the acceptance of messages in an environment of suspicion hosted by cultural critics such as Manthia Diawara, Dominick Head, and Eric Todd Smith. Using my own analogy, in which black African writers and critics echo, reflect, absorb, or avoid the green sound waves rumbling around the globe, I can conclude that a choral response to the green global call is not static (noise). Instead, environmental literature and ecological criticism are a resonating, dynamic signal generated by concern for the health of the earth and its resources. Consistent with Derrida's predication and prediction in the epigraph to this essay, the call of the other is to come – its future is definite – but it will not be univocal.

On the contrary, the call will be equivocal, with all the contradictions and aporias as well as the celebrations of equality and indefiniteness that are heard in equivocation.[11]

Notes

1   The critical work *Toward the Decolonization of African Literature*, by the Nigerian Bolekaja ("come down and fight") troika, Chinweizu, Onwuchekwa Jemie, and Ihechukwu Madubuike, is one of the most controversial and most commonly cited examples of anti-Western literary criticism. Interestingly enough, Chinweizu was a research fellow in environmental economics at the Massachusetts Institute of Technology in 1978–79. The book deals with the economics of African literature and criticism but not with any environmental themes or ideas.

2   In the 1920s proponents of art deco attempted to capture markets for their artisanal goods, made in Paris and Vienna and later New York. This art-and-craft movement attracted middle-class consumer interest by combining new technologies of domestic craft production with an efflorescent botanical style that developed from the exoticized nature popularized by Gauguin and other painters. There are striking similarities between art deco and popular forms of environmental literature in their preservationist aesthetics of a primitivized or primeval nature that nonetheless is highly stylized and rich in detail and color.

3   Harvey analyzes environmentalism as a suspect tool of globalism in his book *Justice, Nature and the Geography of Difference*. Especially pertinent are part 2, "The Nature of Environment," and ch. 13, "The Environment of Justice." It is noteworthy that Harvey's introductory "Thoughts for a Prologue" reproduces part of Adrienne Rich's ecopoem "An Atlas of the Difficult World." Another good monograph that examines the specious discourses of global environmentalism is Kay Milton's *Environmentalism and Cultural Theory*. Ch. 5, "Globalization, Culture and Discourse," and ch. 6, "The Culture of Environmentalist Discourse," offer further arguments about "scientific imperialism," the mythical and mystical natures of globalist discourses, and the abuses that environmentalism lends itself to.

4   Lindfors, a scholar of African literature at the University of Texas, Austin, claims that Osundare has reached number 26 and is rising in Lindfors's ranking of anglophone African writers by interest and importance ("African Literature Request"). Lindfors calculates African literary canons when he compiles the bibliographic publication *Black African Literature in English*. It is interesting to note the "nature numbers" (the counts of subject-guide references to nature, ecology, and the environment) in the next volume of the series, covering 1992–96 and published after this essay was written. The score now reads: "ecology" (no entries), "environment" (twenty-four entries), and "nature" (no entries). Lindfors has no clear notion why the numbers have changed so dramatically ("African Literature Inquiry").

5   A review of *Ogoni's Agonies* reveals no ecocritical essays, only a few ecopoems. In the foreword, Biodun Jeyifo, a prominent Nigerian literary critic, does pay tribute to the "political-ideological seismic shift" that has occurred in the past ten years as a result of concern for the "ecological survival of most of the people of our common earth" (xxiv). Jeyifo considers global ecocriticism a "fad" that nonetheless has important implications for future African literary studies (Personal interview). The poems "Ogoni People, the Oil Wells of Nigeria" (Olafioye) and "Ogoni, the Eagle Birds' Agony in the Delta Woods" (Na'Allah) are the best examples of ecoliterature in the collection. They demonstrate the small but growing interest in this literary approach among Nigerian writers who, because of the sensationalism surrounding the Saro-Wiwa affair, have well-defined personal and political interests in environmental disasters in Nigeria. In addition, there now exists a global audience for literature by Nigerians and others on Big Oil and local ecotragedies suffered by the Ogoni people and its leaders. This is borne out by the publication of

Saro-Wiwa's last work and words *(A Month and a Day)* by Penguin in London. Saro-Wiwa had published most of his work himself through the press he founded and supported, Saros International, in Port Harcourt, Nigeria.

6   Osofisan's play *Many Colors Make the Thunder-King* was commissioned by the Guthrie Theater, in Minneapolis, and performed there in February and March 1997. His interpretive notes for the play, contained in the program, state, "Weaving together a number of Yoruba folk tales, I re-read the whole story from an ecological perspective. And I discover [. . .] that most knowledge about the environment that we moderns are just now 'discovering,' had been written long ago, encapsulated in nuggets of mythical wisdom."

7   Maathai's essay "Foresters without Diplomas" attracted a great deal of attention to her environmental activities and the Kenyan women's Green Belt movement. Subsequently, Maathai along with her fellow Kenyan Michael Werikhe received the Goldman Ecological Prize. Aubrey Wallace's book *Eco-heroes: Twelve Tales of Environmental Victory* provides brief biographies, interviews, and statements that explain the environmental activities and interests of Wallace and the prize recipients. Maathai surfaces fairly regularly in documentaries and interviews that focus on women, the environment, and grassroots self-help movements in Africa and elsewhere.

8   Ngũgĩ and Mazrui have spent much of their careers out of Africa; thus, they write about the margins from the centers (London and New York, mainly) of academic employment and intellectual enterprise. African writers are often alienated from their natural environments and from culturally important events taking place in the regions they call home. They carry the burden of trying to interpret these landscapes and events for themselves and others from spatial and psychological distances. Environmental problems most often become paramount for a writer when they are in the writer's face and backyard, though firsthand experience of such problems did not make Saro-Wiwa focus on them in his literary activities.

9   Environmentalist and ecological movements in South Africa not only developed out of the importation of European views on land and biological preservation and study but also were coupled with nationalist movements and attempts to solidify power and control over large areas through the establishment of parks and preserves. Particularly good studies of the cultural-historical mechanisms of white environmental movements in South Africa can be found in *Ecology and Empire*, edited by Tom Griffiths and Libby Robin. Of special interest in this volume are "Ecology: A Science of Empire," by Robin, and Jane Carruthers's revealing study of the South African park system and its white nationalist roots, "Nationhood and the National Parks: Comparative Examples from the Post-imperial Experience."

10 There are many research studies from the 1980s and 1990s that link development and the environment. Barbara Thomas-Slayter and Dianne Rocheleau's book *Gender, Environment, and Development in Kenya* is one example of them. Particularly obvious is the richness of work linking women's environmental efforts and African development. For example, Rosemary Ruether's essay collection *Women Healing Earth* contains five essays – one-third of the total – by women about women's ecoactivism in eastern and southern Africa. Yet Florence Stratton's book *Contemporary African Literature and the Politics of Gender*, which focuses on the exclusion of the female other and the related under-development of women in African cultures, does not take up the central problem of women's relations to nature, the earth, and nonhuman others. Gay Wilentz's *Binding Cultures* avoids examining the relations of black women and ecology. So does Odile Cazenave's very recent work *Rebellious Women: The New Generation of Female African Novelists*. Neither the novelists Cazenave discusses nor their female creations are rebels and activists in the mold of Maathai and the women of the Kenyan Green Belt movement. However, in a collection edited by Stephanie Newell, *Writing African Women*, there is direct reference to the central relations of women, global ecological movements, and local African environmental issues. Newell's article in the volume, "Anatomy of Masculine Power," takes up the problem, though for Nigerian

nonfiction rather than literature (180–1). There are as yet few African literary critics who attempt to bridge disciplines and worlds – the technical and the literary or the human and the nonhuman – and to link the economics and technologies of development to gender and the environment and their literary representations.

11 Dimock and Derrida offer optimistic readings of confounded and multivoiced collisions between selves and others. For them static as background noise and interference has the positive qualities associated with diversifying the frequencies and amplifying the signals of cultural ideas. Dimock and Derrida often disclose and undermine static as the conceptual position of conservative interpretive communities that refuse to be moved by transformative texts and contexts. Their cultural critiques are, I believe, consistent with what Arjun Appadurai argues in his essay "Disjuncture and Difference in the Global Cultural Economy." He maintains that there is no neat, nonequivocal way to model the chaotic disjunctions that characterize "global flows" of cultural ideas and power. Borrowing techniques and terminology from fractal and chaos theories, Appadurai attempts to set up a lexicon for analyzing disjunctures and differences, though he does not claim to know how information and ideas will continue to shape globalization. For the study of black African ecoliterature and ecocriticism this means that scholars and writers must recognize that while the global green call may be more noise than pure signal and while the impulsive message that drives this fashionable literary approach may attenuate with time, it is nonetheless a genuine, if impure and often self-contradictory, call for information exchanges and interpretive responses to the global environmental crisis.

References

Adams, Anne, and Janis Mayes, eds. *Mapping Intersections: African Literature and Africa's Development.* Trenton: Africa World, 1998.

Amuta, Chidi. *The Theory of African Literature: Implications for Practical Criticism.* London: Zed, 1989.

Appadurai, Arjun. "Disjuncture and Difference in the Global Cultural Economy." *Public Culture* 2.2 (1990): 2–23.

Asante-Darko, Kwaku. "The Flora and Fauna of Negritude Poetry: An Ecocritical Re-reading." Jaccomard.

Attridge, Derek. "Innovation, Literature, Ethics: Relating to the Other." *PMLA* 114 (1999): 20–31.

Bamikunle, Aderemi. "The Development of Niyi Osundare's Poetry: A Survey of Themes and Technique." *Research in African Literatures* 26.4 (1995): 121–37.

Bell, Nigel, and Meg Cowper-Lewis, eds. *Literature, Nature and the Land: Ethics and Aesthetics of the Environment.* N.p.: University of Zululand, Dept. of English, 1993.

Beney, Guy. "'Gaia': The Globalitarian Temptation." *Global Ecology: A New Arena of Political Conflict.* Ed. Wolfgang Sachs. London: Zed, 1993. 179–93.

Buell, Lawrence. *The Environmental Imagination: Thoreau, Nature Writing, and the Formation of American Culture.* Cambridge: Harvard University Press, 1995.

Carruthers, Jane. "Nationhood and the National Parks: Comparative Examples from the Post-imperial Experience." Griffiths and Robin 125–38.

Cazenave, Odile. *Rebellious Women: The New Generation of Female African Novelists.* Boulder: Rienner, 2000.

Chapman, Michael. *Southern African Literatures.* London: Longman, 1996.

Chinweizu, Onwuchekwa Jemie, and Ihechukwu Madubuike. *Toward the Decolonization of African Literature.* Washington: Howard University Press, 1983.

Cope, Michael. "Three Degree Ecosutra." *Scenes and Visions.* 15 Feb. 1999 <http://www.cope.co.za/scenes/s&v.htm#ecosutra>.

Davies, Ioan. "Negotiating African Culture: Toward a Decolonization of the Fetish." Jameson and Miyoshi 125–45.

Dehon, Claire L., ed. *Africa: Literature and Politics*. Spec. issue of *Studies in Twentieth Century Literature* 15.1 (1991): 7–184.

Derrida, Jacques. "From Psyche: Invention of the Other." *Acts of Literature*. Ed. Derek Attridge. New York: Routledge, 1992. 310–43.

Diawara, Manthia. *In Search of Africa*. Cambridge: Harvard University Press, 1998.

——— . Reader's report for *PMLA*. 1999.

——— . "Toward a Regional Imaginary in Africa." Jameson and Miyoshi 103–24.

Dimock, Wai Chee. "A Theory of Resonance." *PMLA* 112 (1997): 1060–71.

Ecocriticism. Spec. issue of *New Literary History* 30.3 (1999): 505–716.

"Forum on Literatures of the Environment." *PMLA* 114 (1999): 1089–1104.

Griffiths, Tom, and Libby Robin, eds. *Ecology and Empire: Environmental History of Settler Societies*. Seattle: University of Washington Press, 1997.

Harvey, David, *Justice, Nature and the Geography of Difference*. Oxford: Blackwell, 1996.

——— . "What's Green and Makes the Environment Go Round?" Jameson and Miyoshi 327–55.

Head, Dominic. "The (Im)Possibility of Ecocriticism." Kerridge and Sammells 27–39.

Hochman, Jhan. *Green Cultural Studies: Nature in Film, Novel, and Theory*. Moscow: University of Idaho Press, 1998.

Jaccomard, Hélène, ed. *Ecologie, écocritique et littérature/ Ecology, Ecocritic and Literature*. Spec. issue of *Mots pluriels* 11 (1999). 2 Nov. 2000 <http://www.arts.uwa.edu.au/motspluriels/MP1199kad.html>.

Jameson, Fredric, and Masao Miyoshi, eds. *The Cultures of Globalization*. Durham: Duke University Press, 1998.

Jeyifo, Biodun. "Ken Saro-Wiwa and the Hour of the Ogoni." Foreword. Na'Allah, *Ogoni's Agonies* xxiii–xxxii.

——— . Personal interview. 3 Sept. 1999.

Jones, Eldred D., ed. *Critical Theory and African Literature Today*. Trenton: Africa World, 1994.

——— . "Land, War, and Literature in Zimbabwe: A Sampling." Jones, *New Trends* 50–61.

——— , ed. *New Trends and Generations in African Literature*. Trenton: Africa World, 1996.

Kerridge, Richard, and Neil Sammells, eds. *Writing the Environment: Ecocriticism and Literature*. London: Zed, 1998.

Kroeber, Karl. *Ecological Literary Criticism: Romantic Imagining and the Biology of Mind*. New York: Columbia University Press, 1994.

Lazarus, Neil. *Resistance in Postcolonial African Fiction*. New Haven: Yale University Press, 1990.

Lindfors, Bernth. "African Literature Inquiry." E-mail to the author. 18 Dec. 2000.

——— . "African Literature Request." E-mail to the author. 15 Apr. 1999.

——— . *Black African Literature in English, 1987–1991*. London: Zell, 1995.

Loflin, Christine. *African Horizons: The Landscapes of African Fiction*. Westport: Greenwood, 1998.

Lohman, Larry. "Resisting Green Globalism." *Global Ecology: A New Arena of Political Conflict*. Ed. Wolfgang Sachs. London: Zed, 1993, 157–69.

Maathai, Wangari. "Foresters without Diplomas." *Ms.* Mar.–Apr. 1991: 74–5.

Martin, Julia. "Long Live the Fresh Air! Long Live Environmental Culture in the New South Africa!" Murphy 337–43.

Mazrui, Ali A. *The Africans*. PBS. WETA, Washington. 1986.

——— . *The Africans: A Triple Heritage*. Boston: Little, 1986.

——— . *Cultural Forces in World Politics*. London: Currey, 1990.

——— . "From Sun-Worship to Time-Worship: Toward a Solar Theory of History." Oruka, *Philosophy* 165–76.

McMurry, Andrew. "Figures in a Ground: An Ecofeminist Study of Olive Schreiner's *The Story of an African Farm*." *English Studies in Canada* 4 (1994): 431–48.

Milton, Kay. *Environmentalism and Cultural Theory: Exploring the Role of Anthropology in Environmental Discourse*. London: Routledge, 1996.

Murphy, Patrick, ed. *Literature of Nature: An International Sourcebook*. Chicago: Fitzroy, 1998.

Na'Allah, Abdul-Rasheed, ed. *Ogoni's Agonies: Ken Saro-Wiwa and the Crisis in Nigeria*. Trenton: Africa World, 1998.

——. "Ogoni, the Eagle Birds' Agony in the Delta Woods." Na'Allah, *Ogoni's Agonies* 101.

Newell, Stephanie. "Anatomy of Masculine Power." Newell, *Writing* 170–90.

——, ed. *Writing African Women: Gender, Popular Culture and Literature in West Africa*. London: Zed, 1997.

Ngũgĩ wa Thiong'O. *Decolonising the Mind: The Politics of Language in African Literature*. London: Currey, 1986.

——. *Matigari*. Trans. Wangũi wa Goro. London: Heinemann, 1989.

——. *Moving the Centre: The Struggle for Cultural Freedoms*. London: Currey, 1993.

——. *Penpoints, Gunpoints, and Dreams: Towards a Critical Theory of the Arts and the State in Africa*. Oxford: Clarendon, 1998.

Nixon, Rob. "Pipedreams: Ken Saro-Wiwa, Environmental Justice, and Micro-minority Rights." *Black Renaissance* 1.1 (1996): 39–55.

Nwachukwu-Agbada, J. O. J. "Lore and Other in Niyi Osundare's Poetry." Jones, *New Trends* 73–86.

Obradovic, Ndezhda, ed. *African Rhapsody: Short Stories of the Contemporary African Experience*. New York: Bantam, 1994.

Olafioye, Tayo. "Ogoni People, the Oil Wells of Nigeria." Na'Allah, *Ogoni's Agonies* 99–100.

Ombaka, Christine. "War and Environment in African Literature." Murphy 327–36.

Oruka, H. Odera. "Ecophilosophy and the Parental Earth Ethics." Oruka, *Philosophy* 115–29.

——, ed. *Philosophy, Humanity and Ecology: Philosophy of Nature and Environmental Ethics*. Nairobi: ACTS, 1994.

Osofisan, Femi. "Reinterpreting the Ancestor's Lore." Program for *Many Colors Make the Thunder-King*, by Osofisan. Guthrie Theater, Minneapolis. Feb.–Mar. 1997. N. pag.

Osundare, Niyi. *The Eye of the Earth*. Ibadan: Heinemann, 1986.

Owomoyela, Oyekan, ed. *A History of Twentieth-Century African Literatures*. Lincoln: University of Nebraska Press, 1993.

Ramphele, Mamphele. "New Day Rising." Ramphele, *Restoring* 1–12.

——, ed. *Restoring the Land: Environment and Change in Post-apartheid South Africa*. London: Panos, 1991.

Robin, Libby. "Ecology: A Science of Empire." Griffiths and Robin 63–75.

Ruether, Rosemary, ed. *Women Healing Earth: Third World Women on Ecology, Feminism, and Religion*. Maryknoll: Orbis, 1996.

Saro-Wiwa, Ken. "Africa Kills Her Sun." Obradovic 290–303.

——. *Basi and Company: A Modern African Folktale*. Port Harcourt: Saros, 1987.

——. *A Forest of Flowers*. Port Harcourt: Saros, 1986.

——. *Genocide in Nigeria: The Ogoni Tragedy*. Port Harcourt: Saros, 1992.

——. *A Month and a Day: A Detention Diary*. London: Penguin, 1995.

Schipper, Mineke. *Beyond the Boundaries: African Literature and Literary Theory*. London: Allison, 1989.

Serote, Mongane Wally. *Come and Hope with Me*. Cape Town: Philip, 1994.

——. "National Liberation Culture, Environment and Literature." *On the Horizon*. Johannesburg: COSAW, 1990. 79–85.

Smith, Eric Todd. "Dropping the Subject: Reflections on the Motives for an Ecological Criticism." *Reading the Earth: New Directions in the Study of Literature and Environment*. Ed. Michael Branch, Rochelle Johnson, Daniel Patterson, and Scott Slovic. Moscow: University of Idaho Press, 1998. 29–39.

Soyinka, Wole. *The Burden of Memory, the Muse of Forgiveness.* New York: Oxford University Press, 1999.

—— . *The Open Sore of a Continent: A Personal Narrative of the Nigerian Crisis.* New York: Oxford University Press, 1996.

Stratton, Florence. *Contemporary African Literature and the Politics of Gender.* London: Routledge, 1994.

Thomas-Slayter, Barbara, and Dianne Rocheleau. *Gender, Environment, and Development in Kenya: A Grassroots Perspective.* Boulder: Rienner, 1995.

Wallace, Aubrey. *Eco-heroes: Twelve Tales of Environmental Victory.* San Francisco: Mercury, 1993.

Wilentz, Gay. *Binding Cultures: Black Women Writers in Africa and the Diaspora.* Bloomington: Indiana University Press, 1992.

Williams, Joy. Postscript. *The Eggs of the Eagle.* By Raymond Williams. London: Chatto, 1990. 318–23. Vol. 2 of *People of the Black Mountains.*

Williams, Raymond. *The Country and the City.* New York: Oxford University Press, 1973.

—— . *Resources of Hope: Culture, Democracy, Socialism.* London: Verso, 1989.

Winkler, Karen. "Inventing a New Field: The Study of Literature about the Environment." *Chronicle of Higher Education* 9 Aug. 1996: A8+.

Wright, Derek, ed. *Contemporary African Fiction.* Vol. 42. Bayreuth: Bayreuth African Studies Breitinger, 1997.

Yearbook of Comparative and General Literature 43 (1995): 5–136. Bloomington: Indiana University Press, 1995.

Chapter 91

Different Shades of Green:
Ecocriticism and African Literature

Byron Caminero-Santangelo

In the past fifteen years, African environmental activism has been brought to the world's attention through the martyrdom of Ken Saro-Wiwa and, more recently, by the awarding of the Nobel Peace Prize to Wangari Maathai. These figures point not only to the ways that Africans have mobilized against environmental degradation, but also to the grave environmental problems faced by Africa which have become, especially in conjunction with social problems, a significant threat to its present and future well-being. (It is no accident, of course, that both Saro-Wiwa and Maathai are also – perhaps primarily – civil rights activists.) Ken Saro-Wiwa's leadership also suggests that African writers can play a significant role in environmental causes, just as they have in other forms of social activism. Might Africanist literary studies more generally have a place in this venture? The new, burgeoning field of ecocriticism would suggest that it could.[1] As Laurence Buell claims, "The success of all environmentalist efforts finally hinges not on 'some highly developed technology, or some arcane new science' but on 'a state of mind': on attitudes, feelings, images, narratives" (*Writing* 1), all of which can be found in "acts of environmental imagination" (2).

In the most extensive discussion to date on African literature and ecocriticism, William Slaymaker argues "that global ecocritical responses to what is happening to the earth have had an almost imperceptible African echo" (138), and calls for both African writers and critics to embrace what he sees as a global ecocritical movement. Yet, although Slaymaker claims that ecocriticism is global, the criteria he uses to determine if a piece of writing is properly environmental come from a primarily Anglo-American ecocritical framework, associated with the application of the sciences to literature and with deep ecology, which focuses on attacking "anthropocentrism."

Now, it is true that if one uses these criteria, there has certainly been little environmental writing – literary or critical – from Africa. The problem, however, is precisely that Slaymaker embraces these criteria and the principles underpinning them – principles which represent a

Unpublished paper.

potential ecocritical orthodoxy, primarily developed in the West using American and British literature, and which have some serious limitations (at least in the African context).[2] Putting these principles in dialogue with African environmental history and literary engagement with that history points to those limitations and might suggest why an ecocritical vision in its more orthodox form has not been and probably will not be embraced by many Africanist critics and/or reflected by African writers. The kind of dialogue I am calling for can result in transformations in the definition of environmental writing in such a way that the list of such writing from Africa might be substantially expanded and revised. Ultimately, my aim is not to create an antagonistic binary (ecocriticism vs. African literature and environmental history) in which the two "sides" are represented as necessarily at odds or in which each "side" is represented as a single, homogenous entity. Rather, I wish to begin examining African literary texts in light of issues raised by ecocriticism and African environmental history (and the relationship between them) in order, on the one hand, to look at those texts and their relationships with each other in new ways and, on the other hand, to enable them to contribute to developing discussions *within* ecocriticism and African environmental history.

Anglo-American ecocriticism frequently embraces the ethical position that humans need to do away with "anthropocentrism" by rejecting the nature–culture dualism which objectifies nature and places the category of culture/humanity at the center of things. If other "political" approaches are concerned with the ways that human difference and relations of dominance are made "natural," an ecocritical approach is focused on anthropocentrism as a way of creating difference between humans and non-human nature and reinforcing the exploitation of the environment. Ecocriticism, therefore, aims to decenter humans, often by giving nature "back" its subjectivity. We must, ecocritics claim, represent nature (speak for *and* about it) as a subject with rights by finding (listening to) nature's voice. Lawrence Buell wants "a mode of vision that . . . opens itself up as well as it can to the perception of the environment as an actual independent party entitled to consideration for its own sake" (77). This call for an "ecocentric" vision encourages a focus on nature as wilderness or outback, since in this form nature appears to be most fully separated from "culture," there to be known and valued for itself. Part of the attack on "anthropocentrism" can also involve a refusal to define environmental problems in terms of effects on humans and in terms of struggles for a more just, equitable set of relationships among humans.

Ecocritical attacks on "anthropocentrism" are often coupled with a sharp castigation of literary studies. For example, ecocritics criticize Marxism and poststructuralism for suggesting that nature itself is always, already, a cultural construct tied to human political interests (Bate; Buell *Environmental*). They insist that in literary studies non-human nature must be treated as having an existence and value beyond the human and that environmental representation is not to be read only as a means of symbolically exploring other, more important (human) concerns or as an ideological tool.[3] The concern with the referential properties of literary representation leads to a focus on the question of mimesis – with asking how and whether a piece of literature is trying to break through cultural constructions of the environment to the thing in itself (nature). Not surprisingly, given the focus on knowing and understanding nature, ecocritics embrace the use of the biological sciences in the study of literature. Finally, using the positions described above, ecocritics have called for a new set of evaluative criteria based on the degree to which a piece of literature strives to represent non-human nature (as opposed, for example, to making it a screen for other concerns), give it a voice, invest it with value, emphasize humans' interdependence with it, decenter the human, and alleviate environmental degradation (Buell 7–8).

Of course, what is being described in broad strokes are some prominent trends in ecocriticism; there are many, many voices within ecocriticism which offer theoretically complex versions of or dissent from the kinds of positions described above.[4] Of particular relevance for the thesis proffered here is David Mazel's focus on the need to recognize that *all* representations of the environment are constructions tied to power and that to ignore this political component of environmental representation is to ignore one's own (interested) position within a power/knowledge matrix. He offers the provocative claim that "American environmentalism be approached as a form of domestic Orientalism... Rather than treating environmentalism as a conceptually 'pure' and unproblematic *resistance* to power, as resistance based upon an objective and disinterested organization of knowledge, I suggest we analyze it as just one of many potential modes for *exercising power*" (144). Mazel goes on to discuss (briefly) the link between literary environmentalism and imperial conquest in the American West (144). In the context of colonial and postcolonial Africa, it is difficult to dismiss this kind of relationship between environmentalism and imperialism. Slaymaker even acknowledges that a primary reason for African resistance to ecocriticism is its potential "imperial" implications: "there is good cause to worry that environmentalism and ecologism are new forms of dominating discourses" (133). Yet, despite this acknowledgment, Slaymaker does not really explore the significance of these imperial implications for the dominant ecocritical paradigm to which he ascribes. I would like to explore both the history of the relationship between imperialism and environmentalism in Africa (this relationship is not "new" as Slaymaker suggests) and the implications of this history for some key ecocritical positions.

Recent scholarship on conservation in Africa shows the links among many Western "environmental" beliefs regarding Africa, conservationist policies, and power in colonial and postcolonial Africa (W. Adams, Anderson and Grove, Bienert, Bonner, Carruthers, Grove, Ranger, Hulme and Murphree, Leach and Mearns, Neumann). This work suggests, for example, that traditional Western "wisdom" about the environment and environmental change in Africa can be a form of colonial discourse which works all the more effectively through claims to its scientific validity and/or its apolitical objectivity. Such "wisdom" celebrates Western environmental knowledge and denigrates indigenous environmental practice, suggesting that (non-Westernized) Africans do not understand and abuse their environment, and that Westerners (or those with Western training) need to protect it. Thus, much recent scholarship in African environmental history represents Western "received wisdom" about African environments, as well as Western conservation in Africa, as determined by the "historical, political and institutional context for science and policy" and, more specifically, by the effort to promote "external intervention in the control and use of natural resources" (20). In order to counter such "wisdom," many environmental historians have argued that what has been seen as a lack of environmental wisdom among African peoples can reflect a more accurate understanding of environment and environmental change. Furthermore, such work suggests, resistance to conservation efforts (past and present) by locals is not necessarily to be understood only as resulting from ignorance or simple self-interest; rather it can be about a political struggle over the meanings of environmental conditions and the policies and power dynamics enabled by such meanings (Grove, Ranger, Neumann).

Some of the most interesting scholarship showing the political underpinnings and implications of conservation policy in Africa has been focused on national parks (W. Adams, Bonner, Carruthers, Ranger, Hulme and Murphree, Neumann). For example, some scholars have claimed that parks serve the symbolic function of reinforcing the notion that the "real" Africa is a natural wilderness untouched by culture. This symbolic resonance comes to reinforce the notion that Africans had no culture before colonization and that Europeans and those who have been Europeanized bring civilization. Perhaps even more importantly, those who create and maintain parks and, more generally, protect Africa's wildlife – colonists, white settlers, post-independence elites – are represented as the proper stewards and thus owners of this "real" Africa. In fact, the supposed lack of civilization among the majority of Africans is marked by their lack both of "nature" appreciation and of desire to "protect" animals. Such ideas both reinforce and are reinforced by the expelling of Africans from the land set aside for conservation purposes.

In general, developments in conservation history lead to very different conclusions and point to different environmental agendas from those encouraged by ecocriticism, which has embraced the vision of deep ecology. What these developments suggest is precisely the need to think about the "anthropocentric" *politics* both of conservation in Africa and of the knowledge on which conservation is based – including scientific knowledge. Recent environmental studies in Africa bring into question those aspects of ecocriticism which would downplay the social and political implications of representations of nature, especially as these representations are related to the claim to speak for and to protect nature. They also bring into bold relief the danger of subordinating human concerns to environmental concerns, revealing how such subordination in the African context has been tied to heinous (hegemonic) political ideologies and goals rather than leading to a liberatory, counter-hegemonic agenda.

The questions posed for the dominant ecocritical paradigm by studies of conservation in Africa can be underscored by exploring the political implications of representations of the African environment and/or environmentalist concerns in European literature about Africa. Karen Blixen's (alias Isak Dinesen) *Out of Africa* offers a particularly good case in point. In many ways, it fulfills the requirements offered by those like Buell and Slaymaker for an environmental text. In significant sections of it, especially "From an Immigrant's Notebook," Blixen focuses on the ways that her experiences in Africa have taught her to value and appreciate non-human nature; this transformative lesson is embodied in a kind of "nature writing" with careful descriptions of nature's wonder and beauty. The text also abhors the abuse of non-human nature by modernity, suggesting in the process that nature has a subjectivity we must respect.

Yet, although the more eco-centered aspects of *Out of Africa* might, in the context of the history of Western environmental degradation, have a potentially counter-hegemonic force, it is important to emphasize that these eco-friendly elements are key parts of the text's colonialist ur-narrative. The narrative develops the notion of a natural aristocracy made up of those Europeans who maintain a non-bourgeois, feudal cultural sensibility; part of this sensibility involves appreciating and being in tune with Africa's wild nature.[5] The more environmentalist sections of the text are tied to this narrative in that they help establish both how Blixen was able to appreciate and value nature in a way the bourgeois, who arbitrarily slaughter wildlife wholesale, were not, and how she maintained enough distance from nature to make her appreciation for it cultured and self-aware in a way impossible for the natives. (Africans, we are told, "have no sense or taste for contrasts, the umbilical cord of Nature has, with them, not been quite cut through" (158), and they "usually have very little feeling for animals" (34).) Blixen's environmental sensibility is directly tied with colonial conservation when she mentions (at least twice) her regret that "the whole of Ngong Mountain was not enclosed in the Game Reserve" (6) so that the "Buffalo, the Eland and the Rhino" would not be killed off and driven away by the "young Nairobi shop-people" (6).

Given that much African literature struggles to offer a different vision from the one produced by colonial discourse, it should be no surprise that the potential challenges posed for ecocriticism by recent African environmental history can also be found in African literature with an anti-colonial agenda. For example, Ngugi wa Thiong'O's classic *A Grain of Wheat* points to the relationship between nature conservation (and appreciation) and colonialism. Most of the British characters in the novel live and work at the "Githima Forestry and Agricultural Research Station." The apparent purpose of the "station" is to develop knowledge of plants, soil, and weather in order to improve agriculture and conservation. However, it is also a colonial institution which reinforces imperial ideology and practice; indeed, it was started "as part of a new colonial development plan" (33). The notion that the British are able to "understand" and institute the proper management of nature reinforces the dispossession of the Gikuyu from their land by formulating the British as its proper stewards and by effacing the forms of knowledge and the kinds of relationships with the land which have been developed over centuries. This idea also positions the Gikuyu as in need of instruction. In a sense, they become part of the African wilderness itself – that which needs to be known and managed. When the representation of the forestry station is put in the context of the novel as a whole, what becomes clear is that the station's purpose – knowledge about and conservation of nature – cannot be separated either from the colonial vision of the relationship between Britain and Africa or from (related) colonial policies of land alienation, political rule, and resource control.

Nevertheless, although *A Grain of Wheat* reminds us of how conservation has been tied to colonial (and neo-colonial) agendas in Africa, Ngugi uses concerns about environmental decline to oppose colonialism and its ideology, implying that to engage in anti-colonial struggle is also to fight against environmental degradation. In the novel, this degradation cannot be separated from the continued colonization of the land, despite the imminence of Uhuru, and the perpetuation of capitalism as a *form* of ownership. The novel suggests that true political and economic liberation will result in a healthy land, since its well-being is determined by a return to the proper economic and political relationships which define its identity. Using nature – and nature's protection – as a means to naturalize its anti-colonial construction of the "people" and the nation, *A Grain of Wheat* can be aligned with much early nationalist and anti-colonial African literature which embraced a pastoral vision of a pre-colonial African order aligned and in tune with nature over and against a corrupting, mechanized European modernity. Although *A Grain of Wheat* would still not really be considered properly "green" when viewed from the perspective of Buell's criteria for an environmental text (since it focuses almost exclusively on human concerns, even in its environmental representations), many ecocritics embrace the kind of vision offered by Ngugi, which assumes an alignment between the fight for environmental preservation and anti-colonial struggle, and which romanticizes pre-colonial (especially animist) societies as in harmony with nature (see Manes, Ombaka, Willoquet-Maricondi).

In a sense, many of the recent studies in African environmental history discussed earlier also could be read as reinforcing a romantic perspective on anti-colonial struggle and indigenous societies by suggesting that colonists, post-independence governments, and conservation agencies have been blinded by their political agendas and have missed the "right" ecological perspective which non-Westernized Africans embrace and which is a legacy of pre-colonial African societies. But this idea, in its turn, has been challenged from within the discipline. William Bienart, citing much recent work in African environmental studies, warns that "Arguments rooted in an anti-colonial and sometimes populist or anti-modernist discourse can present us with an analytic closure, too neat an inversion" (284). In his effort to challenge the continued use, if inversion, of homogenizing binaries (modern/traditional; Western/Indigenous; and so on), Bienert points out that pre-colonial, colonial, and postcolonial African rural communities have been and are in flux, and that their environmental knowledge and practices are not outside relationships of power. Bienert argues that pre-colonial African practices were by no means always in harmony with local ecology, and notes how the long histories of Western influence and of colonialism have transformed local environmental knowledge, attitudes, and practices.

Nuruddin Farah's *Secrets* could also be read as encouraging skepticism regarding an overly romanticized ecological vision, since for Farah *all* environmental knowledge must be viewed as cultural constructions tied to power and open to appropriation for environmentally and socially questionable practices. This postmodern skepticism regarding environmental representation makes *Secrets* a text that many ecocritics would deem insufficiently environmental, especially given that questions about human identity and development remain at the center of the narrative.

Yet, in other ways, *Secrets* is profoundly "environmental," even in Buell's terms. Its skepticism regarding representations of nature is tempered by an intense concern with the process of environmental degradation in Somalia in the last decades of the twentieth century. For example, it offers a vivid representation of the killing off of Somalia's wildlife for the sake of individual profit through international trade. Just as importantly, it emphasizes the importance of the *effort* both to engage with nature as something existing beyond human representation and to represent and value it in new ways. Finally, Farah suggests that human identity is partly constituted by non-human nature, and, in this way, decenters the human in relation to nature. Ultimately, *Secrets'* combination of skepticism towards *all* representations of nature and its ecofriendly vision puts it in line with Buell's notion of the need for dual accountability in environmental representation and imagination – accountability both to the linguistic (constructed) nature of all representations of nature *and* to an extant non-human nature which we must try to represent and with which we are interdependently bound.

This complex situation is often represented when Kalaman, the main protagonist, and his family interact with animals. For example, when a plover perches on a table at which Nonno and Kalaman are talking, the two human characters challenge various human efforts to assign meaning to the bird. Nonno questions a cultural construction of the plover as ill-omened, and both he and Kalaman undermine any absolute distinction between themselves and the bird by treating and describing it as a human visitor. Yet, Nonno himself tries to define the plover, claiming: "Our visitor is no domesticated Hanu [their pet monkey] whom we pamper with a personal name and our affection. This plover is a freeborn, freethinking bird" (155). Carefully observing the bird, Kalaman mentally contradicts Nonno's effort to turn it into the image of a pastoral nature free from human restraint. He notes to himself that there is a "thread tied to the bird's shank" with "a tiny piece of paper": "Was the plover a message-carrying bird in our dining room? Contrary to Nonno's view, the bird was no free agent, roaming the winds at will . . ." (155). As it progresses, this scene of critical observation combines an effort to represent and value non-human nature in ways that exceed existing cultural vocabularies, an effort to represent the (possibly destructive) impact of humans on nature, and an intense skepticism regarding all such efforts.

More generally, in *Secrets* part of Kalaman's development is marked by an awareness of his interdependence with the greater biosphere (the decentering of the human), the need to try to understand (and represent) nature in new ways, *and* the need to recognize that all attempts to speak for nature will be a human appropriation of nature's voice. In other words, development in the novel is related to the acquisition of a more eco-centered sensibility, even as the human is recentered (as agent of change) and environmental representation is brought into question. Dominic Head claims that such a perspective can recuperate the postmodern novel form for ecocriticism even as it brings into question some central ecocritical principles. According to Head, the "environmental" novel pro-motes a more ecological mode of perception in the reader through a rethinking of nature and the self's relationship with it. Human consciousness remains central, in a sense, but it has been recentered through a kind of decentering. Head acknowledges that this kind of recuperation of the novel will still be considered too anthropocentric for many ecocritics. However, he points out that the promotion (expansion) of an ecocritical agenda remains dependent on the transformation of human consciousness. Furthermore, the postmodern novel enables an opening for non-human nature – a pointing towards it and an emphasis on the importance of trying to understand and represent it – while *at the very same time* undermining the truth claims of environmental representation. In this sense, Head sees ecocriticism as having the potential to be aligned with postcolonialism (in its more postmodern manifestation) which tries to open up a space for the voice of the other – including within the self – while maintaining a healthy skepticism about the final recuper-ation of this voice.

My brief discussions of *Secrets* and *A Grain of Wheat* have tried to show, admittedly in a very preliminary fashion, both how ecocriticism might open up some new, important ways of looking at African literary texts in terms of environmental concerns and, at the same time, how these texts might be linked with recent studies of conservation in Africa which suggest a number of limitations to ecocritical orthodoxy, especially in the African context. Yet, in my literary readings and my discussions of ecocriticism and African environmental history, I have pointed to the heterogeneity of each "field." Ultimately, the most productive way of using the latter two "fields" to open up different ways of reading African literature is not to argue which literary texts take the "right" position on a set of issues, but to trace their convergence and divergence with different points of view in ecocriticism and studies of conservation in Africa and with each other. In turn, this mode of reading enables African literary texts to contribute to ecocriticism and African environmental history not simply by offering further examples for already existing frameworks, but by opening out and devel-oping debates and positions within those fields. The ultimate goal, of course, remains to make African literature and its study relevant to environmentalism in Africa by helping us think and rethink the meanings of environment and environmental degradation, as well as their relationships with humans and human history.

Notes

1   As Laurence Coupe defines it, ecocriticism is an approach to literature which "considers the relationship between human and non-human life as represented in literary texts and which theorizes about the place of literature in the struggle against environmental destruction" (302).

2   Michael Lundblad makes a similar point about Slaymaker's overview, claiming that the terms of Slaymaker's "hopes" for an ecocritical revolution in African literature and literary studies "are still flowing outward from the metropole, refusing to *listen* to the messages being generated by activists like Saro-Wiwa and writers like Achebe" (18).

3   For particularly strident attacks on literary studies in this vein, see Love and Howarth.

4   Buell offers a particularly important case in point. In *The Environmental Imagination*, his questioning of trends in literary theory which are skeptical of referentiality is carefully balanced by an acknowledgment of the need to read realist representations as intertextual constructions. Perhaps even more significantly, in his most recent book, *Writing for an Endangered World*, Buell acknowledges that his previous rejection of anthropocentrism as a motive for environmental protection might have gone too far and, concomitantly, notes the need for ecocriticism to move away from too strict a focus on wilderness and outback (8).

5   For an excellent recent reading of *Out of Africa* in terms of the naturalization of a colonial, aristocratic authority through a form of settler pastoral, see Simon Lewis's *White Women Writers and Their African Invention*.

References

Adams, William and David Hulme. "Changing Narratives, Policies & Practices in African Conservation." Hulme and Murphree, 9–23.

Anderson, David and Grove, Richard, eds. *Conservation in Africa: People, Policies, and Practice*. Cambridge: Cambridge University Press, 1987.

Bate, Jonathan. *Romantic Ecology: Wordsworth and the Environmental Tradition*. New York: Routledge, 1991.

Bienert, William. "African History and Environmental History." *African Affairs* 99 (2000): 269–302.

Bonner, Raymond. *At the Hand of Man: Peril and Hope for Africa's Wildlife*. New York, Knopf, 1993.

Buell, Lawrence. *The Environmental Imagination: Thoreau, Nature Writing, and the Formation of American Culture*. Cambridge, MA: Harvard University Press, 1995.

——. *Writing for an Endangered World*. Cambridge, MA: Harvard University Press, 2001.

Carruthers, Jane. "Nationhood and National Parks: Comparative Examples from the Post-imperial Experience." *Ecology and Empire*. Eds. Tom Griffiths and Libby Robin. Seattle: University of Washington Press, 1997, 125–38.

——. *The Kruger National Park: A Social and Political History*. Pietermaritzburg: Natal University Press, 1995.

Coupe, Laurence, ed. *The Green Studies Reader*. New York: Routledge, 2000.

Dineson, Isak. *Out of Africa and Shadows on the Grass*. New York: Random House, 1937.

Farah, Nuruddin. *Secrets*. New York: Penguin, 1998.

Glotfelty, Cheryll and Harold Fromm, eds. *The Ecocriticism Reader: Landmarks in Literary Ecology*. Athens (GA): University of Georgia Press, 1996.

Grove, Richard. *Ecology, Climate and Empire: Colonialism and Global Environmental History, 1400–1940*. Cambridge: White Horse, 1997.

Head, Dominic. "The (Im)possibility of Ecocriticism." *Writing the Environment: Ecocriticism and Litera-ture*. Eds. Richard Kerridge and Neil Sammells. New York: Zed, 1998, 27–39.

——. "Problems in Ecocriticism and the Novel." *Key Words*. 1 (1998), 60–78.

Howarth, William. "Some Principles of Ecocriticism." Glotfelty and Fromm, 69–91.

Hulme, David and Marshall Murphee, eds. *African Wildlife & Livelihoods*. Portsmouth: Heinemann, 2001.

Leach, Melissa and Robin Mearns, eds. *The Lie of the Land: Challenging Received Wisdom on the African Environment*. Portsmouth (NH): Heinemann, 1996.

Lewis, Simon. *White Women Writers and Their African Invention*. Gainesville: University Press of Florida, 2003.

Love, Glen A. "Revaluing Nature: Toward an Ecological Criticism." Glotfelty and Fromm, 225–40.

Lundblad, Michael. "Malignant and Beneficent Fictions: Constructing Nature in Ecocriticism and Achebe's *Arrow of God*." *West Africa Review* 3.1 (2001): 1–22.

Manes, Christopher. "Nature and Silence." Glotfelty and Fromm, 15–29.

Mazel, David. "American Literary Environmentalism as Domestic Orientalism." Glotfelty and Fromm, 137–46.

Neumann, Roderick. *Imposing Wilderness: Struggles over Livelihood and Nature Preservation in Africa*. Berkeley: University of California Press, 1998.

Ngugi wa Thiong'O. *A Grain of Wheat*. Portsmouth: Heinemann, 1967.

Ombaka, Christine. "War and Environment in African Literature." *Literature of Nature: An International Sourcebook*. Ed. Patrick D. Murphy. Chicago: Fitzroy Dearborn, 1998, 327–35.

Ranger, Terence. *Voices from the Rocks: Nature, Culture, and History in the Matopos Hills of Zimbabwe*. Oxford: James Currey, 1999.

Slaymaker, William. "Ecoing the Other(s): The Call of Global Green and Black African Responses." *PMLA* 116 (2001): 129–44.

Willoquet-Maricondi, Paula. "Aimé Césaire's *The Tempest* and Peter Greenaway's *Prospero's Books* as Ecological Readings and Rewritings of Shakespeare's *The Tempest*." *Reading the Earth: New Directions in the Study of Literature and Environment*. Eds. Michael P. Branch, Rochelle Johnson, Daniel Patterson, and Scott Slovic. Moscow (ID): University of Idaho Press, 1998, 209–24.

Chapter 92

Ecological Postcolonialism in African Women's Literature

Juliana Makuchi Nfah-Abbenyi

In *Elle sera de jaspe et de corail* the Cameroonian writer, Werewere Liking states:

> Vraiment, Lunaï est un village fatidique. Ce sont les differences qui caractérisent ce vingtième siècle dit-on. Des differences qui se côtoient de manière si inharmonieuse qu'il a fallu inventer l'écologie: Des super-puissants à côté du tiers-monde les villes à côté des bidons-villes les riches à côté des pauvres.... Tant de misère juste à côté de tant d'opulence c'est inharmonieux à vomir c'est disharmonique à crever...(pp. 44–5)

> [Really, Lunaï is a fateful village. Differences are characteristic of this twentieth century people say. Differences that coexist in such an inharmonious way that ecology had to be invented: Superpowers side by side the third world cities side by side shanty towns the rich side by side the poor.... So much misery alongside so much opulence it's inharmonious one could vomit it's disharmonious to death....] (my translation)

Ecology had to be invented, Werewere Liking maintains. "Why this invention?" one might ask. Liking's statement posits a reality that has either been lost, forgotten, or ignored. It claims a time when people knew their environment. They understood it, respected it, treasured the interdependence and harmonious co-existence with it. Then the seeds of "disharmony" in the form of differences, whether ideological, cultural, political or economic, were planted, nurtured, and have grown deep roots. This "disharmony" is clearly asserted not only by the content of Liking's statement but is also conveyed through her style of writing itself: one that defies conventional syntactic and grammatical norms; that transgresses traditional rules of writing as it combines poetic, prosaic, and dramatic forms of expression throughout the text, inscribing an intertextuality that is unique. It is one that aptly captures the chaos about which she speaks.

First published in *Literature of Nature: An International Sourcebook*, ed. Patrick Murphy, pp. 344–9. Chicago: Fitzroy Dearborn Publishers, 1998.

Liking's fictional village, Lunaï, sometimes stands for her native land, but often symbolically represents Africa, and the world at large. Lunaï embodies the almost total degradation and/or amnesia into which its peoples seem to bury themselves each waking day. They slumber and wallow in this atmosphere of total chaos, whether physical, psychical, or spiritual, as their world falls apart. It is because of their inability or refusal to acknowledge or to integrate traditional ways of knowing with technologically oriented values that "ecology" had to be invented, an invention that would supposedly rid the world of its environmental hazards. The people of Lunaï must therefore snap out of this general state of (dis)ease in order to save themselves, their environment, in short, their humanity. They can achieve this goal by taking the plunge, reimmersing themselves in their traditions and recreating the healthy relationship once shared with their universe.

Liking's text highlights the major issues that other African women writers also address in their writing, as well as the impact of these issues on the lives of their people, and especially, on women's lives. These writers show that African women's roles (and sometimes men's roles), which are often linked to the land, have seen drastic changes following the movement from colonialism, through independence, to the postcolonial era that have (re)shaped African societies, histories, and cultures. They contend that women's lives have tended to be the most affected by these local and global shifts.

Buchi Emecheta's *The Joys of Motherhood* is a case in point. Although we hear the patriarchal Nwokocha Agbadi in this novel scornfully declaring that "only lazy men who could not face farm work went to the coast to work, leaving the land which their parents and great-great-grandparents had worked and cared for" (p. 37), it is the women like Nnu Ego and Cordelia who have married these "lazy men" who complain bitterly, and are constantly comparing life in urban Lagos with life in rural Ibuza. Their complaints are grounded by the fact that when their husbands become part of and are consumed by the (post)colonial economy, the women resent how their positions, roles, and influence are substantially eroded by their non-ownership of land and/or farms in Lagos. As Nnu Ego laments, "In Ibuza, women made a contribution, but in urban Lagos, men had to be the sole providers; this new setting robbed the woman of her useful role" (p. 81). The contribution that women made to the income and welfare of the family partially came from their work on the land thus promoting an acceptable sexual division of labor and creating a balance in gender relations. If Agbadi's criticism of "lazy men" who run away from the land and farm work in favor of modern, (post)colonial "menial" jobs (like becoming cooks or washer men for white men and women) not only robs them of their "manhood," thus redefining concepts of masculinity within Ibuza society and culture; displacement and non-ownership of land and/or farms not only represents the loss of a vital source of power for women, it also reshapes their gender roles and concepts of womanhood and femininity as well. In the minds of the Agbadis and the Nnu Egos, therefore, the urban setting destroys an important and essential link to one's land, one's home, and one's identity. They see the new relation to the urban environment as more destructive and less gratifying than constructive. Although one might argue that working on the land and assuming familial responsibilities does not necessarily always empower women – especially when they are treated as the mules of the earth, for instance, in Delphine Zanga Tsogo's *Vies de femmes* and *L'Oiseau en cage* – African women's writing does show that women and children are those who are the most adversely affected by the (post)colonial relation to the urban environment.

Calixthe Beyala paints just such a picture in *The Sun Hath Looked upon Me* and *Your Name Shall Be Tanga*. She portrays children as those who are primarily crushed by the weight of the migration to, and the living conditions in, urban slums. Through the eyes of her teenage heroines, Ateba Léocadie and Tanga, we are shown how life in the ghettos "kills" children, smothers their dreams, and engenders total disillusionment and often death. Beyala points out how unwary, ignorant, irresponsible, and/or morally bankrupt adults, parents, politicians (who themselves equally wallow in the malaise of post-colonial politics of survival) often watch helplessly as the children fester in poverty, illiteracy, homelessness, delinquency, crime and prostitution. Rural exodus has created untold imbalances that are progressively destroying the environment, contaminating children and especially young women. It is deplorable that local governments have been unable to help children in the stifling milieux that have become fertile ground for the daily violence perpetrated on their minds and bodies. Beyala claims to write for the ordinary people of the ghettos and she maintains that they are the ones who will bring true change to Africa. They are the future of the continent. She therefore points an accusing finger specifically at politicians who, after riding the waves of independence, have lagged into incompetence with the resultant gross mismanagement of their national resources.

Paralleling such incompetence is the corruption of these politicians and post-colonial leaders, as is comically, sarcastically, and cynically portrayed by Aminata Sow Fall in *The Beggars' Strike*. Fall exposes yet another ugly side of postcolonial politics and denounces the dexterity with which power-hungry individuals exploit this global invention called "ecology" with its global economic backing (tourism, development, aid from the so-called first world to the so-called third world) for their own selfish benefit.

The first sentence of *The Beggars' Strike* reads, "This morning there has been another article about it in the newspaper: about how the streets are congested with these beggars, these *talibés*, these lepers and cripples, all these derelicts" (p. 1). The streets of the Capital, we are told, are crying out to be cleansed of these dregs of society, "these parodies of human beings." The Director of the Department of Public Health and Hygiene decides to launch an "effective plan of campaign" to rid the Capital of this plague that stands in the way of hygiene and the city's progress. But Mour Ndiaye is also motivated by other personal and political reasons: "We are now the ones responsible for the destiny of our country. We must oppose anything which harms our economic and tourist development," he tells his personal marabout, Serigne Birama (p. 18). Birama remains unconvinced by this argument and resents the further marginalization of the beggars for reasons of so-called "economic development." His skepticism is well-founded given that the beggars "invade" the Capital because there is a relation of give and take between them and the city folk. City folk give alms to the beggars not out of the goodness of their hearts, not necessarily because religion demands that they give to the poor, but "out of an instinct for self-preservation" (p. 22). They need the beggars' wishes for long life, their wishes for prosperity, their prayers to drive away bad dreams, bring hope, and so they give, "so that they can live in peace" (p. 38).

Ndiaye's enthusiasm, therefore, is fueled by personal political ambition and his ability to exploit first/third-world politics grounded in something as elusive as "economic development." For the question remains: "Who benefits from this monster labeled development?" The campaign to harass the beggars is not undertaken because Ndiaye has the control of "congestion" or the need to limit the destruction of the environment thus promoting its protection at heart. His campaign is geared toward a tourist economy that needs to be developed and maintained. It is therefore the interests of the select, well-to-do foreign tourists and the local politicians like Ndiaye that "justify" this brutal action and not those of the local inhabitants themselves on whose backs ecological imperialism is being practiced. Local and exogenous power and economic politics therefore collude, further marginalizing already dispossessed numbers of African peoples. How, therefore, can one speak of development, of the benefits and values of this global politic called "ecology," of "protecting the environment," when those who inhabit that environmental space, whether geographic and/ or political, are either used as bait, or blatantly excluded from the construction and implementation of policies that govern their land and, consequently, their lives?

Fall clearly discounts such policies/politics and their bearers/enforcers by subverting the entire process itself and putting the power in the hands of the dispossessed. Under the leadership of a woman, Salla Diang, and without the help of the likes of the Ndiayes, the beggars very cleverly solve the problem of "congestion" by moving to the Slum-Clearance Resettlement Area on the outskirts of the city. The tables are turned, for those who were formerly tracked down, flogged, and beaten like dogs, gleefully orchestrate their revenge on ruthless, power-hungry politicians like Mour Ndiaye (if only he had listened to Birama, the "uneducated" traditional leader!). The city folk now have to seek the beggars out and the cycle of dependence is reversed. By moving out of that overcrowded location, the beggars reclaim their identity, their dignity, and assert their humanity. Their ultimate revenge comes when Ndiaye himself is thwarted as the beggars follow Salla's order to continue their strike. "Don't budge from here. No one is to budge from here ever again! Tomorrow, we shall see that he bites dust!" (p. 86). By not returning to the Capital, they rob Ndiaye of the possibility of carrying out the one and only act of benevolence that would have guaranteed him the one thing he had been scheming for all along – an appointment to the post of vice president.

When Ndiaye begins to learn the invaluable lesson of interconnectedness, of the correlation between modern politics and economic development (administrative posts/tourism) and the link between traditional voices and values (Birama/beggars – "who have been here since the time of our great-great-grandparents" [p. 15]), it is almost too late to repair the damage that his campaign has already done. His statements, "We have to find some way of letting them get back their rights as citizens ... create some organisations to which they can be assimilated ... carry out a vast campaign of rehabilitation on their behalf ... " (p. 94), stand in jarring opposition to Birama's question, "You waged war against the beggars ... Who won?" (p. 66, all ellipses in the original). Ndiaye's inability to recognize the dialectical relation between culture, religion, economics and politics; his refusal to combine socio-cultural values with modern values in order to combat and effectively deal with the (dis)ease that "economic development" poses for his people becomes the tool of his own undoing.

But beyond much of the gloom that "development" and mismanagement breed in post-colonial Africa, there is hope, as Bessie Head demonstrates in When Rain Clouds Gather and A Question of Power. It is the coming together of traditional/local ways of knowing and modern science/technologies that can best guarantee a productive but protected environment in African and third-world countries where the drive toward modernization and so-called "progress and civilization" is pushing the limits of environmental degradation and the survival of its people. Their survival will continue to hang in the balance unless "progress and civilization" also means learning to aggressively combine local and exogenous ways of knowing.

Bostwana became Bessie Head's adoptive country, a hospitable place she could call home after she fled South Africa where she had faced rejection, humiliation, dispossession and virulent racism (Head, *Serowe* and *A Woman Alone*). The strong bonds of love and belonging that she developed in Botswana are captured in her novels. The name of the village in *When Rain Clouds Gather* is Golema Mmidi, which means "to grow crops" (p. 28), while the name of the village in *A Question of Power* is Motabeng, which means "the place of sand" (p. 19). It is no accident that the titles of these novels speak of the weather, of crops, of the land, of the environment, and their relationship with the people. Head's fascination with the land and its people comes through as she portrays the intricate webs that are woven between women and men, and between collaborative ventures involving local farming methods and modern scientific methods adapted to the land based on studying the weather and the environment itself. We are told in *When Rain Clouds Gather* that while men are cattle drovers, the women are the agriculturalists. The women are the tillers of the earth and are on the land 365 days of the year: "No one ever worked harder than Botswana women, for the whole burden of providing food for big families rested with them" (p. 104). The arid nature of the land, coupled with unpredictable weather patterns, and women's central role in farming, lead Gilbert Balfour to believe that perhaps, "all change in the long run would depend on the women of the country and perhaps they too could provide a number of solutions to problems he had not yet thought of" (p. 43). They would be women like Paulina Sebeso, who would rally the others and "help open the way for new agricultural developments" (p. 75).

But gender ideologies, and cultural and tribal land practices intertwine in complex ways, raising problems that could stand in the way of new agricultural developments. For instance: although women are the backbone of agriculture, programs for improved techniques in agriculture "were only open to men" (p. 34); the tribal land tenure system, whereby "ownership of the land was vested in the tribe as a whole" (p. 38), posed the problem of fencing parts of the land for controlled grazing. Eating habits grounded in culture and prejudice add (an)other dimension to development. For instance, although the discovery of a drought-resistant millet would not only increase the quantity and add diversity to the Motswana diet, they would rather not eat this millet because it is consumed by the "inferior" Bushman of the Kalahari desert. The solutions to these many and varied problems are carefully laid out by Head in the novel. With the help of the women, and later with the collaboration of the men, Gilbert is able to launch some of the projects and find solutions that are uplifting for himself, the people, and their environment.

Projects are planned in such a way that the ecology is taken into consideration every step of the way. For instance, ways are sought to bring cattle production and crop production together – fencing the land and controlled grazing on cooperatively owned feeding grounds thus preventing overstocking and the spread of diseases. This method also increases the number of better fed beasts thereby increasing their cash value and, consequently, reducing the hardship and the labor of cattle rearing. Cash crop farming like growing Turkish tobacco is practiced alongside subsistence farming. The digging of bore-holes and the making of reservoirs provide each home with water, and a network of small dams are built for irrigation purposes. The philosophy that guides the efforts made through collaborative work and incentives, "the materials were simple and the costs kept low" (p. 136), clearly underlines Head's belief that only when development projects in post-colonial African societies have the interests of the people at heart can these actually have any impact or meaning for all the parties concerned. Ultimately, this interrelationship of respect for the environment, while improving productivity, must have as its aim the "uplift of the poor," consequently uplifting the women whose major role it is to carry the burden of feeding the land. Therefore, "communal systems of development which imposed co-operation and sharing of wealth were much better than the dog-eat-dog policies, take-over bids, and grab-what-you-can of big finance" (p. 156).

Head builds on the idea of communal uplift once again in *A Question of Power*. In Motabeng, Youth Development work groups, represented by young, intelligent, enthusiastic men like Small-Boy and women like Kenosi, provide instruction on the basic tenets of productivity. They construct local industries projects; adapt agriculture to water conservation methods; practice crop rotation following a prescribed formula for success and continued productivity of various kinds of crops and products. Whatever the Motabeng community does is geared toward turning the "people's attention to their natural resources," thus breaking the cycle of dependence on "the goods of the rich manufacturers in South Africa and Rhodesia" (p. 69).

If turning to one's natural resources breaks the cycle of dependence that is not only economic but political, Head posits yet another element in this novel, that of turning to the land as an elixir to feed one's soul, as medicine to heal that which ails one's mind, one's body, as a means to discover and cherish one's and another's humanity (p. 158). "It is impossible," Elizabeth muses, "to become a vegetable gardener without at the same time coming in contact with the wonderful strangeness of human nature" (p. 72). Elizabeth's displacement and her search for a place to belong are captured in the words of the Schoolmaster of Motabeng: "I suffer, too, because I haven't a country and know what it's like. A lot of refugees have nervous breakdowns" (p. 52). Only her connection to the land saves her from literal death when Elizabeth suffers the same fate. Her relationship with Tom and, more importantly, with Kenosi and the garden help her free herself from the physical, psychological prisons, and the mental horrors that are a legacy of her childhood (her white mother's madness and suicide in the asylum where she was locked up for having a child with a black stable boy; the many times Elizabeth was locked up in school on the mere suspicion of her "inherited" insanity) and her growing up in apartheid South Africa. A place, she says, where it was "like living with permanent nervous tension, because you did not know why white people there had to go out of their way to hate you or loathe you" (p. 19).

During the three years of her "journey into hell and darkness" (p. 190), of the almost total collapse of her body, Elizabeth battles the demons that threaten to claim her, body and soul, as her life hangs in the balance while her inner and outer worlds collide. Her anxiety about her work in the garden with Kenosi "would jerk her awake" and bring her swimming back to reality (p. 169). Working with Kenosi serves as potent treatment for her condition, for, "[a]s far as Elizabeth was concerned she was to look back on . . . the Kenosi woman's appearance as one of the miracles or accidents that saved her life" (p. 89). Her work with Kenosi offers her healing that is physical, mental, spiritual and metaphysical (she is often in total contemplation, absorbed by her surroundings). In her quiet but stubborn and respectful attitude, Kenosi never mentions Elizabeth's illness, never invokes the evils that plague her friend's entire existence. Kenosi would sit with Elizabeth, eat with her, chat with her son, and her only reproaches to her friend are made in relation to the garden:

"You must never leave the garden," she said. "I cannot work without you. People are teasing me these days. They say: 'Kenosi, where's your teacher? You are not in school.' People have never seen a garden like our garden. . . . "

Elizabeth struggled to an upright posture. The way this woman brought her back to life and reality! (p. 142)

Kenosi's words say how much their work and their lives are dependent on each other's. But most of all, Kenosi teaches Elizabeth that even in her world of distorted realities, other human beings can be/are dependent on her. She is an important and useful member of Motabeng village. The land, their work, their relationship, bring them together, giving them a sense of belonging, a sense of hope that must and does save Elizabeth. No wonder the last sentence of *A Question of Power* emphatically states: "As [Elizabeth] fell asleep, she placed one soft hand over her land. It was a gesture of belonging" (p. 206).

Belonging to the land, therefore, gives one an identity and a history that is deeply grounded in a culture as well. It is such a history that Nyasha in Tsitsi Dangarembga's *Nervous Conditions* craves. One that she needs to fill in the gaps of what she has lost or revise the "lies" taught by her Anglo-Saxon education. Nyasha's struggle is one of combating the "Englishness" that has erased her Shona self, her African history, and has made her forget who she is. She resents the hybrid she has become and she desperately seeks to redefine her identity. Unlike Nyasha who rebels against those and the discourses of (post)colonialism that threaten to destroy her sense of (Shona) self, Tambudzai does not lack that groundedness in her history. The advantage that Tambu has is one she has gleaned from her grandmother during their work sessions on the land.

Women like Tambu's grandmother are storytellers and custodians of history. Their knowledge of the land and of history is shared, thus making the acquisition of both forms of knowledge complementary for children like Tambudzai. She learns invaluable lessons about her family, the history of her people "that could not be found in the textbooks" from her grandmother. It is important to note how the grandmother subverts work on the farm and uses it as a platform for instruction and the construction of self, for whenever Tambu would plead for more (his)stories, Mbuya, as if teasing her grandchild with the bait, would say, "More work, my child, before you hear more story." And then, "[s]lowly, methodically, throughout the day the field would be cultivated, the episodes of [her] grandmother's own portion of history strung together from beginning to end" (pp. 17–18). It is her relationship with her grandmother, her stories, and their farm work, that give Tambu a sense of belonging, a strong sense of identity. She does not therefore have the same kind of struggle Nyasha has to (re)learn the forgotten. Not forgetting is Tambudzai's trump card. Knowledge of her history better prepares her to confront (an)other colonizing history, to resist assimilation and those oppressive discourses of (post)colonialism that almost consume her cousin, Nyasha. Learning, even if through farm work from Mbuya, more importantly, knowing her self will save her, a point that Werewere Liking also makes throughout *Elle sera de jaspe et de corail*. The people of Lunaï are pitiful because they have reneged on their histories and their traditions. They can only heal as a people when they reclaim and revalue local and traditional knowledge that they must then correlate with imported, modern ways of thinking. Liking optimistically posits that when men and women live in harmony with each other, with their environment and the cosmos, only then shall the new race of people that she maintains, will be of jasper and coral, be born.

References

Beyala, Calixthe, *The Sun Hath Looked upon Me*, translated by Marjolijn de Jager, Portsmouth, New Hampshire, and Oxford: Heinemann, 1996.

——, *Your Name Shall Be Tanga*, translated by Marjolijn de Jager, Portsmouth, New Hampshire, and Oxford: Heinemann, 1996.

Dangarembga, Tsitsi, "Interview," in *Talking with African Writers*, Portsmouth, New Hampshire: Heinemann, 1992; London: James Currey, 1992.

——, *Nervous Conditions*, London: Women's Press, 1988; Seattle, Washington: Seal, 1989.

Emecheta, Buchi, *The Joys of Motherhood*, New York: G. Braziller, 1979; London: Heinemann, 1979.

Fall, Aminata Sow, *The Beggars' Strike, or, The Dregs of Society*, translated by Dorothy S. Blair, Harlow, England: Longman, 1981.

Head, Bessie, *A Question of Power*, London: Davis-Poynter, 1973; New York: Pantheon, 1974.

——, *Serowe: Village of the Rain Wind*, London: Heinemann, 1981.

——, *When Rain Clouds Gather*, New York: Simon & Schuster, 1968; London: Gollancz, 1969.

——, *A Woman Alone: Autobiographical Writings*, Portsmouth, New Hampshire, and Oxford: Heinemann, 1990.

Liking, Werewere, *Elle sera de jaspe et de corail*, Paris: Editions l'Harmattan, 1983.

Mateteyou, Emmanuel, "Calixthe Beyala: entre le terroir et l'exil," *The French Review* 69:4 (1996), pp. 605–15.

Nfah-Abbenyi, Juliana M., *Gender in African Women's Writing: Identity, Sexuality, and Difference*, Bloomington: Indiana University Press, 1997.

Zanga Tsogo, Delphine, *L'Oiseau en cage*, Paris: Edicef, 1983.

Chapter 93

Environmentalism and Postcolonialism

Rob Nixon

What would it mean to bring environmentalism into dialogue with postcolonialism? These are currently two of the most dynamic areas in literary studies, yet their relationship continues to be one of reciprocal indifference or mistrust. A broad silence characterizes most environmentalists' stance toward postcolonial literature and theory, while postcolonial critics typically remain no less silent on the subject of environmental literature. What circumstances have shaped this mutual reluctance? And what kinds of intellectual initiatives might best advance an overdue dialogue?

Let me begin with the events that set my thinking on these issues in motion. In October 1995, the *New York Times* Sunday magazine featured an essay by Jay Parini entitled "The Greening of the Humanities."[1] Parini described the rise to prominence of environmentalism in the humanities, especially in literature departments. At the end of the essay, he named twenty-five writers and critics whose work was central to this environmental studies boom. Something struck me as odd about the list, something that passed unmentioned in the article: all twenty-five writers and critics were American.

This unselfconscious parochialism was disturbing, not least because at that time I was active in the campaign to release Ken Saro-Wiwa, the Ogoni author held prisoner without trial for his environmental and human rights activism in Nigeria.[2] Two weeks after Parini's article appeared, the Abacha regime executed Saro-Wiwa, making him Africa's most visible environmental martyr. Here was a writer – a novelist, poet, memoirist, and essayist – who had died fighting the ruination of his Ogoni people's farmland and fishing waters by European and American oil conglomerates in cahoots with a despotic African regime. Yet, clearly, Saro-Wiwa's writings were unlikely to find a home in the kind of environmental literary lineage outlined by Parini. The more ecocriticism I read, the more this impression was confirmed. I encountered some illuminating books by Lawrence Buell, Cheryll

First published in *Postcolonial Studies and Beyond*, ed. A. Loomba, Suvir Kaul, M. Bunzl, A. Burton, and J. Esty, pp. 233–8, 242–4, 247–8. Durham: Duke University Press, 2005.

Glotfelty, Harold Fromm, Daniel Payne, Scott Slovic, and many others.[3] Yet these authors tended to canonize the same self-selecting genealogy of American writers: Ralph Waldo Emerson, Henry David Thoreau, John Muir, Aldo Leopold, Edward Abbey, Annie Dillard, Terry Tempest Williams, Wendell Berry, and Gary Snyder.[4] All are writers of influence and accomplishment, yet all are drawn from within the boundaries of a single nation. Environmental literary anthologies, college course Web sites, and special journal issues on ecocriticism revealed similar patterns of predominance. Accumulatively, I realized that literary environmentalism was developing de facto as an offshoot of American studies.

The resulting national self-enclosure seemed peculiar: one might surely have expected environmentalism to be more, not less, transnational than other fields of literary inquiry. It was unfortunate that a writer like Saro-Wiwa, who had long protested what he termed "ecological genocide," could find no place in the environmental canon.[5] Was this because he was an African? Was it because his work revealed no special debt to Thoreau, to the wilderness tradition, or to Jeffersonian agrarianism? Instead, the fraught relations between ethnicity, pollution, and human rights animated Saro-Wiwa's writings. As did the equally fraught relations between local, national, and global politics. It was futile, he recognized, to try to understand or protest the despoiling of his people's water, land, and health within a purely national framework. For Ogoniland's environmental ruin resulted from collaborative plunder by those he dubbed Nigeria's "internal colonialists" and by the unanswerable, transnational power of Shell and Chevron.[6]

Saro-Wiwa's canonical invisibility in the United States seemed all the more telling given the role that America played in his emergence as an environmental writer. The United States buys half of Nigeria's oil and Chevron has emerged as a significant Ogoniland polluter.[7] More affirmatively, it was on a trip to Colorado that Saro-Wiwa witnessed a successful environmental campaign to stop corporate logging.[8] This experience contributed to his decision to mobilize international opinion by voicing his people's claims not just in the language of human rights but in environmental terms as well. Yet it was clear from the prevailing ecocritical perspective in literary studies that someone like Saro-Wiwa – whose environmentalism was at once profoundly local and profoundly international – would be bracketed as an African, the kind of writer best left to the postcolonialists.

I became aware, however, of a second irony: that postcolonial literary critics have, in turn, shown scant interest in environmental concerns, regarding them implicitly as, at best, irrelevant and elitist, at worst as sullied by "green imperialism."[9] Saro-Wiwa's distinctive attempt to fuse environmental and minority rights was unlikely to achieve much of a hearing in either camp.

These, then, were the circumstances that got me thinking about the mutually constitutive silences that have developed between environmental and postcolonial literary studies. Broadly speaking, there are four main schisms between the dominant concerns of postcolonialists and ecocritics. First, postcolonialists have tended to foreground hybridity and cross-culturation. Ecocritics, on the other hand, have historically been drawn more to discourses of purity: virgin wilderness and the preservation of "uncorrupted" last great places.[10] Second, postcolonial writing and criticism largely concern themselves with displacement, while environmental literary studies has tended to give priority to the literature of place. Third, and relatedly, postcolonial studies has tended to favor the cosmopolitan and the transnational. Postcolonialists are typically critical of nationalism, whereas the canons of environmental literature and criticism have developed within a national (and often

nationalistic) American framework. Fourth, postcolonialism has devoted considerable attention to excavating or reimagining the marginalized past: history from below and border
histories, often along transnational axes of migrant memory. By contrast, within much
environmental literature and criticism, something different happens to history. It is often
repressed or subordinated to the pursuit of timeless, solitary moments of communion with
nature. There is a durable tradition within American natural history writing of erasing the
history of colonized peoples through the myth of the empty lands. Postcolonialist critics are
wary of the role that this strain of environmental writing (especially wilderness writing) has
played in burying the very histories that they themselves have sought to unearth.

Postcolonial critics understandably feel discomfort with preservationist discourses of
purity, given the role such discourses have played historically in the racially unequal
distribution of post-Enlightenment human rights. In the context of a romantic primordial-
ism, the colonized, especially women, have been repeatedly naturalized as objects of
heritage to be owned, preserved, or patronized rather than as the subjects of their own
land and legacies. Once cultures have been discursively assimilated to nature (not least
through the settler tradition of viewing the United States as "nature's nation"), they have
been left more vulnerable to dispossession – whether in the name of virgin wilderness
preservation or the creation of nuclear test zones.[11]

Autobiographical divergences have doubtlessly sharpened intellectual differences between
postcolonial writers and ecocritics over the politics of purity, place, nation, and history.
The preeminent critics associated with postcolonialism – Kwame Anthony Appiah, Homi
K. Bhabha, Edward Said, Sara Suleri, Gayatri Chakravorty Spivak, and Gauri Viswanathan,
among others – have lived across national boundaries in ways that have given a personal
edge to their intellectual investment in questions of dislocation, cultural syncretism, and
transnationalism. Conversely, the most prominent environmental writers and critics are
mono-nationals with a deep-rooted experiential and imaginative commitment to a particular
American locale: Vermont for John Elder, the Sierra Nevada for Gary Snyder, Appalachian
Kentucky for Wendell Berry, Utah in Terry Tempest Williams's case.

This tension between a postcolonial preoccupation with displacement and an ecocritical
preoccupation with an ethics of place needs to be further situated in terms of cosmopolitanism, on the one hand, and bioregionalism, on the other.[12] Bioregionalism, in Parini's
words, entails a responsiveness to "one's local part of the earth whose boundaries are
determined by a location's natural characteristics rather than arbitrary administrative
boundaries."[13] Gary Snyder and ecocritics like John Elder and David Orr are all vocal
advocates of a bioregional ethic. Orr connects ecological destruction to the way people
can graduate from college "with obligations to no place in particular. Their knowledge is
mostly abstract, equally applicable in New York or San Francisco."[14] Similarly, Elder argues
that "the traditional model in education has been cosmopolitanism. I've come to prefer a
concentric and bioregional approach to learning. . . . It makes sense – educationally – to
begin with local writing; then you expand, adding layers of knowledge."[15]

There is much to be said for this approach: it can help instill in us an awareness of our
impact on our immediate environment, help ground our sense of environmental responsibility. However, from a postcolonial perspective, a bioregional ethic poses certain problems.
For the concentric rings of the bioregionalists more often open out into transcendentalism
than into transnationalism. All too frequently, we are left with an environmental vision that
remains inside a spiritualized and naturalized national frame.

Much of the American imaginative and critical literature associated with bioregionalism tends toward a style of spiritual geography premised on what I call spatial amnesia. Within a bioregional center-periphery model, the specificity and moral imperative of the local typically opens out not into the specificities of the international but into transcendental abstraction. In this way, a prodigious amount of American environmental writing and criticism makes expansive gestures while remaining amnesiac toward non-American geographies that vanish over the intellectual skyline.

The environmentalist advocacy of an ethics of place has, all too often, morphed into hostility toward displaced people. Edward Abbey's rants against Mexican immigrants, Mary Austin's anti-Semitism, and the Sierra Club's disastrous referendum on zero immigration all evidence a xenophobic strain running through ethics-of-place environmentalism.[16] With the Sierra Club in mind, Richard Rodriguez has noted how the weeping Amerindian in the public service commercial first became an environmental talisman and then, in a grim historical irony, was invoked against the immigrant descendants of indigenous populations heading north from Mexico and Central America.[17]

An exclusionary ethics of place can easily lapse into jingoistic transcendentalism, as in an essay that the Montana author, Rick Bass, wrote in defense of southern Utah's Red Rock country. "The unprotected wilderness of the West," Bass declared

> is one of our greatest strengths as a country. Another is our imagination, our tendency to think rather than to accept – to challenge, to ask why and what if, to create rather than to destroy. This questioning is a kind of wildness, a kind of strength, that many have said is peculiarly American. Why place that strength in jeopardy? To lose Utah's wilderness would be to strip westerners and all Americans of a raw and vital piece of our soul, our identity, and our ability to imagine. . . . The print of a deer or lion in the sand, in untouched country, as you sleep – it is these things that allow you, allow us, to continue being American, rather than something else, anything else, everything else.[18]

In trying to rally Americans to a worthy preservationist cause, Bass may be resorting here to what Spivak calls "strategic essentialism."[19] After all, it is the American people's representatives who will determine the fate of Red Rock country. But such essentialism, strategic or otherwise, comes at a cost, for Bass aggrandizes and naturalizes the American national character in ways politically perturbing. How do we square his intimation that creative questioning is "peculiarly American" with Americans' widespread, unquestioning ignorance of the disastrous consequences (not least environmental consequences) of US foreign policy? Bass's position is predicated on, among other things, a failure of geographical imagination – a kind of superpower parochialism.

If your frame is Red Rock country, the United States may seem quintessentially a nation of questioners who seek to "to create rather than to destroy." But from the vantage point of the 1 million Vietnamese still suffering the health consequences of Agent Orange, or from the perspective of vulnerable microminorities in Nigeria, Ecuador, or West Papua, places where American extraction industry giants like Chevron, Texaco, and Freeport McMoran run rampant, a reluctance to destroy may not seem as definitive an American value. We should temper Bass's blinkered econationalism with Aldo Leopold's sobering reminder of what else it means, in environmental terms, to be an American: "When I go birding in my Ford, I am devastating an oil field, and re-electing an imperialist to get me rubber."[20]

Bass's exaltation of the American soul as pure imagination – a higher soul in search of "untouched country" – has, moreover, a dubious settler lineage. It is precisely such thinking that has impeded the American environmental movement's efforts to diversify its support base. From the perspective of North America's First Peoples, the white soul dream of "untouched country" has meant cultural erasure and dispossession. It contributed, classically, to the Ahwahneechee's eviction from Yosemite as part of Yosemite's reinvention as pure wilderness.[21]

For people relegated to the unnatural margins of nature's nation – like gay minority writers Rodriguez and Melvin Dixon – the wilderness experience can look ominously purified (as opposed to pure). In his ironically titled essay "True West," Rodriguez describes how, setting off on a hike, he hears, three minutes beyond the trailhead, rustling in the bushes. Instead of experiencing transcendental uplift, he fears ambush by "Snow White and the seven militias."[22] And in *Ride Out the Wilderness*, poet-critic Dixon has chronicled how African Americans have associated wilderness with the travail of exile: it is more a place of eviction and historical hauntings than of redemptive silences.[23]

Our intellectual challenge, then, is how to draw on the strengths of bioregionalism without succumbing to ecoparochialism. Here one might heed the call by the British natural historian Richard Mabey for a less brittle, less exclusionary environmental ethics. As Mabey writes, "the challenge, in a world where the differences between native and stranger are fading, is to discover veins of local character which are distinctive without being insular and withdrawn."[24] Yet in response to the blurring of the distinction between native and stranger we have frequently witnessed a defensive tendency to naturalize rootedness and stigmatize as alien people who look or talk differently.

[...]

Ecological literary critics have been slow to absorb the kinds of provocative transnational thinking that has gathered strength in other disciplines central to the greening of the humanities, disciplines like history, geography, and anthropology.[25] Postcolonial literary critics, by contrast, have tended to shy away from environmental issues as if they were soft, Western, bourgeois concerns. But the notion that environmental politics are a luxury politics for the world's wealthy is clearly untenable. As Gayatri Spivak, one of the few postcolonial literary scholars to even allude to environmental issues, has argued, "the local in the South directly engages global greed."[26]

Any postcolonialist dismissal of environmentalism as marginal to "real" politics is belied by the current proliferation of indigenous environmental movements across the global South. Saro-Wiwa was not some isolated epic hero: his actions were indicative of a myriad non-Western environmental campaigns locally motivated, locally led, and internationally inflected. We are witnessing, on the environmental front, something similar to the mutation of feminism, which was often dismissed, twenty or thirty years ago, as white, privileged, and irrelevant to the needs of third world women. We have seen what counts as feminism radically changed by the rise of local social movements that have decentered and diversified the agenda of women's rights in ethnic, geographic, religious, sexuality, and class terms. In recent years, we have witnessed a similar decentering in environmentalism, one that has begun to shift the terms of the decisive debates away from issues like purity preservation and Jeffersonian-style agrarianism.

As William Beinart and Peter Coates have argued, "all human activity alters the composition of the natural world which in itself is never static. A critique which regards all change as

decay begs the very legitimacy of human survival."[27] Non-Western environmental movements are typically alert to the interdependence of human survival and environmental
change in situations where the illusion of a static purity cannot be sustained, far less exalted
as an ideal. Such movements are also typically aware of how easily foreign forces –
transnational corporations, the World Bank, or NGOs, often in cahoots with authoritarian
regimes – can destroy the delicate, always mutable, mesh between cultural traditions, social
justice, and ecosystems.

In Ecuador, one such locally led campaign, Acción Ecológica, mobilized the nation's
Confederation of Indigenous Nationalities against Texaco, whose ransacking of the environment echoed the plunder, ten thousand miles away, that generated Nigeria's Movement of
the Survival of the Ogoni People.[28] In India, the corporatizing of biodiversity has proved a
major rallying point: 200,000 Indian farmers descended on Delhi in the so-called Seed
Satyagraha to protest transnational efforts to wrest control over the reproduction and
distribution of seeds from traditional farmers.

Wangari Maathai, Kenya's first woman professor, has been imprisoned and tortured for
helping instigate mass tree plantings to protest rampant deforestation. In 1998, when
Kenya's kleptocractic government began expropriating and selling off the publicly held
Karura Forest to developers of luxury housing, students at the University of Nairobi
and Kenyatta University launched another dissident tree planting. The government's brutal
response produced campus riots that closed down both universities in defense of what
student leader Wycliffe Mwebi called the "moral right to defend the environment against a
corrupt land grab."[29]

If it is no longer viable to view environmentalism as a Western luxury, how are we best to
integrate environmental issues into our approach to postcolonial literature and vice versa?
Among many possible productive starting places, one could turn to the current wave of
interest in Black Atlantic studies and seek to give it an environmental dimension. Black
Atlanticism stands as one of the most energizing paradigms to have emerged in literary and
cultural studies during the past decade. Yet the questions it raises – about transnational
identities, the triangular trade in people and commodities, the multiple passages of modernity – remain cordoned off from environmental considerations. The literary possibilities
are alluring: not just in Kincaid's oeuvre but also in the work of writers like Derek Walcott
(starting with his assertion, "the sea is history"), Aimé Césaire, Wilson Harris, Michelle Cliff,
and Patrick Chamoiseau, among others.[30]

By integrating approaches from environmental and Black Atlantic studies, we might help
bridge the divide between the ecocritical study of America's minority literatures (a recent
growth area) and the ecocritical study of postcolonial literatures, which remains extremely
rudimentary. The recent influential anthology, *Literature and the Environment* evidences the
problems with this divide.[31] In one important regard, this makes for an encouraging volume:
it is the first environmental anthology to include a significant spread of minority writers,
many of them foregrounding issues that the environmental justice movement has priori-
tized. By acknowledging what Langston Hughes, bell hooks, Louis Owens, Clarissa Pinkola
Estes, and Marilou Awiakta (among others) add to environmental debate and testimony, the
anthology marks a shift away from the American ecocritical obsession with wilderness
writing and the literature of Jeffersonian agrarianism. Several of the essays address indigenous land rights, community displacement, and toxicity, often in the context of urban or poor
rural experience. Encouragingly, these are some of the American concerns that most readily

connect with the environmental priorities that predominate in postcolonial writing. It is here that one recognizes the richest possibilities for a more transnational rapprochement.
[. . .]

Ours is an age in which the combined wealth of the world's 550 billionaires exceeds that of the 3 billion humans who constitute the planet's poorest 50 percent. Five hundred corporations command 70 percent of world trade. In an era of giga-mergers and nanosecond transnationalisms, we cannot persist with the kind of isolationist thinking that has, in different ways, impeded both postcolonial and ecocritical responses to globalization.[32] The isolation of postcolonial literary studies from environmental concerns has limited the field's intellectual reach. Likewise, ecocriticism's predominantly American studies frame has proven inadequate, not least because we cannot afford to stop seeing the broader connections. Invisibility has its costs, as Arundhati Roy reminds us: globalization, she observes, is "like a light which shines brighter and brighter on a few people and the rest are in darkness, wiped out. They simply can't be seen. Once you get used to not seeing something, then, slowly, it's no longer possible to see it."[33] In the classroom, in our writing, and in the media, we need to widen that beam.

The dialogue I have sought to outline can help us rethink oppositions between bioregionalism and cosmopolitanism, between transcendentalism and transnationalism, between an ethics of place and the experience of displacement. Through such a rapprochement, we can begin to think, simultaneously, for example, about nature-induced states of transport and the vast, brutal history of humans forcibly transported. In the process, we can aspire to a more historically answerable and geographically expansive sense of what constitutes our environment and which literary works we entrust to voice its parameters. This is an ambitious but crucial task, not least because, for the foreseeable future, literature departments are likely to remain influential players in the greening of the humanities.

Notes

1　Jay Parini, "The Greening of the Humanities," *New York Times* Sunday magazine, October 23, 1995, 52–3.

2　Rob Nixon, "The Oil Weapon," *New York Times*, November 17, 1995. For a fuller discussion of the issues at stake, see Nixon, "Pipedreams: Ken Saro-Wiwa, Environmental Justice, and Micro-Minority Rights," *Black Renaissance/Renaissance Noire* 1.1 (1996): 39–55.

3　Lawrence Buell, *The Environmental Imagination: Thoreau, Nature Writing, and the Formation of American Culture* (Cambridge, MA: Harvard University Press, 1996); Cheryll Glotfelty and Harold Fromm, ed., *The Ecocritical Reader: Landmarks in Literary Ecology* (Athens: University of Georgia Press, 1996); Daniel G Payne, *Voices in the Wilderness: American Nature Writing and Environmental Politics* (Hanover, NH: University Press of New England, 1996); and Scott Slovic, *Seeking Awareness in American Nature Writing: Henry Thoreau, Annie Dillard, Edward Abbey, Wendell Berry, Barry Lopez* (Salt Lake City: University of Utah Press, 1992). Buell does stress the need to give international dimension to environmental literary studies, but, in design and emphasis, *The Environmental Imagination* remains within an Americanist paradigm.

4　For a classic instance of these limitations, see Max Oelschlaeger's *The Idea of Wilderness: Prehistory to the Age of Ecology* (New Haven, CT: Yale University Press, 1991).

5　Ken Saro-Wiwa, *Nigeria: The Brink of Disaster* (Port Harcourt, Nigeria: Saros International Publishers, 1991), 71.

6   Ken Saro-Wiwa, *A Month and A Day: A Detention Diary* (London: Penguin, 1995), 7.

7   Ibid., 80.

8   Ibid., 79.

9   For an influential postcolonial challenge to the American wilderness obsession, see Ramachandra Guha, "Radical American Environmentalism and Wilderness Preservation: A Third World Critique," *Environmental Ethics* II (1989): 71–83.

10 For an invaluable critique of the wilderness tradition of "purity," see William Cronon, "The Trouble with Wilderness; Or, Getting Back to the Wrong Nature," 69–90, in Cronon, ed., *Uncommon Ground: Rethinking the Human Place in Nature* (New York: Norton, 1996).

11 See J. M. Coetzee's terse assessment that "it is certainly true that the politics of expansion has uses for the rhetoric of the sublime," Coetzee, *White Writing: On the Culture of Letters in South Africa* (New Haven, CT: Yale University Press), 62.

12 For an excellent discussion of the dangers of an excessive preoccupation with displacement, see Amitava Kumar, *Passport Photos* (Berkeley: University of California Press, 2000), 13–14. See also, Ian Buruma, "The Romance of Exile," *New Republic*, February 12, 2001, 23–30.

13 Parini, "The Greening of the Humanities," 53.

14 Quoted in ibid., 53

15 Quoted in ibid., 53.

16 On Abbey's anti-immigrant environmentalism, which became more prominent in his later years, see Rick Scarce, *Eco-warriors: Understanding the Radical Environmental Movement* (Chicago: Nobel, 1990), 92. For Austin's anti-Semitism, see Tom Athanasiou, *Divided Planet: The Ecology of Rich and Poor* (Boston: Little, Brown, 1996), 297.

17 Richard Rodriguez, *Days of Obligation: An Argument with My Mexican Father* (New York: Viking, 1992), 5.

18 Rick Bass, "A Landscape of Possibility," *Outside*, December 1995, 100–1.

19 Gayatri C. Spivak, *The Post-colonial Critic: Interviews, Strategies, Dialogues* (New York: Routledge, 1990), 72.

20 Aldo Leopold, "Game and Wildlife Conservation," in Leopold, *Game Management* (1933; Madison: University of Wisconsin Press, 1986), 23.

21 For a brilliant account of this process, see Rebecca Solnit, *Savage Dreams: A Journey into the Landscape Wars of the American West* (Berkeley: University of California Press, 1999), 215–385.

22 Richard Rodriguez, "True West," in *The Anchor Essay Annual: The Best of 1997*, ed. Phillip Lopate (New York: Anchor, 1998: 331).

23 Melvin Dixon, *Ride Out the Wilderness: Geography and Identity in Afro-American Literature* (Urbana: University of Illinois Press, 1987).

24 Richard Mabey, *Landlocked: In Pursuit of the Wild* (London: Sinclair Stevenson, 1994), 71.

25 One thinks here of innovative works like Richard Grove, *Green Imperialism: Colonial Expansion, Tropical Island Edens, and the Origins of Environmentalism, 1600–1860* (Cambridge: Cambridge University Press, 1995); Tom Griffiths and Libby Robin, *Ecology and Empire: Environmental History of Settler Societies* (Seattle: University of Washington Press, 1997); David Arnold and Ramachandra Guha, ed., *Nature, Culture, Imperialism: Essays on the Environmental History of South Asia* (Delhi: Oxford University Press, 1995); and William Beinart and Peter Coates, *Environment and History: The Taming of Nature in the USA and South Africa* (London: Routledge, 1995).

26 Gayatri C. Spivak, "Attention: Postcolonialism!" *Journal of Caribbean Studies* 12.2–3 (1997–98): 166; 159–79.

27 Beinart and Coates, *Environment and History*, 3. This book offers a fine comparative history of national parks in the United States and South Africa.

28 See Joe Kane, *Savages* (New York: Knopf, 1995); Suzana Sawyer, "The Politics of Petroleum: Indigenous Contestation of Multinational Oil Development in the Ecuadorian Amazon,"

MacArthur Consortium Occasional Papers Series, MacArthur Program, University of Minnesota, 1997; and Melina Selverston, "The 1990s Indigenous Uprising in Ecuador: Politicized Ethnicity as Social Movement," *Papers on Latin America*, 32 (New York: Columbia University Institute of Latin American and Iberian Studies, 1993).

29 Quoted in ibid., 18.

30 For the rich possibilities to be found in this kind of intellectual rapprochement, see the Canadian critic Sarah P. Casteel's, "New World Pastoral: The Caribbean Garden and Emplacement in Gisele Pineau and Shani Mootoo," *Interventions* 5.1 (2003): 12–28.

31 Lorraine Anderson, Scott Slovic, and John O'Grady, eds., *Literature and the Environment: A Reader on Nature and Culture* (New York: Longman, 1999). Of the 104 essays and poems included by the editors, twenty-six are by African American, Amerindian, Latina/o, or Asian American writers. This marks a significant advance over the more typical spectrum of Glotfelty and Fromm's influential *Ecocriticism Reader*, which found room for only two "minority" essays out of twenty-six.

32 Clearly, a narrowing of the divides between these two powerful intellectual currents only marks a beginning. In search of a truly international, interdisciplinary response, we would need to move beyond postcolonialism's anglo- and francophone emphases toward more fully global imaginings. But a postcolonial-environmental rapprochement would represent an invaluable start.

33 Roy, quoted in Madeleine Bunting, "Dam Buster," *Guardian* (London), July 28, 2001.

Part XIII

Queer, Postcolonial

Queer criticism is yet to take hold in African literary criticism. This is partly because of what Chris Dunton identifies in his piece as the largely monothematic nature of queer representation in African literary texts. The monothematic representations are themselves reflections of the perception by most Africans that homosexuality is inherently alien to African cultures. However, with increasing recognition of the fact that various traditional African societies have institutionalized homosexual practices among women in particular, queer criticism is drawing on a wider array of resources to re-orient the understanding of the representation of sexualities within African literary texts. The essays in this section address an incipient but no less significant field in African literary studies. Whereas Dunton and Desai's pieces focus on outlining a tentative typology of such representations, Munro and Nfah-Abbenyi attempt more robust analyses drawing on the South African and West African contexts respectively. What is clear from all four pieces is the need for a close reading of African texts to see how they might be made available for discussions of the alternative sexualities that are in evidence all across the continent, from gay bars in Accra to the after-effects of homosexual relations of the male dormitory system in apartheid South Africa, where migrant men lived in the cities separated from their wives, girlfriends and families for long periods and had to explore different sexualities from what was assumed to be the norm.

Chapter 94

"Wheyting be dat?":
The Treatment of Homosexuality in African Literature

Chris Dunton

In an article published in *Peuples Noirs, Peuples Africains* in 1983, Daniel Vignal comments:

> For the majority of [African writers], homophilia is exclusively a deviation introduced by colonialists or their descendants; by outsiders of all kinds: Arabs, French, English, *métis*, and so on. It is difficult for them to conceive that homophilia might be the act of a black African. (74–5)[1]

A more comprehensive survey than Vignal's confirms his findings: in texts dealing with colonial rule, or with the experience of African students living in Europe and the United States, or with conditions in South African prisons, homosexual practice[2] is almost invariably attributed to the detrimental impact made on Africa by the West.[3]

In most cases, even when the treatment of homosexuality is not crudely stereotypical, it remains monothematic: the function that the subject plays in the text's larger thematic and narrative design is restricted and predictable. In some texts, however, homosexual subject matter is utilized in a more complex, though not necessarily more sympathetic manner. Few, if any, of the writers here are known to be homosexual, and the primary concern of the present article is not the identification of texts that take a more liberal approach to the subject. To this extent I am not concerned with the pejorative judgment that African writers apply to homosexuality as being a problem in itself. Rather, I am interested in showing how the treatment of homosexuality provides a convenient reference point – a closely defined narrative element – which helps reveal the general thematic concerns and the larger narrative strategy of the text.

First published in *Research in African Literatures* 20.3 (1989): 422–8, 444–8.

I shall first survey the range of the treatment and then focus on a few texts to illustrate my point. In analyzing novels like Maddy's *No Past, No Present, No Future*, Aidoo's *Our Sister Killjoy*, Soyinka's *The Interpreters*, and Ouologuem's *Bound to Violence*, I hope to clarify the bearing a homosexual subject matter has on the ideology of the text as a whole. In *No Past*, for example, the rather uncertain presentation of Joe Bengoh's homosexuality is a useful indicator of Maddy's general procedures: specifically, of his deliberate projection of moral priorities that differ radically from those of other African novelists. In *The Interpreters* the relevance of the American homosexual, Joe Golder, is not just that he represents one of those characters in the novel who systematically impose demands on others, but that he constitutes another difficult, unpliable entity toward which others (the interpreters) must find a way to respond. The harshly unsympathetic but unusually detailed portrait of this homosexual character is complexly related to Soyinka's romantic assertion of individual vision as a dynamic force in society. *Bound to Violence* projects a homosexual relationship in a way that is unique in the literature to date and does so in the interests of a wide-ranging critique of orthodox modes of articulating African social and historical realities. Ouolo-guem's treatment of the relationship between Raymond and Lambert raises the whole question of irony and parody – of the assault on reader conventions – as being central to the novel's strategy. In these three novels – and in a few other texts, like Aidoo's *Our Sister Killjoy* – the subject of homosexuality becomes liberated, in the special sense that whether or not it is treated sympathetically, it is granted a greater capacity to disturb, to call questions, than in texts where it merely forms part of the data of a social typology.

It remains true that the great majority of texts in which the subject occurs stigmatize homosexual practice as a profoundly "un-African" activity: a perspective succinctly expressed by the grandmother in Maddy's play *Big Berrin* when she inquires: " 'Homosexu-ality? Wheyting be dat?' " (16). Two rare cases where an exclusive identification of homo-sexuality with the West is withheld are Soyinka's *Season of Anomy* and Mariama Bâ's *Scarlet Song*. In the former the Zaki – the traditional head of a Muslim Court within an independent African state – presides over the trial of a suspect dissident, accompanied by a fancy-boy with "long lashes" who giggles at the terror of the accused and who minces out of the room with the Zaki at the end of the hearing (120–8).[4] In *Scarlet Song*, Bâ records a traditional, highly specialized acceptance of homosexual behavior when Yaye Khady comments on one of her neighbor's sons, who is spectacularly effeminate, that he has every prospect of turning into a *gôr djiguène*, a courtesan's pimp-cum-manservant, whose responsibilities may include the provision of sexual favors for clients of a homosexual orientation (70). Yet even if homosex-ual practice is acknowledged in these passages to have been allocated a specialized, legitim-ate role in traditional society, it still is stigmatized: the reference to the *gôr djiguène* in Bâ's novel comes as part of a diatribe by Yaye Khady on unsatisfactory sons (the other three she mentions are a school failure, a pickpocket, and a drug addict), while in *Season of Anomy* the Zaki's liking for boys is marked as one more unsavory aspect of a repressive political system, the function of the Zaki's court within the state being equivalent to that of a colonial power.

These instances apart, the fact that homosexuality is projected as a phenomenon alien to African societies enables it to play a special function in pornographic fiction. In Edia Apolo's short story collection *Lagos Na Waa I Swear*, an anecdote on a lesbian relationship provides exotic relief from the succession of heterosexual liaisons that occupies the remainder of the book: here Apolo simultaneously exploits the erotic possibilities of a homosexual relation-ship and stigmatizes it as "grossly repulsive, un-African and most unlikely" (44). In Dillibe

Onyeama's novel *Sex Is a Nigger's Game*, the stereotypical identification of homosexuality with the West is compounded with a bizarre regurgitation of Western racist myths of black sexual superiority. When Chidi, a male prostitute, is taken up by a voyeuristic homosexual, Sir Brian, the erotic effect of the episode is predicated on an enhanced, specialized emphasis on Chidi's value as sexual commodity (Onyeama refers repeatedly to Chidi's virility and to the size of his organ), while at the same time Sir Brian himself absolves Africa of the stigma of sexual inversion, commenting that this was " 'largely imported by the early colonists and by Westernized Africans' " (76).[5]

The exclusive attribution of homosexual activity to the West is equally commonplace in more substantial African literature. In J. P. Clark's play *The Raft*, for example, Kengide and Ibobo comment that white men are "beastly," indulging in sodomy to "keep sane" in their barracks and boarding schools (127). There is a clear projection here of the alienating effect that the notion of homosexuality is assumed to have on an African society: an effect which is related consistently in other texts to the general experience of alienation faced by Africans living under colonial rule – or when in contact with the West in some other context. Further, if the engagement of the West with the African continent is generally identified as being exploitative, then homosexual activity is seen as being a particularly repugnant aspect of this. In a number of different contexts – the colonial situation; the neocolonial state ruled through collusion with Western advisers; the prison system under apartheid; the situation of the African student living in the West – homosexual activity is identified with exploitation, being enabled by money or power relations, and understood to be all the more disturbing because alien to African society.

In Armah's *Two Thousand Seasons*, the Arab colonization of Africa is characterized by sexual as well as economic exploitation. The Arab "predator" Faisal is, typically, homosexual. Guilty, too, however, is the *askari* employed to sodomize Faisal; Armah's intention here is not only to expose the predatory nature of the colonialists but to emphasize the betrayal of Africa by those who collaborate with them and, in so doing, exploit their own people. Consequently, when the woman Azania assassinates Faisal, enacting a more elaborate symbolic execution than that in Marlowe's *Edward II*, she skewers the Arab through the back of his *askari* (23). Later, Armah emphasizes the central point, that Africa fell in part through its collaborators, as he comments on the African monarch Jonto, "[he] came among us with a spirit caught straight from the white predators from the desert" (64). Like his Arab mentors, Jonto is homosexual, and his oppression of his people is imaged in his brutal violation of young boys (65).

Under Western, as under Arab, colonization, homosexual activity is identified as one facet of a broader process of exploitation. In Sassine's *Wirriyamu*, set in Mozambique under Portuguese rule, the brutal landowner Amigo regularly orders his servant Malick to find him boys as sexual partners (38–9). In Awoonor's *This Earth, My Brother*, the houseboy Yaro has left his white master "because he wanted to turn him into a woman" (24), while in both Caya Makhele's *L'homme au Landau* and Sarif Easmon's short story "For Love of Thérèse," the degeneration of expatriates is marked by their turning away from their wives and developing sexual relationships with boys. Easmon, especially, emphasizes the alien nature of homosexuality in an African context, commenting how the pederast Jacques Lublin's behavior makes him "an object of contempt and ridicule in Susu society" (125). That idea is foregrounded, too, in Beti's *Remember Ruben*, in a discussion between two Cameroonian freedom fighters on the alleged sexual relationship between the European Sandrinelli and the country's future dictator and protégé of the colonial power, Baba Toura (195–6). Here, homosexuality is a weapon in the armory by which Beti discredits Sandrinelli and by which he emphasizes the symbiotic link between indigenous and Western interests in exploiting the African people. This is similar to the technique used by Sony Labou Tansi in satirizing the neocolonial state in *L'état honteux*, when he notes that the European security adviser to the dictator Lopez suffers from the idiotic trait of preferring men to women; it is clear that for Lopez the European's political usefulness far outweighs any importance that might be attached to his deviancy (81; 44).

Under the internal colonization maintained by apartheid in South Africa, dissident blacks may find themselves in prison, where the severity of constraint generates homosexual activity.[6] Again, in the literature on the subject, homosexuality is stigmatized as being alien to traditional mores: its prevalence in South African jails metaphorically stands for the extreme distortions in social organization established by the regime. In South African writing on prison life, then, homosexual activity has a more specialized function than in equivalent writing from Europe or the United States, since it images a rupture – and subsequent alienation – fundamental to the organization of South African society. In Gibson Kente's play *Too Late*, the young man Saduva is arrested after a sequence of episodes that illustrate in graphic detail the appalling constraints under which blacks live; Saduva's life outside is mirrored by his experience inside the prison when the cell boss Matric – rendered an exploiter under an exploitative system – seizes his food and then calls him over to his side of the cell for sex (117). In Dennis Brutus's poem "Letter to Martha: 6," an inmate's need for cigarettes is so great he has to force himself not to think of smoking, knowing that otherwise he may end up by buying them with sex (7). The emphasis on the disfigurement of accepted norms brought about under apartheid is foregrounded again in James Matthews's story "A Case of Guilt," in which a relatively privileged colored man is arrested on a false charge of nonpayment of taxes. The story revolves round his shock at discovering the brutality of prison conditions, which begins with his witnessing the sodomization of one of the prisoners in the toilet block. When he leaves prison, with the charge withdrawn, the narrator comments: "he felt it receding, the nightmare of men turned into beasts, where abnormality was the norm" (164).[7] But the irony here is that the nightmare has only receded in the subjective sense (from the man's immediate consciousness): the system which has spawned the prison remains as inflexible, as damaging, as before. The episode has not opened a window into a world radically distinct from that of daily life under apartheid; it has cast that world in a clearer, harder, light.

That world is depicted with intensified vividness in Bessie Head's *A Question of Power*, where homosexuality is identified as part of a pattern of systematic disintegration, cognate to other violations of normal behavior (in a significant parallel, the narrator points to the South African slums as places where small girls are raped and where homosexuals are "laughingly accepted," 117). Here, as in Kente, Brutus, and Matthews, homosexuality is seen as reflecting the larger identity disorder created by apartheid: after a passage on colored homosexuals – "a disease one had to live with" – the narrator quotes this explanation for the prevalence of deviance:

"How can a man be a man when he is called boy? I can barely retain my own manhood. I was walking down the road the other day with my girl, and the Boer policeman said to be: 'Hey, boy, where's your pass?' Am I a man to my girl or a boy? Another man addressing me as boy. How do you think that I feel?" (45)[8]

Finally, the prevalence of homosexuality is regarded as presenting a dilemma for African students living in the West. In Laye's *A Dream of Africa* (*Dramouss*), Fatoman is propositioned by an old man in a bar in the Latin Quarter; at first he does not understand what is happening and when the girl Liliane explains the incident to him, he protests angrily that nothing like that could happen in his own country (53–4).[9] In Abdoul Doukouré's *Le Déboussolé*, the student Kaydot observes with consternation his employer's affair with a young black American (36 passim), while the student-narrator of Bernard Nanga's *La trahison de Marianne* is himself given the chance (which he refuses) of offering his services to a Parisian man who has "a weakness for the boys" (190).

Again, the treatment of the subject tends to be monothematic; as in the literature on colonial Africa, the emphasis is placed on the theme of exploitation and on the idea that homosexual activity is rare in traditional African society and, therefore, especially alienating in its impact. A more obviously didactic and schematic equivalent to these episodes occurs in Kole Omotoso's *The Edifice*, where a continuum is drawn between the hero, Dele's, experience of sexual exploitation in a colonial mission school and the aspirations that later persuade him to study in the West. When Dele's excellence in English is used by a homosexual teacher at the school as the pretext for an attempted seduction, Omotoso's ironic recounting of the episode makes the point that Dele's absorption in the West is responsible for this entanglement, that it is his just reward for aspiring to be an *oyinbo* (38–40). Those later sections of the book set in Britain are designed to confirm that Dele's years there are as misconceived as is the nature of his relationship with his English teacher; the one is emblematic of the other.

In one other novel of student life, Saidou Bokoum's *Chaîne*, homosexual activity plays a more elaborate, more sophisticated narrative function. Ideologically, however, the treatment of homosexuality in *Chaîne* is not far removed from its treatment by Omotoso or Laye. At the beginning of the novel, Kanaan reveals how he has found himself increasingly alienated from Parisian society, abandoning his studies, breaking off his relationship with his girlfriend and gradually withdrawing from all contact with women. First masturbation, then homosexual activity, provides him with the stimulus he requires.

The marked emphasis Bokoum places on Kanaan's progressive degeneration as he discovers first one, then another means of degrading himself is reminiscent of the gradual descent to perdition of a morality tale. More centrally, however, this narrative strategy is designed to suggest the self-consciousness with which Kanaan engages in his descent. The thrill for Kanaan here lies in the *apprehension* of his own degradation, as he gradually installs himself "in the morbid universe of damnation" (63).

Exciting himself first by reading and writing homosexual graffiti in urinals, Kanaan then attempts an abortive rendezvous. Later, an erotic dream leaves him with an obscure, remembered phrase, *Saint Jean Po*, which he adopts as the name of a new persona.[10]

The idea of self-apprehension now becomes more central, and, for the first time, Kanaan begins to project for himself the identity of passive, homosexual *black*. Jean-Paul Sartre, in his essay "Orphée Noir," describes a poem by Césaire as constantly exploding and turning on itself and then comments on the process by which the negritude poets assert their identity as blacks: "It isn't a matter of coming together again in the calm unity of contraries, but of making stiffen like a sex *one* of the contraries in the pair 'black-white' in its opposition to the other" (xxvi–xxvii). Kanaan's crisis, however, requires just the opposite of this: he needs to see himself not as assertive but as a black abused, affirming the denigratory view of him sustained by the West. Pushing a padded knife into his anus, he announces the act with the words "SAINT JEAN PO violated by..." (typically, the headline style of the announcement *projects* the experience of being sodomized, so Kanaan can apprehend this with an enhanced sense of his degradation). Again, the question of race enters as a major substantiating element: when Kanaan fantasizes about being sodomized by another man, he questions himself what color is the penis that will violate him (63).

It is only after Kanaan is brutally sodomized by four youths that he is able to reclaim a true sense of himself and to escape from denigratory fantasy. Barely able to stumble away after the assault, he comments: "The eunuch miraculously escaped from butchery walks like this. Osiris walked like this searching for a member cut into pieces" (75). The reference to the god Osiris, dismembered, reborn, again recalls Sartre, commenting: "It is a matter...of the black dying at the hands of white culture in order to be reborn into the black spirit" (xxiii). Kanaan realizes that the period of degradation was the product of a crisis in which he was unable to confront the West's dismissal of his value as a black as something external to himself. That recognition constitutes the first step in a process of reclamation, during which he will come to acknowledge his actual condition and to find a way to negotiate this.

From the beginning of the homosexual episode, Kanaan drives himself, stage by stage, into more candid and unambiguous sexual contacts in order to bring himself up against himself in increasingly marked terms: apprehending himself as outcast, as (in the romantic sense) the man depraved, and as black. Illustrating, as it does, the playing out of Kanaan's existential crisis, the role played by homosexual activity in the thematic development of this text is more specialized than in other texts, where it tends to be seen simply, objectively, as part of a pattern of exploitation. As elsewhere, however, homosexuality is conceived as part of the arena of African/Western relations. Further, Bokoum sustains his theme by describing homosexual contacts of a kind that are consistently degrading; another sort of contact – mutual, loving, and not dependent on Kanaan's projection of his own role – would, after all, render Kanaan's neurotic program much more tenuous. In the end, then, the subject of homosexuality is treated as pejoratively in this novel as in most African writing: it is singled out as the worst possible course, adopted by Kanaan when he has rejected all other forms of human contact.

In the texts discussed above, homosexuality is treated as an aspect of the degenerate transformation wrought on Africa through its contact with the West. In a number of other texts, however, the subject is treated nonpejoratively and, in some cases, plays an elaborate and central thematic function.

[...]

Conclusion

Clearly there is a considerable divergence between the texts discussed in the first part of this article and those by Aidoo, Maddy, and Soyinka. The latter exhibit a much deeper imaginative engagement in the condition of homosexuality and in its social psychology. But there is little to be gained from constructing a league-table proposing clear divisions between the defective and the reflective text. Few of the works discussed early in this article are as crude and shallow in broad terms as their stereotypical treatment of homosexuality would suggest. Novels such as *Wirriyamu* or *Remember Ruben* imply the same pejorative assessment of homosexuality as do the majority of African texts, but in so doing they display an ideological foreshortening that is not typical of their larger thematic structures. On the other hand, the more responsive and detailed treatments of homosexual relationships by Maddy, Aidoo, and Ouologuem, are actually *dependent* upon the stereotype in the sense that they are only thematically effective when read against this. Maddy's decision, for instance, to characterize Joe Bengoh as homosexual and at the same time to project Joe's moral priorities as being superior to those of any character in the novel, is only fully significant in a context in which the pairing of homosexuality with moral consciousness would normally be dismissed as absurd. In these texts, then, the presentation of homosexual relationships remains schematic, intentional.

What remains conspicuous in all these works is the abstention among African writers, and even among the most searching and responsive of these, from a fully characterized and nonschematic depiction of a homosexual relationship between Africans. It is true that the treatment of such relationships between African men or between African women would involve more than the transference of the category "homosexual" – which is, as has been seen, a highly marked term – to an African context. A non-schematic treatment of the subject in that context would, after all, have no need to acknowledge Western modes of self-representation. Nonetheless, the practice of homosexuality within African society remains an area of experience that has not been granted a history by African writers, but has been greeted, rather, with a sustained outburst of silence. Whether this has been carried out within or beyond the limits of the stereotype, the identification of homosexuality with the West has helped defend that silence. An "official" history has concealed the reluctance of African writers to admit homosexuality into the bounds of a different kind of discussion.

Notes

1   Translations of this and other quotations are my own unless otherwise stated.
2   The term "homosexual practice" is used in this article to cover a range of sexual practices: male homosexuality, featured in the majority of texts under discussion, masturbation (*Blanket Boy's Moon*), pedophilia ("For Love of Thérèse," *Two Thousand Seasons*) and lesbianism (*Our Sister Killjoy*). The distinctions between these practices would appear not to be relevant to the writers, and so to have little significance in discussing the ideology of these texts. The exception is in the case of *Our Sister Killjoy*, where lesbianism is related to a wider discussion of female identity.
3   The terms "West" and "Westerners" are used throughout the article – the latter in preference to "whites" – so as to incorporate reference to black American homosexual characters, such as Joe Golder (*The Interpreters*) and Jimmy (*Le Déboussolé*). The point is that homosexual practice consistently is projected as being external to African culture.
4   In Soyinka's earlier novel, *The Interpreters*, the American Joe Golder dismisses the idea that homosexuality is exclusively an imposition by the West: " 'Comparatively healthy society my foot. Do you think I know nothing of your Emirs and their little boys? . . . And what about those exclusive coteries in Lagos?' " (200).
5   Onyeama's autobiographical *Nigger at Eton* contains a chapter titled "Homosexuality" in which the chief interest is the determined emphasis with which he marks homosexuality as being a Western phenomenon. "In Nigeria it certainly was very uncommon, and truly I have never heard of any case of serious homosexual practices there" (164).

6 Though not in prison alone: for a description of the sexual exploitation of young boys in a migrant workers' camp, see Mathabane (74); for comments on the incidence of homosexuality among migrant workers, see Mopeli-Paulus and Lanham (36, 95).

7 For comments on sexual exploitation in South African jails, see also Mopeli-Paulus and Lanham (77) and Zwelonke (21, 61).

8 Writing on Europe, Sembène Ousmane also identifies homosexuality as a social problem, identifying it as "a product of the times," engendered by poverty and unemployment. The reductive nature of this approach is clear when he then links homosexuality with "murders, abortions, poisoning, theft, prostitution, alcoholism" (119). For a similar reductive categorization, see Arthur Nortje's "Sonnet three," where homosexuals are among the detritus Nortje wishes to make "sublime" (a wish that is predicated upon identifying them as being in the depths: "homosexuals, bums, rag-pickers so obsessed / me I could watch them all for hours in fascination," 135).

9 Adele King notes that James Kirkup's translation of this passage presents a coarsened version of Laye's reticent original (106).

10 Later he remembers that *Seins Jambes Peau* (breasts, legs, skin) had been a password among himself and Guinean friends, signifying the prospect of conquering white women. But another interpretation of these words comes to mind: *Saint Jean* suggests the title of Sartre's book *Saint [Jean] Genet*; *Po* is (British) English slang for lavatory: derived from the Fr. *pot* (pronounced *po*, meaning chamber pot). Sartre's essay "Orphée Noir" is a clear source for this novel.

References

Aidoo, Ama Ata. *Our Sister Killjoy.* London: Longman, 1977.

Apolo, Edia. *Lagos Na Waa I Swear.* Lagos: Heritage Books, 1982.

Armah, Ayi Kwei. *Two Thousand Seasons.* London: Heinemann, 1979.

——. *Why Are We So Blest?* London: Heinemann, 1974.

Awoonor, Kofi. *This Earth, My Brother.* London: Heinemann, 1972.

Bâ, Mariama. *Scarlet Song.* Trans. Dorothy S. Blair. London: Longman, 1985.

Beti, Mongo. *Remember Ruben.* Trans. Gerald Moore. London: Heinemann, 1980.

Bokoum, Saidou. *Chaîne.* Paris: Denoël, 1974.

Brutus, Dennis. *Letters to Martha.* London: Heinemann, 1969.

Clark, J. P. *Three Plays.* London: Oxford University Press, 1964.

Dipoko, Mbella Sonne. *A Few Nights and Days.* London: Heinemann, 1970.

Doukouré, Abdoul. *Le Déboussolé.* Sherbrooke: Editions Naaman, 1978.

Eagleton, Terry. *Literary Theory.* Oxford: Blackwell, 1983.

Easmon, R. Sarif. *The Feud.* London: Longman, 1981.

Head, Bessie. *A Question of Power.* London: Heinemann, 1974.

Kente, Gibson. "Too Late." *South African People's Plays.* London: Heinemann, 1981.

King, Adele. *The Writings of Camara Laye.* London: Heinemann, 1980.

Laye, Camara. *A Dream of Africa.* Trans. James Kirkup. London: Fontana/Collins, 1970.

McDonald, Robert. "*Bound to Violence*: A Case of Plagiarism." *Transition* 41 (1972): 64–8.

Maddy, Yulissa Amadu. *Big Berrin.* Leeds: Gbakanda, 1984.

——. *No Past, No Present, No Future.* London: Heinemann, 1973.

Makhele, Caya. *L'homme au Landau.* Paris: L'Harmattan, 1988.

Marechera, Dambudzo. *Mindblast.* Harare: College Press, 1984.

Mathabane, Mark. *Kaffir Boy.* London: Pan, 1987.

Matthews, James. *The Park and Other Stories.* Braamfontein: Ravan, 1983.

Mopeli-Paulus, A. S., and Peter Lanham. *Blanket Boy's Moon*. London: Collins, 1953.

Nanga, Bernard. *La trahison de Marianne*. Dakar, Lome, Abidjan: NEA, 1984.

Nortje, Arthur. *Dead Roots*. London: Heinemann, 1973.

Omotoso, Kole. *The Edifice*. London: Heinemann, 1971.

Onyeama, Dillibe. *Nigger at Eton*. London: Leslie Frewen, 1972.

——. *Sex Is a Nigger's Game*. London: Satellite Books, 1976.

Ouologuem, Yambo. *Bound to Violence*. Trans. Ralph Manheim. London: Heinemann, 1971.

——. *Lettre à la France nègre*. Paris: Editions Edmond Nalis, 1968.

Sartre, Jean-Paul. "Orphée Noir. *Anthologie de la nouvelle poésie nègre et malgache de langue française*. Ed. Léopold Sédar Senghor. Paris: Presses Universitaire de France, 1948.

Sassine, Williams. *Wirriyamu*. Trans. John Reed and Clive Wake. London: Heinemann, 1980.

Sellin, Eric. "The Unknown Voice of Yambo Ouologuem." *Yale French Studies* 53 (1976): 137–62.

Sembène Ousmane. *The Black Docker*. Trans. Ros Schwartz. London: Heinemann, 1987.

Soyinka, Wole. *The Interpreters*. London: Fontana / Collins, 1972.

——. *Season of Anomy*. London: Rex Collings, 1973.

Tansi, Sony Labou. *L'etat honteux*. Paris: Editions du Seuil, 1981.

Vignal, Daniel. "L'homophilie dans le roman négro-africain d'expression anglaise et française." *Peuples Noirs, Peuples Africains* 33 (May–June 1983): 63–81.

Whiteman, Kaye. "In Defence of Yambo Ouologuem." *West Africa* 2875. 21 July 1972: 939, 941.

Zwelonke, D. M. *Robben Island*. London: Heinemann, 1973.

Chapter 95

Out in Africa

Gaurav Desai

At one point in Wole Soyinka's novel *The Interpreters*, the African-American homosexual[1] Joe Golder, who incidentally also happens to be a historian of Africa, attempts to discuss indigenous African homosexuality with the Nigerian journalist Sagoe:

> "Do you think I know nothing of your Emirs and their little boys? You forget history is my subject. And what about those exclusive coteries in Lagos?"
> Sagoe gesture[s] defeat. "You seem better informed than I am. But if you don't mind I'll persist in my delusion."[2]

In this brief encounter, Soyinka dramatizes the hitherto dominant narrative of attempts at discussing alternative African sexualities. Typically an "outside"[3] observer, with motivations which are probably too overdetermined to be clearly delineated, ventures into the vexed territory of studying alternative sexualities in a given culture; typically, again, an "insider" says "Leave us alone. We are not interested in talking about these things and it's really none of your business." An impasse – suspicious of the historically ethnocentric renderings of non-Western sexualities as "primitive," the "insider" prefers to draw attention away from any nonnormative sexual practices; at the risk of not being offensive, at the risk of not being unethical, the "outsider" exits. Some necessary questions continue to remain unasked.

In this troubled exchange however, it is not entirely clear where the moral high ground lies. Just as Western feminism finds itself in a "nervous condition" vis-à-vis its negotiations with non-Western practices such as incision and clitoridectomy,[4] an antihomophobic politics finds itself unable to open up gay-affirmative spaces without running the risk of being culturally insensitive. And yet, if no "culture" is so monolithic, so homogeneous, as to be fully recuperable within a singular sexual, aesthetic, economic, moral, or epistemic order, if "culture," that is, always exceeds the limits it seeks to set for itself, then what divides the "culturally sensitive" from the "culturally insensitive?" Could sensitivity to the needs and

First published in *Sex Positives? The Cultural Politics of Dissident Sexualities*, ed. Thomas Foster, Carol Siegel, and Ellen F. Berry, pp. 120–8. New York: New York University Press, 1997.

desires of *some* subjects mean risking insensitivity to the needs and desires of others? If so, to which subjects and voices must such a politics pay heed?

By drawing on a variety of texts – some literary, some historical, some anthropological – I want, in this chapter, to join hands with those African(ist)s[5] who are interested in opening up a space for considerations of African sexual practices in all their fluid forms. In particular I am interested in the ways in which literary works interpellate issues of sexual normativity and transgression. I open with the general problematics surrounding scholarship on non-normative African sexualities and show the discursive continuities in the arguments from colonial to postcolonial times.[6] I then proceed to read Bessie Head's short novel *Maru* against the grain of existing scholarship, which insists on reading it as a traditional hetero-sexual romance. I suggest that my alternative reading of the novel is enabled by, and hopefully in its own small way contributes to, the work of those who are currently struggling to open up the discourses of alternative African sexualities both within and without the continent. I follow the seminal work of Chris Dunton whose essay "'Whetyin be Dat?' The Treatment of Homosexuality in African Literature" remains the single most comprehensive treatment of the subject to date, and the more recent work of Rhonda Cobham on the integral relationship between sexual and national identities in the writings of Nuruddin Farah.[7] While Cobham's work, in its critical interrogation of the construction of masculinity is most directly relevant to my own reading of *Maru*, my interest in Dunton's essay is rooted in the larger question of the conditions of possibility of literary interpretations.

Through critical readings of a variety of African literary texts written since the 1950s, Dunton argues in his essay that with few exceptions, African writers tend to present homo-sexuality monothematically. Homosexuality is, in these texts "almost invariably attributed to the detrimental impact made on Africa by the West" and consequently "the function that it plays in the text's larger thematic and narrative design is restricted and predictable."[8] While Dunton's argument is indeed confirmed by the numerous critical readings of these texts written since the 1960s, the issue of *where* the blindness lies – on the part of the authors or on the part of the critics – is one that needs greater scrutiny. If, as reader-response theorists would have us believe, texts are as much the product of the interpretive practices of readers as they are the product of authorial intentions, then could the supposedly monothematic treatment be a product not of authorial agency but rather of the critic's interpretive limitations?

Consider the case of Joe Golder. Joe, the professor of African history with whom we began this essay, has consistently been read in the critical literature as Soyinka's emblem of everything that is wrong with a Western-based, romanticized Afrocentricity. This critical reading emphasizes Joe's alienation from his Nigerian colleagues who read him as a doubly foreign person – not only is he an American but also one who engages in sexual practices unknown (at least so far as these interpreters are concerned) in indigenous Nigerian society.[9] Joe Golder becomes in this reading an impotent (because homosexual) character who can only poach upon African subjects (such as the young boy Noah) and be the cause of destruction. Read in this manner, the character of Joe Golder confirms Chris Dunton's thesis: he is presented as no more than a scaffold for the larger narrative thematic so that consistent with the dominant theme of the novel, this particular "interpreter," much like his Nigerian counterparts, is unable to be a productive force in the newly independent society. Like philosophers, Joe and his friends can interpret the world but cannot change it. Yet, is there a different Joe Golder in this text who remains to be heard? A Joe Golder who is not predictably lecherous and filled with vice?

In one episode in the novel, the young boy Noah jumps off a balcony to his death, the narrative suggesting that his death is caused by Joe's sexual advances. The unfortunate incident is read by most critics as Soyinka's last straw in his rebuke of Golder. Thus Derek Wright writes "(Noah) is subsequently left at the *mercy* of the *neurotic* American quadroon Joe Golder, whose attraction to blackness is *more sexual than racial* and whose *inevitable* homosexual advances result in the boy's death."[10] Let us note immediately that the supposed *inevitability* of sexual desire and a forthcoming solicitation when a homosexual man finds himself in the company of a young boy speaks more perhaps to the critic's interpretive assumptions and cultural imaginary than to the actual unfolding of the narrative. For there is sufficient reason to believe that Golder doesn't quite understand why the boy jumps to his own death especially since he has assured him that he would not touch or harm him.

What is clear in the narrative, and what is rarely addressed by critics, is the double-bind that Joe consistently finds himself in – on the one hand, he *does* want people to know about his sexual preferences and to be proud of his homosexual identity (as is evident in the exchange with Sagoe), and yet on the other, he hopes that he is not reduced to *just* being a desiring and lecherous body by society, read by his friends, that is, as a foreign parasite whose sole purpose is to prey upon the Nigerian men. Read from Joe's point of view, his implication in Noah's death is less a product of his direct actions than it is of his perceived identity. Much like the famous Marabar Cave scene in Forster's *Passage to India*, the victimization is more the effect of a larger social imaginary than of an actual sexual offense. If to the British, Aziz can be read as no other than the emblem of a desiring Muslim India, then to the Nigerian interpreters, Joe Golder too emerges as a dangerously desiring body. But while Aziz, by the end of Forster's novel and in most literary criticism, is exonerated of his alleged crime, Golder remains to this day in the criticism of this text, the homosexual – and therefore – the accused.

Herein, then, lies Joe Golder's tragedy – attempting to escape both the homophobia within the African American community at home and the insistent hypersexuality ascribed to the black man by the larger predominantly white American society, Joe finds that in Africa too he is no more than a sexual body. Yet, if the possibility of this reading is left open by the narrative, it is one that few critics have pursued. Instead, the critics *replay* the textual tragedy in their own criticism. So, for instance, in Wright's reading, Joe emerges as an odd man, a "neurotic" whose identification with the black race for what it's worth, is "more sexual than racial."

While a more detailed reading of Joe Golder is best left for another occasion, I want to reiterate that it is precisely in addressing his simultaneous negotiations of racial and sexual identities that Soyinka presents Golder as a profoundly sympathetic character. Golder is an individual who has had to claim actively at least two identities which continually threaten to escape him – he is at once a light-skinned black man capable of "passing" as a white man and a homosexual capable of passing as straight. His choice not to pass – his choice to reaffirm at once two identities not only at odds with the hegemonic order of things but also, more importantly, at odds with one another – is a choice that must sober even the most unsympathetic of readers. Furthermore, Joe's decision to study African history and his move to Nigeria, despite its potentially romanticizing implications, is presented by Soyinka as his continual attempt to negotiate the different demands placed upon his identities. Like DuBois, Joe has continually been confronted with a "double consciousness, (the) sense of always looking at one's self through the eyes of others, of measuring one's soul by the tape of a world that looks on in amused contempt and pity."[11] He comes to Africa hoping to erase at least one if not both of these sources of difference. He fails.

It is significant in this context that Soyinka presents us a Joe armed with a copy of James Baldwin's *Another Country*. For here is the suggestion that Golder is not some singular oddity but one with a legacy. Just as Baldwin, a gay black man, felt unable to find a home in the United States and thus sought Paris, Golder too seeks to find a different home in Nigeria. In this new African context, however, Joe Golder is unable to connect either emotionally or physically and remains desperately lonely. Golder then, is a character full of pathos if not tragedy, living through the experience of a transcendental homelessness, of belonging nowhere. To heighten this sense of pathos, towards the end of the novel, Soyinka has Joe Golder sing "Sometimes I Feel Like a Motherless Child," a song whose performance profoundly increases the sense of alienation already being felt by the other Nigerian protagonists. It is important to note that Soyinka's choice of this song is not innocent but draws upon the very same James Baldwin who has affected Joe's life. In his *Notes of a Native Son*, Baldwin, reflecting upon the distance between the African and the African American writes:

> [The African American] begins to conjecture how much he has gained and lost during his long sojourn in the American republic. The African before him has endured privation, injustice, medieval cruelty; but the African has not yet endured the utter alienation of himself from his people and his past. His mother did not sing "Sometimes I Feel Like a Motherless Child" and he has not, all his life long, ached for the acceptance in a culture which pronounced straight hair and white skin the only acceptable beauty.[12]

Soyinka's tragic vision then, appropriates this song from the African American tradition to now include the predicament of a postcolonial nation-state in Africa. Rather than providing a supportive and inviting space for the alienated African American, the postcolonial nation-state too joins hands in the tragic condition.

The Emergence of a Discourse

I have focused on the character of Joe Golder not so much in the interests of promoting him to a heroic type but instead to ask a basic question in the history of literary interpretations. If indeed Joe can be read in a sympathetic manner today (indeed, if as some of my students suggest he could not be read as anything *but* tragic), then how do we account for the fact that he has never so far been read as such? The answer, I suggest, has less to do with any intentional malice on the part of critics than with the nature of critical discourse itself and the contingencies of its production. Simply put, just as literary genres have their histories, so does the genre of criticism, and critical discourses like any other have rules of exclusion and inclusion. Until these rules, both internal as well as external to the discourse, realign themselves to open up different conditions of possibilities, certain kinds of claims remain unthought, or if at all thought, remain unintelligible and unallowable within the dominant discourse.[13] Or, as Michel Foucault puts it, for a claim to be considered true, it must first be "within the truth."[14] What causes realignments within the field of discursive legitimacy are a multiplicity of factors – some relatively external to the discourse, such as political revolutions, others relatively internal to it, such as sheer boredom with existing models of explanation on the part of participants. Most often, of course, the various contingencies work together to form new conditions of possibility and new intellectual configurations. Thus, with the simultaneous growth of gay and lesbian political activism in Africa, and the emergence of gay and lesbian studies as legitimate foci for scholarly research, we find ourselves today in the midst of such a process vis-à-vis the discourse of African sexuality. As such the times are both politically and intellectually exciting.

In addressing the limits and the stakes involved in this newly emergent discursive field it is important to note the complicated issue of the relationship between anticolonial politics, gay-lesbian liberation, and the politics of feminism. If we are embarked on a space-clearing project, the desire to keep it antihomophobic, feminist, and anticolonial at the same time is one which I share and uphold, but it is important to state that the specific lines of alliance between these three nodes will for now have to remain undetermined. While one may expect to find a continuity between certain political positions, such as between feminism and antihomophobia for instance (since both share the project of being critical of patriarchy), these continuities are not natural but rather contingently forged. And if such forging is to take shape in the threshold of a colonial landscape, it is always susceptible to the over-determinations of "race" and "nation."

Take for instance, the seminal work of Ifi Amadiume on the changing construction of gender in Nnobi society. In her work, Amadiume shows how the institution of woman-to-woman marriages in precolonial Nnobi society suggests that there existed in this society a certain fluidity in the gender-sex system so that biological sex did not necessarily determine social gender. Amadiume's compelling insight is that the relative reification and indeed "naturalization" of sex-gender roles which one observes in more contemporary times among the Nnobi was not a precolonial legacy but rather a direct consequence of British colonial practices aimed at regulating the possible gender options available for Nnobi women. In other words, by drawing on a precolonial social institution in which women could marry other women and play the social role of husbands, Amadiume shows that things were not always as they seem today in Nnobi society. Gender roles were not easily tied to biological sex and individual women did indeed have social possibilities that they have no more. So far, her argument is an important historical corrective to those who tend to either essentialize women or to essentialize patriarchy. But the force of Amadiume's argument is lost in her consideration of sexual practices. For having demonstrated gender-mobility in precolonial society, Amadiume proceeds to insist that the phenomenon of woman marriages should not be misread as any kind of institutionalized lesbianism. Such a reading, which Amadiume suggests has been carried on primarily by black lesbians in the West, can only result from the interpreter's "wishes and fantasies" and ultimately reveal nothing more than her "ethnocentrism." Furthermore, she suggests that such a reading would be "shocking and offensive to Nnobi women"[15] for whom lesbianism remains a foreign practice.

While Amadiume's cautionary remarks are indeed ones that any reader must pay heed to, the precise *argument* made in their defense remains elusive – for surely while Amadiume is probably correct in suggesting that contemporary Nnobi women would find any hints of lesbianism "offensive,"[16] her own greatest insight that colonial practices severely disturbed precolonial *gender* possibilities resulting in a different normatization of gender roles may also *potentially* lend itself to sexual practices. In other words, could it be that just as British colonialism radically changed the gender possibilities available to women, it may also have instituted and regulated sexual practices so that "offense" at the thought of lesbianism may be precisely the ideological mark of such intervention? Or to put it differently, can we be reasonably sure that through a historical change in which gender seems to have transformed so much, sexuality could have gone unaffected? *We cannot yet be sure* – more research would have to be done to answer this question, and indeed it may well turn out that Amadiume is right in suggesting that sexual practices were always resolutely heterosexual among the Nnobi.[17] But to silence the question through accusations of ethnocentrism and offense seems an unfortunate way to deal with an uncomfortable question. An unquestionable and unquestioning nativism is no satisfactory response to even the most pervasive ethnocentrism.

My point in singling out Amadiume's work is to show how even the most sophisticated feminists and the most engaging critics of patriarchy can nevertheless lend themselves to a theoretical silence or even downright hostility when issues of homosexuality are raised. But this hostility we must note is, at least in our case, not unconnected to the complex problematics of cultural difference and race which are always informing such accounts. For if Amadiume's anger is directed towards black lesbians primarily in the West who it would seem bring their false desires to bear upon a resolutely heterosexual Africa, then the *hors texte* of this encounter is surely the earlier voice of Frantz Fanon.

It is Frantz Fanon who in *Black Skin, White Masks* provides what for many has become the classic position on the relation between Africa, the West, and homosexuality. Fanon's double move consists not only of associating white racism with homosexuality – as in the statement "the Negrophobic man is a repressed homosexual"[18] – but also simultaneously insisting that no indigenous homosexuality exists in Africa. Fanon suggests that while transvestism may occur among some Martiniquans, these men lead normal sex lives and can "take a punch like any 'he-man.'"[19] In Fanon's account then, homosexuality becomes associated on the one hand with racism and colonial oppression, and on the other with effeminacy. In a context in which the black man's sexuality is read simultaneously as excessive as well as castrated, homosexuality comes into focus here, as Lee Edelman suggests, "only as the conflictual undoing of one man's authority by another; it signifies that is, only as a failed, debased, or inadequate masculinity – a masculinity severed from the ground of its meaning in a phallic 'possession' betokening one's legitimate status as a subject."[20] To be sure, at a historical moment when civilized, normative sexuality was read as one located in the monogamous, heterosexual family, and primitive sexuality in a whole host of what are read as abnormalities and "perversions," it is understandable that Fanon would wish to dissociate Africa from the "primitive" – the sexually "perverse." But, as Diana Fuss notes, it is unfortunate that "Fanon does not think beyond the presuppositions of colonial discourse to examine how colonial domination itself works partially through the social institutionalization of misogyny and homophobia."[21] Could it be that a particular form of heteronormativity was a necessary accomplice to the workings of colonial authority?

If in Fanon's framework nationalist struggle must depend on a simultaneous insistence on the creation of a productive black male subjectivity, a subjectivity that is, which does not allow itself to be symbolically "castrated" through any association with homosexuality, it is not clear that this strategy necessarily speaks to all the experiences of all the subjects within the newly forming nations. Not only does this normative order dictate the sexual construction of masculinity, it also, through the extension in which the demands of race supersede those of gender and sexuality, begins to dictate the sexual lives of women. It is thus that we find in Adrienne Rich's seminal essay "Compulsory Heterosexuality and Lesbian Existence" a letter from a Mozambican woman in exile:

> I am condemned to a life of exile because I will not deny that I am a lesbian, that my primary commitments are, and will always be to other women. In the new Mozambique, lesbianism is considered a left-over from colonialism and decadent Western civilization. Lesbians are sent to rehabilitation camps to learn through self-criticism the correct line about themselves.... If I am forced to denounce my own love for women, if I therefore denounce myself, I could go back to Mozambique and join forces in the exciting and hard struggle of rebuilding a nation, including the struggle for the emancipation of Mozambiquan women. As it is, I either risk the rehabilitation camps, or remain in exile.[22]

Unlike in the contemporary West then, where one may well postulate a lesbian continuum in the midst of a radically discontinuous male homosocial/sexual existence, in colonial-nationalist and postcolonial Africa one often finds both the male as well as female continuums disrupted. Thus, in such a context, just as the national struggle often takes precedence over the women's movement, so it is that the construction of an insistent heteronormativity begins to threaten any existing alternative sexual practices. It is in this sense that one could argue that at least in some African contexts, it was not *homosexuality* that was inherited from the West but rather a more regulatory *homophobia*.
[...]

Notes

1   While at one point in the novel Joe Golder is referred to as being "queer" (236), the term is not used here as it is in contemporary gay politics in the United States. I choose to use the term "homosexual" here because it more accurately conveys the reading of Golder in the newly independent Nigerian context of the novel. As often is the case in such situations, the choice of categories for the intellectual historian are complicated – should one use the word "queer" and insist upon its different signification in the Nigerian context, or should one, instead, shy away from the term, so heavily overdetermined by its contemporary American connotations, and choose a term which currently has relatively less political valence? While the term "queer" is quite appropriately used in discussions of some of the more recent events unfolding in South Africa and elsewhere in sub-Saharan Africa, I find that it is of limited value in claiming it for a 1960s context. Yet, this is a terminological issue in much need of debate.

2   Wole Soyinka, *The Interpreters* (1965; reprint, London: Heinemann, 1970), 199.

3   The quotes are meant to remind us of the always ambiguous relation between any inside-outside relation. In the case of Joe Golder in particular, he is a liminal figure – outsider by virtue of nationality (American) but insider by virtue of "race." Indeed Joe's search is precisely for a better negotiation of this inside–outside position. The fact that Joe Golder is an academic is also of relevance here because it too sets up a familiar dichotomy – that between academic or "bookish" knowledge and lived or "experiential" knowledge. This dichotomy while speaking to the earlier polarity between the inside-outside also looks towards yet another polarity – homosexual versus heterosexual. While in practice all these dichotomies are indeed in flux, my argument is that foundational discourses, whether Eurocentric or Nativist, whether from the political left or the political right, rigidly uphold the dichotomies thereby rendering dialogue impossible.

4   See Alice Walker and Prathiba Parmar, eds., *Warrior Marks: Female Genital Mutilation and the Sexual Blinding of Women* (New York: Harcourt Brace, 1993) for an elaboration of how this problematic works.

5   Elsewhere, I have argued for the use of this term as a more inclusive category than either "African" or "Africanist." In this earlier scenario, the term "African" is usually meant to authenticate a subjective or experiential knowledge while the term "Africanist" is used, either pejoratively or arrogantly, to describe a "learned" (or "bookish") knowledge. But knowledges are neither so easily divided nor is it the case that even if they were, anything would *necessarily* follow from this division. My alternative term African(ist) puts in productive tension the limits of "experiential" knowledge and those of "bookish" knowledge, hence resuming dialogue without erasing tensions.

6   "Why 'Africa' as opposed to the various different cultures of the continent?" is a question that is often asked in African(ist) circles. As indicated in note 1, the level of abstraction used in any discussion is always a factor among other things, of previous discourses on the subject. Since the usual claim is that homosexuality is "un-African" rather than "un-Ibo" or "un-Hausa" or "un-Gikuyu," I have found it best, in my counterargument to stick to the level of abstraction encountered in this claim. Similarly, since historical time periods, whether measured in relation to colonialism (pre-, colonial, post-) or to any other schema are *not* typically factored into these discussions, I have not attempted in any significant way to address them here. It is precisely in these directions (of ethnic and historical specificity) that future scholarship on African sexualities must find its way. As an early effort, I have chosen to retain a wider angle on these matters.

7   See Chris Dunton, " 'Whetyin be Dat?' The Treatment of Homosexuality in African Literature," *Research in African Literatures* 20:3 (Fall 1989): 422–48, and Rhonda Cobham, "Boundaries of the Nation: Boundaries of the Self: African Nationalist Fictions and Nuruddin Farah's *Maps*," in Andrew Parker, Mary Russo, Doris Summer, and Patricia Yaeger, eds., *Nationalisms and Sexualities* (New York: Routledge, 1992), 42–59.

8   Chris Dunton, " 'Whetyin be Dat?,' " 422.

9   Thus for instance, Femi Ojo-Ade writes about Golder, "He is a strange person, full of contradictions and self-hatred." See Femi Ojo-Ade, "Soyinka's Indictment of the Ivory Tower," *Black American Literature Forum* 22:4 (Winter 88): 748.

10   Derek Wright, *Wole Soyinka Revisited* (Boston: Twayne, 1993), 122 (italics mine).

11   W. E. B. DuBois, *The Souls of Black Folk*, intro. by John Edgar Wideman (1903; reprint, New York: Vintage, 1990), 8.

12   James Baldwin, *Notes of a Native Son* (Boston: Beacon, 1955), 122.

13   One could cite several examples of this vis-à-vis the discussion of homosexuality in African(ist) literary criticism. In addition to the example of Joe Golder, the most obvious instantiation of such limitations is the criticism surrounding Yambo Ouologuem's *Bound to Violence* (1968; reprint, London: Heinemann, 1971). In this novel, just about every sexual relationship except one is "bound to violence" – we are presented with incest, bestiality, voyeurism, and rape. Furthermore, none of these sexual encounters are ever presented as loving or tender ones. The one exception is the relationship between Raymond Kassoumi and the Frenchman Lambert. While this relationship is by no means perfect, Ouologuem treats it as a loving relationship and insists on its tenderness. The novel, in other words, leaves open the possibility of reading this same-sex relationship between a black man and a white man as somehow sidestepping the inherent violence of the other relationships. Problematic though its implications might be, critics have chosen to silence the question by suggesting instead that Ouologuem's portrayal of tenderness and love here is either simply a flaw on his part, or else is not inconsistent given the homosexual nature of the relationship. In other words, this latter claim is based on the argument that the relationship is presented no differently from the others in the novel since the *homosexual nature of the relationship itself* is proof positive of the unnaturalness and violence.

14   Michel Foucault, "Appendix: The Discourse on Language," in *The Archaeology of Knowledge* (New York: Tavistock, 1972), 224. One of the external readers of this essay felt that this discussion of Michel Foucault would be familiar to most readers of *Genders*. While shortening and revising it to some extent, I have nevertheless chosen to retain it here. As a writer, I have wanted to be able to write the essay not only for an audience interested primarily in the study of gender and sexuality and only secondarily in African studies, but *also* (and perhaps more politically importantly) for an audience of Africanists who may not otherwise turn to a journal such as *Genders*. If there is to be a dialogue between both these communities, certain ideas taken for granted by each but not intimately familiar to the other must be rehearsed. I feel that the discussion of the production of discourse of African sexuality is thus crucial in such a context.

15   Ifi Amadiume, *Male Daughters, Female Husbands: Gender and Sex in an African Society* (London: Zed Press, 1987), 7.

16   I suggest that it is not enough, in a critical enterprise, to stop an analysis as soon as one encounters such barriers. While being sensitive to that which causes "offense," we need to ask: How does one historicize this condition of being offended? My argument parallels Joan Scott's skepticism of the category of "experience" as the ultimate grounding for historical claims. One has to attempt to understand how "experience" comes to be experienced as such, and the same is true of "offense." See Joan Scott, "Experience," in Judith Butler and Joan Scott, eds., *Feminists Theorize the Political* (New York: Routledge, 1992), 22–40.

17   It may be useful to note here that while I have not been able to locate any other references to the presence or absence of lesbianism among the precolonial Nnobi, there are indeed records indicating that other African societies having similar institutional set-ups did not preclude lesbian possibilities. Thus Melville Herskovits, "A Note on 'Woman Marriage' in Dahomey," *Africa* 10:3 (1937): 335–41 suggests that while lesbianism may not always be a factor in such alliances it sometimes may be. On the other hand, it is clear that even institutions based on heterosexual norms leave a certain amount of space for homosexual activities. Thus Evans-Pritchard reports that lesbianism was practiced by women in some polygamous Azande households. Also of note in this context is Evelyn Blackwood's more comprehensive survey of the construction of lesbianism in anthropological discourse (Evelyn Blackwood, "Breaking the Mirror: The Construction of Lesbianism and the Anthropological Discourse on Homosexuality," in David Suggs and Andrew Miracle, eds., *Culture and Human Sexuality: A Reader* (Pacific Grove, CA: Brooks/Cole, 1993), 328–40. Gill Shepherd's article on homosexuality in Mombasa (Gill Shepherd, "Rank, Gender, and Homosexuality: Mombasa As a Key to Understanding Sexual Options," in Pat Caplan, ed., *The Cultural Construction of Sexuality* (New York: Tavistock Publications, 1987), 240–70, Renee Pittin's article on lesbian sexuality in Katsina ("Houses of Women: A Focus on Alternative Life-Styles in Katsina City," in Christine Oppong, ed., *Female and Male in West Africa* (Boston: George Allen, 1983), 291–302), and Judith Gay's article on "Mummies and Babies" ("'Mummies and Babies' and Friends and Lovers in Lesotho," in David Suggs and Andrew Miracle, eds., *Culture and Human Sexuality: A Reader* (Pacific Grove, CA: Brooks/Cole, 1993), 341–55, all cast lesbian relations in the significantly different light of economics, rank, prestige, and possibilities of upward mobility. Once again, as indicated in note 6, I am aware of the dangers of using any one African society as metonymic for the whole of Africa. My listing of these instances from other African societies is not meant to make any claims about the Nnobi themselves. It is rather to counter the often articulated *generalized* claim that homosexuality is alien to Africa.

18   Frantz Fanon, *Black Skin, White Masks* (New York: Grove Press, 1967), 156.

19   Ibid, 180, note 44.

20   Lee Edelman, *Homographesis: Essays in Gay Literary and Cultural Theory* (New York: Routledge, 1994), 54.

21 Diana Fuss, "Interior Colonies: Frantz Fanon and the Politics of Identification," *diacritics* 24:2–3 (Summer–Fall 1994): 20–42.

22 Adrienne Rich, "Compulsory Heterosexuality and the Lesbian Existence," in Henry Abelove, Michele Aina Barale, and David Halperin, eds., *The Lesbian and Gay Studies Reader* (New York: Routledge, 1993), 240.

Chapter 96

Toward a Lesbian Continuum?
Or Reclaiming the Erotic

Juliana Makuchi Nfah-Abbenyi

In Calixthe Beyala's *Tu t'appelleras Tanga*, Tanga's identity and sexuality are controlled and exploited by individual men, as well as by a patriarchal society, but this control is compounded by the cooperation of her own mother. Tanga's mother, for instance, subjects her daughter to a clitoridectomy. This ritual has among other things economic implications for the mother for whom it is the culmination of her daughter's commercial servitude and, as she puts it, the old age insurance that she expects and demands of her daughter by forcing her into prostitution. Tanga's mother not only reinforces the ritual and cruelty to women and their bodies, but legitimizes her financial demands on her own (female) child. Mothers or other women, on individual basis, prepare their daughters for the ritual and the duties that lie ahead. In *Tanga*, there are only three people present at Tanga's clitoridectomy, the "arracheuse de clitoris" (the woman responsible for "tearing out" the clitoris, "the clitoris snatcher"), Tanga herself, and her mother. Similarly, in *C'est le soleil qui m'a brulée*, when Ada takes her niece, Ateba Léocadie, to the old woman for the egg ritual, these three women are the only ones involved. In *Soleil*, Ada "needs" to prove that her niece is a virgin in order to restore her own honor as a "mother" and caretaker. She wants to show that she has brought up her daughter the right way, i.e., properly prepared for the marriage market. Likewise, Tanga's mother subjects Tanga to the clitoridectomy in order "to prepare" her daughter for the market of prostitution.

Tanga's and Ateba's experiences illustrate how women, and women's sexuality, are constructed and constituted by a ladder of power struggles in such a way that they become accomplices in men's domination. Women become active participants in their own object-ification. The novels demonstrate that men cannot always be blamed for the ways in which the woman's body is written into the cultural script. By criticizing women like Ada and Tanga's mother, the novels position themselves beyond the margins of radical protest and

Excerpted, with two additional paragraphs (supplied by the author), from Juliana Makuchi Nfah-Abbenyi, *Gender in African Women's Writing: Identity, Sexuality, and Difference*, pp. 90–6. Indiana University Press, 1997.

conscious-raising. They are demanding that women assume their responsibilities in the (con)textual writing of this script. They must cease to be the domesticated victims that they make themselves out to be by rejecting what conditions them into subservience. True change can begin with women, one that consequently would invade and subvert the collective consciousness constructed by the Law of the Father, thus exploding the very foundations and boundaries erected by that consciousness.

Calixthe Beyala illustrates this beginning in *Tanga* and *Soleil* by portraying women seeking women-centered spaces and women-grounded relationships that seem to be not as oppressive as the male-centered spaces and relationships within which their sexuality is constructed. In *Tanga*, the seventeen-year-old African woman opens up her soul to the Jewish French woman. This is the first time, during her neglected and exploited existence, that Tanga has ever spoken about herself with anyone. She tells Anna-Claude the story of her life. The story opens with the two women in a prison cell, the ultimate metaphor for the various kinds of prisons that have defined and entrapped their lives and their sexuality. Recounting her story to Anna-Claude becomes the final straw in Tanga's struggle to break her own silences, "silence as a will not to say or a will to unsay and as a language of its own" (Minh-ha 74). Storytelling in this context becomes the medium through which both women explore and subvert the very prison walls within which the experiences of their identities and sexualities have been confined for so long. It becomes the route to self-liberation and the construction of agency, one that enables them to bridge multiple differences of white/black, colonization/colonized, oppressor/oppressed.

Tanga (re)constructs the maternal link with Anna-Claude. I see this reconstruction as the continuation of what began with her adoption and breastfeeding of the little boy, Mala. Both women become what Julia Kristeva has defined as subjects-in-process, as they seek to reactivate the repressed feminine and appropriate a semiotic, maternal link[1] – one that, in the novel, facilitates the shattering of prison walls and patriarchal boundaries. As she haltingly recounts her story, Tanga insists on everything about both women touching: their stories, their minds, their bodies. Tanga begins by asking Anna-Claude to put her hand in her own: "Donne-moi la main, désormais tu seras moi" (*TTT* 18) [Give me your hand. From now on you will be me]. This act is the beginning of something psychological and physical, mental and sensual that ignites the flow of the story. Bodies, not objectified bodies, but revived bodies; bodies in the process of rejuvenation, reconstruction, and reconstitution; bodies that shatter their shields of armor through a persistent reaching out, a touching of hands, without which Tanga feels no warmth or communication. This mental and physical touching recaptures for both women what they interpret as the maternal:

> Leurs corps s'enlacent. Anna-Claude pleure. Tanga trace sur son cou et son flanc des sillons de tendresse. Elle lui dit de ne pas pleurer, qu'elles venaient de connaître le cauchemar mais que le réel était l'étreinte. Elle lui dit qu'elles frotteront leur désespoir et que d'elles jaillira le plus maternel des amours (*TTT* 72).

> [Their bodies embrace. Anna-Claude weeps. Tanga traces furrows of tenderness down her neck and side. She tells her not to cry, that they had just known a nightmare but the embrace was reality. She tells her that they will rub their despair together and from them will spring the most maternal of loves.]

Female bonding develops out of this sensuous, maternal love, and paves the way for both women to shift in and out of their marginality, for their silences to be broken and their stories to be told. Non-heterosexual and women-centered existence is strongly reclaimed and reaffirmed in Beyala's work. But there is a difference in reclaiming these women-centered spaces that does not exclude a male frame of reference – a difference that I see in Beyala's work as compared, for example, with Monique Wittig's *Les guérillères*. There is an active pursuit of sensuous relationships between women, but there is also a tolerance for women seeking pleasures with men, if only the women are not objectified in the process. These women-centered spaces are unlike those portrayed by the other women writers here considered. Though others do affirm women-to-women bonding, what is specific and important in Beyala's work is that it goes beyond mere "bonding" (i.e., the type of bonding within the women's network that pitches in to help other women when they are in need). Calixthe Beyala portrays a specific sensuousness and eroticization of that women-centered existence that can be likened to a modified version of what Adrienne Rich has described as a lesbian continuum. According to Rich, *"lesbian existence* suggests both the fact of the historical presence of lesbians and our continuing creation of the meaning of that existence. I mean the term *lesbian continuum* to include a range – through each woman's life and throughout history – of women-identified experience; not simply the fact that a woman has had or consciously desired genital sexual experience with another woman" (156). I will here modify Rich's definition by inserting in this continuum Alice Walker's definition of a womanist as "a woman who loves other women, sexually and/or nonsexually. . . . Sometimes loves individual men, sexually and/or nonsexually" (xi). The continuum that I see in Beyala reflects both Rich's and Walker's suggestions. The women in Beyala's work do not necessarily reject heterosexuality, nor do they necessarily turn to lesbianism. Walker would say, for example, that these women appreciate women's culture and possess a valuable emotional flexibility. Some of them (especially the main characters, Tanga and Ateba Léocadie) simply seem to find psychological, sensuous, and sometimes sexual fulfilment in other women.

The nineteen-year-old Ateba spends all her life writing letters to women, recreating a women's "world of stars," a mythological world in which women were free before men invited them and then subjugated them. Ateba's "madness" and revolt against patriarchy and the male subordination of women is mediated through this writing, in the same way that Tanga uses storytelling. Women therefore seem to be the best friends, listeners, and confidantes of other women. Women bring out the best in other women, listen to them, kindle their loves not only for living but for enjoying life. They mold each others' desires – desires that, according to Ateba, should be directed toward other women, but that in some instances could also be directed toward men. As Ateba herself puts it: "Quelquefois, je t'ai reproché ton desire de l'homme" (*CSB* 67) [Sometimes I have begrudged you your desire for men]. But then, her own pursuit of these desires and contact with men have only reinforced her closeness to women, in every sense.

The sheer cruelty of the egg ritual on Ateba's body only reinforces this belief and strengthens her friendship with Irène, the prostitute who fills a gap in Ateba's heart. Irène is like the real-life representation of her own mother, Betty, the (ideal) woman whose soul and problematic life Ateba has sought to recreate in her dreams, fantasies, and relentless quest for happiness and self-definition. Irène becomes that woman through whom Ateba's subjectivity and sexuality gain full expression. When she goes with Irène to the midwife for

Irène's abortion, she tries to comfort her frightened but determined friend, telling her that woman's suffering, caused by "man", has become women's strength. As they wait in front of the midwife's office, she tries to reach out to Irène:

> Elle avance une main, elle veut la poser sur le genou d'Irène, elle tremble, son corps lui dit qu'elle pèche, tout son être lui dit qu'elle pèche. Et elle reste le corps tremblant, essayant d'écraser cette chose intérieure qui la dévore. La femme et la femme. Nul ne l'a écrit; nul ne l'a dit. Aucune prévision. Elle pèche et rien ni personne n'explique pourquoi elle pèche. Tout le monde baragouine à ce sujet (*CSB* 158).

> [She reaches out a hand, she wants to place it on Irène's knee, she trembles, her body tells her she is sinning, her entire being tells her she is sinning. And she waits, her body trembling, trying to crush this thing that is devouring her from within. A woman and a woman. It was never written of; neither was it spoken about. No preparation. She sins and nothing, no one, can explain why she sins. Everyone gabbles on this subject.]

This is what I see as the erotic and (un)spoken moment of/for lesbianism in *Soleil*,[2] an issue, among others, that has been highly controversial with some readers and critics.[3] Jean-Marie Volet has rightly suggested that Beyala is "developing into one of the most provocative women writers of her generation."[4] While some reviewers of Beyala's work, like Armelle Nacef, celebrate what she refers to as a feminine way of loving,[5] Richard Bjornson maintains that "Beyala's lesbian approach to the reality of contemporary Cameroon is unusual within the context of the country's literate culture" (420). Ndache Tagne claims that "Ateba's homosexual yearnings . . . will raise an outcry from a number of African readers," and even states that readers will be scandalized by the "pornographic" content of Beyala's first novel (97). But Rangira Gallimore disagrees with critics who label Beyala's work as pornographic when they accuse her of "commercializing African eroticism."[6]

What I see in Beyala's work is an obvious eroticization of the woman's body by another woman. Audre Lorde has described the erotic as

> [A] resource within each of us that lies in a deeply female and spiritual plan, firmly rooted in the power of our unexpressed or unrecognized feeling. In order to perpetuate itself, every oppression must corrupt and distort those very sources of power within the culture of the oppressed that can provide energy for change. For women, this has meant the suppression of the erotic as a considered source of power and information within our lives. (*SO* 53)

Lorde condemns what she sees as the prevalent attempts to separate the spiritual from the political, as well as from the erotic, because she believes that "the bridge which connects them is formed by the erotic – the sensual – those physical, emotional, and psychic expressions of what is deepest and strongest and richest within each of us, being shared: the passions of love in its deepest meanings" (56). Ateba Léocadie tries to make an erotic connection with Irène, but these connections remain frustratingly muted because of their association with and definition as "sin." As Ateba muses, "She sins and nothing, no one, can explain why she sins. Everyone gabbles on this subject." Ateba questions those histories, cultures, and laws that have posited woman-woman (sensuous/sexual) pleasures as "sinning." This questioning puts into perspective Beyala's critique of institutionalized heterosexuality and patriarchal ideologies in the two texts, *Tanga* and *Soleil*. By questioning what this "sin" is, a restriction reserved for women in patriarchal culture, Ateba is, to paraphrase Lorde, making those connections between the spiritual (psychic and emotional), the political, and the erotic (physical and sensual). Women's sexuality and the repression of lesbian contacts become much more than a sensuous and sexual issue. They are a political concern to be reckoned with.

At the end of the novel, Ateba commits a murder that has personal and political ramifications. After Irène bleeds to death from the abortion, Ateba goes to the bar where Irène had always gone to pick up men, and does the same. The man takes her home, rapes her, and forces her to have oral sex on her knees because, "God sculpted woman on her knees at the feet of man" [Dieu a sculpte la femme à genoux aux pieds de l'homme] (*CSB* 173). She spits out his sperm at his feet, kills him by repeatedly hitting him on the skull with a heavy ashtray. In her mind, she destroys that which has forever subjugated her and all women and romanticized her and woman's subjugation. Then in a hallucinatory daze, she embraces, kisses, and fondles this corpse all night, calling it Irène, and professing her love to Irène.

In *Tanga*, the erotic moment of fulfilment for Tanga and Anna-Claude comes when they embrace and share physical, spiritual, and sensuous warmth as the culmination of their self-liberation of and from their her-stories. The affirmation and the use of the erotic as power can therefore be seen as an important and original weapon used by Calixthe Beyala to describe women's sexuality. This use of the erotic as a critical and powerful subverting tool is also seen in Werewere Liking's *Elle sera de jaspe et de corail*, which is interestingly, though pointedly, subtitled *journal d'une misovire* (diary of a man-hater).[7]

The use of the erotic is also deeply embedded in the style of this novel. Liking calls it a "chant roman" (chant-novel), because it is profoundly anchored in Bassa ritual. Although Liking is a novelist, poet, painter, performer, and playwright, this multitalented artist is best known for her *théâtre rituel* (ritual theatre) in which she adopts, transforms, and recreates traditional ritual content of Bassa initiation rites for performance on stage. The performances are meant to serve the same purpose that purification rituals serve in traditional Bassa society. Jeanne Dingome has noted that Liking's parents were

> traditional musicians who introduced her to their art as well as to oral literature in general. But it is after her initiation into esoteric cults as a teenager that she developed an intimate relationship with the living culture around her.... Indeed, it is her initiation at that most sensitive period of her life that later put her in a position to draw more readily on her culture's aesthetic (and essentially its theatrical) resources which are embedded in its myths and rituals.[8]

By combining and fusing traditional and modern elements, and by utilizing these elements to persistently question the mores of modern African society, Werewere Liking has succeeded in creating a new African literary aesthetic that clearly distinguishes itself from Western literary forms. It is within the context of this revolutionary aesthetic/ritual theatre, grounded in Bassa ritual and Liking's creative process, that the "chant roman" *Elle sera de jaspe et de corail* is written.[9] It is therefore the framework within which I read the text.

Liking incorporates many elements from different genres in this chant-novel, giving it a new form and aesthetic. In an interview with Magnier, Liking describes her chant-novel and defends her style of writing in these words:

L'esthétique textuelle négro-africaine est d'ailleurs caractérisée, entre autres, par le mélange des genres. Et ce n'est qu'en mélangeant différents genres qu'il me semble possible d'atteindre différents niveaux de langues, différentes qualités d'émotions et d'approcher différents plans de conscience d'où l'on peut tout exprimer....

Dans mon avant-dernière publication *Elle sera de jaspe et de corail*, tous les genres se rencontrent: poésie, roman, théâtre....[10]

[Negro-African textual aesthetic is for that matter characterized, among other things, by a mixture of genres. And it is only by mixing different genres that I deem it possible to attain different levels of languages, different qualities of emotions, and to come close to different planes of consciousness from which one can express everything.... In my last-but-one publication, *Elle sera de jaspe et de corail*, all genres meet: poetry, novel, theatre....]

It is this new and very innovative form of writing – combining genres, juggling words and phrases, defying conventional syntax, grammar, punctuation, et cetera – that has put Liking's work on a plane all its own. Critics have applauded the unique intertextuality that grounds her work and the heterogeneous voices that are woven into these complex texts.[11]

[...]

Notes

1 Julia Kristeva, "From One Identity to an Other," in *Desire in Language: A Semiotic Approach to Literature and Art*, ed. Leon Roudiez (New York: Columbia University Press, 1980), 136.
2 Calixthe Beyala has been known to adamantly reject the word "lesbian" used in reference to her work by critics on the grounds that this word does not exist in African languages. Granted, but this lack of terminology in no way erases those strong homoerotic feelings that Ateba has for Irène. It seems to me that Beyala wants to distance the limited sexual meanings by which "lesbianism" is often defined for possible cultural, political, or other personal reasons. (I am grateful here to Eloïse Brière for letting me read the manuscript of an interview with Beyala that she co-conducted with Béatrice Gallimore in Paris).
3 See Daniel Atchebro, "Beyala: trop 'brûlante' pour les mecs!" *Regards Africains* 8 (1988): 29; Joseph Ndinda, "Écriture et discours féminin au Cameroun: Trois générations de romancières," *Notre Librairie* 118 (Juillet–Septembre 1994): 12; Doumbi-Fakoly's review of *Tanga* in *Présence Africaine* 148 (1988): 148; Ndache Tagne's review of *Soleil* in *Notre Librairie* 100 (Janvier–Mars 1990): 97.
4 "Calixthe Beyala, or The Literary Success of a Cameroonian Woman Living in Paris," *World Literature Today* 67.2 (Spring 1993): 309.
5 "Sous le signe de l'amour au féminin," *Jeune Afrique* No. 1423 (13 avril, 1988): 55. See also Arlette Chemain, "L'écriture de Calixthe Beyala: Provocation ou révolte généreuse," *Notre Librairie* 99 (Oct.–Déc. 1989): 162–3, and Anny-Claire Jaccard's "Des textes novateurs: La littérature féminine," *Notre Librairie* (Oct.–Déc. 1989): 160.
6 "Le corps: de l'aliénation à la réappropriation, chez les romancières d'Afrique noire francophone," *Notre Librairie* 117 (Avril–Juin 1994): 60.
7 The working title of this novel before publication, as quoted extensively by Marie-José Hourantier in *Du rituel au théâtre rituel: Contribution à une esthétique négro-africaine* (Paris: l'Harmattan, 1984), was simply *Le Journal d'une misovire*.

8   "Ritual and Modern Dramatic Expression in Cameroon: The Plays of Werewere-Liking," in *Semper Aliquid Novi: Littérature Comparée et Littératures d'Afrique* (Tübingen: Gunter Narr Verlag, 1990) 318.

9   See Hourantier, 22–3.

10 *Notre Librairie* 79 (Avril–Juin, 1985): 18. Ellipses in the original.

11 See, for instance, Thécla Midiohouan, "La parole des femmes," *Figures et fantasmes de la violence dans les Littératures francophones de l'Afrique subsaharienne et des Antilles* (Bologna: Cooperativa Libraria Universitaria Editrice Bologna, 1991): 150–2; Madeleine Borgomano, "Les femmes et l'écriture-parole," *Notre Librairie* 117 (Avril–Juin 1994): 88–90; and also in the same issue, see Athleen Ellington, "L'interdépendance, un discours d'avenir: Calixthe Beyala, Werewere Liking et Simone Schwarz-Bart," 103–5.

Chapter 97

Queer Futures:
The Coming-Out Novel in South Africa

Brenna Munro

To come out as a gay African is often understood to be a contradiction in terms. Sexual identity has become caught up in the politics of racial authenticity and postcolonial nationalism, and since the 1990s heads of state from Uganda, Namibia, Zambia, Swaziland, and Kenya have followed Zimbabwean president Robert Mugabe's lead in passing anti-gay laws, and making public statements denigrating homosexuals as both un-Christian and un-African.[1] South Africa is the exception to this trend; its 1996 Constitution was the first in the world to prohibit discrimination on the grounds of sexual orientation. African appropriations of the identities "gay" and "lesbian" do necessitate an engagement with the legacies of colonialism, but in a rather more complex way than the likes of Mugabe would have it. Although never complete or coherent in its effects, colonialism had a transforming impact on African ideologies of gender and sexuality.[2] Administrators and missionaries introduced and enforced heterosexuality and homosexuality as the central axis of sexual definition, and female domesticity within the patriarchal nuclear family as the ideal, healthy template for social organization.[3] Pre-colonial relationships, identities, or practices that did not fit within this framework were often eradicated in the colonial encounter and its aftermath.[4] Meanwhile, what Bessie Head describes as the "astonishing phantom" of imperial modernity had queer effects that were not part of the official "civilizing mission" (87). In Southern Africa, for example, the migrant labor system and the growth of cities produced unruly new sexual cultures, from Cape Town's cross-dressing "moffies" to the systems of temporary male marriage that flourished in the mines.[5] Contemporary same-sex loving Africans must translate themselves through these local queer histories, regional invocations of a "traditional" African heterosexuality, and a Euro-American "gay" identity that has gained wide circulation in the last thirty years, thanks to mass media, tourism, work on HIV/AIDS, the travels of migrants, and the growth of huge urban centers in the global South.

Unpublished paper.

Affirming a gay identity offers postcolonials the prospect of new kinds of national citizenship and political representation, as well as new kinds of vulnerability;[6] it also marks participation in the circuits of globalization. It is thus easy to see the adoption of gay styles of being as a mode of assimilation into individualist Western epistemologies of the self, homogenizing mass-consumer markets, and the neo-liberal economic policies that enable these markets. However, as Dennis Altman says, "the ways in which the new gay groups of Asia, South America, and Africa will adapt ideas of universal discourse and western identity politics to create something new and unpredictable – these will be the interesting developments" (15). Queer postcolonial renditions of gay politics have indeed been at the forefront of radical critiques of the "new world order." From South Africa's Zachie Achmat, a gay rights and anti-apartheid activist who has led the Treatment Action Campaign in their fight for affordable drugs from multinational pharmaceutical companies and government action against HIV/AIDS, to the queer Israeli group Kvisa Shchora/Black Laundry, who flamboyantly protest the occupation of Palestine,[7] and "Salam Pax," the infamous and irreverent gay Iraqi blogger,[8] queer postcolonials are leading the way in inventively forging and embodying Michael Hardt and Antonio Negri's rather inchoate notion of global insurgent "multitudes." Gay modernity might be scripted by the West, but the terms of this modernity are being revised by queer Africans. Emerging black South African writer K. Sello Duiker does just that. In his novels *Thirteen Cents* (2000) and *The Quiet Violence of Dreams* (2001) he appropriates and transforms the coming-out novel, thus engaging with both Western notions of gay identity and the official South African national coming-out narrative.

South Africa's transition to democracy involved the attempt to create a "rainbow" nationalism, markedly different from most postcolonial nationalisms, which is not attached to one ethnic identity and explicitly includes gay people as citizens. The debate over the status of gay identity in the Constitution received a great deal of attention, and millions of people submitted their opinions on the issue to the Constitutional Assembly, as they did on all the clauses. Ultimately, those supporting gay rights greatly outnumbered those against, and South African politicians even used the metaphor of "coming-out" to talk about the nation's emergence from apartheid.[9] A sense of general investment in the idea of gay rights as a symbol of national freedom and the desired nation of the future is exemplified in Mark Gevisser's description of reactions to a Johannesburg gay pride march in 1994:

> The onlookers – ordinary black folk who live in the neighborhood – beamed back delight. "Vivia the moffies!" A young man shouted. . . . On one level, the bonhomie of the onlookers was simply sheer ebullience at a South Africa which no longer compartmentalized and categorized and shut people off from each other. . . . But there was something deeper in the crowd's clear – if bemused – approval of the event. "No, I would not want to see my son or daughter marching there," said one observer to me . . . "but those people have the right to march. This is the New South Africa. When we were voting last April, we weren't just voting for our freedom, we were voting for everyone to be free with who they are" (111).

The public welcoming of gay people becomes a mark of the new nation's ideals – a progressive generosity, and ability to be totally inclusive. The second commentator's somewhat counterintuitive combination of identification with and differentiation from gays reflects the contradictory discourse of South Africa's "rainbow" nationalism.

The coming-out narrative thus offers writers a template for allegories of the new nation, both euphoric and critical.

Duiker's *Thirteen Cents* tells the story of a homeless and orphaned thirteen-year-old boy who sells sex to survive in Cape Town.[10] Its bleak vision of the new South Africa from the perspective of a queer youth challenges the narrative of national progress to which gay identity has been lent. I am going to focus on *The Quiet Violence of Dreams*, however, which extends this attention to economies of sexuality into a more direct engagement with "rainbow" nationalism. This book is a late transition-era meditation on the disorienting effects of becoming "gay" in the new South Africa, which also insists on the possibility of self-fashioning through queer sex. Duiker, now thirty, is of a new generation of writers that came of age as apartheid was ending. He grew up in Soweto, studied journalism and art history at Rhodes University, and worked in advertising until his literary career began. He is not well-known outside South Africa, although he was featured with two other major black male post-apartheid South African novelists, Zakes Mda and Phaswane Mpe, in a 2002 *New York Times* article about how contemporary South African writing is turning away from apartheid to discuss new themes. He has, however, received little critical attention thus far.

The Coming-Out Novel: A Global Genre?

The coming-out narrative first appeared in Europe and America, as a popular gay genre that has now become almost ubiquitous in literature and film. Coming-out stories have been essential for creating a politically "representable" constituency; they might be described as mirrors in which people learn to recognize themselves. As such, they promulgate a quite specific form of identity through the process of reading. The "standard" coming-out novel, exemplified in a text like Edmund White's *A Boy's Own Story* (1982), is a realist coming-of-age novel, often told in the first person, of a young white man who discovers his sexuality through some bitters-weet encounters, faces the difficulty of telling a hostile world, in particular his family, and finishes the book with a hard-won sense of himself.

However, while this has become the template for "coming-out," the genre is far from monolithic. For example, Jeanette Wintersons's equally popular and acclaimed *Oranges Are Not the Only Fruit* (1984) not only deploys myth and fairy tale alongside its realist narrative, but presents the mother's desire to change her lesbian daughter as parallel to her missionary impulse to reform the "heathens" of the world. She listens to the World Service Missionary Program every week, and keeps a map of the world and its "strange tribes" in her kitchen; she even reads her daughter a truncated version of Jane Eyre, in which Jane leaves with St John Rivers and becomes a missionary. The coming-out novel can thus be rewritten as a parody of imperialism. Robert McRuer argues that recent American writing, primarily African-American, Asian-American, and Latino, queers or reinvents the standard paradigm of gay and lesbian identity – for example, Audre Lorde's transformation of the coming-out novel into "biomythography" with *Zami: A New Spelling of My Name* (1982). I suggest that postcolonial literary refashionings of what it means to be gay are a parallel but separate project to these North American efforts to create different selves through the identity-machine of the coming-out novel.

Narrating the Nation

The Quiet Violence of Dreams offers us a panoramic, and lengthy, picture of the post-apartheid cultural landscape, through the story of Tshepo, a young black student in Cape Town. The novel speaks in Tshepo's voice, as well as in the voices of a series of other narrators, primarily his friend Mmabatho, a bisexual actress who is also a sex-worker, an asylum inmate, and a Nigerian migrant couple. These narrators tell their own stories as well as giving their perspectives on Tshepo.

Tshepo begins the novel after having experienced the first of a series of spells of madness. Sent to an institution, he is diagnosed as suffering from cannabis-induced psychosis, but it is clear that he is also wrestling with extremely harrowing childhood trauma, and ultimately with his sexual identity. When he was around seven years old, his father, who is involved in organized crime, arranged to have his mother killed because she threatened to turn him in. Before she was shot, both she and the young Tshepo were raped. It emerges that a fellow inmate of Tshepo's was one of the murderers, and we hear his voice as well; the ghosts of the past literally haunt the asylum. Eventually Tshepo is released, and becomes a waiter, sharing a flat with Chris, a young coloured man who has just left prison.[11]

Tshepo realizes that he is attracted to Chris, but their budding romantic friendship deteriorates; Chris resents the advantages Tshepo's education has given him in life, and is both attracted by Tshepo's gentleness and scornful of it. In a devastating chapter, he rapes Tshepo, and gets him fired from his job. Heartbroken, homeless and unemployed, Tshepo takes a job in a male brothel. Contrary to what one might expect, the multiracial brothel is a place of healing and friendship, in which Tshepo comes to fully accept his desire for other men. Ultimately, and after a seemingly endless series of sexual encounters, he leaves the brothel. Meanwhile, his friendship with Mmabatho has foundered when she becomes caught up in a relationship with a man, which ends after she becomes pregnant. After a confrontation with his dying father, Tshepo once again goes "mad," and wanders the city and the townships in a Dostoyevskian state of despair. He recovers, however, and ends the book in Johannesburg, where he is working in a home for abandoned children, and has bought an easel in order to begin painting, while Mmabtho awaits the birth of her child in Cape Town.

All of this, of course, departs dramatically from what we have come to expect of the coming-out novel. *The Quiet Violence of Dreams* is an epic picaresque, in which the varied national landscape is continually unfolding before the gaze of the protagonist. At the same time, the development of the central character can be read as a corollary to national progress; Tshepo's journey is one of growth out of madness, exorcising the violence of the past. Like South Africa, Tshepo emerges from a tragically divided and abusive family and chooses a (gay) fellowship with people who are not his kin. The novel's concern with a panoply of fragile inter-racial relationships reflects the national project of reconciliation between the races, from Mmabatho's relationships with an Indian-South African woman and the disabled German man who fathers her child, to Tshepo's many encounters, including his unrequited love for an Afrikaaner fellow sex-worker, Karel. Mmabatho's narrative trajectory, from freewheeling bisexuality to conventional heterosexual romance to single motherhood, also opens up the coming-out novel to more than one trajectory of sexual development.

Tshepo, as the central character, however, is the symbolic figure through which the nation's past is exorcized and new national senses of belonging and affiliation forged. He is a character with a great capacity for sympathy, and at certain points in the novel he feels himself inhabited by other people's histories; the anguished memories of a black woman who lost her child to the violence of the apartheid state, and, more surprisingly, memories of Afrikaaners being tortured by the British during the Boer War. His boundaries with others are as permeable as the narrative itself, and it is as if the whole nation has been pulled into "his" story. The multiple narrative voices turn this bildungsroman into a chorus, and the sprawling novel is almost unable to contain its over-population of characters, locations and plots. The novel is in this sense a queer echo of Salman Rushdie's *Midnight's Children* (1980), in which the protagonist, born at the same time as the new nation of India, becomes filled with the voices of all of the "motherland's" other children. In Tshepo's sexual encounters, penetrating and being penetrated becomes a literalization of the breaking down of old boundaries after apartheid.

Tshepo "comes out" in the context of a multiracial community of men – the brothel. The experience of the brothel transforms Tshepo, whose narratives in this section are told under a new name, "Angelo." Tshepo goes from being the resistant subject of treatment in the asylum, to sex-worker-as-therapist: "I usually come out of there feeling like a psychologist, a confidant" (313). His charming and charismatic fellow workers see themselves as part of a brotherhood which transcends race, as Karel explains to him:

> "We're like brothers here. You will see things that not many people get to see in one life. And you will do things you never thought you would do. . . . But I'm telling you with all the things we have done and seen we could do anything. I could be president one day," he says and suddenly looks serious. (244)

The gay sex-worker "seriously" considering political office gives us a sense of the possibilities opened up in the newly invented nation. If sex is "serious work," it is because it is a kind of magically immediate nationalism, connecting people viscerally who otherwise would have nothing in common. Tshepo literally dreams of the rainbow nation as a field of erotic male comradeship:

> In Rockville I come to a stadium. Wild horses are running there, their manes magnificently flapping in the wind. In another field I see a group of bare-chested men playing soccer. But as I get closer they metamorphose into graceful centaurs with long untamed tails. I run towards them and they form a circle around me. They are handsome in a rugged way and are of every color imaginable. I become aroused as I watch this rainbow of muscular torsos. They drink wine and run riot on the field, kicking the ball, sweating, galloping, the earth thudding with their hooves. (*Quiet*, 416)

The stadium, site of both political rallies and the symbolic nation-building of sport, becomes a peaceful "riot" of free play – the new South Africa as mythic gay fantasia. Taking the alliance of gayness and nationalism to radically explicit heights, Tshepo/Angelo says that "the expression on a man's face when he comes, for me it would be the true expression of a patriot when he serenades his land and his people" (389).

This presentation of the gay man and the sex-worker as patriots and possible presidents seems like a direct rebuke to Robert Mugabe's notion that homosexuality is "cultural prostitution" for Africans. At the same time, Duiker takes on the stigmatization of prostitutes themselves in contemporary Africa. Cindy Patton argues that sex-workers in Africa are

seen through the same lens of HIV/AIDS panic in Africa as gay men have been in the West –
as frighteningly mobile and modern creatures, transgressively single and yet promiscuous,
and therefore a good target for blame (227). Duiker's writing of sex work is unusually
nuanced. In *Thirteen Cents*, the boy Azure experiences his body as an object to be traded and
indeed stolen, so that it becomes impossible for him to ascertain his sexual orientation – it is
an un-coming-out novel. In *The Quiet Violence of Dreams*, however, Tshepo has far more
control over his labor and its terms, as well as a queer narrative of patriotism through which
to interpret it. Sex work is the antidote to rape here, while, for the far more vulnerable
Azure, the two are almost interchangeable.

The Broken Temporalities of the New Nation

However, this novel is not simply a "patriotic" celebration of the new South Africa. As
preoccupied with sexual violence as sexual liberation, the novel addresses two post-apartheid
phenomenon that have been read as marks of the nation's failure – rape and HIV/AIDS.
Narratives about sexuality are thus prominent in both the discourse of rainbow nationalism,
and disillusionment with the new South Africa. The novel's queer temporality, its projection
of the relationship between the present and the future, is a disorienting mix of utopian,
apocalyptic, and dystopian. This mixture makes sense in the context of a long-fought-for
demise of a hated regime, disappointment at the ongoing problems of a supposedly post-
liberation society, and the rising crisis of HIV/AIDS. Tshepo, especially in his hallucinatory
phases, is obsessed with apocalyptic occult forces:

> Strange looking people walk amongst us, making precise calculations for our destruction.
> Diseases far deadlier than Aids, more insidious, are germinating, waiting for ideal conditions
> to wreak havoc and death. The ocean and the sky are plotting against us. (426)

The narrative chorus is sometimes a fractured narrative of a divided social landscape, in
which characters repeatedly describe themselves as "broken." Although Tshepo moves
between multiple worlds, and his narrative arguably unifies them all, his madness may be
a sign of their incommensurability within one person's experience, and one nation. There
are drastic differences between, for example, rastafarians in a prison cell and hipsters at Café
Ganesh, the racial mixing in urban dance clubs and the racial tension in a suburban
hardware store, and finally the inequality between the city and the townships:

> A lot of capable looking men hang around corners, their hands idle, frustrated, itchy with
> desperation. Are they plotting their crimes quietly? There is a goldmine in the suburbs, even the
> dustbins eat well. Perhaps inside they are bruised, feeling forgotten, progress going at lightning
> speed while poverty takes them at a snail's pace. No-one knows how shattered we are inside,
> they seem to say with their eyes, how desperate we are. Given a chance we can do anything. We
> lived through '76, Casspirs, detention, Botha, and now this, everyone grabbing as much as they
> can for themselves, they seem to say. . . . A Coca-Cola sign towers on a billboard. What does it
> mean to us, what does it mean to them who have nothing? (430)

Tshepo's grammar and point of view shifts wildly here between "we" and "they," between
division and unity, just as the men in the township experience the disjuncture between the

"snail's pace" temporality of poverty and the speed of national change. Perhaps the most terrifying space in the book is that of the asylum, because, like poor communities cut off from prosperity, the march of history does not seem to touch it. It is a malign state institution in which people can be certified as non-persons mentally, as they used to be racially under apartheid.

Even the utopianism of the rainbow brothel is also ultimately suspect. The owner, a white man, slips up and uses a racist phrase in front of Tshepo, and later fires Karel for refusing to apologize to a client who has underpaid him. Profit is after all the guiding principle, and what makes a profit, as well as who makes it, is structured racially after all. Tshepo says, "I start thinking deeper about the brotherhood itself. Why are Cole and I the only black faces? . . . Surely there are Indian and coloured masseurs out there," (344), questioning his work-place as well as the gay bars of Cape Town:

> My stomach turns as I think deeper about Biloxi, all the black people I have never seen there. They are . . . the ones I would meet in the township or in a squatter camp . . . I feel cornered. I feel my blackness. . . . I get up and make my way to work, heavy with disillusionment. (*Quiet*, 344)

Tshepo leaves the brothel, and sheds the name of Angelo, now perhaps too close to "Anglo."

The brothel-as-nation is also an exclusively male affair. While this fraternity is a radical transformation of the homophobic male collectivity of much South African "protest" writing, it once again leaves women out of the picture. Duiker attempts to make a gender critique of rainbow nationalism; as Tshepo impatiently says to one of his brothel "brothers": " 'Gay men, gay men. You've said nothing about gay women. In fact any woman listening to you would think you're a misogynist, all this pro-male rhetoric,' " (254). In the final passage of the novel, Tshepo attempts to access his creativity through the spirit of his dead, beloved mother in order to begin painting, a queer artistic genealogy rather than a (gay) literary fraternity.[12]

At the beginning of the novel, Tshepo celebrates the cosmopolitan democracy of the dance floor, a space that stands for the new South Africa and the breaking down of old political and racial divisions. The queer possibilities of consumerism and its flexible production of queer new desires are both celebrated and ironized here:

> On the dance floor it doesn't matter which party you voted for in the last election. . . . People only care that you can dance and that you look good. They care that you are wearing Soviet jeans with an expensive Gucci shirt and that you have a cute ass. They care that your girlfriend has a pierced tongue and that sometimes on a Saturday night she goes to bed with another woman and likes you to watch them. . . . Designer labels are the new Esperanto. Dolce and Gabbana kicks more ass than any bill of rights. (34)

A hybrid culture is being forged here, going beyond African and Western, which perhaps harks back to the polyglot jazz life of South Africa's urban cultures of the first half of the twentieth century:

> They want to say ah you're cool and not ah you're black or white. . . . You must know what heita means, what magents are and how to shake hands the African way. You must know what a barmitzvah is, in which direction Mecca faces and who charras are. . . . You must know all these things and more in a culture pushing to be hybrid and past gender and racial lines. (*Quiet*, 34–5)

Duiker seems genuinely invested in this syncretic nationalism; his novel after all includes references as widely ranging as Egyptian and Norse mythology, novelists Ben Okri and Dambudzo Marechera, and the music of Marilyn Manson and Massive Attack. Tshepo asks, "Can I claim Afrikaans, Coloured tsotsi taal, Indian cuisine or English sensibilities as my own? Must I always be apologetic for wanting more than what my culture offers?" (348)

But by the end of the novel Tshepo has experienced being barred from the dance floor during his unkempt periods of madness, and develops a critique of capitalism that takes him from the brothel to Whitmanesque queer encounters that are not for money:

> I always meet special men who come from different places.... They offer me blueprints for survival, for building a new civilization, a new way of life. I have met bankers, architects, poets, builders, miners, diplomats, engineers, labourers, waiters, sailors, firemen, soldiers, farmers, teachers, men worth their salt and men of integrity.... There are better ways, they keep telling me, capitalism is not the only way. We haven't nearly exhausted all the possibilities, they say. (455)

This critique of capitalism marks a departure from South Africa's new dispensation, which has moved South Africa as swiftly as possible into the global economy. Rather than simply extolling and exemplifying the new South Africa, Tshepo chooses to adopt the nation's cast-offs, as a queer "uncle" for homeless children like Azure. His relationship with rainbow nationalism is also complicated by his identification with the nation's new outsiders – immigrants from other African countries. Mmabatho parrots the xenophobia that became a controversial issue in South Africa in the late 1990s:[13]

> Tshepo keeps going to them. Them with their funny smells and accents. I don't like them. A friend of mine who stays in a block of flats dominated by them tells me that they bring strange diseases into the country because they insist on performing their queer rituals even though this isn't really Third World Africa. (*Quiet*, 261)

Tshepo, however, has an affinity with this pan-African "queerness," which represents a different kind of cosmopolitanism than that of "Dolce and Gabbana." At the end of the novel he locates himself in what used to be Johannesburg's gay bohemian neighborhood, and is now full of people from across the continent: "I believe in people, in humankind, in personhood. In Hillbrow I live with foreigners, illegal and legal immigrants.... I feel at home with them because they are trying to find a home in our country" (454).

The Quiet Violence of Dreams is a queer paradox: the narration of a gay subject "finding himself" that is also a jeremiad against consumer labels and ready-made identities. Increasingly, Duiker has performed this paradox in his public self-presentation. His book covers feature handsome, pensive photographs of the author, and the information they provide encourages an autobiographical reading of the texts. Nonetheless, a recent interview with Victor Lakay in the South African *Daily Mail* and in the *Guardian*'s Q-page presents a different version of "the author." Lakay asks him about *The Quiet Violence of Dreams*:

VL: Is there anything autobiographical about this?
KSD: Tshepo and I both went to Rhodes. Everything else is fiction. (Smiles) Could anybody be
       as hectic as Tshepo? Well, I suppose I can vouch for the drug experiences had . . .

VI: I suppose I'm asking whether you are gay... or bisexual?

KSD: I'm a writer and interested in every aspect of human relations and identity. The whole thing is not an issue for me. My first novel, *Thirteen Cents*, did not have a gay character and neither will the third. I really don't want to be pigeonholed.

His response lends itself to several possible interpretations. If Duiker is in fact heterosexual, then the novel marks the centrality of the issue of gay identity for writers of all sexualities. However, his denial is an ambiguous one, especially given that *Thirteen Cents* focuses almost entirely on sex between men, and features several gay-identified characters. If Duiker is not straight, then this interview could mark the difficulty of negotiating a black gay identity in South Africa, despite the official rhetoric, and indeed the waning of the cultural moment the book itself charts.[14] A final possibility is that Duiker does not want to conform to global marketing profiles – he is a "writer," not a "gay man." This may be his mode of resistance to the categories of global capitalism that leave little room for people from the South to articulate their own subjectivities.

Conclusion: Mad Languages, Queer Translations

The novel embodies this conflict in its dialogic form, where two different modes of writing, the realist – in which gay identity is a recognizable way of translating a person – and what we might call the visionary, compete for space. Duiker begins the book by staging an argument about storytelling, when Tshepo tries to tell Mambatho what his first bout of madness was like:

> I still find it hard to explain what really happened, what was really going on in my life. There's a part of me that will never be the same again. I feel like I've lost something or got lost in something too big to describe with easy words.... I had spells. I lost time.... I remember the rain mostly and the disheartening feeling that it would never end, I say to her. That it would rain with so much volition, so much conviction, that it would drown out the memories and cries that are haunting me.... "Uhuh," she says and licks her lips. "Is that all you're going to say?" "Is that it because if it is, it's a bullshit story, Tshepo? Hawu, you can't expect me to go on that stuff, come on." (1–2)

The reader, like Mmabatho, wants Tshepo to escape his madness, which is, by definition, hard to "read." Much of the novel attempts to relay states of mind that resist realist representation – dreams, being high on drugs, conspiracy theories, and occult beliefs. Madness is often described as an alternate language, "the language of the unspoken" (55), just as sex is also a "secret language" (391). These occluded languages might be read as Duiker's attempt to indicate alternative realms of possibility beyond the dominant discourse, even as that attempt disintegrates the narrative of gay brotherhood by which Tshepo has made sense of his life. While madness literally confines Tshepo, it is also presented as having its own validity, and certainly its own beauty, as we can see in this passage of Tshepo's:

> Everything I look at haunts me because it seems to have a life of its own. Trees move and rocks whisper.... The undead and unseen have voices. And the air is as much alive as I am, breeding stories and messages, populating the earth with ideas about things to come.... I must wonder

why I always surround myself with women, why I can never look another man in the eye, why I won't allow my masculinity to blossom. For surely just like a flower a man can blossom. . . . I must know the cold, understand the wetness of rain and the thing the wind complains about when it blows through the streets. . . . I must feel overwhelmed at the expanse and intelligence of life and all the degrees of living. . . . I must become a world to myself, an encyclopedia unfolding. (91–2)

This "mad" and radically open attempt to hear and understand the unspeakable, or unspeaking, stands for sexuality – looking another man in the eye – and for so much more. The simultaneity of opening up to the world and reading oneself like an "encyclopedia" indicates the necessity for a politics of sexuality that addresses more than individual subjectivity. These alternative queer languages inhabit a book which also presents the reader with a variety of untranslated passages in African languages, and in which Tshepo himself navigates multiple lingos, from rasta-talk to *tsotsi-taal* (gangster/street-talk), and feels split between Sotho and English. The question of whether queer postcolonial sexuality can be represented, or indeed translated, what the right national or literary language, and indeed the right genre for it is, lies at the heart of the novel.

Finally, this question is also framed in terms of art and imperialism. During his time as a sex-worker, Tshepo stays over at a rich white client's house, and peruses his bookshelves:

He seems to have a particular interest in Picasso's work. . . . My Art lecturer used to castigate him as being a trickster . . . complain about the way he misappropriated sacred African imagery and reinterpreted it in disguise as his own genius without ever really acknowledging the real artists from whom he stole. . . . Cubism wasn't so much an invention, a natural artistic development, but a blatant type of artistic plagiarism. . . . The other books are mostly novels, with a large contingency of gay literature. . . . After a while I . . . fall into . . . a long conflicting dream. (279–80)

Tshepo's "conflicting dream," and the novel itself, wrestles with whether "gay literature" is part of the imperial cultural formation, or library, in which Picasso apparently belongs. Conversely, is Duiker's use of the coming-out novel also "plagiarism," or indeed mimicry? I would argue that, just as Tshepo is "turning tricks" here, Duiker is something of a queer "trickster" himself, rejecting the idea of "natural artistic development" altogether, and stealing the coming-out novel in order to dream up queer postcolonialities that may yet transform our own notions of sexuality, race and nation.

Notes

1 In the latest instance, Zanzibar's parliament unanimously passed a new law in April 2004 instituting harsh prison sentences for same-sex sex acts; in this case, homosexuality has been pronounced un-African and un-Islamic.

2 See, for example, Stephen Murray and Will Roscoe's *Boy-Wives and Female Husbands: Studies of African Homosexualities*, and Ifi Amadiume's *Male Daughters, Female Husbands: Gender and Sex in an African Society*.

3 In India and in many of the former British colonies in Africa, colonial anti-sodomy laws are still on the books, and are currently being contested as well as hotly defended. See Mark Gevisser's

discussion of Southern Africa in "Mandela's Step-Children" (114), and Suparna Bhaskaran's "The Politics of Penetration: Section 377 of the Indian Penal Code."

4   For example, Kendall's work on Basotho women indicates that in the past, women had relationships with each other that often involved what we would call sex, but which in their conceptual vocabulary were about love, and therefore not a threat to heterosexual marriage. With the advent of the language of homosexual identity, however, these relationships have become stigmatized and are far less common. It remains to be seen whether the great-granddaughters of these women will turn this history into a useable queer past.

5   See Moodie and Achmat.

6   The rape and murder of lesbian activist Fannyann Eddy in September of this year in the offices of the organization she had founded, the Sierra Leone Lesbian and Gay Association, is the latest tragic instance of the targeting such political and sexual identification provokes.

7   Combining nudity and Palestinian kaffiahs at demonstrations, Black Laundry's slogans, which take the insouciance of Act Up to a new level, include "There is No Pride in Occupation," "Free Condoms, Free Palestine," "Jerusalem: One City, Two Capitals, All Genders," and "Transgender not Transfer."

8   "Pax" says of the American occupation, "colonialism isn't the word, but it has the same color scheme."

9   See Tim Trengove Jones's discussion of Supreme Court Justice and long-time ANC activist Albie Sachs's repeated public deployment of this metaphor.

10   *Thirteen Cents* was made into a short film, *Azure*, in 2003, won a Commonwealth Writers Prize for Best First Book, and gained the author a fairly high profile in South Africa. *The Quiet Violence of Dreams* won the Charles Herman Bosman prize for literature.

11   I am using the word "coloured" here with its South African spelling in order to indicate the specificity of the racial appellation, a much-contested nvention of the apartheid regime to mean people of mixed-race.

12   Duiker also talks in interviews about how his mother, an insatiable reader, inspired him to write.

13   See Chris McGreal's "Turning Racism on its Head" for an overview of inter-African xenophobia across the continent.

14   As Vasu Reddy of the NGCLE asserts, the "moment of great social change has come and gone. South Africa is now in its second phase of its post-apartheid context with President Mbeki at the helm" (176).

References

Achmat, Zachie. "'Apostles of Civilized Vice'; 'Immoral Practices' and 'Unnatural Vice' in South African Prisons and Compounds, 1890–1920," *Social Dynamics*, 19/2, Summer 1993.

Altman, Dennis. "Global Gaze/Global Gays." *Postcolonial and Queer Theories: Intersections and Essays.* Ed. John C. Hawley. Westport, Connecticut: Greenwood, 2001, 1–18.

Amadiume, Ife. *Male Daughters, Female Husbands: Gender and Sex in an African Society.* London: Zed Books, 1987.

Bhaskaran, Suparna. "The Politics of Penetration: Section 377 of the Indian Penal Code," in *Queering India: Same-Sex Love and Eroticism in Indian Culture and Society,* ed. Ruth Vanita. New York: Routledge, 2002.

Duiker, K. Sello. *Thirteen Cents.* Cape Town: David Philip New Africa Books, 2000.

——. *The Quiet Violence of Dreams.* Johannesburg: Kwela Books, 2001.

Gevisser, Mark. "Mandela's Step-Children: Homosexual Identity in Post-Apartheid South Africa," in *Different Rainbows*, ed. Peter Drucker. London: Gay Men's Press, 2000.

Head, Bessie. *The Collector of Treasures, and Other Botswana Village Tales.* London: Heinemann Educational, 1977.

Jeppie, Shamil. "Popular Culture and Carnival in Cape Town: The 1940s and 1950s," in *The Struggle for District Six*, eds. Shamil Jeppie and Crain Soudien. Cape Town: Buchu Books, 1990.

Jones, Tim Trengove. "Fiction and the Law: Recent Inscriptions of Gayness in South Africa," in *Modern Fiction Studies*, Spring 2000.

Kendall. " 'When a Woman Loves a Woman' in Lesotho: Love, Sex, and the (Western) Construction of Homophobia," in *Boy-Wives and Female Husbands: Studies of African Homosexualities*, eds. Murray, Stephen O, and Will Roscoe. New York: St Martin's Press, 1998.

Lakay, Victor. "I'm a Traveling Salesman: An Interview with K. Sello Duiker." *South African Daily Mail* and *Guardian* Q-page.

Moodie, T. Dunbar, Ndatshe, Vivian, and British, Sibuye. "Migrancy and Male Sexuality on the South African Gold Mines," *Journal of South African Studies*. 14.1, 1988: 228–56.

Murray, Stephen O. and Will Roscoe, eds. *"Boy-Wives and Female Husbands: Studies of African Homosexualities*. New York: St Martin's Press, 1998.

Pax, Salam. *Salam Pax: The Clandestine Diary of an Ordinary Iraqi.* New York: Grove Press, 2003.

Rickards, Meg. dir. *Azure.* South Africa, 2003.

Index